# Paintings from Europe and the Americas in the Philadelphia Museum of Art

This publication was made possible by the National Endowment for the Arts and a gift from the Women's Committee of the Philadelphia Museum of Art

Research was supported by the Andrew W. Mellon Foundation Endowment Fund for Scholarly Publications and the CIGNA Foundation Endowment Fund for Scholarly Publications

# Paintings from Europe and the Americas in the Philadelphia Museum of Art

# A Concise Catalogue

**Philadelphia Museum of Art**

**Distributed by the University of Pennsylvania Press**

Edited by Curtis R. Scott, Owen Hess Dugan, and John Paschetto
Designed by James A. Scott
Printed in Italy by Stamperia Valdonega, Verona

Produced by the Department of Publications and Graphics
Philadelphia Museum of Art
26th Street and the Benjamin Franklin Parkway
P.O. Box 7646
Philadelphia, Pennsylvania 19101

Distributed by the University of Pennsylvania Press
418 Service Drive
Philadelphia, Pennsylvania 19104-6097

Library of Congress Cataloging-in-Publication Data

Philadelphia Museum of Art.
    Paintings from Europe and the Americas in the Philadelphia
Museum of Art : a concise catalogue
       p.   cm.
    Includes index.
    ISBN 0-87633-093-6 (pbk. : alk. paper). — ISBN 0-8122-7964-6
(cloth : copublication with University of Pennsylvania Press :
alk. paper)
    1. Painting—Pennsylvania—Philadelphia—Catalogs.
2. Philadelphia Museum of Art—Catalogs.  I. Title.
N685.A63  1994
750'.74'74811—dc20               94-23570
                             CIP

# CONTENTS

# PREFACE

Almost thirty years have passed since the publication of the first *Check List of Paintings in the Philadelphia Museum of Art*, a slim unillustrated volume representing much hard work and enterprise on the part of Henry G. Gardiner, then assistant curator of paintings at the Museum, who compiled the information on the 1,298 works included therein. The present volume builds upon his labors and expands enormously the usefulness of such an effort by incorporating the large and celebrated John G. Johnson Collection, which has been on permanent deposit at the Museum since 1933. With 3,921 entries, each illustrated with a small photograph, this catalogue thoroughly documents one of the largest collections of paintings in North America. The paintings are grouped into large sections corresponding to curatorial departments within the Museum so that readers consulting this book for its wealth of specific information may also gain a rough sense of the shape and character of the Museum's holdings.

The process of preparing this volume occupied many members of the curatorial and publications staff over the better part of a decade. It incorporates research already published in the Museum's recent catalogues of British paintings, by Richard Dorment, and Northern European paintings, by Peter C. Sutton, and it presages the appearance of Carl Brandon Strehlke's volumes devoted to Italian paintings in the Johnson Collection, which will also contain much new scholarship. The curators in charge of each major section—Joseph Rishel for European Painting before 1900, Darrel Sewell for American Painting before 1900, and Ann Temkin for Twentieth-Century Painting—have encouraged and benefited from the work of more than eighteen colleagues in their departments, whose dedication to accuracy and completeness was essential to this project. George H. Marcus,

head of publications at the Museum, directed the overall production of the book. The mammoth task of preparing the manuscript for the printer was undertaken first by John Paschetto, then Owen Dugan, and finally Curtis Scott, who brought it to completion. Clarisse Carnell, associate registrar for collections, has had the lion's share of reviewing more than 2,653 names and citations of donors of works of art and of purchase funds. Without the initial and valiant work of Martha Small, assisted by Colin Currie, to inventory and measure every painting, this volume could not have begun to take form.

Two generous grants from the National Endowment for the Arts and a handsome contribution from the Women's Committee of the Philadelphia Museum of Art have made this publication possible. No better example can be imagined of a public-private partnership to support the Museum's fundamental mission of making its collections widely accessible. The endowment funds for scholarly publications created by a grant from the Andrew W. Mellon Foundation and funds from the CIGNA Foundation were also invaluable in support of the detailed research necessary to reexamine many attributions. Distributed by the University of Pennsylvania Press and by our own library exchange program to museums and libraries around the world, this book provides students, scholars, and the museum-going public with the most up-to-date information about the entire paintings collection in a single, comprehensive volume.

Since 1965, when the history of the Museum's collections was ably summarized by Mr. Gardiner in the essay reprinted in the following pages, the heady rate of growth that rapidly filled the Museum's vast neoclassical building (nearly empty when it opened in 1928) has slowed somewhat, though gifts of extraordinary importance have continued to enrich the collections. Not surprisingly, individual gifts and purchases since 1965 have wrought among the most significant changes to the Museum's representation of the art of the latter half of the twentieth century. In 1967, the Samuel S. White 3rd and Vera White Collection added important works by Matisse, Rouault, and the School of Paris. In 1974, the Albert M. Greenfield and Elizabeth M. Greenfield Collection brought a wide array of modern paintings, including the first works by Jackson Pollock and Willem de Kooning to enter the Museum. Also in 1974, Mr. and Mrs. H. Gates Lloyd initiated the gift of their extraordinarily important early masterpiece by Pollock, *Male and Female*, which joins Cézanne's *The Large Bathers* and Duchamp's *The Bride Stripped Bare by Her Bachelors, Even (The Large Glass)* as complex, pivotal works suggesting powerful new directions in twentieth-century art.

The creation of two programs—one national and one enthusiastically local—have helped to emphasize the importance of contemporary acquisitions during the past thirty years. The museum purchase plan program of the National Endowment for the Arts has been a crucial source of matching funds for acquiring works by living American artists, such as Richard Diebenkorn and Philip Pearlstein. The Friends of the Philadelphia Museum of Art, founded in 1964 to raise much-needed purchase funds, gave the Museum its first major painting by Robert Rauschenberg in 1967 and has continued to add strength to strength ever since, contributing works by Sol LeWitt, Frank Stella, Alex Katz, and Ellsworth Kelly, among many others.

Over the past thirty years, Philadelphians have remembered the Museum in their wills with extraordinary generosity. The collections of nineteenth-century painting were substantially strengthened by the 1978 bequest of Charlotte Dorrance Wright, whose love of Impressionism brought important pictures by Monet, Cassatt, Pissarro, and many of their contemporaries. In 1986, a splendid gift from the late Henry P. McIlhenny, former curator, trustee, and chairman of the board, enriched the Museum's nineteenth-century European holdings with his distinguished collection of masterpieces by Ingres, David, Delacroix, Degas, Cézanne, Van Gogh, and Toulouse-Lautrec, as well as a charming group of British Victorian paintings. In 1980, Mr. McIlhenny's longtime friends and fellow benefactors of the Museum, Rodolphe and Willemina Meyer de Schauensee, culminated a lifetime of joint gifts with Mrs. de Schauensee's bequest in 1980 of a splendid late Renoir, a Van Gogh portrait, and the first Tahitian subject by Gauguin to enter the collections.

Over the past fifteen years, a number of spectacular purchases have been made possible by individuals and a foundation with deep roots in Philadelphia. A gift of funds from the bequest of George D. Widener enabled former director Jean Sutherland Boggs to acquire Edgar Degas's late masterpiece *After the Bath*, which she had admired for many years. The generosity of the Mabel Pew Myrin Trust and the gift of an anonymous donor ensured that Charles Willson Peale's five portraits of the family of General John Cadwalader would not leave Philadelphia, where they were painted in the late eighteenth century. Thus was preserved intact for the public a vivid group of personalities revolving about a man who played a notable role in both the arts and the history of the new republic as they were formulated in this city.

Most recently, a munificent gift of purchase funds from the foundation established by Mr. and Mrs. Walter H. Annenberg made possible the Museum's most important Old Master acquisition since Fiske Kimball's brilliant purchases of Poussin's *The Birth of Venus* and Rubens's *Prometheus Bound*. Hendrick Goltzius's exquisitely wrought "pen-painting" *Without Ceres and Bacchus, Venus Would Freeze* will forever alter the character of the Museum's collections, adding an unforgettable image by the master of Northern Mannerism that is, in the true sense of an overused adjective, unique.

On behalf of several generations of curatorial staff at the Philadelphia Museum of Art, whose research and enthusiasm are here reflected, it is a delight and an honor to present this book to the public. It is, in turn, dedicated to the generations of donors of works of art and of acquisition funds whose collective generosity has made the Philadelphia Museum of Art one of the most distinguished institutions of its kind in the world.

**Anne d'Harnoncourt**
*The George D. Widener Director*
*October 1994*

# A HISTORY OF THE COLLECTIONS TO 1965

Reprinted from *Check List of Paintings in the Philadelphia Museum of Art* (1965)

In July 1875, a group of Philadelphians met for the purpose of taking steps toward the establishment of a museum of art in Philadelphia. In February 1876, the Pennsylvania Museum and School of Industrial Art, known since 1937 as the Philadelphia Museum of Art, was chartered, and in May of 1877, the new Museum took up residence in Memorial Hall, which had been part of the Centennial Exposition of 1876 and was intended to survive that exhibition as a functioning museum for the enjoyment of the city. The painting collection, at first, was virtually nonexistent.

In 1882, Mrs. Bloomfield Moore, whose husband had been prominent in lumber and paper circles, gave an extensive collection of objects to the Museum, including half a dozen paintings; in 1883, she augmented that gift by about a hundred more paintings. From this moment the new Museum began to consider itself an art gallery and to seek to enlarge its collections. In 1899, Mrs. Moore gave about twenty additional paintings.

However, as the Museum's holdings have become more and more important, the Moore Collection has become less important. Changing tastes and factors of scholarship have brought about the disposition of a sizable portion of the original gift, which contained many copies and inadequate school pieces.

In 1903, Dr. Robert H. Lamborn gave about seventy-five Mexican–Spanish Colonial religious paintings to the young Museum. He was a businessman who, in 1881 and 1883, went to Mexico City, where he bought these works. In subsequent years he studied and researched his finds. His donation remains to this day one of the most original and surprising aspects of the collections. Little is known about the artists, many of whom are unrecorded, or indeed about the history of the paintings prior to Dr. Lamborn's acquisition of them.

In 1893, a benefactress of the city made an indirect but outstanding and lasting contribution to the growth of the new Museum. Mrs. William P. Wilstach, whose husband had made a fortune in saddlery and hardware, bequeathed nearly one hundred fifty paintings to the Commissioners of Fairmount Park, and the Museum Corporation administered the collection on behalf of the Commissioners. She also left a purchase fund, the collection and the purchases from the fund to be known as the W. P. Wilstach Collection. Since the original gift in 1893, many purchases have been made from this fund; the dates of acquisition are indicated in the accession number of each work in the checklist that follows.

In 1895, thirteen works of art were purchased, among them a Ruisdael, a Gainsborough, a Courbet, an Inness, and a Whistler. The next year, twelve more were acquired, including a Vittore Crivelli altarpiece, a Hondecoeter and a Constable. In 1900 and 1901, works by Zurbarán, Murillo, Ribera, Koninck, and Weenix were added to the seventeenth-century Spanish and Dutch collections as well as others by Marieschi, Rosa Bonheur, and Bouguereau.

In 1921, the fund was used to buy from the Alexander J. Cassatt family a remarkably modern group of paintings, considering the local taste of the day—three Monets, two Pissarros, a Degas, a Manet, and a Renoir, as well as a painting by Mary Cassatt, who had been responsible for her brother's purchasing the other works.

Other outstanding bequests to the City and the Commissioners of Fairmount Park came from a father and his son, and the Museum continues to benefit greatly from this generous family in the third generation. William L. Elkins, who was born in West Virginia and was successful in oil, gas, and, later, in the traction business in Philadelphia, and his son, George W. Elkins, bequeathed their noteworthy collections. In 1924 the care of the two collections passed to the new Museum Corporation, which then partially occupied the new museum building being constructed on the site of the former Fairmount Reservoir, at the end of the new parkway.

William L. Elkins exemplified the characteristic taste of his generation in owning primarily, among the nearly one hundred works bequeathed, examples of seventeenth-century Dutch painting, of eighteenth- and nineteenth-century English painting, and of the nineteenth-century French paintings of the Barbizon school and the then-popular Salon art; his bequest also included three Monets, a Homer, and an Inness. His son, George W. Elkins, left thirty-five works presenting a somewhat later taste—eighteenth-century English portraits as well as four Corots and a work each by Alma-Tadema, Boldini, Sargent, Homer, and Whistler. Subsequent purchases have been made from a fund bequeathed by George W. Elkins.

The exceptional collection of English paintings from Hogarth to Constable, formed by John H. McFadden, was received in 1928 and numbered forty-three outstanding works, among them excellent examples by Romney, Raeburn, Gainsborough, Lawrence, and Constable, as well as an outstanding picture by Turner. Mr. McFadden was internationally known, with his brother, as a cotton merchant. His substantial knowledge about English painting, chiefly portraits, was not generally appreciated at the time but can be well comprehended today.

While these valuable assets were being added to the Museum's responsibilities, although they were technically the property of the City and the Commissioners of Fairmount Park, other lesser collections were being given directly to the growing institution, which was fifty years old in 1925. The Walter Lippincott and the Alex Simpson, Jr., Collections added fifty fashionable and popular late nineteenth-century American artists' works to the galleries, which were nearing completion.

The most outstanding single gift of paintings between 1928 and 1950 was, however, the generous one by Mrs. Thomas Eakins and Miss Mary Adeline Williams of thirty-six oils of superb quality by Thomas Eakins, given in 1929, and, in addition, sixteen sketches for these and other works, given in 1930.

The Museum now could boast a fine collection of European paintings and also the works of Thomas Eakins, perhaps the best artist America had yet produced.

As years passed, other good collections were added, the John D. McIlhenny and the Robert Stockton Johnson Mitcheson Collections among them. The John D. McIlhenny Collection was more distinguished for its furniture and rugs, but it included a few fine paintings. The Christian Brinton Collection, given in 1941, was more unusual. Mr. Brinton lived near West Chester and was an art critic who often spoke out for national schools other than our own. His collection comprised over one hundred fifty oils, drawings, and prints done by Russian artists influenced by the Cubist and other stylistic innovations reaching Moscow from Paris before the First World War. Artists of this period of Russian art never fell under the imposition of "Soviet Realism," for the artists themselves all fled Russia, largely for America, where Mr. Brinton patronized them. This collection is as unusual as Dr. Lamborn's Mexican–Spanish Colonial examples, and both are fascinating revelations of how styles can be copied from totally different and foreign contexts—Mexico from Spain, and Moscow copying or being affected by Paris.

Other than by the work of Thomas Eakins, the American paintings in the collection gave only irregular glimpses into our national past and paid virtually no attention to the twentieth century. In 1949, this was partially corrected by the Alfred Stieglitz Bequest, one of several made to the museums of the United States, which numbered thirteen early oils by Hartley and Dove, many watercolors by Marin, and numerous important works by other artists. Stieglitz, as the founder of the famous "291 Gallery" in New York, had introduced modern art to America through his early exhibitions and his efforts on behalf of the Armory Show of 1913. It is most appropriate, therefore, that by his will this Museum received the initial part of its modern American art collection. Although contemporary art had often been exhibited in the Museum, and the collection was on loan here through the war years, the Stieglitz paintings were among the first permanent acquisitions in this area.

However, they were by no means the last, and the next few years were to see three major modern painting collections added to the rapidly growing Museum. In 1950, Lisa Norris Elkins, a daughter-in-law of George W. Elkins, died, and the Museum received works by Renoir, Pissarro, Toulouse-Lautrec, Van Gogh, Picasso, and Matisse, as well as two exceptional paintings by Edward Hicks, the Bucks County artist of a century earlier, whose discovery was causing such excitement at the time.

The collections of Louise and Walter Arensberg and of Albert E. Gallatin were received in 1950 and 1952, respectively, and from that moment onward Philadelphia was almost unrivaled in the world for its proto-Cubist, Cubist, and abstract collections of the 1905–1925 period. To this day, any general study of art in those years has to turn to Philadelphia for source material, and many detailed studies nearly begin and end in the Museum's collections.

Walter Arensberg was born in Pittsburgh and worked as a lawyer in New York, where he came to know and to admire Marcel Duchamp as an artist and as a wise counselor in building the collection. After the Arensbergs moved to Hollywood, they became interested in pre-Columbian sculpture, as well, and added much of that to their famous collection. All in all, they purchased over two hundred paintings and modern sculptures, most noteworthy being thirty-eight works by Duchamp, including all known versions of the *Nude Descending a Staircase*, especially the version which had caused such a furor at the New York Armory Show of 1913; eighteen works by Constantin Brancusi, the Rumanian-Frenchman whose work in essential forms was to become such an integral part of the twentieth-century vision; as well as seven by Georges Braque; five by Juan Gris; seven by Wassily Kandinsky; thirteen by Paul Klee; nine by Joan Miró; fifteen by Pablo Picasso; and four by Henri Rousseau, including the well-known *Merry Jesters*. This was, indeed, a rich accession to the Museum, then celebrating its seventy-fifth year, or its "Diamond Jubilee."

Two years later the Museum was equally, and in a sense doubly, fortunate to receive the A. E. Gallatin Collection, which had been on loan to New York University as the "Museum of Living Art" for many years. Gallatin, an artist himself, knew many of the men whose work he bought, and his sensitively selected collection has, for that reason, an extra fascination. The strongest representations, among some one hundred seventy-five examples, are those of Jean Arp and Georges Braque, with ten examples each; Juan Gris with twelve; Fernand Léger with fifteen, including his supreme early statement, *The City*, of 1919; and twenty-three by Picasso, including the arresting early *Self-Portrait* and *Three Musicians*, one of the two similar closing statements he made to the synthetic Cubist phase of his art.

The collections had now become predominantly twentieth-century and Cubist, whereas the Wilstach, Elkins, and McFadden paintings represented the seventeenth century in Holland, the eighteenth century in England, and the popular Salon and other art of nineteenth-century France as well as England.

The John G. Johnson Collection, which has been housed in the Museum since the early 1930s as a separate unit, gives a firm foundation through its untold wealth of paintings from the early and later Italian Renaissance, through the North European schools of Flanders, Holland, and Germany in the fifteenth, sixteenth, and seventeenth centuries.

As yet, however, the Museum was not as strong as could be desired in the famous French schools of Impressionism and Post-Impressionism. Mr. and Mrs. Carroll S. Tyson, Jr., who gave many years of devoted service to the boards of the Museum, were to remedy that gap in 1963 by their magnificent bequest of twenty-three major paintings, nearly all of which date from approximately forty years: 1869 to 1906, the year of the death of Paul Cézanne, in whose works Mr. Tyson, an artist in his own right, was particularly interested. They bequeathed five works by Cézanne and five by Renoir, including the world-famous *Bathers*, as well as two Manets, two Monets, and a *Sunflowers* by Van Gogh. This tightly focused chronological representation was accompanied by a classical allegory from the circle of Poussin and two early nineteenth-century portraits.

Almost immediately afterwards, in the same year, the Museum was awarded the highly coveted Louis E. Stern Collection of nearly two hundred fifty objects from all schools and national styles of art, including seventy-five paintings of the last one hundred years, of which twenty-five oils, prints, and drawings were by his close personal friend Marc Chagall. Among the many gems of this very individual collection one can cite *Carnival Evening*, by Henri Rousseau, *Madame Cézanne*, by Paul Cézanne, and *The Polish Woman*, by Amedeo Modigliani.

Louis Stern was long a governor of the Museum and a lawyer in Atlantic City and New York. He collected avidly not only modern painting and sculpture but also modern books and prints. In his later years his interests went also to Oriental and African sculpture. The result is a truly unique and personal vision of man's use of art as a creative force throughout the centuries.

As has been stated, the Wilstach and Elkins Collections were accompanied by purchase funds which have extended the collections significantly over the years. The Wilstach Fund had been periodically employed by the Commissioners of Fairmount Park since the original bequest of 1893. From the early 1930s to the present day, the Wilstach and Elkins funds have been employed to purchase truly noteworthy paintings of which the Museum and the public can justly feel proud. In 1932, Poussin's great *Birth of Venus* was obtained from the Hermitage Collection, having been sold by the Russian government. Two exceptional Cézannes were purchased: *Mont Sainte-Victoire* in 1936 and the *Bathers* in 1937. The Degas *Ballet Class* was bought in 1937, and the Charles Willson Peale *Staircase Group* in 1945. In 1950, on the occasion of the "Diamond Jubilee," many purchases were made: the Claude Gellée, the Le Nain, the Rubens *Prometheus*, a Corot, and a Delacroix, thus notably enriching the collections of the Museum. Since that event, the twelfth-century *Crucifixion*, by a follower of the San Francesco Master, was bought in 1953, a Daumier in 1954, the Titian and a Renoir in 1957, a Magnasco and a Cassatt in 1959, and the Kuhn in 1962.

One of the Museum's very few contemporary paintings was bought in 1963 from the John H. McFadden, Jr., Fund. It was *Lumen Naturale*, by Hans Hofmann. Also purchased from that fund have been a Homer and a Prendergast. In addition, other funds of a restricted nature have been employed from time to time to obtain works of art that were within the limits set by the donor.

In addition to major bequests and acquisitions by Museum purchase, the other important factor in the growth of the paintings collection is the gift of a few objects, or even a single object, which the Museum has repeatedly received from many interested Philadelphians. Mr. and Mrs. R. Sturgis Ingersoll have been particularly generous over many years by continuously giving examples from their outstanding private collection, thus greatly enriching the collections of the Museum. Mr. and Mrs. Herbert C. Morris, Dr. and Mrs. MacKinley Helm, and Mr. and Mrs. Henry Clifford have made contributions to the contemporary Mexican paintings collection and have given other works as well. The children of the late John D. McIlhenny— Bernice Wintersteen and Henry P. McIlhenny—have carried on their parents' interest in the Museum, both by their active participation and by generously presenting handsome paintings to fill important gaps in the collection.

Many other persons, too numerous to specify, have frequently donated one or more paintings to indicate their support and to assist the growth of the collections. It is the wealth of smaller donors that collectively creates a museum and gives character to the collections as a whole. Large bequests can change the emphasis of the total presentation, and purchases can fill gaps or vacancies, but smaller, or single, gifts add up to a totality of taste that so often forms the essence of a museum's collection.

**Henry G. Gardiner**

*Assistant Curator of Paintings*
*January 1965*

## NOTES TO THE USE OF THE CATALOGUE

This catalogue lists all paintings from Europe and the Americas executed entirely or in part in mediums such as oil, tempera, or acrylic that were in the collections of the Philadelphia Museum of Art and the John G. Johnson Collection as of June 30, 1992. Pastels and works on paper are not included. All miniatures, regardless of medium, are included.

The book is divided into four sections—European Painting before 1900, American Painting before 1900, Twentieth-Century Painting, and Miniatures—and further subdivided into national or regional groupings. Within each subsection, the paintings are arranged alphabetically by artist and chronologically within each artist's listings.

Each artist is listed under the name by which he or she is most commonly known. Given names, if different from the primary listing, appear in parentheses. Alternate names and the names of collaborators are also listed, and all names are cross-referenced in the **Index of Artists**. Unknown artists are listed under national school. Qualifiers are used to indicate the strength of attribution:

The artist's name is used alone when the work is known to be by that artist, or when it is believed, with reasonable certainty, that the work was executed by that artist.

**Attributed to** is used when the work is believed to have been executed by the named artist but when some doubt exists, either because the present condition of the work precludes certainty, because the named artist's body of work is insufficiently defined to permit a definite attribution, or because the attribution is subject to continuing scholarly debate.

**Workshop of** or **studio of** is used to indicate that the work is believed to have been executed by a pupil or an assistant under the direction of the named artist. With the earlier paintings, the term *workshop* is used to indicate the social situations then prevalent.

**Follower of** is used for works dependent upon the work of the named artist but not necessarily executed within the general sphere of the artist's influence.

**Imitator of** is used for works dependent upon the work of the named artist, sometimes painted at a much later date, and possibly intended to deceive.

**Copy after** is used for copies after identifiable works of art. Information on the original work or works is included in the entry.

The artist's nationality and dates of activity are listed under the first entry for that artist, regardless of strength of attribution. When the place of birth and places of major activity are different, both locations are given.

Unless otherwise indicated, artists' dates are assumed to be birth and death dates. A solidus is used to indicate *or* in a birth or death date. For example, born 1399/1400 means the artist was born in either 1399 or 1400. Other terms used in dating artists are listed below:

1400–1450 is used if the dates are documented birth and death dates.

documented 1400–1450 is used if the dates are documented dates of activity, but neither is a birth or death date.

first documented 1400, died 1450 is used if the first date is not a birth date, but the death date is known.

first securely documented 1400, died 1450 is used when there are several early possible dates for the artist. Only the first securely documented date is cited.

first recorded 1400, died 1450 is used when the first date comes from a secondary source, not a documented source.

**born 1400, died before 1450** is used when the artist's birth date is known, but the death date is known only from a document stating the artist is dead or referring to his or her heirs.

**dated works 1400–1410** is used in cases where an artist's only documentation is his work.

**Circa (c.)** may be used if a date is deduced from another documented source. For example, a tax record stating that an artist is fifty years old in 1450 means that his birth date, depending on the month of his birth, is c. 1400.

Previous attributions are listed below the artists' dates for all works listed in the Museum's 1965 checklist of paintings and the 1941, 1966, and 1972 catalogues of the John G. Johnson Collection when the attributions have changed in any way. The following abbreviations are used for these sources:

**JGJ 1941** *John G. Johnson Collection: Catalogue of Paintings.* Philadelphia, 1941.

**JI 1966** *John G. Johnson Collection: Catalogue of Italian Paintings.* Philadelphia, 1966.

**JFD 1972** *John G. Johnson Collection: Catalogue of Flemish and Dutch Paintings.* Philadelphia, 1972.

**PMA 1965** *Check List of Paintings in the Philadelphia Museum of Art.* Philadelphia, 1965.

In order to avoid confusion resulting from variant spellings, the artists' names for previous attributions are listed as they are spelled in the present catalogue. The **Index of Previous Attributions** lists those works for which the change in attribution results in a substantive shift from one artist to another, or where the artist is alphabetized differently.

The titles of paintings are given in English unless a particular significance is intended by the artist's use of a foreign language. Alternate titles are given in parentheses. Names of sitters are given as they were at the time the painting was executed, with supplemental identification provided in brackets. The **Index of Named Sitters** lists portraits and silhouettes for which the subject sat (paintings where a subject is named but did

not actually sit are not included). Cross-references for married women and titled persons are also provided.

Additional information is often included about a painting's origin or function, the locations of any known companion paintings, and, in the case of copies, their sources. References to etchings and engravings are identified by entry number in Adam von Bartsch, *Le Peintre graveur*, 21 vols. (Vienna, 1803–21).

Dates of works are assumed to be documented unless preceded by a circa (c.). Inclusive dates are given for works executed over the course of several years. When a work was painted in two or more installments several years apart, or later retouched, the word *and* is used to separate the dates. *By* is used to indicate the date a work was finished, but which may have been started long before. *Before* is used when a painting is referred to in a document, thereby establishing a date before which it must have been completed. For example, if a painting's date is not known, but it is known to have entered a collection in 1892, it may be dated "before 1892."

Signatures and inscriptions in languages using the Latin alphabet are transcribed; those in other alphabets are translated. The transcriptions seek to preserve the spelling and style of the original, including misspellings and grammatical errors, with lacunae and editorial interpolations in brackets. Signatures believed to be spurious or later additions are so identified.

The identification of mediums for most paintings is based upon visual examination. Unusual or mixed media are so designated either by the artist or by scientific analysis. *Panel* indicates a natural wood support. Synthetic fabrications such as cardboard, Masonite, and acrylic are so identified.

Measurements are given both in inches and in centimeters, height preceding width. For irregularly shaped works, dimensions reflect greatest height and greatest width. In some cases, such as multipaneled paintings, overall dimensions are given in addition to the measurements of individual panels.

The names of donors are cited and styled according to their wishes. All donors are listed in the **Index of Donors**.

The last line of each entry is the Museum's accession number, which generally consists of three parts. The first part indicates the year of accession; the second, the place of the painting in the order of gifts within that year; and the third, the item within that gift.  In some cases, the accession number bears a letter prefix indicating that it is part of a named collection (W-Wilstach, E-Elkins, M-McFadden) or was originally given to the City of Philadelphia through the Commissioners of Fairmount Park (F).  Paintings from the John G. Johnson Collection are listed by the catalogue or inventory number corresponding to the previous catalogues of that collection.  All paintings are listed in the **Index of Accession Numbers**.

# ACKNOWLEDGMENTS

This project was completed over the course of a decade with assistance from many people.

In the Department of European Painting before 1900, the John G. Johnson Collection, and the Rodin Museum: Joseph J. Rishel, Senior Curator, Colin Bailey, Brian Clancy, Richard Dorment, Alison Goodyear, Priscilla Grace, Jan Klincewicz, Katherine Luber, Lawrence Nichols, Christopher Riopelle, Carl Strehlke, Peter Sutton, and Jennifer Vanim.

In the Department of American Art: Darrel L. Sewell, the Robert L. McNeil, Jr., Curator of American Art, Andrew Brunk, and Mike Hammer. Kristina Haugland of the Department of Costume and Textiles assisted in the dating of some of the miniatures.

In the Department of Twentieth-Century Art: Ann Temkin, the Muriel and Philip Berman Curator of Twentieth-Century Art, Margaret Kline, John Ravenal, Mark Rosenthal, and Andrew Walker.

In the Department of Conservation: Marigene H. Butler, Head of Conservation, Mark Aaronson, Karen H. Ashworth, Jesse Baker, Paul Cooper, Jonathan Grauer, Stephen Gritt, Teresa Lignelli, Joe Mikuliak, Marie von Möller, Suzanne Penn, Jean F. Rosston, David Skipsey, Michael Stone, and Mark Tucker.

In the Department of the Registrar: Irene Taurins, Registrar, Clarisse Carnell, Colin Currie, and Martha Small.

In the Departments of Rights and Reproductions and Photography: Conna Clark, Manager, Graydon Wood, Senior Photographer, Will Brown, John Costello, Andrew Harkins, Terry Flemming Murphy, Lynn Rosenthal, and Alfred J. Wyatt.

In the Department of Publications and Graphics: George H. Marcus, Head of Publications, Beth Bazar, Owen Dugan, Charles Field, Sandra Klimt, John Paschetto, Alison Rooney, Curtis Scott, James Scott, Catherine Stifel, and Jane Watkins.

Arlene Pagan of the Thomas Eakins House assisted with transcribing the Spanish inscriptions on the Latin American paintings. Katharine Baetjer of the Metropolitan Museum of Art, New York, provided very helpful general advice.

# European Painting before 1900

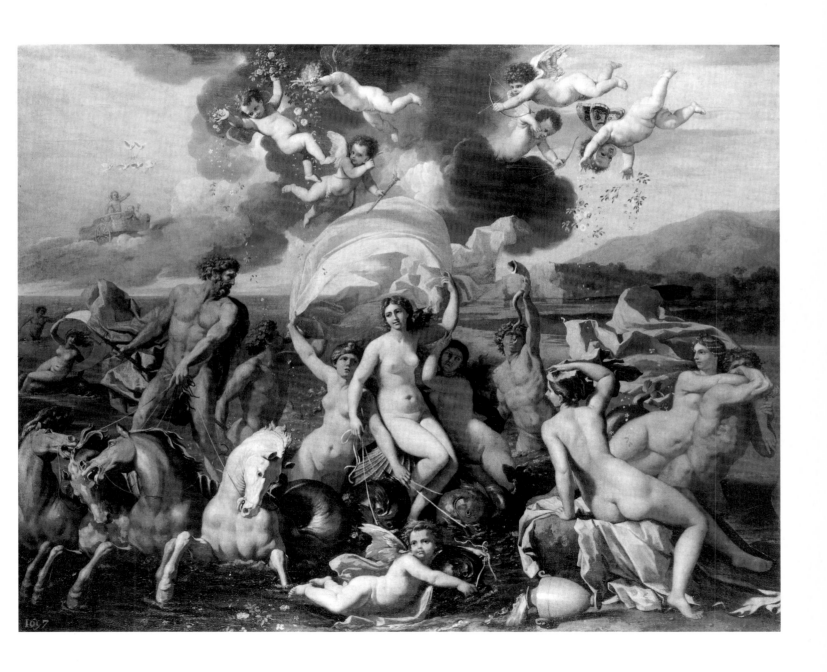

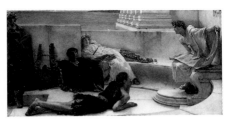

**Alma-Tadema, Sir Lawrence**
English, born Netherlands,
1836–1912
*A Reading from Homer*
1885
Upper right: [Greek for
"HOMER"]; center right:
L. ALMA-TADEMA op. CCLXVII
Oil on canvas
36 1/8 × 72 1/4" (91.8 × 183.5 cm)

The George W. Elkins Collection
E1924-4-1

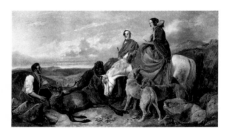

**Ansdell, Richard**
English, 1818–1885
*Mr. and Mrs. John Naylor with a
Keeper and a Dead Stag*
1847
Oil on canvas
41 × 72" (104.1 × 182.9 cm)

The Henry P. McIlhenny
Collection in memory of
Frances P. McIlhenny
1986-26-271

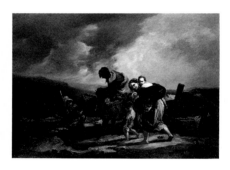

**Barker, Thomas, also called
Thomas Barker of Bath**
English, 1769–1847
Previously attributed to Thomas
Barker (PMA 1965)
*Gypsies on the Heath*
c. 1810–15
Oil on canvas
30 × 41 3/8" (76.2 × 105.1 cm)

Gift of John G. Johnson for the
W. P. Wilstach Collection
W1903-1-5

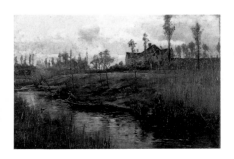

**Bartlett, William H.**
English, 1858–1932
*Stream with a Boat*
1884
Lower left: W H Bartlett. 84.
Oil on canvas
12 5/8 × 18 1/2" (32.1 × 47 cm)

John G. Johnson Collection
cat. 889

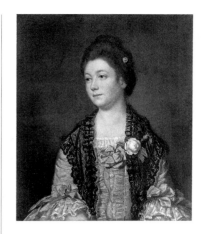

**Beach, Thomas, also called
Thomas Beach of Bath**
English, 1738–1806
*Portrait of the Honorable Mrs.
Edmund Lambert of Boyton Manor,
Wiltshire*
Companion to *Portrait of Edmund
Lambert*, 1771, unknown location
1771
Oil on canvas
30 × 25" (76.2 × 63.5 cm)

Gift of Mrs. Henry W. Breyer
1974-98-1

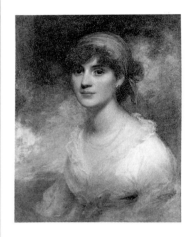

**Beechey, Sir William**
English, 1753–1839
*Portrait of Elizabeth, Lady
Le Despencer*
Cut down on all sides
c. 1795–97
On reverse: Ellsth Lady
Le Despencer / wife of Thomas
22 Baron Le Despencer / about
the year 1795 / by Romney
Oil on canvas
24 3/4 × 19 1/8" (62.9 × 48.6 cm)

Bequest of Helen S. Fennessey in
memory of her stepfather, Horace
Trumbauer
1974-161-1

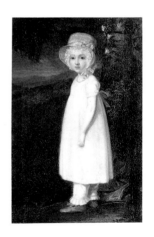

**Beechey, Sir William**
Previously attributed to Sir
William Beechey (PMA 1965)
*Portrait of a Young Girl (Little
Mary)*
Fragment
c. 1810–15
Oil on canvas
42 1/2 × 26" (108 × 66 cm)

Gift of Mrs. John S. Williams
1946-88-1

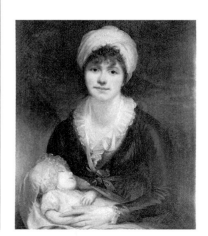

**Beechey, Sir William,
copy after**
*Portrait of Lady Beechey and Her
Child*
After the painting, dated
1800 or 1801, in the Detroit
Institute of Arts (53.387)
19th century
Oil on canvas
29 15/16 × 24 7/16" (76 × 62.1 cm)

Gift of Mrs. S. Emlen Stokes
1973-264-1

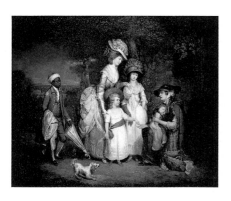

**Bigg, William Redmore**
English, 1755–1828
*A Lady and Her Children Relieving a Cottager*
1781
Lower right: WR Bigg 178[1?]
Oil on canvas
29 5/8 × 35 5/8" (75.2 × 90.5 cm)

Gift of Mr. and Mrs. Harald Paumgarten
1947-64-1

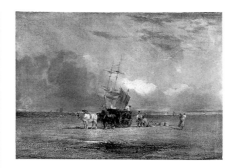

**Bonington, Richard Parkes, follower of**
Previously listed as Richard Parkes Bonington (JGJ 1941)
*Beach with a Cart and Figures*
19th century
Oil on canvas
10 1/4 × 14 1/4" (26 × 36.2 cm)

John G. Johnson Collection
cat. 883

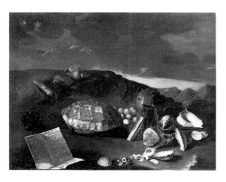

**Black**
English, 18th century
*Still Life with a Tortoise*
1743
On letter: April 1743 / Black pinxit
Oil on canvas
29 1/2 × 38" (74.9 × 96.5 cm)

The Henry P. McIlhenny Collection in memory of Frances P. McIlhenny
1986-26-272

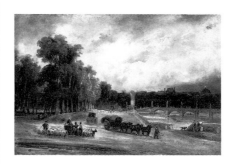

**Bonington, Richard Parkes, imitator of**
*View of the Seine*
19th century
Oil on canvas
13 5/8 × 19 1/4" (34.6 × 48.9 cm)

John G. Johnson Collection
cat. 882

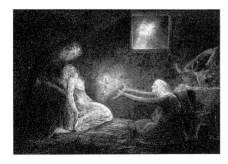

**Blake, William**
English, 1757–1827
*The Nativity*
1799 or 1800
On reverse: Don't place this picture in the sun or near / the fire, or it will crack off the Copper / W.B.S. [William Bell Scott] 1865.
Tempera on copper
10 3/4 × 15 1/16" (27.3 × 38.3 cm)

Gift of Mrs. William Thomas Tonner
1964-110-1

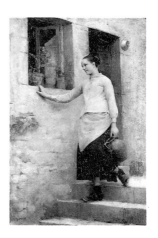

**Brown, Frederick**
English, 1851–1941
*Girl with a Pitcher*
1883
Lower right: FRED BROWN / 1883
Oil on canvas
24 1/4 × 15 3/8" (61.6 × 39.1 cm)

John G. Johnson Collection
cat. 907

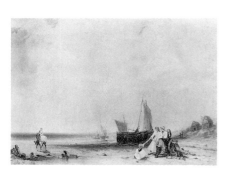

**Bonington, Richard Parkes, follower of**
English, 1802–1828
Previously listed as Richard Parkes Bonington (PMA 1965)
*Coast Scene*
c. 1828–40
Oil on canvas
24 × 33" (61 × 83.8 cm)

The John Howard McFadden Collection
M1928-1-1

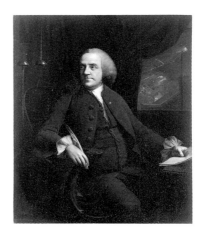

**Chamberlin, Mason**
English, died 1787
*Portrait of Benjamin Franklin*
1762
Lower left: M. Chamberlin. pinxt. 1762.
Oil on canvas
50 3/8 × 40 3/4" (128 × 103.5 cm)

Gift of Mr. and Mrs. Wharton Sinkler
1956-88-1

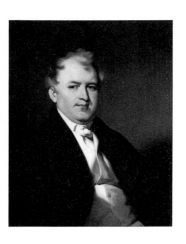

**Chinnery, George, attributed to**
English, 1748–1847
*Portrait of Nathan Dunn*
c. 1830
Oil on canvas
23 ³/₈ × 18" (59.4 × 45.7 cm)

Gift of Mrs. Joseph H. Gaskill
1970-89-1

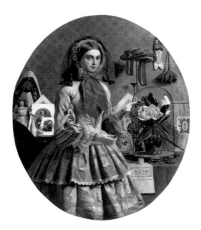

**Collinson, James**
English, c. 1825–1881
*For Sale*
c. 1855–60
Center left, on bottle: Eau / de / Cologne; center right, on box: BRICKS; lower right, on sign: ST BRIDE'S CHURCH / THE ANNUAL / BAZAAR / FOR THE SALE OF / USEFUL AND FANCY ARTICLES / PATRONESS / [RIG]HT HONOUR-ABLE LADY DORCAS / COMMITTEE
Oil on canvas
23 × 18" (58.4 × 45.7 cm)

The Henry P. McIlhenny Collection in memory of Frances P. McIlhenny
1986-26-273

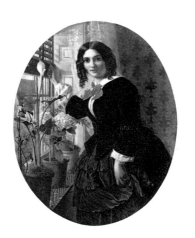

**Collinson, James**
*To Let*
c. 1855–60
Center left, on sign: [reverse of "FURNISH / APARTM"]
Oil on canvas
23 × 18" (58.4 × 45.7 cm)

The Henry P. McIlhenny Collection in memory of Frances P. McIlhenny
1986-26-274

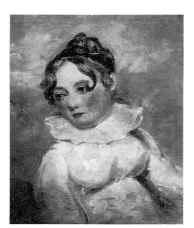

**Constable, John**
English, 1776–1837
Previously attributed to John Constable (JGJ 1941)
*Portrait of a Girl*
c. 1806–10
Oil on paper on panel
9 ¹/₂ × 7 ⁷/₈" (24.1 × 20 cm)

John G. Johnson Collection
cat. 872

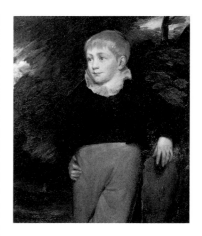

**Constable, John**
*Portrait of Master Crosby*
1808
Lower right: J. Constable. P. 1808.
Oil on canvas
30 ¹/₄ × 25 ¹/₄" (76.8 × 64.1 cm)

John G. Johnson Collection
cat. 873

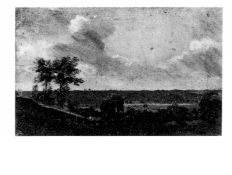

**Constable, John**
*Hilly Landscape*
c. 1808
On reverse: J. Constable / about 1808
Oil on panel
6 ³/₈ × 9 ⁷/₁₆" (16.2 × 24 cm)

John G. Johnson Collection
cat. 859

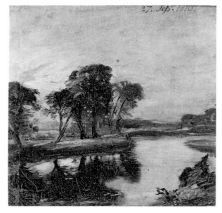

**Constable, John**
*The Stour*
1810
Upper right: 27. Sept. 1810.
Oil on canvas
9 ³/₈ × 9 ¹/₄" (23.8 × 23.5 cm)

John G. Johnson Collection
cat. 857

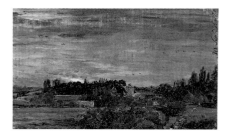

**Constable, John**
*View toward the Rectory, East Bergholt*
1810
Upper right: 30 Sept. / 1810
Bergholt Common
Oil on paper on panel
6 ¹/₈ × 9 ³/₄" (15.6 × 24.8 cm)

John G. Johnson Collection
cat. 856

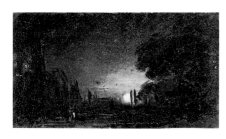

**Constable, John**
*Rising Moon*
c. 1810
Oil on paper on panel
4 1/4 × 7 3/8" (10.8 × 18.7 cm)

John G. Johnson Collection
cat. 868

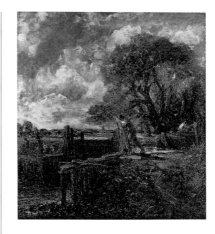

**Constable, John**
*Sketch for "A Boat Passing a Lock"*
For the painting in the Thyssen-
Bornemisza Collection, Madrid
1822–24
Oil on canvas
55 1/2 × 48" (141 × 121.9 cm)

The John Howard McFadden
Collection
M1928-1-2

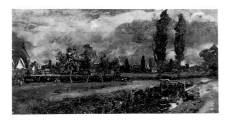

**Constable, John**
*Landscape with a River*
c. 1810–12
Oil on canvas
6 1/4 × 11 1/4" (15.9 × 28.6 cm)

John G. Johnson Collection
cat. 863

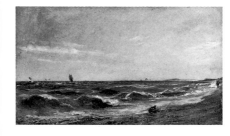

**Constable, John**
*Coast Scene, Brighton*
c. 1824–28
Oil on cardboard
10 × 16 5/8" (25.4 × 42.2 cm)

The Henry P. McIlhenny
Collection in memory of
Frances P. McIlhenny
1986-26-4

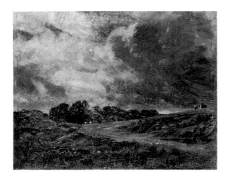

**Constable, John**
*Hampstead Heath*
1821
Oil on paper on canvas
10 × 12 1/4" (25.4 × 31.1 cm)

John G. Johnson Collection
cat. 864

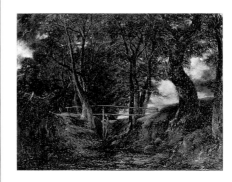

**Constable, John**
*Dell at Helmingham Park*
1825 or 1826, retouched 1833
Oil on canvas
28 × 36" (71.1 × 91.4 cm)

John G. Johnson Collection
cat. 871

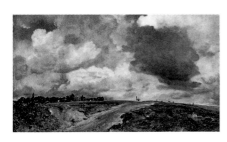

**Constable, John**
*Road to the Spaniards, Hampstead*
1822
On reverse: [Hamp]stead.
Monday 2[?] July 1822 looking
NE 3 PM previous to a thunder
squall wind N West.
Oil on canvas
12 1/8 × 20 1/8" (30.8 × 51.1 cm)

John G. Johnson Collection
cat. 858

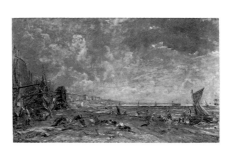

**Constable, John**
*Sketch for "The Marine Parade and
Chain Pier, Brighton"*
For the painting in the Tate
Gallery, London (N 05957)
c. 1826–27
Oil on canvas
23 3/4 × 38 7/8" (60.3 × 98.7 cm)

Purchased with the W. P.
Wilstach Fund
W1896-1-5

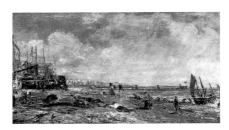

**Constable, John, attributed to**
Previously listed as John Constable (JGJ 1941)
*Chain Pier, Brighton*
After 1826
Oil on paper on canvas
13 1/16 × 24 1/8" (33.2 × 61.3 cm)

John G. Johnson Collection
cat. 869

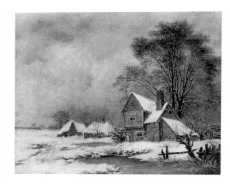

**Constable, John, follower of?**
Previously listed as John Constable (JGJ 1941)
*Gandish Cottage, Suffolk*
Before 1878
On reverse: purchased of Mrs. Newman Webb the Niece / of the Artist at the Cottage 27 February 1878 / where the picture had always hung
Oil on canvas
14 1/16 × 17 9/16" (35.7 × 44.6 cm)

John G. Johnson Collection
cat. 851

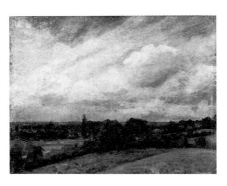

**Constable, John, attributed to**
*Landscape* [possibly the Stour valley]
19th century
Oil on paper on panel
7 7/8 × 10" (20 × 25.4 cm)

John G. Johnson Collection
cat. 853

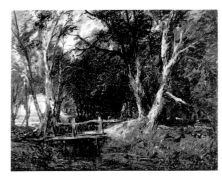

**Constable, John, imitator of**
Previously listed as John Constable (PMA 1965)
*Dell at Helmingham Park*
After 1828
Oil on canvas
30 1/2 × 38 1/2" (77.5 × 97.8 cm)

The John Howard McFadden Collection
M1928-1-4

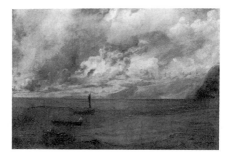

**Constable, John, attributed to**
Previously listed as John Constable (JGJ 1941)
*Weymouth Bay*
19th century
Oil on canvas
21 3/8 × 30 1/8" (54.3 × 76.5 cm)

John G. Johnson Collection
cat. 865

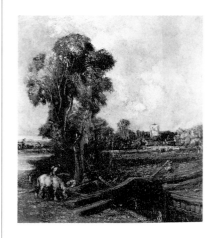

**Constable, John, imitator of**
Previously listed as English, unknown artist, 19th century (PMA 1965)
*Landscape with a Lock*
19th century
Oil on canvas
35 1/4 × 30 5/8" (89.5 × 77.8 cm)

The George W. Elkins Collection
E1924-4-4

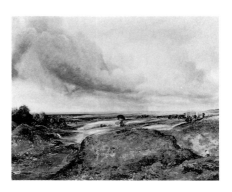

**Constable, John, studio of**
Previously listed as John Constable (PMA 1965)
*Branch Hill Pond, Hampstead Heath*
After 1825
Oil on canvas
23 × 29 1/2" (58.4 × 74.9 cm)

The John Howard McFadden Collection
M1928-1-3

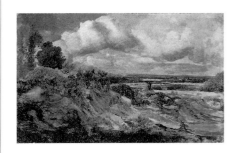

**Constable, John, imitator of**
*Landscape with Brushwood*
19th century
Oil on paper on panel
12 13/16 × 20" (32.5 × 50.8 cm)

John G. Johnson Collection
cat. 855

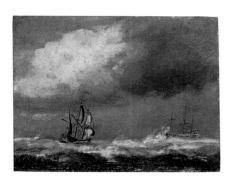

**Constable, John, imitator of**
*Marine*
19th century
Oil on panel
5 3/4 × 7 7/16" (14.6 × 18.9 cm)

John G. Johnson Collection
cat. 861

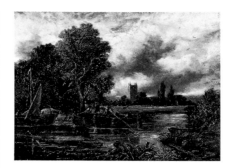

**Constable, John, copy after**
Previously listed as John Constable (JGJ 1941)
*The Stour*
After the painting in the Huntington Library, San Marino, California
19th century
Oil on panel
12 3/8 × 16 7/16" (31.4 × 41.8 cm)

John G. Johnson Collection
cat. 866

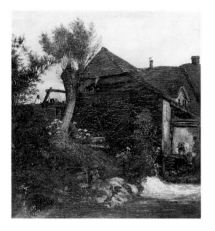

**Constable, John, imitator of**
*Mill*
19th century
Oil on canvas
24 1/2 × 21" (62.2 × 53.3 cm)

John G. Johnson Collection
inv. 2814

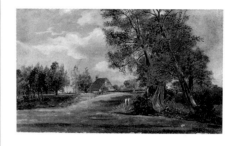

**Constable, Lionel Bicknell**
English, 1828–1887
Previously listed as John Constable (JGJ 1941)
*Cottage on the Stour*
c. 1850
Oil on paper on canvas
10 × 16 5/16" (25.4 × 41.4 cm)

John G. Johnson Collection
cat. 852

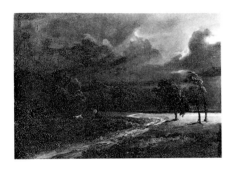

**Constable, John, imitator of**
Previously listed as John Constable (JGJ 1941)
*Near Bergholt Common*
19th century
Oil on canvas
8 1/4 × 11" (21 × 27.9 cm)

John G. Johnson Collection
cat. 860

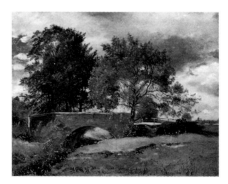

**Constable, Lionel Bicknell**
Previously listed as John Constable (JGJ 1941)
*Bridge on the Mole*
c. 1850–55
Oil on paper on panel
10 3/8 × 12 3/8" (26.4 × 31.4 cm)

John G. Johnson Collection
cat. 854

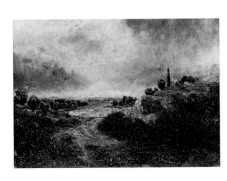

**Constable, John, copy after**
Previously listed as John Constable (JGJ 1941)
*Branch Hill Pond, Hampstead Heath*
After a mezzotint by David Lucas (English, 1802–1881), after a composition by Constable
19th century
Oil on canvas
11 7/8 × 16 1/16" (30.2 × 40.8 cm)

John G. Johnson Collection
cat. 862

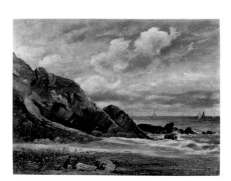

**Constable, Lionel Bicknell, attributed to**
*Beach near Yarmouth*
c. 1850
Oil on canvas
14 1/4 × 18 1/2" (36.2 × 47 cm)

John G. Johnson Collection
cat. 867

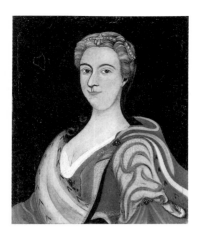

**Cooper, J., attributed to**
English, born c. 1695,
still active 1754
*Portrait of a Lady with a Beaded Headdress*
c. 1718
Oil on canvas
22 3/8 × 18 1/8" (56.8 × 46 cm)

The Edgar William and Bernice Chrysler Garbisch Collection
1969-276-1

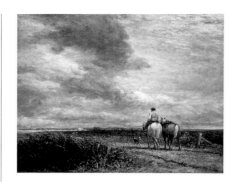

**Cox, David**
English, 1783–1859
*Going to the Hayfield*
1849
Lower right: David Cox / 1849
Oil on canvas
28 × 36" (71.1 × 91.4 cm)

The John Howard McFadden Collection
M1928-1-5

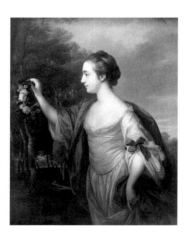

**Cotes, Francis**
English, 1726–1770
*Portrait of Frances Burdette as Emma the Nut-Brown Maid*
1761
Oil on canvas
43 1/2 × 33 1/2" (110.5 × 85.1 cm)

Gift of Muriel and Philip Berman
1989-70-5

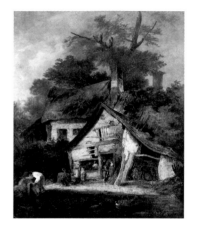

**Crome, John**
English, 1768–1821
*Blacksmith's Shop near Hingham, Norfolk*
c. 1808
Oil on canvas
60 5/8 × 48" (154 × 121.9 cm)

The John Howard McFadden Collection
M1928-1-6

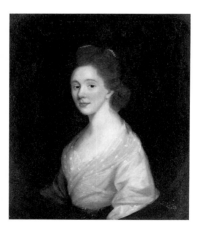

**Cotes, Francis, imitator of**
*Portrait of a Lady*
19th century?
Oil on canvas
30 3/8 × 25 1/4" (77.2 × 64.1 cm)

Gift of Mrs. Henry W. Breyer
1974-98-2

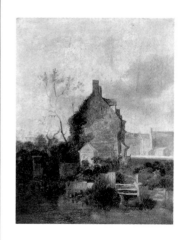

**Crome, John**
*Saint Martin's River near Fuller's Hole, Norwich*
c. 1813–14
On label on reverse: November 12, 1885: I hearby certify that I have known this picture a view on St. Martin's River / near Fullers hole for thirty years & the late Lord Stafford always told me it was by Crome. There were many others of his in the Hall. C. E. Britcher / The Carver [?]
Oil on panel
20 1/8 × 15 1/4" (51.1 × 38.7 cm)

The William L. Elkins Collection
E1924-3-27

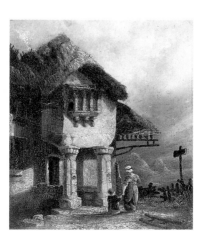

**Cotman, John Sell, imitator of**
English, 1782–1842
Previously listed as an English artist, c. 1820 (JGJ 1941)
*Old House with Pillars*
19th century
Oil on panel
12 × 10" (30.5 × 25.4 cm)

John G. Johnson Collection
cat. 878

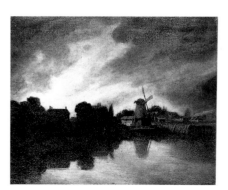

**Crome, John, follower of**
Previously listed as John Crome (PMA 1965)
*Old Mill on the Yare*
c. 1806
Oil on canvas
25 × 30 1/8" (63.5 × 76.5 cm)

The George W. Elkins Collection
E1924-4-9

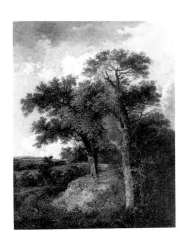

**Crome, John, copy after**
Previously listed as John Crome
(PMA 1965)
*Woody Landscape at Colney*
After Crome's soft-ground
etching *At Colney*, c. 1812
c. 1850–75?
Oil on canvas
22 1/2 × 17" (57.2 × 43.2 cm)

The John Howard McFadden
Collection
M1928-1-7

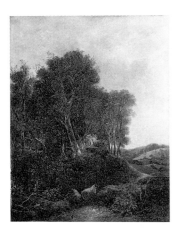

**Crome, John, copy after**
Previously listed as John Crome
(JGJ 1941)
*The Way through the Wood*
After the painting in the
Birmingham Museums and Art
Gallery, England (P.10'50)
19th century
Oil on canvas
23 1/2 × 17 1/2" (59.7 × 44.5 cm)

John G. Johnson Collection
cat. 876

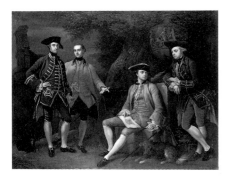

**Dance, Nathaniel**
English, 1735–1811
*Conversation Piece (Portrait of James
Grant of Grant, John Mytton, the
Honorable Thomas Robinson, and
Thomas Wynne)*
Three other versions, for the
various sitters, are in the collection
of the Earl of Seafield, Cullen,
Banffshire; the Yale Center for
British Art (B1976.7.19); and the
collection of Lady Lucas
1760 or 1761
Oil on canvas
37 7/8 × 48 1/2" (96.2 × 123.2 cm)

Gift of John Howard McFadden, Jr.
1946-36-1

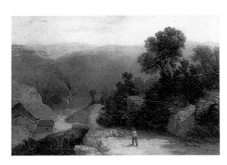

**Dawson, Henry,
attributed to**
English, 1811–1878
Previously listed as Henry
Dawson (JGJ 1941)
*Landscape*
19th century
Oil on canvas
20 3/8 × 29 3/4" (51.8 × 75.6 cm)

John G. Johnson Collection
cat. 885

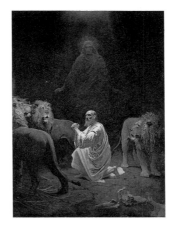

**Dowling, Robert**
English, born Australia,
1827–1886
*Daniel in the Lion's Den*
1882
On reverse: DANIEL IN THE DEN
OF LIONS BY DOWLING / 27
COLEHERNE ROAD / WEST
B[ROMPTON] / 1882
Oil on canvas
72 × 50 1/2" (182.9 × 128.3 cm)

Gift of the Richard and Susan
Levy Art Foundation
1968-181-1

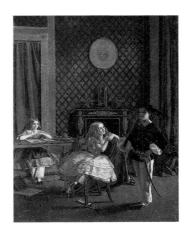

**Egley, William Maw**
English, 1826–1916
*Just as the Twig Is Bent*
Companion to the following
painting
1861
Lower left: W. Maw Egley.
1861.; lower left, on papers: SEE
THE / CONQUERING / HERO /
COMES
Oil on canvas
24 1/4 × 18 1/4" (61.6 × 46.4 cm)

Purchased with the Katharine
Levin Farrell Fund
1970-3-1

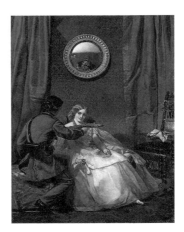

**Egley, William Maw**
*The Tree's Inclined*
Companion to the preceding
painting
1861
Lower right: W. Maw Egley.
1861.
Oil on canvas
24 1/4 × 18 1/4" (61.6 × 46.4 cm)

Purchased with the Katharine
Levin Farrell Fund
1970-3-2

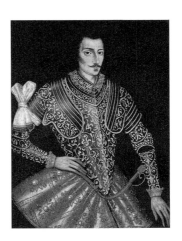

**English, unknown artist**
*Portrait of a Man in Armor*
16th century
Oil on panel
13 7/8 × 10 3/4" (35.2 × 27.3 cm)

Bequest of Carl Otto
Kretzschmar von Kienbusch
1977-167-1044

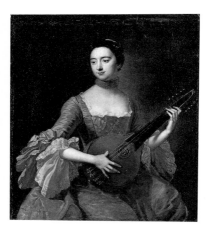

**English or Irish, unknown artist**
*Portrait of a Woman with a Cittern*
c. 1725–50
Oil on canvas
41 1/2 × 36 1/8" (105.4 × 91.8 cm)

Gift of Rodman A. Heeren
1971-262-1

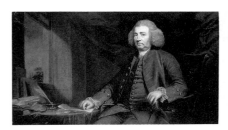

**English, unknown artist**
Previously attributed to Sir
Joshua Reynolds (JGJ 1941)
*Portrait of a Gentleman*
18th century
Oil on canvas
36 5/16 × 63 3/8" (92.2 × 161 cm)

John G. Johnson Collection
cat. 826

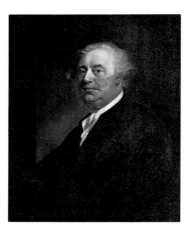

**English, unknown artist**
Previously listed as Sir Joshua
Reynolds (JGJ 1941)
*Portrait of Sir William Yonge*
c. 1750–75
Oil on canvas
30 × 25 1/16" (76.2 × 63.7 cm)

John G. Johnson Collection
cat. 829

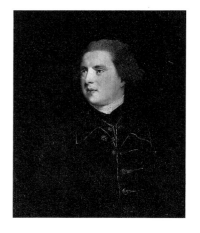

**English, unknown artist**
Previously listed as Sir Joshua
Reynolds (JGJ 1941)
*Portrait of a Gentleman*
18th century
Oil on canvas
30 5/16 × 25 3/8" (77 × 64.5 cm)

John G. Johnson Collection
cat. 828

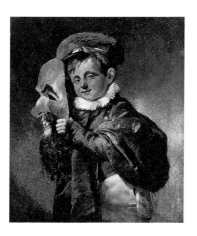

**English, unknown artist**
Previously listed as Sir Henry
Raeburn (JGJ 1941)
*Boy with a Mask*
c. 1775–1800?
Oil on canvas
30 1/16 × 25" (76.4 × 63.5 cm)

John G. Johnson Collection
cat. 840

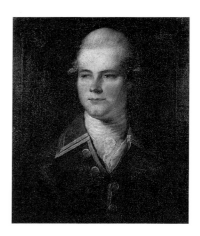

**English, unknown artist**
Previously listed as George
Romney (JGJ 1941)
*Portrait of a Gentleman*
18th century
Oil on canvas
24 1/16 × 20 1/16" (61.1 × 51 cm)

John G. Johnson Collection
cat. 838

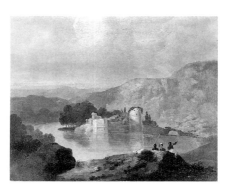

**English, unknown artist**
Previously listed as Richard
Wilson (JGJ 1941)
*Castle by the Sea*
18th century
Oil on canvas
18 1/4 × 22 1/2" (46.4 × 57.2 cm)

John G. Johnson Collection
cat. 824

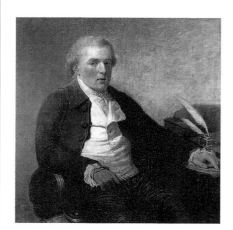

**English, unknown artist**
Previously listed as John
Hoppner (JGJ 1941)
*Portrait of a Gentleman*
18th century
Oil on canvas
37 3/8 × 36 1/2" (94.9 × 92.7 cm)

John G. Johnson Collection
cat. 842

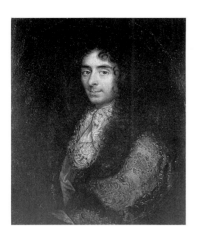

**English?, unknown artist**
*Portrait of a Gentleman*
Originally oval
18th century
Oil on canvas
28 1/2 × 23 3/16" (72.4 × 58.9 cm)

John G. Johnson Collection
inv. 2832

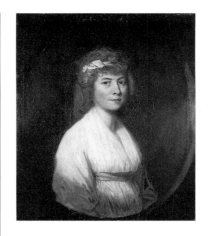

**English, unknown artist**
Previously listed as John
Hoppner (JGJ 1941)
*Portrait of a Woman*
18th century
Oil on canvas
30 1/4 × 25 1/16" (76.8 × 63.7 cm)

John G. Johnson Collection
cat. 843

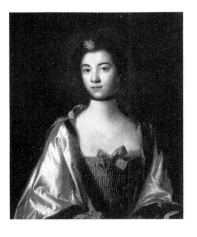

**English, unknown artist**
Previously listed as Sir Joshua
Reynolds (JGJ 1941)
*Portrait of a Lady*
18th century
Oil on canvas
29 3/4 × 24 5/8" (75.6 × 62.6 cm)

John G. Johnson Collection
cat. 830

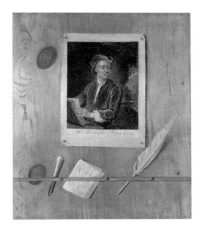

**English, unknown artist**
*Trompe l'Oeil with a Print of
Alexander Pope*
18th century
On print: Mr. Alexander Pope.
AEts. 28. / G. Kneller Pinx.
1716. J. Smith fec. et ex. 1717.;
on letter: To / Mr. Francis Loobell
/ All neigh / Cornwall
Oil on canvas
29 15/16 × 25 1/16" (76 × 63.7 cm)

John G. Johnson Collection
cat. 825

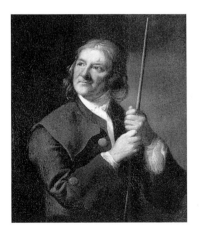

**English, unknown artist**
Previously listed as Thomas
Gainsborough (JGJ 1941)
*Portrait of a Man*
18th century
Oil on canvas
30 × 25 1/8" (76.2 × 63.8 cm)

John G. Johnson Collection
cat. 832

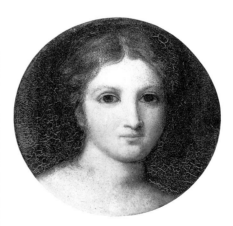

**English or American,
unknown artist**
*Head of a Girl*
c. 1800–25
Oil on academy board
16 × 15 3/4" (40.6 × 40 cm)

John G. Johnson Collection
inv. 2849

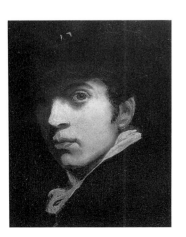

**English, unknown artist**
*Portrait of a Man*
18th century
Oil on panel
16 13/16 × 12 11/16" (42.7 × 32.2 cm)

John G. Johnson Collection
cat. 836

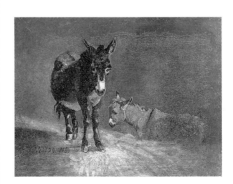

**English, unknown artist**
*Two Donkeys*
1816?
Lower left: feb. 29, 1816
Oil on panel
7 1/2 × 9 7/8" (19.1 × 25.1 cm)

John G. Johnson Collection
inv. 155

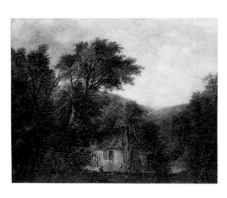

**English, active Norwich, unknown artist**
Previously listed as John Crome (PMA 1965)
*Ringland Hill*
c. 1820–30
Oil on canvas
32 1/2 × 39 3/4" (82.6 × 101 cm)

The William L. Elkins Collection
E1924-3-43

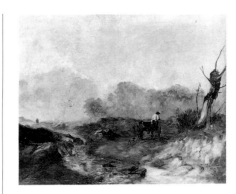

**English, unknown artist**
*Landscape*
19th century
Oil on canvas
25 × 30" (63.5 × 76.2 cm)

Bequest of T. Edward Hanley
1970-76-1

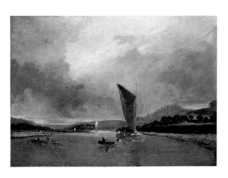

**English, active Norwich, unknown artist**
Previously attributed to John Crome (PMA 1965)
*Hay Barges on the Yare*
c. 1825–50
Oil on canvas
30 1/8 × 40" (76.5 × 101.6 cm)

Purchased with the W. P. Wilstach Fund
W1906-1-4

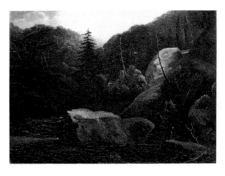

**English?, unknown artist**
Previously listed as Joseph Mallord William Turner (JGJ 1941)
*Landscape*
19th century
Oil on panel
12 3/16 × 16 3/8" (31 × 41.6 cm)

John G. Johnson Collection
cat. 850

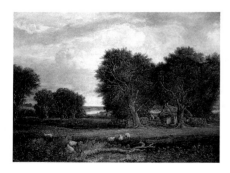

**English, unknown artist**
Previously listed as John Crome (PMA 1965)
*Landscape*
c. 1825–50
Oil on canvas
29 3/4 × 39 1/4" (75.6 × 99.7 cm)

Gift of Mrs. Robert M. Hogue
1943-50-1

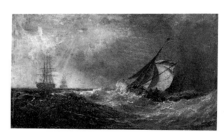

**English, unknown artist**
*Marine*
19th century
Lower left (spurious): Cox; on reverse: Off Flushing / Holland
Oil on cardboard
5 5/8 × 9 5/8" (14.3 × 24.5 cm)

Gift of Joseph K. Eddleman and Mrs. William M. Dunlap in memory of Dr. J. S. Ladd Thomas
1974-160-1

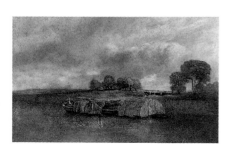

**English, unknown artist**
Previously listed as John Sell Cotman (PMA 1965)
*Barge on a River*
19th century
Oil on canvas
8 7/8 × 14" (22.5 × 35.6 cm)

The William L. Elkins Collection
E1924-3-42

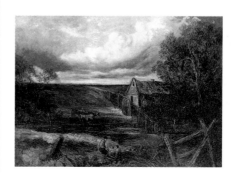

**English, unknown artist**
*Overshot Mill*
19th century
Oil on canvas
39 3/4 × 51 1/2" (101 × 130.8 cm)

The William L. Elkins Collection
E1924-3-1

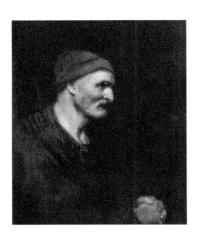

**English, unknown artist**
*Portrait of an Old Man*
19th century?
Oil on canvas
30 × 24 7/8" (76.2 × 63.2 cm)

John G. Johnson Collection
cat. 839

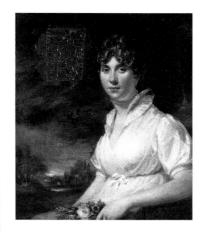

**English, unknown artist**
Previously listed as an English
artist, c. 1790 (JGJ 1941)
*Portrait of a Lady*
In an 18th-century style
19th or 20th century
Oil on canvas
30 3/16 × 24 11/16" (76.7 × 62.7 cm)

John G. Johnson Collection
cat. 841

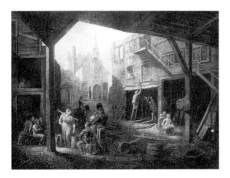

**English, unknown artist**
Previously listed as Joseph
Mallord William Turner (JGJ
1941)
*Winchester Cross*
19th century
Oil on canvas
40 1/8 × 50 1/4" (101.9 × 127.6 cm)

John G. Johnson Collection
cat. 849

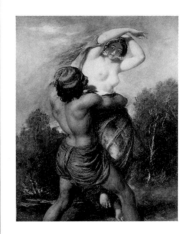

**Etty, William**
English, 1787–1849
*The Corsair*
c. 1846
Oil on canvas on fiberboard
27 3/4 × 21" (70.5 × 53.3 cm)

John G. Johnson Collection
cat. 884

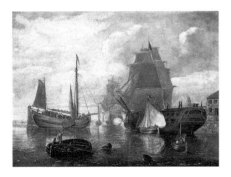

**English, unknown artist**
Previously attributed to John Sell
Cotman (JGJ 1941)
*View of the Yare*
19th century
Oil on canvas
28 × 36 1/8" (71.1 × 91.8 cm)

John G. Johnson Collection
cat. 877

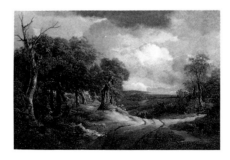

**Gainsborough, Thomas**
English, 1727–1788
*Rest by the Way*
1747
Lower left: Gainsbro:1747
Oil on canvas
40 1/8 × 58" (101.9 × 147.3 cm)

Purchased with the W. P.
Wilstach Fund
W1895-1-4

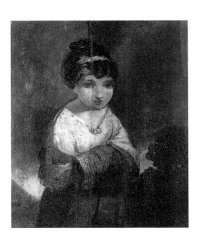

**English, unknown artist**
*Young Girl*
19th century?
Oil on panel
22 1/2 × 18 1/2" (57.2 × 47 cm)

John G. Johnson Collection
inv. 2828

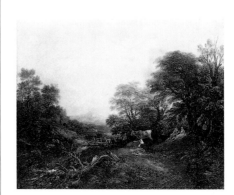

**Gainsborough, Thomas**
*Landscape with Rustic Lovers, Two
Cows, and a Man on a Distant
Bridge*
c. 1755–59
Oil on canvas
25 1/4 × 30" (64.1 × 76.2 cm)

Gift of Mrs. Wharton Sinkler
1964-103-1

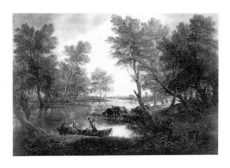

**Gainsborough, Thomas**
*View near King's Bromley, on Trent,
Staffordshire*
1768–70
Oil on canvas
47 × 66 1/8" (119.4 × 168 cm)

The William L. Elkins Collection
E1924-3-6

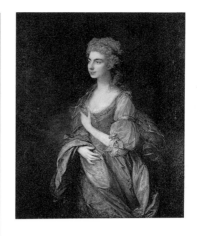

**Gainsborough, Thomas**
*Portrait of Lady Rodney* [née Anne
Harley]
c. 1781
Oil on canvas
50 1/4 × 39 7/8" (127.6 × 101.3 cm)

The John Howard McFadden
Collection
M1928-1-8

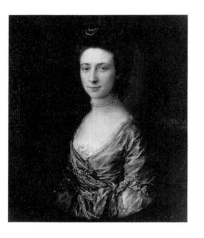

**Gainsborough, Thomas**
*Portrait of Mrs. Clement Tudway*
Companion to *Portrait of Clement
Tudway*, North Carolina Museum
of Art, Raleigh (G.60.11.1)
1773
Oil on canvas
30 1/8 × 25 1/8" (76.5 × 63.8 cm)

The George W. Elkins Collection
E1924-4-12

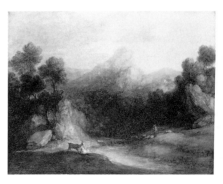

**Gainsborough, Thomas**
*Pastoral Landscape (Rocky Mountain
Valley with a Shepherd, Sheep, and
Goats)*
c. 1783
Oil on canvas
40 3/8 × 50 3/8" (102.6 × 128 cm)

The John Howard McFadden
Collection
M1928-1-9

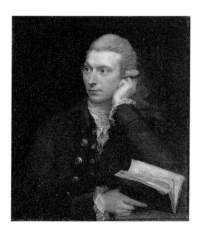

**Gainsborough, Thomas**
*Portrait of John Palmer*
c. 1775
Oil on canvas
30 × 25 1/8" (76.2 × 63.8 cm)

The William L. Elkins Collection
E1924-3-28

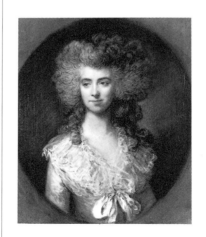

**Gainsborough, Thomas**
*Portrait of a Lady in a Blue Dress*
c. 1783–85
Oil on canvas
30 1/4 × 25" (76.9 × 63.5 cm)

Bequest of George D. Widener
1972-50-1

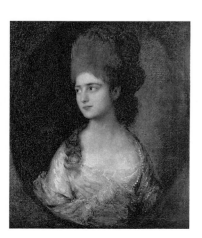

**Gainsborough, Thomas**
*Portrait of Miss Elizabeth Linley*
[later Mrs. Richard Brinsley
Sheridan]
c. 1775
Oil on canvas
30 × 25" (76.2 × 63.5 cm)

The George W. Elkins Collection
E1924-4-13

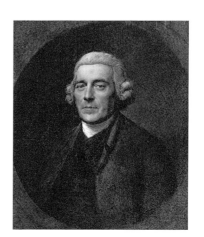

**Gainsborough, Thomas,
attributed to**
Previously listed as Thomas
Gainsborough (JGJ 1941)
*Portrait of George Coyte*
18th century
Oil on canvas
30 1/8 × 25 1/8" (76.5 × 63.8 cm)

John G. Johnson Collection
cat. 833

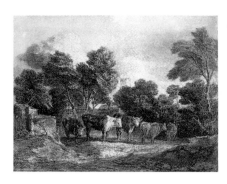

**Gainsborough, Thomas, imitator of**
*Pastoral Landscape*
18th or 19th century
Charcoal, watercolor, and oil on paper on canvas
17 × 21 ³/₄" (43.2 × 55.3 cm)

John G. Johnson Collection
cat. 835

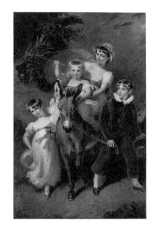

**Harlow, George Henry**
English, 1787–1819
*Portrait of the Leader Children*
1813–14
Oil on canvas
94 ¹/₂ × 58 ¹/₄" (240 × 148 cm)

The John Howard McFadden Collection
M1928-1-11

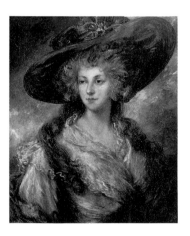

**Gainsborough, Thomas, imitator of**
Previously listed as Gainsborough Dupont (PMA 1965)
*Portrait of a Lady* [possibly Lady Cavendish]
19th century
Oil on canvas
30 × 25 ¹/₈" (76.2 × 63.8 cm)

The Walter Lippincott Collection
1923-59-13

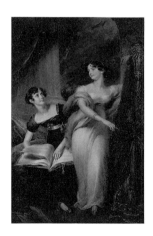

**Harlow, George Henry**
*Portrait of the Misses Leader*
1813–14
Oil on canvas
94 ¹/₄ × 58" (239.4 × 147.3 cm)

The John Howard McFadden Collection
M1928-1-10

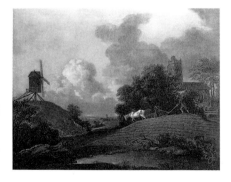

**Gainsborough, Thomas, copy after**
Previously listed as Thomas Gainsborough (JGJ 1941)
*Landscape with a Windmill*
After the painting in the collection of Dr. J. B. Labia, Jersey
18th century
Oil on canvas
23 ¹⁵/₁₆ × 30 ¹/₈" (60.8 × 76.5 cm)

John G. Johnson Collection
cat. 834

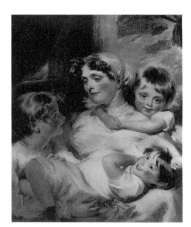

**Harlow, George Henry**
*Portrait of a Mother and Her Children* [possibly Mrs. Weddell]
c. 1816
Oil on canvas
36 × 28 ¹/₄" (91.4 × 71.8 cm)

The John Howard McFadden Collection
M1928-1-12

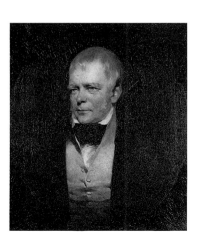

**Gordon, Sir John Watson**
Scottish, 1778–1864
*Portrait of Sir Walter Scott*
c. 1831–35
Oil on canvas
30 × 25" (76.2 × 63.5 cm)

The John Howard McFadden Collection
M1928-1- 42

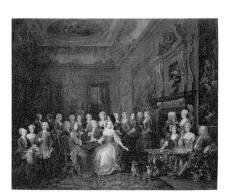

**Hogarth, William**
English, 1697–1764
*Assembly at Wanstead House*
1728–31
Oil on canvas
25 ¹/₂ × 30" (64.8 × 76.2 cm)

The John Howard McFadden Collection
M1928-1-13

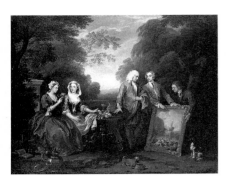

**Hogarth, William**
*Conversation Piece (Portrait of Sir Andrew Fountaine with Other Men and Women)*
c. 1730–35
Oil on canvas
18 3/4 × 23" (47.6 × 58.4 cm)

The John Howard McFadden Collection
M1928-1-14

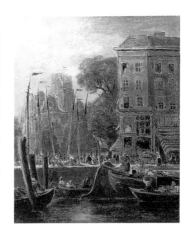

**Holland, James,
attributed to**
Previously listed as James Holland (JGJ 1941)
*View of Delft*
19th century
Oil on fiberboard
14 1/4 × 11 1/16" (36.2 × 28.1 cm)

John G. Johnson Collection
cat. 887

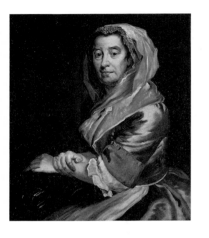

**Hogarth, William,
imitator of**
Previously listed as William Hogarth (JGJ 1941)
*Portrait of a Woman*
18th century
Oil on canvas
29 15/16 × 25 3/16" (76 × 64 cm)

John G. Johnson Collection
cat. 823

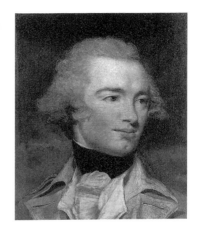

**Hoppner, John,
attributed to**
English, 1758–1810
*Portrait of an Officer*
c. 1795–1800
Oil on canvas
15 3/4 × 13" (40 × 33 cm)

Bequest of Helen S. Fennessy in memory of her stepfather, Horace Trumbauer
1974-161-2

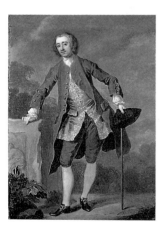

**Hogarth, William,
copy after**
*Portrait of Gustavus Hamilton, 2nd Viscount Boyne*
After the painting in the collection of Viscount Boyne, Burwarton House, Salop
c. 1740
Oil on canvas
21 × 14 5/8" (53.3 × 37.2 cm)

The John D. McIlhenny Collection
1943-40-49

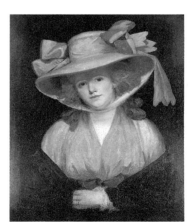

**Hoppner, John, imitator of**
Previously attributed to John Hoppner (PMA 1965)
*Portrait of Mrs. Hoppner*
In the style of c. 1783; probably a copy of an unrecorded picture or an adaptation after the print of Hoppner's *Sophia Western*
c. 1850–1900?
Oil on canvas
30 1/4 × 24 7/8" (76.8 × 63.2 cm)

The John Howard McFadden Collection
M1928-1-15

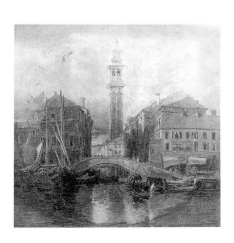

**Holland, James**
English, 1800–1870
*Canal of Venice*
1848
Lower left: The Tower of St. George the Greek / Venice; lower right: James Holland, 1848
Oil and ink on fiberboard
20 1/8 × 20 1/8" (51.1 × 51.1 cm)

John G. Johnson Collection
cat. 886

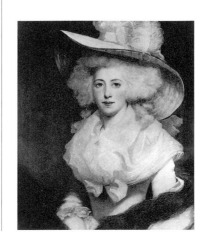

**Hoppner, John, copy after**
Previously listed as John Hoppner (PMA 1965)
*Portrait of Susanna Gyll*
After a lost composition of c. 1779
19th century
On reverse: Susanna Daughter of William Gyll of Wysadsbury. Married 4 Feb. 1779 Thomas Cheadle Sanders Esq[ui]re / Died 7 Sept. 1833 aged 77
Oil on canvas
30 1/8 × 25 1/8" (76.5 × 63.8 cm)

The George W. Elkins Collection
E1924-4-16

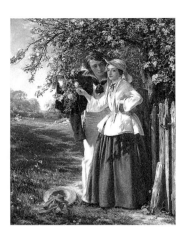

**Horsley, John Calcott**
English, 1817–1903
*Lovers under a Blossom Tree*
By 1859
Oil on canvas
35 1/2 × 27 1/4" (90.2 × 69.2 cm)

The Henry P. McIlhenny
Collection in memory of
Frances P. McIlhenny
1986-26-278

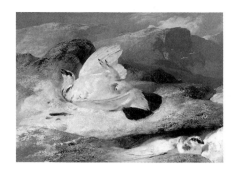

**Landseer, Sir Edwin**
*Ptarmigan in a Landscape*
By 1833
Oil on panel
19 1/2 × 25 3/4" (49.5 × 65.4 cm)

The Henry P. McIlhenny
Collection in memory of
Frances P. McIlhenny
1986-26-280

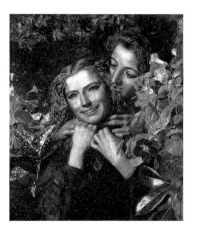

**Houghton, Arthur Boyd**
English, 1836–1875
*The Surprise*
c. 1860
Oil on canvas
9 1/4 × 7 1/2" (23.5 × 19.1 cm)

The Henry P. McIlhenny
Collection in memory of
Frances P. McIlhenny
1986-26-279

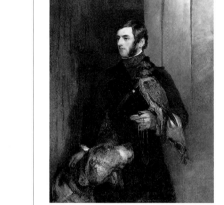

**Landseer, Sir Edwin**
*The Falconer* [possibly a portrait
of William Russell]
1830s
Oil on canvas
54 1/2 × 43 1/2" (138.4 × 110.5 cm)

The Henry P. McIlhenny
Collection in memory of
Frances P. McIlhenny
1986-26-24

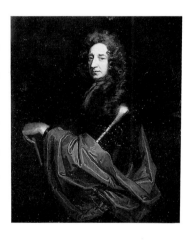

**Kneller, Sir Godfrey**
English, born Germany,
1646–1723
*Portrait of a Soldier*
c. 1690–95
Oil on canvas
49 1/2 × 39 1/2" (125.7 × 100.3 cm)

The William L. Elkins Collection
E1924-3-97

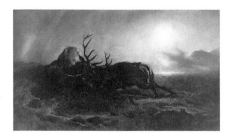

**Landseer, Sir Edwin**
*Night (Two Stags Battling by
Moonlight)*
Pendant to *Morning*
By 1853
Oil on canvas
56 × 103" (142.2 × 261.6 cm)

The Henry P. McIlhenny
Collection in memory of
Frances P. McIlhenny
1986-26-282

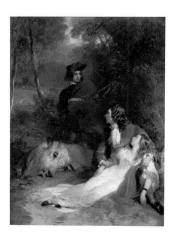

**Landseer, Sir Edwin**
English, 1802–1873
*The Bride of Lammermoor*
By 1830
Oil on panel
12 3/4 × 9 3/4" (32.4 × 24.8 cm)

The Henry P. McIlhenny
Collection in memory of
Frances P. McIlhenny
1986-26-281

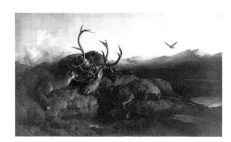

**Landseer, Sir Edwin**
*Morning (Two Dead Stags
and a Fox)*
Pendant to *Night*
By 1853
Oil on canvas
56 × 103" (142.2 × 261.6 cm)

The Henry P. McIlhenny
Collection in memory of
Frances P. McIlhenny
1986-26-283

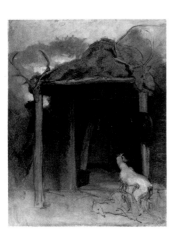

**Landseer, Sir Edwin**
*Duchess of Bedford's Hut, Glenfeshie*
Mid-19th century
Oil on panel
23 1/2 × 17 1/2" (59.7 × 44.5 cm)

The Henry P. McIlhenny
Collection in memory of
Frances P. McIlhenny
1986-26-284

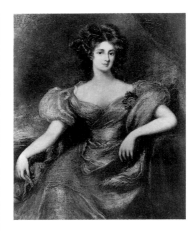

**Lawrence, Sir Thomas,
copy after**
Previously listed as Sir Thomas
Lawrence (PMA 1965)
*Portrait of Lady Harriet Clive*
[later Baroness Windsor]
After the painting, dated c. 1823,
in the collection of the Earl of
Plymouth, Oakley Park, England
19th century
Oil on canvas
49 1/2 × 40 1/2" (125.7 × 102.9 cm)

The Walter Lippincott Collection
1923-59-17

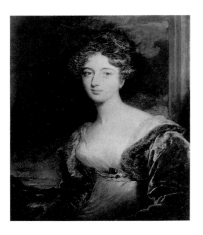

**Lawrence, Sir Thomas**
English, 1769–1830
*Portrait of Mrs. James Fraser of
Castle Fraser*
c. 1817
Oil on canvas
30 1/8 × 25" (76.5 × 63.5 cm)

The George W. Elkins Collection
E1924-4-17

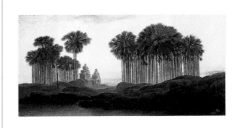

**Lear, Edward**
English, 1812–1888
*Mahabalipooram*
1881
Oil on canvas
9 × 18" (22.9 × 45.7 cm)

The Henry P. McIlhenny
Collection in memory of
Frances P. McIlhenny
1986-26-285

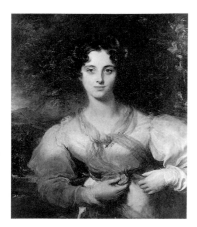

**Lawrence, Sir Thomas**
*Portrait of Harriott West* [later
Mrs. William Woodgate]
c. 1824–25
Oil on canvas
30 1/4 × 25 1/8" (76.8 × 63.8 cm)

The John Howard McFadden
Collection
M1928-1-16

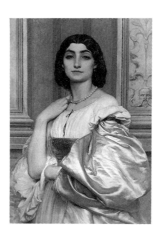

**Leighton, Sir Frederic**
English, 1830–1896
*Portrait of a Roman Lady (La
Nanna)*
1859
Oil on canvas
31 1/2 × 20 1/2" (80 × 52.1 cm)

Purchased with the Henry
Clifford Memorial Fund
1976-34-1

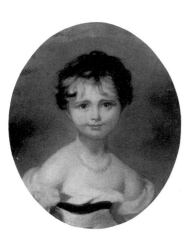

**Lawrence, Sir Thomas,
copy after**
*Portrait of Lady Emily Cowper*
[later Lady Ashley, Countess of
Shaftesbury]
After the painting, dated 1814,
in the collection of the Earl of
Shaftesbury
19th century
Oil on canvas
21 1/8 × 16 7/8" (53.7 × 42.9 cm)

Bequest of Lisa Norris Elkins
1950-92-8

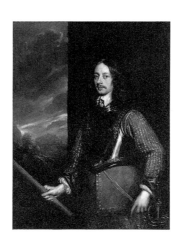

**Lely, Sir Peter
(Pieter van der Faes)**
English, active Netherlands,
1618–1680
*Portrait of James Butler, 12th Earl
and 1st Duke of Ormonde*
1647
Oil on canvas
47 7/8 × 36 1/2" (121.6 × 92.7 cm)

Bequest of Arthur H. Lea
F1938-1-3

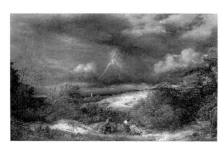

**Linnell, John**
English, 1792–1882
*The Storm (The Refuge)*
1853
Lower right: J. Linnell, 1853
Oil on canvas
35 1/2 × 57 1/2" (90.2 × 146.1 cm)

The John Howard McFadden
Collection
M1928-1-17

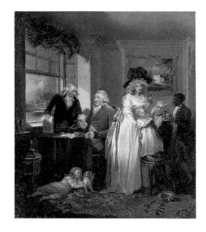

**Morland, George**
English, 1763–1804
*Fruits of Early Industry and Economy*
Pendant to Morland's *Effects of Youthful Extravagance and Idleness*, 1789, location unknown
1789
Oil on canvas
30 1/4 × 25 1/8" (76.8 × 63.8 cm)

The John Howard McFadden
Collection
M1928-1-19

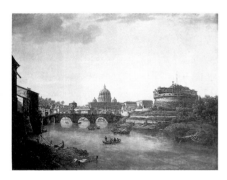

**Marlow, William**
English, 1740–1813
*View of Rome from the Tiber*
c. 1775
Lower left: W. Marlow
Oil on canvas
40 × 50 1/8" (101.6 × 127.3 cm)

Gift of Jay Cooke
1955-2-4

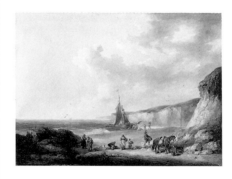

**Morland, George**
*Coast Scene with Smugglers*
1790
Lower right: G. Morland Pinx'
1790
Oil on canvas on panel
38 1/4 × 50 1/2" (97.2 × 128.3 cm)

Gift of Mrs. Edward Browning
1947-99-1

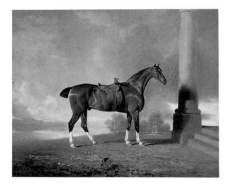

**Marshall, Benjamin**
English, 1768–1835
*Favorite Chestnut Hunter of Lady Frances Stephens [née Lady Frances Pierrepont]*
1799
Lower right: B. Marshall pt.
1799; on label on reverse: The favourite hunter of Lady Frances Stephens, / daughter of the first Lord Manvers, / painted for the family by Ben Marshall 1799
Oil on canvas
24 5/8 × 29 1/2" (62.6 × 74.9 cm)

Centennial gift of Mr. and Mrs.
Charles H. Norris
1977-44-1

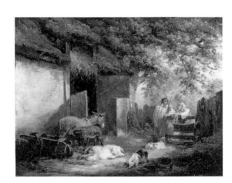

**Morland, George**
*Farmyard*
1790 or 1791
Center right: G Morland
Oil on canvas
28 × 36" (71.1 × 91.4 cm)

Gift of Mrs. Gordon A. Hardwick
and Mrs. W. Newbold Ely in
memory of Mr. and Mrs.
Roland L. Taylor
1944-9-1

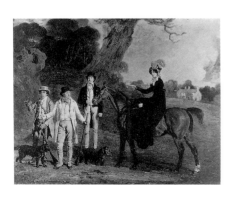

**Marshall, Benjamin**
*Portrait of the Weston Family*
1818
Lower right: B. Marshall / 1818
Oil on canvas
39 7/8 × 50 1/4" (101.3 × 127.6 cm)

Gift of Diana Kendall, Alexandra
Dewey, Linda Jones, and Sheila
Neville in memory of their
grandfather, George D. Widener
1978-40-1

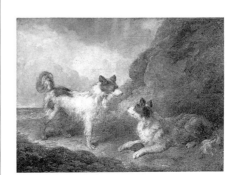

**Morland, George**
*Two Terriers*
c. 1790–91
Oil on canvas
18 × 23 7/8" (45.7 × 60.6 cm)

John G. Johnson Collection
cat. 846

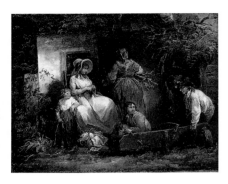

**Morland, George**
*The Happy Cottagers (The Cottage Door)*
A larger version is in the Bass Museum of Art, Miami Beach
c. 1790–92
Oil on canvas
14 1/2 × 18 1/2" (36.8 × 47 cm)

The John Howard McFadden Collection
M1928-1-20

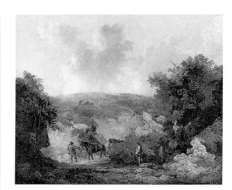

**Morland, George, attributed to**
Previously listed as George Morland (JGJ 1941)
*The Lane*
Early 19th century
Oil on canvas
10 1/4 × 12 3/16" (26 × 31 cm)

John G. Johnson Collection
cat. 845

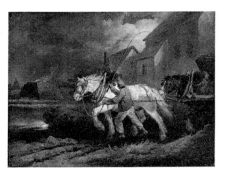

**Morland, George**
*The Carter*
1791
Center right: G. Morland / pinx
Oil on canvas
16 1/16 × 20 9/16" (40.8 × 52.2 cm)

John G. Johnson Collection
cat. 844

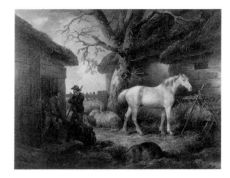

**Morland, George, imitator of**
Previously listed as George Morland (PMA 1965)
*Interior of a Farm*
Early 19th century
Lower left (spurious): G. Morland Pinx.
Oil on canvas
28 × 36 1/4" (71.1 × 92.1 cm)

The William L. Elkins Collection
E1924-3-33

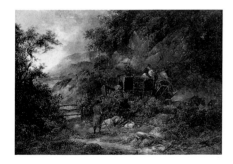

**Morland, George**
*The Stagecoach*
1791
Lower left: G. Morland Pinx. / October 3[?]. 1791
Oil on canvas
34 1/2 × 46 1/2" (87.6 × 118.1 cm)

The John Howard McFadden Collection
M1928-1-18

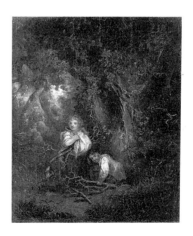

**Morland, George, copy after**
Previously listed as George Morland (PMA 1965)
*Gathering Wood*
After a lost painting dated 1791
After 1791
Lower right (spurious): G. Morland 1795
Oil on canvas
15 1/4 × 12 1/2" (38.7 × 31.8 cm)

The William L. Elkins Collection
E1924-3-44

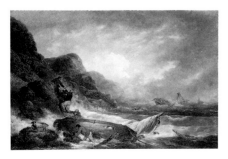

**Morland, George**
*Shipwreck*
1793
Center bottom: G. Morland
Oil on canvas
38 1/8 × 57" (96.8 × 144.8 cm)

The William L. Elkins Collection
E1924-3-98

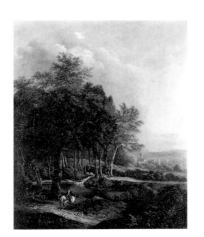

**Nasmyth, Peter**
Scottish, 1787–1831
*View of Lambeth*
Early 19th century
Lower left: P. N.
Oil on canvas
28 9/16 × 23 1/8" (72.6 × 58.7 cm)

John G. Johnson Collection
cat. 880

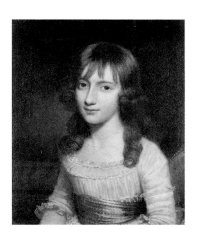

**Opie, John**
English, 1761–1807
Previously attributed to John
Opie (PMA 1965)
*Portrait of Anne Westcott* [later
Mrs. Frederick Waller]
By 1799
Oil on canvas
21 1/8 × 17 1/8" (53.7 × 43.5 cm)

Gift of John S. Williams
1947-100-2

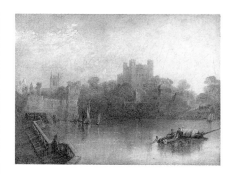

**Pyne, James Baker,
attributed to**
English, 1800–1870
Previously listed as James Baker
Pyne (JGJ 1941)
*Rochester*
19th century
Oil on canvas
9 × 12 1/4" (22.9 × 31.1 cm)

John G. Johnson Collection
cat. 881

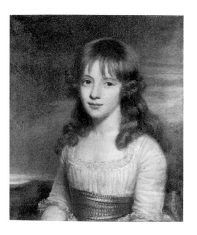

**Opie, John**
Previously attributed to John
Opie (PMA 1965)
*Portrait of Mary Westcott* [later
Mrs. Benjamin Waller]
By 1799
Oil on canvas
21 1/8 × 17 5/8" (53.7 × 44.8 cm)

Gift of John S. Williams
1947-100-1

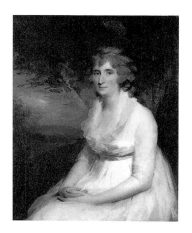

**Raeburn, Sir Henry**
Scottish, 1756–1823
*Portrait of a Woman* [possibly Mrs.
William Stewart of Summer
Bank]
c. 1790
Oil on canvas
35 7/8 × 27 1/8" (91.1 × 68.9 cm)

Bequest of George D. Widener
1972-50-3

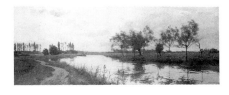

**Parsons, Alfred**
English, 1847–1920
*River and Towpath*
1883
Lower right: ALFRED PARSONS.
1883.
Oil on canvas
24 3/8 × 60 3/8" (61.9 × 153.4 cm)

John G. Johnson Collection
cat. 1054

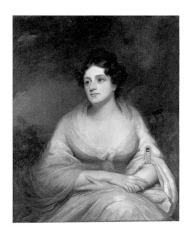

**Raeburn, Sir Henry**
Previously attributed to Sir
Henry Raeburn (PMA 1965)
*Portrait of Lady Belhaven*
Another version is in the New York
Public Library
c. 1790
On reverse: Raeburn [?] C. J.
Raeburn / L. W. Raeburn /
Painted by my Grandfather, Sir
Henry Raeburn
Oil on canvas
36 1/8 × 27 7/8" (91.8 × 70.8 cm)

The John Howard McFadden
Collection
M1928-1-21

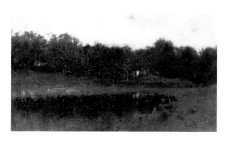

**Paterson, James**
Scottish, 1854–1932
*Landscape*
1890
Lower right: James Paterson. /
Monsoire. 1890.
Oil on canvas
18 1/16 × 30 1/16" (45.9 × 76.4 cm)

John G. Johnson Collection
cat. 1058

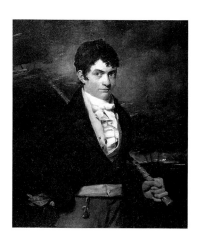

**Raeburn, Sir Henry**
*Portrait of Charles Christie, Esq.*
c. 1800
Oil on canvas
30 1/2 × 25 1/2" (77.5 × 64.8 cm)

The John Howard McFadden
Collection
M1928-1-25

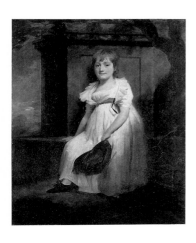

**Raeburn, Sir Henry**
*Portrait of Master John Campbell of Saddell*
c. 1800
Oil on canvas
49 1/4 × 39 3/8" (125.1 × 100 cm)

The John Howard McFadden Collection
M1928-1-24

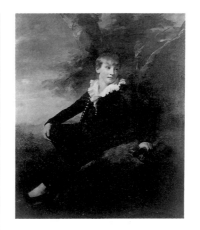

**Raeburn, Sir Henry**
*Portrait of Master Thomas Bissland*
c. 1809
Oil on canvas
56 1/2 × 44 3/8" (143.5 × 112.7 cm)

The John Howard McFadden Collection
M1928-1-23

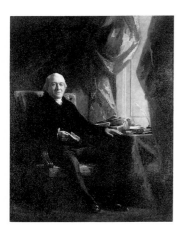

**Raeburn, Sir Henry**
*Portrait of William MacDonald of Saint Martin's*
An earlier version, documented in 1803, is in the collection of the Royal Highland and Agricultural Society of Scotland, Edinburgh
c. 1803
Oil on canvas
78 × 60" (198.1 × 152.4 cm)

Purchased with the W. P. Wilstach Fund
W1895-1-9

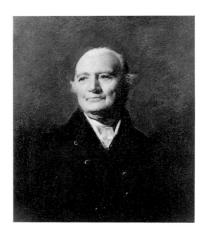

**Raeburn, Sir Henry**
*Portrait of Alexander Shaw*
c. 1810–15
Oil on canvas
30 × 25 1/8" (76.2 × 63.8 cm)

The John Howard McFadden Collection
M1928-1-27

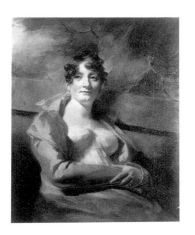

**Raeburn, Sir Henry**
*Portrait of Lady Elibank*
c. 1805
Oil on canvas
36 × 28" (91.4 × 71.1 cm)

The John Howard McFadden Collection
M1928-1-22

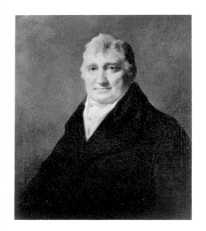

**Raeburn, Sir Henry**
*Portrait of Walter Kennedy Lawrie of Woodhall, Laurieston*
c. 1815
Oil on canvas
30 × 25" (76.2 × 63.5 cm)

The John Howard McFadden Collection
M1928-1-26

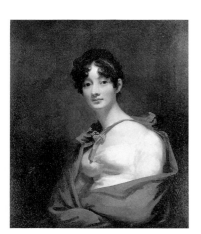

**Raeburn, Sir Henry**
*Portrait of Ellen Cochrane*
c. 1808
Oil on canvas
30 1/8 × 25 1/8" (76.5 × 63.8 cm)

Gift of Mr. and Mrs. John Howard McFadden, Jr.
1952-97-1

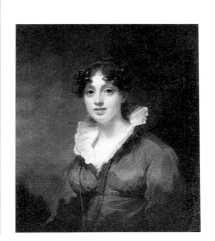

**Raeburn, Sir Henry**
*Portrait of Jane Anne Catharine Fraser of Reelig*
1816
On reverse, covered by relining: Jane Anne Catharine Fraser of Reelick Aet: 19 / Raeburn pinx. 1816
Oil on canvas
30 1/8 × 25 3/4" (76.5 × 65.4 cm)

Gift of Mr. and Mrs. Wharton Sinkler
1963-171-1

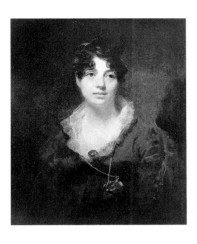

**Raeburn, Sir Henry**
*Portrait of Mrs. John McCall of Ibroxhill*
c. 1820
Oil on canvas
30 × 25" (76.2 × 63.5 cm)

The George W. Elkins Collection
E1924-4-23

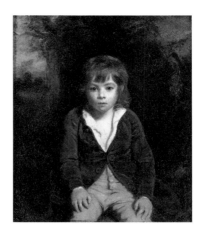

**Reynolds, Sir Joshua**
*Portrait of Master Bunbury*
1780 or 1781
Oil on canvas
30 ⅛ × 25 ⅛" (76.5 × 63.8 cm)

The John Howard McFadden Collection
M1928-1-29

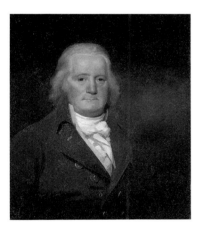

**Raeburn, Sir Henry, follower of**
Previously attributed to Sir Henry Raeburn (PMA 1965)
*Portrait of a Gentleman*
19th century
Oil on canvas
29 ¾ × 25 ¼" (75.6 × 64.1 cm)

The John Howard McFadden Collection
M1928-1-28

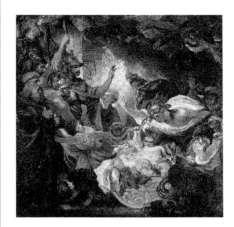

**Reynolds, Sir Joshua, attributed to**
Previously listed as Sir Joshua Reynolds (JGJ 1941)
*Infant Hercules Strangling the Serpents*
Possibly after the large version in the Hermitage, St. Petersburg (inv. no. 6745)
18th century
Oil on paper on canvas
23 ⅞ × 23 ¾" (60.6 × 60.3 cm)

John G. Johnson Collection
cat. 831

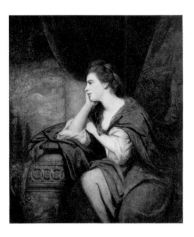

**Reynolds, Sir Joshua**
English, 1723–1792
*Portrait of Lady Mary O'Brien*
[later 3rd Countess of Orkney]
c. 1772
Oil on canvas
50 × 40 ⅛" (127 × 101.9 cm)

Gift of Mr. and Mrs. William H. Donner
1948-95-1

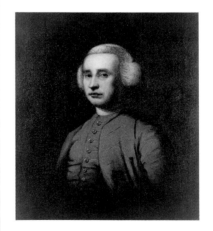

**Reynolds, Sir Joshua, follower of**
Previously attributed to Sir Joshua Reynolds (PMA 1965)
*Portrait of the Right Honorable Edmund Burke*
c. 1756–60
Oil on canvas
30 ⅛ × 25" (76.5 × 63.5 cm)

The John Howard McFadden Collection
M1928-1-30

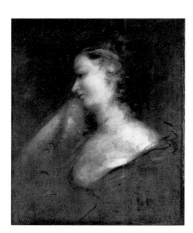

**Reynolds, Sir Joshua**
*Portrait of a Lady*
c. 1780
Oil on canvas
24 ½ × 20" (62.2 × 50.8 cm)

The John D. McIlhenny Collection
1943-40-40

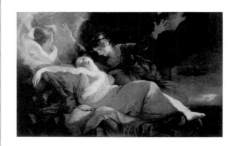

**Reynolds, Sir Joshua, copy after**
*The Death of Dido*
After the painting, dated 1781, in the collection of Her Majesty Queen Elizabeth II (1029)
c. 1781
Oil on canvas
58 ¼ × 94 ⅝" (148 × 240.3 cm)

The William L. Elkins Collection
E1924-3-18

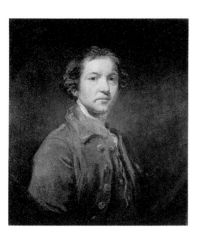

**Reynolds, Sir Joshua,
copy after**
*Portrait of Sir Joshua Reynolds*
After the self-portrait in the Tate
Gallery, London (N 889)
c. 1820
Oil on canvas
30 3/16 × 25 1/4" (76.7 × 64.1 cm)

John G. Johnson Collection
cat. 827

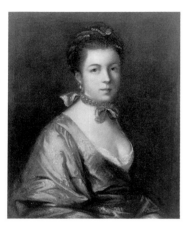

**Reynolds, Sir Joshua,
copy after**
Previously attributed to Sir
Joshua Reynolds (PMA 1965)
*Portrait of Lady Monnoux [née
Elizabeth Riddell]*
After the painting sold at
Christie's, March 28, 1952
(lot 53)
After c. 1860
Oil on canvas
29 7/8 × 24 7/8" (75.9 × 63.2 cm)

The George W. Elkins Collection
E1924-4-24

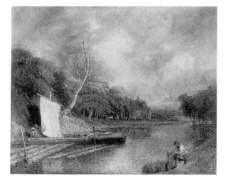

**Reynolds, Samuel William,
attributed to**
English, 1773–1835
*Fisherman*
19th century
Oil on canvas
20 1/16 × 23 7/8" (51 × 60.6 cm)

John G. Johnson Collection
cat. 847

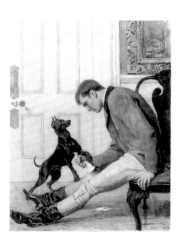

**Riviere, Briton**
English, 1840–1920
*Jilted*
1887
Lower right: [Signed with
monogram and dated 1887]
Oil on canvas
30 1/2 × 23" (77.5 × 58.4 cm)

Gift of Muriel and Philip Berman
1989-70-6

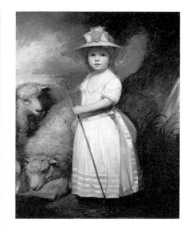

**Romney, George**
English, 1734–1802
*Shepherd Girl (Little Bo-Peep)*
c. 1778
Oil on canvas
46 1/2 × 35 1/2" (118.1 × 90.2 cm)

The John Howard McFadden
Collection
M1928-1-38

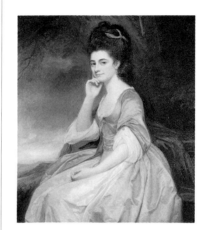

**Romney, George**
*Portrait of Lady Grantham*
1780–81
Lower right: Mary Jemima 2nd /
Daughter Marchioness Grey / and
Wife of Thomas Lord Grantham
Oil on canvas
46 1/2 × 39" (118.1 × 99.1 cm)

The John Howard McFadden
Collection
M1928-1-36

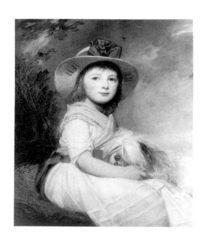

**Romney, George**
*Portrait of Marianne Holbech*
1781–82
On label on reverse: 1781–82, /
Sometime in 1782 Romney
painted the portrait of Mary
Anne Holbech / (afterwards Lady
Mordaunt) / — who was born
1777. See entry in her father's
account — "1782 / Oct: 21
Romney for Mary Anne's picture
£ 21.8.6. / It was paid for, being
sent home / 10 Oct. / CWH"
Oil on canvas
30 × 25" (76.2 × 63.5 cm)

The George W. Elkins Collection
E1924-4-25

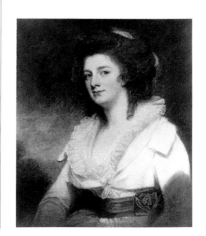

**Romney, George**
*Portrait of the Honorable Mrs.
Beresford*
c. 1785
Oil on canvas
30 1/8 × 24 3/4" (76.5 × 62.9 cm)

The George W. Elkins Collection
E1924-4-26

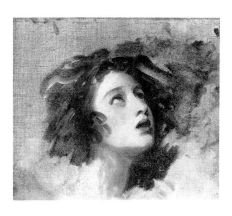

**Romney, George**
*Portrait of Emma Hart as Miranda*
[later Lady Hamilton]
1785 or 1786
Oil on canvas
14 1/8 × 15 1/2" (35.9 × 39.4 cm)

The John Howard McFadden
Collection
M1928-1-34

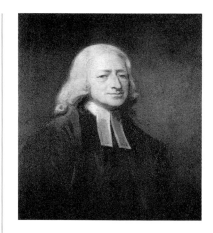

**Romney, George**
*Portrait of John Wesley*
1788–89
Oil on canvas
30 × 25" (76.2 × 63.5 cm)

The John Howard McFadden
Collection
M1928-1-37

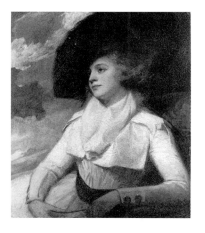

**Romney, George**
*Portrait of a Lady*
c. 1786
Oil on canvas
30 1/8 × 25 1/4" (76.5 × 64.1 cm)

Bequest of George D. Widener
1972-50-2

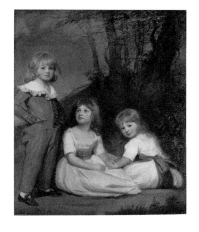

**Romney, George**
*Portrait of Mr. Adye's Children*
*(The Willett Children)*
1789–90
Oil on canvas
60 × 48" (152.4 × 121.9 cm)

The George W. Elkins Collection
E1924-4-27

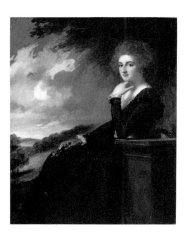

**Romney, George**
*Portrait of Mrs. Champion de*
*Crespigny* [née Dorothy Scott]
1786–90
Oil on canvas
51 1/8 × 40" (129.9 × 101.6 cm)

The John Howard McFadden
Collection
M1928-1-32

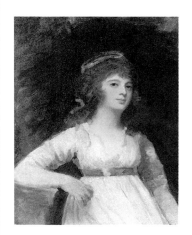

**Romney, George**
*Portrait of Mrs. Finch*
1790
Oil on canvas
35 7/8 × 27 3/4" (91.1 × 70.5 cm)

The John Howard McFadden
Collection
M1928-1-33

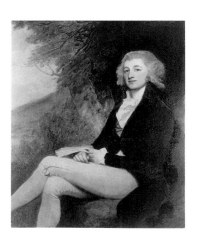

**Romney, George**
*Portrait of Sir John Reade*
1788
Oil on canvas
50 × 39 7/8" (127 × 101.3 cm)

The William L. Elkins Collection
E1924-3-19

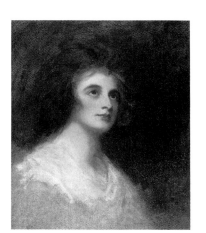

**Romney, George**
*Portrait of Mrs. Tickell*
1791 or 1792
Oil on canvas
24 × 20 1/8" (61 × 51.1 cm)

The John Howard McFadden
Collection
M1928-1-35

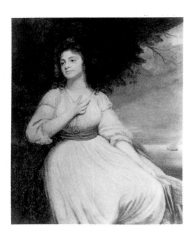

**Romney, George**
*Portrait of Mrs. Crouch*
The original version, dated 1787,
is in the Iveagh Bequest,
Kenwood, London (34)
c. 1793
Lower right, on musical score:
[Hus]h Ev'ry Breeze let /
[nothi]ng [or:] [su]ng by Mrs.
Crouch / composed by Hook /
Andantino Hush ev'ry breeze let
nothing
Oil on canvas
50 1/4 × 39 1/2" (127.6 × 100.3 cm)

The John Howard McFadden
Collection
M1928-1-31

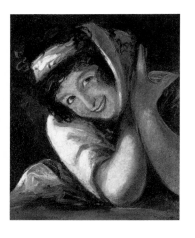

**Romney, George,
copy after**
Previously listed as George
Romney (JGJ 1941)
*Portrait of Lady Hamilton as a
Bacchante*
After the painting in the Tate
Gallery, London (N 00312),
known through numerous
engravings
19th century
Oil on canvas
22 3/16 × 18" (56.4 × 45.7 cm)

John G. Johnson Collection
cat. 837

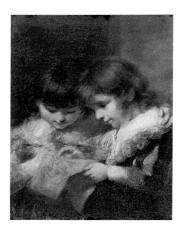

**Russell, William**
English, 1784–1870
Previously listed as John Russell
(PMA 1965)
*Young Artists (Portrait of William
and Thomas Russell)*
After a lost pastel by John Russell
(English, 1745–1806)
After 1793
Oil on canvas
24 × 18" (61 × 45.7 cm)

Gift of John S. Williams
1947-100-3

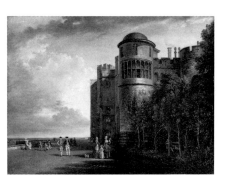

**Sandby, Paul**
English, 1730–1809
*The North Terrace at Windsor
Castle, Looking East*
c. 1775–80
Oil on canvas
39 3/4 × 50" (101 × 127 cm)

Gift of John Howard McFadden, Jr.
1951-125-18

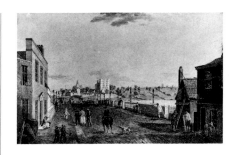

**Scott, Samuel, follower of**
English, c. 1702–1772
Previously listed as Samuel Scott
(PMA 1965)
*Old Rochester Bridge*
c. 1732–40
Oil on canvas
22 5/8 × 34 5/8" (57.5 × 88 cm)

Purchased with the W. P.
Wilstach Fund
W1906-1-5

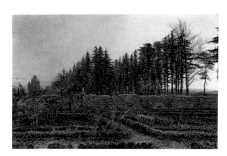

**Scott, William Bell**
Scottish, 1811–1890
*The Gloaming (Manse Garden,
Berwickshire)*
1863
Lower left: WB Scott 1863
Oil on canvas
16 × 24" (40.6 × 61 cm)

Purchased with the John Howard
McFadden, Jr., Fund
1971-164-1

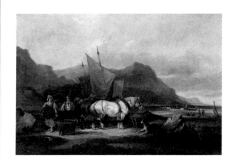

**Shayer, William, Sr.**
English, 1781–1879
Previously listed as George
Morland (PMA 1965)
*Fishing Scene*
c. 1850?
Lower left (spurious): G.
Morland Pinx / 1797
Oil on canvas
26 × 36 1/8" (66 × 91.8 cm)

The Walter Lippincott Collection
1923-59-11

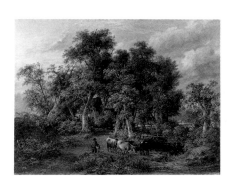

**Stark, James**
English, 1794–1859
*Landscape with Cattle*
c. 1820–30
Oil on panel
16 1/2 × 21 7/8" (41.9 × 55.6 cm)

The John Howard McFadden
Collection
M1928-1-39

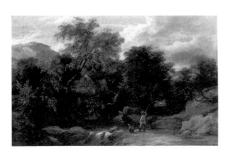

**Stark, James**
*Millstream, Norfolk*
c. 1830–40
Oil on panel
19 3/4 × 29 7/8" (50.2 × 75.9 cm)

The William L. Elkins Collection
E1924-3-46

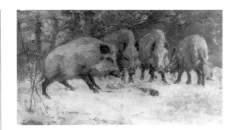

**Swan, John MacAllan**
English, 1847–1910
*Wild Boars*
1879
Lower left: J. M. SWAN. 1879
Oil on panel
4 7/8 × 8 3/8" (12.4 × 21.3 cm)

John G. Johnson Collection
cat. 1086

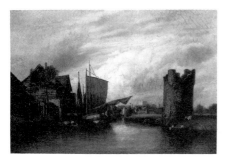

**Stark, James, copy after**
Previously listed as James Stark
(PMA 1965)
*The Devil's Tower*
After 1831
Lower left: J. Stark
Oil on canvas
19 1/4 × 26 1/4" (48.9 × 66.7 cm)

The William L. Elkins Collection
E1924-3-45

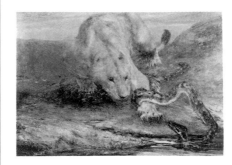

**Swan, John MacAllan**
*A Lioness and a Snake*
Before 1889
Lower left: JOHN. M. SWAN
Oil on canvas
24 1/2 × 34 1/2" (62.2 × 87.6 cm)

John G. Johnson Collection
cat. 1089

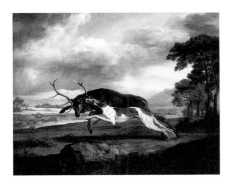

**Stubbs, George**
English, 1724–1806
*Hound Coursing a Stag*
c. 1762
Lower right: Geo. Stubbs / pinx
Oil on canvas
39 3/8 × 49 1/2" (100 × 125.7 cm)

Purchased with the W. P.
Wilstach Fund, the John D.
McIlhenny Fund, and gifts (by
exchange) of Samuel S. White
3rd and Vera White, Mrs. R.
Barclay Scull, and Edna M. Welsh
W1984-57-1

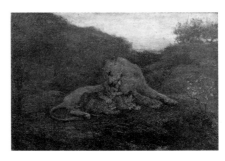

**Swan, John MacAllan**
*A Lioness and Cubs*
c. 1890
Lower left: J. M. Swan
Oil on canvas
17 1/8 × 24 1/2" (43.5 × 62.2 cm)

The William L. Elkins Collection
E1924-3-65

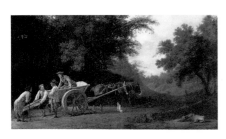

**Stubbs, George**
*Laborers Loading a Brick Cart*
1767
Lower right: Geo: Stubbs / 1767
Oil on canvas
24 × 42" (61 × 106.7 cm)

The John Howard McFadden
Collection
M1928-1-40

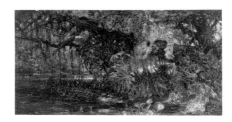

**Swan, John MacAllan**
*Jaguars and a Crocodile*
1891
Lower left: JOHN. M. SWAN. 1891.
Oil on canvas
18 × 35 3/8" (45.7 × 89.9 cm)

John G. Johnson Collection
cat. 1088

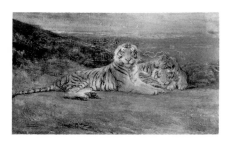

**Swan, John MacAllan**
*Tigers*
Before 1893
Lower left: J. M. SWAN
Oil on canvas
16 3/4 × 27 15/16" (42.6 × 71 cm)

John G. Johnson Collection
cat. 1087

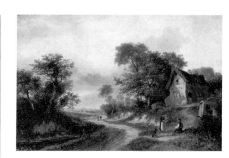

**Vincent, George**
English, 1796–1831
*Cottage on the Roadside*
1831
Lower right: GV 1831
Oil on panel
8 3/4 × 13" (22.2 × 33 cm)

John G. Johnson Collection
cat. 879

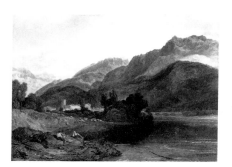

**Swan, John MacAllan**
*In Ambush*
1894
Lower left: John M. Swan / 1894
Oil on canvas
32 1/4 × 52 1/8" (81.9 × 132.4 cm)

The William L. Elkins Collection
E1924-3-81

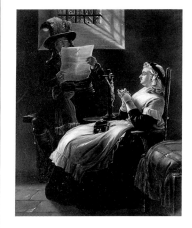

**Ward, Edward Matthew,
copy after**
English, 1816–1879
*Marie Antoinette Listening to the
Act of Accusation, the Day before Her
Trial*
19th century
Lower left: J. M. Baudy
Oil on canvas
36 7/8 × 29 5/8" (93.7 × 75.2 cm)

Bequest of Katherine E. Sheafer
1971-272-1

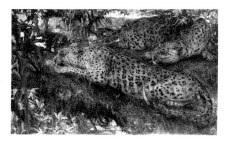

**Turner, Joseph Mallord
William**
English, 1775–1851
*Bonneville, Savoy*
c. 1812
Oil on canvas
36 9/16 × 48 3/4" (92.9 × 123.8 cm)

John G. Johnson Collection
cat. 848

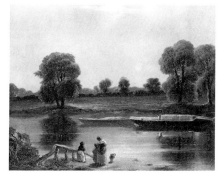

**Watts, Frederick William**
English, 1800–1862
*Landscape with a River and Boats*
1840
Lower left: F. Watts Pintx 1840
Oil on canvas
25 3/8 × 30 3/8" (64.5 × 77.2 cm)

The William L. Elkins Collection
E1924-3-41

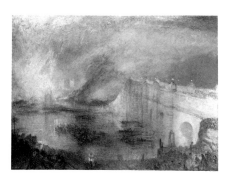

**Turner, Joseph Mallord
William**
*The Burning of the Houses of Lords
and Commons, October 16, 1834*
1834 or 1835
Oil on canvas
36 1/4 × 48 1/2" (92.1 × 123.2 cm)

The John Howard McFadden
Collection
M1928-1-41

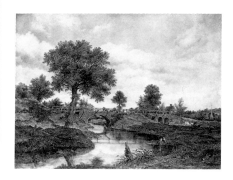

**Watts, William**
English, 1752–1851
*Suffolk Landscape*
Early 19th century
Oil on canvas
34 1/2 × 45 5/8" (87.6 × 115.9 cm)

John G. Johnson Collection
cat. 874

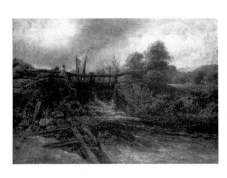

**Watts, William,
attributed to**
Previously listed as William
Watts (JGJ 1941)
*Lock*
19th century
Oil on canvas
24 1/16 × 32" (61.1 × 81.3 cm)

John G. Johnson Collection
cat. 875

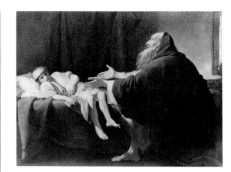

**West, Benjamin**
*Elijah Raising the Widow's Son*
1774, retouched 1819
Center right: Benjamin West
1774 / Retouched 1819
Oil on canvas
64 5/8 × 82 5/8" (164.1 × 209.9 cm)

The Bloomfield Moore Collection
1899-1106

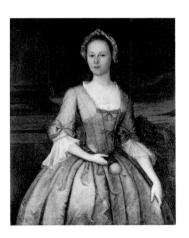

**West, Benjamin**
English, born America,
1738–1820
*Portrait of Miss Mary Keen*
By 1767
Oil on canvas
41 × 32" (104.1 × 81.3 cm)

Gift of Caleb W. Hornor
1956-39-2

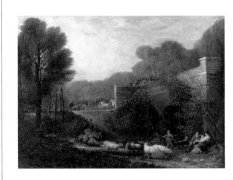

**West, Benjamin**
*Landscape with a Coaching Party*
1791, retouched 1801
Right center: B. West 1791 /
retouched 1801
Oil on canvas
28 × 36" (71.1 × 91.4 cm)

Gift of Mrs. Craig W. Muckle
1991-182-1

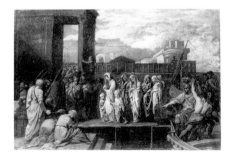

**West, Benjamin**
*Sketch for "Agrippina Landing at
Brundisium with the Ashes of
Germanicus"*
For the following painting
c. 1767
Lower left: B. West / 1766.
Oil on paper on canvas on panel
13 3/8 × 18 7/8" (34 × 47.9 cm)

Gift of the Robert L. McNeil, Jr.,
Trusts
1965-49-1

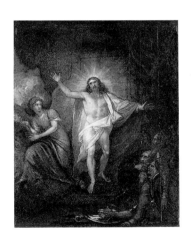

**West, Benjamin**
*The Resurrection*
c. 1808
Oil on slate
15 3/4 × 12 1/16" (40 × 30.6 cm)

Gift of Mr. and Mrs. D. Clifford
Ruth
1967-195-1

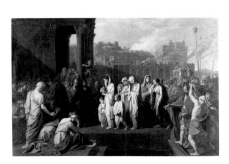

**West, Benjamin**
*Agrippina Landing at Brundisium
with the Ashes of Germanicus*
1770
Center bottom: B. West PINXIT. /
1770.
Oil on canvas
65 × 94" (165.1 × 238.8 cm)

Purchased with the George W.
Elkins Fund
E1972-1-1

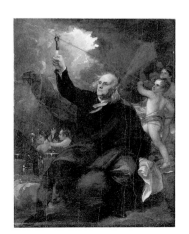

**West, Benjamin**
*Benjamin Franklin Drawing
Electricity from the Sky*
c. 1816
Oil on slate
13 3/8 × 10 1/16" (34 × 25.6 cm)

Gift of Mr. and Mrs. Wharton
Sinkler
1958-132-1

29

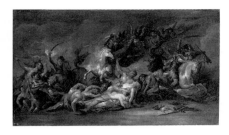

**West, Benjamin, copy after**
Previously listed as Benjamin
West (PMA 1965)
*Death on the Pale Horse*
After the painting in the
Pennsylvania Academy of the
Fine Arts, Philadelphia
Before 1829
Oil on canvas
21 × 36" (53.3 × 91.4 cm)

Gift of Theodora Kimball
Hubbard in memory of Edwin
Fiske Kimball
1928-112-1

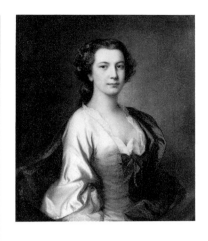

**Wilson, Benjamin,
attributed to**
English, 1721–1788
*Portrait of a Lady*
c. 1745–50
Oil on canvas
29 7/8 × 25" (75.9 × 63.5 cm)

Gift of Sol M. Flock
1966-121-1

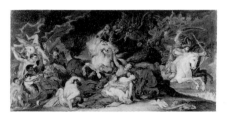

**West, Benjamin, copy after**
Previously listed as Benjamin
West (PMA 1965)
*Death on the Pale Horse*
After the painting in the
Pennsylvania Academy of the
Fine Arts, Philadelphia
19th century
Oil on paper on panel
11 1/4 × 22 1/2" (28.6 × 57.2 cm)

Purchased with the John D.
McIlhenny Fund
1938-11-1

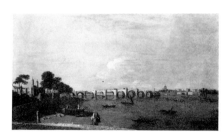

**Wilson, Richard**
Welsh, 1713–1782
*The Thames, Westminster Bridge
under Construction*
1745
Lower left: R. Wilson / 1745
Oil on canvas
32 1/8 × 54" (81.6 × 137.2 cm)

The John Howard McFadden
Collection
M1928-1-43

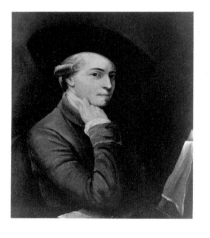

**West, Benjamin, copy after**
*Portrait of Benjamin West*
After the self-portrait in the
National Gallery of Art,
Washington, D.C. (592)
19th century
Oil on canvas
30 × 24 7/8" (76.2 × 63.2 cm)

Gift of Miss Lena Cadwalader
Evans
1935-28-1

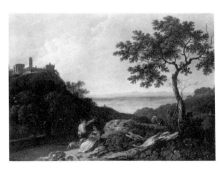

**Wilson, Richard**
Previously listed as an
18th-century copy after Richard
Wilson (PMA 1965)
*Tivoli: Temple of the Sibyl and the
Campagna I*
c. 1760–65
Center bottom: RW
Oil on canvas
25 × 33 1/8" (63.5 × 84.1 cm)

The William L. Elkins Collection
E1924-3-47

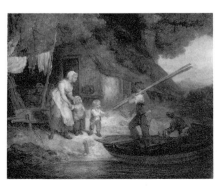

**Wheatley, Francis**
English, 1747–1801
*The Fisherman's Return*
c. 1790
Lower right: F. Wheatley Pinxt
1790
Oil on canvas
18 × 22 1/8" (45.7 × 56.2 cm)

The William L. Elkins Collection
E1924-3-85

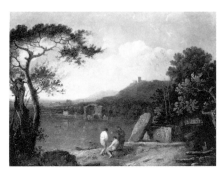

**Wilson, Richard**
Previously listed as an
18th-century copy after Richard
Wilson (PMA 1965)
*Lake Avernus I*
c. 1765
Oil on canvas
27 3/4 × 35 1/4" (70.5 × 89.5 cm)

The William L. Elkins Collection
E1924-3-39

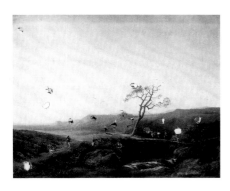

**Wilson, Richard, follower of**
*Landscape with a Horse*
Late 18th century
Lower right: Maninus
Oil on canvas
21 1/2 × 25 1/2" (54.6 × 64.8 cm)

Bequest of Arthur H. Lea
F1938-1-13

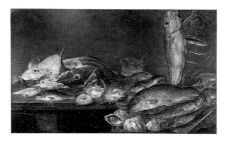

**Adriaenssen, Alexander**
Flemish, active Antwerp,
1587–1661
*Still Life with Fish and Oysters*
1649
Lower left: Alex Adriaenssen
Fecit Ao 1649
Oil on panel
17 1/4 × 27 3/4" (43.8 × 70.5 cm)

John G. Johnson Collection
cat. 646

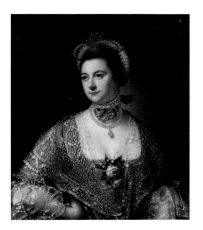

**Wright, Joseph, also called
Joseph Wright of Derby**
English, 1734–1797
*Portrait of Mrs. Andrew Lindington*
c. 1761–63
Oil on canvas
30 × 24 1/8" (76.2 × 61.3 cm)

Gift of Mr. and Mrs. Henry W.
Breyer, Jr.
1968-73-1

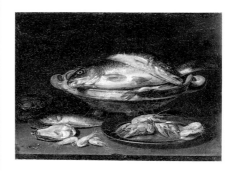

**Adriaenssen, Alexander,
attributed to**
*Still Life with Fish and Shellfish*
17th century
Center bottom: II
Oil on canvas
13 7/8 × 19" (35.2 × 48.3 cm)

John G. Johnson Collection
cat. 647

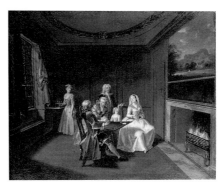

**Aken, Joseph van,
also called Joseph Haecken,
attributed to**
Flemish, active London,
1709–1749
Previously attributed to William
Hogarth (JGJ 1941)
*Conversation Piece (Winter)*
Before 1750
Oil on panel
25 1/8 × 30 3/16" (63.8 × 76.7 cm)

John G. Johnson Collection
cat. 822

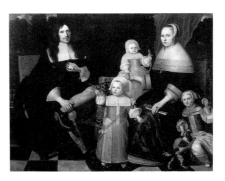

**Aldewerelt, Hermanus van**
Dutch, active Amsterdam,
1628/29–1669
*Family Portrait Group*
1664
Center top: H.V. Alde
[cryptogram] f 1664
Oil on canvas
61 × 77 1/2" (154.9 × 196.8 cm)

Gift of Mrs. Al Paul Lefton
1972-264-1

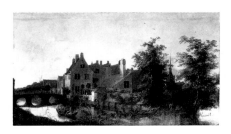

**Asch, Pieter Jansz. van**
Dutch, active Delft, 1603–1678
Previously listed as a Dutch
artist, c. 1650 (JFD 1972)
*Houses beside a Canal*
c. 1650
Oil on canvas
40 1/16 × 69 3/4" (101.8 × 177.2 cm)

John G. Johnson Collection
cat. 503

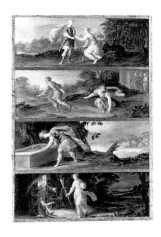

**Balen, Hendrik van,
the Elder**
Flemish, active Antwerp,
1575–1632
*Cephalus and Procris, Atalanta and
Hippomenes, Narcissus, and the
Mocking of Ceres*
c. 1600–25
Oil on panel
Top 3 panels [each]: 2 3/4 × 7 1/4"
(7 × 18.4 cm); bottom panel:
2 1/2 × 7 1/4" (6.3 × 18.4 cm)

John G. Johnson Collection
cat. 653

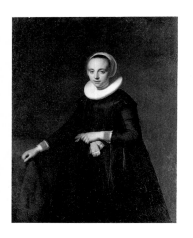

**Backer, Jacob Adriaensz.**
Dutch, active Amsterdam,
1608–1651
*Portrait of a Lady*
c. 1625–50
Center left: [illegible signature]
Oil on canvas
51 5/16 × 39 5/8" (130.3 × 100.6 cm)

John G. Johnson Collection
cat. 484

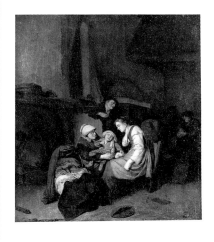

**Bega, Cornelis Pietersz.**
Dutch, active Haarlem,
active 1631/32–1664
*Peasant Family*
Mid-17th century
Oil on panel
16 1/4 × 13 15/16" (41.3 × 35.4 cm)

John G. Johnson Collection
cat. 527

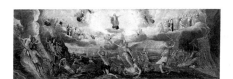

**Backer, Jacob de,
follower of**
Netherlandish, active Antwerp,
1530–1560
Previously listed as a Flemish
artist, late 16th century (JFD
1972)
*The Last Judgment*
Late 16th century
Oil on panel
11 3/16 × 31 1/8" (28.4 × 79.1 cm)

John G. Johnson Collection
cat. 407

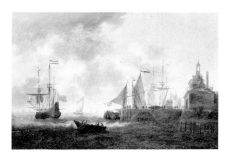

**Bellevois, Jacob Adriaensz.**
Dutch, active Rotterdam,
1621–1676
*The Hoofdpoort, Rotterdam*
Mid-17th century
Center right: Jbelevois
Oil on panel
28 3/4 × 42" (73 × 106.7 cm)

John G. Johnson Collection
cat. 588

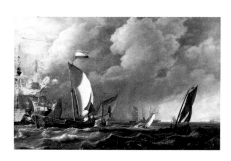

**Backhuysen, Ludolf**
Dutch, active Amsterdam,
1631–1708
*Marine*
Late 17th century
Oil on panel
25 5/8 × 37 7/8" (65.1 × 96.2 cm)

John G. Johnson Collection
cat. 592

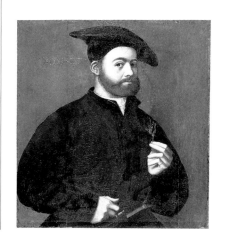

**Benson, Ambrosius**
Netherlandish, active Bruges,
documented 1519–1550
*Portrait of a Man Holding a Rose*
1525
Upper left: ANOS-27;
center top: 1525
Oil on panel
20 9/16 × 18 1/2" (52.2 × 47 cm)

John G. Johnson Collection
cat. 360

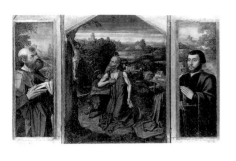

**Benson, Ambrosius, attributed to**
Previously listed as Ambrosius Benson (JFD 1972)
*Penitent Saint Jerome, with Saint Peter and a Donor as Saint Paul*
Triptych possibly assembled later; center panel cut at top corners; donor's hands once in prayer
c. 1525
Oil on panel
Center panel: 17 3/16 × 14 3/8" (43.7 × 36.5 cm); left panel: 18 1/4 × 7 1/4" (46.3 × 18.4 cm); right panel: 18 1/4 × 7 1/8" (46.3 × 18.1 cm)

John G. Johnson Collection
cat. 359

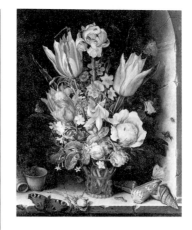

**Berghe, Christoffel van den**
Dutch, active Middelburg, active c. 1617–c. 1642
*Still Life with Flowers in a Vase*
1617
Lower right: CV BERGHE 1617
Oil on copper
14 13/16 × 11 5/8" (37.6 × 29.5 cm)

John G. Johnson Collection
cat. 648

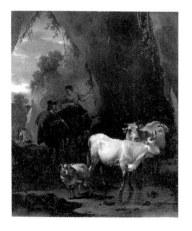

**Berchem, Nicolaes Pietersz.**
Dutch, active Haarlem, Amsterdam, and Italy, 1620–1683
*A Shepherd and a Shepherdess with Animals*
Mid-17th century
Lower left: Berchem
Oil on panel
12 3/8 × 9 3/4" (31.4 × 24.8 cm)

John G. Johnson Collection
cat. 610

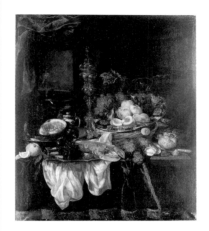

**Beyeren, Abraham van**
Dutch, active The Hague, Leiden, Delft, and Alkmaar, 1620/21–1690
*Banquet Still Life*
c. 1654–67
Oil on canvas
50 5/16 × 42 13/16" (127.8 × 108.7 cm)

The William L. Elkins Collection
E1924-3-23

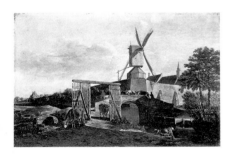

**Berckheyde, Gerrit Adriaensz.**
Dutch, active Haarlem and Amsterdam, 1638–1698
*Mill on the Town Wall, Haarlem*
Late 17th century
Lower left: Heyde
Oil on panel
16 1/4 × 24 3/4" (41.3 × 62.9 cm)

John G. Johnson Collection
cat. 598

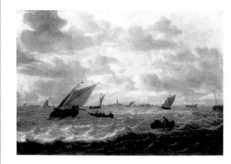

**Beyeren, Abraham van**
*Marine with a Rough Sea*
17th century
Center left: AB
Oil on canvas
32 1/2 × 44 1/2" (82.5 × 113 cm)

John G. Johnson Collection
cat. 637

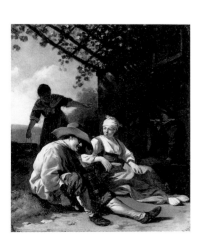

**Berckheyde, Job**
Dutch, active Haarlem and Germany, 1630–1693
*At the Inn*
17th century
Lower right: JHBerckheyde
Oil on panel
12 15/16 × 10 15/16" (32.9 × 27.8 cm)

John G. Johnson Collection
cat. 530

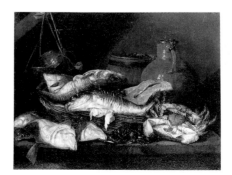

**Beyeren, Abraham van**
*Still Life with Fish*
17th century
Lower right: .AB.f.
Oil on canvas
28 1/8 × 36 3/8" (71.4 × 92.4 cm)

John G. Johnson Collection
cat. 639

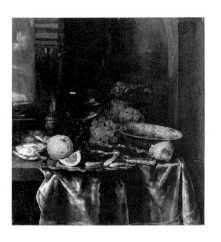

**Beyeren, Abraham van, attributed to**
Previously listed as Abraham van Beyeren (JFD 1972)
*Still Life with Grapes and a Beaker*
17th century
Center left: .AB.f.
Oil on panel
26 1/4 × 23 3/8" (66.7 × 59.4 cm)

John G. Johnson Collection
cat. 638

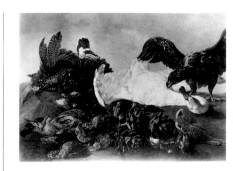

**Boel, Pieter, attributed to**
Previously listed as Frans Snyders (PMA 1965)
*Dead Game with an Eagle*
17th century
Oil on canvas
48 5/8 × 65 3/8" (123.5 × 166 cm)

Purchased with the W. P. Wilstach Fund
W1904-1-35

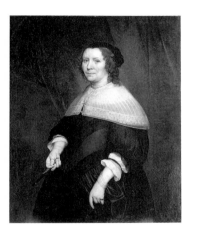

**Bloemaert, Hendrick**
Dutch, active Utrecht, 1601–1672
*Portrait of an Elderly Lady*
1663
Lower left: Henr. Bloemaert Ao 1663
Oil on canvas
43 × 34 1/2" (109.2 × 87.6 cm)

John G. Johnson Collection
cat. 494

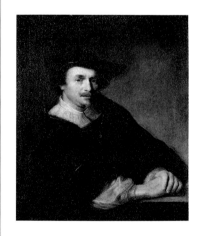

**Boelema de Stomme, Maerten**
Dutch, active Leeuwarden, first documented 1642, died after 1664
*Still Life with a Roemer*
Mid-17th century
Center right: M. B. / de Stomme
Oil on panel
16 3/8 × 20 7/8" (41.6 × 53 cm)

John G. Johnson Collection
cat. 649

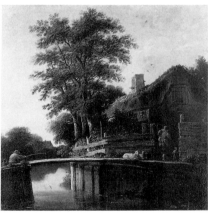

**Bloot, Pieter de**
Dutch, active Rotterdam, c. 1601–1658
*Cottage on the Waterside*
17th century
Oil on panel
13 7/8 × 13 3/16" (35.2 × 33.5 cm)

John G. Johnson Collection
cat. 552

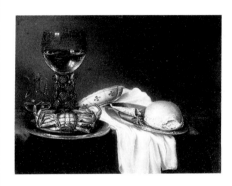

**Bol, Ferdinand, copy after**
Dutch, active Amsterdam, 1616–1680
Previously listed as Ferdinand Bol (PMA 1965)
*Portrait of a Man*
After the painting in the Bayerische Staatsgemäldesammlungen, Alte Pinakothek, Munich (609)
After c. 1648
Oil on canvas
34 15/16 × 28 3/8" (88.7 × 72.1 cm)

Gift of Mr. and Mrs. William H. Donner
1948-95-2

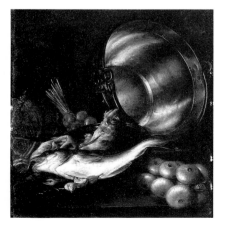

**Boel, Pieter**
Flemish, active Antwerp and Paris, 1622–1674
*Still Life with Fish and a Copper Kettle*
Mid-17th century
Upper right: PBoel
Oil on panel
26 9/16 × 25 3/16" (67.5 × 64 cm)

John G. Johnson Collection
cat. 706

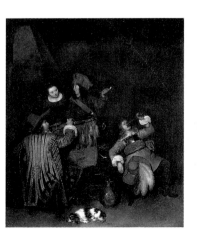

**Borch, Gerard ter**
Dutch, active Deventer after 1654, 1617–1681
*Guardroom*
1658
On cask under table: GTB 1658
Oil on canvas
38 1/2 × 32 1/2" (97.8 × 82.5 cm)

John G. Johnson Collection
cat. 504

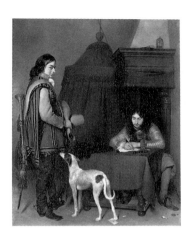

**Borch, Gerard ter**
*Officer Writing a Letter, with a Trumpeter*
c. 1658–59
Lower right: GTBorch
Oil on canvas
22 3/8 × 17 1/4" (56.8 × 43.8 cm)

The William L. Elkins Collection
E1924-3-21

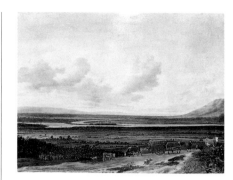

**Borssom, Anthonij van**
Dutch, active Amsterdam,
1630/31–1677
Previously listed as Philips de Koninck (PMA 1965)
*View of Schenkenschanz and the Eltenberg, near Emmerich*
c. 1656
Oil on canvas
39 1/16 × 49 5/16" (99.2 × 125.2 cm)

Purchased with the W. P. Wilstach Fund
W1901-1-2

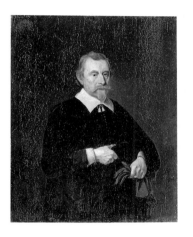

**Borch, Gerard ter, copy after**
*Portrait of a Gentleman*
After a lost painting
17th century
Lower left: [illegible signature]
Oil on panel
10 7/16 × 8" (26.5 × 20.3 cm)

John G. Johnson Collection
cat. 493

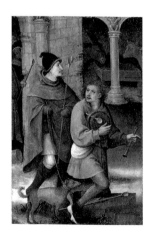

**Bosch, Hieronymus**
Netherlandish, active
's Hertogenbosch, c. 1450–1516
*The Adoration of the Magi*
Early 16th century
Oil on panel
30 1/2 × 22" (77.5 × 55.9 cm)

John G. Johnson Collection
inv. 1321

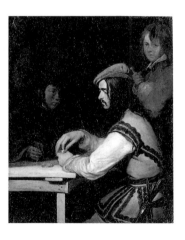

**Borch, Gerard ter, copy after**
*Scene in an Inn*
After a painting in a private collection
17th century
Oil on panel
9 3/16 × 7 1/2" (23.3 × 19 cm)

John G. Johnson Collection
cat. 1177

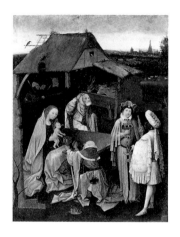

**Bosch, Hieronymus, attributed to**
Previously listed as Hieronymus Bosch (JFD 1972)
*Two Shepherds*
Left wing of a triptych, cut down on all sides; companion to the following painting
Early 16th century
Oil on panel
14 3/4 × 8 7/8" (37.5 × 22.5 cm)

John G. Johnson Collection
inv. 1275

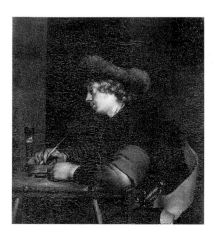

**Borch, Gerard ter, copy after**
*Smoker*
After the painting in the Gemäldegalerie, Staatliche Museen zu Berlin-Preussischer Kulturbesitz (cat. no. 791 F)
17th century
Oil on canvas
15 9/16 × 12 3/4" (39.5 × 32.4 cm)

John G. Johnson Collection
inv. 377

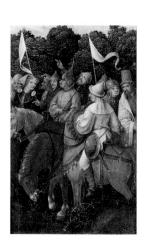

**Bosch, Hieronymus, attributed to**
Previously listed as Hieronymus Bosch (JFD 1972)
*Retinue of the Magi*
Right wing of a triptych, cut down on all sides; companion to the preceding painting
Early 16th century
Oil on panel
14 1/4 × 8 3/8" (36.2 × 21.3 cm)

John G. Johnson Collection
inv. 1276

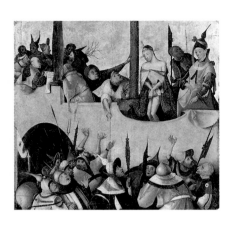

**Bosch, Hieronymus, attributed to**
Previously listed as Hieronymus Bosch (JFD 1972)
*"Ecce Homo"*
16th century
Oil and gold on panel
20 1/2 × 21 1/4" (52.1 × 54 cm)

John G. Johnson Collection
cat. 352

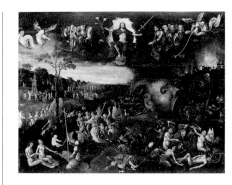

**Bosch, Hieronymus, follower of**
Previously listed as a remote follower of Hieronymus Bosch (JFD 1972)
*The Last Judgment*
Late 16th century
Oil on panel
29 7/8 × 37 3/4" (75.9 × 95.9 cm)

John G. Johnson Collection
cat. 386

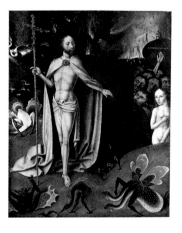

**Bosch, Hieronymus, follower of**
Previously listed as a unique copy after a lost original by Hieronymus Bosch (JFD 1972)
*Christ and the Woman Taken in Adultery*
16th century
Lower right: [illegible]
Oil on panel
29 7/8 × 22" (75.9 × 55.9 cm)

John G. Johnson Collection
inv. 353

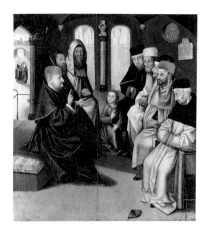

**Bosch, Hieronymus, copy after**
*Christ among the Doctors*
One of several copies after a lost painting
16th century
Oil and gold on panel
27 1/4 × 22 15/16" (69.2 × 58.3 cm)

John G. Johnson Collection
inv. 77

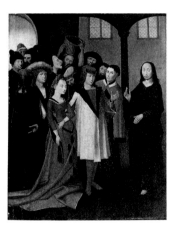

**Bosch, Hieronymus, follower of**
*Christ in Limbo*
A figure to the right of Christ has been painted out
16th century
Upper right: P. CHRISTOPSEN M F
Oil on panel
21 1/2 × 16 5/16" (54.6 × 41.4 cm)

John G. Johnson Collection
inv. 2055

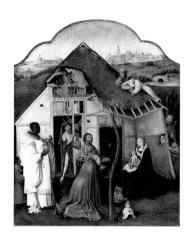

**Bosch, Hieronymus, copy after**
*The Adoration of the Magi*
After the center panel of a triptych in the Museo del Prado, Madrid (2048)
16th century
Oil on panel
37 × 29 5/16" (94 × 74.4 cm)

John G. Johnson Collection
cat. 354

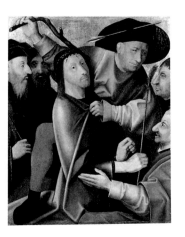

**Bosch, Hieronymus, follower of**
Previously listed as a copy after a lost original by Hieronymus Bosch (JFD 1972)
*The Mocking of Christ*
16th century
Oil and gold on panel
26 5/8 × 20 3/8" (67.6 × 51.7 cm)

John G. Johnson Collection
cat. 353

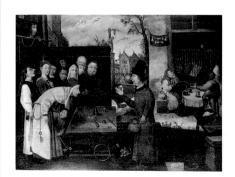

**Bosch, Hieronymus, copy after**
Previously listed as a variation on Hieronymous Bosch (PMA 1965)
*The Conjurer (The Prestidigitator)*
After a lost original of which the best and earliest copy is in the Musée Municipal, Saint-Germain-en-Laye, France (inv. no 872/1/87)
16th century
Oil on panel
41 1/2 × 54 5/8" (105.4 × 138.7 cm)

Purchased with the W. P. Wilstach Fund
W1914-1-2

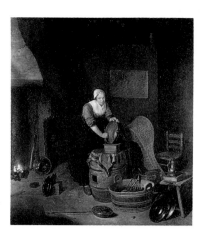

**Bosch, Pieter van den**
Dutch, active Leiden,
Amsterdam, and London,
born 1613, still active 1663
*Maid Scouring a Kettle*
Mid-17th century
Lower right (spurious): QvB.
Oil on panel
26 1/2 × 22 5/8" (67.3 × 57.5 cm)

John G. Johnson Collection
cat. 536

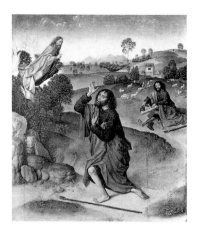

**Bouts, Dierick, attributed to**
Previously listed as Dierick Bouts
(JFD 1972)
*Moses and the Burning Bush, with
Moses Removing His Shoes*
c. 1465–70
Oil on panel
17 5/8 × 14" (44.8 × 35.6 cm)

John G. Johnson Collection
cat. 339

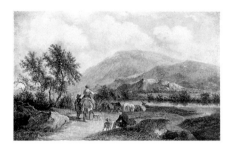

**Both, Andries, imitator of**
Dutch, active Utrecht and Rome,
1612–1641
*Landscape with Cattle, Italy*
17th century
Lower left: ABoth
Oil on panel
9 5/8 × 14 5/8" (24.4 × 37.1 cm)

John G. Johnson Collection
cat. 614

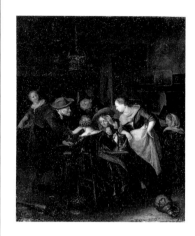

**Brakenburg, Richard**
Dutch, active Haarlem,
1650–1702
*The Dice Players*
Late 17th century
Lower right: R. Bra[k]enburgh
Oil on panel
14 13/16 × 11 11/16" (37.6 × 29.7 cm)

John G. Johnson Collection
cat. 528

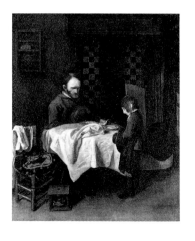

**Boursse, Esaias**
Dutch, active Amsterdam,
1631–1672
*Grace before Meat*
Mid-17th century
Center left: EB
Oil on canvas
23 1/2 × 18 3/4" (59.7 × 47.6 cm)

John G. Johnson Collection
cat. 539

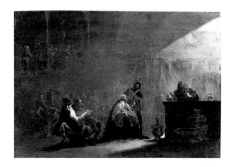

**Bramer, Leonard**
Dutch, active Delft, 1596–1674
*The Presentation of Christ in the
Temple*
17th century
Oil on panel
21 1/4 × 28 3/4" (54 × 73 cm)

John G. Johnson Collection
cat. 489

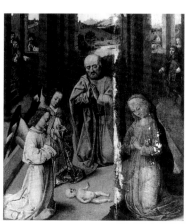

**Bouts, Dierick, attributed to**
Netherlandish, active Louvain,
first securely documented 1447,
died 1475
Previously listed as Dierick Bouts
(JFD 1972)
*The Nativity*
c. 1450–75
Oil on panel
10 1/4 × 8 5/8" (26 × 21.9 cm)

John G. Johnson Collection
cat. 340

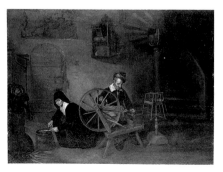

**Brekelenkam, Quirijn
Gerritsz. van**
Dutch, active Leiden,
c. 1620–1668
*A Wool Spinner and His Wife*
c. 1653
Lower right: Q v B
Oil on panel
23 1/4 × 30 11/16" (59 × 77.9 cm)

John G. Johnson Collection
cat. 535

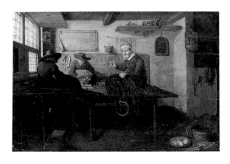

**Brekelenkam, Quirijn Gerritsz. van**
*The Tailor*
c. 1658
Lower left: QB
Oil on panel
22 3/8 × 32 3/8" (56.8 × 82.2 cm)

John G. Johnson Collection
cat. 534

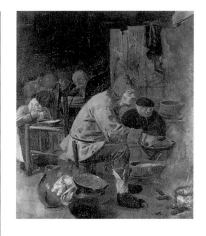

**Brouwer, Adriaen, attributed to**
Previously listed as Adriaen Brouwer (JFD 1972)
*Pancake Baker*
c. 1625
Oil on panel
13 3/8 × 11 3/16" (34 × 28.4 cm)

John G. Johnson Collection
cat. 681

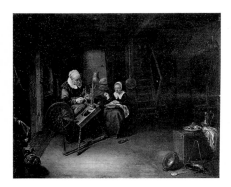

**Brekelenkam, Quirijn Gerritsz. van**
*A Woman and a Girl in a Kitchen*
Mid-17th century
Oil on panel
21 1/8 × 25 7/8" (53.7 × 65.7 cm)

John G. Johnson Collection
cat. 537

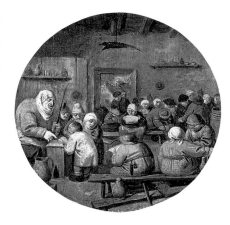

**Brouwer, Adriaen, follower of**
*Interior of a School*
17th century
Oil on panel
10 1/2" (26.7 cm) diameter

John G. Johnson Collection
inv. 1694

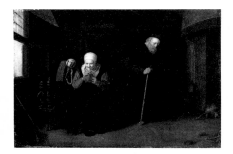

**Brekelenkam, Quirijn Gerritsz. van, follower of**
Previously listed as Quirijn Gerritsz. van Brekelenkam (JFD 1972)
*Interior with an Old Man and His Wife*
17th century
Oil on panel
15 1/2 × 22" (39.4 × 55.9 cm)

John G. Johnson Collection
cat. 538

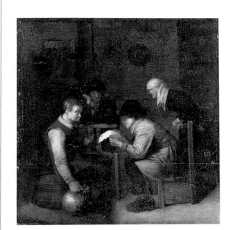

**Brouwer, Adriaen, follower of**
Previously attributed to Adriaen Brouwer (JFD 1972)
*Listening to the News*
17th century
Lower left: AB
Oil on panel
18 3/8 × 17 7/16" (46.7 × 44.3 cm)

John G. Johnson Collection
cat. 1183

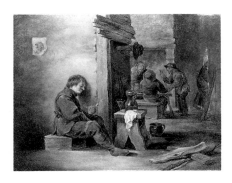

**Brouwer, Adriaen**
Dutch, active Haarlem, Amsterdam, and Antwerp, 1606–1638
*Scene in a Tavern*
17th century
Lower right: AB
Oil on panel
10 5/8 × 13 3/4" (27 × 34.9 cm)

John G. Johnson Collection
cat. 1184

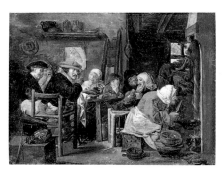

**Brouwer, Adriaen, follower of**
Previously listed as Adriaen Brouwer (JFD 1972)
*Woman Making Pancakes*
17th century
Lower left: AB
Oil on panel
11 3/4 × 15 3/4" (29.8 × 40 cm)

John G. Johnson Collection
cat. 680

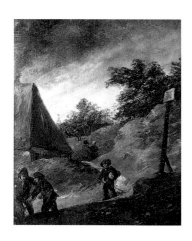

**Brouwer, Adriaen,
copy after?**
Previously listed as Adriaen
Brouwer (JFD 1972)
*Road near a House*
17th century
Lower right: AB
Oil on panel
9 7/8 × 7 1/2" (25.1 × 19 cm)

John G. Johnson Collection
cat. 685

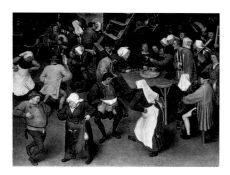

**Bruegel, Pieter, the Elder,
follower of**
Netherlandish, active Antwerp and
Brussels, first documented
1550, died 1569
Previously listed as a composition
of uncertain origin (JFD 1972)
*Wedding Dance*
Probably after a lost painting of
1567–69
c. 1575–1600
Oil on panel
31 5/8 × 41 7/8" (80.3 × 106.4 cm)

John G. Johnson Collection
cat. 420

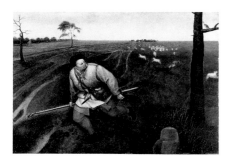

**Bruegel, Pieter, the Elder,
follower of**
Previously listed as a composition
of Pieter Bruegel the Elder,
painted possibly by Marten van
Cleve (JFD 1972)
*The Unfaithful Shepherd*
Probably after a lost painting of
1567–69
c. 1575–1600
On shepherd's staff: VV [ligated];
lower right: CSH [ligated]
Oil on panel
24 1/4 × 34 1/8" (61.6 × 86.7 cm)

John G. Johnson Collection
cat. 419

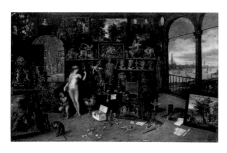

**Brueghel, Jan, the Younger**
Flemish, active Antwerp,
1601–1678
*Allegory of Sight (Venus and Cupid
in a Picture Gallery)*
c. 1660
Lower right: J Breugel
Oil on copper
22 7/8 × 35 5/16" (58.1 × 89.7 cm)

John G. Johnson Collection
cat. 656

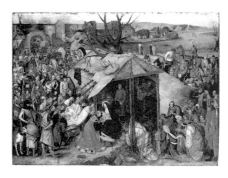

**Brueghel, Pieter, the Younger**
Flemish, active Antwerp,
1564–1637/38
*The Adoration of the Magi*
1595?
Lower left: P. BRUEGEL
Oil on canvas
48 1/2 × 63 3/8" (123.2 × 161 cm)

The Bloomfield Moore Collection
1883-73

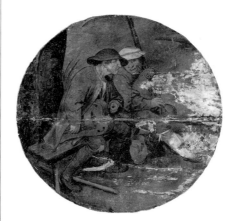

**Brueghel, Pieter, the Younger**
*A Hurdy-Gurdy Player and a
Bagpiper*
c. 1600
Oil on panel
13 9/16" (34.4 cm) diameter

John G. Johnson Collection
cat. 1176

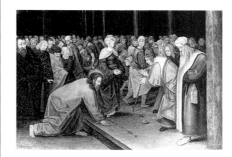

**Brueghel, Pieter, the Younger**
*Christ and the Woman Taken in
Adultery*
Based on the painting, dated
1565, by Pieter Bruegel the
Elder, in the Courtauld Institute
Galleries, London (The Princes
Gate Collection, 9)
c. 1600
Lower left: P BREVGHEL; center
bottom: DIE SONDER SONDE
IS / DIEW
Oil on panel
11 1/16 × 16" (28.1 × 40.6 cm)

John G. Johnson Collection
cat. 423

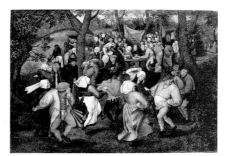

**Brueghel, Pieter, the Younger**
*Wedding Dance in the Open Air*
c. 1600
Oil on panel
14 7/8 × 21 1/8" (37.8 × 53.7 cm)

John G. Johnson Collection
cat. 421

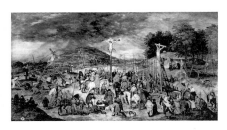

**Brueghel, Pieter, the Younger, attributed to**
Previously listed as Pieter Brueghel the Younger (PMA 1965)
*The Crucifixion*
1617?
On cross: INRI
Oil on panel
25 5/8 × 47 3/4" (65.1 × 121.3 cm)

Purchased with the W. P. Wilstach Fund
W1903-1-6

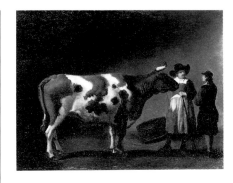

**Calraet, Abraham Pietersz. van**
Dutch, active Dordrecht, 1642–1722
*Bull in a Barn with Two Figures*
Late 17th century
Oil on panel
13 7/8 × 17 1/2" (35.2 × 44.4 cm)

John G. Johnson Collection
cat. 625

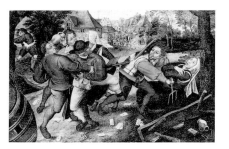

**Brueghel, Pieter, the Younger, imitator of**
Previously listed as Pieter Brueghel the Younger (JFD 1972)
*Fighting Peasants*
One of many versions probably after a lost painting by Pieter Bruegel the Elder
c. 1600
Lower left (spurious): BREVGHEL
Oil on panel
14 × 22 1/4" (35.6 × 56.5 cm)

John G. Johnson Collection
cat. 422

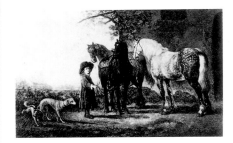

**Calraet, Abraham Pietersz. van**
*Cows in a Stable*
Late 17th century
Lower left: A.C.
Oil on panel
17 9/16 × 23 3/8" (44.6 × 59.4 cm)

John G. Johnson Collection
inv. 424

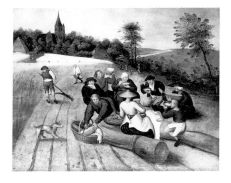

**Brueghel, Pieter, the Younger, imitator of**
*Summer with Peasants at a Meal*
Conflation of several summer scenes by Pieter Brueghel the Younger
19th century
Oil on panel
17 × 21 3/4" (43.2 × 55.2 cm)

John G. Johnson Collection
inv. 2519

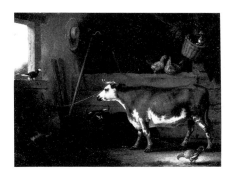

**Calraet, Abraham Pietersz. van**
*Groom with Three Horses and Two Dogs*
Late 17th century
Lower right: A C
Oil on panel
13 7/16 × 21" (34.1 × 53.3 cm)

The William L. Elkins Collection
E1924-3-3

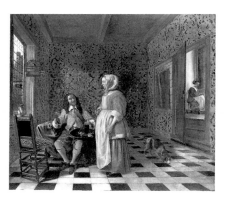

**Burch, Hendrick van der**
Dutch, active Delft and Leiden, born 1627, still active 1666
*An Officer and a Standing Woman*
c. 1665
Oil on canvas
22 3/4 × 25 1/4" (57.8 × 64.1 cm)

The William L. Elkins Collection
E1924-3-51

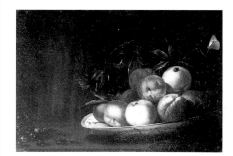

**Calraet, Abraham Pietersz. van**
*Still Life with Peaches*
Late 17th century
Lower left: A.C.
Oil on panel
17 3/8 × 25 1/2" (44.1 × 64.8 cm)

John G. Johnson Collection
cat. 628

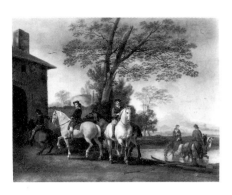

**Calraet, Abraham Pietersz. van, attributed to**
Previously listed as Abraham Pietersz. van Calraet (PMA 1965)
*Horsemen Watering Their Horses*
Late 17th century
Oil on panel
24 1/8 × 29 3/4" (61.3 × 75.6 cm)

The William L. Elkins Collection
E1924-3-74

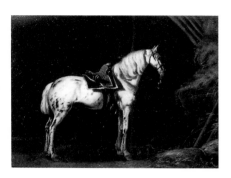

**Calraet, Abraham Pietersz. van, copy after**
Previously listed as Abraham Pietersz. van Calraet (PMA 1965)
*White Horse in a Stable*
After the painting in the Collection of the Trustees of Berkeley Castle, Gloucestershire
Late 17th century
Oil on panel
12 1/2 × 16 3/4" (31.7 × 42.5 cm)

The William L. Elkins Collection
E1924-3-91

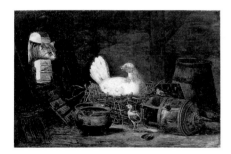

**Camphuysen, Govert**
Dutch, active Amsterdam and Stockholm, 1623/24–1672
*A Sitting Hen and a Cat*
Mid-17th century
Lower left: G Camphuysen
Oil on panel
28 11/16 × 41 7/8" (72.9 × 106.4 cm)

John G. Johnson Collection
cat. 560

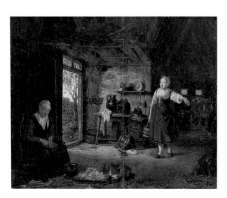

**Camphuysen, Govert**
*A Woman and a Maid in a Barn*
Mid-17th century
Oil on panel
13 7/8 × 16 1/4" (35.2 × 41.3 cm)

John G. Johnson Collection
cat. 559

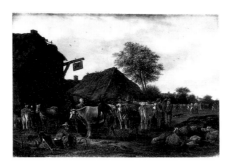

**Camphuysen, Govert**
*Cattle Market*
Mid-17th century
Lower right (spurious): A Cuyp
Oil on panel
22 3/8 × 32 1/4" (56.8 × 81.9 cm)

John G. Johnson Collection
cat. 1179

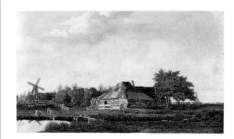

**Camphuysen, Govert**
*Farm near a Village*
Mid-17th century
Center bottom (spurious): Paulus Potter; lower right (spurious): P[?]er
Oil on panel
26 3/8 × 42 3/4" (67 × 108.6 cm)

John G. Johnson Collection
cat. 558

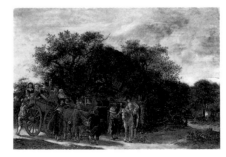

**Camphuysen, Govert**
*The Halt at the Inn*
Mid-17th century
Lower right: G Camphuysen
Oil on panel
26 3/16 × 36 1/4" (66.5 × 92.1 cm)

John G. Johnson Collection
cat. 557

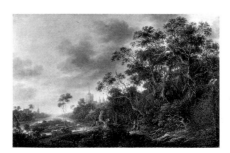

**Camphuysen, Joachim**
Dutch, active Amsterdam and Stockholm, 1602–1659
*Woods beside a Canal*
17th century
Oil on panel
15 11/16 × 24 1/4" (39.8 × 61.6 cm)

John G. Johnson Collection
cat. 556

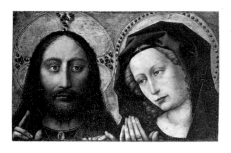

**Campin, Robert, also called the Master of Flémalle**
Netherlandish, active Tournai, first documented 1406, died 1444
*Christ and the Virgin*
Cut down at the top
c. 1430–35
Oil and gold on panel
11 1/4 × 17 15/16" (28.6 × 45.6 cm)

John G. Johnson Collection
cat. 332

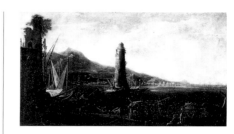

**Casteels, Pieter, II, imitator of**
Flemish, active Antwerp, active c. 1673/74
*Harbor with a Lighthouse*
Late 17th century
Oil on canvas
39 1/2 × 68 1/8" (100.3 × 173 cm)

Bequest of Arthur H. Lea
F1938-1-25

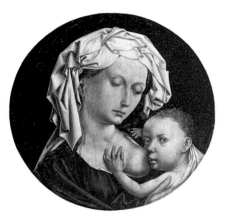

**Campin, Robert, follower of**
Previously listed as a copy after Robert Campin (JFD 1972)
*The Virgin Suckling the Christ Child*
Known in many versions; based on the painting in the Städelsches Kunstinstitut, Frankfurt (inv. no. 939), or a lost painting
Mid-15th century
Oil on panel
10 3/4" (27.3 cm) diameter

John G. Johnson Collection
cat. 331

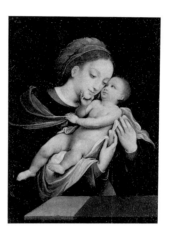

**Cleve, Cornelis van**
Netherlandish, active Antwerp, 1520–1567
*Virgin and Child*
Mid-16th century
Oil on panel
14 1/2 × 10 1/8" (36.8 × 25.7 cm)

John G. Johnson Collection
cat. 403

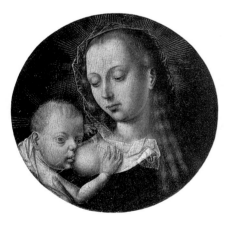

**Campin, Robert, follower of**
Previously listed as a copy after Robert Campin (JFD 1972)
*The Virgin Suckling the Christ Child*
See preceding painting
Mid-15th century
Oil on panel
10 9/16" (26.8 cm) diameter

John G. Johnson Collection
cat. 333

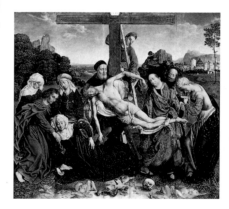

**Cleve, Joos van**
Netherlandish, active Antwerp and France, first documented 1511, died 1540/41
*The Descent from the Cross*
The composition of the figures is based on Rogier van der Weyden's *The Descent from the Cross*, in the Museo del Prado, Madrid (2825)
c. 1518–20
Oil on panel
45 1/4 × 49 3/4" (114.9 × 126.4 cm)

John G. Johnson Collection
cat. 373

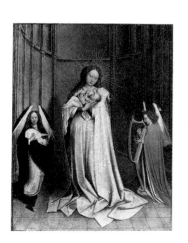

**Campin, Robert, copy after**
*Virgin and Child, with Two Angels in an Apse*
Known in many versions; probably after a lost painting
c. 1475–1500
Oil and gold on panel
19 × 13 7/8" (48.3 × 35.2 cm)

John G. Johnson Collection
inv. 458

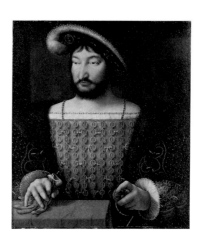

**Cleve, Joos van**
*Portrait of Francis I, King of France*
Known in several versions; this is probably the earliest
c. 1525
Oil on panel
28 3/8 × 23 5/16" (72.1 × 59.2 cm)

John G. Johnson Collection
cat. 769

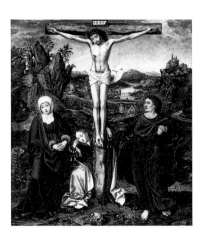

**Cleve, Joos van, workshop of**
*The Crucifixion*
Center panel of a triptych; a companion panel is in the Fitzwilliam Museum, Cambridge, England (1518a, b)
c. 1525
Center top: I N R I
Oil and gold on panel
12 ¾ × 11" (32.4 × 27.9 cm)

John G. Johnson Collection
cat. 374

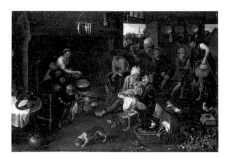

**Cleve, Marten van, follower of**
Previously listed as Marten van Cleve (JFD 1972)
*The Formal Visit*
1624
Upper right: A1624
Oil on panel
29 × 41 ⅜" (73.7 × 105.1 cm)

John G. Johnson Collection
cat. 424

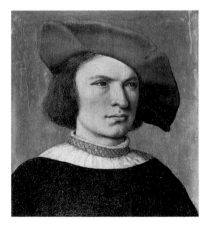

**Cleve, Joos van, imitator of**
Previously listed as Joos van Cleve (JFD 1972)
*Portrait of a Young Man*
16th century
Oil on panel
11 × 9 ½" (27.9 × 24.1 cm)

John G. Johnson Collection
cat. 375

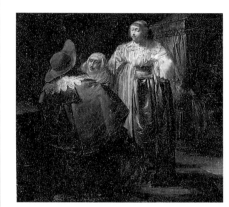

**Codde, Pieter**
Dutch, active Amsterdam, 1599–1678
*A Soldier, an Old Woman, and a Young Woman*
Possibly cut down at the top and left
17th century
Oil on panel
10 ½ × 10 ⅞" (26.7 × 27.6 cm)

John G. Johnson Collection
cat. 443

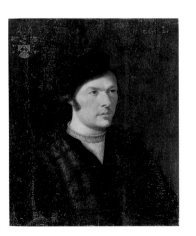

**Cleve, Joos van, copy after**
*Portrait of a Gentleman* [possibly Nicasius Hanneman]
After the painting in the Toledo Museum of Art, Ohio (26.59)
16th century
Upper right: AEt. 25
Oil on panel
26 ½ × 20 ¹³⁄₁₆" (67.3 × 52.9 cm)

John G. Johnson Collection
cat. 431

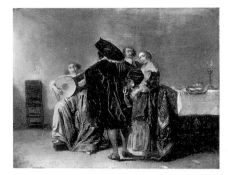

**Codde, Pieter**
*The Lute Player*
17th century
Oil on panel
14 ⅛ × 17 ¾" (35.9 × 45.1 cm)

John G. Johnson Collection
cat. 442

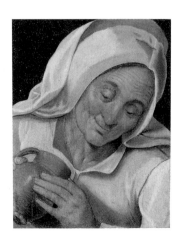

**Cleve, Marten van**
Netherlandish, active Antwerp, 1527–1581
*Peasant Woman Holding a Mug*
Probably a fragment
Mid-16th century
Oil on panel
13 × 9 ¾" (33 × 24.8 cm)

John G. Johnson Collection
cat. 425

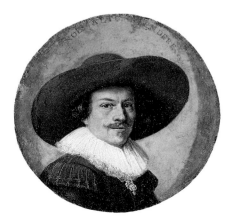

**Codde, Pieter, attributed to**
Previously listed as Pieter Codde (JFD 1972)
*Portrait of a Man*
17th century
Across top: NOL ALT ENDERE
Oil on canvas
5 ⅞" (14.9 cm) diameter

John G. Johnson Collection
cat. 455

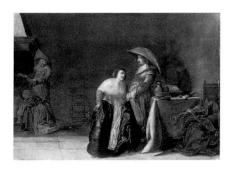

**Codde, Pieter, follower of**
Previously listed as Pieter Codde
(JFD 1972)
*A Lady and a Cavalier*
17th century
Oil on panel
15 5/8 × 20 11/16" (39.7 × 52.5 cm)

John G. Johnson Collection
cat. 444

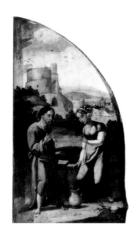

**Coecke van Aelst, Pieter,
follower of**
Previously listed as the workshop
of Pieter Coecke van Aelst
(PMA 1965)
*Christ and the Samaritan Woman*
Upper right outer panel from an
altarpiece; see previous and
following entries
c. 1532–35
Tempera on panel
20 1/2 × 10 3/4" (52 × 27.3 cm)

Purchased from the George Grey
Barnard Collection with Museum
funds
1945-25-117 b

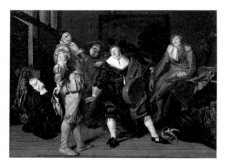

**Codde, Pieter, copy after**
*Company of Actors*
After the painting in the
Gemäldegalerie, Staatliche
Museen zu Berlin-Preussischer
Kulturbesitz (cat. no. 800 A)
17th century
Oil on panel
14 3/8 × 19 5/8" (36.5 × 49.8 cm)

John G. Johnson Collection
cat. 441

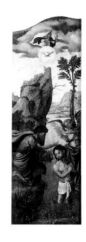

**Coecke van Aelst, Pieter,
follower of**
Previously listed as the workshop
of Pieter Coecke van Aelst
(PMA 1965)
*The Baptism of Christ*
Center far left outer panel from
an altarpiece; see previous and
following entries
c. 1532–35
Tempera on panel
48 5/8 × 16 3/8" (123.5 × 41.6 cm)

Purchased from the George Grey
Barnard Collection with Museum
funds
1945-25-117 c

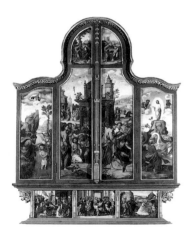

**Coecke van Aelst, Pieter,
follower of**
Netherlandish, active Antwerp,
1502–1550
Previously listed as the workshop
of Pieter Coecke van Aelst
(PMA 1965)
*Altar of the Passion*
Altarpiece with 19 painted and
6 carved panels; view with wings
closed; see following 20 entries
c. 1532–35
Wings: 88 1/2 × 42" (224.8 ×
106.7 cm); predella panels:
15 1/2 × 66" (39.4 × 167.6 cm)

Purchased from the George Grey
Barnard Collection with Museum
funds
1945-25-117

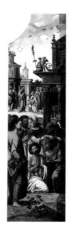

**Coecke van Aelst, Pieter,
follower of**
Previously listed as the workshop
of Pieter Coecke van Aelst
(PMA 1965)
*The Raising of Lazarus*
Center near left outer panel from
an altarpiece; see previous and
following entries
c. 1532–35
Tempera on panel
56 13/16 × 16 5/16" (144.3 × 41.5 cm)

Purchased from the George Grey
Barnard Collection with Museum
funds
1945-25-117 d

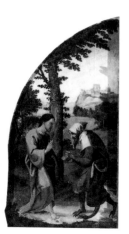

**Coecke van Aelst, Pieter,
follower of**
Previously listed as the workshop
of Pieter Coecke van Aelst
(PMA 1965)
*The Temptation of Christ*
Upper left outer panel from an
altarpiece; see previous and
following entries
c. 1532–35
Tempera on panel
20 1/2 × 10 5/8" (52 × 27 cm)

Purchased from the George Grey
Barnard Collection with Museum
funds
1945-25-117 a

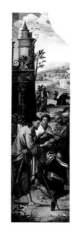

**Coecke van Aelst, Pieter,
follower of**
Previously listed as the workshop
of Pieter Coecke van Aelst
(PMA 1965)
*Christ Healing the Blind*
Center near right outer panel
from an altarpiece; see previous
and following entries
c. 1532–35
Tempera on panel
56 13/16 × 16 3/8" (144.3 × 41.6 cm)

Purchased from the George Grey
Barnard Collection with Museum
funds
1945-25-117 e

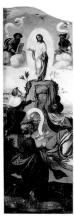

**Coecke van Aelst, Pieter, follower of**
Previously listed as the workshop of Pieter Coecke van Aelst (PMA 1965)
*The Transfiguration*
Center far right outer panel from an altarpiece; see previous and following entries
c. 1532–35
Tempera on panel
49 1/8 × 16 3/8" (124.8 × 41.6 cm)

Purchased from the George Grey Barnard Collection with Museum funds
1945-25-117 f

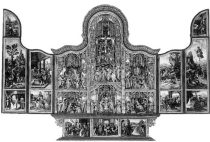

**Coecke van Aelst, Pieter, follower of**
Previously listed as the workshop of Pieter Coecke van Aelst (PMA 1965)
*Altar of the Passion*
Altarpiece with 19 painted and 6 carved panels; view with wings open; see previous and following entries
c. 1532–35
Wings: 88 1/2 × 42" (224.8 × 106.7 cm); predella panels: 15 1/2 × 66" (39.4 × 167.6 cm)

Purchased from the George Grey Barnard Collection with Museum funds
1945-25-117

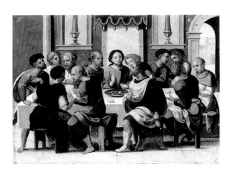

**Coecke van Aelst, Pieter, follower of**
Previously listed as the workshop of Pieter Coecke van Aelst (PMA 1965)
*The Meeting of Abraham and Melchizedek*
Left predella panel from an altarpiece; see previous and following entries
c. 1532–35
Tempera on panel
15 3/16 × 20 1/16" (38.5 × 51 cm)

Purchased from the George Grey Barnard Collection with Museum funds
1945-25-117 g

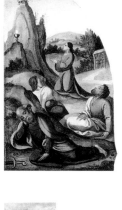

**Coecke van Aelst, Pieter, follower of**
Previously listed as the workshop of Pieter Coecke van Aelst (PMA 1965)
*The Agony in the Garden*
Upper left inner panel from an altarpiece; see previous and following entries
c. 1532–35
Tempera on panel
20 11/16 × 10 7/16" (52.5 × 26.5 cm)

Purchased from the George Grey Barnard Collection with Museum funds
1945-25-117 j

**Coecke van Aelst, Pieter, follower of**
Previously listed as the workshop of Pieter Coecke van Aelst (PMA 1965)
*The Last Supper*
Center predella panel from an altarpiece; see previous and following entries
c. 1532–35
Tempera on panel
15 3/16 × 20 1/16" (38.5 × 51 cm)

Purchased from the George Grey Barnard Collection with Museum funds
1945-25-117 h

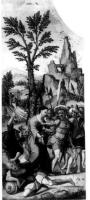

**Coecke van Aelst, Pieter, follower of**
Previously listed as the workshop of Pieter Coecke van Aelst (PMA 1965)
*The Betrayal of Christ*
Center far left inner panel from an altarpiece; see previous and following entries
c. 1532–35
Tempera on panel
41 11/16 × 17 1/8" (105.8 × 43.5 cm)

Purchased from the George Grey Barnard Collection with Museum funds
1945-25-117 k

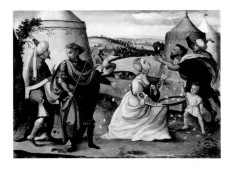

**Coecke van Aelst, Pieter, follower of**
Previously listed as the workshop of Pieter Coecke van Aelst (PMA 1965)
*The Gathering of Manna*
Right predella panel from an altarpiece; see previous and following entries
c. 1532–35
Tempera on panel
15 3/16 × 20 1/2" (38.5 × 52 cm)

Purchased from the George Grey Barnard Collection with Museum funds
1945-25-117 i

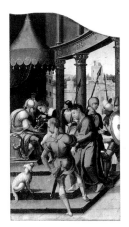

**Coecke van Aelst, Pieter, follower of**
Previously listed as the workshop of Pieter Coecke van Aelst (PMA 1965)
*Christ before Pilate*
Center near left inner panel from an altarpiece; see previous and following entries
c. 1532–35
Tempera on panel
31 × 16 5/8" (78.7 × 42.3 cm)

Purchased from the George Grey Barnard Collection with Museum funds
1945-25-117 l

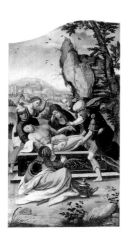

**Coecke van Aelst, Pieter, follower of**
Previously listed as the workshop of Pieter Coecke van Aelst (PMA 1965)
*The Entombment*
Center near right inner panel from an altarpiece; see previous and following entries
c. 1532–35
Tempera on panel
30 11/16 × 16 5/8" (78 × 42.3 cm)

Purchased from the George Grey Barnard Collection with Museum funds
1945-25-117 m

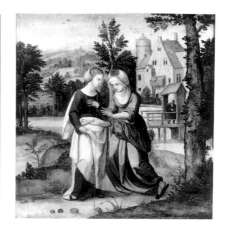

**Coecke van Aelst, Pieter, follower of**
Previously listed as the workshop of Pieter Coecke van Aelst (PMA 1965)
*The Visitation*
Lower near left inner panel from an altarpiece; see previous and following entries
c. 1532–35
Tempera on panel
17 1/2 × 16 7/8" (44.5 × 42.8 cm)

Purchased from the George Grey Barnard Collection with Museum funds
1945-25-117 q

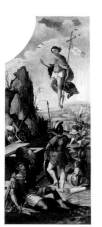

**Coecke van Aelst, Pieter, follower of**
Previously listed as the workshop of Pieter Coecke van Aelst (PMA 1965)
*The Resurrection*
Center far right inner panel from an altarpiece; see previous and following entries
c. 1532–35
Tempera on panel
41 3/4 × 16 7/8" (106 × 42.8 cm)

Purchased from the George Grey Barnard Collection with Museum funds
1945-25-117 n

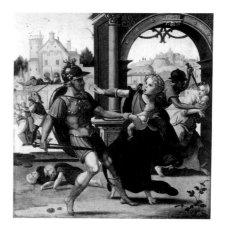

**Coecke van Aelst, Pieter, follower of**
Previously listed as the workshop of Pieter Coecke van Aelst (PMA 1965)
*The Massacre of the Innocents*
Lower near right inner panel from an altarpiece; see previous and following entries
c. 1532–35
Tempera on panel
17 1/2 × 16 9/16" (44.5 × 42 cm)

Purchased from the George Grey Barnard Collection with Museum funds
1945-25-117 r

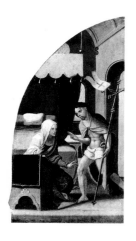

**Coecke van Aelst, Pieter, follower of**
Previously listed as the workshop of Pieter Coecke van Aelst (PMA 1965)
*"Noli Me Tangere"*
Upper right inner panel from an altarpiece; see previous and following entries
c. 1532–35
Tempera on panel
20 1/2 × 10 13/16" (52 × 27.5 cm)

Purchased from the George Grey Barnard Collection with Museum funds
1945-25-117 o

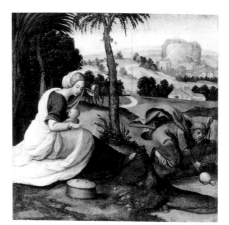

**Coecke van Aelst, Pieter, follower of**
Previously listed as the workshop of Pieter Coecke van Aelst (PMA 1965)
*Rest on the Flight into Egypt*
Lower far right inner panel from an altarpiece; see previous entries
c. 1532–35
Tempera on panel
17 1/2 × 16 3/4" (44.5 × 42.5 cm)

Purchased from the George Grey Barnard Collection with Museum funds
1945-25-117 s

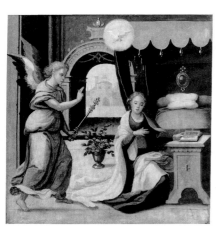

**Coecke van Aelst, Pieter, follower of**
Previously listed as the workshop of Pieter Coecke van Aelst (PMA 1965)
*The Annunciation*
Lower far left inner panel from an altarpiece; see previous and following entries
c. 1532–35
Tempera on panel
17 1/2 × 16 7/8" (44.5 × 42.8 cm)

Purchased from the George Grey Barnard Collection with Museum funds
1945-25-117 p

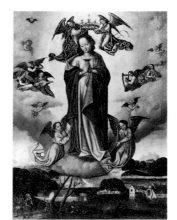

**Coffermans, Marcellus, imitator of**
Netherlandish, active Antwerp, first securely documented 1549, last dated work 1570
Previously listed as Marcellus Coffermans (JFD 1972)
*The Assumption of the Virgin*
16th century
Oil on panel
15 1/2 × 10 7/8" (39.4 × 27.6 cm)

John G. Johnson Collection
cat. 396

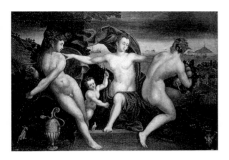

**Coignet, Gillis, copy after**
Flemish, 1538–1599
*Sine Cerere et Baccho friget Venus (Without Ceres and Bacchus, Venus Would Freeze)*
After an engraving by Raphaël Sadeler (Flemish, 1560/61–1628/32) of a lost painting by Coignet
Late 16th century
Center bottom: SINE CERERE ET BACCHO / FRIGET VENVS / B. DOSSI FERRARENSE PIN. 1553
Oil on canvas
24 7/8 × 36 1/4" (63.2 × 92.1 cm)

Purchased with the W. P. Wilstach Fund
W1904-1-10

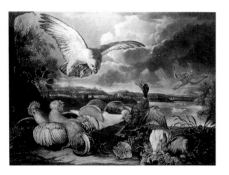

**Coninck, David de**
Flemish, active Antwerp and Brussels, 1636–1699
Previously listed as Pauwel de Vos (JFD 1972)
*Owl Attacking Chickens, Ducks, and Hares*
Known in several versions
17th century
Lower left (spurious): A Cuyp
Oil on canvas
50 7/8 × 69" (129.2 × 175.3 cm)

John G. Johnson Collection
cat. 701

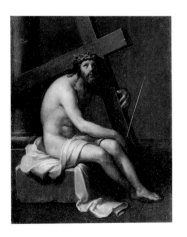

**Cornelis Cornelisz. van Haarlem**
Dutch, active Haarlem, 1562–1638
*The Man of Sorrows*
1597
Lower left: CHaerlemesis Ao. 1597—
Oil on panel
16 3/4 × 12 3/8" (42.5 × 31.4 cm)

Gift of Dr. and Mrs. Richard W. Levy
1968-182-1

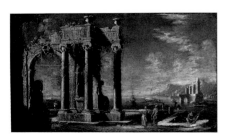

**Cossiau, Jan Joost van**
Dutch, active Germany and Paris?, 1660–1732/34
*Ruins*
Early 18th century
Oil on canvas
12 × 20 3/16" (30.5 × 51.3 cm)

Bequest of Robert Nebinger
1889-139

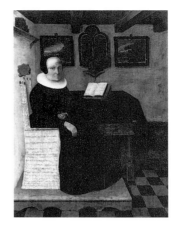

**Coster, Hendrick**
Dutch, active Arnhem, active c. 1642–c. 1659
*Portrait of a Lady*
17th century
Oil on panel
19 1/2 × 14 9/16" (49.5 × 37 cm)

John G. Johnson Collection
cat. 460

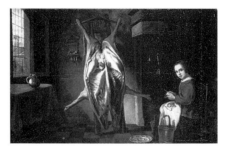

**Coveyn, Reinier**
Flemish, active Antwerp and Dordrecht, born 1636, still active 1674
*Interior with a Slaughtered Pig*
17th century
Oil on panel
17 1/4 × 25 5/8" (43.8 × 65.1 cm)

John G. Johnson Collection
cat. 486

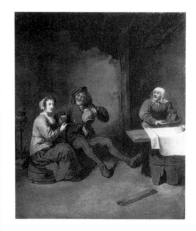

**Craesbeck, Joos van, attributed to**
Flemish, active Antwerp and Brussels, 1605/8–1662
*Peasant Couple Drinking*
17th century
Oil on panel
15 15/16 × 12 7/8" (40.5 × 32.7 cm)

John G. Johnson Collection
cat. 687

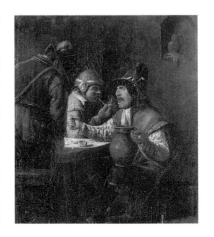

**Craesbeck, Joos van, attributed to**
Previously listed as Joos van Craesbeck (JFD 1972)
*Smokers*
17th century
Lower left: CB
Oil on panel
16 1/8 × 13 1/4" (41 × 33.6 cm)

John G. Johnson Collection
cat. 688

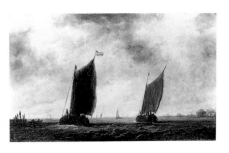

**Cuyp, Aelbert**
Dutch, active Dordrecht,
1620–1691
*Fishing Boats on the Maas*
c. 1641
Lower right: A Cuyp
Oil on panel
18 3/8 × 29" (46.7 × 73.7 cm)

John G. Johnson Collection
cat. 627

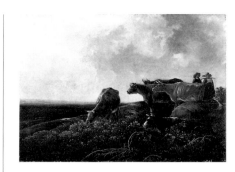

**Cuyp, Aelbert, imitator of**
*Hilly Landscape with Cattle*
17th century
Lower right (spurious): A. cuyp.
Oil on panel
17 5/8 × 24 3/16" (44.8 × 61.4 cm)

John G. Johnson Collection
cat. 624

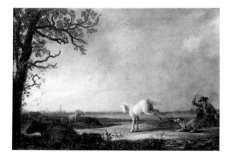

**Cuyp, Aelbert**
*Landscape with Cows and Sheep*
c. 1645
Lower left: A. cuyp.
Oil on panel
12 11/16 × 18 1/4" (32.2 × 46.3 cm)

John G. Johnson Collection
cat. 621

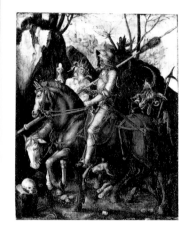

**Dalem, Cornelis van,
attributed to**
Netherlandish, active Antwerp,
first documented 1545, died
1573
Previously listed as Cornelis van
Dalem (JFD 1972)
*A Knight, Death, and the Devil*
After the engraving by Albrecht
Dürer (German, 1471–1528),
dated 1513 (Bartsch 98)
16th century
Oil on panel
10 5/8 × 8 3/16" (27 × 20.8 cm)

John G. Johnson Collection
cat. 405

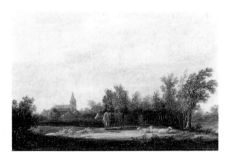

**Cuyp, Aelbert**
*Kicking Horse*
c. 1645–50
Lower right: AL [ligated] cuyp:
Oil on panel
25 7/8 × 36 3/16" (65.7 × 91.9 cm)

John G. Johnson Collection
cat. 622

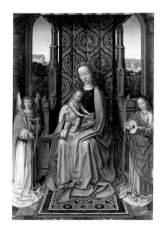

**David, Gerard**
Netherlandish, active Bruges,
first documented 1484, died
1523
*Enthroned Virgin and Child, with
Angels*
c. 1490–95
Oil on panel
39 1/16 × 25 11/16" (99.2 × 65.2 cm)

John G. Johnson Collection
cat. 329

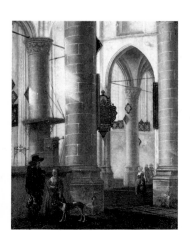

**Cuyp, Aelbert, attributed to**
Previously listed as Aelbert Cuyp
(JFD 1972)
*Interior of the Groote Kerk,
Dordrecht*
c. 1660
Lower left: A. cuyp fecit
Oil on panel
16 5/16 × 12 1/2" (41.4 × 31.7 cm)

John G. Johnson Collection
cat. 1181

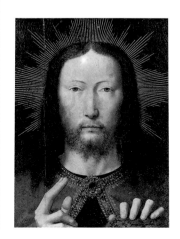

**David, Gerard**
*Salvator Mundi*
c. 1500
Oil on panel
18 1/8 × 13 1/4" (46 × 33.6 cm)

John G. Johnson Collection
cat. 330

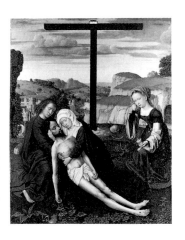

**David, Gerard**
*Lamentation*
c. 1515–20
On cross: INRI; center right, on
ointment jar: [P?]AIS
Oil on panel
34 1/4 × 25 5/8" (87 × 65.1 cm)

John G. Johnson Collection
cat. 328

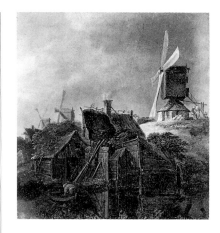

**Decker, Cornelis**
*Windmills and Houses on the
Waterside*
17th century
Oil on panel
14 1/4 × 12 5/8" (36.2 × 32.1 cm)

John G. Johnson Collection
cat. 583

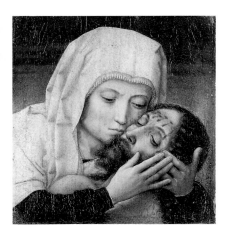

**David, Gerard, follower of**
Previously listed as a copy after
Gerard David (JFD 1972)
*Pietà*
16th century
Oil on panel
7 13/16 × 7 3/16" (19.8 × 18.3 cm)

John G. Johnson Collection
inv. 54

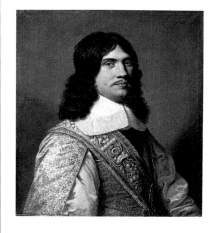

**Delff, Jacob Willemsz., II**
Dutch, active Delft, 1619–1661
*Portrait of a Young Man*
1655
Center left: AEtatis. 25. / JDelff.
1655.
Oil on canvas
27 9/16 × 24 3/16" (70 × 61.4 cm)

John G. Johnson Collection
cat. 496

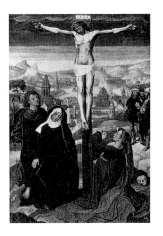

**David, Gerard, follower of**
Previously listed as a late copy
after Gerard David (JFD 1972)
*The Crucifixion*
Another version is in the Bob
Jones University Collection of
Religious Art, Greenville, South
Carolina
16th century
On cross: I N R I
Oil on panel
12 3/8 × 8 1/4" (31.4 × 20.9 cm)

John G. Johnson Collection
cat. 395

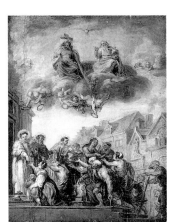

**Diepenbeeck, Abraham van**
Flemish, active Antwerp,
1596–1675
*Saints Roch, Stephen, Lawrence, and
Elizabeth Distributing Alms*
c. 1635
Oil on panel
15 15/16 × 11 3/4" (40.5 × 29.8 cm)

John G. Johnson Collection
cat. 676

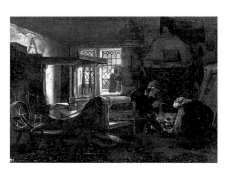

**Decker, Cornelis**
Dutch, active Haarlem, first
documented 1623, died 1678
*The Weaver*
17th century
Oil on panel
12 5/16 × 16 1/4" (31.3 × 41.3 cm)

John G. Johnson Collection
cat. 549

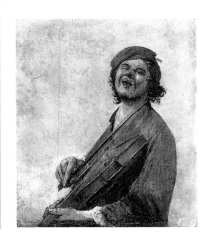

**Diepraem, Abraham,
copy after**
Dutch, active Rotterdam,
1622?–1670?
Previously listed as Abraham
Diepraem (JFD 1972)
*Fiddler*
17th century
Oil on panel
14 3/4 × 12 3/8" (37.5 × 31.4 cm)

John G. Johnson Collection
cat. 533

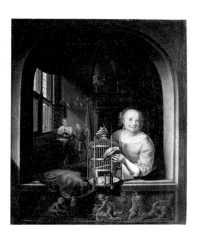

**Dou, Gerard, follower of**
Dutch, active Leiden,
1613–1675
Previously listed as a copy after
Gerard Dou (JFD 1972)
*Girl with a Parrot*
Possibly based on Dou's *Girl with
a Parrot*, formerly in the collection
of Graf Gagarin, St. Petersburg
17th century
Oil on panel
14 3/8 × 11 3/4" (36.5 × 29.8 cm)

John G. Johnson Collection
inv. 432

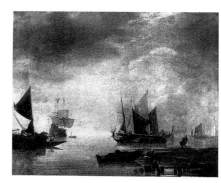

**Dubbels, Hendrick Jacobsz.,
attributed to**
Dutch, active Amsterdam,
1620/21–c. 1676
Previously listed as a copy after
Willem van de Velde the
Younger (JFD 1972)
*Calm Sea*
17th century
Oil on canvas
22 × 27 1/8" (55.9 × 68.9 cm)

John G. Johnson Collection
cat. 585

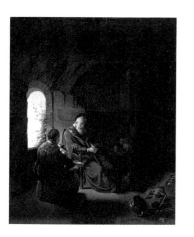

**Dou, Gerard, copy after**
Previously listed as a copy after
Rembrandt Harmensz. van Rijn
(JFD 1972)
*Blind Tobit and His Wife*
After the painting in the
National Gallery, London (4189)
17th century
Upper right (spurious): R
Oil on canvas
26 3/16 × 20 3/8" (66.5 × 51.7 cm)

John G. Johnson Collection
cat. 482

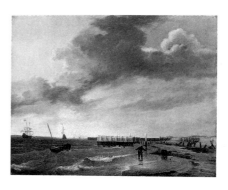

**Dubbels, Hendrick Jacobsz.,
copy after**
*Coast Scene*
After the painting in the Galleria
Palatina, Florence (457)
17th century
Lower right: DVBBELS
Oil on canvas
27 1/2 × 34 3/4" (69.8 × 88.3 cm)

John G. Johnson Collection
cat. 586

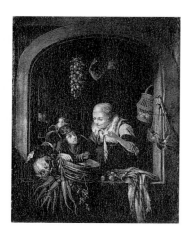

**Dou, Gerard, copy after**
*Fishwife*
After the painting formerly in the
collection of Henry Blank, Glen
Ridge, New Jersey
17th century
Oil on canvas
18 × 13 15/16" (45.7 × 35.4 cm)

John G. Johnson Collection
cat. 548

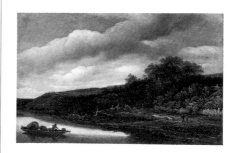

**Dubois, Guillam**
Dutch, active Haarlem,
c. 1610–1680
*River Scene*
1652
Lower left, on boat: G D Bois
1652
Oil on panel
15 1/2 × 23 3/4" (39.4 × 60.3 cm)

John G. Johnson Collection
cat. 562

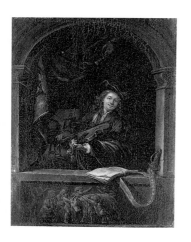

**Dou, Gerard, copy after**
*Violinist*
After the painting in the
Gemäldegalerie Alte Meister,
Staatliche Kunstsammlungen
Dresden (gal. no. 1707)
17th century
Oil on panel
13 × 9 7/8" (33 × 25.1 cm)

John G. Johnson Collection
cat. 545

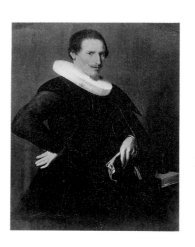

**Dubordieu, Pieter**
Dutch, active Leiden and
Amsterdam, born 1609/10,
still active 1678
*Portrait of Pieter de la Court*
Companion to the following
painting
1635
Upper left: AETATIS 42; upper
right: A N 1635; lower right: PD
[ligated] fecit
Oil on panel
45 1/2 × 33 1/8" (115.6 × 84.1 cm)

Purchased with the W. P.
Wilstach Fund
W1904-1-63

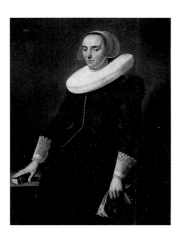

**Dubordieu, Pieter**
*Portrait of Jeanne de Planque*
Companion to the preceding painting
1635
Upper left: AETATIS 43; lower left: PD [ligated]; upper right: A 1635
Oil on panel
44 7/8 × 32 7/8" (114 × 83.5 cm)

Purchased with the George W. Elkins Fund
E1982-1-1

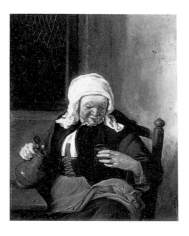

**Dusart, Cornelis**
Dutch, active Haarlem, 1660–1704
*Old Woman Drinking*
17th century
Lower left: Cordousart.
Oil on panel
13 × 10" (33 × 25.4 cm)

John G. Johnson Collection
cat. 529

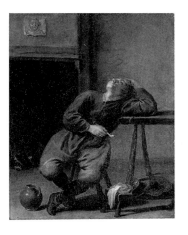

**Duck, Jacob, attributed to**
Dutch, active Utrecht, Haarlem, and The Hague, c. 1600–1667
Previously listed as Adriaen Brouwer (JFD 1972)
*Smoker*
17th century
Center bottom: AB
Oil on panel
12 5/8 × 9 9/16" (32.1 × 24.3 cm)

John G. Johnson Collection
cat. 683

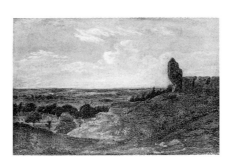

**Dutch, active Haarlem, unknown artist**
Previously attributed to Hercules Seghers (JFD 1972)
*Landscape with Fences*
c. 1600–25
Oil on panel
10 3/4 × 15 3/8" (27.3 × 39 cm)

John G. Johnson Collection
cat. 461

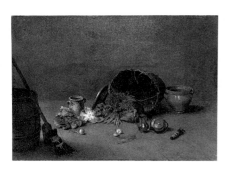

**Duifhuysen, Pieter Jacobsz., also called Colinckhovius**
Dutch, active Rotterdam, 1608–1677
Previously listed as Hendrik Maertensz. Sorgh (JFD 1972)
*Still Life*
17th century
Oil on panel
11 1/16 × 14 7/8" (28.1 × 37.8 cm)

John G. Johnson Collection
cat. 783

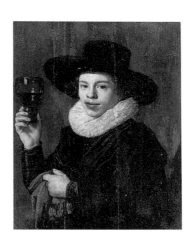

**Dutch, active Amsterdam, unknown artist**
*Portrait of a Nineteen-Year-Old Man*
1623
Upper right: 1623 / AETATIS.SVAE. / 19.
Oil on panel
18 7/8 × 14 3/8" (47.9 × 36.5 cm)

John G. Johnson Collection
cat. 457

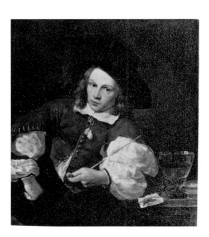

**Dujardin, Karel, attributed to**
Dutch, active Amsterdam and Italy, c. 1622–1678
*Portrait of a Young Man Seated Smoking*
17th century
Oil on canvas
16 7/16 × 14 1/8" (41.7 × 35.9 cm)

John G. Johnson Collection
cat. 609

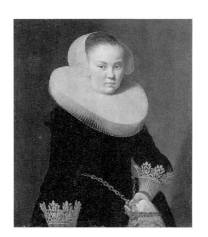

**Dutch, active Amsterdam, unknown artist**
*Portrait of an Eighteen-Year-Old Woman*
1631
Upper left: [AETA]TIS.SVAE.18. / 1631.
Oil on canvas
28 15/16 × 23 9/16" (73.5 × 59.8 cm)

John G. Johnson Collection
cat. 454

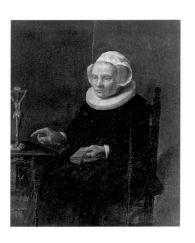

**Dutch, active Haarlem, unknown artist**
*Portrait of a Seventy-Four-Year-Old Woman*
1635
Upper left: AETATIS 74 1635; on crucifix: INRI
Oil on panel
12 3/4 × 10 3/8" (32.4 × 26.3 cm)

The William L. Elkins Collection
E1924-3-75

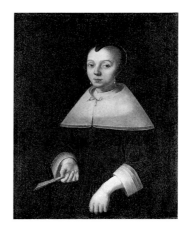

**Dutch, unknown artist**
Previously listed as Ludolf de Jongh (JFD 1972)
*Portrait of a Lady*
c. 1650–1700
Oil on canvas
34 1/2 × 26 7/16" (87.6 × 67.1 cm)

John G. Johnson Collection
inv. 2818

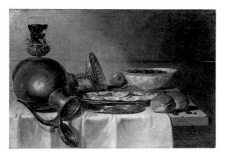

**Dutch, unknown artist**
*Still Life with Metal Cups and Oysters*
1636
Lower right: JS 1636
Oil on panel
22 1/16 × 31 7/8" (56 × 81 cm)

John G. Johnson Collection
cat. 651

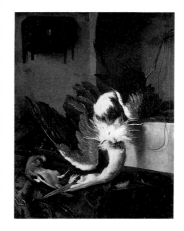

**Dutch, unknown artist**
*Still Life with a Heron*
c. 1660
Lower right (spurious): B. F. / Fytt
Oil on canvas
41 1/2 × 29 7/8" (105.4 × 75.9 cm)

John G. Johnson Collection
cat. 641

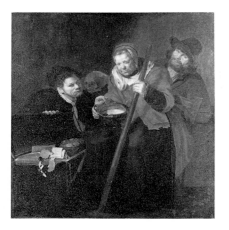

**Dutch, unknown artist**
Previously listed as an unknown artist, 17th century (JFD 1972)
*The Miser*
1646
Oil on canvas
56 1/2 × 52 5/8" (143.5 × 133.7 cm)

John G. Johnson Collection
cat. 436

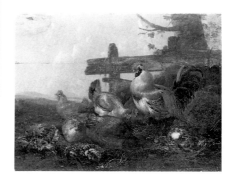

**Dutch, unknown artist**
Previously listed as Aelbert Cuyp (JFD 1972)
*A Cock and Hens*
17th century
Oil on panel
35 9/16 × 45 1/2" (90.3 × 115.6 cm)

John G. Johnson Collection
cat. 623

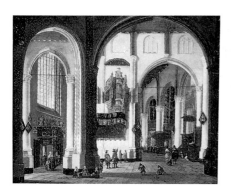

**Dutch, active Rotterdam, unknown artist**
*Interior of the St. Laurenskerk, Rotterdam*
c. 1650–60
Lower left: E. de Gruyter
Oil on panel
26 × 30 3/4" (66 × 78.1 cm)

John G. Johnson Collection
cat. 601

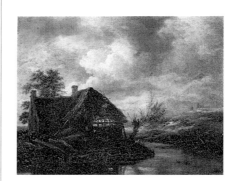

**Dutch, unknown artist**
Previously listed as Jacob Isaacksz. van Ruisdael (JFD 1972)
*Cottage by the Waterside*
17th century
Lower right (spurious): Ruysdael ft
Oil on canvas
11 3/16 × 13 5/8" (28.4 × 34.6 cm)

John G. Johnson Collection
cat. 568

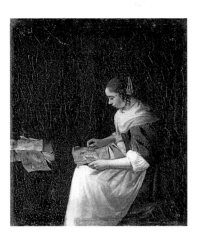

**Dutch, unknown artist**
*Girl Drawing*
17th century
Oil on canvas
10 ⁵/₈ × 8 ⁷/₈" (27 × 22.5 cm)

John G. Johnson Collection
cat. 506

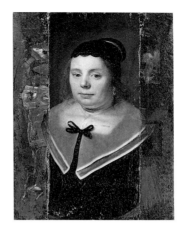

**Dutch, unknown artist**
Previously listed as Aelbert Cuyp
(JFD 1972)
*Portrait of a Lady*
A 4 ¹/₂" strip has been added to
each side
17th century
Oil on panel
27 ⁹/₁₆ × 20 ¹/₄" (70 × 51.4 cm)

John G. Johnson Collection
cat. 1182

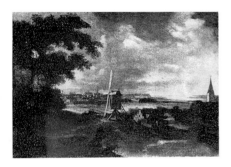

**Dutch, unknown artist**
*Landscape with a Windmill*
17th century
Oil on canvas
10 ⁵/₈ × 14 ³/₄" (27 × 37.5 cm)

John G. Johnson Collection
cat. 579

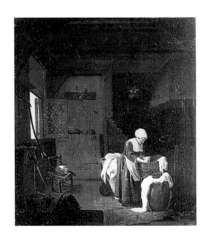

**Dutch, unknown artist**
*Still Life with Fish and a Cat*
The signature "A. B. Beyeren"
came away in cleaning in 1970
17th century
Lower right: [illegible signature]
Oil on canvas
19 ¹/₄ × 24 ¹/₄" (48.9 × 61.6 cm)

John G. Johnson Collection
cat. 640

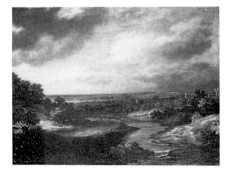

**Dutch, unknown artist**
*Landscape with Dunes*
17th century
Oil on canvas
31 ⁷/₈ × 40 ¹/₄" (81 × 102.2 cm)

John G. Johnson Collection
cat. 578

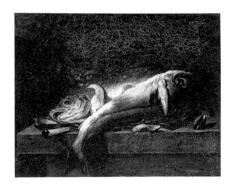

**Dutch, unknown artist**
*Working Woman*
17th century
Oil on canvas
28 ⁹/₁₆ × 24" (72.5 × 61 cm)

John G. Johnson Collection
cat. 540

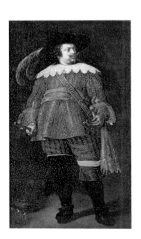

**Dutch, unknown artist**
*Portrait of a Field Marshal*
17th century
Oil on canvas
80 ⁷/₈ × 45 ⁵/₈" (205.4 × 115.9 cm)

Purchased with the W. P.
Wilstach Fund
W1904-1-20

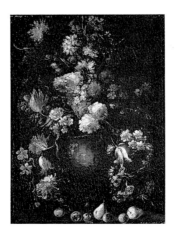

**Dutch or Flemish,
unknown artist**
*Still Life with Flowers*
Companion to the following
painting
18th century
Oil on canvas
38 ¹³/₁₆ × 29 ¹/₈" (98.6 × 74 cm)

The Bloomfield Moore Collection
1883-120

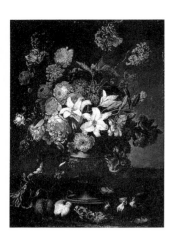

**Dutch or Flemish,
unknown artist**
*Still Life with Flowers*
Companion to the preceding
painting
18th century
Oil on canvas
39 × 29 1/4" (99.1 × 74.3 cm)

The Bloomfield Moore Collection
1883-121

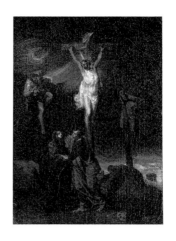

**Dyck, Anthony van,
follower of**
Previously listed as an old copy
after Anthony van Dyck (JFD
1972)
*The Crucifixion*
17th century
Oil on canvas
15 1/4 × 10 1/2" (38.7 × 26.7 cm)

John G. Johnson Collection
cat. 673

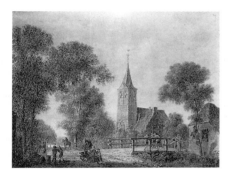

**Dutch, unknown artist**
*Village Church*
18th century
Oil on panel
7 11/16 × 10" (19.5 × 25.4 cm)

John G. Johnson Collection
inv. 2811

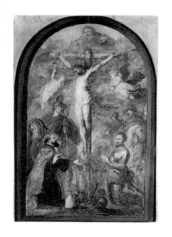

**Dyck, Anthony van,
follower of**
*The Crucifixion, with a Bishop, a
Saint, and a Donor in Armor*
17th century
Oil on panel
13 5/8 × 9 1/16" (34.6 × 23 cm)

Purchased with the W. P.
Wilstach Fund
W1902-1-8

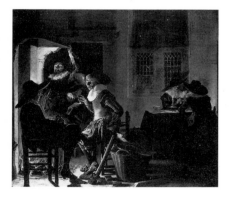

**Duyster, Willem Cornelisz.**
Dutch, active Amsterdam,
1598/99–1635
*Soldiers beside a Fireplace*
c. 1628–32
Oil on panel
16 1/2 × 18 1/2" (41.9 × 47 cm)

John G. Johnson Collection
cat. 445

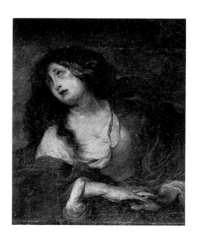

**Dyck, Anthony van,
follower of**
*Saint Mary Magdalene Mourning*
17th century
Oil on panel
29 1/8 × 23 3/8" (74 × 59.4 cm)

John G. Johnson Collection
cat. 670

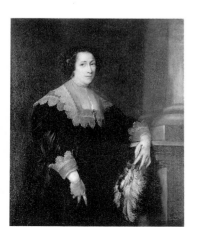

**Dyck, Anthony van,
attributed to**
Flemish, active Italy, Antwerp,
and England, 1599–1641
Previously listed as Anthony van
Dyck (JFD 1972)
*Portrait of a Lady* [possibly Lady
Philadelphia Wharton]
1636
Center right: AETATIS SVAE. /
22. ANNO 1636
Oil on canvas
47 3/4 × 38 1/4" (121.3 × 97.1 cm)

John G. Johnson Collection
cat. 674

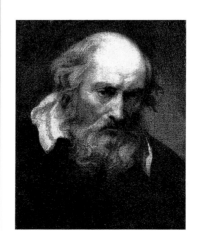

**Dyck, Anthony van,
imitator of**
Previously listed as Anthony van
Dyck (JFD 1972)
*Head of an Old Man*
17th century
Oil on canvas
16 1/2 × 13 3/16" (41.9 × 33.5 cm)

John G. Johnson Collection
cat. 669

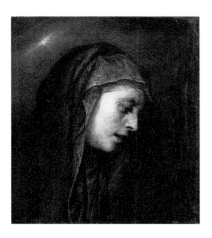

**Dyck, Anthony van, imitator of**
Previously listed as an old copy after Anthony van Dyck (JFD 1972)
*Mater Dolorosa*
17th century
Oil on canvas
18 3/8 × 16 3/8" (46.7 × 41.6 cm)

John G. Johnson Collection
cat. 672

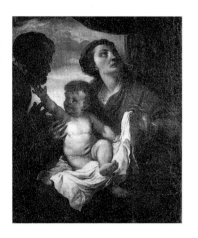

**Dyck, Anthony van, copy after**
*The Holy Family*
After the painting in the Kunsthistorisches Museum, Vienna (inv. no. 1047)
17th century
Oil on canvas
20 1/8 × 15 7/8" (51.1 × 40.3 cm)

John G. Johnson Collection
inv. 2842

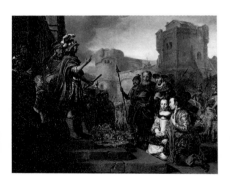

**Eeckhout, Gerbrand van den**
Dutch, active Amsterdam, 1621–1674
*The Continence of Scipio*
1659
Center bottom: G. V. Eeckhout fe. / A 1659
Oil on canvas
52 × 67" (132.1 × 170.2 cm)

Purchased with the George W. Elkins Fund
E1981-1-1

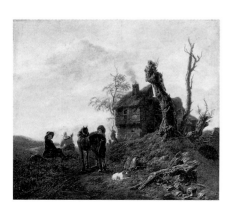

**Eemont, Adriaen van, attributed to**
Dutch, active Dordrecht, c. 1627–1662
Previously listed as Nicolaes Ficke (JFD 1972)
*The Halt at the Cottage*
17th century
Oil on canvas
25 9/16 × 28 3/8" (64.9 × 72.1 cm)

John G. Johnson Collection
cat. 526

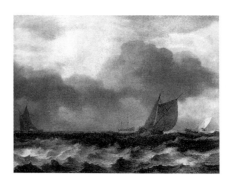

**Everdingen, Allart van**
Dutch, active Alkmaar and Amsterdam, 1621–1675
*Rough Sea*
17th century
Lower right: AVE
Oil on canvas
24 3/4 × 30 15/16" (62.9 × 78.6 cm)

John G. Johnson Collection
cat. 587

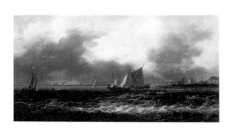

**Everdingen, Allart van, copy after**
*Rough Sea*
After an engraving by Pierre-Charles Canot (French, 1710–1777) of a painting by Everdingen in the Landesmuseum für Kunst und Kulturgeschichte, Oldenburg, Germany
17th century
Lower right (spurious): JRuisdael
Oil on panel
13 3/16 × 23 1/8" (33.5 × 58.7 cm)

John G. Johnson Collection
cat. 470

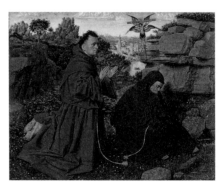

**Eyck, Jan van, attributed to**
Netherlandish, active Bruges, first documented 1422, died 1441
Previously listed as Jan van Eyck (JFD 1972)
*Saint Francis of Assisi Receiving the Stigmata*
c. 1438–40
Oil on vellum on panel
5 × 5 3/4" (12.7 × 14.6 cm)

John G. Johnson Collection
cat. 314

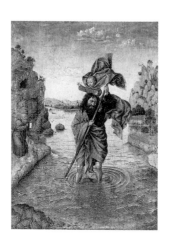

**Eyck, Jan van, follower of**
*Saint Christopher*
c. 1440–50
Oil on panel
11 5/8 × 8 5/16" (29.5 × 21.1 cm)

John G. Johnson Collection
cat. 342

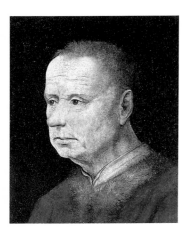

**Eyck, Jan van, follower of**
*Portrait of a Man*
Fragment [?] inlaid in a larger
panel
15th century
Oil on panel
Painting: 5 $\frac{1}{2}$ × 3 $\frac{3}{4}$"
(14 × 9.5 cm)

John G. Johnson Collection
cat. 315

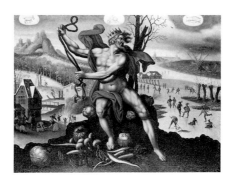

**Flemish, unknown artist**
*Winter*
See previous three entries
c. 1575–1625
Oil on canvas
45 $\frac{1}{4}$ × 57 $\frac{3}{4}$" (114.9 × 146.7 cm)

Bequest of John W. Pepper
1935-10-95

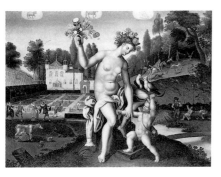

**Flemish, unknown artist**
*Spring*
After an engraving by Adrian
Collaert (Flemish, c. 1560–
1618) after designs by Marten
de Vos (Flemish, 1532–1603);
companion to the following three
paintings
c. 1575–1625
Oil on canvas
45 $\frac{1}{4}$ × 57 $\frac{7}{8}$" (114.9 × 147 cm)

Bequest of John W. Pepper
1935-10-98

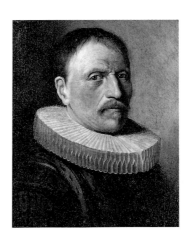

**Flemish, unknown artist**
Previously listed as an unknown
artist, c. 1600–10 (JFD 1972)
*Portrait of a Gentleman*
c. 1600–10
Oil on panel
18 $\frac{1}{8}$ × 14 $\frac{1}{8}$" (46 × 35.9 cm)

John G. Johnson Collection
cat. 458

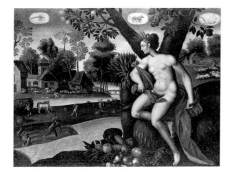

**Flemish, unknown artist**
*Summer*
See previous entry
c. 1575–1625
Oil on canvas
46 $\frac{1}{4}$ × 58" (117.5 × 147.3 cm)

Bequest of John W. Pepper
1935-10-96

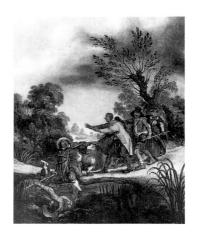

**Flemish, unknown artist**
Previously listed as an imitator of
Pieter Breugel the Elder,
mid-17th century (JFD 1972)
*The Blind Leading the Blind*
c. 1600–50
Oil on panel
16 $\frac{9}{16}$ × 12 $\frac{11}{16}$" (42.1 × 32.2 cm)

John G. Johnson Collection
cat. 472

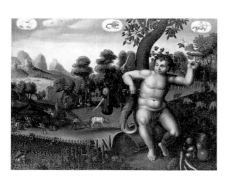

**Flemish, unknown artist**
*Autumn*
See previous two entries
c. 1575–1625
Oil on canvas
43 $\frac{3}{4}$ × 58 $\frac{3}{4}$" (111.1 × 149.2 cm)

Bequest of John W. Pepper
1935-10-97

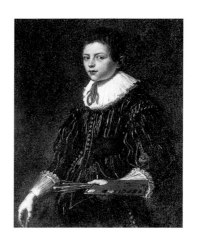

**Flemish, unknown artist**
Previously listed as Peter Paul
Rubens (JFD 1972)
*Portrait of a Young Man with a
Palette and Brushes*
c. 1615–20
Oil on canvas
30 $\frac{3}{16}$ × 23 $\frac{13}{16}$" (76.7 × 60.5 cm)

John G. Johnson Collection
cat. 810

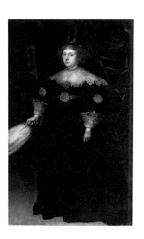

**Flemish or Dutch,
unknown artist**
Previously listed as Flemish,
unknown artist, 17th century
(PMA 1965)
*Portrait of a Lady*
c. 1630–35
Oil on canvas
78 3/4 × 46 3/8" (200 × 117.8 cm)

Purchased with the W. P.
Wilstach Fund
W1899-1-2

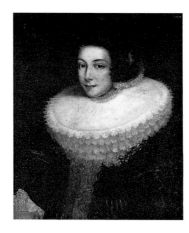

**Flemish, unknown artist**
*Portrait of a Woman in a Ruff*
17th century
Oil on canvas
31 9/16 × 24 1/2" (80.2 × 62.2 cm)

Bequest of Arthur H. Lea
F1938-1-8

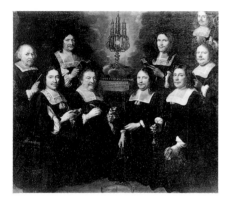

**Flemish, unknown artist**
Previously listed as Lodewyck van
der Helst (PMA 1965)
*Portrait of the Deacons of the
Confraternity of the Holy Sacrament*
1673
Center: LOF SŸ T HEŸLICH,
SACRAMENT / Geen wiin, oft
Ipocras, noch Terwe graen en
Liet— / ons Goodt int Avontmael,
maer 't Broot (Door 't Woort)
herdreven, / Wordt Vleesch, de
Wiin Wordt Bloet: daer en Bleef
anders niet— / als Godt, wiens
Vleesch, en Bloet ons daeghlijckx
Wordt Ge geven; bottom center:
DE-KENS / 1. Peeter Willemans
2. Carel Verhuyck / 3. Iōan de
Haegh  4. Cornelis Peeters / 1673
Oil on canvas
71 1/4 × 81 1/4" (181 × 206.4 cm)

Gift of John G. Johnson for the
W. P. Wilstach Collection
W1904-1-52

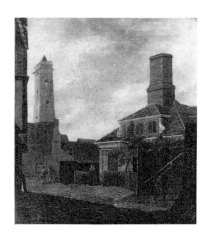

**Flemish, unknown artist**
*Street Scene*
18th century
Oil on canvas
11 15/16 × 10 1/16" (30.3 × 25.6 cm)

John G. Johnson Collection
cat. 541

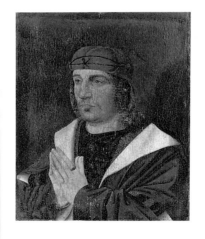

**Franco-Netherlandish,
unknown artist**
*Portrait of a Man in Prayer*
c. 1480?
Oil on panel
9 3/4 × 7 7/8" (24.8 × 20 cm)

John G. Johnson Collection
cat. 1174

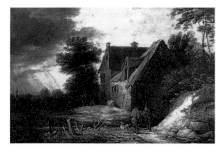

**Flemish, unknown artist**
*Peasant's Cottage*
17th century
Lower right: AB
Oil on panel
9 1/2 × 13 3/4" (24.1 × 34.9 cm)

John G. Johnson Collection
cat. 684

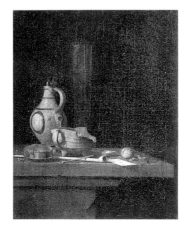

**Fris, Jan**
Dutch, active Amsterdam,
1627–1672
Previously listed as Edwaert
Kollier (JFD 1972)
*Still Life with a Stoneware Jar and
a Brazier*
17th century
Lower left (spurious): Kollier
Oil on canvas
25 1/2 × 19 3/16" (64.8 × 48.7 cm)

John G. Johnson Collection
cat. 643

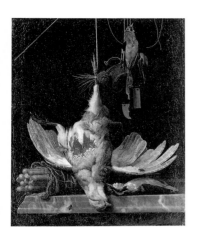

**Fromantiou, Hendrik de**
Dutch, active Maastricht, after
1670 active largely in Berlin,
1633–1694
*Still Life with Birds*
1679
Lower left: H d F 1679
Oil on canvas
21 1/4 × 16 7/8" (54 × 42.9 cm)

John G. Johnson Collection
cat. 645

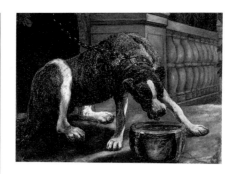

**Fyt, Jan, copy after**
*Watchdog Drinking Water*
Known in several versions
17th century
Oil on canvas
38 3/4 × 51 3/16" (93.4 × 130 cm)

John G. Johnson Collection
cat. 702

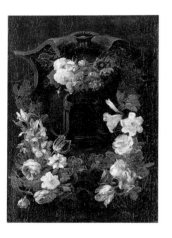

**Fyt, Jan**
Flemish, active Antwerp,
1611–1661
*Flowers Enframing a Relief of the
Virgin*
1643
Center: Johannes Fyt / 1643
Oil on panel
32 5/16 × 22 3/4" (82.1 × 57.8 cm)

John G. Johnson Collection
cat. 704

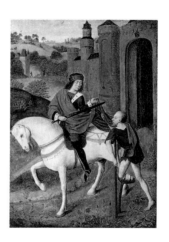

**Geertgen tot Sint Jans,
follower of**
Netherlandish, active Haarlem,
active c. 1480–c. 1490
*Saint Martin of Tours and the
Beggar*
Early 16th century
Oil on panel
17 5/16 × 12 1/8" (44 × 30.8 cm)

John G. Johnson Collection
cat. 346

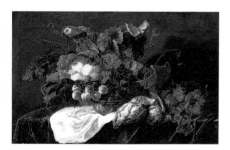

**Fyt, Jan**
*Still Life with Fruit, Dead
Partridges, and a Parrot*
1646
Center right: Joannes Fyt / 1646
Oil on canvas
29 7/8 × 43 3/4" (75.9 × 111.1 cm)

John G. Johnson Collection
cat. 705

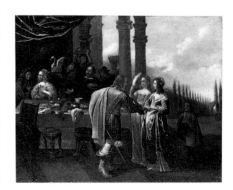

**Geffels, Frans**
Flemish, active Mantua and
environs, first recorded 1635/36,
died c. 1699
Previously listed as a Flemish
artist, c. 1650 (JFD 1972)
*Dinner Party on a Terrace*
17th century
On chair (spurious): P. D. Hoog
Oil on canvas
33 1/2 × 40 3/8" (85.1 × 102.5 cm)

John G. Johnson Collection
cat. 502

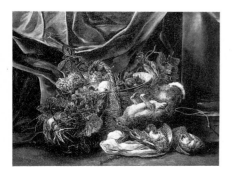

**Fyt, Jan**
Previously attributed to Jan Fyt
(JFD 1972)
*Still Life with Game and Fruit*
17th century
Oil on canvas
36 7/8 × 49 7/8" (93.7 × 126.7 cm)

John G. Johnson Collection
cat. 703

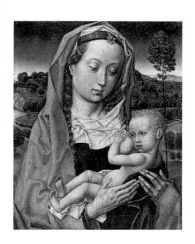

**Goes, Hugo van der,
attributed to**
Netherlandish, active Ghent,
first documented 1467, died 1482
Previously listed as Hugo van der
Goes (JFD 1972)
*Virgin and Child*
c. 1470
Oil on panel
12 3/4 × 10" (32.4 × 25.4 cm)

John G. Johnson Collection
cat. 336

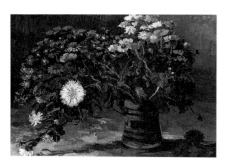

**Gogh, Vincent Willem van**
Dutch, 1853–1890
*Still Life with a Bouquet of Daisies*
1886
Oil on paper on panel
16 3/8 × 22 1/2" (41.6 × 57.1 cm)

Bequest of Charlotte Dorrance
Wright
1978-1-33

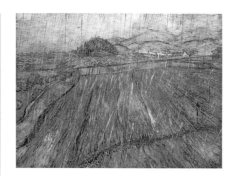

**Gogh, Vincent Willem van**
*Rain*
1889
Oil on canvas
28 7/8 × 36 3/8" (73.3 × 92.4 cm)

The Henry P. McIlhenny
Collection in memory of
Frances P. McIlhenny
1986-26-36

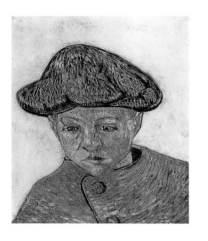

**Gogh, Vincent Willem van**
*Portrait of Camille Roulin*
1888 or 1889
Oil on canvas
17 × 13 3/4" (43.2 × 34.9 cm)

Gift of Mr. and Mrs. Rodolphe
Meyer de Schauensee
1973-129-1

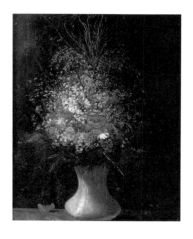

**Gogh, Vincent Willem van,
imitator of**
Previously listed as Vincent van
Gogh (JGJ 1941)
*Still Life with a Vase of Flowers*
c. 1900
Lower right (spurious): Vincent
Oil on canvas
30 3/4 × 25 3/16" (78.1 × 64.3 cm)

John G. Johnson Collection
inv. 2322

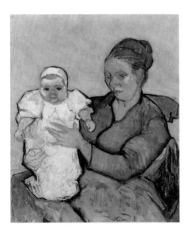

**Gogh, Vincent Willem van**
*Portrait of Madame Augustine Roulin
and Baby Marcelle*
1888 or 1889
Oil on canvas
36 3/8 × 28 15/16" (92.4 × 73.5 cm)

Bequest of Lisa Norris Elkins
1950-92-22

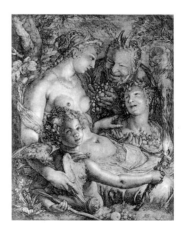

**Goltzius, Hendrick**
Dutch, active Haarlem,
1558–1617
*Sine Cerere et Libero friget Venus
(Without Ceres and Bacchus, Venus
Would Freeze)*
c. 1600–3
Lower right: HG[olt]z[ius] inv.[?]
Ink and oil on canvas
41 3/8 × 31 1/2" (105.1 × 80 cm)

Purchased with the Mr. and Mrs.
Walter H. Annenberg Fund for
Major Acquisitions, the Henry P.
McIlhenny Fund in memory of
Frances P. McIlhenny, bequest (by
exchange) of Mr. and Mrs. Herbert
C. Morris, and gift (by exchange)
of Frank and Alice Osborn
1990-100-1

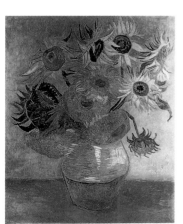

**Gogh, Vincent Willem van**
*Sunflowers*
1888 or 1889
On vase: Vincent
Oil on canvas
36 3/8 × 28" (92.4 × 71.1 cm)

The Mr. and Mrs. Carroll S.
Tyson, Jr., Collection
1963-116-19

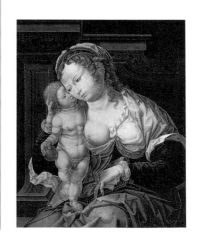

**Gossaert, Jan, also called
Jan Mabuse, follower of**
Netherlandish, active Antwerp,
Mechelen, Utrecht, and
Middelburg, c. 1478–1532
Previously listed as a copy after
Jan Gossaert (JFD 1972)
*Virgin and Child*
Based on the painting in the
Museo del Prado, Madrid (1930)
16th century
Oil on panel
22 1/8 × 16 5/8" (56.2 × 42.2 cm)

John G. Johnson Collection
cat. 390

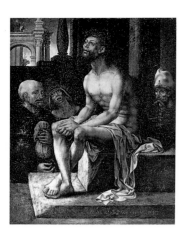

**Gossaert, Jan, copy after**
*"Ecce Homo"*
After a painting known through
several copies
1527
Center bottom: IOANNES,
MALBODIVS, INVENIT; lower
right: 15,27
Oil on panel
9 3/4 × 7 3/8" (24.8 × 18.7 cm)

John G. Johnson Collection
cat. 391

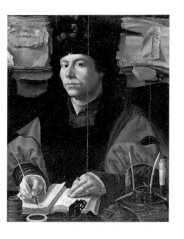

**Gossaert, Jan, copy after**
*Portrait of a Merchant* [possibly
Jerome Sandelin]
After the painting in the
National Gallery of Art,
Washington, D.C. (1967.4.1)
16th century
Upper left: Alrehande Missiven;
upper right: Alrehande Minuten;
on pin in hat: IAS; on ring: IS
Oil on panel
25 1/4 × 19" (64.1 × 48.3 cm)

John G. Johnson Collection
inv. 2051

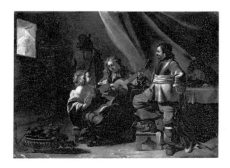

**Goubau, Antoine**
Flemish, active Antwerp and
Rome, 1616–1698
Previously listed as Karel
Dujardin? (JFD 1972)
*Concert*
c. 1645–50
On footstool: KDJ
Oil on copper
8 3/8 × 11 5/16" (21.3 × 28.7 cm)

John G. Johnson Collection
cat. 607

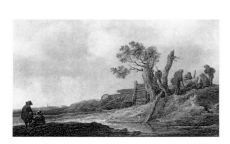

**Goyen, Jan van**
Dutch, active Leiden and
The Hague, 1596–1656
*Peasants near a Pool*
1633
Lower left: VG 1633
Oil on panel
12 1/2 × 21 1/4" (31.7 × 54 cm)

John G. Johnson Collection
cat. 462

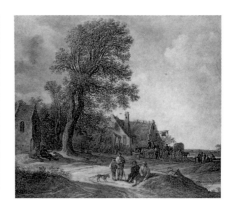

**Goyen, Jan van**
*Peasants Resting before an Inn*
Early 1640s
Oil on canvas
48 1/8 × 53 7/8" (122.2 × 136.8 cm)

The William L. Elkins Collection
E1924-3-30

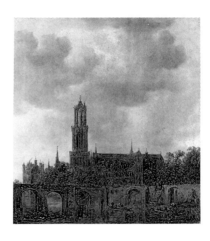

**Goyen, Jan van**
*Cathedral of Utrecht*
1646
Center bottom: v G 1646
Oil on panel
14 3/8 × 12 3/8" (36.5 × 31.4 cm)

John G. Johnson Collection
cat. 463

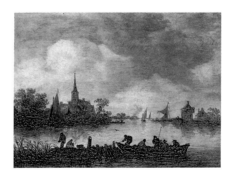

**Goyen, Jan van**
*Landscape with a Canal*
1653
Center bottom: v G 1653
Oil on panel
9 1/2 × 12 1/2" (24.1 × 31.7 cm)

John G. Johnson Collection
cat. 464

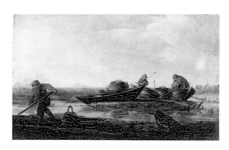

**Goyen, Jan van, imitator of**
Previously listed as in the manner
of Jan van Goyen (JFD 1972)
*Boats on a Beach*
17th century
Oil on panel
8 3/4 × 14 3/16" (22.2 × 36 cm)

John G. Johnson Collection
cat. 469

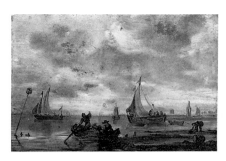

**Goyen, Jan van, imitator of**
Previously listed as Jan van
Goyen (JFD 1972)
*Zuider Zee*
Painted on the back of the plate
for the etching *Lot and His
Daughters*, by Gerard ter Borch
the Elder (Dutch, 1584–1662)
17th century
On reverse: GTBorch F Ano 1632
[in reverse]
Oil on copper
5 5/8 × 8" (14.3 × 20.3 cm)

John G. Johnson Collection
cat. 505

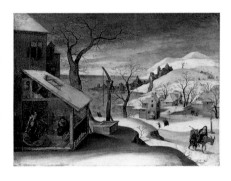

**Grimmer, Abel**
Flemish, active Antwerp,
active 1592–1619
*Winter Landscape with the Angel
Appearing to Saint Joseph, the
Massacre of the Innocents, and the
Flight into Egypt*
c. 1600–19
Lower right: ABEL GRIMER
FECIT
Oil on panel
10 1/8 × 13 1/16" (25.7 × 33.2 cm)

John G. Johnson Collection
cat. 654

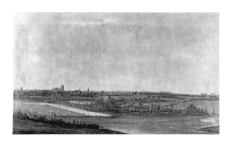

**Haagen, Joris van der,
attributed to**
Dutch, active The Hague and
Arnhem, born 1613–17,
died 1669
*View of Arnhem*
17th century
Oil on canvas
19 3/4 × 32 1/8" (50.2 × 81.6 cm)

John G. Johnson Collection
cat. 574

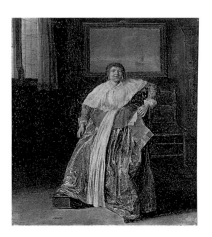

**Hals, Dirck**
Dutch, active Haarlem and
Leiden, 1591–1656
*Seated Woman with a Letter*
1633
Lower left: DHals / 1633
Oil on panel
13 5/16 × 11 1/4" (33.8 × 28.6 cm)

John G. Johnson Collection
cat. 434

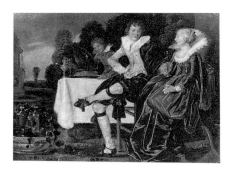

**Hals, Dirck, attributed to**
Previously listed as Dirck Hals
(JFD 1972)
*A Gentleman and a Lady Dining on
a Terrace*
c. 1625
Oil on panel
6 15/16 × 9 3/8" (17.6 × 23.8 cm)

John G. Johnson Collection
cat. 435

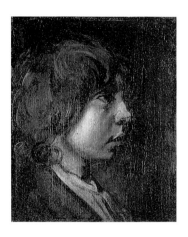

**Hals, Frans, follower of**
Dutch, active Haarlem,
c. 1582–1666
Previously listed as the school of
Frans Hals (JFD 1972)
*Portrait of a Boy*
17th century
Lower right (spurious): FH
Oil on panel
5 3/4 × 4 3/8" (14.6 × 11.1 cm)

John G. Johnson Collection
cat. 432

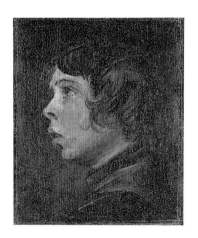

**Hals, Frans, follower of**
Previously listed as the school of
Frans Hals (JFD 1972)
*Portrait of a Boy*
17th century
Lower left (spurious): FH
Oil on panel
5 11/16 × 4 1/2" (14.4 × 11.4 cm)

John G. Johnson Collection
cat. 433

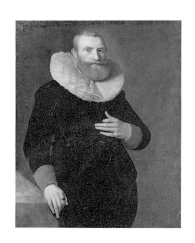

**Harings, Matthijs,
attributed to**
Dutch, active Leeuwarden and
Houbraken, documented
1609–1637
Previously listed as an Amsterdam
artist, c. 1610–15 (JFD 1972)
*Portrait of a Forty-One-Year-Old
Man*
1634
Upper left: AETAT.41 / Ao 1634
Oil on canvas
41 3/8 × 31 3/4" (105.1 × 81.6 cm)

John G. Johnson Collection
cat. 450

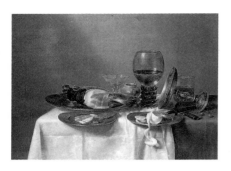

**Heda, Willem Claesz.**
Dutch, active Haarlem,
1594–1680/82
Previously listed as Pieter Claesz.
(JFD 1972)
*Still Life with a Ham and a Roemer*
c. 1631–34
Oil on panel
23 1/4 × 32 1/2" (59 × 82.5 cm)

John G. Johnson Collection
cat. 644

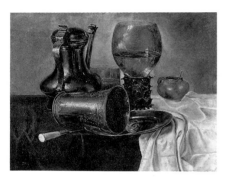

**Heda, Willem Claesz.,
imitator of**
Previously listed as Willem
Claesz. Heda (JFD 1972)
*Still Life with a Roemer, a Covered
Flagon, and a Beaker*
17th century
Oil on panel
16 5/8 × 19 3/4" (42.2 × 50.2 cm)

John G. Johnson Collection
cat. 642

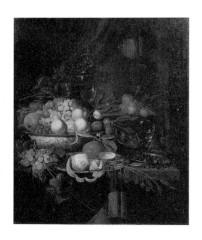

**Heem, Cornelis de,
attributed to**
Flemish, active Leiden and
Antwerp, 1631–1695
Previously listed as a follower of
Jan Davidsz. de Heem (JFD 1972)
*Still Life with Peaches, Grapes, and
Other Fruits*
17th century
Oil on canvas
39 × 31 1/8" (99.1 × 79.1 cm)

John G. Johnson Collection
cat. 631

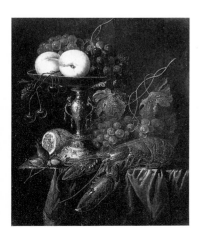

**Heem, Jan Davidsz. de,
follower of**
Flemish, active Utrecht, Leiden,
and Antwerp, 1606–1684
*Still Life with Fruit and a Lobster*
17th century
Lower left (spurious): Joh. Fyt
Oil on panel
17 3/4 × 15 3/8" (45.1 × 39 cm)

John G. Johnson Collection
inv. 421

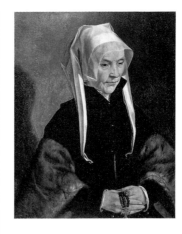

**Heemskerck, Maarten van,
attributed to**
Netherlandish, active Haarlem
and Rome, 1498–1574
Previously listed as the Master of
the 1540s (JFD 1972)
*Portrait of Sophia van Amerongen*
A version lacking the hands and
reversed is in the Rijksmuseum
Twenthe, Enschede (inv. no. 120)
c. 1550
Oil on panel
29 1/2 × 21 3/4" (74.9 × 55.2 cm)

John G. Johnson Collection
cat. 417

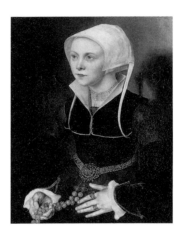

**Heemskerck, Maarten van,
follower of**
Previously listed as the school of
Maarten van Heemskerck (JFD
1972)
*Portrait of a Nineteen-Year-Old
Woman*
1548
Upper left: 1548; upper right: 19
Oil on panel
28 3/16 × 21 1/16" (71.6 × 53.5 cm)

John G. Johnson Collection
cat. 416

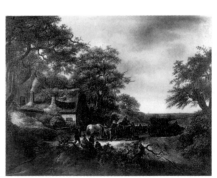

**Hees, Gerrit van**
Dutch, active Haarlem,
active by 1650, died 1670
Previously listed as Isaack van
Ostade (PMA 1965)
*Landscape with Travelers Resting by
an Inn*
1653
Lower right (spurious): I ostade .
f. /1653
Oil on canvas
41 × 51 3/8" (104.1 × 130.5 cm)

The William L. Elkins Collection
E1924-3-35

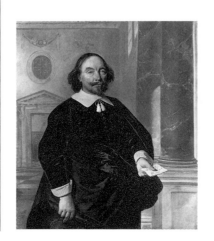

**Helst, Bartholomeus van der**
Dutch, active Amsterdam,
1613–1670
*Portrait of Michiel Heusch*
1653
Lower left: B. van der / Helst, f. /
1653; lower right, on letter: Al
sig. Michiel / Heusch /
Hamborgh in.
Oil on canvas
51 × 44" (129.5 × 111.8 cm)

John G. Johnson Collection
cat. 495

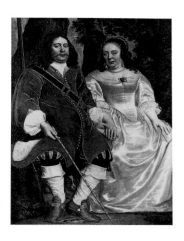

**Helst, Lodewyck van der, attributed to**
Dutch, active Amsterdam, 1642–c. 1684
Previously listed as Bartholomeus van der Helst (PMA 1965)
*Portrait of a Gentleman and a Lady Seated Outdoors*
c. 1670
Oil on canvas
62 1/2 × 46 1/2" (158.7 × 118.1 cm)

Purchased with the W. P. Wilstach Fund
W1904-1-60

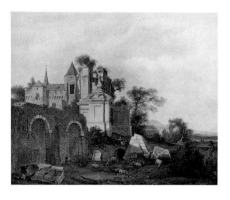

**Heyden, Jan van der**
Dutch, active Amsterdam, 1637–1712
*Ideal Landscape with a Romanesque Church*
17th century
Lower right, on stone: J V. Heyden; on pyramid of stones: [illegible signature]
Oil on panel
16 × 18 3/16" (40.6 × 46.2 cm)

John G. Johnson Collection
cat. 595

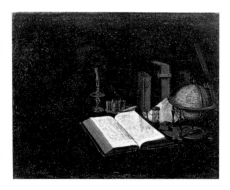

**Heyden, Jan van der**
Previously attributed to Jan van der Heyden (JFD 1972)
*Still Life with Books and a Globe*
17th century
Lower left: J.V. Heyde
Oil on panel
8 15/16 × 10 5/8" (22.7 × 27 cm)

John G. Johnson Collection
cat. 597

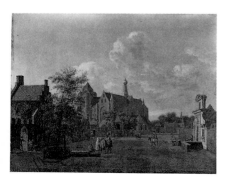

**Heyden, Jan van der**
*View of Veere, Zeeland*
17th century
Lower left: J.V.D Heyde
Oil on panel
16 5/8 × 21 1/8" (42.2 × 53.7 cm)

John G. Johnson Collection
cat. 596

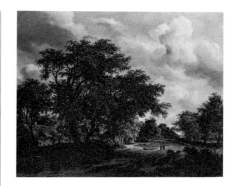

**Hobbema, Meindert**
Dutch, active Amsterdam, 1638–1709
*Landscape with a Wooded Road*
1662
Lower left: m. hobbema.f.166[2]
Oil on canvas
42 1/8 × 51 1/2" (107 × 130.8 cm)

The William L. Elkins Collection
E1924-3-7

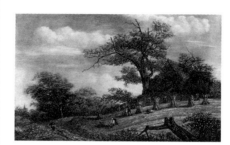

**Hobbema, Meindert, imitator of**
*Sheaf Binders*
17th century
Oil on panel
16 15/16 × 26 3/4" (43 × 67.9 cm)

John G. Johnson Collection
cat. 571

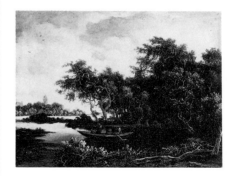

**Hobbema, Meindert, copy after**
*Landscape with a River*
After the painting formerly in the collection of the 2nd Earl of Northbrook
17th century
Oil on panel
11 7/8 × 15 1/8" (30.2 × 38.4 cm)

John G. Johnson Collection
cat. 573

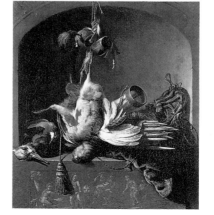

**Hondecoeter, Melchior de**
Dutch, active Utrecht, Amsterdam, and The Hague, 1636–1695
*Still Life with Birds*
17th century
Upper right: M d hondecoeter
Oil on canvas
28 7/8 × 25 1/4" (73.3 × 64.1 cm)

John G. Johnson Collection
cat. 630

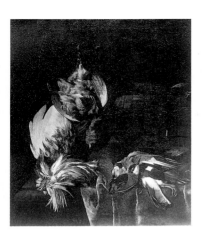

**Hondecoeter, Melchior de, attributed to**
Previously listed as Melchior de Hondecoeter (PMA 1965)
*Still Life with Game Birds*
c. 1665–75
Oil on canvas
31 7/8 × 27 1/2" (81 × 69.8 cm)
Purchased with the W. P. Wilstach Fund
W1902-1-18

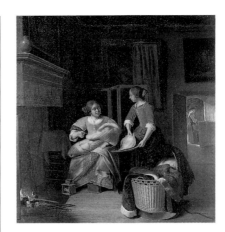

**Hooch, Pieter de**
Previously listed as a copy after Pieter de Hooch (JFD 1972)
*A Lady and a Child with a Serving Maid*
c. 1674–76
Oil on canvas
33 15/16 × 31 3/8" (86.2 × 79.7 cm)

John G. Johnson Collection
cat. 501

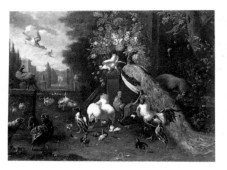

**Hondecoeter, Melchior de, workshop of**
Previously listed as Melchior de Hondecoeter (PMA 1965)
*Poultry Yard*
1680s?
Oil on canvas
84 1/4 × 110 1/4" (214 × 280 cm)

Purchased with the W. P. Wilstach Fund
W1896-1-12

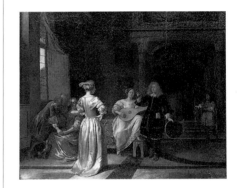

**Hooch, Pieter de**
*Party*
The inscription "P. de Hoogh / 1675" came away in cleaning in 1940
1675
Oil on canvas
32 3/16 × 38 15/16" (81.8 × 98.9 cm)

Purchased with the W. P. Wilstach Fund
W1912-1-7

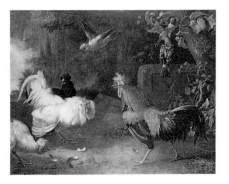

**Hondecoeter, Melchior de, follower of**
*A Rooster and a Hen Fighting*
17th century
Oil on canvas
42 × 51 1/2" (106.7 × 130.8 cm)

John G. Johnson Collection
cat. 629

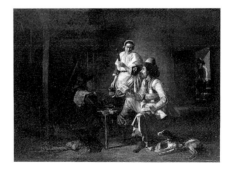

**Hooch, Pieter de, follower of**
Previously listed as Pieter de Hooch (JFD 1972)
*Soldiers with a Serving Maid in a Barn*
17th century
Oil on panel
21 9/16 × 27 3/16" (54.8 × 69.1 cm)

John G. Johnson Collection
cat. 498

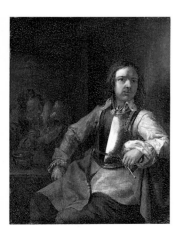

**Hooch, Pieter de**
Dutch, active Delft and Amsterdam, 1629–1684
Previously listed as Hendrik van der Burgh (JFD 1972)
*Soldier Smoking*
c. 1650
On table edge: P. D Hooch
Oil on panel
13 15/16 × 10 5/8" (35.4 × 27 cm)

John G. Johnson Collection
cat. 499

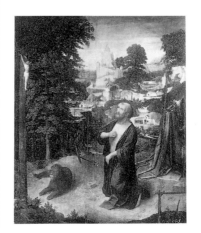

**Isenbrant, Adriaen**
Netherlandish, active Bruges, first documented 1510, died 1551
*Penitent Saint Jerome*
Upper corners have been added
c. 1525–50
Oil on panel
34 1/4 × 27" (87 × 68.6 cm)

John G. Johnson Collection
cat. 357

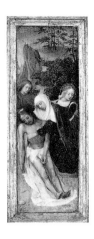

**Isenbrant, Adriaen**
*Lamentation*
Possibly a wing from a triptych
Mid-16th century
Oil on panel
12 1/4 × 4 7/8" (31.1 × 12.4 cm)

John G. Johnson Collection
cat. 358

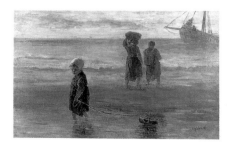

**Israëls, Jozef**
*Children at the Seashore*
c. 1890
Lower right: Jozef Israels
Oil on canvas
21 3/8 × 32 9/16" (54.3 × 82.7 cm)

John G. Johnson Collection
cat. 1010

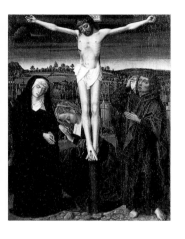

**Isenbrant, Adriaen,
workshop of**
*The Crucifixion*
Mid-16th century
On cross: [I] N R I
Oil on panel
19 9/16 × 14 15/16" (49.7 × 37.9 cm)

John G. Johnson Collection
cat. 356

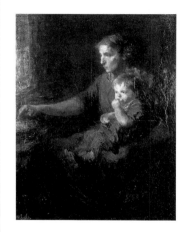

**Israëls, Jozef**
*Mother and Child*
Before 1892
Lower left: Jozef Israels.
Oil on canvas
50 1/4 × 37 1/2" (127.6 × 95.2 cm)

John G. Johnson Collection
cat. 1009

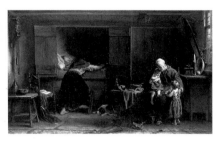

**Israëls, Jozef**
Dutch, active The Hague,
Amsterdam, and Paris,
1824–1911
*The Last Breath*
1872
Lower right: Jozef Israels
Oil on canvas
44 × 69 1/2" (111.8 × 176.5 cm)

Gift of Ellen Harrison McMichael
in memory of C. Emory
McMichael
1942-60-2

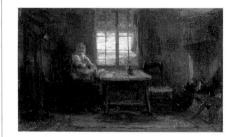

**Israëls, Jozef**
*The Fisherman's Family*
Late 19th century
Lower left: Jozef Israels
Oil on panel
10 7/8 × 17 3/16" (27.6 × 43.7 cm)

The William L. Elkins Collection
E1924-3-79

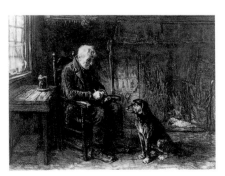

**Israëls, Jozef**
*Old Friends (Silent Conversation)*
Before 1882
Lower left: Jozef Israels
Oil on canvas
52 1/8 × 69 1/16" (132.4 × 175.4 cm)

The William L. Elkins Collection
E1924-3-10

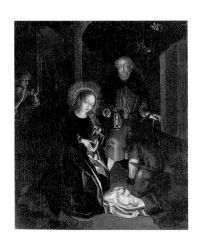

**Joest, Jan, attributed to**
Netherlandish, active Calcar and
Haarlem, first documented 1474,
died 1519
Previously listed as Jan Joest
(JGJ 1941)
*The Nativity, at Night*
Based on an engraving by Martin
Schongauer (German, 1445?–
1491) (Bartsch 4)
Early 16th century
Oil on panel
15 1/2 × 12 1/2" (39.4 × 31.7 cm)

John G. Johnson Collection
cat. 350

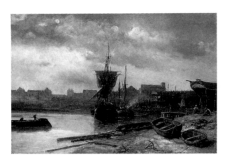

**Jongkind, Johan Barthold**
Dutch, active The Hague, Paris, and Rotterdam, 1819–1891
*Shipyard*
1852
Lower right: Jongkind 52
Oil on canvas
16 7/8 × 23 5/8" (42.9 × 60 cm)

John G. Johnson Collection
cat. 1013

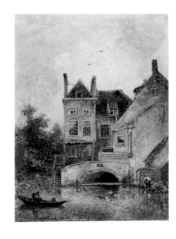

**Jongkind, Johan Barthold**
*The Artist's House, Maassluis*
1871
Lower left: Jongkind 1871
Oil on canvas
18 1/4 × 13 1/4" (46.3 × 33.6 cm)

The William L. Elkins Collection
E1924-3-84

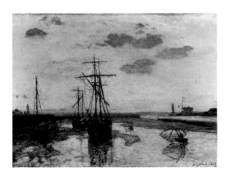

**Jongkind, Johan Barthold**
*Port of Honfleur at Evening*
1863
Lower right: Jongkind 1863
Oil on canvas
16 1/2 × 22 1/4" (41.9 × 56.5 cm)

The William L. Elkins Collection
E1924-3-76

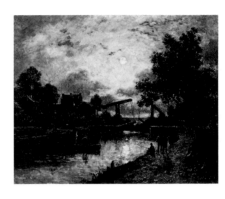

**Jongkind, Johan Barthold,
attributed to**
Previously listed as Johan
Barthold Jongkind (PMA 1965)
*Nocturnal Landscape with a
Drawbridge*
19th century
Lower right: Jongkind.
Oil on canvas
18 × 21 3/4" (45.7 × 55.2 cm)

Gift of Lucie Washington
Mitcheson in memory of Robert
Stockton Johnson Mitcheson for
the Robert Stockton Johnson
Mitcheson Collection
1938-22-7

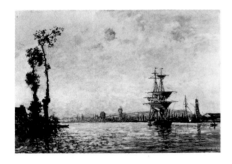

**Jongkind, Johan Barthold**
*The Seine near Rouen*
1865
Lower right: Jongkind 1865
Oil on canvas
20 × 28 3/4" (50.8 × 73 cm)

Gift of Lucie Washington
Mitcheson in memory of Robert
Stockton Johnson Mitcheson for
the Robert Stockton Johnson
Mitcheson Collection
1938-22-8

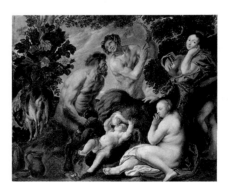

**Jordaens, Jacob, copy after**
Flemish, active Antwerp,
England, The Hague, and
Amsterdam, 1593–1678
*The Infant Jupiter Fed by the Goat
Amalthea*
After the lost original known
through the drawing in the
Hermitage, St. Petersburg
(inv. no. 4200), and a painted
studio replica in the museum in
Kishinev, Moldavia (inv. no. 340)
17th century
Oil on canvas
38 11/16 × 46 3/16" (98.3 ×
117.3 cm)

The Bloomfield Moore Collection
1889-79

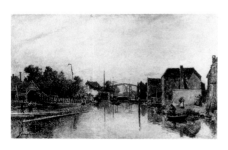

**Jongkind, Johan Barthold**
*Canal*
1869
Lower left: Jongkind 1869
Oil on canvas
16 3/16 × 25 11/16" (41.1 × 65.2 cm)

John G. Johnson Collection
cat. 1012

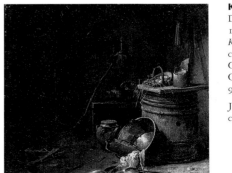

**Kalf, Willem**
Dutch, active Amsterdam,
1619–1693
*Kitchen*
c. 1642
Center right: WK
Oil on panel
9 3/4 × 9 13/16" (24.8 × 24.9 cm)

John G. Johnson Collection
cat. 636

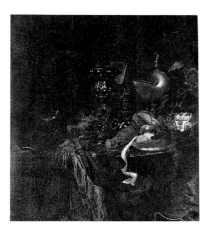

**Kalf, Willem**
*Still Life*
17th century
Oil on canvas
48 × 21 1/2" (121.9 × 54.6 cm)

John G. Johnson Collection
cat. 634

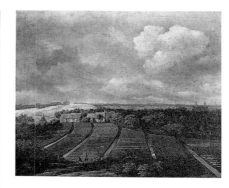

**Kessel, Jan van, III,
copy after**
Previously listed as a follower of
Jan van Kessel III (JFD 1972)
*Dunes near Haarlem*
After the painting formerly in the
National Art Collection, Warsaw
17th century
Oil on canvas
21 3/8 × 25 9/16" (54.3 × 64.9 cm)

John G. Johnson Collection
cat. 582

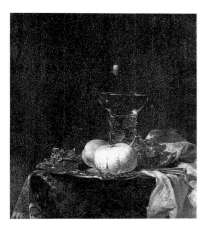

**Kalf, Willem**
*Still Life with a Roemer*
17th century
Lower left: W Kalf
Oil on canvas
19 1/2 × 16 11/16" (49.5 × 42.4 cm)

John G. Johnson Collection
cat. 635

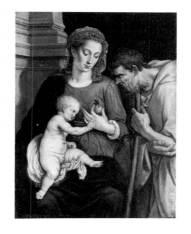

**Key, Adriaen Thomasz.**
Netherlandish, active Antwerp,
first documented 1558, still
active 1589?
*The Holy Family*
Late 16th century
Upper left: ATK
Oil on panel
33 1/4 × 24 1/2" (84.4 × 62.2 cm)

John G. Johnson Collection
cat. 430

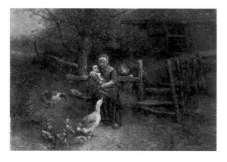

**Kate, Johan Mari Henri ten**
Dutch, active The Hague,
Amsterdam, England, and Paris,
1831–1910
Previously listed as Johannes
Marinus ten Kate (1859–1896)
(PMA 1965)
*A Mother and Two Children with
Geese*
c. 1870–75
Lower right: JM. ten Kate
Oil on canvas
14 15/16 × 21 3/16" (37.9 × 53.8 cm)

The Walter Lippincott Collection
1923-59-8

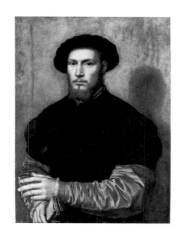

**Key, Willem**
Netherlandish, active Antwerp,
c. 1520–1568
*Portrait of a Gentleman*
Mid-16th century
Oil on panel
26 3/8 × 19" (67 × 48.3 cm)

John G. Johnson Collection
cat. 429

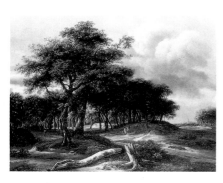

**Kessel, Jan van, III**
Dutch, active Amsterdam,
1641–1680
Previously listed as the school of
Jacob Isaacksz. van Ruisdael (JFD
1972)
*Landscape with a Wood*
c. 1665
Lower right (spurious):
M. Hobbema
Oil on canvas
41 1/4 × 52 7/8" (104.8 × 134.3 cm)

John G. Johnson Collection
cat. 565

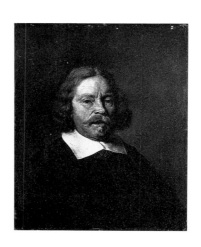

**Keyser, Thomas de,
attributed to**
Dutch, active Amsterdam,
1596/97–1667
Previously listed as Thomas de
Keyser (JFD 1972)
*Portrait of a Gentleman* [possibly
Jacob van Campen]
1659
Upper left: TDKeyser F. /
AETA. 59
Oil on copper
13 1/4 × 10 7/8" (33.6 × 27.6 cm)

John G. Johnson Collection
cat. 456

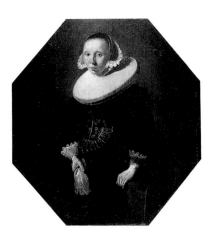

**Keyser, Thomas de, follower of**
Previously listed as Thomas de Keyser (PMA 1965)
*Portrait of a Woman*
c. 1635
Oil on panel
14 1/2 × 12 1/2" (36.8 × 31.7 cm)

The John D. McIlhenny Collection
1943-40-41

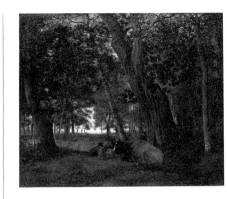

**Koninck, Jacob**
Dutch, active Rotterdam and Amsterdam, born 1614/15, died after 1690
Previously listed as Adriaen van de Velde (JFD 1972)
*Cattle in a Wood*
1656
Lower left: AvVelde / f. 1656
Oil on canvas
14 1/16 × 16" (35.7 × 40.6 cm)

John G. Johnson Collection
cat. 602

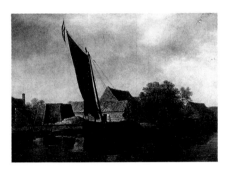

**Knijff, Wouter**
Dutch, active Haarlem, born c. 1607, still active 1693
Previously listed as Jacob Isaacksz. van Ruisdael (PMA 1965)
*River with a Barge and a Limekiln*
1640s
Lower left: [illegible signature?]
Oil on canvas
29 7/8 × 41 3/8" (75.9 × 105.1 cm)

Purchased with the W. P. Wilstach Fund
W1902-1-20

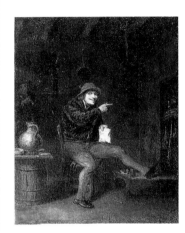

**Koninck, Philips, attributed to**
Dutch, active Amsterdam and Rotterdam, 1619–1688
*Interior with Two Figures*
17th century
Lower right: P. Koninck.
Oil on panel
13 1/8 × 9 1/4" (33.3 × 23.5 cm)

John G. Johnson Collection
inv. 742

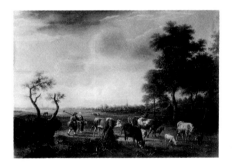

**Kobell, Johannes Baptista, imitator of**
Dutch, active Rotterdam and Gouda, 1756–1833
Previously listed as an imitator of Paulus Potter (JFD 1972)
*Return from the Pasture*
18th century
Oil on panel
20 3/4 × 28 1/8" (52.7 × 71.4 cm)

John G. Johnson Collection
cat. 712

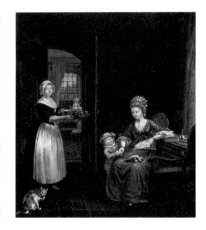

**La Fargue, Maria**
Dutch, active The Hague, 1743–1813
*A Lady and a Servant*
1777
Center left: Marie de / la Fargue / f 77
Oil on canvas
12 5/16 × 10 1/16" (31.3 × 25.6 cm)

John G. Johnson Collection
cat. 709

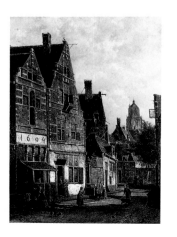

**Koekkoek, Willem**
Dutch, active Amsterdam, 1839–1895
*Street*
19th century
Center left, on building: 1604; lower right: W. Koekkoek
Oil on canvas
23 3/4 × 17 3/4" (60.3 × 45.1 cm)

The Walter Lippincott Collection
1923-59-12

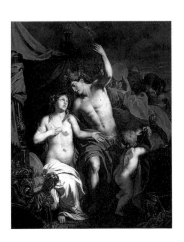

**Lairesse, Gerard de**
Dutch, active Liège, Amsterdam, and The Hague, 1641–1711
*Bacchus and Ariadne*
17th century
Lower left: G. Lairesse
Oil on canvas
26 1/4 × 20" (66.7 × 50.8 cm)

Gift of Mrs. Edgar P. Richardson
1986-83-1

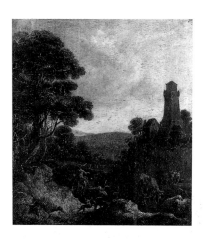

**Lapp, Jan Willemsz.,
follower of**
Dutch, active The Hague,
born c. 1600, died after 1663
*Pastoral Landscape*
17th century
Oil on panel
10 × 8 1/4" (25.4 × 20.9 cm)

Gift of Mrs. Hampton L. Carson
1929-136-148

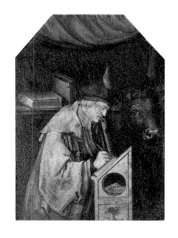

**Leyden, Lucas van,
copy after**
*Saint Luke*
After the engraving (Bartsch 102)
16th century
Oil on copper
6 1/4 × 4 1/2" (15.9 × 11.4 cm)

John G. Johnson Collection
inv. 3

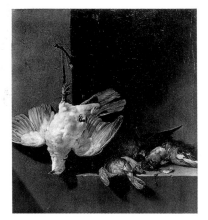

**Lelienbergh, Cornelis**
Dutch, active The Hague,
born c. 1626, died after 1676
*Still Life of Dead Birds*
1654
Lower left: C. Lelienbergh f. /
1654
Oil on canvas
19 1/2 × 16 1/4" (49.5 × 41.3 cm)

Purchased with the W. P.
Wilstach Fund
W1902-1-19

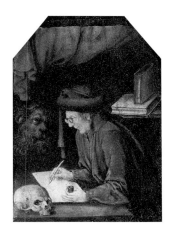

**Leyden, Lucas van,
copy after**
*Saint Mark*
After the engraving (Bartsch 100)
16th century
Oil on copper
6 1/4 × 4 3/8" (15.9 × 11.1 cm)

John G. Johnson Collection
inv. 4

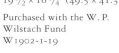
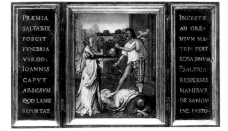

**Leyden, Lucas van,
follower of**
Netherlandish, active Leiden,
c. 1494–1533
Previously listed as Lucas van
Leyden (JFD 1972)
*Salome Receiving the Head of Saint
John the Baptist*
Triptych
Early 16th century
Left wing: PRAEMIA / SALTATRIX
/ POSCIT / FVNEBRIA / VIRGO, /
IOANNIS / CAPVT / ABSCISVM /
QVOD LANCE / REPORTAT.; right
wing: INCESTAE / AD GRE- / MIVM
MA- / TRIS FERT / REGIA DONVM
/ PSALTRIA / RESPERSIS / MANI-
BVS / DE SANGV- / INE IVSTO.
Oil on panel
Center panel: 14 1/4 × 11 9/16"
(36.2 × 29.4 cm); left wing:
14 1/4 × 5 3/4" (36.2 × 14.6 cm);
right wing: 14 1/4 × 5 7/8"
(36.3 × 15 cm)

John G. Johnson Collection
cat. 413

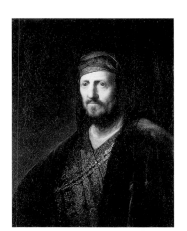

**Leyster, Judith**
Dutch, active Haarlem and
Amsterdam, 1609–1660
*The Last Drop (The Gay Cavalier)*
Possibly a companion to
*The Merry Trio*, in the collection
of P. L. Galjart, Netherlands
c. 1639
Oil on canvas
35 1/16 × 28 15/16" (89.1 × 73.5 cm)

John G. Johnson Collection
cat. 440

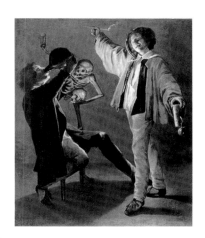

**Lievens, Jan, attributed to**
Dutch, active Leiden and
Amsterdam, 1607–1674
Previously listed as Rembrandt
Harmensz. van Rijn (PMA 1965)
*Portrait of a Man in a Turban*
c. 1629
Oil on canvas
33 7/16 × 25 3/8" (84.9 × 64.4 cm)

Gift of the Reverend Theodore
Pitcairn
1961-195-1

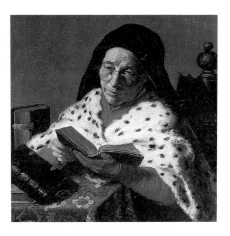

**Lievens, Jan, attributed to**
Previously listed as Jan Lievens
(JFD 1972)
*Old Woman Reading*
17th century
Center left: J. L
Oil on panel
28 1/8 × 26 1/2" (71.4 × 67.3 cm)

John G. Johnson Collection
cat. 487

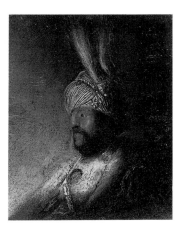

**Lievens, Jan, copy after**
*Portrait of a Turk*
After a painting known in versions
in the collection of D. Hudig,
Rotterdam, and the collection
of Victor Kock, London
17th century
Oil on panel
6 13/16 × 5 1/4" (17.3 × 13.3 cm)

John G. Johnson Collection
cat. 473

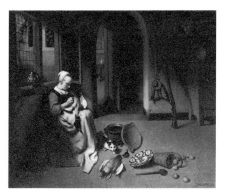

**Maes, Nicolaes**
Dutch, active Amsterdam and
Dordrecht, 1634–1693
*Woman Plucking a Duck*
c. 1655–56
Lower right: N. MAES
Oil on canvas
23 1/2 × 25 3/4" (59.7 × 65.4 cm)

Gift of Mrs. Gordon A. Hardwick
and Mrs. W. Newbold Ely in
memory of Mr. and Mrs.
Roland L. Taylor
1944-9-4

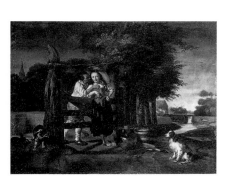

**Maes, Nicolaes,
attributed to**
Previously listed as Nicholaes
Maes (JFD 1972)
*Lovers*
17th century
On gate (spurious): N. MAES
Oil on panel
27 1/2 × 35 9/16" (69.8 × 90.3 cm)

John G. Johnson Collection
cat. 485

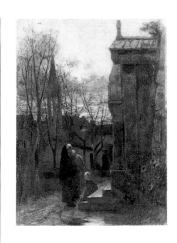

**Maris, Jacob Hendricus**
Dutch, active The Hague and
London, 1837–1899
*Cemetery at Twilight*
1867
Lower right: J. Maris 16[?] 1867
Oil on canvas
22 × 15 1/4" (55.9 × 38.7 cm)

John G. Johnson Collection
cat. 1032

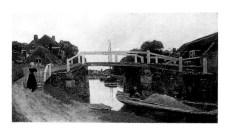

**Maris, Jacob Hendricus**
*Canal near Rijswijk*
1872
Lower left: J Maris 1872
Oil on canvas
32 5/8 × 58" (82.9 × 147.3 cm)

John G. Johnson Collection
cat. 1030

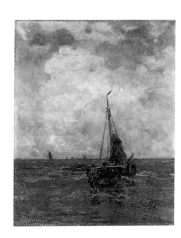

**Maris, Jacob Hendricus**
*A Fishing Boat with a Horse on the
Beach, Sheveningen*
c. 1880–90
Lower right: J. Maris
Oil on canvas
50 × 37 5/8" (127 × 95.6 cm)

The William L. Elkins Collection
E1924-3-12

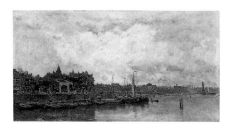

**Maris, Jacob Hendricus**
*The Schreierstoren, Amsterdam*
1882
Lower left: J. Maris
Oil on canvas
32 × 58 1/2" (81.3 × 148.6 cm)

The William L. Elkins Collection
E1924-3-11

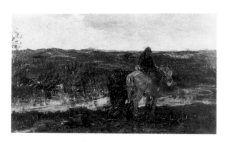

**Maris, Jacob Hendricus**
*Landscape with a Horseman*
c. 1886–92
Oil on canvas
18 11/16 × 30 5/16" (47.5 × 77 cm)

John G. Johnson Collection
cat. 1029

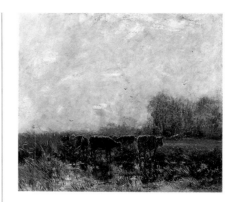

**Maris, Willem**
*Cows in a Marsh*
c. 1897
Lower right: Willem Maris
Oil on canvas
25 1/2 × 29 1/2" (64.8 × 74.9 cm)

Gift of Mrs. Jay Besson Rudolphy
1978-118-1

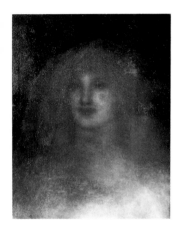

**Maris, Matthijs**
Dutch, active The Hague and
London, 1839–1917
*Head of a Girl*
c. 1888–92
Oil on canvas
22 1/2 × 16 1/4" (57.1 × 41.3 cm)

John G. Johnson Collection
cat. 1033

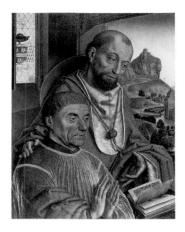

**Marmion, Simon**
Netherlandish, active Amiens,
Lille, Tournai, and Valenciennes,
first documented 1449, died 1489
*Saint Jerome and a Cardinal
Praying*
c. 1475–80
On window: placet / placet / PB
Oil on panel
25 5/8 × 19 1/4" (65.1 × 48.9 cm)

John G. Johnson Collection
inv. 1329

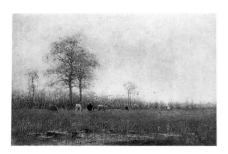

**Maris, Willem**
Dutch, active The Hague,
1844–1910
Previously listed as Jacob
Hendricus Maris (JGJ 1941)
*Landscape with Cows*
1884
Lower right: W Maris.
Oil on canvas on panel
5 7/8 × 8 7/8" (14.9 × 22.5 cm)

John G. Johnson Collection
cat. 1031

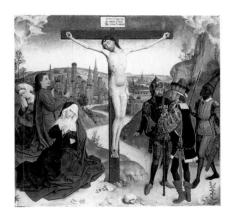

**Marmion, Simon,
attributed to**
Previously listed as Simon
Marmion (JFD 1972)
*The Crucifixion*
1470s
On cross: [Hebrew, Greek, and
Latin for "Jesus of Nazareth,
King of the Jews"]
Oil on panel
35 3/4 × 37 1/2" (90.8 × 95.2 cm)

John G. Johnson Collection
cat. 318

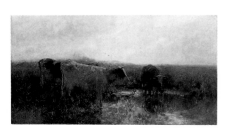

**Maris, Willem**
*Cows in a Marsh*
c. 1890–1900
Oil on canvas
31 1/4 × 57 1/2" (79.4 × 146 cm)

The George W. Elkins Collection
E1924-4-20

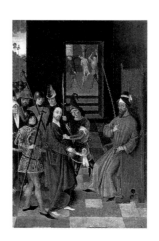

**Marmion, Simon, imitator of**
Previously listed as the school of
Simon Marmion (JFD 1972)
*Christ before Caiaphas, with the
Flagellation*
Early 16th century
Oil on panel
20 × 12 15/16" (50.8 × 32.9 cm)

John G. Johnson Collection
cat. 763

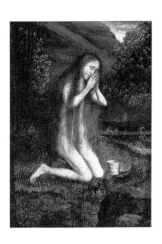

**Massys, Quentin**
Netherlandish, active Antwerp,
1466–1530
*Saint Mary Magdalene*
Companion to the following
painting
c. 1520–30
Oil on panel
12 1/4 × 8 3/8" (31.1 × 21.3 cm)

John G. Johnson Collection
cat. 367

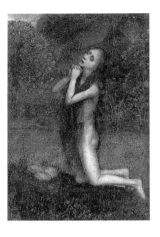

**Massys, Quentin**
*Saint Mary of Egypt*
Companion to the preceding
painting
c. 1520–30
Oil on panel
12 1/4 × 8 3/8" (31.1 × 21.3 cm)

John G. Johnson Collection
cat. 366

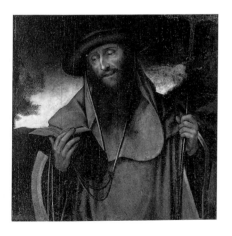

**Massys, Quentin, follower of**
Previously listed as Quentin
Massys (JFD 1972)
*Saint Jerome*
Early 16th century
Oil on panel
27 7/8 × 27" (70.8 × 68.6 cm)

John G. Johnson Collection
cat. 368

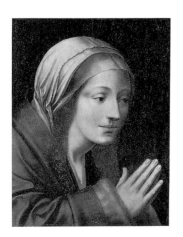

**Massys, Quentin, imitator of**
Previously listed as a Flemish
artist, c. 1600 (JFD 1972)
*Virgin Praying*
A strip has been added to each side
16th century
Oil on panel
18 9/16 × 13 3/8" (47.1 × 34 cm)

John G. Johnson Collection
inv. 1368

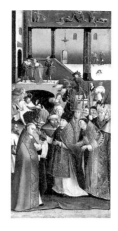

**Master of Alkmaar (Cornelis
Buys?), attributed to**
Netherlandish, active Alkmaar
and Haarlem, active c. 1490–
c. 1520
Previously listed as Cornelis
Buys, the Master of Alkmaar
(JFD 1972)
*The Death of Saint Alexis*
Early 16th century
Oil on panel
29 × 14 1/8" (73.7 × 35.9 cm)

John G. Johnson Collection
cat. 351

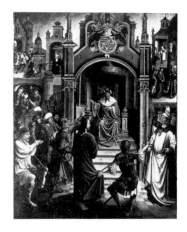

**Master of the Beighem
Altarpiece**
Netherlandish, active Brussels,
active 1520–1540
*Christ before Pilate, with Christ Led
to Annas, the Mocking of Christ, the
Denial by Peter, and Christ before
Caiaphas*
c. 1520–40
Oil and gold on panel
67 7/8 × 50" (172.4 × 127 cm)

John G. Johnson Collection
cat. 362

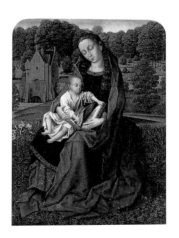

**Master of the Embroidered
Foliage**
Netherlandish, active Brussels,
active c. 1490–c. 1520
*Virgin and Child in a Landscape*
The figures are based on Rogier
van der Weyden's *Virgin and
Child in a Niche*, in the Museo
del Prado, Madrid (2722)
c. 1500
Oil on panel
33 × 23 3/4" (83.8 × 60.3 cm)

John G. Johnson Collection
inv. 2518

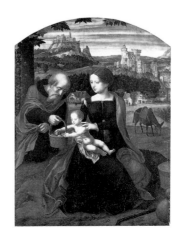

**Master of the Female
Half-Lengths**
Netherlandish, active Antwerp,
active c. 1520–c. 1540
*Rest on the Flight into Egypt*
A 1 × 6" curved piece has been
added to the upper left corner
c. 1520–40
Oil on panel
33 1/8 × 24 7/16" (84.1 × 62.1 cm)

John G. Johnson Collection
cat. 389

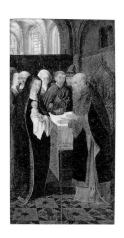

**Master of Hoogstraeten**
Netherlandish, active Antwerp,
active c. 1485–c. 1520
*The Presentation of Christ in the
Temple*
Early 16th century
Center: MHPX
Oil on panel
26 × 13 ³/₈" (66 × 34 cm)

John G. Johnson Collection
cat. 370

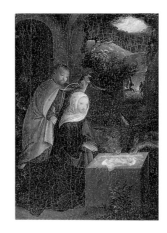

**Master of Hoogstraeten**
*The Nativity*
Panel from an altarpiece; see
previous two entries
Early 16th century
Oil on panel
6 ¹/₈ × 4 ⁵/₁₆" (15.6 × 10.9 cm)

John G. Johnson Collection
inv. 60c

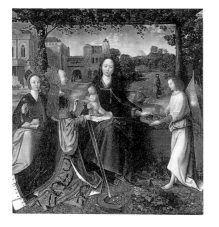

**Master of Hoogstraeten**
*Virgin and Child, with Saint
Catherine of Alexandria, a Female
Saint, and an Angel*
Early 16th century
Oil on panel
31 ¹⁵/₁₆ × 28 ³/₁₆" (81.1 × 71.6 cm)

John G. Johnson Collection
cat. 371

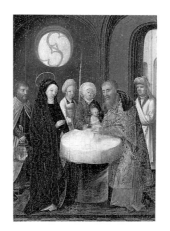
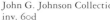

**Master of Hoogstraeten**
*The Presentation of Christ in the
Temple*
Panel from an altarpiece; see
previous three entries
Early 16th century
Oil on panel
6 ¹/₈ × 4 ¹/₄" (15.6 × 10.8 cm)

John G. Johnson Collection
inv. 60d

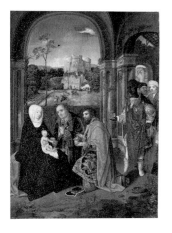

**Master of Hoogstraeten**
*The Adoration of the Magi*
Center panel from an altarpiece;
companion to the following four
panels
Early 16th century
Oil on panel
12 ¹/₂ × 7 ³/₈" (31.7 × 18.7 cm)

John G. Johnson Collection
inv. 60a

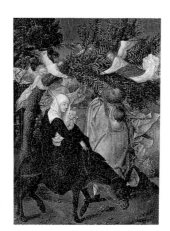

**Master of Hoogstraeten**
*The Flight into Egypt*
Panel from an altarpiece; see
previous four entries
Early 16th century
Oil on panel
6 ¹/₈ × 4 ⁵/₁₆" (15.6 × 10.9 cm)

John G. Johnson Collection
inv. 60e

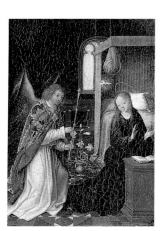

**Master of Hoogstraeten**
*The Annunciation*
Panel from an altarpiece; see
previous entry
Early 16th century
Oil on panel
6 ¹/₈ × 4 ³/₄" (15.6 × 12.1 cm)

John G. Johnson Collection
inv. 60b

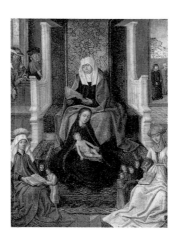

**Master of the Legend of
Saint Anna**
Netherlandish, active Ghent,
active c. 1475–c. 1500
Previously listed as in the manner
of the Master of the Legend of
Saint Ursula (JFD 1972)
*The Holy Kinship*
Late 15th century
Oil on panel
11 × 8" (27.9 × 20.3 cm)

John G. Johnson Collection
cat. 364

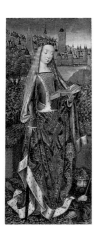

**Master of the Legend of Saint Lucy**
Netherlandish, active Bruges, active c. 1470–c. 1500
*Saint Catherine of Alexandria, with the Defeated Emperor*
Probably the left wing of a triptych
c. 1482
Oil on panel
26 1/4 × 10 5/8" (66.7 × 27 cm)

John G. Johnson Collection
cat. 326

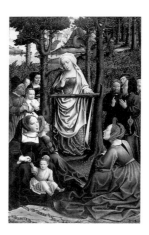

**Master of the Magdalene Legend**
Netherlandish, active Brussels, active c. 1480–c. 1520
*Saint Mary Magdalene Preaching*
Probably a right inner wing from an altarpiece; companion panels in the Statens Museum for Kunst, Copenhagen (Sp. 717); Museum of Fine Arts, Budapest (1338); Staatliches Museum, Schwerin, Germany (G. 196, G. 198); and (formerly) the Kaiser Friedrich Museum, Berlin (2128; destroyed)
c. 1500–20
Oil on panel
48 3/8 × 30 3/16" (122.9 × 76.7 cm)

John G. Johnson Collection
cat. 402

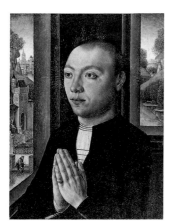

**Master of the Legend of Saint Ursula**
Netherlandish, active Bruges, active c. 1470–c. 1500
*Portrait of a Man Praying*
[possibly Ludovico Portinari]
Right panel from a votive diptych; the companion panel is in the Fogg Art Museum, Cambridge, Massachusetts (1943.07)
c. 1479
On reverse: [coat of arms of the Portinari family] / L P
Oil on panel
17 1/8 × 12 5/8" (43.5 × 32.1 cm)

John G. Johnson Collection
cat. 327

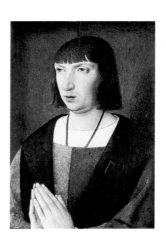

**Master of the Magdalene Legend**
*Portrait of a Man Praying*
Probably the right panel from a votive diptych
c. 1510–20
Oil on panel
14 5/8 × 10 7/8" (37.1 × 27.6 cm)

John G. Johnson Collection
cat. 410

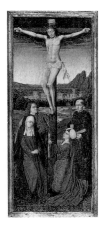

**Master of the Legend of Saint Ursula, attributed to**
*The Crucifixion, with an Abbot Saint*
Wing of a triptych; see following painting for reverse; a companion panel is in the Fitzwilliam Museum, Cambridge, England (1518a, b)
Late 15th century
On cross: INRI
Oil on panel
14 7/8 × 7" (37.8 × 17.8 cm)

John G. Johnson Collection
cat. 322a

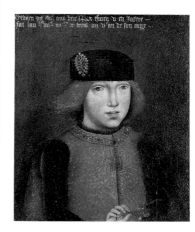

**Master of the Magdalene Legend, attributed to**
Previously listed as the Master of the Magdalene Legend (JFD 1972)
*Portrait of Philip the Fair*
Companion to the portrait of Margaret of Austria in the Musée National du Château de Versailles (MV 4026); 2" strip added at right
1483?
Across top: Gedaen Int Jaer ons here 1483 tsinen v en Jaerre / Fat Lan m. IIII c. IIII xx. z trois ou ve. an de son eage
Oil on panel
11 1/2 × 9 1/2" (29.2 × 24.1 cm)

John G. Johnson Collection
cat. 1175

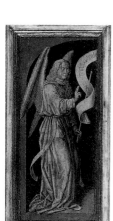

**Master of the Legend of Saint Ursula, attributed to**
*Annunciate Angel*
See previous entry
Late 15th century
On scroll: Ave gratia plena
Oil on panel
14 7/8 × 7" (37.8 × 17.8 cm)

John G. Johnson Collection
cat. 322b

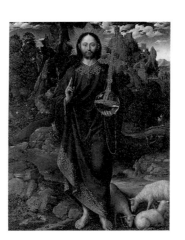

**Master of the Mansi Magdalene**
Netherlandish, active Antwerp, active c. 1510–c. 1530
*Salvator Mundi in a Landscape*
c. 1510–30
Oil and gold on panel
28 15/16 × 21 1/2" (73.5 × 54.6 cm)

John G. Johnson Collection
cat. 388

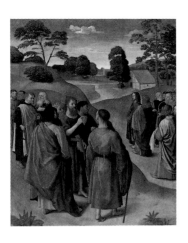

**Master of the Saint John Altarpiece (Hugo Jacobsz.?)**
Netherlandish, active Leiden and Gouda, first securely documented 1478, still active 1534
*Saint John the Baptist Pointing out Christ as the Lamb of God*
Companion panels are in the Museum Boymans–van Beuningen, Rotterdam
c. 1500–10
Oil on panel
48 × 37 5/8" (121.9 × 95.6 cm)

John G. Johnson Collection
cat. 347

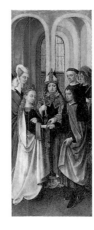

**Master of the Virgin among Virgins, follower of**
Netherlandish, active Delft, active c. 1480–c. 1500
Previously listed as the Master of the Virgin among Virgins (JFD 1972)
*The Marriage of the Virgin*
Late 15th century
Oil on panel transferred to canvas
44 3/8 × 17" (112.7 × 43.2 cm)

John G. Johnson Collection
cat. 349

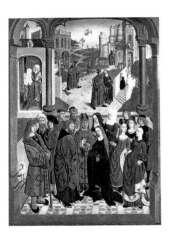

**Master of Sir Thomas Louthe**
Netherlandish, active Bruges or Ghent, active c. 1480
Previously listed as Simon Marmion (JFD 1972)
*Pietà*
Late 15th century
Tempera on vellum on panel
4 5/8 × 3 1/2" (11.7 × 8.9 cm)

John G. Johnson Collection
cat. 343

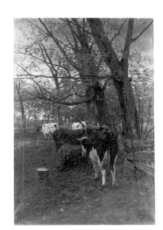

**Master of the Virgin among Virgins, follower of**
Previously listed as the Master of the Virgin among Virgins (JFD 1972)
*Joseph of Arimathea and Nicodemus Asking Pilate for the Body of Christ* [?]
Possibly the right wing from a triptych with the Crucifixion or the Descent from the Cross on its center panel
Late 15th century
Oil on panel
30 5/16 × 15 5/8" (77 × 39.7 cm)

John G. Johnson Collection
cat. 348

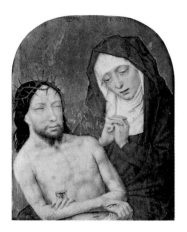

**Master of the Tiburtine Sibyl**
Netherlandish, active Louvain and Haarlem, active c. 1475–c. 1495
*The Marriage of the Virgin, with the Expulsion of Saint Joachim from the Temple, the Angel Appearing to Saint Joachim, the Meeting at the Golden Gate, the Birth of the Virgin, and the Presentation of the Virgin*
c. 1475–95
Oil on panel
57 × 40 1/2" (144.8 × 102.9 cm)

John G. Johnson Collection
cat. 344

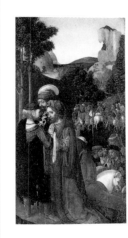

**Mauve, Anton**
Dutch, active Haarlem, Amsterdam, The Hague, and Laren, 1838–1888
*Milking Time*
Late 1870s or 1880s
Lower right: A. Mauve f.
Oil on canvas
40 × 26" (101.6 × 66 cm)

The William L. Elkins Collection
E1924-3-13

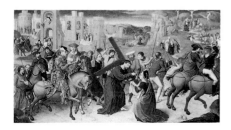

**Master of the Turin Adoration**
Netherlandish, active southern Netherlands, active c. 1490–c. 1510
*Christ Carrying the Cross, with the Entry of Christ into Jerusalem, Christ Driving the Moneychangers from the Temple, the Last Supper, Christ Crowned with Thorns, the Flagellation, "Ecce Homo," the Agony in the Garden, and the Crucifixion*
c. 1500
Upper right, on banner: S P Q R
Oil on panel
37 × 66 1/2" (94 × 168.9 cm)

John G. Johnson Collection
cat. 338

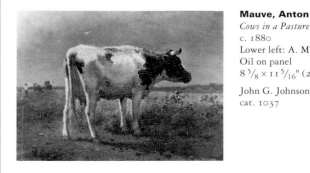

**Mauve, Anton**
*Cows in a Pasture*
c. 1880
Lower left: A. Mauve
Oil on panel
8 5/8 × 11 5/16" (21.9 × 28.7 cm)

John G. Johnson Collection
cat. 1037

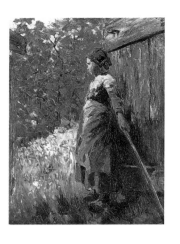

**Mauve, Anton**
*Goose Girl*
c. 1882
Lower right: AM
Oil on panel
18 5/16 × 13 11/16" (46.5 × 34.8 cm)

John G. Johnson Collection
cat. 1036

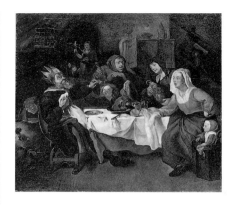

**Metsu, Gabriel, copy after**
*Twelfth Night*
After the painting in the
Bayerische Staatsgemälde-
sammlungen, Alte Pinakothek,
Munich (871)
17th century
Oil on canvas
28 × 31 9/16" (71.1 × 80.2 cm)

John G. Johnson Collection
cat. 508

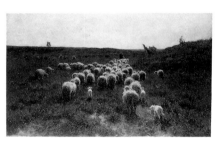

**Mauve, Anton**
*The Return of the Flock, Laren*
c. 1886–87
Lower right: A. Mauve
Oil on canvas
39 7/16 × 63 1/2" (100.2 × 161.3 cm)

The George W. Elkins Collection
E1924-4-21

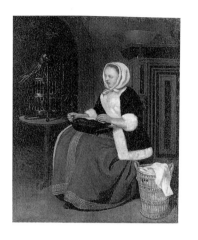

**Metsu, Gabriel, copy after**
*Young Lady Sewing*
After the painting in the State
Museum of A. S. Pushkin,
Moscow
17th century
Oil on canvas on panel
14 1/16 × 11 3/8" (35.7 × 28.9 cm)

John G. Johnson Collection
cat. 507

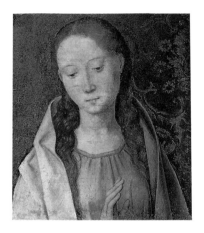

**Memling, Hans**
Netherlandish, active Bruges,
first documented 1465, died 1494
*The Virgin*
Fragment from a painting of the
Annunciation
Late 15th century
Oil on panel
11 1/2 × 9 3/4" (29.2 × 24.8 cm)

John G. Johnson Collection
cat. 324

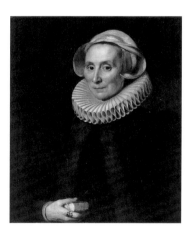

**Mierevelt, Michiel van**
Dutch, active Delft, 1567–1641
*Portrait of a Fifty-Two-Year-Old
Woman*
1618?
Center right: AEtati[s] 52 / Ao
161[8?] / M. Mierevelt.
Oil on panel
28 1/8 × 22 1/2" (71.4 × 57.2 cm)

Gift of the family of J. J. Nevins
(1883–1968) in honor of
Marigene Harrington Butler
1992-41-1

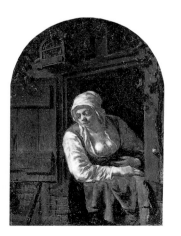

**Metsu, Gabriel**
Dutch, active Leiden and
Amsterdam, 1629–1667
Previously listed as Frans van
Mieris the Elder (JFD 1972)
*Young Woman at a Window*
17th century
Center left: G. Metsu
Oil on panel
9 1/2 × 6 7/8" (24.1 × 17.5 cm)

John G. Johnson Collection
cat. 543

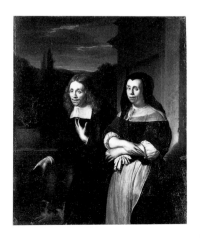

**Mieris, Frans van**
Dutch, active Leiden,
1635–1681
*Portrait of a Husband and Wife*
1675
Lower right: F van Mieris 1675
Oil on panel
10 × 8 1/16" (25.4 × 20.5 cm)

John G. Johnson Collection
inv. 310

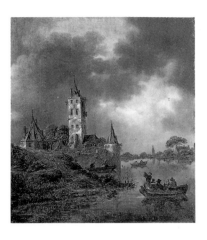

**Molenaer, Claes**
Dutch, active Haarlem,
c. 1630–1676
*Castle near a Canal*
17th century
Lower left: K. Molenaer
Oil on panel
16 1/8 × 13 15/16" (41 × 35.4 cm)

John G. Johnson Collection
cat. 576

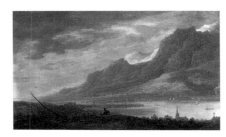

**Momper, Frans de**
Flemish, active Antwerp,
1603–1660
*Mountainous Landscape with a
River*
c. 1640
Oil on panel
14 1/2 × 24 1/2" (36.8 × 62.2 cm)

The Henry P. McIlhenny
Collection in memory of
Frances P. McIlhenny
1986-26-276

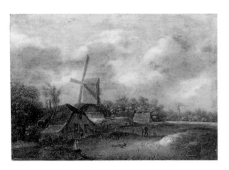

**Molenaer, Claes, imitator of**
Previously listed as Claes
Molenaer (JFD 1972)
*Windmill on the Dunes*
17th century
Oil on panel
19 7/8 × 27 3/8" (50.5 × 69.5 cm)

John G. Johnson Collection
cat. 577

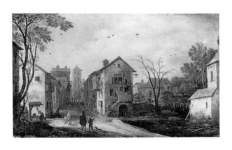

**Momper, Frans de**
*Street in an Italian Village*
17th century
Lower left (spurious): Av. / Neer
Oil on panel
15 1/16 × 24 11/16" (38.3 × 62.7 cm)

John G. Johnson Collection
cat. 655

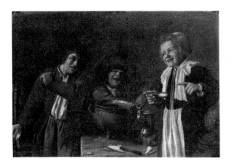

**Molenaer, Jan Miense**
Dutch, active Haarlem and
Amsterdam, c. 1610–1668
*Quarreling Children*
c. 1630
Oil on canvas
18 1/2 × 25 3/8" (47 × 64.4 cm)

John G. Johnson Collection
cat. 438

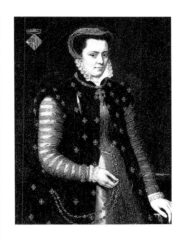

**Mor van Dashorst, Anthonis**
Netherlandish, active Utrecht,
Antwerp, Brussels, Lisbon, and
Madrid, first securely documented
1547, died 1576
*Portrait of Margaret of Parma*
16th century
Oil on panel transferred to canvas
38 1/2 × 28 1/4" (97.8 × 71.7 cm)

John G. Johnson Collection
cat. 428

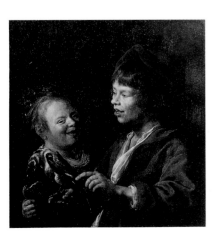

**Molenaer, Jan Miense**
*Two Children Feeding a Bird*
17th century
Oil on panel
22 13/16 × 20 3/16" (57.9 × 51.3 cm)

John G. Johnson Collection
cat. 439

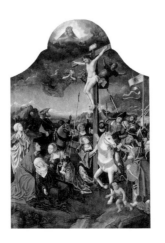

**Mostaert, Jan**
Netherlandish, active Haarlem
and Mechelen, 1472/73–1555/56
*The Crucifixion*
c. 1530
On cross: INRI
Oil on panel
45 1/8 × 29 3/8" (114.6 × 74.6 cm)

John G. Johnson Collection
cat. 411

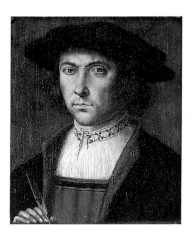

**Mostaert, Jan, follower of**
Previously listed as Jan Mostaert
(PMA 1965)
*Portrait of a Man*
c. 1520–30
Oil on panel
8 15/16 × 7 5/16" (22.7 × 18.6 cm)

The John D. McIlhenny
Collection
1943-40-42

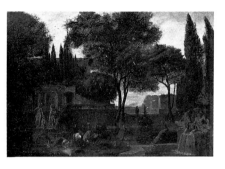

**Moucheron, Isaac de,
imitator of**
Dutch, active Amsterdam,
1667–1744
*Classical Landscape*
Late 17th century
Oil on canvas
38 1/2 × 52" (97.8 × 132.1 cm)

Bequest of Arthur H. Lea
F1938-1-28

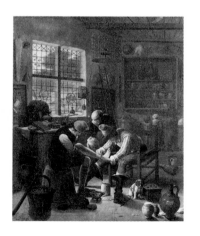

**Natus, Johannes,
attributed to**
Dutch, active Middelburg,
active c. 1658–c. 1662
Previously listed as a Dutch
artist, mid-17th century (JFD
1972)
*Village Surgeon*
Mid-17th century
Lower right: He d
Oil on panel
23 5/8 × 18 7/8" (60 × 47.9 cm)

John G. Johnson Collection
cat. 511

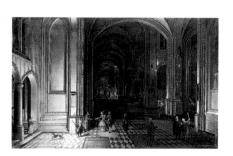

**Neeffs, Peter, the Elder,
attributed to**
Flemish, active Antwerp,
c. 1578–c. 1659
**and Frans Francken III,
attributed to**
Flemish, active Antwerp,
1607–1667
Previously listed as Peter Neeffs
the Younger (JFD 1972)
*Interior of a Church with Torchlight*
c. 1610–60
Oil on panel
10 3/16 × 15 5/8" (25.9 × 39.7 cm)

John G. Johnson Collection
cat. 708

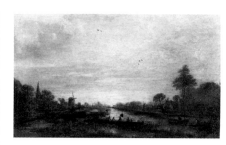

**Neer, Aert van der**
Dutch, active Amsterdam,
1603/4–1677
*Landscape with a River at Twilight*
Late 1640s or early 1650s
Lower left: AVDN
Oil on panel
7 1/4 × 11 1/4" (18.4 × 28.6 cm)

The William L. Elkins Collection
E1924-3-52

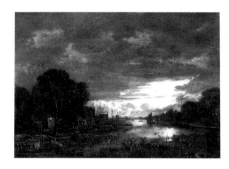

**Neer, Aert van der,
attributed to**
Previously listed as Aert van der
Neer (JFD 1972)
*Moonlight on a Canal*
Mid-17th century
Lower left: AVDN
Oil on canvas
25 9/16 × 33 1/2" (64.9 × 85.1 cm)

John G. Johnson Collection
cat. 553

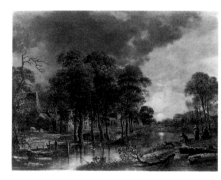

**Neer, Aert van der,
follower of**
Previously listed as Aert van der
Neer (PMA 1965)
*Landscape with a Brook and a
Village in Moonlight*
1650s
Oil on canvas
25 1/2 × 32 1/2" (64.8 × 82.5 cm)

Purchased with the W. P.
Wilstach Fund
W1895-1-7

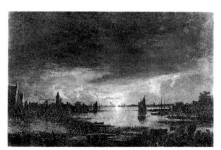

**Neer, Aert van der,
imitator of**
*Harbor*
17th century
Oil on canvas
20 1/8 × 30 1/16" (51.1 × 76.4 cm)

John G. Johnson Collection
inv. 2862

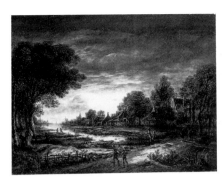

**Neer, Aert van der, imitator of**
Previously listed as a copy after Aert van der Neer (JFD 1972)
*Moonlight on a Canal*
17th century
Lower right (spurious): AVDN
Oil on panel
12 15/16 × 16 1/4" (32.9 × 41.3 cm)

John G. Johnson Collection
cat. 555

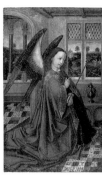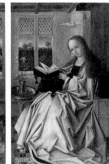

**Netherlandish, active southern Netherlands, unknown artist**
Previously listed as an unknown artist, c. 1460 (JFD 1972)
*The Annunciation*
Diptych
c. 1450–70
Oil on panel
Each panel: 26 1/4 × 15 9/16"
(66.7 × 39.5 cm)

John G. Johnson Collection
cat. 320

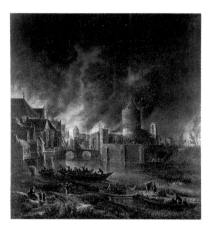

**Neer, Aert van der, copy after**
*Fire at Night*
17th century
Oil on canvas
25 1/4 × 22 3/8" (64.1 × 56.8 cm)

John G. Johnson Collection
cat. 554

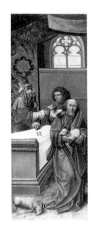

**Netherlandish or German, unknown artist**
Previously listed as a Brussels artist, c. 1470 (JFD 1972)
*The Expulsion of Saint Joachim from the Temple*
Companion to the following painting
c. 1475–1500
Oil on panel
30 7/8 × 11 1/4" (78.4 × 28.6 cm)

John G. Johnson Collection
inv. 339

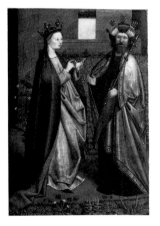

**Netherlandish?, unknown artist**
Previously listed as a Bruges artist, c. 1460 (JGJ 1941)
*Saint Catherine of Alexandria Preaching to the Emperor*
Probably from a series; a companion panel is in the Museum Boymans–van Beuningen, Rotterdam (2468)
c. 1440–60
Oil on panel
14 7/8 × 9 1/2" (37.8 × 24.1 cm)

John G. Johnson Collection
cat. 319

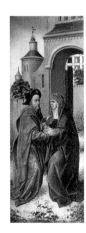

**Netherlandish or German, unknown artist**
Previously listed as a Brussels artist, c. 1470 (JFD 1972)
*The Meeting at the Golden Gate*
Companion to the preceding painting
c. 1475–1500
Oil on panel
30 13/16 × 11" (78.3 × 27.9 cm)

John G. Johnson Collection
inv. 347

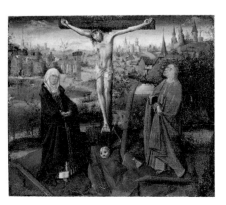

**Netherlandish, active Utrecht?, unknown artist**
Previously listed as an unknown artist, c. 1450 (JFD 1972)
*The Crucifixion*
c. 1440–60
On cross: inri
Oil on panel
7 7/8 × 8 7/8" (20 × 22.5 cm)

John G. Johnson Collection
cat. 316

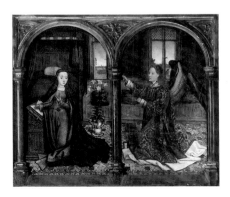

**Netherlandish?, unknown artist**
Previously listed as a Brussels artist, c. 1500 (JGJ 1941)
*The Annunciation*
Diptych
c. 1480–1520
Oil on panel
Each panel: 24 7/8 × 14 1/2"
(63.2 × 36.8 cm)

John G. Johnson Collection
cat. 398 a, b

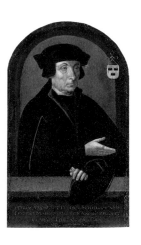

**Netherlandish, active northern Netherlands, unknown artist**
Previously listed as a Dutch artist, c. 1520 (JFD 1972)
*Portrait of Peter Veenlant, Burgomaster of Schiedam*
1489
Across bottom: PETRUS VEEN-LANT CONSUL SCHIEDAMENSIS. / TEMPORE MAXIMILIANI ROMA-NORU REGIS—ET / COMITIS HOLLANDIAE. ANO 1489.
Oil on panel
17 5/8 × 10 1/4" (44.8 × 26 cm)

John G. Johnson Collection
cat. 345

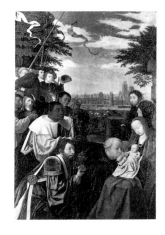

**Netherlandish, active Antwerp, unknown artist**
Previously listed as the Master of the Morrison Triptych (JFD 1972)
*The Adoration of the Magi*
By the same artist who painted a triptych in the National Gallery, London (1085)
c. 1500–10
Oil on panel
65 3/4 × 42 3/4" (167 × 108.6 cm)

John G. Johnson Collection
cat. 369

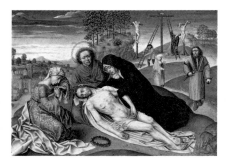

**Netherlandish, active Brussels or Bruges, unknown artist**
Previously listed as a Brussels artist, c. 1500 (JFD 1972)
*Lamentation*
c. 1490–1510
Oil on panel
11 3/8 × 15 5/16" (28.9 × 38.9 cm)

John G. Johnson Collection
cat. 337

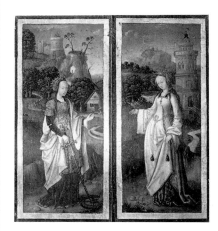

**Netherlandish, active Antwerp?, unknown artist**
Previously listed as an Antwerp Mannerist, c. 1510 (JFD 1972)
*Saints Catherine of Alexandria and Barbara*
Wings from a triptych
c. 1500–20
Oil and gold on panel
Left panel: 13 13/16 × 6 1/8" (35.1 × 15.6 cm); right panel: 13 7/8 × 6 1/8" (35.2 × 15.6 cm)

John G. Johnson Collection
cat. 381

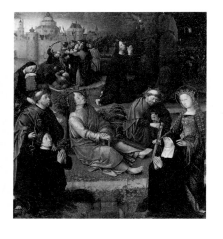

**Netherlandish, active northern Netherlands, unknown artist**
Previously listed as the Amsterdam Master of the Death of the Virgin (JFD 1972)
*The Agony in the Garden, with the Betrayal of Christ, Saints Peter and Catherine of Alexandria, and Two Donors*
c. 1490–1500
Oil and gold on panel
32 5/8 × 28 9/16" (82.9 × 72.5 cm)

John G. Johnson Collection
cat. 751

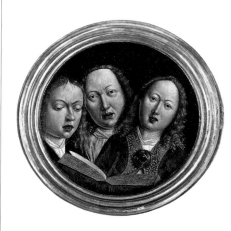

**Netherlandish, unknown artist**
Previously listed as a Bruges artist, c. 1500 (JFD 1972)
*Three Singing Angels*
Based on the panel from the Ghent Altarpiece, by Jan van Eyck, depicting singing angels, in the Cathedral of Saint Bavo, Ghent; see the following painting for reverse
c. 1500–25
Oil on panel
10 11/16" (27.1 cm) diameter

John G. Johnson Collection
cat. 317 a

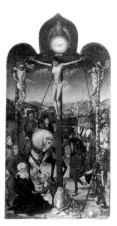

**Netherlandish, active northern Netherlands?, unknown artist**
Previously listed as a Bruges artist, c. 1480 (JFD 1972)
*The Crucifixion*
c. 1490–1510
On cross: INRI; lower right, on caparison of horse: DORO DORO; lower right, on edge of armor: HELGIEO [?] ALV M
Oil on panel
24 1/2 × 12 1/4" (62.2 × 31.1 cm)

John G. Johnson Collection
cat. 323

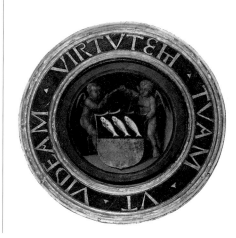

**Netherlandish, unknown artist**
Previously listed as a Bruges artist, c. 1500 (JFD 1972)
*Two Putti Holding a Shield*
Reverse of the preceding painting
c. 1500–25
On frame: VT VIDEAM VIRTVTEM TVAM
Oil on panel
10 11/16" (27.1 cm) diameter

John G. Johnson Collection
cat. 317 b

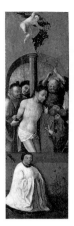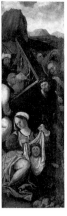

**Netherlandish, active northern Netherlands, unknown artist**
Previously listed as a remote follower of Hieronymous Bosch (JFD 1972)
*The Flagellation, with a Donor, and Christ Carrying the Cross*
Possibly wings from a triptych
c. 1505–15
Oil and gold on panel
Right panel: 41 $^{13}/_{16}$ × 13 $^{1}/_{4}$"
(106.2 × 33.6 cm); left panel:
42 $^{1}/_{16}$ × 13 $^{3}/_{16}$" (106.8 ×
33.5 cm)

John G. Johnson Collection
cat. 408

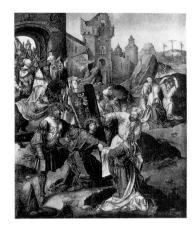

**Netherlandish, active Antwerp, unknown artist**
Previously listed as the Master of the Groote Adoration (JFD 1972)
*Christ Carrying the Cross*
c. 1515–25
Oil and gold on panel
40 × 32 $^{1}/_{4}$" (101.6 × 81.9 cm)

John G. Johnson Collection
cat. 384

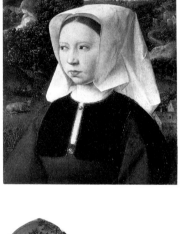

**Netherlandish, active northern Netherlands?, unknown artist**
Previously listed as a Netherlands artist, first half of the 16th century (JFD 1972)
*Portrait of a Woman*
Possibly a fragment of a panel from a diptych or a fragment of the right wing from a triptych
c. 1510–30
Oil on panel
10 $^{1}/_{8}$ × 8 $^{3}/_{16}$" (25.7 × 20.8 cm)

John G. Johnson Collection
cat. 379

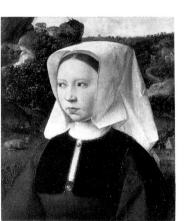

**Netherlandish, active Antwerp, unknown artist**
Previously listed as the Master of the Groote Adoration (JFD 1972)
*The Adoration of the Magi*
c. 1515–25
Oil on panel
27 $^{5}/_{8}$ × 21 $^{1}/_{4}$" (70.2 × 54 cm)

John G. Johnson Collection
cat. 383

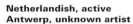

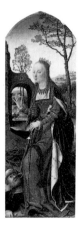

**Netherlandish, active Antwerp?, unknown artist**
Previously listed as an Antwerp Mannerist, c. 1520 (JFD 1972)
*Saint Catherine of Alexandria, with the Defeated Emperor*
Possibly the right wing from a triptych
c. 1510–30
Oil on panel
35 $^{9}/_{16}$ × 12" (90.3 × 30.5 cm)

John G. Johnson Collection
cat. 365

**Netherlandish, active Antwerp, unknown artist**
Previously listed as an Antwerp artist, perhaps to be identified with the Master of 1518 (JFD 1972)
*The Adoration of the Magi*
c. 1515–25
Oil on panel
30 × 21 $^{7}/_{8}$" (76.2 × 55.6 cm)

John G. Johnson Collection
cat. 385

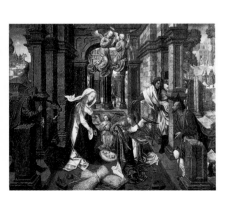

**Netherlandish, active Antwerp, unknown artist**
Previously listed as an Antwerp Mannerist, c. 1520 (JFD 1972)
*The Adoration of the Shepherds*
c. 1510–30
Oil on panel
58 $^{3}/_{8}$ × 69 $^{7}/_{8}$" (148.3 × 177.5 cm)

John G. Johnson Collection
cat. 380

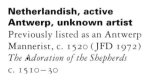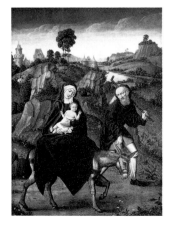

**Netherlandish, unknown artist**
Previously listed as a Flemish artist, mid-16th century (JGJ 1941)
*The Flight into Egypt*
c. 1520
Oil on panel
37 $^{1}/_{2}$ × 24 $^{3}/_{4}$" (95.2 × 62.9 cm)

John G. Johnson Collection
inv. 2840

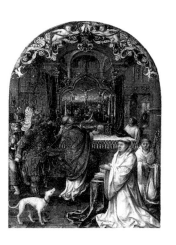

**Netherlandish, active
Antwerp, unknown artist**
*The Seizing of Saint Mark*
c. 1520
Oil and gold on panel
14 5/8 × 11" (37.1 × 27.9 cm)

John G. Johnson Collection
cat. 384a

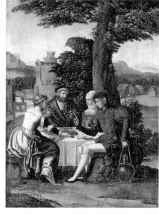

**Netherlandish or German,
unknown artist**
Previously listed as a South
German artist, c. 1560 (JGJ 1941)
*Courtly Scene*
c. 1525–30
Oil on panel
23 3/16 × 16 1/2" (58.9 × 41.9 cm)

John G. Johnson Collection
inv. 3023

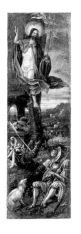

**Netherlandish, active
Antwerp?, unknown artist**
Previously listed as an Antwerp
artist, c. 1510–20 (JFD 1972)
*The Agony in the Garden*
c. 1520–25
Oil on panel
11 11/16 × 7 3/4" (29.7 × 19.7 cm)

John G. Johnson Collection
cat. 382

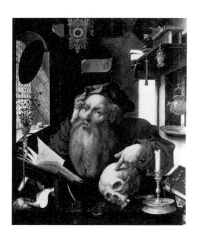

**Netherlandish, active
Antwerp, unknown artist**
Previously listed as an Antwerp
artist, c. 1530 (JFD 1972)
*Saint Jerome in His Study*
Derived from the painting by
Albrecht Dürer (German,
1471–1528) in the Museu
Nacional de Arte Antiga, Lisbon
c. 1530–40
Center: OMNE HOQA.MORICS /
NOSCE SVM
Oil on panel
29 5/8 × 23 9/16" (75.2 × 59.8 cm)

John G. Johnson Collection
cat. 387

**Netherlandish, active
Antwerp, unknown artist**
Previously listed as an Antwerp
Mannerist, c. 1530 (JFD 1972)
*The Resurrection*
Probably the right wing from a
triptych
c. 1520–30
Oil on panel
12 7/16 × 2 3/8" (31.6 × 6 cm)

John G. Johnson Collection
cat. 412

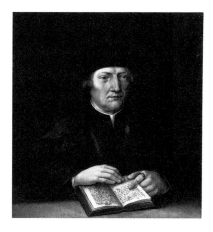

**Netherlandish, active
Antwerp?, unknown artist**
Previously listed as an Antwerp
artist, c. 1530 (JFD 1972)
*Portrait of a Man with a Book of
Hours*
c. 1530–50
On book: [Latin text from the
Gospels of Luke and John]
Oil on panel transferred to canvas
20 1/4 × 17 3/4" (51.4 × 45.1 cm)

John G. Johnson Collection
cat. 376

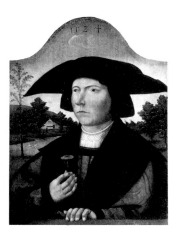

**Netherlandish, active
northern Netherlands,
unknown artist**
Previously listed as the Master of
1518 (JFD 1972)
*Portrait of a Man Holding a Pink*
1524
Center top: 1524
Oil on panel
22 7/8 × 17 1/4" (58.1 × 43.8 cm)

John G. Johnson Collection
inv. 2056

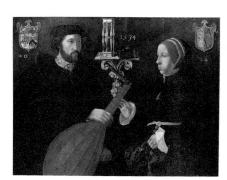

**Netherlandish, active
England?, unknown artist**
Previously listed as an unknown
artist, working 1534 (JFD 1972)
*Portrait of a Husband and Wife*
1534
Upper left: 40; center top: 1534;
upper right: 24; on book: VERBVM
DNI MANET IN ETERNVM
Oil on panel
33 3/4 × 43 3/4" (85.7 × 111.1 cm)

John G. Johnson Collection
cat. 392

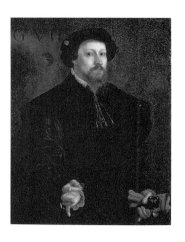

**Netherlandish,
unknown artist**
Previously listed as Johannes
Stephen von Calcar (JFD 1972)
*Portrait of a Gentleman Holding a
Ring*
c. 1545–55
Upper left: G.VIIF / N
Oil on panel
37 3/16 × 27 9/16" (94.5 × 70 cm)

John G. Johnson Collection
cat. 418

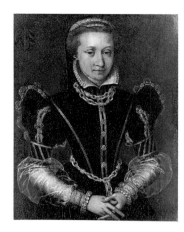

**Netherlandish,
unknown artist**
Previously attributed to François
Clouet (JGJ 1941)
*Portrait of a Lady*
1566
Upper right: 1566
Oil on panel
12 3/8 × 9 1/4" (31.4 × 23.5 cm)

John G. Johnson Collection
cat. 772

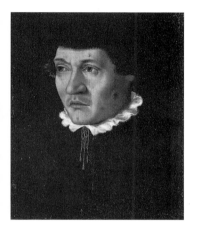

**Netherlandish,
unknown artist**
Previously listed as Nicolaes
Neufchatel (JGJ 1941)
*Portrait of a Man*
c. 1545–55
Oil on panel
19 1/2 × 7 1/4" (49.5 × 18.4 cm)

John G. Johnson Collection
cat. 397

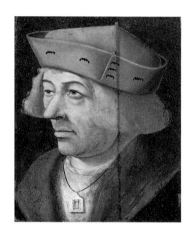

**Netherlandish?,
unknown artist**
Previously listed as a Flemish
artist, second half of the 16th
century (JFD 1972)
*Portrait of a Man in a Red Hat*
16th century
Oil on panel
13 1/8 × 10" (33.3 × 25.4 cm)

John G. Johnson Collection
cat. 426

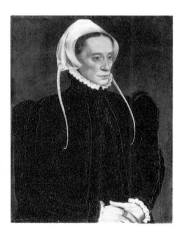

**Netherlandish, active
southern Netherlands,
unknown artist**
Previously attributed to Adriaen
Thomas Key (JFD 1972)
*Portrait of a Lady*
1558
Upper left: 1558
Oil on panel
27 × 20 1/4" (68.6 × 51.4 cm)

John G. Johnson Collection
cat. 427

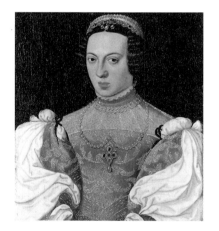

**Netherlandish,
unknown artist**
Previously listed as a Flemish
artist, c. 1530 (JFD 1972)
*Portrait of a Lady*
In a style of c. 1525–35
19th century
Oil on panel
12 1/4 × 10 3/4" (31.1 × 27.3 cm)

John G. Johnson Collection
inv. 387

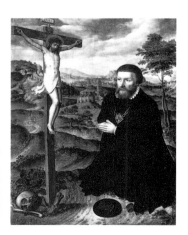

**Netherlandish, active
Bruges, unknown artist**
Previously listed as a Bruges
artist, c. 1570 (JFD 1972)
*Portrait of a Man Kneeling before a
Crucifix in a Landscape*
The medallion worn by the man
indicates that he was a member of
a confraternity of the Holy Cross
c. 1565–75
On cross: INRI
Oil on panel
28 × 21 3/4" (71.1 × 55.2 cm)

John G. Johnson Collection
cat. 363

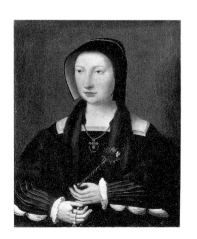

**Netherlandish,
unknown artist**
Previously listed as the school of
Joos van Cleve (JFD 1972)
*Portrait of a Lady with a Nosegay
and a Rosary*
In a style of c. 1520–30
19th century
Oil on panel
13 3/4 × 10 5/8" (34.9 × 27 cm)

John G. Johnson Collection
cat. 372

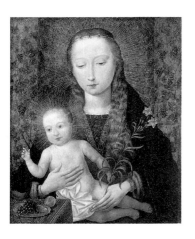

**Netherlandish,
unknown artist**
*Virgin and Child*
In a 15th-century style
19th century
Oil on panel
11 1/2 × 8 7/8" (29.2 × 22.5 cm)

John G. Johnson Collection
inv. 2847

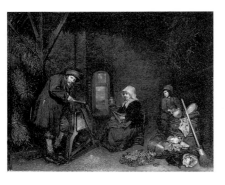

**Netscher, Caspar**
Dutch, active Arnhem, Deventer,
France, and The Hague,
c. 1639–1684
*Chaffcutter with His Wife and Child*
c. 1662–64
On base of cutter (date spurious):
C. Nets 164
Oil on canvas
26 1/8 × 31" (66.4 × 78.7 cm)

John G. Johnson Collection
cat. 544

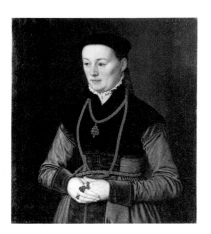

**Neufchatel, Nicolas,
attributed to**
Netherlandish, active
Nuremburg, born c. 1525,
still active c. 1565
*Portrait of a Thirty-Four-Year-Old
Woman*
1562
Upper right: Ao. 1562. /
AETATIS. 34.
Oil on canvas
29 3/4 × 26 1/8" (75.6 × 66.4 cm)

John G. Johnson Collection
inv. 2095

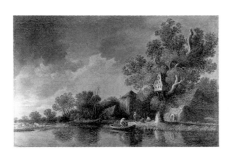

**Neyn, Pieter de**
Dutch, active Leiden,
1597–1639
*Landscape with a Canal*
Early 17th century
On boat (spurious): IVG 1644
Oil on panel
16 1/2 × 25 3/8" (41.9 × 64.4 cm)

John G. Johnson Collection
cat. 465

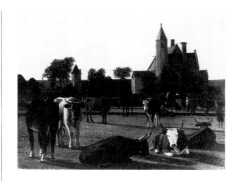

**Oever, Hendrick ten,
attributed to**
Dutch, active Zwolle,
1639–1716
Previously listed as Hendrick ten
Oever (JFD 1972)
*Cattle near a Castle*
17th century
Oil on canvas
21 9/16 × 27" (54.8 × 68.6 cm)

John G. Johnson Collection
cat. 561

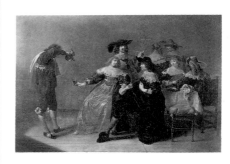

**Olis, Jan**
Dutch, active Rome, Dordrecht,
and Heusden, c. 1610–1676
*Cavaliers and Ladies*
1637
Center right: J Olis fe 1637
Oil on panel
15 9/16 × 23" (39.5 × 58.4 cm)

John G. Johnson Collection
cat. 446

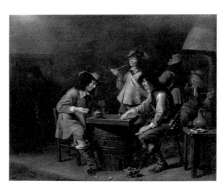

**Olis, Jan**
*Soldiers Playing Draughts*
1646
Lower right: .JOlis . fecit / .Ao .
1646.—
Oil on panel
22 5/8 × 27" (57.5 × 68.6 cm)

John G. Johnson Collection
cat. 447

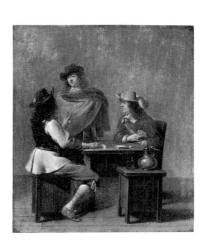

**Olis, Jan**
*Card Players*
Mid-17th century
Center: JO
Oil on panel
14 1/8 × 11 7/8" (35.9 × 30.2 cm)

John G. Johnson Collection
cat. 448

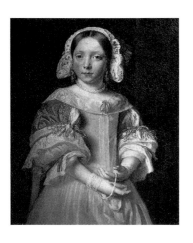

**Oost, Jakob van, the Elder, attributed to**
Flemish, active Italy and Bruges, 1601–1671
Previously listed as a Flemish artist, c. 1660 (JFD 1972)
*Portrait of a Girl*
Early 17th century
Oil on canvas
29 3/8 × 22 3/4" (74.6 × 57.8 cm)

John G. Johnson Collection
inv. 335

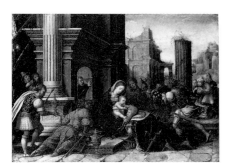

**Oostsanen, Jacob Cornelisz. van, workshop of**
Netherlandish, active Amsterdam, first documented 1507, died 1533
*The Crucifixion*
Early 16th century
On cross: I N R I
Oil on panel
39 × 31 3/4" (99.1 × 80.6 cm)

John G. Johnson Collection
cat. 409

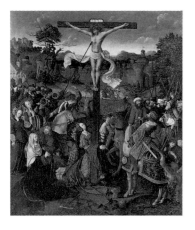

**Orley, Bernard van**
Netherlandish, active Brussels, first documented 1515, died 1542
*The Adoration of the Magi*
c. 1520–40
Center right, on scabbard: MAGI AB ORIENTE
Oil on panel
13 5/16 × 18 1/8" (33.8 × 46 cm)

John G. Johnson Collection
cat. 400

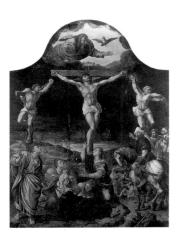

**Orley, Bernard van, copy after**
*The Crucifixion*
After the center panel of a triptych in the church of Onze Lieve Vrouw, Bruges
16th century
On cross: INRI
Oil on panel
44 3/16 × 32 13/16" (112.2 × 83.3 cm)

John G. Johnson Collection
cat. 401

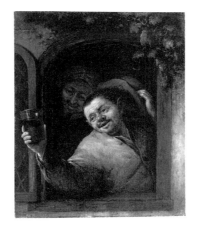

**Ostade, Adriaen van**
Dutch, active Haarlem, 1610–1685
*Peasants Making Merry*
1640
Lower right: A V OSTADE 1640
Oil on panel
8 7/8 × 9 1/16" (22.5 × 23 cm)

John G. Johnson Collection
cat. 521

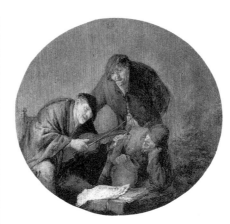

**Ostade, Adriaen van**
*Peasants Drinking at a Window*
c. 1640–70
Center bottom: AV. OSTADE
Oil on panel
11 1/4 × 9 1/8" (28.6 × 23.2 cm)

John G. Johnson Collection
cat. 522

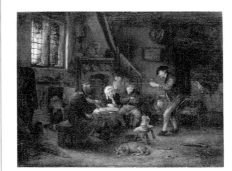

**Ostade, Adriaen van**
*Peasants Drinking and Making Music*
Companion to *Peasants Fighting*, dated 1647, in an unknown location
1647?
Lower right: [illegible signature]
Oil on panel
10 5/8 × 14" (27 × 35.6 cm)

The William L. Elkins Collection
E1924-3-72

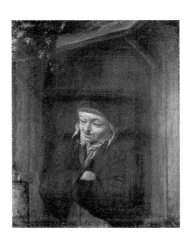

**Ostade, Adriaen van**
*Woman Leaning out a Half-Door*
1660s?
Center bottom: Av Ostade
Oil on panel
10 5/8 × 8 5/8" (27 × 21.9 cm)

The William L. Elkins Collection
E1924-3-71

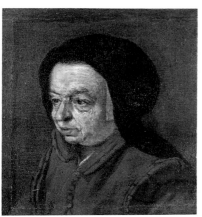

**Ostade, Adriaen van, attributed to**
Previously listed as Adriaen van Ostade (JFD 1972)
*Portrait of an Elderly Lady*
17th century
Center right: A Ostade
Oil on panel
6 × 5 3/8" (15.2 × 13.6 cm)

John G. Johnson Collection
inv. 1258

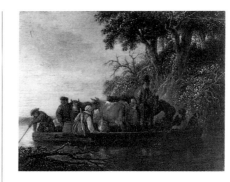

**Ostade, Isaack van, attributed to**
Previously listed as Isaack van Ostade (JFD 1972)
*The Ferry*
Mid-17th century
Oil on panel
9 7/8 × 12 1/4" (25.1 × 31.1 cm)

John G. Johnson Collection
cat. 525

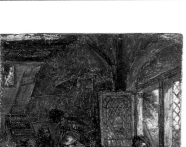

**Ostade, Adriaen van, copy after**
*Interior with Figures*
After the etching (Bartsch 39)
17th century
Oil on panel
3 3/8 × 2 7/8" (8.6 × 7.3 cm)

John G. Johnson Collection
inv. 194a

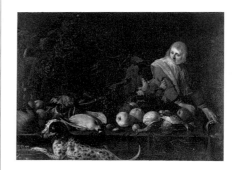

**Palamedesz., Anthonie**
Dutch, active Delft and Amsterdam, 1601–1673
Previously attributed to Anthonie Palamedesz. (PMA 1965)
*Still Life with a Woman, a Boy, and a Dog*
1640s?
Lower left: A. Palamedes
Oil on canvas
48 3/4 × 66" (123.8 × 167.6 cm)

The William L. Elkins Collection
E1924-3-53

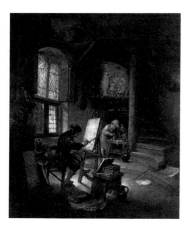

**Ostade, Adriaen van, copy after**
*Painter in His Studio*
After the etching (Bartsch 32)
17th century
Oil on panel
18 1/8 × 14 3/4" (46 × 37.5 cm)

John G. Johnson Collection
cat. 523

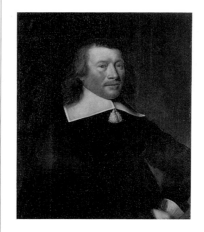

**Palamedesz., Anthonie, attributed to**
Previously listed as Anthonie Palamedesz. (JFD 1972)
*Portrait of a Man*
17th century
Oil on panel
29 1/4 × 23 3/4" (74.3 × 60.3 cm)

John G. Johnson Collection
inv. 1350

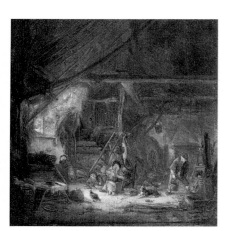

**Ostade, Isaack van**
Dutch, active Haarlem, 1621–1649
*Peasants in a Barn*
c. 1640–49
Center bottom: Isack van Ostade 16
Oil on panel
15 × 14 7/16" (38.1 × 36.7 cm)

John G. Johnson Collection
cat. 524

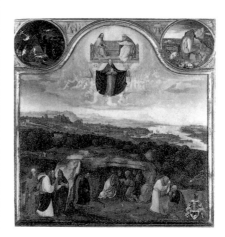

**Patinir, Joachim**
Netherlandish, active Antwerp, c. 1485–1524
*The Assumption of the Virgin, with the Nativity, the Resurrection, the Adoration of the Magi, the Ascension of Christ, Saint Mark and an Angel, and Saint Luke and an Ox*
c. 1510–20
Lower right, on coat of arms of Lucas Rem: ISTZ GVOT SO GEBS GO[T]
Oil on panel
24 1/2 × 23 1/8" (62.2 × 58.7 cm)

John G. Johnson Collection
cat. 378

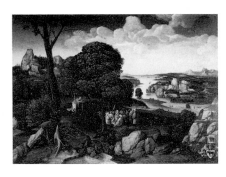

**Patinir, Joachim, workshop of**
Previously listed as Joachim Patinir (PMA 1965)
*Landscape with Saint John the Baptist Preaching*
1516–17?
Lower right, on coat of arms:
POST TENEBRAS / SPERO LUC[EM]
Oil on panel
14 3/4 × 20" (37.5 × 50.8 cm)

Gift of Mrs. Gordon A. Hardwick and Mrs. W. Newbold Ely in memory of Mr. and Mrs. Roland L. Taylor
1944-9-2

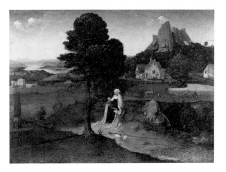

**Patinir, Joachim, workshop of**
*Rest on the Flight into Egypt*
Early 16th century
Oil on panel
18 1/4 × 23 15/16" (46.3 × 60.8 cm)

John G. Johnson Collection
cat. 377

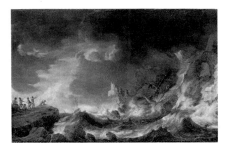

**Peeters, Bonaventura**
Flemish, active Antwerp, 1614–1652
*Shipwreck on a Rocky Coast*
c. 1640
Lower left: B P
Oil on panel
18 13/16 × 28 5/8" (47.8 × 72.7 cm)

Purchased with the Director's Discretionary Fund
1970-2-1

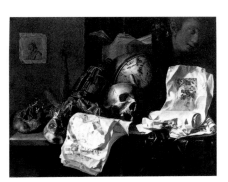

**Peschier, N. L.**
Netherlandish, active 1659–1661
*Vanitas*
1661
Lower left: N vs Le Peschier Fecit / 1661
Oil on canvas
31 1/2 × 40" (80 × 101.6 cm)

The Henry P. McIlhenny Collection in memory of Frances P. McIlhenny
1986-26-287

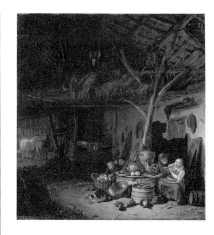

**Poel, Egbert Lievensz. van der**
Dutch, active Delft and Rotterdam, 1621–1664
*The Barn*
1648
Lower right: E V Poel 1648
Oil on panel
23 1/2 × 20" (59.7 × 50.8 cm)

John G. Johnson Collection
cat. 551

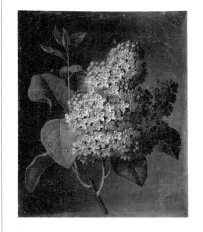

**Pol, Christiaen van**
Dutch, active Antwerp and France, 1752–1813
*Lilac Blossoms*
c. 1800
Lower left: VP
Oil on canvas
10 13/16 × 8 5/8" (27.5 × 21.9 cm)

John G. Johnson Collection
cat. 713

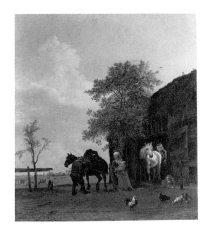

**Potter, Paulus**
Dutch, active The Hague, Delft, and Amsterdam, 1625–1654
*Figures with Horses by a Stable*
1647
Lower left: Paulus Potter. f. 1647
Oil on panel
17 3/4 × 14 3/4" (45.1 × 37.5 cm)

The William L. Elkins Collection
E1924-3-17

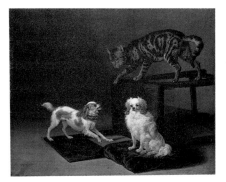

**Potter, Paulus, follower of**
Previously listed as an imitator of Paulus Potter (JFD 1972)
*Cat Playing with Two Dogs*
17th century
Lower right (spurious): Paulus Potter f. 1652
Oil on canvas
36 1/2 × 43" (92.7 × 109.2 cm)

John G. Johnson Collection
cat. 618

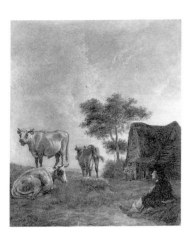

**Potter, Paulus, imitator of**
*Landscape with Cows*
17th century
Lower left (spurious): Paulus
Potter 16[ ]9
Oil on panel
19 ⁵/₈ × 15 ¹/₂" (49.8 × 39.4 cm)

John G. Johnson Collection
inv. 2829

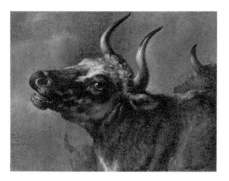

**Potter, Paulus, copy after**
*Bellowing Bull*
After a lost painting
17th century
Oil on canvas
36 ¹/₄ × 45 ¹/₂" (92.1 × 115.6 cm)

John G. Johnson Collection
cat. 619

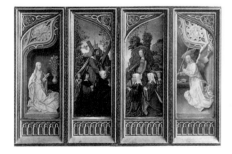

**Provost, Jan**
Netherlandish, active Antwerp
and Bruges, first documented
1493, died 1529
*The Annunciate Virgin, Saint
Andrew with a Donor and His Sons,
Saint Catherine of Alexandria with
a Donor and Her Daughters, and the
Annunciate Angel*
Wings from a triptych, made
into four panels
Early 16th century
Oil on panel
Far left panel: 23 ³/₈ × 8 ³/₈"
(59.4 × 21.3 cm); left panel:
23 ³/₈ × 8 ¹/₄" (59.4 × 20.9 cm);
right panel: 23 ¹/₈ × 8 ⁵/₈"
(58.7 × 21.9 cm); far right panel:
23 ¹/₈ × 8 ¹¹/₁₆" (58.7 × 22.1 cm)

John G. Johnson Collection
cat. 355

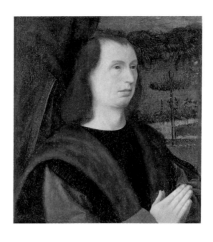

**Provost, Jan, attributed to**
Previously listed as Jan Provost
(JFD 1972)
*Portrait of a Donor Praying*
Fragment from left wing of a trip-
tych from San Colombeno, Genoa,
now in the Galleria di Palazzo
Bianco, on loan from the Ospedale
Civile di San Martino, Genoa; cor-
responding fragment from right
wing is in the Thyssen-Bornemisza
Collection, Madrid (255)
Early 16th century
Oil on panel
21 ⁵/₁₆ × 18 ⁷/₁₆" (54.1 × 46.8 cm)

John G. Johnson Collection
cat. 273

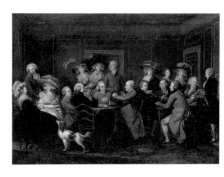

**Puyl, Louis François Gérard
van der**
Dutch, active France, England,
Utrecht, and Amsterdam,
1750–1824
*Portrait of Thomas Payne with His
Family and Friends*
1787
Lower right: L. F. G. van der Puyl
pt / 1787
Oil on canvas
35 × 47" (88.9 × 119.4 cm)

Gift of John Howard McFadden, Jr.
1951-125-17

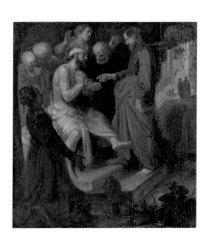

**Pynas, Jan Symonsz.**
Dutch, active Haarlem and
Amsterdam, 1583–1631
*The Raising of Lazarus*
Strips 4" wide have been added to
the top and right
1615?
Oil on panel
22 ³/₄ × 19 ⁷/₈" (57.8 × 50.5 cm)

John G. Johnson Collection
cat. 471

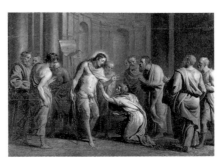

**Quellinus, Erasmus, II**
Flemish, active Antwerp,
1607–1678
*Saint Thomas Touching Christ's
Wounds*
1644
Lower right: Erasmus Quellinus
Delineat Anno 1644
Oil on panel
15 ³/₈ × 21 ⁹/₁₆" (39 × 54.8 cm)

John G. Johnson Collection
cat. 776

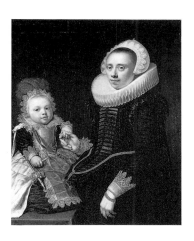

**Ravesteyn, Jan Anthonisz. van**
Dutch, active The Hague,
1572–1657
*Portrait of a Lady and Her Child*
c. 1625
Upper right: Ano [illegible date]
Oil on panel
38 3/8 × 30 11/16" (97.5 ×
77.9 cm)

John G. Johnson Collection
cat. 451

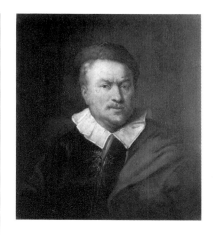

**Rembrandt Harmensz. van Rijn, follower of**
*Portrait of a Gentleman*
17th century
Oil on canvas
29 3/4 × 25 3/4" (75.6 × 65.4 cm)

John G. Johnson Collection
cat. 492

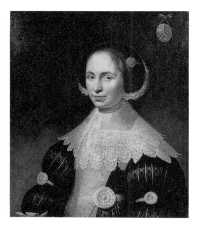

**Ravesteyn, Jan Anthonisz. van**
*Portrait of Gertrude Teding van Berkhout*
1634
Lower left: AEtatis. 23. / Ao.
1634.; on reverse [added later]:
Vrouwe Geertruijt Tedingh / van
Berckhout weduwe wyler /
D'Heer Hugo Brasser Bailla / van
Hovingh Caspel dogter van /
D'Heer Adriaan Tedingh van /
Berckhout en vrouwe Marg / areta
van Berestyn.
Oil on panel
26 7/8 × 22 1/16" (68.3 × 56 cm)

John G. Johnson Collection
cat. 452

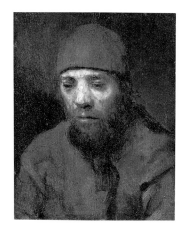

**Rembrandt Harmensz. van Rijn, follower of**
Previously listed as a copy after
Rembrandt Harmensz. van Rijn
(JFD 1972)
*Slaughtered Ox*
17th century
Center bottom (spurious): R.
1637
Oil on panel
19 5/8 × 14 1/2" (49.8 × 36.8 cm)

John G. Johnson Collection
cat. 475

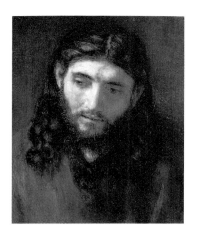

**Rembrandt Harmensz. van Rijn, attributed to**
Dutch, active Leiden and
Amsterdam, 1606–1669
Previously listed as Rembrandt
Harmensz. van Rijn (JFD 1972)
*Head of Christ*
Enlarged on all sides
17th century
Lower right (spurious): Rembran.
/ f. 1656
Oil on panel
9 3/4 × 7 7/8" (24.8 × 20 cm)

John G. Johnson Collection
cat. 480

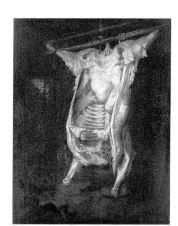

**Rembrandt Harmensz. van Rijn, imitator of**
Previously listed as Carel
Fabritius (JFD 1972)
*Head of an Old Man*
17th century
Oil on panel
9 7/8 × 7 1/2" (25.1 × 19 cm)

John G. Johnson Collection
cat. 479

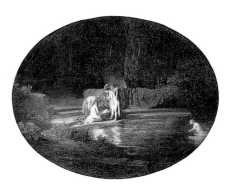

**Rembrandt Harmensz. van Rijn, workshop of**
Previously listed as Rembrandt
Harmensz. van Rijn (JFD 1972)
*The Finding of Moses*
17th century
Oil on canvas
19 1/8 × 23 11/16" (48.6 × 60.2 cm)

John G. Johnson Collection
cat. 474

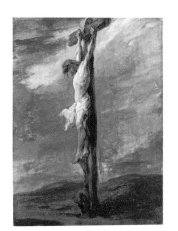

**Rembrandt Harmensz. van Rijn, imitator of**
*The Crucifixion*
17th century
Oil on panel
13 9/16 × 9 5/8" (34.4 × 24.4 cm)

John G. Johnson Collection
cat. 478

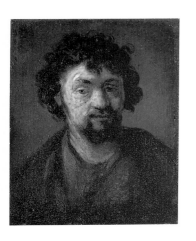

**Rembrandt Harmensz.
van Rijn, copy after**
*Head of a Man*
17th century
Oil on panel
7 ¹³/₁₆ × 6 ³/₁₆" (19.8 × 15.7 cm)

John G. Johnson Collection
cat. 477

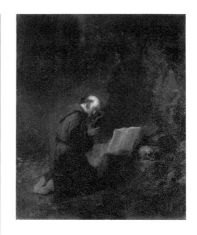

**Rembrandt Harmensz.
van Rijn, copy after**
*Saint Francis of Assisi Praying*
After the Rembrandt School
painting, dated 1637, in the
Columbus Museum of Art,
Ohio (61.2)
17th century
Oil on panel
24 ⁵/₁₆ × 19 ¹/₁₆" (61.7 × 48.4 cm)

John G. Johnson Collection
cat. 481

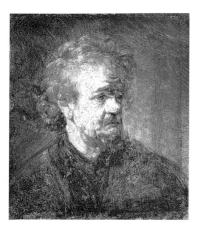

**Rembrandt Harmensz.
van Rijn, copy after**
*Head of an Old Man*
After a painting known through
many copies
17th century
Oil on panel
8 ¹/₄ × 6 ¹⁵/₁₆" (20.9 × 17.6 cm)

John G. Johnson Collection
cat. 476

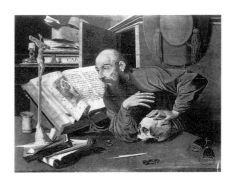

**Reymerswaele, Marinus van,
follower of**
Netherlandish, active Antwerp,
first securely documented 1509,
died c. 1567
*Saint Jerome in His Study*
Mid-16th century
Upper left: CAR; center, on book:
[Latin text of Matthew 25:31–34]
Oil on panel
39 ³/₈ × 50 ¹/₈" (100 × 127.3 cm)

John G. Johnson Collection
cat. 394

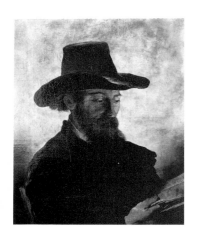

**Rembrandt Harmensz.
van Rijn, copy after**
*Man Reading*
After a painting known through
several copies, the best of which
is in the Sterling and Francine
Clark Art Institute,
Williamstown, Massachusetts
(no. 841)
17th century
Oil on canvas
29 ¹/₁₆ × 23 ¹/₄" (73.8 × 59 cm)

John G. Johnson Collection
cat. 483

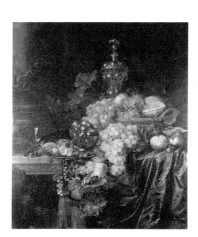

**Ring, Pieter de**
Dutch, active Leiden,
c. 1615–1660
*Still Life with Grapes*
Mid-17th century
Center left: PDR
Oil on canvas
41 ¹/₂ × 33 ¹/₈" (105.4 × 84.1 cm)

John G. Johnson Collection
cat. 632

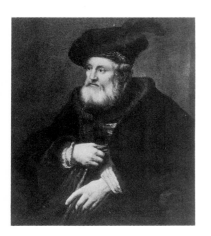

**Rembrandt Harmensz.
van Rijn, copy after**
*Old Man in Fanciful Costume
Holding a Stick*
After the painting, dated 1645,
in the Museu Calouste
Gulbenkian, Lisbon (inv.
no. 1489)
17th century
Oil on canvas
38 ⁷/₈ × 32 ⁷/₈" (98.7 × 83.5 cm)

The William L. Elkins Collection
E1924-3-89

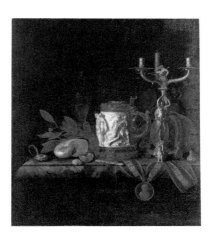

**Roestraten, Pieter Gerritsz.
van**
Dutch, active Haarlem and
England, 1627–1698
*Still Life with an Ivory Cup*
Late 17th century
Oil on canvas
37 ³/₁₆ × 32 ¹/₂" (94.5 × 82.5 cm)

John G. Johnson Collection
cat. 650

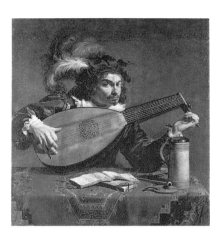

**Rombouts, Theodor**
Flemish, active Antwerp and
Italy, 1597?–1637
*Lute Player*
Known in many versions
c. 1620
Lower right: TR
Oil on canvas
43 3/4 × 39 1/4" (111.1 × 99.7 cm)

John G. Johnson Collection
cat. 679

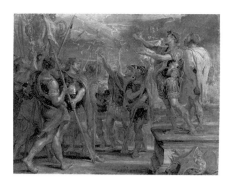

**Rubens, Peter Paul**
*The Emblem of Christ Appearing to
Constantine*
1622
Oil on panel
18 3/16 × 22 1/16" (46.2 × 56 cm)

John G. Johnson Collection
cat. 659

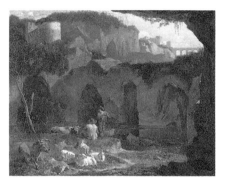

**Romeyn, Willem,
attributed to**
Dutch, active Haarlem,
c. 1624–c. 1694
Previously attributed to Karel
Dujardin (JFD 1972)
*Italian Landscape with Two
Shepherds in a Ravine*
Late 17th century
Oil on canvas
18 × 21 11/16" (45.7 × 55.1 cm)

John G. Johnson Collection
cat. 608

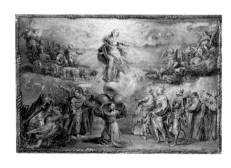

**Rubens, Peter Paul**
*Franciscan Allegory in Honor of the
Immaculate Conception*
1631–32
Oil on panel
21 1/8 × 30 7/8" (53.7 × 78.4 cm)

John G. Johnson Collection
cat. 677

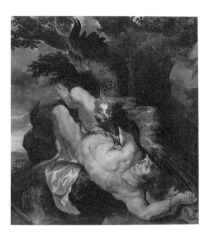

**Rubens, Peter Paul**
Flemish, active Italy, Antwerp,
and England, 1577–1640
**and Frans Snyders**
Flemish, active Antwerp,
1579–1657
*Prometheus Bound*
The eagle was painted by Snyders
Begun c. 1611–12, completed by
1618
Oil on canvas
95 1/2 × 82 1/2" (242.6 × 209.5 cm)

Purchased with the W. P.
Wilstach Fund
W1950-3-1

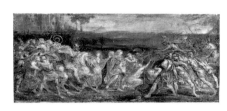

**Rubens, Peter Paul**
*The Reconciliation of the Romans
and Sabines*
1634–36
Oil on panel
11 1/4 × 25 1/8" (28.6 × 63.8 cm)

John G. Johnson Collection
cat. 664

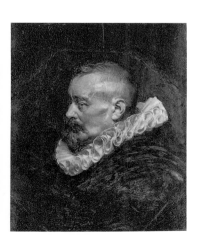

**Rubens, Peter Paul**
*Portrait of a Gentleman* [possibly
Burgomaster Nicholaes Rockox]
Originally octagonal
c. 1615
Oil on panel
15 1/2 × 12 5/16" (39.4 × 31.3 cm)

Gift of Mrs. Gordon A. Hardwick
and Mrs. W. Newbold Ely in
memory of Mr. and Mrs.
Roland L. Taylor
1944-9-9

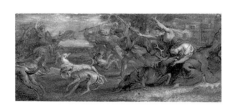

**Rubens, Peter Paul**
*The Death of Silvia's Stag*
c. 1638
Oil on panel
9 1/4 × 20 13/16" (23.5 × 52.9 cm)

John G. Johnson Collection
cat. 663

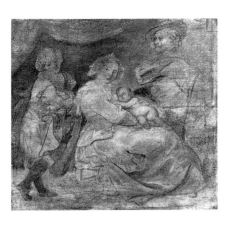

**Rubens, Peter Paul, attributed to**
Previously listed as an imitator of Peter Paul Rubens (JFD 1972)
*Sketch for a Portrait of a Family*
The figures are possibly the family of Rubens
1632–33
Oil on panel
14 × 15" (35.6 × 38.1 cm)

John G. Johnson Collection
cat. 662

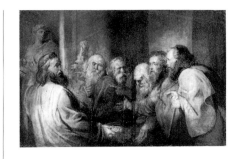

**Rubens, Peter Paul, follower of**
Previously listed as the school of Peter Paul Rubens (JFD 1972)
*The Seven Sages of Greece Disputing over the Tripod*
17th century
Oil on panel
13 5/8 × 19 7/8" (34.6 × 50.5 cm)

John G. Johnson Collection
cat. 658

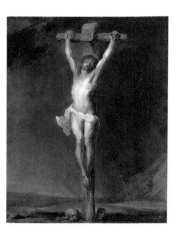

**Rubens, Peter Paul, workshop of**
*The Crucifixion*
17th century
On cross: [Hebrew, Greek, and Latin for "Jesus of Nazareth, King of the Jews"]
Oil on panel
48 1/4 × 36 3/4" (122.5 × 93.3 cm)

John G. Johnson Collection
cat. 657

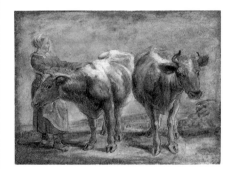

**Rubens, Peter Paul, imitator of**
*Cows*
17th century
Oil on paper on canvas
12 5/8 × 16 3/4" (32.1 × 42.5 cm)

John G. Johnson Collection
cat. 668

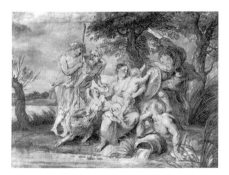

**Rubens, Peter Paul, follower of**
Previously listed as a copy after Peter Paul Rubens (JFD 1972)
*Romulus and Remus*
Based on a painting by a follower of Rubens, formerly in the Staatliche Schlösser und Gärten Potsdam-Sanssouci (7734)
17th century
Oil on panel
13 3/4 × 19 7/8" (34.9 × 50.5 cm)

John G. Johnson Collection
cat. 660

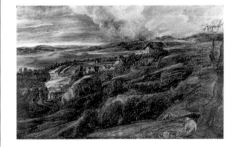

**Rubens, Peter Paul, copy after**
Previously listed as Lucas van Uden (JFD 1972)
*Manzanares Valley*
After a lost painting
c. 1629
Oil on panel
15 1/2 × 23 1/4" (39.4 × 59 cm)

John G. Johnson Collection
cat. 666

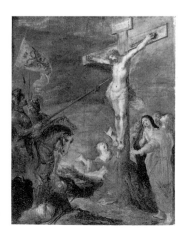

**Rubens, Peter Paul, follower of**
Previously listed as the school of Peter Paul Rubens (PMA 1965)
*The Crucifixion*
17th century
Oil on panel
14 × 10 7/16" (35.6 × 26.5 cm)

The John D. McIlhenny Collection
1943-40-43

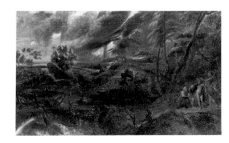

**Rubens, Peter Paul, copy after**
Previously listed as Lucas van Uden (JFD 1972)
*Landscape with Philemon and Baucis*
After the painting in the Kunsthistorisches Museum, Vienna (inv. no. 806)
1630
Oil on panel
16 × 25 1/4" (40.6 × 64.1 cm)

John G. Johnson Collection
cat. 667

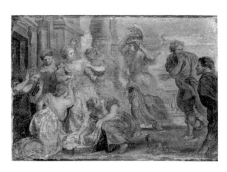

**Rubens, Peter Paul,
copy after**
Previously attributed to Peter
Paul Rubens (PMA 1965)
*Achilles Discovered among the
Daughters of Lycomedes*
After the painting in the Museum
Boymans–van Beuningen,
Rotterdam (2310)
17th century
Oil on panel
14 1/4 × 20 3/8" (36.2 × 51.7 cm)

Purchased with the W. P.
Wilstach Fund
W1902-1-10

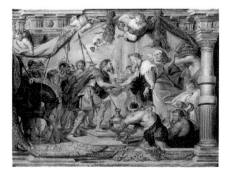

**Rubens, Peter Paul,
copy after**
*The Fall of Icarus*
After the painting in the Musées
Royaux des Beaux-Arts de
Belgique, Brussels (cat. no. 825)
17th century
Oil on panel
12 3/16 × 14 15/16" (31 × 37.9 cm)

John G. Johnson Collection
cat. 665

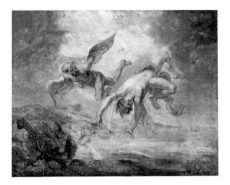

**Rubens, Peter Paul,
copy after**
*The Meeting of Abraham and
Melchizedek*
After the painting in the
National Gallery of Art,
Washington, D.C. (1506)
17th century
Oil on panel
25 3/8 × 32 3/8" (64.4 × 82.2 cm)

John G. Johnson Collection
cat. 661

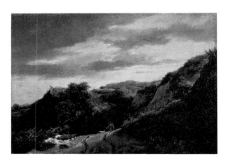

**Ruisdael, Jacob Isaacksz.
van**
Dutch, active Haarlem and
Amsterdam, 1628/29–1682
*Dunes*
c. 1651–55
Lower left: J v R
Oil on panel
13 3/16 × 19 3/8" (33.5 × 49.2 cm)

John G. Johnson Collection
cat. 563

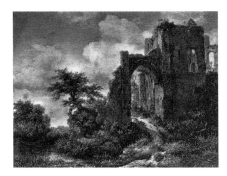

**Ruisdael, Jacob Isaacksz.
van**
*Entrance Gate of the Castle of
Brederode*
c. 1655
Lower right: JVR
Oil on panel
11 7/8 × 14 7/8" (30.2 × 37.8 cm)

John G. Johnson Collection
cat. 564

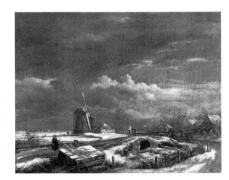

**Ruisdael, Jacob Isaacksz.
van**
*Winter Landscape*
c. 1665
Lower right: JvRuisdael
Oil on canvas
21 3/4 × 27" (55.2 × 68.6 cm)

John G. Johnson Collection
cat. 569

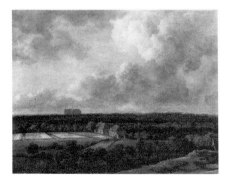

**Ruisdael, Jacob Isaacksz.
van**
*Bleaching Fields to the
North-Northeast of Haarlem*
c. 1670–75
Lower right: [illegible signature]
Oil on canvas
17 1/4 × 21 1/8" (43.8 × 53.7 cm)

The William L. Elkins Collection
E1924-3-90

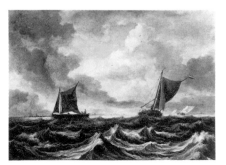

**Ruisdael, Jacob Isaacksz.
van**
*Boats on a Stormy Sea*
After 1670
Lower right (spurious): JvR
Oil on canvas
30 3/16 × 41 3/16" (76.7 × 104.6 cm)

The William L. Elkins Collection
E1924-3-56

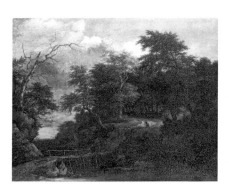

**Ruisdael, Jacob Isaacksz. van**
*Landscape of a Forest with a Wooden Bridge*
After 1670
Lower left: [illegible monogram]
Oil on canvas
41 1/8 × 50 3/8" (104.5 × 127.9 cm)

The William L. Elkins Collection
E1924-3-77

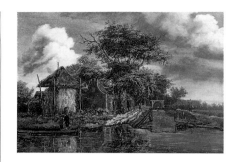

**Ruisdael, Jacob Isaacksz. van, copy after**
*Canal*
After the drawing in the collection of P. and N. de Boer, Amsterdam
17th century
Oil on panel
16 13/16 × 24" (42.7 × 61 cm)

John G. Johnson Collection
cat. 572

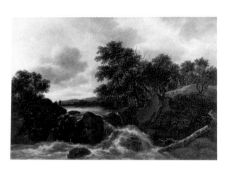

**Ruisdael, Jacob Isaacksz. van**
*Landscape with a Waterfall*
17th century
Lower left: JvRuisdael
Oil on canvas
40 3/4 × 56 1/2" (103.5 × 143.5 cm)

Purchased with the W. P. Wilstach Fund
W1895-1-8

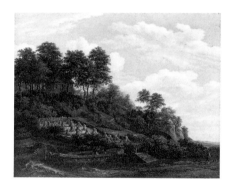

**Ruisdael, Jacob Isaacksz. van, copy after**
*Sloping Field*
After the painting sold at Sotheby's, New York, January 17, 1985 (lot 92)
17th century
Oil on canvas
26 7/16 × 31 3/4" (67.1 × 80.6 cm)

John G. Johnson Collection
cat. 566

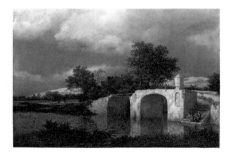

**Ruisdael, Jacob Isaacksz. van**
*Stone Bridge*
17th century
Lower right: JvR
Oil on canvas
14 1/4 × 20 1/2" (36.2 × 52.1 cm)

John G. Johnson Collection
cat. 570

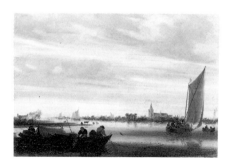

**Ruysdael, Salomon van**
Dutch, active Haarlem, 1600/03?–1670
*Canal*
c. 1650
Lower left: SvR 164
Oil on panel
17 3/16 × 23 3/4" (43.7 × 60.3 cm)

John G. Johnson Collection
cat. 466

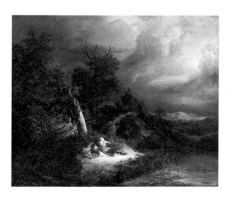

**Ruisdael, Jacob Isaacksz. van**
*Storm on the Dunes*
17th century
Lower right: JRuisdael
Oil on canvas
27 3/8 × 32 1/4" (69.5 × 81.9 cm)

John G. Johnson Collection
cat. 567

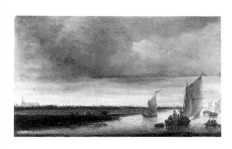

**Ruysdael, Salomon van**
*Evening on the Canal*
c. 1660–70
Lower left: [illegible date]
Oil on panel
12 3/4 × 21 5/16" (32.4 × 54.1 cm)

John G. Johnson Collection
cat. 468

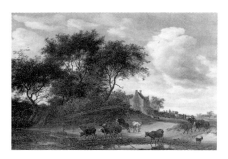

**Ruysdael, Salomon van**
*Landscape with Cattle and an Inn*
1661
Lower left: S. Ruysdael, 1661
Oil on panel
30 × 43 1/2" (76.2 × 110.5 cm)

The William L. Elkins Collection
E1924-3-55

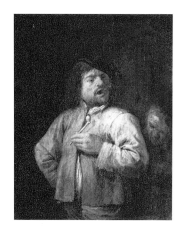

**Ryckaert, David, III**
*Peasant Smoking*
Mid-17th century
Oil on panel transferred to canvas
10 5/16 × 8" (26.2 × 20.3 cm)

John G. Johnson Collection
cat. 698

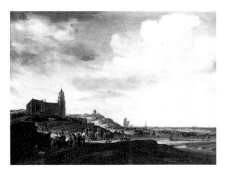

**Ruysdael, Salomon van**
*Beach at Scheveningen*
1665
Lower right: SVRuysdael .1665.
Oil on canvas
34 1/8 × 43 5/8" (86.7 × 110.8 cm)

John G. Johnson Collection
cat. 467

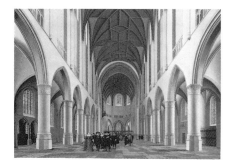

**Saenredam, Pieter Jansz.**
Dutch, active Haarlem and
Utrecht, 1597–1665
*Interior of Saint Bavo, Haarlem*
The figures are attributed to
Pieter Jansz. Post (Dutch,
1608–1669)
1631
Lower left: PSaenredam 1631;
center bottom: 1631
Oil on panel
32 5/8 × 43 1/2" (82.9 × 110.5 cm)

John G. Johnson Collection
cat. 599

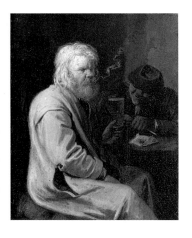

**Ryckaert, David, III**
Flemish, active Antwerp,
1612–1661
*Drinker*
Mid-17th century
Oil on panel
12 5/16 × 9 7/16" (31.3 × 24 cm)

John G. Johnson Collection
cat. 686

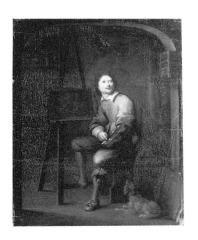

**Saftleven, Cornelis,
copy after**
Dutch, active Rotterdam,
Antwerp, and Utrecht,
c. 1607–1681
*Portrait of Cornelis Saftleven*
After a lost self-portrait
Mid-17th century
Oil on panel
16 3/4 × 13 5/16" (42.5 × 33.8 cm)

John G. Johnson Collection
cat. 546

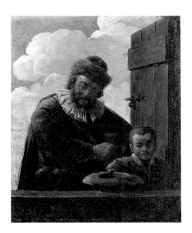

**Ryckaert, David, III**
*Organ Player*
Mid-17th century
Oil on copper
8 3/4 × 7" (22.2 × 17.8 cm)

John G. Johnson Collection
cat. 699

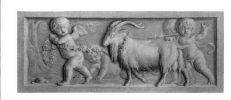

**Sauvage, Piat-Joseph,
attributed to**
Flemish, active Tournai,
1744–1818
Previously listed as Piat-Joseph
Sauvage (PMA 1965)
*Putti Leading a Goat by a Chain of
Flowers*
Late 18th century
Oil on canvas
23 × 57" (58.4 × 144.8 cm)

Gift of Mrs. Morris Hawkes
1942-90-2

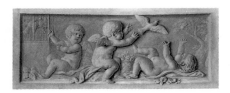

**Sauvage, Piat-Joseph, attributed to**
Previously listed as Piat-Joseph Sauvage (PMA 1965)
*Putti Playing with Birds*
Late 18th century
Oil on canvas
23 × 57" (58.4 × 144.8 cm)

Gift of Mrs. Morris Hawkes
1942-90-1

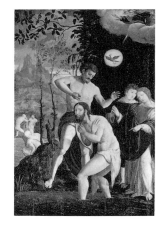

**Scorel, Jan van, workshop of**
Netherlandish, active Utrecht,
1495–1562
Previously listed as the school of
Jan van Scorel (JFD 1972)
*The Baptism of Christ*
Mid-16th century
Oil on panel
49 5/8 × 32" (126 × 81.3 cm)

John G. Johnson Collection
cat. 414

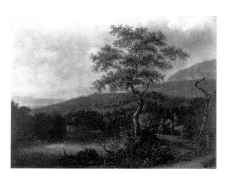

**Schellinks, Willem**
Dutch, active Amsterdam and
London, 1627–1678
*Italian Landscape*
Mid-17th century
Lower left: JR; lower right: WS
Oil on panel
18 5/8 × 24 1/2" (47.3 × 62.2 cm)

John G. Johnson Collection
cat. 613

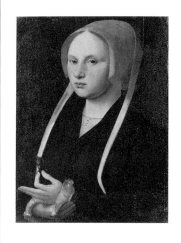

**Scorel, Jan van, follower of**
Previously attributed to Jan van
Scorel (JFD 1972)
*Portrait of a Lady*
Mid-16th century
Oil on panel
19 × 13 9/16" (48.3 × 34.4 cm)

John G. Johnson Collection
cat. 415

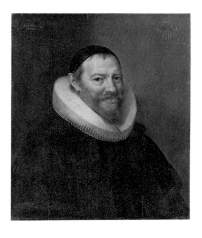

**Schooten, Joris van**
Dutch, active Leiden,
1587–1651
*Portrait of a Clergyman* [possibly
Antonius Thysius]
1635
Upper left: Anno Salutis 1635 /
Aetatis. 70—; upper right:
Scientia et Conscientia / Anno
Salutis 1635. / Aetatis 70.
Oil on panel
26 13/16 × 21 7/8" (68.1 × 55.6 cm)

John G. Johnson Collection
cat. 453

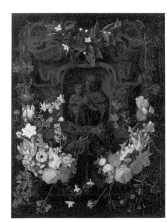

**Seghers, Daniel, copy after**
Flemish, active Antwerp,
1590–1661
Previously listed as Daniel
Seghers (PMA 1965)
*Garland of Flowers with a
Cartouche of the Virgin and Child*
After a painting in a private
collection
Mid-17th century
Oil on canvas
40 × 29" (101.6 × 73.7 cm)

Purchased with the W. P.
Wilstach Fund
W1904-1-54

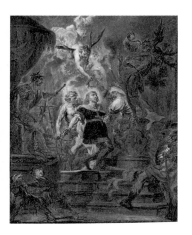

**Schut, Cornelis**
Flemish, active Antwerp,
1597–1655
*The Martyrdom of Saint George*
c. 1640–42
Oil on panel
25 × 19 5/16" (63.5 × 49 cm)

John G. Johnson Collection
cat. 675

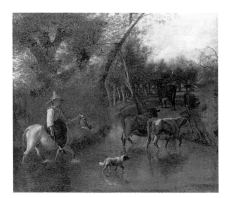

**Siberechts, Jan**
Flemish, active Antwerp and
London, 1627–c. 1703
*Ford*
1670
Lower right: J. Siberechts. /
.1670.
Oil on canvas
29 1/4 × 32 1/2" (74.3 × 82.5 cm)

John G. Johnson Collection
cat. 707

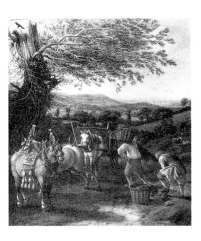

**Siberechts, Jan**
*Horses and a Wagon*
1694
Lower right: J. Siberechts. /
.1694.
Oil on canvas
14 1/8 × 12" (35.9 × 30.5 cm)

John G. Johnson Collection
cat. 1185

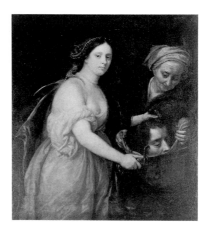

**Soutman, Pieter Claesz.,
attributed to**
Dutch, active Haarlem, Antwerp,
and Poland, c. 1580–1657
Previously attributed to Jacob
Jordaens (PMA 1965)
*Judith with the Head of Holofernes*
Early 17th century
Oil on canvas
46 5/8 × 39 3/8" (118.4 × 100 cm)

Gift of Mrs. George H. Frazier
1936-26-1

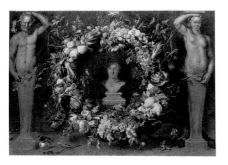

**Snyders, Frans**
Flemish, active Antwerp,
1579–1657
*Still Life with Terms and a Bust of
Ceres*
c. 1630
On bust: CERES; lower right: F.
Snyders fecit
Oil on canvas
67 3/8 × 95" (171.1 × 241.3 cm)

Purchased with the W. P.
Wilstach Fund
W1899-1-4

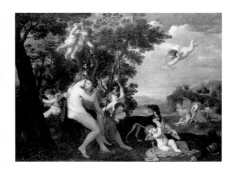

**Spierincks, Karel Philips,
attributed to**
Flemish, active Rome,
1609–1639
Previously listed as the circle of
Nicolas Poussin (PMA 1965)
*Jupiter and Callisto*
Early 17th century
Oil on canvas
53 × 70" (134.6 × 177.8 cm)

The Mr. and Mrs. Carroll S.
Tyson, Jr., Collection
1963-116-12

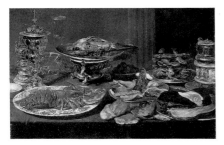

**Snyders, Frans, attributed to**
Previously listed as Frans Snyders
(JFD 1972)
*Still Life with a Lobster*
17th century
Oil on panel
27 3/8 × 41 13/16" (69.5 × 106.2 cm)

John G. Johnson Collection
cat. 700

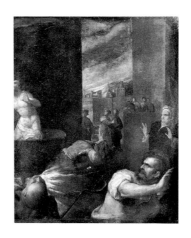

**Spranger, Bartholomeus,
follower of**
Flemish, active Prague and Italy,
1546–1611
Previously listed as Italian,
unknown artist, 17th century
(PMA 1965)
*Saint John the Evangelist at the
Porta Latina*
Fragment
After 1573
Oil on panel
40 × 31" (101.6 × 78.7 cm)

Bequest of Arthur H. Lea
F1938-1-35

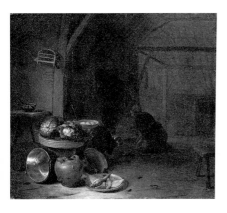

**Sorgh, Hendrick Martensz.**
Dutch, active Rotterdam,
born 1609–11, died 1670
*Woman in a Kitchen*
1648
Center: H Sorgh / 1648
Oil on panel
10 1/2 × 11 1/2" (26.7 × 29.2 cm)

John G. Johnson Collection
cat. 531

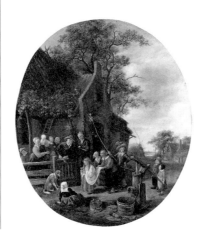

**Steen, Jan**
Dutch, active Leiden, Haarlem,
and The Hague, 1625/26–1679
*The May Queen*
c. 1648–51
Lower left: JSteen
Oil on panel
29 7/8 × 24 1/4" (75.9 × 61.6 cm)

John G. Johnson Collection
cat. 513

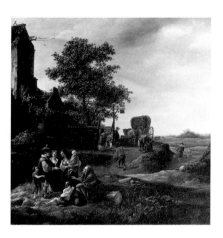

**Steen, Jan**
*The Fortune Teller*
c. 1648–52
Center bottom: JSteen
Oil on canvas
39 × 36" (99.1 × 91.4 cm)

Purchased with the W. P.
Wilstach Fund
W1902-1-21

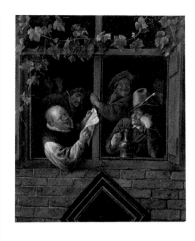

**Steen, Jan**
*Rhetoricians at a Window*
c. 1661–66
Center, on paper: LOF LIET;
center bottom: IVGHT NEMT IN
Oil on canvas
29 7/8 × 23 1/16" (75.9 × 58.6 cm)

John G. Johnson Collection
cat. 512

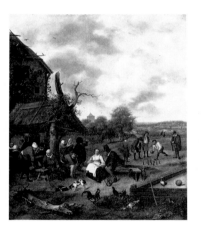

**Steen, Jan**
*Landscape with an Inn and Skittles*
c. 1656–60
Lower right: JSteen
Oil on canvas
24 5/16 × 20 1/8" (61.7 × 51.1 cm)

John G. Johnson Collection
cat. 517

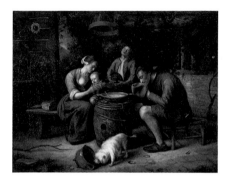

**Steen, Jan**
*Prayer before the Meal*
c. 1667–71
Lower left: JStin
Oil on canvas
24 3/4 × 30 3/4" (62.9 × 78.1 cm)

John G. Johnson Collection
cat. 514

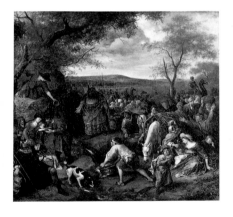

**Steen, Jan**
*Moses Striking the Rock*
c. 1660–61
Lower left: JSteen
Oil on canvas
37 3/8 × 38 3/4" (94.9 × 98.4 cm)

John G. Johnson Collection
cat. 509

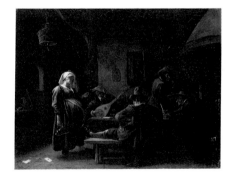

**Steen, Jan**
*Tavern Scene with a Pregnant Hostess*
c. 1670
Lower right: JSteen.
Oil on canvas
17 1/8 × 21 7/16" (43.5 × 54.4 cm)

John G. Johnson Collection
cat. 520

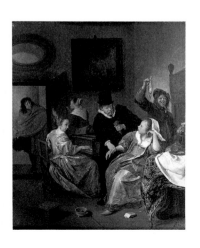

**Steen, Jan**
*The Doctor's Visit*
c. 1660–65
Lower right: JSteen
Oil on panel
18 1/8 × 14 1/2" (46 × 36.8 cm)

John G. Johnson Collection
cat. 510

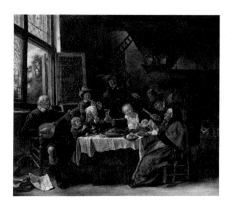

**Steen, Jan**
Previously listed as a copy after
Jan Steen (JFD 1972)
*As the Old Ones Sing, So the Young Ones Pipe*
c. 1670–75
Lower right: JSteen.
Oil on canvas
37 5/8 × 42" (95.6 × 106.7 cm)

John G. Johnson Collection
cat. 519

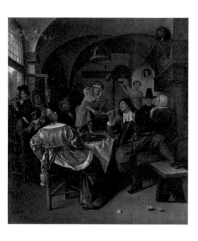

**Steen, Jan, attributed to**
Previously listed as Jan Steen
(JFD 1972)
*Merry Company*
c. 1663–67
Lower left: JSteen.
Oil on canvas
20 7/8 × 17 1/4" (53 × 43.8 cm)

John G. Johnson Collection
cat. 515

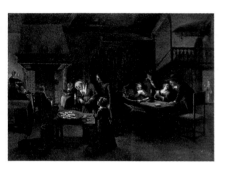

**Steen, Jan, follower of**
Previously listed as Jan Steen
(JFD 1972)
*Tavern Scene by Candlelight*
17th century
Upper left (spurious): JSteen
Oil on panel
17 1/16 × 22 1/2" (43.3 × 57.1 cm)

John G. Johnson Collection
cat. 516

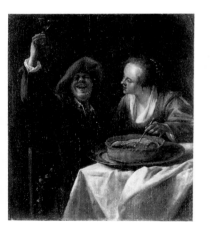

**Steen, Jan, imitator of**
Previously listed as a copy after
Jan Steen (JFD 1972)
*Happy Lovers*
17th century
Oil on panel
9 3/8 × 7 15/16" (23.8 × 20.2 cm)

John G. Johnson Collection
cat. 518

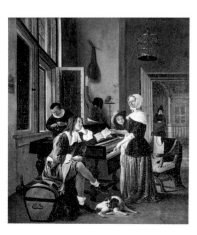

**Steen, Jan, copy after**
Previously listed as Jan Steen
(PMA 1965)
*Lady at a Clavichord*
After a lost painting
After 1661 or 1664
Lower left (spurious): J. Stein /
16[61 or 64]
Oil on canvas
25 1/4 × 21 3/4" (64.1 × 55.2 cm)

The William L. Elkins Collection
E1924-3-37

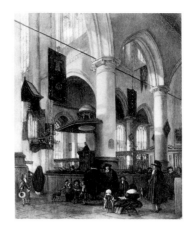

**Streeck, Hendrik van**
Dutch, active Amsterdam,
born 1659, still active 1719
*Interior of the Oude Kerk, Delft*
Late 17th century
Oil on panel
18 3/16 × 13 13/16" (46.2 × 35.1 cm)

John G. Johnson Collection
cat. 600

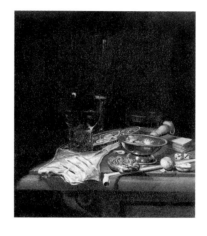

**Streeck, Juriaen van,
copy after?**
Dutch, active Amsterdam,
1632–1687
Previously listed as Juriaen van
Streeck (JFD 1972)
*Still Life with a Flounder and a
Goblet*
17th century
Lower left: J. v Streeck
Oil on canvas
25 7/8 × 21 7/8" (65.7 × 55.6 cm)

John G. Johnson Collection
cat. 652

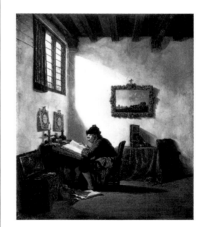

**Strij, Abraham van**
Dutch, active Dordrecht,
1753–1826
*Scholar*
c. 1800
Oil on panel
25 5/16 × 21 1/4" (64.3 × 54 cm)

John G. Johnson Collection
cat. 711

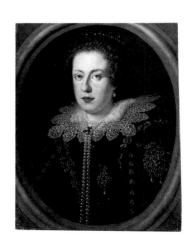

**Sustermans, Justus,
workshop of**
Flemish, active Florence,
1597–1681
Previously listed as Justus
Sustermans (JFD 1972)
*Portrait of Claudia, Daughter of
Ferdinand I, Grand Duke of
Tuscany*
Mid-17th century
Oil on canvas
22 3/4 × 17 1/4" (57.8 × 43.8 cm)

John G. Johnson Collection
cat. 678

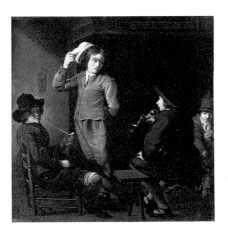

**Sweerts, Michiel, copy after**
Flemish, active Brussels and
Rome, 1624–1664
*Four Youths around a Fire*
After the painting in the
Bayerische Staatsgemälde-
sammlungen, Alte Pinakothek,
Munich (854)
17th century
Oil on canvas
20 5/8 × 20 1/4" (52.4 × 51.4 cm)

John G. Johnson Collection
cat. 550

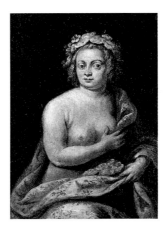

**Teniers, David, II**
*Pomona*
After a painting engraved in
Teniers, *Theatrum Pictorium*
(1660–73), and there attributed
to Palma il Giovane (Italian,
1544–1628)
Late 17th century
Oil on panel
6 3/4 × 4 3/4" (17.1 × 12.1 cm)

John G. Johnson Collection
cat. 694

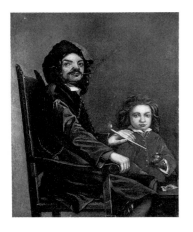

**Sweerts, Michiel, copy after**
*Portrait of a Seated Man with a Boy*
After the painting in the Schloss
Weissenstein der Grafen von
Schönborn, Pommersfelden,
Germany
17th century
Oil on panel
19 1/16 × 14 3/4" (48.4 × 37.5 cm)

John G. Johnson Collection
cat. 1178

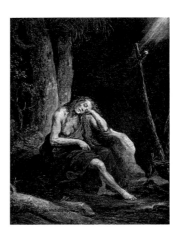

**Teniers, David, II**
*Saint Mary of Egypt in the Desert*
After a painting engraved in
Teniers, *Theatrum Pictorium*
(1660–73), and there attributed
to Palma il Giovane (Italian,
1544–1628)
Late 17th century
Oil on panel
8 7/8 × 6 3/4" (22.5 × 17.1 cm)

John G. Johnson Collection
cat. 693

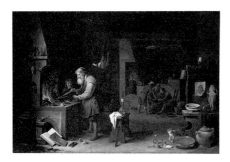

**Teniers, David, II**
Flemish, active Antwerp and
Brussels, 1610–1690
*The Alchemist*
1649
Center right: Ano 1649; lower
right: D. TENIERS. Fec.
Oil on panel transferred to canvas
23 1/2 × 33" (59.7 × 83.8 cm)

John G. Johnson Collection
cat. 689

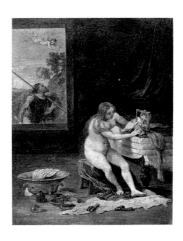

**Teniers, David, II**
*Toilet of Venus*
After a painting engraved in
Teniers, *Theatrum Pictorium*
(1660–73), and there attributed
to Andrea Meldolla, also called
Schiavone (Italian, 1522–
c. 1582)
Late 17th century
Oil on panel
8 7/8 × 6 3/4" (22.5 × 17.1 cm)

John G. Johnson Collection
cat. 696

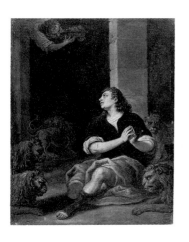

**Teniers, David, II**
*Daniel in the Lion's Den*
After a painting engraved in
Teniers, *Theatrum Pictorium*
(1660–73), and there attributed
to Palma il Giovane (Italian,
1544–1628)
Late 17th century
Oil on panel
9 1/8 × 6 7/8" (23.2 × 17.5 cm)

John G. Johnson Collection
cat. 697

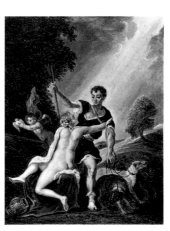

**Teniers, David, II**
*Venus and Adonis*
After a painting engraved in
Teniers, *Theatrum Pictorium*
(1660–73), and there attributed
to Antonio Correggio (Italian,
1494–1534)
Late 17th century
Oil on panel
8 7/8 × 6 3/4" (22.5 × 17.1 cm)

John G. Johnson Collection
cat. 695

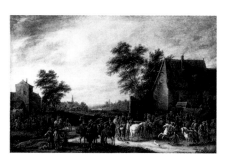

**Teniers, David, II, attributed to**
Previously listed as David Teniers II (JFD 1972)
*Departure of a Troop of Soldiers*
Late 17th century
Center bottom: D Teniers, F.
Oil on canvas
23 1/8 × 33 1/2" (58.7 × 85.1 cm)

John G. Johnson Collection
cat. 690

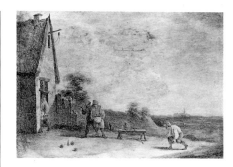

**Teniers, David, II, imitator of**
*Peasants Bowling before an Inn*
Late 17th century
Oil on panel
6 × 8 1/8" (15.2 × 20.6 cm)

John G. Johnson Collection
inv. 162

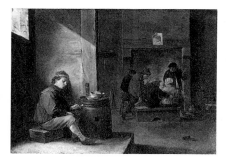

**Teniers, David, II, attributed to**
Previously listed as David Teniers II (JFD 1972)
*Sleeper*
Late 17th century
Oil on panel transferred to canvas
10 13/16 × 15 1/16" (27.5 × 38.3 cm)

John G. Johnson Collection
cat. 691

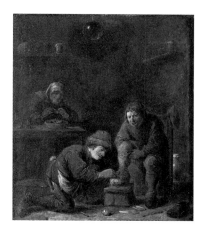

**Teniers, David, II, copy after**
Previously listed as David Teniers II (JFD 1972)
*Operation on the Foot*
After the painting in the Staatliche Kunstsammlungen, Schloss Wilhelmshöhe, Gemäldegalerie Alte Meister, Kassel, Germany
Late 17th century
Oil on panel
14 × 11 7/8" (35.6 × 30.2 cm)

John G. Johnson Collection
cat. 682

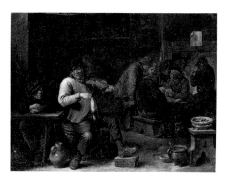

**Teniers, David, II, attributed to**
Previously listed as David Teniers II (JFD 1972)
*Violin Player in a Tavern*
Late 17th century
Center bottom, on footrest:
D. TENIERS. FEC
Oil on panel
11 5/8 × 14 1/2" (29.5 × 36.8 cm)

John G. Johnson Collection
cat. 692

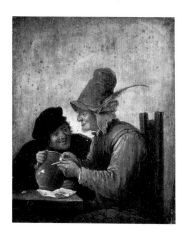

**Teniers, David, II, copy after**
*Two Peasants*
After a lost painting
Late 17th century
Lower left: J. S.
Oil on panel
9 7/8 × 7 5/8" (25.1 × 19.4 cm)

John G. Johnson Collection
cat. 532

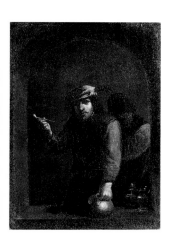

**Teniers, David, II, follower of**
*Peasants in a Niche*
Late 17th century
Lower right (spurious):
D TENIERS F
Oil on canvas
22 5/8 × 16 1/8" (57.5 × 41 cm)

Bequest of Arthur H. Lea
F1938-1-22

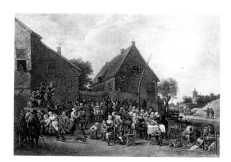

**Teniers, David, II, copy after**
Previously listed as David Teniers II (PMA 1965)
*Wedding Feast*
After the painting, dated 1650, in the Hermitage, St. Petersburg (inv. no. 1719)
Late 17th century
Lower right (spurious):
D TENIERS F
Oil on panel
31 3/8 × 44 5/8" (79.7 × 113.3 cm)

The William L. Elkins Collection
E1924-3-38

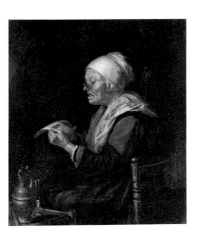

**Tol, Dominicus van**
Dutch, active Leiden,
c. 1635–1676
*Old Woman Reading*
Mid-17th century
Oil on panel
13 3/16 × 10 7/8" (33.5 × 27.6 cm)

John G. Johnson Collection
cat. 547

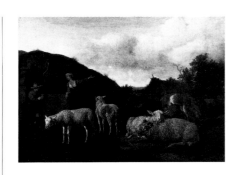

**Velde, Adriaen van de**
*A Shepherd and a Shepherdess with a Flock of Sheep*
Mid-17th century
Lower left: AvVelde
Oil on panel transferred to canvas
16 13/16 × 22 7/16" (42.7 × 57 cm)

John G. Johnson Collection
cat. 606

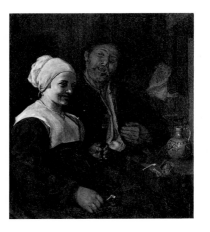

**Toorenvliet, Jacob, attributed to**
Dutch, active Leiden,
1635/36–1719
Previously attributed to Nicolaes Hals (JFD 1972)
*The Happy Lovers*
Late 17th century
Oil on panel
22 7/16 × 19" (57 × 48.3 cm)

John G. Johnson Collection
cat. 437

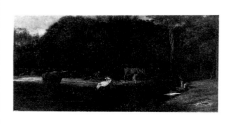

**Velde, Adriaen van de, attributed to**
Previously listed as Adriaen van de Velde (JFD 1972)
*Cattle Grazing in a Wood*
17th century
Oil on canvas
9 1/4 × 18 3/16" (23.5 × 46.2 cm)

John G. Johnson Collection
cat. 604

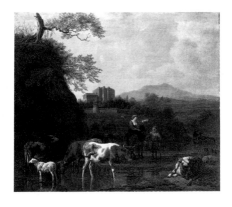

**Velde, Adriaen van de**
Dutch, active Amsterdam,
1632–1672
*Landscape with Cattle*
1659
Lower left: A. v. Velde f. 1659
Oil on canvas
21 15/16 × 23 15/16" (55.7 × 60.8 cm)

John G. Johnson Collection
cat. 605

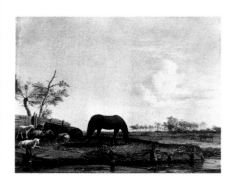

**Velde, Adriaen van de, copy after?**
*Horses and Sheep at Pasture*
17th century
Lower left: A. v. Velde
Oil on canvas
11 7/8 × 15 1/8" (30.2 × 38.4 cm)

John G. Johnson Collection
cat. 1180

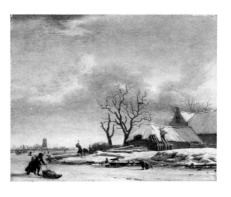

**Velde, Adriaen van de**
*Winter Landscape*
c. 1668
Lower right: AvVelde
Oil on panel
12 1/16 × 14 9/16" (30.6 × 37 cm)

John G. Johnson Collection
cat. 603

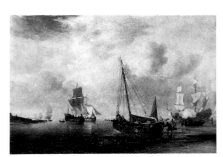

**Velde, Willem van de, the Younger**
Dutch, active Amsterdam and London, 1633–1707
*Calm (A Sloop Aground near the Shore in an Inlet)*
c. 1665
Lower right: W.v.Velde.
Oil on canvas
16 3/8 × 24 1/4" (41.6 × 61.6 cm)

John G. Johnson Collection
cat. 590

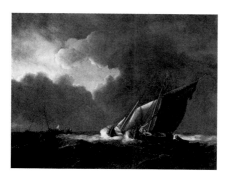

**Velde, Willem van de,
the Younger**
*Two Dutch Vessels Close-Hauled in
a Strong Breeze*
c. 1672
Oil on canvas
17 1/4 × 21 15/16" (43.8 × 55.7 cm)

John G. Johnson Collection
cat. 591

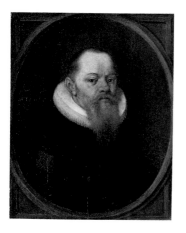

**Venne, Adriaen Pietersz.
van de**
Dutch, active The Hague,
Antwerp, and Middelburg,
1589–1662
*Portrait of a Fifty-Nine-Year-Old
Man*
1624
Center left: Ao 1624 / AETATIS
59
Oil on panel
12 3/8 × 9 1/4" (31.4 × 23.5 cm)

John G. Johnson Collection
inv. 163

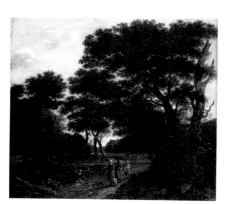

**Verboom, Adriaen
Hendriksz.**
Dutch, active Amsterdam and
Haarlem, c. 1628–c. 1670
*Woods near a Village*
Mid-17th century
Lower left (spurious): Av. Velde
fec. 1638
Oil on canvas
20 3/8 × 22 1/2" (51.7 × 57.1 cm)

John G. Johnson Collection
cat. 575

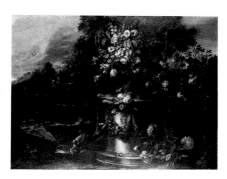

**Verbrugghen, Gaspar Peeter,
II, imitator of**
Flemish, active Antwerp,
1664–1730
Previously listed as Dutch,
unknown artist, 17th century
(PMA 1965)
*Flowers in a Garden*
c. 1700–20
Oil on canvas
58 3/8 × 76 1/2" (148.3 × 194.3 cm)

Gift of Mrs. Chester Dale
1950-121-2

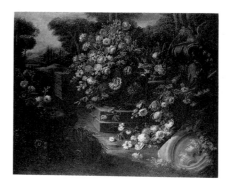

**Verbrugghen, Gaspar Peeter,
II, imitator of**
Previously listed as Dutch,
unknown artist, 17th century
(PMA 1965)
*Flowers in a Garden*
c. 1700–20
Oil on canvas
58 3/8 × 76 1/2" (148.3 × 194.3 cm)

Gift of Mrs. Chester Dale
1950-121-3

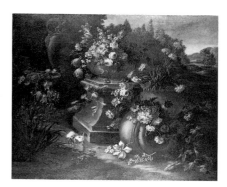

**Verbrugghen, Gaspar Peeter,
II, imitator of**
Previously listed as Dutch,
unknown artist, 17th century
(PMA 1965)
*Flowers in a Garden*
c. 1700–20
Oil on canvas
58 3/8 × 76 1/2" (148.3 × 194.3 cm)

Gift of Mrs. Chester Dale
1950-121-4

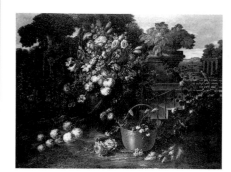

**Verbrugghen, Gaspar Peeter,
II, imitator of**
Previously listed as Dutch,
unknown artist, 17th century
(PMA 1965)
*Flowers on a Terrace*
c. 1700–20
Oil on canvas
58 3/8 × 76 1/2" (148.3 × 194.3 cm)

Gift of Mrs. Chester Dale
1950-121-1

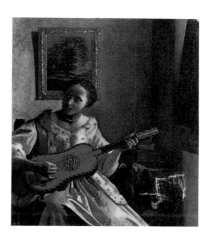

**Vermeer, Johannes,
copy after**
Dutch, active Delft, 1632–1675
*Lady with a Guitar*
After the painting in the Iveagh
Bequest, Kenwood, London (62)
Late 17th century
Oil on canvas
20 11/16 × 17 15/16" (52.5 × 45.6 cm)

John G. Johnson Collection
cat. 497

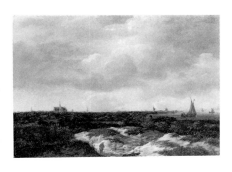

**Vermeer van Haarlem, Jan
(Jan van der Meer)**
Dutch, active Haarlem,
1628–1691
*Dunes near Haarlem*
1667 or 1677
Lower left: J V Meer 16[6 or 7?]7
Oil on panel
23 1/2 × 32 11/16" (59.7 × 83 cm)

The William L. Elkins Collection
E1924-3-95

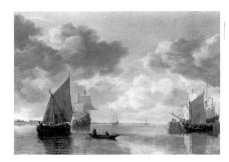

**Vlieger, Simon Jacobsz. de**
Dutch, active Delft and
Amsterdam, c. 1600–1653
*Marine*
c. 1600–50
Oil on panel
23 5/8 × 32 11/16" (60 × 83 cm)

John G. Johnson Collection
cat. 593

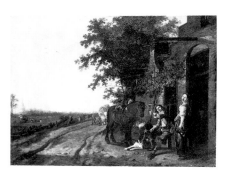

**Vermeer van Utrecht, Johann**
Dutch, active Utrecht,
c. 1640–1692
Previously listed as Ludolf de
Jongh (JFD 1972)
*Halt at the Inn*
Late 17th century
Oil on panel
18 7/8 × 25 1/8" (47.9 × 63.8 cm)

John G. Johnson Collection
cat. 626

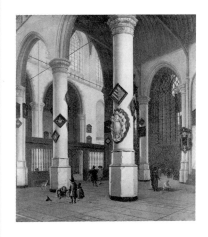

**Vliet, Hendrick Cornelisz.
van**
Dutch, active Delft,
1611/12–1675
*Interior of the Oude Kerk, Delft*
1659
Center bottom: H. van Vliet /
1659
Oil on canvas
31 3/4 × 26 5/8" (80.6 × 67.6 cm)

Purchased with the W. P.
Wilstach Fund
W1902-1-15

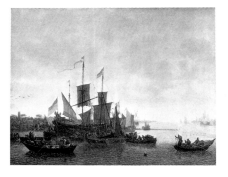

**Verschuier, Lieve Pietersz.**
Dutch, active Rotterdam,
c. 1630–1686
*Marine*
Mid-17th century
Oil on canvas
35 1/8 × 44 11/16" (89.2 ×
113.5 cm)

John G. Johnson Collection
cat. 594

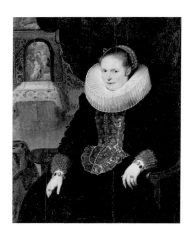

**Vos, Cornelis de**
Flemish, active Antwerp,
1584/85–1651
*Portrait of a Thirty-Year-Old Woman*
1622
Lower right: AET. 30 / Ao 1622
Oil on panel
46 1/4 × 35 7/8" (117.5 × 91.1 cm)

John G. Johnson Collection
cat. 671

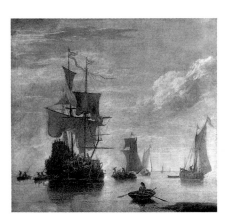

**Verschuier, Lieve Pietersz.,
attributed to**
Previously listed as Lieve
Pietersz. Verschuier (JFD 1972)
*Calm Sea*
17th century
Oil on canvas
20 9/16 × 20 15/16" (52.2 ×
53.2 cm)

John G. Johnson Collection
cat. 589

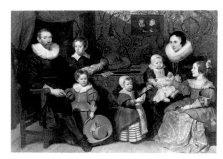

**Vos, Cornelis de**
*Portrait of Anthony Reyniers and
His Family*
1631
Lower left: C. DE VOS. F AO
1631
Oil on canvas
67 × 96 1/2" (170.2 × 245.1 cm)

Purchased with the W. P.
Wilstach Fund
W1902-1-22

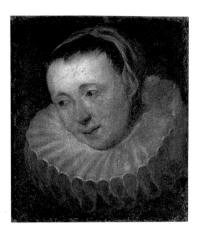

**Vos, Cornelis de, follower of**
*Head of a Woman in a Ruff*
17th century
Oil on canvas
16 × 13 1/2" (40.6 × 34.3 cm)

Gift of Peter D. Krumbhaar
1971-151-1

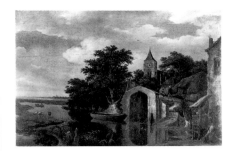

**Vries, Roelof van**
Dutch, active Haarlem and
Amsterdam, born 1630/31,
still active 1681
*Landscape with a Canal*
1652
Lower left: .RV . vries. 1652
Oil on panel
29 7/8 × 43 3/8" (75.9 × 110.2 cm)

John G. Johnson Collection
cat. 581

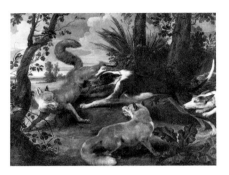

**Vos, Paul de**
Flemish, active Antwerp,
1596–1678
Previously listed as Frans Snyders
(PMA 1965)
*Wolfhounds and Two Foxes*
1630s
Oil on canvas
56 1/2 × 76" (143.5 × 193 cm)

Gift of Nicholas Biddle
1957-130-1

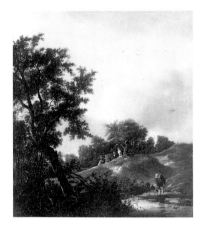

**Vries, Roelof van**
Previously listed as Jacob
Isaacksz. van Ruisdael (PMA
1965)
*Landscape with Men and Dogs*
17th century
Lower left (spurious): JRuisd
Oil on panel
16 1/16 × 13 3/4" (40.8 × 34.9 cm)

The John D. McIlhenny
Collection
1943-40-38

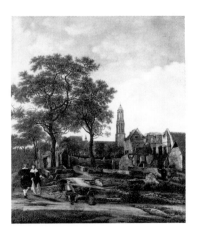

**Vosmaer, Daniel**
Dutch, active Delft,
documented 1650
*View of Delft after the Explosion of
1654*
c. 1654
Oil on canvas
26 5/8 × 21 7/8" (67.6 × 55.6 cm)

John G. Johnson Collection
cat. 500

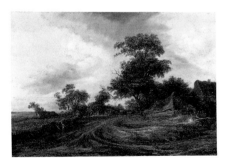

**Vries, Roelof van,
attributed to**
*Landscape with Dunes*
1664
Lower right: [illegible signature],
1664
Oil on panel
16 5/8 × 23 1/2" (42.2 × 59.7 cm)

John G. Johnson Collection
cat. 580

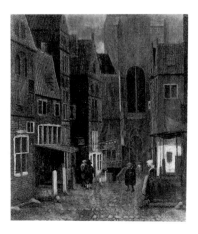

**Vrel, Jacob**
Dutch, active Delft,
active c. 1654–c. 1662
*Street*
Mid-17th century
Oil on panel
19 1/4 × 16 1/2" (48.9 × 41.9 cm)

John G. Johnson Collection
cat. 542

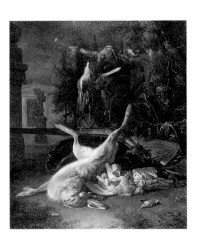

**Weenix, Jan**
Dutch, active Amsterdam,
Utrecht, and Düsseldorf,
1642?–1719
*Still Life with a Hare and Birds*
Late 17th century
Oil on canvas
50 15/16 × 41 7/8" (129.4 ×
106.4 cm)

John G. Johnson Collection
cat. 633

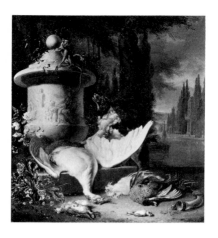

**Weenix, Jan**
*Still Life with Dead Game, a Monkey, and a Spaniel*
1700
Center bottom: J. Weenix f
1700—
Oil on canvas
21 1/2 × 19 3/4" (54.6 × 50.2 cm)

Purchased with the W. P. Wilstach Fund
W1901-1-3

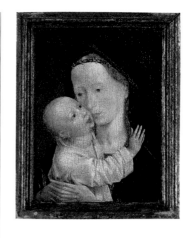

**Weyden, Rogier van der, follower of**
Previously attributed to Hugo van der Goes (JFD 1972)
*Virgin and Child*
c. 1460–1500
Oil on panel
11 13/16 × 8 1/4" (30 × 20.9 cm)

John G. Johnson Collection
cat. 341

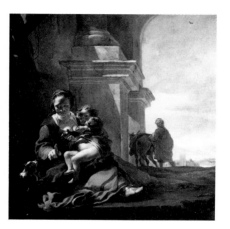

**Weenix, Jan Baptist**
Dutch, active Amsterdam, Rome, and Utrecht, 1621–1660/61
*Rest on the Flight into Egypt*
c. 1647–50
Lower right: Gio Batta Weenix f.
Oil on canvas
21 3/4 × 20" (55.2 × 50.8 cm)

Purchased with the George W. Elkins Fund
E1984-1-1

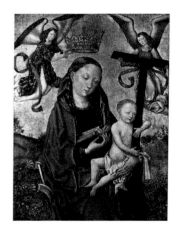

**Weyden, Rogier van der, follower of**
Previously listed as derived from a composition of Rogier van der Weyden (JFD 1972)
*Virgin and Child Holding the Cross*
16th century
On cross: inri; on Virgin's headband: A M ARI A GR ACIA PLEA VE TECU
Oil and gold on panel transferred to canvas
26 × 18 7/8" (66 × 47.9 cm)

John G. Johnson Collection
cat. 321

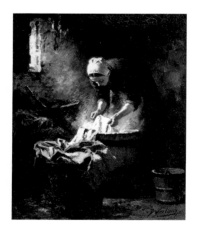

**Weiland, Johannes**
Dutch, active Rotterdam and The Hague, 1856–1909
*The Washerwoman*
c. 1900
Lower right: Weiland
Oil on canvas
19 3/4 × 15 3/4" (50.2 × 40 cm)

The Walter Lippincott Collection
1923-59-9

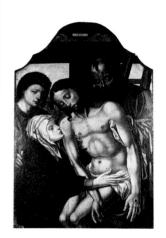

**Weyden, Rogier van der, copy after**
*The Descent from the Cross*
After a lost painting
16th century?
On cross: I N R I
Oil on panel
42 1/2 × 27 1/2" (107.9 × 69.8 cm)

Purchased from the George Grey Barnard Collection with Museum funds
1945-25-124

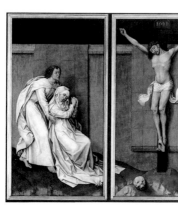

**Weyden, Rogier van der**
Netherlandish, active Tournai and Brussels, 1399/1400–1464
*The Crucifixion, with the Virgin and Saint John the Evangelist Mourning*
Companion paintings
c. 1450–55
On cross: I N R I
Oil and gold on panel
Left panel: 71 × 36 5/16" (180.3 × 92.2 cm); right panel: 71 × 36 7/16" (180.3 × 92.5 cm)

John G. Johnson Collection
cat. 335, cat. 334

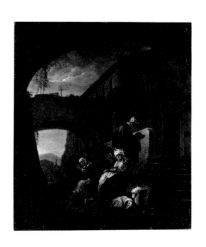

**Wijck, Thomas**
Dutch, active Haarlem and Italy, c. 1616–1677
*Almsgiving*
Mid-17th century
Center left: TWijck
Oil on panel
16 7/16 × 13 9/16" (41.7 × 34.4 cm)

John G. Johnson Collection
cat. 611

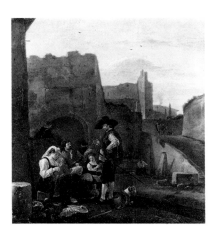

**Wijck, Thomas**
*Italians in a Cloister Court*
Mid-17th century
Lower left: TWijck
Oil on canvas
19 3/8 × 17 1/2" (49.2 × 44.4 cm)

John G. Johnson Collection
cat. 612

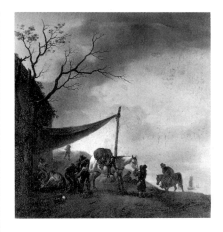

**Wouwermans, Philips**
Dutch, active Haarlem and
Hamburg, 1619–1668
*The Blacksmith's Shop*
Late 1640s
Lower left: PHILS.W
Oil on panel
17 3/8 × 16 1/2" (44.1 × 41.9 cm)

The William L. Elkins Collection
E1924-3-40

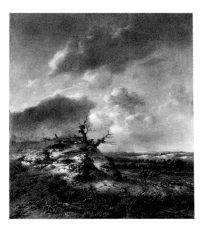

**Wijnants, Jan**
Dutch, active Rotterdam and
Amsterdam, born before 1630,
died 1684
*Dunes*
Mid-17th century
Lower left: J. Wijnants
Oil on canvas
19 1/4 × 16 1/2" (48.9 × 41.9 cm)

John G. Johnson Collection
cat. 584

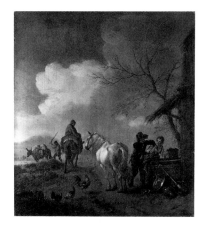

**Wouwermans, Philips**
*The Importunate Groom*
Mid-17th century
Lower right: PHLS.W
Oil on panel
15 1/2 × 13 1/8" (39.4 × 33.3 cm)

John G. Johnson Collection
cat. 616

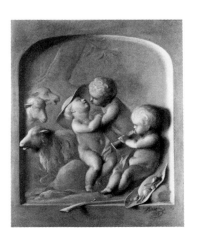

**Wit, Jacob de**
Dutch, active Amsterdam and
Antwerp, 1695–1754
*Putti with Sheep*
1749
Lower right: JdWit / 1749
Oil on canvas
48 1/4 × 39" (122.5 × 99.1 cm)

Gift of Mrs. Gordon A. Hardwick
and Mrs. W. Newbold Ely in
memory of Mr. and Mrs.
Roland L. Taylor
1944-9-5

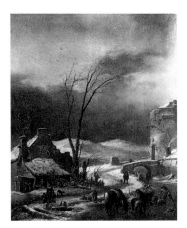

**Wouwermans, Philips,
attributed to**
*Winter Landscape with a Stone
Bridge*
17th century
Lower right: PHLSW
Oil on panel
16 1/4 × 12 1/4" (41.3 × 31.1 cm)

John G. Johnson Collection
cat. 615

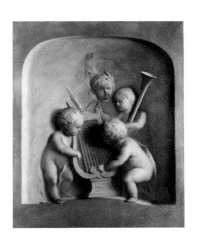

**Wit, Jacob de**
*Putti with Musical Instruments*
1750
Lower right: JdWit / 1750
Oil on canvas
48 7/16 × 39" (123 × 99.1 cm)

Gift of Mrs. Gordon A. Hardwick
and Mrs. W. Newbold Ely in
memory of Mr. and Mrs.
Roland L. Taylor
1944-9-6

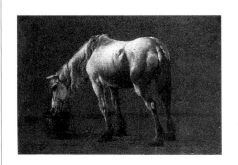

**Wouwermans, Philips,
follower of**
Previously listed as the school of
Philips Wouwermans (JFD 1972)
*White Horse*
17th century
Oil on panel
5 7/8 × 8 1/4" (14.9 × 20.9 cm)

John G. Johnson Collection
cat. 620

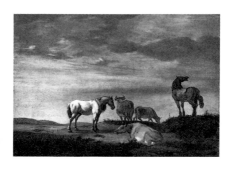

**Wouwermans, Philips, and Paulus Potter, imitator of**
Previously attributed to Philips
Wouwermans (JGJ 1941)
*Horses and Cattle*
Mid-17th century
Lower right: E. D.
Oil on panel
15 11/16 × 21 9/16" (39.8 × 54.8 cm)

John G. Johnson Collection
cat. 617

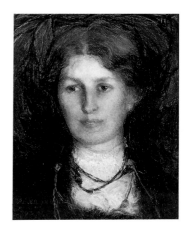

**Aman-Jean, Edmond-François**
French, 1860–1935/36
*Portrait of Mrs. Bosworth*
1904
Lower left: Aman Jean / 1904
Oil on canvas
16 7/8 × 13 3/8" (42.9 × 34 cm)

Gift of Francis Newton,
F. Maurice Newton, and Richard
Newton, Jr., in memory of their
sister, Elizabeth Newton
Bosworth
1962-142-1

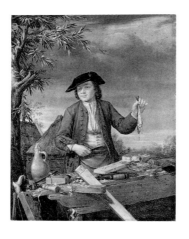

**Zegelaar, Gerrit van**
Dutch, active Amsterdam,
1719–1794
*Carpenter Taking His Meal*
Mid-18th century
Lower right: G. Zegelaar
Oil on panel
14 1/8 × 10 13/16" (35.9 × 27.5 cm)

John G. Johnson Collection
cat. 1186

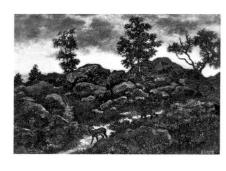

**Barye, Antoine-Louis**
French, 1796–1875
*Rocky Landscape*
c. 1850–75
Lower right: BARYE
Oil on canvas
9 × 12 1/2" (22.9 × 31.7 cm)

John G. Johnson Collection
cat. 890

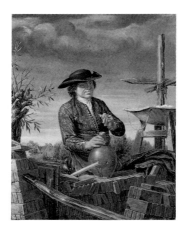

**Zegelaar, Gerrit van**
*Stonemason Resting*
Mid-18th century
Center bottom: G. Zegelaar
Oil on panel
14 1/8 × 10 3/4" (35.9 × 27.3 cm)

John G. Johnson Collection
cat. 1187

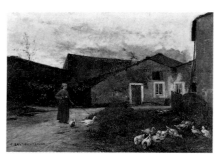

**Bastien-Lepage, Jules**
French, 1848–1884
*Goose Girl*
c. 1875
Lower left: J. BASTIEN-LEPAGE
Oil on canvas
16 5/16 × 23 1/4" (41.4 × 59 cm)

John G. Johnson Collection
cat. 893

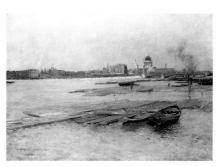

**Bastien-Lepage, Jules**
*Blackfriars Bridge and the Thames,
London*
1881
Lower left: J BASTIEN-LEPAGE /
LONDRES Juillet 81
Oil on canvas
20 1/8 × 27 1/8" (51.1 × 68.9 cm)

John G. Johnson Collection
cat. 891

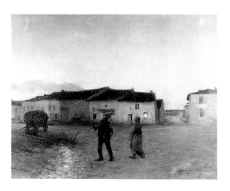

**Bastien-Lepage, Jules**
*Evening at Damvillers*
1882
Lower right: J BASTIEN-LEPAGE
/ Damvillers 1882
Oil on canvas
26 1/8 × 31 5/8" (66.4 × 80.3 cm)

John G. Johnson Collection
cat. 894

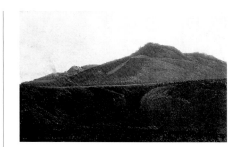

**Bidauld, Jean-Joseph-Xavier**
French, 1758–1846
*Lake Albano*
c. 1785–90
Lower left (spurious): COROT
Oil on canvas
11 1/2 × 17 3/8" (29.2 × 44.1 cm)

John G. Johnson Collection
cat. 937

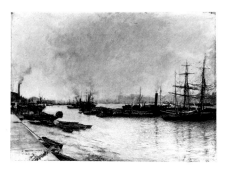

**Bastien-Lepage, Jules**
*The Thames, London*
1882
Lower left: J. BASTIEN-LEPAGE /
Londres 82.
Oil on canvas
22 5/16 × 30 3/8" (56.7 × 77.1 cm)

John G. Johnson Collection
cat. 892

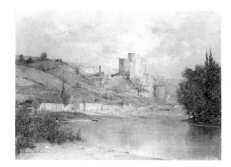

**Billotte, René**
French, 1846–1915
*Château Gaillard des Andelys*
By 1892
Lower left: René Billotte
Oil on canvas
21 1/4 × 28 15/16" (54 × 73.5 cm)

John G. Johnson Collection
cat. 896

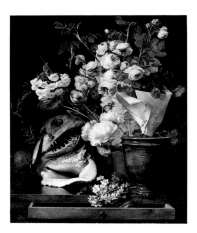

**Berjon, Antoine**
French, 1754–1843
*Still Life with Flowers, Shells, a
Shark's Head, and Petrifications*
1819
Lower right: Berjon / 1819
Oil on canvas
42 1/2 × 34 9/16" (107.9 × 87.8 cm)

Purchased with the Edith H. Bell
Fund
1981-62-1

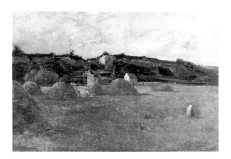

**Billotte, René**
*Landscape*
By 1892
Lower right: René Billotte
Oil on canvas
15 1/16 × 21 5/8" (38.3 × 54.9 cm)

John G. Johnson Collection
inv. 2692

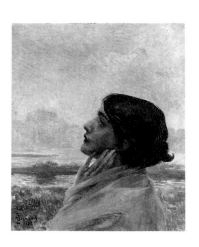

**Besnard, Albert**
French, 1849–1934
*Head of a Woman*
1892
Lower left: ASBesnard / 1892
Oil on panel
24 1/16 × 19 5/8" (61.1 × 49.8 cm)

John G. Johnson Collection
cat. 895

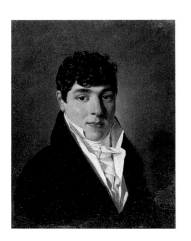

**Boilly, Louis-Léopold,
attributed to**
French, 1761–1845
Previously listed as Louis-
Léopold Boilly (JGJ 1941)
*Portrait of a Young Man*
Early 19th century
Lower right (spurious): L. Boilly
Oil on canvas on panel
9 1/8 × 6 3/4" (23.2 × 17.1 cm)

John G. Johnson Collection
cat. 792

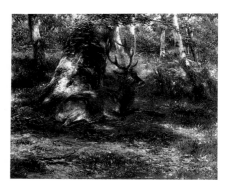

**Bonheur, Marie-Rosalie,
also called Rosa Bonheur**
French, 1822–1899
*Forest with a Buck*
1875
Lower left: Rosa Bonheur / 1875
Oil on canvas
15 × 18 7/16" (38.1 × 46.8 cm)

Gift of Robert Montgomery Scott
1981-116-1

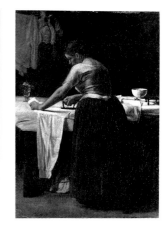

**Bonvin, François**
French, 1817–1887
*Woman Ironing*
1858
Upper right: F. Bonvin. 1858.
Oil on canvas
21 5/8 × 14 5/8" (54.9 × 37.1 cm)

John G. Johnson Collection
cat. 901

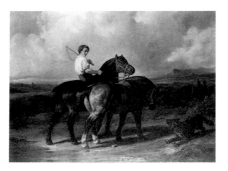

**Bonheur, Marie-Rosalie**
*Two Horses*
1893
Lower right: Rosa Bonheur 1893
Oil on canvas
38 1/2 × 51 1/4" (97.8 × 130.2 cm)

The William L. Elkins Collection
E1924-3-96

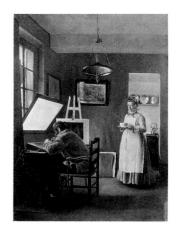

**Bonvin, François**
*The Engraver*
1872
Lower right: F. Bonvin. 1872.
Oil on panel
20 3/4 × 14 5/8" (52.7 × 37.1 cm)

John G. Johnson Collection
cat. 900

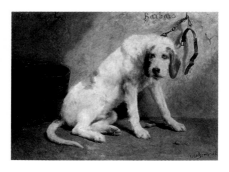

**Bonheur, Marie-Rosalie**
*Barbaro after the Hunt*
Late 19th century
Upper left: FL[rest illegible];
upper right: Barbaro; lower right:
Rosa Bonheur
Oil on canvas
38 × 51 1/4" (96.5 × 130.2 cm)

Gift of John G. Johnson for the
W. P. Wilstach Collection
W1900-1-2

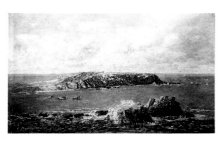

**Boudin, Eugène-Louis**
French, 1824–1898
*Camaret, Le Toulinguet*
c. 1871–73
Lower left: [E]i Boudin
Toulignon
Oil on panel
21 1/4 × 35 1/4" (54 × 89.5 cm)

John G. Johnson Collection
cat. 903

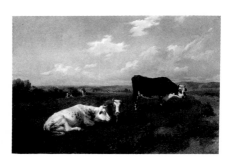

**Bonheur, Marie-Rosalie**
*Landscape with Cattle*
Late 19th century
Lower right: Rosa B
Oil on canvas
33 3/16 × 48 1/4" (84.3 × 122.5 cm)

Gift of Hermann Krumbhaar and
Dr. Edward Krumbhaar
1921-69-1

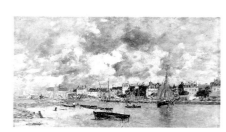

**Boudin, Eugène-Louis**
*View of Deauville*
1873
Lower left: Trouville / E. Boudin
73.
Oil on canvas
12 7/16 × 22 3/4" (31.6 × 57.8 cm)

John G. Johnson Collection
cat. 902

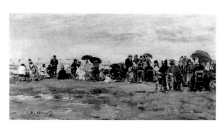

**Boudin, Eugène-Louis**
*Beach at Trouville*
1880
Lower left: E. Boudin; lower
right: Trouville 80.
Oil on canvas
7 × 13 ¹/₂" (17.8 × 34.3 cm)

Bequest of Lisa Norris Elkins
1950-92-2

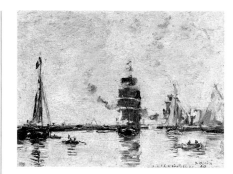

**Boudin, Eugène-Louis**
*Boats in Trouville Harbor*
1894
Lower right: E. Boudin /
[illegible] 94.
Oil on panel
7 ¹/₂ × 9 ¹/₂" (19 × 24.1 cm)

The Louis E. Stern Collection
1963-181-3

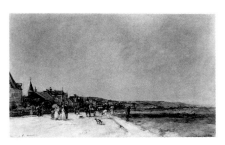

**Boudin, Eugène-Louis**
*Deauville, the Terrace*
1882
Lower left: E. Boudin.; lower
right: Juillet 82
Oil on canvas
14 ¹/₂ × 22 ⁷/₈" (36.8 × 58.1 cm)

The Albert M. Greenfield and
Elizabeth M. Greenfield
Collection
1974-178-20

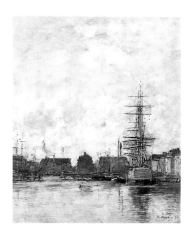

**Boudin, Eugène-Louis**
*The "Bassin du Commerce" at
Le Havre*
1894
Lower right: Le Havre /
E. Boudin 94
Oil on canvas
16 ¹/₈ × 12 ¹¹/₁₆" (41 × 32.2 cm)

Bequest of Mrs. Edna M. Welsh
1982-1-1

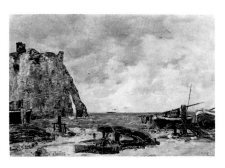

**Boudin, Eugène-Louis**
*Beach at Étretat*
1890
Lower left: E. Boudin 90; lower
right: Etretat.
Oil on canvas
15 ⁷/₈ × 21 ³/₄" (40.3 × 55.2 cm)

The Samuel S. White 3rd and
Vera White Collection
1967-30-3

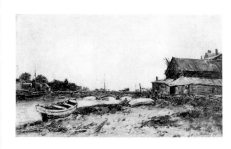

**Boudin, Eugène-Louis**
*The Bridge over the River Touques at
Deauville*
1894
Lower right: Deauville /
E. Boudin 94
Oil on canvas
14 ¹/₄ × 23" (36.2 × 58.4 cm)

The Mr. and Mrs. Carroll S.
Tyson, Jr., Collection
1963-116-1

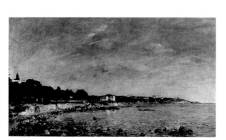

**Boudin, Eugène-Louis**
*Le Cap, Antibes*
1893
Lower left: Le Cap / E. Boudin.
93; lower right: 2 mai 93
Oil on canvas
21 ⁵/₈ × 35 ³/₈" (54.9 × 89.8 cm)

Bequest of Charlotte Dorrance
Wright
1978-1-2

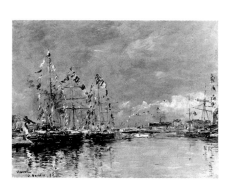

**Boudin, Eugène-Louis**
*Deauville, Flag-Decked Ships in the
Inner Harbor*
1896
Lower left: Deauville / E. Boudin.
96
Oil on panel
12 ³/₄ × 16 ³/₁₆" (32.4 × 41.1 cm)

Bequest of Charlotte Dorrance
Wright
1978-1-3

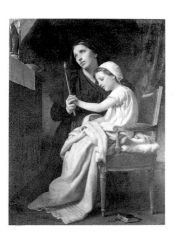

**Bouguereau, William-Adolphe**
French, 1825–1905
*The Thank Offering*
1867
Upper right: W—
BOVGVEREAV—1867.
Oil on canvas
57 15/16 × 42 1/8" (147.2 × 107 cm)

Gift of John G. Johnson for the
W. P. Wilstach Collection
W1900-1-5

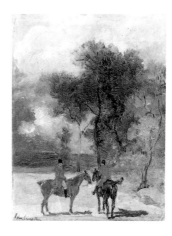

**Brown, John Lewis**
French, 1829–1890
*Two Huntsmen in a Landscape*
Late 19th century
Lower left: John Lewis Brown
Oil on panel
5 5/8 × 3 15/16" (14.3 × 10 cm)

Bequest of Charlotte Dorrance
Wright
1978-1-4

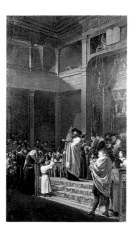

**Brandon, Jacques-Émile-Édouard**
French, 1831–1897
*Scene in a Synagogue*
1869–70
Lower left: Ed. Brandon /
1869–1870.
Oil on canvas
61 3/8 × 34 11/16" (155.9 × 88.1 cm)

John G. Johnson Collection
cat. 904

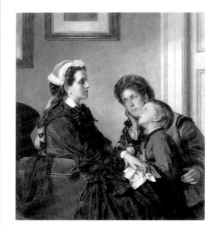

**Cabanel, Alexandre, attributed to**
French, 1823–1889
*The Governess*
c. 1865–70
Lower left: [spurious signature
"A. CABANEL" removed in
restoration in 1979]
Oil on canvas
45 1/4 × 39 3/8" (114.9 × 100 cm)

Purchased with the Edward and
Althea Budd Fund
1977-80-1

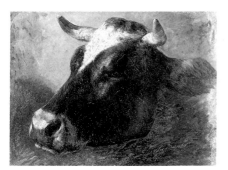

**Brascassat, Jacques-Raymond**
French, 1804–1867
*Head of a Cow*
Mid-19th century
Lower right: JR Brascassat
Oil on canvas
17 1/16 × 21 15/16" (43.3 × 55.7 cm)

John G. Johnson Collection
cat. 905

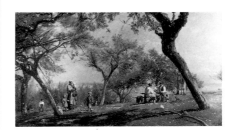

**Cals, Adolphe-Félix**
French, 1810–1880
*The Farm at Saint Simon, Honfleur*
1876
Lower right: Cals Honfleur /
1876
Oil on canvas
14 3/16 × 24 5/8" (36 × 62.5 cm)

John G. Johnson Collection
cat. 909

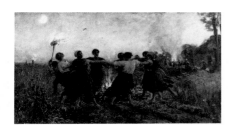

**Breton, Jules-Adolphe-Aimé-Louis**
French, 1827–1905
*The Feast of Saint John*
c. 1875
Lower left: Jules Breton
Oil on canvas
13 1/2 × 24 1/8" (34.3 × 61.3 cm)

John G. Johnson Collection
cat. 906

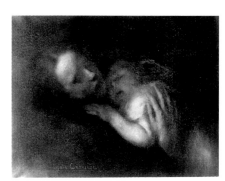

**Carrière, Eugène**
French, 1849–1906
*Mother and Child Sleeping*
c. 1889
Lower left: Eugène Carrière
Oil on canvas
19 3/4 × 24 1/8" (50.2 × 61.3 cm)

John G. Johnson Collection
cat. 910

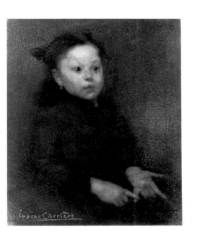

**Carrière, Eugène**
*Young Girl Counting*
Late 19th century
Lower left: Eugène Carrière
Oil on canvas
24 1/4 × 19 13/16" (61.6 × 50.3 cm)

The William L. Elkins Collection
E1924-3-78

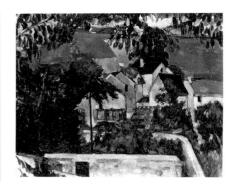

**Cézanne, Paul**
French, 1839–1906
*Quartier Four, Auvers-sur-Oise
(Landscape, Auvers)*
c. 1873
Oil on canvas
18 1/4 × 21 3/4" (46.3 × 55.2 cm)

The Samuel S. White 3rd and
Vera White Collection
1967-30-16

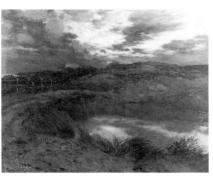

**Cazin, Jean-Charles**
French, 1841–1901
*Pond*
By 1883
Lower left: J. C. CAZIN
Oil on canvas
25 9/16 × 31 15/16" (64.9 × 81.1 cm)

John G. Johnson Collection
cat. 912

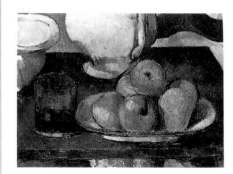

**Cézanne, Paul**
*Still Life with Apples and a Glass
of Wine*
1877–79
Oil on canvas
10 1/2 × 12 7/8" (26.7 × 32.7 cm)

The Louise and Walter Arensberg
Collection
1950-134-32

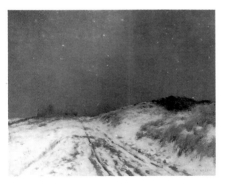

**Cazin, Jean-Charles**
*Solitude*
By 1889
Lower right: J. C. CAZIN
Oil on canvas
23 9/16 × 28 3/4" (59.8 × 73 cm)

John G. Johnson Collection
cat. 911

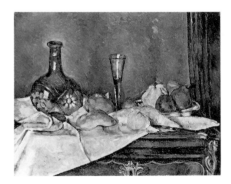

**Cézanne, Paul**
*Still Life with a Dessert*
1877 or 1879
Lower right: P. Cezanne.
Oil on canvas
23 1/4 × 28 11/16" (59 × 72.9 cm)

The Mr. and Mrs. Carroll S.
Tyson, Jr., Collection
1963-116-5

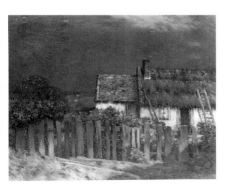

**Cazin, Jean-Charles**
*Fisherman's Cottage*
By 1893
Lower left: J. C. CAZIN
Oil on canvas
18 3/8 × 22 1/8" (46.7 × 56.2 cm)

The George W. Elkins Collection
E1924-4-3

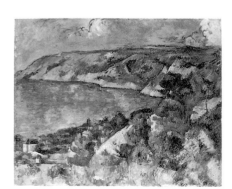

**Cézanne, Paul**
*Bay of l'Estaque*
1879–83
Lower right: PC
Oil on canvas
23 3/4 × 29 1/4" (60.3 × 74.3 cm)

The Mr. and Mrs. Carroll S.
Tyson, Jr., Collection
1963-116-21

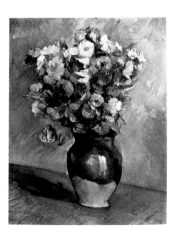

**Cézanne, Paul**
*Still Life with Flowers in an Olive Jar*
c. 1880
Oil on canvas
18 1/4 × 13 1/2" (46.3 × 34.3 cm)

The Mr. and Mrs. Carroll S. Tyson, Jr., Collection
1963-116-2

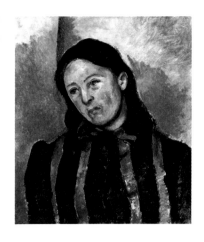

**Cézanne, Paul**
*Portrait of Madame Cézanne*
1890–92
Oil on canvas
24 3/8 × 20 1/8" (61.9 × 51.1 cm)

The Henry P. McIlhenny Collection in memory of Frances P. McIlhenny
1986-26-1

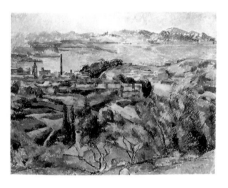

**Cézanne, Paul**
*View of the Bay of Marseilles with the Village of Saint-Henri*
c. 1883
Oil on canvas
25 15/16 × 32" (65.9 × 81.3 cm)

The Mr. and Mrs. Carroll S. Tyson, Jr., Collection
1963-116-3

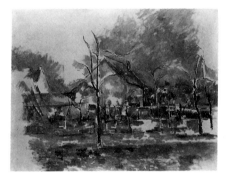

**Cézanne, Paul**
*Winter Landscape near Paris*
1894
Oil on canvas
25 5/8 × 31 7/8" (65.1 × 81 cm)

Gift of Frank and Alice Osborn
1966-68-3

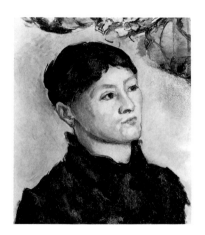

**Cézanne, Paul**
*Portrait of Madame Cézanne*
1885–87
Oil on canvas
18 1/8 × 15 1/16" (46 × 38.3 cm)

The Louis E. Stern Collection
1963-181-6

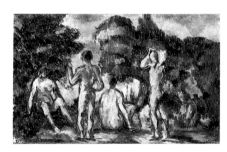

**Cézanne, Paul**
*Group of Bathers*
c. 1895
Oil on canvas
8 1/8 × 12 1/8" (20.6 × 30.8 cm)

The Louise and Walter Arensberg Collection
1950-134-34

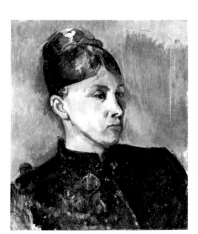

**Cézanne, Paul**
*Portrait of Madame Cézanne*
1886–87
Oil on canvas
18 7/16 × 15 5/16" (46.8 × 38.9 cm)

The Samuel S. White 3rd and Vera White Collection
1967-30-17

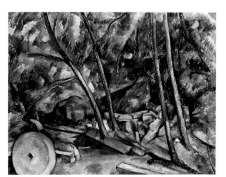

**Cézanne, Paul**
*Millstone in the Park of the Château Noir*
1898–1900
Oil on canvas
28 3/4 × 36 3/8" (73 × 92.4 cm)

The Mr. and Mrs. Carroll S. Tyson, Jr., Collection
1963-116-4

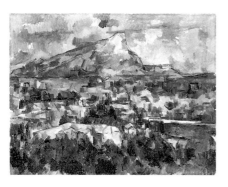

**Cézanne, Paul**
*Mont Sainte-Victoire*
1902–4
Oil on canvas
28 3/4 × 36 3/16" (73 × 91.9 cm)

The George W. Elkins Collection
E1936-1-1

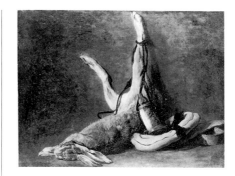

**Chardin, Jean-Baptiste-Siméon**
French, 1699–1779
*Still Life with a Hare*
c. 1730
Center right: chardin.
Oil on canvas
25 5/8 × 32" (65.1 × 81.3 cm)

Gift of Henry P. McIlhenny
1958-144-1

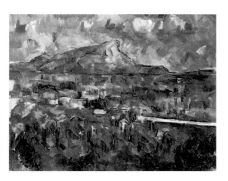

**Cézanne, Paul**
*Mont Sainte-Victoire*
1902–6
Oil on canvas
25 1/2 × 32" (64.8 × 81.3 cm)

Gift of Mrs. Louis C. Madeira
1977-288-1

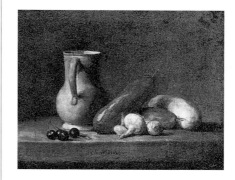

**Chardin, Jean-Baptiste-Siméon, attributed to**
*Still Life with Cherries and Turnips*
18th century
Center bottom: chardin
Oil on canvas
14 3/4 × 17 1/2" (37.5 × 44.4 cm)

John G. Johnson Collection
cat. 785

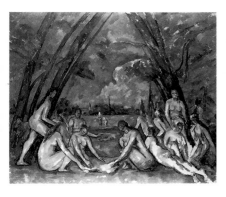

**Cézanne, Paul**
*The Large Bathers*
1906
Oil on canvas
82 7/8 × 98 3/4" (210.5 × 250.8 cm)

Purchased with the W. P. Wilstach Fund
W1937-1-1

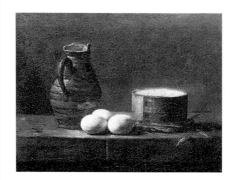

**Chardin, Jean-Baptiste-Siméon, attributed to**
*Still Life with Eggs, Cheese, and a Pitcher*
18th century
Lower left: chardin
Oil on canvas
14 7/8 × 17 15/16" (37.8 × 45.6 cm)

John G. Johnson Collection
cat. 786

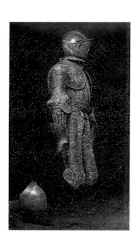

**Chambillan, J., attributed to**
French, active c. 1870
*Suit of Armor*
c. 1870
Oil on canvas
29 × 16 1/2" (73.7 × 41.9 cm)

Bequest of Carl Otto Kretzschmar von Kienbusch
1977-167-1039

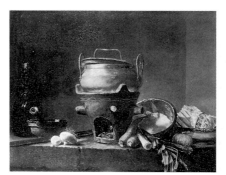

**Chardin, Jean-Baptiste-Siméon, imitator of**
Previously attributed to Jean-Baptiste-Siméon Chardin (JGJ 1941)
*Still Life with a Kettle*
19th century
Oil on canvas
27 3/16 × 33 1/4" (69.1 × 84.4 cm)

John G. Johnson Collection
cat. 788

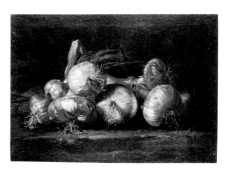

**Chardin, Jean-Baptiste-Siméon, imitator of**
Previously attributed to Jean-Baptiste-Siméon Chardin (JGJ 1941)
*Still Life with Onions*
19th century
Oil on canvas
19 1/8 × 25 3/8" (48.6 × 64.4 cm)

John G. Johnson Collection
cat. 789

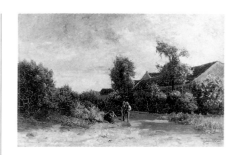

**Chintreuil, Antoine**
*Village Road and Two Figures*
Mid-19th century
Lower right: Chintreuil
Oil on canvas
10 3/4 × 15 15/16" (27.3 × 40.5 cm)

John G. Johnson Collection
cat. 914

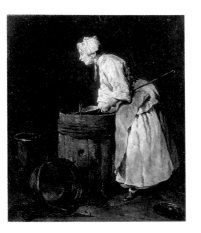

**Chardin, Jean-Baptiste-Siméon, copy after**
*Scullery Maid*
After the painting, dated 1738, in the Hunterian Art Gallery, University of Glasgow
19th century
Oil on canvas
18 1/4 × 15" (46.3 × 38.1 cm)

John G. Johnson Collection
cat. 782

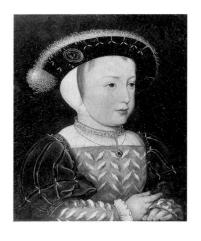

**Clouet, Jean, copy after**
French, c. 1475–1540/41
Previously listed as an old copy after François Clouet (JGJ 1941)
*Portrait of the Dauphin Francis, Son of Francis I*
After the painting in the Koninklijk Museum voor Schone Kunsten, Antwerp (cat. no. 33)
16th century
Oil on panel
12 3/8 × 9 1/8" (31.4 × 23.2 cm)

John G. Johnson Collection
inv. 309

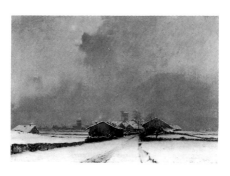

**Chenu, Fleury (Augustin-Pierre-Bienvenu Chenu)**
French, 1833–1875
*Snowy Landscape*
c. 1850–75
Lower right: Fleury Chenu
Oil on canvas on panel
24 1/4 × 32 1/2" (61.6 × 82.5 cm)

John G. Johnson Collection
cat. 913

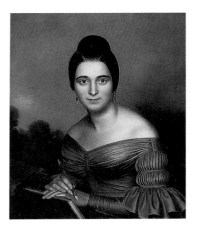

**Collet, Édouard**
French?, active c. 1839
*Portrait of a Woman*
1839
Lower right: Edouard Collet / 1839
Oil on canvas
25 9/16 × 21 5/16" (64.9 × 54.1 cm)

Gift of Mrs. Josiah Marvel
1962-74-1

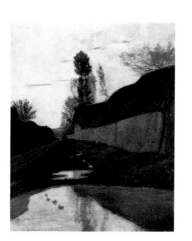

**Chintreuil, Antoine**
French, 1816–1873
*Village Road*
c. 1850–73
Lower right: Chintreuil
Oil on canvas
18 7/8 × 14 1/2" (47.9 × 36.8 cm)

John G. Johnson Collection
cat. 915

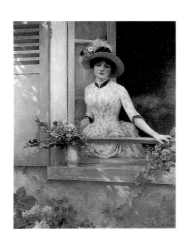

**Collin, Louis-Joseph-Raphaël**
French, 1850–1916
*Morning*
1884
Lower right: R COLLIN 1884
Oil on canvas
59 1/4 × 44 7/8" (150.5 × 114 cm)

John G. Johnson Collection
inv. 2956

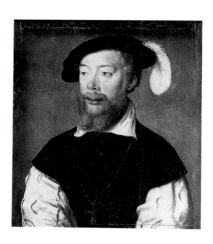

**Corneille de Lyon,
copy after?**
French, born The Hague, active
Lyon, active 1544–1574
Previously attributed to François
Clouet (JGJ 1941)
*Portrait of a Man*
16th century
Oil on panel
7 × 6 1/8" (17.8 × 15.6 cm)

John G. Johnson Collection
cat. 770

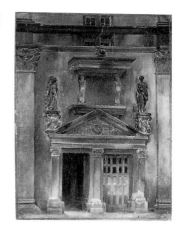

**Corot, Jean-Baptiste-Camille**
*Architectural Study (Door of the
Francis I Staircase, Cour Ovale,
Fontainebleau)*
1831–34
Oil on canvas
12 9/16 × 9 1/8" (31.9 × 23.2 cm)

Purchased with the W. P.
Wilstach Fund
W1897-1-4

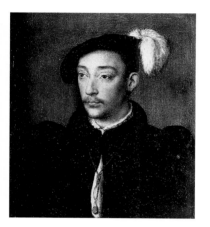

**Corneille de Lyon, copy after**
Previously listed as Corneille de
Lyon (JGJ 1941)
*Portrait of the Dauphin Francis, Son
of Francis I*
After a painting known in four
versions, none the original; other
versions are in the Isabella
Stewart Gardner Museum, Boston
(P21s23); the Musée Condé,
Chantilly (244); and the Musée
du Louvre, Paris (no. 1000)
16th century
Oil on panel
7 1/8 × 6" (18.1 × 15.2 cm)

John G. Johnson Collection
cat. 771

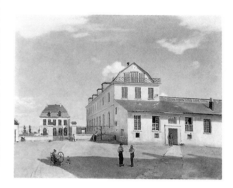

**Corot, Jean-Baptiste-Camille**
*House and Factory of Monsieur Henry*
1833
Lower right: C Corot / 1833
Oil on canvas
32 1/16 × 39 1/2" (81.4 × 100.3 cm)

Purchased with the W. P.
Wilstach Fund
W1950-1-1

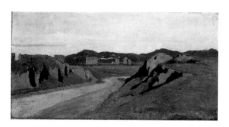

**Corot, Jean-Baptiste-Camille**
French, 1796–1875
*Aqueduct*
c. 1826–28
Lower right: VENTE / COROT
Oil on canvas
9 1/2 × 17 1/4" (24.1 × 43.8 cm)

The Henry P. McIlhenny
Collection in memory of
Frances P. McIlhenny
1986-26-5

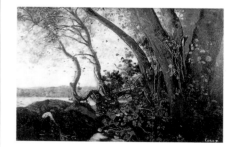

**Corot, Jean-Baptiste-Camille**
*Edge of Lake Nemi*
c. 1843
Lower right: COROT
Oil on canvas
23 5/8 × 36" (60 × 91.4 cm)

John G. Johnson Collection
cat. 940

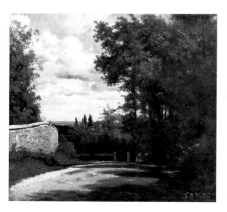

**Corot, Jean-Baptiste-Camille**
*Ville d'Avray*
c. 1828
Lower right: COROT
Oil on paper on canvas
10 7/8 × 11 9/16" (27.6 × 29.4 cm)

John G. Johnson Collection
cat. 931

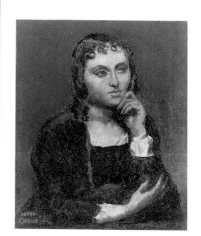

**Corot, Jean-Baptiste-Camille**
*Pensive Young Brunette*
1845–50
Lower left: VENTE / COROT
Oil on canvas
9 1/2 × 7 1/2" (24.1 × 19 cm)

The Louis E. Stern Collection
1963-181-18

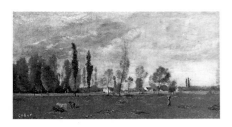

**Corot, Jean-Baptiste-Camille**
*Fields of Saint-Ouen*
1850–55
Lower left: COROT
Oil on canvas
8 1/16 × 14 3/4" (20.5 × 37.5 cm)

John G. Johnson Collection
cat. 918

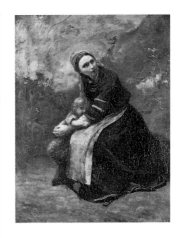

**Corot, Jean-Baptiste-Camille**
*Mother Protecting Her Child*
1855–58
Lower left: COROT
Oil on canvas
19 15/16 × 14 1/4" (50.6 × 36.2 cm)

The John D. McIlhenny
Collection
1943-40-52

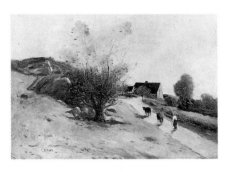

**Corot, Jean-Baptiste-Camille**
*Environs of Gruyères, Switzerland*
c. 1850–65
Lower left: COROT
Oil on canvas
17 1/8 × 23 1/2" (43.5 × 59.7 cm)

John G. Johnson Collection
cat. 916

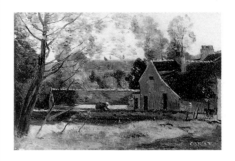

**Corot, Jean-Baptiste-Camille**
*Château Thierry*
1855–65
Lower right: COROT
Oil on canvas
8 7/8 × 13 1/8" (22.5 × 33.3 cm)

The William L. Elkins Collection
E1924-3-26

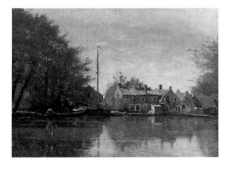

**Corot, Jean-Baptiste-Camille**
*View in Holland*
c. 1854
Lower right: COROT
Oil on canvas
15 7/16 × 20 5/16" (39.2 × 51.6 cm)

The George W. Elkins Collection
E1924-4-6

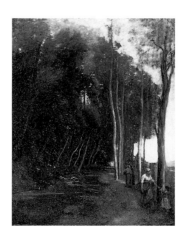

**Corot, Jean-Baptiste-Camille**
*Under Trees, Marcoussy*
c. 1855–65
Lower right: COROT
Oil on canvas
32 1/4 × 24 7/8" (81.9 × 63.2 cm)

John G. Johnson Collection
cat. 921

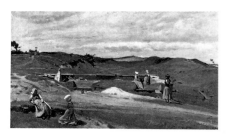

**Corot, Jean-Baptiste-Camille**
*Wall, Côtes-du-Nord, Brittany*
c. 1855
Lower right: COROT
Oil on canvas
12 3/4 × 21 3/4" (32.4 × 55.2 cm)

John G. Johnson Collection
cat. 922

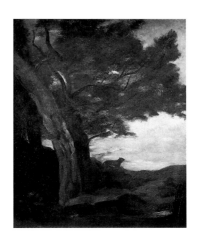

**Corot, Jean-Baptiste-Camille**
*Night Landscape with a Lioness*
1857–73
Lower left: COROT
Oil on canvas
47 1/2 × 39" (120.6 × 99.1 cm)

John G. Johnson Collection
cat. 936

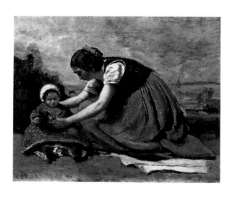

**Corot, Jean-Baptiste-Camille**
*Mother and Child on a Beach*
c. 1860
Lower left: COROT
Oil on canvas
14$^{15}$/$_{16}$ × 18$^{3}$/$_{16}$" (37.9 × 46.2 cm)

John G. Johnson Collection
cat. 930

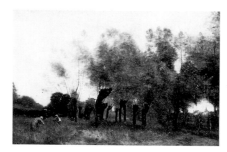

**Corot, Jean-Baptiste-Camille**
*Pollard Willows*
1865–70
Lower left: COROT
Oil on canvas
16$^{3}$/$_{16}$ × 23$^{11}$/$_{16}$" (41.1 × 60.2 cm)

Gift of Elizabeth Donner
Norment
1980-100-1

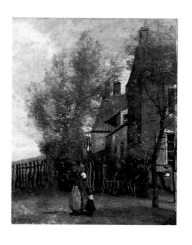

**Corot, Jean-Baptiste-Camille**
*House in the Village of Saint-Martin,
near Boulogne-sur-Mer*
1860–65
Lower left: COROT
Oil on panel
16$^{1}$/$_{8}$ × 12$^{7}$/$_{8}$" (41 × 32.7 cm)

The George W. Elkins Collection
E1924-4-7

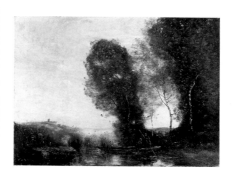

**Corot, Jean-Baptiste-Camille**
*The Ferry*
1865–72
Lower left: COROT
Oil on canvas
17$^{3}$/$_{4}$ × 24" (45.1 × 61 cm)

The George W. Elkins Collection
E1924-4-5

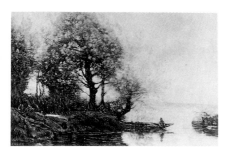

**Corot, Jean-Baptiste-Camille**
*Fisherman*
1865–70
Lower left: COROT
Oil on canvas
19$^{3}$/$_{8}$ × 29$^{3}$/$_{4}$" (49.2 × 75.6 cm)

The William L. Elkins Collection
E1924-3-2

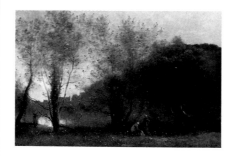

**Corot, Jean-Baptiste-Camille**
*Morning on the Estuary, Ville
d'Avray*
1870
Lower left: 1870; lower right:
COROT
Oil on canvas
22 × 31$^{7}$/$_{8}$" (55.9 × 81 cm)

Bequest of Charlotte Dorrance
Wright
1978-1-7

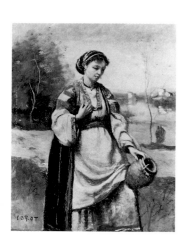

**Corot, Jean-Baptiste-Camille**
*Gypsy Girl at a Fountain*
1865–70
Lower left: COROT
Oil on canvas
22$^{7}$/$_{8}$ × 16$^{7}$/$_{8}$" (58.1 × 42.9 cm)

The George W. Elkins Collection
E1924-4-8

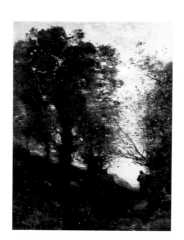

**Corot, Jean-Baptiste-Camille**
*Goatherd of Terni*
c. 1871
Lower right: COROT
Oil on canvas
32$^{3}$/$_{8}$ × 24$^{5}$/$_{8}$" (82.2 × 62.5 cm)

Bequest of Charlotte Dorrance
Wright
1978-1-8

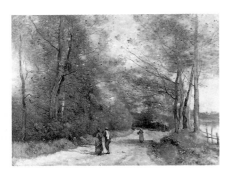

**Corot, Jean-Baptiste-Camille**
*Wooded Path near Ville d'Avray*
1872–74
Lower right: COROT
Oil on canvas
23 ⁷/₈ × 32 ¹/₄" (60.6 × 81.9 cm)

John G. Johnson Collection
cat. 928

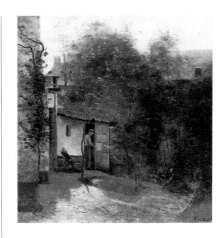

**Corot, Jean-Baptiste-Camille,
attributed to**
Previously listed as Jean-Baptiste-
Camille Corot (JGJ 1941)
*Douai, the House of Alfred Robaut*
1871
Lower right: COROT
Oil on canvas
21 ³/₄ × 19 ³/₄" (55.2 × 50.2 cm)

John G. Johnson Collection
cat. 929

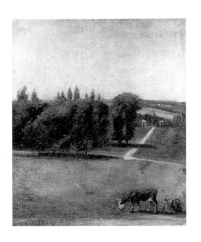

**Corot, Jean-Baptiste-Camille,
attributed to**
*Landscape*
1825
Lower left: COROT 1825
Oil on canvas
16 ¹/₈ × 12 ⁷/₈" (41 × 32.7 cm)

John G. Johnson Collection
cat. 917

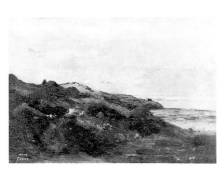

**Corot, Jean-Baptiste-Camille,
attributed to**
Previously listed as Jean-Baptiste-
Camille Corot (JGJ 1941)
*Hilly Coast*
19th century
Lower left: VENTE / COROT
Oil on canvas
10 × 14" (25.4 × 35.6 cm)

John G. Johnson Collection
cat. 926

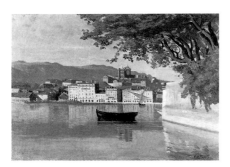

**Corot, Jean-Baptiste-Camille,
attributed to**
Previously listed as Jean-Baptiste-
Camille Corot (JGJ 1941)
*Lake Geneva*
1839
Lower right: COROT
Oil on canvas
10 ¹/₄ × 13 ⁷/₈" (26 × 35.2 cm)

John G. Johnson Collection
cat. 925

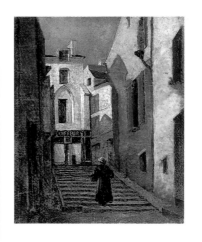

**Corot, Jean-Baptiste-Camille,
imitator of**
*Barbershop*
19th century
Lower left (spurious): COROT; on
sign: COIFFEUR
Oil on canvas
16 ³/₈ × 13 ¹/₄" (41.6 × 33.6 cm)

John G. Johnson Collection
cat. 920

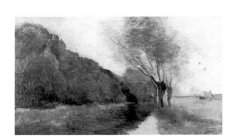

**Corot, Jean-Baptiste-Camille,
attributed to**
Previously listed as Jean-Baptiste-
Camille Corot (JGJ 1941)
*Landscape with a Stream and
Willows near Gisors*
c. 1860
Lower left: VENTE / COROT
Oil on canvas
21 ¹/₈ × 35 ⁷/₈" (53.7 × 91.1 cm)

John G. Johnson Collection
cat. 939

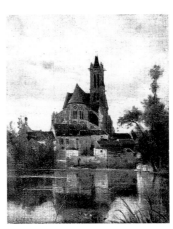

**Corot, Jean-Baptiste-Camille,
imitator of**
*Cathedral of Nîmes*
19th century
Lower left (spurious): COROT
Oil on canvas
14 × 10 ⁵/₈" (35.6 × 27 cm)

John G. Johnson Collection
cat. 927

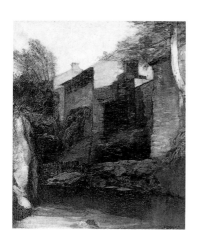

**Corot, Jean-Baptiste-Camille, imitator of**
*Courtyard*
19th century
Lower right (spurious): COROT
Oil on canvas
17 7/16 × 13 7/8" (44.3 × 35.2 cm)

John G. Johnson Collection
cat. 941

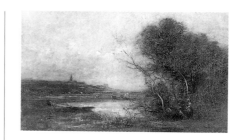

**Corot, Jean-Baptiste-Camille, imitator of**
Previously listed as Jean-Baptiste-Camille Corot ( JGJ 1941)
*Landscape with a Village*
19th century
Lower right (spurious): COROT
Oil on canvas
10 5/8 × 17 3/8" (27 × 44.1 cm)

John G. Johnson Collection
cat. 923

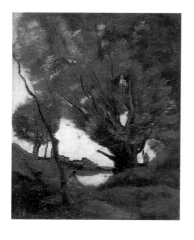

**Corot, Jean-Baptiste-Camille, imitator of**
*Italian Landscape*
19th century
Lower right (spurious): COROT
Oil on canvas
18 5/8 × 14 3/8" (47.3 × 36.5 cm)

John G. Johnson Collection
cat. 924

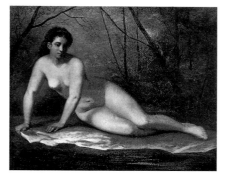

**Corot, Jean-Baptiste-Camille, imitator of**
*Nude Woman*
19th century
Lower left (spurious): COROT
Oil on canvas
21 5/8 × 26 7/8" (54.9 × 68.3 cm)

John G. Johnson Collection
cat. 933

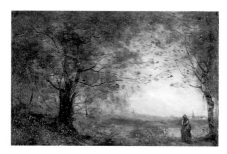

**Corot, Jean-Baptiste-Camille, imitator of**
*Landscape with a Distant Village Spire*
19th century
Lower left (spurious): COROT
Oil on canvas
10 × 14 3/8" (25.4 × 36.5 cm)

John G. Johnson Collection
cat. 932

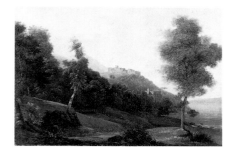

**Corot, Jean-Baptiste-Camille, imitator of**
*Roman Landscape*
19th century
Lower left (spurious): COROT
Oil on canvas
13 × 18 5/8" (33 × 47.3 cm)

John G. Johnson Collection
cat. 935

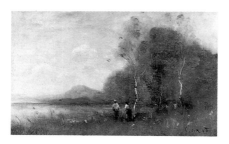

**Corot, Jean-Baptiste-Camille, imitator of**
*Landscape with Two Figures*
19th century
Lower right (spurious): COROT
Oil on canvas
8 1/8 × 13 1/4" (20.6 × 33.6 cm)

John G. Johnson Collection
cat. 934

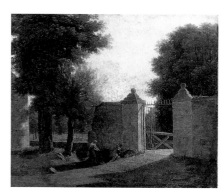

**Corot, Jean-Baptiste-Camille, imitator of**
*Village Lane and Gateway*
19th century
Lower left (spurious): COROT
Oil on canvas
13 1/8 × 15 1/2" (33.3 × 39.4 cm)

John G. Johnson Collection
cat. 938

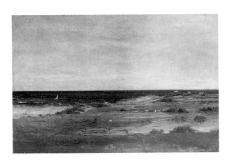

**Courbet, Gustave**
French, 1819–1877
*Coast Scene*
1854
Lower left: G. Courbet
Oil on canvas
37 1/2 × 53 11/16" (95.2 × 136.4 cm)

John G. Johnson Collection
cat. 947

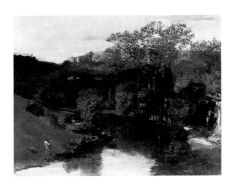

**Courbet, Gustave**
*Valley*
c. 1865
Lower right: G. Courbet
Oil on canvas
25 3/4 × 32" (65.4 × 81.3 cm)

John G. Johnson Collection
cat. 942

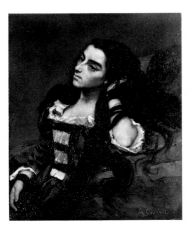

**Courbet, Gustave**
*Spanish Woman*
1855
Lower right: 55 / G. Courbet
Oil on canvas
31 5/8 × 25 1/2" (80.3 × 64.8 cm)

John G. Johnson Collection
inv. 2265

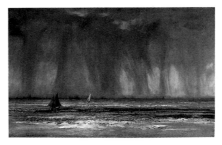

**Courbet, Gustave**
*Marine*
1866
Lower left: 66 / Gustave Courbet
Oil on canvas on gypsum board
17 × 25 7/8" (43.2 × 65.7 cm)

John G. Johnson Collection
cat. 948

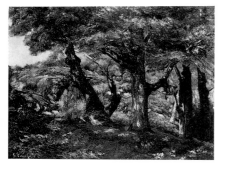

**Courbet, Gustave**
*The Fringe of the Forest*
c. 1856
Lower left: G. Courbet.
Oil on canvas
34 3/4 × 45 3/8" (88.3 × 115.2 cm)

The Louis E. Stern Collection
1963-181-19

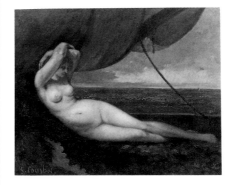

**Courbet, Gustave**
*Nude Reclining by the Sea*
1868
Lower left: 68 / G. Courbet.
Oil on canvas
18 5/16 × 21 7/8" (46.5 × 55.6 cm)

The Louis E. Stern Collection
1963-181-20

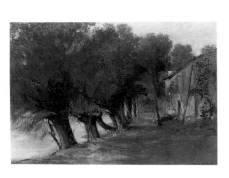

**Courbet, Gustave**
*La Charente, Port-Berteau*
1862
Lower right: G. Courbet
Oil on canvas
16 7/8 × 23 15/16" (42.9 × 60.8 cm)

John G. Johnson Collection
cat. 944

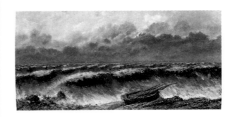

**Courbet, Gustave**
*Waves*
1869
Lower right: G. Courbet
Oil on canvas
29 7/8 × 59 5/8" (75.9 × 151.4 cm)

Gift of John G. Johnson for the
W. P. Wilstach Collection
W1905-1-1

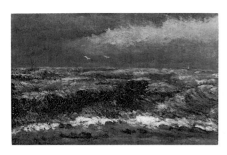

**Courbet, Gustave**
*Waves*
c. 1870
Lower left: G. Courbet.
Oil on canvas
12 3/4 × 19" (32.4 × 48.3 cm)

The Louis E. Stern Collection
1963-181-21

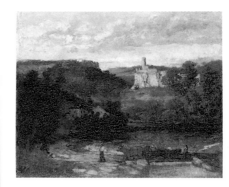

**Courbet, Gustave,
attributed to**
Previously listed as Gustave
Courbet (PMA 1965)
*Landscape at Ornans*
c. 1868
Lower left: G. Courbet
Oil on canvas
18 5/8 × 22 3/16" (47.3 × 56.4 cm)

Purchased with the W. P.
Wilstach Fund
W1895-1-12

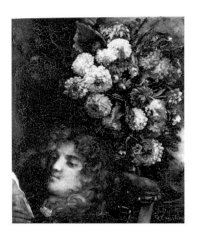

**Courbet, Gustave**
*Head of a Woman and Flowers*
1871
Lower right: .71 Ste. Pelagie /
G. Courbet.
Oil on canvas
21 7/8 × 18 3/8" (55.6 × 46.7 cm)

The Louis E. Stern Collection
1963-181-23

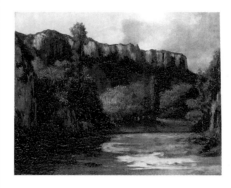

**Courbet, Gustave,
attributed to**
Previously listed as Gustave
Courbet (PMA 1965)
*Landscape at Ornans*
19th century
Lower right: G. Courbet
Oil on canvas
31 7/8 × 39 1/2" (81 × 100.3 cm)

The John D. McIlhenny
Collection
1943-40-55

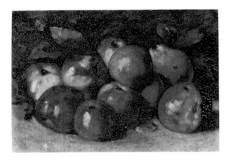

**Courbet, Gustave**
*Still Life with Apples and a Pear*
1871
Lower left: 71 G. Courbet.
Oil on canvas
9 1/2 × 12 5/16" (24.1 × 31.3 cm)

The Louis E. Stern Collection
1963-181-22

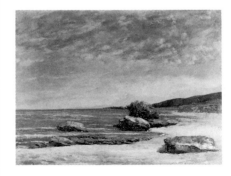

**Courbet, Gustave, studio of**
Previously listed as Gustave
Courbet (JGJ 1941)
*Rocky Coast*
19th century
Lower right: G. Courbet
Oil on canvas
18 5/16 × 23 11/16" (46.5 × 60.2 cm)

John G. Johnson Collection
cat. 943

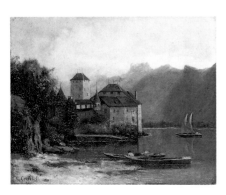

**Courbet, Gustave**
*Château Chillon*
c. 1874
Lower left: G. Courbet.
Oil on canvas on gypsum board
23 9/16 × 28 11/16" (59.8 × 72.9 cm)

John G. Johnson Collection
cat. 945

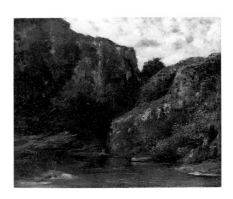

**Courbet, Gustave,
imitator of**
Previously listed as Gustave
Courbet (PMA 1965)
*Rill in the Mountains*
19th century
Lower right (spurious):
G. Courbet. 73
Oil on canvas
21 5/16 × 25 9/16" (54.1 × 64.9 cm)

Gift of John G. Johnson for the
W. P. Wilstach Collection
W1907-1-21

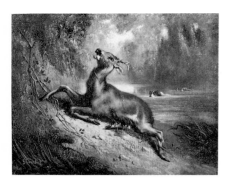

**Courbet, Gustave, imitator of**
*Wounded Stag*
19th century
Lower left (spurious): G. Courbet
Oil on canvas
19 5/8 × 24 9/16" (49.8 × 62.4 cm)

John G. Johnson Collection
cat. 946

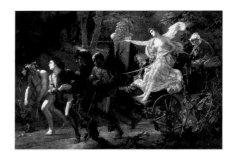

**Couture, Thomas**
*The Thorny Path*
1873
On herm: T. C. / 1873
Oil on canvas
51 1/2 × 75" (130.8 × 190.5 cm)

Purchased with the W. P.
Wilstach Fund, the George W.
Elkins Fund, and the Edith H.
Bell Fund
EW1986-10-1

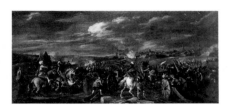

**Courtois, Jacques, also called Il Borgognone, follower of**
French, 1621–1675
*Battle Scene*
17th century
Oil on canvas
29 × 58 7/8" (73.7 × 149.5 cm)

The Bloomfield Moore Collection
1883-140

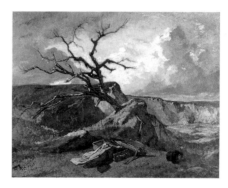

**Couture, Thomas**
*Landscape near the Sea*
1876
Lower left: T. C.
Oil on canvas
18 3/8 × 21 13/16" (46.7 × 55.4 cm)

John G. Johnson Collection
cat. 949

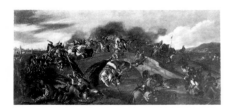

**Courtois, Jacques, follower of**
*Battle Scene*
17th century
Oil on canvas
28 15/16 × 59" (73.5 × 149.9 cm)

The Bloomfield Moore Collection
1883-141

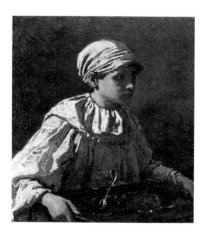

**Couture, Thomas**
*The Little Confectioner*
c. 1878
Center right: T.C.
Oil on canvas
25 7/8 × 21 9/16" (65.7 × 54.8 cm)

The William L. Elkins Collection
E1924-3-67

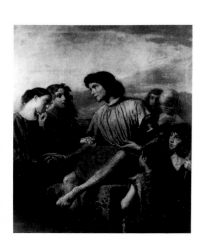

**Couture, Thomas**
French, 1815–1879
*Troubadour*
1843
Center bottom: Tas Couture
Oil on canvas
68 1/8 × 56 1/2" (173 × 143.5 cm)

John G. Johnson Collection
cat. 950

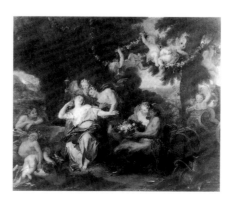

**Coypel, Antoine**
French, 1661–1722
*Bacchus and Ariadne on the Isle of Naxos*
c. 1693
Oil on canvas
28 3/4 × 33 2/3" (73 × 85.5 cm)

Bequest (by exchange) of
Edna M. Welsh and gift of
Mrs. R. Barclay Scull
1990-54-1

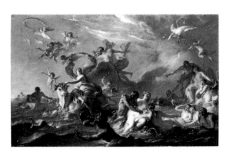

**Coypel, Noël-Nicolas**
French, 1690–1734
*The Rape of Europa*
1726–27
Lower right: Noel Coypel
172[7?]
Oil on canvas
50 1/4 × 76 3/8" (127.6 × 194 cm)

Gift of John Cadwalader
1978-160-1

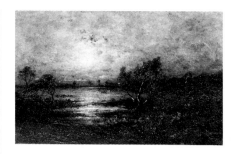

**Daubigny, Charles-François**
*Moonlight*
c. 1860–74
Lower left: Daubigny
Oil on canvas
25 1/2 × 38 3/4" (64.8 × 98.4 cm)

The William L. Elkins Collection
E1924-3-62

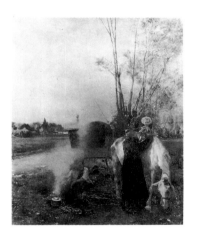

**Dagnan-Bouveret, Pascal-Adolphe-Jean**
French, 1852–1929
*Gypsy Scene*
1883
Lower left: P.A.J. Dagnan / 1883
Oil on canvas
17 3/8 × 14" (44.1 × 35.6 cm)

John G. Johnson Collection
cat. 952

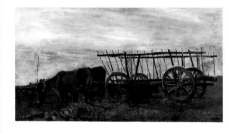

**Daubigny, Charles-François**
*Oxen and a Cart*
1862
Lower left: Daubigny 1862
Oil on canvas
16 15/16 × 28 7/8" (43 × 73.3 cm)

Bequest of Charlotte Dorrance
Wright
1978-1-9

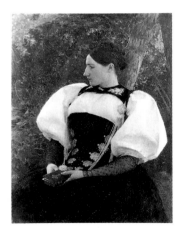

**Dagnan-Bouveret, Pascal-Adolphe-Jean**
*Bernoise*
1887
Lower right: P.A.J. Dagnan.
PB 1887
Oil on canvas
21 7/8 × 16 1/2" (55.6 × 41.9 cm)

John G. Johnson Collection
cat. 953

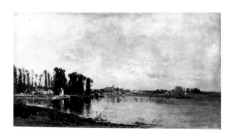

**Daubigny, Charles-François**
*River Scene, Conflans*
1867
Lower left: Daubigny 1867
Oil on panel
17 15/16 × 31 5/8" (45.6 × 80.3 cm)

John G. Johnson Collection
cat. 958

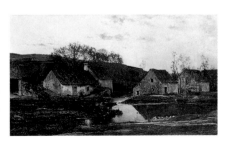

**Daubigny, Charles-François**
French, 1817–1878
*Mill*
1857
Lower right: C. Daubigny 1857
Oil on canvas
34 1/8 × 59 1/4" (86.7 × 150.5 cm)

The William L. Elkins Collection
E1924-3-4

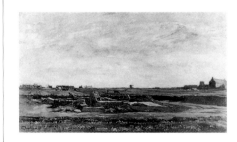

**Daubigny, Charles-François**
*Landscape near Villerville*
1868
Lower left: Daubigny 68
Oil on canvas on gypsum board
18 3/4 × 31 5/8" (47.6 × 80.3 cm)

John G. Johnson Collection
cat. 956

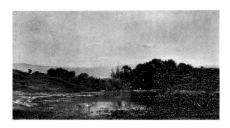

**Daubigny, Charles-François**
*Solitude*
1869
Lower left: Daubigny 1869
Oil on canvas
19 5/8 × 36 9/16" (49.8 × 92.9 cm)

The George W. Elkins Collection
E1924-4-10

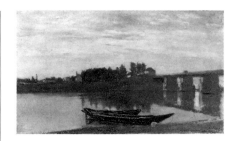

**Daubigny, Charles-François**
*River and Bridge*
Mid-19th century
Lower right: Daubigny
Oil on panel
10 3/8 × 17 7/16" (26.3 × 44.3 cm)

John G. Johnson Collection
cat. 957

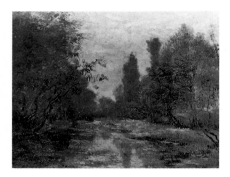

**Daubigny, Charles-François**
*Brook*
Mid-19th century
Lower left: Daubigny
Oil on canvas on gypsum board
10 3/4 × 13 3/4" (27.3 × 34.9 cm)

John G. Johnson Collection
cat. 959

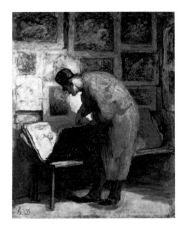

**Daumier, Honoré**
French, 1808–1879
*The Print Collector*
c. 1860
Lower left: h.D
Oil on panel
13 7/16 × 10 1/4" (34.1 × 26 cm)

Purchased with the W. P.
Wilstach Fund
W1954-1-1

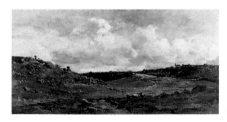

**Daubigny, Charles-François**
*Hilly Landscape*
Mid-19th century
Lower right: Daubigny
Oil on panel
9 3/4 × 18 3/4" (24.8 × 47.6 cm)

John G. Johnson Collection
cat. 955

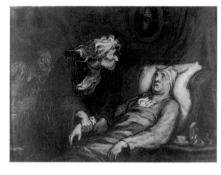

**Daumier, Honoré**
*The Imaginary Illness*
c. 1860–62
Lower right: h. Daumier
Oil on panel
10 1/2 × 13 7/8" (26.7 × 35.2 cm)

Purchased with the Lisa Norris
Elkins Fund and funds
contributed by R. Sturgis
Ingersoll, George D. Widener,
Lessing J. Rosenwald, Henry P.
McIlhenny, Dr. I. S. Ravdin,
Floyd T. Starr, Irving H. Vogel,
Mr. and Mrs. Rodolphe Meyer de
Schauensee, and Mrs. Herbert
Cameron Morris
1954-10-1

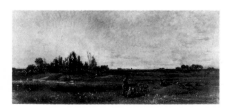

**Daubigny, Charles-François**
*Landscape*
Mid-19th century
Oil on canvas
34 9/16 × 75 11/16" (87.8 ×
192.2 cm)

John G. Johnson Collection
inv. 2976

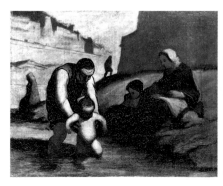

**Daumier, Honoré, imitator of**
*Man Bathing a Child*
Based on the painting in the
Detroit Institute of Arts (70.166)
19th century
Lower right (spurious): h. Daumier
Oil on canvas
12 7/8 × 16 1/4" (32.7 × 41.3 cm)

John G. Johnson Collection
cat. 960

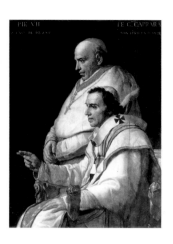

**David, Jacques-Louis**
French, 1748–1825
*Portrait of Pope Pius VII and Cardinal Caprara*
c. 1805
Upper left: PIE VII / A L'AGE DE 63 ANS.; upper right: LE CNAL. CAPRARA / SON LÉGAT EN FRANCE.
Oil on panel
54 3/8 × 37 3/4" (138.1 × 96 cm)

Gift of Henry P. McIlhenny
1971-265-1

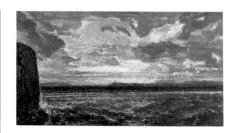

**Decamps, Gabriel-Alexandre**
*Marine with a Stormy Sunset*
c. 1849
Lower left: DC
Oil on canvas
9 1/8 × 15 1/2" (23.2 × 39.4 cm)

John G. Johnson Collection
cat. 965

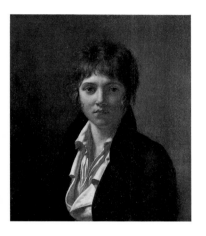

**David, Jacques-Louis, follower of**
Previously listed as Jacques-Louis David (PMA 1965)
*Portrait of Édouard Duval d'Ogne*
c. 1800–10
Oil on canvas
21 7/8 × 18 1/16" (55.6 × 45.9 cm)

The Mr. and Mrs. Carroll S. Tyson, Jr., Collection
1963-116-6

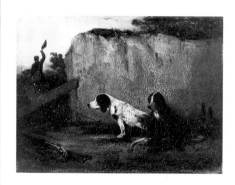

**Decamps, Gabriel-Alexandre**
*Halt during a Hunt*
Mid-19th century
Center bottom: DC.
Oil on canvas
6 3/4 × 8 5/8" (17.1 × 21.9 cm)

The William L. Elkins Collection
E1924-3-58

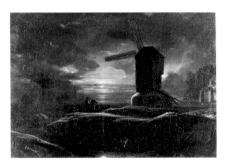

**Decamps, Gabriel-Alexandre**
French, 1803–1860
*Bivouac before Waterloo*
c. 1827
Lower left: DECAMPS.
Oil on canvas
12 5/8 × 17 3/4" (32.1 × 45.1 cm)

John G. Johnson Collection
cat. 967

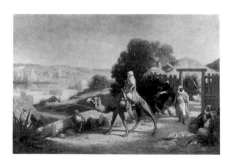

**Decamps, Gabriel-Alexandre**
*Oriental Landscape*
Mid-19th century
Lower right: Decamps
Oil on canvas
16 1/4 × 23 3/8" (41.3 × 59.4 cm)

John G. Johnson Collection
cat. 968

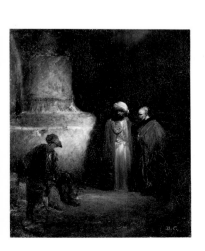

**Decamps, Gabriel-Alexandre**
*Oriental Night Scene*
c. 1836
Lower right: D.C.
Oil on canvas
23 13/16 × 20 3/16" (60.5 × 51.3 cm)

John G. Johnson Collection
cat. 966

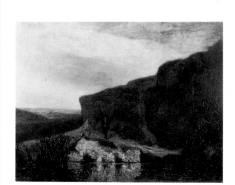

**Decamps, Gabriel-Alexandre, attributed to**
*Syrian Landscape*
19th century
Oil on canvas
19 7/8 × 25 5/8" (50.5 × 65.1 cm)

John G. Johnson Collection
cat. 964

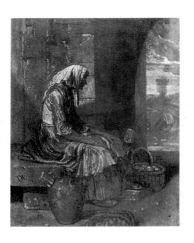

**Decamps, Gabriel-Alexandre, attributed to**
*Vegetable Seller*
19th century
Lower left: DC.
Oil on paper on canvas
26 5/16 × 20 5/16" (66.8 × 51.6 cm)

John G. Johnson Collection
cat. 961

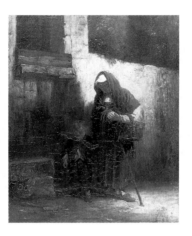

**Decamps, Gabriel-Alexandre, attributed to**
Previously listed as Gabriel-Alexandre Decamps (JGJ 1941)
*Woman and Boy*
19th century
Lower left: DC
Oil on canvas
14 1/8 × 11 1/8" (35.9 × 28.3 cm)

John G. Johnson Collection
cat. 962

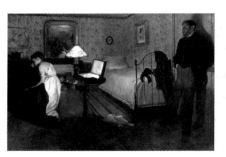

**Degas, Hilaire-Germain-Edgar**
French, 1834–1917
*Interior*
1868 or 1869
Lower right: Degas
Oil on canvas
32 × 45" (81.3 × 114.3 cm)

The Henry P. McIlhenny
Collection in memory of
Frances P. McIlhenny
1986-26-10

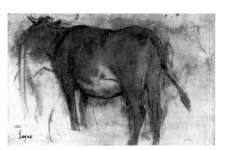

**Degas, Hilaire-Germain-Edgar**
*Cow*
c. 1876
Lower left: Degas
Oil on cigar-box top
8 × 11 5/8" (20.3 × 29.5 cm)

John G. Johnson Collection
cat. 971

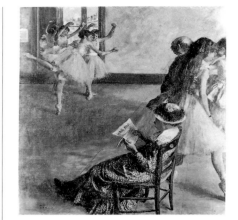

**Degas, Hilaire-Germain-Edgar**
*The Ballet Class*
c. 1880
Lower left: Degas
Oil on canvas
32 3/8 × 30 1/4" (82.2 × 76.8 cm)

Purchased with the W. P.
Wilstach Fund
W1937-2-1

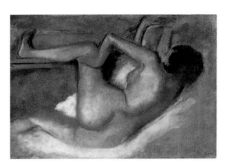

**Degas, Hilaire-Germain-Edgar**
*After the Bath*
c. 1895
Lower right: Degas
Oil on canvas
18 1/4 × 25 3/4" (46.3 × 65.4 cm)

Gift of Mr. and Mrs. Orville H.
Bullitt
1963-117-1

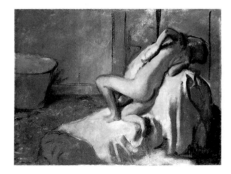

**Degas, Hilaire-Germain-Edgar**
*After the Bath (Woman Drying Herself)*
c. 1896
Lower right: Degas
Oil on canvas
35 1/4 × 46" (89.5 × 116.8 cm)

Purchased with funds from the
estate of George D. Widener
1980-6-1

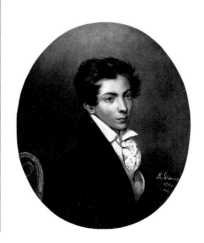

**Delacroix, Ferdinand-Victor-Eugène**
French, 1798–1863
*Portrait of Eugène Berny d'Ouville*
1828
Lower right: Eug. Delacroix /
1828
Oil on canvas
24 × 19 5/16" (61 × 49 cm)

The Henry P. McIlhenny
Collection in memory of
Frances P. McIlhenny
1986-26-18

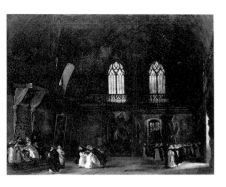

**Delacroix, Ferdinand-Victor-Eugène**
*Interior of a Dominican Convent in Madrid*
1831
Center bottom: EUG. DELACROIX
1831
Oil on canvas
51 1/4 × 63 3/4" (130.2 × 161.9 cm)

Purchased with the W. P. Wilstach Fund
W1894-1-2

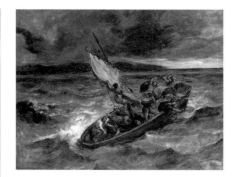

**Delacroix, Ferdinand-Victor-Eugène**
*Christ on the Sea of Galilee*
1853
Lower left: Eug Delacroix
Oil on composition board
18 3/4 × 22 7/8" (47.6 × 58.1 cm)

Gift of Mr. and Mrs. R. Sturgis Ingersoll
1950-6-1

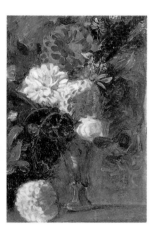

**Delacroix, Ferdinand-Victor-Eugène**
*Still Life with Dahlias*
c. 1833
Oil on canvas
19 11/16 × 13" (50 × 33 cm)

John G. Johnson Collection
cat. 976

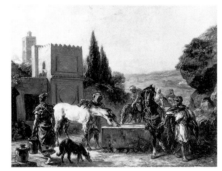

**Delacroix, Ferdinand-Victor-Eugène**
*Horses at a Fountain*
1862
Lower left: Eug. Delacroix 1862.
Oil on canvas
29 × 36 3/8" (73.7 × 92.4 cm)

Purchased with the W. P. Wilstach Fund
W1950-1-2

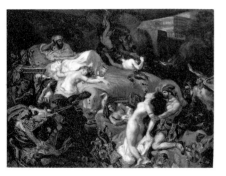

**Delacroix, Ferdinand-Victor-Eugène**
*The Death of Sardanapalus*
1844
Oil on canvas
29 × 32 7/16" (73.7 × 82.4 cm)

The Henry P. McIlhenny Collection in memory of Frances P. McIlhenny
1986-26-17

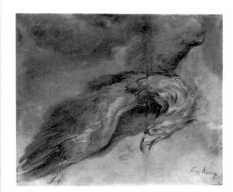

**Delacroix, Ferdinand-Victor-Eugène, imitator of**
Previously listed as Ferdinand-Victor-Eugène Delacroix (JGJ 1941)
*Eagle*
19th century
Lower right (spurious): Eug Delacroix
Oil on canvas
14 3/16 × 16 11/16" (36 × 42.4 cm)

John G. Johnson Collection
cat. 972

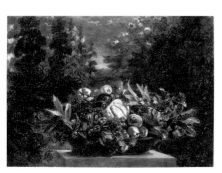

**Delacroix, Ferdinand-Victor-Eugène**
*Still Life with Flowers and Fruit*
1848
Oil on canvas
42 5/8 × 56 3/8" (108.3 × 143.2 cm)

John G. Johnson Collection
cat. 974

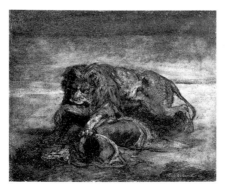

**Delacroix, Ferdinand-Victor-Eugène, imitator of**
Previously listed as Ferdinand-Victor-Eugène Delacroix (JGJ 1941)
*Lion Devouring an Arab*
19th century
Lower right (spurious): Eug. Delacroix
Oil on canvas
21 5/16 × 25 3/4" (54.1 × 65.4 cm)

John G. Johnson Collection
cat. 977

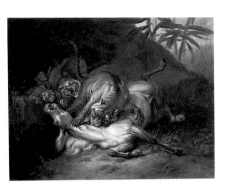

**Delacroix, Ferdinand-Victor-Eugène, imitator of**
*Tigers Devouring a Horse*
19th century
Lower right (spurious): E D.
Oil on canvas
19 1/16 × 23 5/8" (48.4 × 60 cm)

John G. Johnson Collection
inv. 2836

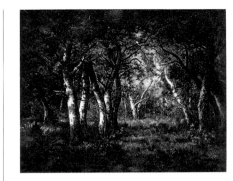

**Diaz de la Peña, Narcisse-Virgile**
*Interior of a Forest*
1862
Lower left: N. DIAZ, 62
Oil on canvas
32 × 39 1/2" (81.3 × 100.3 cm)

The Walter Lippincott Collection
1923-59-16

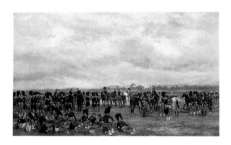

**Detaille, Jean-Baptiste-Édouard**
French, 1848–1912
*Grenadiers at the Camp of Saint-Maur*
1869
Lower right: EDOUARD DETAILLE. / 1869.
Oil on canvas
22 9/16 × 35 5/8" (57.3 × 90.5 cm)

The William L. Elkins Collection
E1924-3-82

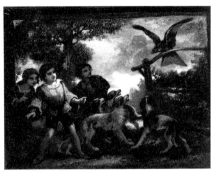

**Diaz de la Peña, Narcisse-Virgile**
*Boys and an Eagle*
1864
Lower right: N. Diaz. 64.
Oil on canvas
15 1/2 × 18 3/4" (39.4 × 47.6 cm)

The William L. Elkins Collection
E1924-3-63

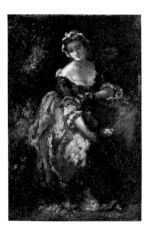

**Diaz de la Peña, Narcisse-Virgile**
French, 1808–1876
*Girl in a Green Dress*
c. 1850–55
Oil on panel
11 7/8 × 7 1/4" (30.2 × 18.4 cm)

Bequest of Arthur H. Lea
F1938-1-31

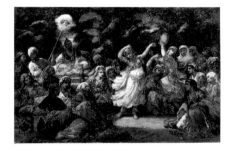

**Diaz de la Peña, Narcisse-Virgile**
*Dance of the Almahs*
1864
Lower right: N. Diaz 64.
Oil on canvas
17 1/2 × 25 11/16" (44.4 × 65.2 cm)

John G. Johnson Collection
cat. 978

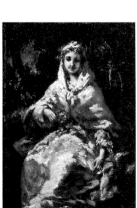

**Diaz de la Peña, Narcisse-Virgile**
*Girl in a White-and-Pink Dress*
c. 1850–55
Oil on canvas
11 7/8 × 7 1/4" (30.2 × 18.4 cm)

Bequest of Arthur H. Lea
F1938-1-20

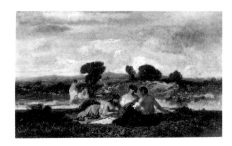

**Diaz de la Peña, Narcisse-Virgile**
*Bathers*
Mid-19th century
Lower left: N. Diaz.
Oil on panel
11 7/16 × 18 5/16" (29 × 46.5 cm)

The William L. Elkins Collection
E1924-3-66

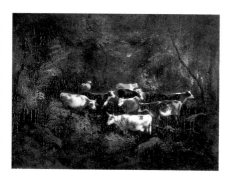

**Diaz de la Peña, Narcisse-Virgile**
*Cows in the Forest*
Mid-19th century
Lower left: N. Diaz
Oil on panel
10 9/16 × 13 13/16" (26.8 × 35.1 cm)

John G. Johnson Collection
cat. 981

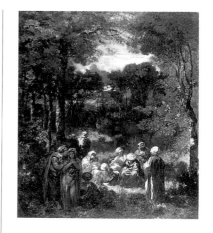

**Diaz de la Peña, Narcisse-Virgile**
*Oriental Fantasy*
Mid-19th century
Lower right: N. Diaz
Oil on canvas
18 3/16 × 15" (46.2 × 38.1 cm)

John G. Johnson Collection
inv. 2585

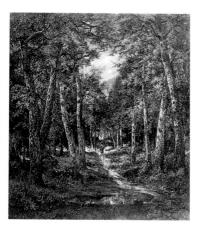

**Diaz de la Peña, Narcisse-Virgile**
*Forest Path*
Mid-19th century
Lower left: N. Diaz
Oil on panel
28 3/16 × 23 1/2" (71.6 × 59.7 cm)

John G. Johnson Collection
cat. 983

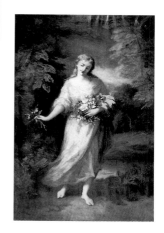

**Diaz de la Peña, Narcisse-Virgile**
*Spring*
Mid-19th century
Oil on canvas
86 7/8 × 58 1/8" (220.7 × 147.6 cm)

The William L. Elkins Collection
E1924-3-70

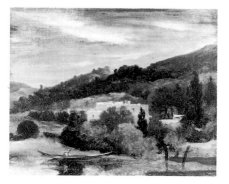

**Diaz de la Peña, Narcisse-Virgile**
*Landscape*
Mid-19th century
Lower right: D.
Oil on canvas
12 11/16 × 16 1/8" (32.2 × 41 cm)

John G. Johnson Collection
cat. 979

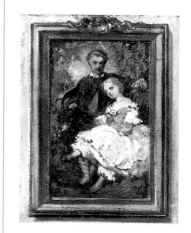

**Diaz de la Peña, Narcisse-Virgile, follower of**
*Picture of a Portrait of a Boy and a Girl*
c. 1860
Lower left: A. M.
Oil on cardboard
11 15/16 × 8 3/4" (30.3 × 22.2 cm)

The Samuel S. White 3rd and
Vera White Collection
1967-30-61

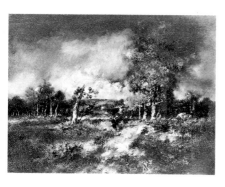

**Diaz de la Peña, Narcisse-Virgile**
*Landscape*
Mid-19th century
Lower left: N. Diaz
Oil on panel
7 3/8 × 9 1/2" (18.7 × 24.1 cm)

John G. Johnson Collection
cat. 982

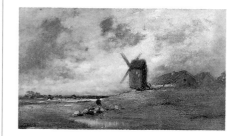

**Dupré, Jules**
French, 1811–1889
*Landscape with a Windmill*
c. 1870
Lower left: Jules Dupré; on card
on reverse: Le tableau ci-contre
representant / —le moulin de
l'Isle-Adam.— / m'a ete
personellement offert / par mon
eminent cofrere et ami / Jules
Dupré / Paris, ce 18 Juin 1870 /
F. Flameng
Oil on panel
11 3/16 × 18 3/4" (28.4 × 47.6 cm)

John G. Johnson Collection
cat. 988

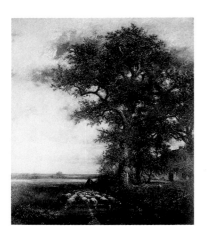

**Dupré, Jules**
*Great Oak*
By 1883
Lower right: Jules Dupré
Oil on canvas
67 1/2 × 56" (171.4 × 142.2 cm)

John G. Johnson Collection
cat. 984

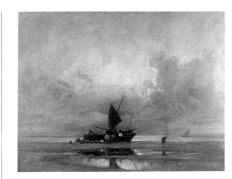

**Dupré, Jules**
*Marine*
Mid-19th century
Lower left: Jules Dupré
Oil on canvas
29 1/8 × 36 9/16" (74 × 92.9 cm)

John G. Johnson Collection
cat. 986

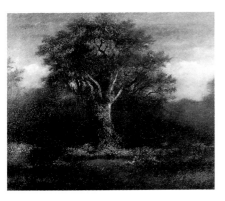

**Dupré, Jules**
*Forest of Compiègne*
Mid-19th century
Lower left: J. Dupré
Oil on panel
25 7/16 × 28 11/16" (64.6 × 72.9 cm)

John G. Johnson Collection
cat. 985

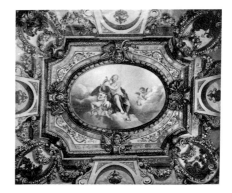

**Dupuis, Pierre**
French, 1610–1682
*Perspectival Ceiling with Apollo Playing the Lyre*
1678
Lower left border, central medallion: Pierre Dupuis 1678
Oil on canvas
204 × 234" (518.2 × 594.4 cm)

Purchased with funds contributed in memory of R. Nelson Buckley
1947-86-1

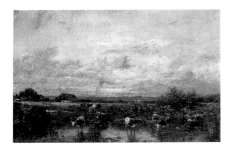

**Dupré, Jules**
*Landscape*
Mid-19th century
Lower right: Jules Dupré
Oil on canvas
20 7/8 × 31 3/4" (53 × 80.6 cm)

The William L. Elkins Collection
E1924-3-5

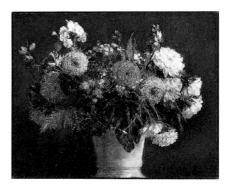

**Fantin-Latour, Ignace-Henri-Jean-Théodore**
French, 1836–1904
*Still Life with Chrysanthemums*
1862
Lower right: Fantin 62
Oil on canvas
18 1/8 × 21 7/8" (46 × 55.6 cm)

John G. Johnson Collection
cat. 990

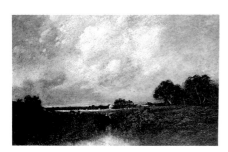

**Dupré, Jules**
*Landscape*
Mid-19th century
Lower right: Jules Dupré
Oil on canvas
23 5/8 × 35 3/8" (60 × 89.8 cm)

The George W. Elkins Collection
E1924-4-11

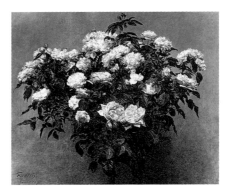

**Fantin-Latour, Ignace-Henri-Jean-Théodore**
*Still Life with White Roses*
1875
Lower left: Fantin / Juillet 1875
Oil on canvas
21 13/16 × 23 1/4" (55.4 × 59 cm)

Bequest of Charlotte Dorrance Wright
1978-1-17

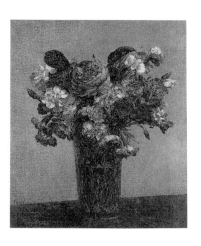

**Fantin-Latour, Ignace-Henri-Jean-Théodore**
*Still Life with Roses and Asters in a Glass*
1877
Lower left: Fantin 77
Oil on canvas
13 3/16 × 10 3/4" (33.5 × 27.3 cm)

Bequest of Charlotte Dorrance Wright
1978-1-13

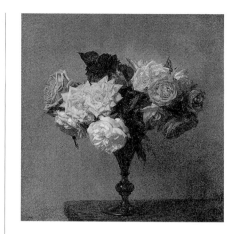

**Fantin-Latour, Ignace-Henri-Jean-Théodore**
*Still Life with Roses in a Vase*
1888
Lower left: Fantin
Oil on canvas
17 1/4 × 18" (43.8 × 45.7 cm)

Bequest of Charlotte Dorrance Wright
1978-1-16

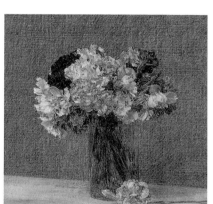

**Fantin-Latour, Ignace-Henri-Jean-Théodore**
*Still Life with Carnations*
1878
Lower left: Fantin—78
Oil on canvas
13 × 11 3/4" (33 × 29.8 cm)

Bequest of Charlotte Dorrance Wright
1978-1-14

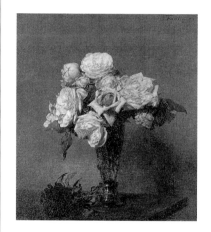

**Fantin-Latour, Ignace-Henri-Jean-Théodore**
*Still Life with Roses in a Fluted Vase*
1889
Upper right: Fantin 89
Oil on canvas
17 1/2 × 15" (44.4 × 38.1 cm)

Bequest of Charlotte Dorrance Wright
1978-1-10

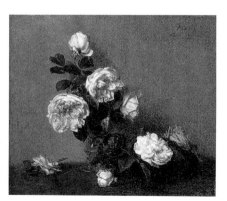

**Fantin-Latour, Ignace-Henri-Jean-Théodore**
*Still Life with Roses of Dijon*
1882
Upper right: Fantin / Bure oct. 1882
Oil on canvas
16 9/16 × 18 5/16" (42.1 × 46.5 cm)

Bequest of Charlotte Dorrance Wright
1978-1-11

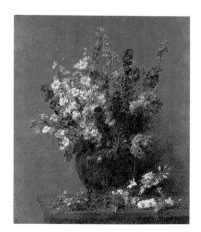

**Fantin-Latour, Ignace-Henri-Jean-Théodore**
*Still Life with Imperial Delphiniums*
1891
Lower left: Fantin—91
Oil on canvas
29 13/16 × 24 5/8" (75.7 × 62.5 cm)

Bequest of Charlotte Dorrance Wright
1978-1-15

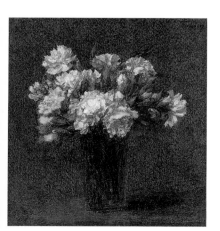

**Fantin-Latour, Ignace-Henri-Jean-Théodore**
*Still Life with White Pinks in a Glass Vase*
c. 1885
Upper right: Fantin
Oil on canvas
13 5/8 × 12 3/4" (34.6 × 32.4 cm)

Bequest of Charlotte Dorrance Wright
1978-1-12

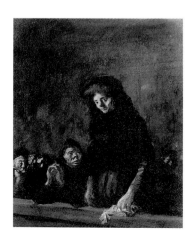

**Forain, Jean-Louis**
French, 1852–1931
*The Hearing*
c. 1900
Lower left: forain
Oil on canvas
29 3/8 × 23 7/8" (74.6 × 60.6 cm)

Gift of Mr. and Mrs. Arthur Wiesenberger
1962-206-1

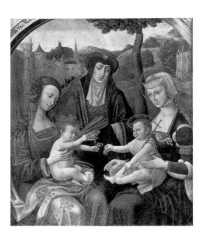

**Franco-Flemish,
unknown artist**
Previously listed as the school of
Jean Bourdichon (JGJ 1941)
*Virgin and Child, with Saints Anne
and Elizabeth, and the Young Saint
John the Baptist*
Center panel of a triptych;
companion to the following two
panels
c. 1500
Oil on panel
36 3/8 × 30" (92.4 × 76.2 cm)

John G. Johnson Collection
cat. 762a

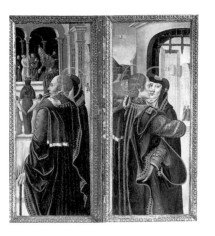

**Franco-Flemish,
unknown artist**
Previously listed as the school of
Jean Bourdichon (JGJ 1941)
*The Presentation of Christ in the
Temple and the Meeting at the
Golden Gate*
Wings of a triptych; companions
to the preceding panel; see
following two panels for reverse
c. 1500
Oil on panel
Each panel: 43 × 18 3/4"
(109.2 × 47.6 cm)

John G. Johnson Collection
cat. 762b, c

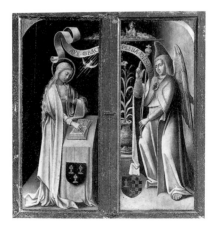

**Franco-Flemish,
unknown artist**
Previously listed as the school of
Jean Bourdichon (JGJ 1941)
*The Annunciation*
Reverse of the preceding two
panels
c. 1500
On banner: AVE GRACI / PLENA
DNS TECVM
Oil on panel
Each panel: 43 × 18 3/4"
(109.2 × 47.6 cm)

John G. Johnson Collection
cat. 762d, e

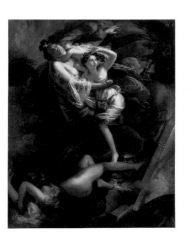

**Franque, Joseph**
French, active Naples,
1774–1833
*Scene during the Eruption of
Vesuvius*
c. 1827
Oil on canvas
116 1/2 × 90" (295.9 × 228.6 cm)

Purchased with the George W.
Elkins Fund
E1972-3-1

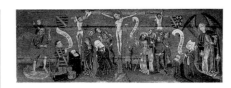

**French, unknown artist**
Previously listed as a South
French artist, c. 1500 (JGJ 1941)
*The Crucifixion, with Saint
Christopher, the Archangel Michael,
and Two Donors*
From the parish church of
Moyencourt
c. 1430
Left: [M]iserere mei deus.; center:
[V]ere filius dei erat iste; right:
[O] filij dei memento mei
Oil on panel
24 1/8 × 65 7/8" (61.3 × 167.3 cm)

John G. Johnson Collection
inv. 1729

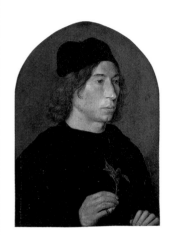

**French, unknown artist**
Previously listed as a French
artist, c. 1490–95 (JGJ 1941)
*Portrait of a Young Man Holding a
Sprig of Coxcomb*
c. 1490–1500
Oil on panel
17 3/4 × 13 1/8" (45.1 × 33.3 cm)

John G. Johnson Collection
cat. 764

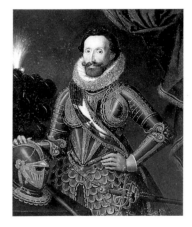

**French, unknown artist**
*Portrait of a Man in Armor*
c. 1575–1625
Oil on canvas
44 1/2 × 35" (113 × 88.9 cm)

Bequest of Carl Otto
Kretzschmar von Kienbusch
1977-167-1085

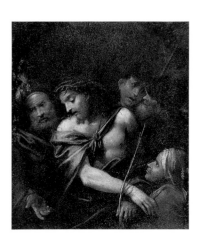

**French, unknown artist**
Previously listed as Jacques Stella
(JGJ 1941)
*The Mocking of Christ*
17th century?
Oil on panel
8 3/8 × 6 13/16" (21.3 × 17.3 cm)

John G. Johnson Collection
cat. 774

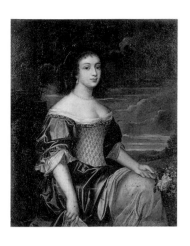

**French, unknown artist**
*Portrait of the Duchess of Chevreuse*
17th century
Oil on canvas
41 3/4 × 32 5/8" (106 × 82.9 cm)

Bequest of Arthur H. Lea
F1938-1-1

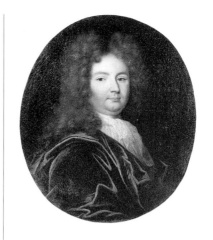

**French, unknown artist**
*Portrait of a Man*
18th century
Oil on canvas
28 3/4 × 23 1/4" (73 × 59 cm)

Bequest of Arthur H. Lea
F1938-1-12

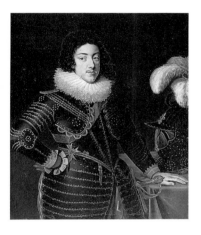

**French, unknown artist**
*Portrait of a Man in Armor*
[possibly Louis XIII, King of
France]
17th century
Oil on canvas on fiberboard
39 1/2 × 33 1/2" (100.3 × 85.1 cm)

Bequest of Carl Otto
Kretzschmar von Kienbusch
1977-167-1084

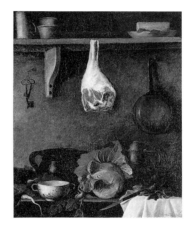

**French, unknown artist**
Previously attributed to Jean-
Baptiste-Simeon Chardin
(JGJ 1941)
*Still Life of Kitchen Shelves with a
Ham*
18th century
Lower right (spurious): Chardin
1774
Oil on canvas
42 1/4 × 33 1/4" (107.3 × 84.4 cm)

John G. Johnson Collection
cat. 787

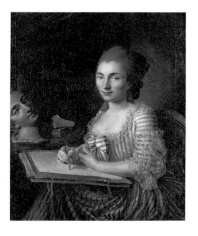

**French?, unknown artist**
Previously listed as a French
artist, c. 1740 (JGJ 1941)
*Portrait of a Woman Drawing*
c. 1750–1800
Oil on canvas
36 3/8 × 29 1/4" (92.4 × 74.3 cm)

John G. Johnson Collection
cat. 780

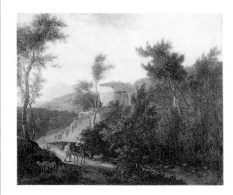

**French, unknown artist**
*Landscape*
c. 1800–25
Oil on canvas
19 3/4 × 23 3/8" (50.2 × 59.4 cm)

John G. Johnson Collection
inv. 2841

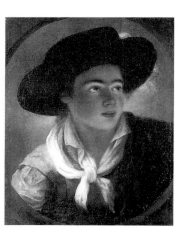

**French, unknown artist**
*Portrait of a Boy*
18th century?
Oil on canvas
19 3/4 × 15 1/2" (50.2 × 39.4 cm)

John G. Johnson Collection
inv. 2926

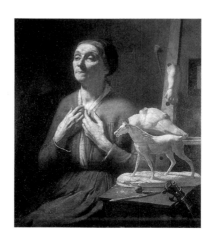

**French, unknown artist**
Previously listed as a French
artist, late 18th century (JGJ
1941)
*Old Woman Seated in an Artist's
Studio*
c. 1800–25
Oil on canvas
42 13/16 × 36 7/8" (108.7 ×
93.7 cm)

John G. Johnson Collection
cat. 779

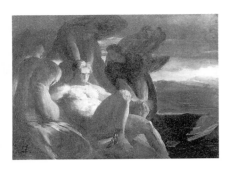

**French, unknown artist**
*Prometheus Bound*
c. 1800–25
Lower left (spurious): E. D.
Oil on paper on canvas
9 3/8 × 12 3/4" (23.8 × 32.4 cm)

John G. Johnson Collection
cat. 975

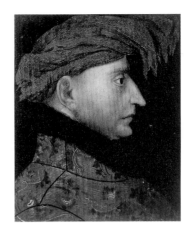

**French, unknown artist**
Previously listed as a French
artist, c. 1600 (JGJ 1941)
*Portrait of Louis II of Anjou, King
of Naples and Sicily*
In a 15th-century style; after an
ink and watercolor drawing in
the Bibliothèque Nationale, Paris
19th century
Upper left: A. Q. F.
Oil on panel
7 5/8 × 5 1/2" (19.4 × 14 cm)

John G. Johnson Collection
inv. 333

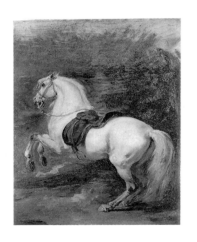

**French, unknown artist**
*Rocky Landscape with a Castle*
c. 1800–25
Oil on panel
9 1/4 × 12 1/2" (23.5 × 31.7 cm)

John G. Johnson Collection
cat. 919

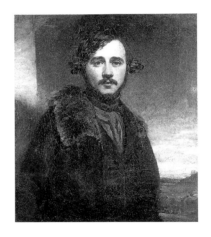

**French, unknown artist**
*Portrait of a Man*
19th century
Oil on canvas
29 1/4 × 24 3/8" (74.3 × 61.9 cm)

John G. Johnson Collection
cat. 973

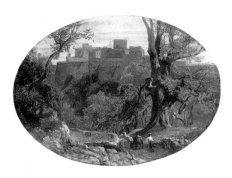

**French, unknown artist**
Previously attributed to Jean-
Louis-André-Théodore Géricault
(PMA 1965)
*Arabian Horse*
c. 1850
Oil on paper on canvas
26 × 20 1/2" (66 × 52.1 cm)

The William L. Elkins Collection
E1924-3-29

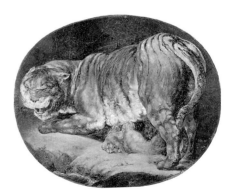

**French, unknown artist**
*A Tigress and Three Cubs*
19th century
Lower left (spurious): E. D.
Oil on canvas
14 1/8 × 16 1/2" (35.9 × 41.9 cm)

John G. Johnson Collection
inv. 2749

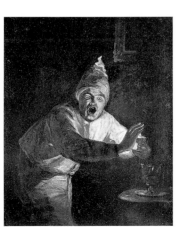

**French, unknown artist**
Previously listed as a French
artist, mid-18th century (JGJ
1941)
*Man Carrying a Light*
19th century
Oil on canvas
32 7/8 × 25 9/16" (83.5 × 64.9 cm)

John G. Johnson Collection
cat. 778

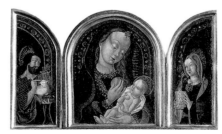

**French, unknown artist**
Previously listed as the school of
Nicolas Froment (JGJ 1941)
*Virgin and Child, with Saints John
the Baptist and Mary Magdalene*
Triptych
Late 15th century
Oil on panel
Center panel: 12 3/8 × 10 3/8"
(31.4 × 26.3 cm); wings [each]:
12 3/8 × 5 1/4" (31.4 × 13.3 cm)

John G. Johnson Collection
cat. 761

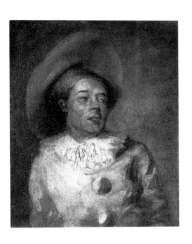

**French, unknown artist**
*Portrait of an Actor Dressed as Harlequin*
In an 18th-century style
Late 19th century
Oil on canvas
12 3/4 × 9 7/8" (32.4 × 25.1 cm)

John G. Johnson Collection
cat. 790

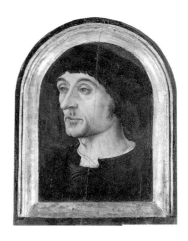

**Froment, Nicolas, follower of**
French, born c. 1425, died 1483–86
Previously listed as a Flemish artist, c. 1550 (JGJ 1941)
*Portrait of a Man*
Late 15th century
Oil on panel
11 13/16 × 8 3/4" (30 × 22.2 cm)

John G. Johnson Collection
cat. 404

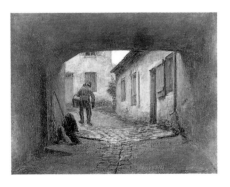

**French, unknown artist**
*Still Life*
Late 19th century
Oil on canvas
10 7/8 × 9 7/8" (27.6 × 25.1 cm)

John G. Johnson Collection
cat. 784

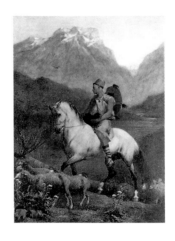

**Fromentin, Eugène (Eugène Fromentin-Dupeux)**
French, 1820–1876
*Arabian Shepherd (Shepherd: High Plateau of Kabylia)*
Reduced-scale replica of a lost painting shown at the Paris Salon of 1861 (cat. no. 1186)
After 1861
Lower right: Eug. Fromentin
Oil on panel
18 × 11 15/16" (45.7 × 30.3 cm)

Bequest of Miss Willian Adger
1933-82-4

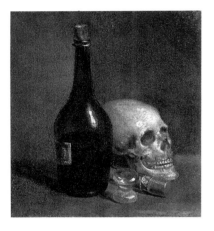

**Frère, Pierre-Édouard**
French, 1819–1886
*Courtyard*
1877
Lower left: Ed. Frère. 77.
Oil on canvas
12 15/16 × 16" (32.9 × 40.6 cm)

John G. Johnson Collection
cat. 993

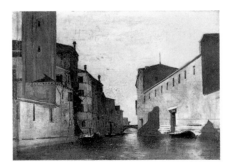

**Fromentin, Eugène**
*Canal in Venice*
c. 1870
Lower right: —Eug. F.—
Oil on panel
11 1/16 × 14 3/8" (28.1 × 36.5 cm)

John G. Johnson Collection
cat. 995

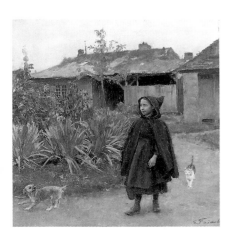

**Friant, Émile**
French, 1863–1932
*The Garden Walk*
1889
Lower right: E. Friant 89
Oil on panel
8 5/16 × 8 1/8" (21.1 × 20.6 cm)

John G. Johnson Collection
cat. 994

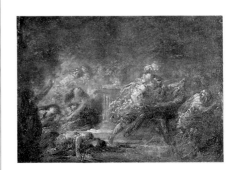

**Gamelin, Jacques, attributed to**
French, 1738–1803
Previously listed as Narcisse-Virgile Diaz de la Peña (JGJ 1941)
*Sketch for "The Death of Priam"*
For the painting in the Musée des Augustins, Toulouse
c. 1785–90
Oil on cardboard
5 1/2 × 7 1/4" (14 × 18.4 cm)

John G. Johnson Collection
cat. 980

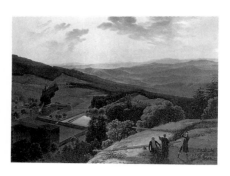

**Gauffier, Louis**
French, 1761–1801
*The Monastery of Vallombrosa and the Arno Valley Seen from Paradisino*
From a series of four paintings of the monastery; companion to the following painting
1797
Lower right: L. Gauffier
Oil on canvas
32 1/2 × 45" (82.5 × 114.3 cm)

Purchased with the W. P. Wilstach Fund
W1975-1-1

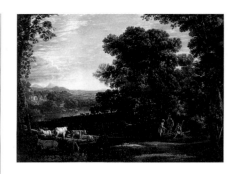

**Gellée, Claude, also called Claude Lorrain**
French, 1600–1682
*Landscape with Cattle and Peasants*
1629
Lower right: CLAUDIO IV ROMA / 1629
Oil on canvas
42 × 58 1/2" (106.7 × 148.6 cm)

The George W. Elkins Collection
E1950-2-1

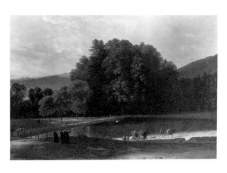

**Gauffier, Louis**
*The Fish Pond at the Monastery of Vallombrosa with Horsemen and Monks*
See previous entry
1797
Lower right: L. Gauffier. 1797.
Oil on canvas
32 1/2 × 45" (82.5 × 114.3 cm)

Purchased with the W. P. Wilstach Fund
W1975-1-2

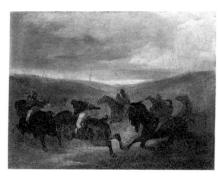

**Géricault, Jean-Louis-André-Théodore, attributed to**
French, 1791–1824
*Horses*
19th century
Oil on canvas
12 3/4 × 16 1/16" (32.4 × 40.8 cm)

Purchased with the W. P. Wilstach Fund
W1912-1-2

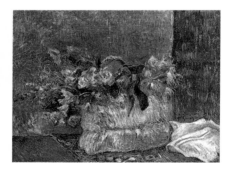

**Gauguin, Paul**
French, 1848–1903
*Still Life with Moss Roses in a Basket*
1886
Lower right: a mon ami Schuffenecker / P. Gauguin
Oil on canvas
19 11/16 × 24 7/8" (50 × 63.2 cm)

Bequest of Charlotte Dorrance Wright
1978-1-18

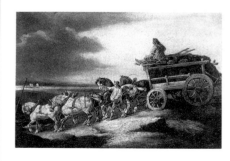

**Géricault, Jean-Louis-André-Théodore, copy after**
*Carbon Wagon*
After the lithograph by Géricault
19th century
Center bottom (spurious): [illegible signature "Géricault"]
Oil on canvas
15 3/4 × 23 1/2" (40 × 59.7 cm)

John G. Johnson Collection
cat. 796

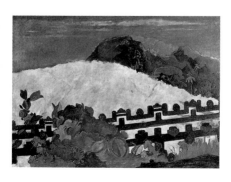

**Gauguin, Paul**
*Sacred Mountain (Parahi Te Marae)*
1892
Lower right: PARAHI TE MARAE / P. Gauguin 92
Oil on canvas
26 × 35" (66 × 88.9 cm)

Gift of Mr. and Mrs. Rodolphe Meyer de Schauensee
1980-1-1

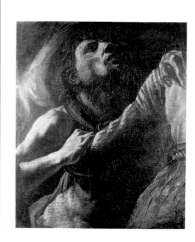

**Géricault, Jean-Louis-André-Théodore, copy after**
Previously listed as Jean-Louis-André-Théodore Géricault (JGJ 1941)
*Figure from "The Raft of the Medusa"*
After the painting in the Musée du Louvre, Paris (inv. 4884)
19th century
Lower right: [illegible]
Oil on canvas
32 1/8 × 25 3/4" (81.6 × 65.4 cm)

John G. Johnson Collection
cat. 795

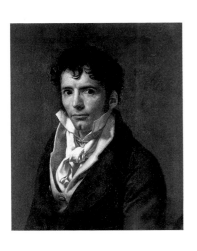

**Girodet de Roucy Trioson, Anne-Louis, attributed to**
French, 1767–1824
*Portrait of a Man*
c. 1810
Lower left: [monogram]
Oil on canvas
25 1/2 × 21" (64.8 × 53.3 cm)

The Henry P. McIlhenny
Collection in memory of
Frances P. McIlhenny
1986-26-35

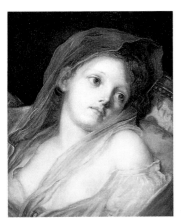

**Greuze, Jean-Baptiste, copy after**
French, 1725–1805
Previously attributed to Jean-Baptiste Greuze (PMA 1965)
*Innocence*
After the painting in the Wallace Collection, London (P. 384)
18th century
Oil on canvas
16 1/8 × 12 7/8" (41 × 32.7 cm)

Gift of Arthur Wiesenberger
1955-109-1

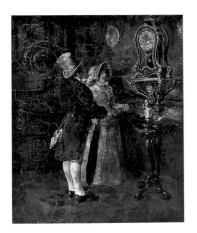

**Grison, François-Adolphe**
French, 1845–1914
*The Chiming Clock*
c. 1900
Lower left: Grison
Oil on panel
10 11/16 × 8 5/8" (27.1 × 21.9 cm)

The William L. Elkins Collection
E1924-3-92

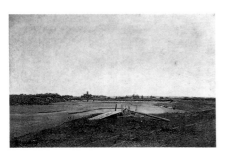

**Harpignies, Henri-Joseph**
French, 1819–1916
*Bank of a Stream*
1857
Lower left: hy harpignies .1857.
Oil on canvas
26 3/16 × 39 1/2" (66.5 × 100.3 cm)

John G. Johnson Collection
cat. 997

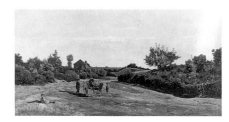

**Harpignies, Henri-Joseph**
*Landscape with a Donkey Cart*
1874
Lower left: hy harpignies . 1874 .
Oil on canvas
11 × 20 1/2" (27.9 × 52.1 cm)

John G. Johnson Collection
cat. 996

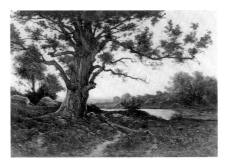

**Harpignies, Henri-Joseph**
*Oak*
1895
Lower left: h. harpignies. 95.
Oil on canvas
46 1/2 × 63 7/16" (118.1 × 161.1 cm)

The William L. Elkins Collection
E1924-3-88

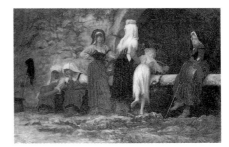

**Hebert, Antoine-Auguste-Ernest**
French, 1817–1908
*Neapolitan Women at a Well*
By 1886
Oil on canvas
13 5/8 × 19 1/2" (34.6 × 49.5 cm)

John G. Johnson Collection
cat. 1003

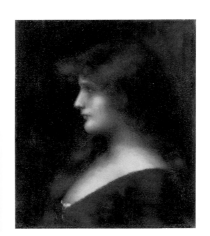

**Henner, Jean-Jacques**
French, 1829–1905
*Head of a Girl*
Late 19th century
Center left: J J HENNER
Oil on canvas
18 3/16 × 15 1/4" (46.2 × 38.7 cm)

The Walter Lippincott Collection
1923-59-4

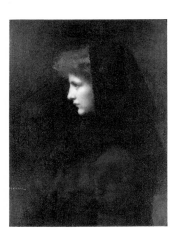

**Henner, Jean-Jacques**
*Head of a Girl*
c. 1900
Lower left: J J HENNER
Oil on canvas
24 1/16 × 18 1/8" (61.1 × 46 cm)

Bequest of Aaron E. Carpenter
1970-75-3

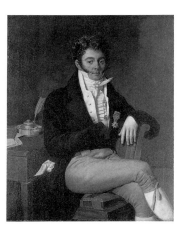

**Hersent, Louis, attributed to**
French, 1777–1860
Previously listed as Jean-Auguste-
Dominique Ingres (JGJ 1941)
*Portrait of Louis-Charles-Mercier
Dupaty*
c. 1810–20
Oil on canvas
45 3/8 × 34 7/8" (115.2 × 88.6 cm)

John G. Johnson Collection
cat. 794

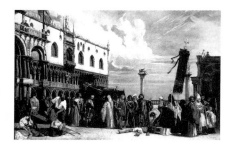

**Hesse, Alexandre-Jean-
Baptiste**
French, 1806–1879
*The Funerary Honors Rendered to
Titian, Who Died in Venice during
the Plague of 1576*
Preparatory sketch for the
painting in the Musée du Louvre,
Paris (R.F. 1985-3), shown at the
Salon of 1833
c. 1833
Oil on canvas
15 3/4 × 23 1/4" (40 × 59 cm)

The Henry P. McIlhenny
Collection in memory of
Frances P. McIlhenny
1986-26-277

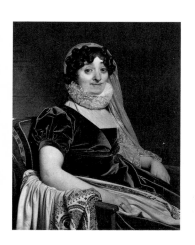

**Ingres, Jean-Auguste-
Dominique**
French, 1780–1867
*Portrait of the Countess of Tournon*
1812
Lower right: Ingres Rome / 1812
Oil on canvas
36 3/8 × 28 13/16" (92.4 × 73.2 cm)

The Henry P. McIlhenny
Collection in memory of
Frances P. McIlhenny
1986-26-22

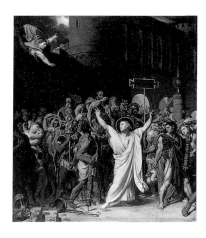

**Ingres, Jean-Auguste-
Dominique**
*The Martyrdom of Saint Symphorien*
1865
Lower right: J. INGRES / 1865
Oil on canvas
14 7/16 × 12 7/16" (36.7 × 31.6 cm)

John G. Johnson Collection
cat. 793

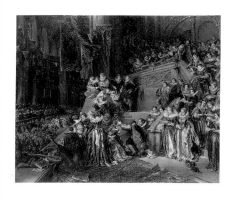

**Isabey, Louis-Gabriel-Eugène**
French, 1803–1886
*The Marriage of Henry IV*
1848
Lower left: E. Isabey / 1848
Oil on canvas
67 3/8 × 80 1/4" (171.1 × 203.8 cm)

The William L. Elkins Collection
E1924-3-86

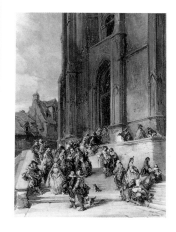

**Isabey, Louis-Gabriel-Eugène**
*Leaving the Cathedral*
1864
Lower right: E. Isabey. 64.
Oil on panel
23 11/16 × 16 5/8" (60.2 × 42.2 cm)

The William L. Elkins Collection
E1924-3-69

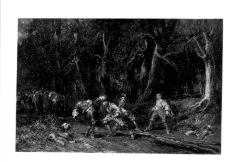

**Isabey, Louis-Gabriel-Eugène**
*The Duel*
1867
Lower left: E. Isabey. 67.
Oil on canvas
17 × 25 7/16" (43.2 × 64.6 cm)

John G. Johnson Collection
inv. 2753

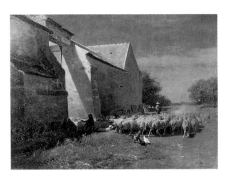

**Jacque, Charles-Émile**
French, 1813–1894
*Sheep Leaving a Farmyard*
1860
Upper left: ch. Jacque. / 1860.
Oil on panel
21 3/4 × 28 5/16" (55.2 × 71.9 cm)

John G. Johnson Collection
cat. 1011

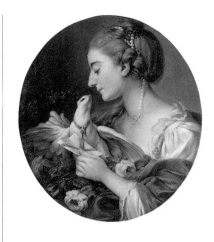

**Lagrenée, Louis, the Elder,
attributed to**
French, 1725–1805
*Young Woman Fastening a Letter to
the Neck of a Pigeon*
c. 1760
On letter: Monsieur / de Fontenet
/ [illegible] / Ponts
Oil on canvas
23 × 19 1/4" (58.4 × 48.9 cm)

Gift of John T. Dorrance
1965-85-1

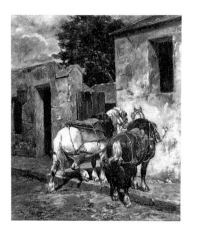

**Jacque, Charles-Émile**
*Percherons at Barbizon*
c. 1880
Lower left: ch. Jacque.
Oil on canvas
32 1/4 × 25 3/16" (81.9 × 64 cm)

Bequest of Charlotte Dorrance
Wright
1978-1-19

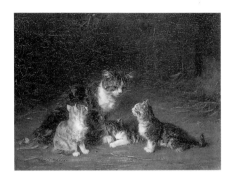

**Lambert, Louis-Eugène**
French, 1825–1900
*A Cat and Three Kittens*
By 1892
Lower left: L Eug Lambert
Oil on canvas
12 3/4 × 16 1/8" (32.4 × 41 cm)

John G. Johnson Collection
cat. 1018

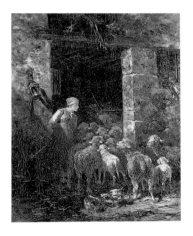

**Jacque, Charles-Émile**
*Sheep in a Stable*
Late 19th century
Lower left: ch. Jacque
Oil on canvas
26 3/4 × 20 3/4" (67.9 × 52.7 cm)

Gift of Walter Lippincott
1923-59-3

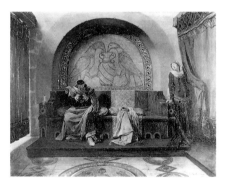

**Laurens, Jean-Paul**
French, 1838–1921
*The Parting of King Robert and
Bertha*
1883
Lower right: Jean Paul Laurens /
1883
Oil on canvas
32 1/8 × 39 1/2" (81.6 × 100.3 cm)

John G. Johnson Collection
inv. 2846

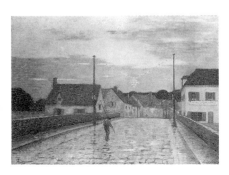

**Lagarde, Pierre**
French, 1853–1910
*Village Street*
c. 1891
Lower right: Pierre Lagarde
Oil on canvas
23 11/16 × 31 3/4" (60.2 × 80.6 cm)

John G. Johnson Collection
cat. 1017

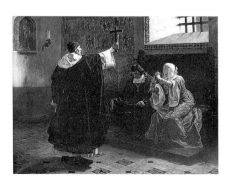

**Laurens, Jean-Paul**
*Torquemada, Grand Inquisitor*
1886
Lower right: Jean-Paul Laurens
1886.
Oil on canvas
45 3/8 × 58 1/4" (115.2 × 147.9 cm)

The William L. Elkins Collection
E1924-3-57

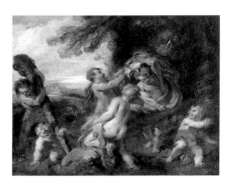

**Lemoyne, François**
French, 1688–1737
*Putti Playing with the Accoutrements of Hercules*
c. 1721–24
Oil on panel
5 1/2 × 7 1/4" (14 × 18.5 cm)

Gift of the Friends of the Philadelphia Museum of Art
1989-3-1

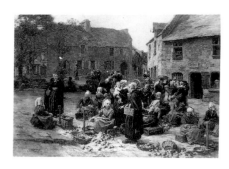

**Lhermitte, Léon-Augustin**
French, 1844–1925
*Apple Market, Landerneau, Brittany*
c. 1878
Lower left: L. Lhermitte
Oil on canvas
33 3/4 × 47 1/4" (85.7 × 120 cm)

The George W. Elkins Collection
E1924-4-18

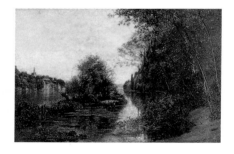

**Lepine, Stanislas-Victor-Édouard**
French, 1835–1892
*The Seine, Paris*
c. 1865
Lower left: S. Lepine
Oil on canvas
17 3/4 × 29 5/8" (45.1 × 75.2 cm)

The William L. Elkins Collection
E1924-3-80

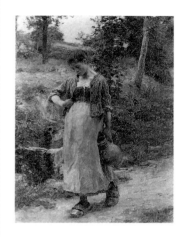

**Lhermitte, Léon-Augustin**
*Woman with a Jug*
1882
Lower right: L. Lhermitte; on jug: 882[?]
Oil on canvas
22 1/8 × 16 1/2" (56.2 × 41.9 cm)

The William L. Elkins Collection
E1924-3-68

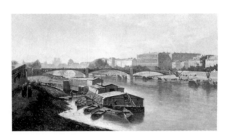

**Lepine, Stanislas-Victor-Édouard**
*Saint-Ouen*
Late 19th century
Lower right: S. Lepine
Oil on canvas on gypsum board
25 7/8 × 38 1/4" (65.7 × 97.1 cm)

John G. Johnson Collection
cat. 1019

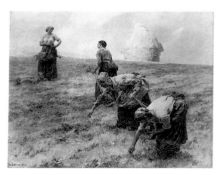

**Lhermitte, Léon-Augustin**
*The Gleaners*
c. 1890–95
Lower left: L. Lhermitte
Oil on canvas
29 1/2 × 37 3/4" (74.9 × 95.9 cm)

The George W. Elkins Collection
E1924-4-19

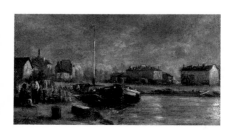

**Lepine, Stanislas-Victor-Édouard**
*The Seine*
Late 19th century
Lower left: S. Lepine
Oil on panel
6 1/4 × 10 3/4" (15.9 × 27.3 cm)

Bequest of Charlotte Dorrance Wright
1978-1-35

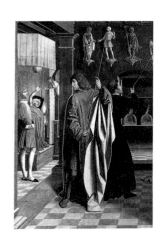

**Lieferinxe, Josse**
French, documented 1493–1505/8
Previously listed as a Rhone Valley artist, c. 1500 (JGJ 1941)
*Saint Sebastian Destroying the Idols*
Panel from the altarpiece of the Saint Sebastian chapel of Notre-Dame-des-Accoules, Marseilles, done in collaboration with Bernardino Simondi (Italian, died 1498); companion to the following three panels and those listed in the following entry
c. 1497
Oil on panel
32 1/8 × 21 1/2" (81.6 × 54.6 cm)

John G. Johnson Collection
cat. 765

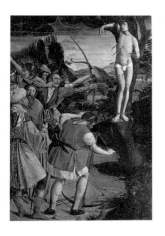

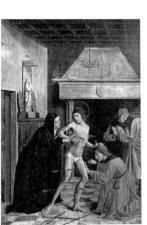

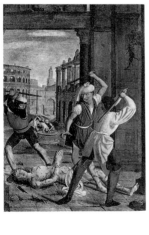

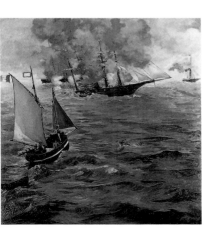

**Lieferinxe, Josse**
Previously listed as a Rhone
Valley artist, c. 1500 (JGJ 1941)
*Saint Sebastian Pierced with Arrows*
See previous entry; companion
panels are in the Walters Art
Gallery, Baltimore (37.1995); the
Hermitage, St. Petersburg (inv.
no. 6745); the Galleria Nazionale
d'Arte Antica, Rome (no. 1590);
and possibly the Musée Royal des
Beaux-Arts, Antwerp (5037)
c. 1497
Oil on panel
32 × 21 5/8" (81.3 × 54.9 cm)

John G. Johnson Collection
cat. 766

**Lieferinxe, Josse**
Previously listed as a Rhone
Valley artist, c. 1500 (JGJ 1941)
*Saint Sebastian Cured by Irene*
See previous two entries
c. 1497
Oil on panel
32 × 21 9/16" (81.3 × 54.8 cm)

John G. Johnson Collection
cat. 767

**Lieferinxe, Josse**
Previously listed as a Rhone
Valley artist, c. 1500 (JGJ 1941)
*The Martyrdom of Saint Sebastian*
See previous three entries
c. 1497
Oil on panel
32 1/2 × 21 3/4" (82.5 × 55.2 cm)

John G. Johnson Collection
cat. 768

**Manet, Édouard**
French, 1832–1883
*The Battle of the "Kearsarge" and
the "Alabama"*
1864
Lower right: manet
Oil on canvas
54 1/4 × 50 3/4" (137.8 × 128.9 cm)

John G. Johnson Collection
cat. 1027

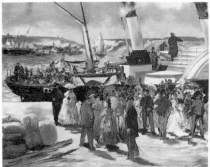

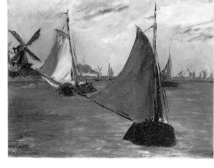

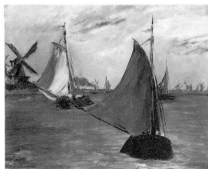

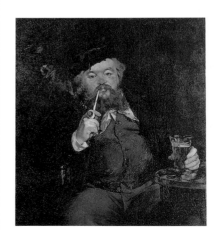

**Manet, Édouard**
*Marine View*
c. 1864
Lower right: Manet
Oil on canvas
32 1/16 × 39 1/2" (81.4 × 100.3 cm)

Bequest of Anne Thomson in
memory of her father, Frank
Thomson, and her mother, Mary
Elizabeth Clarke Thomson
1954-66-3

**Manet, Édouard**
*The Folkestone Boat, Boulogne*
1869
Lower left: Manet
Oil on canvas
23 5/8 × 28 15/16" (60 × 73.5 cm)

The Mr. and Mrs. Carroll S.
Tyson, Jr., Collection
1963-116-10

**Manet, Édouard**
*Marine in Holland*
1872
Lower left: Manet
Oil on canvas
19 3/4 × 23 3/4" (50.2 × 60.3 cm)

Purchased with the W. P.
Wilstach Fund
W1921-1-4

**Manet, Édouard**
*Le Bon Bock*
1873
Lower right: Manet 1873
Oil on canvas
37 1/4 × 32 13/16" (94.6 × 83.3 cm)

The Mr. and Mrs. Carroll S.
Tyson, Jr., Collection
1963-116-9

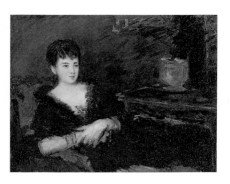

**Manet, Édouard**
*Portrait of Isabelle Lemonnier*
The face has been completely
repainted
c. 1877
Oil on canvas
13 × 16 1/8" (33 × 41 cm)

Bequest of Charlotte Dorrance
Wright
1978-1-21

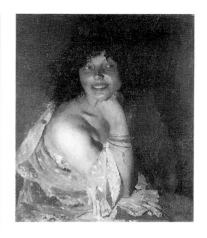

**Martin, Henri-Jean-Guillaume**
French, 1860–1943
*Étude*
1887
Upper left: Henri Martin / 87
Oil on canvas
25 3/4 × 21 1/4" (65.4 × 54 cm)

John G. Johnson Collection
cat. 1035

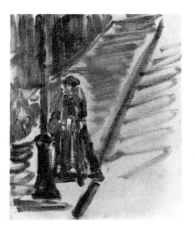

**Manet, Édouard**
*Knife Grinder, Rue Mosnier*
1878
Oil on canvas
16 × 12 7/8" (40.6 × 32.7 cm)

Bequest of Charlotte Dorrance
Wright
1978-1-20

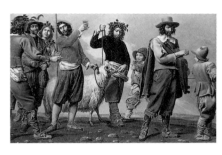

**Master of the Processions**
French, active mid-17th century
Previously listed as Louis and
Mathieu Le Nain (PMA 1965)
*Feast of the Wine (The Procession of
the Ram)*
Companion to *Feast of the Wine
(The Procession of the Fatted Ox)*,
in the Musée Picasso, Paris
Mid-17th century
Oil on canvas
44 × 65" (111.8 × 165.1 cm)

The George W. Elkins Collection
E1950-2-2

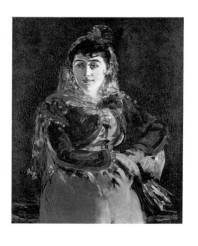

**Manet, Édouard**
*Portrait of Émilie Ambre as Carmen*
c. 1879
Oil on canvas
36 3/8 × 28 15/16" (92.4 × 73.5 cm)

Gift of Edgar Scott
1964-114-1

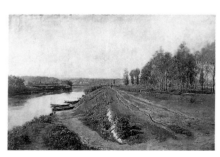

**Meissonier, Jean-Louis-
Ernest**
French, 1815–1891
*The Seine at Poissy*
1884
Lower right: EMeissonier Poissy
1884
Oil on panel
13 11/16 × 20 1/16" (34.8 × 51 cm)

John G. Johnson Collection
cat. 1039

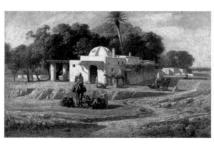

**Marilhat, Prosper**
French, 1811–1847
*Oriental Caravansary*
1835
Lower left: Marilhat, 1835
Oil on panel
10 13/16 × 16 15/16" (27.5 × 43 cm)

John G. Johnson Collection
cat. 1028

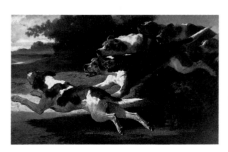

**Melin, Joseph-Urbain**
French, 1814–1886
*In Full Cry*
1861
Lower left: J. Melin / 1861
Oil on canvas
53 × 83 3/4" (134.6 × 212.7 cm)

The William L. Elkins Collection
E1924-3-59

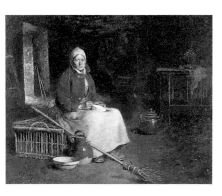

**Mettling, Louis**
French, 1847–1904
*Street Sweeper at Lunch*
By 1886
Lower left: Mettling.
Oil on panel
14 13/16 × 17 5/8" (37.6 × 44.8 cm)

John G. Johnson Collection
cat. 1040

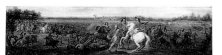

**Meulen, Adam Frans van der, studio of**
French, born Flanders, 1632–1690
Previously listed as Adam Frans van der Meulen (PMA 1965)
*The Passage of the Rhine on June 12, 1672*
c. 1672–90
Lower left: S. 5 E.; on reverse: Peint par van der Meulen. / Passage du Rhin en 1672, par l'Armee Francaise / sous les ordres de Louis XIV. / C. M.
Oil on canvas
20 1/8 × 76 9/16" (51.1 × 194.5 cm)

Gift of James H. Hyde
1948-27-1

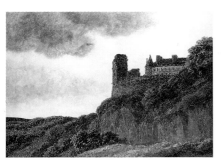

**Michel, Georges**
French, 1763–1843
*Old Château*
c. 1825–43
Lower right (spurious): Eug. Delacroix.
Oil on panel
20 1/4 × 27 7/8" (51.4 × 70.8 cm)

John G. Johnson Collection
cat. 1042

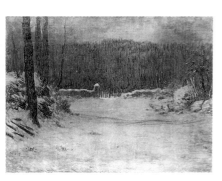

**Millet, Jean-François**
French, 1814–1875
*Solitude*
1853
Lower right: J. F. Millet
Oil on canvas
33 5/8 × 43 1/2" (85.4 × 110.5 cm)

Purchased with the W. P. Wilstach Fund
W1906-1-12

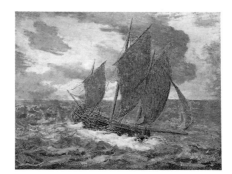

**Millet, Jean-François**
*Bark*
c. 1871
Lower right: J.F. Millet
Oil and crayon on panel
29 × 37" (73.7 × 94 cm)

John G. Johnson Collection
cat. 1047

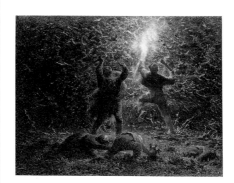

**Millet, Jean-François**
*Bird's-Nesters*
1874
Lower right: J. F. Millet
Oil on canvas
29 × 36 1/2" (73.7 × 92.7 cm)

The William L. Elkins Collection
E1924-3-14

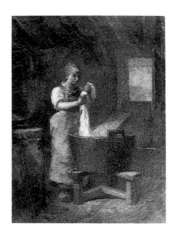

**Millet, Jean-François, imitator of**
Previously listed as Jean-François Millet (JGJ 1941)
*Girl Rinsing Linen*
19th century
Lower right (spurious): J. F. Millet.
Oil on canvas
21 3/8 × 15" (54.3 × 38.1 cm)

John G. Johnson Collection
cat. 1049

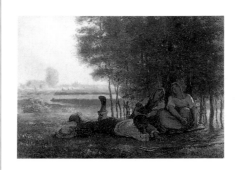

**Millet, Jean-François, imitator of**
Previously listed as Jean-François Millet (JGJ 1941)
*Noonday Rest*
19th century
Lower right (spurious): MILLET
Oil on canvas
10 5/16 × 14 5/8" (26.2 × 37.1 cm)

John G. Johnson Collection
cat. 1043

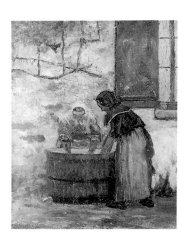

**Millet, Jean-François, imitator of**
*Two Women at a Tub*
19th century
Oil on canvas
14 × 10 3/4" (35.6 × 27.3 cm)

John G. Johnson Collection
cat. 1048

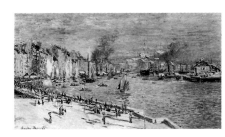

**Monet, Claude**
*Port of Le Havre*
1874
Lower left: Claude Monet
Oil on canvas
23 3/4 × 40 1/8" (60.3 × 101.9 cm)

Bequest of Mrs. Frank Graham
Thomson
1961-48-3

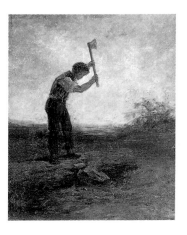

**Millet, Jean-François, imitator of**
Previously listed as Jean-François
Millet (JGJ 1941)
*Woodsman*
19th century
Lower left (spurious): J.F.M.
Oil on canvas
16 5/16 × 12 7/8" (41.4 × 32.7 cm)

John G. Johnson Collection
cat. 1044

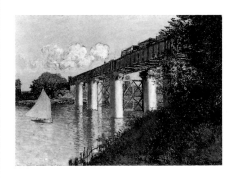

**Monet, Claude**
*Railroad Bridge, Argenteuil*
1874
Lower right: Claude Monet
Oil on canvas
21 3/8 × 28 7/8" (54.3 × 73.3 cm)

John G. Johnson Collection
cat. 1050

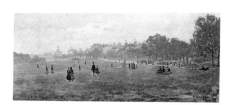

**Monet, Claude**
French, 1840–1926
*Green Park, London*
1870 or 1871
Lower left: Claude Monet
Oil on canvas
13 1/2 × 28 9/16" (34.3 × 72.5 cm)

Purchased with the W. P.
Wilstach Fund
W1921-1-7

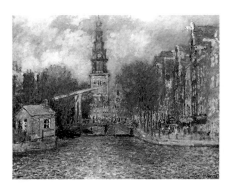

**Monet, Claude**
*The Zuiderkerk, Amsterdam
(Looking up the Groenburgwal)*
c. 1874
Lower right: Claude Monet
Oil on canvas
21 7/16 × 25 3/4" (54.4 × 65.4 cm)

Purchased with the W. P.
Wilstach Fund
W1921-1-6

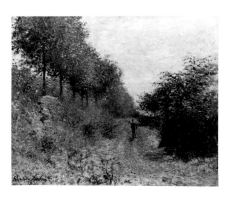

**Monet, Claude**
*The Sheltered Path*
1873
Lower left: Claude Monet / 73
Oil on canvas
21 5/16 × 25 7/8" (54.1 × 65.7 cm)

Gift of Mr. and Mrs. Hughs
Norment in honor of William H.
Donner
1972-227-1

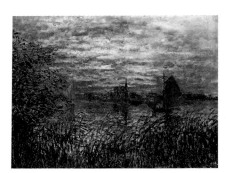

**Monet, Claude**
*Marine View with a Sunset*
c. 1875
Lower left: Claude Monet
Oil on canvas
19 1/2 × 25 5/8" (49.5 × 65.1 cm)

Purchased with the W. P.
Wilstach Fund
W1921-1-5

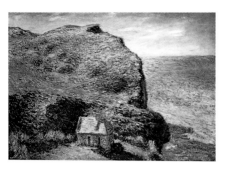

**Monet, Claude**
*Customhouse, Varengeville*
1882
Lower left: Claude Monet 82
Oil on canvas
23 3/4 × 32 1/16" (60.3 × 81.4 cm)

The William L. Elkins Collection
E1924-3-61

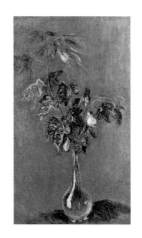

**Monet, Claude**
*Flowers in a Vase*
1888
Lower left: Cl Monet
Oil on canvas
31 1/2 × 17 3/4" (80 × 45.1 cm)

Bequest of Charlotte Dorrance
Wright
1978-1-23

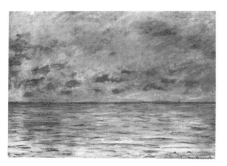

**Monet, Claude**
*Marine near Étretat*
1882
Lower right: Claude Monet
Oil on canvas
21 1/2 × 29 1/16" (54.6 × 73.8 cm)

Bequest of Mrs. Frank Graham
Thomson
1961-48-1

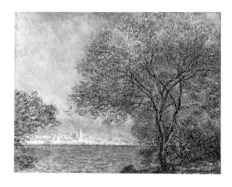

**Monet, Claude**
*Morning at Antibes*
1888
Lower right: Claude Monet 88
Oil on canvas
25 7/8 × 32 5/16" (65.7 × 82.1 cm)

Bequest of Charlotte Dorrance
Wright
1978-1-22

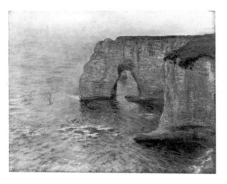

**Monet, Claude**
*Manne-Porte, Étretat*
1885
Lower left: Claude Monet 85
Oil on canvas
25 3/4 × 32" (65.4 × 81.3 cm)

John G. Johnson Collection
cat. 1051

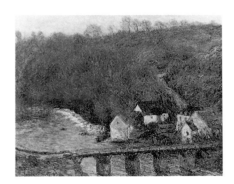

**Monet, Claude**
*The Grande Creuse at Pont de Verry*
1889
Lower left: Claude Monet 89
Oil on canvas
29 1/16 × 36 1/2" (73.8 × 92.7 cm)

The William L. Elkins Collection
E1924-3-32

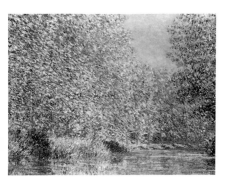

**Monet, Claude**
*Bend in the Epte River near Giverny*
1888
Lower right: Claude Monet 88
Oil on canvas
29 × 36 9/16" (73.7 × 92.9 cm)

The William L. Elkins Collection
E1924-3-16

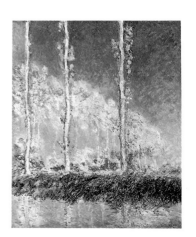

**Monet, Claude**
*Poplars*
1891
Lower right: Claude Monet 91
Oil on canvas
36 5/8 × 29 3/16" (93 × 74.1 cm)

The Chester Dale Collection
1951-109-1

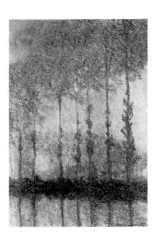

**Monet, Claude**
*Poplars on the Bank of the Epte River*
1891
Lower right: Claude Monet 91
Oil on canvas
39 1/2 × 25 11/16" (100.3 × 65.2 cm)

Bequest of Anne Thomson in memory of her father, Frank Thomson, and her mother, Mary Elizabeth Clarke Thomson
1954-66-8

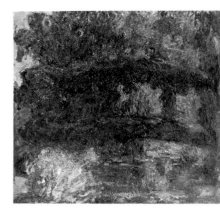

**Monet, Claude**
*Nympheas, Japanese Bridge*
1918–26
Oil on canvas
35 × 36 1/2" (88.9 × 92.7 cm)

The Albert M. Greenfield and Elizabeth M. Greenfield Collection
1974-178-38

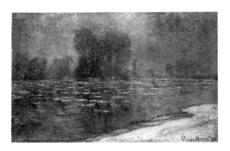

**Monet, Claude**
*Morning Haze*
1894
Lower right: Claude Monet 94
Oil on canvas
25 7/8 × 39 1/2" (65.7 × 100.3 cm)

Bequest of Mrs. Frank Graham Thomson
1961-48-2

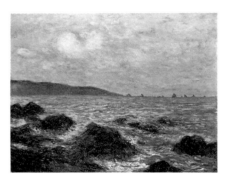

**Monet, Claude, imitator of**
*Coast of Normandy*
19th century
Lower left (spurious): Claude Monet–82
Oil on canvas
25 5/8 × 32 1/8" (65.1 × 81.6 cm)

Gift of Mr. and Mrs. Hughs Norment in honor of William H. Donner
1972-227-2

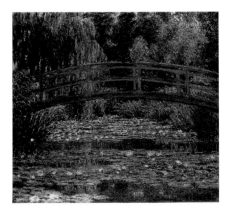

**Monet, Claude**
*The Japanese Footbridge and the Water Lily Pool, Giverny*
1899
Lower right: Claude Monet 99
Oil on canvas
35 1/8 × 36 3/4" (89.2 × 93.3 cm)

The Mr. and Mrs. Carroll S. Tyson, Jr., Collection
1963-116-11

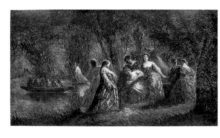

**Monticelli, Adolphe-Joseph-Thomas**
French, 1824–1886
*Boating Party*
1886
Lower right: Monticelli
Oil on panel
18 1/8 × 30 15/16" (46 × 78.6 cm)

Purchased with the W. P. Wilstach Fund
W1897-1-5

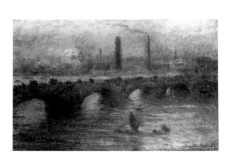

**Monet, Claude**
*Waterloo Bridge, Morning Fog*
1901
Lower right: Claude Monet
Oil on canvas
25 7/8 × 39 7/16" (65.7 × 100.2 cm)

Bequest of Anne Thomson in memory of her father, Frank Thomson, and her mother, Mary Elizabeth Clarke Thomson
1954-66-6

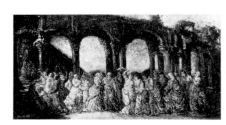

**Monticelli, Adolphe-Joseph-Thomas**
*Masque*
Late 19th century
Lower left: Monticelli
Oil on panel
15 1/4 × 29 5/16" (38.7 × 74.4 cm)

John G. Johnson Collection
cat. 1052

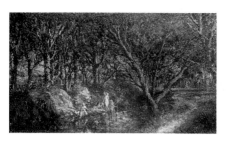

**Monticelli, Adolphe-Joseph-Thomas**
*Nymphs Bathing*
Late 19th century
Lower right: Monticelli
Oil on panel
23 ¹/₈ × 38 ⁷/₁₆" (58.7 × 97.6 cm)

John G. Johnson Collection
cat. 1053

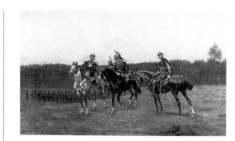

**Neuville, Alphonse-Marie de**
French, 1835–1885
*Orders from Headquarters*
c. 1880
Lower right: A. de Neuville
Oil on canvas
42 × 67 ¹/₂" (106.7 × 171.4 cm)

The William L. Elkins Collection
E1924-3-73

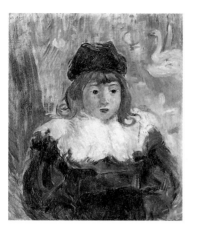

**Morisot, Berthe-Marie-Pauline**
French, 1841–1895
*Portrait of a Child*
1894
Upper left: Berthe Morisot
Oil on canvas
21 ³/₄ × 18 ¹/₄" (55.2 × 46.3 cm)

Bequest of Lisa Norris Elkins
1950-92-10

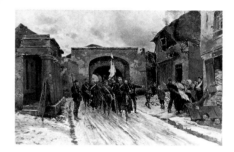

**Neuville, Alphonse-Marie de**
*The Surrender*
c. 1884
Lower left: A. Neuville
Oil on canvas
55 ³/₄ × 82 ³/₄" (141.6 × 210.2 cm)

The William L. Elkins Collection
E1924-3-34

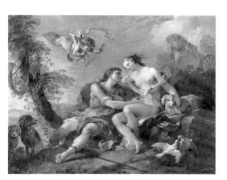

**Natoire, Charles-Joseph**
French, 1700–1777
*Venus and Adonis*
c. 1740
Oil on canvas
37 ³/₈ × 46 ⁷/₈" (94.9 × 119.1 cm)

Gift of the Friends of the
Philadelphia Museum of Art
1989-3-2

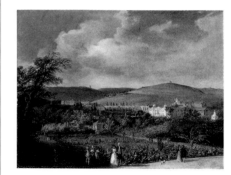

**Noël, Alexandre-Jean**
French, 1752–1834
*Quinta of Gerard de Visme, near Lisbon*
Pendant to the following painting
c. 1785
Oil on canvas
33 ¹¹/₁₆ × 42 ¹/₁₆" (85.6 × 106.8 cm)

Gift of John Howard McFadden, Jr.
1946-36-5

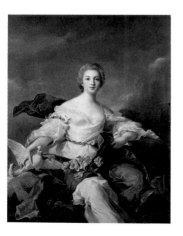

**Nattier, Jean-Marc, studio of**
French, 1685–1766
*Portrait of the Marchioness of Baglion*
Mid-18th century
Oil on canvas
59 × 46" (149.9 × 116.8 cm)

Gift of Mrs. Gordon A. Hardwick
and Mrs. W. Newbold Ely in
memory of Mr. and Mrs.
Roland L. Taylor
1944-9-3

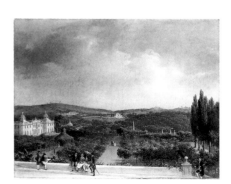

**Noël, Alexandre-Jean**
*Quinta of Gerard de Visme, near Lisbon*
Pendant to the preceding painting
c. 1785
Oil on canvas
33 × 42" (83.8 × 106.7 cm)

Gift of John Howard McFadden, Jr.
1946-36-6

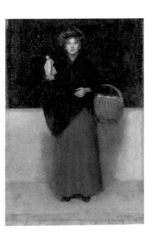

**Picard, Louis**
French, born 1861, still active
1900
*Vendor of Statuettes*
c. 1900
Lower right: LOUIS PICARD
Oil on canvas
21 ⅝ × 13 ⅞" (54.9 × 35.2 cm)

The Walter Lippincott Collection
1923-59-6

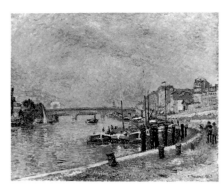

**Pissarro, Camille**
French, 1830–1903
*Quai Napoléon, Rouen*
1883
Lower right: C. Pissarro. 1883
Oil on canvas
21 ⅜ × 25 ⅜" (54.3 × 64.4 cm)

Bequest of Charlotte Dorrance
Wright
1978-1-25

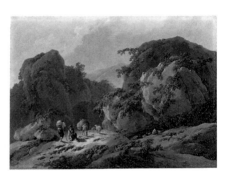

**Pillement, Jean**
French, 1728–1808
*Landscape*
1793
Lower left: Jean Pillement / 1793
Oil on canvas
16 ⅛ × 21 ⅜" (41 × 54.3 cm)

Gift of Mrs. Morris Hawkes
1945-13-59

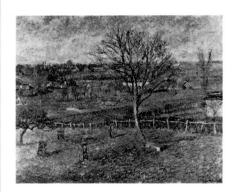

**Pissarro, Camille**
*The Field and the Great Walnut
Tree in Winter, Eragny*
1885
Lower right: C. Pissarro. 1885
Oil on canvas
23 ⅝ × 28 ⅞" (60 × 73.3 cm)

Purchased with the W. P.
Wilstach Fund
W1921-1-9

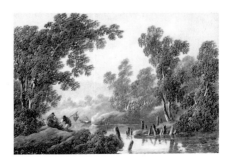

**Pillement, Jean**
*Landscape*
1794
Lower left: J. P. 1794 v
Oil on canvas
6 3/16 × 8 ⅛" (15.7 × 20.6 cm)

Gift of Mrs. Morris Hawkes
1945-13-57

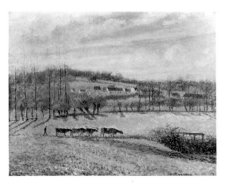

**Pissarro, Camille**
*Summer Landscape, Eragny*
1887 and 1902
Lower right: C. Pissarro. 87 1902
Oil on canvas
22 × 26" (55.9 × 66 cm)

Gift of Mrs. William I. Mirkil
1961-150-1

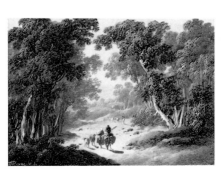

**Pillement, Jean**
*Landscape*
1794
Lower left: J. P. 1794 vs
Oil on canvas
6 3/16 × 8 1/16" (15.7 × 20.5 cm)

Gift of Mrs. Morris Hawkes
1945-13-58

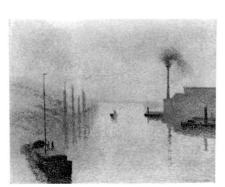

**Pissarro, Camille**
*L'Île Lacroix, Rouen
(The Effect of Fog)*
1888
Lower right: C. Pissarro 1888
Oil on canvas
18 ⅜ × 22" (46.7 × 55.9 cm)

John G. Johnson Collection
cat. 1060

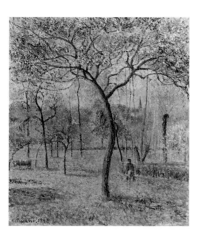

**Pissarro, Camille**
*Landscape (Orchard)*
1892
Lower left: C. Pissarro. 1892
Oil on canvas
25 5/8 × 21 3/8" (65.1 × 54.3 cm)

Purchased with the W. P.
Wilstach Fund
W1921-1-8

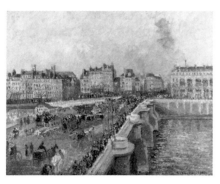

**Pissarro, Camille**
*Afternoon Sunshine, Pont Neuf*
1901
Lower right: C. Pissarro. 1901
Oil on canvas
28 3/4 × 36 1/4" (73 × 92.1 cm)

Bequest of Charlotte Dorrance
Wright
1978-1-24

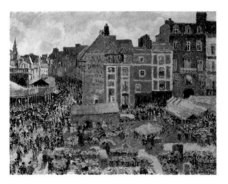

**Pissarro, Camille**
*Fair on a Sunny Afternoon, Dieppe*
1901
Lower right: C. Pissarro. 1901
Oil on canvas
28 15/16 × 36 1/4" (73.5 × 92.1 cm)

Bequest of Lisa Norris Elkins
1950-92-12

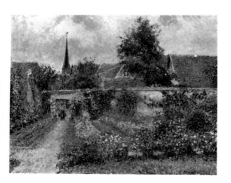

**Pissarro, Camille**
*Vegetable Garden, Overcast
Morning, Eragny*
1901
Lower right: C. Pissarro. 1901
Oil on canvas
25 1/2 × 32" (64.8 × 81.3 cm)

Bequest of Charlotte Dorrance
Wright
1978-1-26

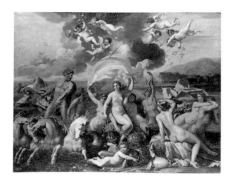

**Poussin, Nicolas**
French, 1594–1665
*The Birth of Venus*
1635 or 1636
Lower left: 1697
Oil on canvas
38 1/4 × 42 1/2" (97.1 × 107.9 cm)

The George W. Elkins Collection
E1932-1-1

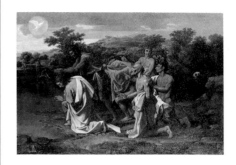

**Poussin, Nicolas**
*The Baptism of Christ*
c. 1658
Oil on canvas
37 7/8 × 53 3/8" (96.2 × 135.6 cm)

John G. Johnson Collection
cat. 773

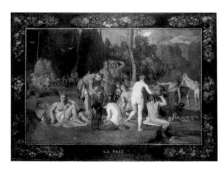

**Puvis de Chavannes, Pierre**
French, 1824–1898
*Peace*
Reduced version of the 1861
painting in the Musée de
Picardie, Amiens; companion to
the following painting and the
paintings *Work* and *Rest*, in the
National Gallery of Art,
Washington, D.C.
1867
Lower left: P. PUVIS DE
CHAVANNES; center bottom: LA
PAIX
Oil on canvas
42 7/8 × 58 1/2" (108.9 × 148.6 cm)

John G. Johnson Collection
cat. 1062

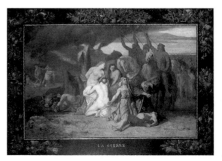

**Puvis de Chavannes, Pierre**
*War*
Reduced version of the 1861
painting in the Musée de
Picardie, Amiens; companion to
the preceding painting and the
paintings *Work* and *Rest*, in the
National Gallery of Art,
Washington, D.C.
1867
Lower left: P. PUVIS DE
CHAVANNES; center bottom: LA
GUERRE
Oil on canvas
43 1/8 × 58 3/4" (109.5 × 149.2 cm)

John G. Johnson Collection
cat. 1063

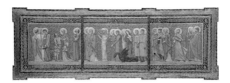

**Puvis de Chavannes, Pierre**
*Legendary Saints of France*
Reduced version of the frieze above
*The Childhood of Saint Geneviève*, in
the church of Saint Geneviève
[The Panthéon], Paris
c. 1879
Oil on canvas
Left canvas: 30 ¼ × 32 ½"
(76.8 × 82.5 cm); center canvas:
30 ¼ × 35" (76.8 × 88.9 cm);
right canvas: 30 ¼ × 32"
(76.8 × 81.3 cm)

Gift of Dr. and Mrs. Richard W.
Levy
1969-167-1

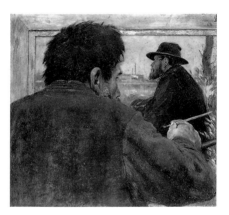

**Raffaëlli, Jean-François**
French, 1850–1924
*Artist Painting*
c. 1879
Lower right: J. F. RAFFAELLI
Oil on panel
20 ½ × 20 ⅞" (52.1 × 53 cm)

John G. Johnson Collection
cat. 1065

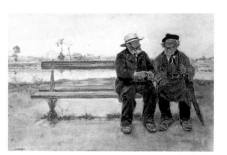

**Raffaëlli, Jean-François**
*Comrades*
1881–83
Lower right: J. F. RAFFAELLI
Oil on paper on panel
15 ⁷⁄₁₆ × 22" (39.2 × 55.9 cm)

John G. Johnson Collection
cat. 1066

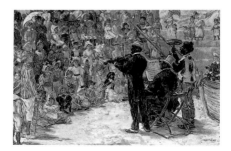

**Raffaëlli, Jean-François**
*The Minstrels*
1887
Lower left: JF RAFFAELLI
Oil on panel
15 ⅞ × 22 ¹⁵⁄₁₆" (40.3 × 58.3 cm)

Gift of Mrs. Francis P. Garvan
1977-257-1

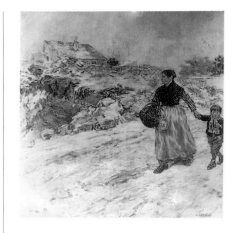

**Raffaëlli, Jean-François**
*Midday, Effect of Frost*
1888
Lower right: J F RAFFAELLI
Oil on canvas
50 ¼ × 45 ¹⁵⁄₁₆" (127.6 ×
116.7 cm)

John G. Johnson Collection
cat. 1064

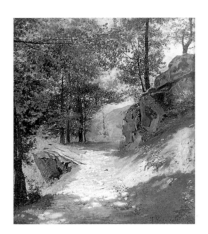

**Regnault, Henri-Georges-
Alexandre**
French, 1843–1871
*The Pyrenees*
c. 1868
Lower right: H. Regnault
Oil on canvas on gypsum board
26 ½ × 21 ¹³⁄₁₆" (67.3 × 55.4 cm)

John G. Johnson Collection
cat. 1067

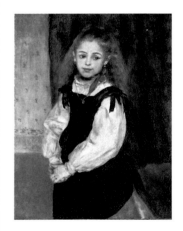

**Renoir, Pierre-Auguste**
French, 1841–1919
*Portrait of Mademoiselle Legrand*
1875
Lower right: Renoir. 75
Oil on canvas
32 × 23 ½" (81.3 × 59.7 cm)

The Henry P. McIlhenny
Collection in memory of
Frances P. McIlhenny
1986-26-28

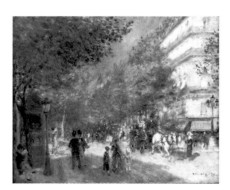

**Renoir, Pierre-Auguste**
*The Grands Boulevards*
1875
Lower right: Renoir. 75
Oil on canvas
20 ½ × 25" (52.1 × 63.5 cm)

The Henry P. McIlhenny
Collection in memory of
Frances P. McIlhenny
1986-26-29

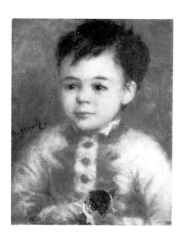

**Renoir, Pierre-Auguste**
*Boy with a Toy Soldier (Portrait of Jean de La Pommeraye)*
c. 1875
Center left: A. Renoir
Oil on canvas
13 ¹⁵/₁₆ × 10 ⁵/₈" (35.4 × 27 cm)

The Mr. and Mrs. Carroll S.
Tyson, Jr., Collection
1963-116-14

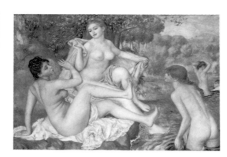

**Renoir, Pierre-Auguste**
*The Great Bathers*
1884–87
Lower left: Renoir. 87.
Oil on canvas
46 ³/₈ × 67 ¹/₄" (117.8 × 170.8 cm)

The Mr. and Mrs. Carroll S.
Tyson, Jr., Collection
1963-116-13

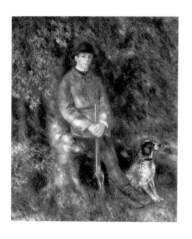

**Renoir, Pierre-Auguste**
*Portrait of Alfred Bérard with His Dog*
1881
Lower left: Renoir. 81.
Oil on canvas
25 ¹¹/₁₆ × 20 ¹/₈" (65.2 × 51.1 cm)

The Mr. and Mrs. Carroll S.
Tyson, Jr., Collection
1963-116-17

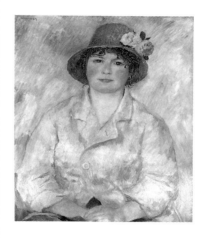

**Renoir, Pierre-Auguste**
*Portrait of Madame Renoir*
c. 1885
Upper left: Renoir
Oil on canvas
25 ³/₄ × 21 ¹/₄" (65.4 × 54 cm)

Purchased with the W. P.
Wilstach Fund
W1957-1-1

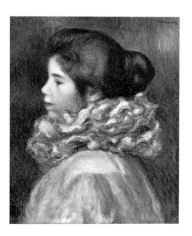

**Renoir, Pierre-Auguste**
*Girl in a Red Ruff*
1884
Upper right: Renoir.
Oil on canvas
16 ¹/₄ × 13 ¹/₈" (41.3 × 33.3 cm)

Bequest of Charlotte Dorrance
Wright
1978-1-28

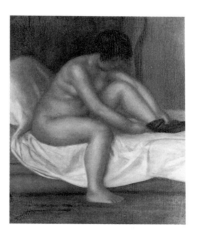

**Renoir, Pierre-Auguste**
*Nude*
1888
Lower right: Renoir.
Oil on canvas
22 × 18 ¹/₄" (55.9 × 46.3 cm)

The Louis E. Stern Collection
1963-181-58

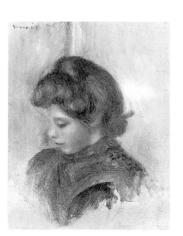

**Renoir, Pierre-Auguste**
*Girl in a Red Scarf*
c. 1884
Upper left: Renoir
Oil on canvas
10 ¹/₄ × 8" (26 × 20.3 cm)

Bequest of Charlotte Dorrance
Wright
1978-1-27

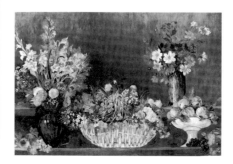

**Renoir, Pierre-Auguste**
*Still Life with Flowers and Fruit*
c. 1890
Lower right: Renoir
Oil on canvas
52 ¹/₂ × 68 ⁷/₈" (133.3 × 174.9 cm)

The Mr. and Mrs. Carroll S.
Tyson, Jr., Collection
1963-116-16

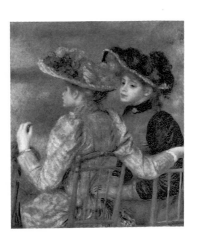

**Renoir, Pierre-Auguste**
*Two Girls*
c. 1892
Lower right: Renoir
Oil on canvas
32 1/4 × 25 13/16" (81.9 × 65.6 cm)

The Mr. and Mrs. Carroll S. Tyson, Jr., Collection
1963-116-15

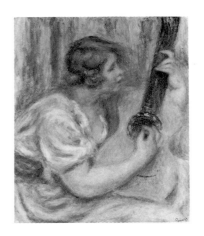

**Renoir, Pierre-Auguste**
*Woman with a Guitar*
c. 1918
Lower right: Renoir.
Oil on canvas
24 3/16 × 19 3/4" (61.4 × 50.2 cm)

Gift of Mr. and Mrs. J. Mahlon Buck
1959-83-1

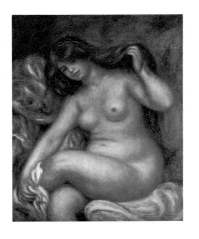

**Renoir, Pierre-Auguste**
*Large Bather*
1905
Lower right: Renoir. 05.
Oil on canvas
38 1/4 × 28 3/4" (97.1 × 73 cm)

Gift of Mr. and Mrs. Rodolphe Meyer de Schauensee
1978-9-1

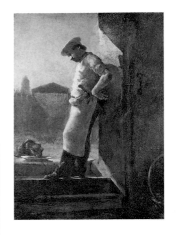

**Ribot, Théodule**
French, 1823–1891
*Poultry Yard*
1861
Lower left: T Ribot 1861
Oil on canvas
18 × 12 3/4" (45.7 × 32.4 cm)

John G. Johnson Collection
cat. 1069

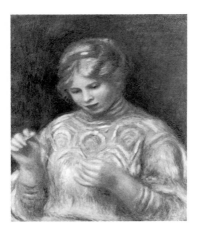

**Renoir, Pierre-Auguste**
*Girl Tatting*
1906–8
Upper right: Renoir.
Oil on canvas
22 1/4 × 18 3/8" (56.5 × 46.7 cm)

The Louis E. Stern Collection
1963-181-59

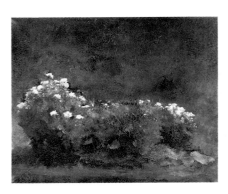

**Ribot, Théodule**
*Chrysanthemums*
Late 19th century
Lower left: T. Ribot.
Oil on canvas
15 × 18" (38.1 × 45.7 cm)

John G. Johnson Collection
cat. 1068

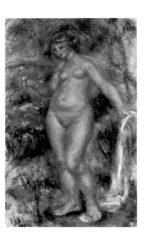

**Renoir, Pierre-Auguste**
*Bather*
c. 1917
Lower left: Renoir.
Oil on canvas
20 3/4 × 13" (52.7 × 33 cm)

The Louise and Walter Arensberg Collection
1950-134-173

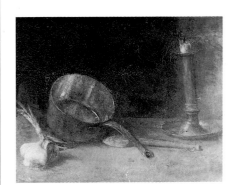

**Ricard, Louis-Gustave**
French, 1823–1873
*Still Life*
19th century
Lower right: GR
Oil on panel
14 11/16 × 18 1/16" (37.3 × 45.9 cm)

John G. Johnson Collection
cat. 1070

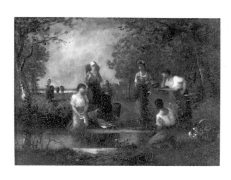

**Richet, Léon**
French, 1847–1907
*The Spring*
1882
Lower left: Leon Richet 1882
Oil on panel
9 1/4 × 13 3/4" (23.5 × 34.9 cm)

The Walter Lippincott Collection
1923-59-7

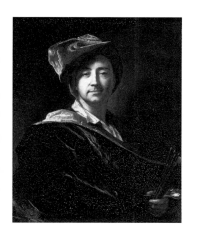

**Rigaud, Hyacinthe,
copy after**
French, 1659–1743
Previously listed as Hyacinthe
Rigaud (JGJ 1941)
*Portrait of Hyacinthe Rigaud*
Known in many versions; the
finest is in the Musée Hyacinthe
Rigaud, Perpignan (inv. D.53.1.1)
18th century
Oil on canvas
31 7/8 × 25 3/4" (81 × 65.4 cm)

John G. Johnson Collection
cat. 777

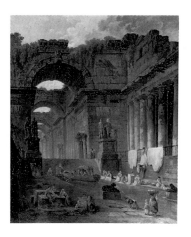

**Robert, Hubert**
French, 1733–1808
*Ruins of a Roman Bath with
Washerwomen*
After 1766
Oil on canvas
54 × 41 1/2" (137.2 × 105.4 cm)

Gift of Dora Donner Ide in
memory of John Jay Ide
1961-215-1

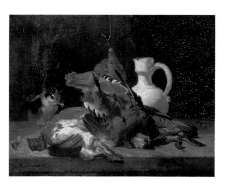

**Rousseau, Philippe**
French, 1816–1887
*Still Life*
1857
Lower left: Ph. Rousseau. 57.
Oil on canvas
19 1/4 × 23 1/2" (48.9 × 59.7 cm)

John G. Johnson Collection
cat. 1077

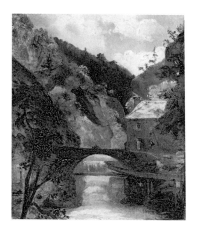

**Rousseau, Pierre-Étienne-
Théodore**
French, 1812–1867
*Water Mill, Thiers*
c. 1830
Lower left: ThR
Oil on canvas
15 7/8 × 12 5/8" (40.3 × 32.1 cm)

Gift of John T. Dorrance
1965-85-2

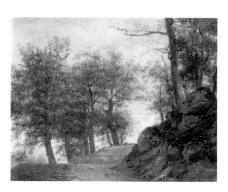

**Rousseau, Pierre-Étienne-
Théodore**
*Mountain Path*
1831
Lower right: T. R. Oct re / 1831.
Oil on canvas
15 × 18 3/16" (38.1 × 46.2 cm)

John G. Johnson Collection
cat. 1075

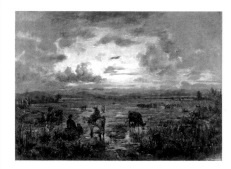

**Rousseau, Pierre-Étienne-
Théodore**
*Landscape with Cattle*
c. 1860
Lower right: T. H. Rousseau
Oil on canvas
35 1/4 × 46" (89.5 × 116.8 cm)

The William L. Elkins Collection
E1924-3-36

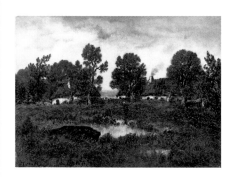

**Rousseau, Pierre-Étienne-
Théodore**
*Landscape*
Mid-19th century
Lower left: Th. Rousseau
Oil on panel
6 1/2 × 8 1/2" (16.5 × 21.6 cm)

John G. Johnson Collection
cat. 1074

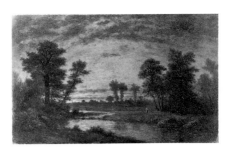

**Rousseau, Pierre-Étienne-Théodore**
*Sunset*
Mid-19th century
Oil on panel
11 × 17 ⅛" (27.9 × 43.5 cm)

John G. Johnson Collection
cat. 1072

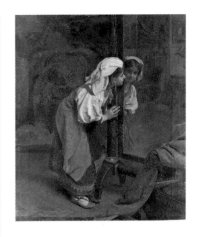

**Schlesinger, Henri-Guillaume**
French, born Germany,
1814–1893
*Alone at the Atelier*
1868
Lower right: H. Schlesinger. 1868
Oil on canvas
36 ½ × 29" (92.7 × 73.7 cm)

The W. P. Wilstach Collection,
bequest of Anna H. Wilstach
W1893-1-93

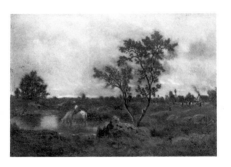

**Rousseau, Pierre-Étienne-Théodore, attributed to**
Previously listed as Pierre-Étienne-Théodore Rousseau
(JGJ 1941)
*Evening Landscape*
19th century
Lower right: Th. Rousseau
Oil on panel
6 ¹¹⁄₁₆ × 9" (17 × 22.9 cm)

John G. Johnson Collection
cat. 1073

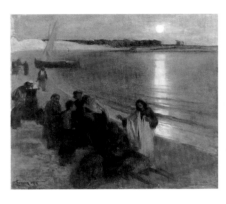

**Simon, Lucien**
French, 1861–1945
*Christ Performing Miracles*
1894
Lower left: LSimon 1894
Oil on canvas
48 ¼ × 55" (122.5 × 139.7 cm)

John G. Johnson Collection
cat. 1081

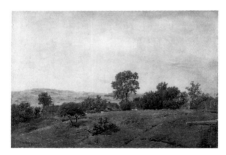

**Rousseau, Pierre-Étienne-Théodore, attributed to**
*Outskirts of a Village*
19th century
Lower left: Th. Rousseau
Oil on paper on canvas
9 ⅜ × 15 ⅜" (23.8 × 39 cm)

John G. Johnson Collection
cat. 1071

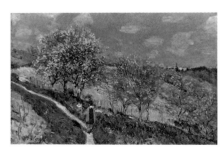

**Sisley, Alfred**
French, 1839–1899
*Landscape (Spring at Bougival)*
c. 1873
Lower left: Sisley.
Oil on canvas
16 × 22 ½" (40.6 × 57.1 cm)

Bequest of Charlotte Dorrance
Wright
1978-1-31

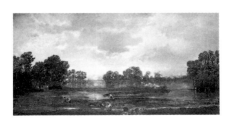

**Rousseau, Pierre-Étienne-Théodore, follower of**
*On the Seine*
19th century
Lower left (spurious): Th. R
Oil on panel
15 ¹⁵⁄₁₆ × 30 ¾" (40.5 × 78.1 cm)

John G. Johnson Collection
cat. 1076

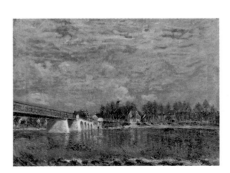

**Sisley, Alfred**
*The Bridge at Saint-Mammes*
1881
Lower right: Sisley.
Oil on canvas
21 ½ × 28 ¹³⁄₁₆" (54.6 × 73.2 cm)

John G. Johnson Collection
cat. 1082

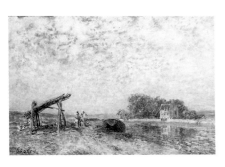

**Sisley, Alfred**
*The Loing River at Saint-Mammes*
1884
Lower left: Sisley.
Oil on canvas
15 × 21 3/4" (38.1 × 55.2 cm)

Bequest of Anne Thomson in
memory of her father, Frank
Thomson, and her mother, Mary
Elizabeth Clarke Thomson
1954-66-9

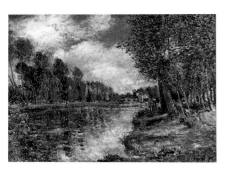

**Sisley, Alfred**
*Banks of the Loing River*
1885
Lower right: Sisley.85
Oil on canvas
21 11/16 × 28 7/8" (55.1 × 73.3 cm)

Bequest of Charlotte Dorrance
Wright
1978-1-30

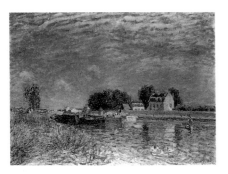

**Sisley, Alfred**
*The Canal at Saint-Mammes*
1885
Lower right: Sisley.85
Oil on canvas
21 3/4 × 29" (55.2 × 73.7 cm)

The Mr. and Mrs. Carroll S.
Tyson, Jr., Collection
1963-116-18

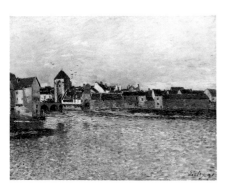

**Sisley, Alfred**
*Bridge at Morny*
1891
Lower right: Sisley 91
Oil on canvas
23 1/2 × 28 1/2" (59.7 × 72.4 cm)

Bequest of Charlotte Dorrance
Wright
1978-1-29

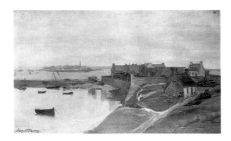

**Stevens, Léopold**
French, 1866–1935
*Coastal Village*
c. 1900
Lower left: .Léopold Stevens.
Oil on canvas
15 × 24" (38.1 × 61 cm)

John G. Johnson Collection
cat. 1084

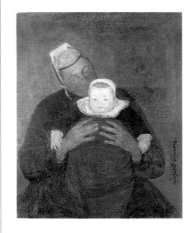

**Stevens, Léopold**
*Mother and Baby*
c. 1900
Lower right: Léopold Stevens.
Oil on canvas
25 5/8 × 19 3/4" (65.1 × 50.2 cm)

John G. Johnson Collection
cat. 1085

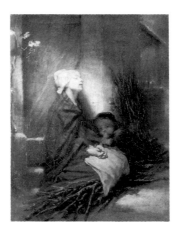

**Tassaert, Octave**
French, 1800–1874
*Poor Children (The Forlorn)*
1855
Lower right: Oct. Tassaert / 1855
Oil on canvas
12 7/8 × 9 3/4" (32.7 × 24.8 cm)

John G. Johnson Collection
cat. 1090

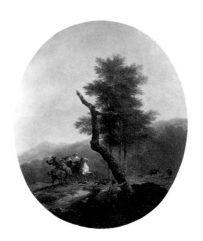

**Taunay, Nicolas-Antoine**
French, 1755–1830
*Landscape with Horsemen*
Companion to the following
painting
Late 18th century
Oil on canvas
21 3/4 × 17 1/2" (55.2 × 44.4 cm)

Gift of Mrs. Van Horn Ely
1971-169-1

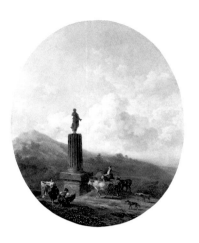

**Taunay, Nicolas-Antoine**
*Landscape with a Ruin and Peasants*
Companion to the preceding
painting
Late 18th century
Oil on canvas
21 7/8 × 17 1/2" (55.6 × 44.4 cm)

Gift of Mrs. Van Horn Ely
1971-169-2

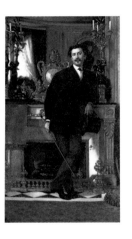

**Tissot, James-Jacques-
Joseph**
French, 1836–1902
*Portrait of Eugène Coppens de
Fontenay*
1867
Lower right: JJ. Tissot / AVRIL
1867
Oil on canvas
27 1/2 × 15 3/8" (69.8 × 39 cm)

Purchased with the W. P.
Wilstach Fund
W1972-2-1

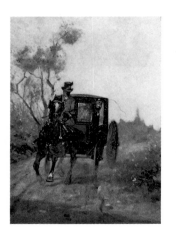

**Toulouse-Lautrec, Henri de**
French, 1864–1901
*Carriage*
c. 1881
Oil on panel
12 3/4 × 9 3/8" (32.4 × 23.8 cm)

Bequest of Charlotte Dorrance
Wright
1978-1-32

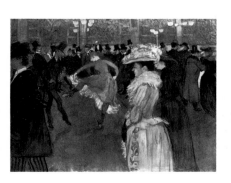

**Toulouse-Lautrec, Henri de**
*At the Moulin Rouge: The Dance*
1890
Upper right: HTLautrec 90
Oil on canvas
45 1/2 × 59" (115.6 × 149.9 cm)

The Henry P. McIlhenny
Collection in memory of
Frances P. McIlhenny
1986-26-32

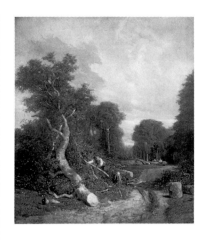

**Troyon, Constant**
French, 1810–1865
*Forest Clearing*
1846?
Lower left: C. TROYON
Oil on canvas
25 9/16 × 21 1/8" (64.9 × 53.7 cm)

John G. Johnson Collection
cat. 1095

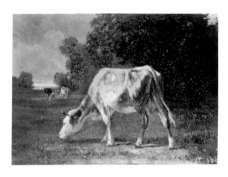

**Troyon, Constant**
*Cows Grazing*
1856
Lower left: C. TROYON. 1856
Oil on canvas
23 9/16 × 32 1/8" (59.8 × 81.6 cm)

John G. Johnson Collection
cat. 1094

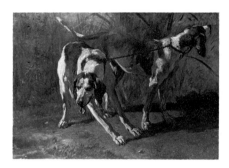

**Troyon, Constant**
*Leashed Hounds*
c. 1860
Lower left: C. TROYON.; lower
right: VENTE / TROYON
Oil on canvas
38 7/8 × 51 1/2" (98.7 × 130.8 cm)

John G. Johnson Collection
cat. 1102

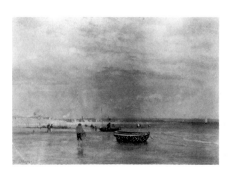

**Troyon, Constant**
*Le Tréport*
1860–62
Lower left: C. TROYON
Oil on panel
10 3/4 × 15" (27.3 × 38.1 cm)

John G. Johnson Collection
cat. 1096

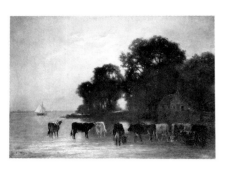

**Troyon, Constant**
*Moerdijk, Holland*
1861
Lower left: C. TROYON. 1861.
Oil on canvas
$36^5/_8 \times 51^7/_{16}$" (93 × 130.6 cm)

The William L. Elkins Collection
E1924-3-22

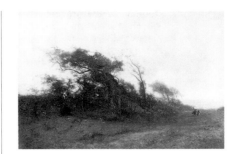

**Troyon, Constant,
attributed to**
Previously listed as Constant
Troyon (JGJ 1941)
*Landscape*
19th century
Oil on canvas
$31^1/_2 \times 46^1/_8$" (80 × 117.2 cm)

John G. Johnson Collection
cat. 1099

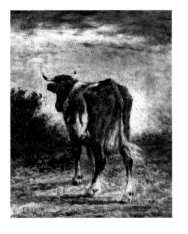

**Troyon, Constant**
*Going to Market*
Mid-19th century
Lower left: C. TROYON
Oil on canvas
$24^3/_4 \times 36^3/_8$" (62.9 × 92.4 cm)

John G. Johnson Collection
cat. 1100

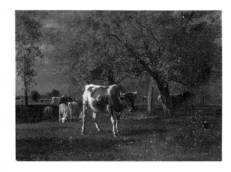

**Troyon, Constant,
attributed to**
Previously listed as Constant
Troyon (PMA 1965)
*Landscape with Cattle and Sheep*
19th century
Lower left: C. TROYON
Oil on canvas
$38^1/_2 \times 51$" (97.8 × 129.5 cm)

The George W. Elkins Collection
E1924-4-29

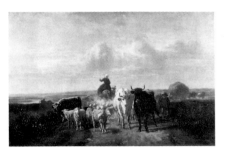

**Troyon, Constant,
attributed to**
*Cow*
19th century
Lower left: C. TROYON
Oil on canvas
$14^1/_2 \times 11^1/_4$" (36.8 × 28.6 cm)

John G. Johnson Collection
cat. 1097

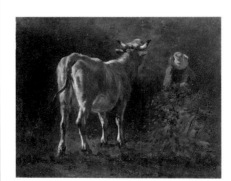

**Troyon, Constant,
attributed to**
Previously listed as Constant
Troyon (PMA 1965)
*Landscape with a Cow and a Figure*
19th century
Lower left: C. TROYON
Oil on panel
$14^3/_4 \times 18^1/_8$" (37.5 × 46 cm)

The George W. Elkins Collection
E1924-4-30

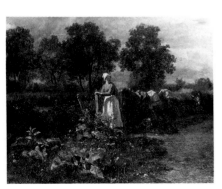

**Troyon, Constant,
attributed to**
Previously listed as Constant
Troyon (JGJ 1941)
*The Garden Gate*
19th century
Lower left: VENTE / TROYON
Oil on canvas
$21^1/_2 \times 25^3/_4$" (54.6 × 65.4 cm)

John G. Johnson Collection
cat. 1098

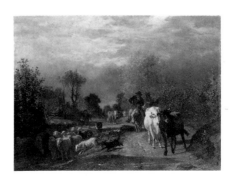

**Troyon, Constant,
attributed to**
Previously listed as Constant
Troyon (PMA 1965)
*Return from the Market*
19th century
Lower left: C. TROYON
Oil on canvas
$28^1/_8 \times 36^1/_4$" (71.4 × 92.1 cm)

The George W. Elkins Collection
E1924-4-31

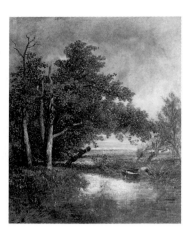

**Troyon, Constant, attributed to**
Previously listed as Constant Troyon (JGJ 1941)
*Stream*
19th century
Lower right: C. TROYON.
Oil on canvas
32 × 25 5/8" (81.3 × 65.1 cm)

John G. Johnson Collection
cat. 1093

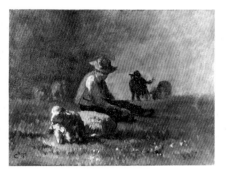

**Troyon, Constant, imitator of**
Previously listed as Constant Troyon (JGJ 1941)
*Man with Sheep*
19th century
Lower left: C T
Oil on canvas
10 5/8 × 13 15/16" (27 × 35.4 cm)

John G. Johnson Collection
cat. 1101

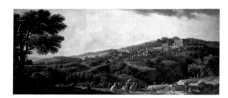

**Vernet, Claude-Joseph**
French, 1714–1789
*Villa at Caprarola*
1746
Lower left: Joseph Vernet fecit Romae / 1746
Oil on canvas
52 3/16 × 121 13/16" (132.6 × 309.4 cm)

Purchased with the Edith H. Bell Fund
1977-79-1

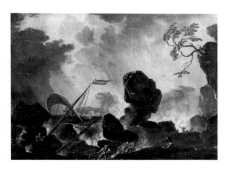

**Vernet, Claude-Joseph, imitator of**
*Coast Scene*
18th century
Oil on canvas
28 3/8 × 38 3/4" (72.1 × 98.4 cm)

The Bloomfield Moore Collection
1883-102

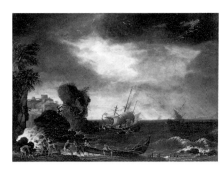

**Vernet, Claude-Joseph, imitator of**
*Coast Scene with a Storm*
18th century
Oil on canvas
39 1/16 × 53" (99.2 × 134.6 cm)

The Bloomfield Moore Collection
1883-83

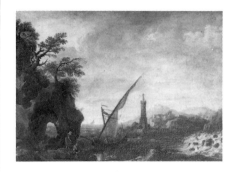

**Vernet, Claude-Joseph, imitator of**
*Marine*
18th century
Oil on canvas
29 3/8 × 38 3/4" (74.6 × 98.4 cm)

The Bloomfield Moore Collection
1883-112

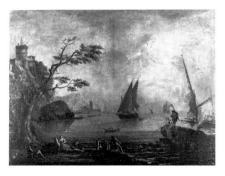

**Vernet, Claude-Joseph, imitator of**
*Marine*
18th century
Oil on canvas
29 5/16 × 38 1/8" (74.4 × 96.8 cm)

The Bloomfield Moore Collection
1883-113

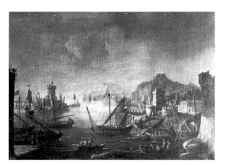

**Vernet, Claude-Joseph, imitator of**
*Marine*
18th century
Oil on canvas
29 3/8 × 38 5/8" (74.6 × 98.1 cm)

The Bloomfield Moore Collection
1883-114

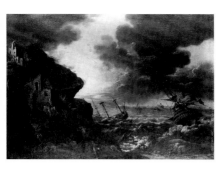

**Vernet, Claude-Joseph, imitator of**
*Shipwreck on a Coast*
Late 18th century
Oil on canvas
38 13/16 × 53 9/16" (98.6 × 136 cm)

The Bloomfield Moore Collection
1883-85

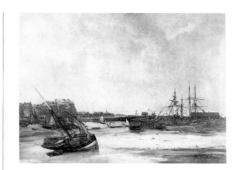

**Vollon, Antoine**
*Le Tréport*
c. 1886
Lower right: A. Vollon
Oil on panel
20 1/4 × 27 3/16" (51.4 × 69.1 cm)

John G. Johnson Collection
cat. 1105

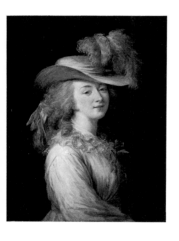

**Vigée-Lebrun, Louise-Elisabeth**
French, 1755–1842
*Portrait of Madame Du Barry*
1781
Oil on panel
27 1/4 × 20 1/4" (69.2 × 51.4 cm)

Gift of Mrs. Thomas T. Fleming
1984-137-1

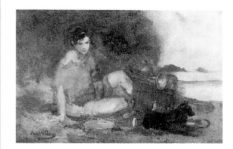

**Vollon, Antoine**
*Musician*
By 1887
Lower left: A. Vollon
Oil on canvas
9 1/2 × 14 1/8" (24.1 × 35.9 cm)

John G. Johnson Collection
cat. 1104

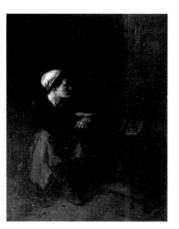

**Vollon, Antoine**
French, 1833–1900
*Woman at a Spinning Wheel*
1867
Lower right: A. Vollon
Oil on canvas
67 1/8 × 51 5/8" (170.5 × 131.1 cm)

John G. Johnson Collection
cat. 1107

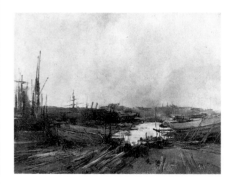

**Vollon, Antoine**
*Dunkirk*
By 1892
Lower right: A. Vollon
Oil on canvas
17 × 21 1/4" (43.2 × 54 cm)

John G. Johnson Collection
cat. 1109

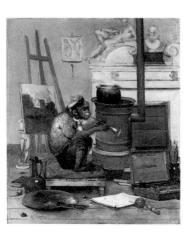

**Vollon, Antoine**
*Monkey in a Studio*
1869
Lower left: A. Vollon
Oil on panel
18 1/8 × 14 5/8" (46 × 37.1 cm)

John G. Johnson Collection
cat. 1108

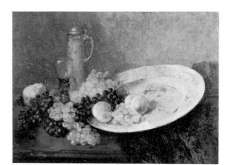

**Vollon, Antoine**
*Still Life*
By 1892
Lower left: A. Vollon
Oil on canvas
23 1/4 × 30 7/8" (59 × 78.4 cm)

John G. Johnson Collection
cat. 1106

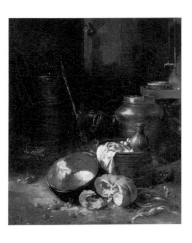

**Vollon, Antoine**
*Still Life*
Late 19th century
Lower left: A. Vollon
Oil on canvas
25 7/8 × 21 1/2" (65.7 × 54.6 cm)

The William L. Elkins Collection
E1924-3-64

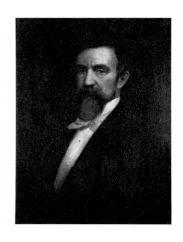

**Weisz, Adolphe**
French, born Hungary,
1819–1878
*Portrait of Bloomfield H. Moore*
Companion to the following
painting
1877
Oil on canvas
28 3/4 × 20 5/8" (73 × 52.4 cm)

The Bloomfield Moore Collection
1882-210

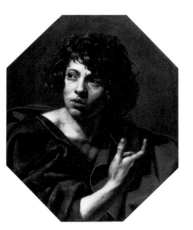

**Vouet, Simon**
French, 1590–1649
*Saint John*
c. 1622–25
Oil on canvas
29 × 23" (73.7 × 58.4 cm)

Purchased with the Henry P.
McIlhenny Fund in memory of
Frances P. McIlhenny, the
Edward and Althea Budd Fund,
the Edith H. Bell Fund, and
bequest (by exchange) of Lisa
Norris Elkins
1987-73-1

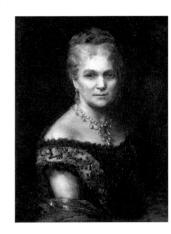

**Weisz, Adolphe**
*Portrait of Mrs. Bloomfield Moore*
Companion to the preceding
painting
1877
Lower left: A. Weisz
Oil on canvas
29 × 20 3/4" (73.7 × 52.7 cm)

The Bloomfield Moore Collection
1899-1099

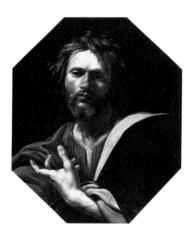

**Vouet, Simon**
*Saint Luke*
c. 1622–25
Oil on canvas
29 × 23" (73.7 × 58.4 cm)

Purchased with the Henry P.
McIlhenny Fund in memory of
Frances P. McIlhenny, the
Edward and Althea Budd Fund,
the Edith H. Bell Fund, and
bequest (by exchange) of Lisa
Norris Elkins
1987-73-2

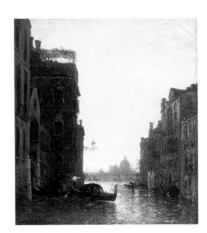

**Ziem, Félix-François-Georges-Philibert**
French, 1821–1911
*Canal in Venice*
Before 1877
Lower left: Ziem.
Oil on canvas
25 9/16 × 21 1/4" (64.9 × 54 cm)

John G. Johnson Collection
cat. 1114

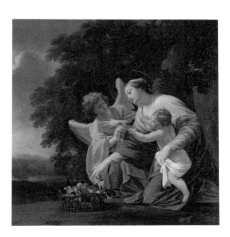

**Vouet, Simon, studio of**
*Virgin and Child, with an Angel*
1642
Oil on canvas
37 × 36" (94 × 91.4 cm)

Purchased with the Fiske
Kimball Fund and the Marie
Kimball Fund
1965-65-1

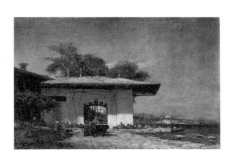

**Ziem, Félix-François-Georges-Philibert**
*The Divine Port, Constantinople*
Late 19th century
Lower left: Ziem
Oil on canvas
27 × 40 3/8" (68.6 × 102.5 cm)

The William L. Elkins Collection
E1924-3-60

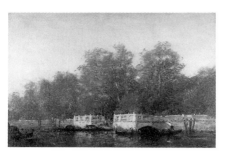

**Ziem, Félix-François-Georges-Philibert**
*Venetian Scene*
Late 19th century
Lower right: Ziem.
Oil on panel
16 11/16 × 25 1/8" (42.4 × 63.8 cm)

John G. Johnson Collection
cat. 1115

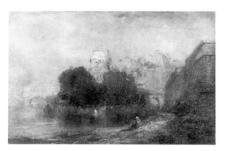

**Ziem, Félix-François-Georges-Philibert, attributed to**
Previously listed as Félix-François-Georges-Philibert Ziem (JGJ 1941)
*View of Paris from the Seine*
19th century
Lower right: Ziem
Oil on panel
8 7/8 × 13 3/4" (22.5 × 34.9 cm)

John G. Johnson Collection
cat. 1116

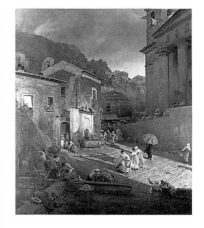

**Achenbach, Oswald**
German, active Italy, 1827–1905
*Street Scene, Naples*
c. 1876–80
Lower right: Osw. Achenbach
Oil on canvas
51 × 43" (129.5 × 109.2 cm)

The W. P. Wilstach Collection, bequest of Anna H. Wilstach
W1893-1-3

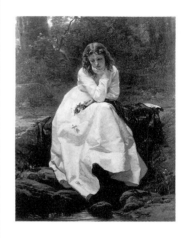

**Amberg, Wilhelm**
German, 1822–1899
*Young Woman Seated by a Stream (Contemplation)*
Before 1886
Lower left: W. Amberg
Oil on canvas
32 1/8 × 24" (81.6 × 61 cm)

The W. P. Wilstach Collection, bequest of Anna H. Wilstach
W1893-1-4

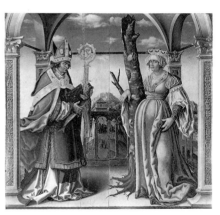

**Beck, Leonhard, attributed to**
German, active Augsburg, c. 1475–1542
*Saints Ulrich and Afra*
Diptych; the monogram of Hans Burgkmair (German, 1473–1531) and the date "1523" came away in cleaning in 1940
1523?
Oil on panel
39 1/4 × 41 1/4" (99.7 × 104.8 cm)

Gift of John G. Johnson for the W. P. Wilstach Collection
W1907-1-25

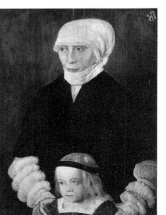

**Beham, Barthel**
German, active Nuremburg, c. 1502–1540
Previously listed as a Swabian artist, c. 1525 (JGJ 1941)
*Portrait of Margaret Urmiller and Her Daughter*
Companion to the portrait of Hans Urmiller and his son, in the Städelsches Kunstinstitut, Frankfurt (inv. no. 919)
c. 1525
Oil on panel
25 3/4 × 18 5/8" (65.4 × 47.3 cm)

John G. Johnson Collection
cat. 728

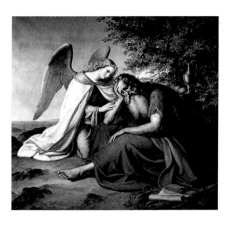

**Berendt, Moritz**
German, born 1803,
died after 1844
*Elijah in the Desert*
1834
Lower right: 1834 M. Berendt.;
on reverse: Berendt / 1834 /
Dusseldorfer / Schule
Oil on canvas
62 $^{11}/_{16}$ × 66 $^{1}/_{16}$" (159.2 ×
167.8 cm)

Gift of Abner Schreiber in
memory of Mary Schreiber
1978-8-1

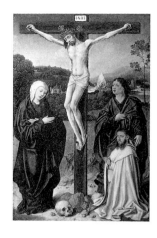

**Bruyn, Bartel, the Elder**
German, active Cologne,
c. 1493–1555
*The Crucifixion, with a Donor*
c. 1525–30
On cross: INRI
Oil on panel
17 × 11" (43.2 × 27.9 cm)

John G. Johnson Collection
cat. 750

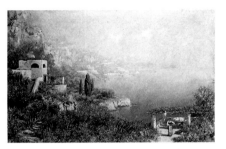

**Berninger, Edmund**
German, born 1843,
still active 1886
*View of Capri*
c. 1877
Lower left: E. BERNINGER
Oil on canvas
21 $^{3}/_{4}$ × 32" (55.2 × 81.3 cm)

Gift of Jay Cooke
1955-2-3

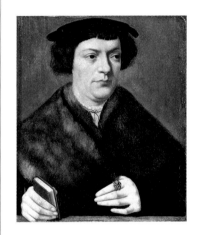

**Bruyn, Bartel, the Elder,
copy after**
Previously listed as Bartel Bruyn
the Elder (JGJ 1941)
*Portrait of a Man*
After a lost painting dated 1536
16th century
Oil on panel
11 $^{15}/_{16}$ × 9 $^{7}/_{16}$" (30.3 × 24 cm)

John G. Johnson Collection
cat. 749

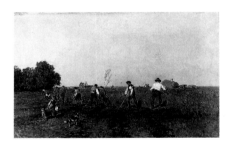

**Bochmann, Alexander
Heinrich Gregor von**
German, 1850–1930
*Landscape with Mowers*
1886
Lower right: G. v Bochmann
Oil on canvas
10 $^{1}/_{2}$ × 17" (26.7 × 43.2 cm)

John G. Johnson Collection
cat. 897

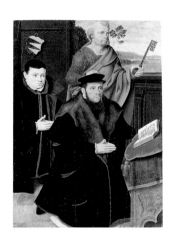

**Bruyn, Bartel, the Younger**
German, active Cologne,
born 1530, died 1607–10
Previously listed as Bartel Bruyn
the Elder (JGJ 1941)
*A Donor and His Son, with Saint
Peter*
Companion to the following
painting
16th century
Oil on panel
30 × 20 $^{1}/_{2}$" (76.2 × 52.1 cm)

John G. Johnson Collection
cat. 747

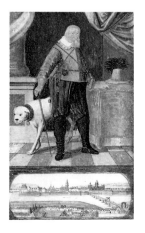

**Bretschneider, Daniel, the
Younger**
German, active Dresden, died 1658
*Portrait of Johann Georg I*
c. 1647
Oil on panel
7 $^{1}/_{8}$ × 4 $^{1}/_{8}$" (18.1 × 10.5 cm)

Bequest of Carl Otto
Kretzschmar von Kienbusch
1977-167-1032

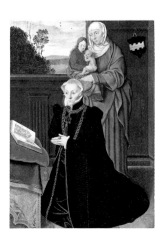

**Bruyn, Bartel, the Younger**
Previously listed as Bartel Bruyn
the Elder (JGJ 1941)
*Female Donor, with Saint Anne and
the Virgin and Child*
Companion to the preceding
painting
16th century
Oil on panel
30 × 20 $^{7}/_{16}$" (76.2 × 51.9 cm)

John G. Johnson Collection
cat. 748

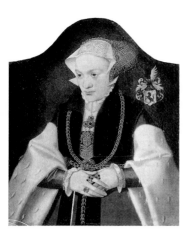

**Bruyn, Bartel, the Younger**
*Portrait of a Lady*
16th century
Oil on panel transferred to canvas
17 3/4 × 14" (45.1 × 35.6 cm)

John G. Johnson Collection
inv. 36

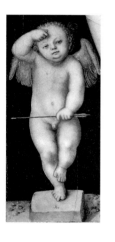

**Cranach, Lucas, the Elder**
German, active Wittenburg,
Vienna, and Weimar, 1472–1553
*Cupid*
Fragment
16th century
Center bottom: [artist's cipher]
Oil on panel
31 1/8 × 15" (79.1 × 38.1 cm)

John G. Johnson Collection
cat. 738

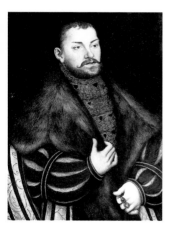

**Cranach, Lucas, the Elder,
attributed to**
Previously listed as Lucas
Cranach the Elder (JGJ 1941)
*Portrait of George the Devout,
Margrave of Brandenburg-Ansbach*
Companion to the portrait of
Margravine Hedwig in the Art
Institute of Chicago (38.310)
1529
Center left: 1529 / [artist's
cipher]
Oil on panel
23 3/8 × 16 3/8" (59.4 × 41.6 cm)

John G. Johnson Collection
cat. 739

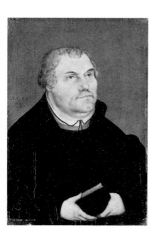

**Cranach, Lucas, the Elder,
workshop of**
*Portrait of Martin Luther*
Based on the painting by
Cranach, dated 1539, in the
collection of Émile Isambert,
Paris
1545
Upper left: 1545 / [artist's
cipher]
Oil on panel
14 1/16 × 9 1/8" (35.7 × 23.2 cm)

John G. Johnson Collection
cat. 740

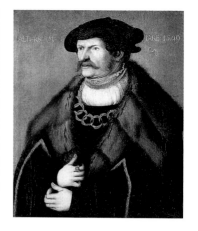

**Doring, Hans**
German, active Laubach and
Wetzlar, first documented 1511,
died 1558
Previously listed as Hans Mielich
(JGJ 1941)
*Portrait of a Nobleman* [possibly a
member of the Solms family]
The date in the inscription may
have been changed
1549
Across top: ALTERS IM I LARE
1549 / Az
Oil on panel
18 3/4 × 15 1/8" (47.6 × 38.4 cm)

John G. Johnson Collection
cat. 736

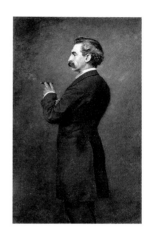

**Encke, Fedor**
German, born 1851,
still active 1913
*Portrait of Edward Stieglitz*
1879
Lower left: Fedor Encke. 1879. /
New York.
Oil on canvas
40 3/4 × 24 13/16" (103.5 × 63 cm)

Gift of Mrs. William Howard
Schubart
1968-45-1

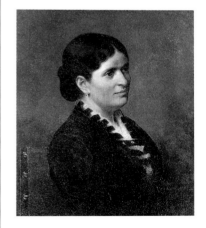

**Encke, Fedor**
*Portrait of Hedwig Stieglitz*
1881–86
Lower right: Fedor Encke / Berlin
Oil on canvas
23 3/4 × 19 5/8" (60.3 × 49.8 cm)

Gift of Mrs. William Howard
Schubart
1968-45-2

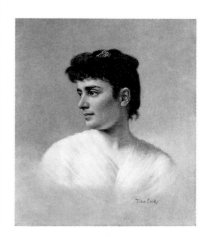

**Encke, Fedor**
*Portrait of Flora Stieglitz*
1880s
Lower right: Fedor Encke.
Oil on canvas
23 1/4 × 19 1/4" (59 × 48.9 cm)

Gift of Sue Davidson Lowe
1968-69-53

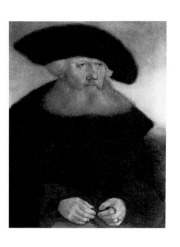

**Faber von Creuznach, Conrad, attributed to**
German, active Frankfurt, c. 1500–1552/53
Previously listed as Conrad Faber von Creuznach (JGJ 1941)
*Portrait of a Man*
c. 1500–50
Oil on panel
21 1/2 × 15" (54.6 × 38.1 cm)

John G. Johnson Collection
cat. 732

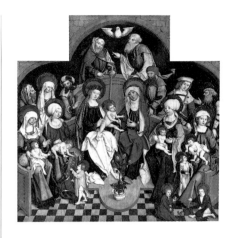

**German, active Swabia, unknown artist**
Previously listed as a Swabian artist, c. 1500 (JGJ 1941)
*The Holy Kinship*
c. 1500
Oil on panel
62 1/2 × 59 1/4" (158.7 × 150.5 cm)

John G. Johnson Collection
cat. 720

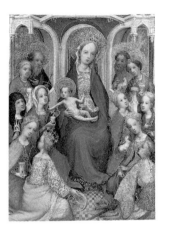

**German, active Cologne, unknown artist**
Previously listed as a Cologne artist, c. 1410 (JGJ 1941)
*Enthroned Virgin and Child, with Saints Paul, Peter, Clare of Assisi, Mary Magdalene, Barbara, Catherine of Alexandria, John the Baptist, John the Evangelist, Agnes, Cecilia, Dorothy, and George*
c. 1430 or after
On halos: S BARBARA /
S CATERINA / S AGNUSM /
S CECILIA / S DOROTHEA
Mixed media and tooled gold on panel
13 1/4 × 9 1/4" (33.6 × 23.5 cm)

John G. Johnson Collection
cat. 742

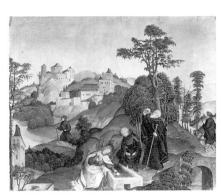

**German, active Ulm or Augsburg, unknown artist,**
Previously listed as an Austrian artist, c. 1500 (JGJ 1941)
*The Separation of the Apostles*
Fragment of an altarpiece; another panel is in the Rosgartenmuseum Konstanz, Germany
c. 1500
Oil on panel
21 1/8 × 24 1/2" (53.7 × 62.2 cm)

John G. Johnson Collection
cat. 726

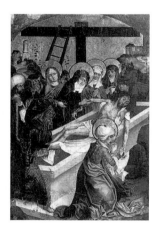

**German, active Swabia, unknown artist**
Previously listed as a Swabian artist, c. 1490 (JGJ 1941)
*The Entombment of Christ*
c. 1490
Oil and tooled gold on panel
30 3/8 × 19" (77.1 × 48.3 cm)

John G. Johnson Collection
cat. 719

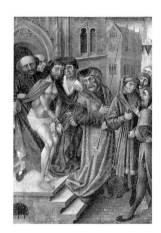

**German, unknown artist**
Previously listed as a follower of the Master of Alkmaar (JGJ 1941)
*"Ecce Homo"*
See following painting for reverse
c. 1500–25
Oil on panel
24 7/8 × 16 1/8" (63.2 × 41 cm)

John G. Johnson Collection
cat. 399a

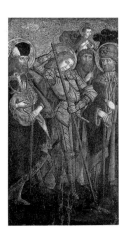

**German or Swiss, unknown artist**
*Saints Eustace, George, Christopher, and Acacius*
Late 15th or early 16th century
Oil on panel
27 × 14 3/4" (68.6 × 37.5 cm)

Bequest of Carl Otto Kretzschmar von Kienbusch
1977-167-1040

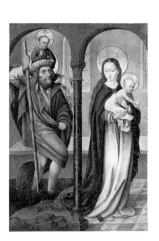

**German, unknown artist**
Previously listed as a follower of the Master of Alkmaar (JGJ 1941)
*Virgin and Child, with Saint Christopher*
Reverse of preceding painting
c. 1500–25
Oil on panel
24 7/8 × 16 1/8" (63.2 × 41 cm)

John G. Johnson Collection
cat. 399b

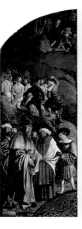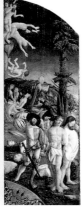

**German, active Bavaria, unknown artist**
Previously listed as a Bavarian artist, c. 1520 (JGJ 1941)
*The Martyrdom of the Ten Thousand*
Companion panels; based on the woodcut, c. 1496, by Albrecht Dürer (German, 1471–1528) (Bartsch 117)
c. 1500–25
Oil on panel
Each panel: 49 1/4 × 17"
(125.1 × 43.2 cm)

John G. Johnson Collection
cat. 730

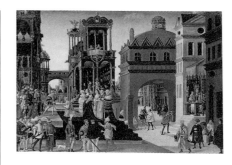

**German, active southern Germany, unknown artist**
Previously listed as a South German artist, c. 1545 (JGJ 1941)
*Scenes from the Book of Esther*
c. 1545
Oil on panel
19 1/16 × 26 1/2" (48.4 × 67.3 cm)

John G. Johnson Collection
cat. 734

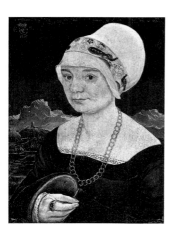

**German, active southern Germany, unknown artist**
Previously listed as Martin Schaffner (JGJ 1941)
*Portrait of a Lady*
c. 1500–50
Upper right (spurious): LC Pinx. / 1505
Oil on panel
12 3/8 × 9 1/2" (31.4 × 24.1 cm)

John G. Johnson Collection
cat. 733

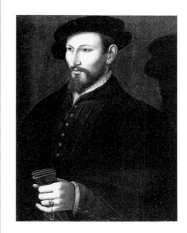

**German, active lower Rhine, unknown artist**
Previously attributed to Ludger Tom Ring the Younger (JGJ 1941)
*Portrait of a Gentleman*
c. 1550
Oil on panel
19 9/16 × 14 11/16" (49.7 × 37.3 cm)

John G. Johnson Collection
cat. 754

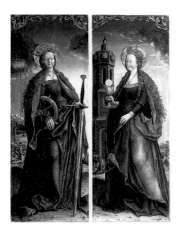

**German, active Swabia, unknown artist**
Previously listed as Hans Goldschmid (JGJ 1941)
*Saints Catherine of Alexandria and Barbara*
Companion panels
c. 1524
On sword: IZ; on tower: 1524 / HG / IZ—
Oil and gold on panel
Left panel: 58 5/8 × 21 7/8"
(148.9 × 55.6 cm); right panel:
58 7/16 × 21 7/8" (148.4 × 55.6 cm)

John G. Johnson Collection
cat. 729

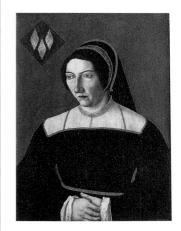

**German, unknown artist**
Previously attributed to Ludger Tom Ring the Younger (JGJ 1941)
*Portrait of a Lady*
c. 1550
Upper left: [coat of arms, possibly of Cambry family]
Oil on panel
18 1/8 × 12 5/8" (46 × 32.1 cm)

John G. Johnson Collection
cat. 755

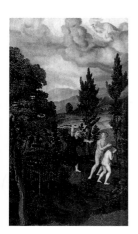

**German, active southern Germany, unknown artist**
Previously listed as a South German artist, c. 1530 (JGJ 1941)
*The Expulsion from Eden*
c. 1530–60
Oil on panel
33 3/8 × 18 1/4" (84.8 × 46.3 cm)

John G. Johnson Collection
cat. 731

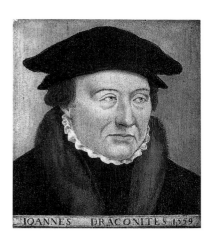

**German, unknown artist**
Previously listed as a Dutch artist, c. 1559 (JGJ 1941)
*Portrait of Johannes Draconites*
1559
Across bottom: IOANNES DRACONITES 1559
Oil on panel
9 7/16 × 8 1/4" (24 × 20.9 cm)

John G. Johnson Collection
inv. 1351

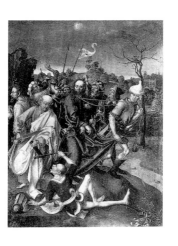

**German, unknown artist**
Previously listed as an old copy after Martin Schongauer (JGJ 1941)
*Christ Taken to Prison*
Based on the print by Martin Schongauer (German, c. 1445–1491) (Bartsch 10)
Early 16th century
Center left (spurious): MS
Oil on panel
13 3/4 × 10 5/16" (34.9 × 26.2 cm)

John G. Johnson Collection
cat. 717

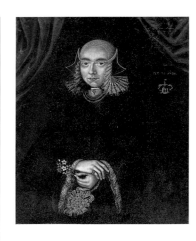

**German, unknown artist**
*Portrait of a Twenty-One-Year-Old Woman*
1721
Upper right: AET. 21, 1721.
Oil on canvas
32 1/8 × 25 11/16" (81.6 × 65.2 cm)

Bequest of Mrs. John Harrison
1921-39-48

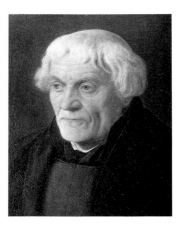

**German, unknown artist**
Previously listed as Christoph Amberger (JGJ 1941)
*Portrait of an Old Man*
16th century
Oil on panel
14 3/8 × 11" (36.5 × 27.9 cm)

John G. Johnson Collection
inv. 220

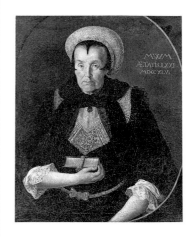

**German, unknown artist**
*Portrait of a Seventy-One-Year-Old Woman*
1745
Upper right: M.W.M. / AETATIS.LXXI / MDCCXLV.
Oil on canvas
34 1/4 × 26 3/4" (87 × 67.9 cm)

Bequest of Mrs. John Harrison
1921-39-49

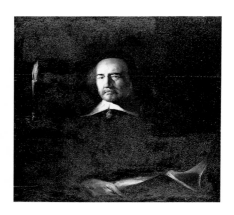

**German?, unknown artist**
Previously listed as the school of Rembrandt Harmensz. van Rijn (JGJ 1941)
*Portrait of a Gentleman*
17th century
Oil on panel
32 × 34 1/8" (81.3 × 86.7 cm)

John G. Johnson Collection
cat. 491

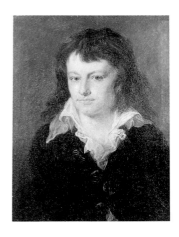

**German, unknown artist**
*Portrait of a Young Man*
c. 1775–1800
Oil on canvas
21 1/4 × 16 5/16" (54 × 41.4 cm)

John G. Johnson Collection
cat. 791

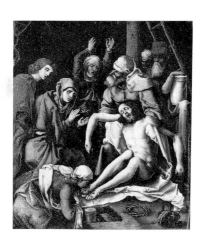

**German, unknown artist**
Previously listed as a German artist, mid-18th century (JGJ 1941)
*The Deposition of Christ*
After a woodcut by Albrecht Dürer (German, 1471–1528) (Bartsch 43)
17th century?
Oil on slate
9 × 7 3/8" (22.9 × 18.7 cm)

John G. Johnson Collection
cat. 406

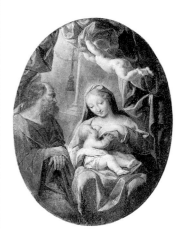

**German?, active Rome, unknown artist**
Previously listed as Raphael Mengs (JGJ 1941)
*The Holy Family*
18th century
Oil on panel
11 7/8 × 8 7/8" (30.2 × 22.5 cm)

John G. Johnson Collection
inv. 2922

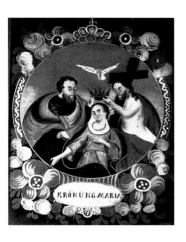

**German, unknown artist**
*The Coronation of the Virgin*
Early 19th century
Center bottom: KRÖNUNG
MARIA
Oil on glass
15 × 12" (38.1 × 30.5 cm)

Purchased with Museum funds
1913-455

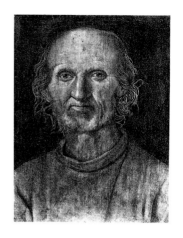

**German, unknown artist**
Previously listed as Albrecht
Dürer (JGJ 1941)
*Portrait of an Old Man*
In a 16th-century style
19th century
Oil on vellum on canvas
15 5/16 × 11" (38.9 × 27.9 cm)

John G. Johnson Collection
cat. 737

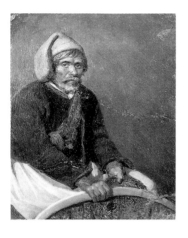

**German?, unknown artist**
*Fisherman*
19th century
Oil on paper on fiberboard
9 1/2 × 7 5/16" (24.1 × 18.6 cm)

John G. Johnson Collection
inv. 2932

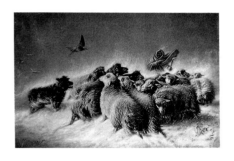

**German, unknown artist**
*Sheep*
19th century
Oil on canvas
18 3/4 × 27 1/8" (47.6 × 68.9 cm)

Bequest of Katherine E. Sheafer
1971-272-2

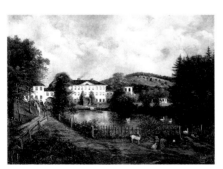

**German, unknown artist**
*The Kienbusch Estate, Unter
Marxgrun*
19th century
Lower right: Forli / Drsd[?]
Oil on canvas
28 × 37" (71.1 × 94 cm)

Bequest of Carl Otto
Kretzschmar von Kienbusch
1977-167-1087

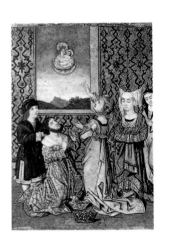

**German, unknown artist**
*The Vision of the Tiburtine Sibyl*
In a 16th-century style;
companion to the following three
paintings
19th century
Oil on panel
7 3/16 × 5 9/16" (18.3 × 14.1 cm)

John G. Johnson Collection
inv. 457a

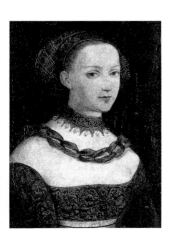

**German, unknown artist**
Previously listed as an old copy
after Lucas Cranach the Elder
(JGJ 1941)
*Portrait of a Girl*
In a 16th-century style
19th century
Oil on panel transferred to canvas
20 13/16 × 14 5/16" (52.9 × 36.3 cm)

John G. Johnson Collection
cat. 741

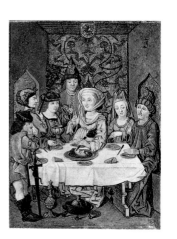

**German, unknown artist**
*The Feast of Herod*
See previous entry
19th century
Upper left: L; upper right: J
Oil on panel
7 1/4 × 5 7/8" (18.4 × 14.9 cm)

John G. Johnson Collection
inv. 457b

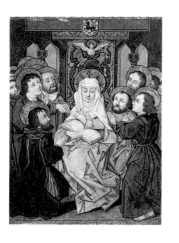

**German, unknown artist**
*Pentecost*
See previous two entries
19th century
Oil on panel
7 1/8 × 5 1/2" (18.1 × 14 cm)

John G. Johnson Collection
inv. 457c

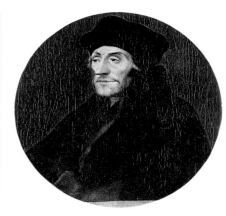

**Holbein, Hans, the Younger, copy after**
*Portrait of Erasmus of Rotterdam*
After the painting in the
Kunstmuseum Basel (inv. no. 324)
16th century
Oil on panel
8 1/8" (20.6 cm) diameter

John G. Johnson Collection
cat. 718

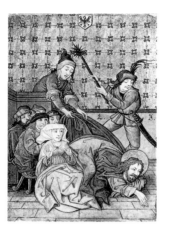

**German, unknown artist**
*The Martyrdom of a Saint*
See previous three entries
19th century
Center right: L. / J.
Oil on panel
7 1/8 × 5 1/2" (18.1 × 14 cm)

John G. Johnson Collection
inv. 457d

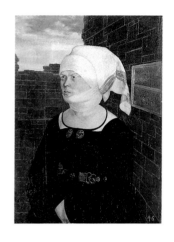

**Huber, Wolf**
German, active Passau,
c. 1485–1553
*Portrait of Margaret Hundertpfundt*
Companion to the portrait of
Antony Hundertpfundt, National
Gallery of Ireland, Dublin (15)
1526
Center right: MARGGRET / HVN-
DERPFV- / NDIN IST AB / GE-
MACHT IRS / ALTER 41 IAR / DA
MANZALT / 1526 IAR AM / 22 TAG
IENNARI / W H; lower right: 46
Oil on panel
27 × 18 5/8" (68.6 × 47.3 cm)

John G. Johnson Collection
inv. 1438

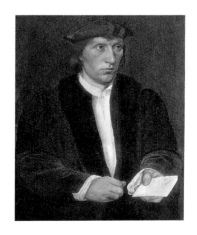

**Holbein, Hans, the Younger, imitator of**
German, active Basel and
England, 1497–1543
Previously listed as Hans
Holbein the Younger (JGJ 1941)
*Portrait of John Godsalve*
Based on a drawing in the
collection of Her Majesty Queen
Elizabeth II (R. L. 12265)
16th century
Oil on panel
12 7/8 × 9 13/16" (32.7 × 24.9 cm)

John G. Johnson Collection
inv. 35

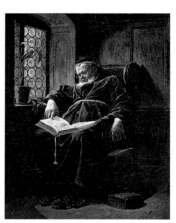

**Kraus, August**
German, 1852–1917
*Interior (Tired Out)*
c. 1900
Lower left: August Kraus.
Oil on canvas
20 3/4 × 16" (52.7 × 40.6 cm)

The Walter Lippincott Collection
1923-59-2

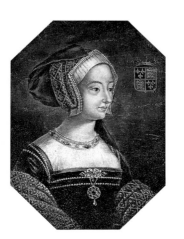

**Holbein, Hans, the Younger, imitator of**
*Portrait of a Woman*
19th century
Oil on panel
6 3/8 × 4 1/2" (16.2 × 11.4 cm)

John G. Johnson Collection
inv. 1855

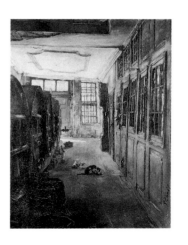

**Kuehl, Gotthardt**
German, 1850–1915
*Wine Room*
1891
Lower right: G Kuehl
Oil on canvas
34 5/8 × 25 3/4" (87.9 × 65.4 cm)

John G. Johnson Collection
cat. 1016

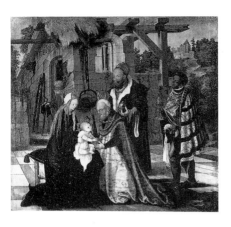

**Kulmbach, Hans Suess von, attributed to**
German, active Nuremburg,
c. 1480–1522
*The Adoration of the Magi*
Early 16th century
Oil on panel
13 5/16 × 13 3/8" (33.8 × 34 cm)

John G. Johnson Collection
cat. 727

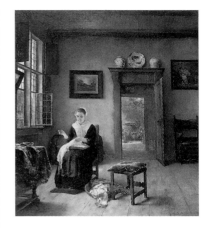

**Löfftz, Ludwig**
German, 1845–1910
*Woman Sewing*
1886
Lower right: L. Loefftz München
1886
Oil on canvas
33 3/8 × 28 1/4" (84.8 × 71.7 cm)

John G. Johnson Collection
cat. 1026

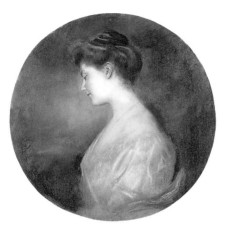

**Lenbach, Franz von**
German, 1836–1904
*Portrait of the Widow Marion Knapp* [née Graham, later Baroness Bateman]
c. 1903
Oil on construction board
28 3/16 × 26 7/8" (71.6 × 68.3 cm)
Gift of Mrs. Henry Clifford
1975-79-3

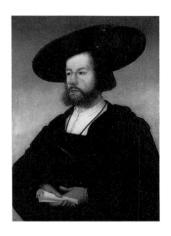

**Maler von Ulm, Hans, attributed to**
German, active Schwaz, born 1470–80, still active c. 1530
*Portrait of a Man*
c. 1500–25
Oil on panel
23 × 16 1/16" (58.4 × 40.8 cm)

John G. Johnson Collection
inv. 2088

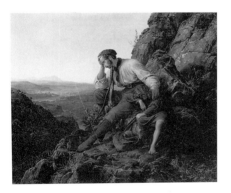

**Lessing, Karl Friedrich**
German, 1808–1880
*The Robber and His Child*
1832
Center bottom: C.F.L. 1832
Oil on canvas
16 5/8 × 19 1/8" (42.2 × 48.6 cm)

The W. P. Wilstach Collection,
bequest of Anna H. Wilstach
W1893-1-65

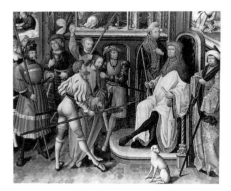

**Master of Cappenberg (Jan Baegart)**
German, active Westphalia,
documented 1465–1515
*Christ before Annas*
Fragment of a panel from an altarpiece; a related fragment was formerly in the collection of H. C. Kruger, Berlin
c. 1500
Oil on panel
49 × 56 1/8" (124.5 × 142.6 cm)

John G. Johnson Collection
cat. 753

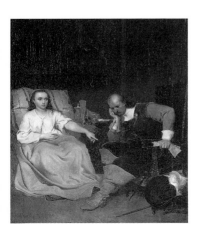

**Leutze, Emanuel**
German, active United States,
1816–1868
*Oliver Cromwell and His Daughter*
1843
Lower left: E. Leutze, Düss f. 1843.
Oil on canvas
29 1/8 × 24 1/2" (74 × 62.2 cm)

The W. P. Wilstach Collection,
bequest of Anna H. Wilstach
W1893-1-67

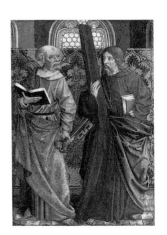

**Master of the Holy Kinship**
German, active Cologne,
c. 1450–c. 1515
*Saints Peter and Andrew*
Panel from an altarpiece; companion panels are in the Rheinisches Landesmuseum, Bonn (141); Museum of Fine Arts, Boston (07.646); collection of Heinz and Gerlinde Kisters, Kreuzlingen, Switzerland; (formerly) the Kulturhistorisches Museum, Magdeburg (GK506, destroyed); and (formerly) the von Schnitzler collection, Cologne
c. 1500
Oil on panel
18 5/8 × 12 5/8" (47.3 × 32.1 cm)

John G. Johnson Collection
cat. 745

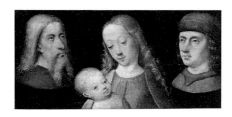

**Master of Liesborn,
workshop of**
German, active Westphalia,
active 1450–1475
Previously listed as the Master of
Liesborn (JGJ 1941)
*Virgin and Child, with Two Male
Figures*
c. 1450–75
Oil on panel
5 15/16 × 11 3/16" (15.1 × 28.4 cm)

John G. Johnson Collection
cat. 752

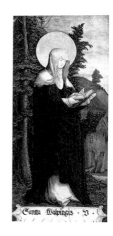

**Master of Messkirch**
*Saint Walpurgis*
See previous two entries
c. 1535–40
Across bottom: Santta
Walpurgis V
Oil and gold on panel
24 3/8 × 11 1/4" (61.9 × 28.6 cm)

John G. Johnson Collection
cat. 723

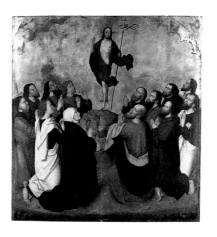

**Master of the Lyversberg
Passion, workshop of**
German, active Cologne,
active c. 1460–c. 1490
Previously listed as the Master of
the Life of the Virgin (JGJ 1941)
*The Ascension of Christ*
Fragment of a panel from an altarpiece commissioned for the church
of Saint Columba, Cologne; companion panels are in the Germanis-
ches Nationalmuseum, Nuremberg (GM 19, GM 20), and Dom-
und Diözesanmuseum, Speyer
c. 1473
Oil and gold on panel
35 7/8 × 31 5/8" (91.1 × 80.3 cm)

John G. Johnson Collection
cat. 743

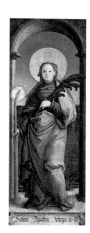

**Master of Messkirch**
*Saint Agatha*
See previous three entries
c. 1535–40
Across bottom: Santta Agatha
Virgo et M
Oil and gold on panel
25 7/8 × 9 3/4" (65.7 × 24.8 cm)

John G. Johnson Collection
cat. 724

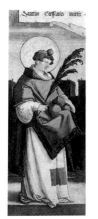

**Master of Messkirch**
German, active 1520–1540
*Saint Stephen*
Panel from an altarpiece
commissioned by Count
Gattfried Werner von Zimmem
for the church of Messkirch,
Baden-Württemberg; companion
to the following four panels
c. 1535–40
Across top: Santtus Steffanus
martir
Oil and gold on panel
25 5/16 × 9 1/2" (64.3 × 24.1 cm)

John G. Johnson Collection
cat. 721

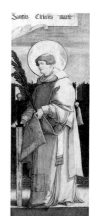

**Master of Messkirch**
*Saint Ciriacus*
See previous four entries
c. 1535–40
Across top: Santtus Ciriacus
martir
Oil and gold on panel
25 1/4 × 9 1/2" (64.1 × 24.1 cm)

John G. Johnson Collection
cat. 725

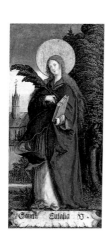

**Master of Messkirch**
*Saint Eulalia*
See previous entry
c. 1535–40
Across bottom: Santta Eulalia V.
Oil and gold on panel
24 5/16 × 10 7/8" (61.7 × 27.6 cm)

John G. Johnson Collection
cat. 722

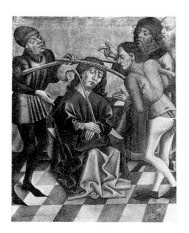

**Master of the Munderkinger
Altar**
German, active Swabia,
dated work 1473
Previously listed as a Swabian
artist, c. 1460 (JGJ 1941)
*Christ Crowned with Thorns*
c. 1475
Oil and gold on panel
22 7/8 × 17" (58.1 × 43.2 cm)

John G. Johnson Collection
cat. 716

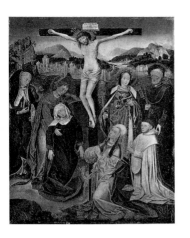

**Master of the Munich
Crucifixion Altarpiece**
German, active Cologne?,
dated work 1517
Previously listed as Pierre des
Mares (JGJ 1941)
*The Crucifixion, with Saints Jerome,
Barbara, and Peter, and a Donor*
Early 16th century
Oil on panel transferred to canvas
24 3/4 × 19" (62.9 × 48.3 cm)

John G. Johnson Collection
cat. 746

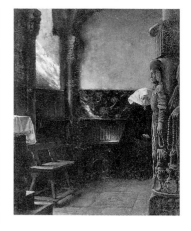

**Meyer, August Eduard
Nicolaus, also called Claus
Meyer**
German, 1856–1919
*Meditation*
1885
Lower right: Claus Meyer / 85.
Oil on panel
10 9/16 × 8 1/16" (26.8 × 20.5 cm)

John G. Johnson Collection
cat. 1041

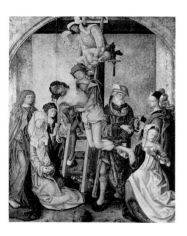

**Master of the Saint
Bartholomew Altar,
follower of**
German, active Cologne,
active c. 1470–c. 1510
Previously listed as a copy after
the Master of the Saint
Bartholomew Altar (JGJ 1941)
*The Descent from the Cross*
Based on the painting in the
Musée du Louvre, Paris (inv. 1445)
Early 16th century
Oil on panel
20 3/16 × 15 9/16" (51.3 × 39.5 cm)

John G. Johnson Collection
cat. 744

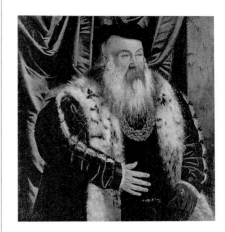

**Mielich, Hans, attributed to**
German, active Munich,
1516–1573
Previously listed as Hans Mielich
(JGJ 1941)
*Portrait of a Nobleman*
16th century
Oil on canvas
38 1/8 × 34 5/8" (96.8 × 87.9 cm)

John G. Johnson Collection
cat. 735

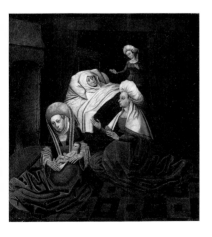

**Master of the Sterzingen
Altar, workshop of**
German, active Swabia,
active c. 1450–c. 1500
Previously listed as a Swabian
artist, c. 1440–50 (JGJ 1941)
*The Birth of the Virgin*
Panel from an altarpiece; see
following entry for companion
panels
c. 1450–1500
Oil on panel
40 1/4 × 36 7/8" (102.2 × 93.7 cm)

John G. Johnson Collection
cat. 714

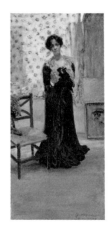

**Oppenheimer, Josef**
German, 1876–1967
*Portrait of Selma Stieglitz Schubart*
1901
Lower right: J. Oppenheimer /
NY. 1901.
Oil on canvas
40 1/8 × 18" (101.9 × 45.7 cm)

Gift of Mrs. William Howard
Schubart
1968-45-4

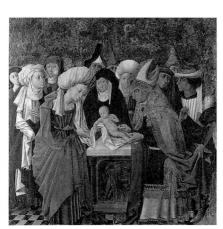

**Master of the Sterzingen
Altar, workshop of**
Previously listed as an Upper
Rhenish artist, c. 1450 (JGJ 1941)
*The Circumcision of Christ*
Panel from an altarpiece;
companion to the preceding panel
and panels in the cloister of
Fischingen, Switzerland; the
Metropolitan Museum of Art,
New York (32.100.38, 32.100.39);
and the Diözesanmuseum
Rottenburg, Germany (B 5, B 6)
Mid-15th century
Oil and gold on panel
40 3/8 × 36 1/4" (102.5 × 92.1 cm)

John G. Johnson Collection
cat. 715

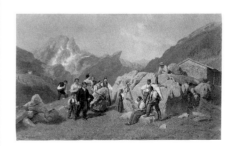

**Riefstahl, Wilhelm Ludwig
Friedrich**
German, 1827–1888
*Return from the Christening*
1865
Lower left: W. Riefstahl. 65
Oil on canvas
27 5/8 × 44 3/4" (70.2 × 113.7 cm)

The W. P. Wilstach Collection,
bequest of Anna H. Wilstach
W1893-1-90

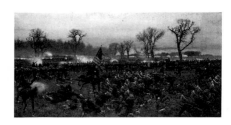

**Röchling, Carl**
German, 1855–1920
*The Battle of Fredericksburg,*
*December 13, 1862*
19th century
Lower right: c RÖCHLING
Oil on canvas
32 1/8 × 59" (81.6 × 149.9 cm)

Commissioners of Fairmount
Park
F1929-1-1

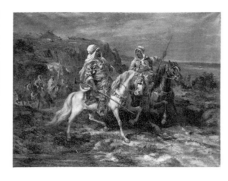

**Schreyer, Adolf**
*Arab Horsemen*
19th century
Lower left: Ad. Schreyer
Oil on canvas
35 1/4 × 45 7/8" (89.5 × 116.5 cm)

The Walter Lippincott Collection
1923-59-1

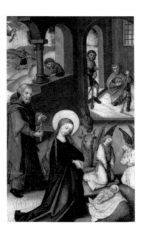

**Schongauer, Ludwig,**
**attributed to**
German, active Colmar, Ulm,
and Augsburg, c. 1440–1494
Previously listed as Bartholomaeus
Zeitblom (PMA 1965)
*The Nativity*
c. 1480–90
Oil on panel
18 1/4 × 11 1/4" (46.3 × 28.6 cm)

The John D. McIlhenny
Collection
1943-40-44

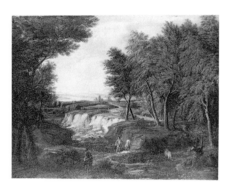

**Weyermann, Jakob Christoph**
German, 1698–1757
Previously listed as Jacob Campo
Weyerman (PMA 1965)
*Ideal Landscape with Figures*
c. 1730–35
Lower right: Weyerma[nn]
Oil on canvas
28 3/16 × 34 13/16" (71.6 × 88.4 cm)

Bequest of Robert Nebinger
1889-113

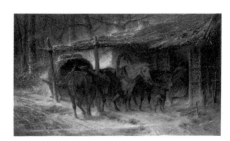

**Schreyer, Adolf**
German, 1828–1899
*Post House, Walachia*
1867
Lower right: Ad. Schreyer. / Paris
1867
Oil on canvas
38 1/4 × 62 1/2" (97.1 × 158.7 cm)

The William L. Elkins Collection
E1924-3-20

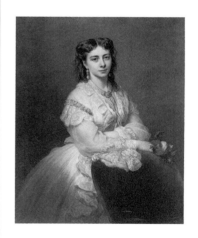

**Winterhalter, Franz Xaver**
German, 1805–1873
*Portrait of Countess Marie Branicka*
*de Bialacerkiew [née Princess*
*Sapicka]*
1865
Lower right: F. Winterhalter /
1865. Paris
Oil on canvas
45 11/16 × 35 5/16" (116 × 89.7 cm)

Purchased with the Edward G.
Budd, Jr., Memorial Fund
1973-252-1

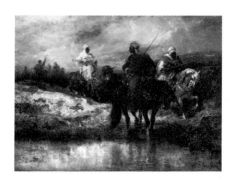

**Schreyer, Adolf**
*Arab Horsemen*
c. 1887–90
Lower right: Ad. Schreyer
Oil on canvas
25 1/4 × 34" (64.1 × 86.4 cm)

Bequest of Chester Waters Larner
1977-258-1

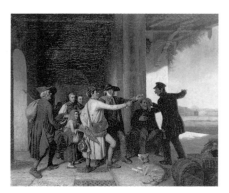

**Zimmermann, Reinhard**
**Sebastian**
German, 1815–1893
Previously listed as August
Richard Zimmermann (PMA
1965)
*Too Late for the Cars*
1855
Lower left: R. S. Zimmermann
1855; on reverse: Vervielfaltigung
vorbehalten / R. S. Zimmermann
Oil on canvas
27 1/2 × 32 5/16" (69.8 × 82.1 cm)

The W. P. Wilstach Collection,
bequest of Anna H. Wilstach
W1893-1-135

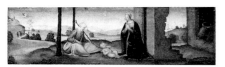

**Albertinelli, Mariotto, workshop of**
Italian, active Florence, 1474–1515
Previously listed as Mariotto Albertinelli (JI 1966)
*The Adoration of the Christ Child*
Predella panel
After 1503
Oil and gold on panel
6 5/8 × 23 3/8" (16.8 × 59.4 cm)

John G. Johnson Collection
cat. 1168

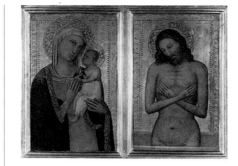

**Allegretto di Nuzio**
*Virgin and Child, and Christ as the Man of Sorrows*
Diptych
c. 1366
Tempera and tooled gold on panel
15 3/8 × 20" (39 × 50.8 cm)
overall

John G. Johnson Collection
cat. 118

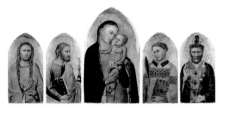

**Allegretto di Nuzio, also called Allegretto Nuzi**
Italian, active Fabriano and Florence, first recorded 1345, died 1373
Previously listed as close to Maso di Banco (JI 1966)
*Virgin and Child, with Saints Mary Magdalene, James the Great, and Stephen, and a Bishop Saint*
Panels from an altarpiece
c. 1345–46
Tempera and tooled gold on panel
Center panel: 28 3/8 × 16 1/2" (72.1 × 41.9 cm); side panels [each]: 23 5/8 × 11 3/4" (60 × 29.8 cm)

John G. Johnson Collection
cat. 5

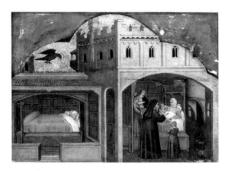

**Altichiero, follower of**
Italian, active Padua and Verona, documented 1369–1384
Previously listed as a Veronese artist, end of the 14th century (JI 1966)
*Saint Eligius's Mother Told of Her Son's Future Fame*
Panel from an altarpiece; companion panels are in the Ashmolean Museum, Oxford (A732); a private collection, England; and an unknown location
1390s
Tempera and gold on panel
20 3/4 × 27 1/2" (52.7 × 69.8 cm)

John G. Johnson Collection
inv. 3024

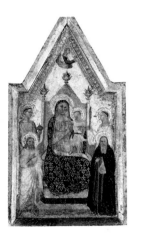

**Allegretto di Nuzio**
*Enthroned Virgin and Child, with Saints Lucy, John the Baptist, and Anthony Abbot, and a Female Martyr*
Panel from a diptych; the companion panel is in the Kerészteny Múzeum, Esztergom, Hungary (55.149)
c. 1350
Oil and tooled gold on panel
17 1/8 × 9 1/4" (43.5 × 23.5 cm)

John G. Johnson Collection
cat. 2

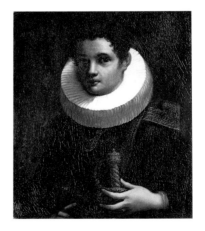

**Amidano, Giulio Cesare**
Italian, active Parma, 1566–1630
Previously attributed to Bartolomeo Schedoni (JI 1966)
*Portrait of a Young Gentleman*
Early 16th century
Across top (spurious): AVGVS MARTELLI AETATIS SVAE XVIII / ANGELVS BRONZINO FECIT ANNO
Oil on panel transferred to canvas
28 1/2 × 24 1/4" (72.4 × 61.6 cm)

John G. Johnson Collection
cat. 282

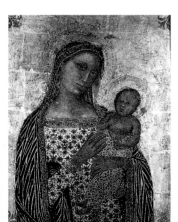

**Allegretto di Nuzio**
*Virgin and Child*
c. 1366
Tempera and tooled gold on panel
14 3/4 × 11 7/8" (37.5 × 30.2 cm)

John G. Johnson Collection
cat. 119

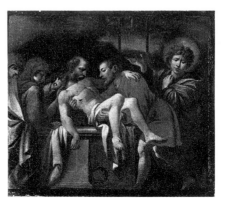

**Amidano, Giulio Cesare, attributed to**
*The Entombment*
Early 16th century
Oil on canvas on panel
8 × 9" (20.3 × 22.9 cm)

John G. Johnson Collection
inv. 198

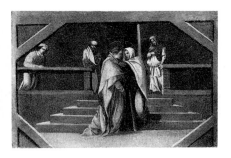

**Andrea del Sarto (Andrea d'Agnolo di Francesco), copy after**
Italian, active Florence, 1486–1530
*The Visitation*
After part of a fresco in the Chiostro del Scalzo, Florence
19th century
Oil on canvas
8 ³/₄ × 12 ⁷/₈" (22.2 × 32.7 cm)

John G. Johnson Collection
inv. 1410

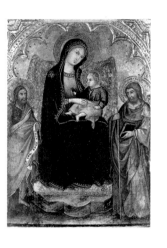

**Andrea di Bartolo**
Italian, active Siena, first documented 1389, died 1428
Previously listed as Taddeo di Bartolo (JI 1966)
*Enthroned Virgin and Child, with Saints John the Baptist and James the Great*
Center panel from a triptych; cut down at the top
c. 1395–1400
On scroll: ECCE A[G]NVS DEI QUI
Tempera and tooled gold on panel
11 ¹/₈ × 8" (28.3 × 20.3 cm)

John G. Johnson Collection
cat. 99

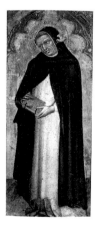

**Andrea di Bartolo**
*Blessed Andrea Sansedoni*
Pilaster panel from an altarpiece; companion to the following panel
After 1413
Tempera and tooled gold on panel
15 × 6 ¹/₂" (38.1 × 16.5 cm)

John G. Johnson Collection
cat. 96

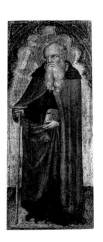

**Andrea di Bartolo**
*Saint Anthony Abbot*
Pilaster panel from an altarpiece; companion to the preceding panel
After 1413
Tempera and tooled gold on panel
16 × 6 ⁵/₈" (40.6 × 16.8 cm)

John G. Johnson Collection
cat. 97

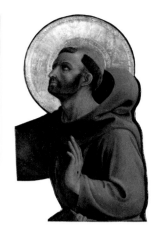

**Fra Angelico (Guido di Pietro), also called Fra Giovanni da Fiesole**
Italian, active Florence and Rome, first securely documented by 1417, died 1455
*Saint Francis of Assisi*
Fragment from *The Crucifixion, with Saints Nicholas of Bari and Francis of Assisi*, in the Confraternity of San Niccolò del Ceppo, Florence
c. 1425–33
Tempera and tooled gold on panel
27 ⁹/₁₆ × 19 ¹/₄" (70 × 48.9 cm)

John G. Johnson Collection
cat. 14

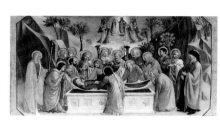
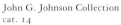

**Fra Angelico**
Previously listed as the studio of Fra Angelico (JI 1966)
*The Dormition of the Virgin*
Predella panel; companion panels are in the Kimbell Art Museum, Fort Worth (AP 1986.03); the Museo Nazionale di San Marco, Florence (Uffizi 1499); and the M. H. de Young Memorial Museum, San Francisco (Kress 289)
c. 1427
Tempera and tooled gold on panel
10 ¹/₄ × 20 ¹³/₁₆" (26 × 52.9 cm)

John G. Johnson Collection
cat. 15

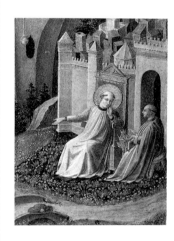

**Fra Angelico, follower of**
*The Papacy Offered to Saint Gregory the Great* [?]
Predella panel; possible companion panels are in the Koninklijk Museum voor Schone Kunsten, Antwerp (117); the Musée Condé, Chantilly (120); the Musée Thomas Henry, Cherbourg (8); and the Museum of Fine Arts, Houston (44-550)
c. 1435
Tempera and gold on panel
11 × 7 ³/₄" (27.9 × 19.7 cm)

John G. Johnson Collection
cat. 1166

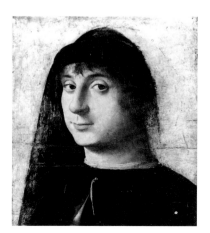

**Antonello da Messina (Antonello di Giovanni di Michele de Antonio)**
Italian, active Messina, Naples, and Venice, first securely documented 1456, died 1479
*Portrait of a Young Gentleman*
c. 1470–74
Oil on panel
12 ⁵/₈ × 10 ¹¹/₁₆" (32.1 × 27.1 cm)

John G. Johnson Collection
cat. 159

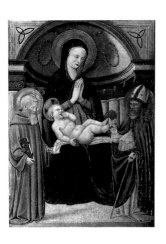

**Apollonio di Giovanni di Tommaso, workshop of**
Italian, active Florence,
born 1415–17, died 1465
**and Marco del Buono di Marco**
Italian, 1403–1489
Previously listed as the Virgil Master (JI 1966)
*Enthroned Virgin and Child, with Saint Benedict and a Bishop Saint*
c. 1460
Tempera and tooled gold on panel
29 3/8 × 19 1/2" (74.6 × 49.5 cm)

John G. Johnson Collection
cat. 26

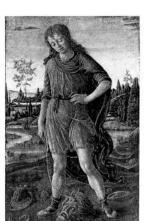

**Argonaut Master**
Italian, active Florence,
active c. 1450–c. 1475
Previously listed as Jacopo del Sellaio (JI 1966)
*David with the Head of Goliath*
c. 1460
Tempera and gold on panel
23 × 15 1/4" (58.4 × 38.7 cm)

John G. Johnson Collection
cat. 51

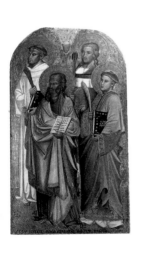

**Arrigo di Niccolò (Master of the Manassei Chapel)**
Italian, active c. 1374–1446
Previously listed as Italian, unknown artist, 14th century (PMA 1965)
*Saints Benedict, Sebastian, Stephen, and John the Evangelist*
Panel from an altarpiece; companion to a panel formerly in a private collection in Milan
c. 1400–10
On Evangelist's book: FILIO / LI [MEI,] .N[ON]. / DILI / GAM[US] / VE[R]BO / NEQUE / LING / UA .S / ET . O / P[ER]E .[E]T / VERI / TATE; across bottom: MRE MMR G ME FECIM MEOT [?]
Tempera and tooled gold on panel
57 5/8 × 32" (146.4 × 81.3 cm)

The Louise and Walter Arensberg Collection
1950-134-528

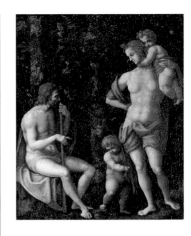

**Bacchiacca (Francesco di Ubertino Verdi)**
Italian, active Florence and Rome, 1494–1557
*Adam and Eve with Cain and Abel*
c. 1516–18
Oil on panel
14 × 11 1/16" (35.6 × 28.1 cm)

John G. Johnson Collection
cat. 80

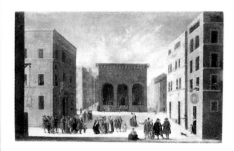

**Badile, Giovanni Antonio, attributed to**
Italian, active Verona,
1518–1560
Previously listed as Giovanni Antonio Badile (JI 1966)
*The Meeting of Solomon and the Queen of Sheba*
Mid-16th century
Oil on canvas
28 1/16 × 43 1/16" (71.3 × 109.4 cm)

John G. Johnson Collection
inv. 729

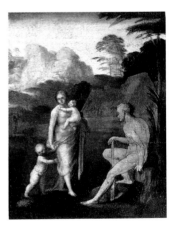

**Fra Bartolomeo (Bartolomeo di Paolo), also called Baccio della Porta**
Italian, active Florence, Venice, and Rome, 1472–1517
*Adam and Eve with Cain and Abel*
By 1512
Oil on panel
12 1/2 × 9 7/8" (31.7 × 25.1 cm)

John G. Johnson Collection
cat. 78

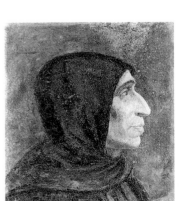

**Fra Bartolomeo, copy after**
*Portrait of Girolamo Savonarola*
After the painting in the Museo Nazionale di San Marco, Florence
19th century
Oil on canvas
16 3/4 × 13 3/16" (42.5 × 33.5 cm)

John G. Johnson Collection
inv. 2059

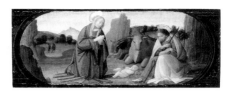

**Bartolomeo di Giovanni**
Italian, active Florence,
documented 1488–1511
*The Adoration of the Christ Child*
Predella panel; companion panels
are in the Gemäldegalerie Alte
Meister, Staatliche Kunstsammlungen Dresden; Ferens Art
Gallery, Hull, Yorkshire; and a
private collection, Fiesole
c. 1485
Oil on panel
7 9/16 × 19" (19.2 × 48.3 cm)

The John D. McIlhenny
Collection
1943-40-53

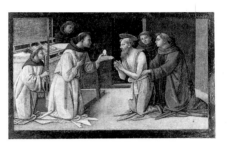

**Bartolomeo di Giovanni**
*The Last Communion of Saint Jerome*
Predella panel
c. 1490–1500
Oil on panel
7 7/8 × 12 11/16" (20 × 32.2 cm)

John G. Johnson Collection
cat. 70

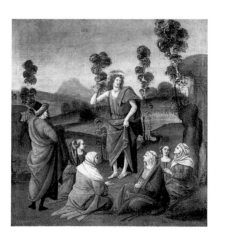

**Bartolomeo di Giovanni**
*Saint John the Baptist Preaching*
c. 1500–10
Oil and gold on canvas
24 1/4 × 21 3/16" (61.6 × 53.8 cm)

John G. Johnson Collection
cat. 71

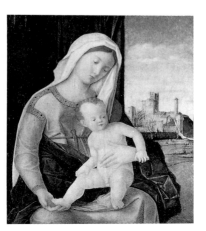

**Bartolomeo Veneto,
follower of**
Italian, active Veneto and
Lombardy, documented
1502–1530
Previously listed as the school of
Giovanni Bellini (JI 1966)
*Virgin and Child before a Landscape*
Based on a composition by
Giovanni Bellini, known through
several copies
Early 16th century
Oil on panel
27 5/8 × 24 1/8" (70.2 × 61.3 cm)

John G. Johnson Collection
cat. 183

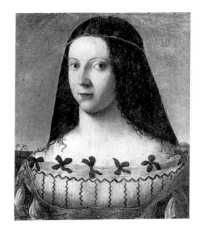

**Bartolomeo Veneto,
copy after**
Previously attributed to
Bernardino de' Conti (JI 1966)
*Portrait of a Woman Once Identified
as Beatrice d'Este*
After the painting in the Snite
Museum of Art, University of
Notre Dame, Indiana (51.4.13)
19th century
Oil on panel
16 1/4 × 13 3/16" (41.3 × 33.5 cm)

John G. Johnson Collection
cat. 270

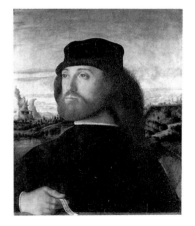

**Basaiti, Marco**
Italian, active Venice,
born c. 1470, still active 1530
*Portrait of a Gentleman*
c. 1500
Center bottom (spurious):
IOHANES BELLI / NVS/1488.
Oil on panel
21 1/2 × 16 7/8" (54.6 × 42.9 cm)

John G. Johnson Collection
cat. 179

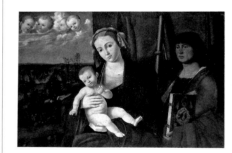

**Basaiti, Marco**
*Virgin and Child, with Saint James
the Great*
c. 1500–1
Center right: MARCVS.B[ ]I /
TI. / .F
Oil on panel transferred to canvas
28 1/4 × 40" (71.7 × 101.6 cm)

John G. Johnson Collection
cat. 180

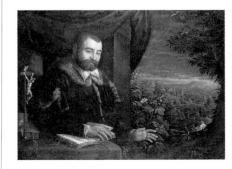

**Bassano, Leandro
(Leandro da Ponte)**
Italian, active Venice and
Bassano, 1557–1622
*Portrait of a Gentleman Seated
before a Landscape*
Early 17th century
Oil on canvas
39 7/8 × 53 3/8" (101.3 × 135.6 cm)

John G. Johnson Collection
cat. 212

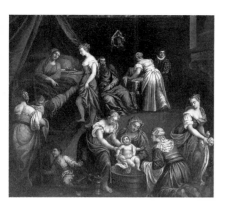

**Bassano, Leandro, follower of**
*The Birth of the Virgin*
Late 16th century
Oil on canvas
61 × 67 1/2" (154.9 × 171.4 cm)

Bequest of Arthur H. Lea
F1938-1-41

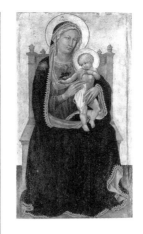

**Battista di Maestro Gerio**
Italian, active Pisa,
documented 1418–1433
Previously listed as the Master of
the Bambino Vispo (JI 1966)
*Enthroned Virgin and Child*
Center panel from an altarpiece;
companion to two panels in
private collections
c. 1426
Tempera and tooled gold on panel
46 5/8 × 25 1/2" (118.4 × 64.8 cm)

John G. Johnson Collection
cat. 12

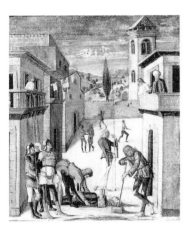

**Bastiani, Lazzaro di Jacopo, follower of**
Italian, active Venice and
environs, first documented 1449,
died 1512
*The Martyrdom of Saint George*
Companion to the following
painting
c. 1495
Oil on panel
21 3/8 × 14 3/4" (54.3 × 37.5 cm)

John G. Johnson Collection
cat. 174

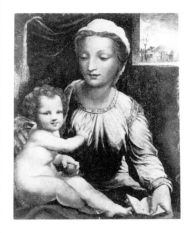

**Beccafumi, Domenico (Domenico di Pace), also called Mecarino, follower of**
Italian, active Siena, 1486–1551
*Virgin and Child*
c. 1535–40
Oil on canvas
28 × 21" (71.1 × 53.3 cm)

Bequest of Arthur H. Lea
F1938-1-43

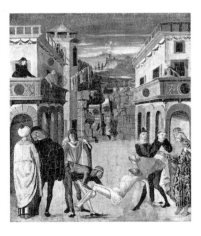

**Bastiani, Lazzaro di Jacopo, follower of**
*The Burial of Saint George*
Companion to the preceding
painting
c. 1495
Oil on panel
21 3/8 × 17 3/4" (54.3 × 45.1 cm)

John G. Johnson Collection
cat. 175

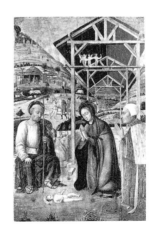

**Bellini, Gentile, follower of**
Italian, active Venice and
Constantinople, first recorded
1460, died 1507
Previously listed as Lazzaro
Bastiani (JI 1966)
*The Nativity, with the Doge
Cristoforo Moro, and the
Annunciation to the Shepherds*
c. 1462–71
Oil on panel
37 1/2 × 23 5/8" (95.2 × 60 cm)

John G. Johnson Collection
cat. 163

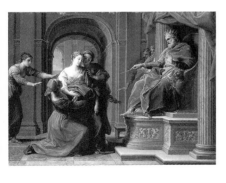

**Batoni, Pompeo Girolamo**
Italian, 1708–1787
*Esther before Ahasuerus*
1738–40
Oil on canvas
29 1/8 × 39 1/16" (74 × 99.2 cm)

Gift of the Women's Committee
of the Philadelphia Museum of
Art in honor of their 100th
anniversary
1982-89-1

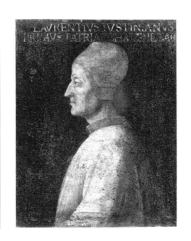

**Bellini, Gentile, copy after**
*Portrait of Lorenzo Giustiniani*
After the full-length portrait,
dated 1465, in the Gallerie
dell'Accademia, Venice
(inv. no. 593, cat. no. 570)
Late 15th century
Across top: LAVRENTIVS
IVSTINIANVS / PRIMVS
PATRIARCHA VENETIAE
Oil on canvas
25 3/4 × 19 3/8" (65.4 × 49.2 cm)

John G. Johnson Collection
cat. 162

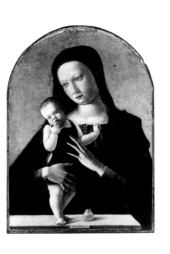

**Bellini, Giovanni,
also called Giambellino**
Italian, active Venice, first
documented 1459, died 1516
*Virgin and Child*
c. 1459–60
Center bottom: [I]OANNES
BELLINVS
Oil on panel
25 3/8 × 17 3/8" (64.4 × 44.1 cm)

John G. Johnson Collection
cat. 165

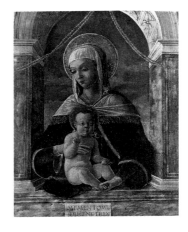

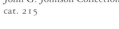

**Benaglio, Francesco,
attributed to**
Italian, active Verona, first
documented 1462, died c. 1492
*Virgin and Child*
c. 1460–70
Center bottom: MEMENTOMEI /
DEIGENETRIX
Oil on panel transferred to canvas
20 1/8 × 16 1/8" (51.1 × 41 cm)

John G. Johnson Collection
cat. 215

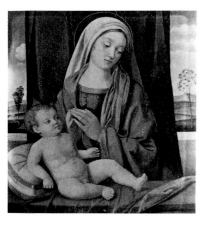

**Bellini, Giovanni,
Emilian follower of**
Previously listed as Gerolamo da
Santacroce (JI 1966)
*Virgin and Child*
Based on the composition by
Giovanni Bellini, in the Galleria
Doria Pamphili, Rome (521)
c. 1500
Oil on panel
20 × 17 5/8" (50.8 × 44.8 cm)

John G. Johnson Collection
cat. 185

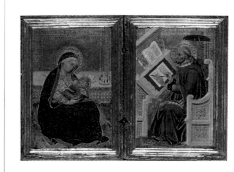

**Benedetto di Bindo,
attributed to**
Italian, active Siena and Perugia,
first securely documented 1410,
died 1417
Previously listed as a Sienese
artist, late 14th century (JI 1966)
*The Virgin of Humility, and Saint
Jerome Translating the Gospel of
John*
Diptych
c. 1400–5
Across lower frame: [ ]OSTRA
DONNA DEL[ ]UM [rest
illegible]; left panel, on book:
[abbreviated Latin text of Psalm
69:2]; right panel, on book:
[abbreviated Latin text of John
1:1–7]
Tempera and tooled gold on panel
11 7/8 × 16 5/8" (30.2 × 42.2 cm)

John G. Johnson Collection
cat. 153

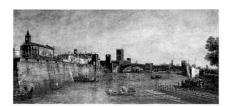

**Bellotto, Bernardo**
Italian, active Veneto,
1721–1780
*View of Verona with the
Castelvecchio and Ponte Scaligero*
c. 1745–46
Oil on canvas
29 × 60 3/4" (73.7 × 154.3 cm)

The William L. Elkins Collection
E1924-3-87

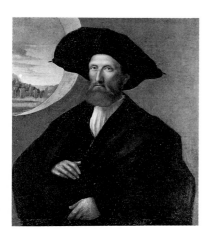

**Bembo, Gian Francesco,
attributed to**
Italian, active Cremona, first
documented 1515, died c. 1526
Previously listed as a Venetian
artist, c. 1520–30 (JI 1966)
*Portrait of an Elderly Gentleman*
c. 1520–25
Oil on canvas
31 1/4 × 27 3/4" (79.4 × 70.5 cm)

John G. Johnson Collection
cat. 181

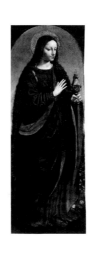

**Bergognone (Ambrogio di
Stefano da Fossano)**
Italian, active Lombardy,
documented 1481–1522
*Saint Mary Magdalene*
Panel from an altarpiece; other
panels are in the Accademia
Carrara, Bergamo; and a private
collection
c. 1515
Oil on panel
49 1/8 × 17 1/16" (124.8 × 43.3 cm)

John G. Johnson Collection
cat. 259

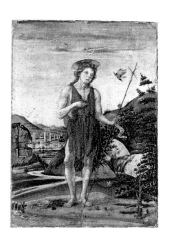

**Biagio d'Antonio da Firenze**
Italian, active Florence, Rome, and Faenza, documented 1476–1504
Previously listed as the school of Piero di Cosimo ( JI 1966)
*Saint John the Baptist in the Wilderness*
Early 1480s
Center right, on banner: EGO VOS CHIAM [ ]
Tempera on panel
11 1/8 × 7 3/4" (28.3 × 19.7 cm)

John G. Johnson Collection
cat. 77

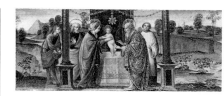

**Binasco, Francesco (Francesco da Lonate)**
Italian, active Milan, active c. 1486–1520
Previously listed as Vincenzo Civerchio ( JI 1966)
*The Circumcision of Christ*
c. 1500
Oil on panel
9 1/4 × 21 3/16" (23.5 × 53.8 cm)

John G. Johnson Collection
cat. 263

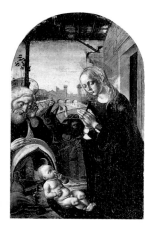

**Biagio d'Antonio da Firenze**
Previously listed as Giovanni Battista Utili da Faenza ( JI 1966)
*The Adoration of the Christ Child*
Late 15th century
Tempera and gold on panel
38 3/8 × 22 3/8" (97.5 × 56.8 cm)

John G. Johnson Collection
cat. 62

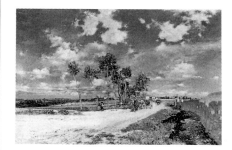

**Boldini, Giovanni**
Italian, 1842–1931
*Highway of Combes-la-Ville*
1873
Lower left: Boldini / 73
Oil on canvas
27 1/4 × 39 15/16" (69.2 × 101.4 cm)

The George W. Elkins Collection
E1924-4-2

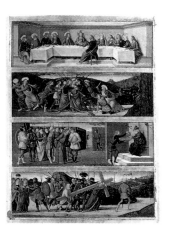

**Biagio d'Antonio da Firenze**
Previously listed as David Ghirlandaio ( JI 1966)
*The Last Supper, the Betrayal of Christ, Christ before Pilate, and Christ Carrying the Cross*
Predella panels; now framed vertically
Late 15th century
Tempera and gold on panel
Each panel: 4 × 12 1/2"
(10.2 × 31.7 cm)

John G. Johnson Collection
cat. 67

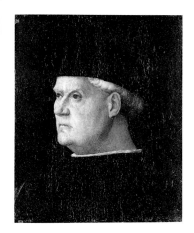

**Bonsignori, Francesco**
Italian, active Verona, c. 1460–1519
*Portrait of an Elderly Gentleman*
c. 1485–90
Oil on panel
16 1/16 × 12 5/8" (40.8 × 32.1 cm)

John G. Johnson Collection
cat. 171

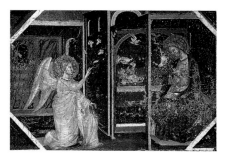

**Bicci di Lorenzo, workshop of**
Italian, active Florence, 1373–1452
Previously listed as the school of Agnolo Gaddi ( JI 1966)
*The Annunciation*
Predella panel
c. 1415
Tempera and tooled gold on panel
9 5/8 × 13 7/8" (24.9 × 35.2 cm)

John G. Johnson Collection
cat. 7

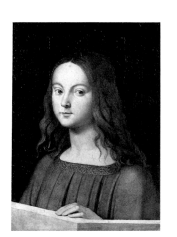

**Bonsignori, Francesco**
*Christ as a Boy*
c. 1510–14
Lower right: F B
Oil on panel
19 5/8 × 14" (49.8 × 35.6 cm)

John G. Johnson Collection
cat. 172

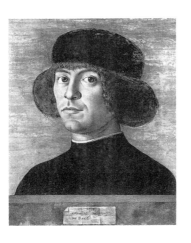

**Bonsignori, Francesco, attributed to**
*Portrait of a Young Gentleman*
c. 1485
Center bottom (spurious): 1477 /
antonellus messaneus / me Pinxit
Oil on panel
11 1/2 × 9 3/8" (29.2 × 23.8 cm)

John G. Johnson Collection
inv. 732

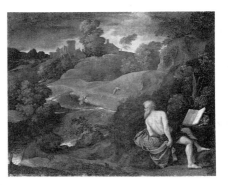

**Bordone, Paris
(Paris Pasqualino)**
Italian, active Venice,
1500–1571
*Saint Jerome in the Wilderness*
c. 1520–25
Oil on canvas
27 5/8 × 34 3/8" (70.2 × 87.3 cm)

John G. Johnson Collection
cat. 206

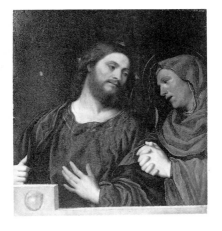

**Bordone, Paris**
*Christ Taking Leave of His Mother*
c. 1530
Oil on canvas transferred from
panel
32 3/4 × 28 3/4" (83.2 × 73 cm)

John G. Johnson Collection
cat. 207

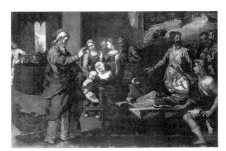

**Boscoli, Andrea**
Italian, active Florence,
c. 1560–1607
Previously listed as Pietro
Mariscalchi (JI 1966)
*Saint John the Evangelist Reviving
Drusiana*
1599
Oil on canvas
30 1/4 × 45 1/4" (76.8 × 114.9 cm)

John G. Johnson Collection
cat. 224

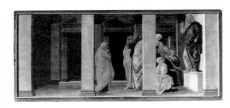

**Botticelli, Sandro (Alessandro
di Mariano Filipepi)**
Italian, active Florence and
Rome, 1445–1510
*Saint Mary Magdalene Listening to
Christ Preach*
Predella panel from an altarpiece
from the convent of Sant'Elisabet-
ta delle Convertite, Florence, the
main panel of which is in the
Courtauld Institute Galleries,
London (The Lee Collection, 61);
companion to the following three
panels
c. 1484–91
Tempera on panel
7 7/8 × 17 1/4" (20 × 43.8 cm)

John G. Johnson Collection
cat. 44

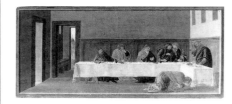

**Botticelli, Sandro**
*The Feast in the House of Simon*
See previous entry
c. 1484–91
Tempera on panel
7 13/16 × 17 3/16" (19.8 × 43.7 cm)

John G. Johnson Collection
cat. 45

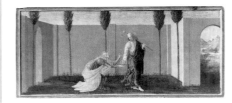

**Botticelli, Sandro**
*"Noli Me Tangere"*
See previous two entries
c. 1484–91
Tempera on panel
7 3/4 × 17 5/16" (19.7 × 44 cm)

John G. Johnson Collection
cat. 46

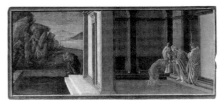

**Botticelli, Sandro**
*The Last Moments of Saint Mary
Magdalene*
See previous three entries
c. 1484–91
Tempera on panel
7 3/16 × 17 1/4" (18.3 × 43.8 cm)

John G. Johnson Collection
cat. 47

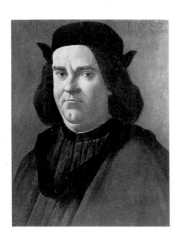

**Botticelli, Sandro**
*Portrait of Lorenzo de' Lorenzi*
c. 1492
Across top: L.LOREN TIANO
Oil on panel
20 × 14 3/8" (50.8 × 36.5 cm)

John G. Johnson Collection
cat. 48

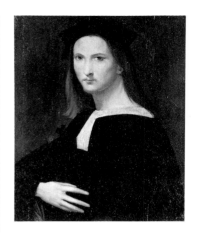

Previously listed as Andrea
Brescianino (JI 1966)
*Portrait of a Young Gentleman*
c. 1510–15
Oil on panel
26 1/4 × 21 5/16" (66.7 × 54.1 cm)

John G. Johnson Collection
cat. 113

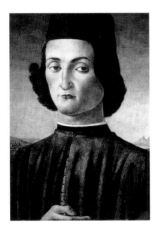

**Botticelli, Sandro,
follower of**
Previously listed as Sandro
Botticelli (JI 1966)
*Portrait of a Young Man*
Late 15th century
Tempera on panel
19 1/16 × 12 7/8" (48.4 × 32.7 cm)

John G. Johnson Collection
cat. 50

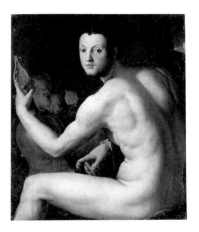

**Bronzino, Agnolo (Agnolo
di Cosimo di Mariano)**
Italian, active Florence,
1503–1572
*Portrait of Cosimo I de' Medici as
Orpheus*
c. 1538–40
Oil on panel
36 7/8 × 30 1/16" (93.7 × 76.4 cm)

Gift of Mrs. John Wintersteen
1950-86-1

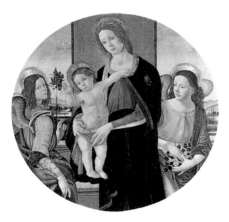

**Botticelli, Sandro,
follower of**
*Virgin and Child, with Two Angels*
c. 1500
Oil on panel
38" (96.5 cm) diameter

John G. Johnson Collection
cat. 49

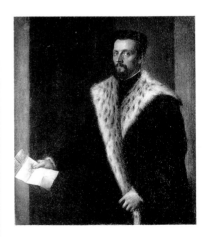

**Brusasorci (Domenico
Riccio), also called Brusasorzi**
Italian, active Verona and
Mantua, c. 1516–1567
Previously listed as the area of
Paolo Veronese–Leandro Bassano
(JI 1966)
*Portrait of a Gentleman with a
Letter*
1551
On letter: MDLI
Oil on canvas
42 3/8 × 35 1/4" (107.6 × 89.5 cm)

John G. Johnson Collection
cat. 229

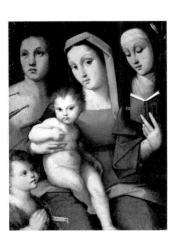

**Brescianino, Andrea
(Andrea di Giovannantonio
di Tommaso Piccinelli)**
Italian, active Siena and Florence,
documented 1506–1525
*Virgin and Child, with the Young
Saint John the Baptist and Saints
Sebastian and Catherine of Siena*
1520s
Center bottom: [E]CCE AGNVS
DEI
Oil on panel
27 1/8 × 20 1/2" (68.9 × 52.1 cm)

John G. Johnson Collection
cat. 114

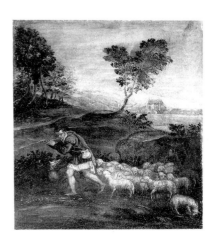

**Brusasorci, attributed to**
*Shepherd with His Flock*
c. 1540–50
Oil on canvas
17 5/8 × 15 3/8" (44.8 × 39 cm)

John G. Johnson Collection
cat. 227

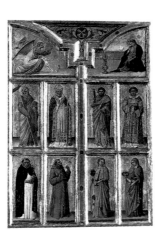

**Bulgarini, Bartolomeo**
Italian, active Siena, first
documented 1337, died 1378
Left panel: *Annunciate Angel, Saint
Andrew, a Bishop Saint, Saint
Dominic, and Saint Francis of
Assisi*; right panel: *Annunciate
Virgin, Saint Bartholomew, a
Deacon Saint, Saint Lucy, and Saint
Agatha*
Wings from a triptych, framed
together; the center panel is in
the Isabella Stewart Gardner
Museum, Boston (P15n8)
c. 1355–60
On angel's scroll: AVE GRATIA
PLENA
Tempera and tooled gold on panel
25 1/8 × 16 7/8" (63.8 × 42.9 cm)
overall

John G. Johnson Collection
cat. 92

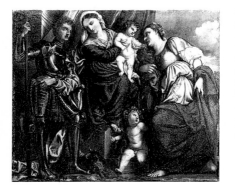

**Campagnola, Domenico**
Italian, active Venice and Padua,
c. 1500–1564
*Virgin and Child, with Saints
George and Catherine of Alexandria,
and a Putto*
c. 1520
Oil on canvas
34 1/2 × 40 1/16" (87.6 × 101.8 cm)

John G. Johnson Collection
cat. 202

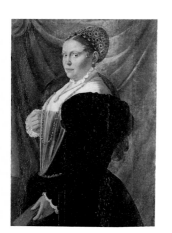

**Campi, Giulio, attributed to**
Italian, active Cremona,
born 1500–2, died 1572
Previously listed as Giulio Campi
(PMA 1965)
*Portrait of a Lady*
Mid-16th century
Oil on panel
40 1/8 × 26 5/8" (101.9 × 67.6 cm)

Purchased with the W. P.
Wilstach Fund
W1896-1-6

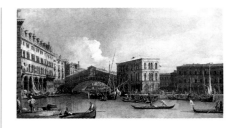

**Canaletto (Giovanni Antonio
Canal)**
Italian, active Venice, Rome,
and England, 1697–1768
*Rialto Bridge*
c. 1730
Oil on canvas
14 9/16 × 25 11/16" (37 × 65.2 cm)

John G. Johnson Collection
inv. 1404

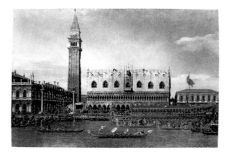

**Canaletto**
*The Bucintoro at the Molo on
Ascension Day*
c. 1745
Oil on canvas
45 1/4 × 64" (114.9 × 162.6 cm)

The William L. Elkins Collection
E1924-3-48

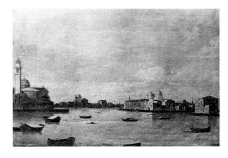

**Canaletto, studio of**
*Bacino of San Marco*
Unfinished
After 1726–28
Oil on canvas
13 1/8 × 19 3/8" (33.3 × 49.2 cm)

John G. Johnson Collection
cat. 1173

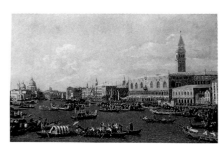

**Canaletto, studio of**
*The Bucintoro at the Molo on
Ascension Day*
Version of the painting in the
collection of the Duke of Bedford,
Woburn
After 1731
Oil on canvas
48 1/8 × 76 1/4" (122.2 × 193.7 cm)

John G. Johnson Collection
cat. 292

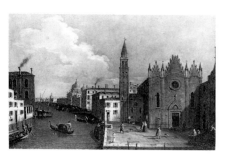

**Canaletto, follower of**
*Grand Canal at Santa Maria della Carità*
After 1726
Oil on canvas
20 5/16 × 30" (51.6 × 76.2 cm)

John G. Johnson Collection
cat. 295

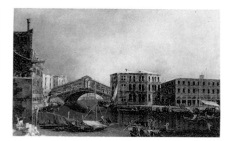

**Canaletto, follower of**
Previously listed as an imitator of Canaletto (PMA 1965)
*Rialto Bridge from the North*
Close to Michele Marieschi; companion to the preceding painting
After 1741?
Oil on canvas
25 × 38 5/8" (63.5 × 98.1 cm)

The William L. Elkins Collection
E1924-3-24

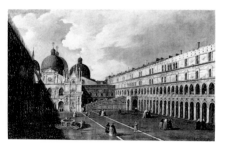

**Canaletto, follower of**
*Court of the Doge's Palace*
1740s
Oil on canvas
29 1/2 × 44 7/8" (74.9 × 114 cm)

John G. Johnson Collection
cat. 293

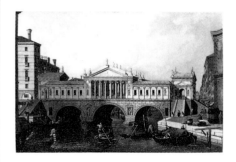

**Canaletto, copy after**
*Capriccio with a Palladian Design for the Rialto Bridge*
After the painting in the collection of Her Majesty Queen Elizabeth II (408)
Soon after 1743–44
Lower right (spurious): ACanal F.
Oil on canvas
35 3/8 × 51 1/8" (89.8 × 129.9 cm)

Purchased with the W. P. Wilstach Fund
W1895-1-3

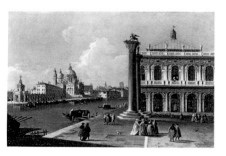

**Canaletto, follower of**
*View from the Piazzetta*
1740s?
Oil on canvas
20 1/4 × 30" (51.4 × 76.2 cm)

John G. Johnson Collection
cat. 294

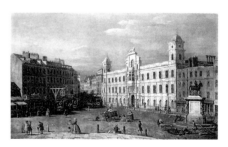

**Canaletto, copy after**
*Northumberland House*
After the painting in the collection of the Duke of Northumberland, Alnwick Castle; possibly by an English copyist; pendant to the following painting
After 1752–53
Oil on canvas
22 1/2 × 35 1/4" (57.1 × 89.5 cm)

Gift of John Howard McFadden, Jr.
1946-36-2

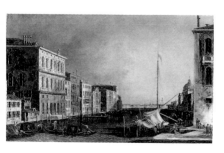

**Canaletto, follower of**
Previously listed as the studio of Canaletto (PMA 1965)
*Grand Canal from Campo di San Vio*
Close to Michele Marieschi; companion to the following painting
After 1741?
Oil on canvas
25 × 38 1/2" (63.5 × 97.8 cm)

The William L. Elkins Collection
E1924-3-25

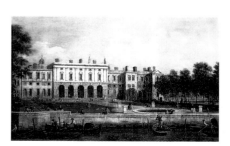

**Canaletto, copy after**
*Old Somerset House from the River Thames*
After a painting in a private collection in the United Kingdom; possibly by an English copyist; pendant to the preceding painting
After 1752–53
Oil on canvas
22 1/2 × 35 1/4" (57.1 × 89.5 cm)

Gift of John Howard McFadden, Jr.
1946-36-3

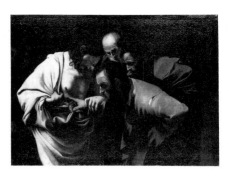

**Caravaggio (Michelangelo Merisi), copy after**
Italian, 1573–1610
*The Incredulity of the Apostle Thomas*
After a painting in the Staatliche Schlösser und Gärten Potsdam-Sanssouci
17th century
Oil on canvas
45 1/4 × 60 5/8" (114.9 × 154 cm)

Bequest of Arthur H. Lea
F1938-1-34

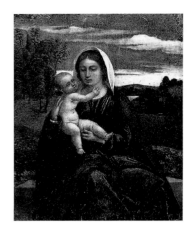

**Cavazzola (Paolo Morando), attributed to**
Italian, active Verona, 1486–1522
*Virgin and Child in a Landscape*
c. 1520–22
Oil on panel
15 5/16 × 12 1/8" (38.9 × 30.8 cm)

John G. Johnson Collection
cat. 220

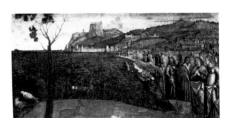

**Carpaccio, Vittore**
Italian, active Venice, first documented 1490, died 1523–26
*The Metamorphosis of Alcyone*
c. 1495–1500
Oil on panel
27 3/8 × 49 9/16" (69.5 × 125.9 cm)

John G. Johnson Collection
cat. 173

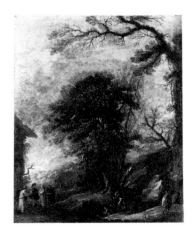

**Cecco Bravo (Francesco Montelatici)**
Italian, active Florence, 1601–1661
*Landscape with Figures*
c. 1635–40
Oil on canvas
31 3/8 × 24 1/2" (79.7 × 62.2 cm)

Bequest of Arthur H. Lea
F1938-1-32

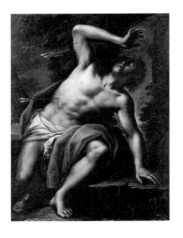

**Carracci, Lodovico, follower of**
Italian, active Bologna, 1555–1619
*Saint Sebastian*
Early 17th century
Oil on canvas
39 1/4 × 29 3/8" (99.7 × 74.6 cm)

Purchased with the W. P. Wilstach Fund
W1904-1-3

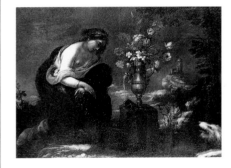

**Cecco Bravo, attributed to**
*Andromeda* [?]
Mid-17th century
Oil on canvas
45 3/16 × 59 5/8" (114.8 × 151.4 cm)

Bequest of Arthur H. Lea
F1938-1-23

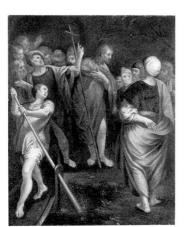

**Carracci, Lodovico, copy after**
Previously listed as a North Italian artist, c. 1600 (JI 1966)
*Saint John the Baptist Preaching*
After the painting in the Pinacoteca Nazionale, Bologna (inv. 458)
Late 17th century?
Oil on canvas
20 3/4 × 16" (52.7 × 40.6 cm)

John G. Johnson Collection
cat. 240

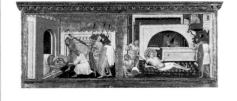

**Cenni di Francesco di Ser Cenni**
Italian, active Florence, Volterra, and San Gimignano, documented 1369–1415
Previously listed as Giovanni del Biondo (JI 1966)
*The Beheading of Saint John the Baptist and the Martyrdom of Saint Lawrence*
Predella panel; companion to the following two panels
c. 1385–90
Tempera and tooled gold on panel
13 × 30 1/2" (33 × 77.5 cm)

John G. Johnson Collection
inv. 1290

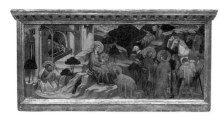

**Cenni di Francesco di Ser Cenni**
Previously listed as Giovanni del Biondo (JI 1966)
*The Adoration of the Magi*
See previous entry
c. 1385–90
Tempera and tooled gold on panel
13 × 25 5/16" (33 × 64.3 cm)

John G. Johnson Collection
inv. 1291

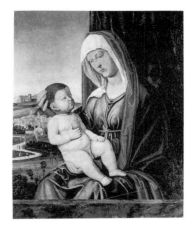

**Cima da Conegliano
(Giovanni Battista Cima)**
Italian, active Venice and Veneto,
1459/60–1517/18
*Virgin and Child before a Landscape*
c. 1485–86
Center bottom: IOANNES
BAPTISTA / DE CONEGLIANO.P
Oil on panel
23 3/4 × 18 3/4" (60.3 × 47.6 cm)

John G. Johnson Collection
cat. 176

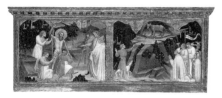

**Cenni di Francesco di Ser Cenni**
Previously listed as Giovanni del Biondo (JI 1966)
*The Martyrdom of Saint Bartholomew and the Archangel Michael with the Bull on Mount Gargano*
See previous two entries
c. 1385–90
Tempera and tooled gold on panel
13 × 30 5/16" (33 × 77 cm)

John G. Johnson Collection
inv. 1292

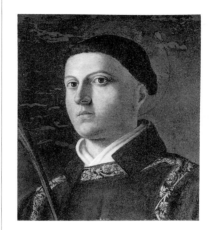

**Cima da Conegliano**
*Head of Saint Stephen*
Fragment
c. 1500–10
Oil on panel transferred to canvas
12 3/4 × 10 7/8" (32.4 × 27.6 cm)

John G. Johnson Collection
cat. 1171

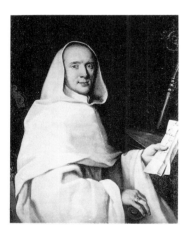

**Chiari, Giuseppe Bartolomeo, attributed to**
Italian, 1654–1727
Previously listed as Alonso Cano (PMA 1965)
*Carthusian Abbot*
1720s
Oil on canvas
38 1/2 × 29 1/2" (97.8 × 74.9 cm)

Purchased with the W. P. Wilstach Fund
W1904-1-2

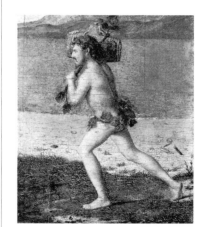

**Cima da Conegliano**
*Bacchant*
Fragment; companion to the following panel and a panel in a private collection in Paris
c. 1505–10
Oil on panel
9 11/16 × 7 5/8" (24.6 × 19.4 cm)

John G. Johnson Collection
cat. 178

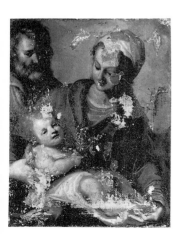

**Cigoli (Lodovico Cardi), copy after**
Italian, active Florence,
1559–1613
*The Holy Family*
After the painting in the Galleria Palatina, Florence
17th century
Oil on canvas
24 7/8 × 18 7/16" (63.2 × 46.8 cm)

Bequest of Arthur H. Lea
F1938-1-19

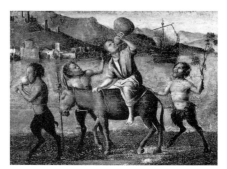

**Cima da Conegliano**
*Silenus and Satyrs*
Fragment; companion to the preceding panel and a panel in a private collection in Paris
c. 1505–10
Oil on panel
12 1/4 × 16 1/8" (31.1 × 41 cm)

John G. Johnson Collection
cat. 177

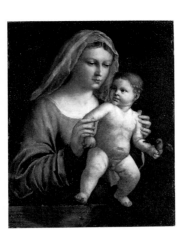

**Cima da Conegliano,
copy after**
*Virgin and Child*
After the painting in the
National Gallery, London (no.
634)
16th century
Oil on panel
22 1/16 × 17 1/16" (56 × 43.3 cm)

John G. Johnson Collection
cat. 192

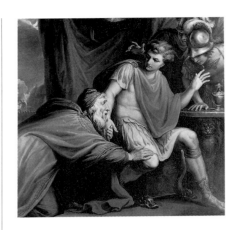

**Cipriani, Giovanni Battista**
*Achilles Besought by Priam for the
Body of His Son Hector*
c. 1776
Oil on canvas
42 1/16 × 41 3/4" (106.8 × 106 cm)

Purchased with the John Howard
McFadden, Jr., Fund
1972-250-4

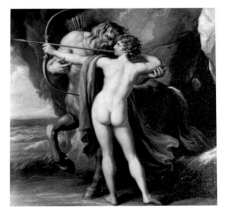

**Cipriani, Giovanni Battista**
Italian, active Florence and
England, 1727–1785
*The Education of Achilles*
c. 1776
Oil on canvas
41 1/16 × 41" (104.3 × 104.1 cm)

Purchased with the John Howard
McFadden, Jr., Fund
1972-250-1

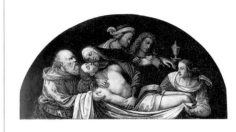

**Coda, Benedetto,
workshop of**
Italian, active Rimini,
first documented 1495–96,
died before 1544
**and Bartolomeo Coda**
Italian, active Rimini,
documented 1516–1565
Previously listed as School of the
Marches, c. 1530 (JI 1966)
*Lamentation*
Lunette of an altarpiece
c. 1540–50
Oil on panel
33 1/8 × 63 1/8" (84.1 × 160.3 cm)

John G. Johnson Collection
cat. 201

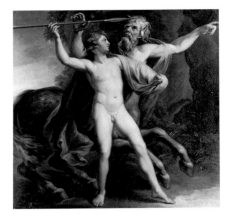

**Cipriani, Giovanni Battista**
*Chiron Instructing Achilles in the
Bow*
c. 1776
Oil on canvas
42 7/16 × 42 1/8" (107.8 × 107 cm)

Purchased with the John Howard
McFadden, Jr., Fund
1972-250-2

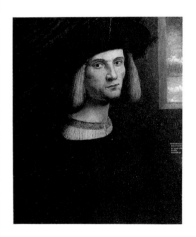

**Conti, Bernardino de'**
Italian, active Milan,
documented 1494–1522
*Portrait of a Gentleman*
c. 1510
Center right: BERNARDINVS /
DE' COMITIBVS / DE CASTRO /
SEPII / FACIEBAT
Oil on panel
23 1/2 × 19 1/2" (59.7 × 49.5 cm)

John G. Johnson Collection
cat. 269

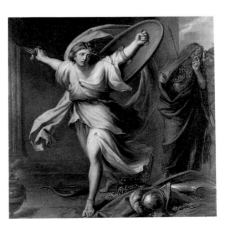

**Cipriani, Giovanni Battista**
*Achilles Discovered by Ulysses among
the Daughters of Lycomedes*
c. 1776
Oil on canvas
42 1/2 × 42 1/4" (107.9 × 107.3 cm)

Purchased with the John Howard
McFadden, Jr., Fund
1972-250-3

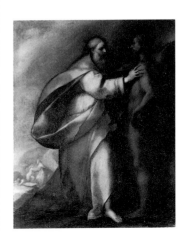

**Cornara, Carlo, attributed to**
Italian, active Milan and
environs, 1605–1673
Previously listed as the school of
Palma il Vecchio (JI 1966)
*The Creation of Adam*
Mid-17th century
Oil on canvas
56 1/2 × 42 1/2" (143.5 × 107.9 cm)

John G. Johnson Collection
cat. 189

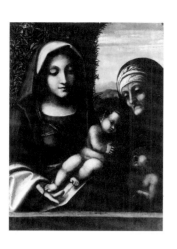

**Correggio (Antonio di Pellegrino Allegri)**
Italian, active Parma,
1489–1534
*Virgin and Child, with Saint Elizabeth and the Young Saint John the Baptist*
c. 1510–12
Oil on panel
23 7/8 × 17 1/4" (60.6 × 43.8 cm)

John G. Johnson Collection
cat. 1173a

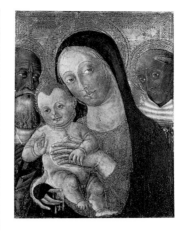

**Cozzarelli, Guidoccio di Giovanni, follower of**
Italian, active Siena, 1450–1517
Previously listed as Guidoccio di Giovanni Cozzarelli (JI 1966)
*Virgin and Child, with Saints Jerome and Bernardino*
Late 15th century
Tempera and tooled gold on panel
22 3/16 × 17 1/8" (56.4 × 43.5 cm)

John G. Johnson Collection
cat. 112

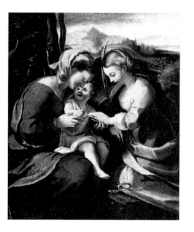

**Correggio, copy after**
*The Mystic Marriage of Saint Catherine of Alexandria*
After the painting in the Museo e Gallerie Nazionali di Capodimonte, Naples (106)
Late 17th century?
Oil on panel
11 1/2 × 9 1/2" (29.2 × 24.1 cm)

John G. Johnson Collection
cat. 254

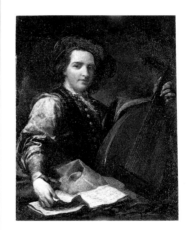

**Crespi, Giuseppe Maria, attributed to**
Italian, active Bologna,
1665–1747
Previously listed as Fra Vittorio Ghislandi (JI 1966)
*Portrait of a Musician*
c. 1740
Oil on canvas
41 3/8 × 30 3/4" (105.1 × 78.1 cm)

John G. Johnson Collection
cat. 291

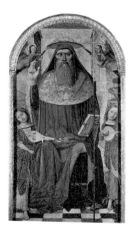

**Corso, Nicolò (Nicolò di Lombarduccio da Pieve di Vico)**
Italian, active Liguria, documented 1469–1503
Previously listed as Giovanni Massone (JI 1966)
*Enthroned Saint Jerome, with Angels*
Panel from the high altarpiece of San Gerolamo di Quarto, Genoa; two side panels are in the Museo e Galleria dell'Accademia Ligustica di Belle Arti, Genoa (inv. 68, 69)
c. 1495
Oil and gold on panel
57 × 29 3/4" (144.8 × 75.6 cm)

John G. Johnson Collection
cat. 262

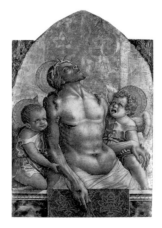

**Crivelli, Carlo**
Italian, active Venice and Marches, first documented 1457, died 1495–1500
*Dead Christ Supported by Two Angels*
Pinnacle from an altarpiece
c. 1472
Tempera and tooled gold on panel
28 × 18 5/8" (71.1 × 47.3 cm)

John G. Johnson Collection
cat. 158

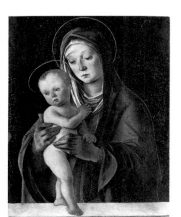

**Costa, Lorenzo di Ottavio**
Italian, active Bologna, Ferrara, and Mantua, c. 1460–1535
*Virgin and Child*
c. 1490
Oil on panel
18 1/4 × 13 1/2" (46.3 × 34.3 cm)

John G. Johnson Collection
cat. 244

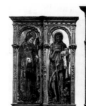

**Crivelli, Vittore**
Italian, active Venice and Marches, active by c. 1481, died c. 1502
*Enthroned Virgin and Child, with Angels and Saints Bonaventure, John the Baptist, Louis of Toulouse, and Francis of Assisi*
Panels from an altarpiece; in a 19th-century frame
1481
On Baptist's scroll: ECCE ANGNVS DEI QVI / TOLLIS PECCATA MVNDI

Tempera on panel
Center panel: 55 ¾ × 30"
(141.6 × 76.2 cm); far left panel:
49 ⅞ × 15 ¼" (126.7 × 38.7 cm);
near left panel: 50 × 15 ⅛"
(127 × 38.4 cm); near right
panel: 49 ⅞ × 15 ¼" (126.7 ×
38.7 cm); far right panel:
49 ⅞ × 15 ⅜" (126.7 × 39 cm)

Purchased with the W. P.
Wilstach Fund
W1896-1-11a–e

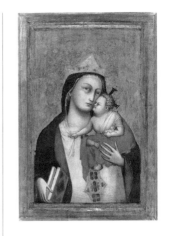

**Dalmasio, attributed to**
Italian, active Bologna, Pistoia,
and Florence, first documented
1342, died before 1377
Previously listed as an immediate
follower of Giotto (JI 1966)
*Virgin and Child, with a Dog*
c. 1330–35
Tempera and tooled gold on panel
18 ⁵⁄₁₆ × 12" (46.5 × 30.5 cm)

John G. Johnson Collection
cat. 3

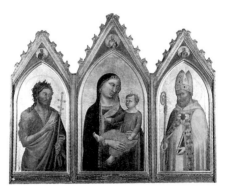

**Daddi, Bernardo**
Italian, active Florence, first
securely documented 1327,
died 1348?
Previously listed as a close
follower of Bernardo Daddi
(JI 1966)
*Virgin and Child, with Saints John
the Baptist and Giles, Two Prophets,
and Christ Blessing*
Panels from an altarpiece;
companion panels are in the Fogg
Art Museum, Cambridge, Mass.
(1936.56), and a private collection
1334
Left panel, bottom of frame: SCS
IOHES BTA; center panel, bottom
of frame: M CCC XXX IIII; right
panel, bottom of frame: SCS
EGIDIUS ABBAS
Tempera and tooled gold and
silver on panel
Left panel: 30 ⅛ × 14 ¼"
(76.5 × 36.2 cm); center panel:
33 ¼ × 17 ¹³⁄₁₆" (84.4 × 45.2 cm);
right panel: 30 ¼ × 14 ¹⁄₁₆"
(76.8 × 35.7 cm)

John G. Johnson Collection
inv. 334

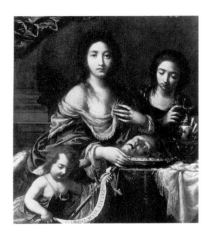

**Dandini, Cesare**
Italian, active Florence,
1596–1657
Previously attributed to Carlo
Dolci (PMA 1965)
*Salome with the Head of Saint John
the Baptist*
1630s
On banner: PARATE VIAM
DOMINI
Oil on canvas
45 ¼ × 36 ¼" (114.9 × 92.1 cm)

Purchased with the W. P.
Wilstach Fund
W1904-1-9

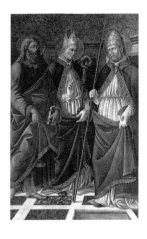

**Fra Diamante
(Diamante di Feo)**
Italian, active Florence, born
c. 1430, last documented 1498
Previously listed as Pesellino
(JI 1966)
*An Apostle Saint, a Bishop Saint,
and a Papal Saint*
Panel from an altarpiece
c. 1480
Tempera and tooled gold on
panel transferred to canvas
71 ½ × 41" (181.6 × 104.1 cm)

John G. Johnson Collection
cat. 55

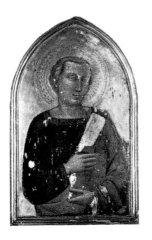

**Daddi, Bernardo**
Previously listed as Allegretto di
Nuzio (JI 1966)
*Saint John the Evangelist*
Panel from an altarpiece;
companion panels are in the
Fondazione Paolo VI, Gazzada
(Milan); the Thyssen-Bornemisza
Collection (1928.11); and Pieve
di San Giovanni Maggiore,
Panicaglia (on deposit Santo
Stefano al Ponte, Florence)
c. 1345–48
Tempera and tooled gold on panel
27 ½ × 16 ⅛" (69.8 × 41 cm)

John G. Johnson Collection
cat. 117

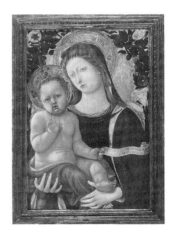

**Domenico di Bartolo (Dome-
nico di Bartolo Ghezzi)**
Italian, active Siena,
documented 1427–1444
*Virgin and Child*
1437
On banner: ME DVLCIS IN TE
NON DESINIT VSQUE PRECLARI /
INGNEM VT NOMINIS PARCE MI-
TIS EGO; on frame: DOMENICUS
DE SENIIS ME PINXIT ANNO D[O-
MINI] MCCCCXXXVII; on Christ's
halo: MV[N]DI EG[O]; on Virgin's
halo: AVE REGI[N]A C[AELO]
Tempera and tooled gold on panel
24 ⅜ × 17 ¼" (61.9 × 43.8 cm)

John G. Johnson Collection
cat. 102

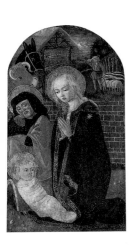

**Domenico di Zanobi (Master of the Johnson Nativity)**
Italian, active Florence, documented 1445–1481
Previously listed as the school of Cosimo Rosselli (JI 1966)
*The Nativity*
c. 1467
Tempera and tooled gold on panel
34 1/2 × 19 1/16" (87.6 × 48.4 cm)

John G. Johnson Collection
cat. 61

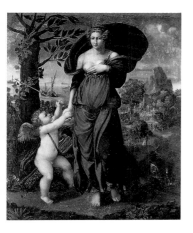

**Dossi, Battista (Battista de' Luteri)**
Italian, active Ferrara, c. 1474–1548
*Venus and Cupid*
c. 1540
Oil on canvas
62 × 50 1/4" (157.5 × 127.6 cm)

Purchased with the George W. Elkins Fund
E1972-2-1

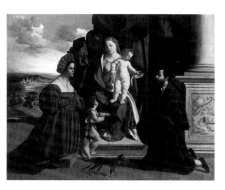

**Dossi, Dosso (Giovanni de' Luteri)**
Italian, active Ferrara, first recorded 1512, died 1542
*The Holy Family, with the Young Saint John the Baptist, a Cat, and Two Donors*
c. 1512–13
Center right: LX
Oil on canvas
38 1/16 × 45 3/4" (96.7 × 116.2 cm)

John G. Johnson Collection
cat. 197

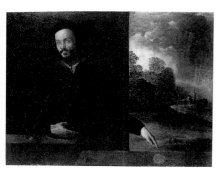

**Dossi, Dosso**
*Portrait of a Gentleman*
c. 1520
Oil on canvas
35 1/16 × 46 1/2" (89.1 × 118.1 cm)

John G. Johnson Collection
cat. 251

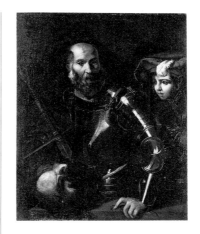

**Dossi, Dosso, copy after**
*Saul and David with the Head of Goliath*
After a painting attributed to Dosso Dossi, in the Galleria Borghese, Rome (inv. no. 181)
16th century?
Oil on canvas
40 × 31 1/2" (101.6 × 80 cm)

John G. Johnson Collection
cat. 252

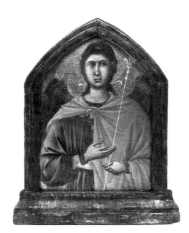

**Duccio di Buoninsegna and workshop**
Italian, active Siena, first documented 1278, died 1318
Previously listed as Duccio di Buoninsegna (JI 1966)
*Half-Length Angel*
Pinnacle from Duccio's *Maestà*, from the Cathedral of Siena; cut and rounded at top; companion pinnacles in collection of J. H. van Heek, 's Heerenberg; Mount Holyoke College Art Museum (P.PI.45.1965); private collection
By 1311
Tempera and tooled gold on panel
9 1/2 × 6 11/16" (24.1 × 17 cm)

John G. Johnson Collection
cat. 88

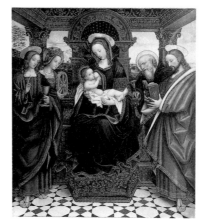

**Ferrari, Defendente**
Italian, active Piedmont, dated works 1510–1535
*Enthroned Virgin and Child, with Saints John the Evangelist, Catherine of Alexandria, and Anthony Abbot, and a Saint Reading a Book*
Altarpiece
1520s
Oil and gold on panel transferred to canvas
53 3/4 × 45 1/4" (136.5 × 114.9 cm)

John G. Johnson Collection
cat. 276

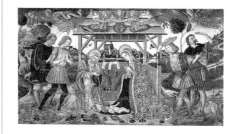

**Folchetti, Stefano**
Italian, active Marches, dated works 1492–1513
*The Nativity and the Annunciation to the Shepherds, with Four Adorants*
Predella panel; companion panel sold at Sotheby's, London, November 30, 1989 (lot 9)
c. 1500
Upper left, on scroll: ANONCIO. VOBIS.GAVDIVM; center top, on scroll: .GLORIA.IN ECELSIS.DEO. ED IN TE[R]RA.PAX.
Tempera and tooled gold on panel
12 5/8 × 19 9/16" (32.1 × 49.7 cm)

John G. Johnson Collection
cat. 134

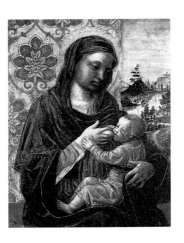

**Foppa, Vincenzo**
Italian, active Milan,
born 1427–30, died 1515/16
*Virgin and Child before a Landscape*
c. 1490
Oil and gold on panel
17 1/4 × 13 5/16" (43.8 × 33.8 cm)

John G. Johnson Collection
cat. 257

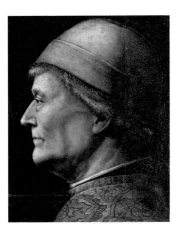

**Foppa, Vincenzo**
Previously listed as Giovanni
Ambrogio de Predis ( JI 1966)
*Portrait of an Elderly Gentleman*
Bottom and right side are later
additions
c. 1495–1500
Oil on panel
13 1/8 × 10 3/4" (33.3 × 27.3 cm)

John G. Johnson Collection
cat. 264

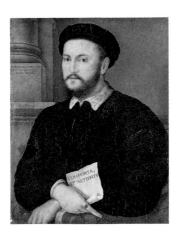

**Foschi, Pier Francesco di
Jacopo**
Italian, active Florence and Pisa,
1502–1567
Previously attributed to
Pontormo ( JI 1966)
*Portrait of Bartolomeo Gualterotti*
1550
Upper left: BART DILOR
GVALTEROTTI / D'ETA DANNI
XLIIII / L'ANNO M D L; center
bottom, on paper: COMPORTA, /
ET ASTIENTI
Oil on panel
30 5/8 × 22 3/4" (77.8 × 57.8 cm)

John G. Johnson Collection
cat. 84

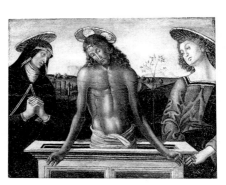

**Francesco da Tolentino**
Italian, active Tolentino and the
environs of Naples, dated works
1525–1531
Previously listed as Giovanni
Battista Bertucci da Faenza the
Elder ( JI 1966)
*The Dead Christ, with the Virgin
and Saint John the Evangelist*
c. 1510
Oil on panel
17 × 21 3/8" (43.2 × 54.3 cm)

John G. Johnson Collection
inv. 716

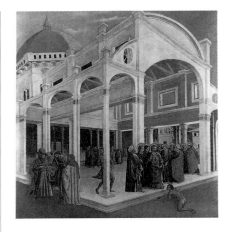

**Francesco di Antonio
(Francesco di Antonio di
Bartolomeo)**
Italian, active Florence,
documented 1393–1433
Previously listed as Andrea di
Giusto ( JI 1966)
*Christ Healing a Lunatic and Judas
Receiving Thirty Pieces of Silver*
Processional banner [?] based on a
design attributed to Masaccio
c. 1424–25
Tempera and gold on canvas
45 3/8 × 41 3/4" (115.2 × 106 cm)

John G. Johnson Collection
cat. 17

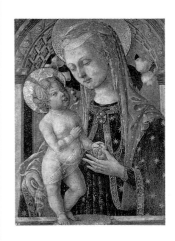

**Francesco di Gentile da
Fabriano**
Italian, active Umbria and
Marches, documented 1497
*Virgin and Child with a
Pomegranate*
Late 15th century
Oil and gold on panel
25 1/4 × 18 13/16" (64.1 × 47.8 cm)

John G. Johnson Collection
cat. 129

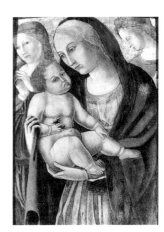

**Francesco di Giorgio
(Francesco di Giorgio
Martini), follower of**
Italian, active Siena, 1439–1502
*Virgin and Child, with Two Angels*
c. 1500
Oil and gold on panel
23 7/8 × 16 3/16" (60.6 × 41.1 cm)

Gift of Dr. Paul G. Ecker
1963-215-1

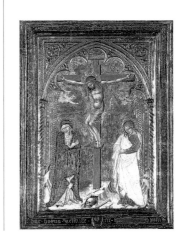

**Francesco di Vannuccio**
Italian, active Siena,
first documented c. 1356,
last documented 1389
*The Crucifixion, with the Virgin,
Saint John the Evangelist, and Angels*
Panel from a diptych; companion
panel is in the Rijksmuseum
Meermanno-Westreenianum,
The Hague (no. 806)
c. 1387–88
On cross: I N R I; on frame: hoc.
hopus.nelmille.CCC.L.[ ] lulii
Tempera and tooled gold on panel
16 7/8 × 12 1/8" (42.9 × 30.8 cm)

John G. Johnson Collection
cat. 94

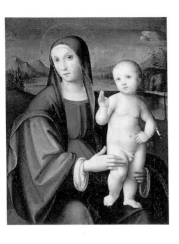

**Francia, Francesco (Francesco di Marco di Giacomo Raiboldini)**
Italian, active Bologna and Ferrara, c. 1450–1517
*Virgin and Child before a Landscape*
c. 1517
Oil and gold on panel
23 × 17 3/16" (58.4 × 43.7 cm)

John G. Johnson Collection
inv. 1282

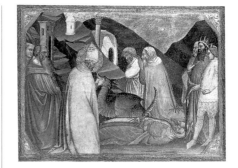

**Gaddi, Agnolo di Taddeo**
Italian, active Florence, first documented 1369, died 1396
Previously listed as a Florentine artist, c. 1400 (JI 1966)
*Saint Sylvester and the Dragon*
Predella panel; a companion panel was sold at Sotheby's, London, July 8, 1981 (lot 87)
c. 1380–85
Tempera and tooled gold on panel
11 1/2 × 15 1/8" (29.2 × 38.4 cm)

John G. Johnson Collection
cat. 9

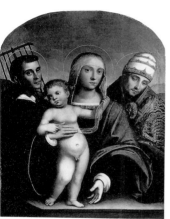

**Francia, Giacomo (Giacomo di Francesco Raiboldini)**
Italian, active Bologna, first documented 1486, died 1557
*Virgin and Child, with Saint Lawrence and a Papal Saint*
Mid-16th century
Oil on canvas
39 5/16 × 28 5/16" (99.8 × 71.9 cm)

John G. Johnson Collection
cat. 250

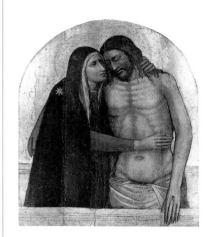

**Gerini, Niccolò di Pietro**
Italian, active Florence, first documented 1368, died 1415
*Pietà*
c. 1377
Tempera and tooled gold on panel
40 5/16 × 33 9/16" (102.4 × 85.2 cm)

John G. Johnson Collection
cat. 8

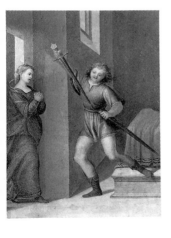

**Franciabigio (Francesco di Cristofano di Francesco), attributed to**
Italian, active Florence and environs, 1484–1524
Previously listed as Francesco Granacci (JI 1966)
*Saint Julian the Hospitaler Meeting His Wife after Killing His Parents*
Fragment of a predella panel
c. 1515
Oil on panel
10 5/16 × 7 5/16" (26.2 × 18.6 cm)

John G. Johnson Collection
inv. 2954

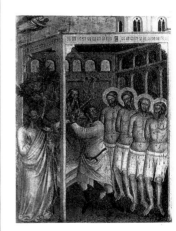

**Gerini, Niccolò di Pietro**
*The Scourging of the Four Crowned Martyrs*
Panel from an altarpiece; companion panels are in the Denver Art Museum (no. E-IT-18-XV-927); the Birmingham Museum of Art, Alabama (no. 1961.119); and a private collection
c. 1385–90
Tempera and tooled gold on panel
23 13/16 × 17" (60.5 × 43.2 cm)

John G. Johnson Collection
cat. 1163

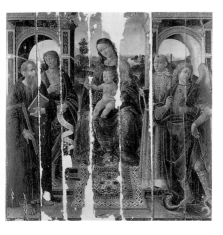

**Frediani, Vincenzo di Antonio (Master of the Lucchese Immaculate Conception)**
Italian, active Lucca, documented 1481–1505
*Enthroned Virgin and Child, with Saint John the Baptist, the Apostle Thomas Didymus, a Deacon Saint, and the Archangel Michael*
Panels from an altarpiece; the predella to this painting is in the Courtauld Institute Galleries, London (The Lee Collection, 65)
Mid-1480s
Oil and tempera on panel
66 1/8 × 63" (168 × 160 cm)

Bequest of Arthur H. Lea
F1938-1-39

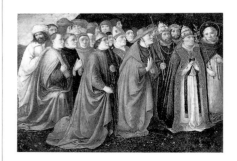

**Gherardo del Fora (Gherardo di Giovanni di Miniato)**
Italian, active Florence, c. 1446–1497
Previously listed as Bastiano Mainardi (JI 1966)
*Group of Men with Rosaries*
Fragment from the same work as the following fragment
Late 15th century
Tempera on panel
11 1/8 × 15 9/16" (28.3 × 39.5 cm)

John G. Johnson Collection
cat. 1167b

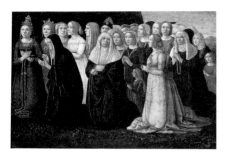

**Gherardo del Fora**
Previously listed as Bastiano
Mainardi (JI 1966)
*Group of Women with Rosaries*
Fragment from the same work as
the preceding fragment
Late 15th century
Tempera on panel
11 ⅛ × 15 ⁹⁄₁₆" (28.3 × 39.5 cm)

John G. Johnson Collection
cat. 1167a

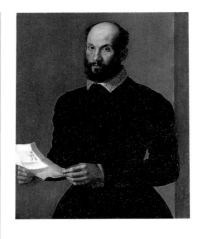

**Ghirlandaio, Ridolfo del
(Ridolfo di Domenico
Bigordi)**
Italian, active Florence,
1483–1561
*Portrait of Andrea Bandini*
An alternative attribution to
Carlo Portelli (Italian, died
1574) has been proposed
Mid-16th century
Lower left, on paper: Dno Andrea
bandini / Infirenze
Oil on panel
35 × 28 ¼" (88.9 × 71.7 cm)

John G. Johnson Collection
cat. 73

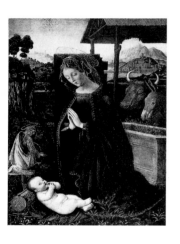

**Ghirlandaio, Benedetto
(Benedetto Bigordi)**
Italian, active Florence,
1459–1497
*The Nativity*
c. 1490
Tempera and gold on panel
31 ⅜ × 22 ¾" (79.7 × 57.8 cm)

John G. Johnson Collection
cat. 68

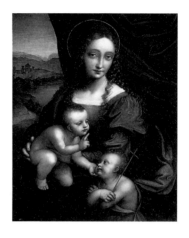

**Giampietrino
(Giovanni Pedrini?)**
Italian, active Milan and
environs, active c. 1510–c. 1540
*Virgin and Child, with the Young
Saint John the Baptist*
c. 1520
Oil on panel
25 ¾ × 18 ⅞" (65.4 × 47.9 cm)

John G. Johnson Collection
cat. 271

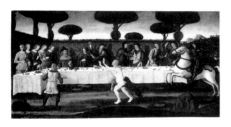

**Ghirlandaio, David
(David Bigordi)**
Italian, active Florence,
1452–1525
Previously listed as Jacopo del
Sellaio (JI 1966)
*Banquet Scene from the Tale of
Nastagio degli Onesti, in Boccaccio's
"Decameron"*
A companion panel is in the
Brooklyn Museum (25.95)
Late 1480s
Tempera on panel
27 ⅝ × 53 ½" (70.2 × 135.9 cm)

John G. Johnson Collection
cat. 64

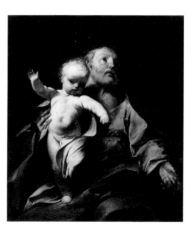

**Giaquinto, Corrado,
attributed to**
Italian, active Naples and Rome,
1703–1766
Previously listed as Corrado
Giaquinto (PMA 1965)
*Saint Joseph and the Christ Child*
1740s
Oil on canvas
46 ¼ × 37 ⁷⁄₁₆" (117.5 × 95.1 cm)

Purchased with the W. P.
Wilstach Fund
W1904-1-7

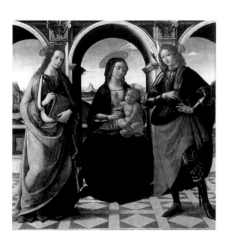

**Ghirlandaio, David**
Previously listed as Bastiano
Mainardi (JI 1966)
*Virgin and Child, with Saints
Apollonia and Sebastian*
Altarpiece
1490s
Tempera on panel
54 ½ × 51 ½" (138.4 × 130.8 cm)

John G. Johnson Collection
cat. 65

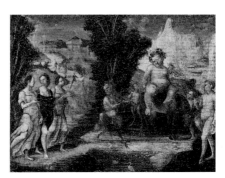

**Giolfino, Niccolò**
Italian, active Verona,
1476–1555
*Triumph of Silenus*
Companion to the following
painting
Early 16th century
Oil on panel
9 ⅞ × 12 ⅜" (25.1 × 31.4 cm)

John G. Johnson Collection
cat. 217

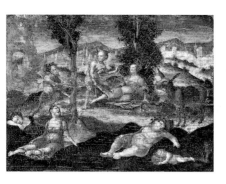

**Giolfino, Niccolò**
*Silenus Sleeping*
Companion to the preceding
painting
Early 16th century
Oil on panel
9 ³/₄ × 12 ³/₈" (24.8 × 31.4 cm)

John G. Johnson Collection
cat. 218

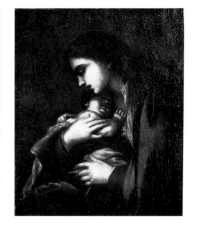

**Giordano, Luca, copy after**
*Virgin and Child*
After the painting in the
Quadreria dei Girolamini,
Naples
Late 17th century
Oil on canvas
29 ¹/₂ × 23 ¹/₂" (74.9 × 59.7 cm)

John G. Johnson Collection
cat. 810a [formerly cat. 281]

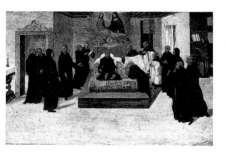

**Giolfino, Niccolò**
Previously listed as Amico
Aspertini (JI 1966)
*The Death of the Blessed Filippo
Benizzi*
Predella panel; a companion
panel is in the Slezské Museum,
Opava, Czech Republic (D5 77)
1515
Oil on panel
12 ⁵/₁₆ × 19 ³/₁₆" (31.3 × 49.7 cm)

John G. Johnson Collection
cat. 247

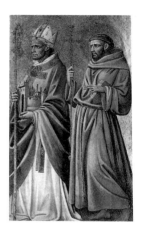

**Giovanni dal Ponte
(Giovanni di Marco)**
Italian, active Florence,
1385–1437
*Saints Geminianus and Francis of
Assisi*
Panel from an altarpiece;
companion panels are in the
M. H. de Young Memorial
Museum, San Francisco, and the
Niedersächsisches Landesmuseum,
Hannover (KM 87)
c. 1434–35
Tempera and tooled gold on panel
38 ¹/₄ × 21 ¹³/₁₆" (97.1 × 55.4 cm)

John G. Johnson Collection
inv. 1739

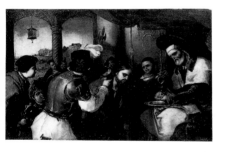

**Giordano, Luca**
Italian, active Italy and Spain,
1632–1705
Previously attributed to Luca
Giordano (JI 1966)
*Christ before Pilate*
1650–55
Oil on panel
17 ⁷/₈ × 27 ¹/₄" (45.4 × 69.2 cm)

John G. Johnson Collection
cat. 249

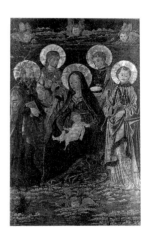

**Giovanni di Francesco del
Cervelliera**
Italian, active Florence, first
documented 1446, died 1459
*Virgin and Child on Clouds, with
Cherubim and Saints Anthony Abbot,
Galganus, Ansanus, and Lawrence*
c. 1454
Tempera and tooled gold on panel
22 ³/₄ × 14 ³/₄" (57.8 × 37.5 cm)

John G. Johnson Collection
cat. 59

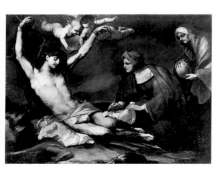

**Giordano, Luca**
Previously listed as Jusepe de
Ribera (PMA 1965)
*Saint Sebastian Cured by Irene*
Painted over Giordano's *Christ
among the Doctors*
c. 1665
Oil on canvas
72 ¹/₂ × 108 ³/₄" (184.1 × 276.2 cm)

Purchased with the W. P.
Wilstach Fund
W1901-1-5

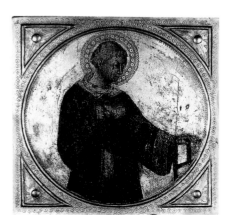

**Giovanni di Paolo (Giovanni
di Paolo di Grazia)**
Italian, active Siena, first securely
documented 1411, died 1482
Previously listed as Italian,
unknown artist, 15th century
(PMA 1965)
*Saint Lawrence*
Predella panel; see following
entry for companion panels
c. 1430–35
Tempera and tooled gold on panel
9 ¹/₂ × 9 ¹/₂" (24.1 × 24.1 cm)

Purchased from the George Grey
Barnard Collection with Museum
funds
1945-25-121

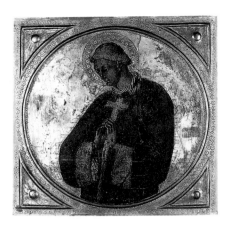

**Giovanni di Paolo**
Previously listed as Italian,
unknown artist, 15th century
(PMA 1965)
*Deacon Saint*
Predella panel; companion to
preceding panel and to two
panels by Martino di Bartolomeo
in the York Art Gallery, England
(no. 779a, 779b)
c. 1430–35
Tempera and tooled gold on panel
9 1/2 × 9 1/2" (24.1 × 24.1 cm)

Purchased from the George Grey
Barnard Collection with Museum
funds
1945-25-122

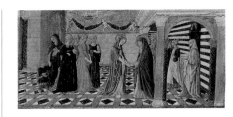

**Giovanni di Pietro**
Previously listed as Pietro di
Giovanni d'Ambrogio (JI 1966)
*The Return of the Virgin to Her
Parents' House*
Predella panel; companion to the
preceding panel and a predella
panel in the Musée du Louvre,
Paris (inv. 814); the main panels
are in San Pietro Ovile, Siena
c. 1455
Tempera and gold on panel
9 1/2 × 18 1/8" (24.1 × 46 cm)

John G. Johnson Collection
cat. 108

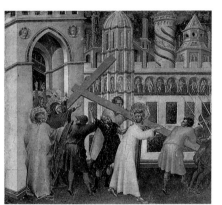

**Giovanni di Paolo**
*Christ on the Road to Calvary*
Predella panel from an altarpiece;
other panels from the predella are
in the Staatliches Lindenau-
Museum, Altenburg, Germany
(78), and the Pinacoteca Vaticana
(no. 124, no. 129)
c. 1430–35
Tempera and tooled gold on panel
12 1/2 × 13 1/8" (31.7 × 33.3 cm)

John G. Johnson Collection
cat. 105

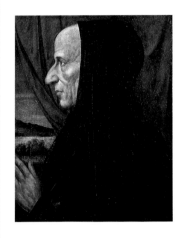

**Fra Girolamo da Brescia**
Italian, born Brescia, active
Florence, first documented 1490,
died 1529
Previously listed as Bartolomeo
Montagna (JI 1966)
*Portrait of a Friar* [possibly
Girolamo Savonarola]
c. 1490–1500
Oil on panel
17 15/16 × 13 1/8" (45.6 × 33.3 cm)

John G. Johnson Collection
cat. 169

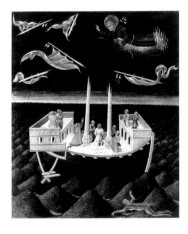

**Giovanni di Paolo**
*Saint Nicholas of Tolentino Saving a
Ship*
Panel from an altarpiece;
companion panels are in the
Gemäldegalerie der Akademie
der Bildenden Künste, Vienna
(inv. no. 1177), and
Sant'Agostino, Montepulciano
1457
Tempera and tooled gold on panel
20 1/2 × 16 5/8" (52.1 × 42.2 cm)

John G. Johnson Collection
inv. 723

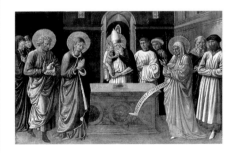

**Gozzoli, Benozzo
(Benozzo di Lese di Sandro)**
Italian, active Florence and
central Italy, born 1420–22,
died 1497
*The Presentation of Christ in the
Temple*
Predella panel from the altarpiece
from the Compagnia di Santa
Maria della Purificazione e di San
Zanobi, Florence, contracted
October 23, 1461; the main
panels from the altarpiece are in
the National Gallery, London
(283); companion predella panels
are in the collection of Her
Majesty Queen Elizabeth II
(132); the Pinacoteca di Brera,
Milan (475); the Gemäldegalerie,
Staatliche Museen zu Berlin-
Preussischer Kulturbesitz (60c);
and the National Gallery of Art,
Washington, D.C. (1086)
c. 1461–62
Tempera and tooled gold on panel
9 3/4 × 14 5/16" (24.8 × 36.3 cm)

John G. Johnson Collection
cat. 38

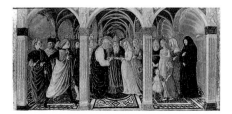

**Giovanni di Pietro, also
called Nanni di Pietro**
Italian, active Siena, first docu-
mented 1432, died before 1479
Previously listed as Pietro di
Giovanni d'Ambrogio (JI 1966)
*The Marriage of the Virgin*
Predella panel from an altarpiece
executed in collaboration with
Matteo di Giovanni, in San Pietro
Ovile, Siena; see following entry
for companion panels
c. 1455
Tempera and gold on panel
9 1/2 × 18 1/8" (24.1 × 46 cm)

John G. Johnson Collection
cat. 107

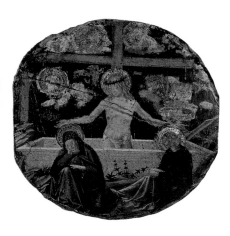

**Gozzoli, Benozzo, attributed to**
*The Man of Sorrows, with the Mourning Virgin, Saint John the Evangelist, and Symbols of the Passion*
Cut down to a circle
c. 1447
Tempera on panel
14 1/4 × 11 1/2" (36.2 × 29.2 cm)

John G. Johnson Collection
inv. 1305

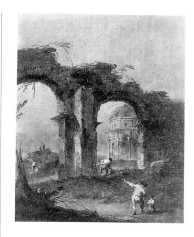

**Guardi, Francesco**
*Capriccio*
c. 1775–80
Oil on panel
7 3/8 × 5 13/16" (18.7 × 14.8 cm)

Gift of an anonymous donor
1974-159-1

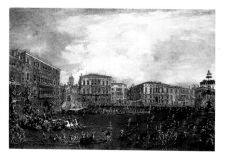

**Guardi, Francesco**
Italian, active Venice,
1712–1793
*Regatta in "Volta di Canal"*
c. 1760–70
Oil on canvas
47 5/16 × 66 1/2" (120.2 × 168.9 cm)

John G. Johnson Collection
cat. 307

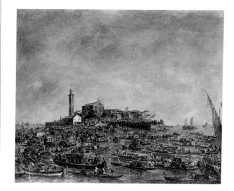

**Guardi, Francesco**
*The Meeting of Pope Pius VI and Doge Paolo Renier at San Giorgio in Alga*
1782
Oil on canvas
28 × 32" (71.1 × 81.3 cm)

The William L. Elkins Collection
E1924-3-49

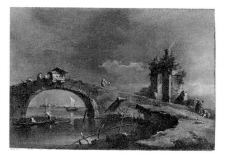

**Guardi, Francesco**
Previously listed as Giacomo Guardi (JI 1966)
*Capriccio with a Bridge*
c. 1770–80
Oil on canvas
7 × 9 5/8" (17.8 × 24.4 cm)

John G. Johnson Collection
cat. 311

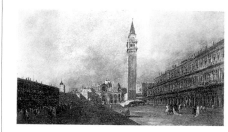

**Guardi, Francesco, attributed to**
*Piazza San Marco*
c. 1770–80
Oil on canvas
16 3/16 × 28" (41.1 × 71.1 cm)

John G. Johnson Collection
cat. 306

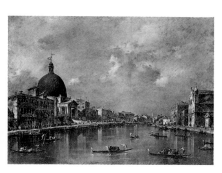

**Guardi, Francesco**
*Grand Canal with San Simeone Piccolo and Santa Lucia*
c. 1770–80
Oil on canvas
26 3/8 × 36 1/16" (67 × 91.6 cm)

John G. Johnson Collection
cat. 303

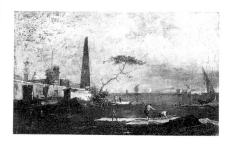

**Guardi, Francesco, attributed to**
Previously listed as Giacomo Guardi (JI 1966)
*Capriccio with an Obelisk on a Lagoon*
1780s
Oil on canvas
8 1/4 × 13 1/4" (20.9 × 33.6 cm)

John G. Johnson Collection
cat. 310

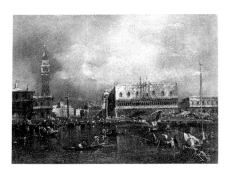

**Guardi, Francesco, follower of**
*Doge's Palace and Libreria from the Laguna*
c. 1785–90
Oil on canvas
15 1/8 × 20 3/8" (38.4 × 51.7 cm)

John G. Johnson Collection
cat. 301

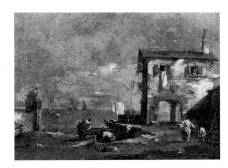

**Guardi, Francesco, follower of**
Previously listed as Francesco Guardi (PMA 1965)
*Venetian View*
Late 18th century
Oil on panel
8 × 10 1/2" (20.3 × 26.7 cm)

The William L. Elkins Collection
E1924-3-50

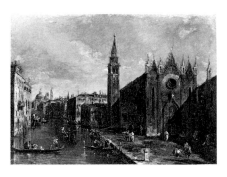

**Guardi, Francesco, follower of**
Previously listed as the school of Francesco Guardi (PMA 1965)
*Santa Maria della Carità*
Late 18th century
Lower right (spurious): F. G.
Oil on canvas
13 × 17 5/8" (33 × 44.8 cm)

The William L. Elkins Collection
E1924-3-31

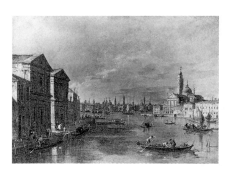

**Guardi, Francesco, follower of**
Previously listed as Giacomo Guardi (JI 1966)
*View between the Giudecca and San Giorgio Maggiore*
Late 18th century?
Oil on canvas
13 × 17 9/16" (33 × 44.6 cm)

John G. Johnson Collection
cat. 308

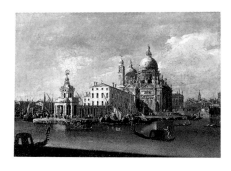

**Guardi, Francesco, follower of**
Previously listed as Giacomo Guardi (JI 1966)
*Santa Maria della Salute and the Dogana*
Late 18th century?
Oil on canvas
13 × 17 9/16" (33 × 44.6 cm)

John G. Johnson Collection
cat. 309

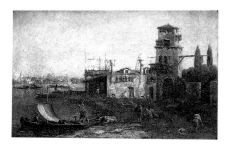

**Guardi, Francesco, imitator of**
*Villa by the Sea*
Late 18th century
Oil on canvas
14 1/2 × 22 1/8" (36.8 × 56.2 cm)

John G. Johnson Collection
cat. 300

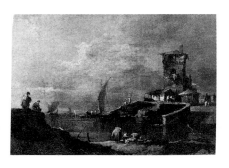

**Guardi, Francesco, follower of**
Previously listed as Giacomo Guardi (JI 1966)
*Seaport with a Castle*
Late 18th century
Oil on canvas
7 × 9 5/8" (17.8 × 24.4 cm)

John G. Johnson Collection
inv. 446

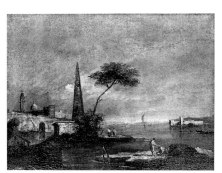

**Guardi, Francesco, imitator of**
*Capriccio with an Obelisk on a Lagoon*
19th century
Oil on canvas
16 9/16 × 21 9/16" (42.1 × 54.8 cm)

John G. Johnson Collection
cat. 312

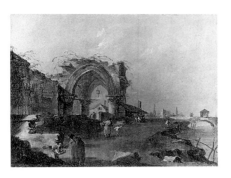

**Guardi, Francesco, imitator of**
*Capriccio with Ruins*
19th century
Oil on canvas
5 3/4 × 7 9/16" (14.6 × 19.2 cm)

John G. Johnson Collection
inv. 415

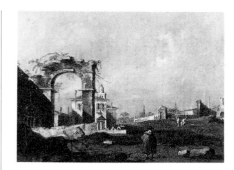

**Guardi, Giacomo, imitator of**
Previously listed as Giacomo
Guardi (JI 1966)
*Ruined Arch*
19th century
Oil on canvas
5 13/16 × 7 13/16" (14.8 × 19.8 cm)

John G. Johnson Collection
cat. 313

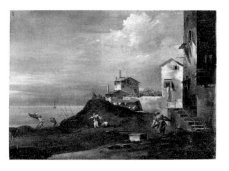

**Guardi, Francesco, imitator of**
*Landscape with Cottages on Dunes*
19th century
Oil on canvas
14 × 18 7/8" (35.6 × 47.9 cm)

John G. Johnson Collection
cat. 304

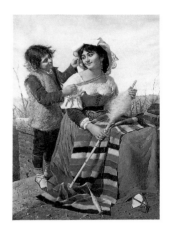

**Indoni, Filippo**
Italian, active Rome,
active late 19th century
*Roman Peasants*
1878
Lower left: Indoni—Roma / 1878
Oil on canvas
66 1/4 × 44 5/8" (168.3 × 113.3 cm)

Gift of Mr. and Mrs. S. F. Houston
1914-26

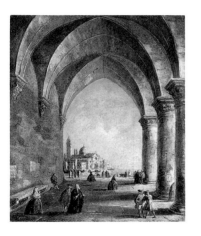

**Guardi, Francesco, imitator of**
*San Giorgio Maggiore Seen through
the Arches of the Doge's Palace*
19th century
Oil on canvas
15 13/16 × 12 7/8" (40.2 × 32.7 cm)

John G. Johnson Collection
cat. 305

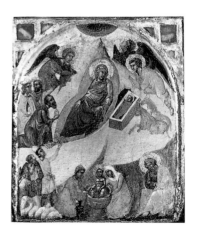

**Italian?, active Venice?, unknown artist**
*The Nativity and the Adoration of
the Magi*
Section of a reliquary
c. 1290–1300
Tempera, tooled gold, and glass
on panel
14 1/4 × 11 3/8" (36.2 × 28.9 cm)

John G. Johnson Collection
cat. 116

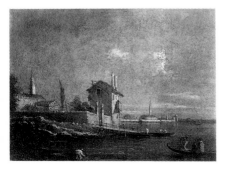

**Guardi, Giacomo, follower of**
Italian, active Venice,
1764–1835
*The Island of San Michele with
Venice in the Background*
After 1782
Oil on canvas
7 1/2 × 9 9/16" (19 × 24.3 cm)

John G. Johnson Collection
cat. 302

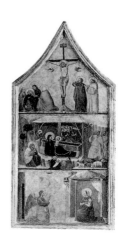

**Italian, active Padua?, unknown artist**
Previously listed as an immediate
follower of Giotto (JI 1966)
*The Crucifixion, the Nativity, and
the Annunciation*
c. 1320–30
Tempera and tooled gold on panel
24 7/8 × 11 7/8" (63.2 × 30.2 cm)

John G. Johnson Collection
cat. 1

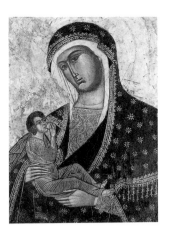

**Italian?, active Adriatic coast, unknown artist**
*Virgin and Child*
c. 1340–50
Oil on panel transferred to canvas
18 5/8 × 13 3/8" (47.3 × 34 cm)

The Louise and Walter Arensberg Collection
1950-134-195

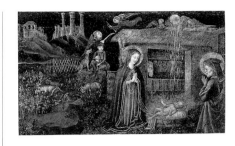

**Italian, active Marches, unknown artist**
Previously listed as an Umbrian follower of Fra Angelico (JI 1966)
*The Nativity*
Later repaintings
c. 1420
Tempera and tooled gold on panel
10 × 15 7/8" (25.4 × 40.3 cm)

John G. Johnson Collection
cat. 16

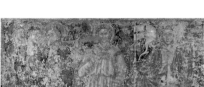

**Italian, active central Italy?, unknown artist**
*The Three Marys at the Sepulcher and the Resurrection*
c. 1375–1400
Detached fresco on canvas
40 1/4 × 87 1/8" (102.2 × 221.3 cm)

Purchased from the George Grey Barnard Collection with Museum funds
1945-25-118

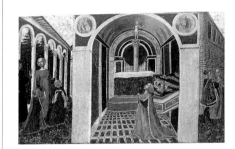

**Italian, active Tuscany, unknown artist**
Previously listed as Andrea di Giusto (JI 1966)
*Scenes from the Book of Esther*
A companion panel is in the Museum of Art, Science and Industry, Bridgeport, Connecticut (K269)
c. 1425–35
Tempera and gold on panel
17 × 26 5/8" (43.2 × 67.6 cm)

John G. Johnson Collection
cat. 20

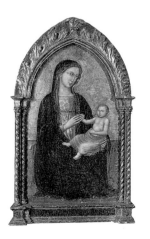

**Italian, active Florence, unknown artist**
Previously listed as an unknown Italian artist, c. 1400 (PMA 1965)
*The Virgin of Humility*
c. 1400
On frame, across bottom: AVE MARIA GRATIA PLENA DO. T.
Tempera and tooled gold on panel
33 5/8 × 20 1/8" (90.5 × 51.1 cm)

The Louise and Walter Arensberg Collection
1950-134-527

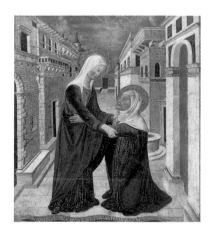

**Italian, active central Italy, unknown artist**
*The Visitation*
c. 1475
Across bottom: [ET] VNDE HOC MIVI [sic] VENIAT MATER DOMINI AD ME BEATA
Oil on panel
33 15/16 × 29" (86.2 × 73.7 cm)

Purchased with the W. P. Wilstach Fund
W1904-1-38

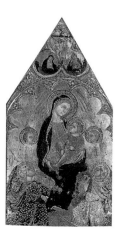

**Italian, active Siena, unknown artist**
Previously listed as Taddeo di Bartolo (JI 1966)
*The Virgin of Humility, with Cherubim, Two Music-Making Angels, and the Crucifixion*
Center panel from a triptych
c. 1400
Tempera and tooled gold on panel
13 3/4 × 7 1/4" (34.9 × 18.4 cm)

John G. Johnson Collection
cat. 100

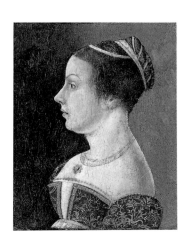

**Italian, active Venice, unknown artist**
Previously listed as a Lombard artist, mid-15th century (JI 1966)
*Portrait of a Lady*
See following painting for reverse
c. 1475–80
Oil on panel
11 1/16 × 8 11/16" (28.1 × 22.1 cm)

John G. Johnson Collection
cat. 164a

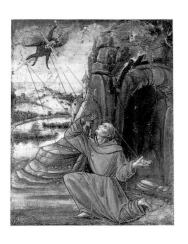

**Italian, active Venice, unknown artist**
Previously listed as a Lombard artist, mid-15th century (JI 1966)
*Saint Francis of Assisi Receiving the Stigmata*
Reverse of preceding painting
c. 1475–80
Oil on panel
11 1/16 × 8 11/16" (28.1 × 22.1 cm)

John G. Johnson Collection
cat. 164b

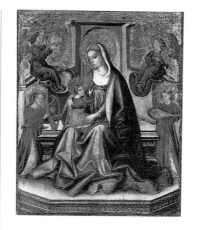

**Italian, active Sicily, unknown artist**
*Enthroned Virgin and Child, with Four Angels*
c. 1480–1500
Oil and tooled gold on panel
17 1/2 × 13 3/4" (44.4 × 34.9 cm)

John G. Johnson Collection
cat. 130

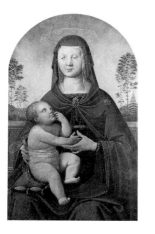

**Italian, active Florence, unknown artist**
Previously listed as David Ghirlandaio (JI 1966)
*Virgin and Child*
c. 1475–1500
Oil and gold on panel transferred to canvas
31 × 18 1/2" (78.7 × 47 cm)

John G. Johnson Collection
cat. 66

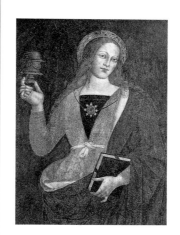

**Italian, active Umbria, unknown artist**
Previously attributed to Lo Spagna (JI 1966)
*Saint Mary Magdalene*
c. 1480–1500
Detached fresco on canvas
37 1/2 × 25 3/4" (95.2 × 65.4 cm)

John G. Johnson Collection
cat. 146

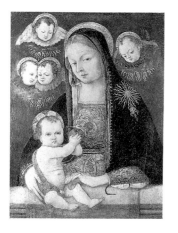

**Italian, active Venice?, unknown artist**
Previously listed as a Sicilian artist, early 16th century (JI 1966)
*Virgin and Child with an Apple and Four Cherubim*
c. 1475–1500
Oil and gold on panel
22 1/2 × 16" (57.1 × 40.6 cm)

John G. Johnson Collection
cat. 161

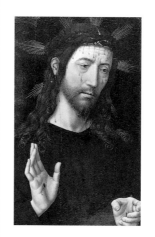

**Italian, active Florence, unknown artist**
Previously listed as a copy after Hans Memling (JFD 1972)
*The Man of Sorrows*
A Florentine copy after a Netherlandish painting in the Galleria di Palazzo Bianco, Genoa
c. 1495
Oil on panel
21 3/8 × 13 1/4" (54.3 × 33.6 cm)

John G. Johnson Collection
cat. 1176a

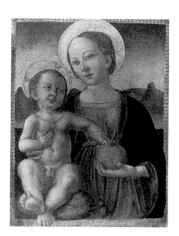

**Italian, active Tuscany, unknown artist**
Previously listed as Giovanni Battista Utili da Faenza (JI 1966)
*Virgin and Child with an Apple before a Landscape*
c. 1480
Tempera and gold on panel
16 3/4 × 12" (42.5 × 30.5 cm)

John G. Johnson Collection
cat. 63

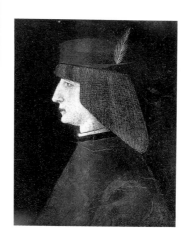

**Italian, active Crema, unknown artist**
*Portrait of a Gentleman*
Ceiling painting
c. 1500
Oil on panel
13 11/16 × 10 5/8" (34.8 × 27 cm)

John G. Johnson Collection
inv. 319

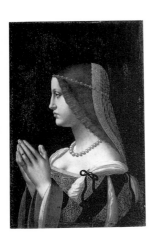

**Italian, active Lombardy, unknown artist**
Previously attributed to
Bernardino de' Conti (JI 1966)
*Portrait of a Lady*
c. 1500
Oil on panel
21 3/4 × 13 3/4" (55.2 × 34.9 cm)

John G. Johnson Collection
cat. 265

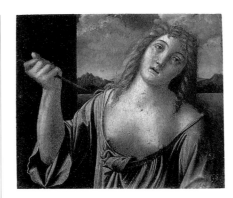

**Italian, active Venice?, unknown artist**
Previously listed as Bramantino
(JI 1966)
*The Suicide of Lucretia*
c. 1500
Oil on panel
11 3/8 × 13 1/8" (28.9 × 33.3 cm)

John G. Johnson Collection
cat. 267

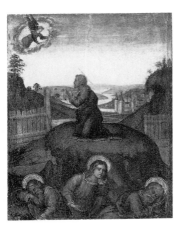

**Italian, active Florence, unknown artist**
*The Agony in the Garden*
c. 1500
Oil and gold on panel
11 3/8 × 8 1/2" (28.9 × 21.6 cm)

John G. Johnson Collection
inv. 1390

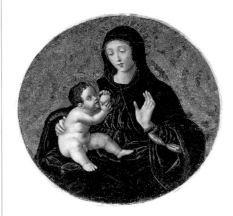

**Italian, active Naples?, unknown artist**
Previously listed as an Umbrian
artist, c. 1500 (JI 1966)
*Virgin and Child*
c. 1500
On Virgin's halo: Ave Gratia
Plena; on Christ's halo: XPOR IHS
Oil and tooled gold on panel
28" (71.1 cm) diameter

John G. Johnson Collection
cat. 133

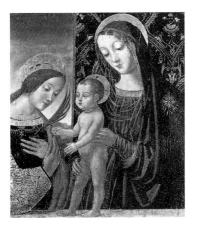

**Italian, active Umbria?, unknown artist**
*The Mystic Marriage of Saint
Catherine of Alexandria*
c. 1500
Oil and gold on panel
14 3/4 × 12 1/16" (37.5 × 30.6 cm)

John G. Johnson Collection
cat. 132

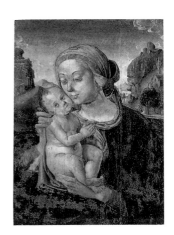

**Italian, active Veneto-Romagna, unknown artist**
Previously listed as a follower of
Piero di Cosimo (JI 1966)
*Virgin and Child*
c. 1500
Oil on panel
17 7/8 × 12 7/8" (45.4 × 32.7 cm)

John G. Johnson Collection
cat. 131

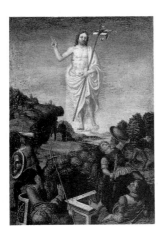

**Italian, active Lombardy, unknown artist**
Previously listed as the school of
Bergognone (JI 1966)
*The Resurrection*
c. 1500
Oil on panel
13 7/16 × 9" (34.1 × 22.9 cm)

John G. Johnson Collection
cat. 258

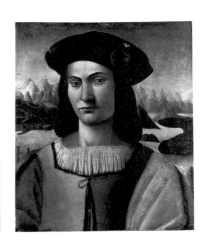

**Italian, active Lombardy, unknown artist**
Previously listed as Giovanni
Antonio Boltraffio (JI 1966)
*Portrait of a Young Gentleman before
a Landscape*
c. 1500–10
Oil on panel
22 1/8 × 17 5/8" (56.2 × 44.8 cm)

John G. Johnson Collection
cat. 268

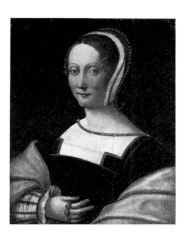

**Italian?, active Milan?, unknown artist**
Previously listed as an imitation of Ambrosius Benson (JFD 1972)
*Portrait of a Lady*
c. 1500–25
Upper left: AB
Oil on panel
18 1/2 × 14 7/8" (47 × 37.8 cm)

John G. Johnson Collection
cat. 361

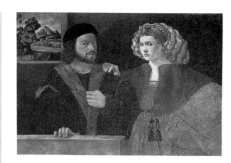

**Italian, active Bergamo, unknown artist**
Previously listed as Cariani (JI 1966)
*Portrait of a Gentleman and a Lady*
c. 1520–30
Oil on panel transferred to canvas
31 5/8 × 44" (80.3 × 111.8 cm)

John G. Johnson Collection
cat. 191

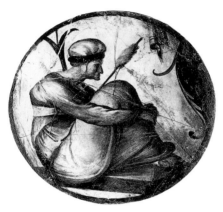

**Italian, active Siena?, unknown artist**
Previously listed as Domenico Beccafumi (JI 1966)
*The Fate Clotho*
c. 1510–30
Detached fresco
14" (35.6 cm) diameter

John G. Johnson Collection
cat. 115

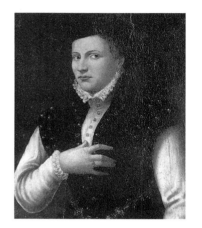

**Italian, active northern Italy, unknown artist**
Previously listed as an Emilian artist, second half of the 16th century (JI 1966)
*Portrait of a Young Gentlewoman*
c. 1525–50
Oil on panel
25 1/16 × 19 1/2" (63.7 × 49.5 cm)

John G. Johnson Collection
cat. 205

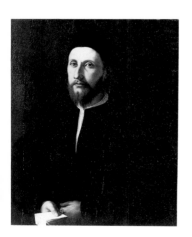

**Italian, active Florence, unknown artist**
Previously attributed to Palma il Vecchio (JI 1966)
*Portrait of a Gentleman*
1512
On letter: 1512; seal on ring
Oil on panel
33 7/16 × 28 1/8" (84.9 × 71.4 cm)

John G. Johnson Collection
cat. 186

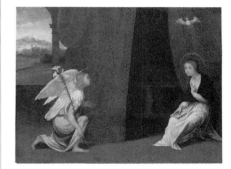

**Italian, active Ferrara, unknown artist**
*The Annunciation*
c. 1530
Oil on panel
14 1/2 × 18 7/8" (36.8 × 47.9 cm)

John G. Johnson Collection
cat. 245

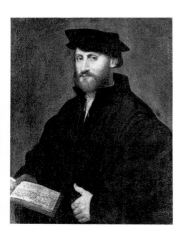

**Italian, active Venice, unknown artist**
Previously listed as the area of Lorenzo Lotto (JI 1966)
*Portrait of a Gentleman with a Musical Score*
c. 1520
On score: A. P. / Spes mea in deo est. [four times]
Oil on canvas
30 3/4 × 23 1/2" (78.1 × 59.7 cm)

John G. Johnson Collection
cat. 182

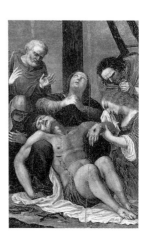

**Italian, active Verona, unknown artist**
Previously listed as Giovanni Francesco Caroto (JI 1966)
*Lamentation*
c. 1550
Oil on panel
19 3/4 × 11 11/16" (50.2 × 29.7 cm)

John G. Johnson Collection
cat. 223

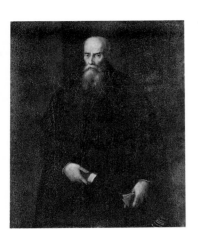

**Italian, active Venice, unknown artist**
Previously listed as Ridolfo del Ghirlandaio (JI 1966)
*Portrait of an Elderly Gentleman* [possibly Oddo degli Oddi]
c. 1550
Oil on panel
49 ⅝ × 40 ⁵/₁₆" (126 × 102.4 cm)

John G. Johnson Collection
cat. 74

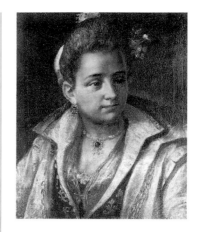

**Italian?, unknown artist**
Previously listed as Leandro Bassano da Ponte (JGJ 1941)
*Portrait of a Lady*
Copy of a portrait in the Statens Museum for Kunst, Copenhagen (no. 1027)
c. 1575–1600
Oil on canvas
21 ⅛ × 16 ⅝" (53.7 × 42.2 cm)

John G. Johnson Collection
inv. 2830

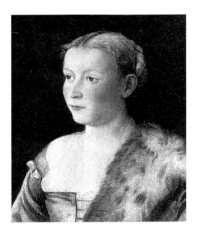

**Italian, active Venice, unknown artist**
Previously listed as after Paolo Veronese (JI 1966)
*Portrait of a Lady*
c. 1550
Oil on canvas
18 ¾ × 15 ⅝" (47.6 × 39.7 cm)

John G. Johnson Collection
cat. 226

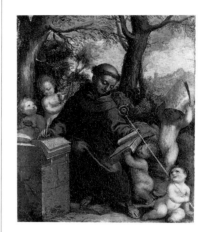

**Italian, active Emilia-Romagna, unknown artist**
Previously listed as a North Italian artist, c. 1590 (JI 1966)
*Saint Bonaventure Writing in a Landscape*
c. 1575–1600
Oil on canvas
9 × 7 ½" (22.9 × 19 cm)

John G. Johnson Collection
cat. 239

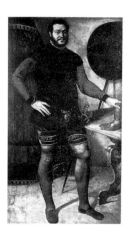

**Italian, active Emilia?, unknown artist**
Previously listed as Giovanni Battista Moroni (JI 1966)
*Portrait of an Officer*
1562
Center bottom: M D LXII
Oil on canvas
77 × 42 ¾" (195.6 × 108.6 cm)

John G. Johnson Collection
cat. 238

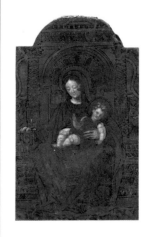

**Italian, active Milan, unknown artist**
*Enthroned Virgin and Child*
Early 16th century
Oil on tooled leather
23 ¾ × 14" (60.3 × 35.6 cm)

Purchased from the George Grey Barnard Collection with Museum funds
1945-25-264

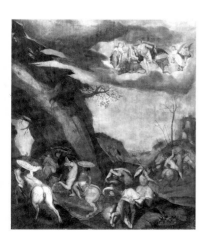

**Italian?, active Rome?, unknown artist**
*The Conversion of Saint Paul*
c. 1570
Oil on panel
32 ½ × 27 ½" (82.6 × 69.9 cm)

Gift of Mr. and Mrs. Edward B. Wilford III
1991-184-1

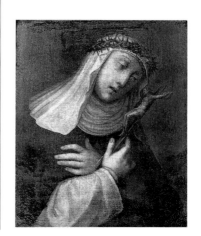

**Italian, active Siena, unknown artist**
*Saint Catherine of Siena with a Crucifix and a Crown of Thorns*
Mid-16th century
Oil on canvas
13 ⅝ × 11 ⁷/₁₆" (34.6 × 29 cm)

Bequest of Arthur H. Lea
F1938-1-21

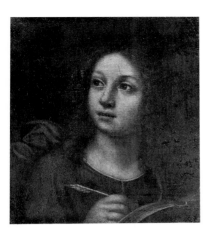

**Italian, unknown artist**
*Saint John the Evangelist*
16th century
Oil on canvas
11 1/16 × 10 1/16" (28.1 × 25.6 cm)

Bequest of Arthur H. Lea
F1938-1-30

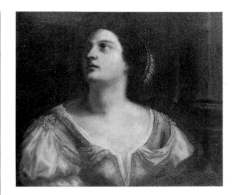

**Italian, active Bologna,
unknown artist**
*Head of an Old Testament Heroine*
c. 1600–25
Oil on canvas
23 × 26 1/2" (58.4 × 67.3 cm)

Bequest of Arthur H. Lea
F1938-1-9

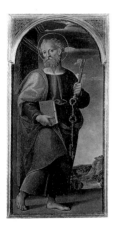

**Italian, active Ferrara?,
unknown artist**
Previously listed as Giulio Campi
(JI 1966)
*Saint Peter*
Panel from an altarpiece
16th century
Oil and gold on panel
31 3/16 × 14 3/16" (79.2 × 36 cm)

John G. Johnson Collection
cat. 235

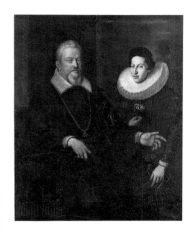

**Italian, unknown artist**
*Portrait of the Grand Duke
Ferdinando I de' Medici and
Probably His Son Cosimo II*
c. 1608
Oil on canvas
56 7/8 × 45 1/4" (144.5 × 114.9 cm)

The Bloomfield Moore Collection
1883-133

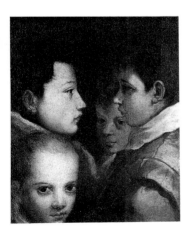

**Italian, active Bologna,
unknown artist**
Previously listed as an Italian
artist, early 17th century
(JI 1966)
*Heads of Four Boys*
c. 1600
Oil on canvas
14 3/4 × 11 7/16" (37.5 × 29 cm)

John G. Johnson Collection
cat. 279

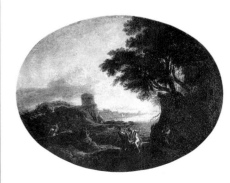

**Italian, active Rome,
unknown artist**
Previously attributed to Claude
Gellée (JGJ 1941)
*Coast Scene with Figures*
c. 1625–50
Oil on canvas
18 1/8 × 23 5/8" (46 × 60 cm)

John G. Johnson Collection
cat. 775

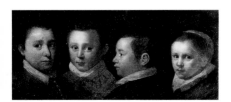

**Italian, active Bologna,
unknown artist**
Previously listed as an Italian
artist, early 17th century
(JI 1966)
*Heads of Three Boys and a Girl*
c. 1600
Oil on panel
13 3/8 × 29 3/4" (34 × 75.6 cm)

John G. Johnson Collection
cat. 280

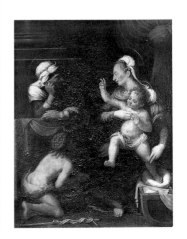

**Italian, unknown artist**
*Virgin and Child, with Saint
Elizabeth and the Young Saint John
the Baptist*
c. 1650–1700
On scroll: ECCE AGNVS DEI
Oil on canvas
69 1/8 × 52 1/2" (175.6 × 133.3 cm)

Bequest of Arthur H. Lea
F1938-1-33

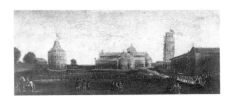

**Italian, unknown artist**
*Religious Procession to the Cathedral of Pisa*
c. 1675–1700
Oil on canvas
13 × 29 1/4" (33 × 74.3 cm)

The Louise and Walter Arensberg Collection
1950-134-529

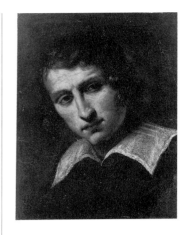

**Italian, active Florence, unknown artist**
*Portrait of a Man with a White Collar*
17th century
Oil on canvas
18 5/8 × 14" (47.3 × 35.6 cm)

Bequest of Arthur H. Lea
F1938-1-15

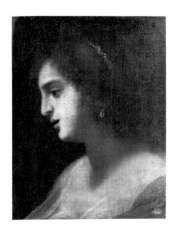

**Italian, unknown artist**
*Head of a Bishop*
17th century
Oil on canvas
21 1/2 × 16 1/4" (54.6 × 41.3 cm)

Bequest of Arthur H. Lea
F1938-1-14

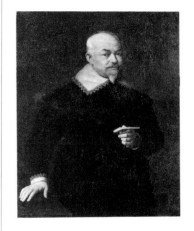

**Italian, unknown artist**
Previously listed as Hieronymus van Kessel (JFD 1972)
*Portrait of an Elderly Gentleman*
17th century
Oil on canvas
39 5/8 × 29 13/16" (100.6 × 75.7 cm)

John G. Johnson Collection
cat. 459

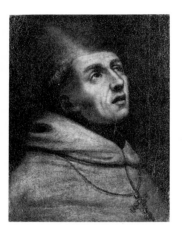

**Italian, active Florence, unknown artist**
*Head of a Woman*
17th century
Oil on canvas
16 5/8 × 12 5/8" (42.2 × 32.1 cm)

Bequest of Arthur H. Lea
F1938-1-29

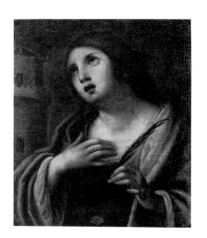

**Italian, active Bologna, unknown artist**
*Saint Barbara*
17th century
Oil on canvas
15 3/8 × 12 7/8" (39 × 32.7 cm)

Bequest of Arthur H. Lea
F1938-1-18

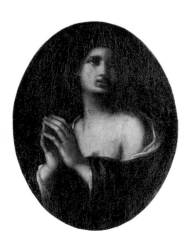

**Italian, unknown artist**
*Penitent Saint Mary Magdalene*
17th century
Oil on canvas
21 3/8 × 16 1/2" (54.3 × 41.9 cm)

Bequest of Arthur H. Lea
F1938-1-17

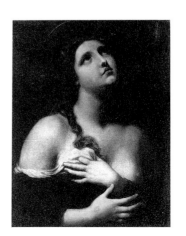

**Italian, active Florence, unknown artist**
*Saint Mary Magdalene*
17th century
Lower right (spurious):
GUERCINO
Oil on canvas
28 × 21 3/4" (71.1 × 55.2 cm)

Bequest of Arthur H. Lea
F1938-1-11

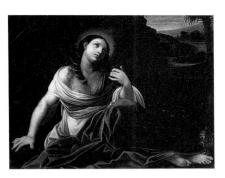

**Italian, unknown artist**
*Saint Mary Magdalene in the Desert*
17th century
Oil on canvas
43 1/2 × 55 1/4" (110.5 × 140.3 cm)

Bequest of Arthur H. Lea
F1938-1-44

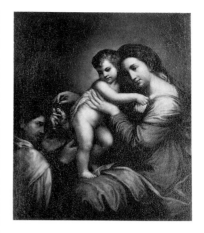

**Italian, unknown artist**
*Virgin and Child, with Saint Vincent Ferrer*
17th century?
Oil on canvas
37 × 30 1/2" (94 × 77.5 cm)

Bequest of Arthur H. Lea
F1938-1-42

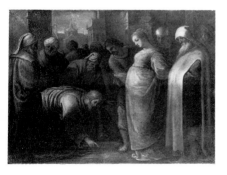

**Italian, active Rome?, unknown artist**
Previously attributed to Andrea Sacchi (JI 1966)
*The Adulteress before Christ*
17th century
Oil on canvas
15 1/8 × 20 5/16" (38.4 × 51.6 cm)

John G. Johnson Collection
cat. 284

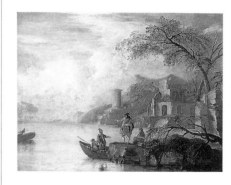

**Italian, unknown artist**
*Landscape with a Lake*
18th century
Oil on canvas
35 1/8 × 42 7/8" (89.2 × 108.9 cm)

Bequest of Arthur H. Lea
F1938-1-47

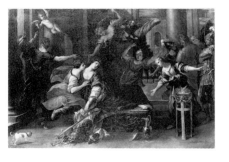

**Italian, active Verona?, unknown artist**
*The Death of Dido*
17th century
Oil on canvas
35 1/8 × 45 3/4" (89.2 × 116.2 cm)

Bequest of Arthur H. Lea
F1938-1-36

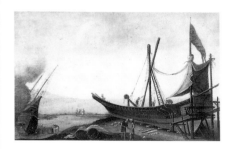

**Italian, unknown artist**
Previously listed as Francesco Fidanza (PMA 1965)
*Marine with a Ship*
Pendant to the following painting
18th century
Oil on canvas
25 × 38 1/4" (63.5 × 97.1 cm)

Bequest of Arthur H. Lea
F1938-1-7

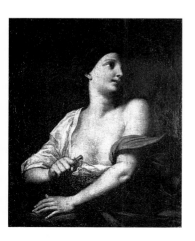

**Italian, active Bologna, unknown artist**
*The Suicide of Lucretia*
17th century
Oil on canvas
35 1/2 × 29 3/4" (90.2 × 75.6 cm)

Bequest of Arthur H. Lea
F1938-1-6

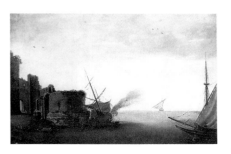

**Italian, unknown artist**
Previously listed as Francesco Fidanza (PMA 1965)
*Marine with Ruins of a Castle*
Pendant to the preceding painting
18th century
Oil on canvas
25 1/4 × 38 3/8" (64.1 × 97.5 cm)

Bequest of Arthur H. Lea
F1938-1-38

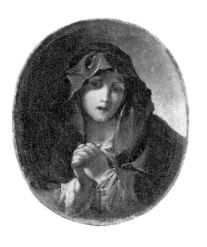

**Italian, active Venice?, unknown artist**
*Mourning Virgin*
18th century
Oil on canvas
9 1/4 × 7 5/8" (23.5 × 19.4 cm)

John G. Johnson Collection
inv. 368

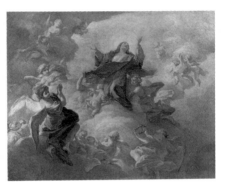

**Italian, active Naples, unknown artist**
*The Assumption of the Virgin*
18th century
Oil on canvas
24 1/8 × 29 1/8" (61.3 × 74 cm)

John G. Johnson Collection
cat. 285

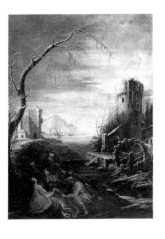

**Italian?, unknown artist**
*Winter Landscape*
18th century
Oil on canvas
62 1/2 × 45" (158.7 × 114.3 cm)

Bequest of Arthur H. Lea
F1938-1-24

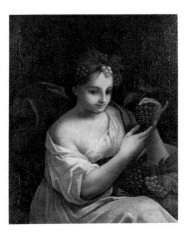

**Italian, unknown artist**
Previously listed as Italian, unknown artist, 17th century (PMA 1965)
*Girl with Grapes*
19th century
Oil on canvas
34 1/2 × 27 3/16" (87.6 × 69.1 cm)

Bequest of Arthur H. Lea
F1938-1-4

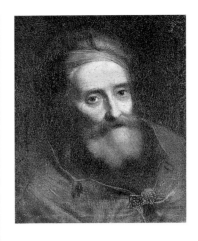

**Italian, unknown artist**
*Portrait of a Man*
In an 18th-century style
19th century?
Oil on canvas
18 3/8 × 14 3/8" (46.7 × 36.5 cm)

John G. Johnson Collection
inv. 2923

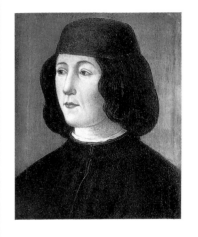

**Italian, unknown artist**
Previously listed as an imitator of Sandro Botticelli (JI 1966)
*Portrait of a Young Gentleman*
In a 15th-century Florentine style
19th century
Oil on panel
13 7/8 × 10 5/8" (35.2 × 27 cm)

John G. Johnson Collection
inv. 705

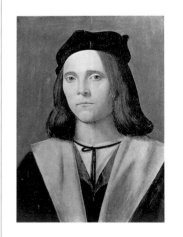

**Italian, unknown artist**
Previously listed as Lorenzo di Credi (JI 1966)
*Portrait of a Young Gentleman*
In a late 15th-century Florentine style
19th century
Oil on panel
17 5/8 × 12 7/8" (44.8 × 32.7 cm)

John G. Johnson Collection
inv. 61

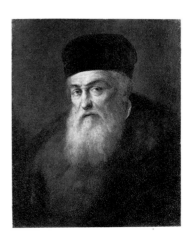

**Italian, active Venice?, unknown artist**
Previously listed as a Venetian artist, 17th century (JI 1966)
*Portrait of an Elderly Gentleman*
19th century?
Oil on canvas
24 11/16 × 19 3/16" (62.7 × 48.7 cm)

John G. Johnson Collection
cat. 228

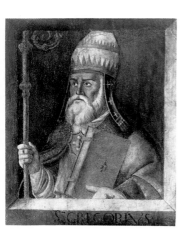

**Italian, unknown artist**
*Saint Gregory the Great*
In a 15th-century style
19th century
Across bottom: S. GREGORIVS
Oil on panel
31 1/4 × 25 3/4" (79.4 × 65.4 cm)

John G. Johnson Collection
inv. 448

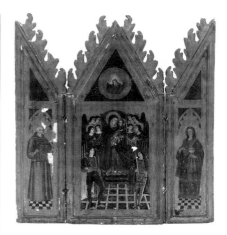

**Italian, unknown artist**
*Enthroned Virgin and Child, with Angels, Candle Bearers, God, and Saints Bernard and Mary Magdalene*
Triptych; in a 14th- and 15th-century Sienese style
c. 1900
Tempera and tooled gold on panel
Center panel: 23 5/8 × 11 1/16" (60 × 28.1 cm); left wing: 23 3/8 × 5 9/16" (59.4 × 14.1 cm); right wing: 23 3/8 × 5 1/2" (59.4 × 14 cm)

Gift of John Harrison, Jr.
1919-447

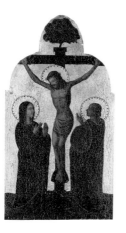

**Italian, unknown artist**
*The Crucifixion*
In a 15th-century style
19th century
Oil and tempera on panel
26 5/8 × 13 3/4" (67.6 × 34.9 cm)

Bequest of Arthur H. Lea
F1938-1-51

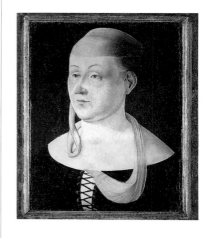

**Jacometto Veneziano, attributed to**
Italian, active Venice, active c. 1472, died c. 1497
Previously listed as Jacometto Veneziano (JI 1966)
*Portrait of a Lady*
Reverse painted with marbleized background and a flower
1470s
On reverse, partially in gold:
VLLLLF / DELITIIS ANIMVM / EXPLE / POST MORTEM / NVLLA VOLVP / TAS
Oil on panel
13 3/8 × 10 13/16" (34 × 27.5 cm)

John G. Johnson Collection
cat. 243

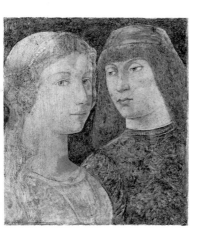

**Italian, unknown artist**
*Two Figures*
In a 15th-century Florentine style
19th century
Oil on panel
17 7/16 × 14 7/8" (44.3 × 37.8 cm)

John G. Johnson Collection
inv. 2856

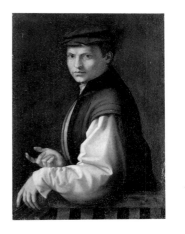

**Jacopino del Conte**
Italian, active Florence and Rome, 1510–1598
*Portrait of a Gentleman*
c. 1535
Oil on panel
26 × 18 3/8" (66 × 46.7 cm)

John G. Johnson Collection
cat. 81

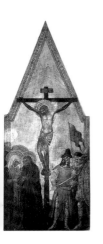

**Italian, unknown artist**
*The Crucifixion*
In a 14th-century Sienese style
Late 19th century
Tempera and tooled gold on panel
22 1/4 × 9 11/16" (56.5 × 24.6 cm)

John G. Johnson Collection
cat. 93

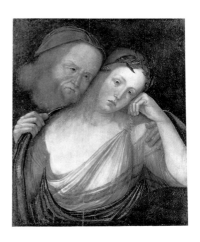

**Jacopo de' Barbari**
Italian, active Venice, Nuremberg, Mechelen, and Brussels, first documented 1497, died before 1515
*An Old Man and a Young Woman (The Nymph Agapes and Her Old Husband)*
1503
Center right: IA.D.BARBARI / M.D.III / [caduceus]
Oil on panel
15 7/8 × 12 3/4" (40.3 × 32.4 cm)

John G. Johnson Collection
cat. 167

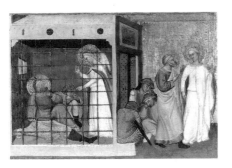

**Jacopo di Cione**
Italian, active Florence,
first documented 1365,
died 1398–1400
*Saint Peter Released from Prison*
Predella panel from the high
altarpiece of San Pier Maggiore,
Florence, designed by Niccolaio
and made in collaboration with
Matteo di Pacino (Italian,
1359–1394); other panels from
the altarpiece are in the National
Gallery, London (569–578); the
Museum of Art, Rhode Island
School of Design, Providence; the
Pinacoteca Vaticana (no. 107,
no. 113, no. 21.04); (formerly)
the Thyssen-Bornemisza
Collection, Lugano, Switzerland;
and (formerly) the Sacerdoti
Collection, Milan
1370–71
Tempera and tooled gold on panel
15 5/16 × 20 5/8" (38.9 × 52.4 cm)

John G. Johnson Collection
cat. 4

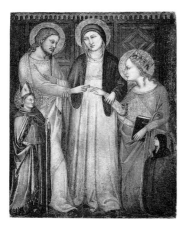

**Jacopo di Cione**
*The Mystic Marriage of Saint
Catherine of Alexandria, with Saint
Louis of Toulouse and a Franciscan
Nun Donor*
c. 1375–80
Tempera and tooled gold on panel
31 15/16 × 24 1/2" (81.1 × 62.2 cm)

John G. Johnson Collection
cat. 6

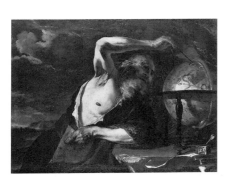

**Langetti, Giovanni Battista,
attributed to**
Italian, active Genoa and Rome,
1625–1676
Previously listed as Luca
Giordano (PMA 1965)
*The Philosopher Anaxagoras*
c. 1660
Oil on canvas
39 1/4 × 52 3/4 (99.7 × 134 cm)

Purchased with the W. P.
Wilstach Fund
W1904-1-25

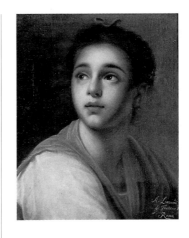

**Leonardi, A.**
Italian, active 19th century
*Portrait of a Girl*
19th century
Lower right: A. Leonardi /
4 Fontane 17 / Roma
Oil on canvas
18 1/4 × 14 1/4" (46.3 × 36.2 cm)

Gift of Jay Cooke
1955-2-5

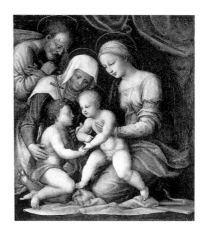

**Leonardo da Pistoia
(Leonardo di Francesco di
Lazzero Malatesta)**
Italian, active Pistoia and
environs and Volterra, born
c. 1483, still active 1518
*The Holy Family with Saint
Elizabeth and the Young Saint John
the Baptist*
Early 16th century
Oil on panel
30 15/16 × 28 13/16" (78.6 × 73.2 cm)

John G. Johnson Collection
cat. 79

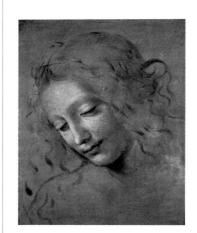

**Leonardo da Vinci,
copy after**
Italian, active Florence, Milan,
Mantua, Rome, and France,
1452–1519
*Head of a Woman*
After the painting in the Galleria
Nazionale, Parma (inv. no. 362)
18th century?
On reverse: Leonardo da Vinci /
[ ] / Parma; on sticker on reverse:
Mar Dogoni cartone / Origle) di
Leonardo. a / Parma. 1797.
Oil on paper mounted on
cardboard backed with twill
9 3/4 × 7 3/8" (24.8 × 18.7 cm)

John G. Johnson Collection
cat. 266

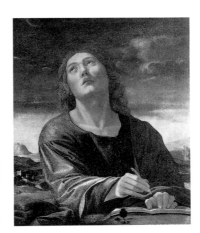

**Liberale da Verona (Liberale
di Jacopo dalla Biava)**
Italian, active Verona, Siena,
and environs, born 1445, died
1525–29
*Saint John the Evangelist on Patmos*
c. 1500
Oil on canvas
28 15/16 × 24 1/2" (73.5 × 62.2 cm)

John G. Johnson Collection
cat. 216

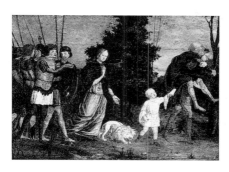

**Libri, Girolamo dai,
follower of**
Italian, active Verona,
1474–1555
*Aeneas Leaving Troy*
Section of a cassone; companion
to the following painting
Mid-16th century
Oil on panel
8 × 11 1/4" (20.3 × 28.6 cm)

John G. Johnson Collection
cat. 221

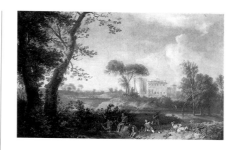

**Locatelli, Andrea, studio of**
*Ideal Landscape*
1730s
Oil on canvas
21 1/2 × 33 1/2" (54.6 × 85.1 cm)

The Bloomfield Moore Collection
1883-98

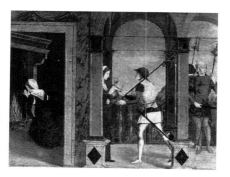

**Libri, Girolamo dai,
follower of**
*The Meeting of Dido and Aeneas*
Section of a cassone; companion
to the preceding painting
Mid-16th century
Oil on panel
8 13/16 × 11 1/2" (22.4 × 29.2 cm)

John G. Johnson Collection
cat. 222

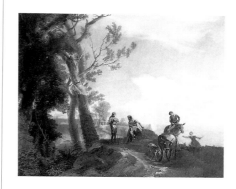

**Locatelli, Andrea, studio of**
Previously listed as Andrea
Locatelli (PMA 1965)
*Pastoral Landscape*
1730s
Oil on canvas
21 3/4 × 34" (55.2 × 86.4 cm)

The Bloomfield Moore Collection
1883-105

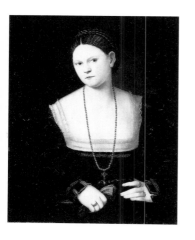

**Licinio, Bernardino di Ser
Antonio**
Italian, active Venice,
documented 1511–1549
*Portrait of a Young Lady*
c. 1530
Oil on panel
27 3/8 × 22" (69.5 × 55.9 cm)

John G. Johnson Collection
cat. 203

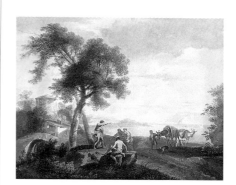

**Locatelli, Andrea, studio of**
Previously listed as Andrea
Locatelli (PMA 1965)
*Pastoral Landscape*
1730s
Oil on canvas
21 1/2 × 33 1/2" (54.6 × 85.1 cm)

The Bloomfield Moore Collection
1883-106

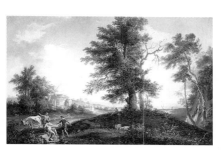

**Locatelli, Andrea, studio of**
Italian, active Rome, 1695–1741
Previously listed as Andrea
Locatelli (PMA 1965)
*Ideal Landscape*
1730s
Oil on canvas
23 3/4 × 29" (60.3 × 73.7 cm)

The Bloomfield Moore Collection
1883-97

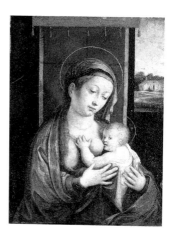

**Longhi, Luca, workshop of**
Italian, active Ravenna,
1507–1580
Previously listed as Luca Longhi
(JGJ 1941)
*Virgin and Child*
Mid-16th century
Oil on canvas on panel
17 1/8 × 12 1/8" (43.5 × 30.8 cm)

John G. Johnson Collection
cat. 256

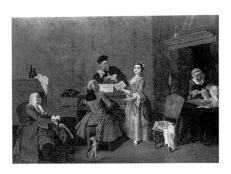

**Longhi, Pietro, copy after**
Italian, 1702–1785
Previously attributed to Pietro
Longhi (PMA 1965)
*The Engagement of a Singer*
After a picture in the Wyndham
Collection, Petworth House,
England
Late 18th or early 19th century
Oil on canvas
21 3/4 × 28 5/16" (55.2 × 71.9 cm)

Purchased with the W. P.
Wilstach Fund
W1916-1-4

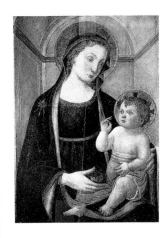

**Lorenzo di Giovanni di Nofri
(Master of San Miniato)**
*Virgin and Child*
c. 1465–70
Tempera and tooled gold on panel
28 5/16 × 19 7/8" (71.9 × 50.5 cm)

John G. Johnson Collection
cat. 37

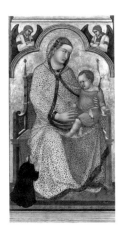

**Lorenzetti, Pietro**
Italian, active Siena, Assisi,
Arezzo, and Florence, first
securely documented 1320,
last documented 1344
*Enthroned Virgin and Child, with a
Monk or Friar Donor and Two
Angels*
Central panel and spandrels from
an altarpiece
1320s
Tempera and tooled gold on panel
Overall: 51 3/4 × 27 1/2"
(131.5 × 69.9 cm); central panel:
49 5/8 × 29 3/4" (126 × 75.6 cm);
spandrels [each]: 9 3/4 × 10 1/2"
(24.8 × 26.7 cm)

John G. Johnson Collection
[central panel]
Purchased with the George W.
Elkins Fund, the W. P. Wilstach
Fund, and the J. Stogdell Stokes
Fund [spandrels]
cat. 91 [central panel]
EW1985-21-1, 2 [spandrels]

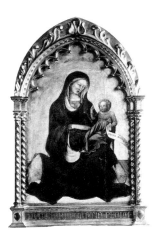

**Lorenzo Monaco (Piero di
Giovanni), workshop of**
Italian, active Florence, first
documented 1390, died 1424?
*The Virgin of Humility*
c. 1413
On scroll: EGO SUM LVX
MV[NDI]; on frame, across
bottom: AVE MARIA GRATIA
PLENA
Tempera and tooled gold on panel
32 3/4 × 19 3/4" (83.2 × 50.2 cm)

John G. Johnson Collection
cat. 10

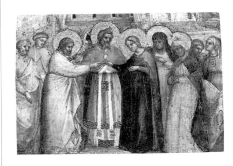

**Lorenzo Veneziano**
Italian, active Veneto and
Bologna, dated works
1356–1372
Previously listed as an Umbro-
Florentine artist, c. 1425 (JI
1966)
*The Marriage of the Virgin*
Predella panel; cut down at top
1360s
Tempera and tooled gold on panel
7 7/8 × 10 1/4" (20 × 26 cm)

John G. Johnson Collection
cat. 128

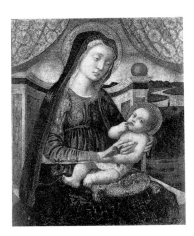

**Lorenzo di Giovanni di Nofri
(Master of San Miniato)**
Italian, active Florence, first
documented 1465, died 1512
Previously listed as the school of
Francesco Botticini (JI 1966)
*Enthroned Virgin and Child*
c. 1465–70
Tempera and tooled gold on panel
17 1/16 × 14 3/8" (43.3 × 36.5 cm)

John G. Johnson Collection
cat. 57

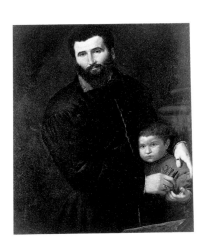

**Lotto, Lorenzo (Lorenzo di
Tommaso Lotto)**
Italian, active Venice, northern
Italy, and Marches, first
documented 1503, died 1556
*Portrait of Gian Giacomo Stuer and
His Son Gian Antonio*
1544
Oil on canvas
35 1/8 × 29 3/8" (89.2 × 74.6 cm)

John G. Johnson Collection
cat. 196

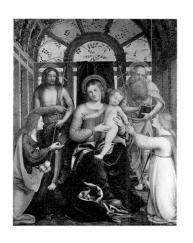

**Lotto, Lorenzo, attributed to**
Previously listed as Lorenzo Lotto
(JI 1966)
*Virgin and Child, with Saints Mary
Magdalene, John the Baptist,
Jerome, and Catherine of Alexandria*
Altarpiece
c. 1517
Oil and gold on panel
60 3/8 × 45 3/4" (153.3 × 116.2 cm)

John G. Johnson Collection
cat. 195

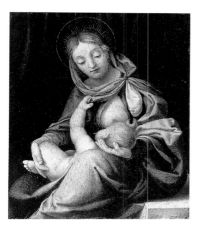

**Lotto, Lorenzo, copy after**
Previously listed as Lorenzo Lotto
(JI 1966)
*Virgin and Child*
Original is in the Hermitage,
St. Petersburg (inv. no. 76)
16th century
Oil on panel
13 1/8 × 10 15/16" (33.3 × 27.8 cm)

John G. Johnson Collection
cat. 194

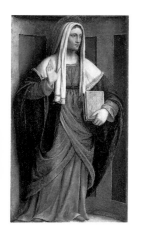

**Luini, Bernardino**
Italian, active Milan and
environs, first documented 1512,
died 1532
*Saint Anne*
Panel from an altarpiece
commissioned in 1523 for San
Sinisio della Torre, Mendrisio,
according to the bequest of
Cristoforo Torriani; companion
panels are in the Di Rovasenda
collection, Turin; the collection
of the Marquess of Normanby,
Whitby; and the Norton Simon
Museum of Art, Pasadena
c. 1523
Oil on panel
24 9/16 × 13 7/16" (62.4 × 34.1 cm)

John G. Johnson Collection
cat. 275

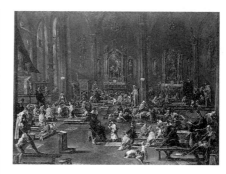

**Magnasco, Alessandro,
also called Lissandro and
Lissandrino**
Italian, active Genoa, Milan,
Venice, and Florence,
c. 1667–1749
*Sermon to Jesuit Novices*
Pendant to the following
painting
After 1711
Oil on canvas
22 11/16 × 15 13/16" (57.6 × 40.2 cm)

Purchased with the Jay Cooke
Fund
1957-2-1

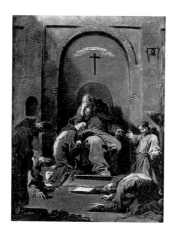

**Magnasco, Alessandro**
*Contrition and Confession of
Capuchin Friars*
Pendant to the preceding
painting
After 1711
On scroll: NII MEMORI IO[ ]
Oil on canvas
22 9/16 × 15 3/4" (57.3 × 40 cm)

Purchased with the Jay Cooke
Fund
1957-2-2

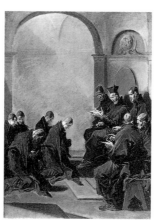

**Magnasco, Alessandro**
*The Catechism in the Cathedral of
Milan*
c. 1725–30
Oil on canvas
47 1/8 × 59" (119.7 × 149.9 cm)

Purchased with the W. P.
Wilstach Fund
W1958-2-1

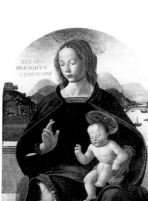

**Mainardi, Sebastiano**
Italian, active San Gimignano,
Pisa, and Florence, documented
1475, died 1513
*Virgin and Child with the Young
Saint John the Baptist*
c. 1500
Upper left: SVB CVM /
PRAESIDIVM / CONFVCIMVS
Oil and gold on panel
36 1/2 × 24 3/8" (92.7 × 61.9 cm)

John G. Johnson Collection
cat. 69

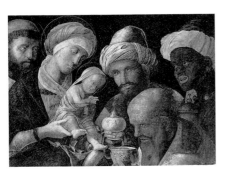

**Mantegna, Andrea, copy after**
Italian, active Padua, Mantua, and Verona, 1431–1506
*The Adoration of the Magi*
After the painting in the J. Paul Getty Museum, Malibu (85.PA.417)
19th century
Oil on canvas
20 1/4 × 29" (51.4 × 73.7 cm)

John G. Johnson Collection
cat. 213

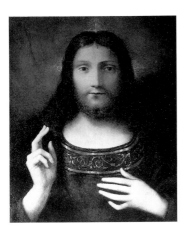

**Marconi, Rocco**
Italian, active Venice, first documented 1504, died 1529
*Christ Blessing*
1520s
Oil on panel
20 11/16 × 16" (52.5 × 40.6 cm)

John G. Johnson Collection
cat. 190

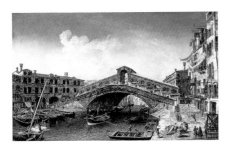

**Marieschi, Michele**
Italian, active Venice, 1710–1744
*Rialto Bridge*
c. 1735–40
Oil on canvas
22 × 33 1/2" (55.9 × 85.1 cm)

John G. Johnson Collection
cat. 298

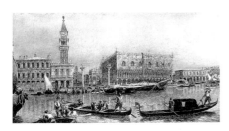

**Marieschi, Michele**
*The Bacino of San Marco*
The figures have been attributed to Francesco Guardi (Italian, 1712–1793) as well as Antonio Guardi (Italian, c. 1698–1760)
c. 1735–40
Oil on canvas
23 11/16 × 44 1/2" (60.2 × 113 cm)

John G. Johnson Collection
cat. 297

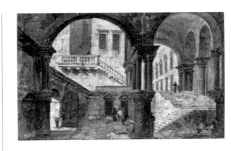

**Marieschi, Michele**
*The Grand Canal at the Scalzi*
Before 1740
Oil on canvas
21 7/8 × 33 3/8" (55.6 × 84.8 cm)

Purchased with the W. P. Wilstach Fund
W1900-1-14

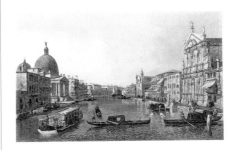

**Marieschi, Michele**
*Courtyard of a Palace*
The figures have been attributed to Francesco Fontebasso (Italian, 1709–1769) as well as Giovanni Battista Tiepolo (Italian, 1696–1770); pendant to a painting in Washington University, St. Louis (no. 2069)
c. 1740
Oil on canvas
14 1/4 × 22 1/4" (36.2 × 56.5 cm)

John G. Johnson Collection
cat. 299

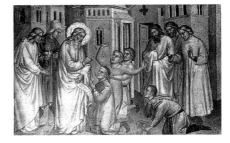

**Martino di Bartolomeo (Martino di Bartolomeo di Biagio)**
Italian, active Siena, first documented 1389, died 1435
Previously listed as Italian, unknown artist, 14th century (PMA 1965)
*Saint Barnabas Curing Cripples*
Predella panel from an altarpiece in the Pinacoteca Nazionale, Siena (160); see following three entries for companion panels
c. 1410
Tempera and tooled gold on panel
10 3/4 × 15 1/2" (27.3 × 39.4 cm)

Purchased from the George Grey Barnard Collection with Museum funds
1945-25-120a

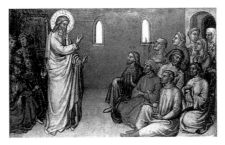

**Martino di Bartolomeo**
Previously listed as Italian, unknown artist, 14th century (PMA 1965)
*Saint Barnabas Preaching*
See previous entry; a fifth predella panel is in the El Paso Museum of Art (K110)
c. 1410
Tempera and tooled gold on panel
10 3/8 × 15 5/8" (26.3 × 39.7 cm)

Purchased from the George Grey Barnard Collection with Museum funds
1945-25-120b

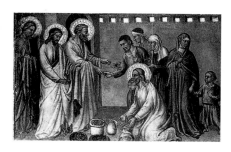

**Martino di Bartolomeo**
Previously listed as Italian, unknown artist, 14th century (PMA 1965)
*Saint Barnabas Laying Money at the Feet of Saints Peter and John the Evangelist*
See previous two entries
c. 1410
Tempera and tooled gold on panel
9 7/8 × 15 1/2" (25.1 × 39.4 cm)

Purchased from the George Grey Barnard Collection with Museum funds
1945-25-120c

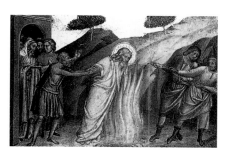

**Martino di Bartolomeo**
Previously listed as Italian, unknown artist, 14th century (PMA 1965)
*The Martyrdom of Saint Barnabas*
See previous three entries
c. 1410
Tempera and tooled gold on panel
9 7/16 × 14 1/8" (24 × 35.9 cm)

Purchased from the George Grey Barnard Collection with Museum funds
1945-25-120d

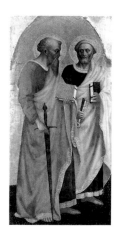

**Masolino (Tommaso di Cristoforo Fini), also called Masolino da Panicale**
Italian, active Florence, Hungary, Rome, Todi, and Castiglione d'Olona, documented 1423–1435
**and Masaccio (Tommaso di Ser Giovanni Cassai)**
Italian, active Florence, 1401–1428
*Saints Paul and Peter*
Panel from an altarpiece from Santa Maria Maggiore, Rome; probably begun by Masaccio and finished after his death by Masolino; see following entry for companion panels
c. 1428
Tempera, oil, and tooled gold on panel
45 × 21 3/8" (114.3 × 54.3 cm)

John G. Johnson Collection
inv. 408

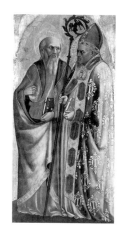

**Masolino and Masaccio**
*Saints John the Evangelist and Martin of Tours*
Companion to the previous panel and panels in the National Gallery, London (5962, 5963); the Museo e Gallerie Nazionali di Capodimonte, Naples (33,35); and the Pinacoteca Vaticana (no. 245, no. 260)
c. 1428
Tempera, oil, and tooled gold on panel
45 × 21 3/8" (114.3 × 54.3 cm)

John G. Johnson Collection
inv. 409

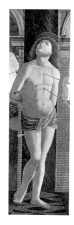

**Master of the Baldraccani**
Italian, active Romagnole, 1480–1510
Previously listed as Francesco Zaganelli (JI 1966)
*Saint Sebastian*
Panel from an altarpiece
c. 1510
Oil on panel
57 × 14 3/4" (144.8 × 37.5 cm)

John G. Johnson Collection
cat. 148

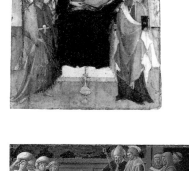

**Master of the Bracciolini Chapel**
Italian, active Pistoia, active c. 1414–c. 1426
Previously listed as Andrea di Giusto (JI 1966)
*Virgin and Child, with Saints Lucy, John the Baptist, Rose, and Bartholomew*
c. 1426
Tempera and tooled gold on panel
22 3/4 × 16" (57.8 × 40.6 cm)

John G. Johnson Collection
cat. 21

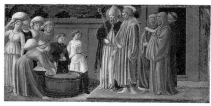

**Master of the Castello Nativity**
Italian, active Florence, active c. 1450–c. 1475
*Saints Justus and Clement Multiplying Grain*
Predella panel from an altarpiece from Santi Giusto e Clemente, Faltignano, now in the Museo Diocesano, Prato; companion to the following panel and a panel in the National Gallery, London (3648)
c. 1460
Tempera and gold on panel
8 1/2 × 18 3/8" (21.6 × 46.7 cm)

John G. Johnson Collection
cat. 24

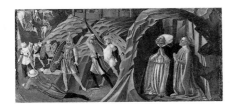

**Master of the Castello Nativity**
*Saints Justus and Clement Praying for Deliverance from the Vandals, and the Departure of the Vandals*
See previous entry
c. 1460
Tempera and gold on panel
8 1/2 × 18 1/2" (21.6 × 47 cm)

John G. Johnson Collection
cat. 25

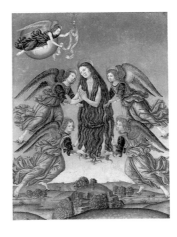

**Master of the Johnson Ascension of Saint Mary Magdalene**
Italian, active Florence,
active c. 1500
Previously listed as Lorenzo di Credi (JI 1966)
*The Ascension of Saint Mary Magdalene*
Based on a painting by Lorenzo di Credi (Italian, 1549–1527), in the Kérészteny Múzeum, Esztergom, Hungary (55.191)
c. 1500
Tempera on panel
20 1/8 × 15 1/16" (51 × 38.2 cm)

John G. Johnson Collection
cat. 75

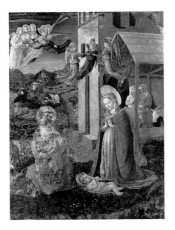

**Master of the Castello Nativity**
*The Adoration of the Christ Child, with the Annunciation to the Shepherds*
c. 1460–70
Tempera and tooled gold on panel
44 5/8 × 32 3/4" (113.3 × 83.2 cm)

John G. Johnson Collection
cat. 23

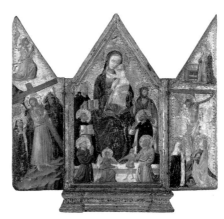

**Master of the Johnson Tabernacle**
Italian, active central Italy,
c. 1420–c. 1465
Previously listed as a follower of Benozzo Gozzoli (JI 1966)
Center panel: *Virgin and Child, with Saints Dominic, John the Baptist, Thomas Aquinas, Peter Martyr, Francis, and Jerome, and an Angel and a Child* [Raphael and Tobias?]; left wing: *Annunciate Angel and Christ Carrying the Cross*; right wing: *Annunciate Virgin and the Crucifixion, with Saints Catherine of Siena and Mary Magdalene*
Triptych
c. 1461
On scroll of Saint John the Baptist: Ecce
Tempera on panel
Center panel: 19 11/16 × 11 1/8" (50 × 28.3 cm); left wing: 19 3/8 × 5 5/8" (49.2 × 14.3 cm); right wing: 19 9/16 × 5 3/8" (49.7 × 13.6 cm)

John G. Johnson Collection
inv. 2034a

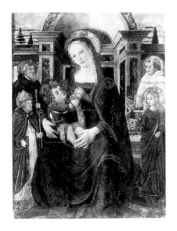

**Master of the Fiesole Epiphany (Filippo di Giuliano Matteo?)**
Italian, active Florence,
active c. 1480–c. 1500
Previously listed as the school of Francesco Botticini (JI 1966)
*Enthroned Virgin and Child, with a Bishop Saint, Saints Benedict, Bernard, and Mary Magdalene*
Late 15th century
Tempera and tooled gold on panel
32 1/8 × 23 1/2" (81.6 × 59.7 cm)

John G. Johnson Collection
cat. 58

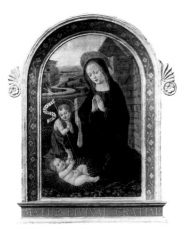

**Master of the Fiesole Epiphany (Filippo di Giuliano Matteo?)**
Previously listed as the school of Francesco Botticini (JI 1966)
*The Virgin and the Young Saint John the Baptist Adoring the Christ Child*
Late 15th century
On scroll: ECE AGNVS DEI;
bottom, on frame [added later]: MATER DIVINAE GRATIAE
Tempera and gold on panel
27 3/4 × 16 3/4" (70.5 × 42.5 cm)

John G. Johnson Collection
cat. 56

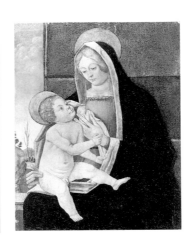

**Master of the Johnson Virgin Lactans**
Italian, active Veneto, active late 15th and early 16th centuries
Previously listed as Benedetto Montagna (JI 1966)
*Virgin and Child before a Landscape*
c. 1500
Oil on panel
16 15/16 × 13 3/16" (43 × 33.5 cm)

John G. Johnson Collection
cat. 170

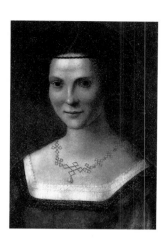

**Master of the Leonardesque Female Portraits**
Italian, active Milan,
active c. 1500–c. 1530
Previously listed as Francesco
Salviati (JI 1966)
*Portrait of a Woman*
Early 16th century
Oil on panel
16 ³/₄ × 11 ³/₄" (42.5 × 29.8 cm)

John G. Johnson Collection
cat. 85

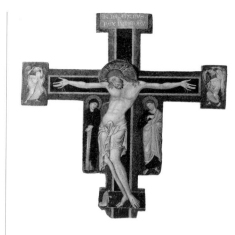

**Master of Montelabate**
Italian, active Perugia,
documented 1285
Previously listed as a follower of
the Master of San Francesco (PMA
1965)
*Crucifix*
c. 1285
Across top: IC .NAZARENVS. /
.REX. IVDEORV.
Tempera on panel
74 × 68 ¹/₄" (188 × 173.3 cm)

Purchased with the W. P.
Wilstach Fund
W1952-1-1

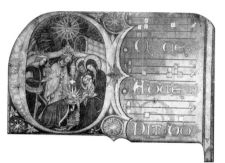

**Master of the Lives of the Emperors**
Italian, active Lombardy,
dated works 1413–1459
*The Adoration of the Magi*
Cut from a manuscript
c. 1440
Text: ECCE / ADVE / NIT
DO[MINUS]; upper left: MONS
VICTORIALIS
Tempera and gold on vellum
9 ¹/₄ × 15" (23.5 × 38.1 cm)

John G. Johnson Collection
cat. 122

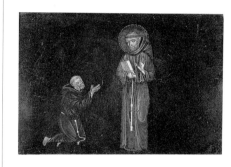

**Master of Montelabate**
Previously listed as Salerno di
Coppo (JI 1966)
*Saint Francis of Assisi and a
Franciscan Devotee*
Valve of a diptych [?]; the other
panel is in a private collection in
Rome
c. 1285
Tempera on panel
6 ¹⁵/₁₆ × 10 ¹/₁₆" (17.6 × 25.6 cm)

John G. Johnson Collection
inv. 325

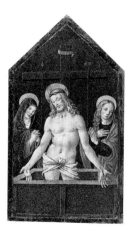

**Master of Marradi**
Italian, active Florence,
1480–1510
Previously listed as Bernardino di
Mariotto (JI 1966)
*The Man of Sorrows, with the Virgin
Mary and Saint John the Evangelist*
c. 1500
On cross: I N R I
Oil and gold on panel
14 ⁵/₈ × 7 ¹³/₁₆" (37.1 × 19.8 cm)

John G. Johnson Collection
cat. 144

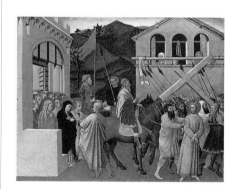

**Master of the Osservanza**
Italian, active Siena,
active c. 1430–c. 1460
Previously listed as Sano di
Pietro (JI 1966)
*Christ on the Road to Calvary*
Predella panel; companion panels
are in the Metropolitan Museum
of Art, New York (1975.1.41);
Fogg Art Museum, Cambridge,
Mass. (1922.172); Pinacoteca
Vaticana (no. 232); Museum of
Western and Oriental Art, Kiev;
Detroit Institute of Arts (60.61)
c. 1440–45
Tempera and tooled gold on panel
14 ¹/₂ × 18 ³/₈" (36.8 × 46.7 cm)

John G. Johnson Collection
inv. 1295

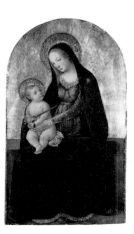

**Master of Marradi**
*Virgin and Child*
c. 1500
On Virgin's halo: AVE MARIA
Tempera and tooled gold on panel
37 ³/₄ × 21" (95.9 × 53.3 cm)

John G. Johnson Collection
cat. 139

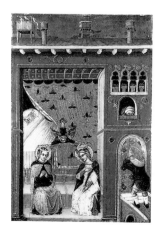
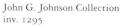

**Master of the Pesaro Crucifix**
Italian, active Venice,
active c. 1375–c. 1400
Previously listed as Jacobello del
Fiore (PMA 1965)
*The Crowning of Saint Cecilia of
Rome and Her Husband, Valerianus*
Panel from an altarpiece
c. 1375–80
Tempera and gold on panel
21 ³/₄ × 14 ³/₁₆" (55.2 × 36 cm)

The John D. McIlhenny
Collection
1943-40-51

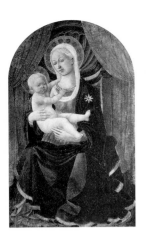

**Master of the Pomegranate**
Italian, active Florence,
active c. 1450–c. 1475
Previously listed as an old copy
after Pesellino (JI 1966)
*Enthroned Virgin and Child*
c. 1460
Tempera and tooled gold on panel
51 × 31 ½" (129.5 × 80 cm)

John G. Johnson Collection
cat. 36

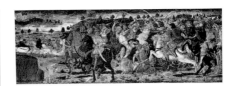

**Matteo di Giovanni,
attributed to**
Previously listed as Guidoccio
Cozzarelli (JI 1966)
*Camilla in Battle*
Panel from a cassone; possibly a
companion to *The Legend of
Cloelia*, in the Metropolitan
Museum of Art, New York
(11.126.2)
1470s
Tempera and tooled gold on panel
15 ⅝ × 41 ⅝" (39.7 × 105.7 cm)

John G. Johnson Collection
cat. 111

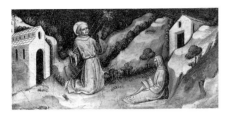

**Master of Staffolo
(Costantino di Francesuccio
di Cecco Ghissi?)**
Italian, active Marches,
documented 1417–1459
Previously listed as the school of
Fabriano (JI 1966)
*Saint Francis of Assisi Receiving the
Stigmata*
Predella panel of a processional
standard; the lower sides are
additions
c. 1420–30
Tempera on panel
6 ⅞ × 12 ½" (17.5 × 31.7 cm)

John G. Johnson Collection
cat. 121

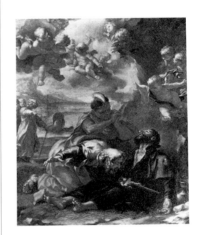

**Mazzanti, Lodovico**
Italian, born Orvieto, active
Rome and Naples, c. 1679–1775
Previously listed as Italian,
unknown artist, 17th century
(PMA 1965)
*The Death of Saint Francis Xavier*
Possibly a sketch for the painting
in the Stadtmuseum Düsseldorf
c. 1740–45
Oil on canvas
17 ⁷⁄₁₆ × 14" (44.3 × 35.6 cm)

The Bloomfield Moore Collection
1883-89

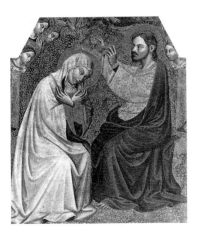

**Master of the Terni
Dormition**
Italian, active Umbria,
active c. 1370–c. 1400
*The Coronation of the Virgin*
Panel from an altarpiece, cut
down at the top; companion
panels are in the Pinacoteca
Capitolina, Rome (353), and the
Kisters Collection, Kreuzlingen,
Switzerland
c. 1390–1400
Tempera and tooled gold on panel
23 ¹⁄₁₆ × 19 ¼" (58.6 × 48.9 cm)

John G. Johnson Collection
cat. 123

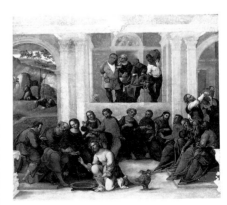

**Mazzolino, Lodovico**
Italian, active Ferrara, first
documented 1504, died 1528–30
*Christ Washing the Feet of the
Disciples*
1527
Lower right: 1527 MESE
Oil on panel
19 ⁷⁄₁₆ × 21 ¹⁄₁₆" (49.4 × 53.5 cm)

John G. Johnson Collection
cat. 248

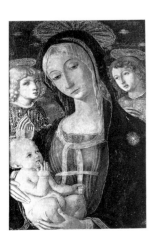

**Matteo di Giovanni (Matteo
di Giovanni di Bartolo)**
Italian, active Siena and environs
and Borgo San Sepolcro, first
documented 1452, died 1495
*Virgin and Child, with Two Angels*
c. 1470
Tempera and tooled gold on panel
23 ⅞ × 15 ¹⁵⁄₁₆" (60.6 × 40.5 cm)

John G. Johnson Collection
cat. 110

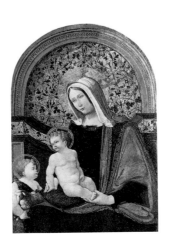

**Melone, Altobello**
Italian, active Cremona,
documented 1516–1518
*Virgin and Child, with the Young
Saint John the Baptist*
c. 1510
Oil and gold on panel
29 ¾ × 19 ¼" (75.6 × 48.9 cm)

John G. Johnson Collection
cat. 151

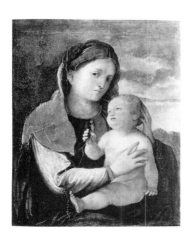

**Melone, Altobello**
*Virgin and Child*
c. 1525
Oil on panel
19 7/8 × 15 1/2" (50.5 × 39.4 cm)

John G. Johnson Collection
cat. 232

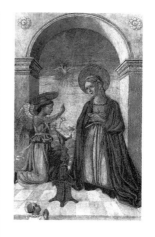

**Morone, Domenico,
workshop of**
Italian, active Verona,
born c. 1442, still active 1517
*The Annunciation, with a Haloed
Donor*
c. 1500
Oil on panel
36 1/4 × 21 1/8" (92.1 × 53.7 cm)

John G. Johnson Collection
cat. 219

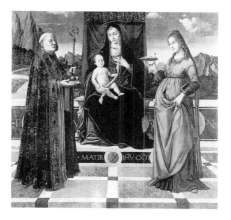

**Montagna, Bartolomeo
(Bartolomeo Cincani)**
Italian, active Veneto, first
documented 1459, died 1523
*Enthroned Virgin and Child, with
Saints Nicholas of Bari and Lucy*
Altarpiece from Santa Maria dei
Servi, Vicenza
c. 1480
Across center: T. V. T. N.; on
step: MATER IHV.CXTI
Oil on panel transferred to canvas
70 1/2 × 71" (179.1 × 180.3 cm)

John G. Johnson Collection
cat. 168

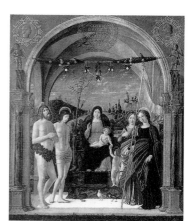

**Morone, Francesco**
Italian, active Verona,
1473–1529
Previously listed as Giovanni
Francesco Caroto (JI 1966)
*Virgin and Child, with Saints
Onuphrius, Sebastian, Justine, and
Ursula*
c. 1500
Center top: GLORIA / IN
EXCELSIS / DEO ET IN TE / RRA
PAX HOM / VOLVNTA / TIS;
center bottom (spurious):
ANDREA MANTEGNA PINGEBAT
Oil on canvas
22 3/8 × 18 3/8" (56.8 × 46.7 cm)

John G. Johnson Collection
cat. 214

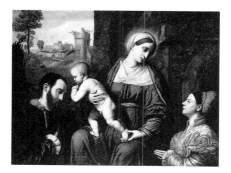

**Moretto da Brescia
(Alessandro Bonvicino)**
Italian, active Brescia,
c. 1498–1554
*Virgin and Child, with Two Donors*
c. 1528–30
Oil on canvas
48 1/2 × 62 1/2" (123.2 × 158.7 cm)

John G. Johnson Collection
cat. 236

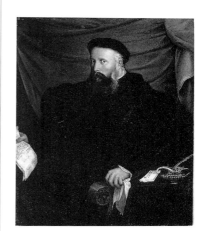

**Moroni, Giovan Battista di
Francesco, attributed to**
Italian, active Brescia,
born c. 1520–25, died 1578
Previously listed as Giovan
Battista di Francesco Moroni
(JI 1966)
*Portrait of a Gentleman*
1547
Center left, on letter: MDXLVII.
G.B.M.; lower right, on envelope:
Al Mageo Signor
Oil on canvas
44 3/4 × 36 3/4" (113.7 × 93.3 cm)

John G. Johnson Collection
cat. 237

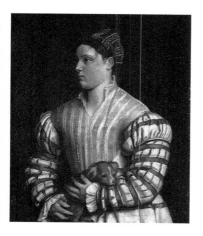

**Moretto da Brescia**
*Portrait of Eleonora Averoldi*
c. 1530
Oil on canvas
33 1/2 × 27 1/8" (85.1 × 68.9 cm)

John G. Johnson Collection
cat. 1172

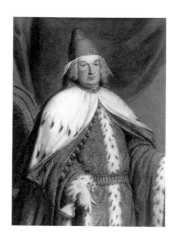

**Nazzari, Nazzario,
attributed to**
Italian, active Bergamo and
Venice, born 1724, still active
1793
*Portrait of Doge Pietro Grimani*
c. 1741–52
Oil on canvas
54 7/8 × 37 3/8" (139.4 × 94.9 cm)

John G. Johnson Collection
cat. 290

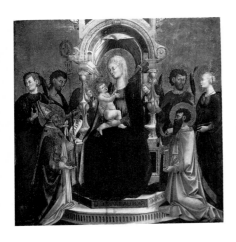

**Neri di Bicci**
Italian, active Florence,
1419–1492
*Enthroned Virgin and Child, with
Two Angels and Saints Nicholas of
Bari, Ansanus, John the Baptist,
Sebastian, Catherine of Alexandria,
and Bartholomew*
Altarpiece
1457
On cartellino: ECCE AGN[US]; on
base of throne: REGINA CELI
LETTARE ALLELVIA QVIA ME P
Tempera and tooled gold on panel
65 × 64 3/8" (165.1 × 163.5 cm)

The Bloomfield Moore Collection
1899-1108

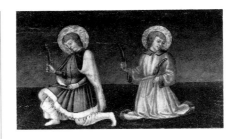

**Neri di Bicci**
*Two Young Martyr Saints*
See previous entry
c. 1476
Tempera and gold on panel
7 × 11" (17.8 × 27.9 cm)

John G. Johnson Collection
cat. 29

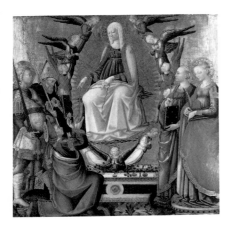

**Neri di Bicci**
*Saint Thomas Receiving the Virgin's
Girdle, with the Archangel Michael,
Saints Augustine, Margaret, and
Catherine of Alexandria, and Angels*
Panel from an altarpiece from San
Michele, Prato, finished in 1467;
the predella is in the Museu
Nacional d'Art de Catalunya,
Barcelona (64972)
1467
Tempera and tooled gold on panel
61 1/4 × 60 7/8" (155.6 × 154.6 cm)

John G. Johnson Collection
cat. 27

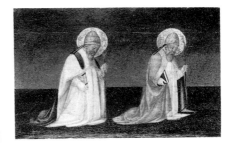

**Neri di Bicci**
*Two Papal Saints*
See previous two entries
c. 1476
Tempera and gold on panel
7 × 11" (17.8 × 27.9 cm)

John G. Johnson Collection
cat. 30

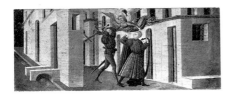

**Neri di Bicci**
*The Archangel Raphael Preventing
an Assassination*
Predella panel; companion panels
are in the Rijksdienst Beelende
Kunst, The Hague (NK1472,
NK2703), and a private
collection in Ferrara
1471?
Oil on panel
8 3/8 × 19 1/8" (21.3 × 48.6 cm)

John G. Johnson Collection
inv. 2073

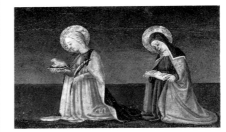

**Neri di Bicci**
*Saint Agnes and a Nun Saint*
See previous three entries
c. 1476
Tempera and gold on panel
7 × 11" (17.8 × 27.9 cm)

John G. Johnson Collection
cat. 31

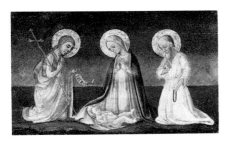

**Neri di Bicci**
*The Virgin and Saints John the
Baptist and Jerome Adoring the
Christ Child*
Predella panel; companion to the
following five panels
c. 1476
On scroll: ECCE AGN[US]
Tempera and gold on panel
7 × 11" (17.8 × 27.9 cm)

John G. Johnson Collection
cat. 28

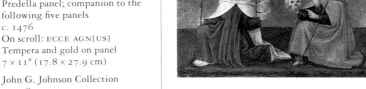

**Neri di Bicci**
*Saints Dominic and Anthony Abbot*
See previous four entries
c. 1476
Tempera and gold on panel
7 × 11" (17.8 × 27.9 cm)

John G. Johnson Collection
cat. 32

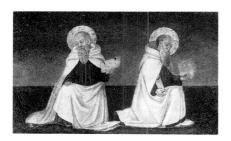

**Neri di Bicci**
*Two Monastic Saints*
See previous five entries
c. 1476
Tempera and gold on panel
7 × 11" (17.8 × 27.9 cm)

John G. Johnson Collection
cat. 33

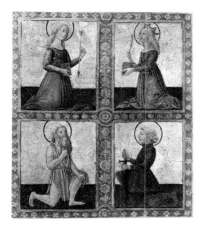

**Neroccio (Neroccio di Bartolomeo di Benedetto de' Landi)**
Italian, active Siena and Lucca, 1447–1500
*Saints Christina of Bolsena [?], Catherine of Alexandria, Jerome, and Galganus*
c. 1470
Tempera and tooled gold on panel
11 3/4 × 10" (29.8 × 25.4 cm)

John G. Johnson Collection
cat. 1169

**Neroccio**
*Virgin and Child, with Saints Jerome and Catherine of Siena*
1470s
Tempera on panel
21 15/16 × 15 1/8" (55.7 × 38.4 cm)

John G. Johnson Collection
cat. 109

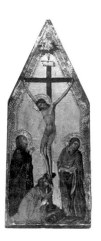

**Niccolò di Segna**
Italian, active Siena, first documented 1331, last signed work 1345
Previously listed as Ugolino di Nerio (JI 1966)
*The Crucifixion*
c. 1330
Tempera and tooled gold on panel
13 5/8 × 5 5/16" (34.6 × 13.5 cm)

John G. Johnson Collection
cat. 90

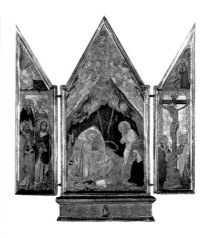

**Niccolò di Tommaso**
Italian, active Florence, Naples, and Pistoia, documented c. 1346–1376
Center panel: *Saint Bridget's Vision of the Nativity*; left wing: *The Annunciate Angel and Saints Anthony Abbot, Catherine of Alexandria, Nicholas of Bari, and James the Great*; right wing: *The Annunciate Virgin and the Crucifixion*
Triptych
c. 1377
On Virgin's halo: AVE MARIA GRATIA; from God the Father: HIC EST FILIVS MEVS; center left: GLORIA IN EXCELSIS DEO; center right: ET IN TERRA PAX HOMINIBVS; from the Virgin: VIAT DEVS MEVS DOMINVS MEVS FILIVS MEVS; on cross: INRI
Tempera and tooled gold on panel
Center panel: 25 × 10 7/16" (63.5 × 26.5 cm); left wing: 21 1/16 × 5" (53.5 × 12.7 cm); right wing: 21 1/16 × 5 1/16" (53.5 × 12.9 cm)

John G. Johnson Collection
cat. 120

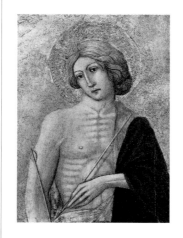

**Nicola d'Ulisse da Siena**
Italian, active Umbria, first documented 1451, still active 1470
Previously attributed to Priamo della Quercia (JI 1966)
*Saint Sebastian*
Panel from an altarpiece; cut down on all sides; companion to the following panel
Mid-15th century
Tempera and tooled gold on panel
16 3/4 × 11 3/4" (42.5 × 29.8 cm)

John G. Johnson Collection
cat. 103

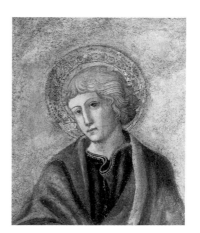

**Nicola d'Ulisse da Siena**
Previously attributed to Priamo della Quercia (JI 1966)
*Saint John the Evangelist [?]*
Panel from an altarpiece; cut down on all sides; companion to the preceding panel
Mid-15th century
Tempera and tooled gold on panel
13 1/2 × 11" (34.3 × 27.9 cm)

John G. Johnson Collection
cat. 104

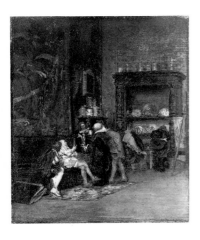

**Nittis, Giuseppe De**
Italian, 1846–1884
*The Connoisseurs*
1869
Lower left: De Nittis 69
Oil on panel
9 ³/₄ × 8" (24.8 × 20.3 cm)

John G. Johnson Collection
inv. 2700

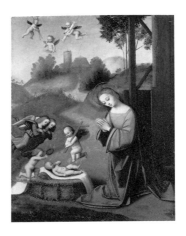

**Ortolano (Giovanni Battista Benvenuti)**
Italian, active Ferrara,
c. 1487–1527
*The Adoration of the Christ Child*
c. 1510
Oil on panel
19 ⁵/₈ × 14 ³/₄" (49.8 × 37.5 cm)

John G. Johnson Collection
cat. 246

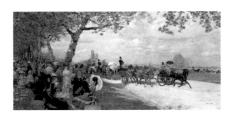

**Nittis, Giuseppe De**
*Return from the Races*
1875
Lower right: D. Nittis '75
Oil on canvas
22 ⁷/₈ × 45 ¹/₈" (58.1 × 114.6 cm)

Gift of John G. Johnson for the
W. P. Wilstach Collection
W1906-1-10

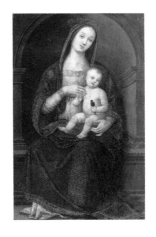

**Pacchiarotti, Giacomo**
Italian, active Siena, 1474–1540
Previously listed as Pietro
Perugino (JI 1966)
*Enthroned Virgin and Child*
c. 1510
Tempera and gold on panel
43 ¹/₂ × 26 ¹/₂" (110.5 × 67.3 cm)

John G. Johnson Collection
cat. 141

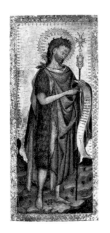

**Orsini, Antonio (Master of
the Carminati Coronation)**
Italian, active Ferrara,
first documented 1432,
died before 1491
Previously listed as a Sienese
artist, c. 1400 (JI 1966)
*Saint John the Baptist*
Companion to the following
painting
c. 1425
On scroll: Ecce / agnus / Dei/E /
cce qui / tollis x / peccha / to mun
/ di/mi / xazeme / nobis
Tempera and tooled gold on panel
12 ³/₈ × 5 ³/₁₆" (31.4 × 13.2 cm)

John G. Johnson Collection
cat. 98a

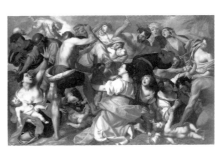

**Pacecco de Rosa
(Francesco de Rosa)**
Italian, active Naples,
c. 1600–1654
*The Massacre of the Innocents*
c. 1640
Oil on canvas
78 × 120 ¹/₄" (198.1 × 305.4 cm)

Purchased with the John D.
McIlhenny Fund
1973-253-1

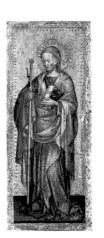

**Orsini, Antonio (Master of
the Carminati Coronation)**
Previously listed as a Sienese
artist, c. 1400 (JI 1966)
*Saint James the Great*
Companion to the preceding
painting
c. 1425
Tempera and tooled gold on panel
12 ³/₈ × 5 ³/₁₆" (31.4 × 13.2 cm)

John G. Johnson Collection
cat. 98b

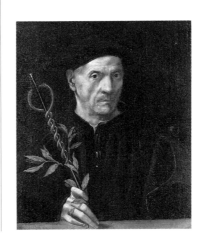

**Pagani, Gaspare,
attributed to**
Italian, active Modena, first
documented 1521, died 1569
Previously listed as a North
Italian artist, 16th- or 17th-
century copy after original of
1500–10 (JI 1966)
*Portrait of an Elderly Physician*
c. 1540
Oil on canvas
26 ¹/₂ × 21 ³/₄" (67.3 × 55.2 cm)

John G. Johnson Collection
cat. 253

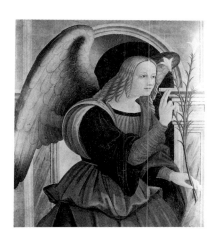

**Pagani, Vincenzo**
Italian, active Marches and
Perugia, c. 1490–1568
*The Annunciate Angel*
Companion to *The Virgin
Annunciate*, in a private collection
c. 1510
Oil on panel
29 5/8 × 26" (75.2 × 66 cm)

John G. Johnson Collection
cat. 198

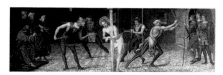

**Pagani, Vincenzo**
*The Flagellation*
Predella panel
1530s
Oil on panel
9 11/16 × 33" (24.6 × 83.8 cm)

John G. Johnson Collection
cat. 199

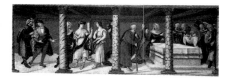

**Pagani, Vincenzo**
*The Presentation of Christ in the
Temple*
Predella panel
1530s
Oil on panel
7 15/16 × 23 5/8" (20.2 × 60 cm)

John G. Johnson Collection
cat. 200

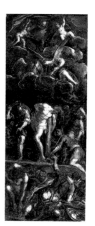

**Palma il Giovane (Jacopo
Negretti), attributed to**
Italian, active Venice,
1544–1628
Previously listed as Italian,
unknown artist, 16th century
(PMA 1965)
*The Flagellation*
Late 16th century
Oil on canvas
34 3/4 × 13 1/2" (88.3 × 34.3 cm)

The Louise and Walter Arensberg
Collection
1950-134-193

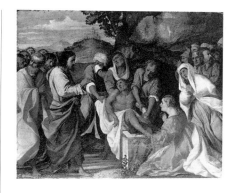

**Palma il Vecchio (Jacopo
d'Antonio Negretti)**
Italian, active Venice, first
documented 1510, died 1528
*The Raising of Lazarus*
c. 1514
Oil on panel
20 7/8 × 24 1/8" (53 × 61.3 cm)

John G. Johnson Collection
cat. 187

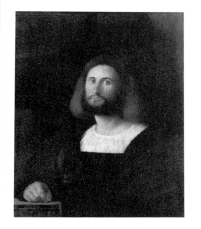

**Palma il Vecchio**
*Portrait of a Gentleman*
c. 1520–25
Oil on panel transferred to canvas
27 3/8 × 21 7/8" (69.5 × 55.6 cm)

John G. Johnson Collection
cat. 188

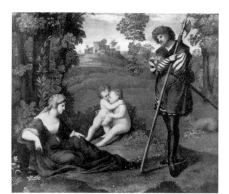

**Palma il Vecchio, follower of**
Previously listed as Palma il
Giovane (PMA 1965)
*Allegory*
c. 1515–20
Oil on canvas
55 7/8 × 62" (141.9 × 157.5 cm)

Purchased with the W. P.
Wilstach Fund
W1922-1-2

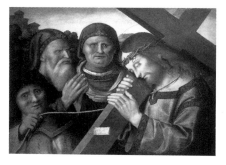

**Palmezzano, Marco (Marco
di Antonio Palmeggiano)**
Italian, active Forlì and Venice,
born c. 1459–63, died by 1539
*Christ Carrying the Cross*
c. 1530–39
Center bottom, on cartellino:
Marcus Palmezianus pictor /
forlienianus faciebat /
Mcccccxxx [ ]
Oil on panel
22 3/8 × 32 3/16" (56.8 × 81.8 cm)

John G. Johnson Collection
inv. 212

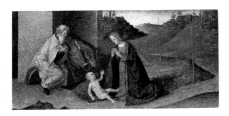

**Palmezzano, Marco**
*The Nativity*
Predella panel
Early 16th century
Oil on panel
9 3/4 × 19 1/2" (24.8 × 49.5 cm)

John G. Johnson Collection
cat. 147

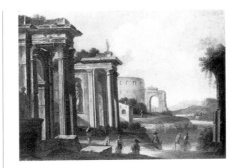

**Pannini, Giovanni Paolo,
imitator of**
Previously listed as the school of
Giovanni Paolo Pannini (PMA
1965)
*Landscape with Classical Ruins and
Figures*
18th century?
Oil on canvas
29 1/8 × 39 1/8" (74 × 99.4 cm)

The Bloomfield Moore Collection
1883-103

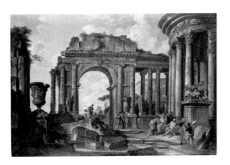

**Pannini, Giovanni Paolo**
Italian, born Piacenza, active
Rome, 1692–1765
*Landscape with Ruins*
1730
Lower left: P. Pannini Rome 1730
Oil on canvas
39 × 53" (99.1 × 134.6 cm)

Gift of Dora Donner Ide in
memory of John Jay Ide
1965-90-1

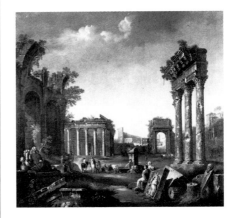

**Pannini, Giovanni Paolo,
imitator of**
Previously attributed to Giovanni
Paolo Pannini (PMA 1965)
*The Roman Forum*
18th century?
Oil on canvas
56 3/16 × 57 1/8" (142.7 × 145.1 cm)

Bequest of Mrs. Harry Markoe
1943-51-101

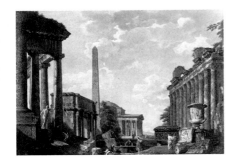

**Pannini, Giovanni Paolo**
*Roman Monuments*
1735?
Lower right: I. P. PANINI /
Roma / 1735[?]; [monuments
also inscribed]
Oil on canvas
38 3/4 × 53 1/4" (98.4 × 135.2 cm)

Purchased with Museum funds
1959-28-1

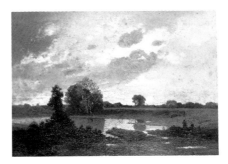

**Pasini, Alberto**
Italian, 1826–1899
*Landscape with a River*
1855
Lower right: A. Pasini. 55
Oil on panel
10 1/4 × 14" (26 × 35.6 cm)

John G. Johnson Collection
cat. 1055

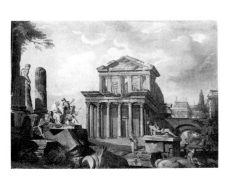

**Pannini, Giovanni Paolo,
imitator of**
Previously listed as Italian,
unknown artist, 18th century
(PMA 1965)
*Architectural Composition*
18th century?
Oil on canvas
28 1/4 × 35 3/8" (71.7 × 89.8 cm)

The Bloomfield Moore Collection
1883-115

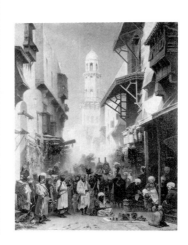

**Pasini, Alberto**
*Street in Constantinople*
1867
Lower right: A Pasini, 1867
Oil on canvas
33 7/8 × 25 3/4" (86 × 65.4 cm)

John G. Johnson Collection
cat. 1056

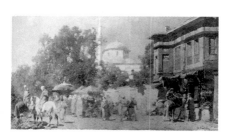

**Pasini, Alberto**
*Street in Damascus*
1871
Lower right: A. Pasini. 1871.
Oil on canvas
9 5/16 × 15 13/16" (23.6 × 40.2 cm)

John G. Johnson Collection
cat. 1057

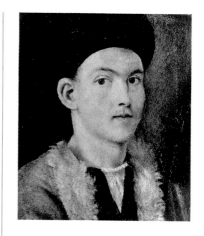

**Piazza, Callisto, attributed to**
Previously listed as Callisto
Piazza (JI 1966)
*Portrait of a Young Man*
Mid-16th century
Oil on panel
12 1/8 × 10 1/8" (30.8 × 25.7 cm)

John G. Johnson Collection
cat. 233

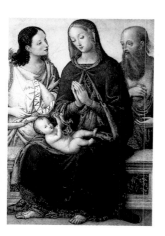

**Pastura (Antonio del Massaro da Viterbo)**
Italian, active central Italy,
documented 1478–1513,
died before 1516
*Virgin and Child, with Saints John
the Baptist and Jerome*
Early 1480s?
On scroll: ECCE ANGNVS DEI
Oil on panel
31 × 21 1/16" (78.7 × 53.5 cm)

John G. Johnson Collection
cat. 143

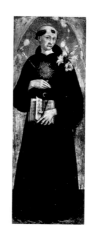

**Piermatteo Lauro de Manfredi da Amelia (Master of the Gardner Annunciation)**
Italian, active central Italy,
documented 1467–1503
*Saint Nicholas of Tolentino*
Panel from an altarpiece;
companion panels are in the
Staatliche Museen zu Berlin-
Preussischer Kulturbesitz (129);
Staatliches Lindenau-Museum,
Altenburg, Germany (110, 111);
and a private collection
1481
On book, first page: ELC / ME /
ET / IN / SO; second page: ET
PRE / CECTA / PATRIS / MEI S /
RVARI; third page: ET MAN / EO
IN E / IVS DILE
Tempera and tooled gold on panel
47 1/2 × 16 1/2" (120.6 × 41.9 cm)

John G. Johnson Collection
cat. 140

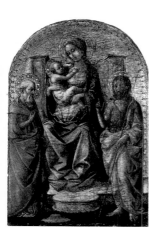

**Pesellino (Francesco di Stefano)**
Italian, active Florence,
c. 1422–1457
*Enthroned Virgin and Child, with
Saints Jerome and John the Baptist*
c. 1448
Tempera and tooled gold on panel
11 3/4 × 7 7/8" (29.8 × 20 cm)

John G. Johnson Collection
cat. 35

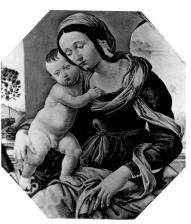

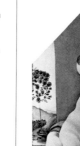

**Piazza, Callisto (Calisto de la Piaza da Lodi)**
Italian, active Lodi and Brescia,
first documented 1524, died 1561
*Musical Group*
1520s
Oil on panel
35 5/8 × 35 3/4" (90.5 × 90.8 cm)

John G. Johnson Collection
cat. 234

**Piero di Cosimo (Piero di Lorenzo), follower of**
Italian, active Florence,
1461/62–1521
Previously listed as Piero di
Cosimo (JI 1966)
*Virgin and Child*
Early 16th century?
Oil on panel
33 1/4 × 27 5/8" (84.4 × 70.2 cm)

John G. Johnson Collection
cat. 76

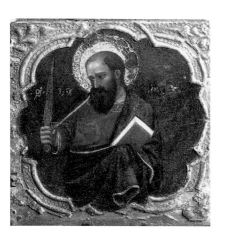

**Pietro di Domenico da Montepulciano**
Italian, active Marches, dated works 1418–1422
Previously listed as a Sienese artist, early 15th century (JI 1966)
*Saint Paul*
Predella panel
c. 1420
Tempera and tooled gold on panel
10 × 9 1/4" (25.4 × 23.5 cm)

John G. Johnson Collection
cat. 1170

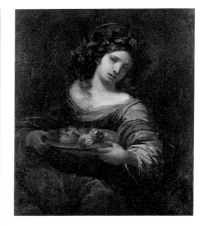

**Pignoni, Simone, follower of**
Previously listed as Italian, unknown artist, 18th century (PMA 1965)
*Saint Dorothy of Cappadocia*
Late 17th century
Oil on canvas
41 1/8 × 34" (104.5 × 86.4 cm)

Bequest of Arthur H. Lea
F1938-1-49

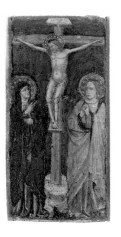

**Piero di Miniato, attributed to**
Italian, active Florence, first documented 1386, died 1430–46
*The Crucifixion*
c. 1430
Tempera and tooled gold on panel
22 5/8 × 10 3/4" (57.5 × 27.3 cm)

The Louise and Walter Arensberg Collection
1950-134-532

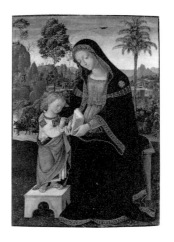

**Pinturicchio (Bernardino di Betto)**
Italian, active central Italy, 1454–1513
*Virgin Teaching Jesus to Read*
c. 1500
Center, on book: Domine l[abia mea] ape[ries]; on Virgin's halo: AVE MARIA GRATIA PLENA DOMINVS TECVM
Oil and gold on panel
24 1/8 × 16 1/2" (61.3 × 41.9 cm)

John G. Johnson Collection
inv. 1336

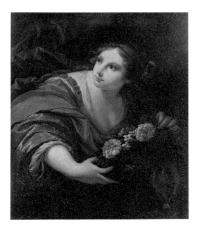

**Pignoni, Simone**
Italian, active Florence, 1611–1698
Previously listed as Italian, unknown artist, 18th century (PMA 1965)
*Saint Rosalie* [?]
Mid to late 17th century
Oil on canvas
34 × 28 1/2" (86.4 × 72.4 cm)

Bequest of Arthur H. Lea
F1938-1-2

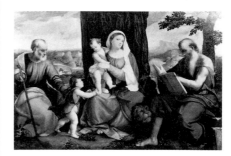

**Pitati, Bonifacio de', also called Bonifacio Veronese**
Italian, c. 1487–1553
*The Holy Family, with the Young Saint John the Baptist and Saint Jerome*
c. 1530
Oil on canvas
55 1/4 × 80 3/4" (140.3 × 205.1 cm)

Purchased with the W. P. Wilstach Fund
W1922-1-1

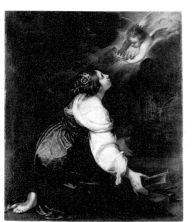

**Pignoni, Simone, follower of**
*Saint Catherine of Alexandria Receiving the Crown of Heaven*
Late 17th century
Oil on canvas
80 1/2 × 63 3/4" (204.5 × 161.9 cm)

Bequest of Arthur H. Lea
F1938-1-40

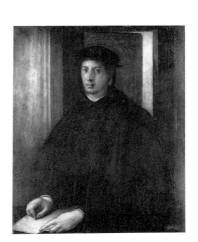

**Pontormo (Jacopo Carucci)**
Italian, active Florence, 1494–1557
*Portrait of Alessandro de' Medici*
1534–35
Oil on panel
39 3/4 × 32 1/16" (101 × 81.4 cm)

John G. Johnson Collection
cat. 83

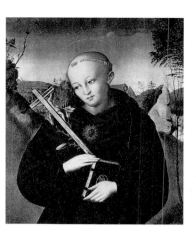

**Pseudo Marco Meloni**
Italian, active Mantua,
active c. 1510–1520
Previously listed as Gerolamo
Marchesi da Cotignola (JI 1966)
*Saint Nicholas of Tolentino*
c. 1510–20
Oil on panel
26 13/16 × 21 7/8" (68.1 × 55.6 cm)

John G. Johnson Collection
cat. 149

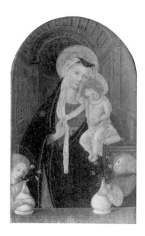

**Pseudo Pier Francesco
Fiorentino, follower of**
Previously listed as a composition
of Pier Francesco Fiorentino
(JI 1966)
*Virgin and Child, with Two Angels*
c. 1450–60
Across bottom: IVSTA PETENTI
GRATIOSA SINT
Tempera and tooled gold on panel
18 1/4 × 10 9/16" (46.3 × 26.8 cm)

John G. Johnson Collection
cat. 42

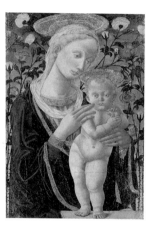

**Pseudo Pier Francesco
Fiorentino**
Italian, active Florence,
active c. 1445–1475
Previously listed as a composition
of Pier Francesco Fiorentino
(JI 1966)
*Virgin and Child before a Rose Hedge*
c. 1455–57
Tempera and tooled gold on panel
29 3/8 × 20 1/2" (74.6 × 52.1 cm)

John G. Johnson Collection
cat. 41

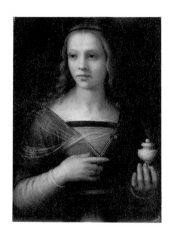

**Puligo, Domenico
(Domenico di Bartolomeo
degli Ubaldini), attributed to**
Italian, active Florence,
born 1492, still active 1527
*Saint Mary Magdalene*
An alternative attribution is to
Jacopino del Conte (Italian,
1510–1598)
Mid-1520s
Oil on panel
21 7/8 × 15 5/16" (55.6 × 38.9 cm)

John G. Johnson Collection
cat. 82

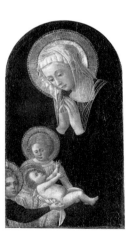

**Pseudo Pier Francesco
Fiorentino**
Previously listed as a composition
of Pier Francesco Fiorentino
(JI 1966)
*Virgin and Child, with Two Angels*
After 1458
Tempera and tooled gold on panel
19 3/16 × 11 1/8" (48.7 × 28.3 cm)

John G. Johnson Collection
cat. 40

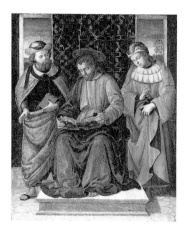

**Raphael (Raffaello Santi),
follower of**
Italian, active central Italy,
1483–1520
Previously listed as Pinturicchio
(JI 1966)
*An Evangelist and Two Saints*
Late 15th century
Oil and gold on panel
17 1/2 × 13 1/16" (44.4 × 33.2 cm)

John G. Johnson Collection
cat. 142

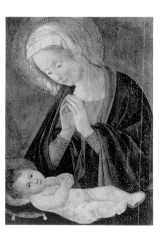

**Pseudo Pier Francesco
Fiorentino**
Previously listed as a composition
of Pier Francesco Fiorentino
(JI 1966)
*Virgin and Child*
After 1460
Tempera and tooled gold on panel
21 1/16 × 14 11/16" (53.5 × 37.3 cm)

John G. Johnson Collection
cat. 39

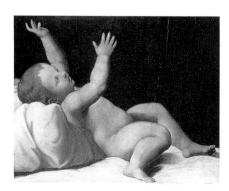

**Raphael, copy after**
*The Christ Child*
After the child in Raphael's
*Madonna di Loreto*, in the Musée
Condé, Chantilly
19th century?
Oil on panel
21 9/16 × 26" (54.8 × 66 cm)

John G. Johnson Collection
cat. 152

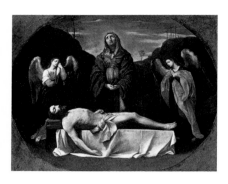

**Reni, Guido, copy after**
Italian, active Bologna and
Rome, 1575–1642
*Lamentation*
After the painting in the
Pinacoteca Nazionale, Bologna
(inv. 445)
19th century?
Oil on canvas
33 7/16 × 43 1/2" (84.9 × 110.5 cm)

John G. Johnson Collection
cat. 283

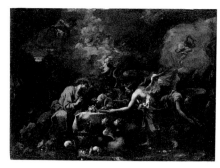

**Ricci, Sebastiano,
attributed to**
Italian, 1659–1734
Previously listed as Alessandro
Magnasco (JI 1966)
*Christ Fed by Angels*
c. 1690–1700
Oil on canvas
22 3/4 × 28 1/2" (57.8 × 72.4 cm)

John G. Johnson Collection
cat. 816

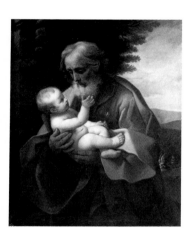

**Reni, Guido, copy after**
*Rest on the Flight into Egypt*
Copy by D. Titov (Russian,
active c. 1913) after the painting
in the Hermitage, St. Petersburg
(inv. no. 58)
1913
On reverse: [Russian for "Copy
from Guido Reni / painted by
D. Titov / from St. Petersburg"]
Oil on canvas
49 1/4 × 40 9/16" (125.1 × 103 cm)

Bequest of Arthur H. Lea
F1938-1-45

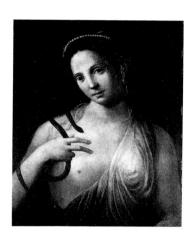

**Riccio (Bartolommeo
Neroni), attributed to**
Italian, active Siena,
born c. 1505–10, died 1571
Previously listed as Francesco
Salviati (JI 1966)
*Cleopatra*
Mid-16th century
Oil on panel
27 1/2 × 21 1/4" (69.8 × 54 cm)

John G. Johnson Collection
cat. 86

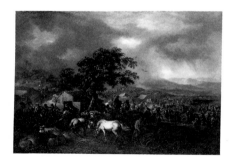

**Reschi, Pandolfo**
Italian, born Poland, active
Florence, 1643–1699
*Encampment in a Storm*
1690–92
Lower right: Pandolfo Reschi
Oil on canvas
57 1/2 × 80 1/2" (146 × 204.5 cm)

Bequest of Arthur H. Lea
F1938-1-46

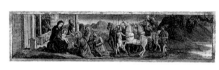

**Riccio, follower of**
Previously listed as Sodoma
(JI 1966)
*The Adoration of the Magi*
Predella panel
c. 1525
Oil on panel
6 1/16 × 21 1/4" (15.4 × 54 cm)

John G. Johnson Collection
cat. 277

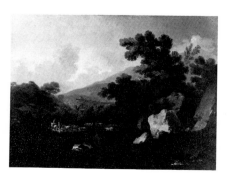

**Ricci, Marco, follower of**
Italian, active Venice, Veneto,
Rome, and England, 1676–1730
Previously listed as Philippe
Jacques de Loutherbourg
(PMA 1965)
*Landscape with Cattle and a
Horseman*
Possibly by an English artist
18th century
Oil on canvas
28 3/4 × 38 3/4" (73 × 98.4 cm)

The Bloomfield Moore Collection
1883-101

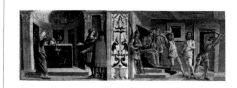

**Rondinelli, Niccolò**
Italian, active Ravenna, Venice,
and Forlì, documented
1495–1502
*The Miracle of the Oil Lamp and the
Flagellation of Saint Bartholomew*
Predella panel of an altarpiece
from San Domenico, Ravenna;
companion predella panels are in
the Musée du Petit Palais, Avignon (210, 211), and an
unknown location; the main section is in the Pinacoteca di Brera,
Milan (453)
After 1496
Oil on panel
14 1/2 × 36" (36.8 × 91.4 cm)

John G. Johnson Collection
cat. 150

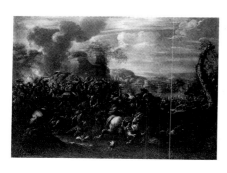

**Rosa, Salvatore, follower of**
Italian, 1615–1673
Previously listed as Salvatore
Rosa (PMA 1965)
*Battle Scene*
c. 1650
Oil on canvas
49 1/16 × 68" (124.6 × 172.7 cm)

Purchased with the W. P.
Wilstach Fund
W1904-1-26

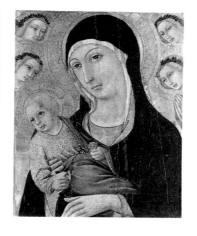

**Sano di Pietro, workshop of**
Italian, active Siena, 1406–1481
Previously listed as Sano di Pietro
(JI 1966)
*Virgin and Child, with Four Angels*
Mid-15th century
On Virgin's halo: AVE GRATI[A]
PLENA DO[MINI]
Tempera and tooled gold on panel
18 1/4 × 14 5/16" (46.3 × 36.3 cm)

John G. Johnson Collection
cat. 106

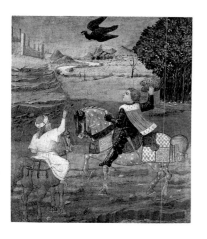

**Rosselli, Bernardo di
Stefano**
Italian, active Florence,
1450–1526
Previously listed as the school of
Paolo Uccello (JI 1966)
*Two Riders Watching a Bird*
Late 15th century
Tempera on panel
16 3/8 × 14 1/8" (41.6 × 35.9 cm)

John G. Johnson Collection
cat. 1165

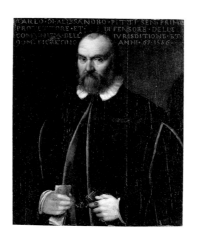

**Santacroce, Gerolamo da
(Gerolamo Galizzi)**
Italian, active Venice, first
recorded 1503, died 1556
*Virgin and Child, with Saints Peter
and Giles*
c. 1512
Oil on panel
28 3/4 × 36 3/8" (73 × 92.4 cm)

John G. Johnson Collection
cat. 184

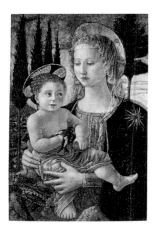

**Rosselli, Cosimo**
Italian, active Florence,
1439–1507
*Virgin and Child*
c. 1470
Tempera and tooled gold on panel
28 3/4 × 19" (73 × 48.3 cm)

John G. Johnson Collection
cat. 60

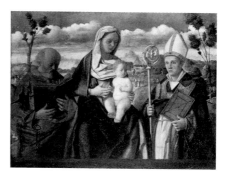

**Santi di Tito, attributed to**
Italian, active Florence and
Rome, 1536–1603
Previously listed as Santi di Tito
(JI 1966)
*Portrait of Carlo Pitti*
1586
Across top: CARLO DI ALESSAN-
DRO PITTI SEN[ATORE] PRIMO /
PROTETTORE ET DIFENSORE
DELLE / COMMVNITA DELLA IV-
RISDITIONE ET / DOM[INIONE]
FIORE[N]TINO ANNI 63 1586
Oil on panel
34 7/16 × 25 3/4" (87.5 × 65.4 cm)

John G. Johnson Collection
cat. 87

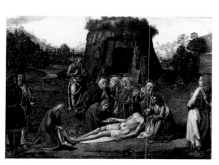

**Rosselli, Cosimo**
*Lamentation*
Predella panel
1480s?
Tempera and gold on panel
13 1/2 × 19 1/4" (34.3 × 48.9 cm)

John G. Johnson Collection
cat. 72

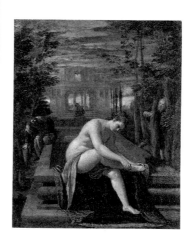

**Scarsellino
(Ippolito Scarsella)**
Italian, active Ferrara,
1551–1620
*Susanna and the Elders*
Early 17th century
Oil on copper
11 11/16 × 9 1/16" (29.7 × 23 cm)

John G. Johnson Collection
cat. 255

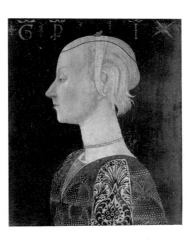

**Scheggia (Giovanni di Ser Giovanni di Mone Cassai)**
Italian, active Florence and environs, 1406–1486
Previously listed as the Master of the Fucecchio Altarpiece (JI 1966)
*Portrait of a Lady*
c. 1440–1450
Across top: G P I
Tempera on panel
17 3/8 × 14 5/16" (44.1 × 36.3 cm)

John G. Johnson Collection
cat. 34

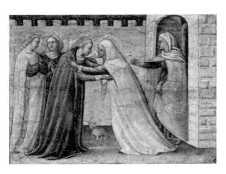

**Schiavo, Paolo (Paolo di Stefano Badaloni)**
Italian, active Florence and environs, 1397–1478
Previously listed as Arcangelo di Cola da Camerino (JI 1966)
*The Visitation*
Predella panel; companion to the following three panels; the main sections of the altarpiece are in the Gemäldegalerie, Staatliche Museen zu Berlin-Preussischer Kulturbesitz (cat. no. 1136, 1123)
Early 1430s
Tempera and tooled gold on panel
8 7/8 × 11 7/8" (22.5 × 30.2 cm)

John G. Johnson Collection
cat. 124

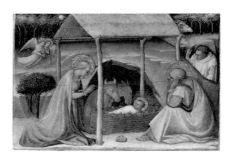

**Schiavo, Paolo**
Previously listed as Arcangelo di Cola da Camerino (JI 1966)
*The Nativity*
See previous entry
Early 1430s
Tempera and tooled gold on panel
8 7/8 × 12 3/4" (22.5 × 32.4 cm)

John G. Johnson Collection
cat. 125

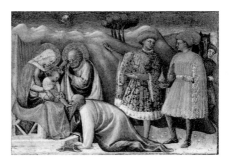

**Schiavo, Paolo**
Previously listed as Arcangelo di Cola da Camerino (JI 1966)
*The Adoration of the Magi*
See previous two entries
Early 1430s
Tempera and tooled gold on panel
8 7/8 × 12 3/4" (22.5 × 32.4 cm)

John G. Johnson Collection
cat. 126

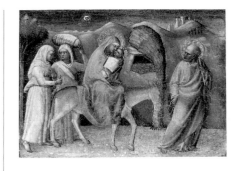

**Schiavo, Paolo**
Previously listed as Arcangelo di Cola da Camerino (JI 1966)
*The Flight into Egypt*
See previous three entries
Early 1430s
Tempera and tooled gold on panel
8 7/8 × 11 7/8" (22.5 × 30.2 cm)

John G. Johnson Collection
cat. 127

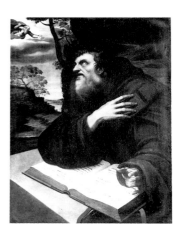

**Sebastiano del Piombo (Sebastiano Luciani), copy after**
Italian, active Venice and Rome, c. 1485–1547
Previously listed as a central Italian artist, late 16th century (JI 1966)
*The Vision of Saint Anthony Abbot*
Possibly by Girolamo Muziano (Italian, 1532–1592); after the painting in the Musée National du Château de Compiègne
Late 16th century
Oil on canvas
51 3/4 × 39" (131.4 × 99.1 cm)

John G. Johnson Collection
cat. 193

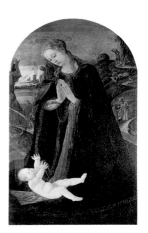

**Sellaio, Jacopo del (Jacopo di Archangelo)**
Italian, active Florence, 1441/42–1493
*The Virgin Adoring the Christ Child, with Saint John the Baptist, the Three Magi, the Annunciation to the Shepherds, and the Penitent Saint Jerome*
1480s
Tempera and gold on panel
41 3/4 × 25" (106 × 63.5 cm)

John G. Johnson Collection
cat. 52

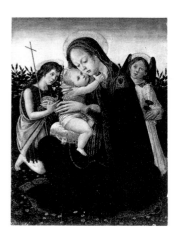

**Sellaio, Jacopo del**
*The Virgin of Humility before a Rose Hedge, with Saint John the Baptist and an Angel*
1480s
On scroll: ECE ANIV DEH ECCE / LOT PEHATA
Tempera and gold on panel
29 × 20" (73.7 × 50.8 cm)

John G. Johnson Collection
cat. 53

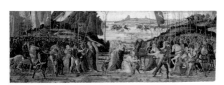

**Sellaio, Jacopo del**
*The Reconciliation of the Romans and Sabines*
Spalliera panel
Late 1480s
Tempera and gold on panel
23 3/4 × 67 1/4" (60.3 × 170.8 cm)

John G. Johnson Collection
cat. 54

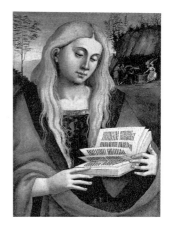

**Signorelli, Luca,
workshop of**
Previously listed as Luca
Signorelli (JI 1966)
*Saint Mary Magdalene*
Fragment
c. 1522–24
On collar: MADALE
Oil on panel transferred to canvas
28 3/8 × 19 7/8" (72.1 × 50.5 cm)

John G. Johnson Collection
cat. 135

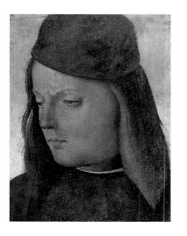

**Signorelli, Luca**
Italian, active central Italy, first
documented 1470, died 1523
*Head of a Boy*
Fragment from an altarpiece
c. 1492–93
Tempera on panel
10 9/16 × 8 1/16" (26.8 × 20.5 cm)

John G. Johnson Collection
cat. 138

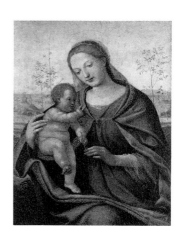

**Sodoma (Giovanni Antonio
Bazzi)**
Italian, active Siena and Rome,
1477–1549
*Virgin and Child*
c. 1508–10
Oil on panel
25 × 18 1/4" (63.5 × 46.3 cm)

John G. Johnson Collection
cat. 278

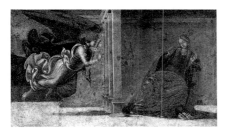

**Signorelli, Luca**
*The Annunciation*
Predella panel
c. 1496–1500
Oil on panel transferred to canvas
9 11/16 × 15 3/4" (24.6 × 40 cm)

John G. Johnson Collection
cat. 136

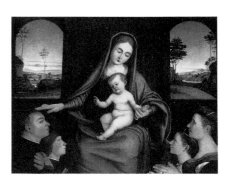

**Solario, Andrea**
Italian, active Venice, Milan,
Normandy, and Rome, first dated
work 1495, died 1524
*Enthroned Virgin and Child, with
Four Donors*
c. 1490–93
Oil on panel transferred to canvas
27 3/8 × 35 7/16" (69.5 × 90 cm)

John G. Johnson Collection
cat. 272

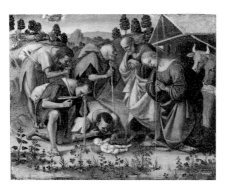

**Signorelli, Luca**
*The Adoration of the Shepherds*
Predella panel; a companion
panel is in the Yale University
Art Gallery (1871.69); they are
possibly from the predella of
Signorelli's *Virgin and Child and
Four Franciscan Saints*, in the
Museo Diocesano, Cortona, Italy
c. 1509–10
Tempera on panel
14 1/8 × 17 1/8" (35.9 × 43.5 cm)

John G. Johnson Collection
cat. 137

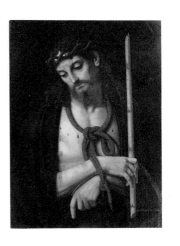

**Solario, Andrea**
*Christ Bound and Crowned with
Thorns*
c. 1509
Lower right: Andreas de Solario
Oil on panel
24 7/8 × 18" (63.2 × 45.7 cm)

John G. Johnson Collection
cat. 274

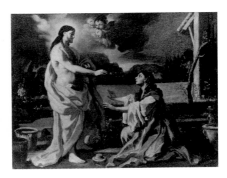

**Solimena, Francesco, workshop of**
Italian, 1657–1747
*"Noli Me Tangere"*
c. 1730
Oil on canvas
19 3/16 × 25 1/16" (48.7 × 63.7 cm)

Purchased with the W. P. Wilstach Fund
W1904-1-46

c. 1408
Tempera and tooled gold on panel
40 7/16 × 35 5/8" (102.7 × 90.5 cm)

John G. Johnson Collection
cat. 13

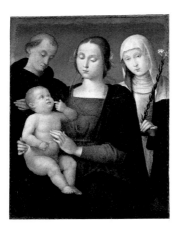

**Lo Spagna (Giovanni di Pietro), workshop of**
Italian, active Umbria and Marches, first documented 1470, died 1528
*Virgin and Child, with a Monk Saint and Saint Catherine of Siena*
A variant is in the National Gallery of Ireland, Dublin (no. 212)
Early 16th century
Oil on panel transferred to canvas
19 5/8 × 14 15/16" (49.8 × 37.9 cm)

John G. Johnson Collection
cat. 145

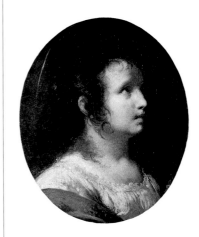

**Strozzi, Bernardo**
Italian, 1581–1644
*Female Saint*
c. 1625
Oil on canvas
22 × 17" (55.9 × 43.2 cm)

Bequest of Arthur H. Lea
F1938-1-16

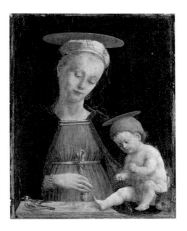

**Spanzotti, Giovanni Martino**
Italian, active Piedmont, documented 1480–1513
Previously listed as the studio of Cosimo Tura (JI 1966)
*Virgin and Child, with a Bird and a Cat*
c. 1475
Oil on panel
17 5/16 × 13 7/16" (44 × 34.1 cm)

John G. Johnson Collection
cat. 242

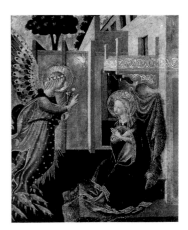

**Strozzi, Zanobi (Zanobi di Benedetto di Caroccio degli Strozzi)**
Italian, active Florence, 1412–1468
Previously listed as Domenico di Michelino (JI 1966)
*The Annunciation*
c. 1453
Tempera and gold on panel
14 9/16 × 11 7/8" (37 × 30.2 cm)

John G. Johnson Collection
cat. 22

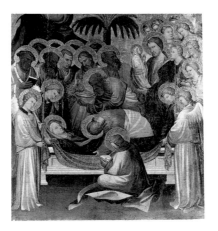

**Starnina (Gherardo di Jacopo di Neri) (Master of the Bambino Vispo)**
Italian, active Florence, Valencia, Toledo, and Empoli, documented 1387–1409, died before 1413
*The Dormition of the Virgin*
From an altarpiece from the Monastero dell'Angelo, Lucca; other panels from the altarpiece are in the Fogg Art Museum, Cambridge, Mass. (1920.1); the Museo Nazionale di Villa Guinigi, Lucca (287, 288); the Nelson-Atkins Museum of Art, Kansas City, Mo. (61-60); and a private collection in Turin

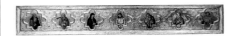

**Taddeo di Bartolo**
Italian, active Siena and environs, Perugia, Pisa, and Genoa, first documented 1383, died 1422
Previously listed as Barna (JI 1966)
*Saint Anthony Abbot, Saint Andrew, the Virgin Mourning, the Man of Sorrows, Saint John the Evangelist Mourning, the Archangel Raphael, and Saint Lawrence*
Predella from an altarpiece once in San Paolo, Collegarli (Pisa)
1389
Tempera, tooled gold, and colored glass on panel
9 1/16 × 82 5/8" (23 × 209.9 cm)

John G. Johnson Collection
cat. 95

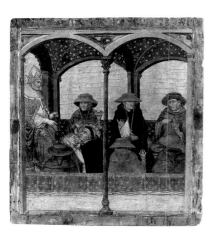

**Taddeo di Bartolo**
*Saint Thomas Aquinas Submitting His Office for Corpus Domini to Pope Urban IV*
Predella panel?; other panels from the altarpiece are in the Smith College Museum of Art, Northampton, Mass. (1958.38); the Marion Koogler McNay Art Museum, San Antonio, Texas (1955.11); and the Pinacoteca Nazionale di Siena (129)
c. 1403
Tempera and tooled gold on panel
16 × 14 ⅛" (40.6 × 35.9 cm)

John G. Johnson Collection
cat. 101

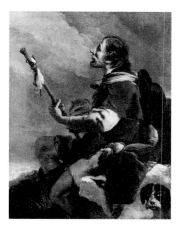

**Tiepolo, Giovanni Battista**
Italian, active Venice, Udine, Würzburg, and Madrid, 1696–1770
*Saint Roch*
1730–35
Oil on paper on canvas
17 ¾ × 13 ⅜" (45.1 × 34 cm)

John G. Johnson Collection
cat. 289

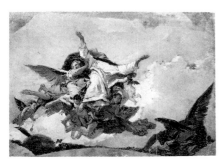

**Tiepolo, Giovanni Battista**
*Sketch for "The Glory of Saint Dominic"*
For the ceiling of the Church of the Gesuati, Venice
1738–39
Oil on canvas
15 ⅛ × 20 ⁹⁄₁₆" (38.4 × 52.2 cm)

John G. Johnson Collection
cat. 286

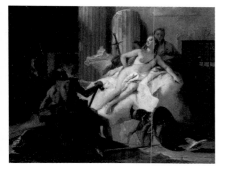

**Tiepolo, Giovanni Battista**
*Sketch for "Venus and Vulcan"*
For the ceiling of the Salón de Alabarderos, Palacio Real, Madrid
1765–66
Oil on paper on canvas
27 ³⁄₁₆ × 34 ⁵⁄₁₆" (69.1 × 87.1 cm)

John G. Johnson Collection
cat. 287

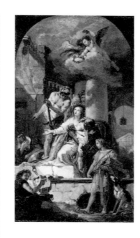

**Tiepolo, Giovanni Battista, copy after**
*The Martyrdom of Saint Agatha*
After the altarpiece in the Basilica di Sant'Antonio, Padua
c. 1750–1800
Oil on canvas
23 ½ × 13 ⅛" (59.7 × 33.3 cm)

The William L. Elkins Collection
E1924-3-94

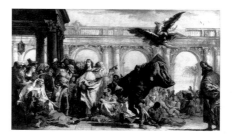

**Tiepolo, Giovanni Domenico**
Italian, active Venice, Würzburg, and Madrid, 1727–1804
*The Miracle of the Pool of Bethesda*
c. 1759
Oil on canvas
28 × 45 ⅝" (71.1 × 115.9 cm)

Purchased with the W. P. Wilstach Fund
W1902-1-12

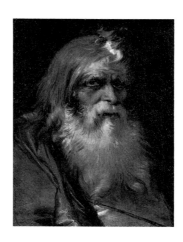

**Tiepolo, Giovanni Domenico, studio of**
*Head of an Old Man*
Variant of an autograph painting in the Museo Civico Malaspina, Pavia
c. 1773–75
Oil on canvas
18 ½ × 15" (47 × 38.1 cm)

John G. Johnson Collection
cat. 288

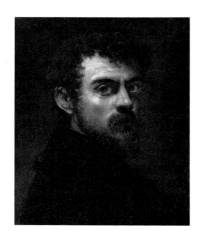

**Tintoretto (Jacopo di Giovanni Battista Robusti)**
Italian, active Venice, 1519–1594
*Self-Portrait*
c. 1546–48
Oil on canvas
17 ¾ × 15" (45.1 × 38.1 cm)

Gift of Marion R. Ascoli and the Marion R. and Max Ascoli Fund in honor of Lessing Rosenwald
1983-190-1

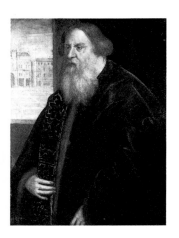

**Tintoretto, follower of**
Previously attributed to
Tintoretto (JI 1966)
*Portrait of a Venetian Senator*
Mid-16th century
Oil on canvas
41 ¾ × 29 ¾" (106 × 75.6 cm)

John G. Johnson Collection
cat. 209

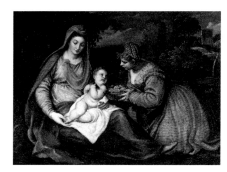

**Titian, studio of**
Previously listed as Titian
(PMA 1965)
*Virgin and Child, with Saint
Dorothy*
c. 1530–40
Oil on canvas
46 ⁷/₁₆ × 60 ¾" (117.9 × 154.3 cm)

The George W. Elkins Collection
E1957-1-1

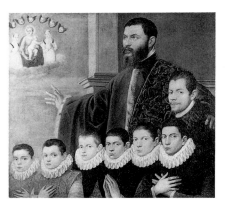

**Tintoretto, follower of**
Previously listed as the school of
Tintoretto (JI 1966)
*Portrait of a Venetian Senator with
Male Members of His Family, the
Virgin and Child with Cherubim,
and Two Female Figures in Glory*
Late 16th century
Oil on canvas
44 × 48 ³/₁₆" (111.8 × 122.4 cm)

John G. Johnson Collection
cat. 210

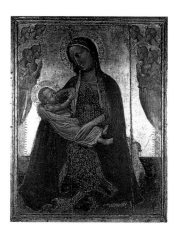

**Todeschini (Giacomo
Francesco Cipper)**
Italian, born Germany or
Switzerland?, active Bergamo,
dated works 1705–1736
*Portrait of a Peasant Girl*
1730s
Oil on canvas
15 ⁵/₈ × 13 ⁷/₁₆" (39.7 × 34.1 cm)

John G. Johnson Collection
cat. 781

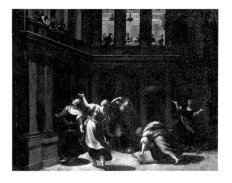

**Tintoretto, copy after**
Previously listed as the school of
Tintoretto (JI 1966)
*The Parable of the Wise and Foolish
Virgins*
After the painting in the Museum
Boymans–van Beuningen,
Rotterdam (2567)
18th century?
Oil on canvas
34 ¼ × 41 ¾" (87 × 106 cm)

John G. Johnson Collection
cat. 211

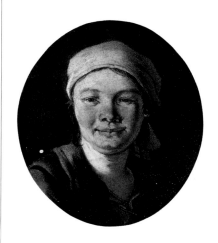

**Tommaso del Mazza
(Master of Santa Verdiana)**
Italian, active Florence,
documented 1377–1375
*The Virgin of Humility, with Eight
Angels*
c. 1370–75
Tempera and tooled gold on panel
32 ½ × 23 ³/₈" (82.5 × 59.4 cm)

Purchased from the George Grey
Barnard Collection with Museum
funds
1945-25-119

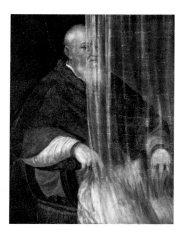

**Titian (Tiziano Vecellio)**
Italian, active Venice, first
securely documented 1508,
died 1576
*Portrait of Cardinal Filippo
Archinto*
1558
Oil on canvas
45 ³/₁₆ × 34 ¹⁵/₁₆" (114.8 ×
88.7 cm)

John G. Johnson Collection
cat. 204

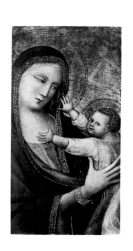

**Toscani, Giovanni (Giovanni
di Francesco Toscani)**
Italian, active Florence,
born 1370–80, died 1430
Previously listed as the Master of
the Griggs Crucifixion (PMA
1965)
*Virgin and Child*
Cut; panel from the altarpiece
from San Bartolomeo, Prato;
companion panels are in the
Museo Diocesano, Prato
c. 1422–23
Tempera and tooled gold on panel
20 ³/₁₆ × 10 ½" (51.3 × 26.7 cm)

The John D. McIlhenny
Collection
1943-40-45

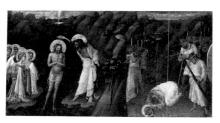

**Toscani, Giovanni**
Previously listed as the Master of the Griggs Crucifixion (JI 1966)
*The Baptism of Christ and the Martyrdom of Saint James the Great*
Predella panel from the altarpiece from the Ardinghelli Chapel in Santa Trinita, Florence; companion panels are in the Galleria dell'Accademia, Florence (no. 3333, no. 6089); the Walters Art Gallery, Baltimore (37.632); the Carandini Collection, Rome; and a private collection in Florence
1423–24
Tempera and tooled gold on panel
16 1/8 × 26 3/8" (41 × 67 cm)

John G. Johnson Collection
cat. 11

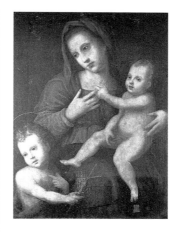

**Tosini, Michele (Michele di Ridolfo del Ghirlandaio), follower of**
Italian, active Florence, 1503–1577
*Virgin and Child, with Saint John the Baptist*
Mid-16th century
Oil on panel
22 3/4 × 17 1/4" (57.8 × 43.8 cm)

Bequest of Arthur H. Lea
F1938-1-10

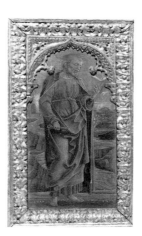

**Trevisani, Francesco, follower of**
Italian, active Rome, 1656–1746
Previously listed as Raphael Mengs (JGJ 1941)
*Dead Christ Supported by Angels*
Based on a painting by Trevisani known in several versions, one of which is in the Kunsthistorisches Museum, Vienna (inv. no. 1564)
c. 1720
Oil on panel
11 7/8 × 8 3/4" (30.2 × 22.2 cm)

John G. Johnson Collection
inv. 2924

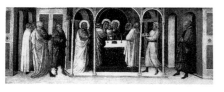

**Toscani, Giovanni**
Previously listed as Andrea di Giusto (JI 1966)
*The Presentation of Christ in the Temple*
Predella panel; companion to the following panel and panels in the National Gallery of Victoria, Melbourne (1731/5)
c. 1427–30
Tempera and gold on panel
7 1/4 × 19 3/8" (18.4 × 49.2 cm)

John G. Johnson Collection
cat. 18

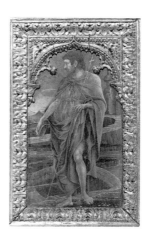

**Tura, Cosimo (Cosmé Tura)**
Italian, active Ferrara, first documented 1430, died 1495
*Saint Peter*
Companion to the following painting
c. 1474
Tempera on panel
9 3/8 × 5 5/8" (23.8 × 14.3 cm)

John G. Johnson Collection
cat. 241a

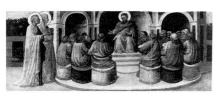

**Toscani, Giovanni**
Previously listed as Andrea di Giusto (JI 1966)
*Christ among the Doctors*
See previous entry
c. 1427–30
Tempera and gold on panel
7 5/8 × 19 3/4" (19.4 × 50.2 cm)

John G. Johnson Collection
cat. 19

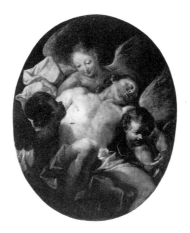

**Tura, Cosimo**
*Saint John the Baptist*
Companion to the preceding painting
c. 1474
Tempera on panel
9 3/8 × 5 5/8" (23.8 × 14.3 cm)

John G. Johnson Collection
cat. 241b

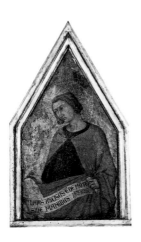

**Ugolino di Nerio**
Italian, active Siena,
documented 1317–27
*Prophet Daniel*
Pinnacle from the high altarpiece
from Santa Croce, Florence;
companion panels are in the
Gemäldegalerie, Staatliche
Museen zu Berlin-Preussischer
Kulturbesitz (cat. no. 1635
A–E); the National Gallery,
London (1188, 1189,
3376–3378, 3473, 4191); the
Los Angeles County Museum of
Art (49.17.40); and the
Metropolitan Museum of Art,
New York (1975.1.7)
c. 1325
On scroll: LAPIS ASCISUS E[ST]
DE MO[N]TE SINE MANIBUS
Tempera and tooled gold on panel
21 1/4 × 12 3/16" (54 × 31 cm)

John G. Johnson Collection
cat. 89

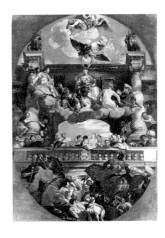

**Veronese, Paolo, copy after**
Previously listed as a Veronese
artist, c. 1600 (JI 1966)
*Triumph of Venice*
After the painting in the Sala del
Maggior Consiglio, Palazzo
Ducale, Venice
18th century
Oil on canvas
42 1/2 × 29" (107.9 × 73.7 cm)

John G. Johnson Collection
cat. 231

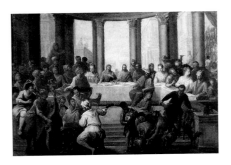

**Veronese, Paolo, copy after**
*The Marriage at Cana*
Based in part on the painting in
the Musée du Louvre, Paris (inv.
142)
19th century
Oil on canvas
38 × 52 1/2" (96.5 × 133.3 cm)

Bequest of Arthur H. Lea
F1938-1-26

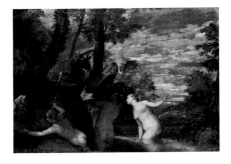

**Veronese, Paolo
(Paolo di Gabriele Caliari)**
Italian, active Verona, Venice,
and environs, 1528–1588
*Diana and Actaeon*
c. 1560
Oil on canvas
47 3/4 × 64 3/4" (121.3 × 164.5 cm)

John G. Johnson Collection
cat. 225

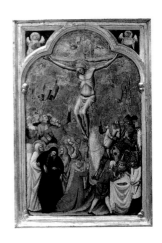

**Vitale da Bologna
(Vitale di Aimo degli Equi)**
Italian, active Bologna and
Udine, documented 1330–1359
Previously listed as a Bolognese
artist, c. 1375–1400 (JI 1966)
*The Crucifixion, with Symbols of
Saints Matthew and John the
Evangelist*
c. 1335
On crucifix: I N R I
Tempera and tooled gold on panel
24 7/16 × 15 3/4" (62.1 × 40 cm)

John G. Johnson Collection
cat. 1164

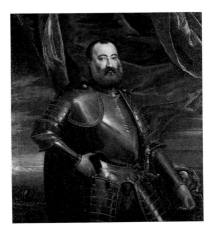

**Veronese, Paolo**
*Portrait of Giuliano Contarini*
1570s
Oil on canvas
49 5/8 × 44 5/8" (126 × 113.3 cm)

John G. Johnson Collection
cat. 208

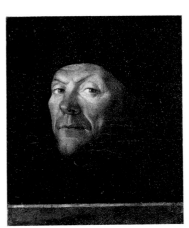

**Vivarini, Alvise**
Italian, active Venice,
c. 1446–c. 1505
*Portrait of an Elderly Gentleman*
c. 1490
Oil on panel transferred to canvas
11 13/16 × 9 5/16" (30 × 23.6 cm)

John G. Johnson Collection
cat. 166

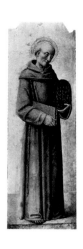

**Vivarini, Antonio**
Italian, active Venice,
born by 1441, died 1476–84
*Saint Bernardino of Siena*
Panel from an altarpiece
c. 1465–70
Oil and tooled gold on panel
44 × 14 1/8" (111.8 × 35.9 cm)

John G. Johnson Collection
cat. 154

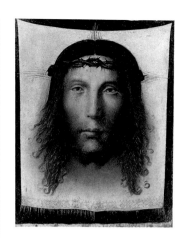

**Zaganelli, Bernardino di
Bosio**
Italian, active Romagna,
c. 1470–c. 1510
Previously listed as Antonello de
Saliba (JI 1966)
*Saint Veronica's Veil*
c. 1500
Oil on panel
10 1/2 × 8" (26.7 × 20.3 cm)

John G. Johnson Collection
cat. 160

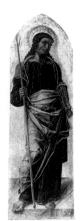

**Vivarini, Bartolomeo**
Italian, active Venice,
signed works 1450–1490
*Saint James the Great*
Panel from an altarpiece;
companion to the following panel
c. 1470–75
Tempera and tooled gold on panel
39 7/8 × 11 15/16" (101.3 × 30.3 cm)

John G. Johnson Collection
cat. 155

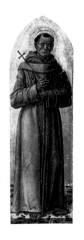

**Vivarini, Bartolomeo**
*Saint Francis of Assisi*
Panel from an altarpiece;
companion to the preceding panel
c. 1470–75
Tempera and tooled gold on panel
39 3/4 × 11 1/2" (101 × 29.2 cm)

John G. Johnson Collection
cat. 156

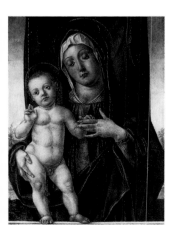

**Vivarini, Bartolomeo**
Previously listed as Jacopo da
Valenza (JI 1966)
*Virgin and Child*
c. 1480
Tempera on panel
26 1/8 × 19 7/16" (66.4 × 49.4 cm)

John G. Johnson Collection
cat. 157

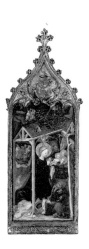

**Alcañiz, Miguel, attributed to**
Spanish, active Valencia and
Majorca, documented 1421–1434
Previously listed as Andreas
Marzal de Sax (JGJ 1941)
*The Nativity*
Panel from an altarpiece;
companion to the following panel
and a panel in the Museo
Provincial de Bellas Artes,
Zaragoza (8)
Early 1420s
Tempera and tooled gold on panel
33 1/2 × 11" (85.1 × 27.9 cm)

John G. Johnson Collection
cat. 756

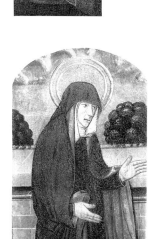

**Espalargues, Pere
(Pere Espalargucs)**
Spanish, active Lérida,
documented 1490
*Saint Peter*
Panel from an altarpiece;
companion to the following five
panels and panels in the
collection of the Hispanic Society
of America, New York (28320),
and an unknown location
c. 1490
On scroll: TIBI DABO CLAVES
REGNUM [ ]UM
Oil and tooled gold on panel
51 1/4 × 22 1/8" (130.2 × 56.2 cm)

John G. Johnson Collection
inv. 170

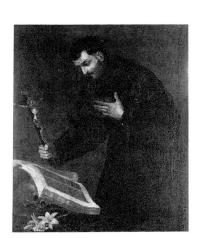

**Alcañiz, Miguel, attributed to**
Previously listed as Andreas
Marzal de Sax (JGJ 1941)
*The Dormition of the Virgin*
See previous entry
Early 1420s
Tempera and tooled gold on panel
33 3/4 × 11 1/8" (85.7 × 28.3 cm)

John G. Johnson Collection
cat. 757

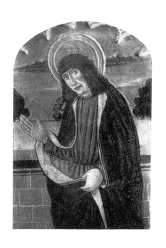

**Espalargues, Pere**
*Mourning Virgin*
See previous entry
c. 1490
Oil and tooled gold on panel
16 3/8 × 10 5/16" (41.6 × 26.2 cm)

John G. Johnson Collection
inv. 171

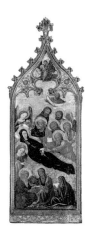

**Cano, Alonso, follower of**
Spanish, active Granada, Seville,
and Madrid, 1601–1667
Previously listed as Bartolomé
Esteban Murillo (PMA 1965)
*Saint Anthony of Padua*
Mid-17th century
Oil on canvas
46 5/8 × 39" (118.4 × 99.1 cm)

Purchased with the W. P.
Wilstach Fund
W1904-1-23

**Espalargues, Pere**
*Saint John the Evangelist Mourning*
See previous two entries
c. 1490
Oil on panel
16 3/8 × 10 5/16" (41.6 × 26.2 cm)

John G. Johnson Collection
inv. 172

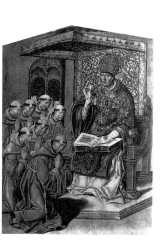

**Castro, Bartolomé del**
Spanish, active Palencia and
environs, died 1507
*Pope Honorius III Approving the
Rule of Saint Francis of Assisi*
Panel from an altarpiece
c. 1500
Tempera and tooled gold on panel
48 5/16 × 33 5/8" (122.7 × 85.4 cm)

John G. Johnson Collection
cat. 800

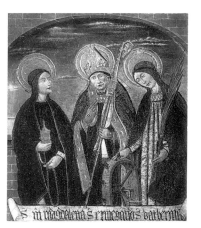

**Espalargues, Pere**
*Saints Mary Magdalene,
Ermengold, and Catherine of
Alexandria*
See previous three entries
c. 1490
On scroll: S M MAGDALENA
S ERMEGAUD S KATHERNIA
Oil and tooled gold on panel
26 3/4 × 22" (67.9 × 55.9 cm)

John G. Johnson Collection
inv. 173

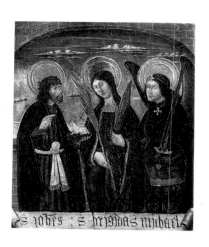

**Espalargues, Pere**
*Saints John the Baptist, Bridget, and the Archangel Michael*
See previous four entries
c. 1490
On scroll: S JOHES S BRIGIDA S MICHAEL
Oil and tooled gold on panel
26 13/16 × 22 1/2" (68.1 × 57.1 cm)

John G. Johnson Collection
inv. 174

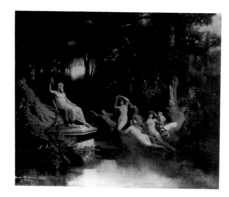

**Fortuny y Carbó, Mariano**
Spanish, 1838–1874
*Statue of Dionysus*
1858
Lower left: Roma 11 Septembre 1858. / M. Fortuny
Oil on canvas
28 1/2 × 32 1/2" (72.4 × 82.5 cm)

John G. Johnson Collection
cat. 991

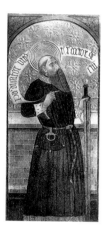

**Espalargues, Pere**
*Saint Paul*
See previous five entries
c. 1490
On scroll: PREDICATOR VITA [ ]T ET DOCTOR GE[ ]CIU[?]
Oil and tooled gold on panel
51 1/4 × 22 1/8" (130.2 × 56.2 cm)

John G. Johnson Collection
inv. 175

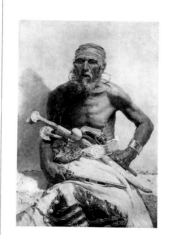

**Fortuny y Carbó, Mariano**
*Arab Chief*
1874
Lower left: Fortuny 74
Oil on canvas
48 3/8 × 31 1/8" (122.9 × 79.1 cm)

John G. Johnson Collection
cat. 992

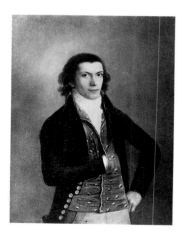

**Esteve y Marques, Agustín**
Spanish, 1753–c. 1820
Previously attributed to Francisco José de Goya y Lucientes (JGJ 1941)
*Portrait of Isidro González Velásquez* [?]
Companion to the following painting
c. 1803–5
Oil on canvas
36 3/4 × 28 1/8" (93.3 × 71.4 cm)

John G. Johnson Collection
cat. 818

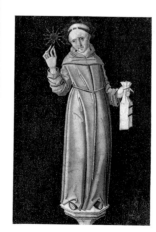

**Gallegos, Fernando, follower of**
Spanish, active Castile, documented 1466–1507
*Saint Bernardino of Siena*
c. 1500
Oil on panel
13 15/16 × 9" (35.4 × 22.9 cm)

John G. Johnson Collection
cat. 325

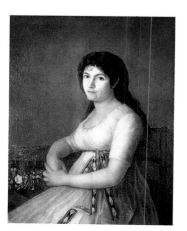

**Esteve y Marques, Agustín**
Previously attributed to Francisco José de Goya y Lucientes (JGJ 1941)
*Portrait of the Wife of Isidro González Velásquez* [?]
Companion to the preceding painting
c. 1803–5
Oil on canvas
36 3/4 × 28 1/8" (93.3 × 71.4 cm)

John G. Johnson Collection
cat. 819

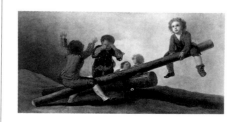

**Goya y Lucientes, Francisco José de**
Spanish, 1746–1828
*The Seesaw*
Cartoon for a tapestry in the Escorial
1791–92
Oil on canvas
32 7/16 × 64 1/4" (82.4 × 163.2 cm)

Gift of Miss Anna Warren Ingersoll
1975-150-1

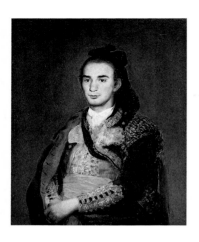

**Goya y Lucientes, Francisco José de**
*Portrait of the Toreador José Romero*
c. 1795
On label on reverse: El celebre torero José Romero, con el / rico vestido que le regaló la Duquesa / de Alva, à que se añade tener el Capote / Terezano, Pañuelo Rondeño al cuello, y / la faxa a lo Sevillano, para denotar / las proezas que en la lid de Toros / hizo en estas tres Ciudades. Este famoso / y diestro torero fue el que de una es— / tocada se dejó a sus pies el terrible toro / que mató al habil / Pepeillo.
Oil on canvas
36 5/16 × 29 7/8" (92.2 × 75.9 cm)

The Mr. and Mrs. Carroll S. Tyson, Jr., Collection
1963-116-8

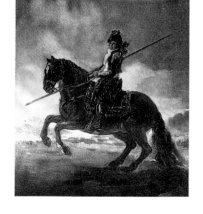

**Goya y Lucientes, Francisco José de, copy after**
Previously attributed to Francisco José de Goya y Lucientes (JGJ 1941)
*Mounted Cavalier with a Javelin*
After the painting in the Museo del Prado, Madrid (744)
Late 19th century
Lower right (spurious): F. Goya
Oil on canvas
16 × 12 7/8" (40.6 × 32.7 cm)

John G. Johnson Collection
cat. 820

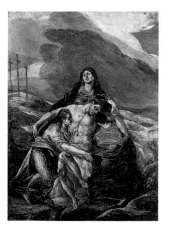

**El Greco (Domenicos Theotocopulos)**
Spanish, born Crete, active Italy and Toledo, 1541–1614
*Lamentation*
c. 1565–70
Oil on copper
11 3/8 × 7 7/8" (28.9 × 20 cm)

John G. Johnson Collection
cat. 807

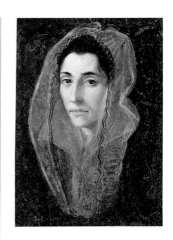

**El Greco, attributed to**
Previously listed as El Greco (JGJ 1941)
*Portrait of a Lady*
c. 1577–80
Oil on panel
15 5/8 × 12 5/8" (39.7 × 32.1 cm)

John G. Johnson Collection
cat. 808

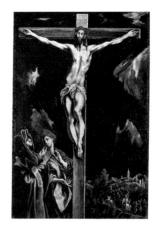

**El Greco, workshop of**
Previously listed as El Greco (JGJ 1941)
*The Crucifixion*
c. 1600–5
On cross: [Hebrew, Greek, and Latin for "Jesus of Nazareth, King of the Jews"]
Oil on canvas
62 3/4 × 38 3/4" (159.4 × 98.4 cm)

John G. Johnson Collection
cat. 809

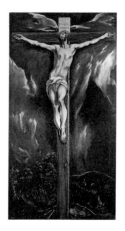

**El Greco, workshop of**
*The Crucifixion*
c. 1605–10
On cross: [Hebrew, Greek, and Latin for "Jesus of Nazareth, King of the Jews"]
Oil on canvas
81 1/4 × 40 3/4" (206.4 × 103.5 cm)

Purchased with the W. P. Wilstach Fund
W1900-1-17

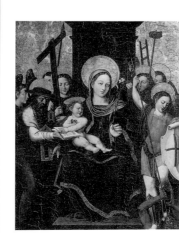

**Juan de Juanes (Juan Vincente Masip the Younger)**
Spanish, active Valencia, c. 1510–1579
*Enthroned Virgin and Child, with Saint Jerome, the Archangel Michael, and Angels Holding Instruments of the Passion*
Mid-16th century
Oil and tooled gold on panel
48 3/4 × 35 1/4" (123.8 × 89.5 cm)

John G. Johnson Collection
cat. 806

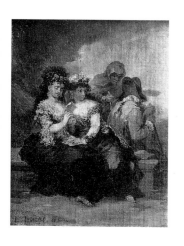

**Lucas Velazquez, Eugenio**
Spanish, 1817–1870
*The Love Letter*
1864
Lower left: Eg. Lucas, 1864.
Oil on canvas
12 5/8 × 9 3/8" (32.1 × 23.8 cm)

John G. Johnson Collection
cat. 821

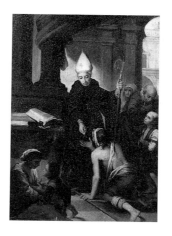

**Murillo, Bartolomé Esteban, copy after**
*Saint Thomas of Villanueva Distributing Alms*
After the painting in the Museo de Bellas Artes, Seville (90)
18th century?
Lower left (spurious): Jan Roldan
Oil on panel
16 1/8 × 11 5/8" (41 × 29.5 cm)

The Bloomfield Moore Collection
1899-1121

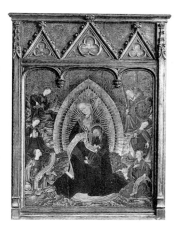

**Martorell, Bernat**
Spanish, active 1427–1452
Previously listed as a South French artist, c. 1450 (JGJ 1941)
*Enthroned Virgin and Child, with the Cardinal Virtues and Two Figures Holding Scrolls*
Center panel from an altarpiece once in the church of Santa María, Monzón (Barcelona)
1437
Tempera and tooled gold on panel
60 3/4 × 42 1/4" (154.3 × 107.3 cm)

John G. Johnson Collection
cat. 759

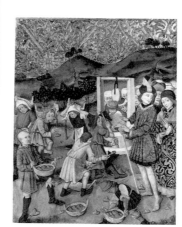

**Olot Master**
Spanish, active Catalonia, active c. 1500
Previously listed as a Castilian artist, c. 1470 (JGJ 1941)
*The Gathering of Manna and the Discovery of the Water of Elim*
Panel from an altarpiece
c. 1500
Tempera and tooled gold on panel
21 15/16 × 17 1/4" (55.7 × 43.8 cm)

John G. Johnson Collection
cat. 801

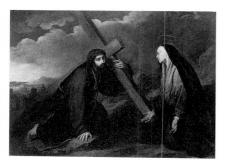

**Murillo, Bartolomé Esteban**
Spanish, active Seville, 1618–1682
*Christ Bearing the Cross*
c. 1665–75
Oil on canvas
60 3/4 × 83" (154.3 × 210.8 cm)

Purchased with the W. P. Wilstach Fund
W1900-1-7

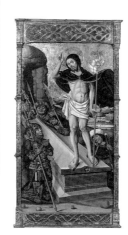

**Oslo Master, attributed to**
Spanish, active Aragon, active c. 1480
*The Resurrection*
Panel from an altarpiece
c. 1480
Oil, silver, and tooled gold on panel
67 3/4 × 35 1/2" (172.1 × 90.2 cm)

Bequest of Carl Otto Kretzschmar von Kienbusch
1977-167-1041

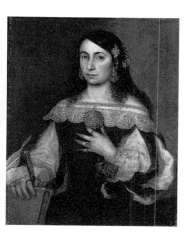

**Murillo, Bartolomé Esteban, attributed to**
Previously listed as Juan Bautista Martínez del Mazo (JGJ 1941)
*Portrait of a Lady*
c. 1655–65
Oil on canvas
31 1/8 × 25" (79.1 × 63.5 cm)

John G. Johnson Collection
cat. 815

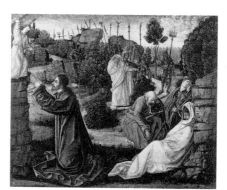

**Osona, Rodrigo de, the Elder**
Spanish, active Valencia, documented 1464–1484
Previously listed as an Aragonese artist, late 15th century (JGJ 1941)
*The Agony in the Garden*
Predella panel; companion to the following two panels
c. 1465
Oil and gold on panel
16 3/4 × 18 3/4" (42.5 × 47.6 cm)

John G. Johnson Collection
cat. 802

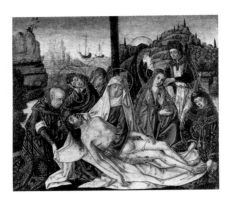

**Osona, Rodrigo de, the Elder**
Previously listed as an Aragonese
artist, late 15th century (JGJ
1941)
*The Lamentation*
Predella panel; see previous entry
c. 1465
Oil and gold on panel
16 3/8 × 18 5/8" (41.6 × 47.3 cm)

John G. Johnson Collection
cat. 803

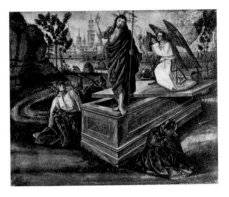

**Osona, Rodrigo de, the Elder**
Previously listed as an Aragonese
artist, late 15th century (JGJ
1941)
*The Resurrection*
Predella panel; see previous two
entries
c. 1465
Oil and gold on panel
16 3/8 × 19" (41.6 × 48.3 cm)

John G. Johnson Collection
cat. 804

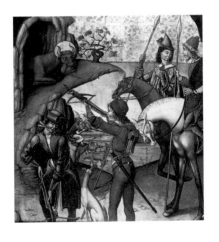

**Palaquinos Master**
Spanish, active León,
active c. 1510–c. 1520
*The Shooting of the Bull on Mount
Gargano*
Panel from an altarpiece;
companion to the following
painting
c. 1515
Tempera and tooled gold on panel
35 1/8 × 30 15/16" (89.2 × 78.6 cm)

John G. Johnson Collection
inv. 2100

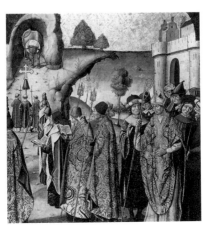

**Palaquinos Master**
*The Episcopal Procession to Mount
Gargano*
Panel from an altarpiece;
companion to the preceding
painting
c. 1515
Tempera and tooled gold on panel
35 1/4 × 31" (89.5 × 78.7 cm)

John G. Johnson Collection
inv. 2101

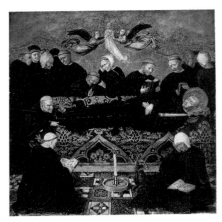

**Rexach, Juan**
Spanish, active Valencia,
documented 1437–1484
*The Death of Saint Giles*
Predella panel
Late 1460s or early 1470s
Oil on panel
24 1/4 × 23 1/4" (61.6 × 59 cm)

John G. Johnson Collection
inv. 337

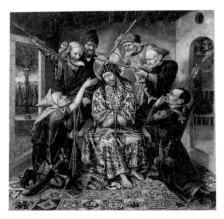

**Rexach, Juan**
*Christ Crowned with Thorns*
Predella panel
c. 1476–80
Oil on panel
15 1/2 × 15 1/4" (39.4 × 38.7 cm)

John G. Johnson Collection
inv. 203

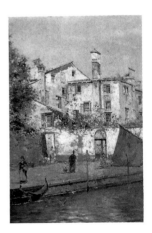

**Reyna, Antonio**
Spanish, born 1861, death date
unknown
*Canal in Venice*
Early 20th century
Lower right: Reyna
Oil on panel
14 1/4 × 9 1/4" (36.2 × 23.5 cm)

The Walter Lippincott Collection
1923-59-10

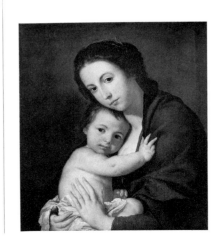

**Ribera, José Jusepe de,
also called Lo Spagnoletto**
Spanish, active Naples,
1591–1652
*Virgin and Child*
1646?
Lower left: Jusepe de Ribera /
español acade / mico Romano /
,F, 1646 [?]
Oil on canvas
27 3/8 × 23 7/16" (69.5 × 59.5 cm)

The William L. Elkins Collection
E1924-3-54

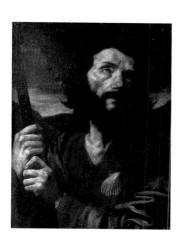

**Ribera, José Jusepe de,
attributed to**
Previously listed as José Jusepe
de Ribera (JGJ 1941)
*Saint James the Great*
Mid-17th century
Oil on canvas
25 ¹/₂ × 19 ³/₈" (64.8 × 49.2 cm)

John G. Johnson Collection
cat. 811

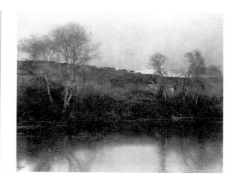

**Sanchez Perrier, Emilio**
Spanish, 1855–1907
*Landscape (Evening in Spain)*
c. 1890
Lower left: E. Sanchez Perrier /
Alcala
Oil on canvas
32 ³/₄ × 40" (83.2 × 101.6 cm)

Gift of Mrs. Joseph A. Henry in
memory of William Robert
White
F1923-4-1

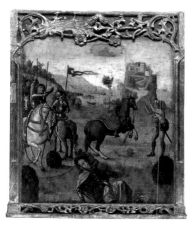

**Rodríguez de Solís, Juan,
attributed to**
Spanish, active León and Zamora,
active early 16th century
*The Conversion of Saint Paul*
Panel from an altarpiece
c. 1525
Oil on panel
32 × 25 ³/₄" (81.3 × 65.4 cm)

Bequest of Carl Otto
Kretzschmar von Kienbusch
1977-167-1042

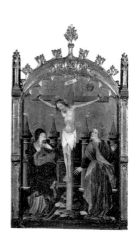

**Spanish, active Catalonia,
unknown artist**
Previously listed as a South
French artist, c. 1430–1450
(JGJ 1941)
*The Crucifixion*
Panel from an altarpiece
c. 1430–50
On cross: INRI
Oil and gold on panel
56 ³/₄ × 30 ⁵/₈" (144.1 × 77.8 cm)

John G. Johnson Collection
cat. 758

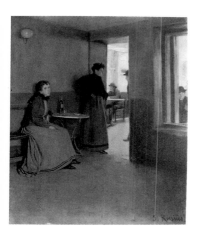

**Rusiñol, Santiago**
Spanish, 1861–1931
*Interior of a Café*
1892
Lower right: S. Rusiñol
Oil on canvas
39 ¹/₂ × 32" (100.3 × 81.3 cm)

John G. Johnson Collection
cat. 1078

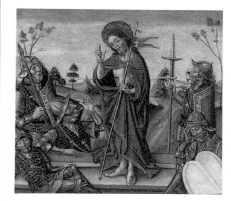

**Spanish, unknown artist**
*The Resurrection*
Predella panel
15th century
Oil on panel
13 × 13 ⁷/₈" (33 × 35.2 cm)

Bequest of Carl Otto
Kretzschmar von Kienbusch
1977-167-1043

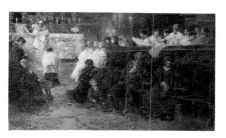

**Salinas, Juan Pablo**
Spanish, 1871–1946
*Interior of a Spanish Church*
c. 1900
Lower left: P. Salinas
Oil on canvas
16 ¹/₄ × 27 ⁵/₈" (41.3 × 70.2 cm)

Gift of Mr. and Mrs. Leon H.
Greenhouse
1973-130-1

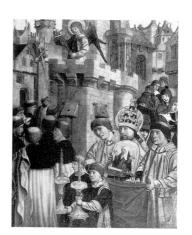

**Spanish, active Aragon,
unknown artist**
Previously listed as a Castilian
artist, second half of the 15th
century (JGJ 1941)
*The Miracle of Castel Sant'Angelo*
Panel from an altarpiece
c. 1500
Tempera and tooled gold on panel
37 × 29 ¹/₈" (94 × 74 cm)

John G. Johnson Collection
cat. 798

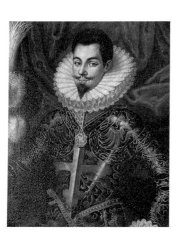

**Spanish, unknown artist**
*Portrait of a Man in Armor*
Late 16th century
Oil on canvas
32 × 24 1/2" (81.3 × 62.2 cm)

Bequest of Carl Otto
Kretzschmar von Kienbusch
1977-167-1083

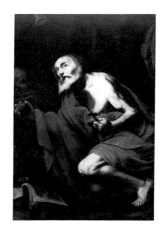

**Spanish, unknown artist**
*Saint Jerome*
17th century
Oil on canvas
61 3/8 × 42 1/4" (155.9 × 107.3 cm)

The Bloomfield Moore Collection
1899-1109

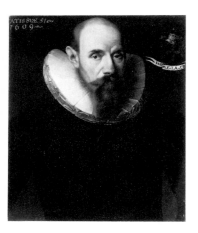

**Spanish, unknown artist**
Previously listed as Michiel van
Mierevelt (PMA 1965)
*Portrait of Jaime la Cruz*
1609
Upper left: [AET]ATIS SVAE. 51 /
1609; upper right: JAIME, LA,
CR[VZ]
Oil on panel
21 1/2 × 17 1/2" (54.6 × 44.4 cm)

Gift of Mrs. J. William White
1922-67-13

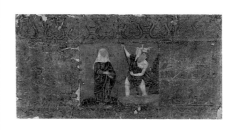

**Spanish, unknown artist**
*Saints Anne and Christopher*
17th century
Center: S. ANNA
Oil on leather
38 × 70 7/8" (96.5 × 180 cm)

Purchased from the George Grey
Barnard Collection with Museum
funds
1945-25-263

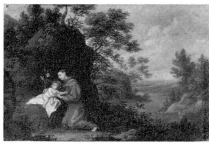

**Spanish, active Madrid,
unknown artist**
Previously listed as Ignacio de
Iriante (JGJ 1941)
*The Vision of Saint Anthony of
Padua*
c. 1650
Oil on canvas
10 5/16 × 15 1/8" (26.2 × 38.4 cm)

John G. Johnson Collection
cat. 817

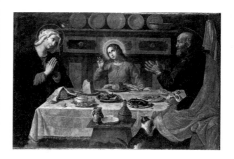

**Spanish, unknown artist**
*The Supper at Emmaus*
17th century
Oil on canvas
51 11/16 × 75 1/4" (131.3 ×
191.1 cm)

Purchased with the W. P.
Wilstach Fund
W1904-1-43

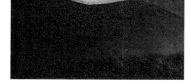

**Spanish, unknown artist**
*Portrait of a Gentleman*
17th century
Oil on canvas
22 7/8 × 17 3/4" (58.1 × 45.1 cm)

John G. Johnson Collection
cat. 813

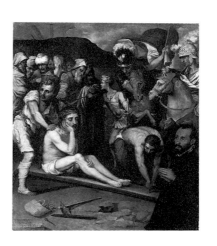

**Vargas, Luis de**
Spanish, active Seville and Rome,
1502–1568
*Preparations for the Crucifixion*
Mid-16th century
Lower right: LVISIVS DE /
VARGAS / FACIEBAT; on banner: P
Oil on panel transferred to canvas
34 5/8 × 30" (87.9 × 76.2 cm)

John G. Johnson Collection
cat. 805

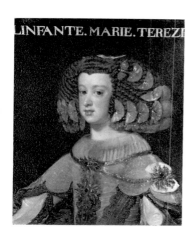

**Velasquez, Diego Rodriguez de Silva y, studio of**
Spanish, active Seville and Madrid, 1599–1660
Previously listed as an old copy after Diego Rodriguez de Silva y Velasquez (JGJ 1941)
*Portrait of the Infanta Maria Teresa*
1650s
Across top: LINFANTE.MARIE. TEREZ[E]
Oil on canvas
26 1/2 × 20 3/4" (67.3 × 52.7 cm)

John G. Johnson Collection
cat. 812

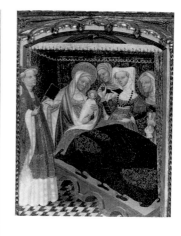

**Villamediana Master**
Previously listed as Luis Borrassá (JGJ 1941)
*The Birth of the Virgin*
Companion to a panel in a private collection in the United States
c. 1450
Tempera and tooled gold on panel
31 × 22 3/4" (78.7 × 57.8 cm)

John G. Johnson Collection
inv. 2493

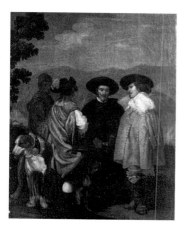

**Velasquez, Diego Rodriguez de Silva y, copy after**
*Cavaliers with a Dog*
Based on a group of figures in the foreground of the painting *Philip IV Hunting Wild Boar ("La Tela Real")*, in the National Gallery, London (197)
19th century
Oil on canvas
19 3/4 × 14 3/4" (50.2 × 37.5 cm)

John G. Johnson Collection
cat. 814

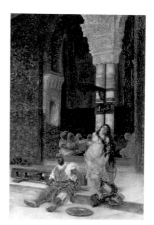

**Villegas y Cordero, José**
Spanish, 1848–1922
*Alhambra Interior*
c. 1875
Lower right: Villegas; center, on curtain: [Arabic for "There is no God but God"]; center, on plaque: [Arabic for "Islam is enriched by God"]
Oil on canvas
29 1/16 × 17 15/16" (73.8 × 45.6 cm)

John G. Johnson Collection
cat. 1103

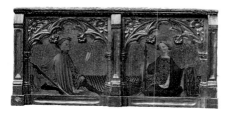

**Villamediana Master**
Spanish, active Palencia, active c. 1430–c. 1460
Previously listed as a Spanish international artist, c. 1450 (JGJ 1941)
*Saints Sebastian and Catherine of Alexandria*
Predella panel from the Saint Ursula altarpiece from San Pablo, Palencia; see following entry for companion panels
c. 1450
Tempera and tooled gold on panel
16 5/8 × 37 3/8" (42.2 × 94.9 cm)

John G. Johnson Collection
cat. 260

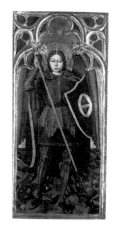

**Ximénez, Juan**
Spanish, active Aragon, first documented 1500, died 1505
Previously listed as a Spanish artist, mid-15th century (JGJ 1941)
*The Archangel Michael*
Panel from an altarpiece from the church of Tamarite de Litera, near Huesca, done in collaboration with Miguel Ximénez
1500–3
Oil and tooled gold on panel
50 1/2 × 22 11/16" (128.3 × 57.6 cm)

John G. Johnson Collection
inv. 183

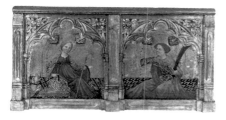

**Villamediana Master**
Previously listed as a Spanish international artist, c. 1450 (JGJ 1941)
*Saints Margaret and Bartholomew*
Predella panel; companion to the preceding panel and panels in the Lady Lever Art Gallery, Port Sunlight Village, England (LL3426–LL3429); the Zornmuseet, Mora, Sweden (Z1460); (formerly) the Gorostiza collection, Bilbao, Spain; and an unknown location
c. 1450
Tempera and tooled gold on panel
16 × 33" (40.6 × 83.8 cm)

John G. Johnson Collection
cat. 261

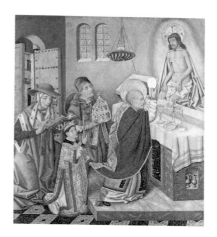

**Ximénez, Miguel, workshop of**
Spanish, active Aragon, first documented 1466, died 1505
**and Martín Bernat**
Spanish, documented 1469–1497
Previously listed as a Castilian artist, second half of the 15th century (JGJ 1941)
*The Mass of Saint Gregory*
c. 1500
Oil and tooled gold on panel transferred to canvas
42 5/8 × 38 5/8" (108.3 × 98.1 cm)

John G. Johnson Collection
cat. 799

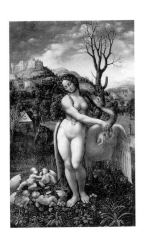

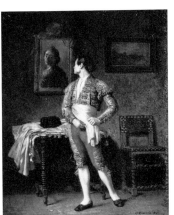

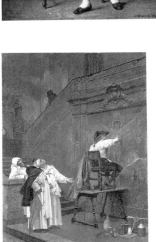

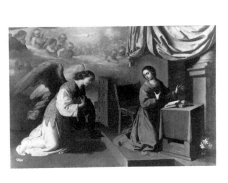

**Yañez, Fernando (Fernando de Almedina), attributed to**
Spanish, active Valencia and Italy, documented 1504/5–1536
Previously listed as a Flemish artist, c. 1540 (JFD 1972)
*Leda and the Swan*
Based on a composition by Leonardo da Vinci (Italian, 1452–1519) known through drawings
After 1508
Oil on panel
51 ⁵/₈ × 30" (131.1 × 76.2 cm)

John G. Johnson Collection
cat. 393

**Zamacois y Zabala, Eduardo**
Spanish, 1842–1871
*Toreador's Toilet*
1866
Lower right: Ed ZAMACOIS. 1866.
Oil on panel
10 × 7 ¹³/₁₆" (25.4 × 19.8 cm)

John G. Johnson Collection
cat. 1113

**Zamacois y Zabala, Eduardo**
*The Decorative Painter (Too Much Blood)*
1868
Lower right: EZ ZAMACOIZ. 68.
Oil on canvas
22 ¹/₈ × 14 ⁷/₈" (56.2 × 37.8 cm)

The W. P. Wilstach Collection, bequest of Anna H. Wilstach
W1893-1-132

**Zurbarán, Francisco de**
Spanish, 1598–1664
*The Annunciation*
1650
Lower left: Franco de Zurbaran 1650
Oil on canvas
85 ⁵/₈ × 124 ¹/₂" (217.5 × 316.2 cm)

Purchased with the W. P. Wilstach Fund
W1900-1-16

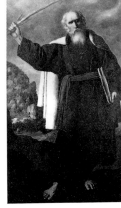

**Zurbarán, Francisco de, workshop of**
*Saint Jerome*
c. 1640–50
Oil on canvas
75 ¹/₄ × 41 ³/₁₆" (191.1 × 104.6 cm)

Bequest of Sally W. Fisher
F1925-1-1

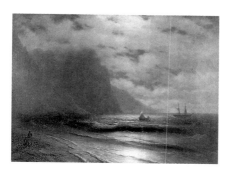

**Aivasovsky, Ivan Konstantinovitsch**
Armenian, 1817–1900
*Rocky Seashore*
1876
Lower left: Aivasovsky 1876
Oil on canvas
21 5/16 × 29 3/8" (54.1 × 74.6 cm)

John G. Johnson Collection
cat. 888

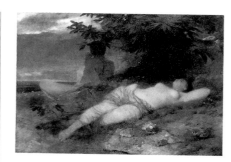

**Böcklin, Arnold**
*Nymph and Satyr*
1871
Lower right: AB
Oil on canvas
42 1/2 × 61" (107.9 × 154.9 cm)

John G. Johnson Collection
cat. 899

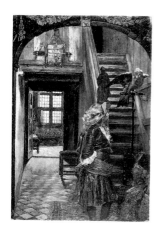

**Beers, Jan van**
Belgian, 1852–1927
*Girl with a Parrot*
1879
Lower left: JAN VAN BEERS / PARIS 1879
Oil on panel
20 3/8 × 12 7/8" (51.7 × 32.7 cm)

John G. Johnson Collection
inv. 2438

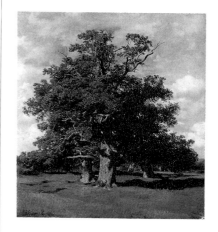

**Calame, Alexandre**
Swiss, 1810–1864
*Oak Trees*
1854
Lower left: A. Calame
Oil on canvas
14 1/2 × 12 7/8" (36.8 × 32.7 cm)

John G. Johnson Collection
cat. 908

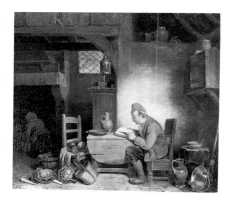

**Belgian, unknown artist**
*Man Reading*
19th century
Oil on panel
14 1/4 × 16 5/8" (36.2 × 42.2 cm)

John G. Johnson Collection
inv. 2843

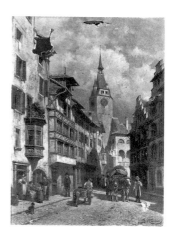

**Carabain, Jacques-François**
Belgian, born Netherlands, born 1834, still active 1891
*Street Scene in Zug, Switzerland*
1891
Lower right: J. Carabain; on reverse: I declare that this picture was painted to the order / of Mr. Craig and Evans / Brussels. 6 Mai 1891. / JS. Carabain
Oil on canvas
23 1/2 × 16 3/4" (59.7 × 42.5 cm)

The Walter Lippincott Collection
1923-59-5

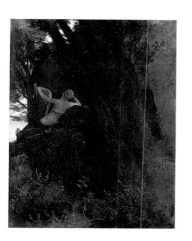

**Böcklin, Arnold**
Swiss, 1827–1901
*Sappho*
1862
Upper right: A Böcklin
Oil on canvas
37 3/8 × 29" (94.9 × 73.7 cm)

John G. Johnson Collection
cat. 898

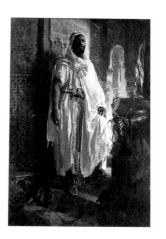

**Charlemont, Eduard**
Austrian, 1848–1906
*The Moorish Chief*
1878
Oil on panel
59 1/8 × 38 1/2" (150.2 × 97.8 cm)

John G. Johnson Collection
cat. 951

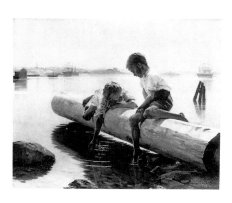

**Edelfelt, Albert Gustaf Aristides**
Finnish, 1854–1905
*Two Boys on a Log (The Little Boat)*
1884
Lower right: A. EDELFELT / 1884
Oil on canvas
35 5/16 × 41 15/16" (89.7 × 106.5 cm)

Purchased with the W. P. Wilstach Fund
W1906-1-9

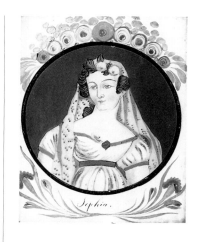

**European, unknown artist**
*Portrait of Sophia*
Companion to the preceding painting
c. 1830–40
Center bottom: Sophia.
Oil on glass
12 9/16 × 10 9/16" (31.9 × 26.8 cm)

Bequest of Lisa Norris Elkins
1950-92-286

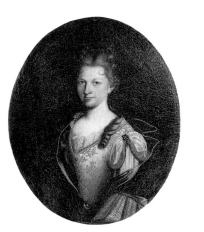

**European, unknown artist**
*Portrait of a Lady*
18th century
Oil on canvas
30 × 23 3/4" (76.2 × 60.3 cm)

Bequest of Arthur H. Lea
F1938-1-5

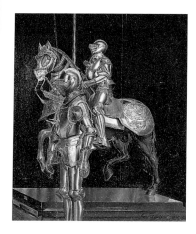

**European, unknown artist**
*Display of Suits of Armor, Musée de l'Armée, Paris*
19th century
Lower right: E. Traverllari
Oil on panel
18 × 14 1/4" (45.7 × 36.2 cm)

Bequest of Carl Otto Kretzschmar von Kienbusch
1977-167-1086

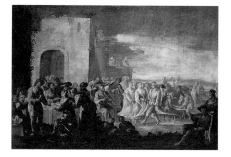

**European, unknown artist**
*Wedding*
c. 1775–1825
Oil on canvas
33 3/16 × 45 3/8" (84.3 × 115.2 cm)

Bequest of Arthur H. Lea
F1938-1-37

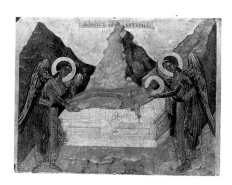

**Greek, unknown artist**
Previously listed as Byzantine, unknown artist, 15th century (PMA 1965)
*The Entombment of Saint Catherine of Alexandria*
Late 15th century
Center top: [Greek for "The Entombment of Saint Catherine"]
Tempera and gold on panel
10 5/8 × 13 1/2" (27 × 34.3 cm)

The Louise and Walter Arensberg Collection
1950-134-194

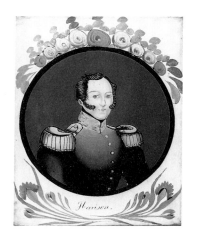

**European, unknown artist**
*Portrait of Harison*
Companion to the following painting
c. 1830–40
Center bottom: Harison.
Oil on glass
12 9/16 × 10 9/16" (31.9 × 26.8 cm)

Bequest of Lisa Norris Elkins
1950-92-285

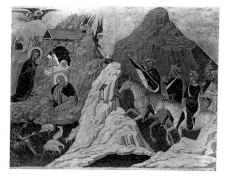

**Greek, active Crete, unknown artist**
Previously listed as Italian, unknown artist, 15th century (PMA 1965)
*The Nativity and the Arrival of the Magi*
Late 15th century
Tempera on panel
13 13/16 × 18 1/8" (35.1 × 46 cm)

The Louise and Walter Arensberg Collection
1950-134-192

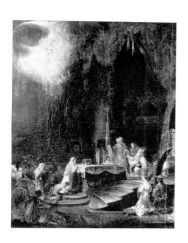

**Jansen, Heinrich**
Danish, 1625–1667
Previously listed as Jacob de
Wett (JFD 1972)
*The Presentation of Christ in the
Temple*
17th century
Oil on panel
22 15/16 × 16 15/16" (58.3 × 43 cm)

John G. Johnson Collection
cat. 490

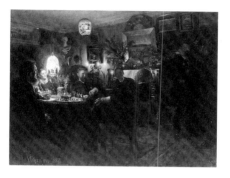

**Johansen, Viggo**
Danish, 1851–1935
*My Friends*
1887
Lower left: V Johansen. 1887.
Oil on canvas
42 7/8 × 54 7/8" (108.9 ×
139.4 cm)

John G. Johnson Collection
cat. 1014

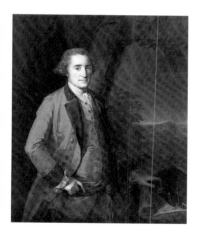

**Kauffman, Angelica**
Swiss, 1741–1807
*Portrait of Lieutenant General
James Cuninghame*
c. 1775
Oil on canvas
72 × 48" (183 × 121.9 cm)

Gift of Mrs. Charles Hamilton
1990-31-1

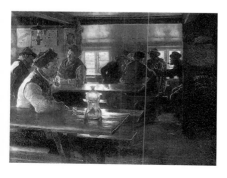

**Krøyer, Peter Severin**
Danish, 1851–1909
*Interior of a Tavern*
1886
Lower left: S Kroyer. SKAGEN
1886.
Oil on canvas
33 3/4 × 45" (85.7 × 114.3 cm)

John G. Johnson Collection
cat. 1015

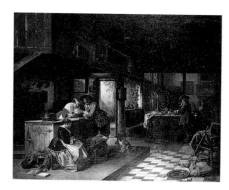

**Leys, Hendrik Jan August**
Belgian, 1815–1869
*Interior of an Inn*
1849
Lower left: H. Leys 1849
Oil on panel
28 7/8 × 35 1/2" (73.3 × 90.2 cm)

John G. Johnson Collection
cat. 1020

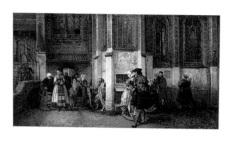

**Leys, Hendrik Jan August**
*Faust and Marguerite*
1856
Lower left: H. Leys f. 1856
Oil on panel
39 1/4 × 69 3/4" (99.7 × 177.2 cm)

The William L. Elkins Collection
E1924-3-83

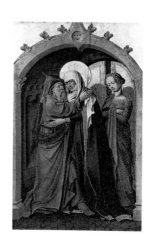

**Master of Schloss
Lichtenstein**
Austrian, active 1440–1445
*The Meeting at the Golden Gate*
Panel from an altarpiece;
companion panels are in the State
Museum of A. S. Pushkin,
Moscow (421); the Bayerische
Staatsgemäldesammlungen, Alte
Pinakothek, Munich (13201);
the State Museum of Art, Tallinn,
Estonia (M1149); Osterreichische
Galerie im Belvedere, Vienna
(inv. 4778, inv. 4904–4906,
inv. 4908); the National Museum,
Warsaw (SR86 MNW); and
(formerly) the Rothschild
collection, Vienna
c. 1440–45
Lower right (spurious):
[Schäufelein monogram]; center
top: [Hebrew letter "sin"]
Oil and gold on panel
32 7/16 × 19 13/16" (82.4 × 50.3 cm)

John G. Johnson Collection
inv. 456

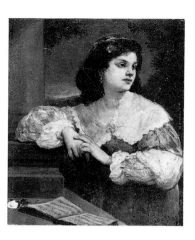

**Max, Gabriel Cornelius von**
Bohemian, 1840–1915
*Girl with Music*
c. 1900
On music: Nachtspiell; lower
right: Gab. Max
Oil on canvas
14 × 11 1/4" (35.6 × 28.6 cm)

John G. Johnson Collection
cat. 1038

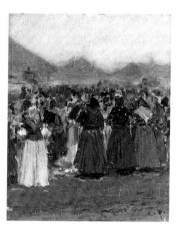

**Pettenkofen, August Xaver
Carl von**
Austrian, 1822–1889
*Market in Hungary*
Before 1888
Lower right: a. p.
Oil on panel
5 1/2 × 4 1/8" (14 × 10.5 cm)

John G. Johnson Collection
cat. 1059

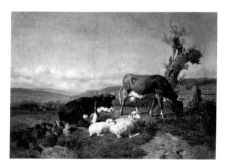

**Robbe, Louis-Marie-
Dominique**
Belgian, 1806–1887
*Pastoral Landscape*
After 1878
Lower left: Robbe
Oil on canvas
31 3/16 × 42 3/4" (79.2 × 108.6 cm)

Gift of Hermann Krumbhaar and
Dr. Edward Krumbhaar
1921-69-2

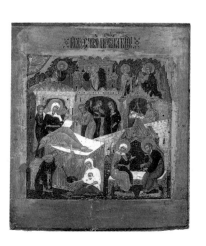

**Russian, unknown artist**
*Episodes from the Life of Saint Anne*
17th century
Across top: [Russian for "The
Nativity of the Mother of God"]
Tempera on panel
12 5/8 × 10 3/4" (32.1 × 27.3 cm)

Gift of Christian Brinton
1941-79-153

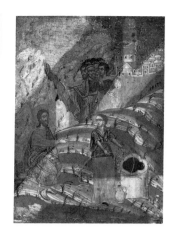

**Russian, unknown artist**
*Christ and the Woman of Samaria*
c. 1750–60
Oil on canvas on panel
21 3/16 × 15 3/8" (53.8 × 39 cm)

The Bloomfield Moore Collection
1883-132

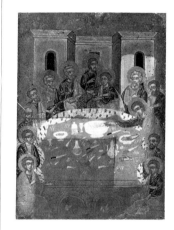

**Russian, unknown artist**
*The Last Supper*
c. 1750–60
Oil on canvas on panel
21 7/8 × 15 1/16" (55.6 × 38.3 cm)

The Bloomfield Moore Collection
1883-131

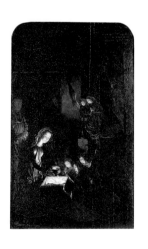

**Sittow, Michel, follower of**
Estonian, 1468–1525/26
Previously listed as Flemish,
unknown artist, early 16th
century (PMA 1965)
*The Nativity, at Night*
Early 16th century
Oil on panel
48 7/8 × 27 5/8" (124.1 × 70.2 cm)

Purchased with the W. P.
Wilstach Fund
W1902-1-13

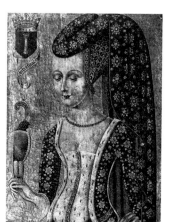

**The Spanish Forger**
European, active c. 1875–1925
*Woman with a Hawk*
c. 1875–1925
On scroll: aetatas suae XVIII
Oil and gold on panel
12 1/4 × 8 7/8" (31.1 × 22.5 cm)

John G. Johnson Collection
cat. 760

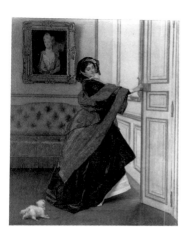

**Stevens, Alfred-Émile-Léopold**
Belgian, 1823–1906
*Departing for the Promenade
(Will You Go Out with Me, Fido?)*
1859
Lower right: Alfred Stevens. 59
Oil on panel
24 1/4 × 19 1/4" (61.6 × 48.9 cm)

The W. P. Wilstach Collection,
bequest of Anna H. Wilstach
W1893-1-106

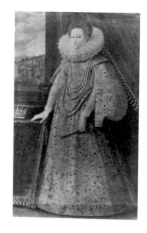

**Swedish?, unknown artist**
*Portrait of a Queen* [?]
c. 1600
Oil on canvas
73 1/4 × 42 1/4" (186 × 107.3 cm)

The Bloomfield Moore Collection
1883-136

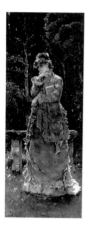

**Stevens, Alfred-Émile-Léopold**
*Reverie*
c. 1875
Lower left: AStevens
Oil on canvas
30 5/8 × 11 1/4" (77.8 × 28.6 cm)

John G. Johnson Collection
cat. 1083

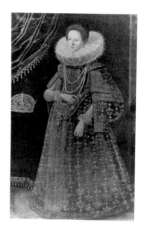

**Swedish?, unknown artist**
*Portrait of a Queen* [?]
c. 1600
Oil on canvas
73 1/4 × 42 1/4" (186 × 107.3 cm)

The Bloomfield Moore Collection
1883-137

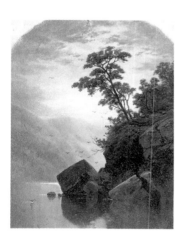

**Stevens, Alfred-Émile-Léopold, follower of**
*Lake*
19th century
Lower left (spurious): ats
Oil on panel
8 × 6" (20.3 × 15.2 cm)

John G. Johnson Collection
inv. 2822

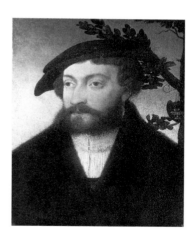

**Swiss, active Basel, unknown artist**
*Portrait of a Man*
c. 1525
Oil on panel
10 1/2 × 8 5/16" (26.7 × 21.1 cm)

John G. Johnson Collection
inv. 1850

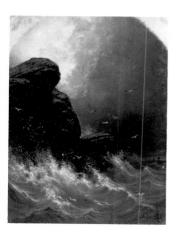

**Stevens, Alfred-Émile-Léopold, follower of**
*Rocks and Waves*
19th century
Lower right (spurious): ATS
Oil on panel
8 × 6" (20.3 × 15.2 cm)

John G. Johnson Collection
inv. 2848

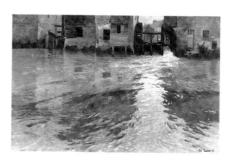

**Thaulow, Frits**
Norwegian, 1847–1906
*Water Mill*
1892
Lower right: Frits Thaulow 92.
Oil on canvas
32 × 47 5/8" (81.3 × 121 cm)

John G. Johnson Collection
cat. 1091

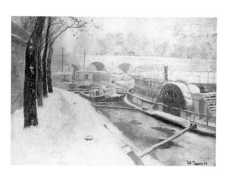

**Thaulow, Frits**
*Snow Scene*
1893
Lower right: Frits Thaulow 93.
Oil on canvas
21 3/8 × 29" (54.3 × 73.7 cm)

John G. Johnson Collection
cat. 1092

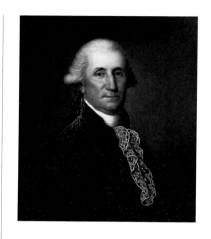

**Wertmüller, Adolph-Ulrich**
Swedish, active United States,
1751–1811
*Portrait of George Washington*
c. 1794
Oil on canvas
25 3/8 × 21 1/8" (64.4 × 53.7 cm)

Gift of Mr. and Mrs. John
Wagner
1986-100-1

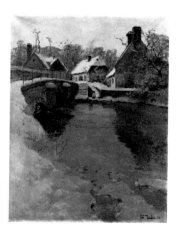

**Thaulow, Frits**
*The Arques River at Ancourt,
Evening*
1895
Lower right: Frits Thaulow. 95.
Oil on canvas
34 1/4 × 25 1/2" (87 × 64.8 cm)

The William L. Elkins Collection
E1924-3-93

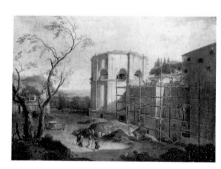

**Wutky, Michael**
Austrian, 1739–1823
*The Sala a Croce Greca of the
Vatican under Construction*
c. 1776
Oil on canvas
39 1/2 × 54 1/4" (100.3 × 137.8 cm)

The Bloomfield Moore Collection
1883-82

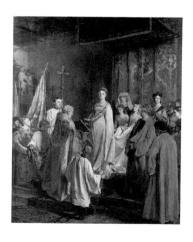

**Wauters, Émile-Charles**
Belgian, 1846–1933
*Mary of Burgundy Granting the
Great Privilege*
By 1878
Lower left: Emile Wauters; top
center, on curtain: [illegible]
Oil on canvas
50 5/8 × 39 3/4" (128.6 × 101 cm)

John G. Johnson Collection
cat. 1110

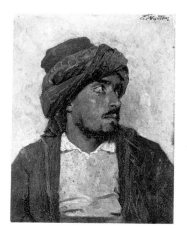

**Wauters, Émile-Charles**
*Head of a Man*
1878
Upper right: E. Wauters
Oil on canvas
12 1/4 × 9 1/8" (31.1 × 23.2 cm)

John G. Johnson Collection
inv. 2943

# American Painting
# before 1900

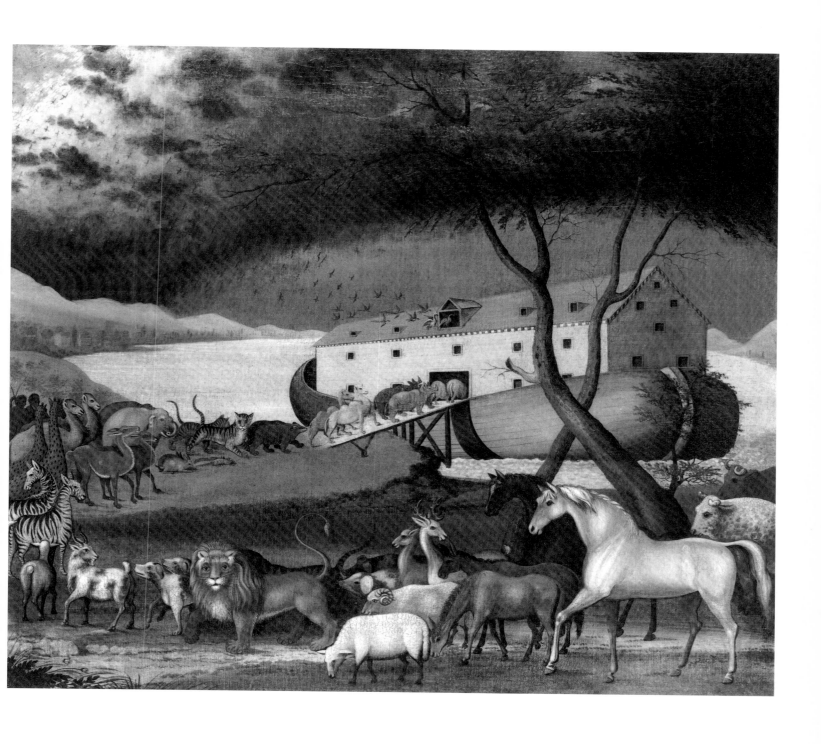

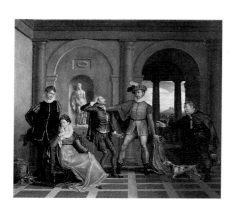

**Allston, Washington**
American, 1779–1843
*Scene from "The Taming of the Shrew"*
1809
Lower left: W. Allston.—
Oil on canvas
27 3/4 × 30 7/8" (70.5 × 78.4 cm)

Purchased with the Edith H. Bell
Fund and the J. Stogdell Stokes
Fund
1987-8-1

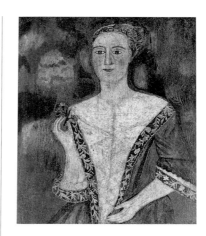

**American, unknown artist**
Previously listed as American,
unknown artist, 18th century
(PMA 1965)
*Portrait of a Woman*
c. 1750
Oil on panel
24 1/4 × 20 1/4" (61.6 × 51.4 cm)

The Louise and Walter Arensberg
Collection
1950-134-198

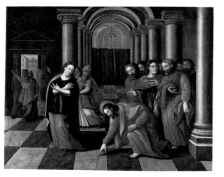

**American, unknown artist**
*Christ and the Scribes*
c. 1725–30
Oil on canvas
41 1/2 × 50 1/2" (105.4 × 128.3 cm)

Bequest of Edgar William and
Bernice Chrysler Garbisch
1980-64-12

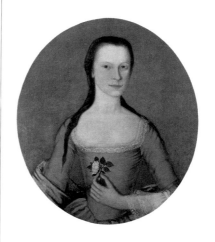

**American, unknown artist**
*Portrait of a Woman*
c. 1750
Oil on canvas
28 3/4 × 24 1/4" (73 × 61.6 cm)

The Louise and Walter Arensberg
Collection
1950-134-196

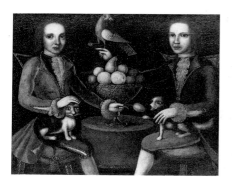

**American, unknown artist**
*Portrait of Two Boys with Pets*
c. 1730
Oil on canvas
31 3/4 × 38 7/8" (80.6 × 98.7 cm)

The Collection of Edgar William
and Bernice Chrysler Garbisch
1967-268-2

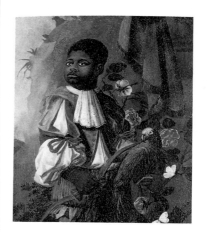

**American, unknown artist**
Previously listed as American,
unknown artist, 19th century
(PMA 1965)
*Young Black Boy with a Parrot*
c. 1760
Oil on canvas
27 3/4 × 22 3/4" (70.5 × 57.8 cm)

Bequest of Lisa Norris Elkins
1950-92-23

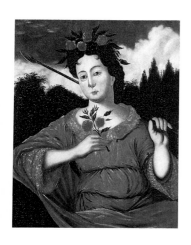

**American, unknown artist**
*Ceres*
c. 1750
Oil on panel
24 3/4 × 18 7/8" (62.9 × 47.9 cm)

Bequest of Edgar William and
Bernice Chrysler Garbisch
1981-1-1

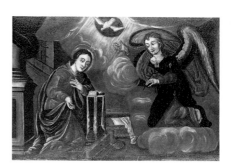

**American, unknown artist**
*The Annunciation*
c. 1775–1800
Oil on panel
23 × 32 7/8" (58.4 × 83.5 cm)

The Collection of Edgar William
and Bernice Chrysler Garbisch
1966-219-1

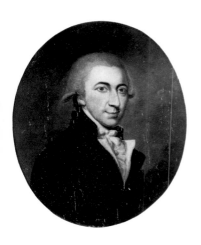

**American, unknown artist**
*Portrait of Thomas Cullum*
Companion to the following
painting
c. 1780
On reverse: Mr. Thomas Cullum /
born February 21st 1751
Oil on panel
9 3/4 × 8 1/8" (24.8 × 20.6 cm)

Bequest of Emily G. Porter
1974-41-4

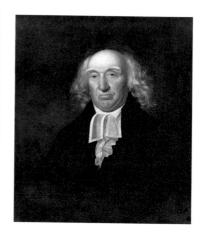

**American, unknown artist**
*Portrait of a Man*
c. 1800
Oil on canvas
30 1/8 × 24 7/8" (76.5 × 63.2 cm)

The Louise and Walter Arensberg
Collection
1950-134-538

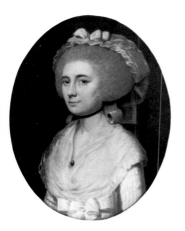

**American, unknown artist**
*Portrait of Mrs. Mary Cullum*
Companion to the preceding
painting
c. 1780
On reverse: Mrs. Mary Cullum
Oil on panel
10 × 8" (25.4 × 20.3 cm)

Bequest of Emily G. Porter
1974-41-5

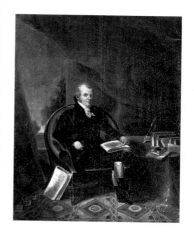

**American, unknown artist**
*Portrait of Paul Beck*
c. 1800
Oil on canvas
22 × 16 15/16" (55.9 × 43 cm)

Gift of Miss Virginia D. Flanagan
1972-201-1

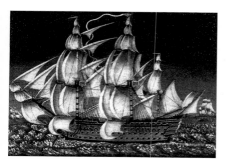

**American, unknown artist**
*First-Rate Ship of the Line*
c. 1790
Oil on panel
18 1/4 × 25 1/4" (46.3 × 64.1 cm)

Bequest of Edgar William and
Bernice Chrysler Garbisch
1981-1-3

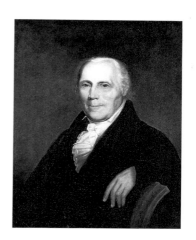

**American, unknown artist**
Previously listed as American,
unknown artist, 19th century
(PMA 1965)
*Portrait of John Paul Schott*
Companion to the following
painting
c. 1805–20
Oil on canvas
29 13/16 × 24 5/8" (75.7 × 62.5 cm)

Gift of Marie Josephine Rozet
and Rebecca Mandeville Rozet
Hunt
1935-13-24

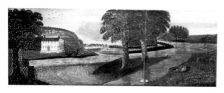

**American, unknown artist**
*Jewett House, Portsmouth,
New Hampshire*
Overmantel from the Jewett
house
c. 1795
Oil on panel
22 11/16 × 52 5/8" (57.6 × 133.7 cm)

Bequest of Edgar William and
Bernice Chrysler Garbisch
1981-1-4

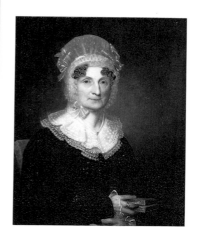

**American, unknown artist**
Previously listed as American,
unknown artist, 19th century
(PMA 1965)
*Portrait of Naomi Sill Schott*
Companion to the preceding
painting
c. 1805–20
Oil on canvas
30 1/8 × 24 13/16" (76.5 × 63 cm)

Gift of Marie Josephine Rozet
and Rebecca Mandeville Rozet
Hunt
1935-13-25

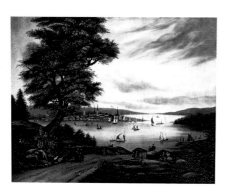

**American, unknown artist**
*View of Baltimore*
c. 1810
Oil on canvas
26 × 31 ¹/₈" (66 × 79 cm)

Bequest of Edgar William and
Bernice Chrysler Garbisch
1980-64-13

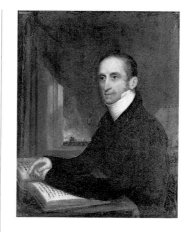

**American, unknown artist**
*Portrait of James Lloyd*
c. 1815–25
Oil on panel
9 ¹/₂ × 7 ⁵/₁₆" (24.1 × 18.6 cm)

Gift of Mrs. C. P. Beauchamp
Jefferys
1966-53-2

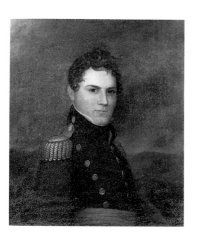

**American, unknown artist**
Previously listed as American,
unknown artist, 18th–19th
century (PMA 1965)
*Portrait of Robert Hector Macpherson*
c. 1810–17
Oil on canvas
29 × 24" (73.7 × 61 cm)

Bequest of Mellicent Story
Garland
1963-75-3

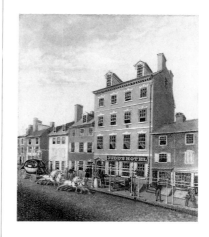

**American, unknown artist**
*Judd's Hotel, Philadelphia*
c. 1820
On signboards: TRENTON
COACH OFFICE; JUDD'S HOTEL;
J. WALNUT HAIR DRESSER
Oil on canvas
30 ¹/₈ × 24 ¹/₂" (76.5 × 62.2 cm)

The Collection of Edgar William
and Bernice Chrysler Garbisch
1968-222-4

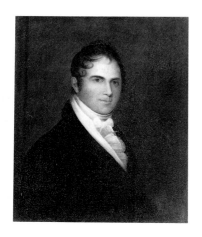

**American, unknown artist**
Previously listed as American,
unknown artist, 18th–19th
century (PMA 1965)
*Portrait of John Montgomery
Macpherson*
c. 1810–20
Oil on canvas
28 ⁷/₈ × 23 ¹³/₁₆" (73.3 × 60.5 cm)

Bequest of Mellicent Story
Garland
1963-75-4

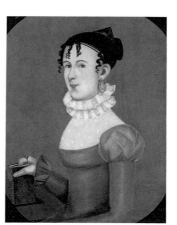

**American, unknown artist**
*Portrait of Adeline Harwood*
c. 1820
Oil on canvas
27 ¹/₄ × 21 ¹/₄" (69.2 × 54 cm)

Bequest of Edgar William and
Bernice Chrysler Garbisch
1980-64-4

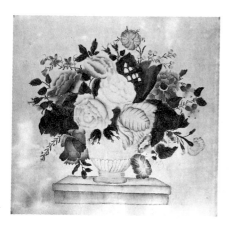

**American, unknown artist**
*Still Life with Flowers*
c. 1810–35
Oil on velvet on panel
16 ¹/₂ × 16 ³/₄" (41.9 × 42.5 cm)

Gift of Mr. and Mrs. Leon C.
Sunstein, Jr.
1969-166-2

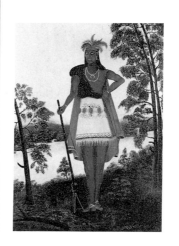

**American, unknown artist**
*Portrait of the Oneida Chieftain
Shikellamy*
c. 1820
Oil on canvas
45 ¹/₈ × 31 ⁷/₈" (114.6 × 81 cm)

The Collection of Edgar William
and Bernice Chrysler Garbisch
1966-219-3

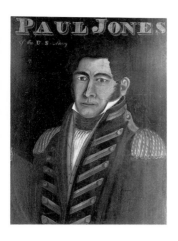

**American, unknown artist**
*Portrait of Paul Jones*
c. 1820–40
Across top: PAUL JONES / of the
U. S. Navy
Oil on panel
29 1/2 × 21 5/8" (74.9 × 54.9 cm)

Gift of Frank and Alice Osborn
1966-68-56

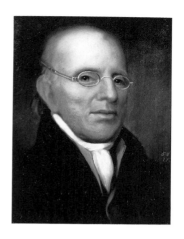

**American, unknown artist**
Previously listed as American,
unknown artist, 19th century
(PMA 1965)
*Portrait of I. W. Morris*
1828
Lower right: 58 / 1828
Oil on panel
10 1/16 × 7 11/16" (25.6 × 19.5 cm)

Gift of Miss Lydia Thompson
Morris
1930-73-4

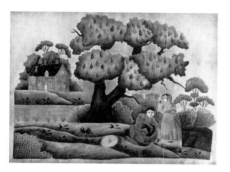

**American, unknown artist**
*Landscape with Figures*
c. 1825
Oil on velvet
16 3/4 × 21 3/4" (42.5 × 55.2 cm)

The Louise and Walter Arensberg
Collection
1950-134-535

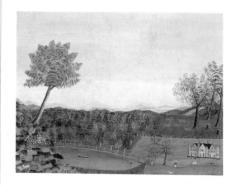

**American, unknown artist**
*Connecticut Landscape*
c. 1830
Oil on ticking
21 1/2 × 26 1/2" (54.6 × 67.3 cm)

Gift of Mrs. Edith Gregor Halpert
1957-4-1

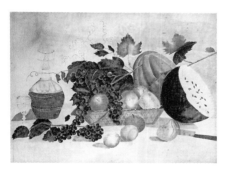

**American, unknown artist**
*Still Life with Fruit*
c. 1825–50
Oil on velvet
19 7/8 × 25 13/16" (50.5 × 65.6 cm)

Gift of Frank and Alice Osborn
1966-68-60

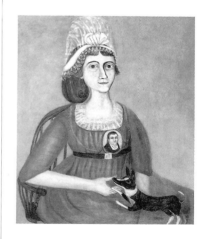

**American, unknown artist**
*Portrait of a Woman Wearing a
Miniature*
c. 1830
Oil on canvas
28 1/16 × 23 9/16" (71.3 × 59.8 cm)

Bequest of Edgar William and
Bernice Chrysler Garbisch
1980-64-5

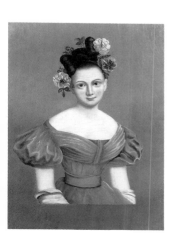

**American, unknown artist**
*Portrait of a Girl of the Lathrop
Family*
1828
On paper on reverse: Given to
Capt. Lathrop / In the year 1828 /
A.D.S. / Dec. 3rd 1875
Oil on panel
15 × 11 1/2" (38.1 × 29.2 cm)

The Collection of Edgar William
and Bernice Chrysler Garbisch
1972-262-2

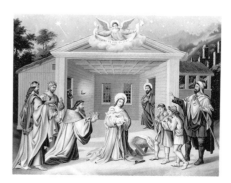
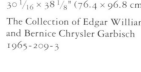

**American, unknown artist**
*The Adoration of the Shepherds and
the Magi*
c. 1830
Center top, on banner: GLORY TO
GOD ON HIGH.
Oil on copper
30 1/16 × 38 1/8" (76.4 × 96.8 cm)

The Collection of Edgar William
and Bernice Chrysler Garbisch
1965-209-3

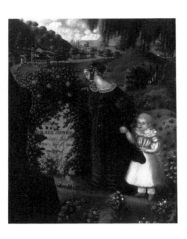

**American, unknown artist**
*A Woman and a Girl at the Tombstone of Israel Jones*
Fragment from the same work as the following two paintings
c. 1831
On tombstone: mot[ ] / ISRAEL JONES / died Jan 6 / 1828
Aged 62
Oil on panel
14 × 11 1/16" (35.6 × 28.1 cm)

Bequest of Edgar William and Bernice Chrysler Garbisch
1980-64-10

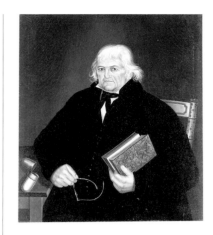

**American, unknown artist**
*Portrait of David Witmer, Sr.*
Companion to the following painting
c. 1835
On reverse: Born December 15th 1752 Old Style / Died August 15 1835 New Style / Aged 82 years 7 mos 19 days.
Oil on canvas on panel
41 5/8 × 35 3/4" (105.7 × 90.8 cm)

The Collection of Edgar William and Bernice Chrysler Garbisch
1970-254-1

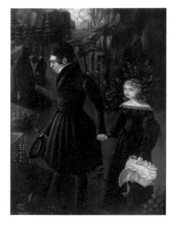

**American, unknown artist**
*A Boy at a Memorial to Sanford and Wealthy Palmer*
See previous entry
c. 1831
On memorial: SACRED TO THE MEMORY / OF / SANFORD PALMER / Who died Octr 14th 1828 / in the 66th year of his age. / AND / WEALTHY his wife / who died June 30th 1831 / in the 63rd year of her age.
Oil on panel
9 7/8 × 9 7/8" (25.1 × 25.1 cm)

Bequest of Edgar William and Bernice Chrysler Garbisch
1980-64-15

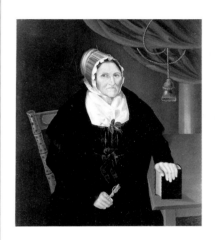

**American, unknown artist**
*Portrait of Mrs. David Witmer, Sr.*
Companion to the preceding painting
c. 1835
Oil on canvas on panel
41 5/8 × 35 3/4" (105.7 × 90.8 cm)

The Collection of Edgar William and Bernice Chrysler Garbisch
1970-254-2

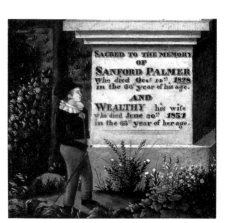

**American, unknown artist**
*A Man and a Girl at a Memorial*
See previous two entries
c. 1831
Oil on panel
14 × 10 1/16" (35.6 × 25.6 cm)

Bequest of Edgar William and Bernice Chrysler Garbisch
1980-64-16

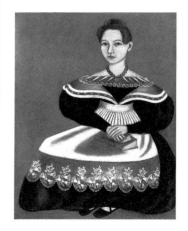

**American, unknown artist**
*Portrait of Sarah Yaw Jones*
c. 1835
Oil on canvas
39 1/2 × 29 1/2" (100.3 × 74.9 cm)

Bequest of Edgar William and Bernice Chrysler Garbisch
1981-1-11

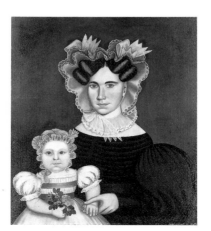

**American, unknown artist**
*Portrait of Agnes Frazee and Her Child*
1834
Oil on canvas
30 × 26" (76.2 × 66 cm)

The Collection of Edgar William and Bernice Chrysler Garbisch
1972-262-1

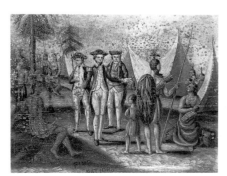

**American, unknown artist**
*Treaty with the Five Nations*
1838?
Lower left: TREATY / with the FIVE / NATIONS; on reverse: 1838
Oil on panel
8 5/8 × 10" (21.9 × 25.4 cm)

Gift of Titus C. Geesey
1969-284-13

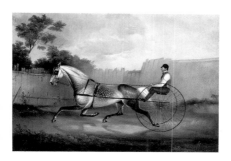

**American, unknown artist**
*In Full Stride*
c. 1840
Oil on canvas
23 ³/₄ × 33 ¹/₄" (60.3 × 84.4 cm)

The Collection of Edgar William
and Bernice Chrysler Garbisch
1965-209-4

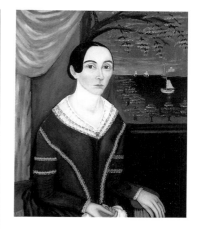

**American, unknown artist**
*Portrait of a Woman in Gray and White*
c. 1840
Oil on canvas
30 ¹/₈ × 25 ¹/₁₆" (76.5 × 63.7 cm)

Bequest of Edgar William and
Bernice Chrysler Garbisch
1980-64-6

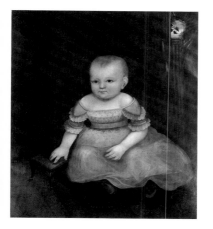

**American, unknown artist**
*Portrait of a Baby, Doylestown, Pennsylvania*
c. 1840
Oil on canvas
33 × 28 ¹/₄" (83.8 × 71.7 cm)

Gift of Mrs. Edith Gregor Halpert
1957-4-2

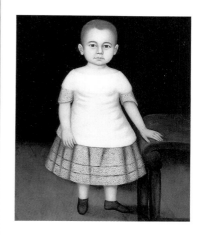

**American, unknown artist**
*Portrait of a Young Girl*
c. 1840
Oil on canvas
30 ¹/₈ × 25 ¹/₁₆" (76.5 × 63.7 cm)

Bequest of Edgar William and
Bernice Chrysler Garbisch
1980-64-7

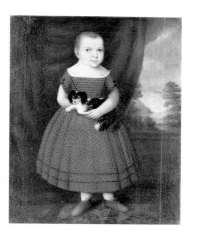

**American, unknown artist**
Previously listed as American,
unknown artist, 19th century
(PMA 1965)
*Portrait of a Child Holding a Dog*
c. 1840
Oil on canvas
36 ¹/₈ × 29" (91.8 × 73.7 cm)

The Louise and Walter Arensberg
Collection
1950-134-533

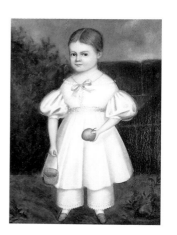

**American, unknown artist**
Previously listed as American,
unknown artist, 19th century
(PMA 1965)
*Portrait of a Young Girl Holding an Apple*
c. 1840
Oil on canvas
34 ¹/₂ × 25" (87.6 × 63.5 cm)

Bequest of Lisa Norris Elkins
1950-92-231

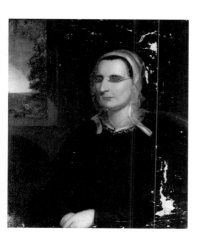

**American, unknown artist**
Previously listed as Jacob
Eichholz (PMA 1965)
*Portrait of a Woman*
c. 1840
On reverse (spurious):
J. Eicholtz [?] / 36
Oil on canvas
30 × 25" (76.2 × 63.5 cm)

Gift of John F. Braun
1949-73-1

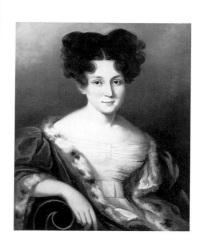

**American, unknown artist**
*Portrait of Cornelia Mandeville*
c. 1840
Oil on canvas
30 × 24 ⁷/₈" (76.2 × 63.2 cm)

Gift of Marie Josephine Rozet
and Rebecca Mandeville Rozet
Hunt
1935-13-26

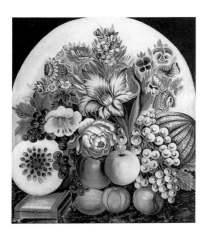

**American, unknown artist**
*Still Life with Fruit, Flowers, and a Jewel Case*
c. 1840
Oil on canvas
23 1/16 × 20 1/2" (58.6 × 52.1 cm)

Bequest of Edgar William and Bernice Chrysler Garbisch
1981-1-8

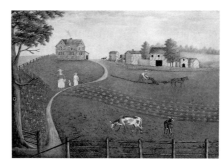

**American, unknown artist**
*"He That Tilleth His Land Shall Be Satisfied"*
c. 1850
Oil on panel
22 7/16 × 29 3/4" (57 × 75.6 cm)

The Collection of Edgar William and Bernice Chrysler Garbisch
1965-209-5

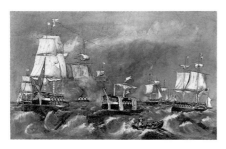

**American, unknown artist**
*The Battle of Lake Erie*
c. 1840
On ships: DETROIT; LAWRENCE; NIAGARA; on banner: DON'T GIVE UP / THE SHIP
Oil on panel
22 3/4 × 35 3/8" (57.8 × 89.8 cm)

The Collection of Edgar William and Bernice Chrysler Garbisch
1973-258-4

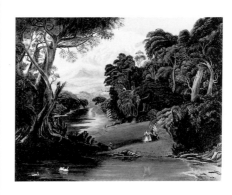

**American, unknown artist**
Previously listed as American, unknown artist, 19th century (PMA 1965)
*Romantic Landscape*
c. 1850
Oil on canvas
25 × 30 1/4" (63.5 × 76.8 cm)

Bequest of Lisa Norris Elkins
1950-92-232

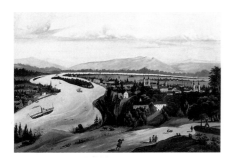

**American, unknown artist**
*View of Reading, Pennsylvania*
c. 1840
Oil on canvas
22 × 30" (55.9 × 76.2 cm)

Bequest of Edgar William and Bernice Chrysler Garbisch
1981-1-5

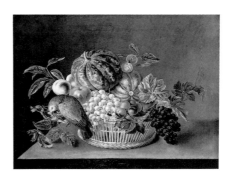

**American, unknown artist**
Previously attributed to James Peale (PMA 1965)
*Still Life*
c. 1850
Oil on canvas
29 1/8 × 37" (74 × 94 cm)

Purchased with Museum funds
1954-31-1

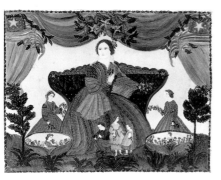

**American, unknown artist**
Previously listed as American, unknown artist, 19th century (PMA 1965)
*A Woman and Children under a Canopy with Flags*
c. 1850
Oil on paper
16 3/4 × 20" (42.5 × 50.8 cm)

Gift of Mrs. Frederick Thurston Mason
1914-365

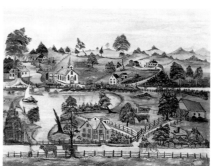

**American, unknown artist**
*View of a Village*
c. 1850
Oil on canvas
35 5/8 × 45 1/8" (90.5 × 114.6 cm)

The Collection of Edgar William and Bernice Chrysler Garbisch
1966-219-4

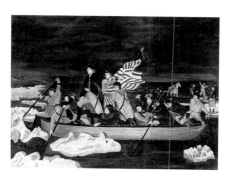

**American, unknown artist**
*Washington Crossing the Delaware*
Based on the painting by Emanuel
Leutze (German, 1816–1868),
dated 1851, in the Metropolitan
Museum of Art, New York (97.34)
After 1851
Oil on canvas
29 3/4 × 39 13/16" (75.6 × 101.1 cm)

The Collection of Edgar William
and Bernice Chrysler Garbisch
1973-258-5

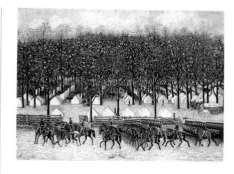

**American, unknown artist**
*Fourth Pennsylvania Cavalry*
1861
Center bottom: Oct 1861; center
right: 4th.PA.CAVALRY
Oil on canvas
36 × 47 7/8" (91.4 × 121.6 cm)

The Collection of Edgar William
and Bernice Chrysler Garbisch
1968-222-3

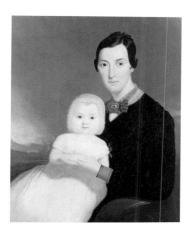

**American, unknown artist**
*Portrait of Caroline Margaret
Seagraves Mensch and Her Son,
John Roseberry Mensch*
c. 1855
Oil on canvas
32 3/4 × 26 1/4" (83.2 × 66.7 cm)

Gift of the Reverend Dr. Franklin
Joiner
1958-92-1

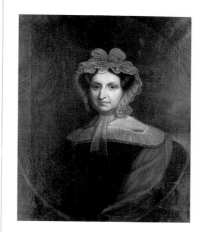

**American, unknown artist**
*Portrait of Sophia Ramsay*
c. 1870
Oil on canvas
35 × 28" (88.9 × 71.1 cm)

Gift of Peter D. Krumbhaar
1969-289-1

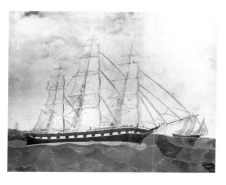

**American, unknown artist**
*Full-Rigged Clipper Ships*
c. 1860
Oil on canvas
26 × 32" (66 × 81.3 cm)

Bequest of Edgar William and
Bernice Chrysler Garbisch
1981-1-2

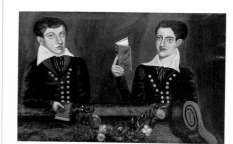

**American, unknown artist**
*Portrait of Two Boys*
c. 1870
Oil on canvas
27 × 42" (68.6 × 106.7 cm)

Gift of Mrs. Edith Gregor Halpert
1957-4-3

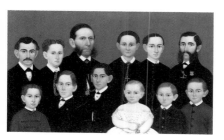

**American, unknown artist**
*Portrait of the Robinson Family*
c. 1860
Oil on canvas
29 1/2 × 49 1/2" (74.9 × 125.7 cm)

The Collection of Edgar William
and Bernice Chrysler Garbisch
1972-262-9

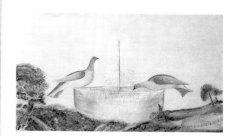

**American, unknown artist**
*Two Doves at a Fountain*
Fireboard
c. 1870
Oil on panel
34 1/4 × 48 1/2" (87 × 123.2 cm)

Bequest of Edgar William and
Bernice Chrysler Garbisch
1980-64-14

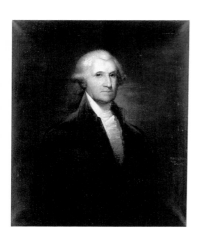

**American, unknown artist**
*Portrait of George Washington*
c. 1876
Center right: E. D. Marchant. /
after / Stuart.
Oil on canvas
36 1/4 × 29 3/8" (92.1 × 74.6 cm)

Gift of the Haas Community
Funds
1968-118-53

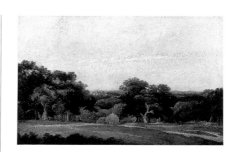

**American, unknown artist**
Previously listed as George Inness
(JGJ 1941)
*Woodland Scene*
Mid-19th century
Oil on panel
10 3/8 × 16 3/8" (26.3 × 41.6 cm)

John G. Johnson Collection
cat. 1008

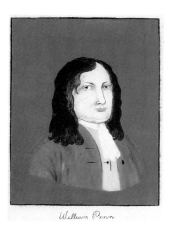

**American, unknown artist**
Previously listed as American,
unknown artist, 19th century
(PMA 1965)
*Portrait of William Penn*
c. 1876
Center bottom: William Penn
Oil on glass
14 1/2 × 10 1/4" (36.8 × 26 cm)

Gift of J. Stogdell Stokes
1927-62-1

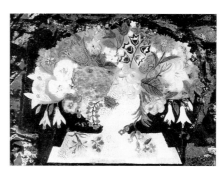

**American, unknown artist**
*Still Life with Flowers*
19th century
Oil and tinfoil on glass
14 × 18" (35.6 × 45.7 cm)

The Louise and Walter Arensberg
Collection
1950-134-534

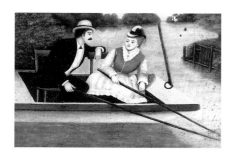

**American, unknown artist**
*Conversation in a Punt*
c. 1880
Oil on canvas
8 1/8 × 12" (20.6 × 30.5 cm)

Gift of Frank and Alice Osborn
1966-68-62

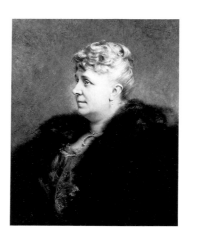

**American, unknown artist**
*Portrait of Mrs. Peter A. B.
Widener* [née Hannah Josephine
Dunton]
c. 1900–10
Oil on canvas
29 1/8 × 23 1/8" (74 × 58.7 cm)

Gift of Peter A. B. Widener III
1971-271-1

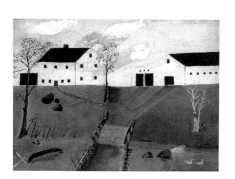

**American, unknown artist**
*Home of John Greenleaf Whittier*
c. 1892
Oil on panel
9 1/4 × 12 1/4" (23.5 × 31.1 cm)

Gift of Frank and Alice Osborn
1966-68-61

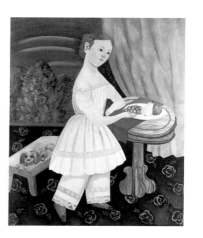

**American, unknown artist**
*Portrait of a Young Girl*
In an early 19th-century style
20th century
Oil on canvas
35 5/8 × 28 7/8" (90.5 × 73.3 cm)

The Collection of Edgar William
and Bernice Chrysler Garbisch
1973-258-6

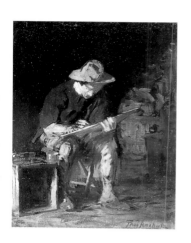

**Anshutz, Thomas Pollock**
American, 1851–1912
*Man Drawing*
c. 1890
Lower right: Thos Anshutz
Oil on canvas
26 1/8 × 20" (66.4 × 50.8 cm)

Bequest of Annie Lovering Perot
1936-1-1

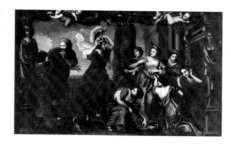

**Benbridge, Henry**
American, 1743–1812
*Achilles among the Daughters of Lycomedes*
c. 1758–64
Oil on canvas
26 1/4 × 42 1/4" (66.7 × 107.3 cm)

Purchased with the J. Stogdell Stokes Fund, the Edith H. Bell Fund, and the Katharine Levin Farrell Fund
1990-88-1

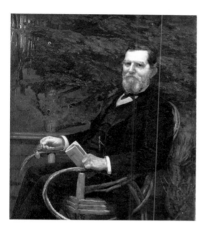

**Beaux, Cecilia**
American, 1855–1942
*Portrait of George Burnham*
1887
Lower right: Cecilia Beaux 87—
Oil on canvas
47 3/4 × 41 3/8" (121.3 × 105.1 cm)

Gift of Mrs. George Burnham III
1986-17-1

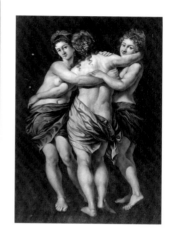

**Benbridge, Henry**
*The Three Graces*
c. 1762–68
Oil on canvas
48 1/2 × 33" (123.2 × 83.8 cm)

Purchased with the J. Stogdell Stokes Fund, the Edith H. Bell Fund, and the Katharine Levin Farrell Fund
1990-88-2

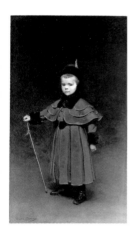

**Beaux, Cecilia**
*Portrait of Cecil Kent Drinker*
1891
Lower left: Cecilia Beaux
Oil on canvas
64 × 34 1/2" (162.6 × 87.6 cm)

Purchased with the Joseph E. Temple Fund
1966-110-1

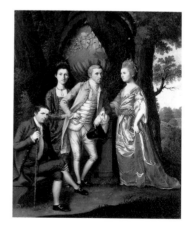

**Benbridge, Henry**
*Portrait of the Enoch Edwards Family*
c. 1783
Oil on canvas
30 × 23 11/16" (76.2 × 60.2 cm)

Gift of Miss Fannie Ringgold Carter
1949-53-1

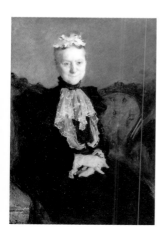

**Beaux, Cecilia**
*Portrait of Mrs. Alexander Biddle*
[née Julia Williams Rush]
1897
Lower left: Cecilia Beaux
Oil on canvas
40 1/4 × 30 3/16" (102.2 × 76.7 cm)

Gift of Horace Brock
1978-35-1

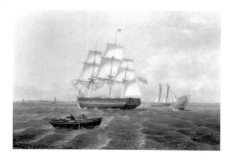

**Birch, Thomas**
American, born England, 1779–1851
*Clipper Ships, New York Harbor*
c. 1830
Lower right: [illegible signature]
Oil on canvas
20 3/4 × 30 1/8" (52.7 × 76.5 cm)

Gift of Caleb W. Hornor and Peter T. Hornor
1968-44-1

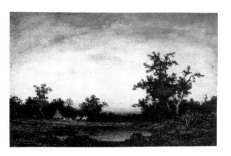

**Blakelock, Ralph A.**
American, 1847–1919
*Indian Encampment*
c. 1890
Lower left: R. A. Blakelock
Oil on canvas
16 × 24" (40.6 × 61 cm)

The Alex Simpson, Jr., Collection
1928-63-2

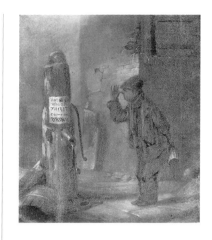

**Blythe, David Gilmour**
American, 1815–1865
*Boy at a Pump*
c. 1858–59
Lower right: Blythe; on pump:
Ho! all ye / who are / THIRSTY /
Come and / DRINK
Oil on canvas
14 1/8 × 12" (35.9 × 30.5 cm)

The W. P. Wilstach Collection,
bequest of Anna H. Wilstach
W1893-1-11

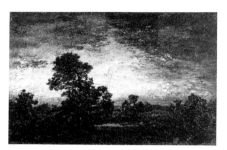

**Blakelock, Ralph A.**
*The Glow, Evening*
c. 1890–98
Lower left: R. A. Blakelock
Oil on panel
15 3/4 × 24 1/8" (40 × 61.3 cm)

Gift of William P. Wood in
memory of Mia Wood
1978-103-1

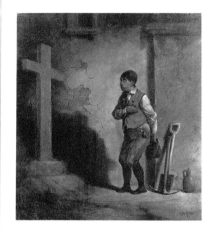

**Blythe, David Gilmour**
*Conscience Stricken*
c. 1860
Lower right: Blythe
Oil on canvas
14 1/8 × 12" (35.9 × 30.5 cm)

The W. P. Wilstach Collection,
bequest of Anna H. Wilstach
W1893-1-12

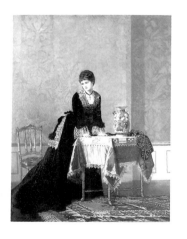

**Blashfield, Edwin Howland**
American, 1848–1936
*The Widow*
1873
Lower left: Edwin H. Blashfield /
1873
Oil on canvas
24 1/8 × 18 1/8" (61.3 × 46 cm)

The Alex Simpson, Jr., Collection
1944-13-1

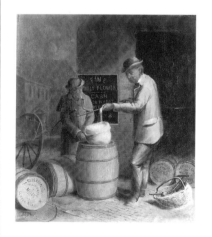

**Blythe, David Gilmour**
*Flour Inspector*
c. 1860
Lower left: Blythe; center, on sign:
FINE / [ ]MILY FLOWER, / CASH /
[F]OR WHEAT / RYE [B]ARLY &;
bottom, on casks: SUPERFINE /
PIGEONCREEK / MILLS;
LISBON & LEE; SUPERFINE /
EXTRA; CONOSTO[GA] / MILLS
Oil on canvas
17 1/8 × 13 15/16" (43.5 × 35.4 cm)

The W. P. Wilstach Collection,
bequest of Anna H. Wilstach
W1893-1-13

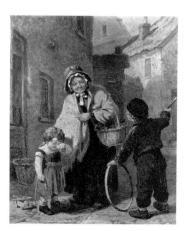

**Blauvelt, Charles F.**
American, 1824–1900
*The Lost Child*
c. 1866
Lower right: C. F. Blauvelt
Oil on canvas
10 1/8 × 8" (25.7 × 20.3 cm)

The W. P. Wilstach Collection,
bequest of Anna H. Wilstach
W1893-1-10

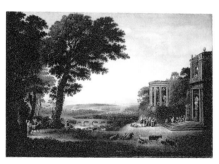

**Bordley, Judge John Beale**
American, 1727–1804
*Temple of Apollo*
After an engraving by William
Woollet (English, 1735–1785)
of the painting *Landscape with the
Father of Psyche Sacrificing at the
Milesian Temple of Apollo*, by
Claude Gellée (French,
1600–1682), in the collection of
Lord Fairhaven
1776
Oil on canvas
16 3/4 × 23 5/8" (42.5 × 60 cm)

Gift of Mr. and Mrs. William F.
Machold
1975-125-1

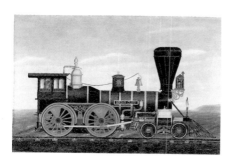

**Bresse, W. L.**
American, active c. 1860
*Locomotive Briar Cliff*
c. 1860
Lower left: WL BRESSE; center:
BRIAR CLIFF
Oil on canvas
24 1/8 × 35 3/4" (61.3 × 90.8 cm)

Gift of Frank and Alice Osborn
1966-68-55

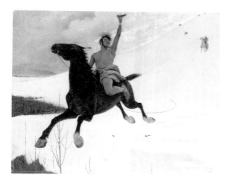

**Britton, William**
American, active c. 1820
*Market Square, Germantown,
Pennsylvania*
c. 1820
Oil on canvas
12 1/4 × 19 7/8" (31.1 × 50.5 cm)

The Collection of Edgar William
and Bernice Chrysler Garbisch
1965-209-2

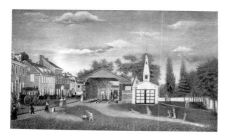

**Brush, George de Forest**
American, 1855–1941
*The Revenge (The Escape)*
1882
Lower right: Geo. de Forest
Brush. / 1882
Oil on canvas
15 1/2 × 19 1/2" (39.4 × 49.5 cm)

The Alex Simpson, Jr., Collection
1944-13-2

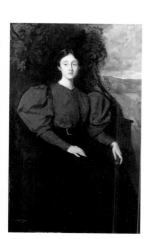

**Brush, George de Forest**
*Portrait of Miss Polly Cabot*
1896
Lower left: Geo. de Forest Brush /
1896
Oil on canvas
61 3/8 × 36 5/8" (155.9 × 93 cm)

Centennial gift of the Friends of
the Philadelphia Museum of Art
1976-156-1

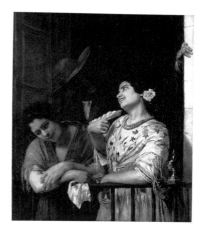

**Cassatt, Mary Stevenson**
American, 1844–1926
*On the Balcony*
1873
Lower left: M.S.C. / a Seville /
1873
Oil on canvas
39 3/4 × 21 1/2" (101 × 54.6 cm)

Gift of John G. Johnson for the
W. P. Wilstach Collection
W1906-1-7

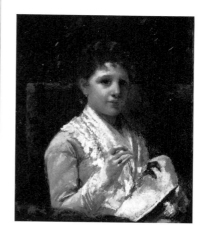

**Cassatt, Mary Stevenson**
*Mary Ellison Embroidering*
1877
Oil on canvas
29 1/4 × 23 1/2" (74.3 × 59.7 cm)

Gift of the children of Jean
Thompson Thayer
1986-108-1

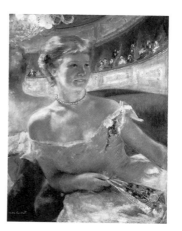

**Cassatt, Mary Stevenson**
*Woman with a Pearl Necklace in a
Loge*
1879
Lower left: Mary Cassatt
Oil on canvas
32 × 23 1/2" (81.3 × 59.7 cm)

Bequest of Charlotte Dorrance
Wright
1978-1-5

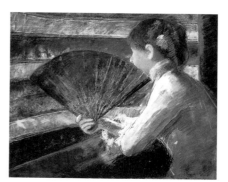

**Cassatt, Mary Stevenson**
*In the Loge*
c. 1879
Pastel and metallic paint on
canvas
25 5/8 × 32" (65.1 × 81.3 cm)

Gift of Mrs. Sargent McKean
1950-52-1

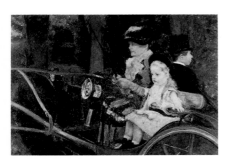

**Cassatt, Mary Stevenson**
*A Woman and a Girl Driving*
1881
Lower right: Mary Cassatt
Oil on canvas
35 5/16 × 51 3/8" (89.7 × 130.5 cm)

Purchased with the W. P.
Wilstach Fund
W1921-1-1

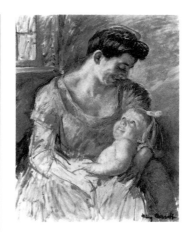

**Cassatt, Mary Stevenson**
*Mother and Child*
1908
Lower right: Mary Cassatt
Oil on canvas
32 × 23 7/8" (81.3 × 60.6 cm)

The Alex Simpson, Jr., Collection
1928-63-3

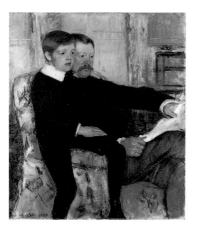

**Cassatt, Mary Stevenson**
*Portrait of Alexander J. Cassatt and
His Son, Robert Kelso Cassatt*
1884
Lower left: Mary Cassatt 1884
Oil on canvas
39 1/2 × 32" (100.3 × 81.3 cm)

Purchased with the W. P.
Wilstach Fund and funds
contributed by Mrs. William
Coxe Wright
W1959-1-1

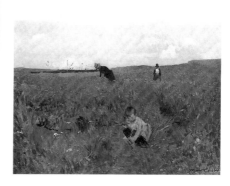

**Cassatt, Mary Stevenson,
attributed to**
*Poppies in a Field*
c. 1874–80
Lower right (spurious): Mary
Cassatt
Oil on panel
10 9/16 × 13 7/8" (26.8 × 35.2 cm)

Bequest of Charlotte Dorrance
Wright
1978-1-6

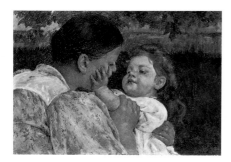

**Cassatt, Mary Stevenson**
*Maternal Caress*
c. 1896
Lower right: Mary Cassatt
Oil on canvas
15 × 21 1/4" (38.1 × 54 cm)

Bequest of Aaron E. Carpenter
1970-75-2

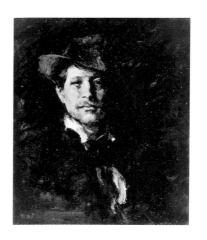

**Chase, William Merritt**
American, 1849–1916
*The Unknown Dane*
c. 1876
Lower right: Chase
Oil on canvas
24 × 20 1/8" (61 × 51.1 cm)

Bequest of Annie Lovering Perot
1936-1-2

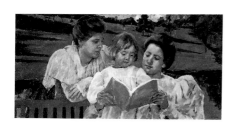

**Cassatt, Mary Stevenson**
*Family Group Reading*
c. 1901
Lower left: Mary Cassatt
Oil on canvas
22 1/4 × 44 1/4" (56.5 × 112.4 cm)

Gift of Mr. and Mrs. J. Watson
Webb
1942-102-1

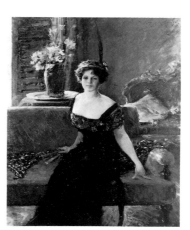

**Chase, William Merritt**
*Portrait of Anna Trequar Lang*
1911
Upper right: Wm M. Chase. /
1911.
Oil on canvas
59 1/2 × 47 3/4" (151.1 × 121.3 cm)

The Alex Simpson, Jr., Collection
1928-63-4

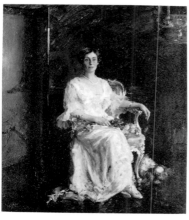

**Chase, William Merritt**
*Portrait of a Lady*
c. 1915
Lower left: Wm. M. Chase
Oil on canvas
70 × 60" (177.8 × 152.4 cm)

Gift of Eldridge R. Johnson
1922-87-1

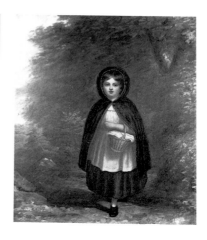

**Conarroe, George W.**
*Little Red Riding Hood*
Mid-19th century
Oil on canvas
30 ¹⁄₈ × 25 ³⁄₈" (76.5 × 64.4 cm)

The W. P. Wilstach Collection,
bequest of Anna H. Wilstach
W1893-1-27

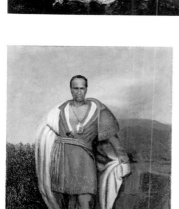

**Cogswell, Charles Nathaniel,
attributed to**
American, 1797–1843
Previously listed as Charles
Nathaniel Cogswell (PMA 1965)
*Portrait of Red Jacket, Chief of the
Six Nations*
c. 1830–40
Lower right: Cog
Oil on canvas
33 ³⁄₄ × 25 ⁷⁄₈" (85.7 × 65.7 cm)

Gift of Peter T. Hornor
1956-40-2

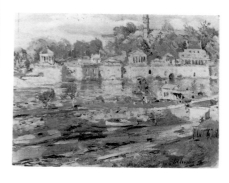

**Cooper, Colin Campbell**
American, 1856–1937
*Sketch for "Old Waterworks,
Fairmount"*
For the following painting
c. 1913
Lower right: C. C. Cooper;
on reverse: Old Waterworks at
Fairmount, Philada
Oil on cardboard
10 ¹⁄₂ × 13 ¹⁵⁄₁₆" (26.7 × 35.4 cm)

Gift of the artist
1936-50-2

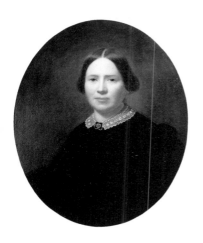

**Conarroe, George W.**
American, born 1803,
died 1882–84
*Portrait of Catharine Benezet Porter*
Companion to following painting
After 1843
On label on reverse: Catharine
Benezet / daughter of Sarah Rod-
man / and John Stephen Benezet /
married to William G. / Porter—
1843—Painted by / Geo. W.
Conarroe. Grand- / mother of
Emily G, Susan H. and Catharine
B. Porter
Oil on canvas
27 ³⁄₈ × 22" (69.5 × 55.9 cm)

Bequest of Emily G. Porter
1974-41-2

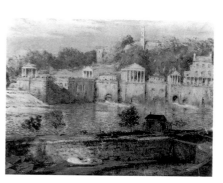

**Cooper, Colin Campbell**
*Old Waterworks, Fairmount*
1913
Lower left: Colin Campbell
Cooper 1913
Oil on canvas
38 × 48" (96.5 × 121.9 cm)

Gift of the artist
1936-50-1

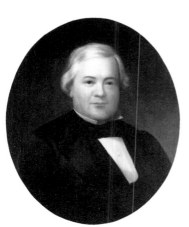

**Conarroe, George W.**
*Portrait of William Gibbs Porter*
Companion to preceding painting
After 1843
Oil on canvas
27 ¹⁄₈ × 22 ¹⁄₈" (68.9 × 56.2 cm)

Bequest of Emily G. Porter
1974-41-3

**Craig, Thomas Bigelow**
American, 1849–1924
*White Mountain Landscape*
1880
Lower left: Thom. B. Craig, 1880
Oil on canvas
30 ¹⁄₈ × 50 ³⁄₈" (76.5 × 127.9 cm)

Gift of Edgar C. Felton
1932-48-1

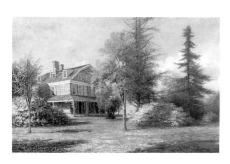

**Craig, Thomas Bigelow**
*Cedar Grove*
1890
Lower left: Thos. B. Craig, 1890;
on reverse: Painted by Thos.
Craig, 1890 for John T. Morris of
Philadelphia Pa.
Oil on canvas
18 1/2 × 26 1/2" (47 × 67.3 cm)

Bequest of Lydia Thompson
Morris
1932-45-117

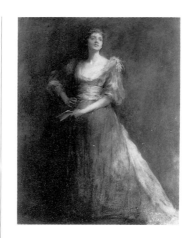

**Dewing, Thomas Wilmer**
American, 1851–1938
*Commedia*
c. 1892–94
Lower left: T W Dewing
Oil on panel
20 1/16 × 15 1/2" (51 × 39.4 cm)

The Alex Simpson, Jr., Collection
1943-74-2

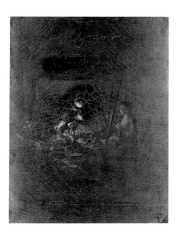

**Culverhouse, Johan Mengels**
American, born Netherlands,
1820–c. 1891
*Night Scene*
1850s
Oil on canvas
25 3/4 × 19 1/8" (65.4 × 48.6 cm)

Gift of Thatcher Longstreth
1975-70-1

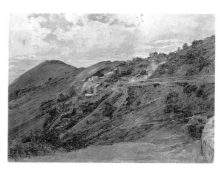

**Dodson, Sarah Paxton Ball**
American, born England,
1847–1906
*The Wyck, Malvern (A Windy Day)*
1892
Oil on canvas
14 × 18" (35.6 × 45.7 cm)

Gift of R. Ball Dodson in
memory of Sarah Ball Dodson
1926-9-1

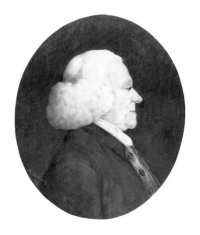

**Dantzig, Meyer**
American, active c. 1897–c. 1904
*Portrait of Captain Samuel Morris*
After the engraving by Charles-
Balthazar-Julien Fevret de Saint-
Mémin (French, 1770–1852)
1897
Lower left: M. Dantzig / 97.; on
reverse: Captain Samuel Morris,
Born 4 mo. 1734—Died 7 mo. 7,
1812.
Oil on canvas
27 × 21 15/16" (68.6 × 55.7 cm)

Bequest of Lydia Thompson
Morris
1932-45-83

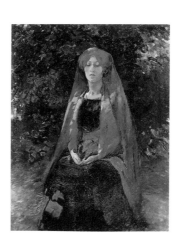

**Dodson, Sarah Paxton Ball**
*Under the Weeping Ash Tree*
1900
Oil on canvas
24 × 18" (61 × 45.7 cm)

Gift of R. Ball Dodson in
memory of Sarah Ball Dodson
1926-9-2

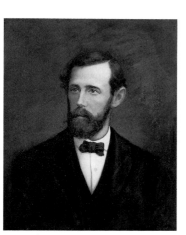

**Dantzig, Meyer**
*Portrait of James Thompson Morris*
1897
Lower right: M. DANTZIG; on
reverse: James t Morris / Born
9 mo. 18 1842 / Died 9 mo. 23
1874
Oil on canvas
27 × 22" (68.6 × 55.9 cm)

Bequest of Lydia Thompson
Morris
1932-45-120

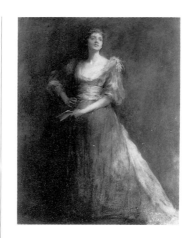

**Drexel, Francis Martin**
American, born Austria,
1792–1863
*Portrait of Edwin Jackson Haas and
His Brother*
c. 1820–25
Oil on canvas
50 1/8 × 39 11/16" (127.3 ×
100.8 cm)

Bequest of Beatrice Pastorius
Turner
1949-16-1

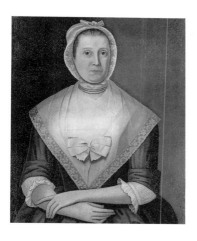

**Durand, John**
American, active 1766–1782
*Portrait of Sarah Whitehead
Hubbard*
1768
Oil on canvas
33 × 27 1/8" (83.8 × 68.9 cm)

The Collection of Edgar William
and Bernice Chrysler Garbisch
1965-209-1

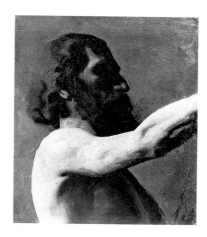

**Eakins, Thomas**
*Study of a Nude Man*
c. 1869
On reverse: T.E.
Oil on canvas
21 1/2 × 18 1/4" (54.6 × 46.4 cm)

Gift of Mrs. Thomas Eakins and
Miss Mary Adeline Williams
1929-184-9

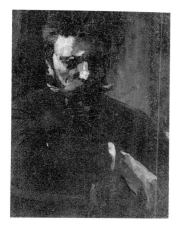

**Duveneck, Frank**
American, 1848–1919
*Portrait of William Merritt Chase*
c. 1876
Oil on canvas
20 1/8 × 15 1/16" (51.1 × 38.3 cm)

Bequest of T. Edward Hanley
1970-76-9

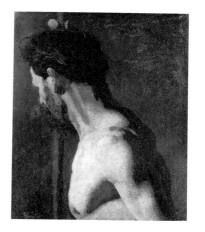

**Eakins, Thomas**
*Study of a Nude Man (The Strong
Man)*
c. 1869
On reverse: T.E.
Oil on canvas
21 1/2 × 17 5/8" (54.6 × 44.8 cm)

Gift of Mrs. Thomas Eakins and
Miss Mary Adeline Williams
1929-184-18

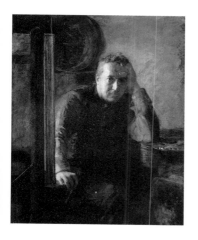

**Eakins, Susan MacDowell**
American, 1851–1938
*Portrait of Thomas Eakins*
c. 1920–25
Oil on canvas
50 × 40" (127 × 101.6 cm)

Gift of Charles Bregler
1939-11-1

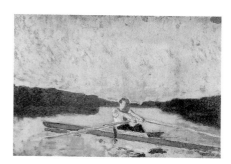

**Eakins, Thomas**
*Sketch of Max Schmitt in a Single
Scull*
c. 1870–71
Oil on canvas
10 × 14 1/4" (25.4 × 36.2 cm)

Gift of Mrs. Thomas Eakins and
Miss Mary Adeline Williams
1930-32-5

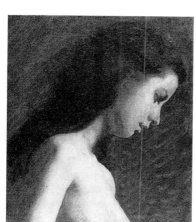

**Eakins, Thomas**
American, 1844–1916
*Study of a Young Woman*
c. 1868
Oil on canvas
17 9/16 × 14 5/16" (44.6 × 36.4 cm)

Gift of Mrs. Thomas Eakins and
Miss Mary Adeline Williams
1929-184-8

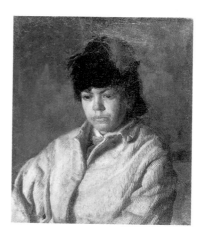

**Eakins, Thomas**
*Portrait of Margaret Eakins in a
Skating Costume*
1871
Lower right: T.E. 1871;
on reverse: Eakins
Oil on canvas
24 1/8 × 20 1/8" (61.3 × 51.1 cm)

Gift of Mrs. Thomas Eakins and
Miss Mary Adeline Williams
1929-184-14

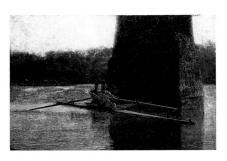

**Eakins, Thomas**
*The Pair-Oared Shell*
1872
Center right: EAKINS / 1872.;
on reverse: Eakins
Oil on canvas
24 × 36" (61 × 91.4 cm)

Gift of Mrs. Thomas Eakins and
Miss Mary Adeline Williams
1929-184-35

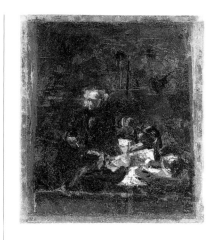

**Eakins, Thomas**
*Sketch for "The Gross Clinic"*
For the painting in the collection
of Jefferson Medical College,
Thomas Jefferson University,
Philadelphia
1875
Signed, lower right: E; lower
right: T.E. 75.; on reverse: T.E.
Oil on canvas
26 × 22" (66 × 55.9 cm)

Gift of Mrs. Thomas Eakins and
Miss Mary Adeline Williams
1929-184-31

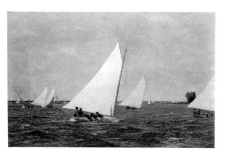

**Eakins, Thomas**
*Sailboats Racing*
1874
Center right: EAKINS / 74.;
on reverse: T.E.
Oil on canvas
24 × 36" (61 × 91.4 cm)

Gift of Mrs. Thomas Eakins and
Miss Mary Adeline Williams
1929-184-28

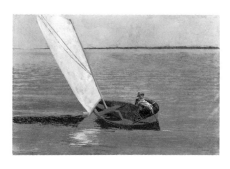

**Eakins, Thomas**
*Sailing*
c. 1875
Lower right: To his friend /
William M. Chase. / Eakins
Oil on canvas
31 ⁷/₈ × 46 ¹/₄" (81 × 117.5 cm)

The Alex Simpson, Jr., Collection
1928-63-6

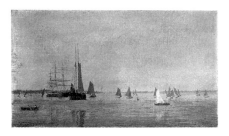

**Eakins, Thomas**
*Ships and Sailboats on the Delaware*
1874
Lower right: EAKINS 74;
on reverse: T.E.
Oil on canvas
10 ¹/₈ × 17 ¹/₈" (25.7 × 43.5 cm)

Gift of Mrs. Thomas Eakins and
Miss Mary Adeline Williams
1929-184-25

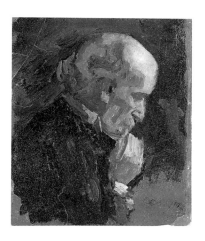

**Eakins, Thomas**
*Portrait of Bertrand Gardel*
*(Study for "The Chess Players")*
For the painting in the
Metropolitan Museum of Art,
New York (81.14)
c. 1875
Lower right: T.E.
Oil on paper on cardboard
12 ¹/₈ × 9 ³/₄" (30.8 × 24.8 cm)

Gift of Mrs. Thomas Eakins and
Miss Mary Adeline Williams
1930-32-6

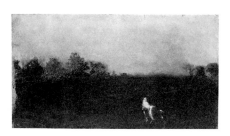

**Eakins, Thomas**
*Landscape with a Dog*
c. 1874
Oil on canvas
17 ⁷/₈ × 32" (45.4 × 81.3 cm)

Gift of Seymour Adelman
1947-96-3

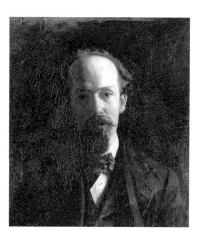

**Eakins, Thomas**
*Portrait of J. Harry Lewis*
1876
Lower right: EAKINS 76.;
on reverse: Eakins
Oil on canvas
23 ⁵/₈ × 19 ³/₄" (60 × 50.2 cm)

Gift of Mrs. Thomas Eakins and
Miss Mary Adeline Williams
1929-184-3

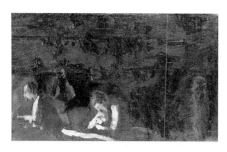

**Eakins, Thomas**
*Interior of a Woodcarver's Shop
(Sketch for "William Rush Carving
His Allegorical Figure of the
Schuylkill River")*
For the following painting
1876–77
Oil on canvas on cardboard
8 5/8 × 13" (21.9 × 33 cm)

Gift of Charles Bregler
1946-19-1

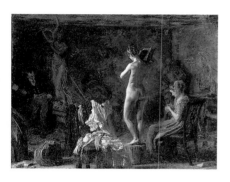

**Eakins, Thomas**
*William Rush Carving His
Allegorical Figure of the Schuylkill
River*
1876–77
Lower right: EAKINS. 77.; on
reverse: T.E.
Oil on canvas on Masonite
20 1/8 × 26 1/8" (51.1 × 66.4 cm)

Gift of Mrs. Thomas Eakins and
Miss Mary Adeline Williams
1929-184-27

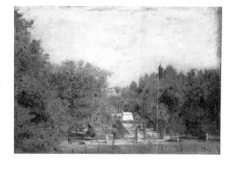

**Eakins, Thomas**
*Sketch of Lafayette Park,
Washington, D.C. (In Washington)*
1877
Lower right: T.E.
Oil on panel
10 1/2 × 14 1/2" (26.7 × 36.8 cm)

Gift of Mrs. Thomas Eakins and
Miss Mary Adeline Williams
1930-32-17

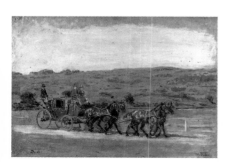

**Eakins, Thomas**
*Sketch for "The Fairman Rogers
Four-in-Hand"*
See following painting for reverse
1879
Lower right: T.E.
Oil on panel
10 1/4 × 14 1/2" (26 × 36.8 cm)

Gift of Mrs. Thomas Eakins and
Miss Mary Adeline Williams
1930-32-18a

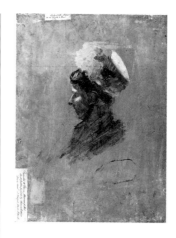

**Eakins, Thomas**
*Portrait of Mrs. Fairman Rogers
(Study for "The Fairman Rogers
Four-in-Hand")*
Reverse of the preceding painting
1879
Upper left, on label: Study of
Mrs. Rogers / for the Coach &
Four / T.E.; lower left, on label:
Presented to Penna. Museum of
Art / Small picture painted by
Thomas Eakins / "Four-in-Hand"
at Newport, Rhode Island
Oil on panel
14 1/2 × 10 1/4" (36.8 × 26 cm)

Gift of Mrs. Thomas Eakins and
Miss Mary Adeline Williams
1930-32-18b

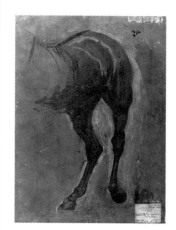

**Eakins, Thomas**
*Study of Hindquarters of Left
Leader Horse for "The Fairman
Rogers Four-in-Hand"*
See following painting for reverse
1879
Lower right, on label: Sketch
other side / "Boat-man" /
Presented to Museum / by Mrs.
Eakins / T. Eakins / Below, Study
of horses for / "Coach & Four"
Oil on panel
14 1/2 × 10 1/4" (36.8 × 26 cm)

Gift of Mrs. Thomas Eakins and
Miss Mary Adeline Williams
1930-32-11a

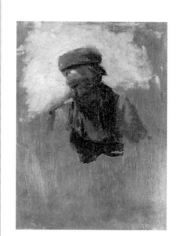

**Eakins, Thomas**
*Study of a Groom*
Reverse of the preceding painting
c. 1879
Oil on panel
14 1/2 × 10 1/4" (36.8 × 26 cm)

Gift of Mrs. Thomas Eakins and
Miss Mary Adeline Williams
1930-32-11b

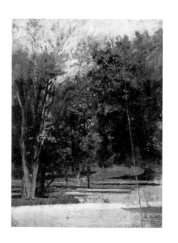

**Eakins, Thomas**
*Fairmount Park (Sketch for "The
Fairman Rogers Four-in-Hand")*
Color samples for the following
painting are on reverse
1879 or 1880
Lower right: Fair Mount Park /
T.E. / Eakins; on reverse: 'Study
in Fairmount Park'/ T.E.; on
reverse, on label: Study of
Fairmount Park / for picture of
Fairman Rogers / Four-in-Hand /
Painted by Thomas Eakins / 1879;

on reverse, on label: Presented to
Penna. Museum of Art / by Mrs.
Thos. Eakins / Study in
Fairmount Park for picture /
"Coach and Four" painted for
Fairman Rogers / by Thomas
Eakins
Oil on panel
14 9/16 × 10 1/4" (37 × 26 cm)

Gift of Mrs. Thomas Eakins and
Miss Mary Adeline Williams
1930-32-10

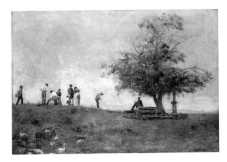

**Eakins, Thomas**
*Mending the Net*
1881
Center right: EAKINS 81.
Oil on canvas
32 1/8 × 45 1/8" (81.6 × 114.6 cm)

Gift of Mrs. Thomas Eakins and
Miss Mary Adeline Williams
1929-184-34

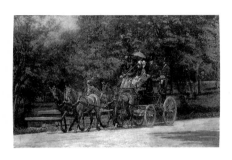

**Eakins, Thomas**
*The Fairman Rogers Four-in-Hand
(A May Morning in the Park)*
1879–80
Lower left: EAKINS. / 79
Oil on canvas
23 3/4 × 36" (60.3 × 91.4 cm)

Gift of William Alexander Dick
1930-105-1

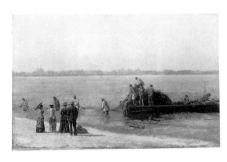

**Eakins, Thomas**
*Shad Fishing at Gloucester on the
Delaware River*
1881
On reverse: T.E.
Oil on canvas
12 1/8 × 18 1/8" (30.8 × 46 cm)

Gift of Mrs. Thomas Eakins and
Miss Mary Adeline Williams
1929-184-33

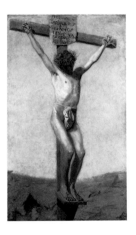

**Eakins, Thomas**
*The Crucifixion*
1880
Center top: [Greek and Latin for
"Jesus of Nazareth, King of the
Jews"]; on reverse, covered by
relining: CHRISTI EFFIGIEM
EAKINS PHIL[ADEL]PHIENSIS
PINXIT MDCCCLXXX
Oil on canvas
96 × 54" (243.8 × 137.2 cm)

Gift of Mrs. Thomas Eakins and
Miss Mary Adeline Williams
1929-184-24

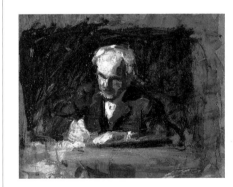

**Eakins, Thomas**
*Portrait of Benjamin Eakins
(Sketch for "The Writing Master")*
For the painting in the
Metropolitan Museum of Art,
New York (17.173); see
following painting for reverse
1882
Oil on panel
8 1/4 × 10 1/8" (20.9 × 25.7 cm)

Gift of Mrs. Thomas Eakins and
Miss Mary Adeline Williams
1930-32-4a

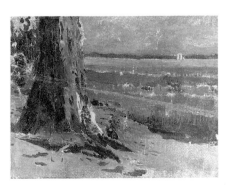

**Eakins, Thomas**
*Landscape Sketch*
c. 1880–90
Oil on canvas on cardboard
6 1/4 × 7" (15.9 × 17.8 cm)

Gift of an anonymous donor
1985-25-1

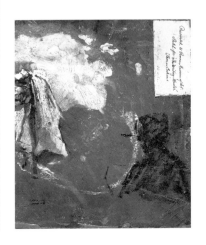

**Eakins, Thomas**
*Sketch of a Man and Study of
Drapery*
Reverse of the preceding painting
c. 1882
Upper right, on label: Presented
to Penna. Museum of Art. /
Sketch for 'The Writing Master' /
Thomas Eakins / Board 8 high 10
wide
Oil on panel
10 1/8 × 8 1/4" (25.7 × 20.9 cm)

Gift of Mrs. Thomas Eakins and
Miss Mary Adeline Williams
1930-32-4b

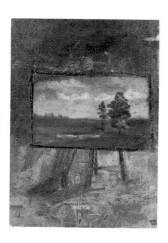

**Eakins, Thomas**
*Sketch of a Landscape*
See following painting for reverse
c. 1882
Oil on cardboard
13 × 8 ³/₄" (33 × 22.2 cm);
composition: 4 ¹/₂ × 7"
(11.4 × 17.8 cm)

Gift of Seymour Adelman
1947-96-1a

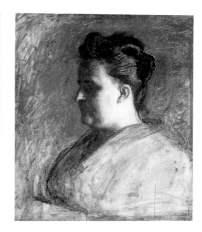

**Eakins, Thomas**
*Portrait of Blanche Hurlbut*
1885 or 1886
Lower right: Thomas Eakins
Oil on canvas
24 × 20" (61 × 50.8 cm)

Gift of Mrs. Thomas Eakins and
Miss Mary Adeline Williams
1929-184-5

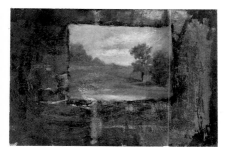

**Eakins, Thomas**
*Sketch of a Landscape*
Reverse of the preceding painting
c. 1882
Oil on cardboard
13 × 8 ³/₄" (33 × 22.2 cm);
composition: 4 ³/₄ × 6 ¹/₂"
(12.1 × 16.5 cm)

Gift of Seymour Adelman
1947-96-1b

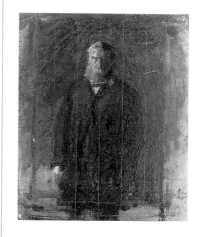

**Eakins, Thomas**
*Sketch for "Portrait of Professor
George F. Barker"*
For the painting in the Mitchell
Museum, Mount Vernon, Illinois
(1973.6.1a, b); see the following
painting for reverse
1886
Oil on cardboard
12 ³/₈ × 10 ¹/₈" (31.4 × 25.7 cm);
composition: 12 ¹/₄ × 7"
(31.1 × 17.8 cm)

Gift of Mrs. Thomas Eakins and
Miss Mary Adeline Williams
1930-32-7a

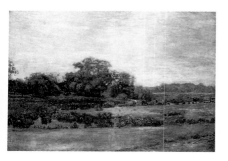

**Eakins, Thomas**
*The Meadows, Gloucester*
c. 1882
On reverse: T. EAKINS
Oil on canvas
31 ¹⁵/₁₆ × 45 ¹/₈" (81.1 × 114.6 cm)

Gift of Mrs. Thomas Eakins and
Miss Mary Adeline Williams
1929-184-32

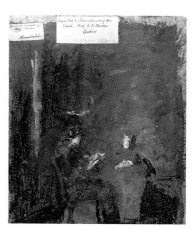

**Eakins, Thomas**
*Seated Figures*
Reverse of the preceding painting
c. 1886
Upper left, on label: Sketch for
portrait of / Prof. Barker /
Thomas Eakins; top center, on
label: Presented to Penna.
Museum of Art, / Sketch—Prof.
G. F. Barker / Eakins / 12 ¹/₈ high.
10 ¹/₈ wide
Oil on cardboard
12 ³/₈ × 10 ¹/₈" (31.4 × 25.7 cm)

Gift of Mrs. Thomas Eakins and
Miss Mary Adeline Williams
1930-32-7b

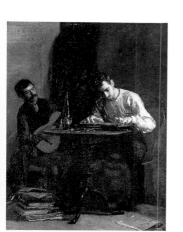

**Eakins, Thomas**
*Professionals at Rehearsal*
1883
Upper left: EAKINS
Oil on canvas
16 × 12" (40.6 × 30.5 cm)

The John D. McIlhenny
Collection
1943-40-39

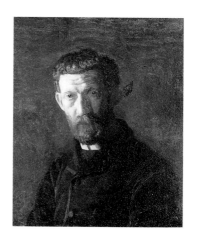

**Eakins, Thomas**
*Portrait of Arthur Burdett Frost*
c. 1886
On reverse: T.E.
Oil on canvas
27 ¹/₁₆ × 21 ¹⁵/₁₆" (68.7 × 55.7 cm)

Gift of Mrs. Thomas Eakins and
Miss Mary Adeline Williams
1929-184-1

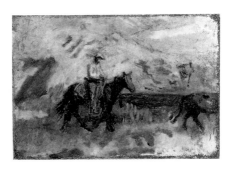

**Eakins, Thomas**
*Cowboy (Sketch for "Cowboys in the Bad Lands")*
For a painting in a private collection
1887
Oil on canvas on Masonite
10 × 14 1/4" (25.4 × 36.2 cm)

Gift of Mrs. Thomas Eakins and Miss Mary Adeline Williams
1930-32-3

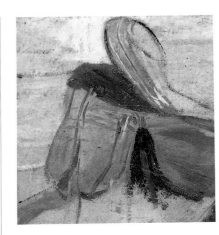

**Eakins, Thomas**
*Saddle (Sketch for "Cowboys in the Bad Lands")*
For a painting in a private collection
1887
Oil on canvas on cardboard
8 5/8 × 9 3/8" (21.9 × 23.8 cm)

Gift of Mr. and Mrs. Chaim Gross
1979-147-1

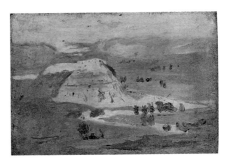

**Eakins, Thomas**
*Landscape (Sketch for "Cowboys in the Bad Lands")*
For a painting in a private collection
1887
Oil on canvas on cardboard
10 1/2 × 14 1/2" (26.7 × 36.8 cm)

Gift of Mrs. Thomas Eakins and Miss Mary Adeline Williams
1930-32-13

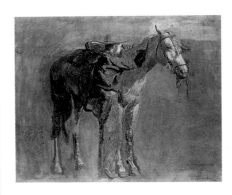

**Eakins, Thomas**
*Cowboy (Study for "Cowboys in the Bad Lands")*
For a painting in a private collection
1887–88
Lower right: Study for picture / 'Cow Boys in Bad Lands' / Eakins
Oil on canvas
20 1/16 × 24 1/16" (51 × 61.1 cm)

Gift of Mrs. Thomas Eakins and Miss Mary Adeline Williams
1930-32-12

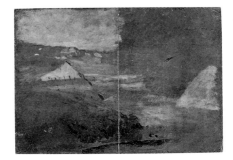

**Eakins, Thomas**
*Landscape (Sketch for "Cowboys in the Bad Lands")*
For a painting in a private collection; originally held the following painting on reverse
1887
Oil on canvas on Masonite
10 7/16 × 14 1/2" (26.5 × 36.8 cm)

Gift of Seymour Adelman
1947-96-2a

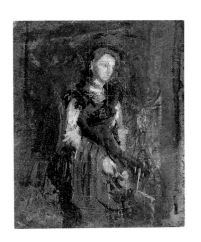

**Eakins, Thomas**
*Sketch for "Portrait of Letitia Wilson Jordan"* [later Mrs. Leonard Woolsey Bacon]
For the painting, dated 1888, in the Brooklyn Museum, New York (27.50)
c. 1888
Lower left: T.E.
Oil on cardboard on Masonite
13 3/4 × 10 3/4" (34.9 × 27.3 cm)

Gift of Mrs. Thomas Eakins and Miss Mary Adeline Williams
1930-32-8

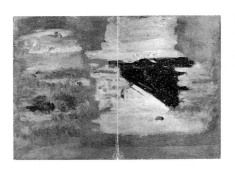

**Eakins, Thomas**
*Landscape (Sketch for "Cowboys in the Bad Lands")*
For a painting in a private collection; originally reverse of the preceding painting
1887
Oil on canvas on Masonite
10 1/4 × 14 1/2" (26 × 36.8 cm)

Gift of Seymour Adelman
1947-96-2b

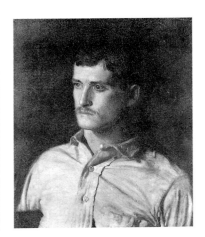

**Eakins, Thomas**
*Portrait of Douglass Morgan Hall*
c. 1889
Oil on canvas
24 × 20" (61 × 50.8 cm)

Gift of Mrs. William E. Studdiford
1975-90-1

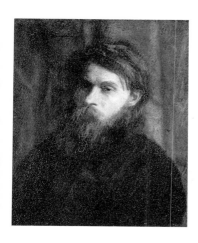

**Eakins, Thomas**
*The Bohemian (Portrait of Franklin Louis Schenck)*
c. 1890
Lower right: EAKINS; on reverse: T.E.
Oil on canvas
23 7/8 × 19 3/4" (60.6 × 50.2 cm)

Gift of Mrs. Thomas Eakins and Miss Mary Adeline Williams
1929-184-15

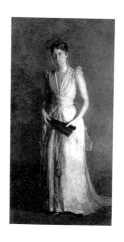

**Eakins, Thomas**
*The Black Fan (Portrait of Mrs. Talcott Williams)*
c. 1891
Oil on canvas
80 1/16 × 40 1/16" (203.4 × 101.8 cm)

Gift of Mrs. Thomas Eakins and Miss Mary Adeline Williams
1929-184-30

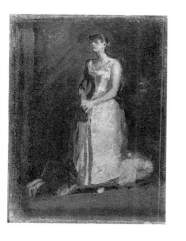

**Eakins, Thomas**
*The Red Shawl*
c. 1890
On reverse: Eakins
Oil on canvas
24 × 20" (61 × 50.8 cm)

Gift of Mrs. Thomas Eakins and Miss Mary Adeline Williams
1929-184-11

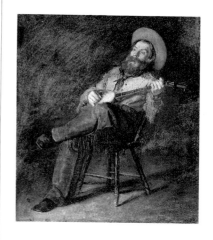

**Eakins, Thomas**
*Cowboy Singing*
c. 1892
Lower right: Eakins
Oil on canvas
24 × 20" (61 × 50.8 cm)

Gift of Mrs. Thomas Eakins and Miss Mary Adeline Williams
1929-184-22

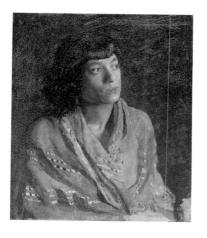

**Eakins, Thomas**
*Sketch for "The Concert Singer"*
For the following painting
c. 1890
Oil on canvas on cardboard
13 3/4 × 10 3/8" (34.9 × 26.4 cm); composition: 13 × 8 1/2" (33 × 21.6 cm)

Gift of Mrs. Thomas Eakins and Miss Mary Adeline Williams
1929-184-20

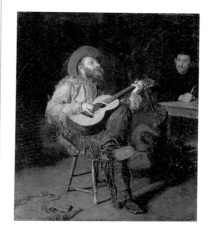

**Eakins, Thomas**
*Home Ranch*
1892
Center right: EAKINS 92; on reverse: T.E.
Oil on canvas
24 × 20" (61 × 50.8 cm)

Gift of Mrs. Thomas Eakins and Miss Mary Adeline Williams
1929-184-12

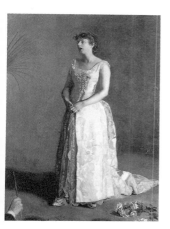

**Eakins, Thomas**
*The Concert Singer*
1890–92
Upper right: EAKINS. / 92.
Oil on canvas
75 1/8 × 54 1/4" (190.8 × 137.8 cm)

Gift of Mrs. Thomas Eakins and Miss Mary Adeline Williams
1929-184-19

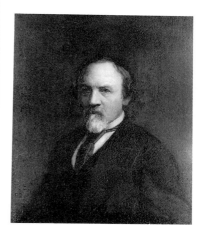

**Eakins, Thomas**
*Portrait of Joshua Ballinger Lippincott*
1892
Lower left: T.E. / 92.
Oil on canvas
30 1/8 × 25" (76.5 × 63.5 cm)

Gift of Mrs. Bertha Coles in memory of Mrs. Stricker Coles
1967-37-1

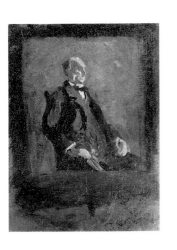

**Eakins, Thomas**
*Sketch for "Portrait of Dr. Jacob Mendez da Costa"*
For the painting in the collection of the Pennsylvania Hospital, Philadelphia
c. 1893
Lower right: Sketch / T.E.
Oil on canvas on cardboard
14 1/2 × 10 1/2" (36.8 × 26.7 cm); composition: 8 3/4 × 7 1/2" (22.2 × 19.1 cm)

Gift of Mrs. Thomas Eakins and Miss Mary Adeline Williams
1930-32-16

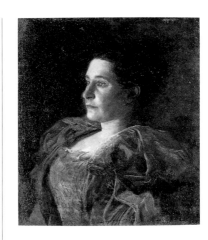

**Eakins, Thomas**
*Portrait of Mrs. James Mapes Dodge* [née Josephine Kern]
1896
Lower right: EAKINS 96 / to his friend / James M. Dodge
Oil on canvas
24 1/8 × 20 1/8" (61.3 × 51.1 cm)

Gift of Mrs. James Mapes Dodge
1951-79-1

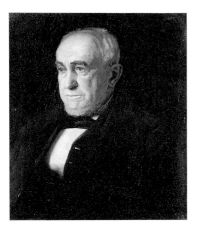

**Eakins, Thomas**
*Portrait of Benjamin Eakins*
c. 1894
Oil on canvas
24 1/8 × 20" (61.3 × 50.8 cm)

Gift of Mrs. Thomas Eakins and Miss Mary Adeline Williams
1929-184-36

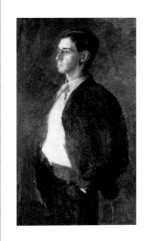

**Eakins, Thomas**
*The Young Man (Portrait of Kern Dodge)*
c. 1898–1902
Oil on canvas
45 3/16 × 26 1/8" (114.8 × 66.4 cm)

Gift of Mrs. Thomas Eakins and Miss Mary Adeline Williams
1929-184-21

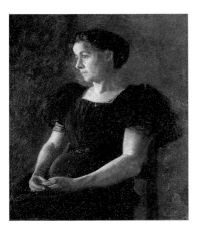

**Eakins, Thomas**
*Portrait of Mrs. Frank Hamilton Cushing*
1895
Lower right: T.E.
Oil on canvas
26 3/16 × 22" (66.5 × 55.9 cm)

Gift of Mrs. Thomas Eakins and Miss Mary Adeline Williams
1929-184-4

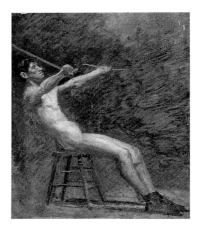

**Eakins, Thomas**
*Portrait of Billy Smith (Study for "Between Rounds")*
For the following painting
c. 1898
On reverse: T.E.
Oil on canvas
20 × 16" (50.8 × 40.6 cm)

Gift of Mrs. Thomas Eakins and Miss Mary Adeline Williams
1929-184-17

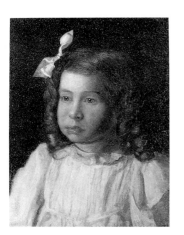

**Eakins, Thomas**
*Portrait of a Little Girl*
c. 1895–1900
Lower right: EAKINS
Oil on canvas
16 1/8 × 12 1/8" (41 × 30.8 cm)

The Louis E. Stern Collection
1963-181-25

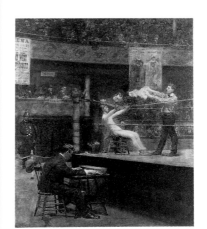

**Eakins, Thomas**
*Between Rounds*
1899
Lower right: EAKINS. 99.
Oil on canvas
50 1/8 × 39 7/8" (127.3 × 101.3 cm)

Gift of Mrs. Thomas Eakins and Miss Mary Adeline Williams
1929-184-16

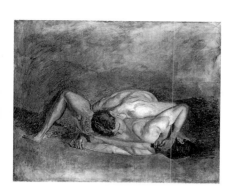

**Eakins, Thomas**
*Wrestlers*
A later, finished version is in the
Columbus Museum of Art, Ohio
(70.38)
1899
Oil on canvas
40 × 50 1/16" (101.6 × 127.2 cm)

Bequest of Fiske and Marie
Kimball
1955-86-14

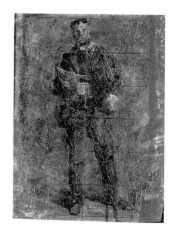

**Eakins, Thomas**
*Sketch for "Portrait of Leslie W.
Miller"*
For the following painting; *Sketch
of Harry* originally on reverse
1901
Oil on cardboard on panel
13 3/8 × 9 5/8" (34 × 24.4 cm);
composition: 13 1/4 × 8"
(33.7 × 20.3 cm)

Gift of Percy Chase Miller
1945-33-1

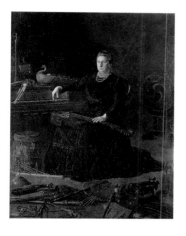

**Eakins, Thomas**
*Portrait of Mrs. William D.
Frishmuth (Antiquated Music)*
1900
Lower right: EAKINS. 1900.
Oil on canvas
97 × 72" (246.4 × 182.9 cm)

Gift of Mrs. Thomas Eakins and
Miss Mary Adeline Williams
1929-184-7

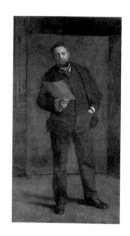

**Eakins, Thomas**
*Portrait of Leslie W. Miller*
1901
Lower right: Eakins / 1901.
Oil on burlap
88 × 44" (223.5 × 111.8 cm)

Gift of Martha Page Laughlin
Seeler in memory of Edgar
Viguers Seeler
1932-13-1

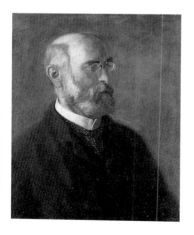

**Eakins, Thomas**
*Portrait of Dr. Edward J. Nolan*
c. 1900
Lower right: EAKINS; on reverse:
T.E.
Oil on canvas
24 × 20" (61 × 50.8 cm)

Gift of Mrs. Thomas Eakins and
Miss Mary Adeline Williams
1929-184-2

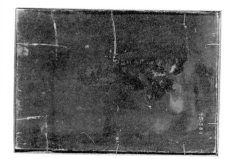

**Eakins, Thomas**
*Sketch of Harry*
Originally on reverse of *Sketch for
"Portrait of Leslie W. Miller"*
c. 1901
Oil on cardboard on hardboard
9 5/8 × 13 3/8" (24.4 × 34 cm)

Gift of Percy Chase Miller
1945-33-2

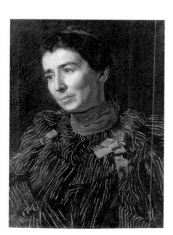

**Eakins, Thomas**
*Portrait of Mary Adeline Williams
(Addie)*
c. 1900
On reverse: T.E.
Oil on canvas
24 1/8 × 18 1/8" (61.3 × 46 cm)

Gift of Mrs. Thomas Eakins and
Miss Mary Adeline Williams
1929-184-10

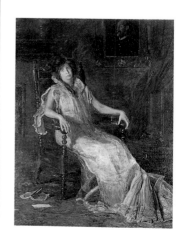

**Eakins, Thomas**
*Actress (Portrait of Suzanne Santje)*
[née Suzanne Keyser]
1903
Lower left: Eakins / 1903; lower
left, on letter: Miss Suzanne
Santje / Roanoke / Va.
Oil on canvas
79 3/4 × 59 7/8" (202.6 × 152.1 cm)

Gift of Mrs. Thomas Eakins and
Miss Mary Adeline Williams
1929-184-23

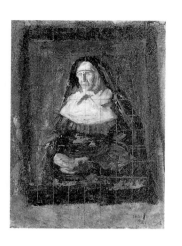

**Eakins, Thomas**
*Sketch for "Portrait of Mother Patricia Waldron"*
For a lost painting
1903
Lower right: Sketch / T.E.
Oil on canvas on Masonite
14 3/8 × 10 1/2" (36.5 × 26.7 cm);
composition: 9 1/2 × 7 1/2"
(24.1 × 19.1 cm)

Gift of Mrs. Thomas Eakins and
Miss Mary Adeline Williams
1930-32-14

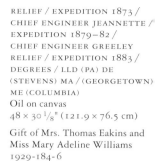

RELIEF / EXPEDITION 1873 /
CHIEF ENGINEER JEANNETTE /
EXPEDITION 1879–82 /
CHIEF ENGINEER GREELEY
RELIEF / EXPEDITION 1883 /
DEGREES / LLD (PA) DE
(STEVENS) MA / (GEORGETOWN)
ME (COLUMBIA)
Oil on canvas
48 × 30 1/8" (121.9 × 76.5 cm)

Gift of Mrs. Thomas Eakins and
Miss Mary Adeline Williams
1929-184-6

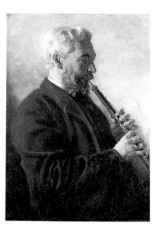

**Eakins, Thomas**
*The Oboe Player (Portrait of Dr. Benjamin Sharp)*
1903
Lower left: EAKINS 1903
Oil on canvas
36 1/8 × 24 1/8" (91.8 × 61.3 cm)

Gift of Mrs. Benjamin Sharp
1946-77-1

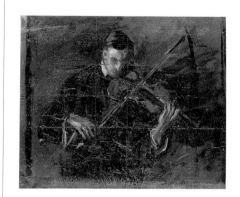

**Eakins, Thomas**
*Sketch for "Music" (The Violinist)*
For the painting in the Albright-
Knox Art Gallery, Buffalo
(inv. no. 55.4)
c. 1904
Oil on canvas on cardboard
13 × 14 7/8" (33 × 37.8 cm)
composition: 11 1/2 × 13 1/2"
(29.2 × 34.3 cm)

Gift of Mrs. Thomas Eakins and
Miss Mary Adeline Williams
1930-32-9

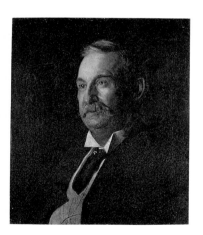

**Eakins, Thomas**
*Portrait of Edward Taylor Snow*
1904
On reverse: TO MY FRIEND /
E. TAYLOR SNOW / THOMAS
EAKINS / 1904
Oil on canvas
24 1/16 × 20 1/8" (61.1 × 51.1 cm)

Bequest of Mrs. Laura Elliot
Harmstad
1953-120-1

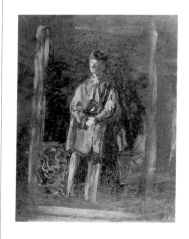

**Eakins, Thomas**
*Sketch for "Portrait of Monsignor James P. Turner"*
For the painting in the Nelson-
Atkins Museum of Art, Kansas
City, Missouri (F38-41); see the
following painting for reverse
c. 1906
Lower right: Sketch / T.E.
Oil on cardboard
14 1/2 × 10 1/2" (36.8 × 26.7 cm);
composition: 12 1/2 × 6 1/2"
(31.8 × 16.5 cm)

Gift of Mrs. Thomas Eakins and
Miss Mary Adeline Williams
1930-32-15a

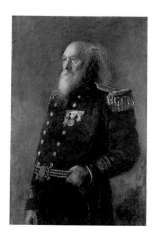

**Eakins, Thomas**
*Portrait of Rear Admiral George Wallace Melville*
1904
Lower right: EAKINS / 1904.;
on reverse: REAR ADMIRAL /
GEORGE WALLACE MELVILLE
U S N / BORN NEW YORK CITY
JANUARY 10 1841 / ENTERED
U S NAVY JULY 29, 1861. / 1881
CHIEF ENGINEER / 1887
ENGINEER IN CHIEF / 1898
REAR ADMIRAL / 1904 RETIRED.
/ MEMBER OF THE HALL

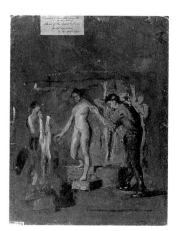

**Eakins, Thomas**
*Sketch for "William Rush and His Model"*
For the painting in the Honolulu
Academy of Arts (548.1); reverse
of the preceding painting
c. 1908
Upper left, on label: Presented to
Penna. Museum of Art. / by Mrs.
Eakins / Sketch of Rev. James P.
Turner / for Life size portrait / by
Thos. Eakins 1906; lower left, on
label: Sketch in studio / 7-5
Oil on cardboard
14 1/2 × 10 1/2" (36.8 × 26.7 cm)

Gift of Mrs. Thomas Eakins and
Miss Mary Adeline Williams
1930-32-15b

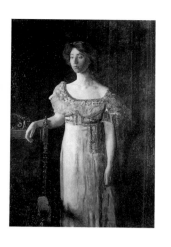

**Eakins, Thomas**
*The Old-Fashioned Dress (Portrait of Helen Parker)*
c. 1908
Lower right: T.E.; on reverse: T. Eakins
Oil on canvas
60 1/8 × 40 3/16" (152.7 × 102.1 cm)

Gift of Mrs. Thomas Eakins and Miss Mary Adeline Williams
1929-184-29

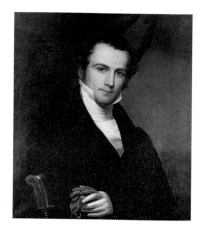

**Eichholtz, Jacob**
*Portrait of Josiah Stewart*
c. 1825
Oil on canvas
29 3/4 × 25" (75.6 × 63.5 cm)

Bequest of Emily Stewart Smith
1951-2-1

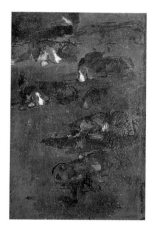

**Eakins, Thomas, attributed to**
*Views of Harry*
c. 1890–1900
Oil on canvasboard
21 × 14" (53.3 × 35.6 cm)

Gift of Mr. and Mrs. Ulrich W. Hiesinger in honor of Bea Garvan
1981-66-1

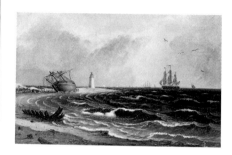

**Eichholtz, Jacob**
*Cape Henlopen*
After the painting by Thomas Birch (American, 1779–1851), in the Museum of Fine Arts, Boston (62.261)
1832
Oil on canvas
20 1/8 × 29 7/8" (51.1 × 75.9 cm)

Gift of Mrs. William M. Wills
1930-50-2

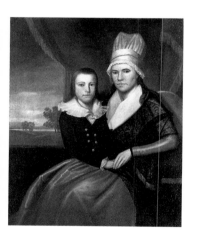

**Earl, Ralph**
American, 1751–1801
*Portrait of Sara Bradley and Her Son*
c. 1788
Oil on canvas
44 × 35 3/4" (111.8 × 90.8 cm)

The Collection of Edgar William and Bernice Chrysler Garbisch
1972-262-7

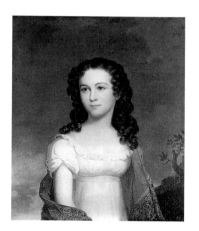

**Eichholtz, Jacob**
*Portrait of Miss Julia Nicklin*
1837
Lower right: J.E / 1837
Oil on canvas
30 1/8 × 25 5/16" (76.5 × 64.3 cm)

Gift of Peter T. Hornor
1956-40-1

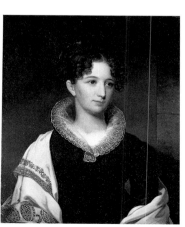

**Eichholtz, Jacob**
American, 1776–1842
*Portrait of Eliza Teackle Montgomery*
1822
Oil on canvas
30 1/8 × 25" (76.5 × 63.5 cm)

Purchased for the Cadwalader Collection with funds contributed by the Mabel Pew Myrin Trust and the gift of an anonymous donor
1983-90-11

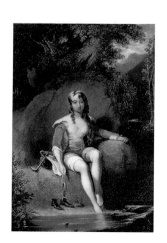

**Eichholtz, Jacob**
*Dorothea*
1841
Lower right: J. E. / 1841
Oil on canvas
20 1/16 × 13 3/4" (51 × 34.9 cm)

Gift of Mrs. William M. Wills
1930-50-3

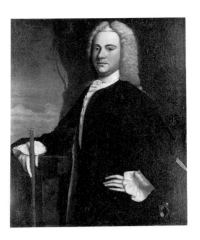

**Feke, Robert**
American, born c. 1705,
still active 1750
*Portrait of Dr. Phineas Bond*
1750
Oil on canvas
40 × 32 1/2" (101.6 × 82.5 cm)

Gift of Phyllis Cochran Denby in
memory of her uncle, George
Bond Cochran
1963-191-1

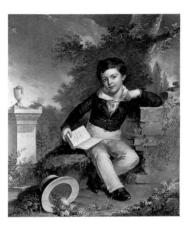

**França, Manuel Joachim de**
American, born Portugal,
1808–1865
*Portrait of Matthew Hinzinga
Messchert*
1839
On monument: SACRED / To the
Memory of / ELIZABETH A.
MESSCHERT / Born Sept 14 1809
/ Died May 20 1839; on book:
To / M. H. Messchert / a
Remembrance / from his /
Mother; on reverse: M. J. de
Franca / Pinxit Aug' 9 1839 /
Matthew Hinzinga Messchert /
Aged 8 years and 5 months /
Born March 1831
Oil on canvas
50 1/8 × 40 1/4" (127.3 × 102.2 cm)

Gift of Dr. and Mrs. Harold Lefft
1965-214-1

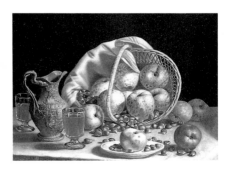

**Francis, John F.**
American, c. 1808–1886
*Still Life with Apples*
1858
Lower left: J. F. Francis. pt. 1858.
Oil on canvas
22 7/8 × 30 1/8" (58.1 × 76.5 cm)

Gift of the Haas family in
memory of Joseph S. Haas
1979-32-1

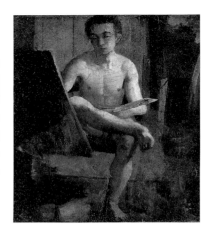

**Fussell, Charles Lewis**
American, 1840–1909
*A Young Art Student (Portrait of
Thomas Eakins)*
c. 1860–65
Oil on paper on canvas
15 × 13" (38.1 × 33 cm)

Gift of Seymour Adelman
1946-73-1

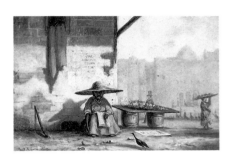

**Gifford, Robert Swain**
American, 1840–1905
*Our American Cousin*
1860
Lower left: R. S. Gifford 1860;
center: OUR AMERICAN COUSIN
Oil on millboard
6 13/16 × 10" (17.3 × 25.4 cm)

The W. P. Wilstach Collection,
bequest of Anna H. Wilstach
W1893-1-46

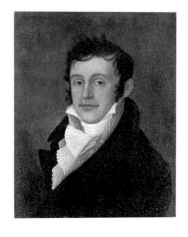

**Greenwood, Ethan Allen**
American, 1779–1856
*Portrait of a Man Wearing a
Brown-and-White Striped Vest*
Companion to the following
painting
1810
Lower left: E. A. Greenwood /
Pinxit 1810
Oil on canvas
24 1/8 × 18" (61.3 × 45.7 cm)

The Collection of Edgar William
and Bernice Chrysler Garbisch
1972-262-3

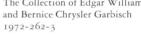

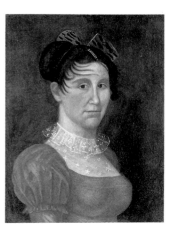

**Greenwood, Ethan Allen**
*Portrait of a Woman Wearing a Red
Dress and Combs*
Companion to the preceding
painting
1810
Lower right: E. A. Greenwood /
Pinxit 1810
Oil on canvas
24 1/8 × 18" (61.3 × 45.7 cm)

The Collection of Edgar William
and Bernice Chrysler Garbisch
1972-262-4

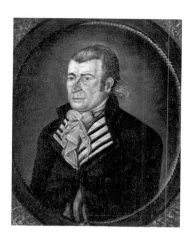

**Gullager, Christian, attributed to**
American, born Denmark, 1759–1826
*Portrait of Ebenezer Bancroft*
c. 1785–90
Oil on canvas
29 × 23 9/16" (73.7 × 59.8 cm)

Centennial gift of Mrs. Francis P. Garvan
1976-164-4

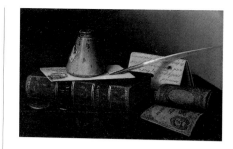

**Harnett, William Michael**
*Still Life with a Writing Table*
1877
Lower left: WMHARNETT / 1877
Oil on canvas
8 1/16 × 12 13/16" (20.5 × 32.5 cm)

The Alex Simpson, Jr., Collection
1943-74-4

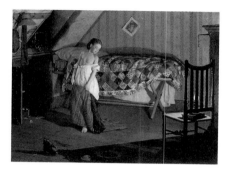

**Guy, Seymour Joseph**
American, born England, 1824–1910
*Making a Train*
1867
Lower left: SJGuy. 1867
Oil on canvas
18 1/8 × 24 1/8" (46 × 61.3 cm)

The George W. Elkins Collection
E1924-4-14

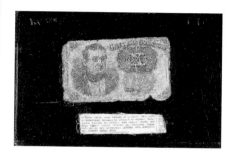

**Harnett, William Michael**
*Still Life with a Ten-Cent Bill (Shinplaster)*
1879
Upper left: WMHARNETT; upper right: 1879
Oil on cardboard
5 9/16 × 7 5/8" (14.1 × 19.4 cm)

The Alex Simpson, Jr., Collection
1943-74-6

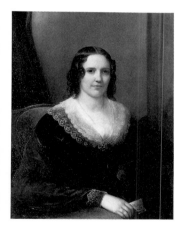

**Harding, Chester**
American, 1792–1866
*Portrait of Fanny Hayes*
1840s
Oil on canvas
36 1/4 × 28 1/8" (92.1 × 71.4 cm)

Bequest of T. Edward Hanley
1970-76-3

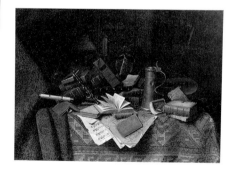

**Harnett, William Michael**
*Still Life*
1882
Lower left: WMHARNETT / MUNCHEN / 1882
Oil on canvas
7 1/4 × 11 7/8" (18.4 × 30.2 cm)

The Albert M. Greenfield and Elizabeth M. Greenfield Collection
1974-178-32

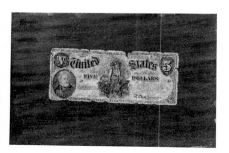

**Harnett, William Michael**
American, 1848–1892
*Still Life—Five-Dollar Bill*
1877
Upper left: WMHarnett / 1877
Oil on canvas
8 × 12 1/8" (20.3 × 30.8 cm)

The Alex Simpson, Jr., Collection
1943-74-5

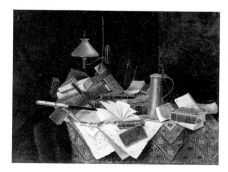

**Harnett, William Michael, copy after**
Previously listed as William Michael Harnett (PMA 1965)
*Still Life*
After the painting, dated 1882, in the Munson-Williams-Proctor Institute Museum of Art, Utica, New York (57.67)
After 1882
Lower right (spurious): WMHARNETT
Oil on canvas
12 × 16" (30.5 × 40.6 cm)

The Gertrude Schemm Binder Collection
1951-84-1

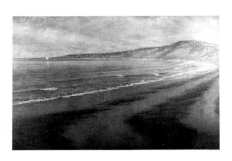

**Harrison, Alexander**
American, 1853–1930
*Coast Scene*
1882
Lower right: A. Harrison
Oil on canvas
24 1/8 × 36 1/4" (61.3 × 92.1 cm)

John G. Johnson Collection
cat. 998

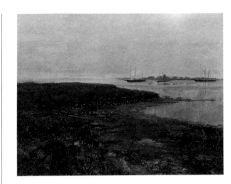

**Harrison, Alexander**
*Three Schooners at Anchor*
c. 1890–1913
Lower left: Alex–Harrison
Oil on canvas on panel
25 3/8 × 32 1/8" (64.4 × 81.6 cm)

John G. Johnson Collection
cat. 1000

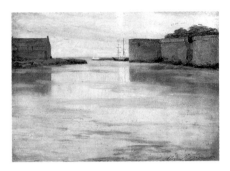

**Harrison, Alexander**
*Harbor of Concarneau*
c. 1882–92
Lower right: Alex Harrison
Oil on panel
10 1/4 × 13 3/4" (26 × 34.9 cm)

John G. Johnson Collection
cat. 1001

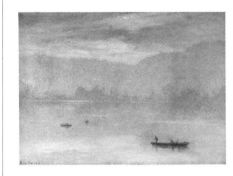

**Harrison, Lowell Birge**
American, 1854–1929
*Misty Morn*
c. 1900–15
Lower left: Birge Harrison
Oil on canvas
17 × 23 1/4" (43.2 × 59 cm)

The Alex Simpson, Jr., Collection
1943-74-3

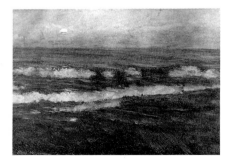

**Harrison, Alexander**
*Moonlight Marine*
c. 1882–92
Lower left: Alex Harrison
Oil on canvas
23 1/2 × 32" (59.7 × 81.3 cm)

John G. Johnson Collection
cat. 999

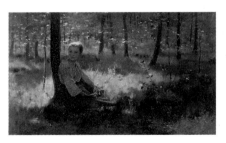

**Harrison, Lowell Birge**
*Girl in a Wood*
1920
On reverse: M. Chabod / Md. de
Couleurs / & Toiels a Tableaux /
Re Jacob, 20
Oil on canvas
19 5/8 × 30 3/4" (49.8 × 78.1 cm)

John G. Johnson Collection
cat. 1002

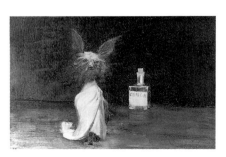

**Harrison, Alexander**
*Caricature of John G. Johnson as a
Sick Dog*
c. 1883–1908
Lower left: To Mrs. Johnson;
lower right: With kind regards /
Alex Harrison; on bottle: COUGH
Oil on canvas
15 7/8 × 24 1/8" (40.3 × 61.3 cm)

John G. Johnson Collection
inv. 2827

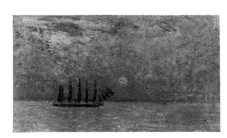

**Hassam, Childe**
American, 1859–1935
*Boat off East Hampton*
1909
On reverse: Childe Hassam /
1909
Oil on panel
5 5/8 × 9 1/4" (14.3 × 23.5 cm)

The Louis E. Stern Collection
1963-181-32

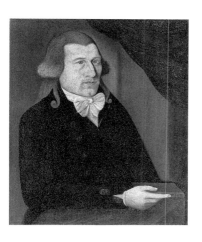

**Hathaway, Rufus**
American, 1770–1822
*Portrait of the Reverend Nehemiah Thomas*
1794
On reverse: Nehemiah Thomas age 28, June 10th 1794—/ Ordained Nov. 12th, 1792 this likeness / was taken by Dr. Rufus Hathaway of Duxbury / June 10th, 1794.
Oil on canvas on panel
29 1/4 × 24 1/4" (74.3 × 61.6 cm)

The Collection of Edgar William and Bernice Chrysler Garbisch
1972-262-10

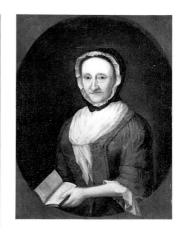

**Hesselius, Gustavus**
American, born Sweden,
1682–1755
*Portrait of a Woman*
1751
On book: O Lord I give / thee praise / for health / strength / length of / days my Age / Being Seventy- / two years and / five days April / the 25 : 1751
Oil on canvas
32 7/8 × 24 11/16" (83.5 × 62.7 cm)

Gift of Mr. and Mrs. William F. Machold
1978-100-1

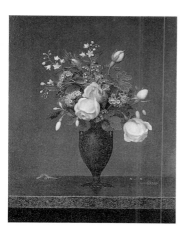

**Heade, Martin Johnson**
American, 1819–1904
*Still Life with Flowers*
c. 1865–70
Oil on canvas
18 1/4 × 14 5/16" (46.3 × 36.3 cm)

Bequest of Lisa Norris Elkins
1950-92-5

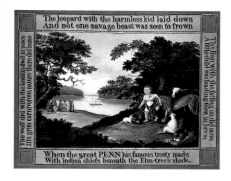

**Hicks, Edward**
American, 1780–1849
*The Peaceable Kingdom*
1826
On border: The wolf did with the lambkin dwell in peace / His grim carnivorous nature there did cease / The leopard with the harmless kid laid down / And not one savage beast was seen to frown / The lion with the fatling on did move / A little child was leading them in love; / When the great PENN his famous treaty made / With indian chiefs beneath the Elm-tree's shade.; on reverse: Edw. Hicks painter / New-town Bucks County / Penna. 8 moth. 26th / 1826
Oil on canvas
32 7/8 × 41 3/4" (83.5 × 106 cm)

Bequest of Charles C. Willis
1956-59-1

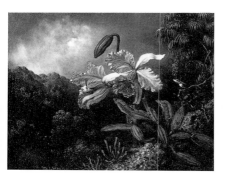

**Heade, Martin Johnson**
*Orchids in a Jungle*
1870s
Lower left: M J. Heade
Oil on canvas
16 3/16 × 20 1/4" (41.1 × 51.4 cm)

Bequest of Charlotte Dorrance Wright
1978-1-48

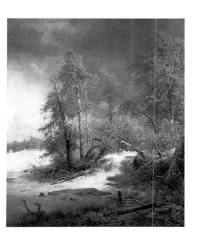

**Herzog, Hermann**
American, born Germany,
1832–1932
*Goat Island, Niagara Falls*
1878
Lower left: H. Herzog, 1878
Oil on canvas
56 × 47 3/4" (142.2 × 121.3 cm)

Bequest of Arthur H. Lea
F1938-1-117

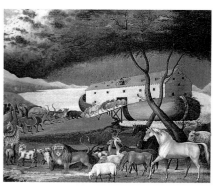

**Hicks, Edward**
*Noah's Ark*
1846
Oil on canvas
26 5/16 × 30 3/8" (66.8 × 77.1 cm)

Bequest of Lisa Norris Elkins
1950-92-7

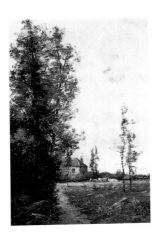

**Hilliard, William Henry**
American, 1836–1905
*Pasturage near Rapendrecht,
Holland*
c. 1880–1900
Lower right: W.H. Hilliard
Oil on canvas
24 1/8 × 16 1/8" (61.3 × 41 cm)

The Walter Lippincott Collection
1923-59-15

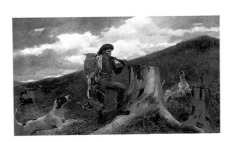

**Homer, Winslow**
*A Huntsman and Dogs*
1891
Lower right: Winslow Homer
1891
Oil on canvas
28 1/8 × 48" (71.4 × 121.9 cm)

The William L. Elkins Collection
E1924-3-8

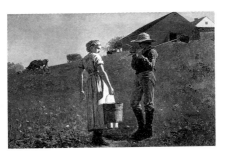

**Homer, Winslow**
American, 1836–1910
*Farm at Gloucester*
1874
Lower right: WINSLOW HOMER.
N. A / 1874
Oil on canvas
20 3/8 × 30 1/8" (51.7 × 76.5 cm)

Purchased with the John Howard
McFadden, Jr., Fund
1956-118-1

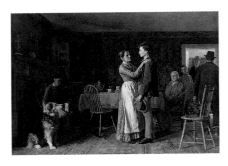

**Hovenden, Thomas**
American, born Ireland,
1840–1895
*Breaking Home Ties*
1890
Lower right: T HOVENDEN 1890
/ COPYRIGHTED 1891
Oil on canvas
52 1/8 × 72 1/4" (132.4 × 183.5 cm)

Gift of Ellen Harrison McMichael
in memory of C. Emory
McMichael
1942-60-1

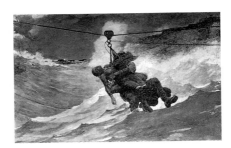

**Homer, Winslow**
*The Life Line*
1884
Lower right: WINSLOW HOMER /
1884
Oil on canvas
28 5/8 × 44 3/4" (72.7 × 113.7 cm)

The George W. Elkins Collection
E1924-4-15

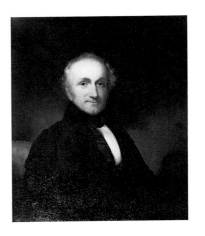

**Inman, Henry**
American, 1801–1846
*Portrait of Moses Seixas*
1837
Oil on canvas
30 1/8 × 25 3/16" (76.5 × 64 cm)

Gift of an anonymous donor
1941-78-1

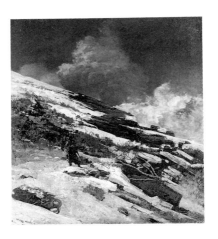

**Homer, Winslow**
*Winter Coast*
1890
Lower left: Winslow Homer /
1890
Oil on canvas
36 1/8 × 31 11/16" (91.8 × 80.5 cm)

John G. Johnson Collection
cat. 1004

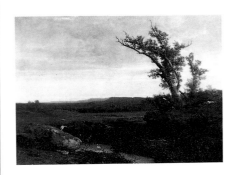

**Inness, George**
American, 1825–1894
*Twilight on the Campagna*
Early 1850s
Oil on canvas
37 7/8 × 53 5/8" (96.2 × 136.2 cm)

The Alex Simpson, Jr., Collection
1945-5-1

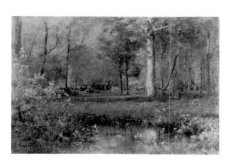

**Inness, George**
*Landscape with Yellow Bushes*
1865
Lower left: G. Inness 1865
Oil on canvas on panel
12 1/16 × 18 1/8" (30.6 × 46 cm)

John G. Johnson Collection
cat. 1005

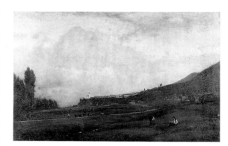

**Inness, George**
*Valley of Cadore, Italy*
1873
Lower right: G. Inness Rome
1873
Oil on canvas
16 3/16 × 24 5/16" (41.1 × 61.7 cm)

John G. Johnson Collection
cat. 1007

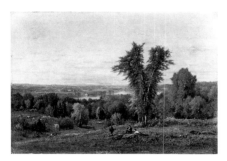

**Inness, George**
*Landscape near Medfield,*
*Massachusetts*
1868
Lower right: G. Inness 1868
Oil on panel
12 1/4 × 17 1/4" (31.1 × 43.8 cm)

The John D. McIlhenny
Collection
1943-40-48

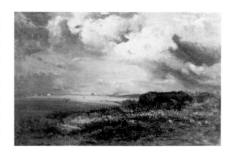

**Inness, George**
*Roman Campagna (Passing Shower)*
1875
Lower right: G. Inness 1875
Oil on canvas
20 1/8 × 31 1/2" (51.1 × 80 cm)

Gift of Lucie Washington
Mitcheson in memory of Robert
Stockton Johnson Mitcheson for
the Robert Stockton Johnson
Mitcheson Collection
1938-22-9

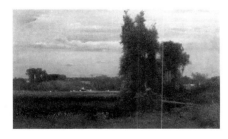

**Inness, George**
*Evening Landscape*
c. 1868
Lower right: G. Inness
Oil on canvas
14 3/4 × 23 1/2" (37.5 × 59.7 cm)

Bequest of R. Nelson Buckley
1943-85-1

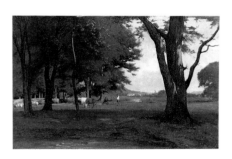

**Inness, George**
*Summer Landscape*
1876
Lower right: G. Inness 1876
Oil on canvas
30 1/4 × 45 1/4" (76.8 × 114.9 cm)

The William L. Elkins Collection
E1924-3-9

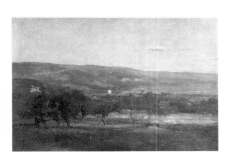

**Inness, George**
*Landscape*
c. 1871
Lower right: G. Inness
Oil on canvas
14 1/2 × 21 1/2" (36.8 × 54.6 cm)

Gift of Miss Anna Catherine
Stinson in memory of Mary
Arthur Burnham
1930-7-1

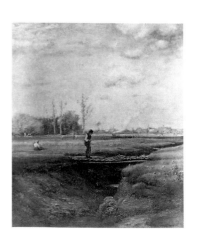

**Inness, George**
*Short Cut, Watchung Station,*
*New Jersey*
1883
Lower right: G. Inness 1883
Oil on canvas
37 5/8 × 29 1/8" (95.6 × 74 cm)

Purchased with the W. P.
Wilstach Fund
W1895-1-5

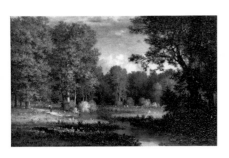

**Inness, George**
*Landscape with a Stream*
1885
Lower left: Inness
Oil on canvas
12 1/16 × 18 3/16" (30.6 × 46.2 cm)

John G. Johnson Collection
cat. 1006

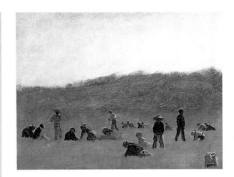

**Johnson, Eastman**
*Cranberry Pickers*
c. 1879
Oil on cardboard
13 15/16 × 17 1/2" (35.4 × 44.4 cm)

Gift of Mr. and Mrs. Arthur U.
Crosby
1974-229-1

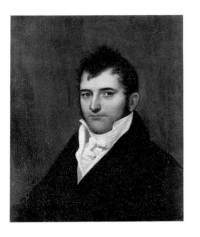

**Jarvis, John Wesley**
American, 1780–1840
*Self-Portrait*
c. 1810
Oil on canvas
23 7/8 × 19 5/8" (60.6 × 49.8 cm)

Bequest of T. Edward Hanley
1970-76-6

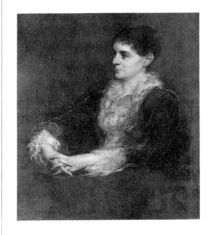

**Johnson, Eastman**
*Portrait of Mrs. Allen Shelden*
c. 1885
Lower left: E. J.
Oil on canvas
36 1/4 × 30 1/8" (92.1 × 76.5 cm)

The Alex Simpson, Jr., Collection
1928-63-7

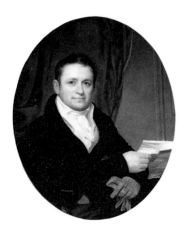

**Jarvis, John Wesley**
*Portrait of William Norris*
1813
On label on reverse: Willm
Norris / Son of Joseph / Born in
Lancaster County / Virginia in
the year of our / Lord 1774 the 21
March / this likeness is taken by
Jarvis in the year of our / Lord
1813 being 39 years old
Oil on panel
34 × 26 1/8" (86.4 × 66.4 cm)

Bequest of G. Heide Norris
1944-1-1

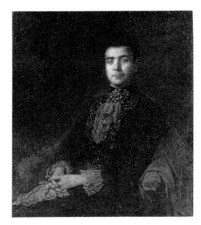

**Johnson, Eastman**
*Portrait of Mrs. Ellen Inslee
Eichholtz*
c. 1885
Lower left: E. Johnson
Oil on canvas
36 × 30" (91.4 × 76.2 cm)

Gift of Paul Denckla
1958-94-1

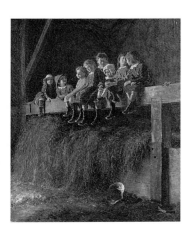

**Johnson, Eastman**
American, 1824–1906
*Barn Swallows*
1878
Lower right: Eastman Johnson /
1878; on reverse: Barn
Swallows—Mary K. Johnson
from E.J.
Oil on canvas
27 3/16 × 22 3/16" (69.1 × 56.4 cm)

Gift of Mrs. John Wintersteen in
memory of John Wintersteen
1953-111-1

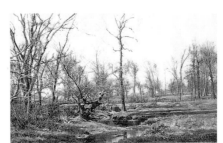

**Jones, H. Bolton**
American, 1848–1927
*Landscape with a Stream through
Fields*
1889
Lower right: H. BOLTON JONES
1889
Oil on canvas
16 × 24 1/8" (40.6 × 61.3 cm)

Bequest of Lydia Thompson
Morris
1932-45-116

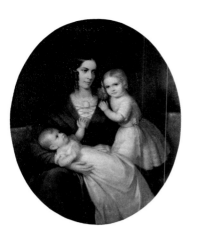

**Lambdin, James Reid**
American, 1807–1889
*Portrait of Mrs. Miles and Her
Children*
1840s
Oil on canvas
50 × 37 ¾" (127 × 95.9 cm)

Gift of W. Parsons Todd and
Miss Mary J. Todd
1938-25-1

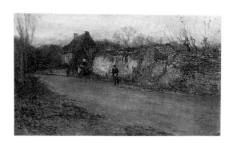

**Martin, Homer D.**
American, 1836–1897
*Beach Road, Normandy*
c. 1885
Lower right: Homer Martin
Oil on canvas
35 ³/₁₆ × 44 ¹/₁₆" (89.4 × 111.9 cm)

Bequest of T. Edward Hanley
1970-76-7

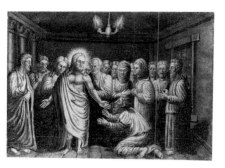

**Landis, John**
American, born 1805,
still active 1851
*Christ in the Upper Room*
1836
On reverse: Jno. Landis, /
Pinxit / 1836
Oil on canvas
13 ⁷/₈ × 18 ⁷/₈" (35.2 × 47.9 cm)

The Titus C. Geesey Collection
1953-125-20

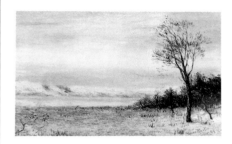

**Martin, Homer D.**
*Sand Dunes*
1887
Lower right: Homer Martin / 1887
Oil on canvas
14 × 22 ¹/₁₆" (35.6 × 56 cm)

The Alex Simpson, Jr., Collection
1944-13-5

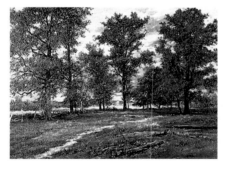

**Linford, Charles**
American, 1846–1897
*Landscape*
1888
Lower left: C. LINFORD. 1888
Oil on canvas
22 ⅛ × 30 ³/₁₆" (56.2 × 76.7 cm)

Bequest of Lydia Thompson
Morris
1932-45-121

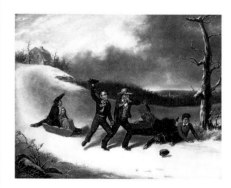

**Mason, William Sanford**
American, 1824–1864
*Sledding*
1854
Lower left: W. Sanford Mason /
1854
Oil on canvas
25 × 30 ⁵/₁₆" (63.5 × 77 cm)

Centennial gift of Mr. and Mrs.
Stuart P. Feld
1976-168-1

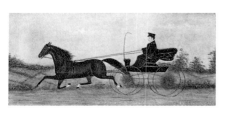

**Lovejoy, E. W.**
American, active c. 1840
*Road Master*
c. 1840
Center bottom: ROAD MASTER;
lower right: E. W. LOVEJOY. P.R.
Oil on cardboard
10 ⁵/₈ × 23 ³/₈" (27 × 59.4 cm)

The Collection of Edgar William
and Bernice Chrysler Garbisch
1972-262-8

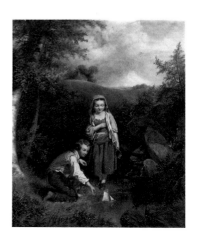

**Mason, William Sanford**
*Two Children Sailing a Boat*
1857
Lower right: Wm Sanford Mason
/ 1857
Oil on canvas
30 ⅛ × 25" (76.5 × 63.5 cm)

Bequest of Katherine E. Sheafer
1971-272-3

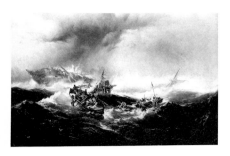

**Moran, Edward**
American, born England,
1829–1901
*Shipwreck*
1858
Lower left: E. Moran
Oil on canvas
40 1/8 × 60 1/8" (101.9 × 152.7 cm)

Gift of E. H. Butler
1894-276

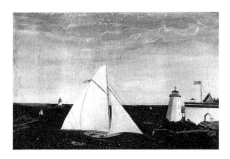

**Moses, Thomas**
American, born England,
1856–1934
*Portsmouth Harbor*
Late 19th or early 20th century
Oil on canvas
18 1/16 × 20 1/8" (45.9 × 51.1 cm)

Gift of Frank and Alice Osborn
1966-68-30

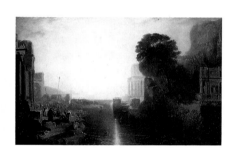

**Moran, Edward**
*Windy Day, Coney Island*
1871
Lower left: Edward Moran 1871
Oil on canvas
18 1/2 × 30 1/2" (47 × 77.5 cm)

Gift of Harry S. Dion
1979-105-1

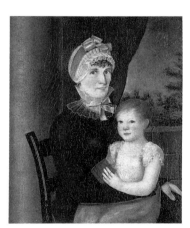

**Moulthrop, Reuben**
American, 1763–1814
*Portrait of John Broadbent and
His Son*
Companion to the following
painting
c. 1795
Lower left, on paper: Sheffield
Oil on canvas
31 5/16 × 25 5/16" (79.5 × 64.3 cm)

The Collection of Edgar William
and Bernice Chrysler Garbisch
1972-262-5

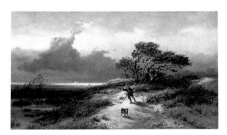

**Moran, Thomas**
American, 1837–1926
*The Building of Carthage*
After Joseph Mallord William
Turner's *Dido Building Carthage;
or the Rise of the Carthaginian
Empire*, dated 1815, in the
National Gallery, London (498)
1862
Lower left: T. MORAN After
J.M.W. TURNER 1862
Oil on canvas
40 1/4 × 60 1/4" (102.2 × 153 cm)

Gift of Bradford S. Magill in
memory of Matthew Baird
1977-174-1

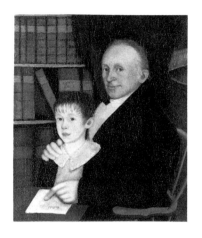

**Moulthrop, Reuben**
*Portrait of Mrs. John Broadbent and
Her Child*
Companion to the preceding
painting
c. 1795
Oil on canvas
31 5/16 × 25 5/16" (79.5 × 64.3 cm)

The Collection of Edgar William
and Bernice Chrysler Garbisch
1972-262-6

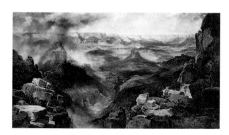

**Moran, Thomas**
*Grand Canyon of the Colorado River*
1892 and 1908
Lower right: TMORAN.
1892–1908 Copyright
Oil on canvas
53 × 94" (134.6 × 238.8 cm)

Gift of Graeme Lorimer
1975-182-1

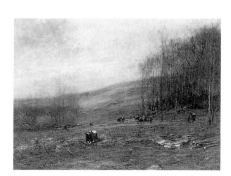

**Murphy, John Francis**
American, 1853–1921
*Landscape*
1901
Lower left: J FRANCIS MURPHY.
1901—
Oil on canvas
14 × 19" (35.6 × 48.3 cm)

Gift of Lucie Washington
Mitcheson in memory of Robert
Stockton Johnson Mitcheson for
the Robert Stockton Johnson
Mitcheson Collection
1938-22-1

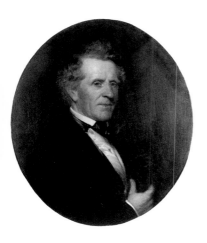

**Neagle, John**
American, 1796–1865
*Portrait of Samuel Vaughan*
Companion to the following
painting
c. 1820–30
Oil on canvas
30 1/4 × 25" (76.8 × 63.5 cm)

Gift of Mrs. Samuel M. Baker
1925-83-2

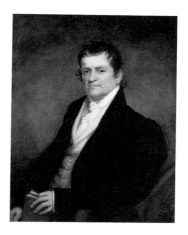

**Otis, Bass**
*Portrait of Newberry Smith*
1820s
Oil on canvas
36 1/2 × 28 1/16" (92.7 × 71.3 cm)

Gift of Mrs. Mary Stockton
Taylor
1944-77-1

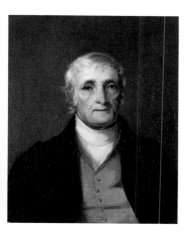

**Neagle, John**
*Portrait of Susan Hoffman Vaughan*
Companion to the preceding
painting
c. 1820–30
Oil on canvas
29 3/4 × 24 3/4" (75.6 × 62.9 cm)

Gift of Mrs. Samuel M. Baker
1925-83-1

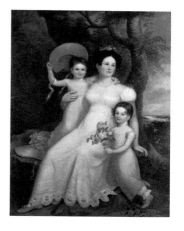

**Otis, Bass**
*Portrait of a Philadelphian and Her
Two Children*
1823
Center left: B. OTIS pinxt. AD 1823
Oil on canvas
66 3/8 × 50 1/4" (168.6 × 127.6 cm)

Purchased with the Edgar V.
Seeler Fund
1965-48-1

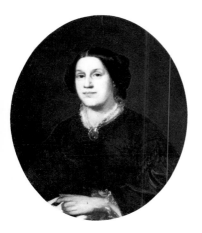

**Ord, Joseph Biays**
American, 1805–1865
*Portrait of John McMullin*
1834
Oil on canvas
16 1/4 × 13 1/2" (41.3 × 34.3 cm)

Purchased with Museum funds
1950-13-1

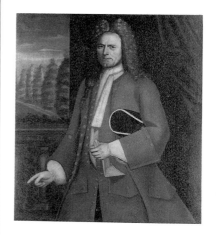

**Partridge, Nehemiah**
American, 1683–c. 1737
*Portrait of Johannes ten Broeck*
Companion to the following
painting
1720
Center left: Etas. Sue. 37. 1720
Oil on ticking
46 3/8 × 39 9/16" (117.8 × 100.5 cm)

Gift of the Runk family
1972-124-1

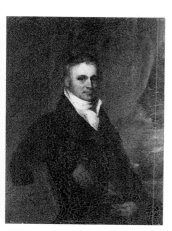

**Otis, Bass**
American, 1784–1861
*Portrait of Samuel Breck*
c. 1816
On reverse: Portrait of Samuel
Breck / of Sweetbriar, taken by
Otis, / when Mr. Breck was about
forty / five. It is a good likeness.
Oil on panel
9 1/16 × 6 7/8" (23 × 17.5 cm)

Gift of Mrs. C. P. Beauchamp
Jefferys
1966-53-1

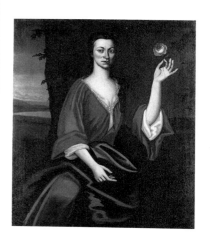

**Partridge, Nehemiah**
*Portrait of Catryna van Rensselaer
ten Broeck*
Companion to the preceding
painting
1720
Lower right: Etats. Suae. / 29.
years / 1720:
Oil on ticking
46 1/4 × 39 7/16" (117.5 × 100.2 cm)

Gift of the Runk family
1972-124-2

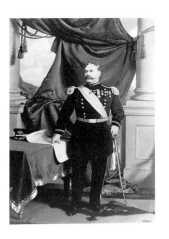

**Paxton, William McGregor**
American, 1869–1941
*Portrait of General Wendell Phillips
Bowman*
1930s
Lower right: PAXTON
Oil on canvas
101 × 66 ½" (256.5 × 168.9 cm)

Gift of Elizabeth Malcolm
Bowman in memory of Wendell
Phillips Bowman
1936-17-1

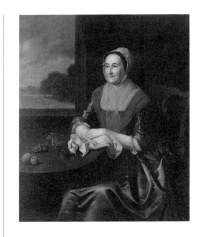

**Peale, Charles Willson**
*Portrait of Hannah Lambert
Cadwalader*
c. 1772
Oil on canvas
50 × 40" (127 × 101.6 cm)

Purchased for the Cadwalader
Collection with funds
contributed by the Mabel Pew
Myrin Trust and the gift of an
anonymous donor
1983-90-2

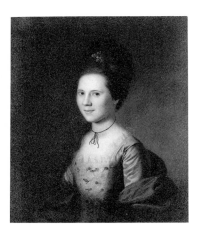

**Peale, Charles Willson**
American, 1741–1827
*Portrait of Mary Benezet*
1772
Lower left: Chas. Wn. Peale /
pinxt: 1772
Oil on canvas
30 ⅛ × 25 ³/₁₆" (76.5 × 64 cm)

Gift of Mrs. Thomas Evans
1962-126-1

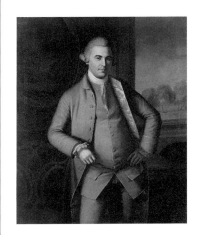

**Peale, Charles Willson**
*Portrait of Colonel Lambert
Cadwalader*
c. 1772
Oil on canvas
50 × 40" (127 × 101.6 cm)

Purchased for the Cadwalader
Collection with funds
contributed by the Mabel Pew
Myrin Trust and the gift of an
anonymous donor
1983-90-4

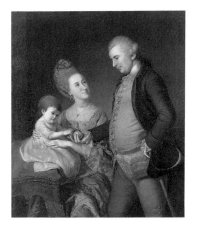

**Peale, Charles Willson**
*Portrait of John and Elizabeth Lloyd
Cadwalader and Their Daughter
Anne*
1772
Oil on canvas
51 ½ × 41 ¼" (130.8 × 104.8 cm)

Purchased for the Cadwalader
Collection with funds
contributed by the Mabel Pew
Myrin Trust and the gift of an
anonymous donor
1983-90-3

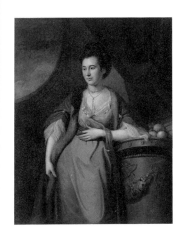

**Peale, Charles Willson**
*Portrait of Martha Cadwalader
Dagworthy*
c. 1772
Center right: C Peale pinxit 1771
Oil on canvas
50 × 40" (127 × 101.6 cm)

Purchased for the Cadwalader
Collection with funds
contributed by the Mabel Pew
Myrin Trust and the gift of an
anonymous donor
1980-135-1

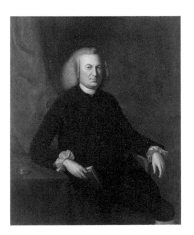

**Peale, Charles Willson**
*Portrait of Dr. Thomas Cadwalader*
c. 1772
Oil on canvas
50 × 40" (127 × 101.6 cm)

Purchased for the Cadwalader
Collection with funds
contributed by the Mabel Pew
Myrin Trust and the gift of an
anonymous donor
1983-90-1

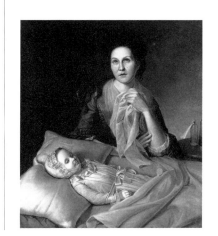

**Peale, Charles Willson**
*Rachel Weeping*
Enlarged in 1776; repainted in
1818
1772, 1776, and 1818
Oil on canvas
36 ¹³/₁₆ × 32 ¹/₁₆" (93.5 × 81.4 cm)

Gift of the Barra Foundation, Inc.
1977-34-1

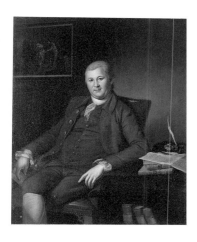

**Peale, Charles Willson**
*Portrait of John B. Bayard*
Companion to the following
painting
1780
On reverse: John Bayard / Chas.
Peale pinxit / 1780
Oil on canvas
50 1/4 × 40 1/2" (127.6 × 102.9 cm)

Gift of Mrs. T. Charlton Henry
1964-105-2

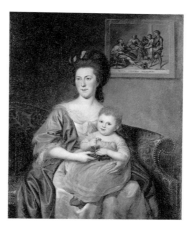

**Peale, Charles Willson**
*Portrait of Mrs. Thomas McKean
and Her Daughter, Sophia Dorothea*
Companion to the preceding
painting
1787
Lower right: C. W Peale pinxit
1787; on print: DATE OBOLUM
BELISARIO
Oil on canvas
50 5/8 × 41 1/16" (128.6 × 104.3 cm)

Bequest of Phebe Warren
McKean Downs
1968-74-2

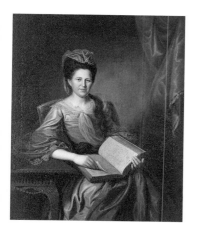

**Peale, Charles Willson**
*Portrait of Mrs. John B. Bayard*
Companion to the preceding
painting
1780
On book: PROVERBS / CHAP.
XXXI; on reverse: Chas. Peale
pinxit, 1780
Oil on canvas
50 1/4 × 40 1/2" (127.6 × 102.9 cm)

Gift of Mrs. T. Charlton Henry
1964-105-3

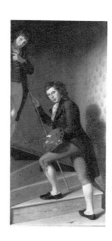

**Peale, Charles Willson**
*Staircase Group (Portrait of
Raphaelle Peale and Titian
Ramsey Peale)*
1795
Center bottom, on card: [illegible
signature]
Oil on canvas
89 1/2 × 39 3/8" (227.3 × 100 cm)

The George W. Elkins Collection
E1945-1-1

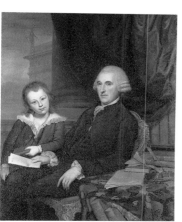

**Peale, Charles Willson**
*Portrait of Thomas Wharton*
c. 1781–1805
Oil on canvas
23 5/16 × 19 1/2" (59.2 × 49.5 cm)

Gift of the children of Marianna
Lippincott O'Neill in her memory
1967-216-1

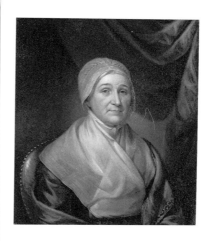

**Peale, Charles Willson**
*Portrait of Mrs. Leonard Nutz*
c. 1815–20
Oil on canvas
26 1/8 × 22 1/8" (66.4 × 56.2 cm)

Gift of the Frescoln family
1969-266-1

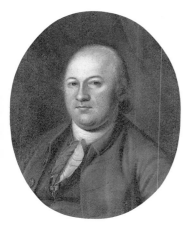

**Peale, Charles Willson**
*Portrait of Governor Thomas
McKean and His Son, Thomas
McKean, Jr.*
Companion to the following
painting
1787
Center right: C. W Peale, 1787
Oil on canvas
50 5/8 × 41 1/8" (128.6 × 104.5 cm)

Bequest of Phebe Warren
McKean Downs
1968-74-1

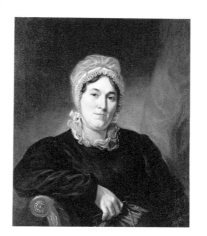

**Peale, Charles Willson**
Previously listed as Rembrandt
Peale (PMA 1965)
*Portrait of Polly S. Royal*
1821
Oil on canvas
29 1/2 × 24 3/8" (74.9 × 61.9 cm)

Gift of Eliza Royal Finckel
1956-66-5

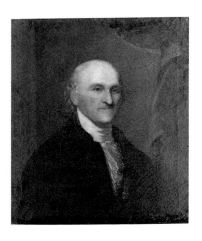

**Peale, Charles Willson, attributed to**
*Portrait of Colonel Samuel Miles*
c. 1790–1800
Oil on canvas
28 1/2 × 23 3/4" (72.4 × 60.3 cm)

Gift of Mrs. Catherine M. G. Dinges
1930-54-1

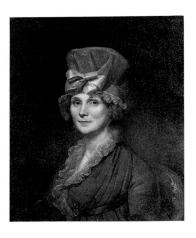

**Peale, Charles Willson, attributed to**
*Portrait of Mary Ann MacNeal Macpherson*
1799
On reverse, covered by relining:
[ ] Peale / pted 1799
Oil on canvas
29 × 24 1/2" (73.7 × 62.2 cm)

Bequest of Mellicent Story Garland
1963-75-2

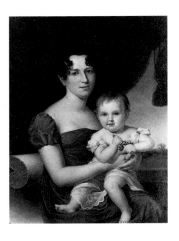

**Peale, James**
American, 1749–1831
*Portrait of Mrs. Nathaniel Waples and Her Daughter, Sarah Ann*
1817
Lower right: Jas. Peale / 1817
Oil on canvas
36 × 28" (91.4 × 71.1 cm)

Gift of Mrs. C. Emory McMichael
1950-51-1

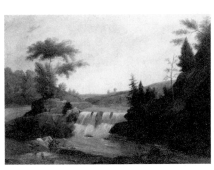

**Peale, James**
*Wissahickon Creek*
1830
On reverse: S. Olivia S. Morris /
Pa. / and / Painted by Jn. Peale
Sen. in the year of his / Age 81 /
Philada. 1830.
Oil on canvas
20 1/8 × 27" (51.1 × 68.6 cm)

Gift of T. Edward Hanley
1964-210-1

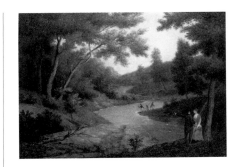

**Peale, James**
*Wissahickon Creek*
1830
On reverse: S. Olivia S. Morris /
Pa. / and / Painted by Jn. Peale
Sen. in the year of his / Age 81 /
Philada. 1830.
Oil on canvas
20 1/8 × 27" (51.1 × 68.6 cm)

Gift of T. Edward Hanley
1964-210-2

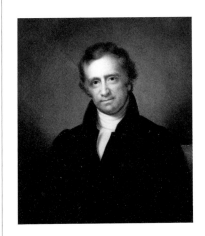

**Peale, Rembrandt**
American, 1778–1860
*Portrait of Bartholomew Wistar*
c. 1820
Oil on canvas
30 1/8 × 24 7/8" (76.5 × 63.2 cm)

Gift of Mrs. J. Morris Wistar
1976-223-3

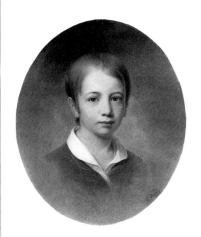

**Peale, Rembrandt**
*Portrait of a Boy in a Red Jacket*
1845
Lower left: R. Peale. / 1845.
Oil on canvas
24 × 18 5/16" (61 × 46.5 cm)

Purchased with the W. P. Wilstach Fund
W1918-3-1

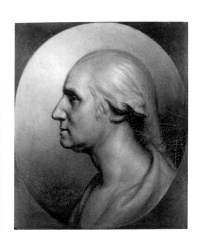

**Peale, Rembrandt**
*Bust of Washington*
After a bust by Jean-Antoine
Houdon (French, 1741–1828)
1857
Lower right: Painted by
Rembrandt Peale from Houdon
Oil on canvas
36 1/8 × 29 1/8" (91.8 × 74 cm)

The W. P. Wilstach Collection,
bequest of Anna H. Wilstach
W1893-1-84

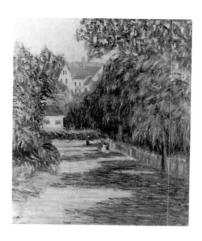

**Perot, Annie Lovering**
American, 1854–1931
*Little Lane, East Gloucester*
c. 1900–25
Lower left: A. L. Perot
Oil on canvas
29 3/4 × 25" (75.6 × 63.5 cm)

Bequest of Annie Lovering Perot
1936-1-3

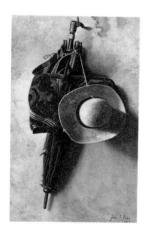

**Peto, John Frederick**
American, 1854–1907
*Still Life with a Hat, an Umbrella,
and a Bag*
1905
Lower right: John F. Peto / 1905;
on reverse: J.F.Peto / 1905 /
ISLAND HEIGHTS / N.J.
Oil on canvas
20 1/8 × 12 1/16" (51.1 × 30.6 cm)

The Albert M. Greenfield and
Elizabeth M. Greenfield
Collection
1974-178-40

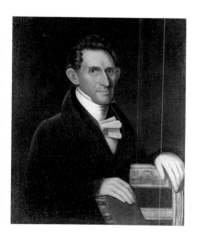

**Phillips, Ammi**
American, 1788–1865
*Portrait of Mr. Warburton of
Rockboro, Virginia*
Companion to the following
painting
c. 1825
On book: WARBURTON'S /
LETTERS
Oil on canvas
28 7/8 × 23 13/16" (73.3 × 60.5 cm)

The Collection of Edgar William
and Bernice Chrysler Garbisch
1973-258-1

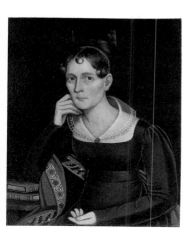

**Phillips, Ammi**
*Portrait of Mrs. Warburton of
Rockboro, Virginia*
Companion to the preceding
painting
c. 1825
On books: NEWTON'S / WORKS;
MILTON'S WORKS
Oil on canvas
29 13/16 × 23 7/8" (75.8 × 60.6 cm)

The Collection of Edgar William
and Bernice Chrysler Garbisch
1973-258-2

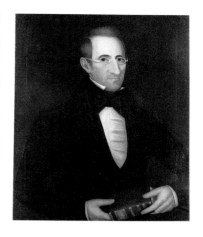

**Phillips, Ammi**
*Portrait of a Man*
Companion to the following
painting
c. 1830
On book: HOLY- / BIBLE.
Oil on canvas
33 1/2 × 28" (85.1 × 71.1 cm)

Gift of Mr. and Mrs. John B.
Schorsch
1973-263-1

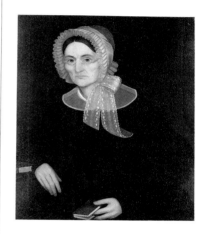

**Phillips, Ammi**
*Portrait of a Woman*
Companion to the preceding
painting
c. 1830
Oil on canvas
33 5/8 × 23 1/8" (85.4 × 58.7 cm)

Gift of Mr. and Mrs. John B.
Schorsch
1973-263-2

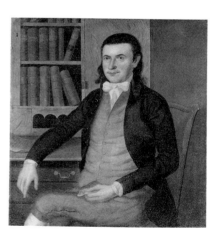

**Polk, Charles Peale**
American, 1767–1822
*Portrait of John Hart*
Companion to following painting
c. 1795
On books: COOK'S / [V]OYAGE;
HERVEY / MEDITATIONS;
MCEWEN / ON THE / TYPES;
PAINE'S / WORKS; BLAIR'S /
LECTURES; WORLD; BELKNAP'S
/ AMERICAN / BIOGRAPHY;
ROBERTSON / INDIA; NATUREAL
/ HISTORY; POPES WORKS;
on paper: Invoice / of / Books
Oil on canvas
37 1/2 × 33 5/8" (95.2 × 85.4 cm)

The Collection of Edgar William
and Bernice Chrysler Garbisch
1968-222-1

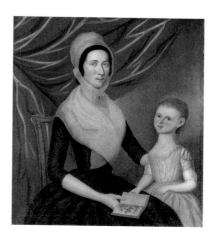

**Polk, Charles Peale**
*Portrait of Mrs. John Hart and Her
Daughter*
Companion to preceding painting
c. 1795
Oil on canvas
37 1/8 × 33 1/8" (94.3 × 84.1 cm)

The Collection of Edgar William
and Bernice Chrysler Garbisch
1968-222-2

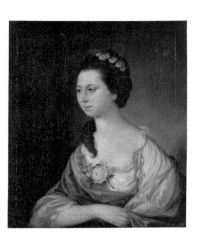

**Pratt, Matthew**
American, 1734–1805
*Portrait of Mrs. Samuel Powel*
[née Elizabeth Willing]
1768–70
Oil on canvas
29 7/8 × 25" (75.9 × 63.5 cm)

Purchased with the George W.
Elkins Fund
E1973-1-1

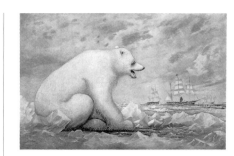

**Raleigh, Charles Sidney**
American, born England,
1830–1925
*Chilly Observation*
1889
Lower left: C. S. Raleigh / 1889
Oil on canvas
29 13/16 × 43 7/8" (75.7 × 111.4 cm)

The Collection of Edgar William
and Bernice Chrysler Garbisch
1965-209-6

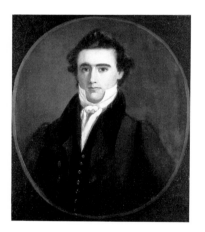

**Prior, William Matthew**
American, 1806–1873
*Portrait of a Man*
1829
On reverse: Wm. M. Prior / 1829
Oil on canvas
26 3/8 × 22 1/16" (67 × 56 cm)

Bequest of Edgar William and
Bernice Chrysler Garbisch
1980-64-8

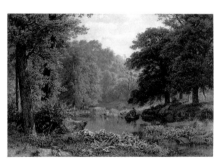

**Richards, William Trost**
American, 1833–1905
*Landscape*
1864
Lower left: Wm. T. Richards.
1864
Oil on canvas
16 × 22 3/8" (40.6 × 56.8 cm)

Centennial gift of Dr. and Mrs.
Bernard J. Ronis and family
1976-222-1

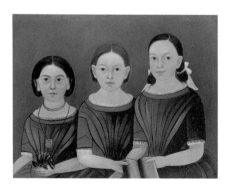

**Prior, William Matthew**
*Portrait of Three Girls*
c. 1850
Oil on canvas
21 13/16 × 26 3/4" (55.4 × 67.9 cm)

The Collection of Edgar William
and Bernice Chrysler Garbisch
1973-258-3

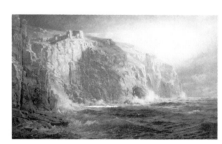

**Richards, William Trost**
*Marine*
1886
Lower left: Wm. T. Richards
1886
Oil on canvas
28 1/4 × 44" (71.7 × 111.8 cm)

Bequest of Arthur H. Lea
F1938-1-48

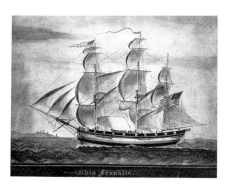

**Ralb, G. E.**
American, active 19th century
*The Ship "Franklin"*
c. 1830
Center bottom: Ship Franklin;
lower right: G. E. RALB.
Oil on panel
15 3/4 × 20 1/8" (40 × 51.1 cm)

Bequest of Edgar William and
Bernice Chrysler Garbisch
1980-64-11

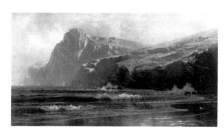

**Richards, William Trost**
*Marine with a View of the English
Coast*
1891
Oil on canvas
44 × 65" (111.7 × 165.1 cm)

Gift of the estate of Katharine C.
Wharton
1986-76-4

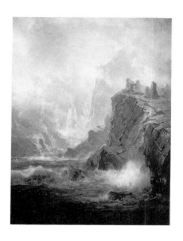

**Richards, William Trost**
*Fast Castle*
1892
Lower left: W. T. Richards, 92.
Oil on canvas
48 × 36 ³/₈" (121.9 × 92.4 cm)

Bequest of Arthur H. Lea
F1938-1-27

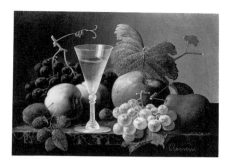

**Roesen, Severin**
*Still Life with Fruit and a Wine Glass*
c. 1850–70
Lower right: Roesen
Oil on canvas
11 ³/₄ × 16" (29.8 × 40.6 cm)

Purchased with the Joseph E. Temple Fund
1969-259-1

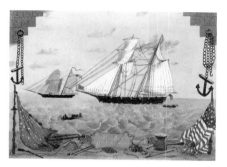

**Roath, H. A.**
American, active c. 1825
*US Revenue Cutter*
c. 1825
Center bottom: U S / REVENUE CUTTER; on capstan: U S / MORRIS; lower right: H A ROATH
Oil on canvas
15 ¹/₂ × 21 ⁷/₈" (39.4 × 53.3 cm)

The Collection of Edgar William and Bernice Chrysler Garbisch
1967-268-3

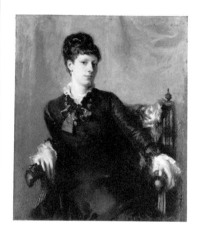

**Sargent, John Singer**
American, active London, Florence, and Paris, 1856–1925
*Portrait of Frances Sherborne Ridley Watts*
1877
Upper right: John S. Sargent
Oil on canvas
41 ¹¹/₁₆ × 32" (105.9 × 81.3 cm)

Gift of Mr. and Mrs. Wharton Sinkler
1962-193-1

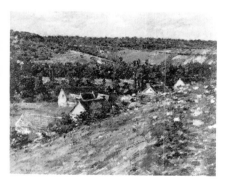

**Robinson, Théodore**
American, 1852–1896
*Giverny*
c. 1888
Lower left: Th. Robinson
Oil on canvas
18 ¹/₈ × 21 ⁷/₈" (46 × 55.6 cm)

Gift of Lucie Washington Mitcheson in memory of Robert Stockton Johnson Mitcheson for the Robert Stockton Johnson Mitcheson Collection
1938-22-10

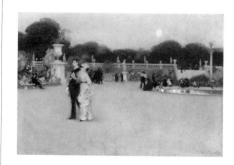

**Sargent, John Singer**
*In the Luxembourg Gardens*
1879
Lower right: John S. Sargent, Paris / 1879
Oil on canvas
25 ⁷/₈ × 36 ³/₈" (65.7 × 92.4 cm)

John G. Johnson Collection
cat. 1080

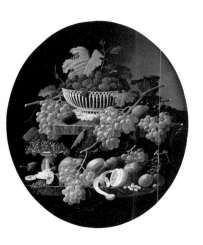

**Roesen, Severin**
American, born Germany, 1848–1871
*Still Life with Fruit*
c. 1850–70
Lower right: Roesen
Oil on canvas
30 ¹/₄ × 25" (76.8 × 63.5 cm)

This painting by Severin Roesen, known as the pauper painter of Williamsport, Pennsylvania, was given by Theodore Wiedemann in memory of his wife, Letha M. Wiedemann, a native of that city
1980-63-1

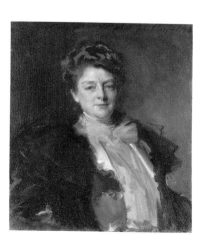

**Sargent, John Singer**
*Portrait of Mrs. J. William White*
1903
Across top: To my friend Mrs. White  John S. Sargent, 1903
Oil on canvas
30 ¹/₁₆ × 25 ¹/₁₆" (76.4 × 63.7 cm)

Commissioners of Fairmount Park
F1925-5-1

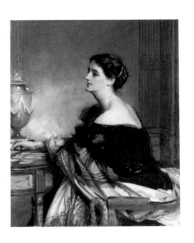

**Sargent, John Singer**
*Portrait of Lady Eden*
1906
Upper left: John S. Sargent;
upper right: 1906
Oil on canvas
43 9/16 × 34 1/16" (110.6 × 86.5 cm)

Purchased with the W. P.
Wilstach Fund
W1920-2-1

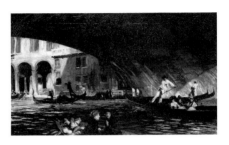

**Sargent, John Singer**
*The Rialto, Venice*
c. 1911
Lower left: John S. Sargent
Oil on canvas
22 × 36 1/4" (55.9 × 92.1 cm)

The George W. Elkins Collection
E1924-4-28

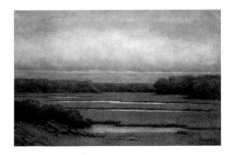

**Sartain, William**
American, 1843–1924
*Green Meadow*
c. 1880–1900
Lower right: W. SARTAIN.
Oil on canvas
22 1/8 × 32" (56.2 × 81.3 cm)

Gift of Miss Harriet Sartain
1947-81-1

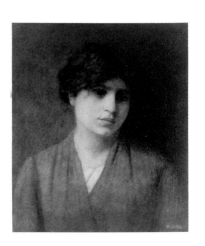

**Sartain, William**
*Rosa*
c. 1880–1900
Lower right: W. SARTAIN
Oil on canvas
20 1/8 × 16 1/16" (51.1 × 40.8 cm)

Gift of Lucie Washington
Mitcheson in memory of Robert
Stockton Johnson Mitcheson for
the Robert Stockton Johnson
Mitcheson Collection
1938-22-6

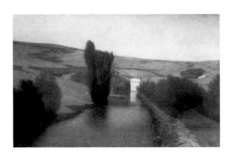

**Sartain, William**
*The Royal Mill on the Eresma River,
Segovia, Spain*
c. 1880–1900
Lower right: W. Sartain.
Oil on canvas
30 × 45 1/8" (76.2 × 114.6 cm)

Purchased with the Edward and
Althea Budd Fund
1977-114-1

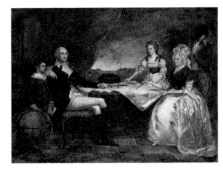

**Savage, Edward, copy after**
American, 1761–1817
*Portrait of George Washington and
His Family*
After the engraving, dated 1798,
by Edward Savage and David
Edwin (American, 1776–1841),
of the painting by Savage, in the
Henry Francis du Pont
Winterthur Museum,
Winterthur, Delaware (61.708)
c. 1850
Oil on canvas
28 × 36" (71.1 × 91.4 cm)

Bequest of F. King Wainwright
1952-65-1

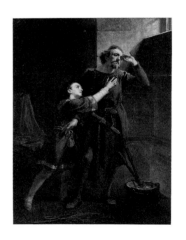

**Schussele, Christian**
American, 1824?–1879
*Hubert and Arthur*
1858
Lower right: C. Schuessele /
Philada. / 1858
Oil on canvas
62 5/8 × 46" (159.1 × 116.8 cm)

Gift of R. A. Ellison
1979-146-1

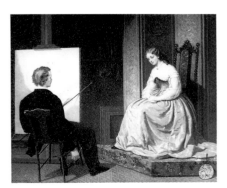

**Smith, T. Henry**
American, active c. 1861–1896
*With Love (Con Amore)*
1866
Lower left: T. HENRY SMITH /
1866
Oil on canvas
20 1/8 × 24" (51.1 × 61 cm)

The W. P. Wilstach Collection,
bequest of Anna H. Wilstach
W1893-1-100

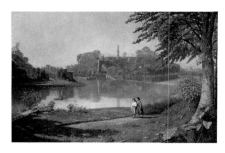

**Smith, T. Henry**
*Fairmount Waterworks*
1871
Lower left: T. Henry Smith. /
1871; on reverse: Fairmount /
Painted by / T. Henry Smith /
1871
Oil on canvas
30 ¹³/₁₆ × 47 ¹/₁₆" (78.3 ×
119.5 cm)

Purchased with the Bloomfield
Moore Fund
1966-4-1

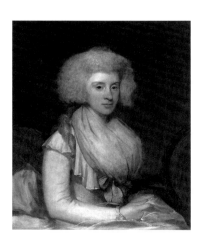

**Street, Robert**
*Portrait of Joseph Mount*
Companion to the preceding
painting
1835
Center right: R. STREET / 1835
Oil on canvas on panel
30 × 25 ¹/₁₆" (76.2 × 63.7 cm)

Gift of Miss Eleanor Bispham
1975-40-1

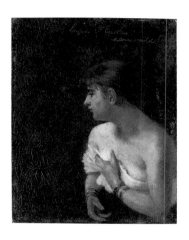

**Stieglitz, Edward**
American, born Germany,
1833–1909
*Portrait of a Young Woman*
After a painting by Fedor Encke
(German, born 1851, still active
1913), in an unknown location
1885
Upper right: Copie F. Encke, /
Mittenwald Sept / 85 / ES; on
reverse: Copy of picture by Fedor
Encke, Mittenwald, September
'85 by Edward Stieglitz
Oil on panel
7 ¹/₁₆ × 5 ³/₈" (17.9 × 13.6 cm)

Gift of Katherine Kuh
1972-100-1

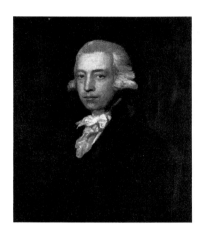

**Stuart, Gilbert Charles**
American, 1755–1828
*Portrait of Phineas Bond*
c. 1780
Oil on canvas
29 ⁹/₁₆ × 25 ¹/₈" (75.1 × 63.8 cm)

Purchased for the Cadwalader
Collection with funds
contributed by the Mabel Pew
Myrin Trust and the gift of an
anonymous donor
1983-90-5

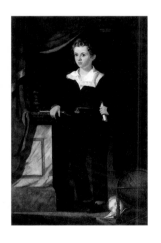

**Street, Robert**
American, 1796–1865
*Portrait of William H. Klapp*
1820
Lower left: R. Street 1820
Oil on canvas
72 × 48" (182.9 × 121.9 cm)

Purchased with the J. Stogdell
Stokes Fund
1992-60-1

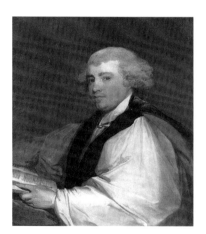

**Stuart, Gilbert Charles**
*Portrait of Dean Christopher Bertson*
Companion to the following
painting
c. 1788–92
Oil on canvas
30 × 25" (76.2 × 63.5 cm)

Gift of Muriel and Philip Berman
1992-15-1

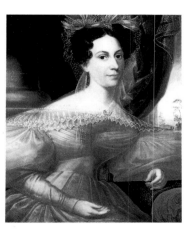

**Street, Robert**
*Portrait of Susan Baker Mount*
Companion to the following
painting
1834
Upper left: R. STREET / 1834
Oil on canvas on panel
30 ¹/₈ × 25 ¹/₁₆" (76.5 × 63.7 cm)

Gift of Miss Eleanor Bispham
1975-40-2

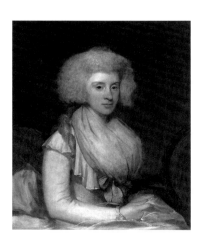

**Stuart, Gilbert Charles**
*Portrait of Mrs. Christopher Bertson*
Companion to the preceding
painting
c. 1788–92
Oil on canvas
30 × 25" (76.2 × 63.5 cm)

Gift of Muriel and Philip Berman
1992-15-2

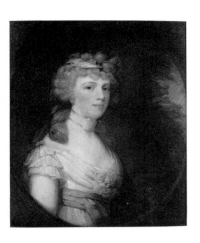

**Stuart, Gilbert Charles**
*Portrait of Ann Penn Allen*
Replica of the painting in the
Metropolitan Museum of Art,
New York (43.86.3)
c. 1795
Oil on canvas
30 × 25 1/8" (76.2 × 63.8 cm)

Gift of Mr. and Mrs. Wharton
Sinkler
1959-79-1

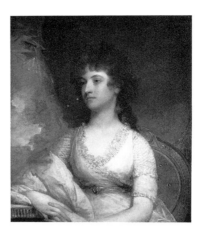

**Stuart, Gilbert Charles**
*Portrait of Frances Cadwalader
Montagu, Lady Erskine*
Companion to the preceding
painting
1802
Oil on canvas
29 5/16 × 24 1/8" (74.4 × 61.3 cm)

Purchased for the Cadwalader
Collection with funds
contributed by the Mabel Pew
Myrin Trust and the gift of an
anonymous donor
1983-90-7

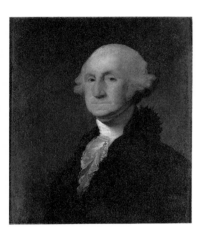

**Stuart, Gilbert Charles**
*Portrait of George Washington
(The Mount Vernon Washington)*
After the painting, dated 1796,
jointly owned by the Museum of
Fine Arts, Boston, and the
National Portrait Gallery,
Washington, D.C.
1796
Oil on canvas
28 1/8 × 24 3/16" (71.4 × 61.4 cm)

Gift of Mr. and Mrs. Wharton
Sinkler
1957-67-1

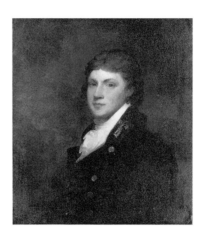

**Stuart, Gilbert Charles,
attributed to**
Previously listed as Gilbert
Charles Stuart (PMA 1965)
*Portrait of John Browne Davy*
c. 1815
Oil on canvas
29 1/8 × 21 1/16" (74 × 53.5 cm)

Purchased with the Katharine
Levin Farrell Fund
1960-109-1

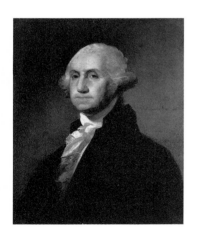

**Stuart, Gilbert Charles**
*Portrait of George Washington*
After the painting, dated 1796,
jointly owned by the Museum of
Fine Arts, Boston, and the
National Portrait Gallery,
Washington, D.C.
After 1796
Oil on canvas
30 × 24 1/8" (76.2 × 61.3 cm)

Gift of Mrs. T. Charlton Henry
1964-105-1

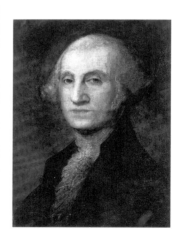

**Stuart, Gilbert Charles,
copy after**
*Portrait of George Washington*
After a painting known in many
versions
Mid-19th century
Oil on canvas
22 × 16 1/8" (55.9 × 41 cm)

Gift of Mrs. Robert F. Beard
1961-21-1

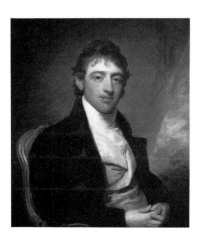

**Stuart, Gilbert Charles**
*Portrait of David Montagu,
2nd Baron Erskine*
Companion to the following
painting
1802
Oil on canvas
29 1/8 × 24 1/8" (74 × 61.3 cm)

Purchased for the Cadwalader
Collection with funds
contributed by the Mabel Pew
Myrin Trust and the gift of an
anonymous donor
1983-90-6

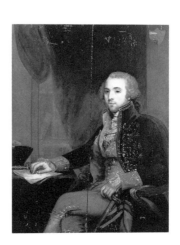

**Stuart, Gilbert Charles,
copy after**
*Portrait of Don Josef de Jaudenes y
Nebot*
After the painting, dated 1794,
in the Metropolitan Museum of
Art, New York (07.75);
companion to the following
painting
19th century
Oil on panel
25 13/16 × 19 1/8" (65.6 × 48.6 cm)

Gift of Mr. and Mrs. Rowland
Evans
1956-61-1

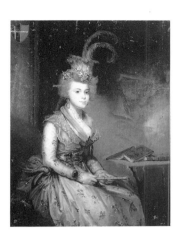

**Stuart, Gilbert Charles, copy after**
*Portrait of Doña Matilda Stoughton de Jaudenes y Nebot*
After the painting, dated 1794, in the Metropolitan Museum of Art, New York (07.76); companion to the preceding painting
19th century
Oil on panel
25 ³/₄ × 19 ¹/₂" (65.4 × 49.5 cm)

Gift of Mr. and Mrs. Rowland Evans
1956-61-2

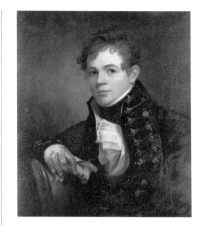

**Sully, Thomas**
*Portrait of Dr. William P. C. Barton*
1809
Oil on canvas
29 × 24" (73.7 × 61 cm)

Gift of Dr. William Barton Brewster for the W. P. Wilstach Collection
W1919-2-1

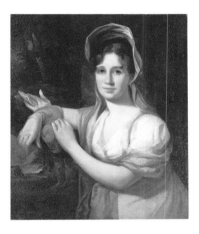

**Sully, Thomas**
American, born England, 1783–1872
*Portrait of Sarah Sully, Wife of the Artist*
1806, retouched 1856
On reverse: Painted in 1806 / Retouched 1856 / TS / Sarah wife of / Thos Sully
Oil on canvas
30 × 25 ¹/₈" (76.2 × 63.8 cm)

Gift of Mr. and Mrs. Wharton Sinkler
1962-193-2

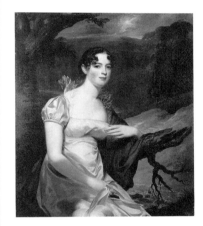

**Sully, Thomas**
*Portrait of Mrs. Mary Siddons Whelen*
1812
Oil on canvas
44 ¹/₂ × 37 ¹/₄" (113 × 94.6 cm)

Gift of Mrs. Thomas J. Dolan
1943-53-1

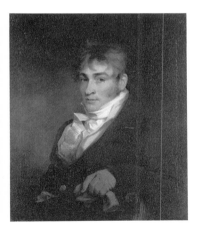

**Sully, Thomas**
*Portrait of Redwood Fisher*
1808, retouched 1847
Oil on canvas
29 ¹/₄ × 24 ¹/₈" (74.3 × 61.3 cm)

Gift of the estate of Lydia Fisher Warner
1949-54-1

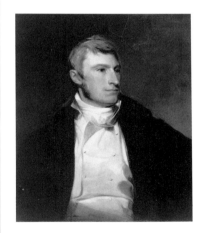

**Sully, Thomas**
*Portrait of Charles Willing Hare*
1814
Oil on canvas
29 × 24" (73.7 × 61 cm)

Bequest of Elizabeth C. Hare
1938-8-1

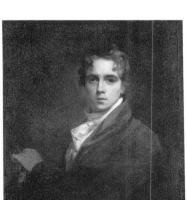

**Sully, Thomas**
*Self-Portrait*
1808, retouched 1856
Lower left: TS. 1808 / AE 25; on reverse: [pa]inted 1808 / retouched & / repai[n]ted / 1856 / Thos. Sully
Oil on canvas
30 ¹/₈ × 25 ³/₁₆" (76.5 × 64 cm)

Gift of Mr. and Mrs. Wharton Sinkler
1961-171-1

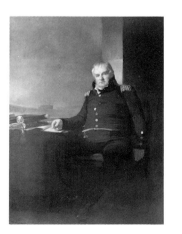

**Sully, Thomas**
*Portrait of Colonel Jonathan Williams*
1815
Lower left: TS 1815
Oil on canvas on plywood
81 × 58" (205.7 × 147.3 cm)

Gift of Alexander Biddle
1964-111-1

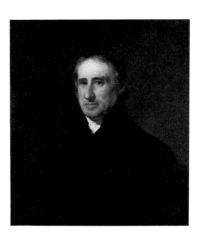

**Sully, Thomas**
*Portrait of John Teackle*
1815
Oil on canvas
30 5/16 × 25 5/16" (77 × 64.3 cm)

Purchased for the Cadwalader
Collection with funds
contributed by the Mabel Pew
Myrin Trust and the gift of an
anonymous donor
1983-90-8

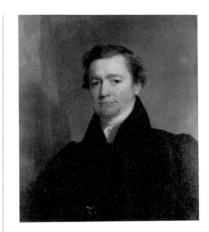

**Sully, Thomas**
*Portrait of William Norris*
Companion to the following
painting
1830
Lower left: TS. 1830.
Oil on canvas
30 1/8 × 25 3/16" (76.5 × 64 cm)

Bequest of G. Heide Norris
1960-78-1

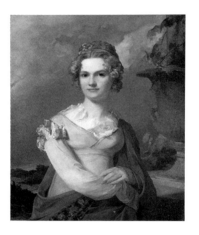

**Sully, Thomas**
*Portrait of Maria Donath Koecker*
1820
Center right: TS. 1820
Oil on canvas
35 1/2 × 27 1/2" (90.2 × 69.8 cm)

Bequest of Leonora L. Koecker
1942-37-2

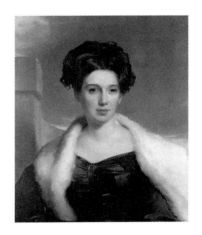

**Sully, Thomas**
*Portrait of Mary Anne Heide Norris*
Companion to the preceding
painting
1830
Lower left: TS 1830.
Oil on canvas
30 5/16 × 25 1/4" (77 × 64.1 cm)

Bequest of G. Heide Norris
1960-78-2

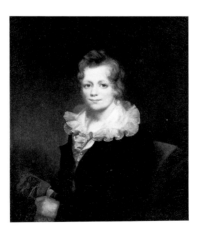

**Sully, Thomas**
Previously attributed to Thomas
Sully (PMA 1965)
*Portrait of William Pitt Bedlock*
c. 1825–30
Oil on canvas
30 3/16 × 25 3/16" (76.7 × 64 cm)

Gift of Maria Godey Bedlock
Thomas
1943-90-1

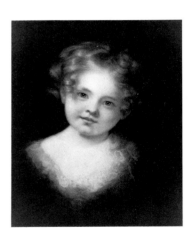

**Sully, Thomas**
Previously attributed to Thomas
Sully (PMA 1965)
*Head of a Girl*
c. 1830–50
Oil on cardboard
21 1/4 × 17 1/16" (54 × 43.3 cm)

Bequest of Bertha H. Giles
1935-9-1

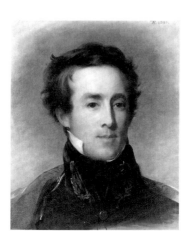

**Sully, Thomas**
*Portrait of Captain Hartman Bache*
1826
Upper right: TS. 1826.
Oil on canvas
19 1/16 × 15 1/8" (48.4 × 38.4 cm)

Bequest of Henrietta D. Pepper
1958-28-1

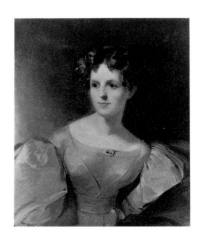

**Sully, Thomas**
*Portrait of Mrs. Robert Ewing*
1831
Lower left: T.S. 1831
Oil on canvas
30 1/8 × 25 1/4" (76.5 × 64.1 cm)

Gift of Mrs. Harvey Nelson
Carpenter
1936-10-1

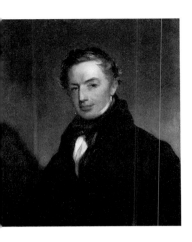

**Sully, Thomas**
*Portrait of General Thomas Cadwalader*
1833
Lower left: TS. 1833
Oil on canvas
30 5/16 × 25" (77 × 63.5 cm)

Purchased for the Cadwalader Collection with funds contributed by the Mabel Pew Myrin Trust and the gift of an anonymous donor
1983-90-10

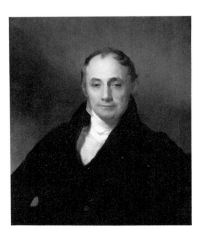

**Sully, Thomas**
Previously attributed to Thomas Sully (PMA 1965)
*Portrait of Amos Pennebaker, Jr.*
See previous two entries
c. 1835–40
Oil on canvas
30 × 24 1/2" (76.2 × 62.2 cm)

Bequest of Susan B. Pennebaker in memory of Sophie E. Pennebaker
1942-31-3

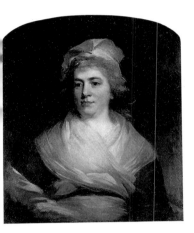

**Sully, Thomas**
*Portrait of Sarah Franklin Bache, Daughter of Benjamin Franklin*
After the painting by John Hoppner (English, 1758–1810), in the Metropolitan Museum of Art, New York (01.20)
1834
On reverse: TS 1834 / Portrait / Copied from Hoppner
Oil on canvas
30 × 25" (76.2 × 63.5 cm)

Bequest of Caroline D. Bache
1958-27-1

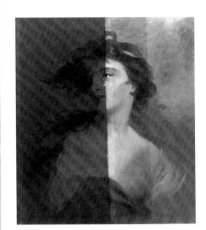

**Sully, Thomas**
*Portrait of Lady Hamilton as Ariadne*
Possibly after a painting by Sir Joshua Reynolds (English, 1723–1792)
1837
Oil on canvas
24 × 20" (61 × 50.8 cm)

Bequest of Mrs. Mary Frances Nunns
1959-59-1

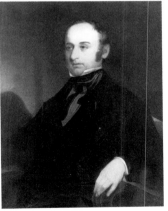

**Sully, Thomas**
Previously attributed to Thomas Sully (PMA 1965)
*Portrait of Amos Pennebaker*
Pendant to the following two paintings
c. 1835–40
Oil on canvas
36 1/8 × 29" (91.8 × 73.7 cm)

Bequest of Susan B. Pennebaker in memory of Sophie E. Pennebaker
1942-31-1

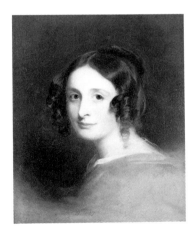

**Sully, Thomas**
*Portrait of Maria Markoe Wharton*
1837
Center bottom: TS. 1837
Oil on cardboard
21 1/8 × 17 1/8" (53.7 × 43.5 cm)

Bequest of Mrs. Maria McKean Allen
1951-44-1

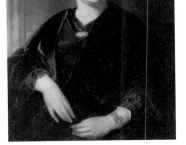

**Sully, Thomas**
Previously attributed to Thomas Sully (PMA 1965)
*Portrait of Susan Campbell Pennebaker*
See previous entry
c. 1835–40
Oil on canvas
36 × 28 3/4" (91.4 × 73 cm)

Bequest of Susan B. Pennebaker in memory of Sophie E. Pennebaker
1942-31-2

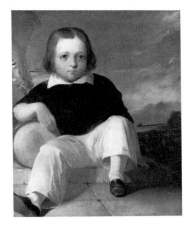

**Sully, Thomas**
*Portrait of Charles Nicoll Bancker*
1850
Oil on canvas
30 1/16 × 25 1/4" (76.4 × 64.1 cm)

Purchased for the Cadwalader Collection with funds contributed by the Mabel Pew Myrin Trust and the gift of an anonymous donor
1983-90-9

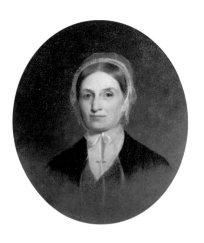

**Sully, Thomas**
*Portrait of Mrs. Evan Poultney*
1857
On reverse: TS 1857
Oil on canvas
24 × 20" (61 × 50.8 cm)

Gift of Brig. Gen. Bryan Conrad
1964-31-1

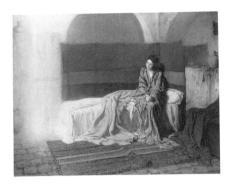

**Tanner, Henry Ossawa**
American, active France,
1859–1937
*The Annunciation*
1898
Lower left: H. O. TANNER / 1898
Oil on canvas
57 × 71 1/4" (144.8 × 181 cm)

Purchased with the W. P.
Wilstach Fund
W1899-1-1

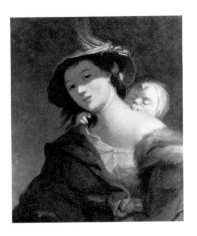

**Sully, Thomas**
*Gypsy Woman and Child*
After a painting possibly by
Bartolomeo Morelli (Italian,
died 1703)
1859
On reverse: TS 1859 / copied
from Morelli
Oil on canvas
30 1/16 × 25 3/16" (76.4 × 64 cm)

The W. P. Wilstach Collection,
bequest of Anna H. Wilstach
W1893-1-107

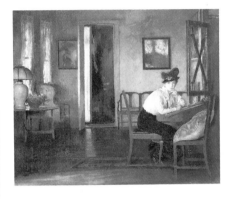

**Tarbell, Edmund Charles**
American, 1862–1938
*Girl Writing*
1917
Lower right: Tarbell 17
Oil on canvas
32 7/16 × 36 1/2" (82.4 × 92.7 cm)

The Alex Simpson, Jr., Collection
1944-13-6

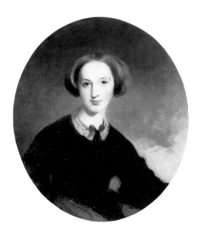

**Sully, Thomas**
*Portrait of Virginia Earp*
1859
On reverse: Virginia Earp / April
12, 1859 / Lillie Estelle Earp's /
private property / Sep. 23rd,
1892 / TS 1859 April
Oil on canvas
30 1/8 × 25" (76.5 × 63.5 cm)

Bequest of Anne Tucker Earp
1953-11-18

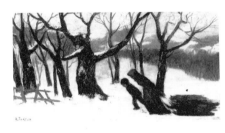

**Thayer, Abbott Handerson**
American, 1849–1921
*Winter 1890*
1890
Lower left: A. THAYER
Oil on canvas
10 1/4 × 18 1/8" (26 × 46 cm)

Centennial gift of Mrs. Francis P.
Garvan
1976-164-1

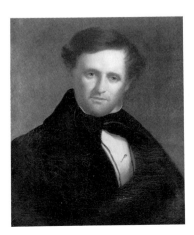

**Sully, Thomas, follower of**
Previously listed as in the manner
of Thomas Sully (PMA 1965)
*Portrait of Isaac Paschal Morris*
c. 1835–40
Oil on canvas
24 × 20 1/4" (61 × 51.4 cm)

Gift of Miss Lydia Thompson
Morris
1928-7-121

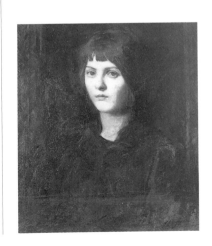

**Thayer, Abbott Handerson**
*My Daughter Mary (Portrait of
Mary Thayer)*
c. 1894
Lower right: Abbott H. Thayer
Oil on canvas
24 1/8 × 20 1/8" (61.3 × 51.1 cm)

The Alex Simpson, Jr., Collection
1928-63-9

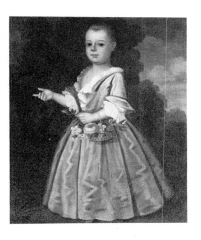

**Theus, Jeremiah**
American, born Switzerland,
c. 1719–1774
*Portrait of Ellinor Cordes*
c. 1746
Oil on canvas
29 7/8 × 24 3/8" (75.9 × 61.9 cm)

The Collection of Edgar William
and Bernice Chrysler Garbisch
1967-268-1

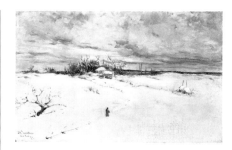

**Twachtman, John Henry**
American, 1853–1902
*Japanese Winter Landscape*
1879
Lower left: J. H. Twachtman /
New York / 79
Oil on canvas
12 3/4 × 20 1/8" (32.4 × 51.1 cm)

The Alex Simpson, Jr., Collection
1946-5-3

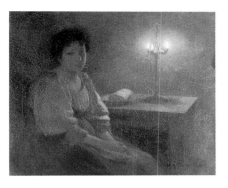

**Trotter, Mary K.**
American, active France and
United States, active 1888–1901
*Lamplight*
1888
Lower right: M K Trotter 1888
Oil on canvas
20 1/8 × 24 3/8" (51.1 × 61.9 cm)

John G. Johnson Collection
inv. 2773

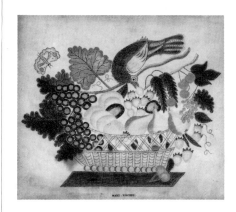

**Vincent, Mary**
American, active c. 1800–c. 1830
*Still Life with a Basket of Fruit*
Center bottom: MARY . VINCENT.
Oil on velvet
15 13/16 × 18" (40.2 × 45.7 cm)

Gift of Frank and Alice Osborn
1966-68-54

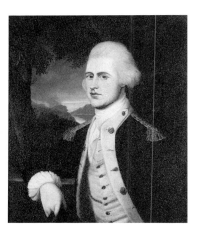

**Trumbull, John, attributed to**
American, 1756–1843
*Portrait of Major John Macpherson*
c. 1775–85
Oil on canvas on panel
30 × 25" (76.2 × 63.5 cm)

Gift of Caleb W. Hornor
1956-39-1

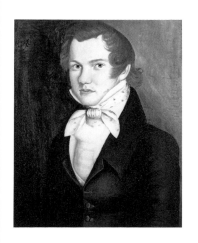

**Wale, T., attributed to**
American, active c. 1810–c. 1820
*Portrait of Edwin Sturdevant of
Hartland, Vermont*
Companion to the following
painting
c. 1810
Oil on panel
25 7/8 × 20 3/8" (65.7 × 51.7 cm)

Bequest of Edgar William and
Bernice Chrysler Garbisch
1981-1-6

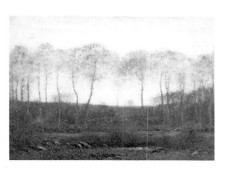

**Tryon, Dwight W.**
American, 1849–1925
*Autumn Evening*
1919–20
Lower right: D. W. TRYON;
on reverse: Autumn Evening /
D W Tryon / 1919–20
Oil on panel
13 7/8 × 20" (35.2 × 50.8 cm)

The Alex Simpson, Jr., Collection
1945-5-2

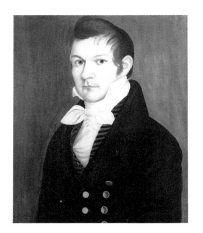

**Wale, T., attributed to**
*Portrait of Cullen Sturdevant of
Hartland, Vermont*
Companion to the preceding
painting
c. 1810
Oil on panel
25 15/16 × 21 9/16" (65.9 × 54.8 cm)

Bequest of Edgar William and
Bernice Chrysler Garbisch
1981-1-7

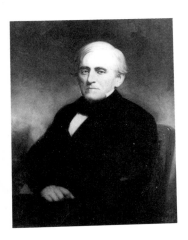

**Waugh, Samuel Bell**
American, 1814–1885
*Portrait of Isaac Paschal Morris*
1873
Lower right: 1873. / S. B.
Waugh.
Oil on canvas
36 1/8 × 29" (91.8 × 73.7 cm)

Bequest of Lydia Thompson
Morris
1932-45-119

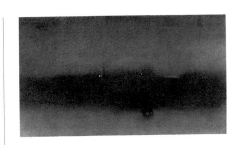

**Whistler, James Abbott
McNeill**
*Nocturne*
c. 1875–80
Oil on canvas
12 1/4 × 20 3/8" (31.1 × 51.7 cm)

John G. Johnson Collection
cat. 1111

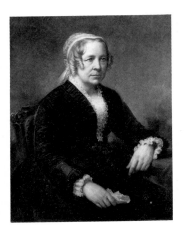

**Waugh, Samuel Bell,
follower of**
Previously listed as Samuel Bell
Waugh (PMA 1965)
*Portrait of Rebecca Thompson Morris*
After 1873
Oil on canvas
39 × 29 1/8" (99.1 × 74 cm)

Bequest of Lydia Thompson
Morris
1932-45-118

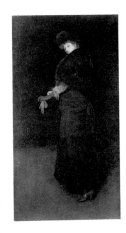

**Whistler, James Abbott
McNeill**
*Arrangement in Black (The Lady in
the Yellow Buskin)*
c. 1883
Oil on canvas
86 × 43 1/2" (218.4 × 110.5 cm)

Purchased with the W. P.
Wilstach Fund
W1895-1-11

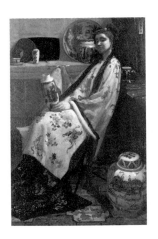

**Wayne, Hattie**
American, active c. 1864
*Portrait of Abraham Lincoln*
1864
Oil on canvas
30 1/8 × 25 1/16" (76.5 × 63.7 cm)

Gift of Mrs. Richard Waln Meirs
1933-11-2

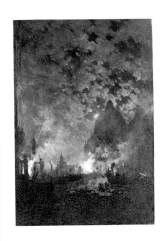

**Whistler, James Abbott
McNeill, imitator of**
Previously listed as James Abbott
McNeill Whistler (PMA 1965)
*Grand Canal, Venice (Moonlight)*
After 1890
Lower right (spurious): Whistler,
1890.
Oil on canvas
33 1/8 × 21 3/8" (84.1 × 54.3 cm)

The George W. Elkins Collection
E1924-4-32

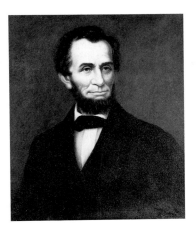

**Whistler, James Abbott
McNeill**
American, active England,
1834–1903
*The Lady of the Lang Lijsen*
1864
Upper right: Whistler 1864
Oil on canvas
36 3/4 × 24 1/8" (93.3 × 61.3 cm)

John G. Johnson Collection
cat. 1112

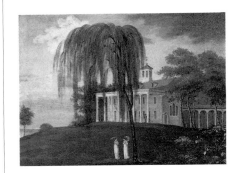

**Wiess, J.**
American, active c. 1797
*Home of George Washington*
1797
Oil on canvas
15 13/16 × 20 11/16" (40.2 × 52.5 cm)

The Collection of Edgar William
and Bernice Chrysler Garbisch
1966-219-2

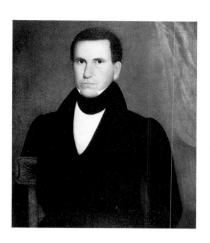

**Wilkie, John**
American, active c. 1830–c. 1840
*Portrait of a Man*
1836
On reverse: John Wilkie Pinxit /
Hamilton 20 Dec-1836
Oil on canvas
29 7/8 × 25" (75.9 × 63.5 cm)

The Louise and Walter Arensberg
Collection
1950-134-523

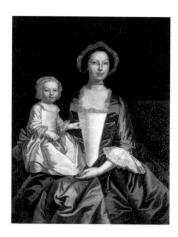

**Wollaston, John,
attributed to**
American, born England,
active c. 1736–c. 1767
Previously listed as John
Wollaston (PMA 1965)
*Portrait of Mrs. Perry and Her
Daughter Anna*
c. 1758
Oil on canvas
49 15/16 × 37 1/4" (126.8 × 94.6 cm)

Gift of the Robert L. McNeil, Jr.,
Trusts
1961-226-1

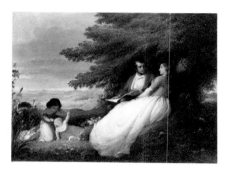

**Winner, William E.**
American, c. 1815–1883
*Domestic Felicity*
c. 1845–50
Oil on canvas
20 × 26 5/8" (50.8 × 67.6 cm)

The W. P. Wilstach Collection,
bequest of Anna H. Wilstach
W1893-1-125

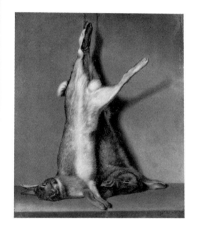

**Woodside, John Archibald, Sr.**
American, 1781–1852
*Still Life with Rabbits*
1827
Lower right: J. A. Woodside
1827
Oil on canvas
23 7/16 × 17 7/16" (59.5 × 44.3 cm)

Bequest of Robert Nebinger
1889-110

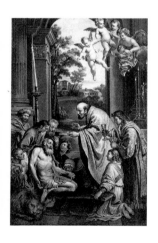

**Winner, William E.**
*The Last Communion of Saint Jerome*
Copy after the painting by
Domenichino (Italian,
1581–1641), in the Vatican
c. 1850
Lower left: WM E WINNER
Oil on canvas
29 × 19 1/8" (73.7 × 48.6 cm)

Gift of Mr. and Mrs. Samuel
James
1975-86-1

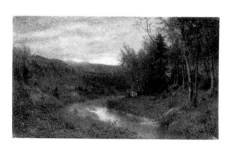

**Wyant, Alexander Helwig**
American, 1836–1892
*The Gathering Storm*
c. 1875–90
Lower right: A. H. Wyant
Oil on canvas
15 3/8 × 25" (39 × 63.5 cm)

The Alex Simpson, Jr., Collection
1928-63-11

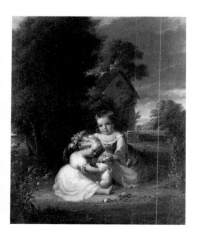

**Winner, William E.**
*Landscape with Figures*
c. 1855–65
On reverse: Winner Pinxit
Oil on canvas
30 1/4 × 25 1/4" (76.8 × 64.1 cm)

The W. P. Wilstach Collection,
bequest of Anna H. Wilstach
W1893-1-126

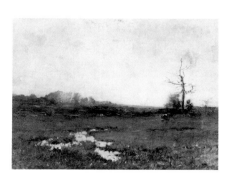

**Wyant, Alexander Helwig**
*Pastureland, Kaaterskill*
1880s
Lower left: A. H. Wyant
Oil on canvas
14 × 19 1/4" (35.6 × 48.9 cm)

Gift of Lucie Washington
Mitcheson in memory of Robert
Stockton Johnson Mitcheson for
the Robert Stockton Johnson
Mitcheson Collection
1938-22-4

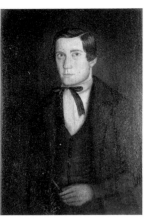

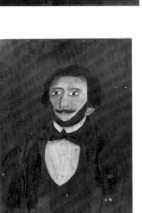

**Wyckoff, Sylvester**
American, active 19th century
*Self-Portrait*
See following painting for reverse
c. 1825
Oil on panel
29 1/4 × 19 1/4" (74.3 × 48.9 cm)

The Louise and Walter Arensberg
Collection
1950-134-526a

**Wyckoff, Sylvester**
*Portrait of a Man*
Reverse of the preceding painting
c. 1825
Oil on panel
29 1/4 × 19 1/4" (74.3 × 48.9 cm)

The Louise and Walter Arensberg
Collection
1950-134-526b

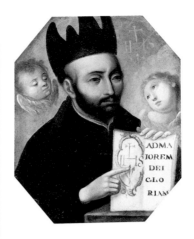

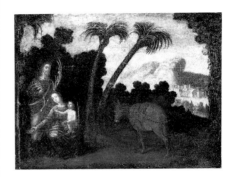

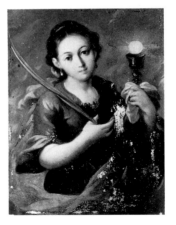

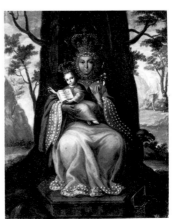

**Arellano**
Mexican, active c. 1774
Previously listed as Juan de
Arellano (PMA 1965)
*Portrait of an Ecclesiastic*
1774
Upper right: IHS; lower right:
IHS / ADMA / IOREM / DEI / GLO
/ RIAM / Arellano. f. 1774
Oil on copper
13 5/8 × 10 1/2" (34.6 × 26.7 cm)

The Robert H. Lamborn
Collection
1903-904

**Becerra, Fray Diego**
Mexican, active c. 1640–c. 1699
*Rest on the Flight into Egypt*
c. 1640–50
Center bottom: S. P. De Becerra
Oil on canvas
18 5/8 × 24 1/4" (47.3 × 61.6 cm)

The Robert H. Lamborn
Collection
1903-935

**Cabrera, Miguel**
Mexican, 1695–1768
*Martyr*
c. 1740
Oil on canvas
8 3/8 × 6 1/8" (20.3 × 15.6 cm)

The Robert H. Lamborn
Collection
1903-879

**Cabrera, Miguel**
*Crowned Virgin and Child*
1762
Center bottom: Mich Cabrera,
pinxit 1762; on book held by
Christ child: Volvio / christo / el
Ros- / tro por / no ver / vo sacri- /
legio.
Oil on copper
16 9/16 × 12 1/2" (42.1 × 31.7 cm)

The Robert H. Lamborn
Collection
1903-897

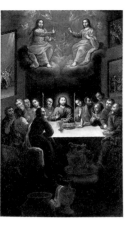

**Cabrera, Miguel, attributed to**
Previously listed as Mexican, unknown artist, 18th century (PMA 1965)
*The Last Supper*
After 1719
Oil on canvas
77 1/8 × 44" (195.9 × 111.8 cm)

The Robert H. Lamborn Collection
1903-915

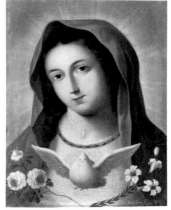

**Caro, Manuel**
Mexican, active c. 1781–c. 1820
*The Virgin*
c. 1781
Lower right: Manl. Caro. F.
Oil on canvas
16 1/2 × 12 1/2" (41.9 × 31.7 cm)

The Robert H. Lamborn Collection
1903-872

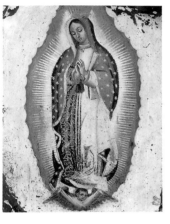

**Cabrera, Miguel, attributed to**
*Virgin of Guadalupe*
c. 1740
Oil on copper
15 1/2 × 11 5/8" (39.4 × 29.5 cm)

The Louise and Walter Arensberg Collection
1950-134-817

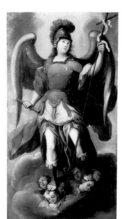

**Correa, Juan, the Younger**
Mexican, active c. 1731–1760
*The Virgin*
c. 1735
Lower right: Juan Correa / F.
Oil on canvas
8 3/8 × 6 1/8" (21.3 × 15.6 cm)

The Robert H. Lamborn Collection
1903-877

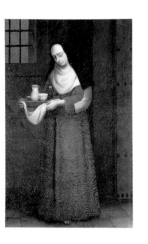

**Cabrera, Miguel, follower of**
Previously listed as Mexican, unknown artist, 19th century (PMA 1965)
*Capuchin Nun Carrying Food*
Companion to the following painting
c. 1775–1800
Oil on canvas
70 × 42" (177.8 × 106.7 cm)

The Robert H. Lamborn Collection
1903-938

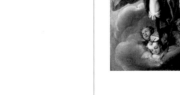

**Correa, Juan, the Younger**
*The Archangel Michael*
1739
Upper right, on banner: QUIS UT DE US; lower right: Juan Correa, 1739
Oil on canvas
71 1/2 × 36 5/16" (181.6 × 92.2 cm)

The Robert H. Lamborn Collection
1903-919

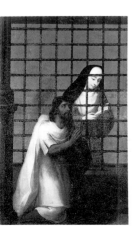

**Cabrera, Miguel, follower of**
Previously listed as Mexican, unknown artist, 19th century (PMA 1965)
*Capuchin Nun Reading to an Indian Visitor through the Gates of a Convent*
Companion to the preceding painting
c. 1775–1800
Oil on canvas
70 3/8 × 41 3/4" (178.7 × 106 cm)

The Robert H. Lamborn Collection
1903-933

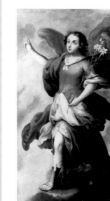

**Correa, Juan, the Younger**
*The Archangel Gabriel*
1739
Lower right: Juan Correa f. 1739.
Oil on canvas
71 3/4 × 36 3/8" (182.2 × 92.4 cm)

The Robert H. Lamborn Collection
1903-923

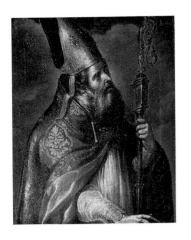

**Echave Orio, Baltasar de**
Mexican, born c. 1548, last dated
work 1612
*Saint Augustine*
c. 1600
Oil on canvas
19 11/16 × 15" (50 × 38.1 cm)

The Robert H. Lamborn
Collection
1903-934

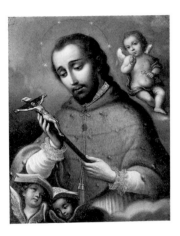

**Enriquez, Nicolas**
Mexican, active c. 1730–c. 1768
*Saint John Nepomuck*
1738
Lower right: N. Enriquz. Fct.;
on book: Pro Sigillo / Confes- /
sion.; on crucifix: INRI
Oil on copper
11 1/4 × 8 1/4" (28.6 × 20.9 cm)

The Robert H. Lamborn
Collection
1903-889

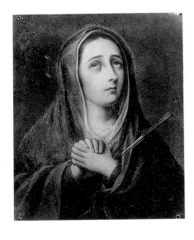

**Enriquez, Nicolas**
*The Suicide of Lucretia*
c. 1750
Center right: Nicolas / Enriq /
Fecit
Oil on copper
10 7/8 × 8 3/8" (27.6 × 21.3 cm)

The Robert H. Lamborn
Collection
1903-891

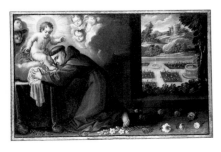

**Herrera, Fray Miguel de**
Mexican, active c. 1725–c. 1780
*Saint Anthony in Prayer before the
Christ Child*
1725
Lower right: Fr. Miguel de
Herrera, Augustino, fect. / 1725
ad.
Oil on canvas
43 1/4 × 66 3/8" (109.8 × 168.6 cm)

The Robert H. Lamborn
Collection
1903-943

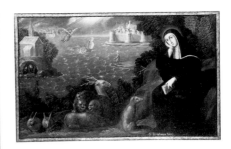

**Herrera, Fray Miguel de**
*Saint Limbania the Virgin and
Sympathetic Wild Animals*
1725
Lower left: A. Migl. de Herrera, /
Aug. Anno fait. 1725 ad; lower
right: SCTA. Limbania Virg.
Oil on canvas
43 × 66 1/8" (109.2 × 168 cm)

The Robert H. Lamborn
Collection
1903-906

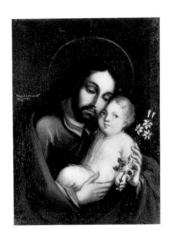

**Herrera, Fray Miguel de**
*Christ and a Child*
1778
Center left: Miguel de Herrera.
Ft. / Megco. 1778.
Oil on canvas
16 3/8 × 11 1/2" (41.6 × 29.2 cm)

The Robert H. Lamborn
Collection
1903-894

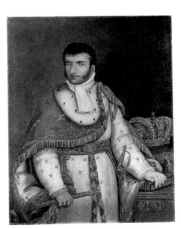

**Huerta, Josephus Arias,
attributed to**
Mexican, active 19th century
*Portrait of Agustín de Iturbide,
Emperor of Mexico*
Companion to the following
painting
1822
On book: CONSTI / TUCION /
AMERI / [CA]NA; on robe: A / I.;
on belt buckle: AP.
Oil on canvas
44 1/16 × 33 1/2" (111.9 × 85.1 cm)

Gift of an anonymous donor
1922-89-2

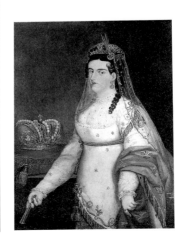

**Huerta, Josephus Arias,
attributed to**
*Portrait of Anna Maria Iturbide,
Empress of Mexico*
Companion to the preceding
painting
1822
Oil on canvas
44 1/8 × 33 1/2" (112.1 × 85.1 cm)

Gift of an anonymous donor
1922-89-1

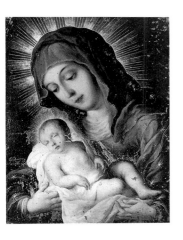

**Juarez, Juan Rodriguez**
Mexican, c. 1675–1728
*Virgin and Child*
c. 1700
Center left: Ju Rodriguez /
Xuarez f.a
Oil on copper
11 × 8 1/2" (27.9 × 21.6 cm)

The Robert H. Lamborn
Collection
1903-878

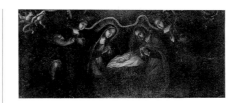

**Martínez, Francisco**
Mexican, active by c. 1718,
died 1758
*The Nativity*
c. 1750
On scroll: GLORIA IN
EXCELS[IS] [DEO] ET IN TERRA
PAX HOMINIBUS BONAE
VOLUNTATIS [N]OBIS HODIE
Oil on canvas
23 1/16 × 51 9/16" (58.6 × 131 cm)

The Robert H. Lamborn
Collection
1903-939

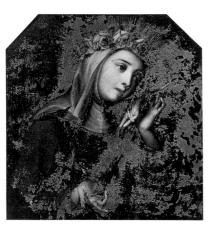

**Juarez, Juan Rodriguez**
*Saint Rose of Lima*
c. 1710
Lower right: Juan Juarez; on
reverse: Santa Rosalia de Lima,
Convent of St. Catherine of Siena,
Juan Juarez, Mexico
Oil on copper
13 1/2 × 12 3/4" (34.3 × 32.4 cm)

The Robert H. Lamborn
Collection
1903-901

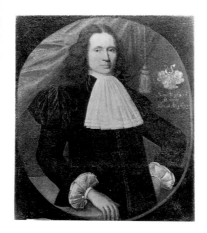

**Mexican?, unknown artist**
Previously listed as Spanish,
unknown artist, 17th century
(PMA 1965)
*Portrait of a Gentleman*
1679
Center right: Natg Ao 1643 d /
18 Aprilus / Pietg est Ao 1679
Oil on canvas
35 3/16 × 29" (89.4 × 73.7 cm)

The Bloomfield Moore Collection
1899-1120

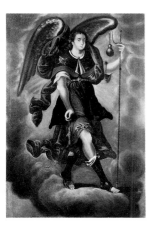

**Jurado, Juan José**
Mexican, active c. 1727
*The Archangel Raphael*
1727
Lower left: Juan Joseph. Jurado.
fa. / Año 1727
Oil on canvas
64 1/8 × 42 1/16" (162.9 × 106.8 cm)

The Robert H. Lamborn
Collection
1903-914

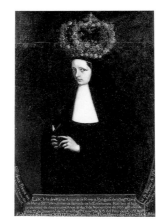

**Mexican, unknown artist**
Previously listed as Mexican,
unknown artist, 18th century
(PMA 1965)
*Portrait of the Reverend Mother
Maria Antonia de Rivera*
Retable
c. 1775
Lower left: Fue electa Priora en- /
Relecta e la misma fha. y / el dia
Miercoles 12. de 94. Fallecio / del
Marzo 1806.; lower right: 24 de
Marzo de 1791 / mes de año de
94 Falleció / de Marzo 1806.;
bottom center: La Ra. Madre
Maria Antonia de Rivera,
Religiosa de la Sagda. Compa. /
de Maria SSma. comunmente
llamada de la Enseñanza. Resibió
el habi- / to de edad de
diezynueve Años, el dia 9. de
Noviembre de 1755. y Professo /
el dia 12. de Diziembe. de 57. en
el Sagdo. Convto. de N. S. del
Pilar de la Ciud. de Mexco. / En
Manos del ylustrisimo. Sr. Dr.
Dn. Manuel Ant. Rojo del Rio. y
Bieyra dignimo. Arsovpo. de la
Ciud. de Mania.
Oil on canvas
49 × 31 5/8" (124.5 × 80.3 cm)

The Robert H. Lamborn
Collection
1903-920

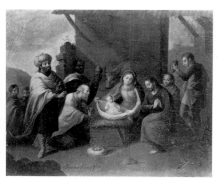

**López, Andreas**
Mexican, active 1777–1805
*The Adoration of the Magi*
c. 1800
Center bottom: Andreas Lopez
fecit.
Oil on canvas
36 3/4 × 43 1/4" (93.3 × 109.8 cm)

The Robert H. Lamborn
Collection
1903-932

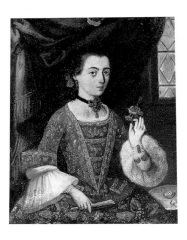

**Mexican, unknown artist**
Previously listed as Mexican, unknown artist, 17th century (PMA 1965)
*Portrait of a Lady*
18th century
Oil on copper
6 1/8 × 4 5/8" (15.6 × 11.7 cm)

The Robert H. Lamborn Collection
1903-874

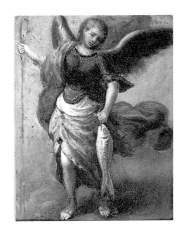

**Mexican, unknown artist**
*The Archangel Raphael*
18th century
Oil on copper
5 3/4 × 4 1/8" (14.6 × 10.5 cm)

The Robert H. Lamborn Collection
1903-875

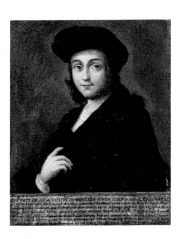

**Mexican, unknown artist**
Previously listed as Mexican, unknown artist, 17th century (PMA 1965)
*Virgin and Child, with Saints*
Escudo
18th century
Oil on vellum
5 15/16" (15.1 cm) diameter

The Robert H. Lamborn Collection
1903-900

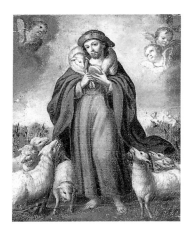

**Mexican, unknown artist**
*The Divine Shepherd*
18th century
Oil on canvas
9 1/4 × 7 1/2" (23.5 × 19 cm)

The Robert H. Lamborn Collection
1903-876

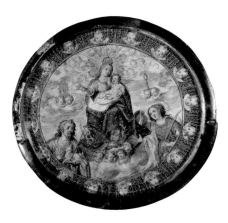

**Mexican, unknown artist**
*Saint Augustine as a Youth*
18th century
Across bottom: RETRATO DE S.S. AUGUSTIN QVANDO ERA JOVEN. CONFORME AL ORIGINAL. Q' / entre las cosas raras del Principe Aresio, se conserva en grande estimacion en Milan: donde hay / una continua tradicion, que Sn. Ambrosio Hizo añadir en las Letanias publicas De la Logica de- / Augustino libranos Señor; pero de quanta ventaja haya sido para la Iglesia esta Logica / despues de catolico Augustino lo publican tantos hereges convencidos, confundidos, conver- / tidos a si en su tiempo soma despues; por lo que el intimo Sn Augustino lo Uoma Filorofo Aibri- / [    ] y otro lo aclaman Principe de toi Filorofos. Manuel Villa en Año de 1784.
Oil on paper
6 3/8 × 4 3/4" (16.2 × 12.1 cm)

The Robert H. Lamborn Collection
1903-873

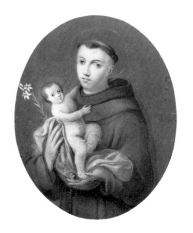

**Mexican, unknown artist**
*Saint Anthony Abbot*
18th century
Oil on copper
6 7/8 × 5 5/16" (17.5 × 13.5 cm)

The Robert H. Lamborn Collection
1903-880

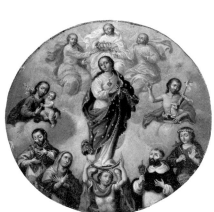

**Mexican, unknown artist**
*The Assumption of the Virgin*
18th century
Lower right: Faxfan de / los Go / F
Oil on copper
6 1/2" (16.5 cm) diameter

The Robert H. Lamborn Collection
1903-882

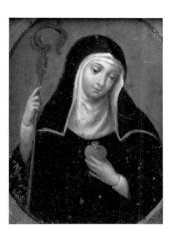

**Mexican, unknown artist**
*Saint Gertrude*
18th century
Lower right: Br. Alva
Oil on copper
4 × 3" (10.2 × 7.6 cm)

The Robert H. Lamborn
Collection
1903-883

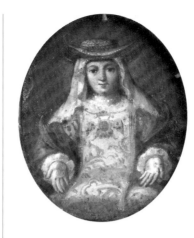

**Mexican, unknown artist**
*The Divine Shepherd*
Reverse of the preceding painting
18th century
Oil on copper
2 3/16 × 1 11/16" (5.6 × 4.3 cm)

The Robert H. Lamborn
Collection
1903-886b

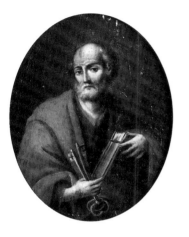

**Mexican, unknown artist**
*Saint Peter*
18th century
Oil on panel
5 × 3 5/8" (12.7 × 9.2 cm)

The Robert H. Lamborn
Collection
1903-884

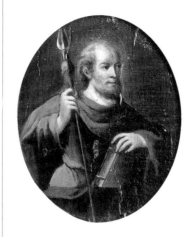

**Mexican, unknown artist**
*Apostle*
18th century
Oil on panel
4 15/16 × 3 11/16" (12.5 × 9.4 cm)

The Robert H. Lamborn
Collection
1903-887

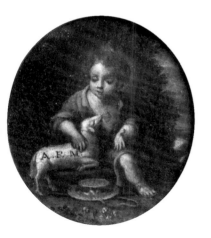

**Mexican, unknown artist**
*The Lamb of God*
18th century
Lower left: A.F.M.
Oil on copper
2 3/16 × 1 13/16" (5.6 × 4.6 cm)

The Robert H. Lamborn
Collection
1903-885

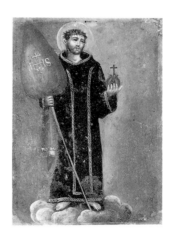

**Mexican, unknown artist**
*Saint John of God*
See following painting for reverse
18th century
Upper left, on cloth covering
staff: JHS
Oil on copper
7 1/2 × 6 1/2" (19 × 16.5 cm)

The Robert H. Lamborn
Collection
1903-888a

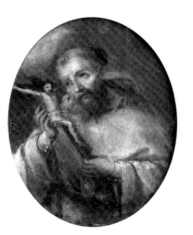

**Mexican, unknown artist**
*Saint Peter Nolasco*
See following painting for reverse
18th century
Oil on copper
2 3/16 × 1 11/16" (5.6 × 4.3 cm)

The Robert H. Lamborn
Collection
1903-886a

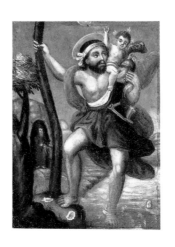

**Mexican, unknown artist**
*Saint Christopher*
Reverse of the preceding painting
18th century
Oil on copper
7 1/2 × 6 1/2" (19 × 16.5 cm)

The Robert H. Lamborn
Collection
1903-888b

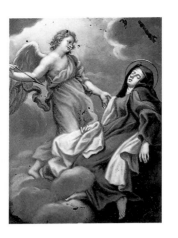

**Mexican, unknown artist**
*Saint Theresa in Ecstasy*
Based on the sculpture, dated
1644–52, by Gian Lorenzo
Bernini (Italian, 1598–1680), in
Santa Maria della Vittoria, Rome
18th century
Oil on copper
9 1/2 × 6 7/8" (24.1 × 17.5 cm)

The Robert H. Lamborn
Collection
1903-892

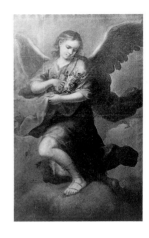

**Mexican, unknown artist**
*Angel with Flowers*
18th century
Oil on canvas
65 1/4 × 39 1/4" (165.7 × 99.7 cm)

The Robert H. Lamborn
Collection
1903-908

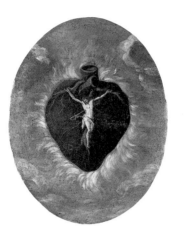

**Mexican, unknown artist**
*Christ Crucified on the Sacred Heart*
18th century
Oil on canvas
18 3/8 × 13 1/2" (46.7 × 34.3 cm)

The Robert H. Lamborn
Collection
1903-902

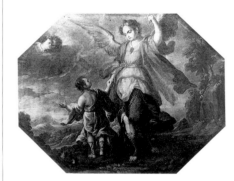

**Mexican, unknown artist**
*Guardian Angel*
18th century
Oil on canvas
32 15/16 × 40 5/8" (83.7 × 103.2 cm)

The Robert H. Lamborn
Collection
1903-909

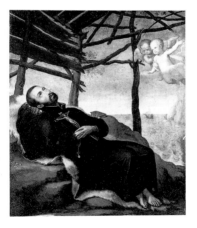

**Mexican, unknown artist**
*Saint Francis Xavier*
18th century
Oil on copper
12 1/2 × 10 1/8" (31.7 × 25.7 cm)

The Robert H. Lamborn
Collection
1903-903

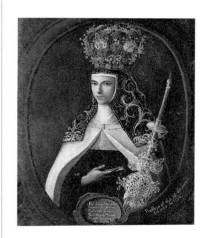

**Mexican, unknown artist**
*Portrait of a Nun (Sister Inés Jopha)*
18th century
Center bottom, in medallion: Sor
Ines Jopha del / Corason de Jesus /
Relixiosa Profesa / En el Conto.
Nuedo. / de Sta Theresa / de
Mexico; lower right: Profleso el
dia 25 de Junio / del año de 1756
Oil on canvas
36 13/16 × 30 1/8" (93.5 × 76.5 cm)

The Robert H. Lamborn
Collection
1903-911

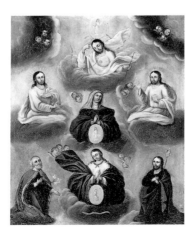

**Mexican, unknown artist**
*The Holy Trinity, with the Virgin
and Saints*
18th century
Center top: IDEA / DIVINA / IN
CRISTALO ENTIS MEI INTACTAM
TE LABE PREPARO
Oil on copper
12 5/8 × 10 1/8" (32.1 × 25.7 cm)

The Robert H. Lamborn
Collection
1903-905

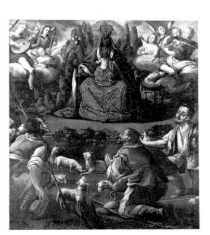

**Mexican, unknown artist**
*Black Virgin and Child*
18th century
Oil on canvas
60 1/4 × 53 3/16" (153 × 135.1 cm)

The Robert H. Lamborn
Collection
1903-912

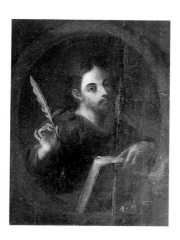

**Mexican, unknown artist**
*Saint John the Evangelist*
18th century
Oil on burlap
32 3/4 × 26 1/16" (83.2 × 66.2 cm)

The Robert H. Lamborn
Collection
1903-913

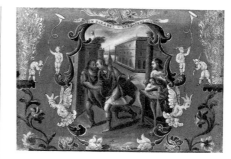

**Mexican, unknown artist**
*Figures on a Street*
Decorative panel; companion to
the following three paintings
18th century
Center top: NADA ES CON
PARABLE VERDADERO AMIGO
Oil on canvas
15 3/4 × 22 1/2" (40 × 57.1 cm)

The Robert H. Lamborn
Collection
1903-922

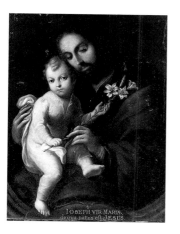

**Mexican, unknown artist**
*Saint Joseph with the Christ Child*
18th century
Center bottom: IOSEPH VIR
MARIAE, / dequa natus est
JESUS.
Oil on canvas
33 1/8 × 24 7/8" (84.1 × 63.2 cm)

The Robert H. Lamborn
Collection
1903-916

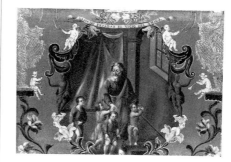

**Mexican, unknown artist**
*Old Man Led by Children*
See previous entry
18th century
Center top: NO HA DE ENFADAR
EL VICIO DEL AMIGO.
Oil on canvas
15 3/4 × 21 7/8" (40 × 55.6 cm)

The Robert H. Lamborn
Collection
1903-924

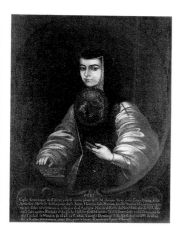

**Mexican, unknown artist**
*Portrait of Sister Juana Inés de la
Cruz*
After a self-portrait
18th century
Across bottom: FIEL / Copia de
otra que de si hizo, y de su mano
pintò la R. M. Juana Ynés de la
Cruz Fenix de la / America,
Glorioso desempeño de su Sexo,
Honrra de la Nacion de este
Nuevo Mundo, y argu- / mento
de las admiraciones, y elogios de
el Antiguo. Naciò el dia 12. de
Nove. de el año de 1651. á las /
onse de la noche. Reciuiò el
Sagrado Habito de el Maximo Dr.
Sr. Sn. Geronimo en su Convento
de / esta Ciudad de Mexico. de
edad / 40. y 4. años, cinco mezes,
cinco dias. y cinco horas.
Requiescat in pace. Amen.; on
book: Obras de la Unica Poetisa /
Soror Juana Ynés / de la Cruz.
Oil on canvas
41 1/2 × 32 1/2" (105.4 × 82.5 cm)

The Robert H. Lamborn
Collection
1903-918

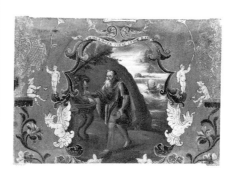

**Mexican, unknown artist**
*Old Man at a Fountain*
See previous two entries
18th century
Center top: NADA DESSEA
QUIEN TIENE LO QUE BASTA
Oil on canvas
15 3/4 × 21 7/8" (40 × 55.6 cm)

The Robert H. Lamborn
Collection
1903-925

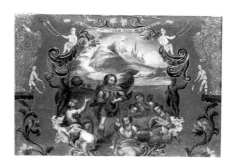

**Mexican, unknown artist**
*Allegorical Figures in a Landscape*
See previous three entries
18th century
Center top: EL VIRTUOSO
TRADAXO FIDE SU REPOSO.
Oil on canvas
15 1/2 × 22 1/2" (39.4 × 57.1 cm)

The Robert H. Lamborn
Collection
1903-926

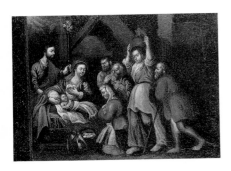

**Mexican, unknown artist**
*The Adoration of the Shepherds*
18th century
Oil on canvas
11 ⁵/₈ × 16 ¹/₁₆" (29.5 × 40.8 cm)

The Robert H. Lamborn
Collection
1903-927

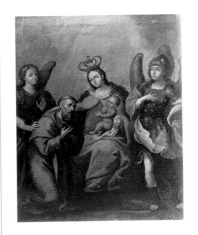

**Mexican, unknown artist**
*Virgin and Child Guarded by Angels*
18th century
Oil on canvas
23 ¹/₄ × 18 ¹/₂" (59 × 47 cm)

The Robert H. Lamborn
Collection
1903-940

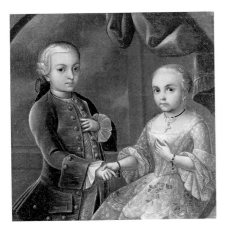

**Mexican, unknown artist**
*Portrait of Two Children of the Aristocracy*
18th century
Oil on canvas
31 ⁵/₈ × 29 ⁷/₈" (80.3 × 75.9 cm)

The Robert H. Lamborn
Collection
1903-929

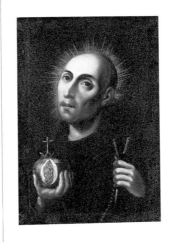

**Mexican, unknown artist**
*Saint John of God with a Pomegranate Surmounted by a Cross*
18th century
Oil on canvas
24 ³/₁₆ × 16 ⁷/₁₆" (61.4 × 41.7 cm)

The Robert H. Lamborn
Collection
1903-942

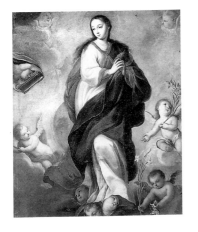

**Mexican, unknown artist**
*The Assumption of the Virgin*
18th century
Oil on canvas
51 × 40 ³/₄" (129.5 × 103.5 cm)

The Robert H. Lamborn
Collection
1903-930

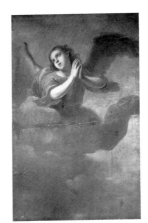

**Mexican, unknown artist**
*Angel in Clouds*
18th century
Oil on canvas
65 ³/₈ × 39 ⁵/₈" (166 × 100.6 cm)

The Robert H. Lamborn
Collection
1903-944

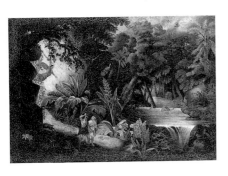

**Mexican, unknown artist**
*The Expulsion from Eden*
18th century
Oil on canvas
19 ³/₁₆ × 26 ¹/₂" (48.7 × 67.3 cm)

The Robert H. Lamborn
Collection
1903-936

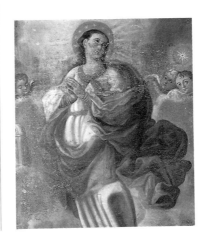

**Mexican, unknown artist**
*The Virgin with Cherubim*
18th century
Oil on burlap
40 × 33 ⁹/₁₆" (101.6 × 85.2 cm)

The Robert H. Lamborn
Collection
1903-946

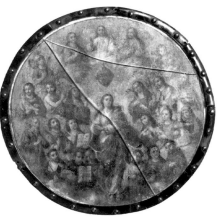

**Mexican, unknown artist**
*The Assumption of the Virgin*
Escudo
18th century
Oil on vellum
7 1/2" (19 cm) diameter

Gift of Mrs. John Harrison
1915-196

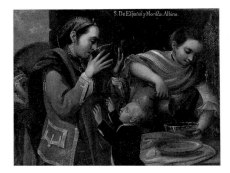

**Mexican, unknown artist**
*Racial Examples*
From an untraced series;
companion to the preceding
painting
c. 1840
Upper right: 8. De Español, y
Morisca. Albino.
Oil on canvas
31 × 39 3/4" (78.7 × 101 cm)

Gift of the nieces and nephews of
Wright S. Ludington in his honor
1980-139-2

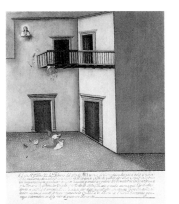

**Mexican, unknown artist**
*Fall from a Balcony*
Retable
After c. 1803
Across bottom: El Dia Martes 22.
de Febrero del año de 1803.
tercero de Carnestolendas entre
ocho y nueve / de la mañana,
estando la Criada Barbara Rico
con el Niño de edad de dos años y
medio en los bra- / zos
improvisamente, y sin haber
causa se desquició, y undió un
pedazo del Corredor de la Casa
Estanco; / y haviendo caido
abrazados Criada, y niño do la
altitud de seis y media varas, que
hày desde / donde si undiò à el
empedrado del suelo, al dar el
golpe, quedaron apartados, pero
sin daño, ni / lesion alguna, à
causa de haver invocado la Criada
à el Alma de Maria Santisima, por
/ cuya intercecion se deja vèr el
presente Portento.
Oil on canvas
33 3/4 × 24 1/2" (85.7 × 62.2 cm)

The Louise and Walter Arensberg
Collection
1950-134-492

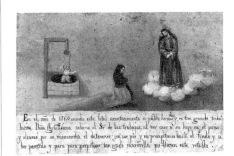

**Mexican, unknown artist**
*Accident in a Well*
Retable
After 1864
Across bottom: En el año de 1864
sucedio este fatal acontecimiento
á pablo hernandez y en tan grande
tribu- / lacion Doña Gerbaca
Licea aclamo al Sr de los trabajos,
al ver caer á su hijo en el pozo:
y alcanzó por su micericordia
el detenerse con un pie y no
precipitarse hastá el fondo
y á- / ber perecido y para para
perpetuar tan gra[n]de maravilla
pu-blican este retablo.
Oil on tin
7 × 10" (17.8 × 25.4 cm)

The Louise and Walter Arensberg
Collection
1950-134-824

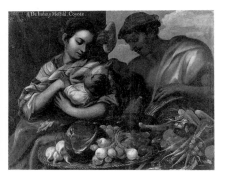

**Mexican, unknown artist**
*Racial Examples*
From an untraced series;
companion to the following
painting
c. 1840
Upper left: 4. De Indio, y
Mestisa. Coyote.
Oil on canvas
31 × 39 3/4" (78.7 × 101 cm)

Gift of the nieces and nephews of
Wright S. Ludington in his honor
1980-139-1

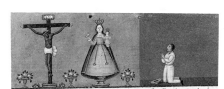

**Mexican, unknown artist**
*Recovery from an Illness*
Retable
After 1865
On crucifix: INRI; across bottom:
En el año de 1865 en el mes de
Junio, enpeso a estar grabemente
enfermo Juan Ebangelista
Gonsales, de / una inflamasion
de vientre y mal de Orina, que
lo cual se bido a la muerte,
tanto que duro en cama / dies
meses catorce dias, y mirandose
en esta aflision tan grande, dicho
enfermo y su Sra. Madre / Maria
Bustamante, lo encomendo con

todos las beras de su corazon, al Sor. del Ospital de la villa / de Salamanca, y a Nra. Sra. de la SALUD; que le diera el alibio si le conbenia.—por lo que lo consiguio / milagrosamente, y por este beneficio tan singular le dedican este cuadrito a dichas Ymagenes. / y tanbien para demostrar que es mui grande su / misericordia.
Oil on panel
5 7/8 × 9 1/4" (14.9 × 23.5 cm)

The Louise and Walter Arensberg Collection
1950-134-823

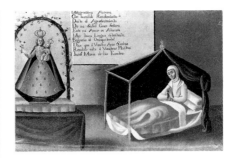

**Mexican, unknown artist**
*Joseph Maria de las Fuentes*
Retable
19th century
Center top: Milagrosisima Aurora / Con humilde Rendimiento / Doite el Agradecimiento / De mi Salud Gran Señora / Enti mi Amor se Atesora / Mas tosca Lengua detentente. / ¿Balgame el Omnipotente? / Dios que a Vuestrs Aras Santas / Rendido esta a Vuestras Plantas / Josef Maria de las Fuentes.
Oil on canvas
11 7/8 × 16 7/8" (30.2 × 42.9 cm)

The Louise and Walter Arensberg Collection
1950-134-815

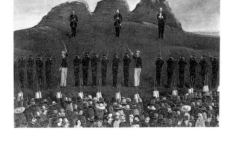

**Mexican, unknown artist**
*The Execution of Maximilian*
After 1867
Oil on canvas
14 7/8 × 20 1/4" (37.8 × 51.4 cm)

The Louise and Walter Arensberg Collection
1950-134-827

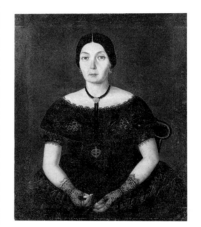

**Mexican, unknown artist**
*Portrait of the Countess of Canal*
19th century
Oil on canvas
25 3/16 × 20" (64 × 50.8 cm)

Gift of Mrs. René d'Harnoncourt
1969-273-1

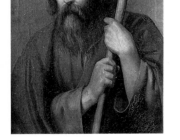

**Mexican, unknown artist**
*Head of a Pilgrim*
19th century
Oil on canvas
30 3/8 × 22" (77.1 × 55.9 cm)

The Robert H. Lamborn Collection
1903-907

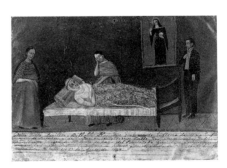

**Middle American, unknown artist**
*Recovery from an Illness*
Retable
1849
Across bottom: Doña Josefa Aguilera y Billalobos Hayandose grabemente Enferma de Una Enfla / macion de Bientre y allandose en los ultimos Casie Instantes de Bida, Inboco a / la Milagrosa Imagen de Sta. Rita de Casia del Recinto de Guadalupe y Milagrosamente / Consignio la Salud Despues de 3 Meses de padeser: y en Memoria de tan grande beneficio / Dedica Este Retablo en 13. de Agosto de 1849.
Oil on tin
10 1/8 × 14" (25.7 × 35.6 cm)

The Louise and Walter Arensberg Collection
1950-134-814

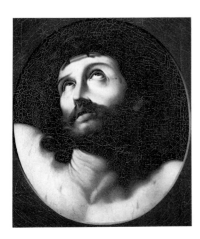

**Mexican, unknown artist**
*Christ as the Man of Sorrows*
19th century
After a painting by Guido Reni (Italian, 1575–1642) known in many versions
Oil on canvas
21 × 15 3/16" (53.3 × 38.6 cm)

The Robert H. Lamborn Collection
1903-941

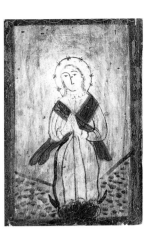

**Middle American,
unknown artist**
*Figure Praying*
19th century
Oil on panel
13 × 8 5/8" (33 × 21.9 cm)

The Louise and Walter Arensberg
Collection
1950-134-826

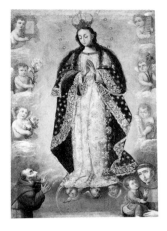

**Peruvian, unknown artist**
Previously listed as Peruvian,
unknown artist, 17th century
(PMA 1965)
*The Virgin Glorified with Virtues,
with Saints Francis of Assisi and
Anthony Abbot*
c. 1775–1825
Oil on canvas
51 3/8 × 34 1/2" (130.5 × 87.6 cm)

Gift of Mr. and Mrs. Leopold
Tschirky
1956-112-3

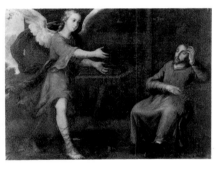

**Pérez, Diego**
Mexican, active c. 1720
*The Revelation to Saint Joseph*
1720
Center bottom: Diego Pérez
fta. 1720.
Oil on canvas
42 7/8 × 57" (108.9 × 144.8 cm)

The Robert H. Lamborn
Collection
1903-910

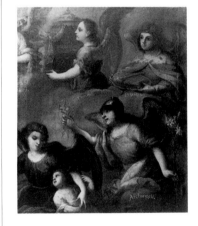

**Vallejo, Francisco Antonio**
Mexican, active c. 1770–c. 1800
*Angels Bearing Ecclesiastical
Insignia*
Fragment from the same original
as the following painting
c. 1780
Center: Cherubini. Throni.
Poteltates.; lower left: Angeli.;
lower right: Archangeli.
Oil on canvas
33 7/8 × 27 3/8" (86 × 69.5 cm)

The Robert H. Lamborn
Collection
1903-928

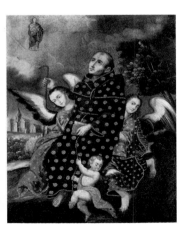

**Peruvian, unknown artist**
Previously listed as Peruvian,
unknown artist, 17th century
(PMA 1965)
*Saint Francis of Assisi*
c. 1775–1825
Oil on canvas
50 3/16 × 39 3/4" (127.5 × 101 cm)

Gift of Mr. and Mrs. Leopold
Tschirky
1956-112-2

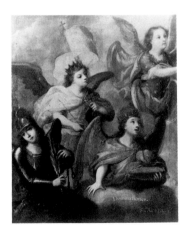

**Vallejo, Francisco Antonio**
*Angels Bearing Ecclesiastical
Insignia*
Fragment from the same original
as the preceding painting
c. 1780
Center top: Principatus.; center
right: Seraphini.; lower right:
Dominationes. / Francus Anto. à
Vallejo ft.
Oil on canvas
33 7/8 × 27 3/8" (86 × 69.5 cm)

The Robert H. Lamborn
Collection
1903-931

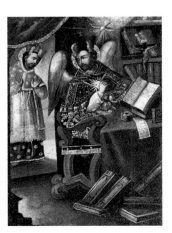

**Peruvian, unknown artist**
Previously listed as Peruvian,
unknown artist, 17th century
(PMA 1965)
*Saint Thomas Aquinas in His Study*
c. 1775–1825
Oil on canvas
32 3/4 × 24 1/16" (83.2 × 61.1 cm)

Gift of Mr. and Mrs. Leopold
Tschirky
1956-112-1

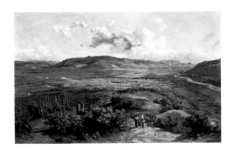

**Velasco, José Maria**
Mexican, 1840–1912
*Valley of Oaxaca*
1888
Lower right: José M. Velasco. /
Mexico 1888.
Oil on canvas
41 7/8 × 63 1/4" (106.4 × 160.6 cm)

Gift of the Mauch Chunk
National Bank
1949-56-1

# Twentieth-Century Painting

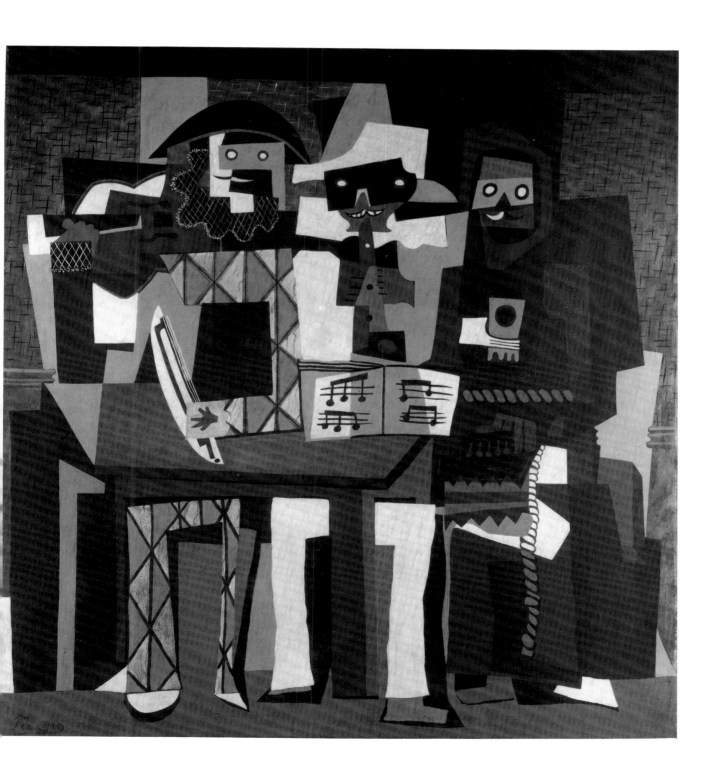

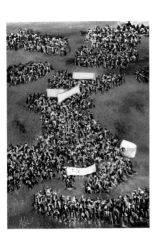

**Abidine (Abidine Dino)**
Turkish, born 1911
*Parade*
c. 1957
Lower left: Abidine
Oil on canvas
76 5/8 × 51 1/16" (194.6 × 129.7 cm)

Gift of Frederick Chait
1980-150-1

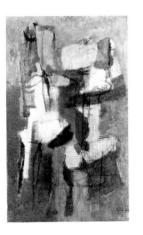

**Afro (Afro Basaldella)**
Italian, born 1912
*Abstraction of Two Figures*
1954
Lower right: Afro. 54
Oil on canvas
32 5/8 × 18 1/2" (82.9 × 47 cm)

Gift of Mr. and Mrs. James P.
Magill
1957-127-1

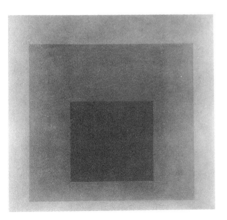

**Albers, Josef**
American, born Germany,
1888–1976
*Homage to the Square (It Seems)*
1963
Lower right: A 63
Oil on panel
39 7/8 × 40" (101.3 × 101.6 cm)

Gift of the Friends of the
Philadelphia Museum of Art
1968-183-1

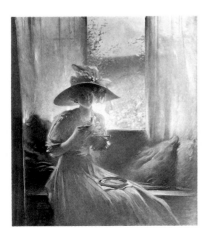

**Alexander, John White**
American, 1856–1915
*The Gossip*
1912
Lower left: John W. Alexander
1912
Oil on canvas
63 5/16 × 54" (160.8 × 137.2 cm)

The Alex Simpson, Jr., Collection
1928-63-1

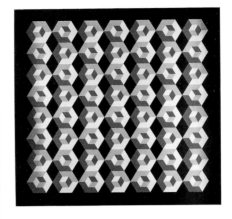

**Andrade, Edna**
American, born 1917
*Hot Blocks*
1966–67
Lower left: EA
Acrylic on canvas
60 × 60" (152.4 × 152.4 cm)

Purchased with the Philadelphia
Foundation Fund
1967-65-1

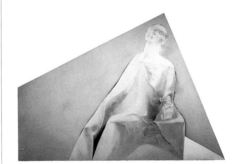

**Andrade, Edna**
*Night Sea*
1977
Lower left: EA
Acrylic on canvas
72 × 71 15/16" (182.9 × 182.7 cm)

Gift of the Philadelphia Arts
Exchange
1978-13-1

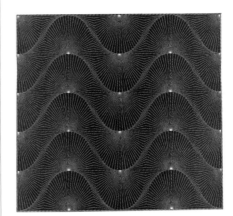

**André, Françoise**
American, born France,
born 1926
*Untitled*
1975
Lower left: Fr. Andre. 75.
Oil on canvas
68 3/4 × 85 3/4" (174.6 × 217.8 cm)

Purchased with funds contributed
by the friends of Charles
Stegeman and Françoise André
1975-165-2

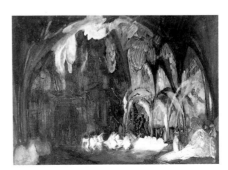

**Anisfeld, Boris**
Russian, active United States,
1879–1973
*Sketch for "Egyptian Nights"*
Sketch for a backdrop for the
ballet *Egyptian Nights*, by Michel
Fokine, based on a story by
Aleksander Pushkin and music by
Nikolai Rimski-Korsakov
1913
Lower left: Boris Anisfeld / 1913
Tempera on composition board
27 × 36" (68.6 × 91.4 cm)

Gift of Christian Brinton
1941-79-144

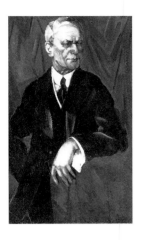

**Anisfeld, Boris**
*Portrait of Christian Brinton*
1920
Oil on canvas
41 × 25 3/4" (104.1 × 65.4 cm)

Gift of Mrs. Otis Chatfield-
Taylor
1985-112-4

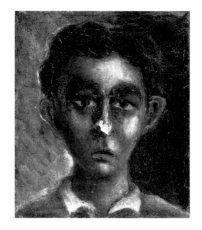

**Ara**
*Self-Portrait*
c. 1940
On reverse: Self Portrait by
B.D.K. Ara the Abbacuch Cook
Book painted in the time of
harvest
Oil on canvas
10 × 8 1/8" (25.4 × 20.6 cm)

The Louise and Walter Arensberg
Collection
1950-134-506

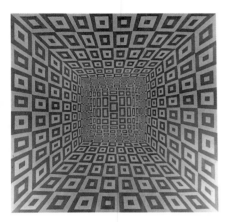

**Anuszkiewicz, Richard**
American, born 1930
*Knowledge and Disappearance*
1961
Oil on canvas
50 1/8 × 49 1/16" (127.3 × 124.6 cm)

Purchased with the Adele Haas
Turner and Beatrice Pastorius
Turner Memorial Fund
1968-77-1

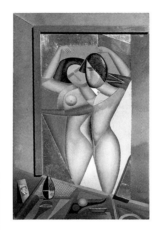

**Archipenko, Alexander
Porfirevich**
American, born Ukraine,
1887–1964
*In the Boudoir (Before the Mirror)*
1915
Lower right: A. Archipenko.
Oil, graphite, photograph, and
metal on panel
18 × 12" (45.7 × 30.5 cm)

Gift of Christian Brinton
1941-79-119

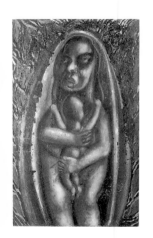

**Ara (Benjamin Dusanovich
Kosich)**
Mexican, active c. 1935
*Mother and Child Standing*
1935
Lower right: Ara; on reverse:
Benjamin Dusanovich Kosich
ARA / 1935 Boom Boom Barabas
Oil on gypsum board
20 3/16 × 11 7/8" (51.3 × 30.2 cm)

The Louise and Walter Arensberg
Collection
1950-134-505

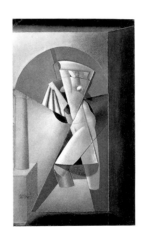

**Archipenko, Alexander
Porfirevich**
*The Bather*
1915
Lower left: A. Archipenko / Nice
1915
Oil, graphite, paper, and metal
on panel
20 × 11 1/2" (50.8 × 29.2 cm)

The Louise and Walter Arensberg
Collection
1950-134-1

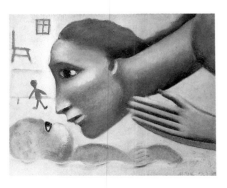

**Ara**
*Mother and Child Stooping*
c. 1940
Lower right: BDK ara; on reverse:
Benjamin Dusanovich Kosich
ARA
Oil on gypsum board
10 3/4 × 13 7/16" (27.3 × 34.1 cm)

The Louise and Walter Arensberg
Collection
1950-134-504

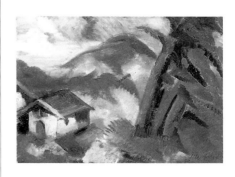

**Archipenko, Gela Forster**
American, born Russia,
1887–1957
*Autumn*
1928
Lower right: Gela Forster; on
reverse: gela forster to / Christian
Brinton / with love / gela /
N.Y.C. / feb. 7th 1928
Oil on canvas
18 1/16 × 24" (45.9 × 61 cm)

Gift of Christian Brinton
1941-79-77

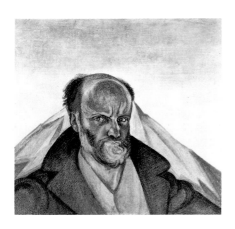

**Dr. Atl (Gerardo Murillo)**
Mexican, 1877–1964
*Self-Portrait with Popocatépetl*
1928
Lower left: Dr. Atl; lower right:
1928
Atl color [oil, wax, dry resin, and gasoline] on canvas
26 3/4 × 26 3/4" (67.9 × 67.9 cm)

Gift of Dr. MacKinley Helm
1949-30-1

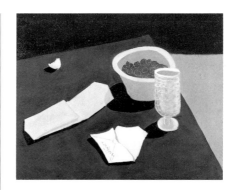

**Avery, Milton**
*Still Life (Blue Bowl with Nuts)*
1945
Center bottom: Milton Avery /
1945
Oil on canvas
25 1/8 × 30" (63.8 × 76.2 cm)

Gift of Mrs. Herbert Cameron
Morris
1946-13-1

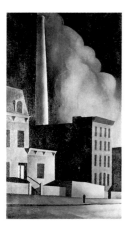

**Ault, George C.**
American, 1891–1948
*Factory Chimney, Brooklyn*
1924
Lower left: G. C. Ault '24.
Oil on canvas
30 × 16" (76.2 × 40.6 cm)

Gift of Dr. Samuel W. Fernberger
1950-5-1

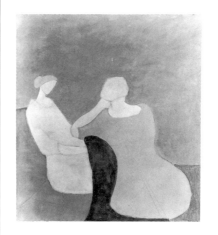

**Avery, Milton**
*Interlude*
1960
Lower right: Milton Avery 1960;
on reverse: "Interlude" / by /
Milton Avery / 68" × 58" / 1960
Oil on canvas
68 × 58" (172.7 × 147.3 cm)

Centennial gift of the Woodward
Foundation
1975-81-1

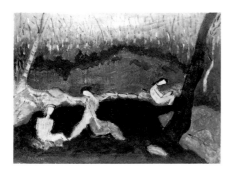

**Avery, Milton**
American, 1893–1965
*Brook Bathers*
1938
Lower left: Milton Avery;
on reverse: "Brook Bathers" /
Milton Avery / 1938 / 30 × 40
Oil on canvas
30 1/8 × 39 7/8" (76.5 × 101.3 cm)

Gift of Dr. and Mrs. Paul Todd
Makler
1971-170-1

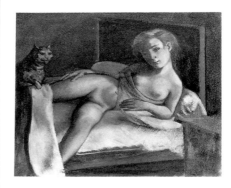

**Balthus (Balthazar
Klossowski de Rola)**
French, born 1908
*Girl on a Bed*
c. 1950
Lower right: Balthus
Oil on canvas
18 × 21 3/4" (45.7 × 55.2 cm)

The Albert M. Greenfield and
Elizabeth M. Greenfield
Collection
1974-178-17

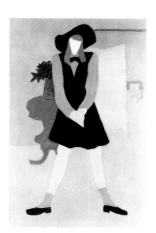

**Avery, Milton**
*Black Jumper*
1944
Center right: Milton Avery /
1944
Oil on canvas
54 3/16 × 33 3/4" (137.6 × 85.7 cm)

Bequest of Mrs. Maurice J. Speiser
in memory of Raymond A. Speiser
1968-177-1

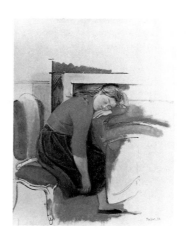

**Balthus**
*Young Girl Asleep (Frédérique)*
1955
Lower right: Balthus.55.
Oil on canvas
45 7/8 × 34 7/8" (116.5 × 88.6 cm)

The Albert M. Greenfield and
Elizabeth M. Greenfield
Collection
1974-178-18

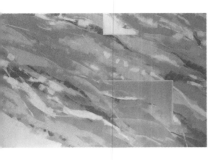

**Bannard, Walter Darby**
American, born 1934
*Amazon No. 3*
1968
Acrylic on canvas
65 15/16 × 99 1/8" (164.5 × 251.8 cm)

Gift of Mr. and Mrs. J. Welles Henderson
1973-259-2

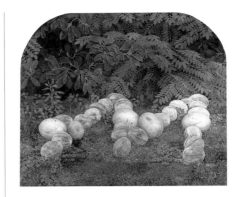

**Bateman, Ronald C.**
American, born Wales, born 1947
*Still Life with Melons*
1975
Oil on canvas
56 1/2 × 66 1/8" (143.5 × 168 cm)

Gift of the Cheltenham Art Centre
1976-35-1

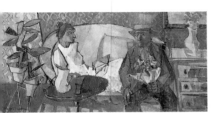

**Barnett, William**
American, 1911–1992
*Widow in White*
1956
Lower left: William Barnett—56
Oil on canvas
37 1/4 × 75 5/8" (94.6 × 192.1 cm)

Purchased with the Adele Haas Turner and Beatrice Pastorius Turner Memorial Fund
1959-12-1

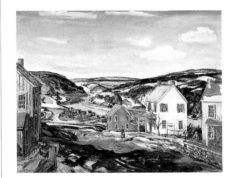

**Baum, Walter Emerson**
American, 1884–1956
*Hill Houses*
1942
Lower left: W.E.BAUM
Oil on canvas
32 1/4 × 40 1/8" (81.9 × 101.9 cm)

Gift of Luther A. Harr
1943-43-1

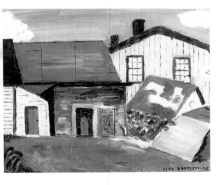

**Bartlett, Frederic Clay**
American, 1873–1953
*Open Door*
1935
Lower right: CLAY BARTLETT—35
Oil on canvas board
8 15/16 × 10 7/8" (22.7 × 27.6 cm)

Gift of Frank and Alice Osborn
1966-68-20

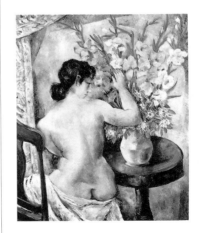

**Baylinson, Abraham S.**
American, born Russia, 1882–1950
*Girl with Gladioli*
1942
Lower right: A.S.Baylinson / 1942
Oil on canvas
41 15/16 × 34" (106.5 × 86.4 cm)

Gift of the Shilling Foundation
1946-46-1

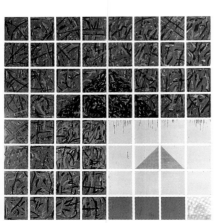

**Bartlett, Jennifer**
American, born 1941
*2 Priory Walk*
1977
Baked enamel, silk-screened ink, and enamel on sixty-four steel plaques
Each plaque: 12 × 12" (30.5 × 30.5 cm); overall: 103 × 103" (261.6 × 261.6 cm)

Purchased with the Adele Haas Turner and Beatrice Pastorius Turner Memorial Fund
1979-14-1

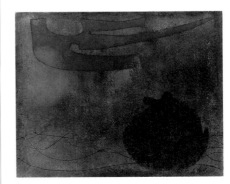

**Baziotes, William**
American, 1912–1963
*Night*
1953
Lower right: Baziotes
Oil on canvas
19 3/4 × 24 3/16" (50.2 × 61.4 cm)

Gift of Anne d'Harnoncourt Rishel
1982-103-1

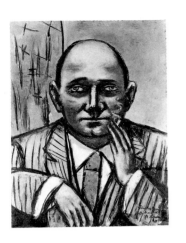

**Beckmann, Max**
German, active United States,
1884–1950
*Portrait of John S. Newberry*
1947
Lower right: John Newberry /
Beckmann / St. Louis / 47
Oil on canvas
29 × 21 $^{15}/_{16}$" (73.7 × 55.7 cm)

Gift of the Barry and Marilyn
Peril Foundation and gifts (by
exchange) of Fiske and Marie
Kimball and Mr. and Mrs. Joseph
Slifka
1972-267-1

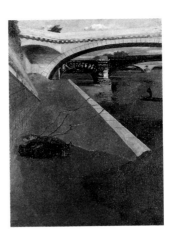

**Berman, Eugène**
American, born Russia,
1899–1972
*Bridges of Paris*
1932
Lower right: E. B. / 1932; on
reverse: E. Berman / Paris Sept.
1932 / Perspective de Ponts
Oil on canvas
36 $^{3}/_{16}$ × 25 $^{1}/_{2}$" (91.9 × 64.8 cm)

Gift of Briggs W. Buchanan
1945-85-1

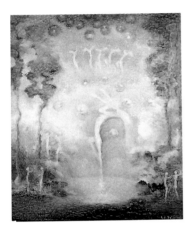

**Belmont, Ira Jean**
American, born Lithuania,
1885–1964
*An Expression from "Moment
Musicale," by Franz Schubert*
c. 1920
Lower right: I. J. Belmont
Oil on canvas
36 × 30 $^{1}/_{4}$" (91.4 × 76.8 cm)

Gift of Mrs. I. J. Belmont
1977-203-1

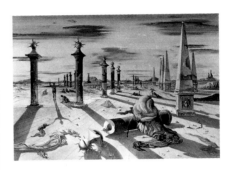

**Berman, Eugène**
*View in Perspective of a Perfect
Sunset*
1941
Lower right: E. B. / 1941; on
reverse: E. Berman / Hollywood:
May–October 1941. View in
Perspective of a Perfect Sunset /
(Avanzi della Citta Perfetta.)
Oil on canvas
36 $^{1}/_{16}$ × 50" (91.6 × 127 cm)

Gift of Mr. and Mrs. Henry
Clifford
1951-28-1

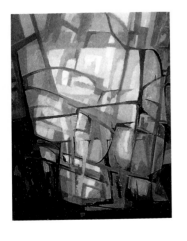

**Bérard, Marius-Honoré**
French, born 1896
*English Suite*
1934
Lower right: HM Berard 34
Oil on canvas
28 $^{3}/_{4}$ × 21 $^{5}/_{16}$" (73 × 54.1 cm)

Gift of the artist
1949-33-1

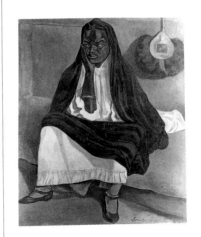

**Bernard, Émile**
French, 1868–1941
*Portrait of a Woman*
1919
Lower right: Emile Bernard
Oil on canvas
43 $^{1}/_{4}$ × 33 $^{1}/_{2}$" (109.8 × 85.1 cm)

Gift of Samuel Pesin and Morris
Lerner
1973-76-1

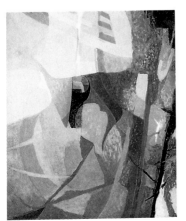

**Bérard, Marius-Honoré**
*Negro Spirituals*
1944
Lower right: HM Berard 44
Oil on canvas
31 $^{3}/_{4}$ × 25 $^{3}/_{8}$" (80.6 × 64.4 cm)

Gift of the artist
1949-33-2

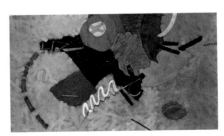

**Bershad, Helen**
American, born 1934
*Middle Field*
1984
Acrylic and pastel on canvas
49 × 85" (124.5 × 215.9 cm)

Gift of Mr. and Mrs. Edwin P.
Rome
1984-69-1

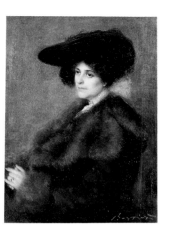

**Bertieri, Pilade**
American, born Italy,
born 1874, death date unknown
*Portrait of Selma Stieglitz Schubart*
c. 1900
Lower right: Bertieri
Oil on canvas
36 1/8 × 26 1/8" (91.8 × 66.4 cm)

Gift of Mrs. William Howard
Schubart
1968-45-3

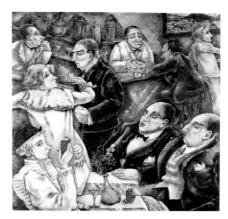

**Biddle, George**
*Whoopee at Sloppy Joe's*
1933
Lower left: Biddle 1933
Oil on canvas
40 1/2 × 40 3/8" (102.9 × 102.5 cm)

Gift of the artist
1972-121-1

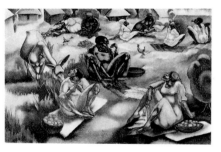

**Biddle, George**
American, 1885–1973
*Mango Market, Haiti*
1927
Lower right: Biddle, 1927.
Oil on canvas
20 1/4 × 30 1/4" (51.4 × 76.8 cm)

Gift of Bernard Davis
1942-64-1

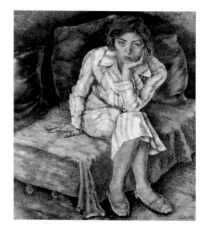

**Biddle, George**
*Portrait of Hélène Sardeau*
1934
Lower right: Biddle 1934; on
reverse: Biddle / 309 / HELENE
SARDEau
Oil on canvas
30 1/16 × 25 1/8" (76.4 × 63.8 cm)

Gift of the artist
1972-121-3

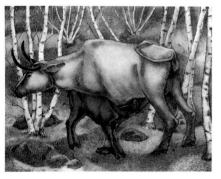

**Biddle, George**
*Cow and Calf*
1929
Lower left: Biddle / 1929; on
reverse: Biddle 199 Cow and Calf
Oil on canvas
21 1/2 × 25 1/2" (54.6 × 64.8 cm)

Bequest of Anne Hinchman
1952-82-12

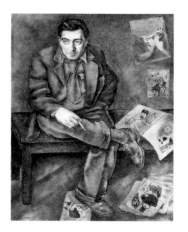

**Biddle, George**
*Portrait of William Gropper*
1938
Lower left: Biddle 1938; on
reverse: Biddle / 373 / "Bill
Gropper"
Oil on canvas
40 1/16 × 30 1/8" (101.8 × 76.5 cm)

Gift of Mr. and Mrs. R. Sturgis
Ingersoll
1942-1-1

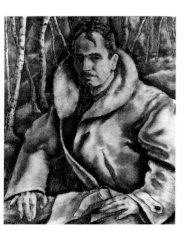

**Biddle, George**
*Self-Portrait*
1933
Lower left: Biddle 1933; on
reverse: Biddle 298 Self Portrait
Oil on canvas
31 1/8 × 25 1/4" (79.1 × 64.1 cm)

Bequest of Margaretta S.
Hinchman
1955-96-1

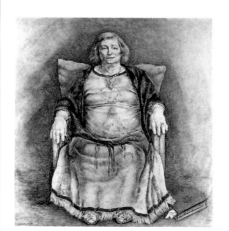

**Biddle, George**
*Portrait of Frieda Lawrence*
1941
Lower left: Biddle 1941; on
reverse: Biddle / Frieda Lawrence
/ No. 471
Oil on canvas
44 1/16 × 40 1/8" (111.9 × 101.9 cm)

Gift of the artist
1972-121-2

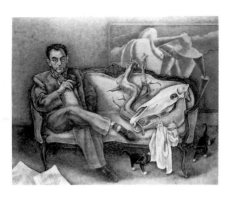

**Biddle, George**
*Portrait of Man Ray*
1941
Lower right: Biddle 41
Oil on canvas
50 × 60 1/16" (127 × 152.6 cm)

Gift of the artist
1972-121-4

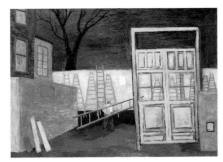

**Blackburn, Morris Atkinson**
*The Blue Door*
1950
Center bottom: Morris Blackburn
Oil on canvas
24 × 32" (61 × 81.3 cm)

Purchased with the Bloomfield
Moore Fund
1951-31-1

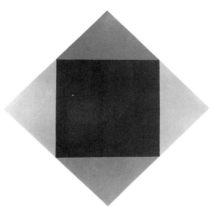

**Bill, Max**
Swiss, born 1908
*Diffusion of Light Green*
1959–69
On reverse: Bill / 1959–69 / max
bill haut oben top zerstrah lung
von hellgrun 1959–69
Oil on canvas
15 7/8 × 15 13/16" (40.3 × 40.2 cm)
diagonal

Gift of Dr. and Mrs. Paul Todd
Makler
1971-170-2

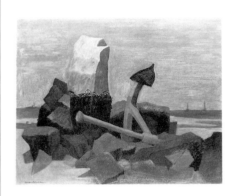

**Blackburn, Morris Atkinson**
*Rock and Anchor*
c. 1961
Lower left: Morris Blackburn
Oil on canvas
30 × 36 1/8" (76.2 × 91.8 cm)

Gift of Dr. Faith S. Fetterman
1961-64-1

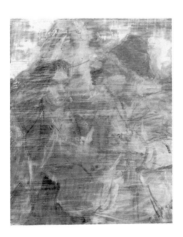

**Bishop, Isabel**
American, 1902–1988
*Sketch for "Eve in the Underground"*
c. 1955
Oil, tempera, and gesso on
Masonite
21 7/8 × 17 3/8" (55.6 × 44.1 cm)

Gift of Mrs. Henry W. Breyer
1977-204-1

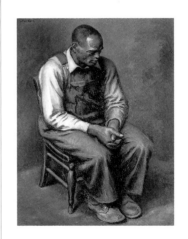

**Bloch, Julius T.**
American, born Germany,
1888–1966
*The Stevedore*
1936
Upper left: Julius Bloch
Oil on canvas
29 3/4 × 22 1/8" (75.6 × 56.2 cm)

Gift of the Committee on
Painting and Sculpture
1947-32-1

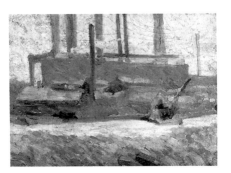

**Blackburn, Morris Atkinson**
American, 1902–1979
*Factory by the Delaware*
c. 1923
On reverse: Morris Blackburn /
1923 approx.
Oil on cardboard
9 1/8 × 12" (23.2 × 30.5 cm)

Gift of the artist
1975-164-1

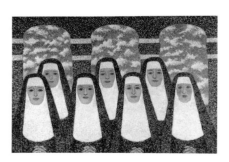

**Bloch, Julius T.**
*Sisters*
1954–55
Upper left: Bloch; on reverse:
November 1954–January 1955
"SISTERS" 1954–55 Julius Bloch
10 So. 18- St Philadelphia
Oil on canvas
40 × 60 1/4" (101.6 × 153 cm)

Gift of Mrs. Lina B. Schwab, Miss
Flora B. Bloch, and Miss Clara B.
Bloch, the sisters of Julius T.
Bloch
1955-33-1

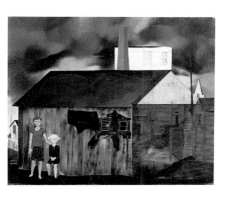

**Blume, Peter**
American, born Belorussia,
born 1906
*The Sheds (Frankie and Johnny)*
c. 1928
Lower left: PETER / BLUME
Oil on canvas
20 3/16 × 24 1/8" (51.3 × 61.3 cm)

Gift of Mr. and Mrs. R. Sturgis
Ingersoll
1941-103-1

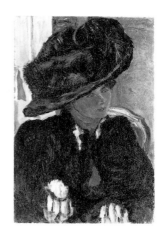

**Bonnard, Pierre**
*Portrait of Madame Franc-Nohain*
c. 1905
Upper right: Bonnard
Oil on canvas
25 × 16 5/16" (63.5 × 41.4 cm)

Gift of Maurice Newton
1966-220-1

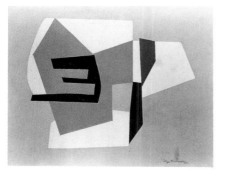

**Bolotowsky, Ilya**
American, born Russia,
1907–1981
*Abstraction in Light Blue*
1940
Lower right: Ilya Bolotowsky 40
Oil on panel
8 × 10" (20.3 × 25.4 cm)

A. E. Gallatin Collection
1946-70-7

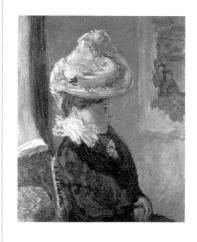

**Bonnard, Pierre**
*Woman in a White Hat*
c. 1908
Upper right: Bonnard
Oil on paper on panel
27 15/16 × 21 13/16" (71 × 55.4 cm)

Bequest of Charlotte Dorrance
Wright
1978-1-1

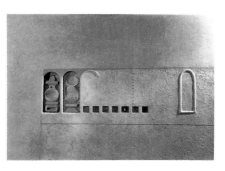

**Bonevardi, Marcelo**
Argentine, active United States,
born 1929
*Landscape with Figures*
1965
On reverse: Bonevardi 65
"Landscape with Figures" no. 190
Oil and painted wood on canvas
39 1/4 × 55 1/4" (99.7 × 140.3 cm)

Gift of Mrs. John Wintersteen
1969-245-1

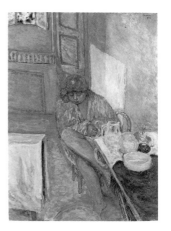

**Bonnard, Pierre**
*After the Shower*
1914
Upper right: Bonnard / 1914
Oil on canvas
37 3/8 × 26 3/16" (94.9 × 66.5 cm)

The Louis E. Stern Collection
1963-181-1

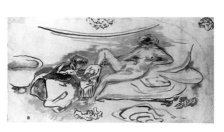

**Bonnard, Pierre**
French, 1867–1947
*Nude with a Maid Attending*
c. 1895
Lower left: PB
Oil and graphite on canvas
15 × 27 1/2" (38.1 × 69.8 cm)

Gift of Mrs. Samuel Brady
1976-242-1

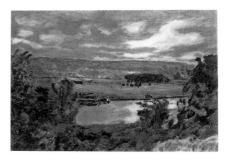

**Bonnard, Pierre**
*Landscape with a River in Stormy
Weather, Vernon*
1914
Lower right: Bonnard / 14
Oil on canvas
15 3/4 × 22 3/8" (40 × 56.8 cm)

Gift of Frank and Alice Osborn
1966-68-2

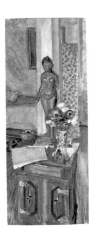

**Bonnard, Pierre**
*Homage to Maillol*
1917
Upper right: Bonnard
Oil on canvas
48 × 18 1/2" (121.9 × 47 cm)

The Louis E. Stern Collection
1963-181-2

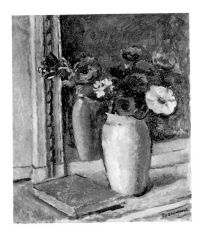

**Borie, Adolphe**
*Still Life with a Vase of Flowers*
c. 1910
Lower right: BORIE
Oil on composition board
21 1/4 × 17 3/8" (54 × 44.1 cm)

Bequest of Marguerite Lahalle
Cret
1965-117-10

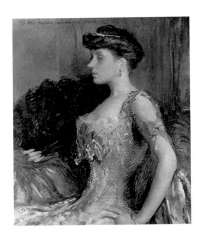

**Bonnard, Pierre**
*Still Life with a Bowl of Fruit*
1933
Lower left: Bonnard
Oil on canvas
22 13/16 × 20 7/8" (57.9 × 53 cm)

Bequest of Lisa Norris Elkins
1950-92-1

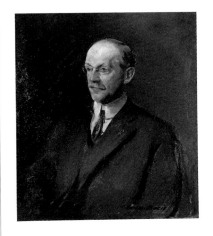

**Borie, Adolphe**
*Portrait of John D. McIlhenny*
1918
Lower right: Adolphe Borie
Oil on canvas
30 × 24 7/8" (76.2 × 63.2 cm)

The John D. McIlhenny
Collection
1943-40-54

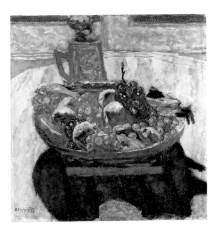

**Borie, Adolphe**
American, active France,
1877–1934
*Portrait of Mrs. Betty Campbell
Madeira*
1907
Upper left: To Mrs. Madeira from
Adolphe Borie—April 1907.
Oil on canvas
36 1/8 × 29 1/4" (91.8 × 74.3 cm)

Gift of Mrs. Brannan Reath II
1931-64-1

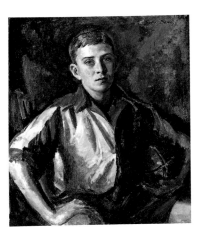

**Borie, Adolphe**
*Portrait of Jack*
1924
Upper right: Adolphe Borie.
Oil on canvas
30 3/16 × 25" (76.7 × 63.5 cm)

Gift of Samuel R. Rosenbaum
1941-22-1

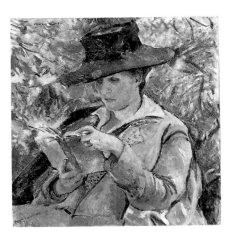

**Borie, Adolphe**
*Woman Reading*
1907
Upper left: Adolphe Borie.
Oil on canvas
26 3/16 × 25 3/16" (66.5 × 64 cm)

Purchased with funds contributed
by a group of ninety-two painters
and sculptors
1935-6-1

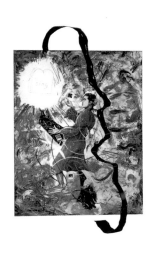

**Borofsky, Jonathan**
American, born 1942
*2,841,777 Sing*
1978–83
Acrylic on canvas, three Polaroid
prints, painted aluminum, and a
stereo cassette with a tape loop
127 × 96" (322.6 × 243.8 cm)

Purchased with the Edward and
Althea Budd Fund, the Adele
Haas Turner and Beatrice
Pastorius Turner Memorial Fund,
and funds contributed by Marion
Boulton Stroud, Mr. and Mrs.
Harvey Gushner, Ella B. Schaap,
Mrs. H. Gates Lloyd, Eileen and
Peter Rosenau, Frances and

Bayard Storey, Dr. and Mrs.
William Wolgin, Mrs. Donald A.
Petrie, Mark Rosenthal, Harold P.
Starr, and two anonymous donors
1984-79-1

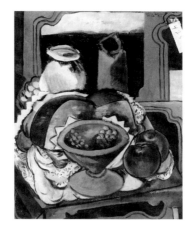

**Bouche, Louis**
*Still Life*
1921
Upper right: LOUIS BOUCHE /
PARIS 1921
Oil on canvas
20 × 16 1/8" (50.8 × 41 cm)

Gift of Frank and Alice Osborn
1966-68-22

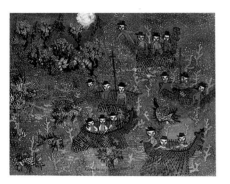

**Bosos**
Unknown nationality,
active 20th century
*The Japanese Fishermen*
1954
Center bottom: les pêcheurs
japonais Bosos 54
Oil on paperboard
12 7/8 × 15 15/16" (32.7 × 40.5 cm)

The Albert M. Greenfield and
Elizabeth M. Greenfield
Collection
1974-178-19

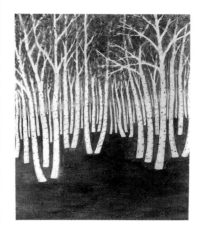

**Branchard, Emile Pierre**
American, 1881–1938
*Midsummer Night's Dream*
c. 1920
Lower right: EMILE /
BRANCHARD
Oil on panel
16 5/8 × 13 1/2" (42.2 × 34.3 cm)

Gift of an anonymous donor
1964-61-1

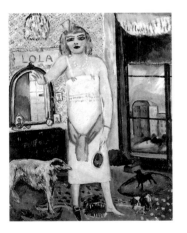

**Bouche, Louis**
American, 1896–1969
*Lola*
c. 1918
Oil on canvas
26 × 20" (66 × 50.8 cm)

The Louise and Walter Arensberg
Collection
1950-134-507

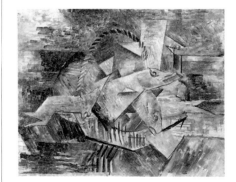

**Braque, Georges**
French, 1882–1963
*Basket of Fish*
c. 1910
Oil on canvas
19 13/16 × 24" (50.3 × 61 cm)

The Samuel S. White 3rd and
Vera White Collection
1967-30-7

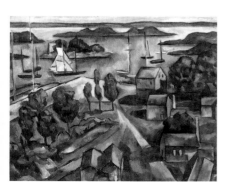

**Bouche, Louis**
*Landscape*
1919
Lower left: L BOUCHE 1919
Oil on canvas
19 7/8 × 24 1/8" (50.5 × 61.3 cm)

Gift of George Biddle
1945-16-36

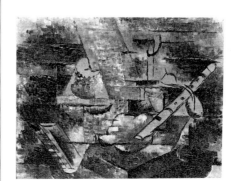

**Braque, Georges**
*Harmonica and Flageolet*
1910–11
On reverse: G. Braque
Oil on canvas
13 1/8 × 16 1/4" (33.3 × 41.2 cm)

A. E. Gallatin Collection
1952-61-4

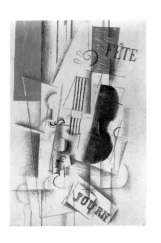

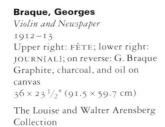

**Braque, Georges**
*Violin and Newspaper*
1912–13
Upper right: FÊTE; lower right:
JOURN[AL]; on reverse: G. Braque
Graphite, charcoal, and oil on
canvas
36 × 23 1/2" (91.5 × 59.7 cm)

The Louise and Walter Arensberg
Collection
1950-134-26

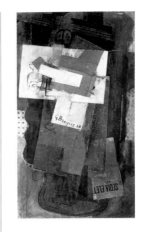

**Braque, Georges**
*Still Life*
See following painting for reverse
1918
Center: G. Braque 18
Oil, gouache, paper, and charcoal
on canvas
52 5/16 × 29 3/4" (132.9 × 75.6 cm)

The Louise and Walter Arensberg
Collection
1950-134-29a

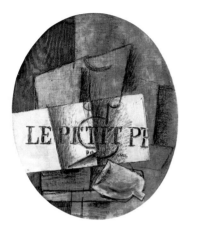

**Braque, Georges**
*Still Life (Newspaper and Lemon)*
1913
Center: LE PETIT PE[ ];
on reverse: G. Braque
Oil, graphite, and charcoal on
canvas
13 11/16 × 10 1/2" (34.8 × 26.7 cm)

A. E. Gallatin Collection
1952-61-5

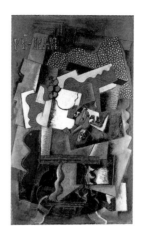

**Braque, Georges**
*The Table*
Reverse of the preceding painting
1918
Upper left: FÉ-BAR
Oil on canvas
52 5/16 × 29 3/4" (132.9 × 75.6 cm)

The Louise and Walter Arensberg
Collection
1950-134-29b

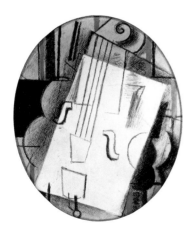

**Braque, Georges**
*Still Life (Violin)*
1913
On reverse: G. Braque
Graphite, charcoal, and oil on
canvas
13 7/8 × 10 7/8" (35.2 × 27.6 cm)

The Louise and Walter Arensberg
Collection
1950-134-25

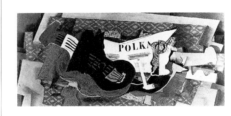

**Braque, Georges**
*Violin and Pipe*
1920–21
Center: POLKA; on reverse:
G. BRAQUE
Oil and sand on canvas
17 × 36 3/8" (43.2 × 92.4 cm)

The Louise and Walter Arensberg
Collection
1950-134-30

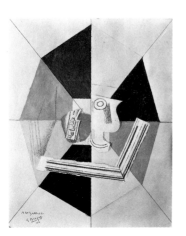

**Braque, Georges**
*The Cup*
1917–18
Lower left: A M.Gallatin /
G Braque / 1918
Oil and graphite on cardboard
25 × 18 7/8" (63.5 × 47.9 cm)

A. E. Gallatin Collection
1952-61-6

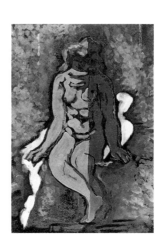

**Braque, Georges**
*Seated Bather*
1925
Lower right: G. Braque / 25
Oil on canvas
15 7/8 × 10 5/8" (40.3 × 27 cm)

Gift of Miss Anna Warren
Ingersoll
1950-27-1

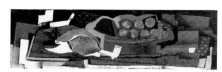

**Braque, Georges**
*Still Life with Fruit*
c. 1926
On reverse: G Braque
Oil on canvas
7 ³/₄ × 25 ¹/₂" (19.7 × 64.8 cm)

Gift of Miss Anna Warren
Ingersoll
1964-108-1

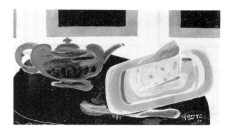

**Braque, Georges**
*A Teapot and a Plate of Cheese*
1942
Lower right: G Braque / 42
Oil on canvas
13 ⁵/₁₆ × 21 ¹³/₁₆" (33.8 × 55.4 cm)

The Louis E. Stern Collection
1963-181-4

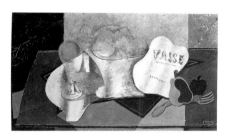

**Braque, Georges**
*Still Life (Compote and Fruit)*
1926–28
Center right: VALSE; lower right:
G Braque
Oil on canvas
17 ³/₁₆ × 28 ⁷/₈" (43.7 × 73.3 cm)

A. E. Gallatin Collection
1952-61-8

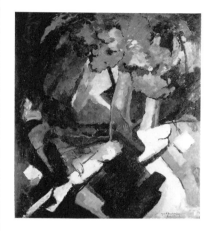

**Breckenridge, Hugh Henry**
American, 1870–1937
*Autumn*
c. 1931
Lower right: Hugh H.
Breckenridge
Oil on canvas
43 ¹/₁₆ × 37 ¹/₁₆" (109.4 × 94.1 cm)

Gift of Mrs. Hugh H.
Breckenridge
1936-35-1

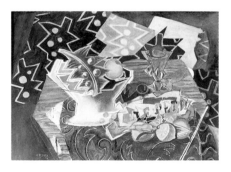

**Braque, Georges**
*Still Life with a Fruit Dish*
1936
Lower left: G Braque / 36;
center right: LE PETI[T]
Oil on canvas
23 ³/₄ × 32" (60.3 × 81.3 cm)

The Samuel S. White 3rd and
Vera White Collection
1967-30-9

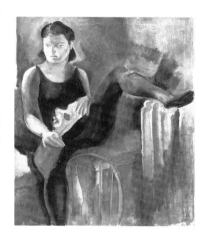

**Brodhead, Quita**
American, born 1901
*Girl with a Mask*
1935
Oil on canvas
36 × 30" (91.4 × 76.2 cm)

Gift of Bill Scott in memory of
Jane Piper
1991-141-1

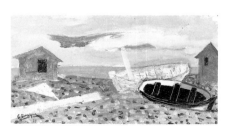

**Braque, Georges**
*Stormy Beach*
1938
Lower left: G Braque / 38
Oil on panel
8 ¹/₁₆ × 15" (20.5 × 38.1 cm)

The Samuel S. White 3rd and
Vera White Collection
1967-30-10

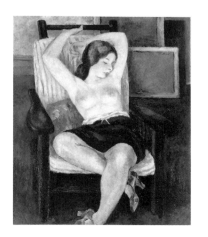

**Brook, Alexander**
American, 1898–1980
*Sleeping Woman*
1929
Upper right: A. Brook
Oil on canvas
36 ³/₈ × 29 ³/₄" (92.4 × 75.6 cm)

The Louis E. Stern Collection
1963-181-5

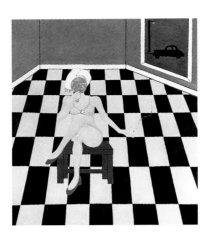

**Brown, Joan**
American, 1938–1990
*Woman in Room*
1975
On reverse: Joan Brown / Woman
in Room / 5/16/75
Acrylic on canvas
72 × 62" (182.9 × 157.5 cm)

Gift of Ernie and Lynn Mieger
1988-33-7

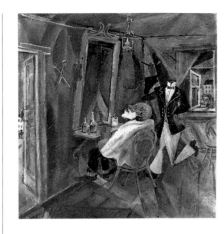

**Burliuk, David Davidovich**
American, born Ukraine,
1882–1967
*A Close Shave*
1910
Lower right: BURLIUK / 1910.
Oil on canvas
13 1/16 × 12 1/8" (33.2 × 30.8 cm)

Gift of Christian Brinton
1941-79-47

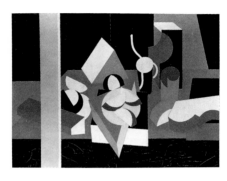

**Bruce, Patrick Henry**
American, active France,
1880–1937
*Still Life*
c. 1921
On reverse: [The inscription
"116 × 89 50F grande barre bleu
verticale #13 fond sombre" was
removed during relining in the
1960s]
Oil on canvas
34 3/4 × 45 1/4" (88.3 × 114.9 cm)

Centennial gift of the Woodward
Foundation
1975-81-2

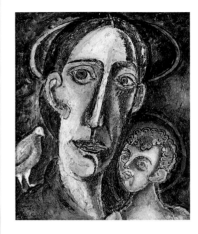

**Burliuk, David Davidovich**
*Icon after the Revolution*
c. 1920
Oil on cardboard
20 × 16" (50.8 × 40.6 cm)

Gift of Christian Brinton
1941-79-95

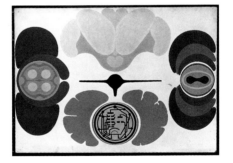

**Bubenik, Gernot**
German, born 1942
*Realization III*
1966
On reverse: Bubenik 66
Acrylic on panel
35 1/2 × 47 1/4" (90.2 × 120 cm)

Gift of Dr. and Mrs. William
Wolgin
1967-41-1

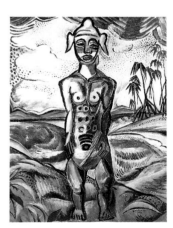

**Burliuk, David Davidovich**
*Pacific Island Totem Pole*
1923
Lower right: Burliuk. / 1923.
Oil on canvas
24 1/4 × 18 1/4" (61.6 × 46.3 cm)

Gift of Christian Brinton
1941-79-76

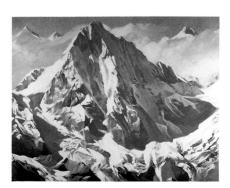

**Burko, Diane**
American, born 1945
*Nevada Ulta*
1975
On reverse: Diane Burko / 12/75
/ "Nevada Ulta"
Acrylic on canvas
60 × 72" (152.4 × 182.9 cm)

Gift of Rachel Seymour
1977-260-1

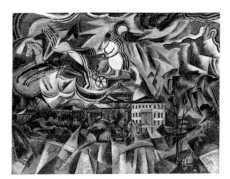

**Burliuk, David Davidovich**
*Elijah the Prophet*
1924
Lower left: Burliuk / 1924.
Oil on burlap
30 × 37 7/8" (76.2 × 96.2 cm)

Gift of Christian Brinton
1941-79-112

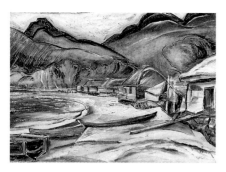

**Burliuk, David Davidovich**
*Island Village, Bonin Archipelago*
1924
Lower right: Burliuk / 1924
Oil on canvas
13 × 17" (33 × 43.2 cm)

Gift of Christian Brinton
1941-79-48

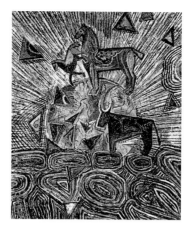

**Burliuk, David Davidovich**
*Dawn, Russia*
c. 1925
Lower left: Burliuk
Oil on canvas
30 1/8 × 24" (76.5 × 61 cm)

Gift of Christian Brinton
1941-79-69

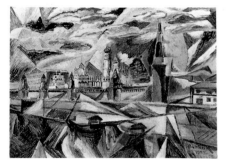

**Burliuk, David Davidovich**
*Moscow in Revolution*
1924
Lower right: Burliuk / 1924.
Oil on canvas
13 × 17" (33 × 43.2 cm)

Gift of Christian Brinton
1941-79-89

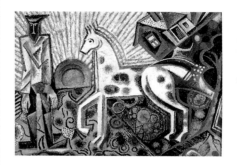

**Burliuk, David Davidovich**
*End of the Day*
c. 1925
Oil on burlap
13 × 18" (33 × 45.7 cm)

Gift of Christian Brinton
1941-79-38

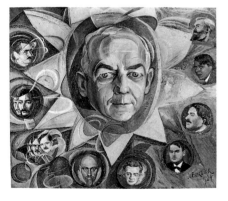

**Burliuk, David Davidovich**
*Portrait of Christian Brinton and Nine Artists*
1924
Lower right: D. Burliuk / 1924
Oil on canvas
25 × 28" (63.5 × 71.1 cm)

Gift of Christian Brinton
1941-79-106

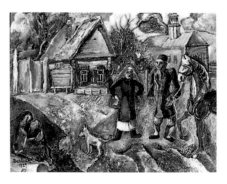

**Burliuk, David Davidovich**
*Bashkir Family, Kargalinskaya Steppe*
1927
Lower left: Burliuk / 1927 / NY.
Oil on canvas
16 1/16 × 20" (40.8 × 50.8 cm)

Gift of Christian Brinton
1941-79-94

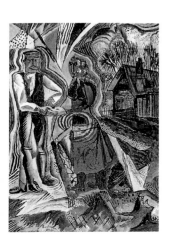

**Burliuk, David Davidovich**
*Russian Village Boy and Girl*
1925
Lower left: Burliuk / 1925.
Oil on canvas
14 × 10" (35.6 × 25.4 cm)

Gift of Christian Brinton
1941-79-82

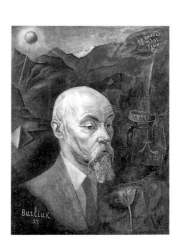

**Burliuk, David Davidovich**
*Portrait of Professor Nicholas K. Roerich, First President of the World of Art Group*
1929
Lower left: Burliuk / 29; upper right: [Greek for "to have fulfillment in itself"]; center right: COR ARDENS
Oil on canvas
24 1/8 × 18" (61.3 × 45.7 cm)

Gift of Christian Brinton
1941-79-3

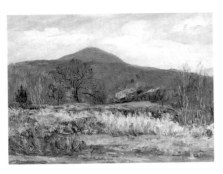

**Butler, Mary**
American, 1865–1946
*The Catskills, December*
1919
Lower right: MARY BUTLER
Oil on canvas
24 × 32 1/8" (61 × 81.6 cm)

Gift of the Fellowship of the
Pennsylvania Academy of the
Fine Arts
1945-38-1

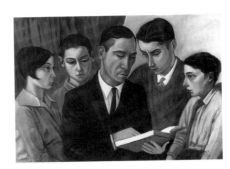

**Canadé, Vincent**
American, born Italy,
1879–1961
*Family Group Reading*
c. 1930
Lower left: To my Friend G. Biddle
/ VINCENT CANADÉ
Oil on canvas
17 7/8 × 25 1/4" (45.4 × 64.1 cm)

Gift of George Biddle
1945-16-37

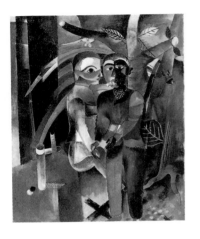

**Campendonk, Heinrich**
German, 1889–1957
*Love in the Forest*
c. 1920
Oil on canvas
29 × 23 1/8" (73.7 × 58.7 cm)

Gift of Christian Brinton
1941-79-70

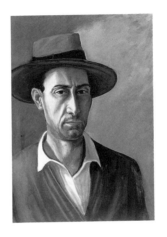

**Canadé, Vincent**
*Self-Portrait*
c. 1930
Oil on canvas
19 1/8 × 13 1/4" (48.6 × 33.6 cm)

Gift of an anonymous donor
1948-53-1

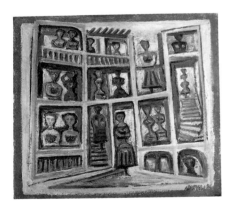

**Campigli, Massimo**
Italian, 1895–1971
*Theater*
1956
Lower right: CAMPIGLI 56
Oil on canvas
19 5/8 × 21 5/8" (49.8 × 54.9 cm)

Gift of Mr. and Mrs. William P.
Wood
1981-58-1

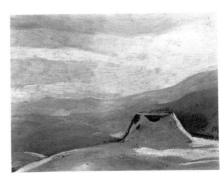

**Canadé, Vincent**
*Winter Landscape*
c. 1930
Oil on panel
8 × 10" (20.3 × 25.4 cm)

Gift of Carl Zigrosser
1972-237-5

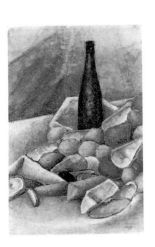

**Canadé, Eugene George**
American, born 1914
*Still Life with Fruit and a Bottle*
c. 1940
Lower right: E. CANADÉ / 604
Oil on canvas
25 5/8 × 15 7/8" (65.1 × 40.3 cm)

Gift of Carl Zigrosser
1972-237-6

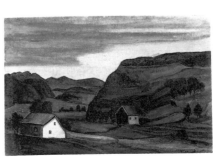

**Canadé, Vincent**
*Dark Landscape with Two Houses*
c. 1935
Lower right: V. CANADÉ
Oil on composition board
13 1/4 × 19 3/8" (33.6 × 49.2 cm)

Gift of Carl Zigrosser
1972-237-1

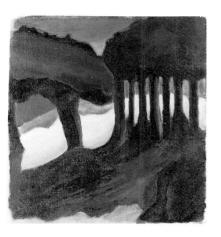

**Canadé, Vincent**
*River Landscape with Trees*
c. 1935
Oil on canvas board
13 1/2 × 10 1/8" (34.3 × 25.7 cm)

Gift of Carl Zigrosser
1972-237-4

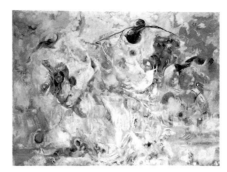

**Capraro, Vincent**
American, born 1924
*Hawks and Doves (Abstraction)*
c. 1955
Oil on canvas
54 3/4 × 71 1/2" (139.1 × 181.6 cm)

The Albert M. Greenfield and
Elizabeth M. Greenfield
Collection
1974-178-21

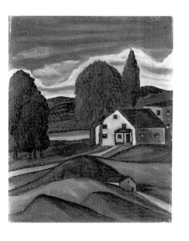

**Canadé, Vincent**
*River Landscape with Trees and Houses*
c. 1935
Lower left: V. CANADÉ
Oil on canvas on panel
13 5/8 × 10 1/8" (34.6 × 25.7 cm)

Gift of Carl Zigrosser
1972-237-2

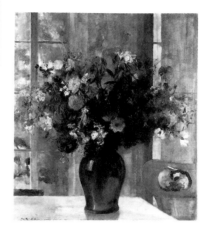

**Carles, Arthur Beecher**
American, 1882–1952
*Bouquet in a Blue Vase*
1914
Lower left: CARLES
Oil on canvas
48 × 40" (121.9 × 101.6 cm)

Gift of Mr. and Mrs. David
Bortin
1956-37-1

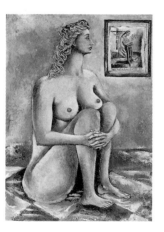

**Cantú, Federico**
Mexican, born 1908
*Sacred and Profane Love*
1937
On picture on wall: federico
Cantú. / "Amour Sacré et Amour
Profane." ad.37.
Oil on canvas
18 × 13" (45.7 × 33 cm)

Gift of Mr. and Mrs. Joseph J.
Gersten
1951-120-1

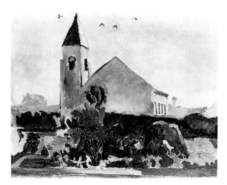

**Carles, Arthur Beecher**
*French Village Church*
c. 1914
Lower left: CARLES
Oil on canvas
23 5/8 × 28 5/8" (60 × 72.7 cm)

The Samuel S. White 3rd and
Vera White Collection
1967-30-11

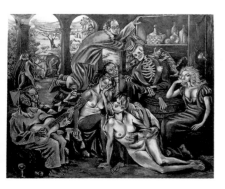

**Cantú, Federico**
*Triumph of Death*
1938
Lower left: Federico Cantú /
A.d. MCMXXXVIII
Oil on canvas
58 1/4 × 72 5/8" (147.9 × 184.5 cm)

Gift of Dr. and Mrs. MacKinley
Helm
1943-44-1

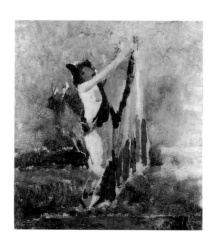

**Carles, Arthur Beecher**
*Study for "The Marseillaise"*
See following painting for reverse
1918
Lower left: To Dorziat / with
appreciation / Carles
Oil on cardboard
13 15/16 × 12 1/16" (35.4 × 30.6 cm)

Gift of John T. Dorrance
1969-140-1a

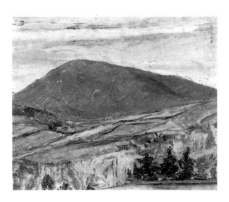

**Carles, Arthur Beecher**
*Autumn Landscape with Blue Mountains*
Reverse of the preceding painting
c. 1918
Oil on cardboard
12 1/16 × 13 15/16" (30.6 × 35.4 cm)

Gift of John T. Dorrance
1969-140-1b

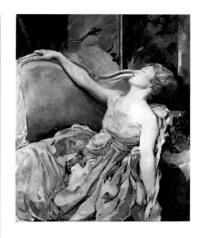

**Carles, Arthur Beecher**
*Portrait of Vera White*
1922
Lower right: CARLES
Oil on canvas
39 1/2 × 32" (100.3 × 81.3 cm)

The Samuel S. White 3rd and Vera White Collection
1967-30-13

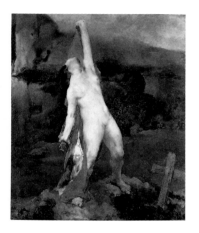

**Carles, Arthur Beecher**
*The Marseillaise*
c. 1918
Center bottom: CARLES
Oil on canvas
77 1/4 × 63 1/8" (196.2 × 160.3 cm)

Purchased with subscription funds
1930-67-1

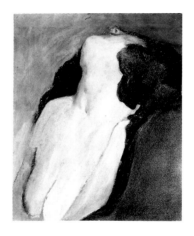

**Carles, Arthur Beecher**
*Redheaded Woman*
1922
Lower right: CARLES
Oil on canvas
16 1/8 × 13" (41 × 33 cm)

The Samuel S. White 3rd and Vera White Collection
1967-30-15

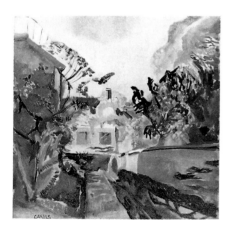

**Carles, Arthur Beecher**
*Steichen's Garden*
c. 1921
Lower left: CARLES
Oil on canvas
24 7/8 × 24 1/8" (63.2 × 61.3 cm)

The Samuel S. White 3rd and Vera White Collection
1967-30-12

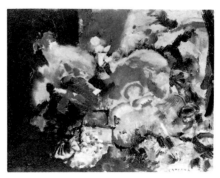

**Carles, Arthur Beecher**
*Abstract of Flowers*
c. 1922
Lower right: CARLES
Oil on canvas
21 1/4 × 25 1/2" (54 × 64.8 cm)

The Samuel S. White 3rd and Vera White Collection
1967-30-14

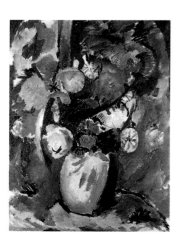

**Carles, Arthur Beecher**
*Composition of Flowers*
1922
Oil on canvas
49 3/8 × 36 3/8" (125.4 × 92.4 cm)

Gift of Mrs. Earle Horter
1950-40-1

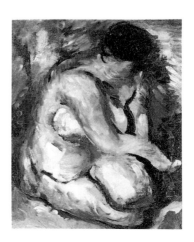

**Carles, Arthur Beecher**
*Nude*
c. 1923
Oil on canvas
16 3/8 × 13" (41.6 × 33 cm)

Gift of Benjamin D. Bernstein
1964-106-1

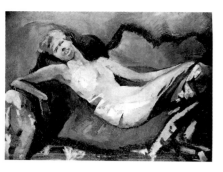

**Carles, Arthur Beecher**
*Figure on a Couch*
1924–25
Upper left: CARLES
Oil on canvas
45 1/8 × 60" (114.6 × 152.4 cm)

Gift of Mr. and Mrs. David
Bortin
1956-37-2

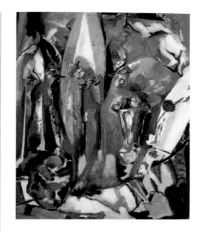

**Carles, Arthur Beecher**
*Blue Abstraction*
c. 1929
Lower right: CARLES
Oil on canvas
40 1/4 × 33 3/16" (102.2 × 84.3 cm)

Gift of Mr. and Mrs. Robert
McLean
1977-202-1

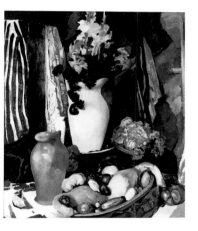

**Carles, Arthur Beecher**
*Still Life*
c. 1926
Oil on canvas
47 1/16 × 40" (119.5 × 101.6 cm)

Gift of Mr. and Mrs. Charles C. G.
Chaplin in memory of Mia Wood
1978-149-1

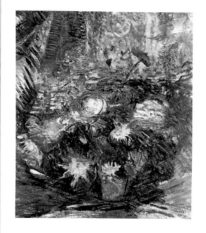

**Carles, Arthur Beecher**
*Flowers*
c. 1930
Oil on canvas
28 7/8 × 23 3/4" (73.3 × 60.3 cm)

The Albert M. Greenfield and
Elizabeth M. Greenfield
Collection
1974-178-22

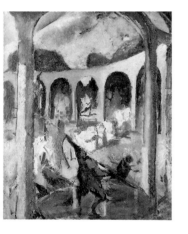

**Carles, Arthur Beecher**
*Through the Arch (Procession)*
1927
On reverse: Arthur B. Carles /
Through the Arch—Carles
Oil on canvas
52 1/4 × 40 1/4" (132.7 × 102.2 cm)

Gift of Mr. and Mrs. C. Earle
Miller
1970-15-1

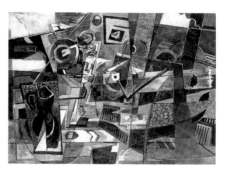

**Carles, Arthur Beecher**
*Abstraction (Composition No. 5)*
c. 1935
Lower left: CARLES
Oil on canvas
38 3/8 × 51 1/2" (97.5 × 130.8 cm)

Gift of Mr. and Mrs. R. Sturgis
Ingersoll
1941-103-4

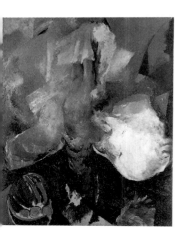

**Carles, Arthur Beecher**
*Turkey*
1927
Lower right: CARLES
Oil on canvas
56 1/2 × 44 1/2" (143.5 × 113 cm)

Gift of Mr. and Mrs. R. Sturgis
Ingersoll
1941-103-5

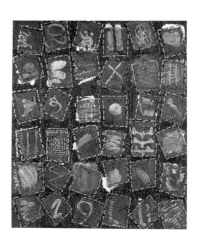

**Carlson, Cynthia J.**
American, born 1942
*Moonlight*
1976
On reverse: Cynthia Carlson 1976/
ACRYlic and OIL ON CANVAS /
"MOONLIGHT" 48" × 60"
Acrylic and oil on canvas
60 1/8 × 48 1/16" (152.7 × 122.1 cm)

Gift of Dr. and Mrs. Lorenzo
Margini
1980-131-1

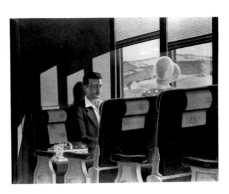

**Carter, Clarence Holbrook**
American, born 1904
*Poor Man's Pullman*
1930
Lower right: Clarence H. Carter
30.
Oil on canvas
35 15/16 × 44 5/16" (91.3 × 112.5 cm)

Purchased with the Edith H. Bell
Fund
1979-163-1

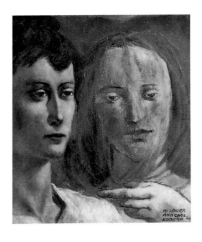

**Castellon, Federico**
American, born Spain,
1914–1971
*Two Heads, One with a Red Veil*
1946
Lower right: TO LAURA / AND
CARL / FEDERO 46
Oil on canvas
12 1/16 × 10 1/8" (30.6 × 25.7 cm)

Gift of Carl Zigrosser
1974-179-1

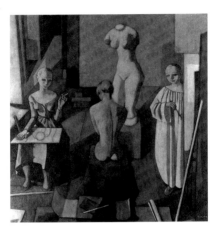

**Casorati, Felice**
Italian, 1883–1963
*The Studio*
c. 1956
Lower right: .F.CASORATI.
Oil on canvas
55 1/4 × 51" (140.3 × 129.5 cm)

Gift of Mrs. Arthur Barnwell
1957-25-1

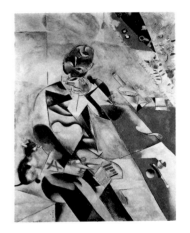

**Chagall, Marc**
French, born Belorussia,
1887–1985
*Half Past Three (The Poet)*
1911
Lower left: Chagall / Paris 1911
Oil on canvas
77 1/8 × 57" (195.9 × 144.8 cm)

The Louise and Walter Arensberg
Collection
1950-134-36

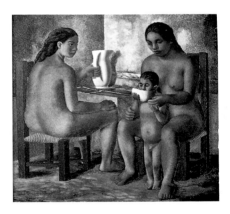

**Castellanos, Julio**
Mexican, 1905–1947
*Three Nudes (The Aunts)*
1930
Oil on canvas
51 15/16 × 55 1/2" (131.9 × 141 cm)

Gift of the Committee on
Painting and Sculpture
1943-45-1

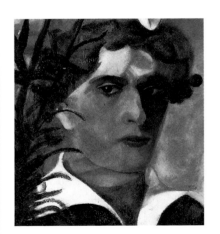

**Chagall, Marc**
*Self-Portrait*
1914
Lower right: Chagall / 1914
Oil on cardboard
11 1/2 × 10 1/8" (29.2 × 25.7 cm)

The Louis E. Stern Collection
1963-181-9

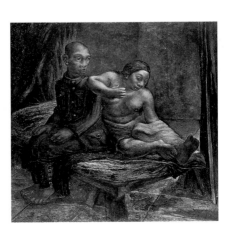

**Castellanos, Julio**
*A Soldier and a Woman (The
Dialogue)*
c. 1936
Oil and wax on canvas
47 3/8 × 47 3/8" (120.3 × 120.3 cm)

Gift of Mr. and Mrs. Henry
Clifford
1947-29-1

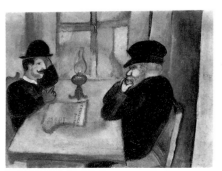

**Chagall, Marc**
*The Smolensk Newspaper*
1914
Center: [Russian for "Smolensk
News / War"]; center right:
[Yiddish for "Smolensk News /
War"]; lower right: Chagall /
Chagall 1914
Oil on cardboard
14 15/16 × 19 3/4" (37.9 × 50.2 cm)

The Louis E. Stern Collection
1963-181-13

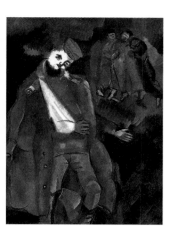

**Chagall, Marc**
*Wounded Soldier*
1914
Oil, watercolor, and gouache on cardboard
19 1/4 × 14 7/8" (48.9 × 37.8 cm)

Gift of Mary Katharine Woodworth in memory of Allegra Woodworth
1986-124-1

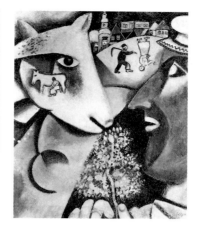

**Chagall, Marc**
*I and the Village*
A larger version, dated 1911, is in the Museum of Modern Art, New York
c. 1924
Lower right: Marc / Chagall.
Oil on canvas
21 15/16 × 18 1/4" (55.7 × 46.3 cm)

Gift of Mr. and Mrs. Rodolphe Meyer de Schauensee
1944-36-1

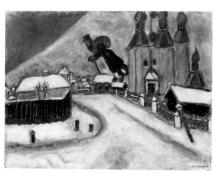

**Chagall, Marc**
*Over Vitebsk*
c. 1914
Lower right: Marc Chagall
Oil, gouache, graphite, and ink on paper
12 3/8 × 15 3/4" (31.4 × 40 cm)

The Louis E. Stern Collection
1963-181-10

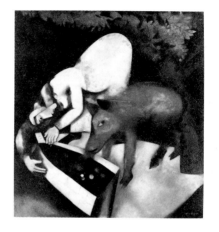

**Chagall, Marc**
*The Watering Trough*
c. 1925
Lower right: Marc Chagall.
Oil on canvas
39 1/4 × 34 11/16" (99.7 × 88.1 cm)

The Louis E. Stern Collection
1963-181-14

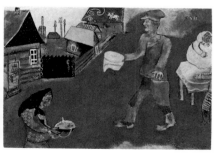

**Chagall, Marc**
*Purim*
1916–18
Lower right: Marc / Chagall.
Oil on canvas
19 7/8 × 28 5/16" (50.5 × 71.9 cm)

The Louis E. Stern Collection
1963-181-11

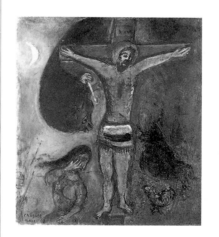

**Chagall, Marc**
*The Crucifixion*
1940
Lower left: Chagall / Marc
Oil on canvas
13 3/8 × 11 9/16" (34 × 29.4 cm)

The Samuel S. White 3rd and Vera White Collection
1959-133-1

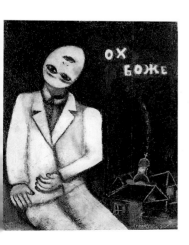

**Chagall, Marc**
*Oh God*
1919
Upper right: [Russian for "Oh God"]; lower left: Marc / 1919; lower right: Chagall
Oil, tempera, crayon, and distemper on paper mounted on cardboard on panel
22 3/4 × 18 5/16" (57.8 × 46.5 cm)

The Louis E. Stern Collection
1963-181-12

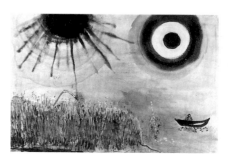

**Chagall, Marc**
*A Wheatfield on a Summer's Afternoon*
Backdrop for Scene III of the ballet *Aleko*, by Léonide Massine, based on a poem by Aleksander Pushkin and music by Peter Ilyich Tchaikovsky
1942
Tempera on fabric
360 × 600" (914.4 × 1524 cm)

Gift of Leslie and Stanley Westreich
1986-173-1

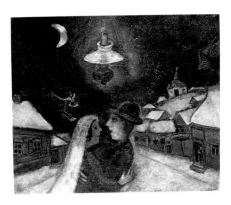

**Chagall, Marc**
*In the Night*
1943
Lower right: MARC CHAGALL / 43
Oil on canvas
18 1/2 × 20 5/8" (47 × 52.4 cm)

The Louis E. Stern Collection
1963-181-16

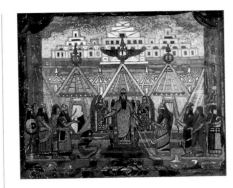

**Chernoff, Vadim Anatolievich**
Ukrainian, 1887–1954
*Sketch for Act I of "Judith"*
Sketch for a backdrop for the play
*Judith*, by Friedrich Hebbel
c. 1920
Lower left: V. CHERNOFF; on
reverse: TO MY DEAR FRIEND /
DR. CHRISTIAN BRINTON /
FROM / VADIM CHERNOFF /
DECEMBER 25 / 1929 / "Judith"
/ ACT I / FRIEDERICK GEBEL /
PRODUCED / REVAL / APRIL 1920
Tempera on canvas
24 × 29" (61 × 73.7 cm)

Gift of Christian Brinton
1941-79-80

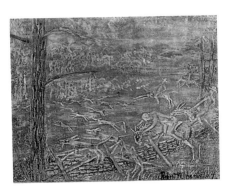

**Chanler, Robert Winthrop**
American, 1872–1930
*The Rokeby Hunt*
1924
Lower right: Robert W. Chanler
1924
Gesso on panel
14 1/2 × 18" (36.8 × 45.7 cm)

Gift of Christian Brinton
1941-79-74

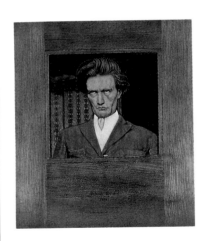

**Chimes, Thomas**
American, born 1921
*Portrait of Alfred Jarry*
1974
Across top: Doctor Alfred Jarry
as he appeared in the year 1896. /
Pa Pa Ebé; center left: Thomas
Chimes / 1974
Oil on panel
12 × 11 11/16" (30.5 × 29.7 cm)

Purchased with the Adele Haas
Turner and Beatrice Pastorius
Turner Memorial Fund
1975-82-1

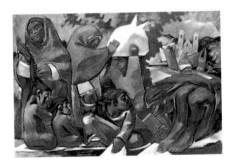

**Charlot, Jean**
Mexican, born France,
1898–1979
*Bathers*
1943
Lower right: Jean Charlot / 43
Oil on canvas
50 × 69 3/4" (127 × 177.2 cm)

Gift of an anonymous donor
1956-26-1

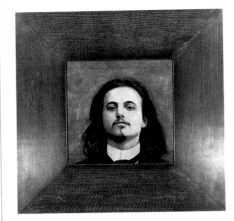

**Chimes, Thomas**
*Portrait of Antonin Artaud*
1974
Upper left: Chimes 1974; center
bottom, on frame: Antonin
Artaud / 1920
Oil on panel
9 1/8 × 9 1/8" (23.2 × 23.2 cm)

Gift of the artist
1975-78-1

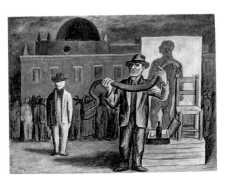

**Chavez-Morado, José**
Mexican, born 1909
*The Charlatan*
1942
Lower left: CHAVEZ / MORADO /
42
Oil on canvas
22 × 28 3/8" (55.9 × 72.1 cm)

Gift of Dr. MacKinley Helm
1947-30-1

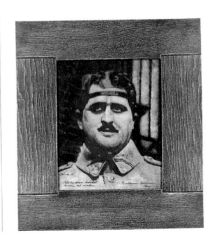

**Chimes, Thomas**
*Portrait of Apollinaire*
1974
Lower left: Chimes 74 / Près du
passé luisant / demain est
incolore; lower right: Guillaume
Apollinaire / Paris
Oil on panel
12 × 9 3/8" (30.5 × 23.8 cm)

Purchased with the Adele Haas
Turner and Beatrice Pastorius
Turner Memorial Fund
1975-82-2

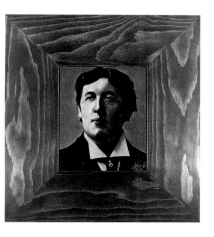

**Chimes, Thomas**
*Portrait of Oscar Wilde*
1975
Lower right: Chimes / 75
Oil on panel
11 × 9 ¼" (27.9 × 23.5 cm)

Gift of the artist
1976-154-1

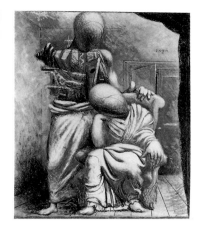

**Chirico, Giorgio de**
*The Poet and His Muse*
1921
Upper right: G. de Chirico / 21
Oil and tempera on canvas
35 ⅞ × 29" (91.1 × 73.7 cm)

The Louise and Walter Arensberg
Collection
1950-134-39

**Chimes, Thomas**
*Faustroll (L'Infini)*
1988
Center: Faustroll
Oil on linen
48 × 68" (121.9 × 172.7 cm)

Purchased with the Julius Bloch
Memorial Fund
1988-42-1

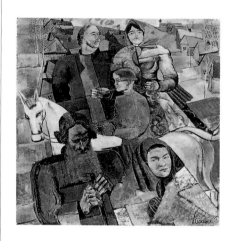

**Cickowsky, Nikolai
Stepanovich**
American, born Belorussia,
born 1894, death date unknown
*Russia*
1925
Lower right: 1925 / N. Cickowsky
Oil on canvas
40 ⅛ × 37" (101.9 × 94 cm)

Gift of Christian Brinton
1941-79-116

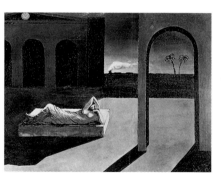

**Chirico, Giorgio de**
Italian, born Greece,
1888–1978
*The Soothsayer's Recompense*
1913
Lower left: Giorgio de Chirico /
M.CM.XIII.
Oil on canvas
53 ⅜ × 70 ⅞" (135.6 × 180 cm)

The Louise and Walter Arensberg
Collection
1950-134-38

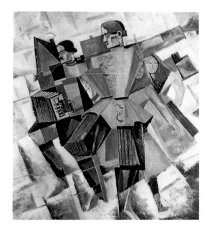

**Cickowsky, Nikolai
Stepanovich**
*Russian Dancer*
c. 1926
Lower right: N. Cickowsky
Oil on canvas
35 ⅛ × 30 ⅛" (89.2 × 76.5 cm)

Gift of Christian Brinton
1941-79-149

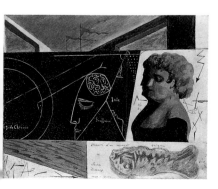

**Chirico, Giorgio de**
*The Fatal Temple*
c. 1913?
Center left: G. de Chirico; center:
Joie / Souffrance; center bottom:
éternité d'un moment / chose /
étrange / non-sens; lower right:
énigme / vie
Oil on canvas
13 ⅛ × 16 ⅛" (33.3 × 41 cm)

A. E. Gallatin Collection
1947-88-14

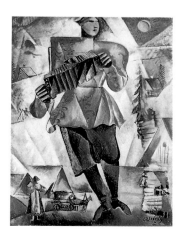

**Cickowsky, Nikolai
Stepanovich**
*Russian Legend*
c. 1926
Lower right: Cickowsky
Oil on canvas
33 × 26" (83.8 × 66 cm)

Gift of Christian Brinton
1941-79-108

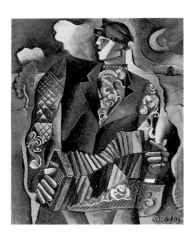

**Cickowsky, Nikolai Stepanovich**
*Young Man from Penza*
By 1931
Lower right: NCickowsky.
Oil on canvas
33 × 26" (83.8 × 66 cm)

Gift of Christian Brinton
1941-79-107

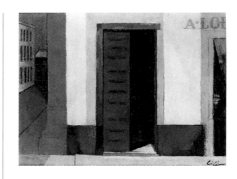

**Coiner, Charles Toucey**
American, born 1897
*The Blue Door*
c. 1959
Lower right: C. C.
Oil on canvas
22 1/2 × 29 5/8" (57.1 × 75.2 cm)

Purchased with the Adele Haas Turner and Beatrice Pastorius Turner Memorial Fund
1959-12-2

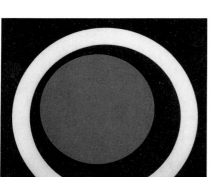

**Claisse, Geneviève**
French, born 1935
*H.*
1969
On reverse: Claisse 1969
Oil on canvas
31 1/2 × 31 1/2" (80 × 80 cm)

Gift of Dr. and Mrs. Paul Todd Makler
1979-186-3

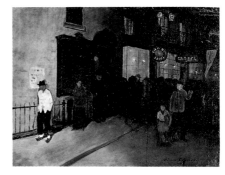

**Coleman, Glenn O.**
American, 1887–1932
*Street Scene, Chinatown, New York City*
c. 1910–15
Lower right: Glenn Coleman
Oil on panel
23 1/2 × 29 7/8" (59.7 × 75.9 cm)

Gift of Mrs. John Wintersteen
1942-66-1

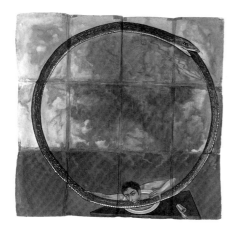

**Clemente, Francesco**
Italian, born 1952
*Hunger*
1980
Gouache on Pondicherry paper, joined by cotton strips
93 1/2 × 96 1/2" (237.5 × 245.1 cm)

Gift of Marion Boulton Stroud
1991-142-1

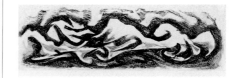

**Cook, Howard Norton**
American, 1901–1980
*Sangre de Cristo Mountains*
1958
Lower right: HOWARD COOK
Oil on panel
5 7/8 × 18 1/8" (14.9 × 46 cm)

Gift of Carl Zigrosser
1972-237-8

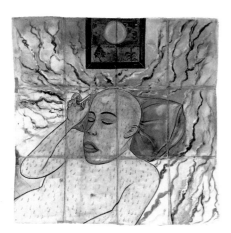

**Clemente, Francesco**
*Sun*
1980
Gouache on twelve sheets of paper, joined by cotton strips
95 × 91" (241.3 × 231.1 cm)

Purchased with the Edward and Althea Budd Fund, the Katharine Levin Farrell Fund, and funds contributed by Mrs. H. Gates Lloyd
1984-118-1

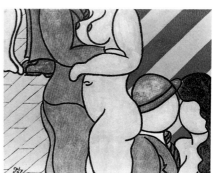

**Copley, William Nelson**
American, born 1919
*Tendresse*
See following painting for reverse
1969
Lower left: CpLy / 69
Liquitex on canvas
26 × 32 3/16" (66 × 81.8 cm)

Gift of an anonymous donor
1970-204-1a

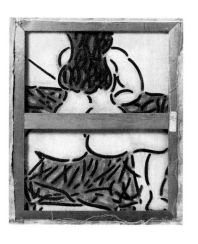

**Copley, William Nelson**
*Nude Woman*
Reverse of the preceding painting
c. 1969
Liquitex on canvas
26 × 32 3/16" (66 × 81.8 cm)

Gift of an anonymous donor
1970-204-1b

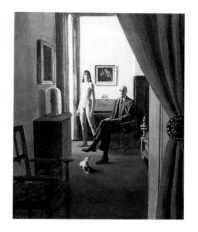

**Crimmins, Jerry**
American, born 1940
*The Ambassador and Her Assistant*
1973
Lower right: G. CRIMMINS. 73
Oil on Masonite
16 1/4 × 13 1/4" (33.6 × 41.3 cm)

Gift of the Cheltenham Art
Centre
1979-30-1

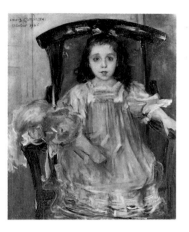

**Corinth, Lovis**
German, 1858–1925
*Portrait of Sophie Cassirer*
1906
Upper left: LOVIS CORINTH. /
October 1906
Oil on canvas
37 11/16 × 29 5/8" (95.7 × 75.2 cm)

Purchased with the George W.
Elkins Fund
E1975-1-1

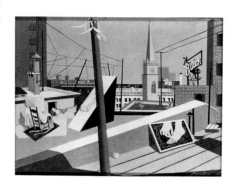

**Criss, Francis H.**
American, 1901–1973
*Words and Music of Two
Hemispheres*
c. 1940
Lower right: Francis Criss
Oil on Masonite
14 1/8 × 18 9/16" (35.9 × 47.1 cm)

Gift of Dr. Herman Lorber
1944-95-1

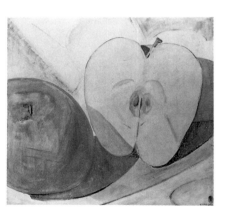

**Covert, John R.**
American, 1882–1960
*Hydro Cell*
1918
Lower right: HYDRO CELL; on
reverse: Hydro Cell / John R.
Covert / NYC—1918
Oil on cardboard
24 1/4 × 26 1/2" (61.6 × 67.3 cm)

The Louise and Walter Arensberg
Collection
1950-134-509

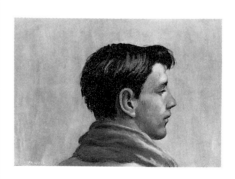

**Crowell, Lucius**
American, 1911–1988
*Profile of a Young Man*
1949
Lower left: L CROWELL
Oil on canvas
10 × 14" (25.4 × 35.6 cm)

Bequest of Lisa Norris Elkins
1950-92-4

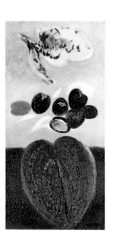

**Cox, Jan**
American, born Netherlands,
born 1919
*Good Night Black Olive*
1959
On reverse: 18 JANUARY 59
Oil and mother-of-pearl on panel
23 13/16 × 11" (60.5 × 27.9 cm)

Gift of Dr. and Mrs. Joseph N.
Epstein
1963-192-1

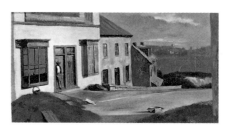

**Crowell, Lucius**
*From Tunnel Hill*
c. 1955
Lower right: L CROWELL
Oil on canvas
16 × 28 1/4" (40.6 × 71.7 cm)

Purchased with the Adele Haas
Turner and Beatrice Pastorius
Turner Memorial Fund
1959-12-3

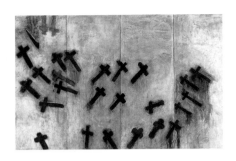

**Cucchi, Enzo**
Italian, born 1950
*Entry into Port of a Ship with a Red Rose Aboard*
1985–86
Fresco
110 × 157" (279.4 × 398.8 cm)

Gift of Mr. and Mrs. David N. Pincus
1991-140-1

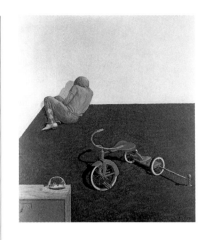

**Danziger, Fred**
American, born 1946
*Playroom Portrait*
1972
Lower right: DANZIGER 72
Oil on canvas
70 × 56 9/16" (177.8 × 143.7 cm)

Gift of Fidelity Bank
1973-131-1

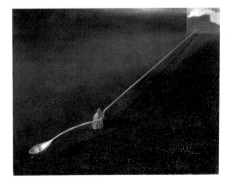

**Curtiss, Deborah**
American, born 1937
*Too*
1972
Lower right: Curtiss
Acrylic on unprimed canvas
50 × 48 1/8" (127 × 122.2 cm)

Centennial gift of the friends of Deborah Curtiss
1976-98-1

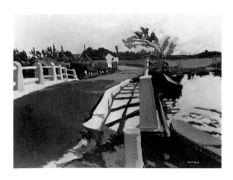

**Dash, Robert**
American, born 1934
*Autumn Bridge*
1971
Lower right: Robert Dash
Acrylic on canvas
30 × 40" (76.2 × 101.6 cm)

Gift of Barbara Kulicke
1973-71-1

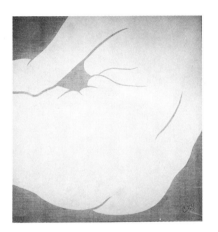

**Dalí, Salvador**
Spanish, 1904–1989
*Agnostic Symbol*
1932
Lower right: gala salvador Dali 1932
Oil on canvas
21 1/4 × 25 11/16" (54 × 65.2 cm)

The Louise and Walter Arensberg Collection
1950-134-40

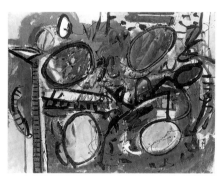

**Davie, Alan**
Scottish, born 1920
*Egg Rocker*
c. 1952
On reverse: ALAN DAVIE
Oil on canvas
47 7/8 × 60" (121.6 × 152.4 cm)

Gift of Mr. and Mrs. David N. Pincus
1971-263-1

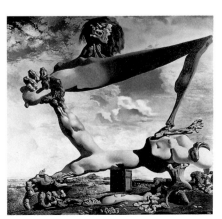

**Dalí, Salvador**
*Soft Construction with Boiled Beans (Premonition of Civil War)*
1936
Oil on canvas
39 5/16 × 39 3/8" (99.8 × 100 cm)

The Louise and Walter Arensberg Collection
1950-134-41

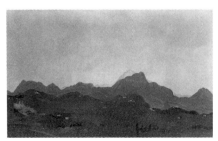

**Davies, Arthur Bowen**
American, 1862–1928
*Apuan, Many-Folded Mountains*
1907
Lower left: A. B. Davies 07
Oil on canvas
26 × 40" (66 × 101.6 cm)

Gift of Mr. and Mrs. Philip S. Collins
1929-79-2

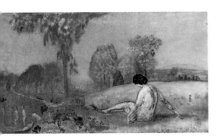

**Davies, Arthur Bowen**
*Autumn—Enchanted Salutation*
1907
Lower left: A. B. Davies
Oil on canvas
18 1/8 × 30 1/4" (46 × 76.8 cm)

Gift of Mr. and Mrs. Meyer P.
Potamkin (reserving life interest)
1964-116-3

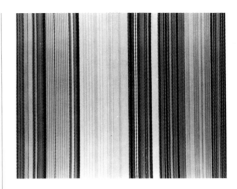

**Davis, Gene**
*Study for "Franklin's Footpath"*
See previous two entries
1971
Liquitex on canvas
99 3/16 × 120 1/8" (251.9 × 305.1 cm)

Gift of the artist and Dr. and
Mrs. William Wolgin
1972-54-1

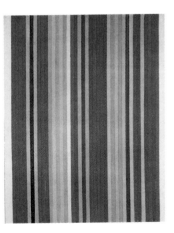

**Davies, Arthur Bowen**
*Daphnes of the Ravine*
1922
Lower left: A / B / Davies
Oil on canvas
32 1/8 × 24 1/8" (81.6 × 61.3 cm)

Gift of Mr. and Mrs. Philip S.
Collins
1929-79-1

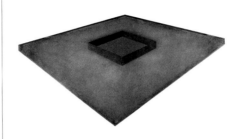

**Davis, Ron**
American, born 1937
*One-Ninth Green*
1966
Plastic, fiberglass, wood, and
polyester
70 × 130" (177.8 × 330.2 cm)

Centennial gift of the Woodward
Foundation
1975-83-3

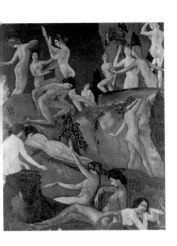

**Davis, Gene**
American, 1920–1985
*Study for "Franklin's Footpath"*
For the painting executed on the
Benjamin Franklin Parkway,
Philadelphia, in 1971 and
removed in 1976
1971
Liquitex on canvas
29 3/4 × 24 1/8" (75.6 × 61.3 cm)

Gift of the artist and Dr. and
Mrs. William Wolgin
1972-30-1

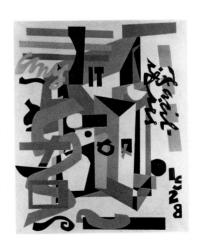

**Davis, Stuart**
American, 1892–1964
*Something on the Eight Ball*
1953–54
Lower right: Stuart Davis.; on
reverse: Something on the 8 Ball,
1953–4
Oil on canvas
56 × 45" (142.2 × 114.3 cm)

Purchased with the Adele Haas
Turner and Beatrice Pastorius
Turner Memorial Fund
1954-30-1

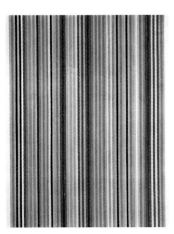

**Davis, Gene**
*Study for "Franklin's Footpath"*
See previous entry
1971
Liquitex on canvas
29 × 22 1/2" (73.7 × 57.1 cm)

Gift of the artist and Dr. and
Mrs. William Wolgin
1972-30-2

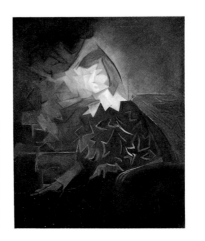

**Dawson, Manierre**
American, 1887–1969
*Eugenia*
1911
Lower right: M Dawson 11
Oil on canvas
36 × 28 1/8" (91.4 × 71.4 cm)

Purchased with the Edith H. Bell
Fund
1975-169-1

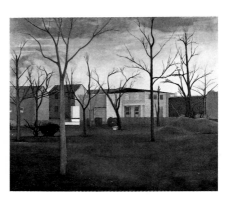

**Day, Larry**
American, born 1921
*Suburban Landscape*
1976
Lower right: Day
Oil on canvas
60 1/2 × 71 1/2" (153.7 × 181.6 cm)

Purchased with funds contributed
by Dr. and Mrs. Stephen D.
Silberstein
1977-201-1

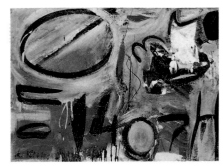

**de Kooning, Willem**
*Open Road*
1950
Lower left: de Kooning; on
reverse: OPEN ROAD 1950
Oil and enamel on cardboard on
Masonite
29 7/8 × 39 15/16" (75.9 × 101.4 cm)

The Albert M. Greenfield and
Elizabeth M. Greenfield
Collection
1974-178-25

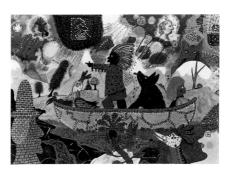

**De Forest, Roy**
American, born 1930
*Canoe of Fate*
1974
On reverse: POLYMER / ROY DE
FOREST 1974 / "CANOE OF
FATE" / VARNISH B-72
Acrylic on canvas
66 3/4 × 90 1/4" (169.5 × 229.2 cm)

Purchased with the Adele Haas
Turner and Beatrice Pastorius
Turner Memorial Fund
1975-83-1

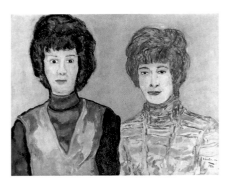

**Delaney, Beauford**
American, 1901–1979
*Portrait of Marian and Betty*
1970
Lower right: B. Delaney / 1970
Oil on canvas
25 × 31" (63.5 × 78.7 cm)

Gift of Gene Locks
1991-139-1

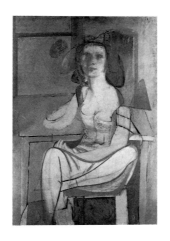

**de Kooning, Willem**
American, born Netherlands,
born 1904
*Seated Woman*
c. 1940
Oil and charcoal on Masonite
54 1/16 × 36" (137.3 × 91.4 cm)

The Albert M. Greenfield and
Elizabeth M. Greenfield
Collection
1974-178-23

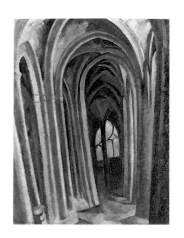

**Delaunay, Robert**
French, 1885–1941
*Saint Séverin*
See following painting for reverse
1909
Lower left: r. delaunay 1909
Oil on canvas
38 × 27 3/4" (96.5 × 70.5 cm)

The Louise and Walter Arensberg
Collection
1950-134-42a

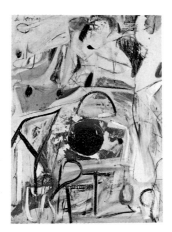

**de Kooning, Willem**
*Noon*
c. 1947
Upper left: de Kooning
Oil and enamel on Masonite
48 × 13 15/16" (121.9 × 35.4 cm)

The Albert M. Greenfield and
Elizabeth M. Greenfield
Collection
1974-178-24

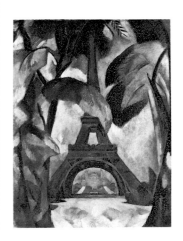

**Delaunay, Robert**
*Eiffel Tower*
Reverse of the preceding painting
c. 1909
Oil on canvas
38 × 27 3/4" (96.5 × 70.5 cm)

The Louise and Walter Arensberg
Collection
1950-134-42b

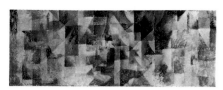

**Delaunay, Robert**
*Three-Part Windows*
1912
Lower left: r delaunay 1912
Oil on canvas
13 7/8 × 36 1/8" (35.2 × 91.8 cm)

A. E. Gallatin Collection
1952-61-13

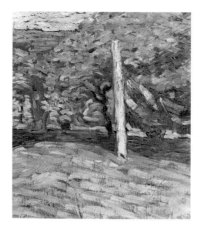

**Demuth, Charles**
*Trees*
1908
On reverse: Demuth
Oil on canvas
12 1/8 × 10 1/8" (30.8 × 25.7 cm)

Gift of Mr. and Mrs. Herman
Finklestein
1962-205-2

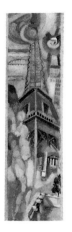

**Delaunay, Robert**
*Eiffel Tower*
See following painting for reverse
c. 1925
Lower left: r. delaunay
Oil on burlap
51 1/2 × 12 1/2" (130.8 × 31.7 cm)

The Louise and Walter Arensberg
Collection
1950-134-43a

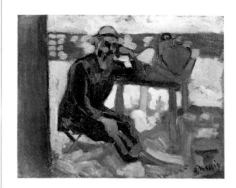

**Derain, André**
French, 1880–1954
*Portrait of Henri Matisse*
c. 1905
Lower right: A. Derain
Oil on canvas
13 × 16 1/8" (33 × 41 cm)

A. E. Gallatin Collection
1952-61-22

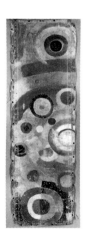

**Delaunay, Robert**
*Untitled*
Reverse of the preceding painting
c. 1925
Oil on burlap
51 1/2 × 12 1/2" (130.8 × 31.7 cm)

The Louise and Walter Arensberg
Collection
1950-134-43b

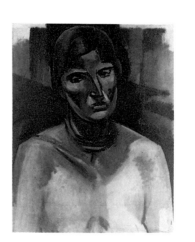

**Derain, André**
*Woman*
c. 1914
Oil on canvas
24 1/8 × 18 1/2" (61.3 × 47 cm)

The Louise and Walter Arensberg
Collection
1950-134-47

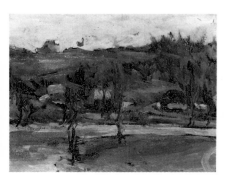

**Demuth, Charles**
American, 1883–1935
*River Scene*
1908
Oil on cardboard
8 × 9 7/8" (20.3 × 25.1 cm)

Gift of Mr. and Mrs. Herman
Finklestein
1962-205-1

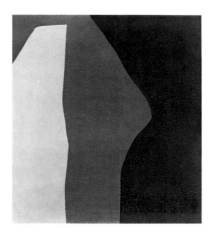

**Dessner, Murray**
American, born 1934
*Oranges for Red Rodney*
1969
Acrylic on canvas
88 1/8 × 76 5/8" (223.8 × 194.6 cm)

Gift of the Cheltenham Art
Centre
1969-88-1

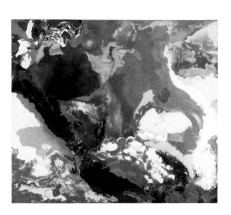

**Dessner, Murray**
*Xanadu*
1972
Acrylic on canvas
108 7/16 × 100 7/8" (275.4 × 256.2 cm)

Purchased with the Philadelphia Foundation Fund
1973-134-1

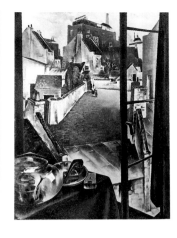

**Dickinson, Preston**
American, 1891–1930
*Old Street, Quebec*
c. 1928
Lower right: P. DICKINSON
Oil on canvas
34 1/16 × 23 7/8" (86.5 × 60.6 cm)

Gift of Mr. and Mrs. R. Sturgis Ingersoll
1941-103-2

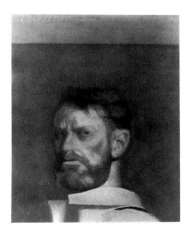

**Dickinson, Edwin Walter**
American, 1891–1979
*Self-Portrait*
1940
Upper left: EW Dickinson; upper right: 1940
Oil on canvas
20 × 15 1/8" (50.8 × 38.4 cm)

Bequest of T. Edward Hanley
1970-76-2

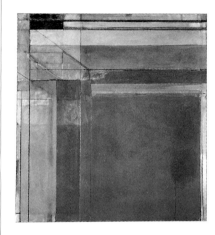

**Diebenkorn, Richard**
American, 1922–1993
*Ocean Park No. 79*
1975
Lower right: R D 75; on reverse: R. DIEBENKORN / Ocean Park #79 1975
Oil on canvas
93 × 81" (236.2 × 205.7 cm)

Purchased with a grant from the National Endowment for the Arts and with funds contributed by private donors
1977-28-1

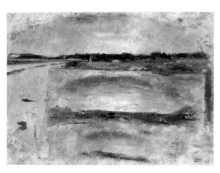

**Dickinson, Edwin Walter**
*Simba and Three in One (Mayo's Beach from Indian Neck)*
1951
Upper left: E W Dickinson; center left: SIMBA; lower left: Wellfleet; center bottom: 1951 / SIMBA
Oil on panel
12 1/16 × 15 13/16" (30.6 × 40.2 cm)

The Albert M. Greenfield and Elizabeth M. Greenfield Collection
1974-178-27

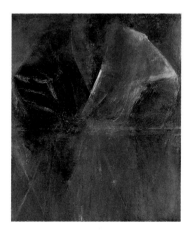

**Dine, Jim**
American, born 1935
*Balcony*
1979
On reverse: BALCONY / Jim Dine 1979
Oil on canvas
102 1/2 × 81" (260.3 × 205.7 cm)

Gift of the Friends of the Philadelphia Museum of Art
1981-56-1

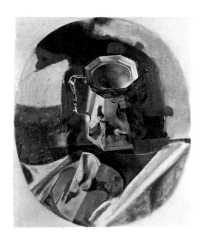

**Dickinson, Edwin Walter**
*Still Life, Lascaux*
1953
Upper left: E W Dickinson / 1953 / Grotte de Lascaux; lower right: 1953 EW Dickinson
Oil on canvas
37 × 30 1/8" (94 × 76.5 cm)

The Albert M. Greenfield and Elizabeth M. Greenfield Collection
1974-178-26

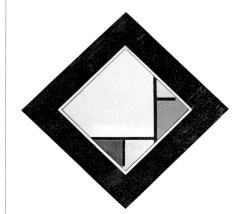

**Doesburg, Theo van (Christian Emil Marie Kupper)**
Dutch, 1883–1931
*Composition*
1929
On reverse: Theo van / Doesburg '29
Oil on canvas
11 13/16 × 11 7/8" (30 × 30.2 cm)
diagonal

A. E. Gallatin Collection
1952-61-124

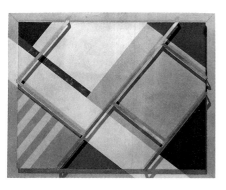

**Domela, César**
Dutch, active France, born 1900
*Construction*
c. 1929
Oil and metal on panel
18 1/4 × 22 1/4" (46.3 × 56.5 cm)

A. E. Gallatin Collection
1952-61-23

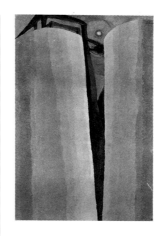

**Dove, Arthur Garfield**
*Silver Tanks and Moon*
1930
Lower right: Dove
Oil and silver paint on canvas
28 3/16 × 18 1/16" (71.6 × 45.9 cm)

The Alfred Stieglitz Collection
1949-18-3

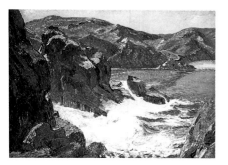

**Dougherty, Paul**
American, 1877–1947
*Cove*
1912
Lower left: Paul Dougherty
Oil on canvas
36 3/4 × 48 1/4" (93.3 × 122.5 cm)

The Alex Simpson, Jr., Collection
1928-63-5

**Dowell, John E., Jr.**
American, born 1941
*Trane Scape*
1972
On reverse: "Trane / Scape" /
John Dowell / '72
Acrylic on canvas
83 3/4 × 63 13/16" (212.7 × 162.1 cm)

Gift of Dr. Luther W. Brady, Jr.
1984-109-1

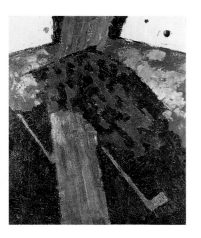

**Dove, Arthur Garfield**
American, 1880–1946
*No. 1*
c. 1915–20
Oil on canvas
21 5/16 × 18" (54.1 × 45.7 cm)

The Alfred Stieglitz Collection
1949-18-1

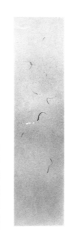

**Dowell, John E., Jr.**
*To Weave through Time*
1979
On reverse: Dowell / 1979 / TO
WEAVE / THROUGH / TIME /
John E. Dowell "R" / 1979
Oil on canvas
84 1/8 × 20 1/8" (213.7 × 51.1 cm)

Gift of Dr. Luther W. Brady, Jr.
1980-57-1

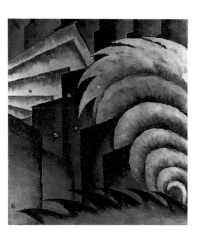

**Dove, Arthur Garfield**
*Chinese Music*
1923
Oil on panel
21 11/16 × 18 1/8" (55.1 × 46 cm)

The Alfred Stieglitz Collection
1949-18-2

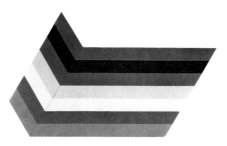

**Downing, Tom**
American, born 1928
*Fan on the Pharaoh*
1966
Oil on canvas
76 5/8 × 106 1/4" (194.6 ×
269.9 cm)

Gift of Vincent Melzac
1967-39-1

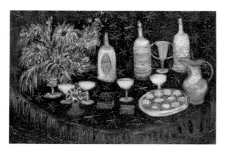

**Drew-Bear, Jessie**
American, born England,
1880–1962
*Still Life: Cocktails*
c. 1960
Center bottom: DREW-BEAR; on
bottles: GILBEYS / GIN; NOILLY-
PRAT / EXTRA-DRY /
VERMOUTH; SEAGRAMS / 7
Oil on canvas
24 3/16 × 35 7/8" (61.4 × 91.1 cm)

Gift of Mrs. William Thomas
Tonner
1960-57-1

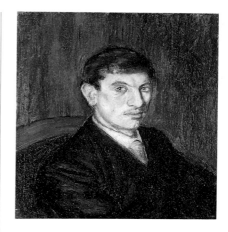

**Duchamp, Marcel**
*Portrait of Marcel Lefrançois*
1904
On reverse: 1904 / J'ATTESTE
QUE CETTE TOILE EST BIEN
DE / MON FRÈRE MARCEL
DUCHAMP / Jacques Villon / 29
Dec. 1949; Portrait de Marcel /
Lefrançois / Marcel Duchamp /
1904 / Signé en 1950
Oil on canvas
25 5/8 × 23 15/16" (65.1 × 60.8 cm)

The Louise and Walter Arensberg
Collection
1950-134-80

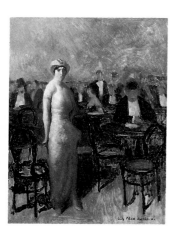

**du Bois, Guy Pène**
American, 1884–1958
*Cabaret*
1915
Lower right: Guy Pène du Bois.
Oil on panel
20 × 14 3/4" (50.8 × 37.5 cm)

The Chester Dale Collection
1946-50-3

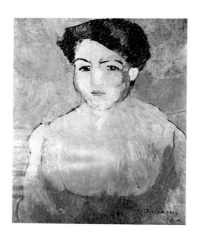

**Duchamp, Marcel**
*Brunette in a Green Blouse (Portrait
of Nana)*
1910
Lower right: Duchamp / 10
Oil on canvas
24 1/4 × 19 15/16" (61.6 × 50.6 cm)

The Louise and Walter Arensberg
Collection
1950-134-48

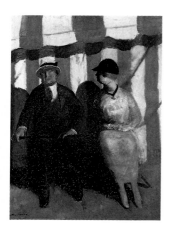

**du Bois, Guy Pène**
*Sporting Life*
1915
Lower left: Guy Pène du Bois.
1915.
Oil on panel
20 × 15" (50.8 × 38.1 cm)

The Chester Dale Collection
1946-50-2

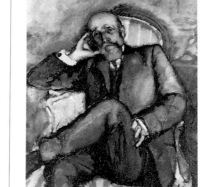

**Duchamp, Marcel**
*Portrait of the Artist's Father*
1910
Center bottom: Marcel Duchamp
10
Oil on canvas
36 3/8 × 28 7/8" (92.4 × 73.3 cm)

The Louise and Walter Arensberg
Collection
1950-134-49

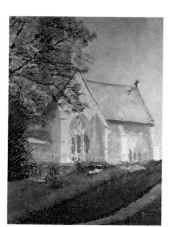

**Duchamp, Marcel**
American, born France,
1887–1968
*Church at Blainville*
1902
Lower right: M Duchamp / 02
Oil on canvas
24 1/8 × 16 7/8" (61.3 × 42.9 cm)

The Louise and Walter Arensberg
Collection
1950-134-81

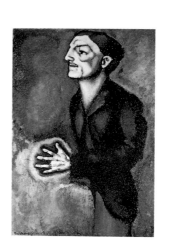

**Duchamp, Marcel**
*Portrait of Dr. Dumouchel*
1910
Lower left: Duchamp / 10; on
reverse: à propos de ta "figure" /
mon cher Dumouchel / Bien
cordialement / Duchamp.
Oil on canvas
39 1/2 × 25 7/8" (100.3 × 65.7 cm)

The Louise and Walter Arensberg
Collection
1950-134-508

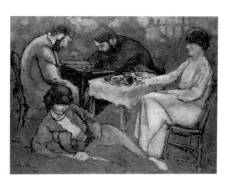

**Duchamp, Marcel**
*The Chess Game*
1910
Lower left: Duchamp / 10—
Oil on canvas
44 7/8 × 57 11/16" (114 × 146.5 cm)

The Louise and Walter Arensberg
Collection
1950-134-82

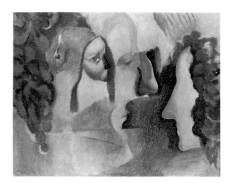

**Duchamp, Marcel**
*Yvonne and Magdeleine Torn in Tatters*
1911
Lower left: Dchp / Sept. 11;
on reverse: Marcel Duchamp /
Yvonne et Magdeleine /
déchiquetées 1911
Oil on canvas
23 3/4 × 28 7/8" (60.3 × 73.3 cm)

The Louise and Walter Arensberg
Collection
1950-134-53

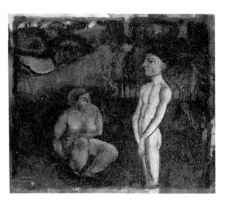

**Duchamp, Marcel**
*Paradise (Adam and Eve)*
Painted on reverse of *The King
and Queen Surrounded by Swift
Nudes*
1910–11
Lower left [added later by the
artist]: MARCEL DUCHAMP /
(PAINTED 1910).
Oil on canvas
45 1/8 × 50 3/4" (114.6 × 128.9 cm)

The Louise and Walter Arensberg
Collection
1950-134-63b

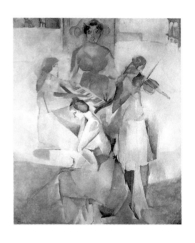

**Duchamp, Marcel**
*Sonata*
1911
Lower left: MARCEL DUCHAMP /
11; on reverse: Sonate / MARCEL
DUCHAMP / 11
Oil on canvas
57 1/8 × 44 5/8" (145.1 × 113.3 cm)

The Louise and Walter Arensberg
Collection
1950-134-52

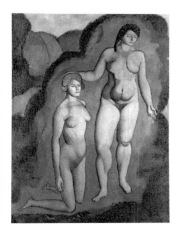

**Duchamp, Marcel**
*The Bush*
1910–11
Lower right: MARCEL
DUCHAMP / 11
Oil on canvas
50 1/8 × 36 3/16" (127.3 × 91.9 cm)

The Louise and Walter Arensberg
Collection
1950-134-51

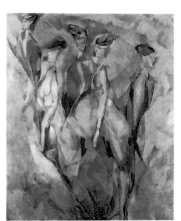

**Duchamp, Marcel**
*Portrait (Dulcinea)*
1911
Lower left: MARCEL DUCHAMP /
11; on reverse: Duchamp Marcel /
Portrait
Oil on canvas
57 5/8 × 44 7/8" (146.4 × 114 cm)

The Louise and Walter Arensberg
Collection
1950-134-54

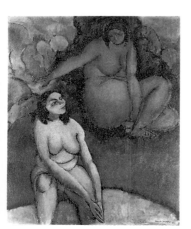

**Duchamp, Marcel**
*Baptism*
1911
Lower right: MARCEL
DUCHAMP / 11; on reverse,
covered by relining: Au cher
Tribout Carabin / j'offre ce
"Baptême": M.D.
Oil on canvas
36 × 25 5/8" (91.5 × 72.7 cm)

The Louise and Walter Arensberg
Collection
1950-134-50

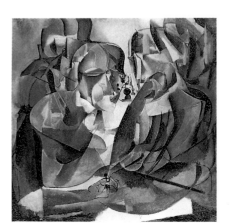

**Duchamp, Marcel**
*Portrait of Chess Players*
1911
Lower left: MARCEL DUCHAMP /
11; on reverse: Marcel Duchamp /
Portrait de joueurs d'échecs
Oil on canvas
39 5/8 × 39 9/16" (100.6 × 100.5 cm)

The Louise and Walter Arensberg
Collection
1950-134-56

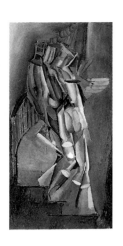

**Duchamp, Marcel**
*Nude Descending a Staircase (No. 1)*
1911
Lower left: MARCEL DUCHAMP /
11 / NU DESCENDANT UN
ESCALIER
Oil on cardboard on panel
37 3/4 × 23 3/4" (95.9 × 60.3 cm)

The Louise and Walter Arensberg
Collection
1950-134-58

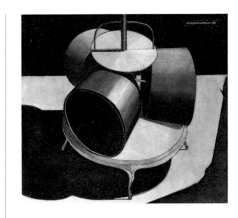

**Duchamp, Marcel**
*Chocolate Grinder (No. 1)*
1913
Upper right, on leather strip:
BROYEUSE DE CHOCOLAT—
1913; on reverse: Broyeuse de
Chocolat 1913 / appartenant à
Marcel Duchamp
Oil on canvas
24 3/8 × 25 3/8" (61.9 × 64.4 cm)

The Louise and Walter Arensberg
Collection
1950-134-69

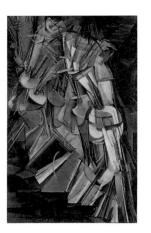

**Duchamp, Marcel**
*Nude Descending a Staircase (No. 2)*
1912
Center bottom: MARCEL
DUCHAMP 12; lower left: NU
DESCENDANT UN ESCALIER; on
reverse: Marcel Duchamp 12
Oil on canvas
57 7/8 × 35 1/8" (147 × 89.2 cm)

The Louise and Walter Arensberg
Collection
1950-134-59

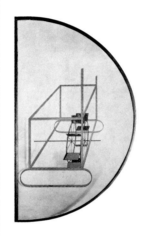

**Duchamp, Marcel**
*Glider Containing a Water Mill in
Neighboring Metals*
1913–15
On reverse: GLISSIERE /
contenant / un MOULIN à Eau /
(en métaux voisins) / appartenant
à / Marcel Duchamp / —1913–
14-15—
Oil and lead wire on glass
59 3/8 × 32 15/16" (150.8 × 83.7 cm)

The Louise and Walter Arensberg
Collection
1950-134-68

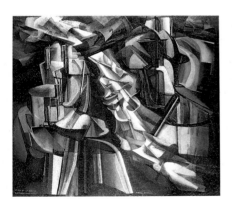

**Duchamp, Marcel**
*The King and Queen Surrounded by
Swift Nudes*
Painted on reverse of *Paradise
(Adam and Eve)*
1912
Lower left: LE ROI ET LA REINE
/ ENTOURES DE NUS VITES;
center bottom: MARCEL
DUCHAMP 12
Oil on canvas
45 1/8 × 50 3/4" (114.6 × 128.9 cm)

The Louise and Walter Arensberg
Collection
1950-134-63a

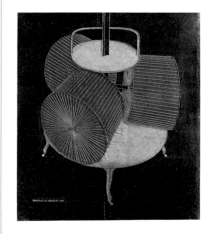

**Duchamp, Marcel**
*Chocolate Grinder (No. 2)*
1914
Lower left, on leather strip:
BROYEUSE DE CHOCOLAT—1914
Oil, graphite, and thread on
canvas
25 3/4 × 21 3/8" (65.4 × 54.3 cm)

The Louise and Walter Arensberg
Collection
1950-134-70

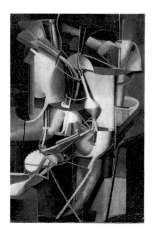

**Duchamp, Marcel**
*Bride*
1912
Lower left: MARIÉE MARCEL
DUCHAMP / august 12
Oil on canvas
35 1/4 × 21 7/8" (89.5 × 55.6 cm)

The Louise and Walter Arensberg
Collection
1950-134-65

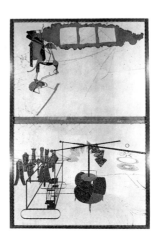

**Duchamp, Marcel**
*The Bride Stripped Bare by Her
Bachelors, Even (The Large Glass)*
1915–23
On reverse: LA MARIEE MISE A
NU PAR / SES CELIBATAIRES,
MEME / MARCEL DUCHAMP /
1915–1923 / —inachevé /
—cassé 1931 / —réparé 1936
Oil, varnish, lead foil, lead wire,
and dust on two glass panels
109 1/4 × 69 1/4" (277.5 × 175.9 cm)

Bequest of Katherine S. Dreier
1952-98-1

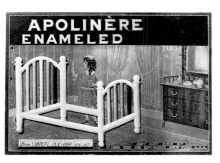

**Duchamp, Marcel**
*Apolinère Enameled*
1916–17
Across top: APOLINÈRE /
ENAMELED; lower left: [from]
MARCEL DUCHAMP 1916 1917;
lower right: ANY ACT RED BY /
HER TEN OR EPERGNE, NEW
YORK, U.S.A.
Graphite on cardboard and
painted tin (Readymade)
9 5/8 × 13 3/8" (24.4 × 34 cm)

The Louise and Walter Arensberg
Collection
1950-134-73

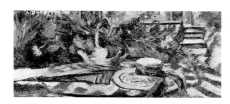

**Dunoyer de Segonzac,
André**
French, 1884–1974
*On the Table*
c. 1926
Upper left: A D de Segonzac
Oil on canvas
13 1/4 × 31 1/2" (33.6 × 80 cm)

Bequest of Lisa Norris Elkins
1950-92-16

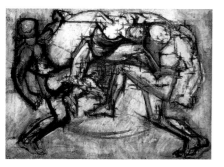

**Duchamp-Villon, Raymond
(Pierre-Maurice-Raymond
Duchamp)**
French, 1876–1918
*Untitled (Three Figures Dancing)*
1913
Center bottom: Rduchamp
Oil on canvas
23 5/8 × 32" (60 × 81.3 cm)

Purchased with the Edward and
Althea Budd Fund
1984-22-1

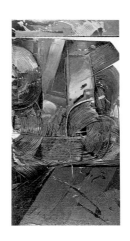

**Dupree, James**
American, born 1950
*Theme 5, Part 1*
1976–77
On reverse: James Dupree 76/77
Acrylic on canvas
72 5/8 × 36 3/4" (184.5 × 93.3 cm)

Gift of the Friends of the Junior
League of Philadelphia
1979-97-1

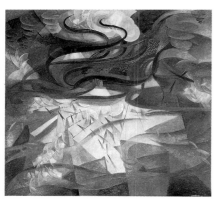

**Dudreville, Leonardo**
Italian, 1885–1975
*Daily Domestic Arguments*
1913
Lower right: L. DUDREVILLE
1913
Oil on canvas
90 3/4 × 98 7/8" (230.5 × 251.1 cm)

Gift of Mr. and Mrs. N. Richard
Miller
1969-265-1

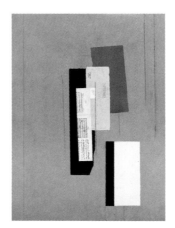

**Edlich, Stephen**
American, born 1944
*Untitled (German Academic
Exchange Service)*
1977
On reverse: Edlich. "Deutscher
Akademicher Austauschdienst"
84 × 60", 1977. Mixed media:
acrylic polymer, / paper and jute
on primed canvas. LES MARTINS
PAR GORDES
Charcoal, acrylic polymer, paper,
and jute on canvas
84 1/4 × 60 3/16 (214 × 152.9 cm)

Gift of Mr. and Mrs. David N.
Pincus
1980-147-1

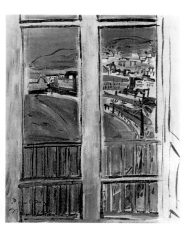

**Dufy, Raoul**
French, 1877–1953
*Window on the Promenade des
Anglais, Nice*
1938
Lower left: Raoul Dufy / Nice
1938
Oil on canvas
18 1/8 × 15 1/16" (46 × 38.3 cm)

The Samuel S. White 3rd and
Vera White Collection
1967-30-36

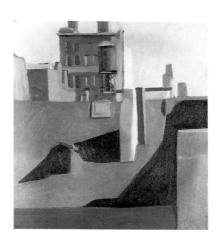

**Egnal, Stuart**
American, 1940–1966
*Roof Tops*
1962
On reverse: Stuart Egnal 1962
#29
Oil on canvas
18 × 16 1/8" (45.7 × 41 cm)

Gift of Mr. and Mrs. Michael H.
Egnal in memory of their son,
Stuart Egnal
1967-193-2

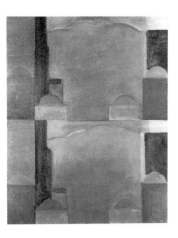

**Egnal, Stuart**
*Still Life*
1966
Oil on canvas
38 1/16 × 28 3/16" (96.7 × 71.6 cm)

Gift of Mr. and Mrs. Michael H.
Egnal in memory of their son,
Stuart Egnal
1967-193-1

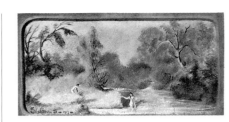

**Eilshemius, Louis Michel**
*Landscape*
1917
Lower left: Eilshemius—1917—
Oil on Masonite
11 5/8 × 22 3/8" (29.5 × 56.8 cm)

The Louise and Walter Arensberg
Collection
1950-134-510

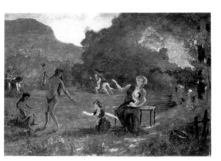

**Eilshemius, Louis Michel**
American, 1864–1941
*Early American Story*
1908
Lower left: Elshemus. / 1908;
on reverse: He called it / "Early
American Story" / This painting
I bought from Eilshemius / in
1935 J Zirinsky
Oil on canvas
27 13/16 × 38 3/4" (70.6 × 98.4 cm)

Gift of James N. Rosenberg in
memory of Felix M. Warburg
1944-96-1

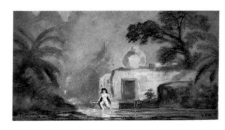

**Eilshemius, Louis Michel**
*Bather in an Architectural
Landscape*
1919
Lower left: Eilshemius—; lower
right: 1919—
Oil on cardboard
12 1/4 × 22" (31.1 × 55.9 cm)

Gift of Frank and Alice Osborn
1966-68-14

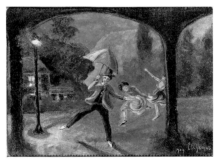

**Eilshemius, Louis Michel**
*Vaudeville*
1909
Lower right: 1909 Elshemus
Oil on Masonite
19 1/8 × 25 11/16" (48.6 × 65.2 cm)

Gift of Mr. and Mrs. Henry
Clifford
1973-256-4

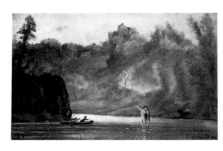

**Eilshemius, Louis Michel**
*Bather in a Wooded Landscape*
1919
Lower left: 1919—; lower right:
Eilshemius—
Oil on cardboard
14 1/8 × 22 1/4" (35.9 × 56.5 cm)

Gift of Frank and Alice Osborn
1966-68-13

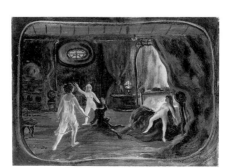

**Eilshemius, Louis Michel**
*Jealousy*
c. 1915
Lower left: Eilshemius.
Oil on cardboard
21 7/8 × 30" (55.6 × 76.2 cm)

Gift of Mr. and Mrs. Henry
Clifford
1973-256-5

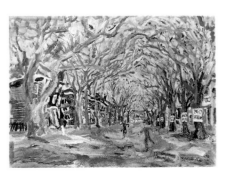

**Eisenstat, Ben**
American, born 1915
*Late Afternoon*
c. 1965
Lower right: Eisenstat
Oil and casein on cardboard
15 × 19 7/8" (38.1 × 50.5 cm)

Gift of Mr. and Mrs. Paul M.
Ingersoll
1967-158-1

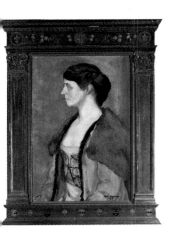

**Emerson, Edith**
American, 1888–1981
*Portrait of Violet Oakley*
1919
Lower right: Edith Emerson /
1919
Oil on canvas
30 1/16 × 20" (76.4 × 50.8 cm)

Bequest of Edith Emerson
1984-66-1

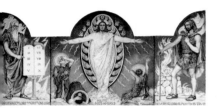

**Emerson, Edith**
*Traveling Altarpiece*
Triptych
1942
Left wing, upper left: MOSES; left
wing, bottom: HEAR O ISRAEL
THE LORD OUR GOD IS ONE
LORD; center panel, top: THIS IS
MY BELOVED SON IN WHOM I
AM WELL PLEASED HEAR YE
HIM; center panel, bottom: ARISE
/ BE NOT AFRAID; right wing,
upper right: ELIAS; right wing,
bottom: THE WORD OF THE
LORD IN THY MOUTH IS TRUTH;
left wing, on reverse: the
Citizen's Committee / for the
Army & Navy
Oil on panel
Center panel: 47 7/8 × 47 15/16"
(121.6 × 121.8 cm); wings [each]:
47 7/8 × 23 7/8" (121.6 × 60.6 cm)

Gift of Joseph Flom and Martin
Horwitz
1975-180-2

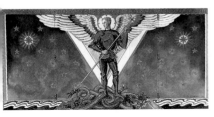

**Emerson, Edith**
*Traveling Altarpiece*
Triptych
1945
Across top: AS CAPTAIN OF THE
HOST OF THE LORD AM I NOW
COME; right wing, upper right:
JOSHUA 5:14; right wing, lower
right: Edith Emerson 1945; left
wing, on reverse: PRESENTED TO
THE / U.S.S. YORKTOWN; right
wing, on reverse: THE /
CITIZEN'S COMMITTEE / FOR
THE / ARMY AND NAVY /
INCORPORATED / NEW YORK
Oil on metal

Center panel: 36 × 36"
(91.4 × 91.4 cm); wings [each]:
36 × 17 15/16" (91.4 × 45.6 cm)

Gift of Joseph Flom and Martin
Horwitz
1976-245-1

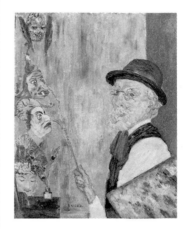

**Ensor, James**
Belgian, 1860–1949
*Self-Portrait with Masks*
1937
Center bottom: ENSOR
Oil on canvas
12 1/4 × 9 5/8" (31.1 × 24.4 cm)

The Louis E. Stern Collection
1963-181-26

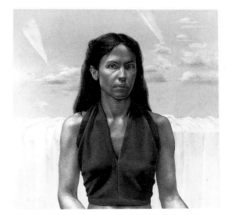

**Erlebacher, Martha Mayer**
American, born 1937
*Self-Portrait*
1975
Lower left: M.M.E.; lower right:
1975
Oil on Masonite
23 7/8 × 23 7/8" (60.6 × 60.6 cm)

Purchased with funds contributed
by Henry Strater
1981-93-1

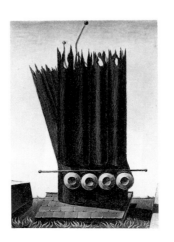

**Ernst, Max**
American, born Germany,
1891–1976
*The Forest*
1923
Lower right: max ernst
Oil on canvas
28 3/4 × 19 13/16" (73 × 50.3 cm)

The Louise and Walter Arensberg
Collection
1950-134-85

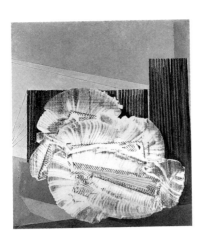

**Ernst, Max**
*Seashell*
1928
Lower right: max ernst
Oil on canvas
25 ¹/₂ × 21 ¹/₄" (64.8 × 54 cm)

The Louise and Walter Arensberg
Collection
1950-134-86

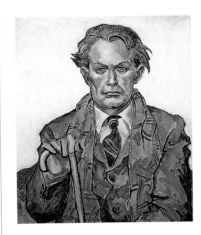

**Etting, Emlen**
American, 1905–1993
*Portrait of Andrew Dasburg*
1939
Lower right: Etting
Oil on canvas
21 ⁵/₈ × 18 ¹/₈" (54.9 × 46 cm)

Centennial gift of Mrs. Herbert
Cameron Morris
1977-27-1

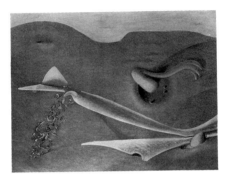

**Ernst, Max**
*Garden Plane Trap*
1934–35
Lower right: Max Ernst 34–35
Oil on canvas
23 ⁷/₈ × 28 ⁷/₈" (60.6 × 73.3 cm)

The Louise and Walter Arensberg
Collection
1950-134-87

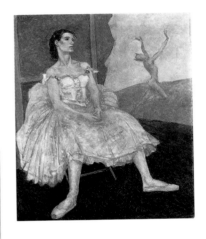

**Etting, Emlen**
*Reverie*
1939
Lower right: Etting
Oil on canvas
23 × 19" (58.4 × 48.3 cm)

The Henry P. McIlhenny
Collection in memory of
Frances P. McIlhenny
1986-26-402

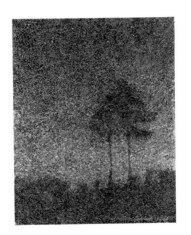

**Esherick, Wharton**
American, 1887–1970
*Moonlight*
1921
Lower right: Wharton Esherick
1921
Oil on canvas
24 ¹/₁₆ × 8 ¹/₈" (61.1 × 20.6 cm)

Purchased with the Director's
Discretionary Fund
1968-226-1

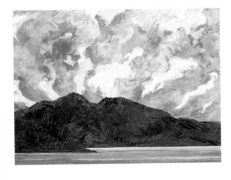

**Etting, Emlen**
*View from Glenveagh (Mount
Dooish)*
1958
Lower right: Etting
Oil on canvas
22 × 28" (55.9 × 71.1 cm)

Centennial gift of Mrs. Herbert
Cameron Morris
1977-27-2

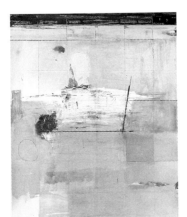

**Estock, Stephen**
American, born 1942
*Babylon*
1978
On reverse: S. Estock Babylon
1978
Acrylic on canvas
84 × 65" (213.4 × 165.1 cm)

Gift of the Cheltenham Art
Centre
1978-58-1

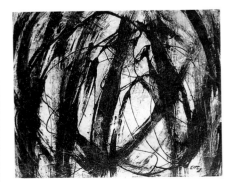

**Etting, Emlen**
*The Forest*
1961
Lower right: Etting
Oil on cardboard on plywood
8 × 9 ³/₄" (20.3 × 24.8 cm)

The Albert M. Greenfield and
Elizabeth M. Greenfield
Collection
1974-178-28

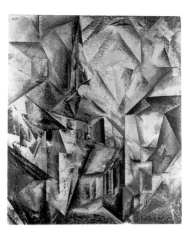

**Feininger, Lyonel**
American, active Germany,
1871–1956
*Umpferstedt II*
1914
Upper left: Feininger; on reverse:
Kiste L. F. VIII Umpferstedt II
1914
Oil on canvas
39 5/8 × 31 5/8" (100.6 × 80.3 cm)

The Louise and Walter Arensberg
Collection
1950-134-88

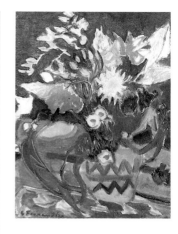

**Ferrandier, Gisele**
French, born 1909
*Flowers in a Vase*
c. 1945
Lower left: G. Ferrandier
Oil on panel
24 × 18 1/8" (61 × 46 cm)

The Albert M. Greenfield and
Elizabeth M. Greenfield
Collection
1974-178-29

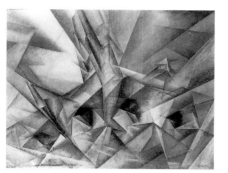

**Feininger, Lyonel**
*Bridge V*
1919
Lower right: Feininger / 1919;
on reverse: Brucke V 1919
Oil on canvas
31 5/8 × 39 1/2" (80.3 × 100.3 cm)

Purchased with the Bloomfield
Moore Fund
1951-31-2

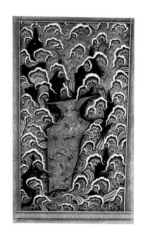

**Ferris, John**
American, born 1952
*Vase with Black Figures*
1984
Lower left: 1984; lower right:
JOHN FERRIS
Oil on linen
54 1/16 × 30 1/8" (137.3 × 76.5 cm)

Purchased with the Julius Bloch
Memorial Fund and with funds
contributed in memory of
Maurice J. Hammond
1984-119-1

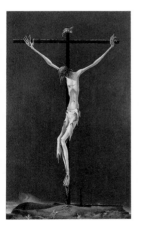

**Ferguson, William H.**
American, born 1905
*Agnus Dei*
1934
Lower right: W. H. FERGUSON
Oil on panel
53 9/16 × 31" (136 × 78.7 cm)

Gift of Henry Clifford
1943-42-1

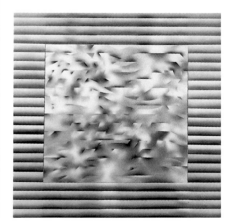

**Ferszt, Ed**
American, born 1947
*Inset No. 1*
1974
On reverse: ED FERSZT / INSET
#1 1974
Acrylic on canvas
54 × 54" (137.2 × 137.2 cm)

Gift of the Cheltenham Art
Centre
1975-54-1

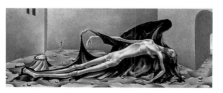

**Ferguson, William H.**
*Pietà*
1934
Lower left: Wm H Ferguson
Oil on panel
11 × 27 15/16" (27.9 × 71 cm)

Gift of Henry Clifford
1943-42-2

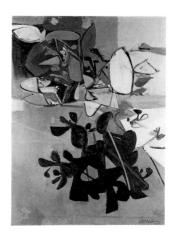

**Finkelstein, Louis**
American, born 1923
*Variations on a Provençal Theme*
c. 1959
Lower right: Louis
Oil on canvas
70 × 49 3/8" (177.8 × 125.4 cm)

Purchased with the Adele Haas
Turner and Beatrice Pastorius
Turner Memorial Fund
1959-12-4

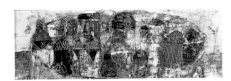

**Foppiani, Gustavo**
Italian, born 1925
*Ancient City No. 4*
1954
Oil on panel
5 5/8 × 15 5/8" (14.3 × 39.7 cm)

Gift of Mr. and Mrs. N. Richard
Miller
1978-151-1

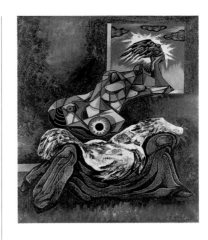

**Francés, Esteban**
Mexican, 1914–1976
*Cock on Block*
1944
Lower right: Esteban Francés /
1944
Oil on canvas
21 3/4 × 17 7/8" (55.2 × 45.4 cm)

Gift of Mr. and Mrs. Henry
Clifford
1973-256-8

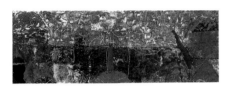

**Foppiani, Gustavo**
*Cafeteria*
1954
Lower right: FOPPIANI
Oil on panel
5 9/16 × 15 1/4" (14.1 × 38.7 cm)

Gift of Mr. and Mrs. N. Richard
Miller
1978-151-2

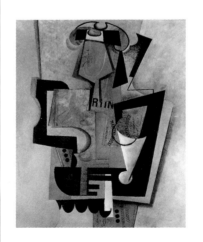

**Frankenthaler, Helen**
American, born 1928
*White Sage*
1962
Lower right: Frankenthaler '62;
on reverse: "WHITE SAGE"—
top—frankenthaler '62
Oil on canvas
54 × 70 7/8" (137.2 × 180 cm)

Centennial gift of the Woodward
Foundation
1975-81-4

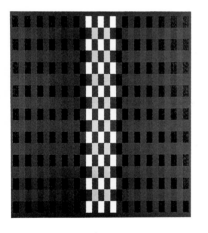

**Formicola, John**
American, born 1941
*Meditative Series*
1973
On reverse: Formicola / —73—
Oil on canvas
72 × 60" (182.9 × 152.4 cm)

Gift of Benjamin D. Bernstein
1973-70-1

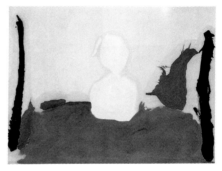

**Frelinghuysen, Suzy (Estelle
Condit Frelinghuysen)**
American, 1912–1988
*Composition (Toreador Drinking)*
See following painting for reverse
1940
Oil and paper on composition
board
39 1/2 × 31 3/8" (100.3 × 79.7 cm)

A. E. Gallatin Collection
1952-61-26a

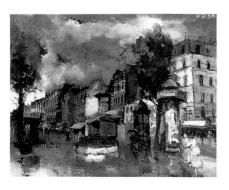

**Foss, Olivier**
French, 1920–1957?
*Street Scene*
c. 1955
Upper right: O FOSS
Oil on canvas
19 1/2 × 23 3/4" (49.5 × 60.3 cm)

The Albert M. Greenfield and
Elizabeth M. Greenfield
Collection
1974-178-30

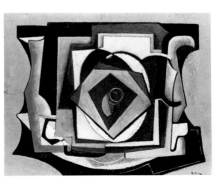

**Frelinghuysen, Suzy**
*Composition*
Reverse of the preceding painting
1940
Lower right: S. F. 1940
Oil and sand on composition
board
39 1/2 × 31 3/8" (100.3 × 79.7 cm)

A. E. Gallatin Collection
1952-61-26b

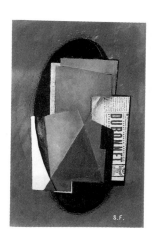

**Frelinghuysen, Suzy**
*Dubonnet*
1942
Lower right: S.F.
Oil, gouache, ink, and paper on panel
15 × 9 1/2" (38.1 × 24.1 cm)

The Samuel S. White 3rd and Vera White Collection
1960-23-3

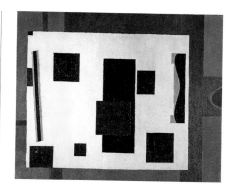

**Gallatin, Albert Eugene**
*Untitled No. 106*
1949
On reverse: A. E. Gallatin / March 1949.
Oil on canvas
20 × 24" (50.8 × 61 cm)

Gift of Mrs. Virginia M. Zabriskie
1980-149-1

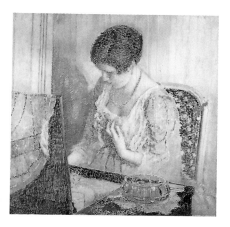

**Frieseke, Frederick Carl**
American, active France, 1874–1939
*The Rose Peignoir*
c. 1915
Lower left: F. C. Frieseke.
Oil on canvas
32 1/4 × 32" (81.9 × 81.3 cm)

The Alex Simpson, Jr., Collection
1943-74-1

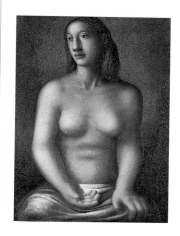

**Galván, Jesús Guerrero**
American, 1910–1973
*Nude Figure*
1939
Lower left: GUERRERO Galván / 1939
Oil on canvas
31 5/8 × 23 3/4" (80.3 × 60.3 cm)

Gift of Daniel Goldberg
1945-37-1

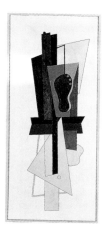

**Gallatin, Albert Eugene**
American, 1881–1952
*Composition*
1942
On reverse: A. E. Gallatin / January / 1942
Oil on canvas
59 7/8 × 25" (152.1 × 63.5 cm)

A. E. Gallatin Collection
1952-61-29

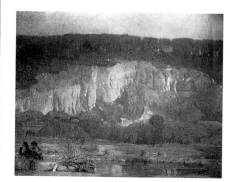

**Garber, Daniel**
American, 1880–1958
*Quarry, Evening*
1913
Lower right: DANIEL GARBER
Oil on canvas
50 × 60" (127 × 152.4 cm)

Purchased with the W. P. Wilstach Fund
W1921-1-3

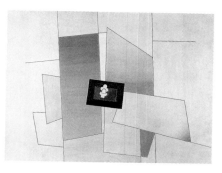

**Gallatin, Albert Eugene**
*Painting*
1944
On reverse: A. E. Gallatin Jan'y 1944
Oil on canvas
37 × 50" (94 × 127 cm)

A. E. Gallatin Collection
1952-61-28

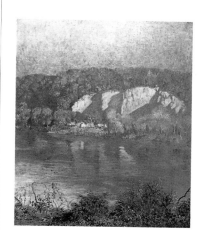

**Garber, Daniel**
*Quarry, Lumberton*
1918
Lower left: DANIEL GARBER
Oil on canvas
29 1/2 × 24" (74.9 × 61 cm)

Gift of Mr. and Mrs. J. Stogdell Stokes
1940-18-1

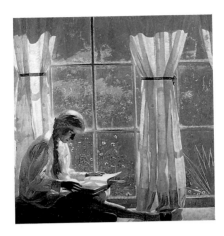

**Garber, Daniel**
*The Orchard Window*
1918
Center bottom: DANIEL GARBER
Oil on canvas
56 7/16 × 52 1/4" (143.3 × 132.7 cm)

Centennial gift of the family of
Daniel Garber
1976-216-1

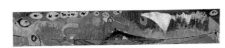

**Gatch, Lee**
American, 1909–1968
*Crow Country*
1953
Lower right: GATCH
Oil on canvas on panel
5 5/16 × 32" (13.5 × 81.3 cm)

The Louis E. Stern Collection
1963-181-29

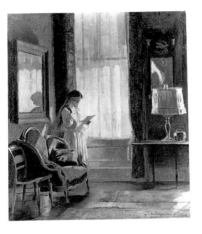

**Garber, Daniel**
*Morning Light, Interior*
1923
Lower right: Daniel Garber
Oil on canvas
30 1/16 × 25 1/8" (76.4 × 63.8 cm)

The Sallie Crozer Hilprecht
Collection, gift of her
granddaughter, Elsie
Robinson Paumgarten
1945-57-191

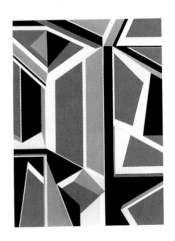

**Gatch, Lee**
*Lambertville Pietà*
1958
Lower right: GATCH
Oil on canvas
34 1/4 × 50 3/16" (87 × 127.5 cm)

Gift of Mr. and Mrs. William P.
Wood
1980-148-1

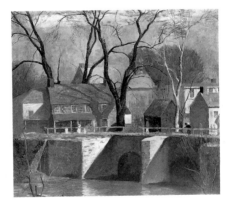

**Garber, Daniel**
*Landscape*
c. 1925
Lower left: Daniel Garber
Oil on canvas
28 1/4 × 30 1/4" (71.7 × 76.8 cm)

Gift of Mrs. Mary B. Mucci
1973-201-1

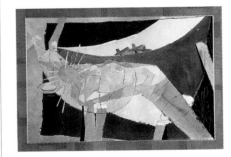

**Gaughan, Tom**
American, born 1923
*Structure*
1973
On reverse: Gaughan '73
Acrylic on canvas
72 × 50 1/8" (182.9 × 127.3 cm)

Gift of the friends of Tom
Gaughan
1975-53-1

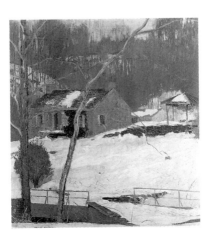

**Garber, Daniel**
*The Glen—Winter*
1926
Lower left: Daniel Garber; on
reverse: "The Glen—Winter" by
Daniel Garber
Oil on canvas
20 1/4 × 18 1/4" (51.4 × 46.3 cm)

The Sallie Crozer Hilprecht
Collection, gift of her
granddaughter, Elsie
Robinson Paumgarten
1945-57-196

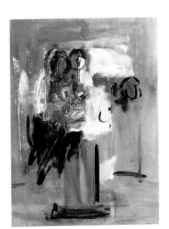

**Gest, Margaret**
American, 1900–1965
*Torch Bouquet*
c. 1955
Oil on canvas
36 1/8 × 25 3/4" (91.8 × 65.4 cm)

Gift of Miss Miriam H. Thrall
1966-221-1

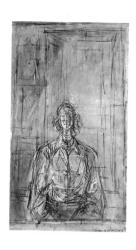

**Giacometti, Alberto**
Swiss, 1901–1966
*Annette in a Red Blouse*
1954
Lower right: Alberto Giacometti
Oil on canvas
22 1/2 × 12 1/2" (57.1 × 31.7 cm)

The Albert M. Greenfield and
Elizabeth M. Greenfield
Collection
1974-178-31

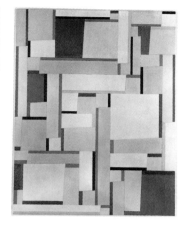

**Glarner, Fritz**
*Relational Painting No. 75*
1955
Center bottom: GLARNER. 1955
Oil on canvas
56 × 42" (142.2 × 106.7 cm)

Centennial gift of Mrs. Henry
Clifford
1975-79-1

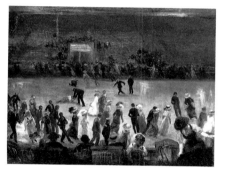

**Glackens, William**
American, 1870–1938
*Skating Rink, New York City*
c. 1906
Oil on canvas
26 × 33" (66 × 83.8 cm)

Gift of Mr. and Mrs. Meyer P.
Potamkin (reserving life interest)
1964-116-7

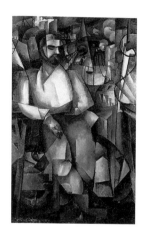

**Gleizes, Albert**
French, 1881–1953
*Man on a Balcony (Portrait of Dr. Morinaud)*
1912
Lower left: Albert Gleizes / 12
Oil on canvas
77 × 45 1/4" (195.6 × 114.9 cm)

The Louise and Walter Arensberg
Collection
1950-134-91

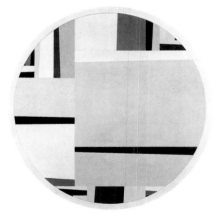

**Glarner, Fritz**
American, born Switzerland,
1899–1972
*Tondo No. 6*
1948
Lower right: F. GLARNER 48
Oil on Masonite
51 1/2" (130.8 cm) diameter

Gift of Mr. and Mrs. Henry
Clifford
1973-256-1

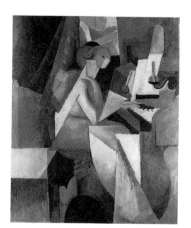

**Gleizes, Albert**
*Woman at the Piano*
1914
Lower right: Albert Gleizes / 14
Oil on canvas
57 5/8 × 44 3/4" (146.4 × 113.7 cm)

The Louise and Walter Arensberg
Collection
1950-134-93

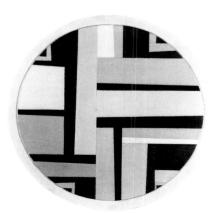

**Glarner, Fritz**
*Tondo No. 8*
1948
Lower right: F. GLARNER 48
Oil on composition board
17 1/2 × 17 3/8" (44.4 × 44.1 cm)

A. E. Gallatin Collection
1949-22-1

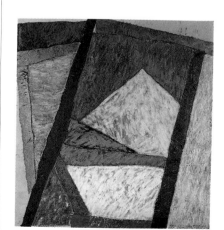

**Goldberg, Michael**
American, born 1924
*Le Grotte Vecchie VII*
1981
On reverse: GOLDBERG '81 / LE
GROTTE VECCHIE VII
Bronze powders, clear alkyd,
pastel, and Liquitex mat medium
on canvas
83 7/8 × 75" (213 × 190.5 cm)

Gift of the artist and gift (by
exchange) of Ronald Stark
1982-3-1

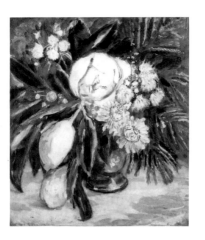

**Goldthwaite, Anne Wilson**
American, 1869–1944
*Magnolia and Passion Flowers*
c. 1938
Lower left: ANNE GOLDTHWAITE
Oil on canvas
24 × 20" (61 × 50.8 cm)

Gift of the estate of Anne
Goldthwaite
1945-83-2

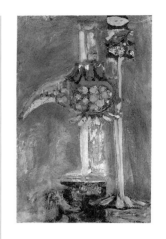

**Gorchov, Ron**
American, born 1930
*Stele*
1959
Upper left: Gorchov 1959
Oil on panel
13 5/8 × 8 5/8" (34.6 × 21.9 cm)

Gift of the Kulicke family in
memory of Lt. Frederick W.
Kulicke III
1969-86-5

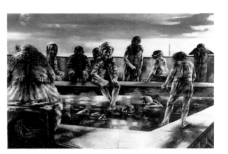

**Goodman, Sidney**
American, born 1936
*Swimming Pool*
1961
Lower left: GOODMAN 61
Oil on canvas
50 × 74" (127 × 188 cm)

Centennial gift of Mr. and Mrs.
David N. Pincus
1976-246-1

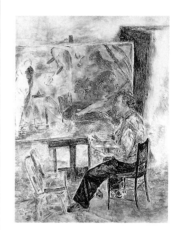

**Gordey, Ida**
French, born 1916
*Portrait of Marc Chagall*
1944
Lower left: For L. Stern / my
papa. / Ida Gordey / 1944
Oil and charcoal on canvas board
24 3/16 × 18 1/8" (61.4 × 46 cm)

The Louis E. Stern Collection
1963-181-30

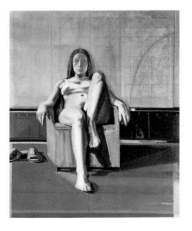

**Goodman, Sidney**
*Seated Woman*
1965
On reverse: GOODMAN 65
"SEATED WOMAN"
Oil on canvas
43 5/8 × 34 5/8" (110.8 × 87.9 cm)

Gift of the American Academy
and Institute of Arts and Letters,
and the Hassam and Speicher
Purchase Funds
1980-56-1

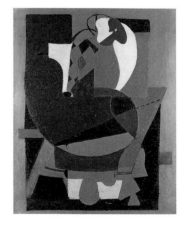

**Gorky, Arshile**
American, born Armenia,
1904–1948
*Abstraction with a Palette*
c. 1930
Oil on canvas
48 × 35 15/16" (121.9 × 91.3 cm)

Gift of Bernard Davis
1942-64-3

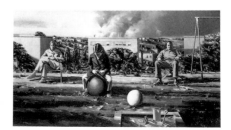

**Goodman, Sidney**
*Figures in a Landscape*
1972–73
Lower left: GOODMAN—/ 72–73
Oil on canvas
55 × 96" (139.7 × 243.8 cm)

Purchased with the Philadelphia
Foundation Fund (by exchange)
and the Adele Haas Turner and
Beatrice Pastorius Turner
Memorial Fund
1974-112-1

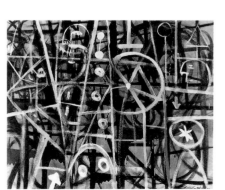

**Gottlieb, Adolph**
American, 1903–1974
*The Cadmium Sound*
1954
Lower right: Adolph Gottlieb 54
Oil on canvas
60 1/16 × 72 1/4" (152.6 × 183.5 cm)

Purchased with the Edward and
Althea Budd Fund
1980-60-1

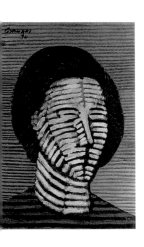

**Graham, John D.
(Ivan Dabrowsky)**
American, born Ukraine,
1891–1961
*Study for "Ikon of the Modern Age"*
1930
Upper left: GRAHAM / 30; on
reverse: To Dr Brinton / with
my / regards / Graham.
Oil on canvas
24 1/8 × 15" (61.3 × 38.1 cm)

Gift of Christian Brinton
1941-79-66

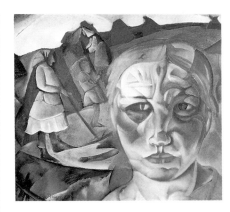

**Grigoriev, Boris Dmitryevich**
*Woman of the Fields*
1920
Lower left: Boris Grigorieff 1920
Oil on cardboard
20 × 24" (50.8 × 61 cm)

Gift of Christian Brinton
1941-79-29

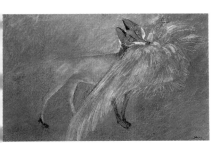

**Graves, Morris Cole**
American, born 1910
*Fox with a Phoenix Wing*
1952
Lower right: Graves '52
Oil on canvas on Masonite
32 × 48" (81.3 × 121.9 cm)

Purchased with the Adele Haas
Turner and Beatrice Pastorius
Turner Memorial Fund
1956-11-1

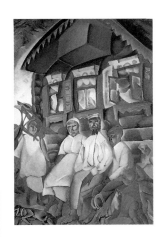

**Grigoriev, Boris Dmitryevich**
*Peasant Family before an Isba*
c. 1920
Upper right: Boris Grigoriev
Tempera on cardboard
37 × 25" (94 × 63.5 cm)

Gift of Christian Brinton
1941-79-99

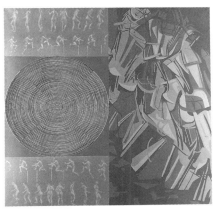

**Graziani, Sante**
American, born 1920
*A Play in Three Acts Titled Motion*
1965
Acrylic on canvas
48 × 48" (121.9 × 121.9 cm)

Gift of an anonymous donor
1968-224-1

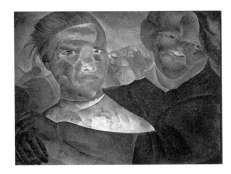

**Grigoriev, Boris Dmitryevich**
*End of the Harvest*
1921
Lower right: Boris Grigorieff / 21.
Tempera and oil on canvas
28 3/4 × 36 1/4" (73 × 92.1 cm)

Gift of Christian Brinton
1941-79-150

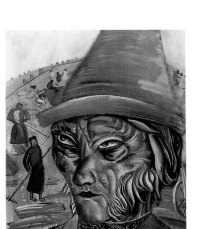

**Grigoriev, Boris Dmitryevich**
Russian, 1886–1939
*Portrait of the Peasant Poet Nikolai
Alexeyevich Kluyev*
1918
Lower left: Boris Grigoriev
Oil, gouache, and ink on
composition board
24 × 20" (61 × 50.8 cm)

Gift of Christian Brinton
1941-79-120

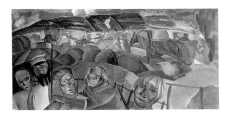

**Grigoriev, Boris Dmitryevich**
*End of the Harvest (Faces of Russia)*
1923
Lower right: Boris Grigorieff 23
Tempera and oil on canvas on
cardboard
28 5/8 × 36" (72.7 × 91.9 cm)

Gift of Christian Brinton
1941-79-68

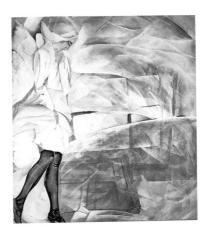

**Grigoriev, Boris Dmitryevich**
*White Nights, Petrograd*
c. 1923
On reverse: Boris Grigoryev
Oil on composition board
33 3/8 × 29 3/8" (84.8 × 74.6 cm)

Gift of Christian Brinton
1941-79-147

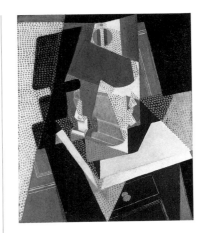

**Gris, Juan**
*Lamp*
1916
On reverse: Juan Gris / 3-16 / 4e
Oil on canvas
31 7/8 × 25 1/2" (81 × 64.8 cm)

The Louise and Walter Arensberg
Collection
1950-134-96

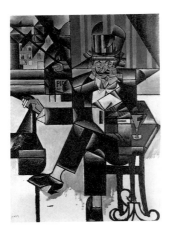

**Gris, Juan (José Victoriano
González Pérez)**
Spanish, 1887–1927
*Man in a Café*
1912
Lower left: Juan Gris
Oil on canvas
50 1/4 × 34 3/4" (127.6 × 88.3 cm)

The Louise and Walter Arensberg
Collection
1950-134-94

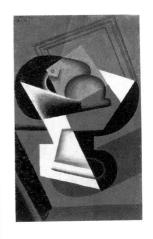

**Gris, Juan**
*Dish of Fruit*
1916
Upper left: Juan Gris / 11-16
Oil on panel
16 × 9 1/2" (40.6 × 24.1 cm)

A. E. Gallatin Collection
1952-61-36

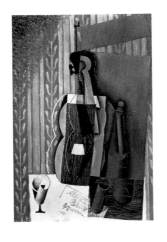

**Gris, Juan**
*Violin*
Pencil sketch on reverse
1913
On reverse: Juan Gris 7-13
Oil on canvas
36 1/4 × 23 5/8" (92.1 × 60 cm)

A. E. Gallatin Collection
1952-61-34

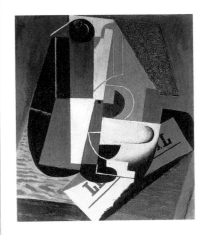

**Gris, Juan**
*Coffeepot*
1916
Upper left: juan gris / 12-1916
Oil on panel
18 1/2 × 15 3/8" (47 × 39 cm)

A. E. Gallatin Collection
1952-61-35

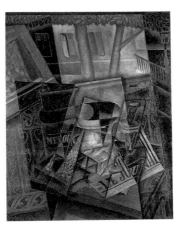

**Gris, Juan**
*Still Life before an Open Window,
Place Ravignan*
1915
Lower left: Juan Gris / 6-1915;
center: MEDOC / LE JOURNAL
Oil on canvas
45 5/8 × 35" (115.9 × 88.9 cm)

The Louise and Walter Arensberg
Collection
1950-134-95

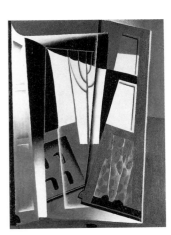

**Gris, Juan**
*Open Window*
1917
Lower right: Juan Gris / 3-1917
Oil, mixed media, and wax on
panel
39 9/16 × 28 13/16" (100.5 ×
73.2 cm)

The Louise and Walter Arensberg
Collection
1950-134-97

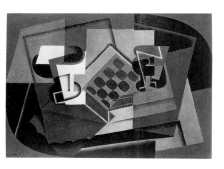

**Gris, Juan**
*Chessboard, Glass, and Dish*
1917
Lower left: Juan Gris / 6-17
Oil on panel
28 7/8 × 40 5/8" (73.3 × 103.2 cm)

The Louise and Walter Arensberg
Collection
1950-134-98

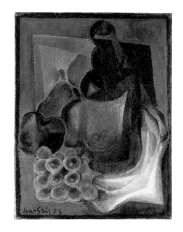

**Gris, Juan**
*A Bottle and Fruit*
1923
Lower left: Juan Gris 23
Oil on canvas
13 × 9 1/2" (33 × 24.1 cm)

A. E. Gallatin Collection
1952-61-40

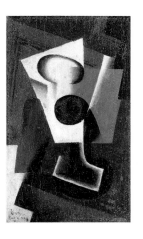

**Gris, Juan**
*Still Life with a Glass*
See following painting for reverse
1917
Lower left: Juan Gris / Paris
9-1917
Oil on panel
13 × 7 1/2" (33 × 19 cm)

A. E. Gallatin Collection
1952-61-38a

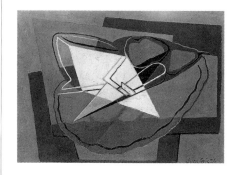

**Gris, Juan**
*Knife*
1926
Lower right: Juan Gris 26
Oil on canvas
10 3/4 × 13 3/4" (27.3 × 34.9 cm)

A. E. Gallatin Collection
1952-61-41

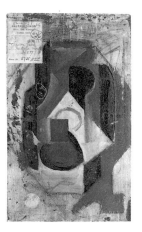

**Gris, Juan**
*Untitled*
Reverse of the preceding painting
1917
Oil on panel
13 × 7 1/2" (33 × 19 cm)

A. E. Gallatin Collection
1952-61-38b

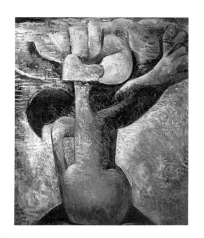

**Gromaire, Marcel**
French, 1892–1971
*Still Life*
1920
Lower right: 20 / Gromaire
Oil on canvas
21 1/2 × 18 1/8" (54.6 × 46 cm)

Bequest of Fiske and Marie
Kimball
1955-86-18

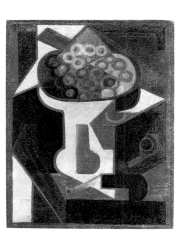

**Gris, Juan**
*A Dish of Grapes and a Pipe on a
Table*
1918
Upper left: Juan Gris / 5-18
Oil on panel
14 1/8 × 10 7/8" (35.9 × 27.6 cm)

A. E. Gallatin Collection
1952-61-39

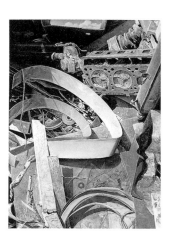

**Grow, Allan**
American, born 1940
*Junkyard*
1983
Lower left: Allan Grow
Acrylic on canvas
44 7/8 × 33 7/8" (114 × 86 cm)

Purchased with the Julius Bloch
Memorial Fund
1984-80-1

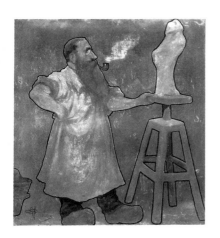

**Guillaume, Albert**
French, 1873–1942
*Portrait of Auguste Rodin*
c. 1915
Lower left: APGuillaume
Oil on canvas
31 1/8 × 28 1/4" (79.1 × 71.7 cm)

Gift of Jules E. Mastbaum
F1929-7-205

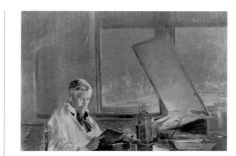

**Hamilton, John McLure**
American, 1853–1936
*Portrait of Joseph Pennell*
c. 1910
Oil on canvas
30 × 42" (76.2 × 106.7 cm)

Gift of Gustavus Wynne Cook
1937-18-1

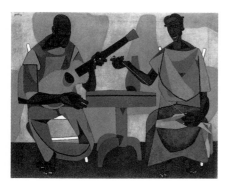

**Gwathmey, Robert**
American, 1903–1988
*Singing and Mending*
1948
Upper left: gwathmey
Oil on canvas
25 3/16 × 30 1/8" (64 × 76.5 cm)

Gift of Edna Beron
1984-159-1

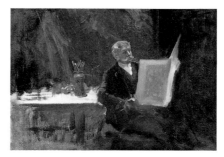

**Hamilton, John McLure**
*Portrait of Charles E. Dana*
c. 1915
Oil on canvas
18 × 24 1/4" (45.7 × 61.6 cm)

Gift of the Philadelphia
Watercolor Club
1941-99-19

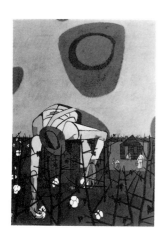

**Gwathmey, Robert**
*Sunup*
c. 1955
Lower right: gwathmey
Oil on canvas
16 × 11" (40.6 × 27.9 cm)

The Louis E. Stern Collection
1963-181-31

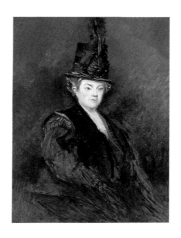

**Hamilton, John McLure**
*Portrait of Mrs. Hamilton*
c. 1915
Oil on canvas
40 × 30 1/16" (101.6 × 76.4 cm)

Gift of George Earle Raiguel
1938-14-1

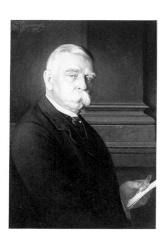

**Haeseler, Conrad F.**
American, active c. 1917
*Portrait of John G. Johnson*
1917
Upper left: CONRAD / F.
HAESELER / 1917
Oil on panel
34 × 24" (86.4 × 61 cm)

Gift of Miss Julia W. Frick and
Sidney W. Frick
1971-36-1

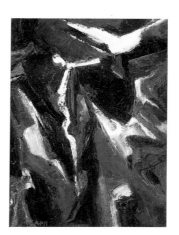

**Hankins, Abraham P.**
American, born Belorussia,
1900–1963
*Tribute to El Greco*
c. 1940
Lower left: APH
Oil on cardboard
12 1/4 × 9 1/16" (31.1 × 23 cm)

Gift of Mrs. James Clark
1964-117-3

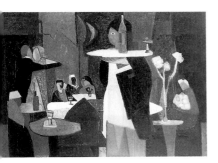

**Hankins, Abraham P.**
*Nightclub*
1942
Lower left: Hankins
Oil on panel
29 ¹⁵/₁₆ × 40 ³/₄" (76 × 103.5 cm)

Gift of Mrs. James Clark
1964-117-1

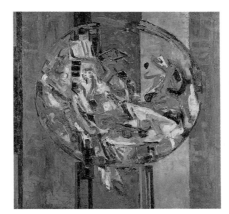

**Hankins, Abraham P.**
*Private Aquarium*
1959
Lower left: A Hankins
Oil on canvas
42 ¹/₁₆ × 42" (106.8 × 106.7 cm)

Gift of the students and friends
of Abraham P. Hankins
1964-32-1

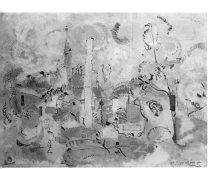

**Hankins, Abraham P.**
*Conshohocken*
c. 1942
Lower right: A P Hankins; on
reverse: 1942 / Victory Show /
Metropolitan Museum / 1943.
Oil on panel
24 × 30" (61 × 76.2 cm)

Gift of Mrs. James Clark
1964-117-5

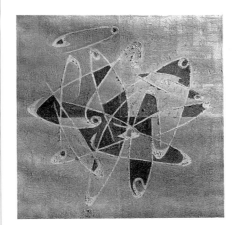

**Hankins, Abraham P.**
*Aux Enfants*
c. 1960
Center bottom: A.P.H.
Oil on canvas
22 ¹/₈ × 21 ³/₁₆" (56.2 × 53.8 cm)

Gift of the estate of Estelle
Hankins
1968-40-3

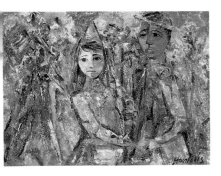

**Hankins, Abraham P.**
*Anniversary*
1949
Lower right: Hankins
Oil on canvas
27 ⁷/₈ × 36 ¹/₈" (70.8 × 91.8 cm)

Gift of Mrs. James Clark
1964-117-4

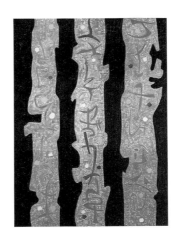

**Hankins, Abraham P.**
*Squicker Cove, Monhegan, Maine*
c. 1960
Oil on canvas
33 × 24 ¹/₈" (83.8 × 61.3 cm)

Gift of the estate of Estelle
Hankins
1968-40-1

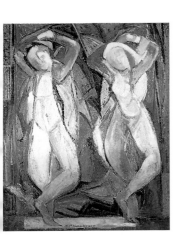

**Hankins, Abraham P.**
*Dancers*
c. 1949
Center bottom: A. P. Hankins
Oil on cardboard
34 ⁵/₈ × 27" (87.9 × 68.6 cm)

Gift of Mrs. James Clark
1964-117-2

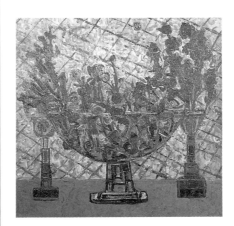

**Hankins, Abraham P.**
*Flowers by the Window*
c. 1960–63
Center top: APH; on reverse:
[date?]
Oil on canvas
29 × 29" (73.7 × 73.7 cm)

Gift of the estate of Estelle
Hankins
1968-40-2

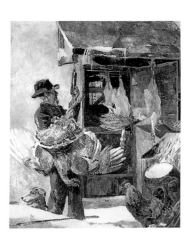

**Harding, George**
American, 1882–1959
*December*
c. 1950–55
Lower left: GEORGE HARDING
Oil on canvas
50 1/2 × 40" (128.3 × 101.6 cm)

Gift of Mrs. John S. Kistler and George M. Harding, Jr., in memory of their father, George Harding
1967-99-1

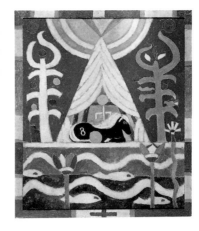

**Hartley, Marsden**
*Painting No. 4 (A Black Horse)*
1915
Oil on canvas
39 1/4 × 31 5/8" (99.7 × 80.3 cm)

The Alfred Stieglitz Collection
1949-18-8

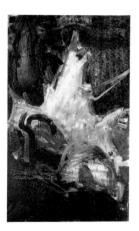

**Hartigan, Grace**
American, born 1922
*Essex and Hester*
1958
Lower right: Hartigan '58
Oil on canvas
71 5/8 × 40 1/4" (181.9 × 102.2 cm)

Gift of Dr. and Mrs. Richard Kaplan
1967-271-1

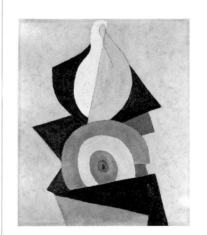

**Hartley, Marsden**
*Movement No. 1 (Provincetown)*
1916
Oil on panel
20 × 15 13/16" (50.8 × 40.2 cm)

The Alfred Stieglitz Collection
1949-18-9

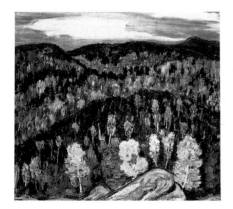

**Hartley, Marsden**
American, 1877–1943
*Maine Landscape No. 27*
1909
Oil on cardboard
12 × 12" (30.5 × 30.5 cm)

The Alfred Stieglitz Collection
1949-18-6

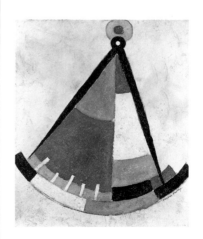

**Hartley, Marsden**
*Sextant*
c. 1917
Lower right: Marsden Hartley.
Oil on panel
20 × 16" (50.8 × 40.6 cm)

Gift of Dr. Herman Lorber
1944-95-2

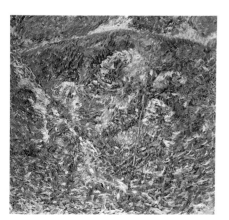

**Hartley, Marsden**
*Winter Chaos (Blizzard)*
1909–11?
Oil on canvas
33 15/16 × 34" (86.2 × 86.4 cm)

The Alfred Stieglitz Collection
1949-18-7

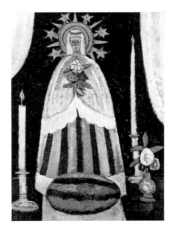

**Hartley, Marsden**
*Blessing the Melon (The Indians Bring the Harvest to Christian Mary for Her Blessing)*
c. 1918
On reverse: Blessing the Melon / by Marsden Hartley / Blessing the Melon / The indians bring the harvest / To Christian Mary for her / blessing
Oil on panel
32 3/8 × 23 7/8" (82.2 × 60.6 cm)

The Alfred Stieglitz Collection
1949-18-13

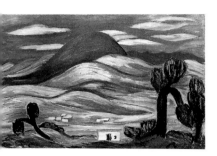

**Hartley, Marsden**
*New Mexico Landscape*
1919
Oil on canvas
17 7/8 × 26" (45.4 × 66 cm)

The Alfred Stieglitz Collection
1949-18-4

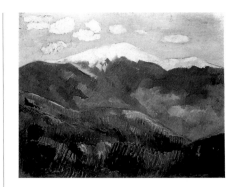

**Hartley, Marsden**
*New Hampshire Mountains*
c. 1928
Oil on Masonite
30 1/8 × 36 1/8" (76.5 × 91.8 cm)

Bequest of T. Edward Hanley
1970-76-4

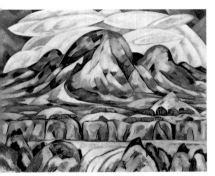

**Hartley, Marsden**
*New Mexico Landscape*
1919
On reverse: Marsden Hartley
1919
Oil on canvas
30 × 36" (76.2 × 91.4 cm)

The Alfred Stieglitz Collection
1949-18-10

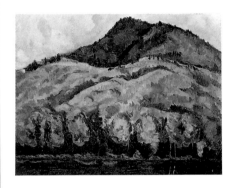

**Hartley, Marsden**
*Landscape No. 35 (Beaver Lake,
Lost River Region)*
c. 1930
Oil on canvas
25 1/2 × 31 3/4" (64.8 × 80.6 cm)

The Alfred Stieglitz Collection
1949-18-5

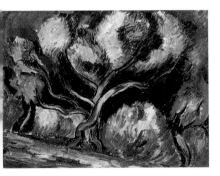

**Hartley, Marsden**
*Landscape No. 1 (Trees, France)*
1919
Oil on panel
14 5/8 × 18 1/8" (37.1 × 46 cm)

The Alfred Stieglitz Collection
1949-18-11

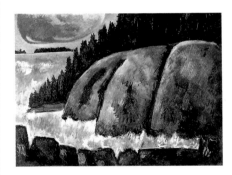

**Hartley, Marsden**
*Hurricane Island, Vinalhaven,
Maine*
1942
Center right: MH / 42
Oil on Masonite
30 × 39 15/16" (76.2 × 101.4 cm)

Gift of Mrs. Herbert Cameron
Morris
1943-5-1

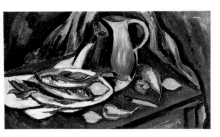

**Hartley, Marsden**
*Still Life with Fish*
1921
Oil on canvas
23 × 39 1/8" (58.4 × 99.4 cm)

The Alfred Stieglitz Collection
1949-18-12

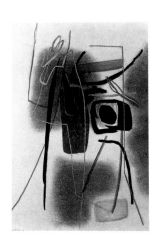

**Hartung, Hans**
French, born Germany,
born 1904
*Composition*
1936
Lower left: Hartung 36
Oil on canvas
33 3/16 × 22 1/8" (84.3 × 56.2 cm)

A. E. Gallatin Collection
1952-61-46

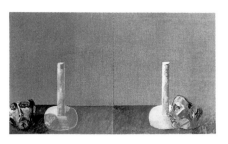

**Hatten, Thomas**
American, born 1946
*Tomhattenxochital*
Diptych; companion to the
following three paintings
1973
Oil and Rhoplex on linen
Left panel: 22 × 18 1/8"
(55.9 × 46 cm); right panel:
22 1/8 × 18 1/8" (56.2 × 46 cm)

Purchased with the Julius Bloch
Memorial Fund
1981-95-1

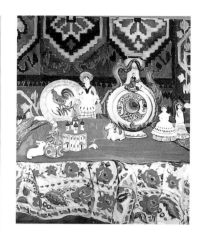

**Hausch, Aleksandr F.**
Russian, born 1873, death date
unknown
*Russian Carpets and Toys*
c. 1926
Lower right: A. Tayen[?]
Oil on canvas
42 3/16 × 35 1/2" (107.2 × 90.2 cm)

Gift of Christian Brinton
1941-79-102

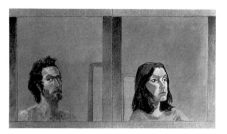

**Hatten, Thomas**
*X.T.H.*
Diptych; see previous entry
1974
Oil and Rhoplex on linen
Each panel: 22 1/8 × 18"
(56.2 × 46 cm)

Purchased with the Julius Bloch
Memorial Fund
1981-95-2

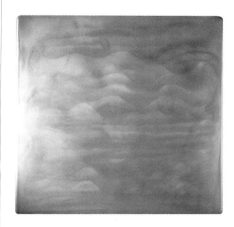

**Havard, James**
American, born 1937
*Wapello III*
1970
Acrylic and lacquer on plexiglass
57 1/2 × 57 1/2" (146 × 146 cm)

Purchased with the Philadelphia
Foundation Fund
1971-9-1

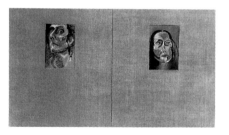

**Hatten, Thomas**
*T.H.X.*
Diptych; see previous two entries
1975
Oil and Rhoplex on linen
Left panel: 22 1/8 × 18"
(56.2 × 45.7 cm); right panel:
22 1/4 × 18" (56.5 × 45.7 cm)

Purchased with the Julius Bloch
Memorial Fund
1981-95-3

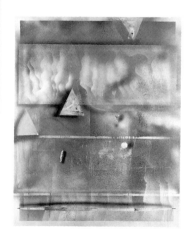

**Havard, James**
*Drink the Juice of the Stone*
1973
Acrylic on canvas
96 × 72" (243.8 × 182.9 cm)

Purchased with the Philadelphia
Foundation Fund
1973-133-1

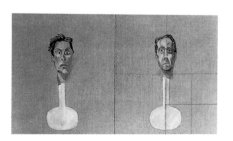

**Hatten, Thomas**
*T.H.X.*
Diptych; see previous three
entries
1975
Oil and Rhoplex on linen
Each panel: 22 × 18"
(55.9 × 45.7 cm)

Purchased with the Julius Bloch
Memorial Fund
1981-95-4

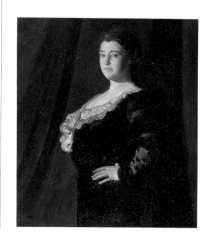

**Hawthorne, Charles Webster**
American, 1872–1930
*Portrait of Georgiana Goddard King*
c. 1905
Oil on canvas
36 1/4 × 30 1/8" (92.1 × 76.5 cm)

Gift of Miss Georgiana Goddard
King
1934-10-1

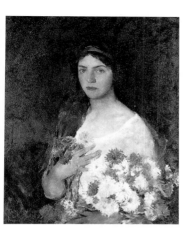

**Hawthorne, Charles Webster**
*Girl with Asters*
c. 1920
Lower left: C. W. Hawthorne
Oil on panel
30 1/8 × 25" (76.5 × 63.5 cm)

Gift of Dr. and Mrs. George
Woodward
1939-7-16

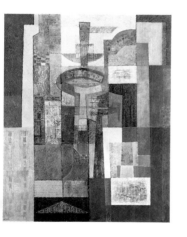

**Heliker, John Edward**
American, born 1909
*Monréale*
1950
Lower left: HELIKER.
Oil on Masonite
28 × 22" (71.1 × 55.9 cm)

Purchased with the Bloomfield
Moore Fund
1951-31-3

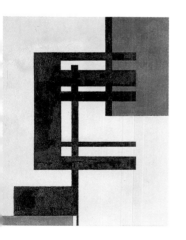

**Hélion, Jean**
French, 1904–1987
*Composition*
1932
On reverse: Jean / Hélion
Oil on canvas
25 7/16 × 19 13/16" (64.6 × 50.3 cm)

A. E. Gallatin Collection
1945-91-1

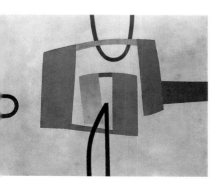

**Hélion, Jean**
*Composition*
1933
On reverse: Hélion / 33
Oil on canvas
25 7/8 × 32" (65.7 × 81.3 cm)

A. E. Gallatin Collection
1945-91-2

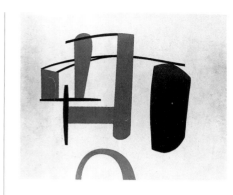

**Hélion, Jean**
*Red Tensions*
1933
On reverse: Jean / Hélion /
painted in / Virginia / 1933 /
(Tensions / Rouges)
Oil on canvas
23 3/4 × 28 5/8" (60.3 × 72.7 cm)

The Louise and Walter Arensberg
Collection
1950-134-99

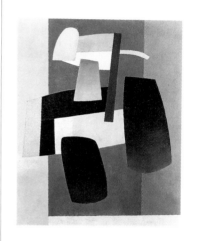

**Hélion, Jean**
*Composition*
1934
On reverse: Hélion / Paris 34
Oil on canvas
14 × 10 3/4" (35.6 × 27.3 cm)

A. E. Gallatin Collection
1945-91-3

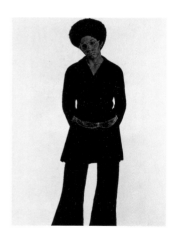

**Hendricks, Barkley**
American, born 1945
*Miss T*
1969
Lower right: B. Hendricks 69
Oil on canvas
66 1/8 × 48 1/8" (168 × 122.2 cm)

Purchased with the Philadelphia
Foundation Fund
1970-134-1

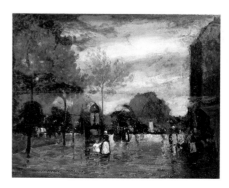

**Henri, Robert**
American, 1865–1929
*Boulevard in Wet Weather, Paris*
1899
Lower left: Robert Henri Paris
'99
Oil on canvas
25 × 32" (63.5 × 81.3 cm)

Gift of Mr. and Mrs. Meyer P.
Potamkin (reserving life interest)
1964-116-6

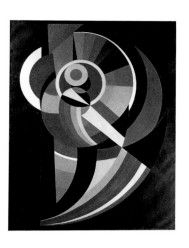

**Herbin, Auguste**
French, 1882–1960
*Composition*
1940
Lower right: Herbin 1940
Oil on canvas
45 5/8 × 35" (115.9 × 88.9 cm)

Gift of Lady George Weidenfeld
1972-125-1

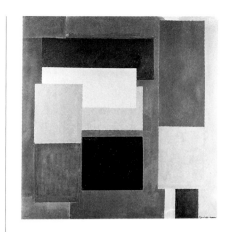

**Hofmann, Hans**
American, born Germany,
1880–1966
*Lumen Naturale*
1962
Lower right: Hans Hofmann '62
Oil on canvas
84 × 77 11/16" (213.4 × 197.3 cm)

Purchased with the John Howard
McFadden, Jr., Fund
1963-180-1

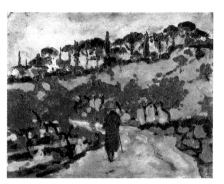

**Hill, Derek**
English, born 1916
*Bernard Berenson in the Snow at
Bagazzano*
1951
Oil on panel
11 × 13" (27.9 × 33 cm)

The Henry P. McIlhenny
Collection in memory of
Frances P. McIlhenny
1986-26-403

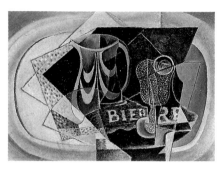
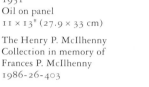

**Horter, Earl**
American, 1881–1940
*Still Life with a Pitcher*
c. 1930
Center: BIER RE; lower right:
E Horter
Oil on canvas
10 1/2 × 13 7/8" (26.7 × 35.2 cm)

Gift of the Honorable Joseph E.
Gold
1974-231-2

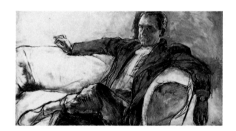

**Hill, Derek**
*Portrait of Henry P. McIlhenny*
c. 1962
Oil on canvas
27 1/4 × 47 1/2" (69.2 × 120.6 cm)

The Henry P. McIlhenny
Collection in memory of
Frances P. McIlhenny
1986-26-404

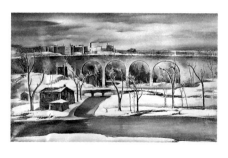

**Horter, Earl**
*Wissahickon Creek*
1938
Lower right: E. Horter 38
Oil on canvas
26 × 40 1/2" (66 × 102.9 cm)

Gift of R. Sturgis Ingersoll and
Carroll S. Tyson, Jr.
1939-53-1

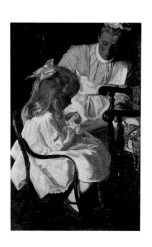

**Hinchman, Margaretta S.**
American, died 1955
*The String of Beads (Portrait of
Conti La Boiteaux Drake)*
1903
Oil on panel
38 1/8 × 23 3/8" (96.8 × 59.4 cm)

Gift of Mrs. Thomas E. Drake
1947-31-1

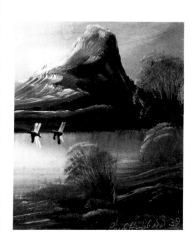

**Hullond, Paul**
American, active c. 1939
*Landscape*
1939
Lower right: Paul Hullond 39
Oil on cardboard
13 3/4 × 10 7/8" (34.9 × 27.6 cm)

Gift of Frank and Alice Osborn
1966-68-26a

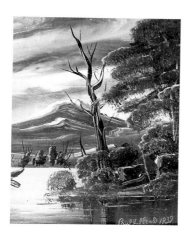

**Hullond, Paul**
*Landscape*
1939
Lower right: Paul Hullond 1939
Oil on cardboard
13 5/8 × 10 7/8" (34.6 × 27.6 cm)

Gift of Frank and Alice Osborn
1966-68-26b

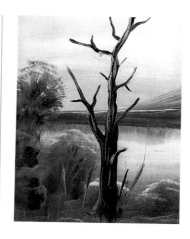

**Hullond, Paul**
*Landscape*
c. 1940
Oil on cardboard
13 3/4 × 10 7/8" (34.9 × 27.6 cm)

Gift of Frank and Alice Osborn
1966-68-26f

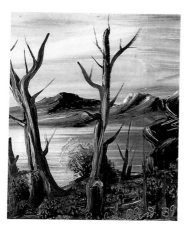

**Hullond, Paul**
*Landscape*
1939
Lower right: Paul Hullond 39
Oil on cardboard
13 3/4 × 11" (34.9 × 27.9 cm)

Gift of Frank and Alice Osborn
1966-68-26d

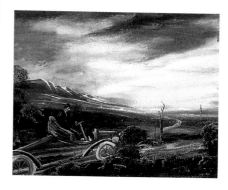

**Hullond, Paul**
*Landscape*
c. 1940
Oil on cardboard
10 5/8 × 13 3/4" (27 × 34.9 cm)

Gift of Frank and Alice Osborn
1966-68-26g

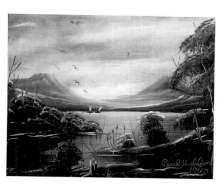

**Hullond, Paul**
*Landscape*
1940
Lower right: Paul Hullond /
1940
Oil on cardboard
10 7/8 × 14" (27.6 × 35.6 cm)

Gift of Frank and Alice Osborn
1966-68-26c

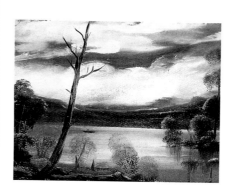

**Hullond, Paul**
*Landscape*
c. 1940
Lower right: Paul Hullond
Oil on cardboard
10 5/8 × 13 1/2" (27 × 34.3 cm)

Gift of Frank and Alice Osborn
1966-68-26h

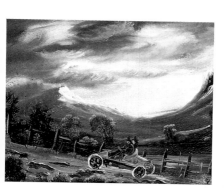

**Hullond, Paul**
*Landscape*
c. 1940
Oil on cardboard
10 5/8 × 14" (27 × 35.6 cm)

Gift of Frank and Alice Osborn
1966-68-26e

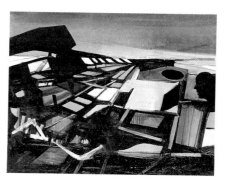

**Hultberg, John**
American, born 1922
*Against the Sky*
1962
On reverse: J. Hultberg / 1962 /
AGAINST THE SKY
Oil on Masonite
25 3/8 × 31 1/2" (64.4 × 80 cm)

Gift of Mr. and Mrs. Barry R.
Peril
1967-269-4

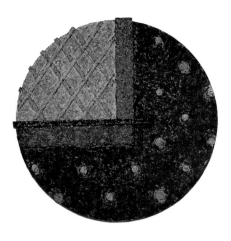

**Humphrey, Ralph**
American, born 1932
*Slice of Life*
1980
On reverse: SLICE OF LIFE /
RALPH 1980 / HUMPHREY
48 DIAM.
Acrylic, modeling paste, and
casein on panel
48 1/4" (122.5 cm) diameter

Purchased with the Adele Haas
Turner and Beatrice Pastorius
Turner Memorial Fund
1981-40-1

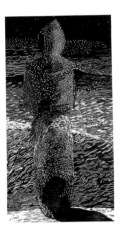

**Hyder, Frank**
American, born 1951
*Sea Watcher*
1986
Acrylic and pastel on carved
wood
96 × 48" (243.8 × 121.9 cm)

Purchased with the Julius Bloch
Memorial Fund
1986-73-1

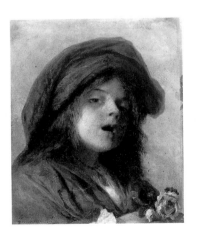

**Innocenti, Camillo**
Italian, 1871–1961
*Head of a Child*
c. 1900
Lower left: Innocenti
Oil on canvas
16 × 13" (40.6 × 33 cm)

John G. Johnson Collection
inv. 2944

**Irwin, Robert**
American, born 1928
*Untitled*
From the series "Venice"
c. 1963–65
Oil on canvas
82 1/2 × 84 1/2" (209.5 × 214.6 cm)

Centennial gift of the Woodward
Foundation
1975-81-5

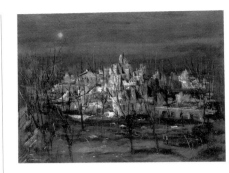

**Jackson, Martin**
American, 1919–1986
*Moon Poem*
1948
Lower left: MARTIN JACKSON 48
Oil on Masonite
29 × 38" (73.7 × 96.5 cm)

Gift of the Honorable Joseph E.
Gold
1973-200-1

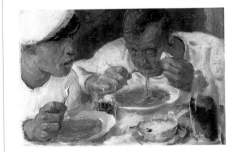

**Jacovleff, Alexander**
Russian, active France,
1887–1938
*Chinese Masks*
c. 1925
Tempera on canvas
31 1/8 × 33 3/4" (79.1 × 85.7 cm)

Gift of Christian Brinton
1941-79-100

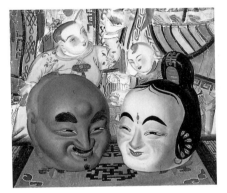

**Jacovleff, Alexander**
*Spaghetti*
1936
Lower right: A Jacovliff Capri /
1936
Oil on burlap on cardboard
21 1/2 × 31 5/8" (54.6 × 80.3 cm)

Gift of Martin Birnbaum in
memory of Mr. and Mrs. John D.
McIlhenny
1944-94-1

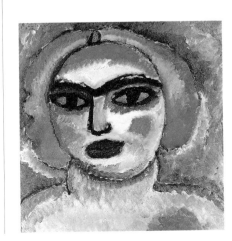

**Jawlensky, Alexey von**
Russian, active Germany,
1864–1941
*Portrait*
See following painting for reverse
1912
Upper left: A.Jawlensky; upper
right: Jawlensky 12
Oil on cardboard
21 1/8 × 19 1/2" (53.7 × 49.5 cm)

The Louise and Walter Arensberg
Collection
1950-134-512a

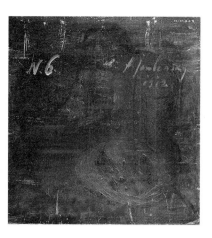

**Jawlensky, Alexey von**
*Seated Woman*
Reverse of the preceding painting
1912
Upper left: N. 6; upper right:
A. Jawlensky / 1912
Oil on cardboard
21 1/8 × 19 1/2" (53.7 × 49.5 cm)

The Louise and Walter Arensberg
Collection
1950-134-512b

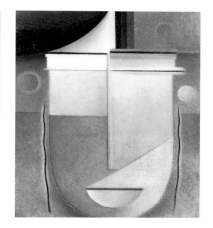

**Jawlensky, Alexey von**
*Looking Within: Rosy Light*
1926
Lower left: A.j.; lower right: V.
26; on reverse: A. v. jawlensky /
Inneres Schauen / "Rosiges Licht /
Annunciator"
Oil on cardboard
21 1/4 × 18 3/4" (54 × 47.6 cm)

The Louise and Walter Arensberg
Collection
1950-134-511

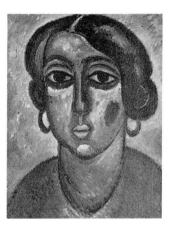

**Jawlensky, Alexey von**
*Earth*
See following painting for reverse
1913
Lower left: Jawlensky. / 1913
Oil on cardboard
26 7/8 × 19 7/8" (68.3 × 50.5 cm)

The Louise and Walter Arensberg
Collection
1950-134-100a

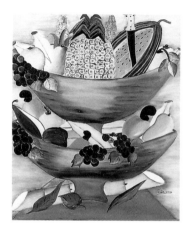

**Jean, Felix**
French, active 20th century
*Bowl of Fruit*
c. 1955
Lower right: Felix Jean
Oil on panel
29 7/8 × 24" (75.9 × 61 cm)

The Albert M. Greenfield and
Elizabeth M. Greenfield
Collection
1974-178-33

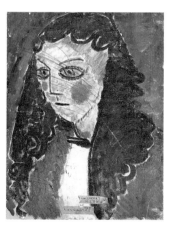

**Jawlensky, Alexey von**
*Head of a Woman*
Reverse of the preceding painting
c. 1913
Oil and graphite on cardboard
26 7/8 × 19 7/8" (68.3 × 50.5 cm)

The Louise and Walter Arensberg
Collection
1950-134-100b

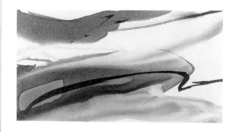

**Jenkins, Paul**
American, born 1923
*Phenomena: Break Rope*
1961
Lower right: Paul Jenkins
Oil on canvas
20 × 36 1/16" (50.8 × 91.6 cm)

Gift of Mr. and Mrs. Barry R.
Peril
1967-269-2

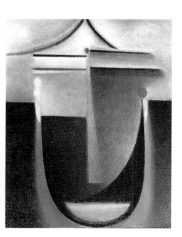

**Jawlensky, Alexey von**
*Looking Within: Night*
1923
Lower left: A.j.; upper right:
Nacht / A jawlensky. / 1923.;
lower right: 1923; on reverse:
Inneres Schauen / Nacht
Oil on cardboard
16 5/8 × 12 3/4" (42.2 × 32.4 cm)

The Louise and Walter Arensberg
Collection
1950-134-101

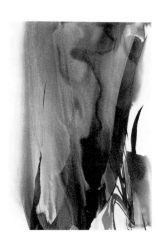

**Jenkins, Paul**
*Phenomena: Guide Polestar,
New York*
1964
Lower left: Paul Jenkins; on
reverse: Paul Jenkins
"Phenomena Guide Pole Star"
New York, 1964 / Phenomena
Guide Pole Star Paul Jenkins—
New York, 1964
Oil on canvas
60 × 39 7/8" (152.4 × 101.3 cm)

Gift of Mr. and Mrs. Barry R.
Peril
1969-282-6

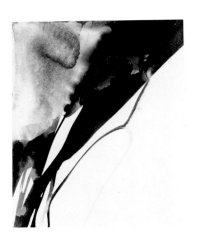

**Jenkins, Paul**
*Phenomena: Shadow Fall*
1964
Lower right: Paul Jenkins
Oil on canvas
20 1/8 × 16 1/16" (51.1 × 40.8 cm)

Gift of Mr. and Mrs. Barry R.
Peril
1967-269-3

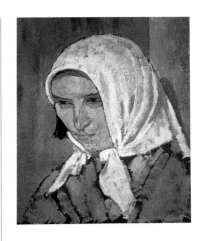

**John, Augustus**
English, 1878–1961
*Head of a Woman (The White
Kerchief)*
1913
Oil on panel
16 × 12 3/4" (40.6 × 32.4 cm)

Gift of Mr. and Mrs. Charles C. G.
Chaplin
1978-173-2

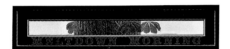

**Jenkins, Paul**
*Phenomena: West Specter*
1964
Lower right: Jenkins
Oil on canvas
20 × 36" (50.8 × 91.4 cm)

Gift of Mr. and Mrs. Barry R.
Peril
1967-269-1

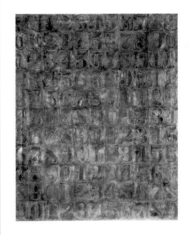

**Johns, Jasper**
American, born 1930
*Sculpmetal Numbers*
1963
On reverse: J Johns / 1963
Sculpmetal on canvas
57 7/8 × 43 7/8" (147 × 111.4 cm)

Centennial gift of the Woodward
Foundation
1975-81-6

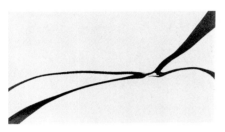

**Jenney, Neil**
American, born 1945
*Meltdown Morning*
1975
Across bottom: MELTDOWN
MORNING
Oil on panel
25 3/4 × 112 1/2" (65.4 × 285.7 cm)

Gift (by exchange) of Samuel S.
White 3rd and Vera White, with
additional funds contributed by
the Daniel W. Dietrich
Foundation in honor of Mrs. H.
Gates Lloyd
1985-23-1

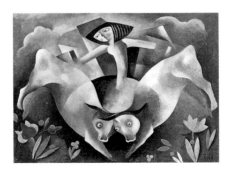

**Kádár, Béla**
Hungarian, 1877–1956
*Angel of Peace*
c. 1925
Lower right: KÁDÁR / BÉLA
Oil on canvas
28 1/8 × 38 3/8" (71.4 × 97.5 cm)

Gift of Christian Brinton
1941-79-103

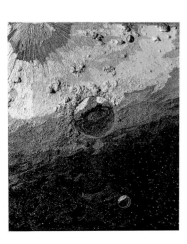

**Jess (Jess Collins)**
American, born 1923
*Ex. 6, No Traveller's Borne
(Translation No. 13)*
1965
Across bottom: EX. 6—NO—
Traveller's Borne; on reverse: 172
Jess '65
Oil on canvas on panel
36 1/4 × 29 1/4" (92.1 × 74.3 cm)

Purchased with the Edith H. Bell
Fund
1979-74-1

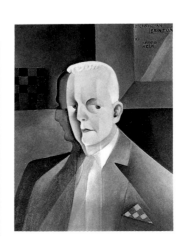

**Kádár, Béla**
*Portrait of an Art Critic (Portrait of
Christian Brinton)*
c. 1925
Upper right: Dr. CHRISTIAN /
BRINTON / BY / KÁDÁR / BÉLA
Oil on canvas
29 1/8 × 22 1/8" (74 × 56.2 cm)

Gift of Christian Brinton
1941-79-105

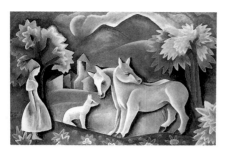

**Kádár, Béla**
*Sunset-Moonrise*
c. 1925
Lower left: KÁDÁR / BÉLA
Oil on canvas
20 1/16 × 29 11/16" (51 × 75.4 cm)

Gift of Christian Brinton
1941-79-138

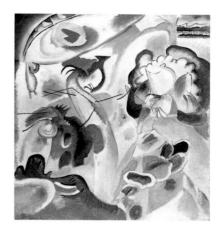

**Kandinsky, Wassily**
Russian, active Germany,
1866–1944
*Improvisation No. 29 (The Swan)*
1912
Lower left: KANDINSKY / 1912.
Oil on canvas
41 3/4 × 38 3/16" (106 × 97 cm)

The Louise and Walter Arensberg
Collection
1950-134-102

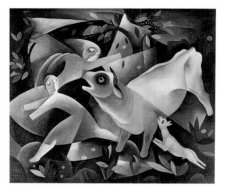

**Kádár, Béla**
*The Impromptu Visitor*
1928
Lower left: KÁDÁR / BÉLA
Oil on canvas
31 3/4 × 36 3/4" (80.6 × 93.3 cm)

Gift of Christian Brinton
1941-79-101

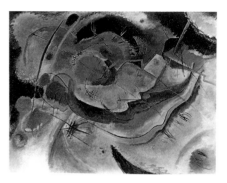

**Kandinsky, Wassily**
*Little Painting with Yellow
(Improvisation)*
1914
Lower right: KANDINSKY / 1914.
Oil on canvas
31 × 39 5/8" (78.7 × 100.6 cm)

The Louise and Walter Arensberg
Collection
1950-134-103

**Kahn, Wolf**
American, born Germany,
born 1927
*Landscape*
1960
Lower right: W. Kahn
Oil on canvas
9 1/8 × 14 1/8" (23.2 × 35.9 cm)

Gift of Barbara Kulicke
1973-71-2

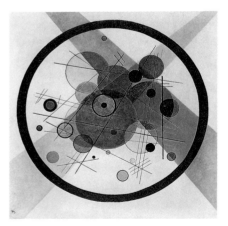

**Kandinsky, Wassily**
*Circles in a Circle*
1923
Lower left: WK 23; on reverse:
N 26i / 1923 / Kreise im Kreis
Oil on canvas
38 7/8 × 37 5/8" (98.7 × 95.6 cm)

The Louise and Walter Arensberg
Collection
1950-134-104

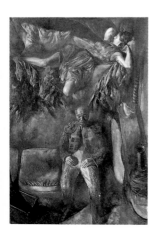

**Kamihira, Ben**
American, born 1925
*Faded Suit of Lights*
1966
Lower right: KAMIHIRA
Oil on canvas
64 1/2 × 42 3/16" (163.8 × 107.2 cm)

Purchased with funds contributed
by Dr. Luther W. Brady, Jr., and
anonymous donors
1978-14-1

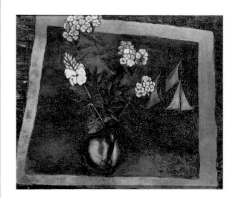

**Kantor, Morris**
American, born Belorussia,
1896–1974
*Vase of Flowers*
1928
Lower left: M. Kantor 1928
Oil on canvas
24 1/2 × 28" (62.2 × 71.1 cm)

Bequest of Anne Hinchman
1952-82-13

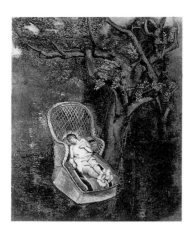

**Kantor, Morris**
*Apple Trees with a Girl in a Chair*
1929
Lower right: M. Kantor / 1929
Oil on canvas
36 1/8 × 29 1/8" (91.8 × 74 cm)

Bequest of Anne Hinchman
1952-82-15

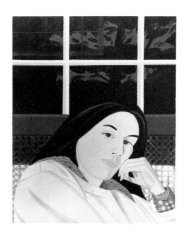

**Katz, Alex**
American, born 1927
*West Interior*
1979
Oil on canvas
96 × 72" (243.8 × 182.9 cm)

Gift of the Friends of the
Philadelphia Museum of Art
1979-145-1

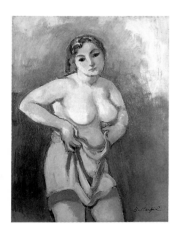

**Kantor, Morris**
*Vase of Flowers*
c. 1930
Lower right: M. Kantor
Oil on canvas
27 1/2 × 21 1/2" (69.8 × 54.6 cm)

Bequest of Anne Hinchman
1952-82-14

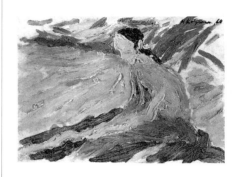

**Katzman, Herbert**
American, born 1923
*Duny*
1960
Upper right: H. Katzman, 60
Oil on canvas
8 1/16 × 11 1/8" (20.5 × 28.3 cm)

Gift of the Kulicke family in
memory of Lt. Frederick W.
Kulicke III
1969-86-1

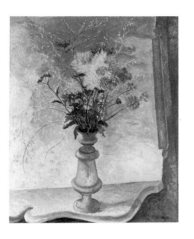

**Karfiol, Bernard**
American, born Hungary,
1886–1952
*The Yellow Slip*
c. 1938
Lower right: B. Karfiol; on
reverse: BERNARD KARFIOL /
THE YELLOW SLIP / THE
DOWNTOWN GALLERY /
32 E. 51st St., NY
Oil on canvas board
16 × 12" (40.6 × 30.5 cm)

Gift of Bryant W. Langston
1961-77-1

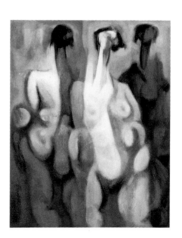

**Keene, Paul**
American, born 1920
*Three Graces*
c. 1960
Oil on canvas
30 × 24" (76.2 × 61 cm)

Gift of Benjamin D. Bernstein
1964-106-2

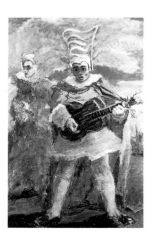

**Karp, Leon**
American, 1903–1951
*New-Year Shooters*
1940
Lower right: Leon Karp
Oil on canvas
48 1/8 × 30" (122.2 × 76.2 cm)

Gift of H. A. Batten, George W.
Cecil, C. T. Coiner, Paul Darrow,
Mrs. Elizabeth Kidd, Gerald M.
Lauck, Leonard Lionni, Walter
Reinsel, Harry Rosin, Granville E.
Toogood, and Edward Zern
1942-65-1

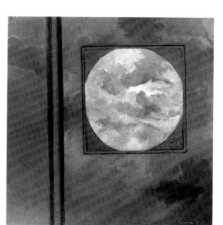

**Keene, Paul**
*Untitled*
From the "Sky Windows" series
1984
Lower right: Keene 84
Oil on canvas
9 3/8 × 9" (23.8 × 22.9 cm)

Purchased with the Julius Bloch
Memorial Fund
1990-119-5

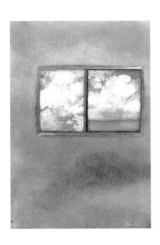

**Keene, Paul**
*Untitled*
From the "Sky Windows" series
1984
Lower right: Keene 84
Oil on canvas
12 × 8" (30.5 × 20.3 cm)

Purchased with the Julius Bloch
Memorial Fund
1990-119-7

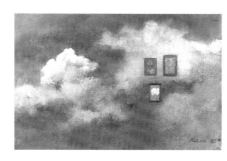

**Keene, Paul**
*Untitled*
From the "Sky Windows" series
1985
Lower right: Keene 85
Oil on canvas
8 3/8 × 12" (21.3 × 30.5 cm)

Purchased with the Julius Bloch
Memorial Fund
1990-119-6

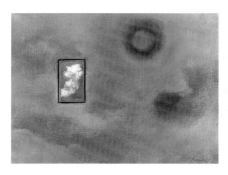

**Keene, Paul**
*Untitled*
From the "Sky Windows" series
1985
Lower right: Keene 85
Oil on canvas
10 × 13" (25.4 × 33 cm)

Purchased with the Julius Bloch
Memorial Fund
1990-119-1

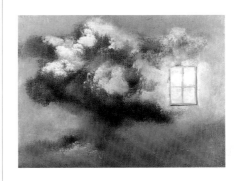

**Keene, Paul**
*Untitled*
From the "Sky Windows" series
c. 1985
Oil on canvas
9 × 12" (22.9 × 30.5 cm)

Purchased with the Julius Bloch
Memorial Fund
1990-119-3

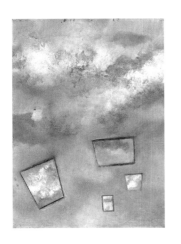

**Keene, Paul**
*Untitled*
From the "Sky Windows" series
1985
Lower right: Keene 85
Oil on canvas
14 × 10" (35.6 × 25.4 cm)

Purchased with the Julius Bloch
Memorial Fund
1990-119-2

**Kelly, Ellsworth**
American, born 1923
*Diagonal with Curve III*
1978
Oil on canvas
135 × 99" (342.9 × 251.5 cm)

Gift of the Friends of the
Philadelphia Museum of Art
1979-99-1

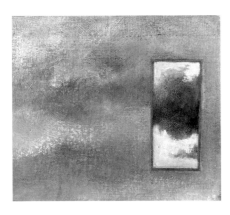

**Keene, Paul**
*Untitled*
From the "Sky Windows" series
1985
Lower right: 85
Oil on canvas
10 × 11" (25.4 × 28 cm)

Purchased with the Julius Bloch
Memorial Fund
1990-119-4

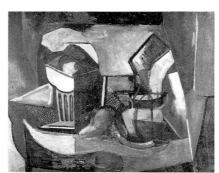

**Kelly, Leon**
American, born France,
1901–1982
*Abstraction*
1922
Lower right: Leon Kelly; on
reverse: Leon Kelly / 1922
Oil on canvas
23 × 29" (58.4 × 73.7 cm)

Gift of Bernard Davis
1942-64-2

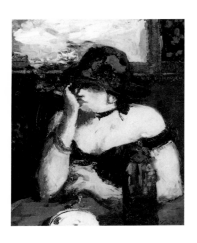

**Kelly, Leon**
*Au Café*
c. 1930
Lower right: Leon Kelly
Oil on canvas
25 5/8 × 21 5/16" (65.1 × 54.1 cm)

Gift of Bernard Davis
1942-14-1

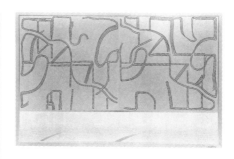

**Keyser, Robert**
American, born 1927
*Ur Landscape*
1974
Lower right: Robert Keyser / '74
Oil on canvas
44 1/8 × 66" (112.1 × 167.6 cm)

Gift of the Women's Committee
of the Philadelphia Museum of
Art in memory of Mrs. Morris
Wenger, with additional funds
contributed by Gene Locks and
Frederick R. McBrien
1975-120-1

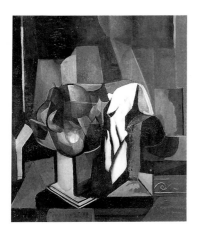

**Kelly, Leon**
*Abstraction*
1937
Upper left: Leon Kelly; on
reverse: Leon Kelly / Vernis
Vibert / April 1937
Oil on canvas
21 3/4 × 18 1/8" (55.2 × 46 cm)

Bequest of Margaretta S.
Hinchman
1955-96-7

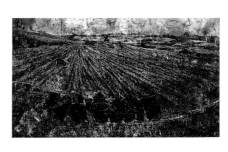

**Kiefer, Anselm**
German, born 1945
*Nigredo*
1984
Upper left: Nigredo
Oil, acrylic, emulsion, shellac,
and straw on photograph on
canvas, with woodcut
130 × 218 1/2" (330.2 × 555 cm)

Gift of the Friends of the
Philadelphia Museum of Art in
celebration of their 20th
anniversary
1985-5-1

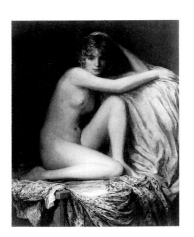

**Kendall, William Sergeant**
American, 1869–1938
*Penumbra*
1917
Lower left: Sergeant Kendall /
1917
Oil on canvas
48 1/2 × 36 3/8" (123.2 × 92.4 cm)

The Walter Lippincott Collection
1923-59-14

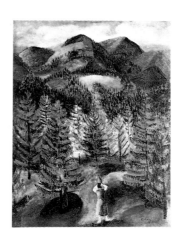

**Kisling, Moïse**
French, born Poland,
1891–1953
*Landscape (Woman with a Jug)*
c. 1920
Lower right: Kisling
Oil on canvas
31 13/16 × 23 5/8" (80.8 × 60 cm)

Gift of George Biddle
1945-16-38

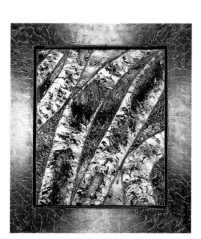

**Kessler, Michael**
American, born 1954
*Swamp Grove*
1984
Oil on panel
32 × 28" (81.3 × 71.1 cm)

Purchased with the Julius Bloch
Memorial Fund
1986-136-1

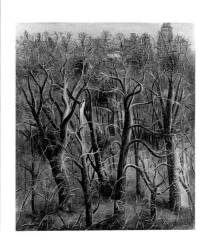

**Kisling, Moïse**
*Central Park, New York City*
1941
Lower left: Kisling; lower right:
New York 1941
Oil on canvas
26 3/8 × 22 3/8" (67 × 56.8 cm)

Gift of Mr. and Mrs. Fredric R.
Mann
1955-24-1

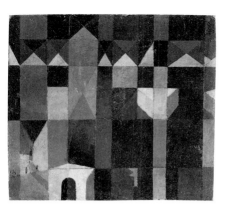

**Klee, Paul**
Swiss, 1879–1940
*City of Towers*
1916
Lower left: Klee / 1916 40; on
reverse: 1916.40. Stadt der
Türme / Klee
Oil on canvas on panel
12 7/8 × 14 1/8" (32.7 × 35.9 cm)

The Louise and Walter Arensberg
Collection
1950-134-109

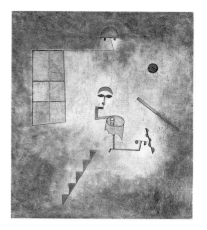

**Klee, Paul**
*Prestidigitator (Conjuring Trick)*
1927
Upper left: Klee 1927 Omega. 7;
on reverse: 1927 Omega 7 /
Zauber Kunst Stuck Klee
Oil on canvas on Masonite
19 9/16 × 16 7/16" (49.7 × 41.7 cm)

The Louise and Walter Arensberg
Collection
1950-134-118

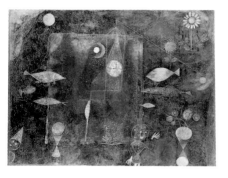

**Klee, Paul**
*Fish Magic*
1925
Lower left: Klee / 1925 R. 5; on
reverse: 1925 R.5 Fischzauber
Klee
Oil and watercolor on canvas on
panel
30 3/8 × 38 3/4" (77.1 × 98.4 cm)

The Louise and Walter Arensberg
Collection
1950-134-112

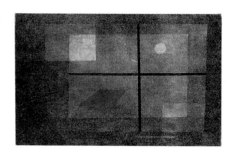

**Klee, Paul**
*But the Red Roof*
1935
Upper left: Klee
Glue tempera on jute-and-flax
fabric
23 3/4 × 35 11/16" (60.3 × 90.6 cm)

The Louise and Walter Arensberg
Collection
1950-134-121

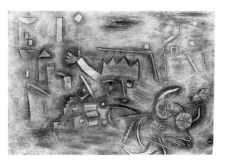

**Klee, Paul**
*Animal Terror*
1926
Upper right: Klee 1926 U. 4.;
on reverse: 1926 U. 4 Der Tie
Schreck Klee
Tempera on canvas
13 7/8 × 19 1/16" (35.2 × 48.4 cm)

The Louise and Walter Arensberg
Collection
1950-134-113

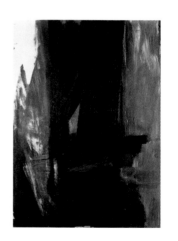

**Kline, Franz**
American, 1910–1962
*Torches Mauve*
1960
On reverse: Franz Kline 60, R 14,
NY, Made in Belgium / Torches
Mauve / Kline
Oil on canvas
120 1/8 × 81 1/8" (305.1 × 206.1 cm)

Gift of the artist
1961-223-1

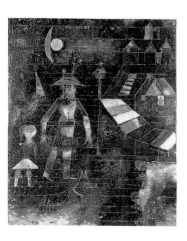

**Klee, Paul**
*Village Carnival*
1926
Center top: Klee 1926 D 5; on
reverse: D 5 Dorf-Carnaval Klee
Oil on canvas on panel
25 11/16 × 17 5/16" (65.2 × 44 cm)

The Louise and Walter Arensberg
Collection
1950-134-115

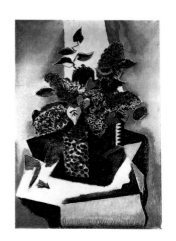

**Knaths, Karl**
American, 1891–1971
*Still Life*
1927
Lower right: KNATHS
Oil on canvas
30 1/8 × 20" (76.5 × 50.8 cm)

A. E. Gallatin Collection
1952-61-51

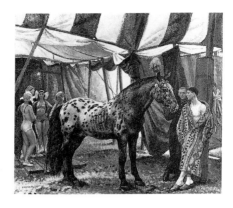

**Knight, Dame Laura**
English, 1877–1970
*The Knap Stroppers*
c. 1925
Lower left: Laura Knight
Oil on canvas
27 1/4 × 30 1/4" (69.2 × 76.8 cm)

Bequest of Charlotte Dorrance
Wright
1978-1-37

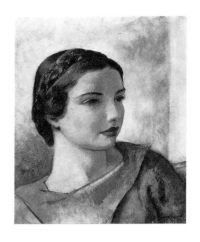

**Kroll, Leon**
American, 1884–1974
*Head of a Girl in a Red Dress*
c. 1930
Lower right: Leon Kroll
Oil on Masonite
18 × 15" (45.7 × 38.1 cm)

The Louis E. Stern Collection
1963-181-38

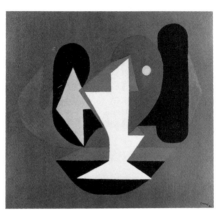

**Konolyi, Mary Barnwell**
American, active c. 1954
*The Spy*
1954
Lower right: KONOLYI / 54
Oil on canvas
36 7/8 × 36 5/8" (93.7 × 93 cm)

Gift of an anonymous donor
1962-49-1

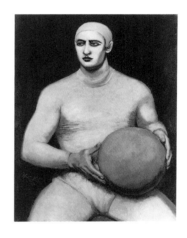

**Kuhn, Walt**
American, 1880–1949
*Athlete in Whiteface*
1934
Lower left: Walt Kuhn / 1934
Oil on canvas
40 1/8 × 30 1/8" (101.9 × 76.5 cm)

Purchased with the W. P.
Wilstach Fund
W1962-1-1

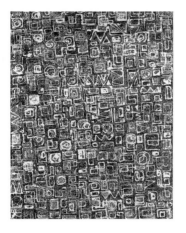

**Krasner, Lee**
American, 1908–1984
*Composition*
1949
On reverse: Lee KRASNER—
'49 / 1949
Oil on canvas
38 1/16 × 27 13/16" (96.7 × 70.6 cm)

Gift of the Aaron E. Norman
Fund, Inc.
1959-31-1

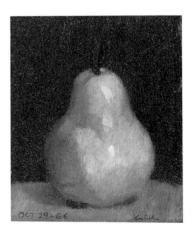

**Kulicke, Robert**
American, born 1924
*Pear*
1966
Lower left: OCT 29-66; lower
right: Kulicke
Oil on panel
9 1/2 × 7 1/8" (24.1 × 18.1 cm)

Gift of the Kulicke family in
memory of Lt. Frederick W.
Kulicke III
1969-86-2

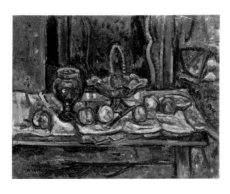

**Kremegne, Pinchus**
Russian, born 1890, death date
unknown
*Still Life with a Fruit Dish*
1958
Lower left: Kremegne
Oil on canvas
25 5/8 × 31 7/8" (65.1 × 81 cm)

Gift of Dr. and Mrs. Paul Todd
Makler
1970-92-1

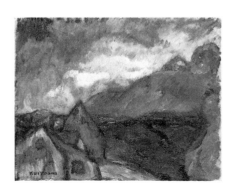

**Kuniyoshi, Yasuo**
American, born Japan,
1893–1953
*Landscape*
c. 1919
Lower left: KUIYOSHI
Oil on panel
8 1/4 × 10 3/8" (20.9 × 26.3 cm)

Gift of Frank and Alice Osborn
1966-68-16

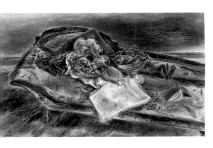

**Kuniyoshi, Yasuo**
*Odd Objects on a Couch*
1930
Lower left: Yasuo Kuniyoshi /
1930
Oil on canvas
40 × 65 ³/₈" (101.6 × 166 cm)

Gift of Mrs. Frank C. Osborn
1957-65-1

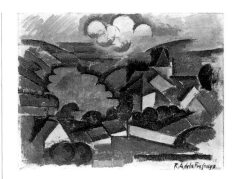

**La Fresnaye, Roger de**
*Landscape*
1912
Lower right: 12 / R. A. de la
Fresnaye
Oil on canvas
18 ³/₄ × 23 ³/₄" (47.6 × 60.3 cm)

The Louise and Walter Arensberg
Collection
1950-134-90

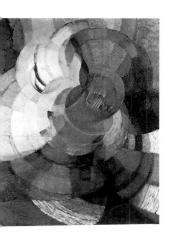

**Kupka, Frank (Frantisek
Kupka)**
Czech, active France,
1871–1957
*Disks of Newton (Study for "Fugue
in Two Colors")*
1912
Lower left: Kupka; on reverse:
Frank Kupka "Disque de
Newton" Etude pour: "La fugue à
2 couleurs"—1912—
Oil on canvas
39 ¹/₂ × 29" (100.3 × 73.7 cm)

The Louise and Walter Arensberg
Collection
1950-134-122

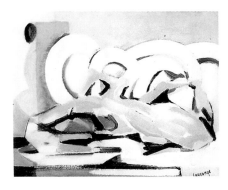

**Lagrange, Jacques**
French, born 1917
*Still Life with a Goose*
c. 1950
Lower right: Lagrange
Oil on canvas
19 ³/₄ × 24" (50.2 × 61 cm)

Gift of John Wanamaker
1951-69-1

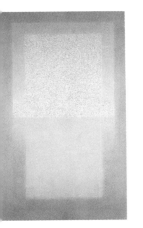

**Kurtz, Elaine**
American, born 1928
*Incandescent Cool*
1982
Acrylic on canvas
84 × 48" (213.4 × 121.9 cm)

Gift of the artist and gift (by
exchange) of James Lee
1982-32-1

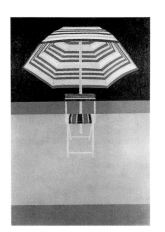

**Lam, Jennett**
American, born 1911
*Chair Plus, Night*
1964
Lower right: Jennett Lam 1964
Oil on canvas
61 × 39" (154.9 × 99.1 cm)

Gift of Haig Tashjian
1966-227-1

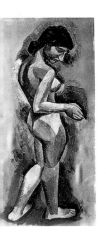

**La Fresnaye, Roger de**
French, 1885–1925
*Nude*
1911
Lower right: mai 1911 / LA
FRESNAYE
Oil on cardboard
50 ¹¹/₁₆ × 22 ¹/₄" (128.7 × 56.5 cm)

The Louise and Walter Arensberg
Collection
1950-134-89

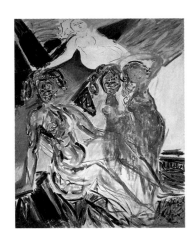

**Lansner, Fay**
American, born 1921
*Metamorphosis*
1954
Lower left: Fay Lansner July / 54;
on reverse: Fay Lansner / 1954
Oil on canvas
89 ³/₄ × 69" (228 × 175.3 cm)

The Albert M. Greenfield and
Elizabeth M. Greenfield
Collection
1974-178-34

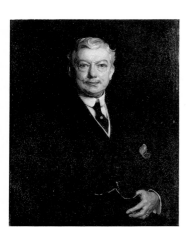

**László, Philip A. de**
English, born Hungary,
1869–1937
*Portrait of John H. McFadden*
1916
Lower left: Laszlo / LONDON /
1916.XI.I
Oil on canvas
35 3/4 × 27 1/2" (90.8 × 69.8 cm)

Gift of Mr. and Mrs. John
Howard McFadden, Jr.
1956-13-1

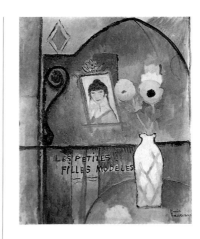

**Laurencin, Marie**
French, 1885–1956
*Young Girl Models*
c. 1913
Lower right: Marie / Laurencin;
center: LES PETITES / FILLES
MODÈLES
Oil on panel
21 × 16 1/2" (53.3 × 41.9 cm)

A. E. Gallatin Collection
1944-12-1

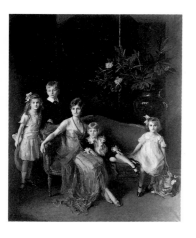

**László, Philip A. de**
*Portrait of Mrs. Francis P. Garvan
and Her Four Children*
1921
Lower left: de Laszlo / Roslyn
House 1921. august.
Oil on canvas
110 × 88" (279.4 × 223.5 cm)

Gift of Mrs. Francis P. Garvan
1965-208-1

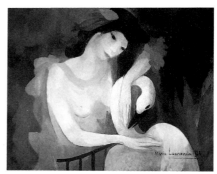

**Laurencin, Marie**
*Leda and the Swan*
1923
Lower right: Marie Laurencin
1923
Oil on canvas
26 1/2 × 32" (67.3 × 81.3 cm)

Gift of Mr. and Mrs. Charles C. G.
Chaplin
1978-173-1

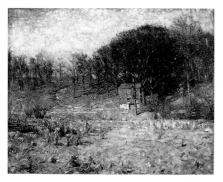

**Lathrop, William Langson**
American, 1859–1938
*Landscape*
1915
Lower right: WL LATHROP / '15
Oil on canvas
25 × 30 3/16" (63.5 × 76.7 cm)

Gift of Lucie Washington
Mitcheson in memory of Robert
Stockton Johnson Mitcheson for
the Robert Stockton Johnson
Mitcheson Collection
1938-22-5

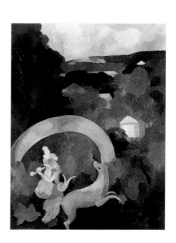

**Laurencin, Marie**
*Nymph and Hind*
1925
Lower right: Marie Laurencin
1925
Oil on canvas
28 5/8 × 21 3/8" (72.7 × 54.3 cm)

Gift of Mr. and Mrs. Herbert
Cameron Morris
1951-104-1

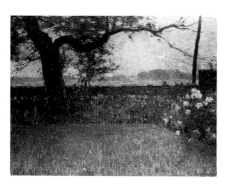

**Lathrop, William Langson**
*Spring Landscape*
c. 1915
Lower right: WL LATHROP
Oil on canvas
32 3/16 × 40 1/16" (81.8 × 101.8 cm)

The Alex Simpson, Jr., Collection
1944-13-3

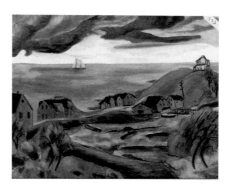

**Lawson, Adelaide**
American, born 1889,
still active 1940
*Ogunquit*
c. 1925
Lower right: A. LAWSON
Oil on canvas
24 3/16 × 30" (61.4 × 76.2 cm)

Gift of Frank and Alice Osborn
1966-68-29

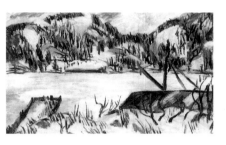

**Lawson, Adelaide**
*Winter*
1926
On reverse: Painted by / Adelaide
Lawson / (Mrs. Wood Taylor)
Glenwood Landing / Long Island
N.Y. / 1926
Oil on cardboard
10 1/8 × 16 1/16" (25.7 × 40.8 cm)

Gift of Frank and Alice Osborn
1966-68-28

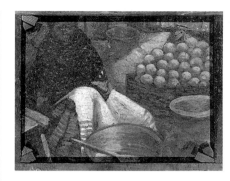

**Lawson, Ernest**
*Woman at a Marketplace*
Reverse of the preceding painting
c. 1913
Oil on canvas
18 × 22" (45.7 × 55.9 cm)

The Alex Simpson, Jr., Collection
1944-13-4b

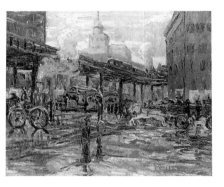

**Lawson, Ernest**
American, 1873–1939
*Chatham Square*
c. 1910
Lower right: E. LAWSON
Oil on canvas
20 1/16 × 26 1/16" (51 × 66.2 cm)

Bequest of T. Edward Hanley
1970-76-8

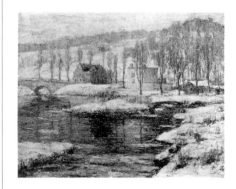

**Lawson, Ernest**
*Winter Landscape*
c. 1925
Lower left: E. Lawson
Oil on canvas on Masonite
25 × 29 15/16" (63.5 × 76 cm)

Gift of Lucie Washington
Mitcheson in memory of Robert
Stockton Johnson Mitcheson for
the Robert Stockton Johnson
Mitcheson Collection
1938-22-3

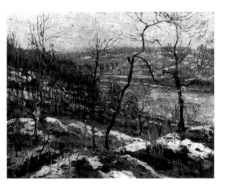

**Lawson, Ernest**
*Landscape near the Harlem River*
c. 1913
Oil on cardboard
25 1/2 × 21 1/2" (64.8 × 54.6 cm)

Gift of Mr. and Mrs. Meyer P.
Potamkin (reserving life interest)
1964-116-4

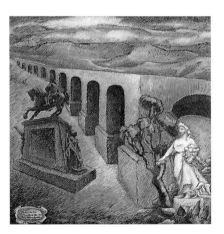

**Lazo, Agustin**
Mexican, born 1900
*View of the City of Morelia*
1938
Lower left: Vista de la / Ciudad
de Mo / relia par Agustin / Lazo.
1938
Oil on canvas
27 1/2 × 25 3/4" (69.8 × 65.4 cm)

Gift of Dr. and Mrs. MacKinley
Helm
1952-57-3

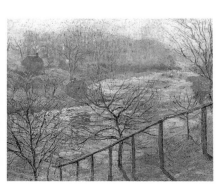

**Lawson, Ernest**
*River*
See following painting for reverse
c. 1913
Lower left: E. LAWSON
Oil on canvas
18 × 22" (45.7 × 55.9 cm)

The Alex Simpson, Jr., Collection
1944-13-4a

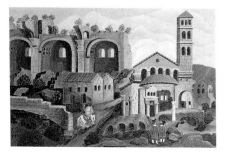

**Lebduska, Lawrence H.**
American, 1894–1966
*Temple of Venus*
1932
Lower right: L. H. Lebduska 32
Oil on canvas
21 × 30" (53.3 × 76.2 cm)

The Louise and Walter Arensberg
Collection
1950-134-513

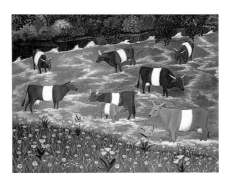

**Lebduska, Lawrence H.**
*White-Belted Cattle*
1937
Upper right: Lebduska / 37
Oil on canvas
24 1/16 × 30 3/16" (61.1 × 76.7 cm)

The Louise and Walter Arensberg
Collection
1950-134-514

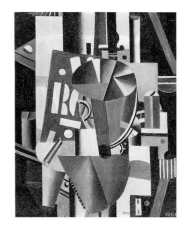

**Léger, Fernand**
*Typographer (Final State)*
1919
Lower right: F. LEGER; on
reverse: LE TYPOGRAPHE ETAT
DEFinitif / F LEGER / 19
Oil on canvas
51 5/16 × 38 3/8" (130.3 × 97.5 cm)

The Louise and Walter Arensberg
Collection
1950-134-125

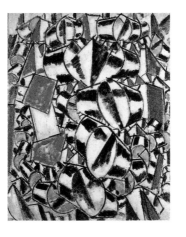

**Léger, Fernand**
French, 1881–1955
*Contrast of Forms*
1913
On reverse: F LEGER / (1913)
Oil on burlap
51 1/4 × 38 7/16" (130.2 × 97.6 cm)

The Louise and Walter Arensberg
Collection
1950-134-123

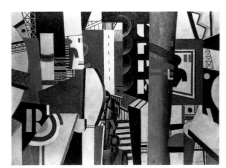

**Léger, Fernand**
*The City*
1919
Lower right: F. LÉGER /
PARIS—19; on reverse: LA VILLE /
1919–20 / F. LEGER
Oil on canvas
91 × 117 1/2" (231.1 × 298.4 cm)

A. E. Gallatin Collection
1952-61-58

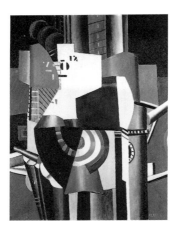

**Léger, Fernand**
*The City (Fragment, Third State)*
1919
Lower right: F. LEGER; on
reverse: LA VILLE (fraGMENT). /
3e ETAT / F. LEGER / 19.
Oil on canvas
51 1/8 × 38 1/4" (129.9 × 97.1 cm)

The Louise and Walter Arensberg
Collection
1950-134-124

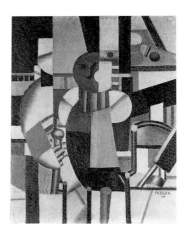

**Léger, Fernand**
*Man with a Cane (First State)*
1920
Lower right: F. LEGER / 20; on
reverse: L'Homme à la Canne /
Ie ETAT / F. LEGER / 20
Oil on burlap
25 5/8 × 19 9/16" (65.1 × 49.7 cm)

The Louise and Walter Arensberg
Collection
1950-134-126

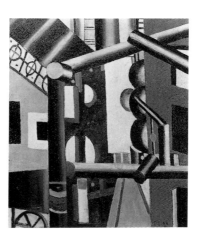

**Léger, Fernand**
*The Scaffolding (First State)*
1919
Lower right: F. LEGER / 19;
on reverse: L'Echafaudage I état
F. Léger —19
Oil on canvas
25 9/16 × 21 3/16" (64.9 × 53.8 cm)

A. E. Gallatin Collection
1952-61-57

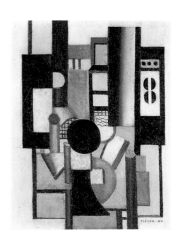

**Léger, Fernand**
*Mechanical Element*
1920
Lower right: F. LÉGER. 20; on
reverse: Elément / Mécanique /
1920 / F. LEGER
Oil on canvas
25 5/8 × 19 3/4" (65.1 × 50.2 cm)

Gift of Miss Anna Warren
Ingersoll
1958-12-1

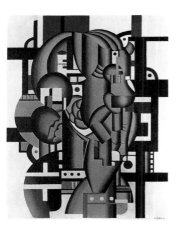

**Léger, Fernand**
*Composition*
1923–27
Lower right: F. LÉGER. 27; on
reverse: Composition / F. LEGER /
23–27
Oil on canvas
50 1/2 × 38 1/4" (128.3 × 97.1 cm)

A. E. Gallatin Collection
1952-61-63

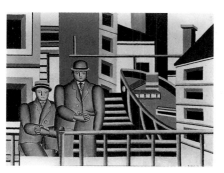

**Léger, Fernand**
*Animated Landscape*
1924
Lower right: F. LEGER. 24.; on
reverse: Paysage Animé—24
F. Leger
Oil on canvas
19 1/2 × 25 5/8" (49.5 × 65.1 cm)

Gift of Bernard Davis
1950-63-1

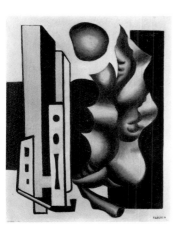

**Léger, Fernand**
*Green Foliage*
1930
Lower right: F. LÉGER. 30;
on reverse: L. Feuille Verte /
F. LEGER. 30
Oil on canvas
25 5/8 × 19 3/4" (65.1 × 50.2 cm)

A. E. Gallatin Collection
1952-61-64

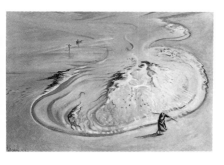

**Leonid (Leonid Berman)**
French, born Russia,
1896–1976
*Fishermen at Belle-Île-sur-Mer*
1949
Lower left: Leonid. 49.
Oil on canvas
25 × 36" (63.5 × 91.4 cm)

Gift of Mme Florence de
Montferrier
1961-180-1

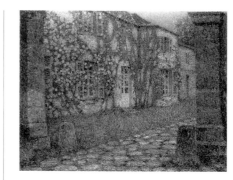

**Le Sidaner, Henri-Eugène-
Augustin**
French, 1862–1939
*House of Roses*
By 1917
Lower left: Le SIDANER
Oil on canvas
32 1/8 × 39 1/2" (81.6 × 100.3 cm)

Purchased with the W. P.
Wilstach Fund
W1917-1-10

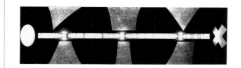

**LeWitt, Sol**
American, born 1928
*On a Blue Ceiling, Eight Geometric
Figures: Circle, Trapezoid,
Parallelogram, Rectangle, Square,
Triangle, Right Triangle, X (Wall
Drawing No. 548)*
Executed on a gallery ceiling in
the museum
1981
Chalk and latex paint on plaster
186 × 655" (472.4 × 1663.7 cm)

Purchased with a grant from the
National Endowment for the Arts
and with funds contributed by
Mrs. H. Gates Lloyd, Mr. and
Mrs. N. Richard Miller, Mrs.
Donald A. Petrie, Eileen and
Peter Rosenau, Mrs. Adolf
Schaap, Frances and Bayard
Storey, Marion Boulton Stroud,
and two anonymous donors (by
exchange), with additional funds
from Dr. and Mrs. William
Wolgin, the Daniel W. Dietrich
Foundation, and the Friends of
the Philadelphia Museum of Art
1982-121-1

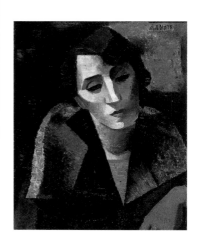

**Lhôte, André**
French, 1885–1962
*Head of a Woman*
c. 1921
Upper right: A. LHOTE
Oil on canvas
24 × 18 1/8" (61 × 46 cm)

Gift of Benjamin D. Bernstein
1978-172-3

**Liberman, Alexander**
American, born Ukraine,
born 1912
*Great Mysteries IV*
1962
Acrylic on canvas
112 × 50" (284.5 × 127 cm)

Centennial gift of the Woodward
Foundation
1975-81-8

**Louis, Morris**
American, 1912–1962
*Beth*
1960
Acrylic resin on canvas
105 × 106 ¼" (266.7 × 269.9 cm)

Purchased with the Adele Haas
Turner and Beatrice Pastorius
Turner Memorial Fund
1966-172-1

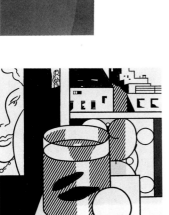

**Lichtenstein, Roy**
American, born 1923
*Still Life with Goldfish*
1974
Oil and Magna on canvas
80 × 60" (203.2 × 152.4 cm)

Purchased with the Edith H. Bell
Fund
1974-110-1

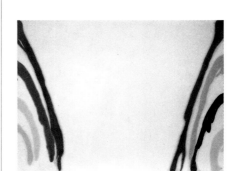

**Louis, Morris**
*Delta*
1960
Acrylic resin on canvas
105 × 141 ½" (266.7 × 359.4 cm)

Centennial gift of the Woodward
Foundation
1975-81-9

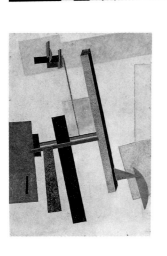

**Lissitzky, El (Eleazar Lissitzky)**
Russian, 1890–1941
*Proun 2 (Construction)*
"Proun" is a Russian acronym for
"Project for the Establishment of
a New Art"
1920
On reverse: [Russian for "El
Lissitzky"], 1920 Proun 2c 1920
Oil, paper, and metal on panel
23 ⁷/₁₆ × 15 ¹¹/₁₆" (59.5 × 39.8 cm)

A. E. Gallatin Collection
1952-61-72

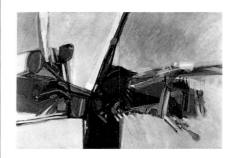

**Lueders, Jimmy C.**
American, born 1927
*Ascension*
Diptych
1965
Lower left: Lueders
Acrylic on canvas
85 ⁷/₈ × 125 ¼" (218.1 × 318.1 cm)

Purchased with the Philadelphia
Foundation Fund
1965-158-1

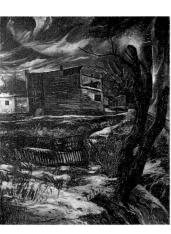

**Loper, Edward**
American, born 1916
*Backyards*
c. 1935
Lower right: Edw. L. Loper
Oil on canvas
30 ¹/₈ × 23 ⁷/₈" (76.5 × 60.6 cm)

Gift of Sam A. Lewisohn
1944-85-1

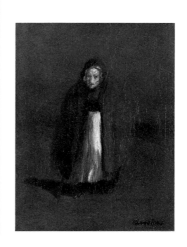

**Luks, George B.**
American, 1867–1933
*Old Beggar Woman*
1907
Lower right: George Luks; on
reverse: Beggar Woman by
George Luks 1907
Oil on canvas
24 ¹/₈ × 18 ¹/₈" (61.3 × 46 cm)

Gift of Mr. and Mrs. Meyer P.
Potamkin (reserving life interest)
1964-116-2

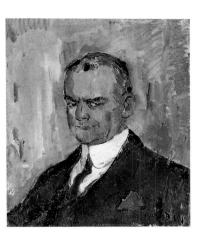

**Lund, Henrik**
Norwegian, 1879–1935
*Portrait of Christian Brinton*
1912
Lower right: Henrik Lund 1912
Oil on composition board
21 ⅝ × 18" (54.9 × 45.7 cm)

Gift of Christian Brinton
1941-79-336

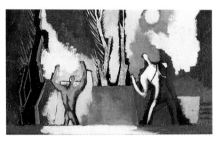

**Lurçat, Jean**
French, 1892–1966
*Composition No. 2*
1925
Lower right: Lurçat / 25
Oil on canvas
15 × 24 ¼" (38.1 × 61.6 cm)

Bequest of Fiske and Marie
Kimball
1955-86-19

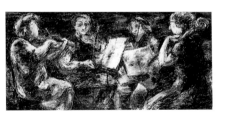

**Lutz, Dan**
American, 1906–1978
*String Quartet*
c. 1940
Lower right: DAN LUTZ
Oil on canvas
18 × 36" (45.7 × 91.4 cm)

Gift of Mrs. Herbert Cameron
Morris
1946-40-1

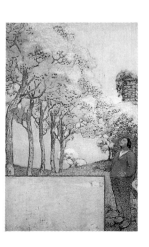

**McCarter, Henry**
American, 1866–1942
*Trees in Bloom*
c. 1930
Oil on cardboard
20 ½ × 12 ⅝" (52.1 × 32.1 cm)

Bequest of Henry McCarter
1944-44-2

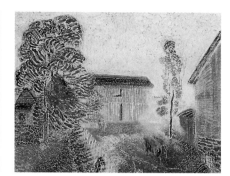

**McCarter, Henry**
*Farm Scene*
c. 1940
Lower left: H.M.C
Oil on canvas
29 ¹³⁄₁₆ × 35 ¹⁵⁄₁₆" (75.7 × 91.3 cm)

Gift of Miss Anna Warren
Ingersoll and R. Sturgis Ingersoll
1942-45-1

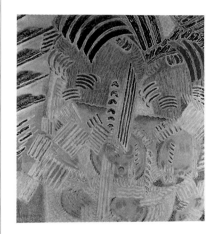

**McCarter, Henry**
*Bells No. 6*
c. 1941
Oil on canvas
48 ⁵⁄₁₆ × 41 ¹⁵⁄₁₆" (122.7 ×
106.5 cm)

Bequest of Henry McCarter
1944-44-3

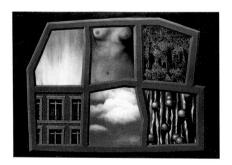

**Magritte, René**
Belgian, 1898–1967
*The Six Elements*
1929
Upper left: Magritte
Oil on canvas
28 ¾ × 39 ⁵⁄₁₆" (73 × 99.8 cm)

The Louise and Walter Arensberg
Collection
1950-134-127

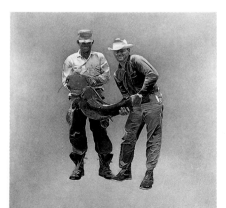

**Mahaffey, Noel**
American, born 1944
*Catfish*
1969
Lower right: N Mahaffey '69
Oil on canvas
72 ¼ × 72 ¼" (183.5 × 183.5 cm)

Gift of the Cheltenham Art
Centre
1970-91-1

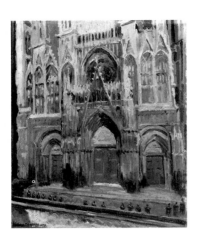

**Malherbe, William**
American, born France,
died 1951
*Rouen Cathedral*
1929
Lower left: WILLIAM MALHERBE.
1929.
Oil on canvas
25 3/4 × 21 3/8" (65.4 × 54.3 cm)

Gift of Mrs. A. W. Erickson
1945-69-1

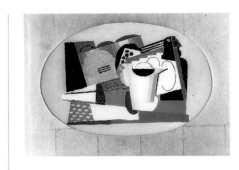

**Marcoussis, Louis (Louis Casimir Ladislas Markus)**
Polish, active France,
1883–1941
*Still Life*
1920
Lower right: LM 1920
Oil on glass
13 1/8 × 18 1/8" (33.3 × 46 cm)

Gift of Richard Davis
1945-40-2

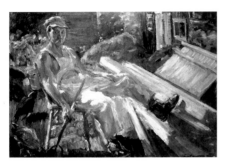

**Malherbe, William**
*The Farmer, Lynne, New Hampshire (Portrait of Bill Stevens)*
1940
Lower right: WILLIAM
MALHERBE. 1940
Oil on canvas
18 × 24" (45.7 × 61 cm)

Gift of Mrs. A. W. Erickson
1945-69-2

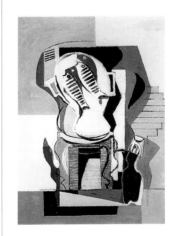

**Marcoussis, Louis**
*Still Life with Fish*
1928
Lower left: Marcoussis 28
Oil on canvas
36 1/4 × 25 1/2" (92.1 × 64.8 cm)

Bequest of Fiske and Marie
Kimball
1955-86-17

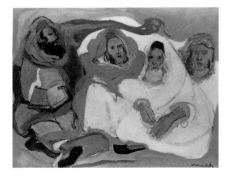

**Mané-Katz**
French, born Ukraine,
1894–1962
*Men at Prayer*
c. 1950
Lower right: Mané-Katz
Oil on canvas
31 7/8 × 39 1/4" (81 × 99.7 cm)

Bequest of Rosaline B. Feinstein
1972-239-1

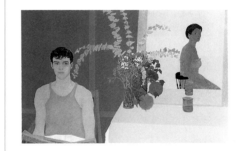

**Marcus, Marcia**
American, born 1928
*Double Portrait with Still Life*
1960
Oil and newspaper on canvas
42 × 59 7/8" (106.7 × 152.1 cm)

Centennial gift of the Woodward
Foundation
1975-81-10

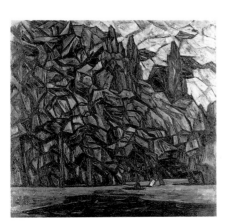

**Manievich, Abraham Anshelovich**
American, born Belorussia,
1881–1942
*Park Fantasy, Autumn, Kiev*
c. 1918
Oil on canvas
36 × 35 13/16" (91.4 × 91 cm)

Gift of Christian Brinton
1941-79-98

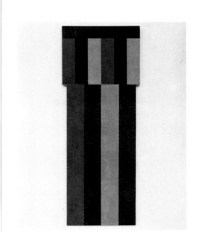

**Marden, Brice**
American, born 1938
*Coda*
1983–84
Oil and wax on canvas
120 × 39 × 9"
(304.8 × 99.1 × 22.9 cm)

Purchased with funds contributed
by the Daniel W. Dietrich
Foundation in honor of Mrs. H.
Gates Lloyd, and gifts (by
exchange) of Samuel S. White
3rd and Vera White and Mr. and
Mrs. Charles C. G. Chaplin
1985-22-1

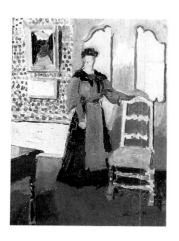

**Marinot, Maurice**
French, 1882–1960
*Helen by a Chair*
1904
On reverse: MARINOT / 1904 /
HELENE / A LA CHAISE
Oil on panel
13 × 9 1/4" (33 × 23.5 cm)

Gift of Mlle Florence Marinot
1967-98-1

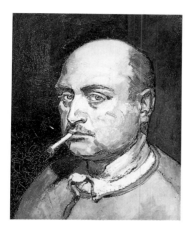

**Marinot, Maurice**
*Self-Portrait*
1927
On reverse: 626 / MARINOT /
1927 / AUTO PORTRAIT
Oil on canvas
16 1/4 × 13 1/8" (41.3 × 33.3 cm)

Gift of Mlle Florence Marinot
1967-98-2

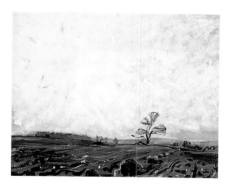

**Marinot, Maurice**
*Landscape*
1953
Lower right: Marinot
Oil on cardboard
13 × 16 3/16" (33 × 41.1 cm)

Gift of Mlle Florence Marinot
1967-98-3

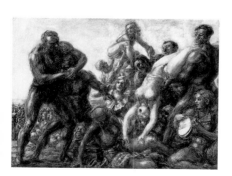

**Marsh, Reginald**
American, 1898–1954
*Coney Island Beach*
1932
Lower right: Marsh / 1932
Tempera on Masonite
36 1/8 × 48 1/8" (91.8 × 122.2 cm)

Gift of the estate of Felicia Meyer
Marsh
1979-98-1

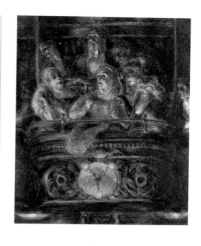

**Marsh, Reginald**
*They Pay to Be Seen*
1934
Lower right: REGINALD MARSH
1934
Oil on canvas
23 3/4 × 19 15/16" (60.3 × 50.6 cm)

Bequest of Margaretta S.
Hinchman
1955-96-8

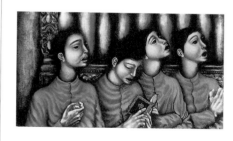

**Martin, Agnes**
American, born Canada,
born 1912
*The Rose*
1965
On reverse: "The Rose" / Acryllic
72" × 72" / a. martin '65
Acrylic on canvas
72 × 72" (182.9 × 182.9 cm)

Centennial gift of the Woodward
Foundation
1975-81-11

**Martínez de Hoyos, Ricardo**
Mexican, born 1918
*Choir Boys*
1942
Lower right: Ricardo Martínez /
de Hoyos 7-42
Oil on canvas
20 1/2 × 34 5/8" (52.1 × 87.9 cm)

Gift of Mr. and Mrs. Henry
Clifford
1947-29-2

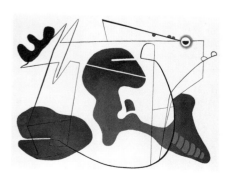

**Mason, Alice Trumbull**
American, 1904–1971
*Brown Shapes White*
1941
On reverse: Alice Trumbull
Mason / 40 Monroe St., / New
York City, / Oil Painting 1941
Oil on panel
23 15/16 × 31 3/4" (60.8 × 80.6 cm)

A. E. Gallatin Collection
1952-61-76

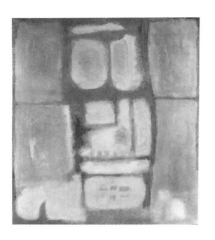

**Massey, John L.**
American, born 1925
*Boy and Balloon*
c. 1958
Oil on canvas
50 × 43" (127 × 109.2 cm)

Purchased with the Adele Haas
Turner and Beatrice Pastorius
Turner Memorial Fund
1959-12-5

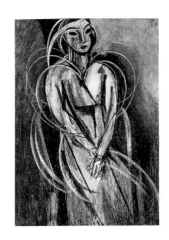

**Matisse, Henri**
*Mademoiselle Yvonne Landsberg*
1914
Lower left: Henri-Matisse 1914
Oil on canvas
58 × 38 3/8" (147.3 × 97.5 cm)

The Louise and Walter Arensberg
Collection
1950-134-130

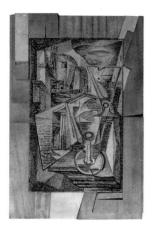

**Masson, André**
French, 1896–1987
*Italian Postcard*
The frame was made by Pierre
Legrain (French, 1889–1929)
1925
On reverse: André Masson
Oil on canvas
16 1/4 × 9 7/16" (41.3 × 24 cm)

A. E. Gallatin Collection
1952-61-77

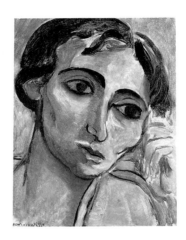

**Matisse, Henri**
*Head of a Woman*
1917
Lower left: Henri.Matisse
Oil on panel
13 3/4 × 10 5/8" (34.9 × 27 cm)

The Samuel S. White 3rd and
Vera White Collection
1967-30-52

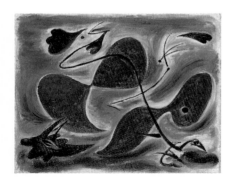

**Masson, André**
*Cockfight*
1930
On reverse: André Masson
Oil on canvas
8 9/16 × 10 5/8" (21.7 × 27 cm)

A. E. Gallatin Collection
1952-61-78

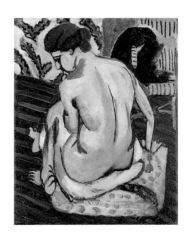

**Matisse, Henri**
*Seated Nude, Back Turned*
1917
Lower left: Henri.Matisse
Oil on canvas
24 1/2 × 18 9/16" (62.2 × 47.1 cm)

The Samuel S. White 3rd and
Vera White Collection
1967-30-53

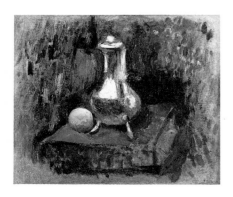

**Matisse, Henri**
French, 1869–1954
*Still Life*
c. 1901
Lower right: Henri-Matisse
Oil on canvas
18 1/4 × 22" (46.3 × 55.9 cm)

The Albert M. Greenfield and
Elizabeth M. Greenfield
Collection
1974-178-35

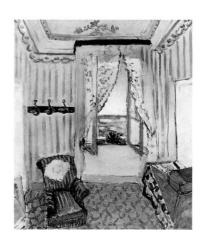

**Matisse, Henri**
*Interior at Nice (Room at the
Beau Rivage)*
1917–18
Lower right: Henri-Matisse
Oil on canvas
29 × 23 3/4" (73.7 × 60.3 cm)

A. E. Gallatin Collection
1952-61-79

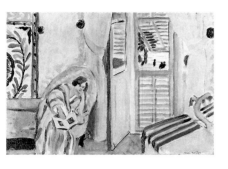

**Matisse, Henri**
*Interior at Nice (Woman Seated in an Armchair)*
1919 or 1920
Lower right: Henri.Matisse
Oil on canvas
18 × 25 ³/₄" (45.7 × 65.4 cm)

Gift of Mr. and Mrs. R. Sturgis Ingersoll
1944-88-1

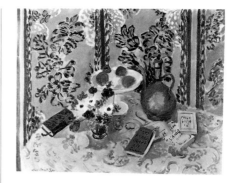

**Matisse, Henri**
*Still Life (Histoire Juive)*
1924
Lower left: Henri-Matisse; on books: HISTOIR[E] / JUIVE; L'AMO / ROMA; PHILO / SOPH / IE
Oil on canvas
32 ¹/₈ × 39 ¹/₂" (81.6 × 100.3 cm)

The Samuel S. White 3rd and Vera White Collection
1967-30-56

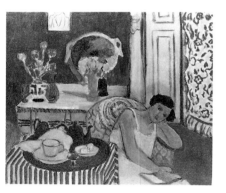

**Matisse, Henri**
*Breakfast*
1921
Lower right: Henri Matisse
Oil on canvas
25 ¹/₄ × 29 ¹/₁₆" (64.1 × 73.8 cm)

The Samuel S. White 3rd and Vera White Collection
1967-30-55

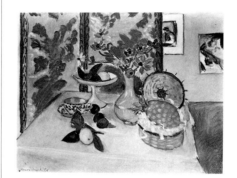

**Matisse, Henri**
*Still Life on a Table*
1925
Lower left: Henri-Matisse
Oil on canvas
31 ³/₄ × 39 ¹/₄" (80.6 × 99.7 cm)

Gift of Henry P. McIlhenny
1964-77-1

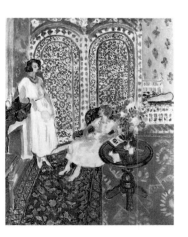

**Matisse, Henri**
*The Moorish Screen*
1921
Lower right: Henri Matisse; on reverse: Les Jeunes filles au paravent, Nice, 1922, Henri Matisse
Oil on canvas
36 ³/₁₆ × 29 ¹/₄" (91.9 × 74.3 cm)

Bequest of Lisa Norris Elkins
1950-92-9

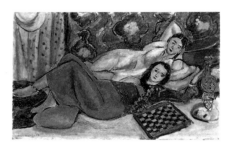

**Matisse, Henri**
*Two Models Resting*
1928
Lower left: Henri-Matisse 28
Oil on canvas
18 ¹/₂ × 28 ⁷/₈" (47 × 73.3 cm)

Gift of Mrs. Frank Abercrombie Elliott
1964-107-1

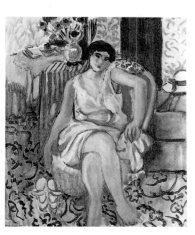

**Matisse, Henri**
*Woman Seated in an Armchair*
1923
Lower left: Henri.Matisse
Oil on canvas
18 ¹/₄ × 15 ¹/₂" (46.3 × 39.4 cm)

The Louis E. Stern Collection
1963-181-45

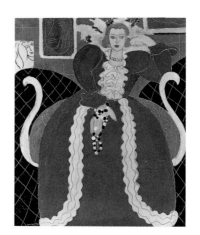

**Matisse, Henri**
*Woman in Blue*
1937
Lower left: Henri Matisse / 37
Oil on canvas
36 ¹/₂ × 29" (92.7 × 73.7 cm)

Gift of Mrs. John Wintersteen
1956-23-1

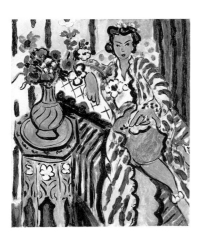

**Matisse, Henri**
*Yellow Odalisque*
1937
Lower right: 37 / Henri Matisse
Oil on canvas
21 3/4 × 18 1/8" (55.2 × 46 cm)

The Samuel S. White 3rd and
Vera White Collection
1967-30-57

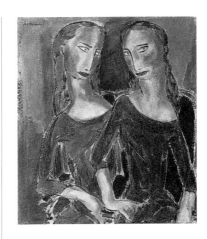

**Maurer, Alfred Henry**
*Two Figures*
c. 1925
Upper left: A. H. Maurer
Oil on composition board
21 5/8 × 18" (54.9 × 45.7 cm)

Gift of Carl Zigrosser
1942-15-1

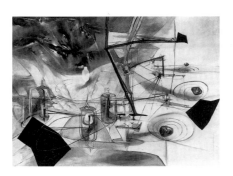

**Matta, Roberto**
Chilean, born 1911
*The Bachelors Twenty Years After*
1943
Oil on canvas
38 × 40" (96.52 × 101.6 cm)

Purchased with the Edith H. Bell
Fund, the Edward and Althea
Budd Fund, gifts (by exchange)
of Mr. and Mrs. William P. Wood
and Bernard Davis, and bequest
(by exchange) of Miss Anna
Warren Ingersoll
1989-51-1

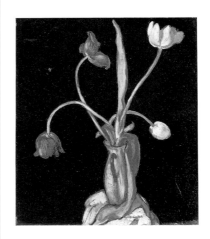

**Maurer, Alfred Henry**
*Vase of Flowers*
c. 1925
Center bottom: A.H. Maurer
Oil on canvas on panel
22 × 18 1/8" (55.9 × 46 cm)

Gift of Carl Zigrosser
1972-237-7

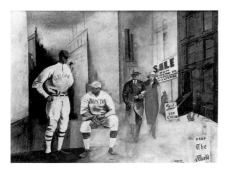

**Mauny, Jacques**
French, 1893–1962
*New York*
1925
Lower right: MAUNY / NEW
YORK; on figures: CHICAG[O];
BOSTON; on signs: SALE / NOW /
GOING ON / BIGGEST BARGAINS
/ OF A LIFETIME; Reid's / IT'S
THE BEST / ICE / CREAM; READ
/ The World
Oil on canvas
17 × 21 3/8" (43.2 × 54.3 cm)

A. E. Gallatin Collection
1945-14-1

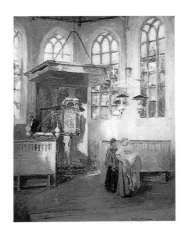

**Melchers, Julius Gari**
American, 1860–1932
*Baptism (Church Interior)*
c. 1900
Lower right: Gari Melchers
Oil on canvas
43 1/2 × 33 3/16" (110.5 × 84.3 cm)

The Alex Simpson, Jr., Collection
1946-5-1

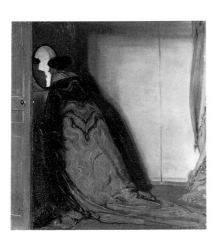

**Maurer, Alfred Henry**
American, 1868–1932
*The Peacock (Portrait of a Woman)*
c. 1903
Lower left: Alfred H. / Maurer
Oil on canvas
36 1/16 × 32 3/8" (91.6 × 82.2 cm)

Purchased with the W. P.
Wilstach Fund
W1903-1-7

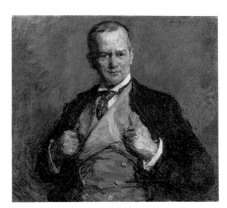

**Melchers, Julius Gari**
*Portrait of a Friend (Portrait of Christian Brinton)*
1910
Upper right: Gari Melchers.
Oil on canvas
27 1/8 × 29 15/16" (68.9 × 76 cm)

Gift of Christian Brinton
1941-79-81

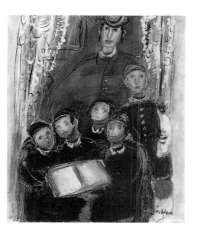

**Menkès, Sigmund**
American, born Poland,
born 1896
*Family Group*
c. 1935
Lower right: Menkes
Oil on canvas
25 ⅝ × 21 ¼" (65.1 × 54 cm)

Gift of Bernard Davis
1950-43-2

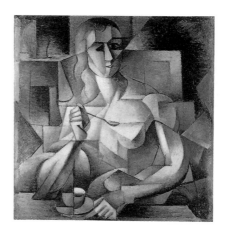

**Metzinger, Jean**
*Tea Time (Woman with a Teaspoon)*
1911
Lower right: 1911 / J. Metzinger
Oil on cardboard
29 ⅞ × 27 ⅝" (75.9 × 70.2 cm)

The Louise and Walter Arensberg
Collection
1950-134-139

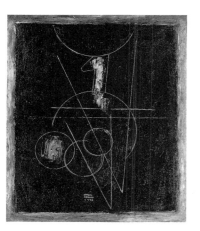

**Merida, Carlos**
Guatemalan, 1891–1984
*Deer Dance*
1935
Center bottom: CARLOS /
MERIDA / 1935
Oil on canvas
24 ³⁄₁₆ × 20 ³⁄₁₆" (61.4 × 51.3 cm)

The Louise and Walter Arensberg
Collection
1950-134-134

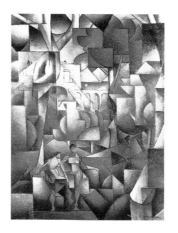

**Metzinger, Jean**
*The Bathers*
1913
Lower right: J. Metzinger; on
reverse: Metzinger "Les
Baigneuses" / Meudon, 1913
Oil on canvas
58 ⅜ × 41 ⅞" (148.3 × 106.4 cm)

The Louise and Walter Arensberg
Collection
1950-134-140

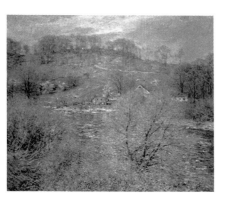

**Metcalf, Willard Leroy**
American, 1858–1925
*Blossoming Willows*
c. 1920
Lower left: W. L. METCALF
Oil on canvas
26 ¼ × 29 ⅛" (66.7 × 74 cm)

The Alex Simpson, Jr., Collection
1946-5-2

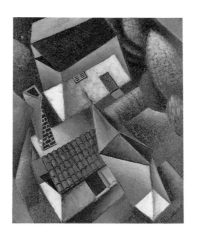

**Metzinger, Jean**
*Landscape with Roofs*
c. 1914
Lower right: JMetzinger
Oil on panel
16 ⅛ × 12 ⅞" (41 × 32.7 cm)

The Louise and Walter Arensberg
Collection
1950-134-138

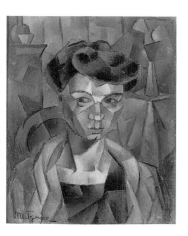

**Metzinger, Jean**
French, 1883–1956
*Portrait of Madame Metzinger*
1911
Lower left: JMetzinger
Oil on canvas board on panel
10 ¾ × 8 ½" (27.3 × 21.6 cm)

A. E. Gallatin Collection
1952-61-81

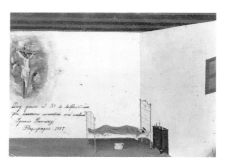

**Mexican, unknown artist**
*Recovery from an Illness*
Retable
1927
Center left: Doy gracias al Sr. de
la Penitencia / por haverme
consedido me salud / Ignacio
Ramirez, / Flaquepaque 1927
Oil on tin
7 × 9 ⅞" (17.8 × 25.1 cm)

The Louise and Walter Arensberg
Collection
1950-134-493

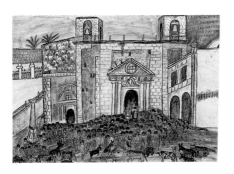

**Mexican, unknown artist**
*The Blessing of the Animals*
c. 1930
Upper right: LA BENDICION /
DE LOS ANIMALES / EN EL
EXCOMVENTO / DE TAXCO,
EDO. GRO. / EL 17 DE ENERO
DE / 1930.
Oil on panel
9 7/8 × 13 3/8" (25.1 × 34 cm)

Gift of Carl Zigrosser
1972-237-11

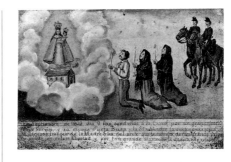

**Middle American, unknown artist**
*Delivery from Prison*
Retable
After 1902
Across bottom: En Septiembre de
1902 dia 9 sue conducido a la
Carcel por un gran crimen. /
Felipe Servin, y su esposa Justa
Busa y la Sra Madre lo
encomendaron a la / Milagrosa
Imagen de la Madre Sma de
Loreto que lo salvara de tan
grande pelig[ro] / y quedo en
entera libertad y por tan grande
maravailla le dedica este retablo.
Oil on tin
7 × 10" (17.8 × 25.4 cm)

The Louise and Walter Arensberg
Collection
1950-134-813

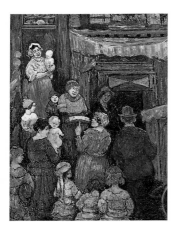

**Meyers, Jerome**
American, 1867–1940
*The Tambourine (East Side New York)*
c. 1905
Lower left: JEROME MEYERS
Oil on canvas
15 15/16 × 12" (40.5 × 30.5 cm)

Centennial gift of Mrs. Francis P.
Garvan
1976-164-2

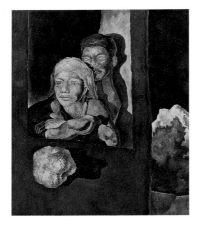

**Meza, Guillermo**
Mexican, born 1917
*Saints Monica and Augustine*
c. 1940
Lower right: G. MEZA
Oil on paper on Masonite
18 × 15 1/8" (45.7 × 38.4 cm)

Gift of Dr. and Mrs. MacKinley
Helm
1951-33-1

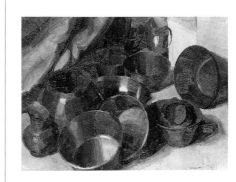

**Mingorance, Juan**
Spanish, active Mexico,
active 20th century
*Coppers*
c. 1960
Lower right: Mingorance
Oil on canvas
27 3/8 × 35 3/8" (69.5 × 89.8 cm)

Gift of Victor Sanchez-Mesas
1963-214-1

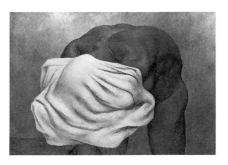

**Meza, Guillermo**
*The White Shirt*
1946
Lower right: G. Meza. a. / 1946
Oil on canvas
30 1/8 × 43 5/8" (76.5 × 110.8 cm)

Gift of Mrs. Herbert Cameron
Morris
1948-11-1

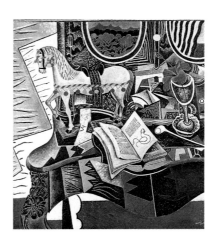

**Miró, Joan**
Spanish, 1893–1983
*Horse, Pipe, and Red Flower*
1920
Lower right: Miró / 1920
Oil on canvas
32 1/2 × 29 1/2" (82.5 × 74.9 cm)

Gift of Mr. and Mrs. C. Earle
Miller
1986-97-1

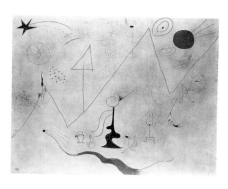

**Miró, Joan**
*The Hermitage*
1924
Lower left: Miró. / 1924.; on reverse: Joan Miró / L'Ermitage / 1924
Oil?, crayon, and graphite on canvas
45 × 57 9/16" (114.3 × 146.2 cm)

The Louise and Walter Arensberg Collection
1950-134-141

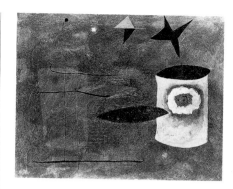

**Miró, Joan**
*Painting*
1926
Lower right: Miró. / 1926.; on reverse: Joan Miró. / 1926.
Oil and aqueous medium on canvas
8 5/8 × 10 5/8" (21.9 × 27 cm)

A. E. Gallatin Collection
1952-61-83

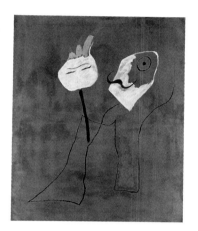

**Miró, Joan**
*Man and Woman*
1925
Lower right: Miró. / 1925.; on reverse: Joan Miró / 1925
Oil? on canvas
39 3/8 × 31 13/16" (100 × 80.8 cm)

The Louise and Walter Arensberg Collection
1950-134-142

**Miró, Joan**
*Painting (Fratellini)*
1927
On reverse: Joan Miró / 1927
Oil and aqueous medium on canvas
51 1/4 × 38 1/4" (130.2 × 97.1 cm)

A. E. Gallatin Collection
1952-16-1

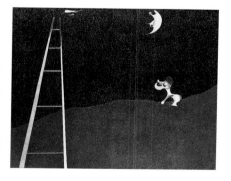

**Miró, Joan**
*Dog Barking at the Moon*
1926
Lower left: Miró. / 1926.; on reverse: Joan Miró / Chien aboyant la lune / 1926
Oil on canvas
28 3/4 × 36 1/4" (73 × 92.1 cm)

A. E. Gallatin Collection
1952-61-82

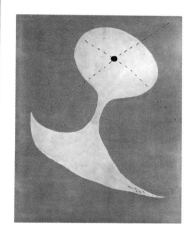

**Miró, Joan**
*Head*
1927
Lower right: Miró. / 1927.; on reverse: Joan Miró / 1927
Oil? and graphite on canvas
57 1/2 × 44 5/8" (146 × 113.3 cm)

The Albert M. Greenfield and Elizabeth M. Greenfield Collection
1974-178-37

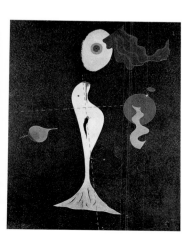

**Miró, Joan**
*Nude*
1926
Center bottom: Miró. / 1926.; on reverse: Joan Miró / Nu / 1926
Oil on canvas
36 3/8 × 29" (92.4 × 73.7 cm)

The Louise and Walter Arensberg Collection
1950-134-143

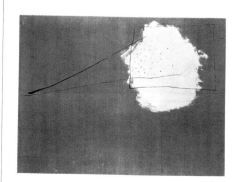

**Miró, Joan**
*Untitled Painting*
1927
Lower left: Miró. / 1927.; on reverse: Joan Miró / 1927
Oil? on canvas
44 11/16 × 57 1/2" (113.5 × 146 cm)

The Albert M. Greenfield and Elizabeth M. Greenfield Collection
1974-178-36

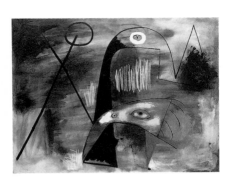

**Miró, Joan**
*Man, Woman, and Child*
1931
Center bottom: Miró. / 2-31.; on
reverse: Homme, femme et enfant
Oil and/or aqueous medium on
canvas
35 3/16 × 45 3/4" (89.4 × 116.2 cm)

The Louise and Walter Arensberg
Collection
1950-134-144

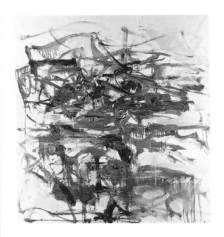

**Mitchell, Joan**
American, 1926–1992
*Untitled*
c. 1960
Oil on canvas
70 3/4 × 63" (179.7 × 160 cm)

Gift of Mr. and Mrs. Joseph
Slifka
1971-264-1

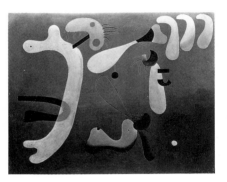

**Miró, Joan**
*Painting*
1933
On reverse: Miró 8-3-33
Oil and aqueous medium on
canvas
51 3/8 × 64 1/4" (130.5 × 163.2 cm)

A. E. Gallatin Collection
1952-61-85

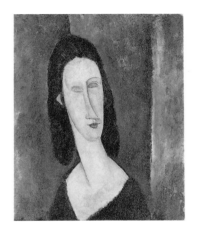

**Modigliani, Amedeo**
Italian, 1884–1920
*Blue Eyes (Portrait of Madame
Jeanne Hebuterne)*
1917
Upper right: Modigliani
Oil on canvas
21 1/2 × 16 7/8" (54.6 × 42.9 cm)

The Samuel S. White 3rd and
Vera White Collection
1967-30-59

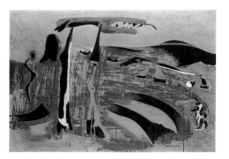

**Miró, Joan**
*Person in the Presence of Nature*
1935
Oil and aqueous medium on
panel
29 5/16 × 41 3/16" (74.9 × 104.6 cm)

The Louise and Walter Arensberg
Collection
1950-134-149

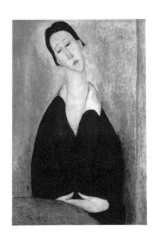

**Modigliani, Amedeo**
*Portrait of a Polish Woman*
1919
Upper right: Modigliani
Oil on canvas
39 1/2 × 25 1/2" (100.3 × 64.8 cm)

The Louis E. Stern Collection
1963-181-48

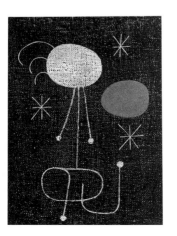

**Miró, Joan**
*Woman in Front of the Sun*
1944
On reverse: Miró. / 1944
Oil and aqueous medium on
burlap
13 1/8 × 9 5/8" (33.3 × 24.4 cm)

The Louis E. Stern Collection
1963-181-47

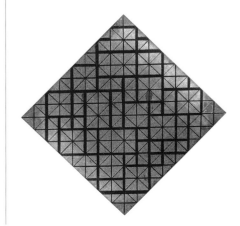

**Mondrian, Piet**
Dutch, 1872–1944
*Composition in Black and Gray*
1919
Center bottom: PM / 19
Oil on canvas
23 5/8 × 23 11/16" (60 × 60.2 cm)
diagonal

The Louise and Walter Arensberg
Collection
1950-134-151

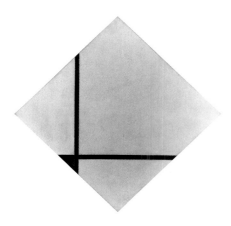

**Mondrian, Piet**
*Composition with Blue*
1926
Lower left: PM 26
Oil on canvas
24 1/16 × 24 1/16" (61.1 × 61.1 cm)
diagonal

A. E. Gallatin Collection
1952-61-87

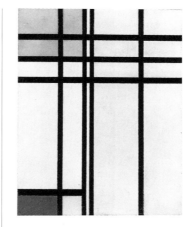

**Mondrian, Piet**
*Opposition of Lines, Red and Yellow*
1937
Lower left: 37; lower right: PM;
on reverse: PIET MONDRIAN '37.
/ Opposition de lignes, / de rouge
et jaune.
Oil on canvas
17 1/8 × 13 1/4" (43.5 × 33.6 cm)

A. E. Gallatin Collection
1952-61-90

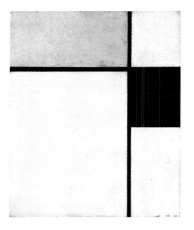

**Mondrian, Piet**
*Composition with Blue and Yellow*
1932
Lower right: P M 32; on reverse:
PIET MONDRIAN
Oil on canvas
16 3/8 × 13 1/8" (41.6 × 33.3 cm)

A. E. Gallatin Collection
1952-61-88

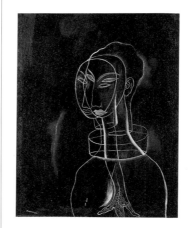

**Montenegro, Roberto**
Mexican, 1881–1968
*The Double*
1938
Lower left: MONTENEGRO.
Oil on panel
26 × 20" (66 × 50.8 cm)

The Louise and Walter Arensberg
Collection
1950-134-153

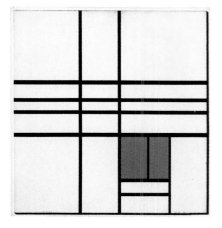

**Mondrian, Piet**
*Composition*
1936
Lower right: PM 36; on reverse:
P MONDRIAN
Oil on canvas
28 3/4 × 26 1/16" (73 × 66.2 cm)

The Louise and Walter Arensberg
Collection
1950-134-152

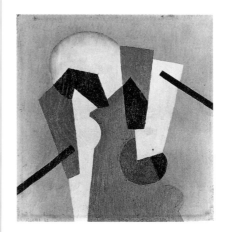

**Morris, George Lovett
Kingsland**
American, 1905–1975
*Composition*
1936
On reverse: George L. K. / Morris
/ 1936
Oil on canvas
8 7/8 × 8 1/8" (22.5 × 20.6 cm)

A. E. Gallatin Collection
1946-70-14

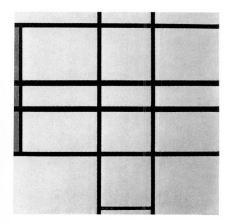

**Mondrian, Piet**
*Composition with White and Red*
1936
Center bottom: P M 36; on
reverse: P. MONDRIAN—PARIS /
Composition—blanc et rouge
Oil on canvas
19 7/8 × 20 1/4" (50.5 × 51.4 cm)

A. E. Gallatin Collection
1952-61-89

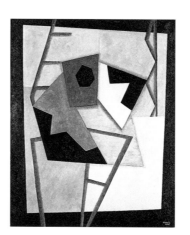

**Morris, George Lovett
Kingsland**
*Composition*
1940
Lower right: Morris / 1940
Oil on canvas
30 3/16 × 23 1/8" (76.7 × 58.7 cm)

A. E. Gallatin Collection
1946-70-15

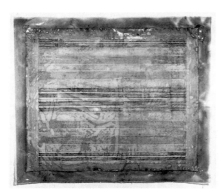

**Moses, Ed**
American, born 1926
*Ill. Hegemann 63*
1972
Pigment and resin on canvas
61 × 74" (154.9 × 188 cm)

Purchased with the Adele Haas
Turner and Beatrice Pastorius
Turner Memorial Fund
1975-38-1

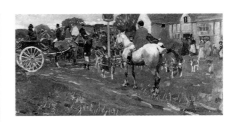

**Munnings, Sir Alfred**
*The Meet*
1902
Lower left: A. J. MUNNINGS /
1902
Oil on canvas
10 ³/₈ × 20" (26.3 × 50.8 cm)

Bequest of Charlotte Dorrance
Wright
1978-1-42

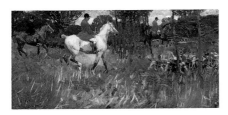

**Munnings, Sir Alfred**
English, 1878–1959
*Going Out*
1902
Lower left: A. J. MUNNINGS /
1902
Oil on canvas
10 ³/₈ × 20 ¹/₈" (26.3 × 51.1 cm)

Bequest of Charlotte Dorrance
Wright
1978-1-41

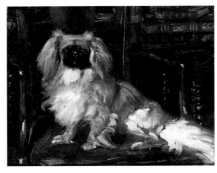

**Munnings, Sir Alfred**
*Pekingese*
1909
Center right: A. J. MUNNINGS /
1909.
Oil on panel
12 ⁷/₈ × 16" (32.7 × 40.6 cm)

Bequest of Charlotte Dorrance
Wright
1978-1-39

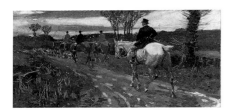

**Munnings, Sir Alfred**
*Homeward Bound*
1902
Lower left: A. J. MUNNINGS /
1902
Oil on canvas
10 ¹/₂ × 20 ¹/₄" (26.7 × 51.4 cm)

Bequest of Charlotte Dorrance
Wright
1978-1-43

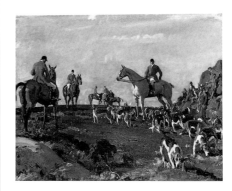

**Munnings, Sir Alfred**
*Hunting on Zennor Hill*
c. 1910
Lower left: A. J. MUNNINGS
Oil on canvas
30 ⁵/₈ × 35 ¹/₂" (77.8 × 90.2 cm)

Bequest of Charlotte Dorrance
Wright
1978-1-47

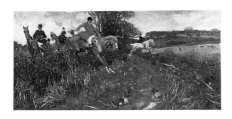

**Munnings, Sir Alfred**
*Racing for the Kill*
1902
Lower right: A. J. MUNNINGS /
1902
Oil on canvas
10 ¹/₂ × 20 ¹/₄" (26.7 × 51.4 cm)

Bequest of Charlotte Dorrance
Wright
1978-1-44

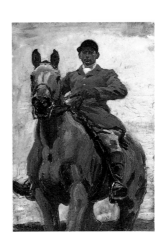

**Munnings, Sir Alfred**
*Portrait of Ned Osborne on Grey Tick*
c. 1910
Lower right: A. J. MUNNINGS
Oil on canvas
30 × 20" (76.2 × 50.8 cm)

Bequest of Charlotte Dorrance
Wright
1978-1-46

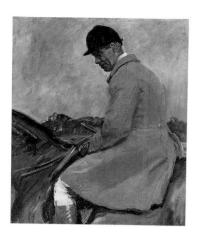

**Munnings, Sir Alfred**
*Portrait of Nobby Grey*
c. 1910
Lower right: A. J. MUNNINGS
Oil on canvas
24 3/16 × 20 1/8" (61.4 × 51.1 cm)

Bequest of Charlotte Dorrance
Wright
1978-1-40

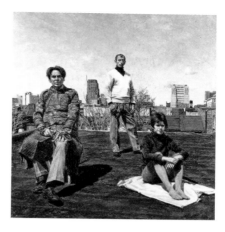

**Neff, Edith**
American, born 1943
*The Magi*
1978
On reverse: Neff
Oil on canvas
71 × 67 1/2" (180.3 × 171.4 cm)

Purchased with the Julius Bloch
Memorial Fund
1983-1-1

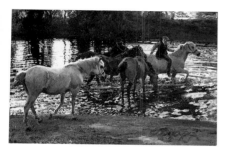

**Munnings, Sir Alfred**
*Welsh Ponies*
1911
Lower right: A. J. MUNNINGS /
1911
Oil on canvas
47 × 67" (119.4 × 170.2 cm)

Bequest of Charlotte Dorrance
Wright
1978-1-38

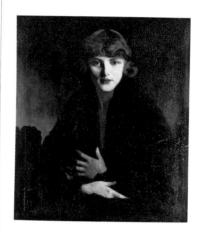

**Neilson, Raymond Perry
Rodgers**
American, 1881–1964
*Portrait of a Woman*
c. 1925
Lower left: Raymond Neilson
Oil on canvas
30 × 24" (76.2 × 61 cm)

Gift of Rodman A. Heeren
1970-255-20

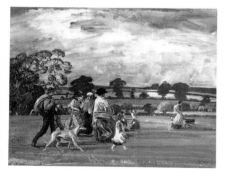

**Munnings, Sir Alfred**
*Hop Pickers, Hampshire*
c. 1913
Lower right: A. J. MUNNINGS
Oil on canvas
28 1/8 × 36" (71.4 × 91.4 cm)

Bequest of Charlotte Dorrance
Wright
1978-1-45

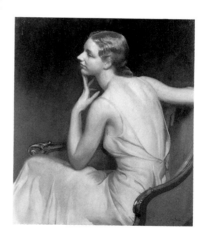

**Neilson, Raymond Perry
Rodgers**
*Portrait of Miss Margaret Wall*
c. 1925
Lower right: Raymond P. R
Neilson
Oil on canvas
36 × 30 1/8" (91.4 × 76.5 cm)

Gift of Rodman A. Heeren
1972-252-21

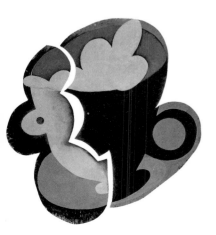

**Murray, Elizabeth**
American, born 1940
*Just in Time*
1981
Oil on canvas
106 × 97" (269.2 × 246.4 cm)

Purchased with the Edward and
Althea Budd Fund, the Adele
Haas Turner and Beatrice
Pastorius Turner Memorial Fund,
and funds contributed by Marion
Boulton Stroud and Lorine E.
Vogt
1981-94-1a, b

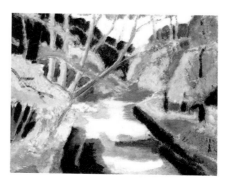

**Newman, Carl**
American, 1858–1932
*Landscape*
c. 1915
Oil on canvas
25 1/8 × 30 1/8" (63.8 × 76.5 cm)

Gift of Dr. and Mrs. Milton Luria
in memory of Mr. and Mrs.
Samuel Herman
1976-37-1

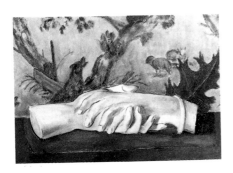

**Newton, Alice M.**
American, active c. 1930–c. 1940
*Clasped Hands*
1930
Lower right: ALICE M. NEWTON
Oil on canvas
12 × 16" (30.5 × 40.6 cm)

Gift of Frank and Alice Osborn
1966-68-32

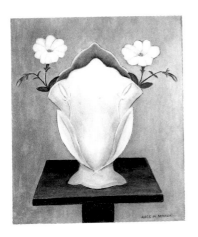

**Newton, Alice M.**
*White Vase*
c. 1930
Lower right: ALICE M. NEWTON
Oil on canvas
20 × 16 1/8" (50.8 × 41 cm)

Gift of Frank and Alice Osborn
1966-68-31

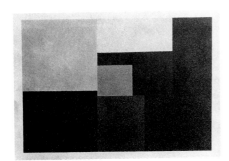

**Nicholson, Ben**
English, 1894–1982
*Painting*
1936
On reverse: Ben Nicholson 1936
Oil on canvas on panel
15 × 20" (38.1 × 50.8 cm)

A. E. Gallatin Collection
1945-91-4

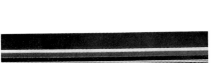

**Noland, Kenneth**
American, born 1924
*Continue*
1967
On reverse: Continue 1967 /
Kenneth Noland
Acrylic on canvas
32 5/8 × 203 1/16" (82.9 × 515.8 cm)

Centennial gift of the Woodward
Foundation
1975-81-12

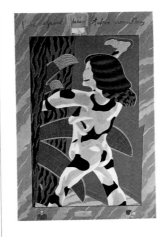

**Nutt, Jim (James Tureman)**
American, born 1938
*The Cards Were in His Favor*
1970–71
Across top: I'm afraid he's taken
something; bottom: time will
tell; on reverse: "The [cards] /
were in his / favour, un. . . ." /
hand-delt and reshuffled By / Jim
Nutt
Acrylic on panel
42 1/2 × 27" (107.9 × 68.6 cm)

Gift of Marion Boulton Stroud
1980-59-1

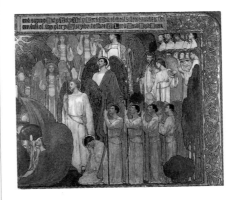

**Oakley, Violet**
American, 1874–1961
*Sketch for the Right Mural of "The
Heavenly Host"*
For the mural in All Angels
Church, New York
c. 1900
Across top: and saying Holy Holy
Holy Lord God of hosts heaven
and earth / are full of thy glory
Glory be to thee O Lord Most
High Amen
Oil and charcoal on paper on
canvas
45 1/4 × 55 1/2" (114.9 × 141 cm)

Purchased with the Lola Downin
Peck Fund
1981-59-1

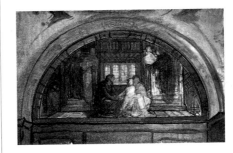

**Oakley, Violet**
*Sketch for "The Child and
Tradition"*
For the lunette in the Charlton
Yarnall house, Philadelphia
1910–11
Oil on canvas
36 × 54" (91.4 × 137.2 cm)

Gift of the Violet Oakley
Memorial Foundation
1984-67-3

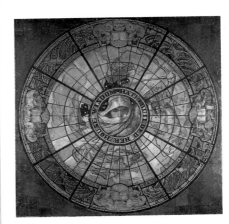

**Oakley, Violet**
*Sketch for "Wisdom"*
For the stained-glass dome in the
Charlton Yarnall house,
Philadelphia
1910–11
Center: WISDOM HATH BUILDED
HER HOUSE; outer circle:
WHOSO FINDETH ME FINDETH
LIFE FOR BY ME THY DAYS
SHALL BE MULTIPLIED
Oil on canvas
101" (256.5 cm) diameter

Gift of the Violet Oakley
Memorial Foundation
1984-67-2

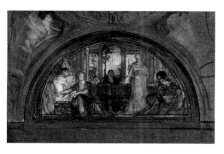

**Oakley, Violet**
*Sketch for "Youth and the Arts"*
For the lunette in the Charlton
Yarnall house, Philadelphia
1910–11
Oil on canvas
36 × 54 3/16" (91.4 × 137.6 cm)

Gift of the Violet Oakley
Memorial Foundation
1984-67-4

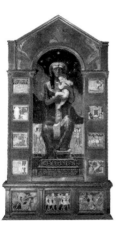

**Oakley, Violet**
*Sketch for "The Life of Moses"*
For the painting in the Samuel S.
Fleisher Art Memorial,
Philadelphia (F29-1)
1927–29
Bottom center: AND THE CHILD
GREW AND HE BECAME HER
SON / AND SHE CALLED HIS
NAME MOSES & SHE SAID /
BECAVSE I DREW HIM OVT OF
THE WATER
Oil on canvas
67 5/8 × 33 7/8" (171.7 × 86 cm)

Gift of the Violet Oakley
Memorial Foundation
1984-67-1

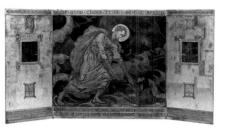

**Oakley, Violet**
*Traveling Altarpiece*
Triptych
1944
Oil on metal
Center panel: 36 × 36 1/4"
(91.4 × 92.1 cm); wings [each]:
36 × 18" (91.4 × 45.7 cm)

Gift of Joseph Flom and Martin
Horwitz
1975-180-1

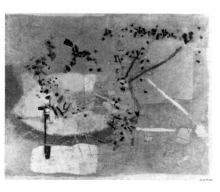

**Okada, Kenzo**
American, born Japan,
1902–1982
*Blue Abstraction*
c. 1952
Lower right: Kenzo Okada
Oil on canvas
57 1/8 × 69 7/8" (145.1 × 177.5 cm)

The Albert M. Greenfield and
Elizabeth M. Greenfield
Collection
1974-178-39

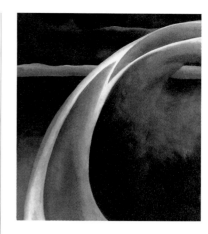

**O'Keeffe, Georgia**
American, 1887–1986
*Orange and Red Streak*
1919
Oil on canvas
27 × 23" (68.6 × 58.4 cm)

Bequest of Georgia O'Keeffe for
the Alfred Stieglitz Collection
1987-70-3

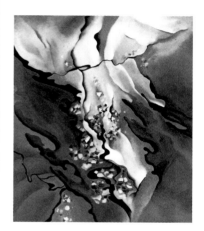

**O'Keeffe, Georgia**
*From the Lake No. 3*
1924
Oil on canvas
36 × 30" (91.4 × 76.2 cm)

Bequest of Georgia O'Keeffe for
the Alfred Stieglitz Collection
1987-70-2

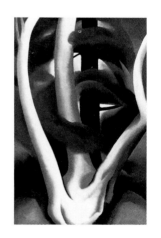

**O'Keeffe, Georgia**
*Birch and Pine Tree No. 1*
1925
Oil on canvas
35 × 22" (88.9 × 55.9 cm)

Bequest of Georgia O'Keeffe for
the Alfred Stieglitz Collection
1987-70-1

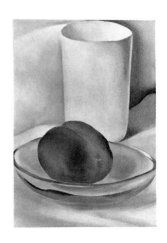

**O'Keeffe, Georgia**
*Peach and Glass*
1927
Oil on canvas
9 1/8 × 6 1/16" (23.2 × 15.4 cm)

Gift of Dr. Herman Lorber
1944-95-4

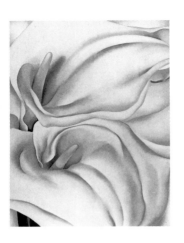

**O'Keeffe, Georgia**
*Two Calla Lilies on Pink*
1928
Oil on canvas
40 × 30" (101.6 × 76.2 cm)

Bequest of Georgia O'Keeffe for
the Alfred Stieglitz Collection
1987-70-4

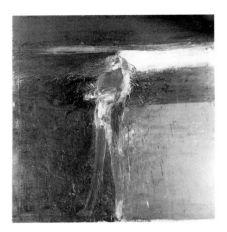

**Oliveira, Nathan**
American, born 1928
*Standing Figure*
1960
Center bottom: Oliveira 60
Oil on canvas
77 1/2 × 71 7/8" (196.8 × 182.6 cm)

Gift of Mr. and Mrs. David N.
Pincus
1968-223-1

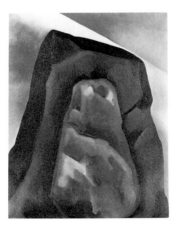

**O'Keeffe, Georgia**
*After a Walk Back of Mabel's*
1929
Oil on canvas
40 × 30" (101.6 × 76.2 cm)

Gift of Dr. and Mrs. Paul Todd
Makler
1967-38-1

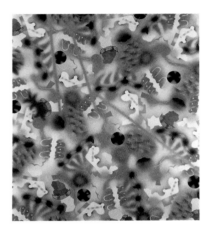

**Omwake, Leon William, Jr.
(EO Omwake)**
American, born 1946
*Recodilam Mullic*
1972
On reverse: Omwake '72
Recodilam Mullic
Acrylic on canvas
72 1/8 × 61 7/8" (183.2 × 157.2 cm)

Gift of the Cheltenham Art
Centre in memory of Tobeleah
Wechsler
1972-131-1

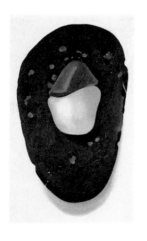

**O'Keeffe, Georgia**
*Three Small Rocks Big*
1937
Oil on canvas
20 × 12" (50.8 × 30.5 cm)

Gift of George Howe
1949-57-1

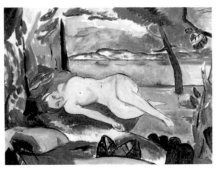

**Osborn, Frank**
American, 1887–1948
*Reclining Nude*
1930
Lower right: Frank Osborn
Oil on canvas
16 × 20 9/16" (40.6 × 52.2 cm)

Gift of Frank and Alice Osborn
1966-68-40

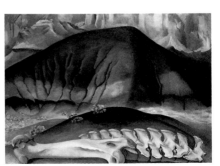

**O'Keeffe, Georgia**
*Red Hills and Bones*
1941
Oil on canvas
29 3/4 × 40" (75.6 × 101.6 cm)

The Alfred Stieglitz Collection
1949-18-109

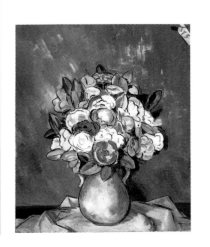

**Osborn, Frank**
*Flowers*
1933
Lower right: FRANK OSBORN /
1933.
Oil on canvas
23 7/8 × 20 1/8" (60.6 × 51.1 cm)

Gift of Frank and Alice Osborn
1966-68-33

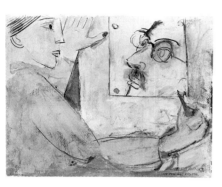

**Osborn, Frank**
*The Poor Man's Picasso*
See following painting for reverse
c. 1935
Lower right: BY F. OSBORN /
THE POOR MAN'S PICASSO.
Oil on canvas
16 × 20" (40.6 × 50.8 cm)

Gift of Frank and Alice Osborn
1966-68-41a

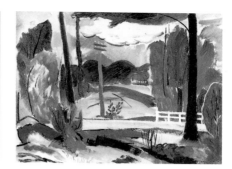

**Osborn, Frank**
*Equinox*
1937
Lower right: FRANK OSBORN—
37
Oil on canvas
12 × 16" (30.5 × 40.6 cm)

Gift of Frank and Alice Osborn
1966-68-36

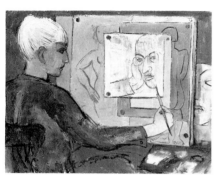

**Osborn, Frank**
*Woman Painting a Portrait*
Reverse of the preceding painting
c. 1935
Oil on canvas
16 × 20" (40.6 × 50.8 cm)

Gift of Frank and Alice Osborn
1966-68-41b

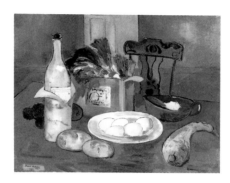

**Osborn, Frank**
*Still Life No. 2*
1937
Lower left: Frank Osborn / 1937
Oil on canvas
16 × 20" (40.6 × 50.8 cm)

Gift of Frank and Alice Osborn
1966-68-39

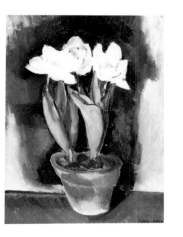

**Osborn, Frank**
*Tulips in a Pot*
c. 1935
Lower right: FRANK OSBORN
Oil on canvas
16 × 12" (40.6 × 30.5 cm)

Gift of Frank and Alice Osborn
1966-68-38

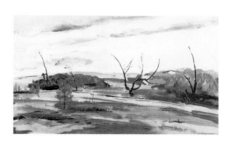

**Osborn, Frank**
*Landscape*
c. 1937
Oil on canvas
12 1/16 × 20" (30.6 × 50.8 cm)

Gift of Frank and Alice Osborn
1966-68-42

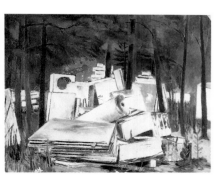

**Osborn, Frank**
*Abandoned Marble*
1936
Lower right: FRANK OSBORN—
36
Oil on canvas
16 × 20" (40.6 × 50.8 cm)

Gift of Frank and Alice Osborn
1966-68-34

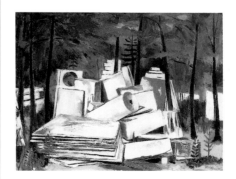

**Osborn, Frank**
*Abandoned Marble*
1940
Lower right: FRANK OSBORN
1940
Oil on canvas
26 × 32 1/8" (66 × 81.6 cm)

Gift of Frank and Alice Osborn
1966-68-37

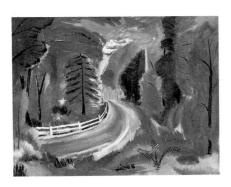

**Osborn, Frank**
*Landscape with a Road*
c. 1940
Oil on canvas
16 × 20" (40.6 × 50.8 cm)

Gift of Frank and Alice Osborn
1966-68-59

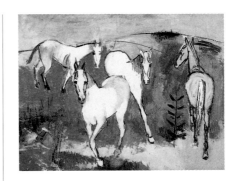

**Osborn, Frank**
*Untitled (Four Horses in a Pasture)*
c. 1948
Oil on canvas
16 ⅛ × 20" (41 × 50.8 cm)

Gift of Frank and Alice Osborn
1966-68-58

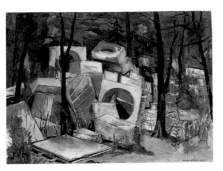

**Osborn, Frank**
*Marble Remainders*
1942
Lower right: FRANK OSBORN
1942
Oil on canvas
26 ⅛ × 34" (66.4 × 86.4 cm)

Gift of Frank and Alice Osborn
1966-68-12

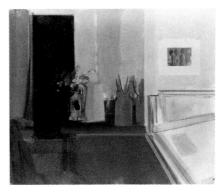

**Osborne, Elizabeth**
American, born 1936
*January Still Life*
1967
Lower right: OSBORNE
Oil on canvas
50 × 57 ⁵/₁₆" (127 × 145.6 cm)

Gift of the Women's Committee
of the Philadelphia Museum of
Art
1968-39-1

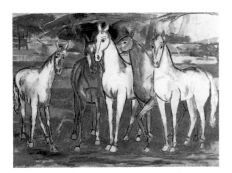

**Osborn, Frank**
*Five Horses*
1948
Lower right: FRANK OSBORN
1948
Oil on canvas
16 × 20" (40.6 × 50.8 cm)

Gift of Frank and Alice Osborn
1966-68-43

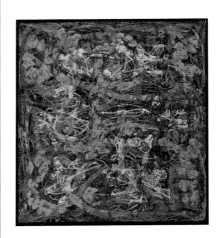

**Ossorio, Alfonso**
American, born Philippines,
1916–1990
*Time Present*
c. 1950
Oil on cardboard collage
36 × 32 ¼" (91.4 × 81.9 cm)

Gift of Mrs. Dorothy Norman
1959-30-1

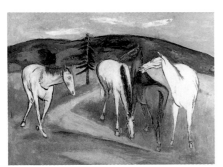

**Osborn, Frank**
*Untitled (Four Horses in a Pasture)*
c. 1948
Oil on canvas
26 × 33 ⅞" (66 × 86 cm)

Gift of Frank and Alice Osborn
1966-68-57

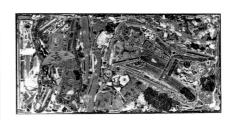

**Ossorio, Alfonso**
*Rescue*
1961–62
Mixed media on panel
47 ¹⁵/₁₆ × 96 ⅛" (121.8 ×
244.2 cm)

Gift of the artist
1969-294-4

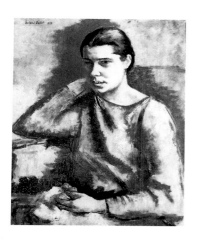

**Oudot, Roland**
French, born 1897
*Portrait of a Young Woman*
1929
Upper left: Roland Oudot 1929
Oil on canvas
28 5/8 × 23 5/8" (72.7 × 60 cm)

The Chester Dale Collection
1946-50-4

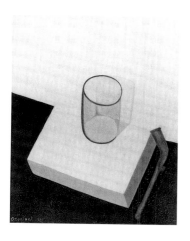

**Ozenfant, Amédée**
French, 1886–1966
*Still Life with a Glass and a Pipe*
1919
Lower left: Ozenfant 1919
Oil on canvas
13 3/4 × 10 5/8" (34.9 × 27 cm)

A. E. Gallatin Collection
1952-61-91

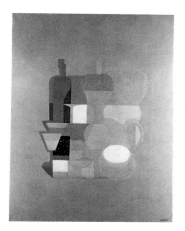

**Ozenfant, Amédée**
*Nacres No. 2*
1923–26
Lower right: ozenfant
Oil on canvas
51 5/16 × 38" (130.3 × 96.5 cm)

Purchased with the Edith H. Bell
Fund and the Edward and Althea
Budd Fund
1975-170-1

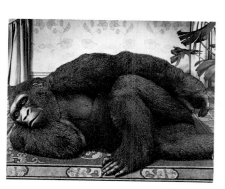

**Palmore, Tommy Dale**
American, born 1944
*Reclining Nude*
1976
On reverse: Palmore 76 /
"Reclining Nude"
Acrylic on canvas
66 × 84" (167.6 × 213.4 cm)

Purchased with the Adele Haas
Turner and Beatrice Pastorius
Turner Memorial Fund and with
funds contributed by Marion
Boulton Stroud
1976-99-1

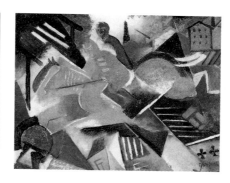

**Palmov, Viktor Nikandrovich**
Russian, 1887–1929
*Impression of Red Cavalry Driving
Petlura from Kiev*
1923
Lower right: [Russian for
"Palmov"]; on reverse: 1923
Oil on panel
8 7/8 × 11 3/8" (22.5 × 28.9 cm)

Gift of Christian Brinton
1941-79-4

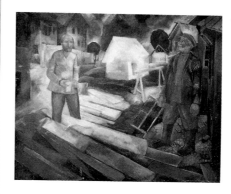

**Palmov, Viktor Nikandrovich**
*Village Carpenters*
c. 1923
Tempera and oil on panel
40 5/8 × 48 5/8" (103.2 × 123.5 cm)

Gift of Christian Brinton
1941-79-115

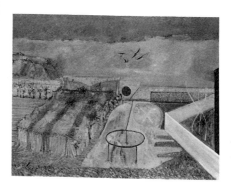

**Paone, Peter**
American, born 1936
*Italian Landscape*
1958
Lower left: Paone '58; on reverse:
Italian Landscape Paone
Oil on canvas
40 1/4 × 51" (102.2 × 129.5 cm)

Purchased with the Adele Haas
Turner and Beatrice Pastorius
Turner Memorial Fund
1959-12-6

**Parker, Raymond**
American, born 1922
*Untitled*
1960
Lower right: Parker; on reverse:
R. Parker / 1960
Oil on canvas
71 × 47 15/16" (180.3 × 121.8 cm)

Gift of Mr. and Mrs. Joseph
Slifka
1971-264-2

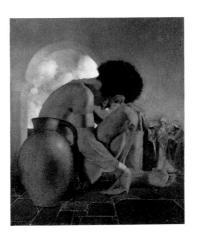

**Parrish, Maxfield**
American, 1870–1966
*Sinbad Plots against the Giant*
1907
Oil on cardboard
20 1/8 × 16 1/8" (51.1 × 41 cm)

Centennial gift of Mrs. Francis P.
Garvan
1976-164-3

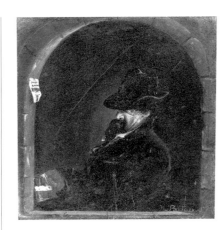

**Paxton, W.**
American, active c. 1925–c. 1957
*Portrait (Bum Bock)*
1957
Lower right: Paxton 57
Oil on cardboard
9 × 8 5/8" (22.9 × 21.9 cm)

Gift of Mrs. Louis C. Madeira
and Charles R. Tyson
1965-205-23

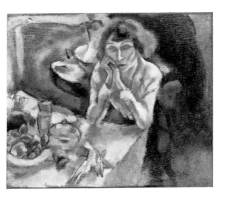

**Pascin, Jules**
American, born Bulgaria,
1885–1930
*Portrait of Madame Pascin* [née
Hermine David]
1915–16
Upper left: Pascin
Oil on canvas
21 × 24" (53.3 × 61 cm)

The Samuel S. White 3rd and
Vera White Collection
1967-30-66

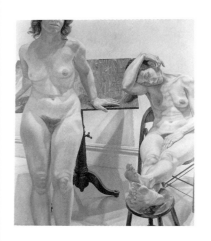

**Pearlstein, Philip**
American, born 1924
*Two Female Models with a Drawing
Table*
1973
Oil on canvas
72 × 60" (182.9 × 152.4 cm)

Purchased with a grant from the
National Endowment for the Arts
and with funds contributed by
private donors
1974-111-1

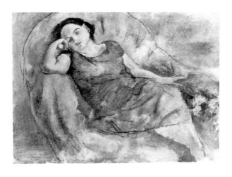

**Pascin, Jules**
*Woman on a Couch*
c. 1925
Lower left: Pascin; on reverse:
PASCIN—Bergere endormie.
Oil on canvas
28 7/8 × 38 1/4" (73.3 × 97.1 cm)

The Samuel S. White 3rd and
Vera White Collection
1967-30-67

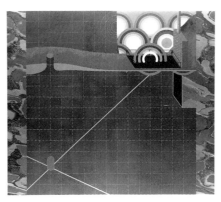

**Pease, David**
American, born 1932
*Don't Drink the Water*
1968
Acrylic on canvas
67 15/16 × 75" (172.6 × 190.5 cm)

Purchased with the Philadelphia
Foundation Fund
1969-7-1

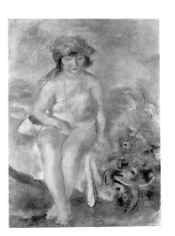

**Pascin, Jules**
*Nude in a Blue Turban (Girl in a
Blue Bonnet)*
c. 1928
Lower right: Pascin
Oil and crayon on canvas
36 5/8 × 26" (93 × 66 cm)

The Louis E. Stern Collection
1963-181-51

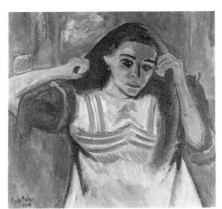

**Pechstein, Max**
German, 1881–1955
*Girl Combing Her Hair*
1910
Lower left: Pechstein / 1910;
on reverse: Pechstein / Berlin /
Mädchen
Oil on canvas
28 9/16 × 28 13/16" (72.5 × 73.2 cm)

Purchased with the J. Stogdell
Stokes Fund
1980-61-1

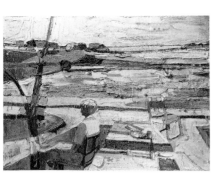

**Petersen, Roland Conrad**
American, born Denmark,
born 1926
*Summer Landscape*
1964
Lower left: Roland Petersen
Acrylic on canvas
47 1/4 × 62 1/8" (120 × 157.8 cm)

Purchased with the Adele Haas
Turner and Beatrice Pastorius
Turner Memorial Fund
1968-76-1

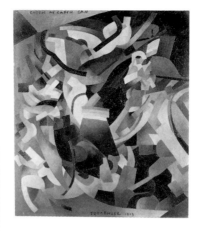

**Picabia, Francis**
*Catch as Catch Can*
1913
Upper left: CATCH AS CATCH
CAN; center bottom: EDTAONISL
1913; on reverse: Picabia / 1913
Oil on canvas
39 5/8 × 32 1/8" (100.6 × 81.6 cm)

The Louise and Walter Arensberg
Collection
1950-134-156

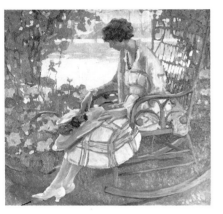

**Peterson, Jane**
American, 1876–1965
*Summertime*
c. 1921
Lower right: JANE PETERSON
Oil on canvas
32 1/4 × 32 3/16" (81.9 × 81.8 cm)

Gift of Martin Horwitz
1976-244-1

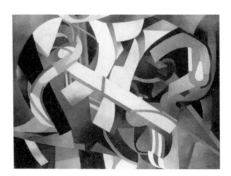

**Picabia, Francis**
*Physical Culture*
1913
On reverse: Picabia / 1913
Oil on canvas
35 1/4 × 45 7/8" (89.5 × 116.5 cm)

The Louise and Walter Arensberg
Collection
1950-134-157

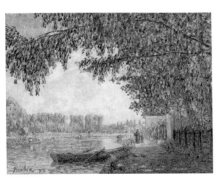

**Picabia, Francis**
French, 1879–1953
*Sunlight on the Banks of the Loing
River, Moret*
1905
Lower left: Picabia 1905; on
reverse: Picabia. effet de Soleil
sur les bords du Loing Moret
1908
Oil on canvas
28 13/16 × 36 3/8" (73.2 × 92.4 cm)

The Gertrude Schemm Binder
Collection
1951-84-2

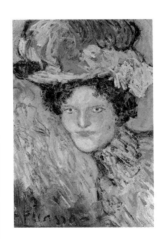

**Picasso, Pablo Ruiz**
Spanish, 1881–1973
*Head of a Woman*
1901
Lower left: Picasso
Oil on millboard
18 1/2 × 12" (47 × 30.5 cm)

Bequest of Lisa Norris Elkins
1950-92-11

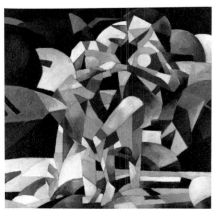

**Picabia, Francis**
*Dances at the Spring*
1912
Upper right: DANSES A LA
SOURCE; lower right: Picabia
1912
Oil on canvas
47 7/16 × 47 1/2" (120.5 × 120.6 cm)

The Louise and Walter Arensberg
Collection
1950-134-155

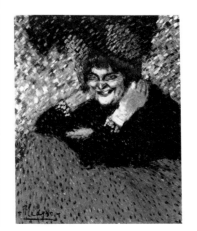

**Picasso, Pablo Ruiz**
*Old Woman (Woman with Gloves)*
1901
Lower left: Picasso
Oil on panel
26 3/8 × 20 1/2" (67 × 52.1 cm)

The Louise and Walter Arensberg
Collection
1950-134-158

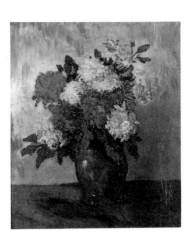

**Picasso, Pablo Ruiz**
*Chrysanthemums*
1901
Lower right: Picasso
Oil on canvas
31 15/16 × 25 5/8" (81.1 × 65.1 cm)

Gift of Mrs. John Wintersteen
1964-46-1

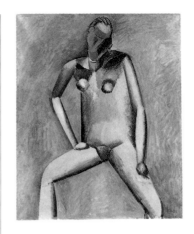

**Picasso, Pablo Ruiz**
*Seated Female Nude*
1908–9
Lower right: Picasso
Oil on canvas
45 7/8 × 35 3/16" (116.5 × 89.4 cm)

The Louise and Walter Arensberg
Collection
1950-134-164

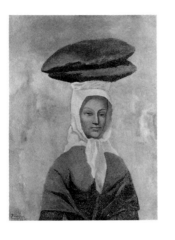

**Picasso, Pablo Ruiz**
*Woman with Loaves*
1906
Lower left [added later by the
artist]: Picasso / 1905
Oil on canvas
39 3/16 × 27 1/2" (99.5 × 69.8 cm)

Gift of Charles E. Ingersoll
1931-7-1

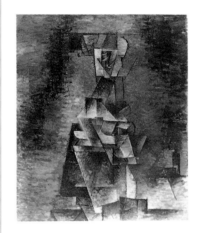

**Picasso, Pablo Ruiz**
*Female Nude*
1910
On reverse: Picasso
Oil on canvas
39 7/8 × 30 9/16" (101.3 × 77.6 cm)

The Louise and Walter Arensberg
Collection
1950-134-166

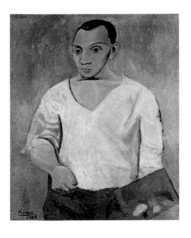

**Picasso, Pablo Ruiz**
*Self-Portrait*
1906
Lower left: Picasso / 1906
Oil on canvas
36 3/16 × 28 7/8" (91.9 × 73.3 cm)

A. E. Gallatin Collection
1950-1-1

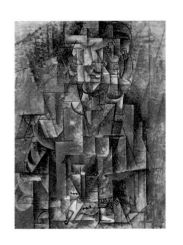

**Picasso, Pablo Ruiz**
*Man with a Violin*
1911–12
On reverse [date spurious]:
Picasso / 1910
Oil on canvas
39 3/8 × 28 13/16" (100 × 73.2 cm)

The Louise and Walter Arensberg
Collection
1950-134-168

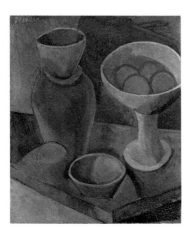

**Picasso, Pablo Ruiz**
*Still Life with Bowls and a Jug*
1908
Upper left: Picasso
Oil on canvas
32 1/4 × 25 7/8" (81.9 × 65.7 cm)

A. E. Gallatin Collection
1952-61-93

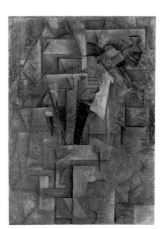

**Picasso, Pablo Ruiz**
*Man with a Guitar*
1912
On reverse: Homme Avec une /
guitare / SORGUES 1912 /
Sorgues / Picasso
Oil on canvas
51 13/16 × 35 1/16" (131.6 × 89.1 cm)

The Louise and Walter Arensberg
Collection
1950-134-169

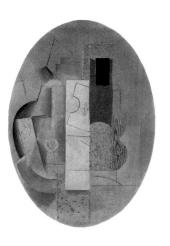

**Picasso, Pablo Ruiz**
*Still Life with a Violin and a Guitar*
1913
On reverse: Picasso / 1913
Graphite, plaster, oil, and other
material on canvas
36 1/16 × 25 3/8" (91.6 × 64.4 cm)

The Louise and Walter Arensberg
Collection
1950-134-170

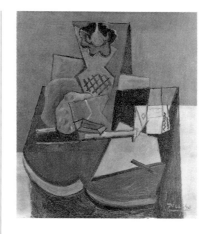

**Picasso, Pablo Ruiz**
*Still Life with a Vase, a Pipe, and a
Package of Tobacco*
1919
Lower right: Picasso / 19
Oil on canvas
25 5/8 × 21 1/4" (65.1 × 54 cm)

The Samuel S. White 3rd and
Vera White Collection
1967-30-71

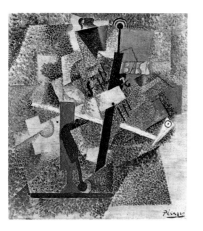

**Picasso, Pablo Ruiz**
*Still Life with a Pipe, a Violin, and
a Bottle of Bass*
1914
Center: BASS; lower right: Picasso
Oil on canvas
21 13/16 × 18 1/8" (55.4 × 46 cm)

A. E. Gallatin Collection
1952-61-94

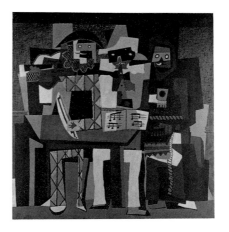

**Picasso, Pablo Ruiz**
*Three Musicians*
1921
Center left: Fontainebleau /
1921; lower left: Picasso
Oil on canvas
80 1/2 × 74 1/8" (204.5 × 188.3 cm)

A. E. Gallatin Collection
1952-61-96

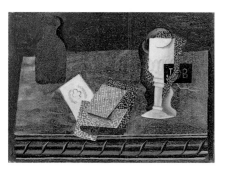

**Picasso, Pablo Ruiz**
*Still Life with a Bottle, Playing
Cards, and a Wineglass on a Table*
1914
Center: J B; upper right: Picasso /
Avignon / 1914
Oil on panel
12 1/2 × 16 7/8" (31.7 × 42.9 cm)

A. E. Gallatin Collection
1952-61-95

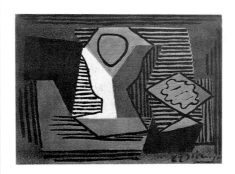

**Picasso, Pablo Ruiz**
*Still Life with a Glass and a
Package of Tobacco (Composition)*
1922
Lower right: 22 Picasso
Oil on canvas
6 3/8 × 8 5/8" (16.2 × 21.9 cm)

A. E. Gallatin Collection
1952-61-97

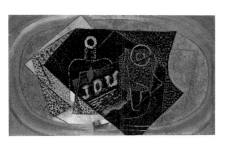

**Picasso, Pablo Ruiz**
*Still Life with a Bottle, a
Newspaper, and a Glass*
c. 1914
Center: JOU
Oil, graphite, tempera, and cork
on cardboard
11 3/8 × 18 5/8" (28.9 × 47.3 cm)

The Samuel S. White 3rd and
Vera White Collection
1967-30-70

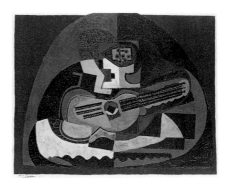

**Picasso, Pablo Ruiz**
*Still Life with a Guitar and a
Compote (The Mandolin)*
1923
Lower left: Picasso 23
Oil on canvas
31 3/4 × 39 7/16" (80.6 × 100.2 cm)

A. E. Gallatin Collection
1952-61-98

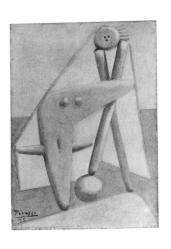

**Picasso, Pablo Ruiz**
*Bather, Design for a Monument (Dinard)*
1928
Lower left: Picasso / 28
Oil on canvas
9 1/2 × 6 3/8" (24.1 × 16.2 cm)

A. E. Gallatin Collection
1952-61-99

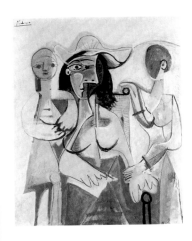

**Picasso, Pablo Ruiz**
*Woman and Children*
1961
Upper left: Picasso
Oil on canvas
57 1/2 × 44 3/4" (146 × 113.7 cm)

Gift of Mrs. John Wintersteen
1964-109-1

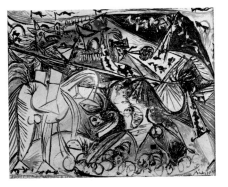

**Picasso, Pablo Ruiz**
*Bullfight*
1934
Lower left: Boisgeloup 9
September XXXIV; lower right:
Picasso
Oil and sand on canvas
13 × 16 1/8" (33 × 41 cm)

Gift of Henry P. McIlhenny
1957-125-1

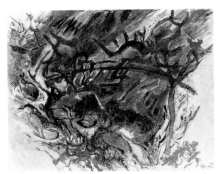

**Pignon, Édouard**
French, 1905–1993
*Olive Trees*
1959
Lower right: 59 / Pignon
Oil on canvas
25 5/8 × 32 1/16" (65.1 × 81.4 cm)

Gift of Dr. and Mrs. Paul Todd
Makler
1969-174-1

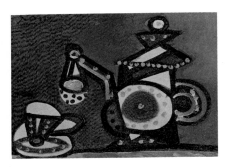

**Picasso, Pablo Ruiz**
*Still Life with a Teapot and a Cup*
1953
Upper left: Picasso; on reverse:
1er Juillet 53
Oil on canvas
9 1/2 × 12 15/16" (24.1 × 32.9 cm)

The Louis E. Stern Collection
1963-181-53

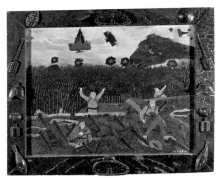

**Pippin, Horace**
American, 1888–1946
*The End of the War: Starting Home*
1930–33
Lower right: H. PIPPIN; on
reverse: S-SEP 15TH 1930 /
BY—HORACE PIPPIN / 327
W. GAY. ST / WEST CHESTER
P.A. / F-DEC 21TH. 1933
Oil on canvas
26 × 30 1/16" (66 × 76.4 cm)

Gift of Robert Carlen
1941-2-1

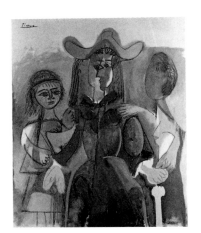

**Picasso, Pablo Ruiz**
*Woman and Children*
1961
Upper left: Picasso; on reverse:
20.4.61
Oil on canvas
63 3/4 × 51 3/16" (161.9 × 130 cm)

Gift of Mrs. Herbert Cameron
Morris
1964-89-1

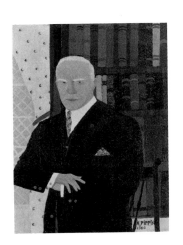

**Pippin, Horace**
*A Chester County Art Critic
(Portrait of Christian Brinton)*
1940
Lower right: H. PIPPIN / 1940
Oil on canvas
21 1/2 × 15 7/8" (54.6 × 40.3 cm)

Gift of Christian Brinton
1941-79-139

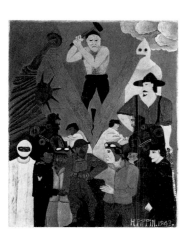

**Pippin, Horace**
*Mr. Prejudice*
1943
Lower right: H. PIPPIN, 1943.
Oil on canvas
18 1/8 × 14 1/8" (46 × 35.9 cm)

Gift of Dr. and Mrs. Matthew T.
Moore
1984-108-1

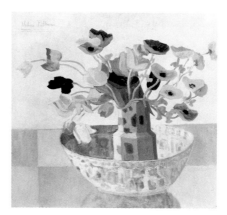

**Pittman, Hobson L.**
*Still Life with Anemones in a Pitcher*
c. 1960
Upper left: Hobson Pittman
Oil on cardboard
30 × 30 1/8" (76.2 × 76.5 cm)

Bequest of Hobson L. Pittman
1972-238-15

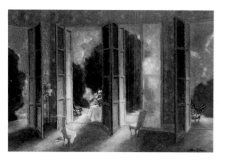

**Pittman, Hobson L.**
American, 1899–1972
*Full Moon*
1947–50
Lower right: Hobson Pittman
Oil on cardboard
30 × 40" (76.2 × 101.6 cm)

Purchased with the Bloomfield
Moore Fund
1951-31-4

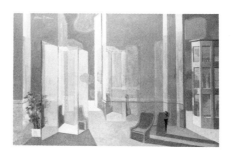

**Pittman, Hobson L.**
*Conversation*
1967–69
Upper left: Hobson Pittman
Oil on canvas
48 × 71 5/8" (121.9 × 181.9 cm)

Bequest of Hobson L. Pittman
1972-238-3

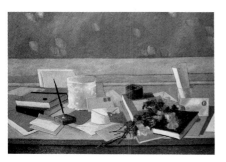

**Pittman, Hobson L.**
*Still Life with Letters and a
Container*
c. 1955
Oil on cardboard
30 × 42" (76.2 × 106.7 cm)

Bequest of Hobson L. Pittman
1972-238-18

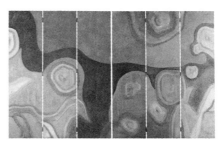

**Pittman, Hobson L.**
*Clouds and Petals*
Two three-panel screens
c. 1968
Right screen, upper right:
Hobson Pittman
Oil on Masonite
Each panel: 67 3/4 × 17 3/4"
(172.1 × 45.1 cm)

Gift of an anonymous donor
1969-87-1a, b

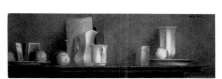

**Pittman, Hobson L.**
*Still Life with Cards, a White
Pitcher, a Cup, and an Orange*
1960
Upper right: Hobson Pittman
Oil on Masonite
12 1/8 × 36 13/16" (30.8 × 93.5 cm)

Bequest of Hobson L. Pittman
1972-238-13

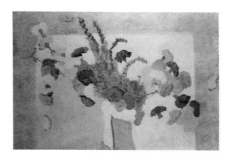

**Pittman, Hobson L.**
*Carnations No. 3*
1969
Lower left: Hobson Pittman
Oil on Masonite
30 × 42" (76.2 × 106.7 cm)

Bequest of Hobson L. Pittman
1972-238-189

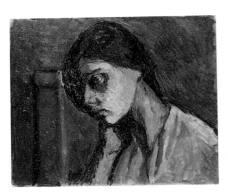

**Pogany, Margit**
Hungarian, 1879/80–1964
*Self-Portrait*
1913
Lower right: Pogany
Oil on cardboard
14 7/8 × 18 1/16" (37.8 × 45.9 cm)

Purchased with the Thomas
Skelton Harrison Fund
1966-173-1

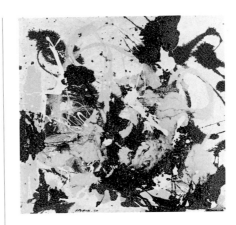

**Pollock, Jackson**
*No. 22*
1950
Center bottom: J. Pollock. 50
Enamel on Masonite
22 3/16 × 22 3/16" (56.4 × 56.4 cm)

The Albert M. Greenfield and
Elizabeth M. Greenfield
Collection
1974-178-41

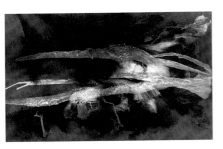

**Polke, Sigmar**
German, born 1941
*Ginkgo*
1989
Gold, graphite, natural pigments,
and synthetic resin on woven
polyester
102 × 160" (259.1 × 406.4 cm)

Gift of the Friends of the
Philadelphia Museum of Art
1990-39-1

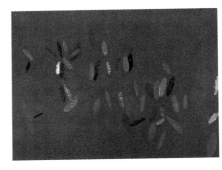

**Poons, Larry**
American, born 1937
*Brown Sound*
1968
Acrylic on canvas
96 1/16 × 125 1/4" (244 × 318.1 cm)

Centennial gift of the Woodward
Foundation
1975-81-13

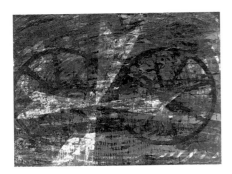

**Pollock, Bruce**
American, born 1951
*Cart*
1987
On reverse: Pollock / 1987 /
'Cart'
Acrylic on panel
6 1/2 × 46 1/2" (16.5 × 118.1 cm)

Purchased with the Julius Bloch
Memorial Fund
1988-41-1

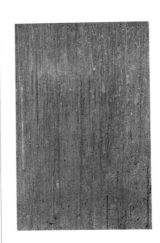

**Poons, Larry**
*At Last*
1970
On reverse: L. Poons / '72 /
"Hornwell"
Oil on canvas
87 5/8 × 54 5/8" (222.6 × 138.7 cm)

Gift of Mr. and Mrs. J. Welles
Henderson
1983-161-1

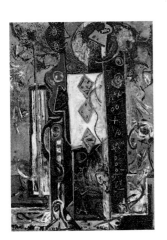

**Pollock, Jackson**
American, 1912–1956
*Male and Female*
c. 1942
Oil on canvas
73 1/4 × 48 15/16" (186 × 124.3 cm)

Gift of Mr. and Mrs. H. Gates
Lloyd
1974-232-1

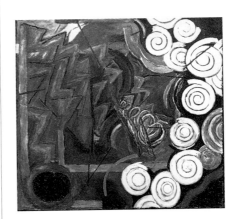

**Porter, Katherine**
American, born 1941
*Truth Rescued from Romance*
1980
On reverse: Truth Rescued From
Romance
Oil on canvas
86 3/8 × 88 5/8" (219.4 × 225.1 cm)

Purchased with the Edward and
Althea Budd Fund
1981-44-1

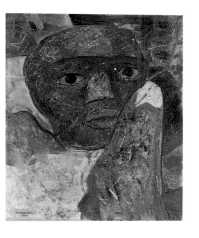

**Portinari, Candido**
Brazilian, 1903–1962
*Discovery of Brazil*
1941
Lower left: PORTINARI / 1941
Oil on canvas
28 ³/₄ × 23 ¹/₂" (73 × 59.7 cm)

Gift of Dr. Robert C. Smith
1970-253-1

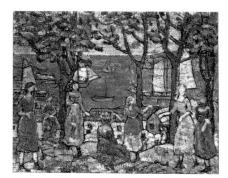

**Prendergast, Maurice B.**
*The Harbor*
1914
Lower left: Prendergast
Oil on canvas
24 ⁵/₁₆ × 30 ¹/₄" (61.7 × 76.8 cm)

Gift of Mr. and Mrs. Philip
Newman
1983-64-1

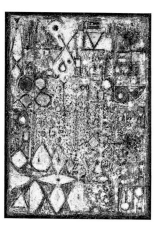

**Pousette-Dart, Richard**
American, 1916–1992
*White Gothic No. 3*
1957
Oil on canvas
97 ³/₁₆ × 64 ⁷/₈" (246.9 × 164.8 cm)

The Albert M. Greenfield and
Elizabeth M. Greenfield
Collection
1974-178-42

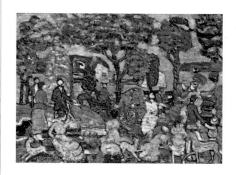

**Prendergast, Maurice B.**
*Sunday Promenade*
1922
Lower left: Prendergast
Oil on canvas
24 × 32" (61 × 81.3 cm)

Gift of Mr. and Mrs. Meyer P.
Potamkin (reserving life interest)
1964-116-1

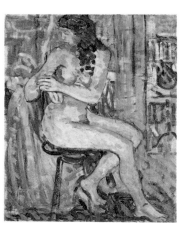

**Prendergast, Maurice B.**
American, 1859–1924
*Seated Nude*
c. 1905
Oil on canvas
24 × 19" (61 × 48.3 cm)

Gift of Mrs. Eugénie Prendergast
1964-104-1

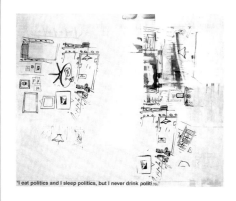

**Prince, Richard**
American, born 1949
*Untitled*
1991
Across bottom: "I eat politics and
I sleep politics, but I never drink
politics."
Acrylic, silk screen, and graphite
on canvas
99 ¹/₂ × 116" (252.7 × 294.6 cm)

Purchased with a grant from the
National Endowment for the Arts,
with matching funds from various
donors, and funds from the Adele
Haas Turner and Beatrice Pastorius
Turner Memorial Fund
1991-51-1

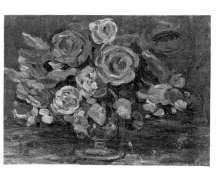

**Prendergast, Maurice B.**
*Night Study of Flowers*
1912
Lower right: Prendergast; on
reverse: "NIGHT STUDY OF
FLOWERS" / MAURICE B.
PRENDERGAST. / 1912
Oil on panel
10 ¹/₂ × 13 ⁷/₈" (26.7 × 35.2 cm)

Gift of Mrs. Charles Prendergast
in memory of Henry Clifford
1975-119-1

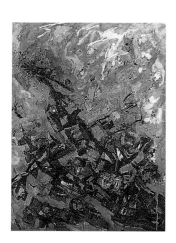

**Rattner, Abraham**
American, 1895–1978
*Gargoyle in Flames No. 2*
1961
Center bottom: RATTNER '61
Oil on canvas
51 ¹/₄ × 38 ¹/₄" (130.2 × 97.1 cm)

Gift of Mr. and Mrs. Barry R.
Peril
1971-266-1

**Rauschenberg, Robert**
American, born 1925
*K 24976 S*
1952
On reverse: RAUSCHENBERG
1952 I of 4 3' by 3' [three times]
/ 61 FULTON STREET—N.Y.C. /
RAUSCHENBERG PAINTING—
1952.
Oil, cloth, metal, paper, and
wood on four canvases
72 × 72" (182.9 × 182.9 cm)
overall

Gift of Mr. and Mrs. N. Richard
Miller
1967-217-1

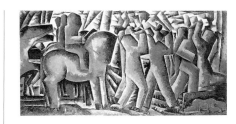

**Ray, Man**
*A.D. 1914*
1914
Lower right: ADMCMXIV /
man ray
Oil on canvas
36 7/8 × 69 3/4" (93.7 × 177.2 cm)

A. E. Gallatin Collection
1944-90-1

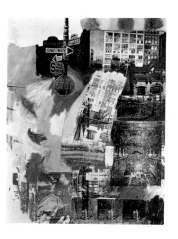

**Rauschenberg, Robert**
*Estate*
1963
Lower left, on space capsule:
UNITED / [S]TATES; center, on
signs: NASSAU ST; PINE ST.;
ONE WAY; ONE; PUBLIC /
SHELTER; STOP; on reverse:
Robert Rauschenberg, 1963
Oil and silk-screened inks on
canvas
96 × 69 13/16" (243.8 × 177.3 cm)

Gift of the Friends of the
Philadelphia Museum of Art
1967-88-1

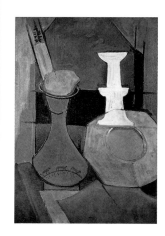

**Ray, Man**
*Still Life*
1915
Lower right: Man Ray / 1915
Oil on cardboard
18 1/2 × 12 1/4" (47 × 31.1 cm)

A. E. Gallatin Collection
1946-70-17

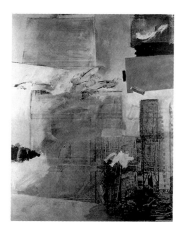

**Rauschenberg, Robert**
*Flush*
1964
Oil and silk-screened inks on
canvas
95 3/16 × 71 5/16" (241.8 × 181.1 cm)

Centennial gift of the Woodward
Foundation
1975-81-14

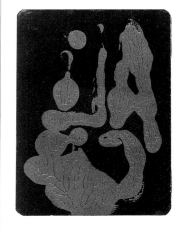

**Ray, Man**
*Ecila for Alice*
1962–64
Acrylic on cardboard
9 3/4 × 7" (24.8 × 17.8 cm)

Gift of John Rewald
1985-62-1

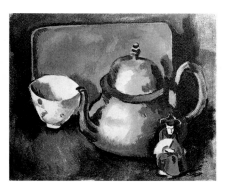

**Ray, Man**
American, active France,
1890–1976
*Still Life with a Teapot*
c. 1910
Lower left: man / ray
Oil on canvas board
8 1/4 × 10 5/16" (20.9 × 26.2 cm)

Gift of Frank and Alice Osborn
1966-68-15

**Ray, Rudolf**
American, 1891–1984
*Nanda Devi (Almora, Himalayas)*
1959
On reverse: Nanda DEVI / Rudolf
Ray / Almora Himalyas / 1959
Burned charcoal and ground
white rock on panel
15 1/4 × 41" (38.7 × 104.1 cm)

Gift of an anonymous donor
1978-123-2

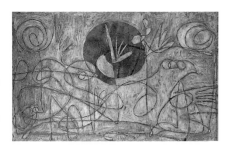

**Ray, Rudolf**
*Sarita*
1968–69
On reverse: Rudolf Ray /
Tepoztlan / 1968/9
Oil on canvas on panel
39 1/16 × 61 1/16" (99.2 × 155.1 cm)

Gift of an anonymous donor
1983-213-1

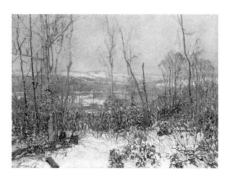

**Redfield, Edward Willis**
*Overlooking the Delaware*
c. 1919
Lower left: E. W. REDFIELD
Oil on canvas
38 × 50 1/4" (96.5 × 127.6 cm)

Gift of Mr. and Mrs. J. Stogdell
Stokes
1931-40-1

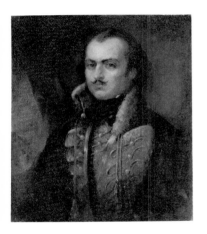

**Reckless, Stanley L.
(Stanley L. Zbytneiwski)**
American, born 1892, death date
unknown
*Portrait of Brigadier General
Casimir Pulaski*
c. 1915–25
Lower right: STAN
ZBYTNEIWSKI / RECKLESS
Oil on canvas
24 × 21 3/16" (61 × 53.8 cm)

Commissioners of Fairmount
Park
F1926-3-1

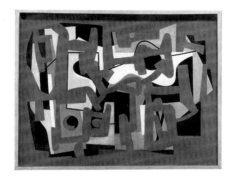

**Reinhardt, Ad**
American, 1913–1967
*Abstraction*
c. 1940
Lower right: REINHARDT
Oil on panel
24 7/8 × 30 3/4" (63.2 × 78.1 cm)

A. E. Gallatin Collection
1946-70-2

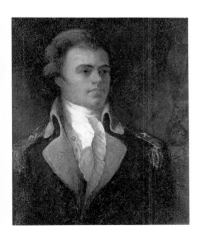

**Reckless, Stanley L.**
*Portrait of Colonel Thaddeus
Kosciusko*
1926
Lower right: STAN Zbytneiwski /
Reckless; on reverse: STANLEY L.
/ RECKLESS / 1926.
Oil on canvas
24 1/8 × 20 1/16" (61.3 × 51 cm)

Commissioners of Fairmount
Park
F1926-3-2

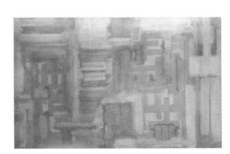

**Reinhardt, Ad**
*Abstraction No. 12*
1950
Lower right: REINHARDT '50;
on reverse: AD REINHARDT
Oil on canvas
40 1/16 × 59 7/8" (101.8 × 152.1 cm)

Gift of Mr. and Mrs. Gerrish H.
Milliken
1978-177-1

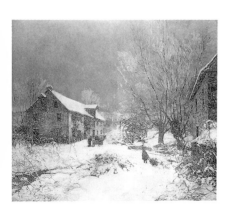

**Redfield, Edward Willis**
American, 1869–1965
*The Day before Christmas*
1919
Lower right: E. W. REDFIELD
DEC. 24, 19.
Oil on canvas
50 × 55 13/16" (127 × 141.8 cm)

Gift of the Art Club of
Philadelphia
1928-37-1

**Reinhardt, Ad**
*Black Cross*
1967
Oil on panel
11 3/8 × 10 1/8" (28.9 × 25.7 cm)

Gift of the Kulicke family in
memory of Lt. Frederick W.
Kulicke III
1969-86-4

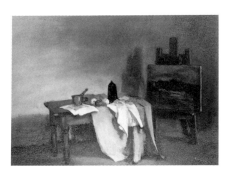

**Remenick, Seymour**
American, born 1923
*Still Life, Artist's Studio*
1951
Lower right: REMENICK
Oil on canvas
18 1/8 × 24" (46 × 61 cm)

Gift of Benjamin D. Bernstein
1964-106-5

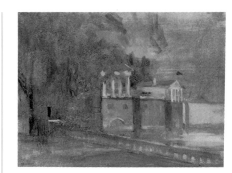

**Remenick, Seymour**
*Fairmount Waterworks*
c. 1962
Lower left: REMENICK
Oil on panel
14 × 18" (35.6 × 45.7 cm)

Gift of Benjamin D. Bernstein
1964-106-4

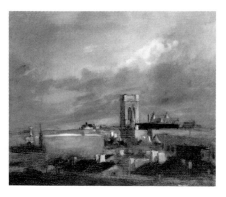

**Remenick, Seymour**
*Rooftops, Philadelphia*
1954
Lower right: REMENICK
Oil on canvas
28 × 32" (71.1 × 81.3 cm)

Gift of Benjamin D. Bernstein
1964-106-3

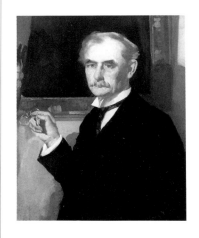

**Ricciardi, Cesare A.**
American, born Italy,
born 1892, still active 1925
*Portrait of Joshua Cope*
c. 1930
Lower right: C. A. Ricciardi
Oil on canvas
30 × 24" (76.2 × 61 cm)

Gift of Mrs. Cesare Ricciardi
1974-233-1

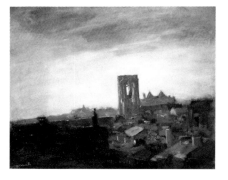

**Remenick, Seymour**
*Church Tower*
c. 1954
Lower left: REMENICK
Oil on canvas
21 × 25 7/8" (53.3 × 65.7 cm)

The Albert M. Greenfield and
Elizabeth M. Greenfield
Collection
1974-178-44

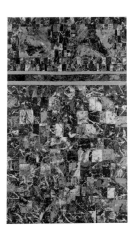

**Richenberg, Robert**
American, born 1917
*Untitled*
1962
On reverse: Robert Richenberg
1962
Oil and newspaper on panel
72 × 40 1/8" (182.9 × 101.9 cm)

Gift of Mr. and Mrs. David N.
Pincus
1965-218-1

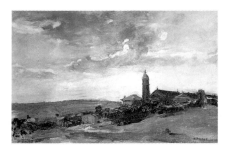

**Remenick, Seymour**
*Holy Family Church, Manayunk*
c. 1957
Lower right: REMENICK
Oil on panel
10 × 15 7/16" (25.4 × 39.2 cm)

The Albert M. Greenfield and
Elizabeth M. Greenfield
Collection
1974-178-43

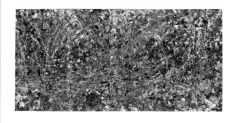

**Riopelle, Jean-Paul**
Canadian, 1923–1990
*Abstraction (Orange)*
1952
Lower right: Riopelle; on reverse:
Riopelle, J. P. 5-52
Oil on canvas
37 3/4 × 76 5/8" (95.9 × 194.6 cm)

Gift of Mr. and Mrs. R. Sturgis
Ingersoll
1964-30-1

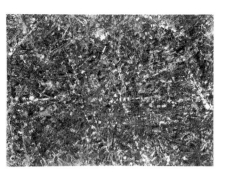

**Riopelle, Jean-Paul**
*Abstraction (Green)*
1952
On reverse: Riopelle, 1952
Oil on canvas
59 × 78 ³/₄" (150 × 200 cm)

Gift of Mr. and Mrs. R. Sturgis
Ingersoll
1966-190-1

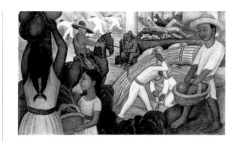

**Rivera, José Diego Maria**
*Sugar Cane*
1931
Fresco
57 ¹/₈ × 94 ¹/₈" (145.1 × 239.1 cm)

Gift of Mr. and Mrs. Herbert
Cameron Morris
1943-46-2

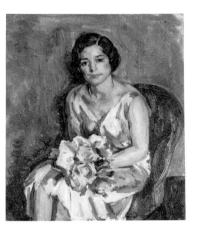

**Ritman, Louis**
American, born Ukraine,
1889–1963
*Portrait of Irene Hudson (Mrs. Louis
E. Stern)*
c. 1930
Lower right: RITMAN
Oil on panel
18 ¹/₄ × 15 ³/₈" (46.3 × 39 cm)

The Louis E. Stern Collection
1963-181-60

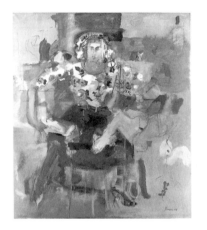

**Rivers, Larry**
American, born 1923
*Blue (The Byzantine Empress)*
1958
Lower right: Rivers '58
Oil on canvas
70 × 69" (177.8 × 175.3 cm)

The Albert M. Greenfield and
Elizabeth M. Greenfield
Collection
1974-178-45

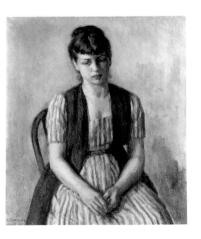

**Ritman, Louis**
*Woman in a Striped Dress*
c. 1930
Lower left: L RITMAN
Oil on canvas
35 ⁷/₈ × 30" (91.1 × 76.2 cm)

Gift of Louis E. Stern
1945-15-1

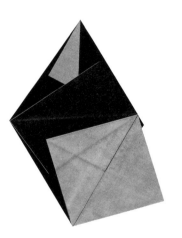

**Rockburne, Dorothea**
American, born Canada,
born 1934
*Robe Series, the Descent*
1976
Gesso, varnish, glue, and oil on
linen
52 × 29" (132.1 × 73.7 cm)

Purchased with the Adele Haas
Turner and Beatrice Pastorius
Turner Memorial Fund
1978-68-1

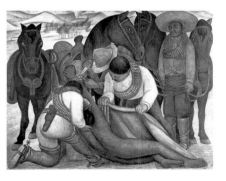

**Rivera, José Diego Maria**
Mexican, 1886–1957
*Liberation of the Peon*
1931
Fresco
73 × 94 ¹/₄" (185.4 × 239.4 cm)

Gift of Mr. and Mrs. Herbert
Cameron Morris
1943-46-1

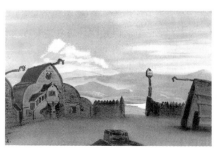

**Roerich, Nicholas
Konstantinovich**
Russian, 1874–1947
*Village of the Berendey*
c. 1919
Lower left: [artist's monogram in
Russian]
Oil on linen
24 ¹/₂ × 36 ¹⁵/₁₆" (62.2 × 93.8 cm)

Gift of Christian Brinton
1941-79-71

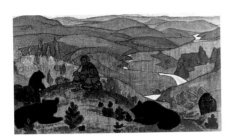

**Roerich, Nicholas Konstantinovich**
*Our Forefathers*
c. 1920
Lower left: [artist's monogram in Russian]
Tempera on burlap
18 7/8 × 31 1/8" (47.9 × 79.1 cm)

Gift of Christian Brinton
1941-79-67

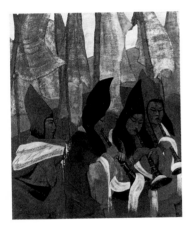

**Roerich, Svyatoslav Nikolaievich**
Russian, born 1904
*Tibetan Red-Sect Lamas at a Ceremony*
c. 1925
Lower left: [artist's monogram in Russian]; on reverse: TO DR. CHRISTIAN BRINTON. / TIBETAN RED SECT MUSICIANS AT CEREMONY / BY SVYATOSLAV NIKOLAIEVICH / ROERICH
Oil on composition board
37 × 24 3/8" (94 × 61.9 cm)

Gift of Christian Brinton
1941-79-148

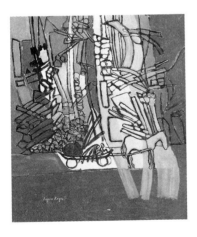

**Roger, Suzanne**
French, born 1899/1900
*Wedding amid Ruins*
1952
Lower left: Suzanne Roger
Oil on canvas
28 1/2 × 23 3/8" (72.4 × 59.4 cm)

The Albert M. Greenfield and Elizabeth M. Greenfield Collection
1974-178-46

**Rohrer, Warren**
American, born 1927
*November*
1973
On reverse: 'November' W. Rohrer 1973
Oil on canvas
66 × 66 1/4" (167.6 × 168.3 cm)

Gift of Rachel Seymour and Gene Locks
1974-77-1

**Rohrer, Warren**
*Settlement Magenta*
1980
On reverse: "Settlement Magenta" 1980 W. Rohrer
Oil on canvas
72 1/16 × 72 1/8" (183 × 183.2 cm)

Purchased with funds contributed by Henry Strater and Marion Boulton Stroud
1982-46-1

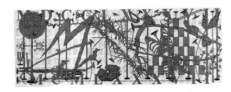

**Rollins, Tim**
American, born 1955
**and K.O.S. (Kids of Survival)**
*Amerika VII*
1986–87
Metallic paint, opaque watercolor, and black crayon on paper with printed text mounted on linen
64 × 169" (162.6 × 429.3 cm)

Purchased with funds contributed by Mr. and Mrs. Harvey Gushner, Mr. and Mrs. Leonard Korman, Mr. and Mrs. David N. Pincus, and Marion Boulton Stroud
1987-31-1

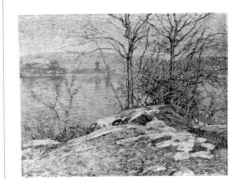

**Rosen, Charles**
American, 1878–1950
*The Delaware in Winter*
c. 1918
Lower left: CHARLES ROSEN
Oil on canvas
31 7/8 × 40" (81 × 101.6 cm)

The Alex Simpson, Jr., Collection
1928-63-8

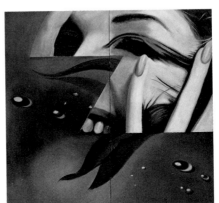

**Rosenquist, James**
American, born 1933
*Zone*
1961
Oil on two canvas sections
Each section: 95 × 47 11/16" (241.3 × 121.1 cm)

Purchased with the Edith H. Bell Fund
1982-9-1

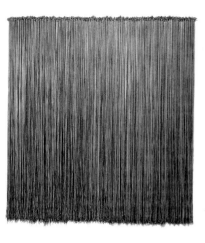

**Roth, David**
American, born 1942
*Full Color Painting*
1970
Acrylic on string
84 × 74" (213.4 × 188 cm)

Gift of Mr. and Mrs. N. Richard
Miller
1985-86-1

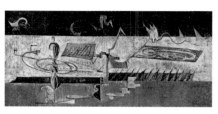

**Rothko, Mark**
American, born Latvia,
1903–1970
*Gyrations on Four Planes*
1944
Lower right: MARK ROTHKO
Oil on canvas
24 × 48" (61 × 121.9 cm)

Gift of the Mark Rothko
Foundation, Inc.
1985-19-3

**Rothko, Mark**
*Untitled*
1955
Oil on canvas
68 ¹/₁₆ × 45 ¹/₄" (172.9 × 114.9 cm)

Gift of the Mark Rothko
Foundation, Inc.
1985-19-2

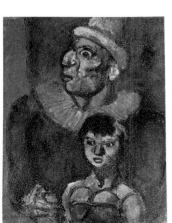

**Rouault, Georges**
French, 1871–1958
*At the Circus (The Mad Clown)*
1907
Oil on cardboard
29 ⁹/₁₆ × 22 ¹/₂" (75.1 × 57.1 cm)

The Louis E. Stern Collection
1963-181-61

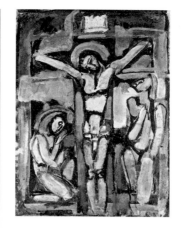

**Rouault, Georges**
*The Crucifixion*
c. 1918
Lower right: G Rouault
Oil and gouache on paper
41 ¹/₄ × 29 ⁵/₈" (104.8 × 75.2 cm)

Gift of Henry P. McIlhenny
1964-77-2

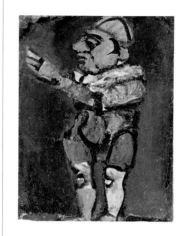

**Rouault, Georges**
*Polichinelle*
c. 1930
Oil on paper on canvas
28 ³/₄ × 20 ⁹/₁₆" (73 × 52.2 cm)

The Louise and Walter Arensberg
Collection
1950-134-174

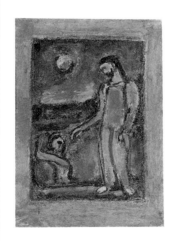

**Rouault, Georges**
*Scene from the Life of Christ*
1935–38
Oil on panel
16 ³/₈ × 11 ⁵/₈" (41.6 × 29.5 cm)

The Louis E. Stern Collection
1963-181-62

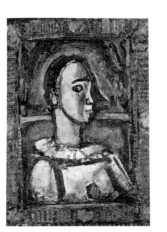

**Rouault, Georges**
*Pierrot with a Rose*
c. 1936
Oil on canvas
36 ¹/₂ × 24 ⁵/₁₆" (92.7 × 61.7 cm)

The Samuel S. White 3rd and
Vera White Collection
1967-30-76

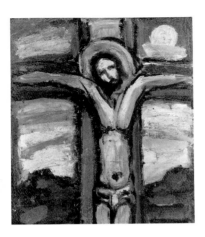

**Rouault, Georges**
*Christ*
c. 1938
Lower right: G. Rouault
Oil on canvas
19 3/8 × 15 7/8" (49.2 × 40.3 cm)

The Samuel S. White 3rd and
Vera White Collection
1967-30-79

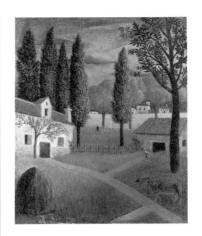

**Rousseau, Henri-Julien-Félix**
*Farm*
c. 1899
Lower left: H. Rousseau
Oil on canvas
13 × 10 3/8" (33 × 26.3 cm)

The Samuel S. White 3rd and
Vera White Collection
1967-30-80

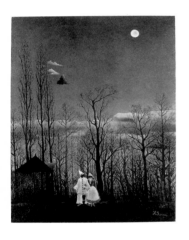

**Rousseau, Henri-Julien-Félix**
French, 1844–1910
*Carnival Evening*
1886
Lower right: H. Rousseau
Oil on canvas
46 3/16 × 35 1/4" (117.3 × 89.5 cm)

The Louis E. Stern Collection
1963-181-64

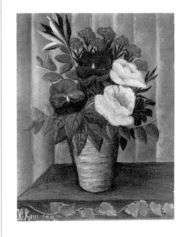

**Rousseau, Henri-Julien-Félix**
*Still Life with Flowers*
c. 1905
Lower left: H Rousseau.
Oil on paper on canvas
13 × 9 1/2" (33 × 24.1 cm)

The Louis E. Stern Collection
1963-181-65

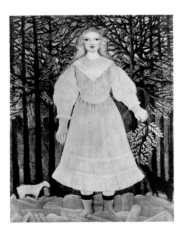

**Rousseau, Henri-Julien-Félix**
*Young Girl in Pink*
1893–95
Oil on canvas
24 × 18" (61 × 45.7 cm)

Gift of Mr. and Mrs. R. Sturgis
Ingersoll
1938-38-1

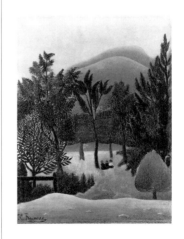

**Rousseau, Henri-Julien-Félix**
*Landscape*
1905–10
Lower left: H. Rousseau
Oil on canvas
18 1/4 × 12 3/4" (46.3 × 32.4 cm)

The Louise and Walter Arensberg
Collection
1950-134-177

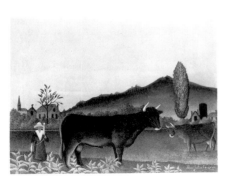

**Rousseau, Henri-Julien-Félix**
*Landscape with Cattle*
1895–1900
Lower right: Henri Julien
Rousseau
Oil on canvas
20 1/16 × 26" (51 × 66 cm)

The Louise and Walter Arensberg
Collection
1950-134-175

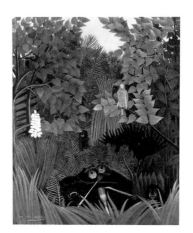

**Rousseau, Henri-Julien-Félix**
*The Merry Jesters*
1906
Lower left: Henri Julien Rousseau
Oil on canvas
57 3/8 × 44 5/8" (145.7 × 113.3 cm)

The Louise and Walter Arensberg
Collection
1950-134-176

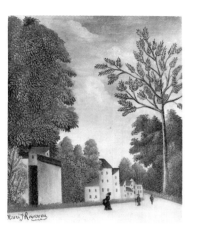

**Rousseau, Henri-Julien-Félix**
*Village Street*
1909–10
Lower left: Henri J. Rousseau
Oil on canvas
17 1/8 × 14 1/8" (43.5 × 35.9 cm)

The Louise and Walter Arensberg
Collection
1950-134-178

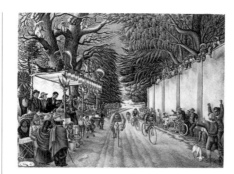

**Ruiz, Antonio**
Mexican, 1897–1964
*Bicycle Race*
1938
Lower right: A. Ruiz 1938
Oil on canvas
13 1/8 × 17" (33.3 × 43.2 cm)

Purchased with the Nebinger
Fund
1949-24-1

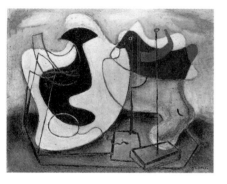

**Roux, Gaston-Louis**
French, born 1904
*Composition*
1927
Lower right: G. L. ROUX.
Oil on canvas
14 15/16 × 18 1/16" (37.9 × 45.9 cm)

A. E. Gallatin Collection
1946-70-5

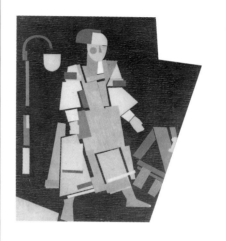

**Russian, unknown artist**
*Milkmaid and Model Barn*
Painted by students at the
Leningrad Institute
c. 1925–35
Tempera on paper on panel
27 3/8 × 22 1/4" (69.5 × 56.5 cm)

Gift of Christian Brinton
1941-79-2

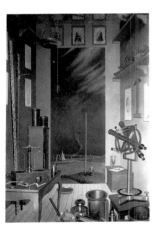

**Roy, Pierre**
French, 1880–1950
*Metric System*
c. 1933
Across top, on portraits:
DELAMERE; MECHAIN;
lower right: P. Roy
Oil on canvas
57 5/8 × 39" (146.4 × 99.1 cm)

The Louise and Walter Arensberg
Collection
1950-134-179

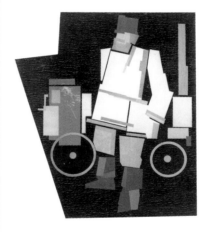

**Russian, unknown artist**
*Muzhik and Tractor*
Painted by students at the
Leningrad Institute
c. 1925–35
Tempera on paper on panel
27 1/2 × 22 1/2" (69.8 × 57.1 cm)

Gift of Christian Brinton
1941-79-1

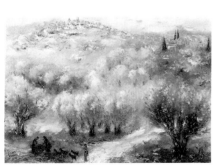

**Rubin, Reuven**
Israeli, born Rumania,
1893–1974
*The Road to Bethlehem*
1939
Lower left: RIKI / Rubin; on
reverse: RUBIN—The Road to
Bethlehem 1939
Oil on canvas
21 3/8 × 28 3/4" (54.3 × 73 cm)

The Louis E. Stern Collection
1963-181-66

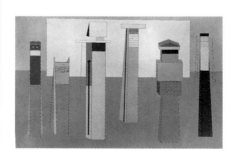

**Salemme, Attilio**
American, 1911–1955
*The Oracle*
1950
Lower right: Attilio Salemme /
'50
Oil on canvas
48 × 72" (121.9 × 182.9 cm)

Gift of Mrs. H. Gates Lloyd
1956-5-1

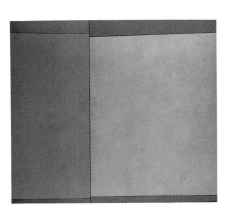

**Sander, Ludwig**
American, 1906–1975
*Adirondacks I*
1971
On reverse: Sander / 1971 /
# L. S 312
Oil on canvas
40 1/8 × 44 1/8" (101.9 × 112.1 cm)

Gift of the Childe Hassam Fund
of the American Academy and
Institute of Arts and Letters
1974-10-1

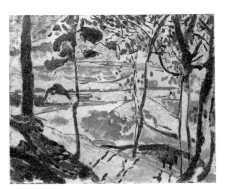

**Saÿen, Henry Lyman**
American, 1875–1918
*Fir Trees*
1915–16
On reverse: H. Lyman Sayen.
S. 312
Oil on canvas
25 × 30" (63.5 × 76.2 cm)

Gift of the National Collection of
Fine Arts
1972-123-1

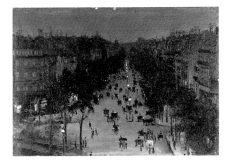

**Schamberg, Morton
Livingston**
American, 1881–1918
*Boulevard in Paris*
1908
On reverse: Paris 1908 /
Schamberg
Oil on cardboard
6 × 8" (15.2 × 20.3 cm)

Bequest of Jean L. Whitehill
1986-9-1

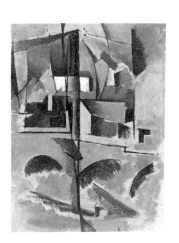

**Schamberg, Morton
Livingston**
*Landscape Bridge*
1915
Oil on panel
13 3/4 × 10" (34.9 × 25.4 cm)

Gift of Dr. and Mrs. Ira Leo
Schamberg
1969-228-1

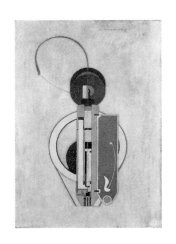

**Schamberg, Morton
Livingston**
*Painting IV (Mechanical
Abstraction)*
See following painting for reverse
1916
Lower right: Schamberg / 1916
Oil on panel
13 3/4 × 10 3/4" (34.9 × 27.3 cm)

The Louise and Walter Arensberg
Collection
1950-134-180a

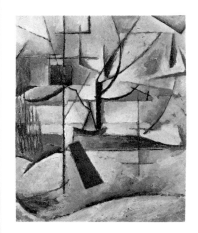

**Schamberg, Morton
Livingston**
*Landscape*
Reverse of the preceding painting
c. 1916
Oil on canvas
13 3/4 × 10 3/4" (34.9 × 27.3 cm)

The Louise and Walter Arensberg
Collection
1950-134-180b

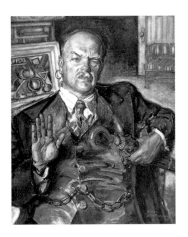

**Schamberg, Morton
Livingston**
*Painting VIII (Mechanical
Abstraction)*
1916
Upper right: Schamberg / 1916
Oil on canvas
30 1/8 × 20 1/4" (76.5 × 51.4 cm)

The Louise and Walter Arensberg
Collection
1950-134-181

**Schattenstein, Nikol
Ovseyvich**
American, born Lithuania,
1879–1954
*Portrait of David Davidovich
Burliuk, Father of Russian Cubo-
Futurism*
c. 1930
Lower right: Nikol. /
Schattenstein / N.Y.
Oil on canvas
37 × 27 3/4" (94 × 70.5 cm)

Gift of Christian Brinton
1941-79-111

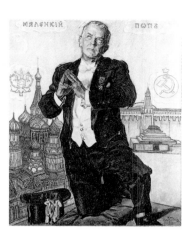

**Schattenstein, Nikol Ovseyvich**
*Adoration of Moscow (Portrait of Christian Brinton)*
1932
Across top: [Russian for "The Little Pope"]; lower right: Nikol. / Schattenstein / N.Y. / 1932.
Oil on canvas
49 15/16 × 40 1/8" (126.8 × 101.9 cm)

Gift of Christian Brinton
1941-79-335

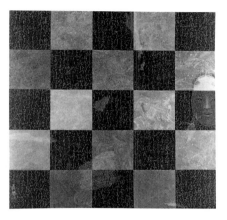

**Schock, Maya**
American, born Japan, 1928–1975
*Fantasia No. 5*
1973
Lower left: [artist's signature in Japanese]
Oil on canvas
29 15/16 × 29 7/8" (76 × 75.9 cm)

Gift of Benjamin D. Bernstein
1975-163-1

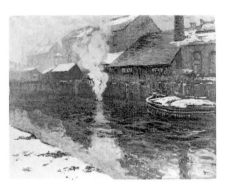

**Schofield, Walter Elmer**
American, active England, 1869–1944
*Winter in Picardy*
1907
Lower right: Schofield— / '07
Oil on canvas
38 1/2 × 48" (97.8 × 121.9 cm)

Gift of Dr. and Mrs. George Woodward
1939-7-18

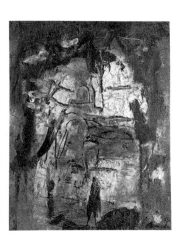

**Schumacher, Emil**
German, born 1912
*Nambit*
1959
Lower right: 59 / E. Schumacher
Oil on canvas
31 9/16 × 23 5/8" (80.2 × 60 cm)

Gift of Mr. and Mrs. Arthur A. Goldberg
1971-218-1

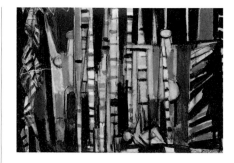

**Schwartz, Manfred**
American, born Poland, 1909–1970
*The Finding of Moses*
c. 1955
Lower right: Manfred Schwartz
Oil on canvas
26 × 36 1/8" (66 × 91.8 cm)

Gift of the M. L. Annenberg Foundation
1955-51-1

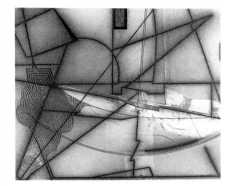

**Schwedler, William**
American, 1942–1982
*Bad Reception*
1976
On reverse: WM. SCHWEDLER / 1976 / "BAD / RECEPTION"
Oil, acrylic, and charcoal on canvas
60 × 70 1/8" (152.4 × 178.1 cm)

Gift of Frederic Mueller
1978-29-1

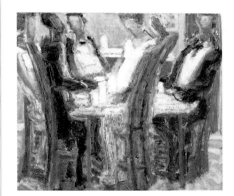

**Sefarbi, Harry**
American, born 1917
*Group at a Table*
c. 1960
Lower left: Sefarbi
Oil on Masonite
14 × 16" (35.6 × 40.6 cm)

Gift of Young America Preserves, Inc.
1976-152-2

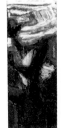

**Sefarbi, Harry**
*Triptych*
c. 1960
Oil on Masonite
Center panel: 16 × 11 15/16" (40.6 × 30.3 cm); left wing: 16 × 6" (40.6 × 15.2 cm); right wing: 16 × 5 7/8" (40.6 × 14.9 cm)

Gift of Young America Preserves, Inc.
1976-152-1

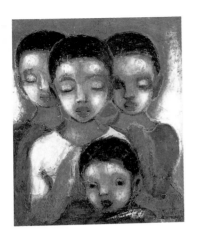

**Sekoto, G.**
American?, active 20th century
*Four Children*
c. 1955
Lower right: G. SEKOTO
Oil on canvas
24 × 19 ⅝" (61 × 49.8 cm)

The Albert M. Greenfield and
Elizabeth M. Greenfield
Collection
1974-178-48

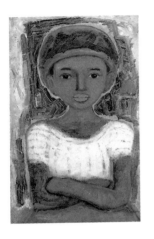

**Sekoto, G.**
*Young Girl*
c. 1955
Lower right: G. SEKOTO
Oil on canvas
24 × 15" (61 × 38.1 cm)

The Albert M. Greenfield and
Elizabeth M. Greenfield
Collection
1974-178-47

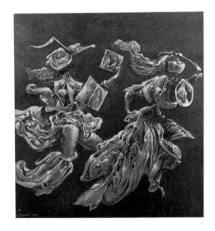

**Seligmann, Kurt**
Swiss, active United States,
1900–1961
*Flight to the Sabbath*
1956
Lower left: Seligmann 1956
Oil on canvas
30 ⅛ × 27" (76.5 × 68.6 cm)

Gift of George Dix
1980-58-1

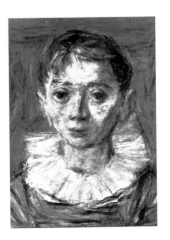

**Serisawa, Sueo**
American, born Japan,
born 1910
*Pierrot*
c. 1947
Lower right: Serisawa
Oil on canvas
12 × 9" (30.5 × 22.9 cm)

Bequest of Lisa Norris Elkins
1950-92-17

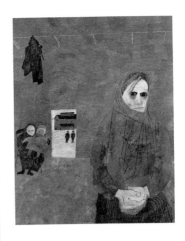

**Shahn, Ben**
American, born Lithuania,
1898–1969
*Miners' Wives*
c. 1948
Center bottom: Ben Shahn
Tempera on panel
48 × 36" (121.9 × 91.4 cm)

Gift of Wright S. Ludington
1951-3-1

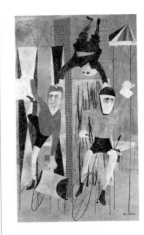

**Shahn, Ben**
*Epoch*
c. 1950
Center left, on card: NO; center
right, on card: YES; lower right:
Ben Shahn; on reverse: from Shahn
Roosevelt N.J. / to B. Shahn / c/o
Rose / 2425 6th St. / Boulder /
Colorado
Tempera on panel
52 × 31 ¼" (132.1 × 79.4 cm)

Purchased with the Bloomfield
Moore Fund
1951-31-5

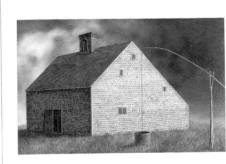

**Sharp, John**
American, born 1926
*The Jethro Coffin House, Nantucket*
1950
Lower right: J. Sharp. '50; on
reverse: "THE JETHRO COFFIN
HOUSE—NANTUCKET" / JOHN
SHARP
Oil on canvas
19 ¹⁵/₁₆ × 29 ¹⁵/₁₆" (50.6 × 76 cm)

Gift of the American Academy of
Arts and Letters
1951-105-1

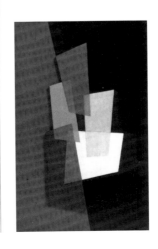

**Shaw, Charles Green**
American, 1892–1974
*Plastic Polygon*
1938
On reverse: CHARLES G. SHAW /
APRIL—1938 / PLASTIC
POLYGON
Oil and wood on panel
42 ¾ × 26 ¹³/₁₆" (108.6 × 68.1 cm)

A. E. Gallatin Collection
1946-70-18

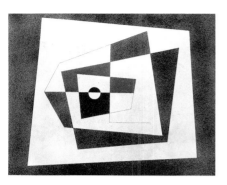

**Shaw, Charles Green**
*Composition*
1942
On reverse: C. G. SHAW / 1942
Oil on canvas
18 1/16 × 22 1/16" (45.9 × 56 cm)

A. E. Gallatin Collection
1946-70-20

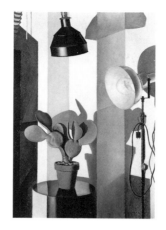

**Sheeler, Charles**
*Cactus*
1931
Lower right: Sheeler. 1931.
Oil on canvas
45 1/8 × 30 1/16" (114.6 × 76.4 cm)

The Louise and Walter Arensberg
Collection
1950-134-186

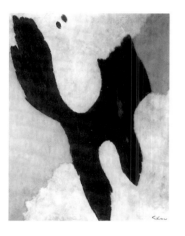

**Shaw, Charles Green**
*Ascent*
c. 1964
Lower right: Shaw
Oil on canvas
61 1/16 × 58" (155.1 × 147.3 cm)

Gift of Bertha Schaefer
1968-43-1

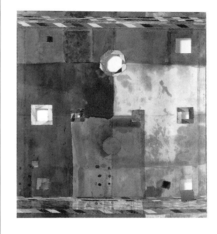

**Shields, Alan**
American, born 1944
*N. D. T. N. A. R. I. A. A. S. H.*
1971
Acrylic on canvas
94 × 83" (238.8 × 210.8 cm)

Gift of the Friends of the
Philadelphia Museum of Art
1972-53-1

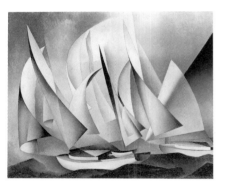

**Sheeler, Charles**
American, 1883–1965
*Pertaining to Yachts and Yachting*
1922
On reverse: Pertaining to Yachts
and Yachting / Charles Sheeler /
1922
Oil on canvas
20 × 24 1/16" (50.8 × 61.1 cm)

Bequest of Margaretta S.
Hinchman
1955-96-9

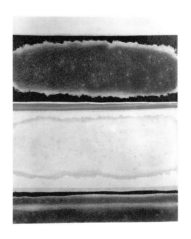

**Simpson, David**
American, born 1928
*After the Storm, Stars and Stripes,
No. 2*
c. 1959
Oil on canvas
65 3/8 × 49 3/4" (166 × 126.4 cm)

Gift of N. Richard Miller in
memory of his parents, Samuel
and Tobie Miller
1966-180-1

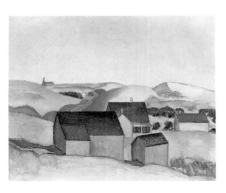

**Sheeler, Charles**
*Pennsylvania Landscape*
1925
Lower right: Sheeler 1925
Oil on canvas
10 × 12 1/16" (25.4 × 30.6 cm)

The Louis E. Stern Collection
1963-181-68

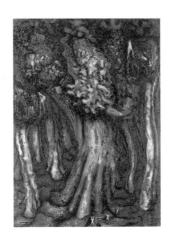

**Siqueiros, David Alfaro**
Mexican, 1896–1974
*The Giants*
1939
Lower left: SIQUIROS / 7-1939
Duco on Masonite
46 3/4 × 33" (118.7 × 83.8 cm)

Gift of Dr. and Mrs. MacKinley
Helm
1944-87-1

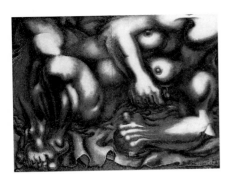

**Siqueiros, David Alfaro**
*War*
1939
Lower left: SIQUEIROS; lower
right: SIQUEIROS / 39
Duco on two panels
Each panel: 48 × 31 ⁵/₈"
(121.9 × 80.3 cm)

Gift of Ines Amor
1945-84-1

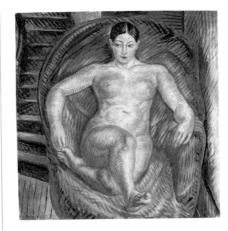

**Sloan, John**
*Arachne*
c. 1940
Lower left: John Sloan
Tempera glazed with oil on
Masonite
27 ¹⁵/₁₆ × 26" (71 × 66 cm)

Gift of Mr. and Mrs. R. Sturgis
Ingersoll
1941-103-3

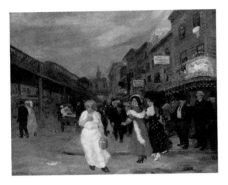

**Sloan, John**
American, 1871–1951
*Sixth Avenue and Thirtieth Street,
New York City*
1907
Lower left: John Sloan 1907
Oil on canvas
24 ¹/₄ × 32" (61.6 × 81.3 cm)

Gift of Mr. and Mrs. Meyer P.
Potamkin (reserving life interest)
1964-116-5

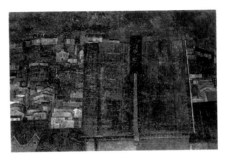

**Sloan, Louis Baynard**
American, born 1932
*Manayunk*
1959
Lower right: SLOAN / 1959
Oil on canvas
42 × 60" (106.7 × 152.4 cm)

Gift of Mr. and Mrs. Theodor
Siegl
1969-50-1

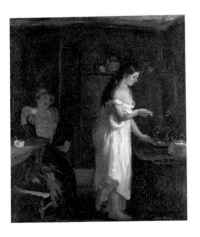

**Sloan, John**
*Three A.M.*
1909
Lower right: John Sloan; on
reverse: THREE A.M. / John Sloan
/ Painted in New York / 1909
Oil on canvas
32 ¹/₈ × 26 ¹/₄" (81.6 × 66.7 cm)

Gift of Mrs. Cyrus McCormick
1946-10-1

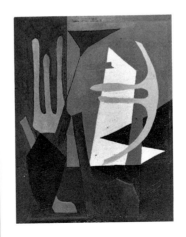

**Slobodkina, Esphyr**
American, born Russia,
born 1908
*Composition*
1940
Lower right: E. S.
Oil on Masonite
12 ¹/₄ × 9 ¹/₄" (31.1 × 23.5 cm)

A. E. Gallatin Collection
1946-70-19

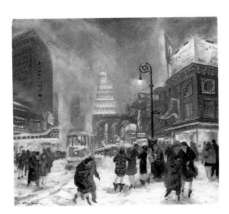

**Sloan, John**
*The White Way*
c. 1926
Lower left: John Sloan
Oil on canvas
30 ¹/₈ × 32 ¹/₄" (76.5 × 81.9 cm)

Gift of Mrs. Cyrus McCormick
1946-10-2

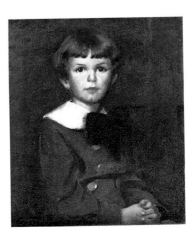

**Smith, Jessie Wilcox**
American, 1863–1935
*Child in a Blue Suit (Portrait of
Henry P. McIlhenny)*
1916
Oil on canvas
22 × 18" (55.9 × 45.7 cm)

The Henry P. McIlhenny
Collection in memory of
Frances P. McIlhenny
1986-26-405

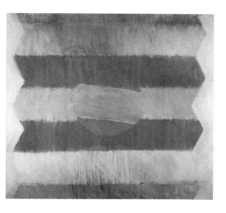

**Smith, Richard**
English, born 1931
*Capsule*
1960–61
On reverse: R. Smith / 1961 /
Capsule
Oil on canvas
84 1/8 × 90 1/4" (213.7 × 229.2 cm)

Centennial gift of the Woodward
Foundation
1975-81-15

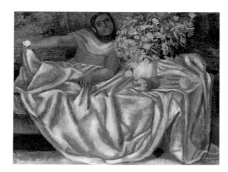

**Soriano, Juan**
*Girl with a Bouquet*
1946
Upper left: J. Soriano / 46.
Oil on canvas
18 1/2 × 23 3/4" (47 × 60.3 cm)

Gift of Mr. and Mrs. Herbert
Cameron Morris
1957-94-1

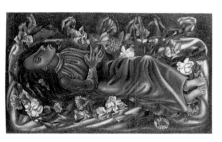

**Soriano, Juan**
Mexican, born 1920
*The Dead Girl*
1938
Lower right: J. Soriano / 38.
Oil on panel
18 1/2 × 31 1/2" (47 × 80 cm)

Gift of Mr. and Mrs. Henry
Clifford
1947-29-3

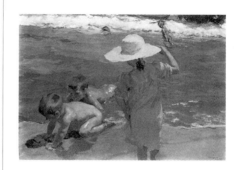

**Sorolla y Bastida, Joaquin**
Spanish, 1863–1923
*The Young Amphibians*
1903
Lower right: J. Sorolla y Bastida /
1903 / Valencia
Oil on canvas
37 7/8 × 51 3/8" (96.2 × 130.5 cm)

Purchased with the W. P.
Wilstach Fund
W 1904-1-55

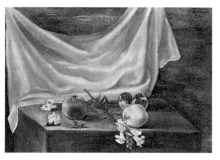

**Soriano, Juan**
*Still Life*
1942
Upper right: J. Soriano. / 42
Oil on canvas
19 5/8 × 27 5/8" (49.8 × 70.2 cm)

Gift of Mr. and Mrs. Joseph J.
Gersten
1951-120-4

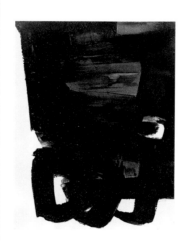

**Soulages, Pierre**
French, born 1919
*Painting November 9, 1966*
1966
Lower right: Soulages
Oil on canvas
51 × 38" (129.5 × 96.5 cm)

Gift of Benjamin D. Bernstein
1978-172-4

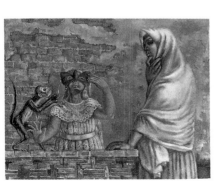

**Soriano, Juan**
*Girl with a Mask*
1945
Upper left: J. Soriano. / 45.
Oil on canvas
31 5/8 × 39 1/2" (80.3 × 100.3 cm)

Gift of Mrs. Herbert Cameron
Morris
1947-24-1

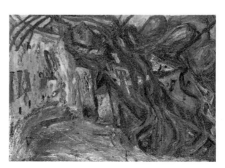

**Soutine, Chaim**
French, born Lithuania,
1894–1943
*Landscape, Céret*
1921
Oil on canvas
26 1/4 × 35 3/4" (66.7 × 90.8 cm)

Gift of Mr. and Mrs. R. Sturgis
Ingersoll
1953-136-1

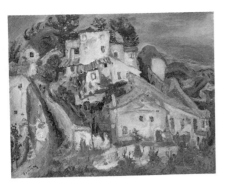

**Soutine, Chaim**
*Landscape, Chemin des Caucourts,
Cagnes-sur-Mer*
c. 1924
Lower left: Soutine
Oil on canvas
21 1/8 × 25 1/2" (53.7 × 64.8 cm)

The Louis E. Stern Collection
1963-181-71

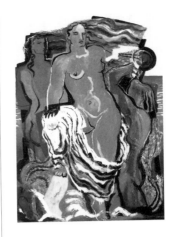

**Souverbie, Jean**
French, born 1891, death date
unknown
*Composition*
c. 1926
Lower right: Souverbie
Oil on canvas
36 1/8 × 25 5/8" (91.8 × 65.1 cm)

Bequest of Fiske and Marie
Kimball
1955-86-16

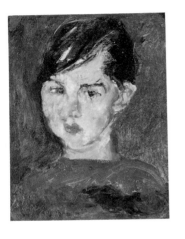

**Soutine, Chaim**
*Girl in Green*
c. 1925–28
On reverse: Chaim Soutine
Oil on canvas
14 5/16 × 11 1/16" (36.3 × 28.1 cm)

The Louis E. Stern Collection
1963-181-72

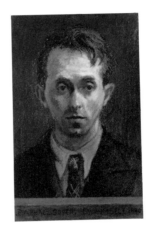

**Soyer, Raphael**
American, 1899–1987
*Self-Portrait*
1940
Across bottom: .RAPHAEL.SOYER.
BY.HIMSELF.1940
Oil on canvas
15 15/16 × 9 7/8" (40.5 × 25.1 cm)

The Louis E. Stern Collection
1963-181-69

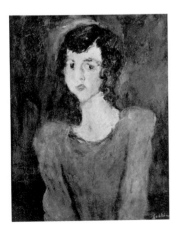

**Soutine, Chaim**
*Woman in Red*
c. 1927–30
Lower right: Soutine
Oil on canvas
25 9/16 × 19 3/4" (64.9 × 50.2 cm)

The Louis E. Stern Collection
1963-181-73

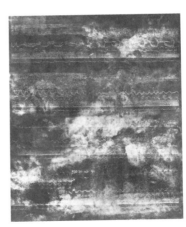

**Spandorfer, Merle**
American, born 1934
*Echo G*
1976
On reverse: Merle / Spandorfer /
"Echo G"
Acrylic and mixed media on
canvas
77 1/8 × 62 7/8" (195.9 × 159.7 cm)

Gift of the Cheltenham Art
Centre
1977-81-1

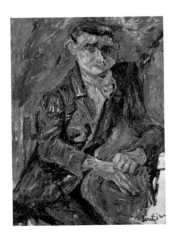

**Soutine, Chaim**
*Portrait of Moïse Kisling*
c. 1930
Lower right: Soutine
Oil on cardboard on Masonite
39 × 27 1/4" (99.1 × 69.2 cm)

Gift of Arthur Wiesenberger
1943-101-1

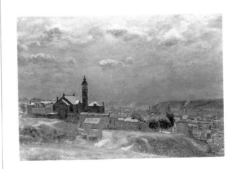

**Speight, Francis**
American, 1896–1989
*Industrial Area*
c. 1952
Lower right: Francis Speight
Oil on canvas
36 3/16 × 50 1/4" (91.9 × 127.6 cm)

Gift of Walter Stuempfig
1961-78-1

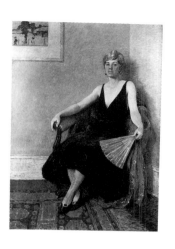

**Spencer, Robert**
American, 1879–1931
*Portrait of Brenda Biddle*
1926
Lower left: Robert Spencer /
1926; on reverse: Portrait of
Mrs. Moncure Biddle by Robert
Spencer
Oil on canvas
60 1/8 × 42 9/16" (152.7 × 108.1 cm)

Gift of Owen Biddle and
Peyton R. Biddle
1978-12-1

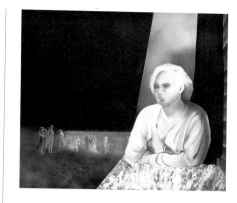

**Stegeman, Charles**
Canadian, born Netherlands,
born 1924
*Untitled*
1975
Lower left: C. Stegeman 75
Oil on canvas
70 × 82" (177.8 × 208.3 cm)

Purchased with funds contributed
by the friends of Charles
Stegeman and Françoise André
1975-165-1

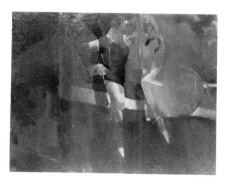

**Sprinchorn, Carl**
Swedish, 1887–1971
*Nijinsky and Pavlova in
"Les Sylphides"*
c. 1920
Upper left: C. Sprinchorn
Oil on canvas
31 1/8 × 39 1/8" (79.1 × 99.4 cm)

Gift of Christian Brinton
1941-79-151

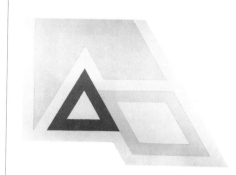

**Stella, Frank**
American, born 1936
*Sanbornville IV*
1966
Acrylic on canvas
104 1/2 × 144" (265.4 × 365.8 cm)

Gift of the Friends of the
Philadelphia Museum of Art
1968-183-2

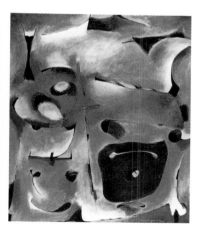

**Springer, Charles**
American, born 1950
*The Majestic*
1985
Lower right: chaspringer 1985;
on reverse: CHARLES SPRINGER /
"THE MAJESTIC" 1985 ACRYLIC
/ CANVAS / 56 × 66 inches
Acrylic on canvas
66 1/16 × 56 3/8" (167.8 × 143.2 cm)

Purchased with the Julius Bloch
Memorial Fund and funds
contributed by the Cheltenham
Art Centre
1986-72-1

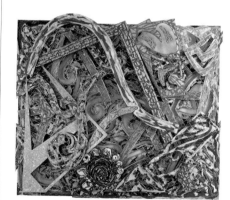

**Stella, Frank**
*Hockenheim*
1982
Oil stick, urethane enamel,
fluorescent alkyd, and Magna on
etched magnesium
124 × 128 × 19"
(315 × 325.1 × 48.3 cm)

Purchased with funds contributed
by Muriel and Philip Berman and
gift (by exchange) of the
Woodward Foundation
1982-48-1

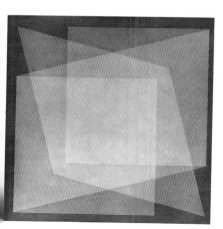

**Stanczak, Julian**
American, born Poland,
born 1928
*Obedient Square*
1970
On reverse: JULIAN STANCZAK /
"OBEDIENT SQUARE"
Acrylic on canvas
73 × 73" (185.4 × 185.4 cm)

Gift of Mr. and Mrs. Paul M.
Ingersoll
1980-129-1

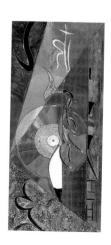

**Stella, Joseph**
American, born Italy,
1880–1946
*Chinatown*
c. 1917
Oil on glass
20 × 8 11/16" (50.8 × 22.1 cm)

The Louise and Walter Arensberg
Collection
1950-134-519

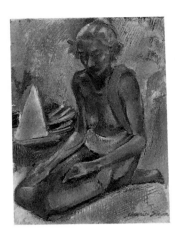

**Sterne, Maurice**
American, born Latvia,
1878–1957
*Bali Priestess*
c. 1913
Lower right: Maurice Sterne
Oil on canvas
24 1/8 × 20 3/8" (61.3 × 51.7 cm)

The Louis E. Stern Collection
1963-181-70

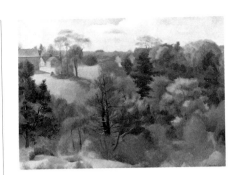

**Strater, Henry**
American, born 1896
*Autumn at Henderson's*
1927
Lower right: Strater '27.
Oil on canvas
30 × 39 15/16" (76.2 × 101.4 cm)

Gift of David Strater
1965-170-1

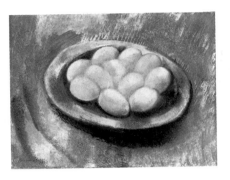

**Sterne, Maurice**
*Eggs*
1930
Lower left: Maurice Sterne / 1930
Oil on panel
14 5/8 × 18 5/8" (37.1 × 47.3 cm)

Bequest of Margaretta S.
Hinchman
1955-96-11

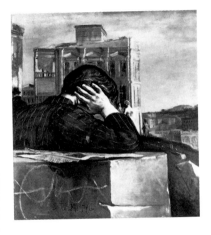

**Stuempfig, Walter, Jr.**
American, 1914–1970
*Back of a Man (Self-Portrait)*
1945
Bottom center: STUEMPFIG
Oil on canvas
24 × 18" (61 × 45.7 cm)

The Henry P. McIlhenny
Collection in memory of
Frances P. McIlhenny
1986-26-401

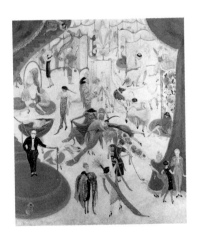

**Stettheimer, Florine**
American, 1871–1948
*Spring Sale at Bendel's*
1921
On reverse: BENDEL—SPRING
SALE BY Florine Stettheimer
1921
Oil on canvas
50 × 40" (127 × 101.6 cm)

Gift of Miss Ettie Stettheimer
1951-27-1

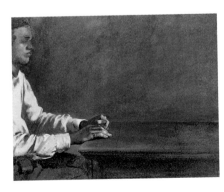

**Stuempfig, Walter, Jr.**
*Meditation*
1946
Oil on canvas
30 1/8 × 36" (76.5 × 91.4 cm)

Bequest of Lisa Norris Elkins
1950-92-18

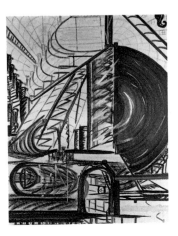

**Stevens, Frances Simpson**
American, 1894–1976
*Dynamic Velocity of Interborough
Rapid Transit Power Station*
c. 1915
Oil and charcoal on canvas
48 3/8 × 35 7/8" (122.9 × 91.1 cm)

The Louise and Walter Arensberg
Collection
1950-134-520

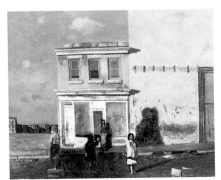

**Stuempfig, Walter, Jr.**
*The Reprimand*
1946
Lower left: STUEMPFIG; center,
on window: NELSON'S
Oil on canvas
24 3/4 × 30" (62.9 × 76.2 cm)

Gift of the Committee on
Painting and Sculpture
1947-33-1

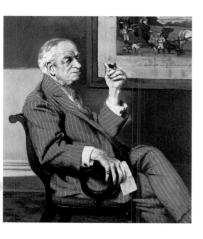

**Stuempfig, Walter, Jr.**
*Portrait of John C. Norris*
1949
Center bottom, on envelope: John
C. Norris / from his friend /
Stuempfig / 1949
Oil on canvas
39 7/8 × 36 1/8" (101.3 × 91.8 cm)

Bequest of Lisa Norris Elkins
1950-92-20

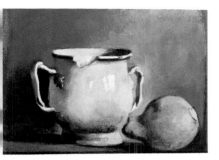

**Stuempfig, Walter, Jr.**
*Still Life with a Sugar Bowl and a
Green Fruit*
1949
Oil on canvas
8 × 10" (20.3 × 25.4 cm)

Bequest of Lisa Norris Elkins
1950-92-19

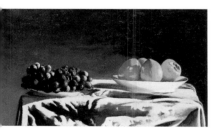

**Stuempfig, Walter, Jr.**
*Still Life with Persimmons and
Grapes*
1949
Oil on canvas
19 1/4 × 33 1/2" (48.9 × 85.1 cm)

Bequest of Lisa Norris Elkins
1950-92-32

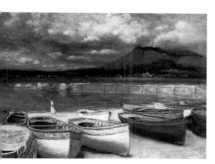

**Stuempfig, Walter, Jr.**
*View of Naples*
1954
Lower left: STUEMPFIG / 1954
Oil on canvas
20 1/8 × 28" (51.1 × 71.1 cm)

Bequest of Mrs. Edna M. Welsh
1982-1-9

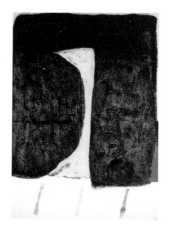

**Sugai, Kumi**
Japanese, active France,
born 1919
*Maison du Diable*
1961
Lower right: SUGAI 61
Oil on canvas
63 5/8 × 44 3/4" (161.6 × 113.7 cm)

Gift of Keith Wellin
1971-219-1

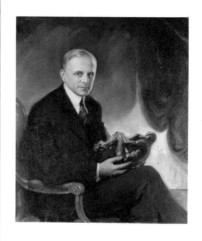

**Susan, Robert**
American, born Netherlands,
1888–1957
*Portrait of Jules E. Mastbaum*
1923
Upper left: Robert Susan / 1923
Oil on canvas
30 × 25 1/8" (76.2 × 63.8 cm)

Gift of Mrs. Charles Solomon,
Mrs. Jefferson Dickson, and Mrs.
Patrick Dinehart, the daughters of
Mr. and Mrs. Jules E. Mastbaum
1953-119-1

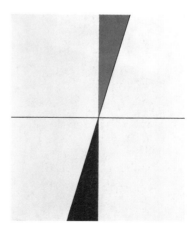

**Taeuber-Arp, Sophie**
Swiss, 1889–1943
*Point on Point*
1931–34
On reverse: SH Taeuber-Arp /
1931/4
Oil on canvas
25 1/2 × 21 1/4" (64.8 × 54 cm)

A. E. Gallatin Collection
1952-61-120

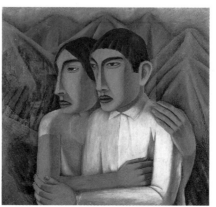

**Tamayo, Rufino**
Mexican, 1899–1991
*Man and Woman*
1926
Lower right: Tamayo / "1926"
Oil on canvas
27 1/2 × 27 5/8" (69.8 × 70.2 cm)

Gift of Mr. and Mrs. James P.
Magill
1957-127-6

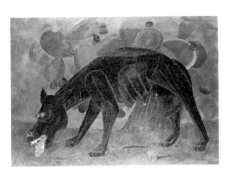

**Tamayo, Rufino**
*The Mad Dog*
1943
Lower right: Tamayo / 0.43
Oil on canvas
32 × 43" (81.3 × 109.2 cm)

Gift of Mrs. Herbert Cameron
Morris
1945-2-1

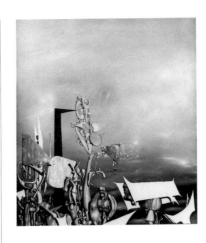

**Tanguy, Yves**
*Explosions of Fire*
1950
Lower right: YVES TANGUY 50
Oil on canvas
28 × 23" (71.1 × 58.4 cm)

Bequest of Kay Sage Tanguy
1964-181-1

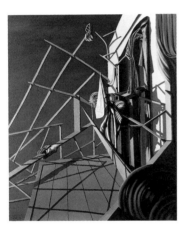

**Tanguy, Kay Sage**
American, 1898–1963
*Unicorns Came Down to the Sea*
1948
Lower left: Kay Sage '48
Oil on canvas
36 1/4 × 28 1/4" (92.1 × 71.7 cm)

Bequest of Hobson L. Pittman
1964-151-1

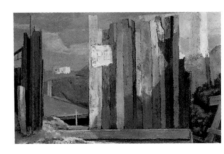

**Taylor, Charles**
American, born 1910
*Shoring*
c. 1958
Lower left: Charles Taylor
Oil on canvas
23 15/16 × 35 7/8" (60.8 × 91.1 cm)

Purchased with the Adele Haas
Turner and Beatrice Pastorius
Turner Memorial Fund
1959-12-7

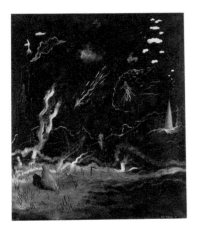

**Tanguy, Yves**
American, born France,
1900–1955
*The Storm (Black Landscape)*
1926
Lower right: YVES TANGUY 26
Oil on canvas
32 1/8 × 25 3/4" (81.6 × 65.4 cm)

The Louise and Walter Arensberg
Collection
1950-134-187

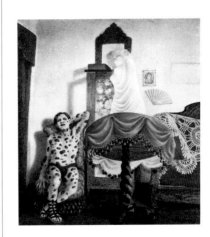

**Tchelitchew, Pavel**
Russian, active United States,
1898–1957
*Leopard Boy*
1935
Lower right: P. Tchelitchew / 35
Oil on canvas
21 5/8 × 18" (54.9 × 45.7 cm)

Gift of Mr. and Mrs. Henry
Clifford
1973-256-3

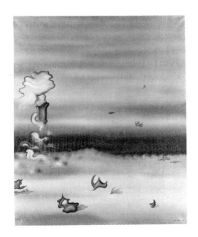

**Tanguy, Yves**
*The Parallels*
1929
Lower right: YVES TANGUY 29
Oil on canvas
36 5/16 × 28 3/4" (92.2 × 73 cm)

The Louise and Walter Arensberg
Collection
1950-134-188

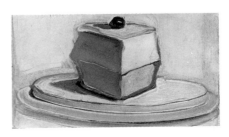

**Thiebaud, Wayne**
American, born 1920
*Cake*
1963
Upper left: Thiebaud 1963
Oil on canvas on panel
5 × 8 5/8" (12.7 × 21.9 cm)

Gift of the Kulicke family in
memory of Lt. Frederick W.
Kulicke III
1969-86-3

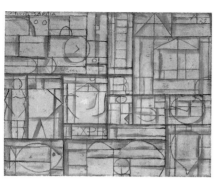

**Torres-Garcia, Joaquin**
Uruguayan, 1874–1949
*Composition*
1929
Upper left: J. Torres-GARCIA;
upper right: 29
Oil on burlap
32 × 39 ⁷/₁₆" (81.3 × 100.2 cm)

A. E. Gallatin Collection
1952-61-121

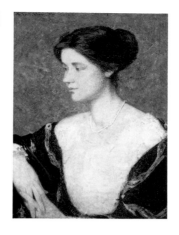

**Turner, Helen Maria**
American, 1858–1958
*Arrangement in Dark and Light*
1912
Upper left: Helen M. Turner
1912
Oil on canvas
24 × 18" (61 × 45.7 cm)

Gift of Dr. and Mrs. George
Woodward
1939-7-17

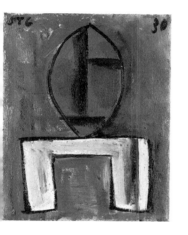

**Torres-Garcia, Joaquin**
*Head*
1930
Upper left: JTG; upper right: 30;
on reverse: J. Torres GARCIA / 30
Oil on canvas
13 ³/₄ × 10 ⁵/₈" (34.9 × 27 cm)

A. E. Gallatin Collection
1952-61-122

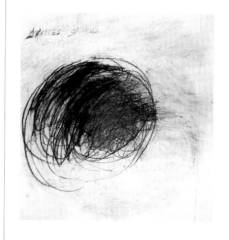

**Twombly, Cy**
American, born 1928
*Fifty Days at Iliam: Shield of
Achilles*
First of ten parts; see following
nine paintings
1978
Upper left: ACHILLES' SHIELD
Oil, oil crayon, and graphite on
canvas
75 ¹/₂ × 67" (191.8 × 170.2 cm)

Gift (by exchange) of Samuel S.
White 3rd and Vera White
1989-90-1

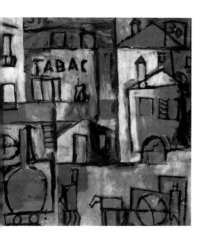

**Torres-Garcia, Joaquin**
*Street*
1930
Upper left: JTG; upper right: 30;
on reverse: J. Torres-Garcia 30
Oil on cardboard
13 × 11 ¹³/₁₆" (33 × 30 cm)

A. E. Gallatin Collection
1937-31-1

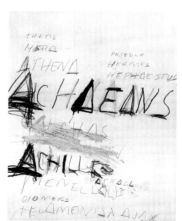

**Twombly, Cy**
*Fifty Days at Iliam: Heroes of the
Achaeans*
Second of ten parts
1978
Top: THETIS / HERA / ATHENA /
POSEDON / HERMES /
HEPHAESTUS; center: ACHAEANS;
bottom: CALCHAS / AG[AMEMNO]N
/ ACHILLES / PATROCLUS /
MENELLAUS / DIOMEDES /
TELAMONIAN AJAX
Oil, oil crayon, and graphite on
canvas
75 ¹/₂ × 59" (191.8 × 149.9 cm)

Gift (by exchange) of Samuel S.
White 3rd and Vera White
1989-90-2

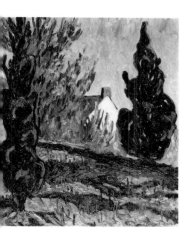

**Tucker, Allen**
American, 1866–1939
*Landscape*
c. 1935
Oil on canvas
24 ¹/₁₆ × 20 ¹/₈" (61.1 × 51.1 cm)

Gift of Mrs. F. Taylor Gauze
1939-3-1

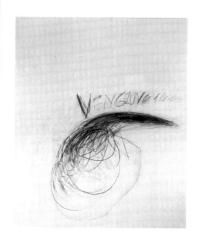

**Twombly, Cy**
*Fifty Days at Iliam: Vengeance of
Achilles*
Third of ten parts
1978
Center: VENGEANCE of
ACHILLES
Oil, oil crayon, and graphite on
canvas
118 × 94 ¹/₄" (299.7 × 239.4 cm)

Gift (by exchange) of Samuel S.
White 3rd and Vera White
1989-90-3

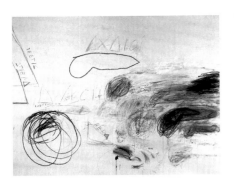

**Twombly, Cy**
*Fifty Days at Iliam: Achaeans in Battle*
Fourth of ten parts
1978
Top center: AXAIOI [Greek for "Achaeans"]; left: THETIS / ATHENA; center: VENUS / DIOMEDES / ACHILLES / AGAMEMNON / AJAX / ACHILLES / PATROCLUS / MENELAUS / HERA; bottom: ARTIST [ ] [ ]
Oil, oil crayon, and graphite on canvas
118 × 149 1/2" (299.7 × 379.7 cm)

Gift (by exchange) of Samuel S. White 3rd and Vera White
1989-90-4

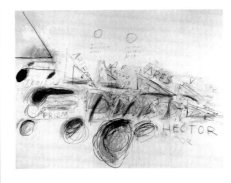

**Twombly, Cy**
*Fifty Days at Iliam: Ilians in Battle*
Eighth of ten parts
1978
Top center: APOLLO / APHRODITE / ARES; ARTEMIS / XANTHUS / LETO; left: PARIS / ANTIPHUS / TROILUS / POLITES / PRIAM; center: ARTEMIS; APOLLO; ARES; Aphrodite / VENUS; right: HECTOR / HEKTOR
Oil, oil crayon, and graphite on canvas
118 × 149 1/2" (299.7 × 379.7 cm)

Gift (by exchange) of Samuel S. White 3rd and Vera White
1989-90-8

**Twombly, Cy**
*Fifty Days at Iliam: The Fire that Consumes All before It*
Fifth of ten parts
1978
Center: Like a fire that consumes all before it
Oil, oil crayon, and graphite on canvas
118 1/8 × 75 5/8" (300 × 192 cm)

Gift (by exchange) of Samuel S. White 3rd and Vera White
1989-90-5

**Twombly, Cy**
*Fifty Days at Iliam: Shades of Eternal Night*
Ninth of ten parts
1978
Center: SHADES OF ETERNAL NIGHT
Oil, oil crayon, and graphite on canvas
118 × 94 1/4" (299.7 × 239.4 cm)

Gift (by exchange) of Samuel S. White 3rd and Vera White
1989-90-9

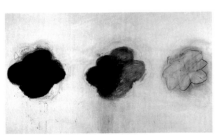

**Twombly, Cy**
*Fifty Days at Iliam: Shades of Achilles, Patroclus, and Hector*
Sixth of ten parts
1978
Left to right, above shades: ACHILLES; PATROCLUS; HECTOR
Oil, oil crayon, and graphite on canvas
118 × 193 1/2" (299.7 × 491.5 cm)

Gift (by exchange) of Samuel S. White 3rd and Vera White
1989-90-6

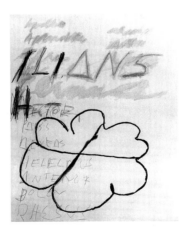

**Twombly, Cy**
*Fifty Days at Iliam: Heroes of the Ilians*
Tenth of ten parts
1978
Top: Apollo / Aphrodite / Ares / Artemis / Xanthus / Leto; center: ILIANS; bottom: HECTOR / PARIS / AENEAS / HELELNUS / ANTENOR / DOLON / RHESUS
Oil, oil crayon, and graphite on canvas
63 3/4 × 59" (161.9 × 149.9 cm)

Gift (by exchange) of Samuel S. White 3rd and Vera White
1989-90-10

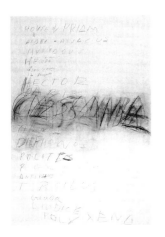

**Twombly, Cy**
*Fifty Days at Iliam: House of Priam*
Seventh of ten parts
1978
Top to bottom: HOUSE OF PRIAM / ARISBE − AESACUS / HYRTACUS / HECUBA / (50 19 SONS by Hecuba / 12 Daughter / HECTOR / PARIS / CASSANDRA / HELENUS / DIEPHONOS / POLITES / POLYDOROS / ANTIPHUS / TROILUS / Creusa / LAODICE / POLYXENA
Oil, oil crayon, and graphite on canvas
118 × 149 1/2" (299.7 × 379.7 cm)

Gift (by exchange) of Samuel S. White 3rd and Vera White
1989-90-7

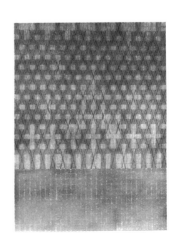

**Tworkov, Jack**
American, born Poland, 1900−1982
*Untitled*
1973
On reverse: Tworkov / 73
Oil on canvas
96 1/4 × 68" (244.5 × 172.7 cm)

Gift of Mr. and Mrs. N. Richard Miller
1979-160-1

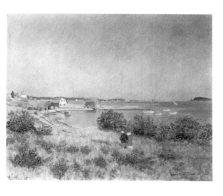

**Tyson, Carroll Sargent, Jr.**
American, 1877–1956
*Before Moonrise*
1912
Lower right: Carroll S. Tyson Jr.
1912.
Oil on canvas
25 × 30 3/16" (63.5 × 76.7 cm)

The Alex Simpson, Jr., Collection
1946-5-4

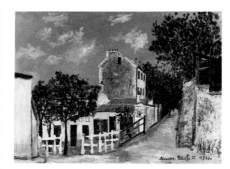

**Utrillo, Maurice**
*The Ancestral Property of Gabrielle d'Estrees (Le Lapin Agile)*
1913
Center: AGILE; lower right:
Maurice. Utrillo. V. 1913.
Oil on panel
23 5/16 × 31 3/16" (59.2 × 79.2 cm)

Bequest of Charlotte Dorrance
Wright
1978-1-36

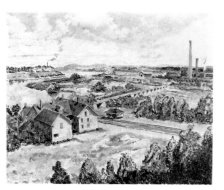

**Tyson, Carroll Sargent, Jr.**
*Inland Maine*
1931
Lower right: Carroll Tyson 1931
Oil on canvas
29 15/16 × 36 1/8" (76 × 91.8 cm)

Gift of an anonymous donor
1932-49-1

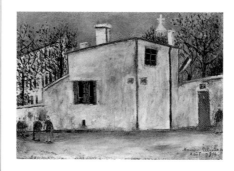

**Utrillo, Maurice**
*Berlioz's House*
1914
Lower right: Maurice Utrillo. /
AOÛT 1914.
Oil on canvas
28 3/4 × 39 3/8" (73 × 100 cm)

The Samuel S. White 3rd and
Vera White Collection
1967-30-84

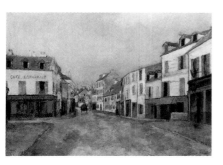

**Utrillo, Maurice**
French, 1883–1955
*Place du Pont, Sarcelles*
1911
Center left: CAFE RESTAURANT /
VINS, CAFE, LIQUEURS; center
right: HOTEL / RESTAURANT;
lower right: Maurice Utrillo, V.
Oil on paper on panel
21 1/2 × 29 3/8" (54.6 × 74.6 cm)

The Louis E. Stern Collection
1963-181-74

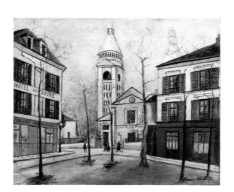

**Utrillo, Maurice**
*Place du Tertre, Montmartre*
c. 1925
Center left: HÔTEL DU TERTRE /
VINS CAFÉ RESTAURANT; lower
right: Maurice. Utrillo. V.
Oil on canvas
21 1/4 × 25 9/16" (54 × 64.9 cm)

Gift of Mr. and Mrs. Cummins
Catherwood
1983-160-1

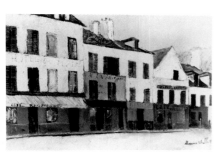

**Utrillo, Maurice**
*Place du Tertre, Montmartre*
c. 1912
Center left: HÔTEL DU TERTRE;
lower right: Maurice Utrillo. V.
Oil on cardboard on panel
19 1/2 × 28 1/2" (49.5 × 72.4 cm)

The Samuel S. White 3rd and
Vera White Collection
1967-30-83

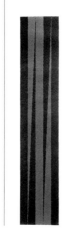

**Valledor, Leo**
American, born 1936
*The Calm*
1966
On reverse: L.V. '66
Acrylic on canvas
15 1/16 × 84 7/16" (38.3 × 214.5 cm)

Purchased with the Adele Haas
Turner and Beatrice Pastorius
Turner Memorial Fund
1967-261-1

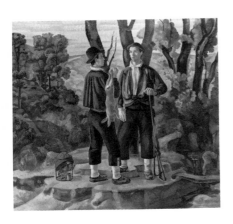

**Valverde, Joaquin**
Spanish, born 1896
*The Hunters*
1931
Lower right: J. VALVERDE /
ALBERCA 930
Oil on canvas
59 × 62 15/16" (149.9 × 159.9 cm)

Gift of Mr. and Mrs. Henry
Clifford
1973-256-9

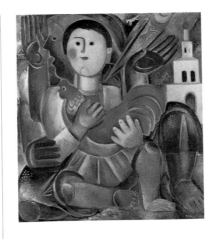

**Vasilieff, Nicholas**
*Young Russia (Child with a Rooster)*
1926
Lower right: N. Vassileff 26; on
reverse: N. Vassileff / 111 W.
122 st
Oil on canvas
40 11/16 × 35 1/8" (103.3 × 89.2 cm)

Gift of Christian Brinton
1941-79-113

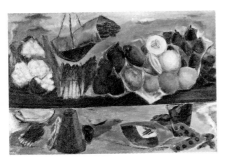

**Van Loan, Dorothy**
American, active c. 1927–c. 1962
*Hercules Cluster*
c. 1944
Lower right: van Loan
Oil on canvas
22 1/8 × 31 7/8" (56.2 × 81 cm)

Gift of John J. Raskob
1945-39-1

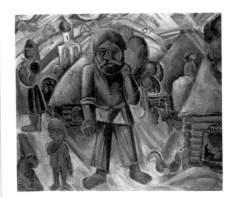

**Vasilieff, Nicholas**
*Return from Work*
1926?
Lower left: Vassileff / 26 [?]
Oil on canvas
21 1/8 × 23 7/8" (53.7 × 60.6 cm)

Gift of Christian Brinton
1941-79-79

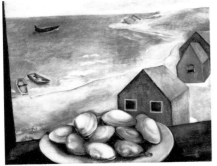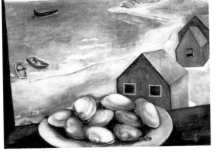

**Varian, Dorothy**
American, born 1895
*Ogunquit*
c. 1930
Lower right: D. Varian
Oil on canvas
15 × 18" (38.1 × 45.7 cm)

Gift of Frank and Alice Osborn
1966-68-53

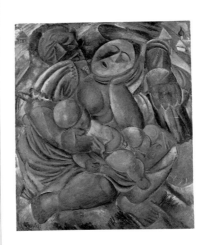

**Vasilieff, Nicholas**
*Rest at Midday*
c. 1926
Lower left: N. Vassileff
Oil on canvas
42 7/8 × 35" (108.9 × 88.9 cm)

Gift of Christian Brinton
1941-79-117

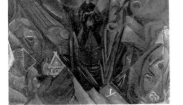

**Vasilieff, Nicholas**
American, born Russia,
1892–1970
*Modern Icon*
c. 1925
Lower left: N. Vassileff
Oil on canvas
40 × 29 7/8" (101.6 × 75.9 cm)

Gift of Christian Brinton
1941-79-110

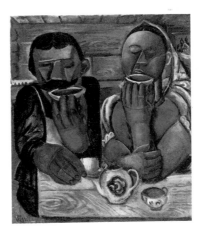

**Vasilieff, Nicholas**
*Tea for Two*
c. 1926
Lower left: Vassileff
Oil on canvas
33 13/16 × 28" (85.9 × 71.1 cm)

Gift of Christian Brinton
1941-79-109

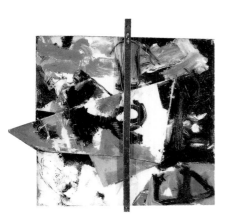

**Vedova, Emilio**
Italian, born 1919
*Plurimi*
1964
Oil on plywood
54 × 56 × 24"
(137.2 × 142.2 × 61 cm)

Gift of Mr. and Mrs. N. Richard
Miller
1972-204-1

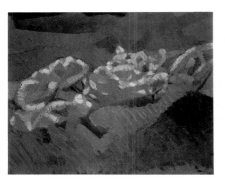

**Villon, Jacques
(Gaston Duchamp)**
French, 1875–1963
*Sketch for "Puteaux (Smoke and
Trees in Bloom No. 2)"*
1912
Lower right: Jacques Villon
Oil on canvas
18 1/4 × 21 3/4" (46.3 × 55.2 cm)

The Louise and Walter Arensberg
Collection
1950-134-189

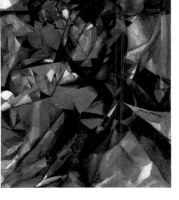

**Villon, Jacques**
*Young Girl*
1912
Center right: Jacques Villon
Oil on canvas
57 9/16 × 45" (146.2 × 114.3 cm)

The Louise and Walter Arensberg
Collection
1950-134-190

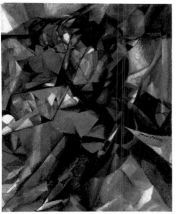

**Villon, Jacques**
*Abstraction*
1932
Lower left: JACQUES VILLON /
32; on reverse: "Abstraction"
Jacques Villon
Oil on canvas
21 7/8 × 26 3/16" (55.6 × 66.5 cm)

The Louise and Walter Arensberg
Collection
1950-134-191

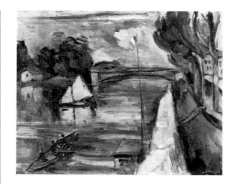

**Vlaminck, Maurice de**
French, 1876–1958
*The Seine at Châtou*
c. 1908
Lower right: Vlaminck
Oil on panel
14 1/2 × 18 1/4" (36.8 × 46.3 cm)

A. E. Gallatin Collection
1944-12-3

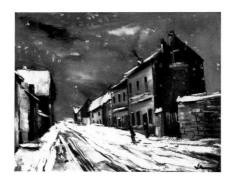

**Vlaminck, Maurice de**
*Winter Scene*
c. 1925
Lower right: Vlaminck
Oil on canvas
28 3/4 × 36" (73 × 91.4 cm)

Gift of Mr. and Mrs. Charles C. G.
Chaplin
1978-149-3

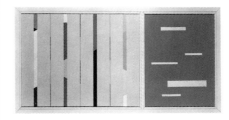

**Vordemberge-Gildewart,
Friedel**
Dutch, born Germany,
1899–1963
*Composition No. 169 (Diptychon)*
1934–48
Right panel, across top:
VORDEMBERGE-GILDEWART /
COMPOSITION No 169 /
1934–1948; on reverse:
VORDEMBERGE-GILDEWART
Composition No. 169 /
1934–1948 DIPTYCHON
Oil on canvas
31 3/4 × 39 7/16" (80.6 × 100.2 cm)
overall

Gift of Mr. and Mrs. Henry
Clifford
1973-256-7

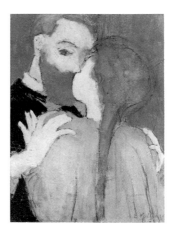

**Vuillard, Édouard**
French, 1868–1940
*Self-Portrait with Sister*
c. 1892
Lower right: E. Vuillard
Oil on paper on cardboard
9 × 6 1/2" (22.9 × 16.5 cm)

The Louis E. Stern Collection
1963-181-76

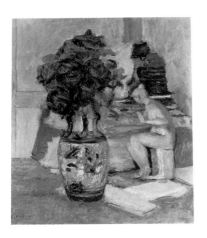

**Vuillard, Édouard**
*Flowers with Leda*
1898–1900
Lower left: E. Vuillard
Oil on cardboard
19 9/16 × 17 3/16" (49.7 × 43.7 cm)

The Louis E. Stern Collection
1963-181-77

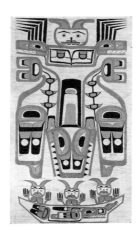

**Wallace, John**
American, born c. 1862, death
date unknown
*Untitled*
Wall panel
1939
Oil on panel
36 × 19 3/4" (91.4 × 50.2 cm)

A. E. Gallatin Collection
1952-61-126

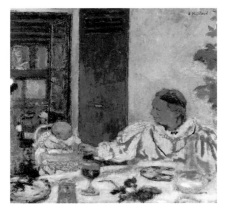

**Vuillard, Édouard**
*The Meal*
c. 1899
Upper right: E. Vuillard
Oil on cardboard
18 1/2 × 18 3/4" (47 × 47.6 cm)

Gift of Henry P. McIlhenny
1964-77-3

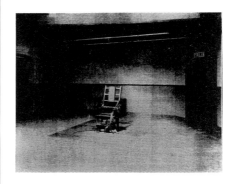

**Warhol, Andy**
American, 1928–1987
*Electric Chair (Red)*
1964
On reverse: Andy Warhol
Silk-screened synthetic polymer
on canvas
22 × 28" (55.9 × 71.1 cm)

Gift of Mr. and Mrs. David N.
Pincus
1979-161-1

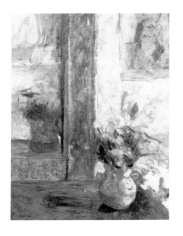

**Vuillard, Édouard**
*Flowers in the Salon*
c. 1905
Lower left: E. Vuillard
Oil on cardboard on canvas
24 7/16 × 18 5/8" (62.1 × 47.3 cm)

Bequest of Charlotte Dorrance
Wright
1978-1-34

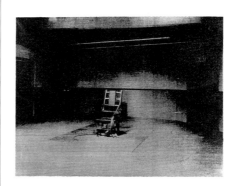

**Warhol, Andy**
*Electric Chair (Gray)*
1964
On reverse: Andy Warhol
Silk-screened synthetic polymer
on canvas
22 1/8 × 28 1/8" (56.2 × 71.4 cm)

Gift of Mr. and Mrs. David N.
Pincus
1979-161-2

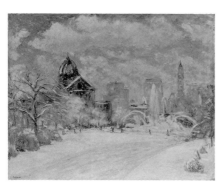

**Wagner, Frederick**
American, 1864–1940
*Logan Circle, Winter*
c. 1920
Lower left: F. WAGNER
Oil on canvas
40 1/8 × 50 3/16" (101.9 × 127.5 cm)

Purchased with subscription
funds
1939-12-1

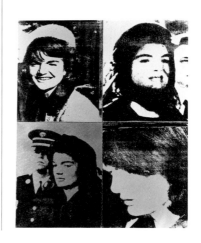

**Warhol, Andy**
*Jackie (Four Jackies) (Portraits of
Mrs. Jacqueline Kennedy)*
1964
On reverse: WARHOL 64 / ANDY
WARHOL '4
Silk-screened acrylic on four
canvas panels
Each panel: 20 × 16" (50.8 ×
40.6 cm)

Gift of Mrs. H. Gates Lloyd
1966-57-1–4

**Wasserman, Burton**
American, born 1929
*1966–67B*
1966–67
On reverse: BURTON
WASSERMAN / 1966/1967-PB
Oil on composition board
30 1/8 × 60" (76.5 × 152.4 cm)

Gift of Mr. and Mrs. Josef Jaffe
1971-220-1

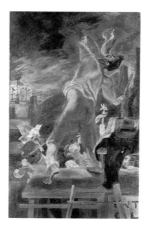

**Watkins, Franklin Chenault**
*The Fire-Eater*
1933–34
On reverse: WATKINS
Oil on canvas
64 3/16 × 37 1/2" (163 × 95.2 cm)

Purchased with subscription
funds
1935-46-1

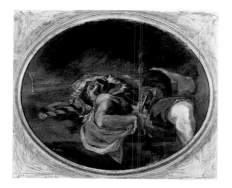

**Watkins, Franklin Chenault**
American, 1894–1972
*Suicide in Costume*
1931–34
Lower left: Watkins
Oil on canvas
36 7/8 × 45 1/16" (93.7 × 114.5 cm)

Purchased with subscription
funds
1942-17-1

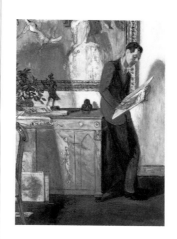

**Watkins, Franklin Chenault**
*Portrait of Henry P. McIlhenny*
1941
Oil on canvas
47 × 33" (119.4 × 83.8 cm)

The Henry P. McIlhenny
Collection in memory of
Frances P. McIlhenny
1986-26-38

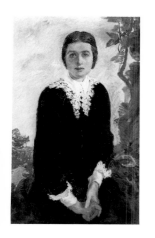

**Watkins, Franklin Chenault**
*Portrait of Mrs. McCarthy*
c. 1932
Oil on canvas
37 1/16 × 22" (94.1 × 55.9 cm)

Gift of Dr. and Mrs. Daniel J.
McCarthy
1942-87-1

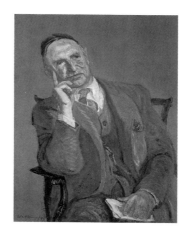

**Watkins, Franklin Chenault**
*Portrait of J. Stogdell Stokes*
1943
Lower left: Watkins/43
Oil on canvas
35 × 27 1/4" (88.9 × 69.2 cm)

Gift of the Board of Trustees
1943-72-1

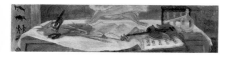

**Watkins, Franklin Chenault**
*Art and Science*
c. 1933
Lower left: FW
Tempera and gesso on panel
11 5/16 × 47" (28.7 × 119.4 cm)

Gift of Dr. and Mrs. Matthew T.
Moore
1964-45-1

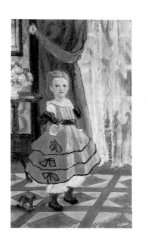

**Watkins, Franklin Chenault**
*Portrait of Sophie Pennebaker*
1943
Lower right: Watkins; on reverse:
derived from a photo taken about
1855. F.C Watkins 1943
Oil on canvas
48 × 27 3/4" (121.9 × 70.5 cm)

Bequest of Susan B. Pennebaker
in memory of Sophie E.
Pennebaker
1944-5-1

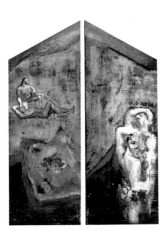

**Watkins, Franklin Chenault**
*Adam and Eve*
Two-panel screen
c. 1947
Silver leaf, tempera, and charcoal
on plywood
Each panel: 79 3/4 × 27 1/2"
(202.6 × 69.8 cm)

Bequest of R. Sturgis Ingersoll
1973-254-1

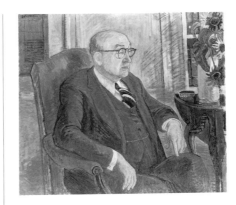

**Watkins, Franklin Chenault**
*Portrait of Albert M. Greenfield*
1959
Upper left: Watkins
Oil on canvas
36 × 40" (91.4 × 101.6 cm)

The Albert M. Greenfield and
Elizabeth M. Greenfield
Collection
1974-178-50

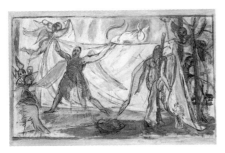

**Watkins, Franklin Chenault**
*Sketch for "The Resurrection"*
For the following painting
c. 1947
Oil on canvas
40 × 60" (101.6 × 152.4 cm)

Bequest of Miss Anna Warren
Ingersoll
1985-85-2

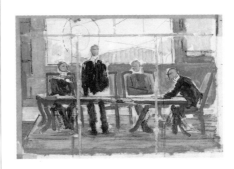

**Watkins, Franklin Chenault**
*Sketch for "Annual Meeting of the
Budd Company"*
For the following painting
c. 1960
Oil, graphite, and newspaper on
panel
16 × 19 1/2" (40.6 × 49.5 cm)

Bequest of Mrs. Edward G.
Budd, Jr.
1973-202-38

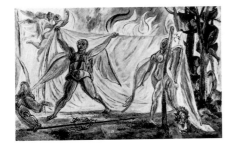

**Watkins, Franklin Chenault**
*The Resurrection*
1948–49
On reverse: Watkins 1948–49
Oil and tempera on canvas
108 × 172" (274.3 × 436.9 cm)

Gift of Henry P. McIlhenny
1955-113-1

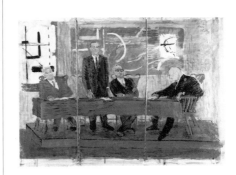

**Watkins, Franklin Chenault**
*Annual Meeting of the Budd
Company*
1960
Upper right: for Ed / from /
Watty
Oil on canvas
24 × 32" (61 × 81.3 cm)

Bequest of Mrs. Edward G.
Budd, Jr.
1973-202-50

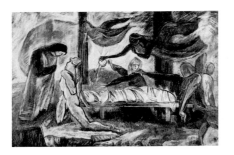

**Watkins, Franklin Chenault**
*Death*
1948–49
On reverse: Watkins 1948–49
Oil and tempera on canvas
108 × 172" (274.3 × 436.9 cm)

Gift of Henry P. McIlhenny
1956-107-1

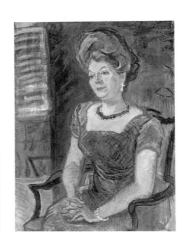

**Watkins, Franklin Chenault**
*Portrait of Elizabeth Greenfield*
1967–68
Upper right: Watkins / 67–68
Oil on canvas
38 1/8 × 28 1/4" (96.8 × 71.7 cm)

Gift of an anonymous donor
1970-52-1

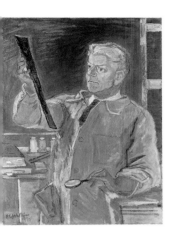

**Watkins, Franklin Chenault**
*Portrait of Henri Marceau*
1970
Lower left: F.C. Watkins / 1970
Oil on canvas
39 1/16 × 29" (99.2 × 73.7 cm)

Purchased with funds contributed
in memory of Henri Marceau
1970-169-1

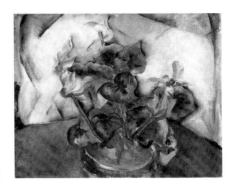

**White, Vera M.**
American, 1888–1966
*Still Life: Cyclamen*
c. 1925
Oil on canvas
8 × 10 1/2" (20.3 × 26.7 cm)

Gift of Salander-O'Reilly
Galleries, Inc.
1988-114-1

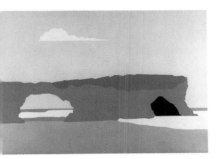

**Weinstone, Howard**
American, born 1928
*Natural Bridge, Pacific Coast*
1971
On reverse: Howard Weinstone
1971 / NATURAL BRIDGES—
PACIFIC COAST #3
Acrylic on canvas
52 1/4 × 72 1/4" (132.7 × 183.5 cm)

Gift of Mr. and Mrs. Walter S.
Marine
1971-222-1

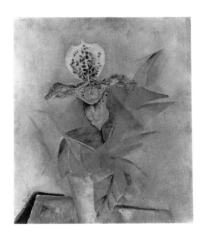

**White, Vera M.**
*Orchid*
1928
On reverse: Vera M. White /
1928
Oil on canvas
12 1/16 × 10" (30.6 × 25.4 cm)

The Samuel S. White 3rd and
Vera White Collection
1967-30-90

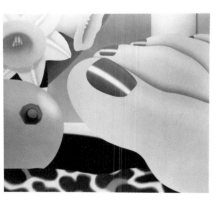

**Wesselmann, Tom**
American, born 1931
*Bedroom Painting No. 7*
1967–69
On reverse: OIL PAINT /
Wesselman 69
Oil on canvas
78 × 87 1/4" (198.1 × 221.6 cm)

Purchased with the Adele Haas
Turner and Beatrice Pastorius
Turner Memorial Fund
1972-156-1

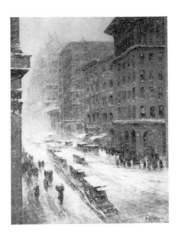

**Wiggins, Guy Carleton**
American, 1883–1962
*Snowstorm, Fifth Avenue*
c. 1935
Lower right: Guy C. Wiggins;
on reverse: "Snow Storm Fifth
Avenue" Guy C. Wiggins
Oil on canvas
40 × 30" (101.6 × 76.2 cm)

The Alex Simpson, Jr., Collection
1946-5-5

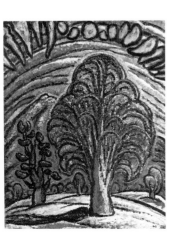

**Weston, Harold**
American, 1894–1972
*The Elm Tree*
1922
Lower right: W. 22
Oil on canvas
24 × 18" (61 × 45.7 cm)

Gift of Mrs. S. Emlen Stokes
1979-13-1

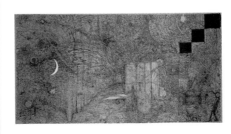

**Wiley, William T.**
American, born 1937
*Known Ooze*
1981
Acrylic and charcoal on canvas
88 × 161" (223.5 × 408.9 cm)

Purchased with the Adele Haas
Turner and Beatrice Pastorius
Turner Memorial Fund and the
Edward and Althea Budd Fund
1982-120-1

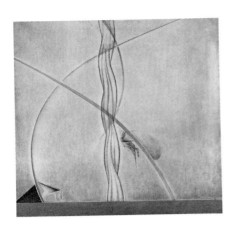

**Williams, Edith Clifford**
American, 1880–1971
*Two Rhythms*
1916
On reverse: Two Rhythms—
1916 / Clifford Williams
Oil on canvas
29 × 28 15/16" (73.7 × 73.5 cm)

The Louise and Walter Arensberg
Collection
1950-134-524

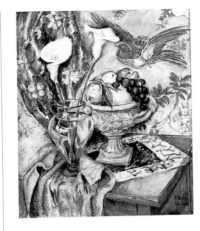

**Wood, Edith Longstreth**
*Still Life with Calla Lilies and Fruit*
c. 1940
Lower right: EDITH / WOOD
Oil on canvas
30 × 25" (76.2 × 63.5 cm)

Gift of Walter Longstreth
1968-41-1

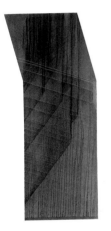

**Williams, Neil**
American, born 1934
*The Return*
1968
Acrylic on canvas
71 5/16 × 24" (181.1 × 61 cm)

Purchased with the Adele Haas
Turner and Beatrice Pastorius
Turner Memorial Fund
1968-119-1

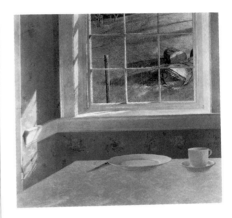

**Wyeth, Andrew Newell**
American, born 1917
*Groundhog Day*
1959
Center right: Andrew Wyeth
Tempera on Masonite
31 3/8 × 32 1/8" (79.7 × 81.6 cm)

Gift of Henry F. du Pont and
Mrs. John Wintersteen
1959-102-1

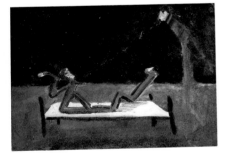

**Wood, Beatrice**
American, born 1896
*Nuit Blanche*
1917
Lower right: Beatrice Wood
Oil on canvas board
10 × 14" (25.4 × 35.6 cm)

Gift of the artist
1978-98-1

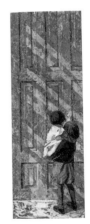

**Yerxa, Thomas**
American, born 1923
*City Children*
1959
Lower left: YERXA 59
Oil on canvas
48 3/16 × 15 15/16" (122.4 × 40.5 cm)

Purchased with the Adele Haas
Turner and Beatrice Pastorius
Turner Memorial Fund
1959-12-8

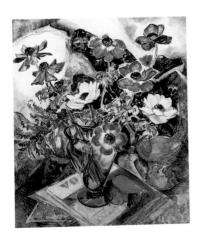

**Wood, Edith Longstreth**
American, 1885–1967
*Still Life with Anemones*
c. 1940
Lower right: E. L. WOOD
Oil on canvas
30 1/4 × 25 1/8" (76.8 × 63.8 cm)

Gift of Miss Miriam H. Thrall
1968-42-1

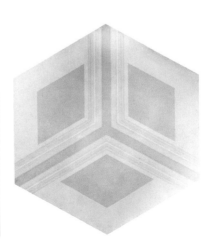

**Zakanitch, Robert**
American, born 1935
*Hexagon Series VI*
1968
Acrylic on canvas
87 3/4 × 76 3/16" (222.9 × 193.5 cm)

Gift of an anonymous donor
1973-73-2

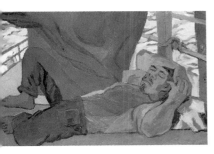

**Zalce, Alfredo**
Mexican, born 1908
*Yucatán, Sleeping on the Deck of a Small Boat*
1945
Lower right: ALFREDO / ZALCE
1945
Oil on canvas
22 1/2 × 33 1/2" (57.1 × 85.1 cm)

Gift of Mr. and Mrs. James P. Magill
1957-127-7

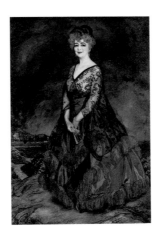

**Zuloaga y Zabaleta, Ignacio**
Spanish, 1870–1945
*Portrait of Mrs. William Fahnestock*
1923
Lower left: I. Zuloaga
Oil on canvas
82 1/4 × 54 1/16" (208.9 × 137.3 cm)

Gift of Julia G. Fahnestock in memory of her husband, William Fahnestock
1940-17-27

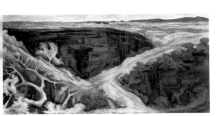

**Zalce, Alfredo**
*Barrancas de Cuernavacas*
1953
Lower left: ALFREDO / ZALCE.53.
Oil on Masonite
23 × 47 5/8" (58.4 × 121 cm)

Gift of Mrs. Beryl Price
1982-104-1

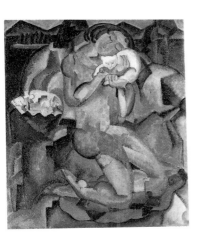

**Zorach, Marguerite Thompson**
American, 1887–1968
*Girl and Cat*
c. 1917
Oil on canvas
24 1/16 × 20 1/16" (61.1 × 51 cm)

Gift of George Biddle
1945-16-39

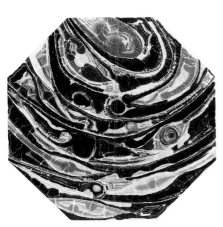

**Zucker, Joe**
American, born 1941
*Porthole No. 3*
1981
Acrylic, cotton, and Rhoplex on canvas
72" (182.9 cm) diameter

Gift of Trisha Brown
1988-80-1

# Miniatures

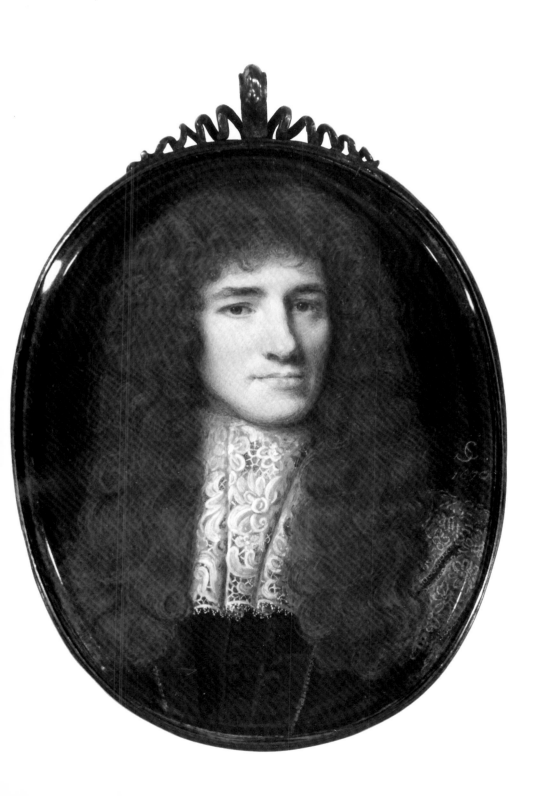

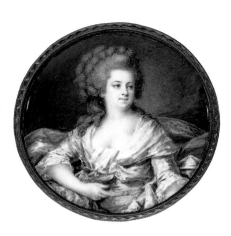

**Augustin, Jean-Baptiste-Jacques**
French, 1759–1832
*Portrait of a Woman*
c. 1800
Watercolor and gouache on cardboard
2 13/16 × 2 7/8" (7.1 × 7.3 cm)

Gift of Mrs. Daniel J. McCarthy
1953-142-2

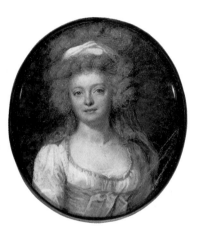

**Augustin, Jean-Baptiste-Jacques**
*Portrait of a Woman*
c. 1800
Watercolor and gouache on cardboard
2 3/8 × 2" (6 × 5.1 cm)

Gift of Mrs. Daniel J. McCarthy
1953-142-3

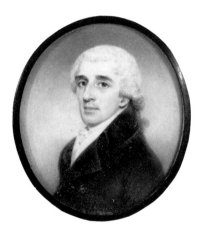

**Barry, John**
English, active 1784–1827
*Portrait of a Man*
Early 19th century
On reverse of frame: Ozias Humphrey / b. 1742 d. 1810
Watercolor on ivory
2 11/16 × 2 3/16" (6.8 × 5.6 cm)

Gift of Mrs. Daniel J. McCarthy
1954-21-11

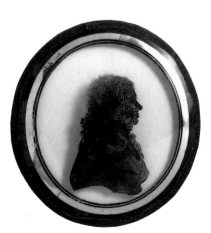

**Beetham, Isabella Robinson, attributed to**
English, 1744–c. 1819
*Silhouette of a Man*
c. 1800
Watercolor reverse-painted on glass
4 1/8 × 3 3/4" (10.5 × 9.5 cm)

Gift of Sarah McLean Williams in memory of Mrs. William L. McLean
1942-101-34

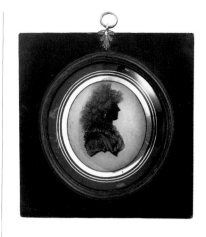

**Beetham, Isabella Robinson, attributed to**
*Silhouette of a Woman*
c. 1800
Watercolor reverse-painted on glass
4 1/2 × 4" (11.4 × 10.2 cm)

Gift of Sarah McLean Williams in memory of Mrs. William L. McLean
1942-101-32

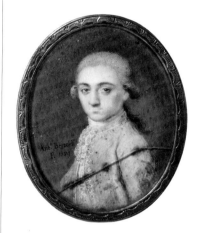

**Bertoldi, Antonio**
Italian, active late 18th century
*Portrait of a Gentleman*
1779
Center left: Ante. Bertoldi / F. 1779
Watercolor on ivory
2 1/8 × 1 5/8" (5.4 × 4.1 cm)

The Bloomfield Moore Collection
1899-966

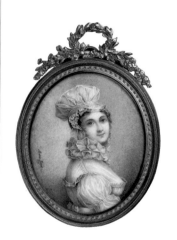

**Bigot, Andrée**
French, active 18th century
*Portrait of a Woman*
18th century
Center left: Andrée Bigot.
Watercolor on ivory
3 5/8 × 2 15/16" (9.2 × 7.5 cm)

Gift of Sarah McLean Williams in memory of Mrs. William L. McLean
1942-101-22

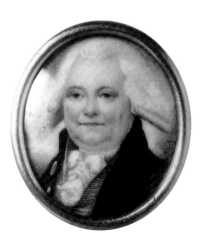

**Bogle, John, attributed to**
Scottish, active England, active c. 1746–c. 1803
*Portrait of a Man*
c. 1800
Center right: JB
Watercolor on ivory
1 9/16 × 1 1/4" (4 × 3.2 cm)

The Bloomfield Moore Collection
1899-968

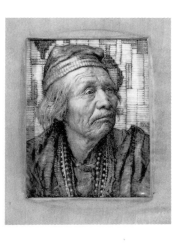

**Brunton, Violet**
English, 1878–1951
*Portrait of an Old Chief*
20th century
Watercolor on ivory
3 ⁵/₈ × 2 ³/₄" (9.2 × 7 cm)

Gift of Mrs. Daniel J. McCarthy
1953-142-8

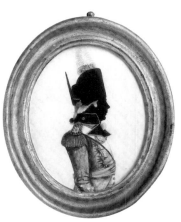

**Buncombe, John**
English, active c. 1790–c. 1800
*Silhouette of an Officer*
c. 1790
Watercolor on cardboard
3 ⁷/₈ × 3" (9.8 × 7.6 cm)

Gift of Sarah McLean Williams
in memory of Mrs. William L.
McLean
1942-101-26

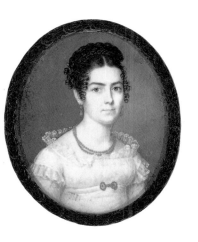

**Collas, Louis-Antoine**
French, born 1775, death date
unknown
*Portrait of Antoinette Melizet*
c. 1820–30
Watercolor on ivory
2 ⁹/₁₆ × 2 ¹/₁₆" (6.5 × 5.2 cm)

Bequest of Leonora L. Koecker
1942-37-5

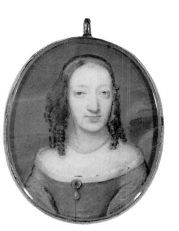

**Cooper, Samuel**
English, 1609–1672
*Portrait of a Woman*
c. 1650–60
Watercolor and gouache on
vellum
1 ¹/₄ × 1" (3.2 × 2.5 cm)

Gift of Mrs. Daniel J. McCarthy
1953-142-13

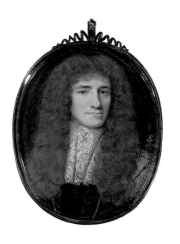

**Cooper, Samuel**
*Portrait of Anthony Ashley Cooper,
2nd Earl of Shaftesbury*
1670
Center right: SC. / 1670
Watercolor on vellum
3 ³/₁₆ × 2 ¹/₂" (8.1 × 6.3 cm)

Gift of Mrs. Daniel J. McCarthy
1953-142-10

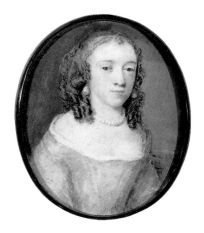

**Cooper, Samuel, attributed to**
*Portrait of Mary, Daughter of
Oliver Cromwell*
17th century
Center right: SC
Watercolor and gouache on
vellum
2 ⁵/₈ × 2 ¹/₈" (6.7 × 5.4 cm)

Gift of Mrs. Daniel J. McCarthy
1953-142-12

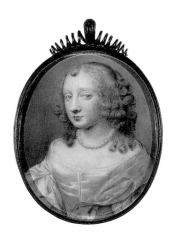

**Cooper, Samuel, copy after**
*Portrait of the Countess of
Shaftesbury*
After 1672
On reverse of frame: Countess of
Shaftesbury, / Samuel Cooper. /
ob. 1672
Watercolor on vellum
2 ¹⁵/₁₆ × 2 ³/₈" (7.5 × 6 cm)

Gift of Mrs. Daniel J. McCarthy
1953-142-11

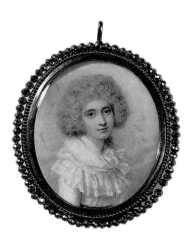

**Cosway, Richard**
English, 1742–1821
*Portrait of the Princess Lubomirska*
1789
On card on reverse: Rdus.
Cosway / R.A. / Primarius Pictor /
Serenissimi Walliae / Principis /
Pinxit / 1789
Watercolor on ivory
2 ⁷/₈ × 2 ³/₈" (7.3 × 6 cm)

Gift of Mrs. Daniel J. McCarthy
1953-142-14

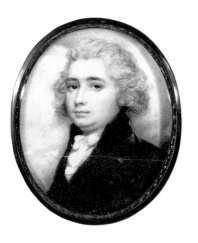

**Cosway, Richard**
*Portrait of a Man in a Black Coat*
c. 1790
Watercolor on ivory
2 1/16 × 1 5/8" (5.2 × 4.1 cm)

Gift of Mrs. Daniel J. McCarthy
1953-142-18

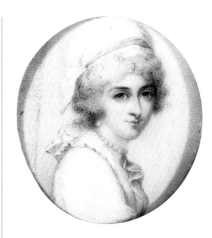

**Cosway, Richard**
*Portrait of Mrs. Jackson*
1794
On paper on reverse: Mrs.
Jackson / 1794
Watercolor on ivory
2 1/2 × 2 3/16" (6.3 × 5.6 cm)

Gift of Mrs. Daniel J. McCarthy
1953-142-19

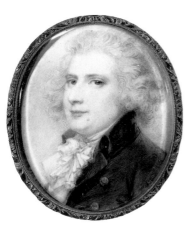

**Cosway, Richard**
*Portrait of a Man in a Blue Coat*
c. 1790
Watercolor on ivory
2 1/16 × 1 5/8" (5.2 × 4.1 cm)

Gift of Mrs. Daniel J. McCarthy
1953-142-17

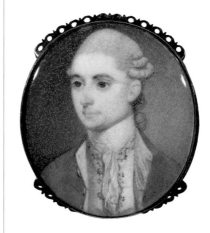

**Crosse, Richard, attributed to**
English, 1742–1810
*Portrait of a Man*
c. 1800
Watercolor on ivory
1 7/16 × 1 1/4" (3.6 × 3.2 cm)

The Bloomfield Moore Collection
1899-969

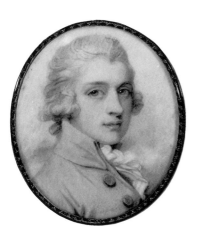

**Cosway, Richard**
*Portrait of a Man in a White Coat*
c. 1790
Watercolor on ivory
2 1/16 × 1 5/8" (5.2 × 4.1 cm)

Gift of Mrs. Daniel J. McCarthy
1953-142-16

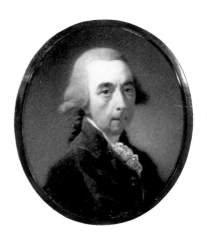

**Daniel of Bath, Joseph,
attributed to**
English, c. 1760–1803
**or Abraham Daniel of Bath,
attributed to**
English, died 1806
*Portrait of Joseph Galloway*
c. 1790–1803
Watercolor on ivory
2 3/8 × 1 15/16" (6 × 4.9 cm)

Purchased with the John D.
McIlhenny Fund
1966-20-3

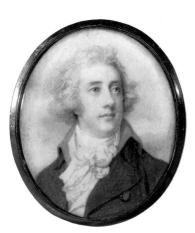

**Cosway, Richard**
*Portrait of the Honorable Andrew
James Cochrane*
1793
On card on reverse: Rdus.
Cosway / R.A. / Primarius Pictor /
Serenissimi Walliae / Principis /
Pinxit / 1793
Watercolor on ivory
2 15/16 × 2 5/16" (7.5 × 5.9 cm)

Gift of Mrs. Daniel J. McCarthy
1953-142-15

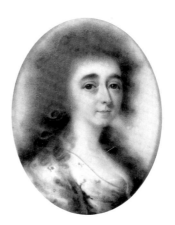

**Daniel of Bath, Joseph,
attributed to**
**or Abraham Daniel of Bath,
attributed to**
*Portrait of Mrs. Roberts* [née
Galloway]
c. 1790–1803
Watercolor on ivory
1 13/16 × 1 3/8" (4.6 × 3.5 cm)

Purchased with the John D.
McIlhenny Fund
1966-20-6

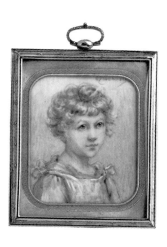

**Debillemont-Chardon, Gabrielle**
French, 1860?–1957
*Portrait of a Girl*
1929
Upper right: G. Debillemont-Chardon
Watercolor on ivory
$2\,^3/_4 \times 2\,^1/_8$" (7 × 5.4 cm)

Gift of the Pennsylvania Society of Miniature Painters in memory of Emily Drayton Taylor
1954-42-25

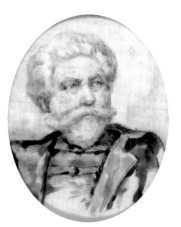

**Debillemont-Chardon, Gabrielle**
*Portrait of an Old, One-Armed, Italian Veteran*
1929
On reverse: June 1929
Watercolor on ivory
$3\,^7/_{16} \times 2\,^5/_8$" (8.7 × 6.7 cm)

Gift of the Pennsylvania Society of Miniature Painters in memory of Emily Drayton Taylor
1954-42-24

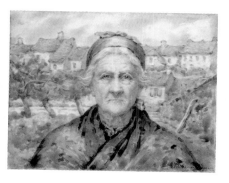

**Debillemont-Chardon, Gabrielle**
*La Mère Melv*
20th century
Lower right: G. Debillemont-Chardon
Watercolor on ivory substitute
$3\,^1/_2 \times 4\,^1/_2$" (8.9 × 11.4 cm)

Gift of Mrs. Daniel J. McCarthy
1953-142-20

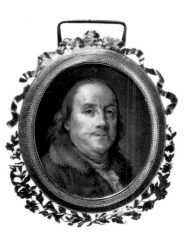

**Duplessis, Joseph-Siffred, attributed to**
French, 1725–1802
*Portrait of Benjamin Franklin*
18th century
Watercolor on ivory
$1\,^5/_8 \times 1\,^3/_8$" (4.1 × 3.5 cm)

Gift of Mrs. Edward S. Harkness
1932-8-1

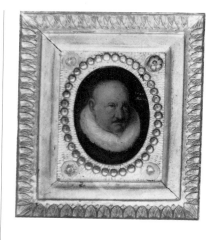

**Dutch, unknown artist**
*Portrait of a Man*
Companion to the following miniature
1626
Upper right: 1626 / AET. 62
Oil on copper
$2\,^9/_{16} \times 1\,^{15}/_{16}$" (6.5 × 4.9 cm)

Bequest of A. Manderson Troth
1927-52-37

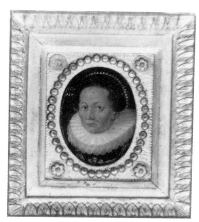

**Dutch, unknown artist**
*Portrait of a Woman*
Companion to the preceding miniature
1626
Upper left: 1626 / AE [illegible]
Oil on copper
$2\,^9/_{16} \times 1\,^{15}/_{16}$" (6.5 × 4.9 cm)

Bequest of A. Manderson Troth
1927-52-38

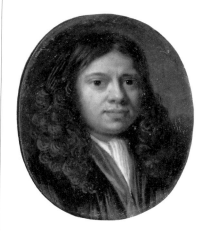

**Dutch, unknown artist**
Previously attributed to Nicolaes Maes (JFD 1972)
*Portrait of a Man*
c. 1675–1700
Oil on copper
$2\,^1/_4 \times 1\,^7/_8$" (5.7 × 4.8 cm)

John G. Johnson Collection
cat. 488

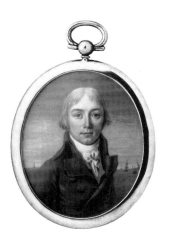

**Dutch or English, unknown artist**
*Portrait of Samuel Hunter Eakin*
18th century
Watercolor on ivory
$2\,^1/_2 \times 2\,^1/_8$" (6.4 × 5.4 cm)

Bequest of Constance A. Jones
1988-27-114

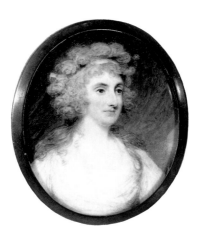

**Edridge, Henry**
English, 1769–1821
*Portrait of Mrs. Berridge*
c. 1790
Watercolor on ivory
2 1/2 × 2" (6.3 × 5.1 cm)

Gift of Mrs. Daniel J. McCarthy
1954-21-7

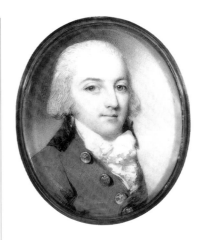

**Engleheart, George**
*Portrait of a Man*
c. 1800
Watercolor on ivory
2 1/16 × 1 5/8" (5.2 × 4.1 cm)

Gift of Mrs. Daniel J. McCarthy
1953-142-25

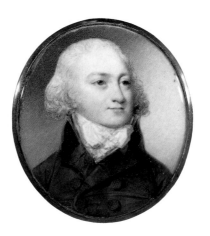

**Engleheart, George**
English, 1752–1829
*Portrait of a Man*
c. 1795
Lower right: E
Watercolor on ivory
2 7/16 × 2 1/16" (6.2 × 5.2 cm)

Gift of Mrs. Daniel J. McCarthy
1953-142-23

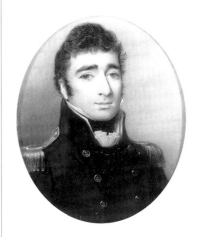

**Engleheart, George**
*Portrait of Captain Roger Curtis, R.N.*
1811
On paper on reverse: George
Engleheart / Hartford Street
Mayfair / Pinxit / 1811
Watercolor on ivory
3 3/4 × 2 7/8" (9.5 × 7.3 cm)

Gift of Mrs. Daniel J. McCarthy
1953-142-21

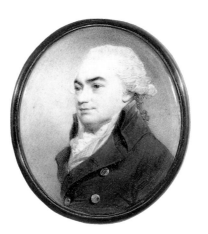

**Engleheart, George**
*Portrait of a Man*
c. 1795
Watercolor on ivory
2 3/8 × 1 15/16" (6 × 4.9 cm)

Gift of Mrs. Daniel J. McCarthy
1953-142-24

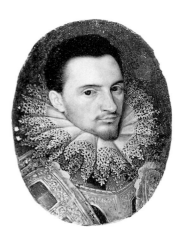

**English, unknown artist**
Previously listed as an English
artist, c. 1650 (JGJ 1941)
*Portrait of a Man*
c. 1600
Oil on copper
3 13/16 × 2 15/16" (9.7 × 7.5 cm)

John G. Johnson Collection
cat. 449

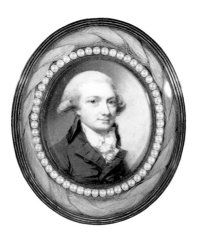

**Engleheart, George**
*Portrait of Lord Northhampton*
c. 1795
Watercolor on ivory
1 15/16 × 1 5/8" (4.9 × 4.1 cm)

Gift of Mrs. Daniel J. McCarthy
1953-142-22

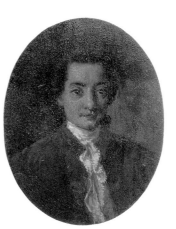

**English, unknown artist**
*Portrait of a Man*
c. 1740
Oil on copper
3 9/16 × 2 5/8" (9 × 6.7 cm)

The Bloomfield Moore Collection
1899-957

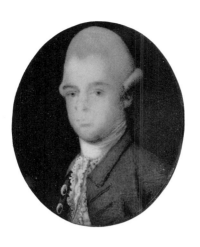

**English, unknown artist**
*Portrait of a Man*
c. 1750
Lower right: JD
Watercolor on ivory
1 9/16 × 1 1/4" (4 × 3.2 cm)

The Bloomfield Moore Collection
1899-965

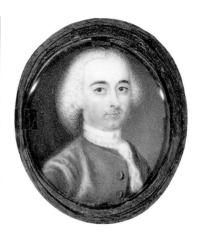

**English, unknown artist**
*Portrait of a Man of the Galloway
Family*
c. 1775
Watercolor on ivory
1 9/16 × 1 1/4" (4 × 3.2 cm)

Purchased with the John D.
McIlhenny Fund
1966-20-4

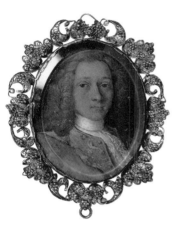

**English?, unknown artist**
*Portrait of a Man*
c. 1750–75
Watercolor and gouache on
cardboard
1 13/16 × 1 7/16" (4.6 × 3.6 cm)

The Bloomfield Moore Collection
1899-1029

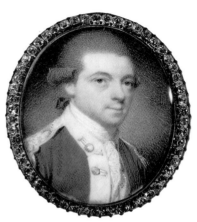

**English, unknown artist**
*Portrait of Joseph Galloway*
c. 1775
Watercolor on ivory
1 7/16 × 1 3/16" (3.6 × 3 cm)

Purchased with the John D.
McIlhenny Fund
1966-20-2

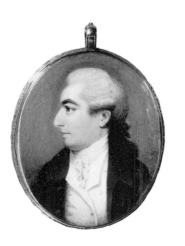

**English, unknown artist**
*Portrait of a Man*
c. 1770
Watercolor on ivory
1 3/4 × 1 3/8" (4.4 × 3.5 cm)

Gift of W. Parsons Todd and
Miss Mary J. Todd
1938-29-6

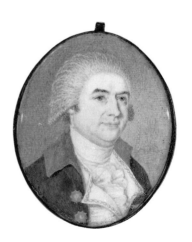

**English, unknown artist**
*Portrait of a Man*
c. 1780–1800
Watercolor on ivory
2 × 1 9/16" (5.1 × 4 cm)

The Bloomfield Moore Collection
1899-964

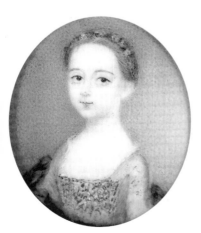

**English, unknown artist**
*Portrait of Miss Roberts*
c. 1770
Watercolor on ivory
1 1/2 × 1 1/4" (3.8 × 3.2 cm)

Purchased with the John D.
McIlhenny Fund
1966-20-5

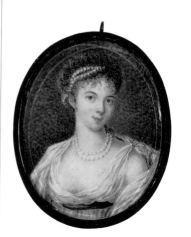

**English, unknown artist**
*Portrait of a Woman*
c. 1780–1800
Watercolor on cardboard
3 × 2 1/4" (7.6 × 5.7 cm)

The Bloomfield Moore Collection
1882-1175

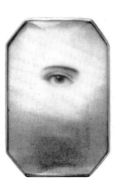

**English, unknown artist**
*Portrait of a Right Eye*
c. 1790–1800
Watercolor on ivory
1 1/8 × 11/16" (2.9 × 1.7 cm)

Gift of Joseph Carson, Hope
Carson Randolph, John B.
Carson, and Anna Hampton
Carson in memory of their
mother, Mrs. Hampton L. Carson
1935-17-6

**English, unknown artist**
*Portrait of Mr. Keppel's Left Eye*
c. 1790–1800
Watercolor on ivory
1/2 × 3/4" (1.3 × 1.9 cm)

Gift of Joseph Carson, Hope
Carson Randolph, John B.
Carson, and Anna Hampton
Carson in memory of their
mother, Mrs. Hampton L. Carson
1935-17-18

**English, unknown artist**
*Portrait of a Woman's Left Eye*
c. 1790–1800
Watercolor on ivory
5/8 × 3/4" (1.6 × 1.9 cm)

Gift of Joseph Carson, Hope
Carson Randolph, John B.
Carson, and Anna Hampton
Carson in memory of their
mother, Mrs. Hampton L. Carson
1935-17-20

**English, unknown artist**
*Portrait of Part of Mr. Keppel's Face*
c. 1790–1800
Watercolor on ivory
5/8 × 13/16" (1.6 × 2.1 cm)

Gift of Joseph Carson, Hope
Carson Randolph, John B.
Carson, and Anna Hampton
Carson in memory of their
mother, Mrs. Hampton L. Carson
1935-17-19

**English, unknown artist**
*Portrait of a Woman's Left Eye*
c. 1790–1800
Watercolor on ivory
9/16 × 3/4" (1.4 × 1.9 cm)

Gift of Joseph Carson, Hope
Carson Randolph, John B.
Carson, and Anna Hampton
Carson in memory of their
mother, Mrs. Hampton L. Carson
1935-17-21

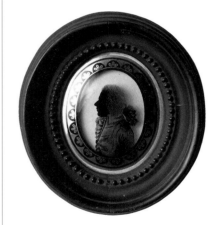

**English, unknown artist**
*Silhouette of a Man*
18th century
Watercolor reverse-painted on
glass
4 3/8 × 3 1/2" (11.1 × 8.9 cm)

Gift of Sarah McLean Williams
in memory of Mrs. William L.
McLean
1942-101-33

**English, unknown artist**
*Portrait of a Woman's Right Eye*
c. 1790–1800
Watercolor on ivory
9/16 × 11/16" (1.4 × 1.7 cm)

Gift of Joseph Carson, Hope
Carson Randolph, John B.
Carson, and Anna Hampton
Carson in memory of their
mother, Mrs. Hampton L. Carson
1935-17-22

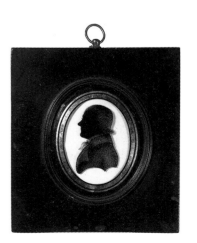

**English, unknown artist**
*Silhouette of a Man*
18th century
Watercolor reverse-painted on
glass
2 7/8 × 2 1/4" (7.3 × 5.7 cm)

Gift of Sarah McLean Williams
in memory of Mrs. William L.
McLean
1942-101-35

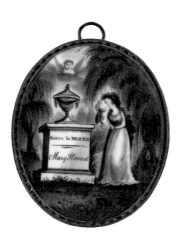

**English, unknown artist**
*Mourner by a Monument*
c. 1800
On plinth: GONE TO BLISS /
Mary Howard; on reverse: MB
Watercolor on ivory
1 7/8 × 1 1/2" (4.8 × 3.8 cm)

Gift of Miss Sara A. Swain in
memory of Mrs. Sara S. Swain
1909-142

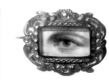

**English, unknown artist**
*Portrait of a Left Eye*
c. 1800
Watercolor on ivory
3/8 × 5/8" (0.9 × 1.6 cm)

Gift of Mrs. Charles Francis
Griffith in memory of Dr. L.
Webster Fox
1936-6-1

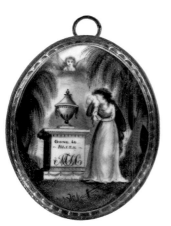

**English, unknown artist**
*Mourner by a Monument*
c. 1800
On plinth: Gone to BLISS / MH;
on reverse: RB
Watercolor on ivory
1 7/8 × 1 1/2" (4.8 × 3.8 cm)

Gift of Miss Sara A. Swain in
memory of Mrs. Sara S. Swain
1909-143

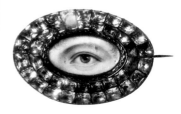

**English, unknown artist**
*Portrait of a Left Eye*
c. 1800
Watercolor on ivory
1/2 × 15/16" (1.3 × 2.4 cm)

Gift of Mrs. Charles Francis
Griffith in memory of Dr. L.
Webster Fox
1936-6-5

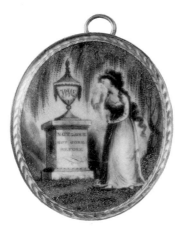

**English, unknown artist**
*Mourner by a Monument*
c. 1800
On urn: WME; on plinth: NOT
LOST / BUT GONE / BEFORE
Watercolor on ivory
1 7/8 × 1 1/2" (4.8 × 3.8 cm)

The Ozeas, Ramborger, Keehmle
Collection
1921-34-119

**English, unknown artist**
*Portrait of a Left Eye*
c. 1800
Watercolor on ivory
1/4 × 1/2" (0.6 × 1.3 cm)

Gift of Mrs. Charles Francis
Griffith in memory of Dr. L.
Webster Fox
1936-6-8

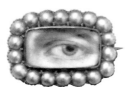

**English, unknown artist**
*Portrait of a Left Eye*
c. 1800
Watercolor on ivory
1/4 × 1/2" (0.6 × 1.3 cm)

Gift of Joseph Carson, Hope
Carson Randolph, John B.
Carson, and Anna Hampton
Carson in memory of their
mother, Mrs. Hampton L. Carson
1935-17-14

**English, unknown artist**
*Portrait of a Left Eye*
c. 1800
Watercolor on ivory
5/16 × 1/2" (0.8 × 1.3 cm)

Gift of Mrs. Charles Francis
Griffith in memory of Dr. L.
Webster Fox
1936-6-14

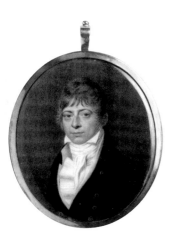

**English, unknown artist**
*Portrait of a Man*
c. 1800
Watercolor on ivory
2 ¹³/₁₆ × 2 ³/₈" (7.1 × 6 cm)

Gift of Mrs. Daniel J. McCarthy
1954-63-11

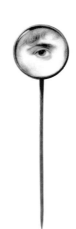

**English, unknown artist**
*Portrait of a Right Eye*
c. 1800
Watercolor on ivory
³/₄" (1.9 cm) diameter

Gift of Joseph Carson, Hope
Carson Randolph, John B.
Carson, and Anna Hampton
Carson in memory of their
mother, Mrs. Hampton L. Carson
1935-17-13

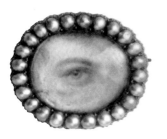

**English, unknown artist**
*Portrait of a Man's Right Eye*
c. 1800
Watercolor on ivory
⁵/₈ × ³/₄" (1.6 × 1.9 cm)

Gift of Joseph Carson, Hope
Carson Randolph, John B.
Carson, and Anna Hampton
Carson in memory of their
mother, Mrs. Hampton L. Carson
1935-17-9

**English, unknown artist**
*Portrait of a Right Eye*
c. 1800
Watercolor on ivory
1 × ⁵/₈" (2.5 × 1.6 cm)

Gift of Joseph Carson, Hope
Carson Randolph, John B.
Carson, and Anna Hampton
Carson in memory of their
mother, Mrs. Hampton L. Carson
1935-17-16

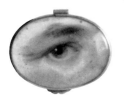

**English, unknown artist**
*Portrait of a Man's Right Eye*
c. 1800
Watercolor on ivory
¹/₂ × ¹¹/₁₆" (1.3 × 1.7 cm)

Gift of Joseph Carson, Hope
Carson Randolph, John B.
Carson, and Anna Hampton
Carson in memory of their
mother, Mrs. Hampton L. Carson
1935-17-17

**English, unknown artist**
*Portrait of a Right Eye*
c. 1800
Watercolor on ivory
⁵/₁₆ × ¹/₂" (0.8 × 1.3 cm)

Gift of Mrs. Charles Francis
Griffith in memory of Dr. L.
Webster Fox
1936-6-2

**English, unknown artist**
*Portrait of a Man's Right Eye*
c. 1800
Watercolor on ivory
⁵/₁₆ × ⁵/₈" (0.8 × 1.6 cm)

Gift of Mrs. Charles Francis
Griffith in memory of Dr. L.
Webster Fox
1936-6-4

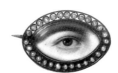

**English, unknown artist**
*Portrait of a Right Eye*
c. 1800
Watercolor on ivory
¹/₂ × ⁷/₈" (1.3 × 2.2 cm)

Gift of Mrs. Charles Francis
Griffith in memory of Dr. L.
Webster Fox
1936-6-3

**English, unknown artist**
*Portrait of a Right Eye*
c. 1800
Watercolor on ivory
³/₈ × ⁵/₈" (0.9 × 1.6 cm)

Gift of Mrs. Charles Francis
Griffith in memory of Dr. L.
Webster Fox
1936-6-12

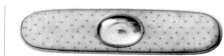

**English, unknown artist**
*Portrait of a Woman's Left Eye*
c. 1800
Watercolor on ivory
⁷/₁₆ × ⁵/₈" (1.1 × 1.6 cm)

Gift of Joseph Carson, Hope
Carson Randolph, John B.
Carson, and Anna Hampton
Carson in memory of their
mother, Mrs. Hampton L. Carson
1935-17-2

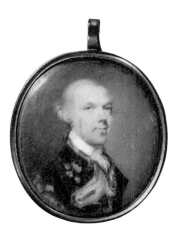

**English, unknown artist**
*Portrait of a Soldier*
c. 1800
Watercolor on ivory
1 ¹/₄ × 1 ¹/₁₆" (3.2 × 2.7 cm)

Gift of W. Parsons Todd and
Miss Mary J. Todd
1938-29-7

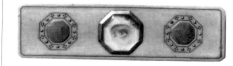

**English, unknown artist**
*Portrait of a Woman's Left Eye*
c. 1800
Watercolor on ivory
⁵/₈ × ⁵/₈" (1.6 × 1.6 cm)

Gift of Joseph Carson, Hope
Carson Randolph, John B.
Carson, and Anna Hampton
Carson in memory of their
mother, Mrs. Hampton L. Carson
1935-17-3

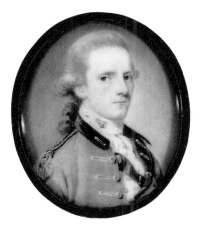

**English, unknown artist**
*Portrait of a Soldier*
c. 1800
Watercolor on ivory
1 ⁷/₁₆ × 1 ³/₁₆" (3.6 × 3 cm)

Gift of Mrs. Daniel J. McCarthy
1955-1-17

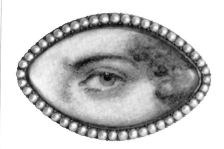

**English, unknown artist**
*Portrait of a Woman's Left Eye*
c. 1800
Watercolor on ivory
³/₄ × 1 ¹/₄" (1.9 × 3.2 cm)

Gift of Joseph Carson, Hope
Carson Randolph, John B.
Carson, and Anna Hampton
Carson in memory of their
mother, Mrs. Hampton L. Carson
1935-17-5

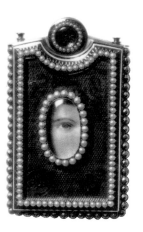

**English, unknown artist**
*Portrait of a Woman's Left Eye*
c. 1800
Watercolor on ivory
¹⁵/₁₆ × ⁹/₁₆" (2.4 × 1.4 cm)

Gift of Joseph Carson, Hope
Carson Randolph, John B.
Carson, and Anna Hampton
Carson in memory of their
mother, Mrs. Hampton L. Carson
1935-17-1

**English, unknown artist**
*Portrait of a Woman's Left Eye*
c. 1800
Watercolor on ivory
³/₈ × ⁹/₁₆" (0.9 × 1.4 cm)

Gift of Joseph Carson, Hope
Carson Randolph, John B.
Carson, and Anna Hampton
Carson in memory of their
mother, Mrs. Hampton L. Carson
1935-17-8

**English, unknown artist**
*Portrait of a Woman's Left Eye*
c. 1800
Watercolor on ivory
$3/8 \times 9/16$" (0.9 × 1.4 cm)

Gift of Mrs. Charles Francis
Griffith in memory of Dr. L.
Webster Fox
1936-6-10

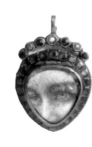

**English, unknown artist**
*Portrait of Part of a Woman's Face*
c. 1800
Watercolor on ivory
$3/8 \times 3/8$" (0.9 × 0.9 cm)

Gift of Joseph Carson, Hope
Carson Randolph, John B.
Carson, and Anna Hampton
Carson in memory of their
mother, Mrs. Hampton L. Carson
1935-17-15

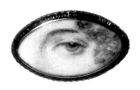

**English, unknown artist**
*Portrait of a Woman's Left Eye*
c. 1800
Watercolor on ivory
$13/16 \times 1\,5/16$" (2.1 × 3.3 cm)

Gift of Mrs. Charles Francis
Griffith in memory of Dr. L.
Webster Fox
1936-6-13

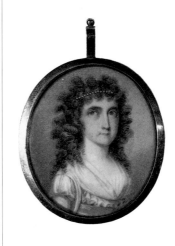

**English, unknown artist**
*Portrait of Catherine Warner Hosach*
c. 1800
Watercolor on ivory
$2\,1/8 \times 1\,3/4$" (5.4 × 4.4 cm)

Gift of Mrs. H. Gates Lloyd
1973-154-1

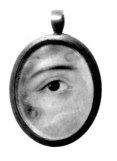

**English, unknown artist**
*Portrait of a Woman's Right Eye*
c. 1800
Watercolor on cardboard
$1\,5/8 \times 1\,3/16$" (4.1 × 3 cm)

Gift of Joseph Carson, Hope
Carson Randolph, John B.
Carson, and Anna Hampton
Carson in memory of their
mother, Mrs. Hampton L. Carson
1935-17-4

**English, unknown artist**
*Portrait of a Left Eye*
c. 1800–10
Watercolor on ivory
$1/4 \times 9/16$" (0.6 × 1.4 cm)

Gift of Mrs. Charles Francis
Griffith in memory of Dr. L.
Webster Fox
1936-6-6

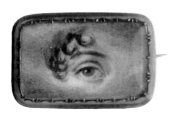

**English, unknown artist**
*Portrait of a Woman's Right Eye*
c. 1800
Watercolor on ivory
$9/16 \times 15/16$" (1.4 × 2.4 cm)

Gift of Joseph Carson, Hope
Carson Randolph, John B.
Carson, and Anna Hampton
Carson in memory of their
mother, Mrs. Hampton L. Carson
1935-17-12

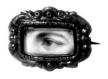

**English, unknown artist**
*Portrait of a Left Eye*
c. 1800–10
Watercolor on ivory
$3/8 \times 5/8$" (0.9 × 1.6 cm)

Gift of Mrs. Charles Francis
Griffith in memory of Dr. L.
Webster Fox
1936-6-11

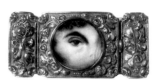

**English, unknown artist**
*Portrait of a Man's Right Eye*
c. 1800–10
Watercolor on ivory
⁵⁄₈" (1.6 cm) diameter

Gift of Mrs. Charles Francis Griffith in memory of Dr. L. Webster Fox
1936-6-15

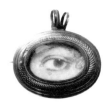

**English, unknown artist**
*Portrait of a Woman's Left Eye*
c. 1800–10
Watercolor on ivory
⁹⁄₁₆ × ⁷⁄₈" (1.4 × 2.2 cm)

Gift of Joseph Carson, Hope Carson Randolph, John B. Carson, and Anna Hampton Carson in memory of their mother, Mrs. Hampton L. Carson
1935-17-23

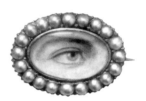

**English, unknown artist**
*Portrait of a Right Eye*
c. 1800–10
On reverse of frame: Ann Saner / died 5 Oct. / 1797. / Aged 66. / Adam Saner / died 30 Nov / 1805 / Aged 7
Watercolor on ivory
³⁄₈ × ⁹⁄₁₆" (0.9 × 1.4 cm)

Gift of Joseph Carson, Hope Carson Randolph, John B. Carson, and Anna Hampton Carson in memory of their mother, Mrs. Hampton L. Carson
1935-17-10

**English, unknown artist**
*Portrait of E. Vestell's Left Eye*
c. 1800–10
On reverse: Eliza Hunt / E. Vestell
Watercolor on ivory
⁵⁄₁₆ × ¹⁄₂" (0.8 × 1.3 cm)

Gift of Mrs. Charles Francis Griffith in memory of Dr. L. Webster Fox
1936-6-9

**English, unknown artist**
*Portrait of a Right Eye*
c. 1800–10
Watercolor on ivory
¹⁄₄ × ¹⁄₂" (0.6 × 1.3 cm)

Gift of Mrs. Charles Francis Griffith in memory of Dr. L. Webster Fox
1936-6-7

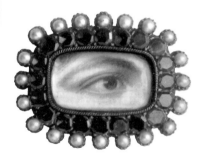

**English, unknown artist**
*Portrait of Sarah Best's Right Eye*
c. 1800–10
On reverse of frame: Sarah Best / Obt July 6; / 1833 / Aet 79
Watercolor on ivory
⁷⁄₁₆ × ³⁄₄" (1.1 × 1.9 cm)

Gift of Joseph Carson, Hope Carson Randolph, John B. Carson, and Anna Hampton Carson in memory of their mother, Mrs. Hampton L. Carson
1935-17-11

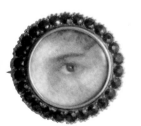

**English, unknown artist**
*Portrait of a Woman's Left Eye*
c. 1800–10
Watercolor on ivory
⁹⁄₁₆" (1.4 cm) diameter

Gift of Joseph Carson, Hope Carson Randolph, John B. Carson, and Anna Hampton Carson in memory of their mother, Mrs. Hampton L. Carson
1935-17-7

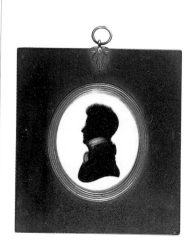

**English, unknown artist**
*Silhouette of Thomas Campbell*
c. 1800–25
Watercolor reverse-painted on glass
3 × 2 ¹⁄₂" (7.6 × 6.3 cm)

Gift of Sarah McLean Williams in memory of Mrs. William L. McLean
1942-101-36

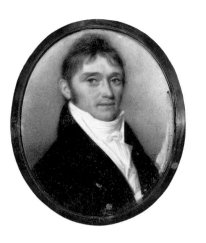

**English, unknown artist**
*Portrait of Alexander Reed of Reading, Pennsylvania*
c. 1830
Watercolor on ivory
3 × 2 3/8" (7.6 × 6 cm)

Gift of Mrs. Edward A. White
1945-64-1

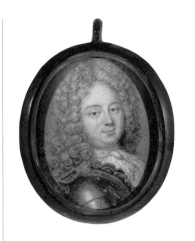

**European, unknown artist**
*Portrait of John Churchill, Duke of Marlborough*
c. 1700
Watercolor on cardboard
1 1/4 × 1 1/8" (3.2 × 2.9 cm)

Bequest of A. Manderson Troth
1927-52-209

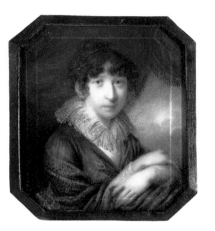

**English, unknown artist**
*Portrait of a Woman*
c. 1830
Watercolor on ivory
2 5/8 × 2 1/4" (6.7 × 5.7 cm)

Gift of Mrs. Daniel J. McCarthy
1955-1-26

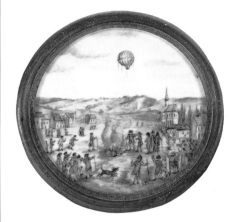

**European, unknown artist**
*Balloon Ascension, Annonay, France*
18th century
Lower right: Rotte
Watercolor on ivory
1 7/8" (4.8 cm) diameter

Gift of the Pennsylvania Society of Miniature Painters in memory of Emily Drayton Taylor, bequest of Berta Carew
1959-91-9

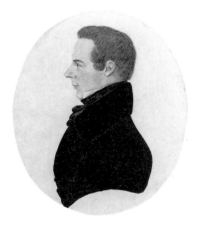

**English, unknown artist**
*Portrait of Isaac Tapping*
c. 1830
Watercolor on cardboard
3 5/16 × 2 5/8" (8.4 × 6.7 cm)

Gift of Mrs. Hampton L. Carson
1929-126-14

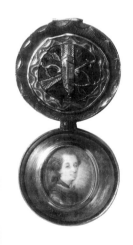

**European, unknown artist**
*Portrait of a Man*
18th century
Watercolor on ivory
9/16 × 1/2" (1.4 × 1.3 cm)

The Bloomfield Moore Collection
1882-1168

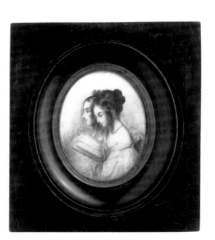

**English, unknown artist**
*Portrait of Two Girls*
c. 1840
Lower right: C [illegible]
Watercolor on ivory
2 15/16 × 2 1/4" (7.5 × 5.7 cm)

Gift of the Pennsylvania Society of Miniature Painters in memory of Emily Drayton Taylor, bequest of Berta Carew
1959-91-1

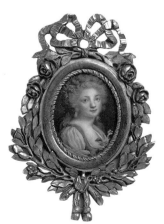

**European, unknown artist**
*Portrait of a Woman*
Late 18th century
Watercolor on ivory
2 × 1 1/2" (5.1 × 3.8 cm)

Gift of Sarah McLean Williams in memory of Mrs. William L. McLean
1942-101-25

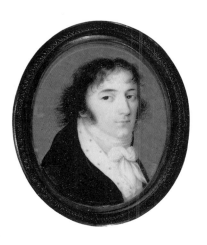

**European, unknown artist**
*Portrait of a Man*
c. 1800
Watercolor on ivory
2 3/8 × 1 7/8" (6 × 4.8 cm)

Gift of the Pennsylvania Society
of Miniature Painters in memory
of Emily Drayton Taylor, bequest
of Berta Carew
1959-91-2

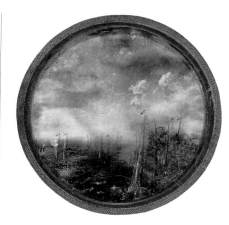

**European, unknown artist**
*Ships at Sea*
19th century
Oil on panel
1 15/16" (4.9 cm) diameter

Gift of the Pennsylvania Society
of Miniature Painters in memory
of Emily Drayton Taylor, bequest
of Berta Carew
1959-91-13

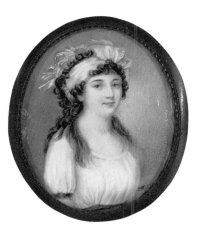

**European, unknown artist**
*Portrait of a Woman*
c. 1800
Watercolor on ivory
2 3/8 × 1 15/16" (6 × 4.9 cm)

Gift of Sarah McLean Williams
in memory of Mrs. William L.
McLean
1942-101-29

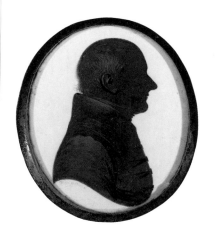

**Field, John**
English, 1771–1841
*Silhouette of Dr. Maltby, Bishop of
Chichester and Durham*
c. 1810
Lower left: Field, 11 Strand
Watercolor on plaster
2 × 1 5/8" (5.1 × 4.1 cm)

Gift of Sarah McLean Williams
in memory of Mrs. William L.
McLean
1942-101-38

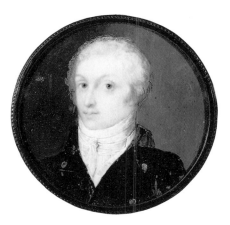

**European, unknown artist**
*Portrait of a Man*
c. 1800–10
Watercolor on ivory
2 3/8" (6 cm) diameter

Gift of the Pennsylvania Society
of Miniature Painters in memory
of Emily Drayton Taylor, bequest
of Berta Carew
1959-91-6

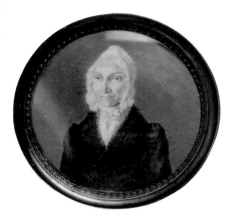

**French, unknown artist**
*Portrait of a Woman*
c. 1790
Watercolor on ivory
2 5/16" (5.9 cm) diameter

The Bloomfield Moore Collection
1882-1171

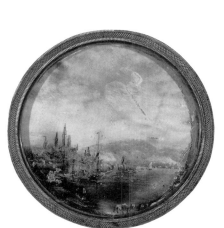

**European, unknown artist**
*Landscape with Ships*
19th century
Watercolor on ivory
1 7/8" (4.8 cm) diameter

Gift of the Pennsylvania Society
of Miniature Painters in memory
of Emily Drayton Taylor, bequest
of Berta Carew
1959-91-14

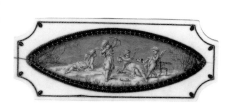

**French, unknown artist**
*Putti with Attributes of Hunters*
Cover of a patch box
c. 1790
Watercolor on ivory
1 × 2 7/8" (2.5 × 7.3 cm)

The Bloomfield Moore Collection
1899-1011

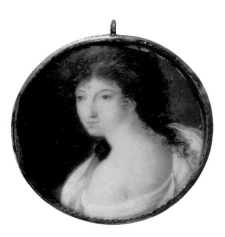

**French, unknown artist**
*Portrait of a Woman*
c. 1790–1800
Watercolor on ivory
2 1/4" (5.7 cm) diameter

The Bloomfield Moore Collection
1899-1030

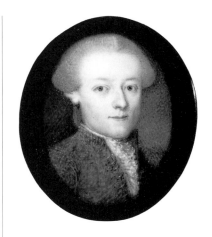

**French?, unknown artist**
*Portrait of a Man*
c. 1800
Watercolor on ivory
1 1/16 × 7/8" (2.7 × 2.2 cm)

Gift of the Pennsylvania Society
of Miniature Painters in memory
of Emily Drayton Taylor, bequest
of Berta Carew
1959-91-4

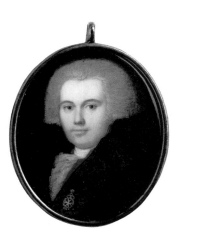

**French, unknown artist**
*Portrait of a Man*
1791
On reverse: 1791
Oil on ivory
2 1/16 × 1 5/8" (5.2 × 4.1 cm)

Bequest of A. Manderson Troth
1927-52-212

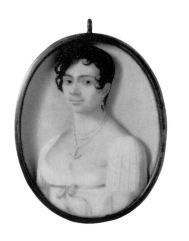

**French, unknown artist**
*Portrait of a Woman*
c. 1800
Watercolor on ivory
2 1/4 × 1 7/16" (5.7 × 3.6 cm)

The Bloomfield Moore Collection
1899-976

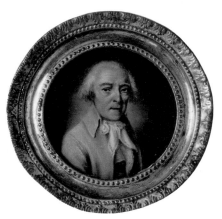

**French, unknown artist**
*Portrait of a Man*
c. 1800
Oil on linen
2 3/8" (6 cm) diameter

The Bloomfield Moore Collection
1899-967

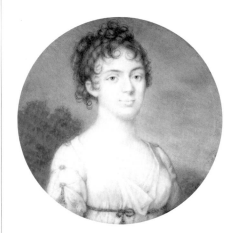

**French, unknown artist**
*Portrait of a Woman*
Companion to the following
miniature
c. 1800
Watercolor on ivory
2 11/16" (6.8 cm) diameter

Gift of Sarah McLean Williams
in memory of Mrs. William L.
McLean
1942-101-27a

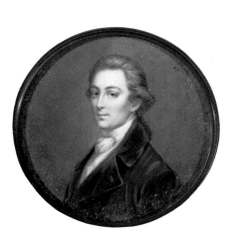

**French, unknown artist**
*Portrait of a Man*
c. 1800
Lower right: K. Feriet
Watercolor on ivory
2 5/8" (6.7 cm) diameter

Gift of Sarah McLean Williams
in memory of Mrs. William L.
McLean
1942-101-30

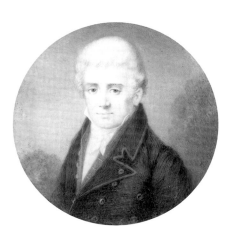

**French, unknown artist**
*Portrait of a Man*
Companion to the preceding
miniature
c. 1800
Watercolor on ivory
2 5/8" (6.7 cm) diameter

Gift of Sarah McLean Williams
in memory of Mrs. William L.
McLean
1942-101-27b

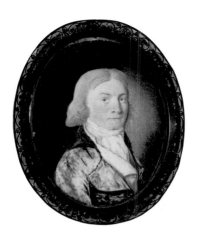

**French, unknown artist**
*Portrait of a Man*
c. 1800–10
Watercolor on ivory
2 $^{11}/_{16}$ × 2 $^{1}/_{16}$" (6.8 × 5.2 cm)

The Bloomfield Moore Collection
1882-1176

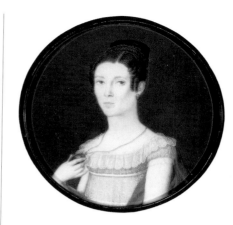

**French, unknown artist**
*Portrait of a Woman*
Companion to the following
miniature
c. 1840
Watercolor on ivory
2 $^{5}/_{8}$" (6.7 cm) diameter

Gift of Mrs. Daniel J. McCarthy
1955-1-27a

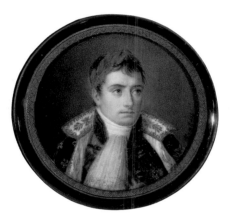

**French, unknown artist**
*Portrait of Napoleon Bonaparte*
c. 1804
Center right (spurious): Isabey
Watercolor on ivory
2 $^{1}/_{8}$" (5.4 cm) diameter

Bequest of A. Manderson Troth
1927-52-206

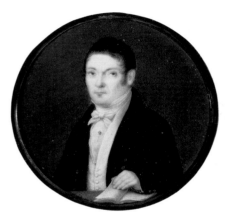

**French?, unknown artist**
*Portrait of a Man*
Companion to the preceding
miniature
c. 1840
Watercolor on ivory
2 $^{5}/_{8}$" (6.7 cm) diameter

Gift of Mrs. Daniel J. McCarthy
1955-1-27b

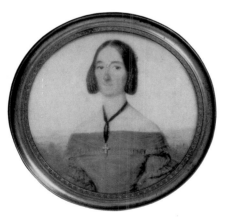

**French?, unknown artist**
*Portrait of Matilda de Burlo-Ramborger*
c. 1820–40
Watercolor on ivory
2 $^{11}/_{16}$ × 2 $^{5}/_{8}$" (6.8 × 6.7 cm)

The Ozeas, Ramborger, Keehmle
Collection
1921-34-96

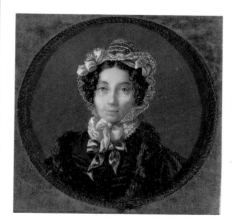

**French?, unknown artist**
*Portrait of a Woman*
Companion to the following
miniature
c. 1850
Watercolor on ivory
3 $^{1}/_{2}$" (8.9 cm) diameter

Gift of Sarah McLean Williams
in memory of Mrs. William L.
McLean
1942-101-28a

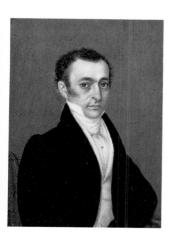

**French, unknown artist**
*Portrait of Henry D. Mandeville*
1822
Oil on mother-of-pearl
3 $^{3}/_{16}$ × 2 $^{3}/_{8}$" (8.1 × 6 cm)

Gift of Marie Josephine Rozet
and Rebecca Mandeville Rozet
Hunt
1935-13-47

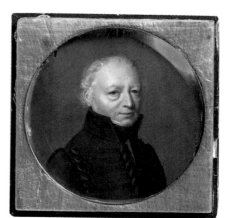

**French?, unknown artist**
*Portrait of a Man*
Companion to the preceding
miniature
c. 1850
Watercolor on ivory
3 $^{1}/_{2}$" (8.9 cm) diameter

Gift of Sarah McLean Williams
in memory of Mrs. William L.
McLean
1942-101-28b

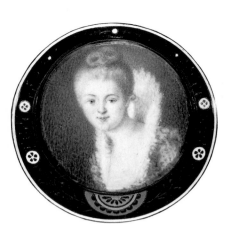

**French, unknown artist**
*Portrait of Madame Guimard*
Possibly based on *L'Étude*, by
Jean-Honoré Fragonard (French,
1732–1806), in the Musée du
Louvre, Paris (cat. no. 297)
19th century
Watercolor on ivory
1" (2.5 cm) diameter

Gift of Mrs. Daniel J. McCarthy
1954-21-2

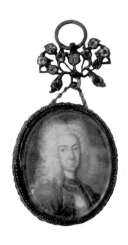

**German, unknown artist**
*Portrait of a Man*
18th century
Watercolor on cardboard
1 ³⁄₈ × 1 ¹⁄₈" (3.5 × 2.9 cm)

The Bloomfield Moore Collection
1882-1170

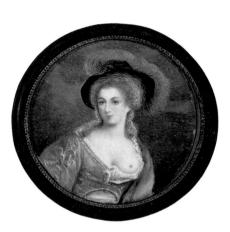

**French, unknown artist**
*Portrait of a Woman*
Late 19th century
Watercolor on ivory
2 ⁵⁄₈" (6.7 cm) diameter

The Bloomfield Moore Collection
1882-1177

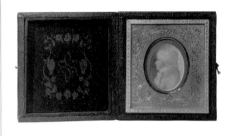

**German, unknown artist**
*Portrait of Wilhelm Christian Stoll*
c. 1800–10
Graphite and wash on cardboard
1 ⁷⁄₈ × 1 ³⁄₈" (4.8 × 3.5 cm)

Gift of Mrs. Charles V. Hemsley
and Miss Helen A. Kimmig
1961-179-1

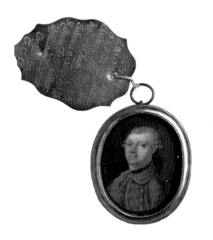

**German, unknown artist**
*Portrait of Johannes Hommel*
1626
Upper left: 1626 / AJS; on metal
tag: Ao. 1760. / d. 26. Octbr.
Morg. zw. / 5.u.6. Uhr ist
gebohren / Johannes Hommel,
Gev. / bey der H. Tauff, Tit. Hr. /
Johan[n]es v. Schütz, dess G. /
Raths, u. Tit. Fr. Cathar. / Ursula
v. Schelhornin / Consulentin. /
G.G.G
Oil on ivory
1 ⁵⁄₈ × 1 ¹⁄₄" (4.1 × 3.2 cm)

Bequest of A. Manderson Troth
1927-52-42

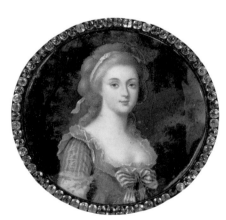

**Giraud, D.**
French, active late 18th and
early 19th centuries
*Portrait of a Woman*
1785
Lower right: Giraud / 1785
Watercolor on ivory
2 ⁷⁄₁₆" (6.2 cm) diameter

Bequest of A. Manderson Troth
1927-52-218

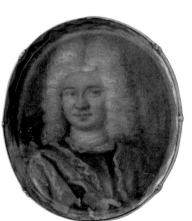

**German, unknown artist**
*Portrait of a Man*
18th century
Watercolor and gouache on
cardboard
1 ³⁄₈ × 1 ³⁄₁₆" (3.5 × 3 cm)

The Bloomfield Moore Collection
1882-1169

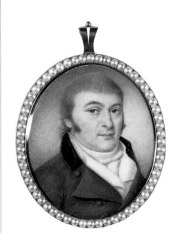

**Henri, Pierre**
English, born France, active
United States c. 1790–1812
*Portrait of Louis Marie Clapier*
c. 1800
Watercolor on ivory
2 ³⁄₄ × 2 ¹⁄₈" (7 × 5.4 cm)

Bequest of Miss Fanny Norris in
memory of Louis Marie Clapier
1940-46-1

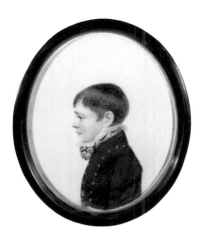

**Hervé, Henry**
English, active 1801–1817
*Portrait of a Boy*
c. 1817
Watercolor on cardboard
3 × 2 ⅜" (7.6 × 6 cm)

Gift of Mrs. Hampton L. Carson
1929-126-15

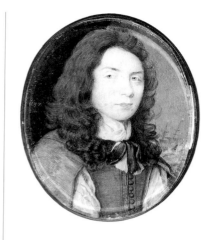

**Hoskins, John**
English, c. 1595–1664/65
*Portrait of a Man*
1657
Center left: 1657 / JH
Watercolor on cardboard
2 ¹⁵⁄₁₆ × 2 ⁵⁄₁₆" (7.5 × 5.9 cm)

Gift of Mrs. Daniel J. McCarthy
1954-21-9

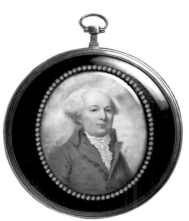

**Hoin, Claude-Jean-Baptiste**
French, 1750–1817
*Portrait of a Man*
1790s
Lower right: Hoin
Watercolor on ivory
2 ⅜ × 1 ¹⁵⁄₁₆" (6 × 4.9 cm)

Gift of the Pennsylvania Society
of Miniature Painters in memory
of Emily Drayton Taylor, bequest
of Berta Carew
1959-91-7

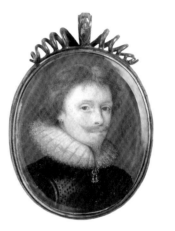

**Hoskins, John, attributed to**
*Portrait of a Man*
c. 1625
Watercolor on cardboard
1 ⅝ × 1 ⁵⁄₁₆" (4.1 × 3.3 cm)

Gift of Mrs. Daniel J. McCarthy
1954-21-8

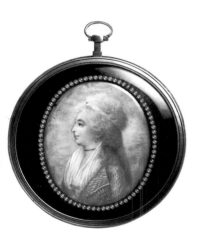

**Hoin, Claude-Jean-Baptiste**
*Portrait of a Woman*
1790s
Lower right: Hoin
Watercolor on ivory
2 ⁷⁄₁₆ × 2" (6.2 × 5.1 cm)

Gift of the Pennsylvania Society
of Miniature Painters in memory
of Emily Drayton Taylor, bequest
of Berta Carew
1959-91-8

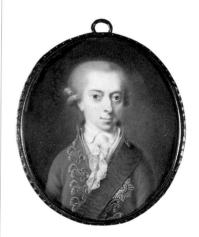

**Høyer, Cornelius**
Danish, 1741–1804
*Portrait of Christian VII, King of
Denmark and Norway*
c. 1784
Watercolor on ivory
2 ¹³⁄₁₆ × 2 ⅜" (7.1 × 6 cm)

Gift of Mrs. Daniel J. McCarthy
1954-21-10

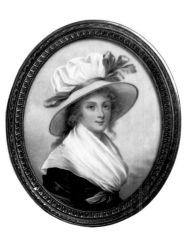

**Hoppner, John, attributed to**
English, 1758–1810
*Portrait of the Princess of Wales*
1787
Lower right: Hoppner / 1787
Watercolor on ivory
3 ¾ × 3 ⅛" (9.5 × 7.9 cm)

Gift of Sarah McLean Williams
in memory of Mrs. William L.
McLean
1942-101-24

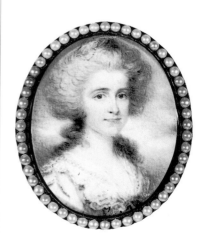

**Humphrey, Ozias**
English, 1742–1810
*Portrait of a Woman*
c. 1800
Center bottom: [illegible
monogram]
Watercolor on ivory
2 ¹⁄₁₆ × 1 ⅝" (5.2 × 4.1 cm)

Gift of Mrs. Daniel J. McCarthy
1954-21-12

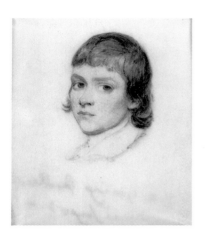

**Humphrey, Ozias**
*Portrait of Mr. Joyot*
c. 1800
Watercolor on ivory
1 $\frac{7}{8}$ × 1 $\frac{3}{4}$" (4.8 × 4.4 cm)

Gift of Mrs. Daniel J. McCarthy
1954-63-5

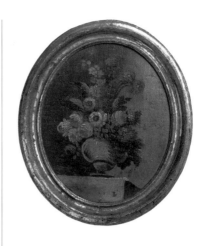

**Italian, unknown artist**
*Still Life with Flowers in a Vase*
18th century
Oil on panel
8 × 6 $\frac{1}{4}$" (20.3 × 15.9 cm)

Gift of the Pennsylvania Society
of Miniature Painters in memory
of Emily Drayton Taylor, bequest
of Berta Carew
1959-91-52

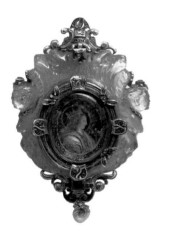

**Italian, active northern
Italy?, unknown artist**
*Annunciate Virgin*
See following miniature for
reverse
16th century
Watercolor reverse-painted on
glass
1 $\frac{1}{16}$ × $\frac{7}{8}$" (2.7 × 2.2 cm)

Purchased with Museum funds
1949-40-1a

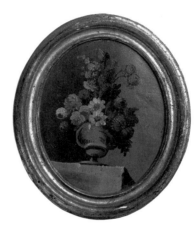

**Italian, unknown artist**
*Still Life with Flowers in a Vase*
18th century
Oil on panel
7 $\frac{3}{4}$ × 6 $\frac{1}{8}$" (19.7 × 15.6 cm)

Gift of the Pennsylvania Society
of Miniature Painters in memory
of Emily Drayton Taylor, bequest
of Berta Carew
1959-91-53

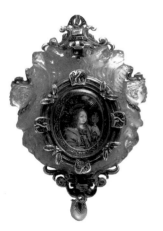

**Italian, active northern
Italy?, unknown artist**
*Saint John the Evangelist with a
Chalice*
Reverse of the preceding
miniature
16th century
Upper left: S.G.
Watercolor reverse-painted on
glass
1 $\frac{1}{16}$ × $\frac{7}{8}$" (2.7 × 2.2 cm)

Purchased with Museum funds
1949-40-1b

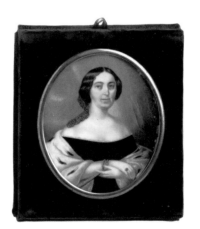

**Italian, unknown artist**
*Portrait of Mrs. Jane Cunningham
Drake*
c. 1850
Watercolor on ivory
3 $\frac{3}{4}$ × 3" (9.5 × 7.6 cm)

Gift of Miss Millicent J. Drake
1935-14-2

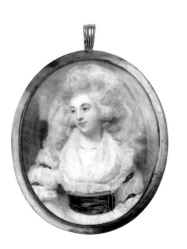

**Italian, unknown artist**
*Portrait of the Duchess of Leinster*
18th century
Watercolor on ivory
3 $\frac{7}{16}$ × 2 $\frac{3}{4}$" (8.7 × 7 cm)

Gift of the Pennsylvania Society
of Miniature Painters in memory
of Emily Drayton Taylor, bequest
of Berta Carew
1959-91-3

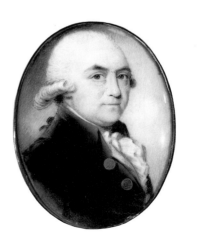

**Jean, Philip**
English, 1755–1802
*Portrait of John Tyers*
1787
Watercolor on ivory
1 $\frac{9}{16}$ × 1 $\frac{1}{4}$" (4 × 3.2 cm)

Gift of Mrs. Daniel J. McCarthy
1954-21-14

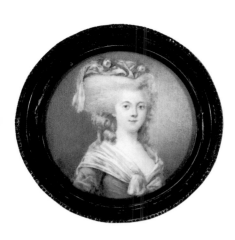

**Joffray**
French, 18th century
*Portrait of a Woman*
18th century
Lower left: Joffray
Watercolor on ivory
2 1/4" (5.7 cm) diameter

Bequest of A. Manderson Troth
1927-52-192

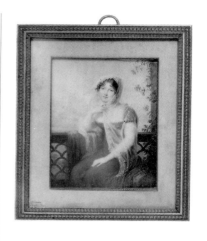

**Leguay, Étienne-Charles, attributed to**
French, 1762–1846
*Portrait of Caroline Bonaparte Murat, Queen of Naples*
c. 1812
Center left: E. Le Guay
Watercolor on ivory
4 7/16 × 3 11/16" (11.3 × 9.4 cm)

Bequest of Elizabeth Ellen Keating
F1920-1-2

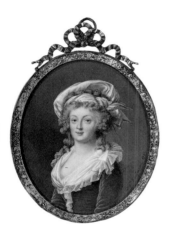

**Kauffmann, Angelica**
Swiss, 1741–1807
*Portrait of Marie Caroline, Queen of Naples*
1780
Lower right: Angca Kaufmann 1780.
Watercolor on ivory
3 5/8 × 2 15/16" (9.2 × 7.5 cm)

Gift of Sarah McLean Williams in memory of Mrs. William L. McLean
1942-101-23

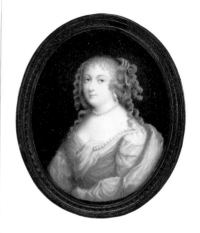

**Lemoine, Jacques-Antoine-Marie**
French, 1751–1824
*Portrait of Henrietta Maria, Queen of England*
After an earlier portrait
1769
Lower left: Lemoine
Watercolor on ivory
3 1/4 × 2 1/2" (8.2 × 6.3 cm)

Gift of Mr. and Mrs. John Harrison
1952-46-1

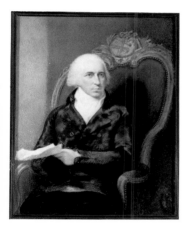

**Lane, John**
English, 1788–1868
*Portrait of Benjamin West, President of the Royal Academy*
After 1792
Watercolor on ivory
6 3/16 × 4 7/8" (15.7 × 12.4 cm)

Gift of Mrs. Daniel J. McCarthy
1954-21-16

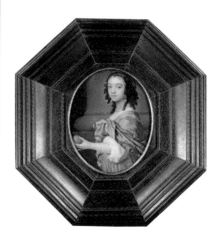

**Luttichuys, Isaac**
Dutch, born England, 1616–1673
*Portrait of a Young Woman Holding an Orange*
c. 1646–50
Oil on copper
4 1/2 × 3 1/4" (11.4 × 8.2 cm)

Purchased with the Director's Discretionary Fund
1968-97-1

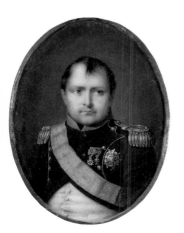

**Larue, André-Léon, also called Mansion, attributed to**
French, 1785–c. 1834
*Portrait of Napoleon Bonaparte*
c. 1810
Center left: Mansion.
Watercolor on ivory
4 1/16 × 3" (10.3 × 7.6 cm)

Gift of Mrs. Jacob Riegel and Mrs. Daniel Whitney
1952-3-1

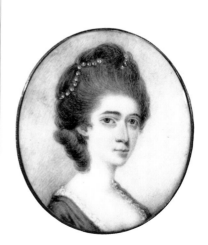

**McMoreland, Patrick John, attributed to**
Scottish, born 1741, still active 1809
*Portrait of Mrs. Joseph Galloway [née Grace Growden]*
c. 1770
Watercolor on ivory
1 1/2 × 1 1/4" (3.8 × 3.2 cm)

Purchased with the John D. McIlhenny Fund
1966-20-7

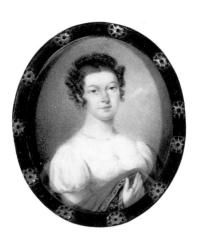

**Mason**
French?, active c. 1849
*Portrait of a Woman*
1849
Lower right: Mason 1849
Watercolor on ivory
1 3/4 × 1 3/8" (4.4 × 3.5 cm)

Gift of the Pennsylvania Society
of Miniature Painters in memory
of Emily Drayton Taylor, bequest
of Berta Carew
1959-91-5

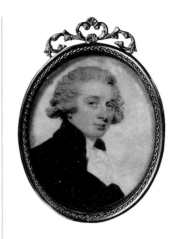

**Miles, Edward**
*Portrait of a Man*
c. 1790
Watercolor on ivory
2 × 1 9/16" (5.1 × 4 cm)

Gift of W. Parsons Todd and
Miss Mary J. Todd
1938-29-11

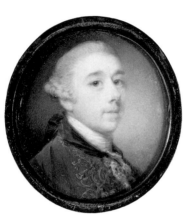

**Meyer, Jeremiah**
English, born Germany,
1735–1789
*Portrait of a Man*
c. 1775
Watercolor on ivory
1 3/8 × 1 1/8" (3.5 × 2.9 cm)

Gift of Mrs. Daniel J. McCarthy
1954-63-4

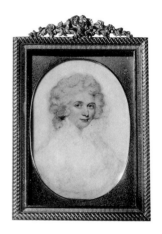

**Miles, Edward**
*Portrait of a Woman*
c. 1790
Watercolor on ivory
3 × 2" (7.6 × 5.1 cm)

Gift of W. Parsons Todd and
Miss Mary J. Todd
1938-29-12

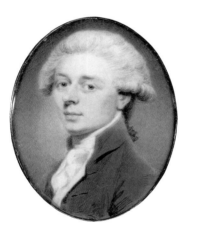

**Meyer, Jeremiah**
*Portrait of Mr. Pilkington*
c. 1775–80
Watercolor on ivory
1 11/16 × 1 5/16" (4.3 × 3.3 cm)

Gift of Mrs. Daniel J. McCarthy
1953-142-4

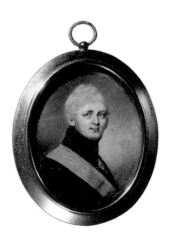

**Miles, Edward**
*Portrait of Alexander I, Czar of
Russia*
Companion to the following
miniature
c. 1797–1807
Watercolor on ivory
2 3/4 × 2" (7 × 5.1 cm)

Gift of W. Parsons Todd and
Miss Mary J. Todd
1938-29-2

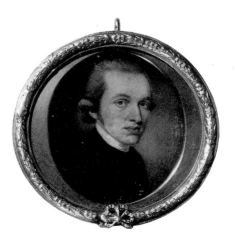

**Miles, Edward**
English, 1752–1828
*Portrait of a Man*
1773
Lower right: EM / 1773
Watercolor on ivory
1 5/8 × 1 3/8" (4.1 × 3.5 cm)

Gift of W. Parsons Todd and
Miss Mary J. Todd
1938-29-17

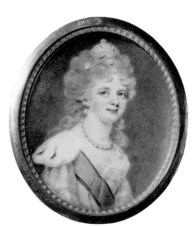

**Miles, Edward**
*Portrait of Louise Marie, Empress of
Russia*
Companion to the preceding
miniature
c. 1797–1807
Watercolor on ivory
2 11/16 × 2 1/8" (6.8 × 5.4 cm)

Gift of W. Parsons Todd and
Miss Mary J. Todd
1938-29-1

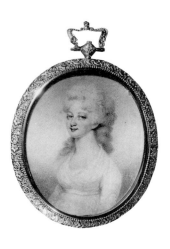

**Miles, Edward**
*Portrait of a Lady of the Imperial Court*
c. 1797–1807
Watercolor on ivory
2 3/4 × 2 3/16" (7 × 5.6 cm)

Gift of W. Parsons Todd and
Miss Mary J. Todd
1938-29-9

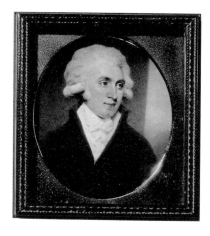

**Miles, Edward**
*Portrait of a Man*
c. 1800
Watercolor on ivory
2 13/16 × 2 5/16" (7.1 × 5.9 cm)

Gift of W. Parsons Todd and
Miss Mary J. Todd
1938-29-14

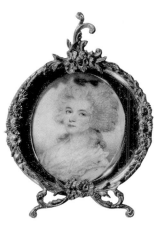

**Miles, Edward**
*Portrait of a Russian Princess*
c. 1797–1807
Watercolor on ivory
1 15/16 × 1 1/2" (4.9 × 3.8 cm)

Gift of W. Parsons Todd and
Miss Mary J. Todd
1938-29-13

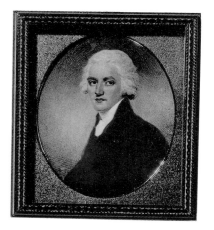

**Miles, Edward**
*Portrait of a Man*
c. 1800
Watercolor on ivory
2 13/16 × 2 5/16" (7.1 × 5.9 cm)

Gift of W. Parsons Todd and
Miss Mary J. Todd
1938-29-15

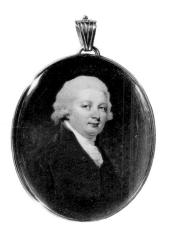

**Miles, Edward**
*Portrait of a Man*
c. 1800
Watercolor on ivory
2 3/4 × 2 1/4" (7 × 5.7 cm)

Gift of W. Parsons Todd and
Miss Mary J. Todd
1938-29-5

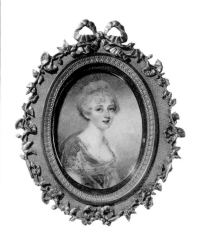

**Miles, Edward**
*Portrait of a Woman*
c. 1800
Watercolor on ivory
2 7/8 × 2 5/16" (7.3 × 5.9 cm)

Gift of W. Parsons Todd and
Miss Mary J. Todd
1938-29-3

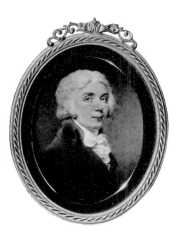

**Miles, Edward**
*Portrait of a Man*
c. 1800
Watercolor on ivory
2 3/4 × 2 1/16" (7 × 5.2 cm)

Gift of W. Parsons Todd and
Miss Mary J. Todd
1938-29-10

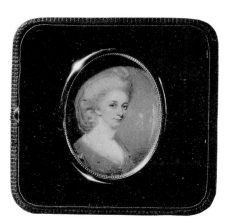

**Miles, Edward**
*Portrait of a Woman*
c. 1800
Watercolor on ivory
1 3/4 × 1 1/2" (4.4 × 3.8 cm)

Gift of W. Parsons Todd and
Miss Mary J. Todd
1938-29-4

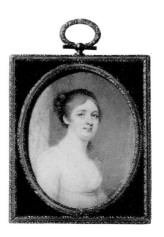

**Miles, Edward**
*Portrait of a Woman*
c. 1800
Watercolor on ivory
3 1/16 × 2 5/16" (7.8 × 5.9 cm)

Gift of W. Parsons Todd and
Miss Mary J. Todd
1938-29-8

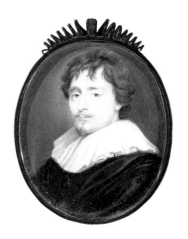

**Oliver, Isaac, copy after**
*Self-Portrait*
17th century
Watercolor and gouache on
cardboard
2 1/2 × 2" (6.3 × 5.1 cm)

Gift of Mrs. Daniel J. McCarthy
1954-21-22

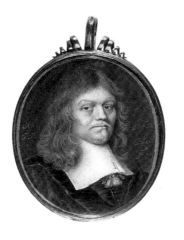

**Miles, Edward**
*Portrait of Bishop William White*
c. 1810
Watercolor on ivory
3 1/16 × 2 1/8" (7.8 × 5.4 cm)

Gift of W. Parsons Todd and
Miss Mary J. Todd
1938-29-16

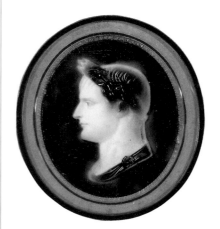

**Parant, Louis-Bertin**
French, 1768–1851
*Portrait of Napoleon Bonaparte*
c. 1810
Lower right: LbParant
Watercolor on ivory
2 × 1 5/8" (5.1 × 4.1 cm)

The Bloomfield Moore Collection
1899-1007

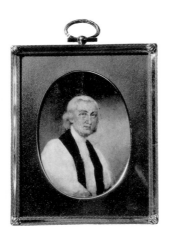

**Monogrammist P. D.**
English, active c. 1665
*Portrait of Edward Hyde,
1st Earl of Clarendon*
1665
Center left: An: / 55.; center
right: 1665. / P.D. / Ft.
Watercolor on vellum
1 7/8 × 1 9/16" (4.8 × 4 cm)

Gift of Mrs. Daniel J. McCarthy
1954-21-1

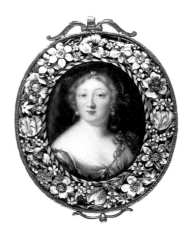

**Petitot, Jean**
French, 1607–1691
*Portrait of Catherine-Henriette
d'Angennes, Countess d'Olonne, as
Diana*
c. 1680
Oil on copper
1 1/2 × 1 1/4" (3.8 × 3.2 cm)

Gift of Mrs. Lessing J. Rosenwald
1961-37-1

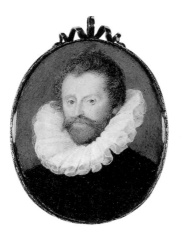

**Oliver, Isaac, attributed to**
English, born France,
born 1551–56, died 1617
*Portrait of Robert Devereux,
2nd Earl of Essex*
c. 1590
Watercolor and gouache on
vellum
2 × 1 5/8" (5.1 × 4.1 cm)

Gift of Mrs. Daniel J. McCarthy
1954-21-23

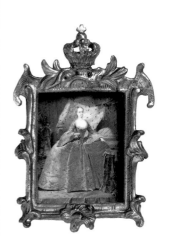

**Pilo, Carl Gustav,
attributed to**
Swedish, 1712–1792
*Portrait of Sophie Magdalene,
Queen of Denmark and Norway*
c. 1740
Watercolor on ivory
4 1/8 × 3 1/16" (10.5 × 7.8 cm)

Gift of Mrs. Daniel J. McCarthy
1955-1-1

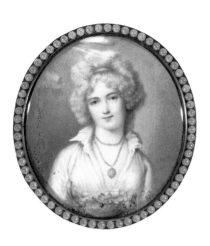

**Plimer, Andrew**
English, 1763–1837
*Portrait of a Woman*
Companion to the following miniature
c. 1800
Watercolor on ivory
2 3/8 × 2" (6 × 5.1 cm)

Gift of Sarah McLean Williams in memory of Mrs. William L. McLean
1942-101-31a

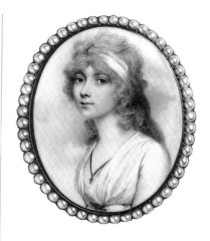

**Plimer, Andrew**
*Portrait of the Honorable Anne Rushout*
c. 1800
Watercolor on ivory
3 1/16 × 2 3/8" (7.8 × 6 cm)

Gift of Mrs. Daniel J. McCarthy
1955-1-2

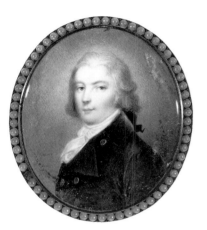

**Plimer, Andrew**
*Portrait of a Man*
Companion to the preceding miniature
c. 1800
Center left: A Plimer
Watercolor on ivory
2 7/16 × 2 1/16" (6.2 × 5.2 cm)

Gift of Sarah McLean Williams in memory of Mrs. William L. McLean
1942-101-31b

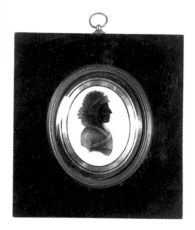

**Readhead, H.**
English, active 18th century
*Silhouette of a Woman*
18th century
On paper on reverse: Mr H Readhead / Profilest / No 54 Upper Norton Street / Fitzroy Ignace / London, V / time of sitting 5 Minutes
Watercolor reverse-painted on glass
3 × 2 1/2" (7.6 × 6.3 cm)

Gift of Sarah McLean Williams in memory of Mrs. William L. McLean
1942-101-37

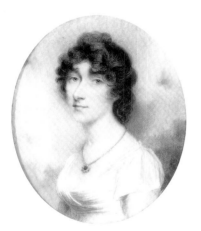

**Plimer, Andrew**
*Portrait of a Woman*
c. 1800
Watercolor on ivory
3 3/16 × 2 9/16" (8.1 × 6.5 cm)

Gift of Mrs. Daniel J. McCarthy
1955-1-4

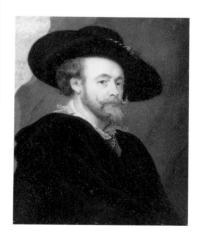

**Richter, Christian**
Swedish, active England, 1678–1732
*Portrait of Peter Paul Rubens*
After a self-portrait in the collection of Her Majesty Queen Elizabeth II, Windsor Castle (157)
c. 1702
Watercolor on cardboard
3 1/8 × 2 9/16" (7.9 × 6.5 cm)

Gift of Mrs. Daniel J. McCarthy
1955-1-6

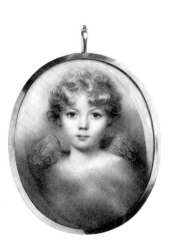

**Plimer, Andrew**
*Portrait of Selina Plimer, Daughter of the Artist*
c. 1800
Watercolor on ivory
3 1/16 × 2 7/16" (7.8 × 6.2 cm)

Gift of Mrs. Daniel J. McCarthy
1955-1-3

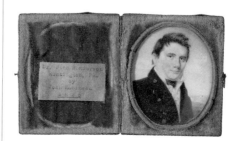

**Robinson, John**
English, active United States, active 1817–1829
*Portrait of Dr. John Henderson*
1825
Lower right: JR / 1825
Watercolor on ivory
2 9/16 × 2" (6.5 × 5.1 cm)

Gift of Dr. William A. Jaquette, Jr.
1962-219-1

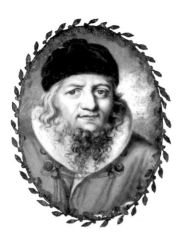

**Rota, Giuseppe, copy after**
Italian, 1777–1821?
*Portrait of Michael Leman*
Companion to the following
miniature
c. 1825
Watercolor on ivory
2 3/4 × 2" (7 × 5.1 cm)

Gift of Mrs. George A. Saportas
1955-66-1

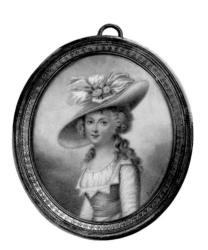

**Rota, Giuseppe, copy after**
*Portrait of Zipporah Leman*
Companion to the preceding
miniature
c. 1825
Watercolor on ivory
2 3/4 × 2" (7 × 5.1 cm)

Gift of Mrs. George A. Saportas
1955-66-2

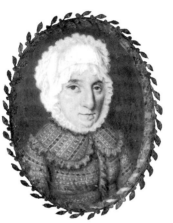

**Rowlandson, Thomas,
attributed to**
English, 1756–1827
*Portrait of the Duchess of Cambridge*
1785
Lower right: Rowlandson. 1785
Watercolor on ivory
3 3/4 × 3 1/8" (9.5 × 7.9 cm)

Gift of Sarah McLean Williams
in memory of Mrs. William L.
McLean
1942-101-21

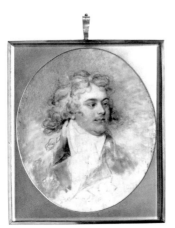

**Russell, John, attributed to**
English, 1745–1806
*Portrait of George Augustus
Frederick, Prince of Wales*
c. 1788
Watercolor on ivory
5 3/8 × 4 1/2" (13.6 × 11.4 cm)

Gift of Mrs. Daniel J. McCarthy
1955-1-8

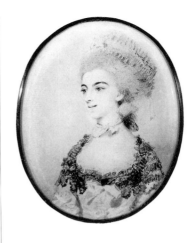

**Rymsdyck, Andreas van**
Dutch, active England, died 1786
*Portrait of Miss Bedingfield*
c. 1767–86
Watercolor on paper
4 3/8 × 3 7/16" (11.1 × 8.7 cm)

Gift of Mrs. Daniel J. McCarthy
1954-21-4

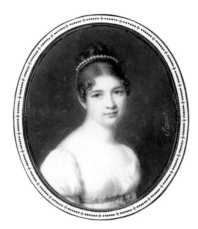

**Saint, Daniel**
French, 1778–1847
*Portrait of a Woman*
c. 1810
Center right: Saint.
Watercolor on ivory
2 3/4 × 2 3/16" (7 × 5.6 cm)

Gift of Mrs. Daniel J. McCarthy
1955-1-9

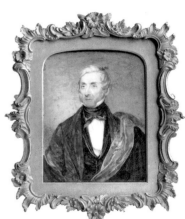

**Saunders, George
Lethbridge**
English, 1807–1863
*Portrait of Benjamin Chew Wilcock*
Companion to the following
miniature
c. 1840
Watercolor on ivory
5 1/4 × 4" (13.3 × 10.2 cm)

Bequest of Dorothy Fisher Reath
1988-72-18

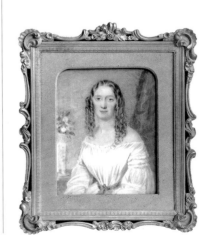

**Saunders, George
Lethbridge**
*Portrait of Sally Waln Wilcock*
Companion to the preceding
miniature
c. 1840
Watercolor on ivory
4 5/16 × 3 5/16" (11 × 8.4 cm)

Bequest of Dorothy Fisher Reath
1988-72-19

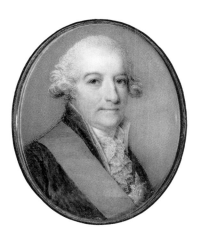

**Shelley, Samuel**
English, c. 1750–1808
*Portrait of the Marquess of Waterford*
c. 1800
Watercolor on ivory
2 1/16 × 1 11/16" (5.2 × 4.3 cm)

Gift of Mrs. Daniel J. McCarthy
1955-1-5

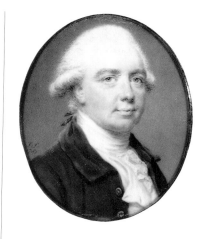

**Smart, John**
*Portrait of a Man*
1781
Lower left: JS / 1781
Watercolor on ivory
1 7/16 × 1 1/8" (3.6 × 2.9 cm)

Gift of Mrs. Daniel J. McCarthy
1955-1-16

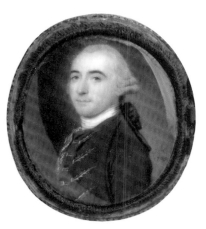

**Smart, John**
English, 1742/43–1811
*Portrait of Colonel Valentine Morris,
Governor of Saint Vincent*
1765
Lower right: J. S. / 1765.
Watercolor on ivory
1 1/4 × 1 1/16" (3.2 × 2.7 cm)

Gift of Mrs. Daniel J. McCarthy
1955-1-15

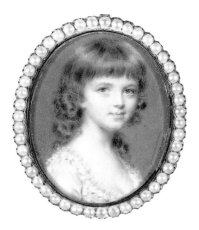

**Smart, John**
*Portrait of Elizabeth Townsend*
1784
Lower left: JS / 1784
Watercolor on ivory
1 7/16 × 1 1/8" (3.6 × 2.9 cm)

Gift of Mrs. Daniel J. McCarthy
1955-1-13

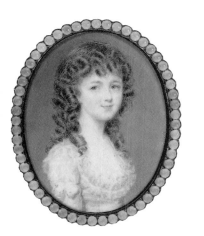

**Smart, John**
*Portrait of Elizabeth Townsend*
1770
Watercolor on ivory
2 3/8 × 1 13/16" (6 × 4.6 cm)

Gift of Mrs. Daniel J. McCarthy
1955-1-12

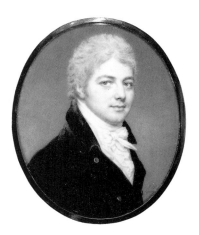

**Smart, John**
*Portrait of Lieutenant Colonel John
Wingfield*
Companion to the following
miniature
1803
Lower right: JS / 1803
Watercolor on ivory
3 1/16 × 2 1/2" (7.8 × 6.3 cm)

Gift of Mrs. Daniel J. McCarthy
1955-1-10

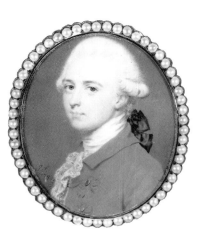

**Smart, John**
*Portrait of a Man*
1779
Lower left: JS. / 1779
Watercolor on ivory
1 5/8 × 1 1/4" (4.1 × 3.2 cm)

Gift of Mrs. Daniel J. McCarthy
1955-1-14

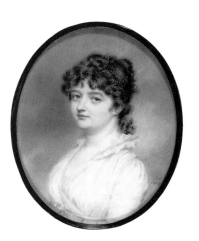

**Smart, John**
*Portrait of the Honorable Mrs. John
Wingfield*
Companion to the preceding
miniature
1803
Lower right: JS / 1803
Watercolor on ivory
3 1/16 × 2 3/8" (7.8 × 6 cm)

Gift of Mrs. Daniel J. McCarthy
1955-1-11

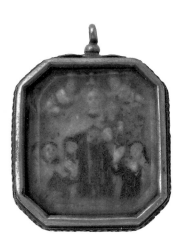

**Spanish, unknown artist**
*Virgin and Child, with a Nun and a Monk*
See following miniature for reverse
c. 1600
Upper left: .S.G.
Watercolor on ivory
2 × 2" (5.1 × 5.1 cm)

Purchased from the George Grey Barnard Collection with Museum funds
1945-25-261a

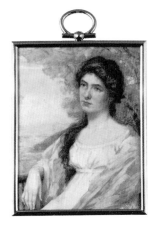

**Ahrens, Ellen Wetherald**
American, 1859–1953
*Day Dreams*
1902
Lower right: EWA 1902
Watercolor on ivory
4 9/16 × 3 7/16" (11.6 × 8.7 cm)

Gift of the Pennsylvania Society of Miniature Painters in memory of Emily Drayton Taylor
1954-42-1

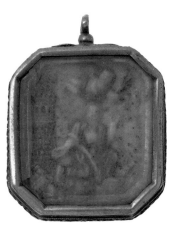

**Spanish, unknown artist**
*Saint Barbara Crowned by an Angel*
Reverse of the preceding miniature
c. 1600
Watercolor on ivory
2 × 2" (5.1 × 5.1 cm)

Purchased from the George Grey Barnard Collection with Museum funds
1945-25-261b

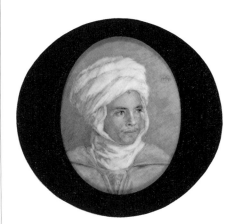

**Ahrens, Ellen Wetherald**
*Portrait of an Arab Guide*
1911
Upper right: EWA 1911
Watercolor on ivory
2 5/8 × 2" (6.7 × 5.1 cm)

Gift of Mrs. Daniel J. McCarthy
1953-142-1

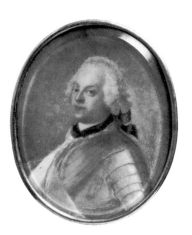

**Swedish, unknown artist**
*Portrait of Adolphus Frederick, King of Sweden*
c. 1751–71
Watercolor on cardboard
3 × 2 1/4" (7.6 × 5.7 cm)

The Bloomfield Moore Collection
1882-1174

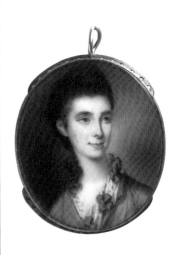

**American, unknown artist**
*Portrait of Frances Strettel*
c. 1765–75
Watercolor on ivory
1 1/4 × 1 1/8" (3.2 × 2.9 cm)

Gift of an anonymous donor in memory of Elizabeth Wheatley Bendiner
1991-76-2

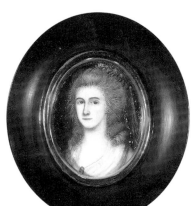

**American, unknown artist**
*Portrait of Lydia Williamson of Virginia*
c. 1775–1800
Watercolor on ivory
2 1/2 × 2 3/16" (6.3 × 5.6 cm)

Gift of the Pennsylvania Society of Miniature Painters in memory of Emily Drayton Taylor
1954-42-103

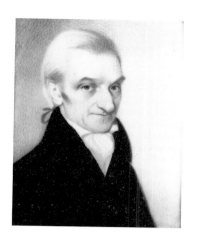

**American, unknown artist**
*Portrait of a Man*
c. 1780–1800
Watercolor on ivory
3 3/8 × 2 3/4" (8.6 × 7 cm)

Bequest of Mrs. Edna M. Welsh
1982-1-2

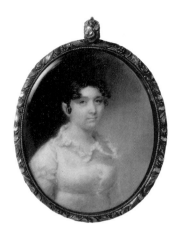

**American, unknown artist**
*Portrait of Elizabeth Ozeas Ramborger*
c. 1800
Watercolor on ivory
2 3/4 × 2 3/16" (7 × 5.6 cm)

The Ozeas, Ramborger, Keehmle Collection
1921-34-101

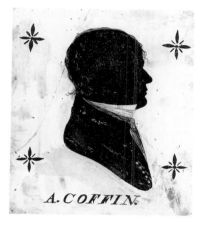

**American, unknown artist**
*Silhouette of Captain Abel Coffin*
c. 1780–1800
Center bottom: A. COFFIN.
Watercolor reverse-painted on glass
5 × 4" (12.7 × 10.2 cm)

Gift of Miss Evelyn L. Whitaker in memory of her mother
1930-46-16

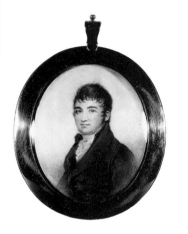

**American, unknown artist**
*Portrait of Erasmus J. Pierce*
c. 1810
Watercolor on ivory
2 3/4 × 2 1/4" (7 × 5.7 cm)

Gift of William Drown Phelps
1938-2-1

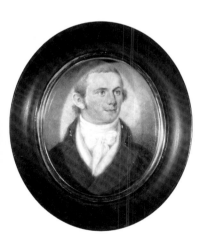

**American, unknown artist**
*Portrait of Captain John Terris of Philadelphia*
1797
Center right: John S[?] Pt 1797.
Watercolor on ivory
2 3/4 × 2 5/16" (7 × 5.9 cm)

Gift of the Pennsylvania Society of Miniature Painters in memory of Emily Drayton Taylor
1954-42-104

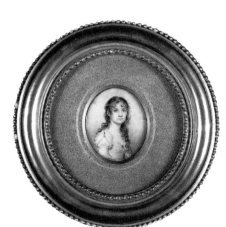

**American, unknown artist**
*Portrait of Julia Macpherson Nicklin*
Companion to the following miniature
c. 1810–20
Watercolor on ivory
2 3/4 × 2 3/16" (7 × 5.6 cm)

Gift of Caleb W. Hornor and Peter T. Hornor
1967-79-5

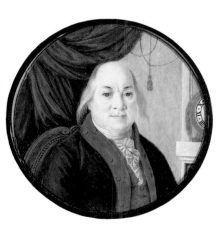

**American, unknown artist**
*Portrait of Benjamin Franklin*
c. 1800
Watercolor and gouache on ivory
2 1/2" (6.3 cm) diameter

Gift of Mrs. Daniel J. McCarthy
1955-1-25

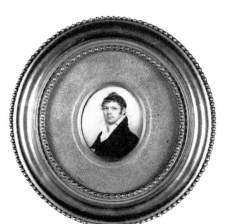

**American, unknown artist**
*Portrait of Philip Nicklin*
Companion to the preceding miniature
c. 1810–20
Watercolor on ivory
2 3/4 × 2 1/4" (7 × 5.7 cm)

Gift of Caleb W. Hornor and Peter T. Hornor
1967-79-6

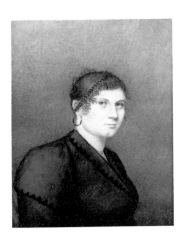

**American, unknown artist**
*Portrait of Mrs. T. T. Heartte*
Companion to the following
miniature
c. 1811
Watercolor on ivory
3 3/8 × 2 1/4" (8.6 × 5.7 cm)

The Ozeas, Ramborger, Keehmle
Collection
1921-34-99

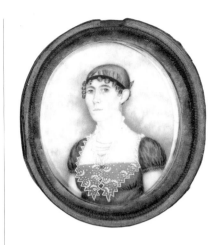

**American, unknown artist**
*Portrait of a Woman*
Companion to the preceding
miniature
c. 1820–30
Watercolor and gouache on ivory
2 3/4 × 2 1/8" (7 × 5.4 cm)

Gift of Mrs. Daniel J. McCarthy
1955-1-28b

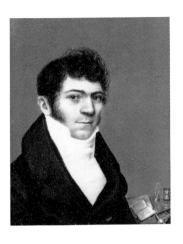

**American, unknown artist**
*Portrait of T. T. Heartte*
Companion to the preceding
miniature
c. 1811
Watercolor on ivory
3 3/8 × 2 1/4" (8.6 × 5.7 cm)

The Ozeas, Ramborger, Keehmle
Collection
1921-34-100

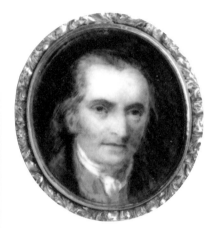

**American, unknown artist**
*Portrait of Dr. Philip Syng Physick*
c. 1820–40
Watercolor on ivory
15/16 × 3/4" (2.4 × 1.9 cm)

Gift of Mrs. Daniel J. McCarthy
1954-63-6

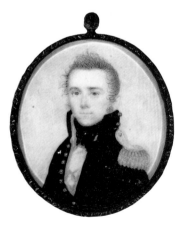

**American, unknown artist**
*Portrait of Lieutenant Horace L.
Broughton*
c. 1812
Watercolor on ivory
2 1/2 × 2 1/8" (6.3 × 5.4 cm)

Gift of Miss D. M. Broughton
1899-1151

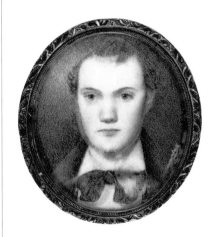

**American, unknown artist**
*Portrait of a Cape Cod Sea Captain*
c. 1830
Watercolor on ivory
1 5/8 × 1 5/16" (4.1 × 3.3 cm)

Gift of the Pennsylvania Society
of Miniature Painters in memory
of Emily Drayton Taylor, bequest
of Berta Carew
1959-91-11

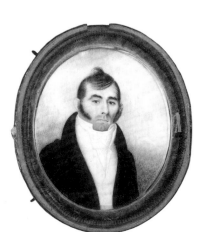

**American, unknown artist**
*Portrait of a Man*
Companion to the following
miniature
c. 1820–30
Watercolor and gouache on ivory
2 11/16 × 2 3/16" (6.8 × 5.6 cm)

Gift of Mrs. Daniel J. McCarthy
1955-1-28a

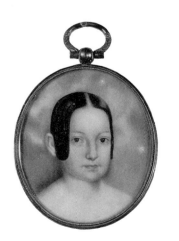

**American, unknown artist**
*Portrait of a Girl*
c. 1830
Watercolor on ivory
1 13/16 × 1 5/8" (4.6 × 4.1 cm)

Gift of the Pennsylvania Society
of Miniature Painters in memory
of Emily Drayton Taylor
1954-42-105

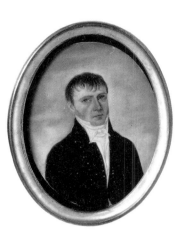

**American, unknown artist**
*Portrait of a Man*
c. 1830
Watercolor on cardboard
$2^{13}/_{16} \times 2^{1}/_{4}$" (7.1 × 5.7 cm)

The Ozeas, Ramborger, Keehmle
Collection
1921-34-223

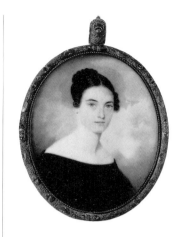

**American, unknown artist**
*Portrait of Mrs. W. C. Keehmle*
c. 1830
Watercolor on ivory
$2^{9}/_{16} \times 2^{1}/_{8}$" (6.5 × 5.4 cm)

The Ozeas, Ramborger, Keehmle
Collection
1921-34-97

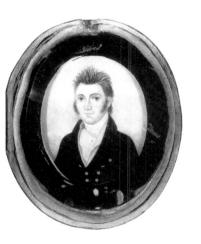

**American, unknown artist**
*Portrait of a Man*
c. 1830
Watercolor on ivory
$3^{9}/_{16} \times 2^{3}/_{4}$" (9 × 7 cm)

Gift of Miss Pauline Townsend
Pease
1979-108-7

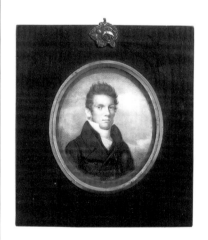

**American, unknown artist**
*Portrait of Ozeas Heartte*
c. 1830
Watercolor on cardboard
$2^{5}/_{8} \times 2^{3}/_{16}$" (6.7 × 5.6 cm)

The Ozeas, Ramborger, Keehmle
Collection
1921-34-104

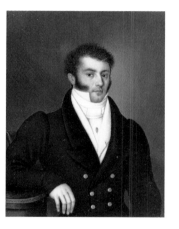

**American, unknown artist**
*Portrait of Dr. Ellis Harland*
c. 1830
Watercolor on ivory
$2^{5}/_{8} \times 2^{1}/_{4}$" (6.7 × 5.7 cm)

Gift of Mrs. John Morton
McIlvain
1929-48-2

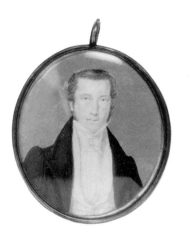

**American, unknown artist**
*Portrait of Samuel Thompson*
c. 1830
Watercolor on ivory
$3^{1}/_{8} \times 2^{5}/_{8}$" (7.9 × 6.7 cm)

Bequest of Lydia Thompson
Morris
1932-45-18

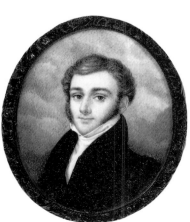

**American, unknown artist**
*Portrait of John Paul Schott III*
c. 1830
Watercolor on ivory
$2^{3}/_{16} \times 1^{7}/_{8}$" (5.6 × 4.8 cm)

Gift of Marie Josephine Rozet
and Rebecca Mandeville Rozet
Hunt
1935-13-34

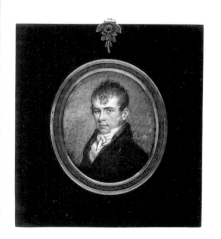

**American, unknown artist**
*Portrait of William C. Poultney*
c. 1830
Watercolor on ivory
$3 \times 2^{3}/_{8}$" (7.6 × 6 cm)

Bequest of Lydia Thompson
Morris
1932-45-19

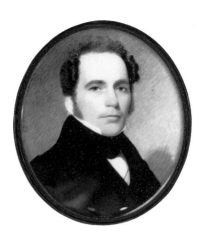

**American, unknown artist**
*Portrait of Henry Ash*
1839
On reverse: May 9th (1839)
Watercolor on ivory
2 1/2 × 2" (6.3 × 5.1 cm)

Gift of Mrs. Frances C. Ely
1944-58-1

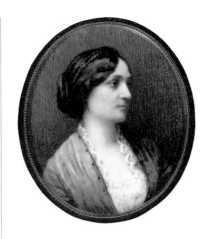

**American, unknown artist**
*Portrait of Josephine Mandeville
Rozet*
c. 1860
Lower left: York
Watercolor on ivory
2 1/2 × 2" (6.3 × 5.1 cm)

Gift of Marie Josephine Rozet
and Rebecca Mandeville Rozet
Hunt
1935-13-33

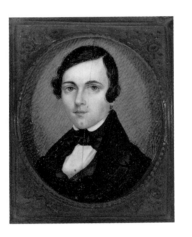

**American, unknown artist**
*Portrait of Samuel R. Marshall*
c. 1839
Watercolor on ivory
2 3/8 × 2" (6 × 5.1 cm)

Bequest of Harold S. Truitt
1927-5-12

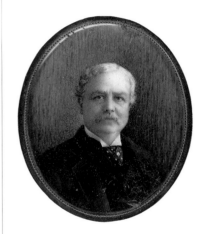

**American, unknown artist**
*Portrait of George H. Rozet*
c. 1880
Watercolor on ivory
2 1/2 × 2" (6.3 × 5.1 cm)

Gift of Marie Josephine Rozet
and Rebecca Mandeville Rozet
Hunt
1935-13-46

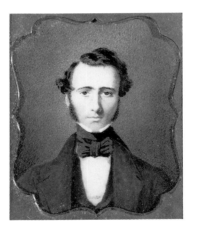

**American, unknown artist**
*Portrait of a Man*
c. 1840
Watercolor on ivory
2 3/4 × 2 1/8" (7 × 5.4 cm)

Gift of Miss Pauline Townsend
Pease
1979-108-8

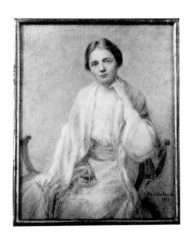

**Archambault, Anna
Margaretta**
American, 1856–1956
*Portrait of Miss Lillian R. Reed*
1915
Lower right: Archambault / 1915
Watercolor on ivory
4 15/16 × 3 15/16" (12.5 × 10 cm)

Gift of the Pennsylvania Society
of Miniature Painters in memory
of Emily Drayton Taylor
1954-42-2

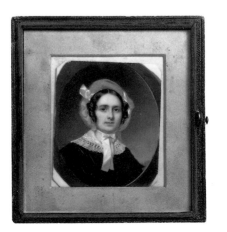

**American, unknown artist**
*Portrait of a Woman*
c. 1850
Watercolor on ivory
3 1/8 × 2 1/2" (7.9 × 6.3 cm)

Bequest of Leonora L. Koecker
1942-37-3

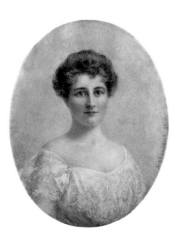

**Archambault, Anna
Margaretta**
*Portrait of Mrs. Clyde Beaumont
Cunningham*
1919
Center right: Archambault. 1919.
Watercolor on ivory
3 5/16 × 2 1/2" (8.4 × 6.3 cm)

Gift of the Pennsylvania Society
of Miniature Painters in memory
of Emily Drayton Taylor
1954-42-3

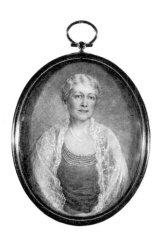

**Archambault, Anna Margaretta**
*Portrait of Mrs. J. Madison Taylor*
{née Emily Drayton}
1924
Center left: Archambault 1924
Watercolor on ivory
4 ³/₁₆ × 3 ³/₁₆" (10.6 × 8.1 cm)

Gift of an anonymous donor
1955-53-1

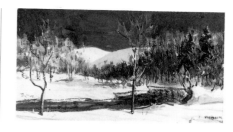

**Baum, Walter Emerson**
*Pennsylvania Hills*
Early to mid-20th century
Lower right: WEBAUM
Gouache on beaverboard
2 ⁷/₈ × 5" (7.3 × 12.7 cm)

Gift of Mrs. Daniel J. McCarthy
1954-63-1

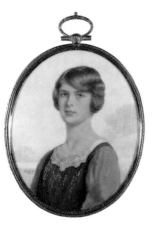

**Baer, William Jacob**
American, 1860–1941
*Portrait of Mrs. H. A. Ashforth*
1924
Lower left: W J. Baer / 1924
Watercolor on ivory
4 × 3 ¹/₈" (10.2 × 7.9 cm)

Gift of the Pennsylvania Society
of Miniature Painters in memory
of Emily Drayton Taylor
1954-42-4

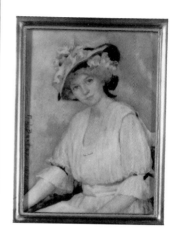

**Baxter, Martha Wheeler**
American, 1869–1955
*Portrait of a Woman in White*
1915
Center left: M. W. Baxter—1915
Watercolor on ivory
4 ³/₁₆ × 3 ¹/₁₆" (10.6 × 7.8 cm)

Gift of the Pennsylvania Society
of Miniature Painters in memory
of Emily Drayton Taylor
1954-42-7

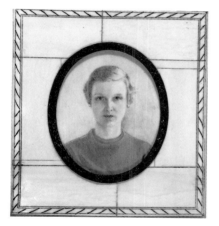

**Barrett, Lisbeth S.**
American, born 1904
*Self-Portrait*
1930s
Lower left: LSB
Watercolor on ivory
2 ¹/₂ × 1 ¹⁵/₁₆" (6.3 × 4.9 cm)

Gift of the Pennsylvania Society
of Miniature Painters in memory
of Emily Drayton Taylor
1954-42-5

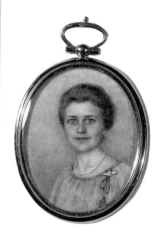

**Baxter, Martha Wheeler**
*Portrait of a Woman*
1926
Center right: M. W. Baxter—/
1926
Watercolor on ivory
2 ³/₈ × 1 ¹³/₁₆" (6 × 4.6 cm)

Gift of the Pennsylvania Society
of Miniature Painters in memory
of Emily Drayton Taylor
1954-42-9

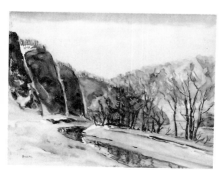

**Baum, Walter Emerson**
American, 1884–1956
*Delaware River*
Early to mid-20th century
Lower left: BAUM
Watercolor on ivory
3 ⁵/₁₆ × 4 ¹/₁₆" (8.4 × 10.3 cm)

Gift of the Pennsylvania Society
of Miniature Painters in memory
of Emily Drayton Taylor
1954-42-6

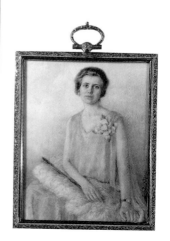

**Baxter, Martha Wheeler**
*Portrait of a Woman with a Fan*
1926
Lower right: M. W. Baxter—/
1926
Watercolor on ivory
4 ³/₁₆ × 3 ³/₁₆" (10.6 × 8.1 cm)

Gift of the Pennsylvania Society
of Miniature Painters in memory
of Emily Drayton Taylor
1954-42-8

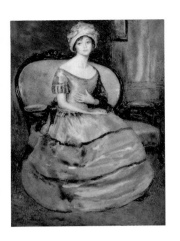

**Becker, Eulabee Dix**
American, 1878–1961
*A Visitor One Hundred Years Ago*
1922
Lower right: E. Dix 1922
Watercolor on ivory
8 1/8 × 6 3/16" (20.6 × 15.7 cm)

Gift of Mrs. Daniel J. McCarthy
1954-63-2

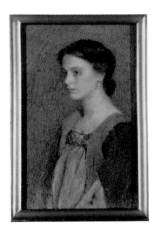

**Beckington, Alice**
American, 1868–1942
*Study in Blues and Greens (Self-Portrait)*
c. 1900
Watercolor on ivory
4 × 2 1/2" (10.2 × 6.3 cm)

Gift of the Pennsylvania Society
of Miniature Painters in memory
of Emily Drayton Taylor
1954-42-10

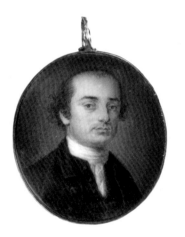

**Benbridge, Henry,
attributed to**
American, 1743–1812
*Portrait of Cadwalader Morris*
c. 1765–75
Watercolor on ivory
1 5/8 × 1 1/4" (4.1 × 3.2 cm)

Gift of an anonymous donor in
memory of Elizabeth Wheatley
Bendiner
1991-76-4

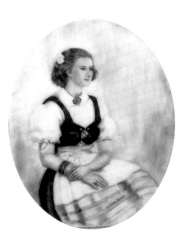

**Benton, Margaret Peake**
American, active by 1944,
died 1975
*The Swiss Costume*
c. 1945–60
Lower right: M. Peake Benton
Watercolor on ivory substitute
3 15/16 × 3" (10 × 7.6 cm)

Gift of the Pennsylvania Society
of Miniature Painters in memory
of Emily Drayton Taylor
1954-42-11

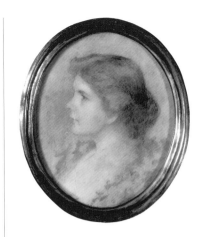

**Bill, Sally Cross**
American, 1874–1950
*Portrait of Mrs. Edwin Blashfield*
c. 1910–20
Watercolor on ivory
2 15/16 × 2 1/4" (7.5 × 5.7 cm)

Gift of the Pennsylvania Society
of Miniature Painters in memory
of Emily Drayton Taylor
1954-42-12

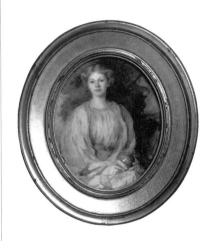

**Bill, Sally Cross**
*Portrait of Miss Dora Wetherbee*
1931
Lower right: SALLY CROSS 31
Watercolor on ivory
5 3/16 × 4 1/8" (13.2 × 10.4 cm)

Gift of the Pennsylvania Society
of Miniature Painters in memory
of Emily Drayton Taylor
1954-42-13

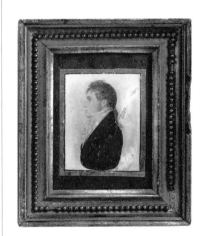

**Birch, Thomas**
American, born England,
1779–1851
*Portrait of Dr. George S. Schott III*
c. 1800–10
Watercolor on cardboard
6 × 4 1/4" (15.2 × 10.8 cm)

Gift of Marie Josephine Rozet
and Rebecca Mandeville Rozet
Hunt
1935-13-22

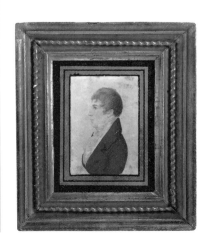

**Birch, Thomas**
*Portrait of Charles Schott*
c. 1808
Watercolor on cardboard
7 1/4 × 5 3/4" (18.4 × 14.6 cm)

Gift of Marie Josephine Rozet
and Rebecca Mandeville Rozet
Hunt
1935-13-21

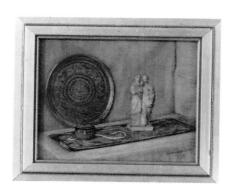

**Bliss, Alma Hirsig**
American, born Switzerland,
born 1875, still active 1956
*Blue and Ivory*
1937
Lower right: ALMA H. BLISS /
1937
Watercolor on ivory
2 11/16 × 3 5/16" (6.8 × 8.4 cm)

Gift of the Pennsylvania Society
of Miniature Painters in memory
of Emily Drayton Taylor
1954-42-14

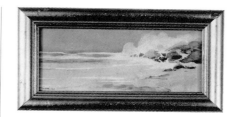

**Boericke, Johanna
Magdalene**
*Rocky Shore*
Early 20th century
Lower left: J. M. Boericke
Watercolor on ivory
2 1/16 × 5" (5.2 × 12.7 cm)

Gift of the Pennsylvania Society
of Miniature Painters in memory
of Emily Drayton Taylor
1954-42-17

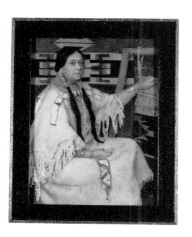

**Boardman, Rosina Cox**
American, 1878–1970
*Chinquilla Weaving*
1927
Upper left: 1927
Watercolor on ivory
4 5/8 × 3 1/2" (11.7 × 8.9 cm)

Gift of the Pennsylvania Society
of Miniature Painters in memory
of Emily Drayton Taylor
1954-42-15

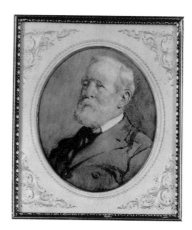

**Bonsall, Mary Waterman**
American, born 1868,
still active 1915
*Portrait of Amos Bonsall*
1903
Lower right: Mary W. Bonsall /
Dec., 1903
Watercolor on ivory substitute
3 × 2 5/8" (7.6 × 6.7 cm)

Gift of the Pennsylvania Society
of Miniature Painters in memory
of Emily Drayton Taylor
1954-42-18

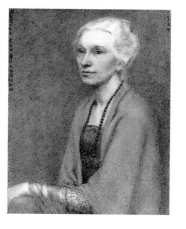

**Boardman, Rosina Cox**
*Portrait of Miss Lydia Longacre*
1929
Upper left: ROSINA COX
BOARDMAN; upper right: 1929
Watercolor on ivory
3 5/8 × 2 7/8" (9.2 × 7.3 cm)

Bequest of Rosina Cox Boardman
1971-199-4

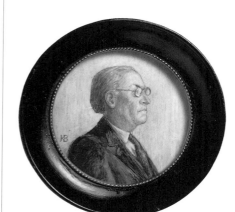

**Borda, Katharine K.**
American, born 1886,
still active 1946
*Portrait of Harry L. Johnson*
1947
Lower left: KB / 1947
Watercolor on ivory substitute
3 1/8" (7.9 cm) diameter

Gift of the Pennsylvania Society
of Miniature Painters in memory
of Emily Drayton Taylor
1954-42-19

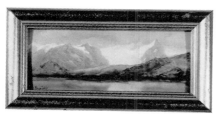

**Boericke, Johanna
Magdalene**
American, born 1868,
still active 1915
*Alaska Coast*
Early 20th century
Lower left: J. M. Boericke
Watercolor on ivory
2 × 4 7/8" (5.1 × 12.4 cm)

Gift of the Pennsylvania Society
of Miniature Painters in memory
of Emily Drayton Taylor
1954-42-16

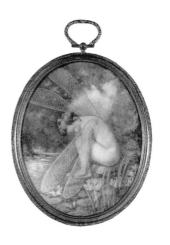

**Boyle, Sarah Yocum
McFadden**
American, active 1909–1940
*Little Sleepy Dragonfly*
1920s
Lower right: TMcF
Watercolor on ivory
4 1/2 × 3 9/16" (11.4 × 9 cm)

Gift of the Pennsylvania Society
of Miniature Painters in memory
of Emily Drayton Taylor
1954-42-20

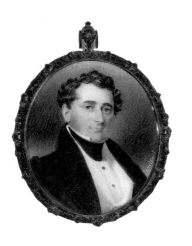

**Bridport, Hugh**
American, born England,
1794–c. 1869
*Portrait of a Man*
c. 1810
Lower right: Bridport
Watercolor on ivory
2 $^{11}/_{16}$ × 2 $^{1}/_{4}$" (6.8 × 5.7 cm)

Gift of Mrs. Daniel J. McCarthy
1953-142-6

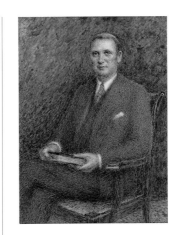

**Bush, Ella Shepard**
American, 1863–c. 1950
*Portrait of Herman Livezey*
c. 1930–50
Lower right: E. S. BUSH
Watercolor on ivory
5 $^{1}/_{2}$ × 3 $^{13}/_{16}$" (14 × 9.7 cm)

Gift of the Pennsylvania Society
of Miniature Painters in memory
of Emily Drayton Taylor
1954-42-21

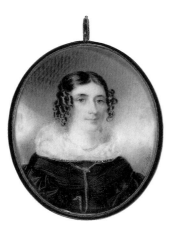

**Bridport, Hugh**
*Portrait of Mrs. Jacob Broom*
c. 1830
Lower right: Bridport
Watercolor on ivory
3 × 2 $^{1}/_{2}$" (7.6 × 6.3 cm)

Gift of Mrs. Daniel J. McCarthy
1953-142-7

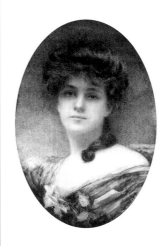

**Carew, Berta**
American, 1878–1956
*The Rose*
1904
Lower right: Berta Carew '04
Watercolor on ivory
3 $^{7}/_{8}$ × 2 $^{1}/_{2}$" (9.8 × 6.3 cm)

Gift of the Pennsylvania Society
of Miniature Painters in memory
of Emily Drayton Taylor, bequest
of Berta Carew
1959-91-31

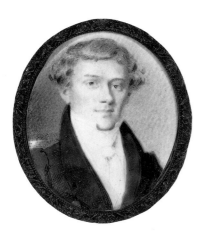

**Bridport, Hugh**
*Portrait of W. C. Keehmle*
c. 1830
On reverse: H Bridport
Watercolor on ivory
2 $^{3}/_{8}$ × 1 $^{15}/_{16}$" (6 × 4.9 cm)

The Ozeas, Ramborger, Keehmle
Collection
1921-34-98

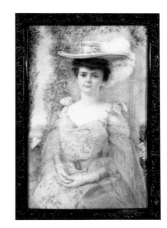

**Carew, Berta**
*Self-Portrait*
c. 1905
Watercolor on ivory
5 $^{7}/_{8}$ × 3 $^{13}/_{16}$" (14.9 × 9.7 cm)

Gift of the Pennsylvania Society
of Miniature Painters in memory
of Emily Drayton Taylor, bequest
of Berta Carew
1959-91-16

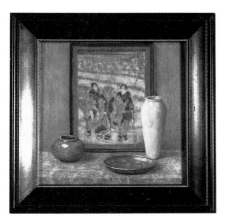

**Brugger, Dorothy**
American, active 1938–1947
*The Japanese Print*
c. 1940
Upper left: DOROTHY BRUGGER
Watercolor on ivory
3 $^{3}/_{4}$ × 3 $^{3}/_{4}$" (9.5 × 9.5 cm)

Gift of the Pennsylvania Society
of Miniature Painters in memory
of Emily Drayton Taylor, bequest
of Berta Carew
1959-91-47

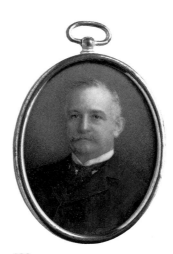

**Carew, Berta**
*Portrait of Mr. Emerson*
c. 1905–10
Lower right: Berta Carew
Watercolor on ivory
3 × 2 $^{3}/_{8}$" (7.6 × 6 cm)

Gift of the Pennsylvania Society
of Miniature Painters in memory
of Emily Drayton Taylor, bequest
of Berta Carew
1959-91-35

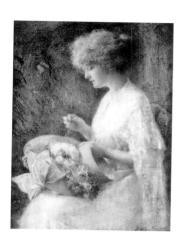

**Carew, Berta**
*Portrait of Silvia Jewel Clay*
c. 1910
Lower right: Berta Carew
Watercolor on ivory
6 × 4 $\frac{1}{2}$" (15.2 × 11.4 cm)

Gift of the Pennsylvania Society of Miniature Painters in memory of Emily Drayton Taylor, bequest of Berta Carew
1959-91-20

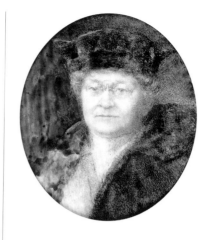

**Carew, Berta**
*My Mother (Portrait of Laura Adelaide Colman)*
1918
Lower right: Berta Carew / Oct. 1918
Watercolor on ivory
2 $\frac{7}{8}$ × 2 $\frac{1}{4}$" (7.3 × 5.7 cm)

Gift of the Pennsylvania Society of Miniature Painters in memory of Emily Drayton Taylor, bequest of Berta Carew
1959-91-21

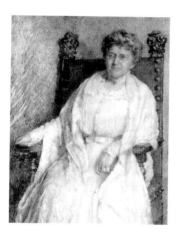

**Carew, Berta**
*My Mother (Portrait of Laura Adelaide Colman)*
c. 1910–20
Lower right: Berta Carew
Watercolor on ivory
5 $\frac{15}{16}$ × 4 $\frac{7}{16}$" (15.1 × 11.3 cm)

Gift of the Pennsylvania Society of Miniature Painters in memory of Emily Drayton Taylor, bequest of Berta Carew
1959-91-22

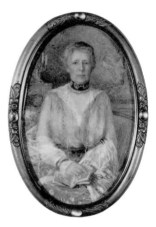

**Carew, Berta**
*Portrait of Mrs. David Rutter* [née Mary Elizabeth McMurtrie]
c. 1920
Upper right: Berta Carew
Watercolor on ivory
5 $\frac{1}{4}$ × 3 $\frac{1}{4}$" (13.3 × 8.2 cm)

Gift of the Pennsylvania Society of Miniature Painters in memory of Emily Drayton Taylor
1954-42-22

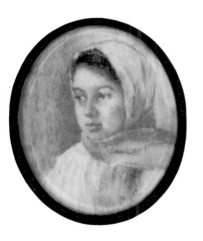

**Carew, Berta**
*Portrait of a Girl in a Pink-and-Green Scarf*
1917
On reverse: Berta Carew / 1917
Watercolor on ivory
2 $\frac{1}{4}$ × 1 $\frac{7}{8}$" (5.7 × 4.8 cm)

Gift of the Pennsylvania Society of Miniature Painters in memory of Emily Drayton Taylor, bequest of Berta Carew
1959-91-34

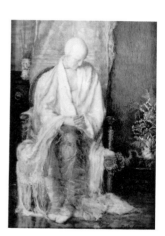

**Carew, Berta**
*Studio Properties*
c. 1920–50
Lower right: Berta Carew
Watercolor on ivory
5 $\frac{9}{16}$ × 3 $\frac{13}{16}$" (14.1 × 9.7 cm)

Gift of the Pennsylvania Society of Miniature Painters in memory of Emily Drayton Taylor, bequest of Berta Carew
1959-91-32

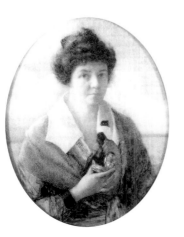

**Carew, Berta**
*Self-Portrait (The Crystal Box)*
1917
Lower right: Berta Carew / 1917
Watercolor on ivory
4 × 3" (10.2 × 7.6 cm)

Gift of the Pennsylvania Society of Miniature Painters in memory of Emily Drayton Taylor, bequest of Berta Carew
1959-91-15

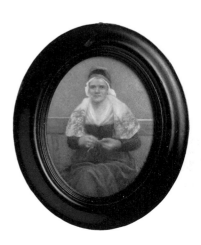

**Carew, Berta**
*Portrait of a French Peasant*
1921
Lower right: Berta Carew / 21
Watercolor on ivory
4 $\frac{1}{2}$ × 3 $\frac{3}{8}$" (11.4 × 8.6 cm)

Gift of the Pennsylvania Society of Miniature Painters in memory of Emily Drayton Taylor, bequest of Berta Carew
1959-91-36

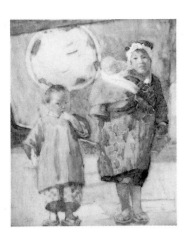

**Carew, Berta**
*Children of Japan*
1928
Watercolor on ivory
3 1/8 × 2 9/16" (7.9 × 6.5 cm)

Gift of the Pennsylvania Society
of Miniature Painters in memory
of Emily Drayton Taylor, bequest
of Berta Carew
1959-91-39

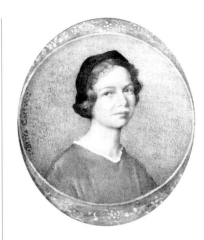

**Carew, Berta**
*Portrait of Mary Catherine Kerwin*
c. 1930
Center left: Berta Carew
Watercolor on ivory
4 1/8 × 3 3/8" (10.5 × 8.6 cm)

Gift of the Pennsylvania Society
of Miniature Painters in memory
of Emily Drayton Taylor, bequest
of Berta Carew
1959-91-27

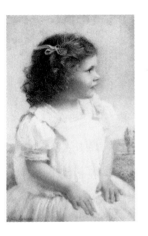

**Carew, Berta**
*Little Mary (Portrait of Mary)*
1920s
Lower left: Berta Carew
Watercolor on ivory
4 7/8 × 2 3/4" (12.4 × 7 cm)

Gift of the Pennsylvania Society
of Miniature Painters in memory
of Emily Drayton Taylor, bequest
of Berta Carew
1959-91-28

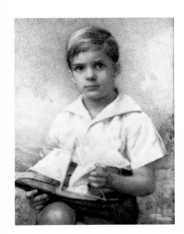

**Carew, Berta**
*Portrait of a Young Sailor*
1937
Lower right: Berta Carew / 1937
Watercolor on ivory
3 5/8 × 2 13/16" (9.2 × 7.1 cm)

Gift of the Pennsylvania Society
of Miniature Painters in memory
of Emily Drayton Taylor, bequest
of Berta Carew
1959-91-29

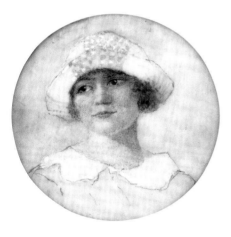

**Carew, Berta**
*Portrait of Virginia*
1920s
Watercolor on ivory
1 3/4" (4.4 cm) diameter

Gift of the Pennsylvania Society
of Miniature Painters in memory
of Emily Drayton Taylor, bequest
of Berta Carew
1959-91-33

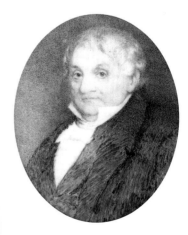

**Carew, Berta**
*Portrait of Josiah Bardwell*
Early 20th century
Lower right: Berta Carew
Watercolor on ivory
3 3/8 × 2 5/8" (8.6 × 6.7 cm)

Gift of the Pennsylvania Society
of Miniature Painters in memory
of Emily Drayton Taylor, bequest
of Berta Carew
1959-91-30

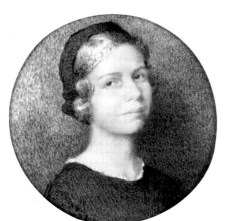

**Carew, Berta**
*Portrait of Mary Catherine Kerwin*
c. 1930
Watercolor on ivory
2 1/4" (5.7 cm) diameter

Gift of the Pennsylvania Society
of Miniature Painters in memory
of Emily Drayton Taylor, bequest
of Berta Carew
1959-91-26

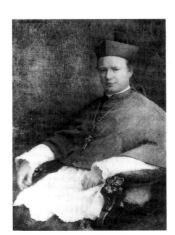

**Carew, Berta**
*Portrait of the Late Archbishop
Corrigan*
Early 20th century
Upper left: Berta Carew
Watercolor on ivory
5 3/4 × 4 1/4" (14.6 × 10.8 cm)

Gift of the Pennsylvania Society
of Miniature Painters in memory
of Emily Drayton Taylor, bequest
of Berta Carew
1959-91-23

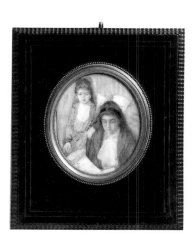

**Carew, Berta**
*The Sisters*
Early 20th century
Watercolor on ivory
4 1/16 × 3 3/8" (10.3 × 8.6 cm)

Gift of the Pennsylvania Society
of Miniature Painters in memory
of Emily Drayton Taylor, bequest
of Berta Carew
1959-91-19

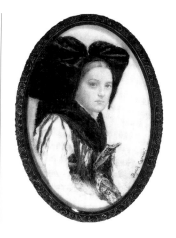

**Carew, Berta**
*Portrait of an Alsacienne*
Early 20th century
Lower right: Berta Carew
Watercolor on ivory
3 7/8 × 2 1/2" (9.8 × 6.3 cm)

Gift of the Pennsylvania Society
of Miniature Painters in memory
of Emily Drayton Taylor, bequest
of Berta Carew
1959-91-17

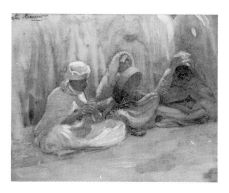

**Carew, Berta**
*Arab Musicians, Tunis*
Early 20th century
Upper left: Berta Carew
Watercolor on ivory
2 1/8 × 2 9/16" (5.4 × 6.5 cm)

Gift of the Pennsylvania Society
of Miniature Painters in memory
of Emily Drayton Taylor, bequest
of Berta Carew
1959-91-45

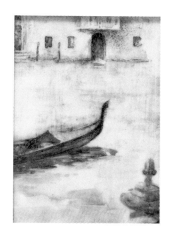

**Carew, Berta**
*Venetian Memories*
Early 20th century
Watercolor on ivory
2 11/16 × 1 3/4" (6.8 × 4.4 cm)

Gift of the Pennsylvania Society
of Miniature Painters in memory
of Emily Drayton Taylor, bequest
of Berta Carew
1959-91-41

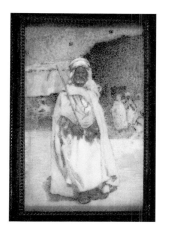

**Carew, Berta**
*Portrait of the Arab Bou Saada*
Early 20th century
Lower left: B. C.
Watercolor on ivory
2 1/2 × 1 9/16" (6.3 × 4 cm)

Gift of the Pennsylvania Society
of Miniature Painters in memory
of Emily Drayton Taylor, bequest
of Berta Carew
1959-91-38

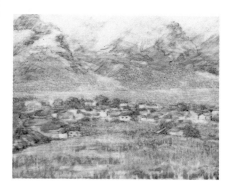

**Carew, Berta**
*Aigle, Switzerland*
Early to mid-20th century
Watercolor on ivory
2 5/8 × 3 1/4" (6.7 × 8.2 cm)

Gift of the Pennsylvania Society
of Miniature Painters in memory
of Emily Drayton Taylor, bequest
of Berta Carew
1959-91-42

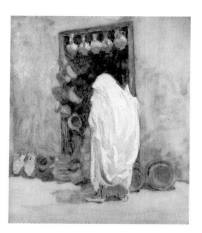

**Carew, Berta**
*Shopping in Tunis*
Early 20th century
Lower left: Berta Carew
Watercolor on ivory
2 5/8 × 2 1/8" (6.7 × 5.4 cm)

Gift of the Pennsylvania Society
of Miniature Painters in memory
of Emily Drayton Taylor, bequest
of Berta Carew
1959-91-44

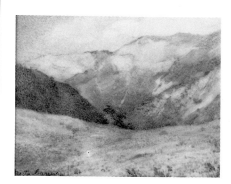

**Carew, Berta**
*French Alps*
Early to mid-20th century
Lower left: Berta Carew
Watercolor on ivory
2 5/8 × 3 1/4" (6.7 × 8.2 cm)

Gift of the Pennsylvania Society
of Miniature Painters in memory
of Emily Drayton Taylor, bequest
of Berta Carew
1959-91-43

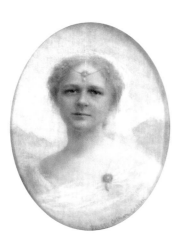

**Carew, Braley Colman**
American, active 20th century
*Portrait of a Woman in White
(Portrait of Cora Braley Venturini)*
Early 20th century
Lower right: BRALEY Colman.
CAREW.
Watercolor on ivory
3 1/16 × 2 5/16" (7.8 × 5.9 cm)

Gift of the Pennsylvania Society
of Miniature Painters in memory
of Emily Drayton Taylor, bequest
of Berta Carew
1959-91-46

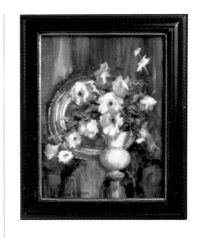

**Collier, Grace**
American, active c. 1940
*White Petunias*
Mid-20th century
Lower left: Grace Collier
Watercolor on ivory
5 5/8 × 4 1/8" (14.3 × 10.5 cm)

Gift of the Pennsylvania Society
of Miniature Painters in memory
of Emily Drayton Taylor
1954-42-27

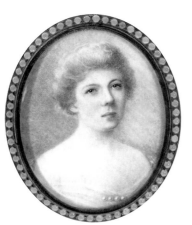

**Cariss, Marguerite
Feldpauche**
American, 1883–1959
*Self-Portrait (Mrs. John Mundell
Hutchinson)*
c. 1905
Watercolor on ivory
2 7/16 × 1 15/16" (6.2 × 4.9 cm)

Gift of the Pennsylvania Society
of Miniature Painters in memory
of Emily Drayton Taylor
1954-42-23

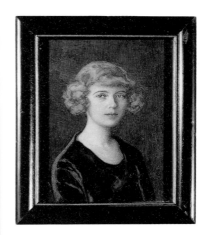

**Coolidge, Bertha**
American, 1880–1934
*Portrait of a Girl*
1923
Lower left: B. Coolidge 1923
Watercolor on ivory
3 1/16 × 2 7/16" (7.8 × 6.2 cm)

Gift of the Pennsylvania Society
of Miniature Painters in memory
of Emily Drayton Taylor
1954-42-28

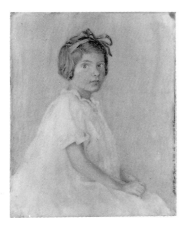

**Chase, Violet Thompson**
American, active 1926–1929
*Portrait of Elizabeth MacNeill*
1929
Lower right: VIOLET T SMITH
1929
Watercolor on ivory
3 11/16 × 2 7/8" (9.4 × 7.3 cm)

Gift of the Pennsylvania Society
of Miniature Painters in memory
of Emily Drayton Taylor
1954-42-26

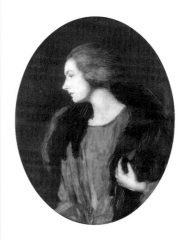

**Coolidge, Bertha**
*Portrait of Poppy*
1926
Center bottom: Coolidge 1926
Watercolor on ivory
4 3/4 × 3 3/4" (12.1 × 9.5 cm)

Gift of the Pennsylvania Society
of Miniature Painters in memory
of Emily Drayton Taylor
1954-42-29

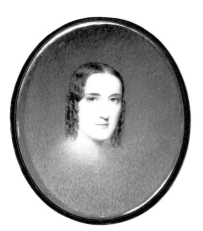

**Clark, Alvan, Jr.**
American?, 1804–1887
*Portrait of Mrs. Goddard*
1840s
Watercolor on ivory
2 13/16 × 2 3/8" (7.1 × 6 cm)

Gift of Mrs. Daniel J. McCarthy
1953-142-9

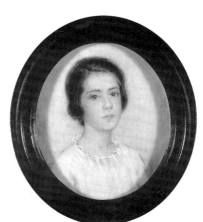

**Cowan, Sarah Eakin**
American, 1875–1958
*Portrait of Emily*
1920s
Watercolor on ivory
2 15/16 × 2 7/16" (7.5 × 6.2 cm)

Gift of the Pennsylvania Society
of Miniature Painters in memory
of Emily Drayton Taylor
1954-42-30

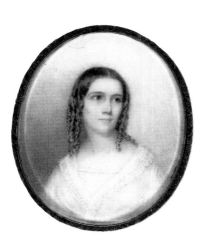

**Cushman, George Hewitt**
American, 1814–1876
*Portrait of Susan Wetherill Cushman*
1840s
On reverse of frame: Susan
Wetherill Cushman / Painted by /
Her Husband / George Hewitt
Cushman
Watercolor on ivory
2 7/16 × 2" (6.2 × 5.1 cm)

Gift of Miss Alice Cushman
1940-10-2

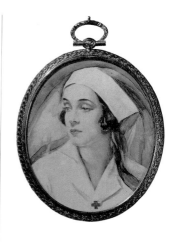

**Dalrymple, Lucille
Stevenson**
American, 1882–1955
*The Red Cross Nurse (Portrait of
Dorothy Diane Dalrymple)*
c. 1917–19
Upper left: L. S. Dalrymple
Watercolor on ivory
3 11/16 × 3 1/16" (9.4 × 7.8 cm)

Gift of the Pennsylvania Society
of Miniature Painters in memory
of Emily Drayton Taylor
1954-42-32

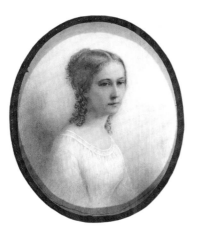

**Cushman, George Hewitt**
*Portrait of Susan Wetherill Cushman*
1850s
Watercolor on vellum
7 3/4 × 6 1/8" (19.7 × 15.6 cm)

Gift of Miss Alice Cushman
1940-10-1

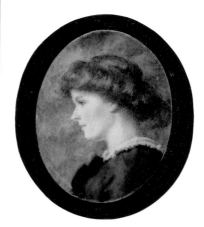

**Day, Martha B. Willson**
American, born 1885,
still active 1978
*Portrait of a Girl*
c. 1910
Watercolor on ivory
1 3/4 × 1 5/16" (4.4 × 3.3 cm)

Gift of the Pennsylvania Society
of Miniature Painters in memory
of Emily Drayton Taylor
1954-42-33

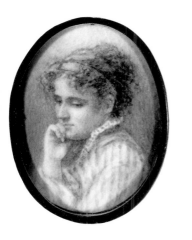

**Cushman, George Hewitt**
*Portrait of Alice Cushman*
c. 1860
Watercolor on ivory
1 3/16 × 7/8" (3 × 2.2 cm)

Bequest of Janet B. Fine
1973-250-1

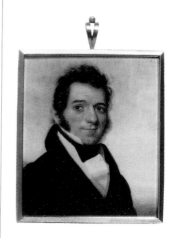

**Dickinson, Anson**
American, 1779–1852
*Portrait of Captain T. T. Heartte*
Companion to the following
miniature
Early 1820s
Watercolor on ivory
3 1/4 × 2 5/8" (8.2 × 6.7 cm)

The Ozeas, Ramborger, Keehmle
Collection
1919-163

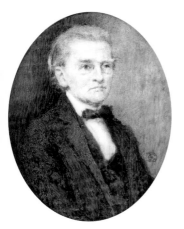

**Daggett, Grace E.**
American, born 1867,
still active 1947
*Portrait of Frank Tiernan*
Early 20th century
Lower right: GED
Watercolor on ivory
3 1/16 × 2 3/8" (7.8 × 6 cm)

Gift of the Pennsylvania Society
of Miniature Painters in memory
of Emily Drayton Taylor
1954-42-31

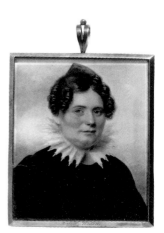

**Dickinson, Anson**
*Portrait of Mary E. Heartte*
Companion to the preceding
miniature
Early 1820s
Watercolor on ivory
3 1/4 × 2 7/16" (8.2 × 6.2 cm)

The Ozeas, Ramborger, Keehmle
Collection
1919-164

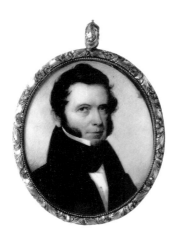

**Dickinson, Anson**
*Portrait of John J. Ramborger*
c. 1830
Watercolor on ivory
2 5/8 × 2 3/16" (6.7 × 5.6 cm)

The Ozeas, Ramborger, Keehmle
Collection
1921-34-102

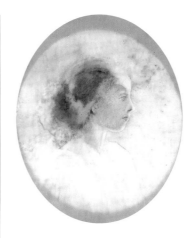

**Ely, Frances Campbell**
American, 1868–1952
*Mornings at Seven*
Early 20th century
Watercolor on ivory
3 × 2 1/4" (7.6 × 5.7 cm)

Gift of the Pennsylvania Society
of Miniature Painters in memory
of Emily Drayton Taylor
1954-42-35

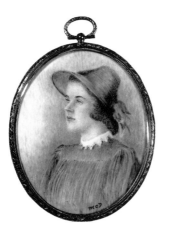

**Dunn, Marjorie Cline**
American, born 1894
*Portrait of Barbara*
c. 1940–60
Lower right: M C D
Watercolor on ivory
4 3/16 × 3 3/16" (10.6 × 8.1 cm)

Gift of the Pennsylvania Society
of Miniature Painters in memory
of Emily Drayton Taylor
1954-42-34

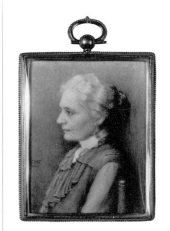

**Fenderson, Annie M.**
American, died 1934
*Portrait of Mrs. M. J. Moffett*
1924
Center left: AMF / 1924
Watercolor on ivory
2 15/16 × 2 1/4" (7.5 × 5.7 cm)

Gift of the Pennsylvania Society
of Miniature Painters in memory
of Emily Drayton Taylor
1954-42-37

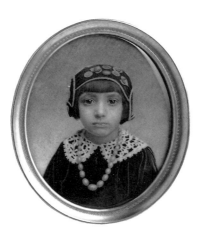

**Durante, M.**
American, active 20th century
*Portrait of an Italian Girl*
1924
Center right: Durante. M. 1924
Watercolor on ivory
3 3/8 × 2 5/8" (8.6 × 6.7 cm)

Gift of the Pennsylvania Society
of Miniature Painters in memory
of Emily Drayton Taylor, bequest
of Berta Carew
1959-91-18

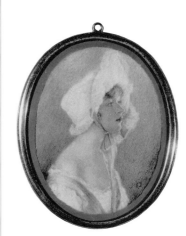

**Fenderson, Annie M.**
*In Fancy Dress*
1920s
Lower right: AMF
Watercolor on ivory
2 15/16 × 2 3/16" (7.5 × 5.6 cm)

Gift of the Pennsylvania Society
of Miniature Painters in memory
of Emily Drayton Taylor
1954-42-36

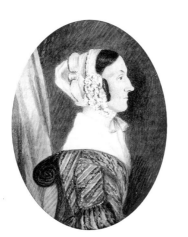

**Ellsworth, James Sanford**
American, 1802–1873/74
*Portrait of Mrs. S. B. Webb*
1840s
On paper on reverse: Sanford
Ellsworth / Guilford Conn. / Mrs.
S. B. Webb / of Wethersfield /
Conn.
Watercolor on paper
3 3/8 × 2 5/16" (8.6 × 5.9 cm)

The Samuel S. White 3rd and
Vera White Collection
1967-30-38

**Fenderson, Annie M.**
*Portrait of Mrs. Fenderson
(Grandmother Fenderson)*
Early 20th century
Center right: AMF
Watercolor on ivory
3 1/4 × 2 7/16" (8.2 × 6.2 cm)

Gift of the Pennsylvania Society
of Miniature Painters in memory
of Emily Drayton Taylor
1954-42-38

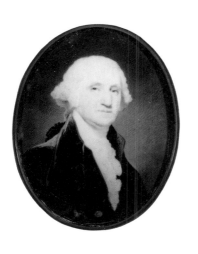

**Field, Robert**
American, born England,
active by 1794, died 1819
*Portrait of George Washington*
After a painting by Gilbert
Stuart (American, 1755–1828)
known in many versions
After 1796
Watercolor on ivory
3 ¹¹/₁₆ × 2 ¹³/₁₆" (9.4 × 7.1 cm)

Gift of Mrs. Daniel J. McCarthy
1953-142-26

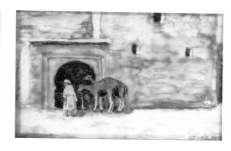

**Fisher, Howell Tracy**
*Young Camels Drinking at the Base
of the Kutubia Mosque, Marrakech*
1929
Lower right: HTFisher 1929
Watercolor on ivory
2 ³/₁₆ × 3 ³/₈" (5.6 × 8.6 cm)

Gift of the Pennsylvania Society
of Miniature Painters in memory
of Emily Drayton Taylor
1954-42-39

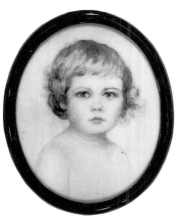

**Fisher, Howell Tracy**
American, active by 1929,
died 1938
*Portrait of Claire*
1920s
Watercolor on ivory
2 ¹/₂ × 1 ¹⁵/₁₆" (6.3 × 4.9 cm)

Gift of the Pennsylvania Society
of Miniature Painters in memory
of Emily Drayton Taylor
1954-42-42

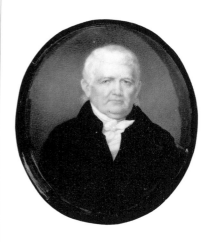

**Fraser, Charles**
American, 1782–1860
*Portrait of Judge Daniel O'Hara*
Mid-19th century
Watercolor on ivory
4 ¹/₂ × 3 ⁷/₈" (11.4 × 9.8 cm)

Gift of Mrs. Daniel J. McCarthy
1954-21-3

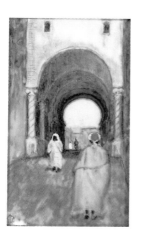

**Fisher, Howell Tracy**
*Street in Tétouan, Spanish Morocco*
1929
Lower left: HTFisher
Watercolor on ivory
3 ⁷/₈ × 2 ⁵/₁₆" (9.8 × 5.9 cm)

Gift of the Pennsylvania Society
of Miniature Painters in memory
of Emily Drayton Taylor
1954-42-41

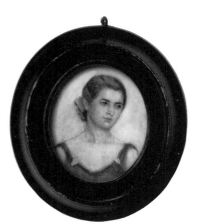

**Gilpin, Blanche R.**
American, active 20th century
*Portrait of Miss Santa Maria*
1930s
Watercolor on ivory
2 ³/₄ × 2 ¹/₄" (7 × 5.7 cm)

Gift of the Pennsylvania Society
of Miniature Painters in memory
of Emily Drayton Taylor
1954-42-43

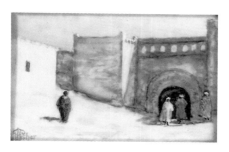

**Fisher, Howell Tracy**
*Sultan's Gate, Marrakech*
1929
Lower left: HTFisher 1929
Watercolor on ivory
2 ¹/₈ × 3 ⁵/₁₆" (5.4 × 8.4 cm)

Gift of the Pennsylvania Society
of Miniature Painters in memory
of Emily Drayton Taylor
1954-42-40

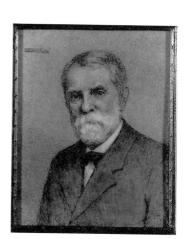

**Graham, Elizabeth
Sutherland**
American, died 1938
*Of the Old School (Portrait of
John S. Graham)*
c. 1915–35
Upper left: E. S. Graham
Watercolor on ivory
4 ¹/₈ × 3 ¹/₈" (10.5 × 7.9 cm)

Gift of the Pennsylvania Society
of Miniature Painters in memory
of Emily Drayton Taylor
1954-42-44

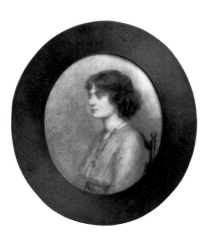

**Harris, Alexandrina Robertson**
American, born Scotland, born 1886, still active 1962
*Meditation*
1920s
Lower left: Alexandrina. R. Harris.
Watercolor on ivory
3 $^{15}/_{16}$ × 3 $^{3}/_{16}$" (10 × 8.1 cm)

Gift of the Pennsylvania Society of Miniature Painters in memory of Emily Drayton Taylor
1954-42-46

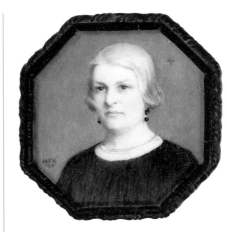

**Hawley, Margaret Foote**
American, 1880–1963
*Portrait of Madame C.*
1925
Lower left: MFH / '25
Watercolor on ivory
1 $^{11}/_{16}$ × 1 $^{13}/_{16}$" (4.3 × 4.6 cm)

Gift of Mrs. Daniel J. McCarthy
1954-21-5

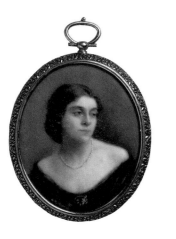

**Harris, Alexandrina Robertson**
*Portrait of a Woman*
Early to mid-20th century
Lower left: A R. Harris
Watercolor on ivory
3 $^{1}/_{2}$ × 2 $^{11}/_{16}$" (8.9 × 6.8 cm)

Gift of the Pennsylvania Society of Miniature Painters in memory of Emily Drayton Taylor
1954-42-45

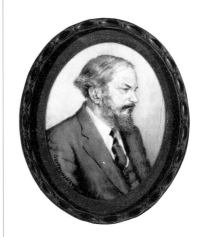

**Hays, Gertrude V.**
American, active 20th century
*Portrait of Mr. Osborne*
Early to mid-20th century
Lower left: GERTRUDE HAYS
Watercolor on ivory
3 $^{1}/_{4}$ × 2 $^{7}/_{16}$" (8.2 × 6.2 cm)

Gift of the Pennsylvania Society of Miniature Painters in memory of Emily Drayton Taylor
1954-42-49

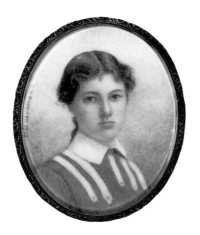

**Harrison, Catherine Norris**
American, active c. 1903–c. 1914
*Portrait of Sophy B. Norris*
1903
Center left: C. N. Harrison 1903
Watercolor on ivory
3 $^{1}/_{8}$ × 2 $^{7}/_{16}$" (7.9 × 6.2 cm)

Gift of the Pennsylvania Society of Miniature Painters in memory of Emily Drayton Taylor
1954-42-48

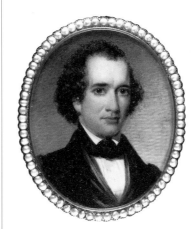

**Hewitt, William K.**
American, 1817–1893
*Portrait of Major Daniel M. Fox*
c. 1840
Watercolor on ivory
2 $^{11}/_{16}$ × 2 $^{1}/_{8}$" (6.8 × 5.4 cm)

Gift of the Pennsylvania Society of Miniature Painters in memory of Emily Drayton Taylor
1954-42-107

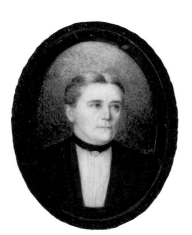

**Harrison, Catherine Norris**
*Portrait of Agnes Irwin*
Early 20th century
Center right: CNH
Watercolor on ivory
2 $^{1}/_{2}$ × 1 $^{13}/_{16}$" (6.3 × 4.6 cm)

Gift of the Pennsylvania Society of Miniature Painters in memory of Emily Drayton Taylor
1954-42-47

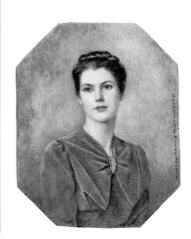

**Hildebrandt, Cornelia Trumbull Ellis**
American, 1878–1962
*Portrait of Sallie Moon*
c. 1945
Center right: Cornelia E Hildebrandt
Watercolor on ivory
3 $^{11}/_{16}$ × 2 $^{7}/_{8}$" (9.4 × 7.3 cm)

Gift of the Pennsylvania Society of Miniature Painters in memory of Emily Drayton Taylor
1954-42-50

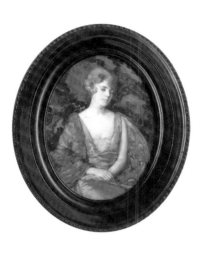

**Hills, Laura Coombs**
American, 1859–1952
*Blue and Crimson*
1920s
Center bottom: Laura Hills
Watercolor on ivory
5 3/4 × 4 3/8" (14.6 × 11.1 cm)

Gift of the Pennsylvania Society
of Miniature Painters in memory
of Emily Drayton Taylor
1954-42-51

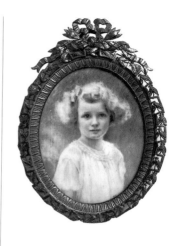

**Huey, Florence Greene**
American, 1872–1961
*Portrait of Marion Pettit*
c. 1905–25
Lower right: F. G. Huey
Watercolor on ivory
3 × 2 3/8" (7.6 × 6 cm)

Gift of the Pennsylvania Society
of Miniature Painters in memory
of Emily Drayton Taylor
1954-42-52

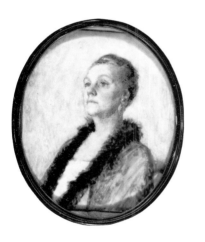

**Hills, Laura Coombs**
*The Green Hat*
1920s
Center bottom: Laura Hills
Watercolor on ivory
5 5/8 × 4 1/8" (14.3 × 10.5 cm)

Gift of Mrs. Daniel J. McCarthy
1954-21-6

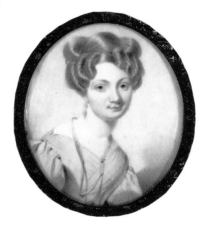

**Inman, Henry**
American, 1801–1846
*Portrait of a Woman*
c. 1830
Watercolor on ivory
2 11/16 × 2 3/16" (6.8 × 5.6 cm)

Gift of Mrs. Daniel J. McCarthy
1954-21-13

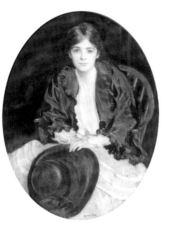

**Hitchner, Mary**
American, born 1884,
still active 1924
*Portrait of Mrs. Howell Tracy Fisher*
1924
Watercolor on ivory
2 15/16 × 2 3/8" (7.5 × 6 cm)

Gift of the Pennsylvania Society
of Miniature Painters in memory
of Emily Drayton Taylor
1954-42-110

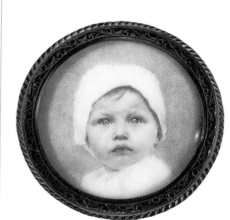

**Irvin, Virginia Hendrickson**
American, born 1904
*Baby Oliver (Portrait of Oliver)*
Early to mid-20th century
Watercolor on ivory
1" (2.5 cm) diameter

Gift of the Pennsylvania Society
of Miniature Painters in memory
of Emily Drayton Taylor
1954-42-53

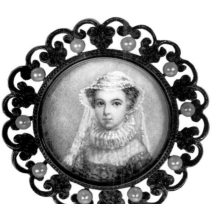

**Holme, Lucy D.**
American, 1848–1928
*Portrait of a Woman in Elizabethan Dress*
Late 19th or early 20th century
Watercolor on ivory
3/4" (1.9 cm) diameter

Gift of Miss Elizabeth D. Hoffman
1976-199-1

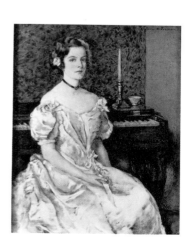

**Jackson, Annie Hurlburt**
American, 1877–1959
*Rosewood and Old Satin*
1930s
Upper right: Annie H. Jackson
Watercolor on ivory
5 7/16 × 4 3/8" (13.8 × 11.1 cm)

Gift of the Pennsylvania Society
of Miniature Painters in memory
of Emily Drayton Taylor
1954-42-54

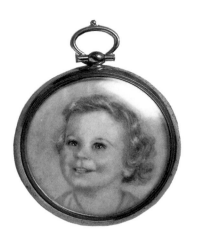

**Jackson, Nathalie L'Hommedieu**
American, born 1883, still active 1940
*Portrait of Daniel N. Phillips*
c. 1930–50
Watercolor on ivory
2" (5.1 cm) diameter

Gift of the Pennsylvania Society of Miniature Painters in memory of Emily Drayton Taylor
1954-42-55

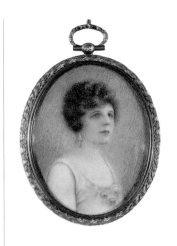

**Kellett, Edith**
Canadian, born England, born 1877, still active 1928
*Portrait of Madame R.*
Mid-1920s
Lower right: Edith Kellet
Watercolor on ivory
2 13/16 × 2 1/8" (7.1 × 5.4 cm)

Gift of the Pennsylvania Society of Miniature Painters in memory of Emily Drayton Taylor
1954-42-58

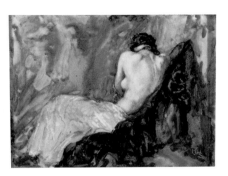

**Johnson, Harry L.**
American, active c. 1940
*La Vie*
1930s
Lower right: HLJ
Watercolor on ivory substitute
3 5/8 × 4 1/2" (9.2 × 11.4 cm)

Gift of the Pennsylvania Society of Miniature Painters in memory of Emily Drayton Taylor
1954-42-56

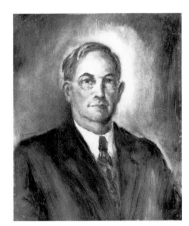

**King, Angelica**
American, active 1941–1951
*Portrait of Dr. Morland King*
1951
Center left: Angelica King—'51
Oil on paper
5 × 4" (12.7 × 10.2 cm)

Gift of the Pennsylvania Society of Miniature Painters in memory of Emily Drayton Taylor
1954-42-59

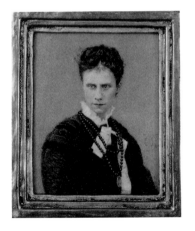

**Johnson, Harry L.**
*Portrait of Miss Julia Waters*
Early 20th century
Center right: HLJ
Watercolor on ivory
3 5/8 × 2 3/4" (9.2 × 7 cm)

Gift of the Pennsylvania Society of Miniature Painters in memory of Emily Drayton Taylor
1954-42-57

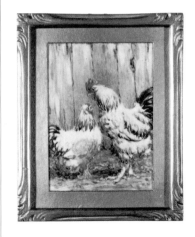

**Knowles, Elizabeth A. McGillivray**
American, born Canada, 1866–1928
*The Explanation*
Early 20th century
Lower left: Elizabeth A. McG. Knowles
Watercolor on ivory
3 7/16 × 2 1/2" (8.7 × 6.3 cm)

Gift of the Pennsylvania Society of Miniature Painters in memory of Emily Drayton Taylor
1954-42-60

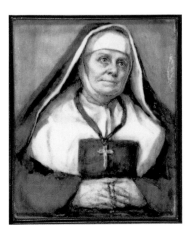

**Johnson, Jeanne Payne**
American, 1887–1958
*Portrait of Sister Madelaine*
Mid-20th century
Watercolor on ivory
3 1/8 × 2 1/2" (7.9 × 6.3 cm)

Gift of Mrs. Daniel J. McCarthy
1954-21-15

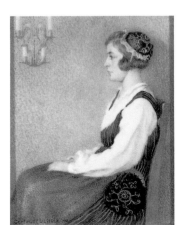

**Little, Gertrude L.**
American, active 1924–1962
*Signe*
1934
Lower left: Gertrude L. Little '34
Watercolor on ivory
4 7/8 × 3 3/4" (12.4 × 9.5 cm)

Gift of the Pennsylvania Society of Miniature Painters in memory of Emily Drayton Taylor
1954-42-61

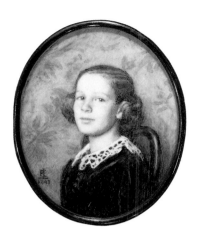

**Longacre, Lydia Eastwick**
American, 1870–1951
*Portrait of Judy*
1943
Lower left: LEL / 1943
Watercolor on ivory
3 1/8 × 2 9/16" (7.9 × 6.5 cm)

Gift of the Pennsylvania Society
of Miniature Painters in memory
of Emily Drayton Taylor
1954-42-62

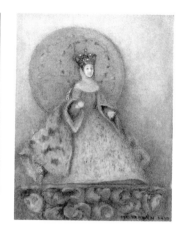

**McKerwin**
American, active c. 1935
*Virgin del Rayo*
1935
Lower right: MCKERWIN 1935
Watercolor on ivory
2 1/2 × 1 15/16" (6.3 × 4.9 cm)

Gift of the Pennsylvania Society
of Miniature Painters in memory
of Emily Drayton Taylor, bequest
of Berta Carew
1959-91-40

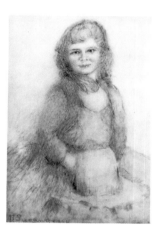

**Lugano, Ines Somenzini**
American, born Italy,
active 1930–1959
*The Little Bridesmaid*
1954
Lower left: I. Lugano 1954
Watercolor and graphite on ivory
substitute
5 11/16 × 4 3/16" (14.4 × 10.6 cm)

Gift of the Pennsylvania Society
of Miniature Painters in memory
of Emily Drayton Taylor
1954-42-63

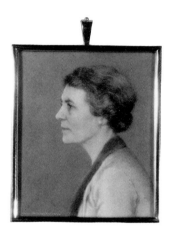

**McMillan, Mary**
American, 1895–1958
*Profile*
1934
Lower left: MARY MCMILLAN 1934
Watercolor on ivory
3 × 2 7/16" (7.6 × 6.2 cm)

Gift of the Pennsylvania Society
of Miniature Painters in memory
of Emily Drayton Taylor
1954-42-65

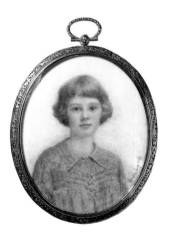

**Lynch, Anna**
American, active by 1915,
died 1940
*Portrait of Charlotte Vanderlip*
1920s
Lower right: Anna Lynch
Watercolor on ivory
3 13/16 × 3" (9.7 × 7.6 cm)

Gift of the Pennsylvania Society
of Miniature Painters in memory
of Emily Drayton Taylor
1954-42-64

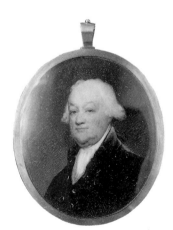

**Malbone, Edward Greene**
American, 1777–1807
*Portrait of Colonel John Nixon*
1790
Lower left: Malbone—90
Watercolor on ivory
3 × 2 1/2" (7.6 × 6.3 cm)

Bequest of Elizabeth Ellen
Keating
F1920-1-1

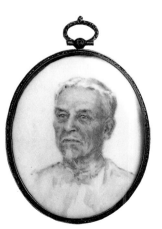

**McCarthy, Elizabeth White**
American, 1891–1952
*Portrait of Dr. Judson Deland*
Mid-20th century
Watercolor on ivory
3 1/4 × 2 1/2" (8.2 × 6.3 cm)

Gift of Mrs. Daniel J. McCarthy
1954-63-7

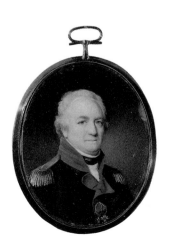

**Malbone, Edward Greene**
*Portrait of General Anne-Louis de
Tousard*
c. 1790
Watercolor on ivory
3 5/8 × 2 3/4" (9.2 × 7 cm)

Gift of Mrs. Daniel J. McCarthy
1954-21-18

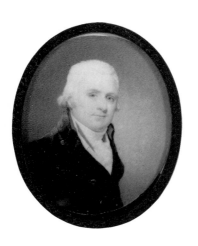

**Malbone, Edward Greene**
*Portrait of J. Higbie*
Companion to the following
miniature
c. 1795–1800
Lower right: E. G. Malbone
Watercolor on ivory
3 × 2 1/2" (7.6 × 6.3 cm)

Gift of Mrs. Daniel J. McCarthy
1954-21-19

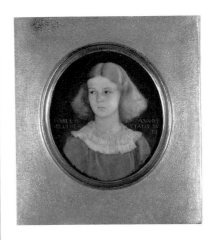

**Melcher, Betsy Flagg**
American, born 1900,
still active 1946
*Portrait of Pamela Melcher*
1939
Lower left: 1939 Betsy.Flagg.
Melcher.; center left: PAMELA /
MELCHER; center right: ANNO
1939 / ETATIS SUAE / 12
Watercolor on ivory
3 5/8 × 3 1/4" (9.2 × 8.2 cm)

Gift of the Pennsylvania Society
of Miniature Painters in memory
of Emily Drayton Taylor
1954-42-66

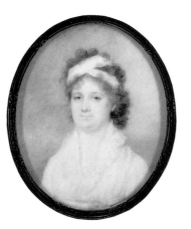

**Malbone, Edward Greene**
*Portrait of Mrs. J. Higbie*
Companion to the preceding
miniature
c. 1795–1800
Watercolor on ivory
3 1/8 × 2 3/8" (7.9 × 6 cm)

Gift of Mrs. Daniel J. McCarthy
1954-21-20

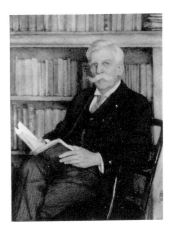

**Murray, Grace Harper**
American, 1872–1944
*Portrait of Justice Oliver Wendell
Holmes*
1920s
Lower right: GHM
Watercolor on ivory
5 1/2 × 4 1/8" (14 × 10.5 cm)

Gift of the Pennsylvania Society
of Miniature Painters in memory
of Emily Drayton Taylor
1954-42-67

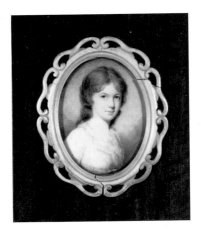

**Malbone, Edward Greene**
*Portrait of Caroline Fenno*
c. 1800
Watercolor on ivory
3 3/16 × 2 3/8" (8.1 × 6 cm)

Gift of Mrs. Daniel J. McCarthy
1954-21-17

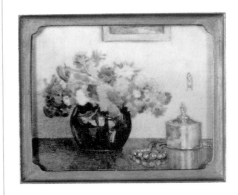

**Murray, Grace Harper**
*Still Life*
c. 1920–40
Center right: GHM
Watercolor on ivory
2 7/8 × 3 1/2" (7.3 × 8.9 cm)

Gift of the Pennsylvania Society
of Miniature Painters in memory
of Emily Drayton Taylor
1954-42-68

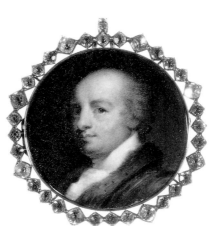

**Marchant, Edward Dalton**
American, 1806–1887
*Portrait of Chancellor Kent of
New York*
Mid-19th century
Watercolor on cardboard
1 13/16" (4.6 cm) diameter

Gift of Mrs. Daniel J. McCarthy
1954-21-21

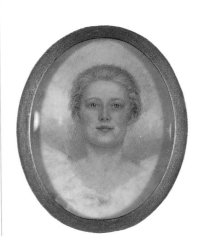

**Otis, Amy**
American, active 1926–1940
*A College Girl (Portrait of Dorothy
Gifford)*
c. 1920–40
Lower left: Amy Otis
Watercolor on ivory
3 3/8 × 2 9/16" (8.6 × 6.5 cm)

Gift of the Pennsylvania Society
of Miniature Painters in memory
of Emily Drayton Taylor
1954-42-69

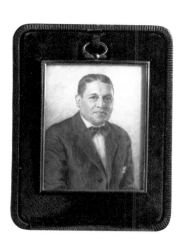

**Page, Polly**
American, active c. 1937
*Portrait of Caspar Wistar Hacker*
c. 1920–40
Lower right: Polly Page
Watercolor on ivory
$3 \, 5/8 \times 2 \, 13/16$" (9.2 × 7.1 cm)

Gift of the Pennsylvania Society
of Miniature Painters in memory
of Emily Drayton Taylor
1954-42-109

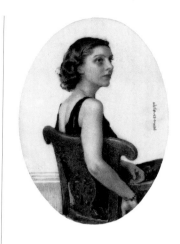

**Pattee, Elsie Dodge**
*Portrait of Eleanor*
1930s
Center right: E. D. PATTEE
Watercolor on ivory
$5 \, 1/4 \times 3 \, 3/4$" (13.3 × 9.5 cm)

Bequest of Rosina Cox Boardman
1971-199-1

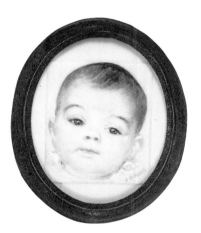

**Parke, Jessie Burns**
American, 1889–1964
*Portrait of Martha Peabody Parke*
Mid-20th century
Lower right: J. B. PARKE
Watercolor on ivory
$1 \, 13/16 \times 1 \, 1/2$" (4.6 × 3.8 cm)

Gift of the Pennsylvania Society
of Miniature Painters in memory
of Emily Drayton Taylor
1954-42-70

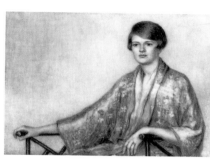

**Patterson, Rebecca Burd Peale**
American, 1881–1952
*The Japanese Coat*
1920s
Watercolor on ivory
$3 \, 1/8 \times 4 \, 5/16$" (7.9 × 10.9 cm)

Gift of the Pennsylvania Society
of Miniature Painters in memory
of Emily Drayton Taylor
1954-42-73

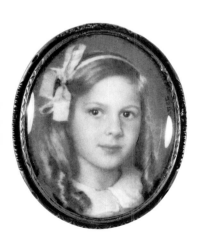

**Pattee, Elsie Dodge**
American, born 1876,
still active 1940
*Little Betsy (Portrait of Betsy)*
c. 1920–40
Center right: E. D. PATTEE
Watercolor on ivory substitute
$1 \, 13/16 \times 1 \, 1/2$" (4.6 × 3.8 cm)

Gift of the Pennsylvania Society
of Miniature Painters in memory
of Emily Drayton Taylor
1954-42-72

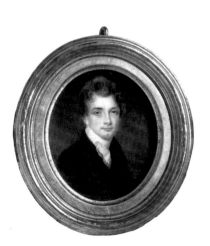

**Peale, Anna Claypoole**
American, 1791–1878
*Portrait of a Man*
1812
Lower right: Anna C. / Peale /
1812
Watercolor on ivory
$2 \, 5/8 \times 2 \, 1/8$" (6.7 × 5.4 cm)

Gift of George W. Norris
1937-14-1

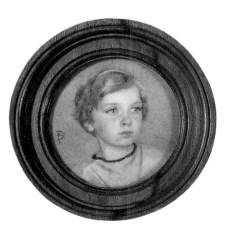

**Pattee, Elsie Dodge**
*Portrait of Lillian*
c. 1920–50
Center left: EDP
Watercolor on ivory substitute
$2 \, 1/4$" (5.7 cm) diameter

Gift of the Pennsylvania Society
of Miniature Painters in memory
of Emily Drayton Taylor
1954-42-71

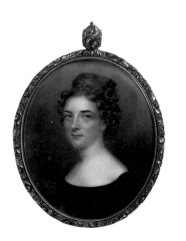

**Peale, Anna Claypoole**
*Portrait of Ellen Matlack Price*
1822
Lower left: Anna C. / Peale / 1822
Oil on ivory
$2 \, 7/8 \times 2 \, 5/16$" (7.3 × 5.9 cm)

Bequest of Constance A. Jones
1988-27-50

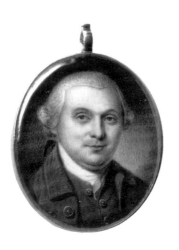

**Peale, Charles Willson**
American, 1741–1827
*Portrait of Benjamin Randolph*
c. 1775–80
Watercolor on ivory
1 1/4 × 1" (3.2 × 2.5 cm)

Gift of Mr. and Mrs. Timothy
Johnes Westbrook
1990-21-1

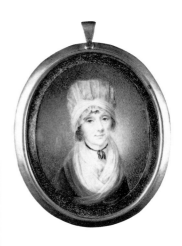

**Peale, James**
*Portrait of Mollie Callahan*
1799
Lower left: JP / 1799
Watercolor on ivory
2 5/8 × 2 1/8" (6.7 × 5.4 cm)

Gift of Mrs. Daniel J. McCarthy
1954-21-25

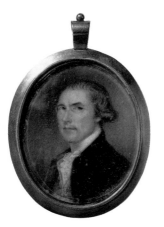

**Peale, Charles Willson**
*Portrait of Captain John
MacPherson*
c. 1787–92
Watercolor on ivory
2 1/8 × 1 11/16" (5.4 × 4.3 cm)

Bequest of Mellicent Story
Garland
1963-75-1

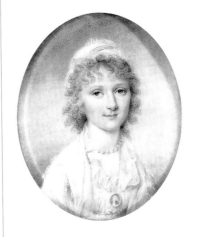

**Peale, James**
*Portrait of Maria Bassett*
1801
Lower right: P / 1801
Oil on ivory
2 3/4 × 2 1/8" (7 × 5.4 cm)

Bequest of Jane Barbour Charles
1980-101-1

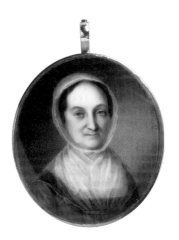

**Peale, Charles Willson,
attributed to**
*Portrait of Hannah Cadwalader
Morris*
c. 1765–75
Watercolor on ivory
1 1/2 × 1 1/4" (3.8 × 3.2 cm)

Gift of an anonymous donor in
memory of Elizabeth Wheatley
Bendiner
1991-76-3

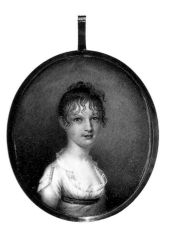

**Peale, James**
*Portrait of a Woman*
1805
Lower right: JP / 1805
Watercolor on ivory
2 15/16 × 2 7/16" (7.5 × 6.2 cm)

Gift of Jeanette Stern Whitebook
in memory of Louise Stern Shanis
1984-102-1

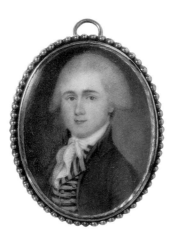

**Peale, James**
American, 1749–1831
*Portrait of a Man*
c. 1790
Watercolor on ivory
1 7/8 × 1 3/8" (4.8 × 3.5 cm)

The Ozeas, Ramborger, Keehmle
Collection
1919-162

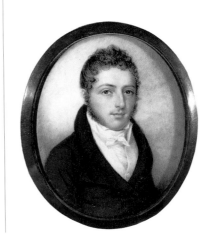

**Peale, James**
*Portrait of a Man*
1812
Lower right: JP / 1812
Watercolor on ivory
2 5/8 × 2" (6.7 × 5.1 cm)

Gift of Mrs. Frederick W. W.
Graham in memory of Mrs.
George H. Earle, Jr.
1944-47-1

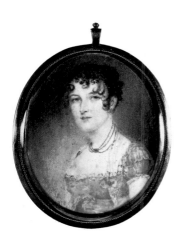

**Peale, James**
*Portrait of Sarah Maria McClintock*
1813
Lower left: J P. / 1813
Watercolor on ivory
3 3/16 × 2 1/2" (8.1 × 6.3 cm)

Bequest of Anne Maria Meeteer
1938-4-1

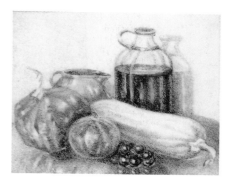

**Pinter, Dora**
American, active c. 1950
*Halloween*
Mid-20th century
Watercolor on ivory
1 5/8 × 2" (4.1 × 5.1 cm)

Gift of the Pennsylvania Society
of Miniature Painters in memory
of Emily Drayton Taylor
1954-42-75

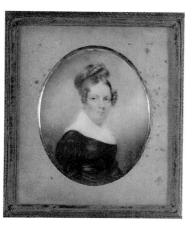

**Peale, Raphaelle**
American, 1774–1825
*Portrait of Catherine Mellish*
c. 1810–20
Watercolor on ivory
2 3/4 × 2 1/4" (7 × 5.7 cm)

Gift of Mrs. Daniel J. McCarthy
1954-21-26

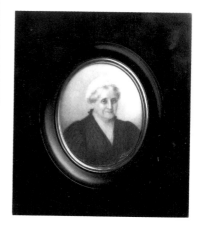

**Pollock, L.**
American, active 20th century
*Portrait of a Woman with a White Cap*
Early 20th century
Lower right: L. Pollock
Watercolor on ivory
3 7/16 × 2 11/16" (8.7 × 6.8 cm)

Gift of the Pennsylvania Society
of Miniature Painters in memory
of Emily Drayton Taylor, bequest
of Berta Carew
1959-91-24

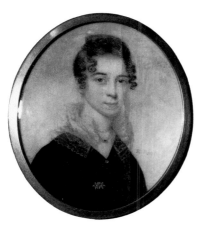

**Peale, Raphaelle**
*Portrait of a Woman*
c. 1810–20
Lower right: R Peale
Watercolor on ivory
2 5/8 × 2 1/4" (6.7 × 5.7 cm)

Gift of Mrs. Daniel J. McCarthy
1954-21-27

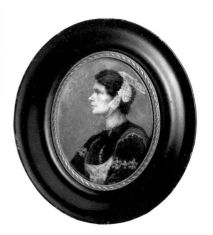

**Purdie, Evelyn**
American, born Turkey,
1858–1943
*Portrait of a Brittany Woman*
Early 20th century
Watercolor on ivory
3 7/8 × 2 7/8" (9.8 × 7.3 cm)

Gift of the Pennsylvania Society
of Miniature Painters in memory
of Emily Drayton Taylor
1954-42-76

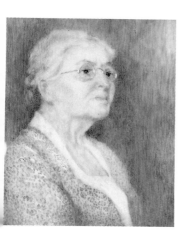

**Phillips, Josephine Neall**
American, 1887–1953
*Model*
c. 1930–50
Watercolor on ivory
3 1/4 × 2 1/2" (8.2 × 6.3 cm)

Gift of the Pennsylvania Society
of Miniature Painters in memory
of Emily Drayton Taylor
1954-42-74

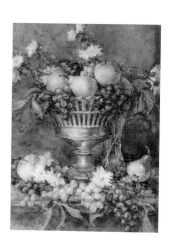

**Purdie, Evelyn**
*Still Life with Flowers and Fruit*
Mid-20th century
Watercolor on ivory
5 1/8 × 3 3/16" (13 × 8.1 cm)

Gift of the Pennsylvania Society
of Miniature Painters in memory
of Emily Drayton Taylor
1954-42-77

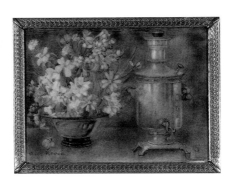

**Reece, Dora**
American, active 1936–1962
*Still Life with Flowers and a Samovar*
Mid-20th century
Lower left: Dora Reece
Watercolor on ivory
3 ¹³⁄₁₆ × 4 ¹⁵⁄₁₆" (9.7 × 12.5 cm)

Gift of the Pennsylvania Society of Miniature Painters in memory of Emily Drayton Taylor
1954-42-78

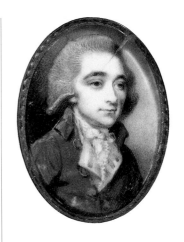

**Robertson, Archibald**
American, born Scotland, 1765–1835
*Portrait of a Man*
c. 1790
Watercolor on ivory
1 ⁵⁄₈ × 1 ¹⁄₈" (4.1 × 2.9 cm)

Gift of Mrs. Daniel J. McCarthy
1955-1-7

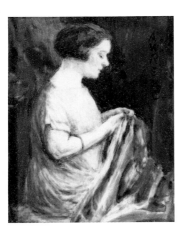

**Reid, Aurelia Wheeler**
American, 1876–1969
*Portrait of Elizabeth Meldrum Reid*
c. 1930
Upper right: A. W. REID.
Watercolor on ivory
3 ¹³⁄₁₆ × 2 ¹⁵⁄₁₆" (9.7 × 7.5 cm)

Gift of the Pennsylvania Society of Miniature Painters in memory of Emily Drayton Taylor
1954-42-79

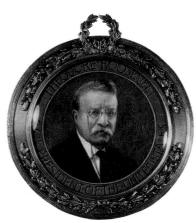

**Saint-Gaudens, Carlota**
American, 1884–1927
*Portrait of Theodore Roosevelt*
Early 20th century
On border: .THEODORE. ROOSEVELT. /.26th. PRESIDENT. OF.THE.UNITED.STATES.
Watercolor on ivory
2 ⁵⁄₈" (6.7 cm) diameter

Gift of the Pennsylvania Society of Miniature Painters in memory of Emily Drayton Taylor
1954-42-82

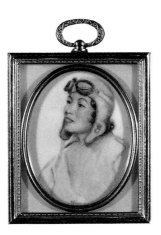

**Rhome, Lily Blanche Peterson**
American, 1874–1943
*Portrait of Sui Fun (Katherine) Cheung*
1939
Center bottom: —Rhome— / L. B. P. Rhome / 1939
Watercolor on ivory substitute
2 ⁷⁄₈ × 2 ¹⁄₈" (7.3 × 5.4 cm)

Gift of the Pennsylvania Society of Miniature Painters in memory of Emily Drayton Taylor
1954-42-80

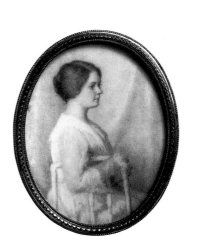

**Sawyer, Edith**
American, active 1926–1933
*Portrait of a Woman in White*
c. 1920
Watercolor on ivory
4 ⁵⁄₁₆ × 3 ¹⁄₄" (10.9 × 8.2 cm)

Gift of the Pennsylvania Society of Miniature Painters in memory of Emily Drayton Taylor
1954-42-83

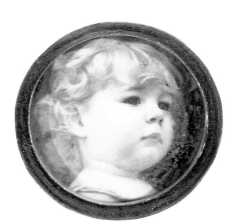

**Richards, Glenora**
American, born 1909
*Portrait of Henry Tracy Richards*
Mid-20th century
Watercolor on ivory substitute
1 ⁵⁄₈" (4.1 cm) diameter

Gift of the Pennsylvania Society of Miniature Painters in memory of Emily Drayton Taylor
1954-42-81

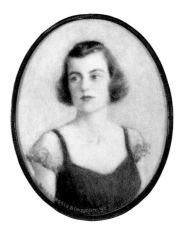

**Simpson, Edna Huestis**
American, 1882–1964
*Portrait of Mrs. Francis H. Brinkley*
1940
Lower left: Edna Huestis Simpson '40
Watercolor on ivory
4 × 3" (10.2 × 7.6 cm)

Gift of the Pennsylvania Society of Miniature Painters in memory of Emily Drayton Taylor
1954-42-84

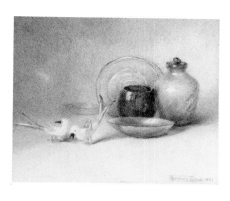

**Sims, Florence**
American, born 1891,
still active 1962
*Still Life with Blue Glass*
1951
Lower right: Florence Sims—1951
Watercolor on ivory
2 1/2 × 3 1/4" (6.3 × 8.2 cm)

Gift of the Pennsylvania Society
of Miniature Painters in memory
of Emily Drayton Taylor
1954-42-85

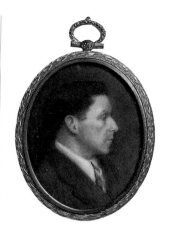

**Starr, Lorraine Webster**
American, born 1887,
still active 1962
*An Actor (Portrait of Arthur Rowe)*
Mid-20th century
Center left: L. W. Starr
Watercolor on ivory
2 3/4 × 2 1/16" (7 × 5.2 cm)

Gift of the Pennsylvania Society
of Miniature Painters in memory
of Emily Drayton Taylor
1954-42-88

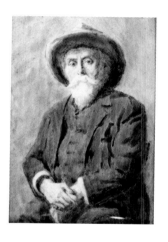

**Springer, Eva**
American, born 1882,
died 1962–64
*Portrait of Count Volney de Saint-Aignau*
1913
Lower right: EVA SPRINGER. /
Paris 1913
Watercolor on ivory
5 7/16 × 4" (13.8 × 10.2 cm)

Gift of the Pennsylvania Society
of Miniature Painters in memory
of Emily Drayton Taylor
1954-42-86

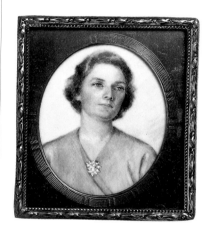

**Stedman, Margaret Weir**
American, born 1882,
still active 1937
*Portrait of Miss Santa Maria*
c. 1950
Watercolor on ivory
2 3/4 × 2 1/4" (7 × 5.7 cm)

Gift of the Pennsylvania Society
of Miniature Painters in memory
of Emily Drayton Taylor
1954-42-89

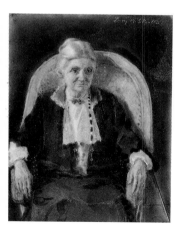

**Stanton, Lucy May**
American, 1875–1931
*Portrait of Miss Jule Moss*
c. 1920
Upper right: Lucy M. Stanton
Watercolor on ivory
5 15/16 × 4 1/2" (15.1 × 11.4 cm)

Gift of Mrs. Daniel J. McCarthy
1955-1-18

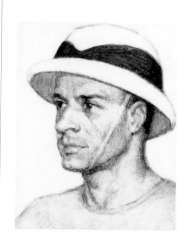

**Stout, Virginia Hollinger**
American, born 1903
*Portrait of a Polo Player*
1950
Watercolor on ivory
2 3/8 × 1 13/16" (6 × 4.6 cm)

Gift of the Pennsylvania Society
of Miniature Painters in memory
of Emily Drayton Taylor
1954-42-90

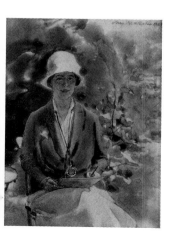

**Stanton, Lucy May**
*Self-Portrait in the Garden*
1928
Upper right: Lucy M. Stanton
1928
Watercolor on ivory
5 11/16 × 4 7/16" (14.4 × 11.3 cm)

Gift of the Pennsylvania Society
of Miniature Painters in memory
of Emily Drayton Taylor
1954-42-87

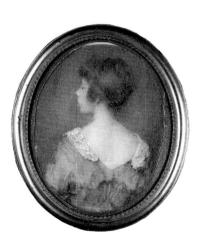

**Strean, Maria Judson**
American, 1865–1949
*Portrait of a Red-Haired Girl*
c. 1915–20
Lower left: M. J. Strean
Watercolor on ivory
3 13/16 × 2 7/8" (9.7 × 7.3 cm)

Bequest of Rosina Cox Boardman
1971-199-2

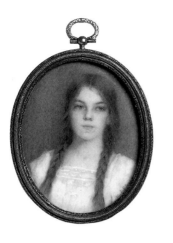

**Strean, Maria Judson**
*Portrait of Dorothy*
1920
Lower right: M. J. Strean
Watercolor on ivory
3 3/4 × 2 7/8" (9.5 × 7.3 cm)

Gift of the Pennsylvania Society
of Miniature Painters in memory
of Emily Drayton Taylor
1954-42-91

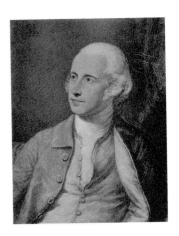

**Stuart, Gilbert, copy after**
*Portrait of Benjamin West*
After the painting, dated c. 1785,
in the National Gallery, London
(no. 895)
c. 1900–25
Upper left (spurious): G. S. / 1792
Watercolor on ivory
4 5/8 × 3 1/2" (11.7 × 8.9 cm)

Gift of Miss Lena Cadwalader
Evans
1936-22-9

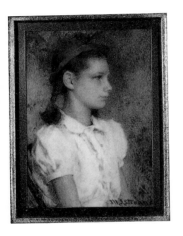

**Strean, Maria Judson**
*The Red Hat*
1940s
Lower right: M. J. Strean
Watercolor on ivory
3 3/4 × 2 5/8" (9.5 × 6.7 cm)

Gift of the Pennsylvania Society
of Miniature Painters in memory
of Emily Drayton Taylor
1954-42-92

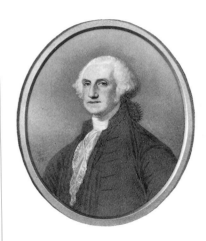

**Stuart, Gilbert, copy after**
*Portrait of George Washington*
A composite of several portraits
by Stuart
c. 1900–25
Lower left (spurious): G. S / 1793
Watercolor on ivory
5 1/8 × 4 1/4" (13 × 10.8 cm)

Gift of Miss Lena Cadwalader
Evans
1936-22-10

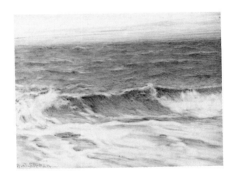

**Strean, Maria Judson**
*Sea*
Early to mid-20th century
Lower left: M. J. Strean
Watercolor on ivory
2 11/16 × 3 3/16" (6.8 × 8.1 cm)

Gift of Mrs. Daniel J. McCarthy
1955-1-19

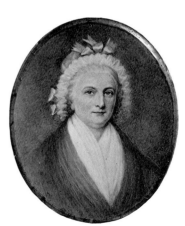

**Stuart, Gilbert, copy after**
*Portrait of Martha Washington*
Possibly after *Portrait of Martha
Washington*, in the Museum of
Fine Arts, Boston (1980.2)
c. 1900–25
Center right (spurious): G. S.
Watercolor on ivory
4 3/8 × 3 1/2" (11.1 × 8.9 cm)

Gift of Miss Lena Cadwalader
Evans
1936-22-12

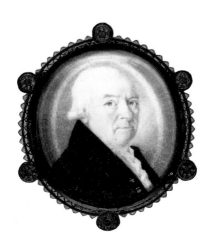

**Stuart, Gilbert, attributed to**
American, 1755–1828
*Portrait of Paul Revere*
Early 19th century
Watercolor on ivory
1 3/4 × 1 9/16" (4.4 × 4 cm)

Gift of Mrs. Daniel J. McCarthy
1955-1-20

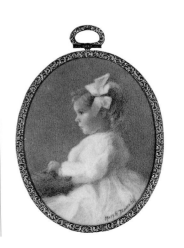

**Tannahill, Mary H.**
American, born 1868,
still active 1940
*Portrait of Elizabeth*
Early 20th century
Lower right: Mary H. Tannahill
Watercolor on ivory
3 7/8 × 3" (9.8 × 7.6 cm)

Gift of the Pennsylvania Society
of Miniature Painters in memory
of Emily Drayton Taylor
1954-42-93

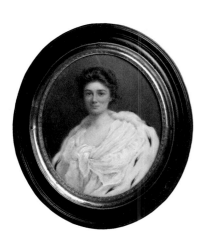

**Taylor, Emily Drayton**
American, 1860–1952
*Portrait of Mrs. Richard Berridge*
[née Eulalie Lesley]
1906
Center left: E. D. Taylor / 1906
Watercolor on ivory
4 3/8 × 3 9/16" (11.1 × 9 cm)

Gift of the Pennsylvania Society
of Miniature Painters in memory
of Emily Drayton Taylor
1954-42-94

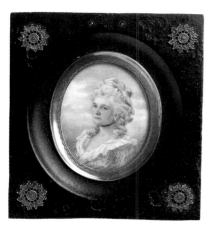

**Taylor, Emily Drayton**
*Portrait of Mrs. John Innes Kane*
1911
Lower right: E. D. Taylor / 1911
Watercolor on ivory
3 1/8 × 2 5/8" (7.9 × 6.7 cm)

Gift of Edith M. Patterson in
memory of her mother, Emily
Drayton Taylor
1956-36-1

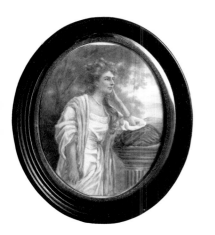

**Taylor, Emily Drayton**
*Portrait of a Woman Leaning on a
Cushion*
Early 20th century
Lower right: E. D. Taylor
Watercolor on ivory
5 × 3 15/16" (12.7 × 10 cm)

Gift of Edith M. Patterson in
memory of her mother, Emily
Drayton Taylor
1956-36-2

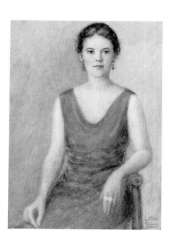

**Thomas, Lillian M.**
American, active c. 1946
*Portrait of a Woman in Red*
1930s
Lower right: Lillian / Thomas
Watercolor on ivory
3 7/8 × 2 13/16" (9.8 × 7.1 cm)

Gift of the Pennsylvania Society
of Miniature Painters in memory
of Emily Drayton Taylor
1954-42-95

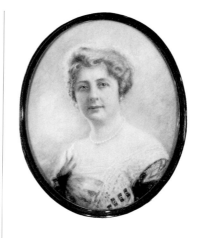

**Tolman, Nelly Summerill
McKenzie**
American, 1877–1961
*Portrait of Elizabeth C. Wickersham*
c. 1915–25
Center right: Nelly McK. Tolman.
Watercolor on ivory
3 1/2 × 2 11/16" (8.9 × 6.8 cm)

Gift of the Pennsylvania Society
of Miniature Painters in memory
of Emily Drayton Taylor
1954-42-96

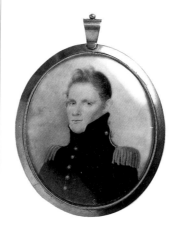

**Trott, Benjamin**
American, c. 1770–1843
*Portrait of Colonel William King*
c. 1800
Watercolor on ivory
2 5/8 × 2 3/16" (6.7 × 5.6 cm)

Gift of Mrs. Daniel J. McCarthy
1954-63-8

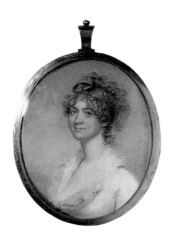

**Trott, Benjamin**
*Portrait of Mary Catherine Sprogell*
c. 1800
Watercolor on ivory
3 × 2 3/8" (7.6 × 6 cm)

Gift of John J. Jaquette
1962-218-1

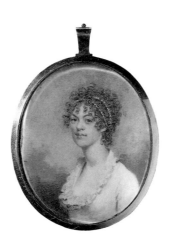

**Trott, Benjamin**
*Portrait of Mary Catherine Sprogell*
1805
Watercolor on ivory
3 1/16 × 2 7/16" (7.8 × 6.2 cm)

Gift of Mrs. William A. Jaquette
1962-217-1

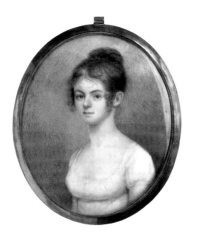

**Trott, Benjamin**
*Portrait of Mrs. Walter Livingston*
c. 1820
Watercolor on ivory
3 × 2 1/4" (7.6 × 5.7 cm)

Gift of Mrs. Daniel J. McCarthy
1955-1-21

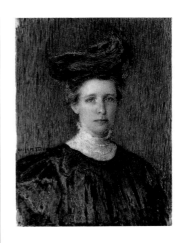

**Turner, Helen Maria**
American, 1858–1958
*Portrait of Lettie Turner*
c. 1903–5
Center left: Helen M. Turner
Watercolor on ivory
4 1/4 × 3 1/4" (10.8 × 8.2 cm)

Bequest of Rosina Cox Boardman
1971-199-3

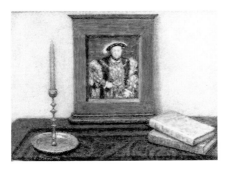

**Trueworthy, Jessie**
American, born 1891,
still active 1962
*Still Life*
Early 20th century
Lower left: J. Trueworthy
Watercolor on ivory
3 1/4 × 4 1/4" (8.2 × 10.8 cm)

Gift of the Pennsylvania Society
of Miniature Painters in memory
of Emily Drayton Taylor, bequest
of Berta Carew
1959-91-37

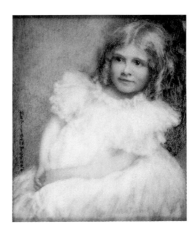

**Turner, Matilda Hutchinson**
American, born 1869,
still active 1959
*Portrait of Mildred Louise Otto*
Early 20th century
Center left: Matilda H Turner;
lower right: M H Turner
Watercolor on ivory
3 5/16 × 2 5/8" (8.4 × 6.7 cm)

Gift of the Pennsylvania Society
of Miniature Painters in memory
of Emily Drayton Taylor
1954-42-106

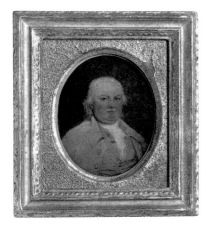

**Trumbull, John**
American, 1756–1843
*Portrait of Robert Morris*
Companion to the following
miniature
1790
Oil on panel
4 × 3 1/4" (10.2 × 8.2 cm)

Gift of Mrs. Philip Livingston
Poe
1981-99-1

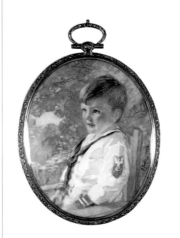

**Tuttle, Adrianna**
American, 1870–1941
*Portrait of James A. Coe III*
1922
Center right: A. Tuttle 1922
Watercolor on ivory
3 3/4 × 2 7/8" (9.5 × 7.3 cm)

Gift of the Pennsylvania Society
of Miniature Painters in memory
of Emily Drayton Taylor
1954-42-97

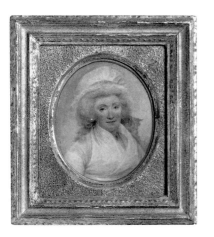

**Trumbull, John**
*Portrait of Mary White Morris*
Companion to the preceding
miniature
1790
Oil on panel
4 × 3 1/4" (10.2 × 8.2 cm)

Gift of Mrs. Philip Livingston
Poe
1981-99-2

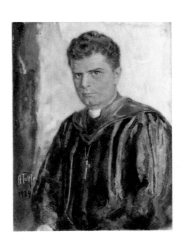

**Tuttle, Adrianna**
*Portrait of the Reverend
Alexander N. Keedwell*
1929
Lower left: A Tuttle / 1929
Watercolor on ivory
4 1/8 × 3 1/4" (10.5 × 8.2 cm)

Gift of Mrs. Albert Keedwell
1972-43-1

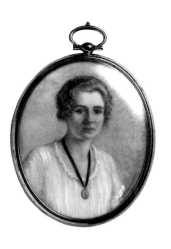

**Washington, Elizabeth Fisher**
American, 1872–1953
*The Blue Locket*
c. 1920–25
Lower right: E. F. WASHINGTON
Watercolor on ivory
3 3/4 × 3" (9.5 × 7.6 cm)

Gift of the Pennsylvania Society
of Miniature Painters in memory
of Emily Drayton Taylor
1954-42-98

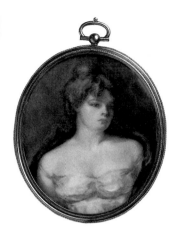

**Wilde, Ida M.**
American, active 1926–1940
*Portrait of Leslie Hall*
1930s
Lower right: Ida M. Wilde.
Watercolor on ivory
3 3/4 × 3" (9.5 × 7.6 cm)

Gift of Mrs. Sylvia Wilde
Cornwell
1954-42-108

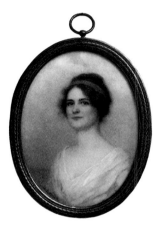

**Welch, Mabel R.**
American, active by 1915,
died 1959
*Portrait of Mrs. Hahn*
c. 1915
Lower left: M. R. Welch.
Watercolor on ivory
4 × 3" (10.2 × 7.6 cm)

Gift of the Pennsylvania Society
of Miniature Painters in memory
of Emily Drayton Taylor
1954-42-99

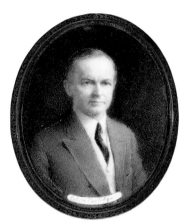

**Williams, Alyn**
American, born Wales,
1865–1955
*Portrait of Calvin Coolidge*
1925
Lower left: Alyn Williams R M S /
1925; center bottom: Calvin
Coolidge
Watercolor on ivory
4 1/8 × 3 1/8" (10.5 × 7.9 cm)

Gift of Mrs. Daniel J. McCarthy
1955-1-23

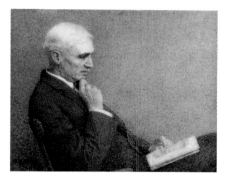

**Welch, Mabel R.**
*Portrait of William J. Baer*
1923
Lower left: M. R. Welch / 1923
Watercolor on ivory
3 7/16 × 4 3/8" (8.7 × 11.1 cm)

Gift of Mrs. Daniel J. McCarthy
1955-1-22

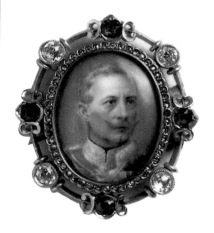

**Williams, Alyn**
*Portrait of Kaiser Wilhelm II*
Early 20th century
Watercolor on ivory
1 3/4 × 9/16" (4.4 × 1.4 cm)

Gift of Mrs. Daniel J. McCarthy
1954-63-9

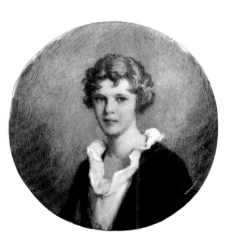

**Whittemore, William John**
American, 1860–1955
*Portrait of Marion*
c. 1925
Lower right: WHITTEMORE
Watercolor on ivory
3 7/8" (9.8 cm) diameter

Gift of the Pennsylvania Society
of Miniature Painters in memory
of Emily Drayton Taylor
1954-42-100

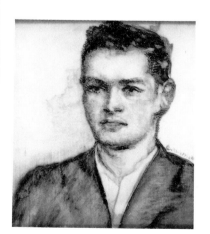

**Wright, Catherine Morris**
American, 1899–1988
*Portrait of Jim Emlen*
1945
Center right: C. M. Wright / 1945
Watercolor on ivory
3 × 2 1/2" (7.6 × 6.3 cm)

Gift of the Pennsylvania Society
of Miniature Painters in memory
of Emily Drayton Taylor
1954-42-101

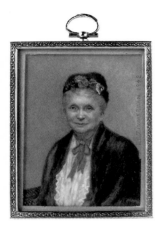

**Zimmerman, Elinor Carr**
American, born 1878,
still active 1947
*The Old-Fashioned Bonnet*
1942
Center right: E. C. ZIMMERMAN
1942
Watercolor on ivory
3 7/8 × 2 7/8" (9.8 × 7.3 cm)

Gift of the Pennsylvania Society
of Miniature Painters in memory
of Emily Drayton Taylor
1954-42-102

# Indexes

The Aaron E. Norman Fund, Inc.
Gift 1959-31-1
Adelman, Seymour
Gift 1946-73-1–3
Adger, Miss Willian
Bequest 1933-82-4
A group of ninety-two painters and sculptors
Funds contributed 1935-6-1
Allen, Mrs. Maria McKean
Bequest 1951-44-1
The American Academy and Institute of Arts
and Letters
Gift 1980-56-1
The American Academy of Arts and Letters
Gift 1951-105-1
Amor, Ines
Gift 1945-84-1
André, Françoise (friends of)
Funds contributed 1975-165-1–2
Annenberg, Mr. and Mrs. Walter H.
Fund for Major Acquisitions 1990-100-1
Anonymous donor
Funds contributed 1984-79-1
Gift 1922-89-1–2, 1932-49-1, 1941-78-1, 1948-
53-1, 1955-53-1, 1956-26-1, 1962-49-1, 1964-
61-1, 1968-224-1, 1969-87-1a–b, 1970-52-1,
1970-204-1a–b, 1973-73-2, 1974-159-1, 1978-
123-2, 1982-121-1, 1983-213-1, 1985-25-1,
1991-76-2–4
Arensberg, Louise and Walter
Collection 1950-134-1, 25–26, 29–30, 32, 34,
36, 38–43, 47–54, 56, 58–59, 63, 65, 68–70, 73,
80–82, 85–91, 93–99, 100–104, 109, 112–113,
115, 118, 121–27, 130, 134, 138–44, 149, 151–
53, 155–58, 164, 166, 168–70, 173–81, 186–96,
198, 492–93, 504–14, 519–20, 523–24, 526–
29, 532–35, 538, 813–15, 817, 823–24, 826–27
The Art Club of Philadelphia
Gift 1928-37-1
Ascoli, Marion R.
Gift 1983-190-1
Ascoli, Marion R. and Max
Fund 1983-190-1
Bache, Caroline D.
Bequest 1958-27-1
Baker, Mrs. Samuel M.
Gift 1925-83-1–2
Barnard, George Grey
Collection (purchased from) 1945-25-117–22,
124, 261, 263–64
Barnwell, Mrs. Arthur
Gift 1957-25-1
The Barra Foundation, Inc.
Gift 1977-34-1
The Barry and Marilyn Peril Foundation
Gift 1972-267-1
Batten, H. A.
Gift 1942-65-1
Beard, Mrs. Robert F.
Gift 1961-21-1
Bell, Edith H.
Fund 1974-110-1, 1975-169-1, 1975-170-1,
1977-79-1, 1979-163-1, 1979-74-1, 1981-62-1,
1982-9-1, EW1986-10-1, 1987-8-1, 1987-73-1-2,
1989-51-1, 1990-88-1–2
Belmont, Mrs. I. J.
Gift 1977-203-1
Bendiner, Elizabeth Wheatley
Gift of an anonymous donor in memory of 1991-
76-2–4
Bérard, Marius-Honoré
Gift of the artist 1949-33-1–2

Berman, Muriel and Philip
Funds contributed 1982-48-1
Gift 1989-70-5–6, 1992-15-1–2
Bernstein, Benjamin D.
Gift 1964-106-1–5, 1973-70-1, 1975-163-1,
1978-172-3–4
Beron, Edna
Gift 1984-159-1
Biddle, Alexander
Gift 1964-111-1
Biddle, George
Gift 1945-16-36–39
Gift of the artist 1972-121-1–4
Biddle, Nicholas
Gift 1957-130-1
Biddle, Owen, and Peyton R. Biddle
Gift 1978-12-1
Binder, Gertrude Schemm
Collection 1951-84-1–2
Birnbaum, Martin
Gift 1944-94-1
Bispham, Miss Eleanor
Gift 1975-40-1–2
Blackburn, Morris Atkinson
Gift of the artist 1975-164-1
Bloch, Miss Clara B.
Gift 1955-33-1
Bloch, Miss Flora B.
Gift 1955-33-1
Bloch, Julius
Memorial Fund 1981-95-1–4, 1983-1-1, 1984-80-
1, 1984-119-1, 1986-72-1, 1986-73-1, 1986-136-
1, 1988-41-1, 1988-42-1, 1990-119-1–7
Boardman, Rosina Cox
Bequest 1971-199-1–4
The Board of Trustees
Gift 1943-72-1
Bortin, Mr. and Mrs. David
Gift 1956-37-1–2
Bowman, Elizabeth Malcolm
Gift 1936-17-1
Brady, Dr. Luther W., Jr.
Funds contributed 1978-14-1
Gift 1980-57-1, 1984-109-1
Brady, Mrs. Samuel
Gift 1976-242-1
Braun, John F.
Gift 1949-73-1
Breckenridge, Mrs. Hugh H.
Gift 1936-35-1
Bregler, Charles
Gift 1939-11-1, 1946-19-1
Brewster, Dr. William Barton
Gift W1919-2-1
Breyer, Mrs. Henry W.
Gift 1974-98-1–2, 1977-204-1
Breyer, Mr. and Mrs. Henry W., Jr.
Gift 1968-73-1
Brinton, Christian
Gift 1941-79-1–4, 29, 47–48, 66–71, 74, 76–
77, 79–82, 89, 94–95, 98–103, 105–13, 115–
17, 119–20, 138–39, 144, 147–51, 153, 335–36
Brock, Horace
Gift 1978-35-1
Broughton, Miss D. M.
Gift 1899-1151
Brown, Trisha
Gift 1988-80-1
Browning, Mrs. Edward
Gift 1947-99-1
Buchanan, Briggs W.
Gift 1945-85-1

Buck, Mr. and Mrs. J. Mahlon
Gift 1959-83-1
Buckley, R. Nelson
Bequest 1943-85-1
Funds contributed in memory of 1947-86-1
Budd, Edward and Althea
Fund 1975-170-1, 1977-80-1, 1977-114-1, 1980-
60-1, 1981-44-1, 1981-94-1a–b, 1982-120-1,
1984-22-1, 1984-79-1, 1984-118-1, 1987-73-1–2,
1989-51-1
Budd, Edward G., Jr.
Memorial Fund 1973-252-1
Budd, Mrs. Edward G., Jr.
Bequest 1973-202-38, 50
Bullitt, Mr. and Mrs. Orville H.
Gift 1963-117-1
Burnham, Mrs. George, III
Gift 1986-17-1
Butler, E. H.
Gift 1894-276
Cadwalader, John
Gift 1978-160-1
Cadwalader Collection
Gift of an anonymous donor 1980-135-1,
1983-90-1–11
Carew, Berta
Bequest 1959-91-1–9, 11, 13–24, 26–47, 52–53
Carlen, Robert
Gift 1941-2-1
Carpenter, Aaron E.
Bequest 1970-75-2–3
Carpenter, Mrs. Harvey Nelson
Gift 1936-10-1
Carson, Mrs. Hampton L.
Gift 1929-126-14–15, 1929-136-148
Carson, Joseph, Hope Carson Randolph, John B.
Carson, and Anna Hampton Carson
Gift 1935-17-1–23
Carter, Miss Fannie Ringgold
Gift 1949-53-1
Catherwood, Mr. and Mrs. Cummins
Gift 1983-160-1
Cecil, George W.
Gift 1942-65-1
Chait, Frederick
Gift 1980-150-1
Chaplin, Mr. and Mrs. Charles C. G.
Gift 1978-149-1, 3, 1978-173-1–2, 1985-22-1
Charles, Jane Barbour
Bequest 1980-101-1
Chatfield-Taylor, Mrs. Otis
Gift 1985-112-4
The Cheltenham Art Centre
Funds contributed 1986-72-1
Gift 1969-88-1, 1970-91-1, 1972-131-1,
1975-54-1, 1976-35-1, 1977-81-1, 1978-58-1,
1979-30-1
The Childe Hassam Fund of the American Academy
and Institute of Arts and Letters
Gift 1974-10-1
Chimes, Thomas
Gift of the artist 1975-78-1, 1976-154-1
Clark, Mrs. James
Gift 1964-117-1–5
Clifford, Henry
Gift 1943-42-1–2
Memorial Fund 1976-34-1
Clifford, Mr. and Mrs. Henry
Gift 1947-29-1–3, 1951-28-1, 1973-256-1, 3–5,
7–9
Clifford, Mrs. Henry
Gift 1975-79-1, 3

Gersten, Mr. and Mrs. Joseph J.
Gift 1951-120-1–4
Giles, Bertha H.
Bequest 1935-9-1
Gold, Hon. Joseph E.
Gift 1973-200-1, 1974-231-2
Goldberg, Mr. and Mrs. Arthur A.
Gift 1971-218-1
Goldberg, Daniel
Gift 1945-37-1
Goldberg, Michael
Gift of the artist 1982-3-1
Goldthwaite, Anne
Gift of the estate 1945-83-2
Graham, Mrs. Frederick W. W.
Gift 1944-47-1
Greenfield, Albert M., and Elizabeth M. Greenfield
Collection 1974-178-17–50
Greenhouse, Mr. and Mrs. Leon H.
Gift 1973-130-1
Griffith, Mrs. Charles Francis
Gift 1936-6-1–15
Gross, Mr. and Mrs. Chaim
Gift 1979-147-1
Gushner, Mr. and Mrs. Harvey
Funds contributed 1984-79-1, 1987-31-1
Haar, Luther A.
Gift 1943-43-1
The Haas Community Funds
Gift 1968-118-53
Haas family
Gift 1979-32-1
Halpert, Mrs. Edith Gregor
Gift 1957-4-1–3
Hamilton, Mrs. Charles
Gift 1990-31-1
Hammond, Maurice J.
Funds contributed in memory of 1984-119-1
Hankins, Abraham P. (students and friends of)
Gift 1964-32-1
Hankins, Estelle
Gift of the estate 1968-40-1–3
Hanley, T. Edward
Bequest 1970-76-1–4, 6–9
Gift 1964-210-1–2
Harding, George M., Jr.
Gift 1967-99-1
Hardwick, Mrs. Gordon A.
Gift 1944-9-1–6, 9
Hare, Elizabeth C.
Bequest 1938-8-1
Harkness, Mrs. Edward S.
Gift 1932-8-1
Harmstad, Mrs. Laura Elliot
Bequest 1953-120-1
Harrison, Mr. and Mrs. John
Gift 1952-46-1
Harrison, Mrs. John
Bequest 1921-39-48–49
Gift 1915-196
Harrison, John, Jr.
Gift 1919-447
Harrison, Thomas Skelton
Fund 1966-173-1
The Hassam and Speicher Purchase Funds
Gift 1980-56-1
Hawkes, Mrs. Morris
Gift 1942-90-1–2, 1945-13-57–59
Heeren, Rodman A.
Gift 1970-255-20, 1971-262-1, 1972-252-21
Helm, Dr. MacKinley
Gift 1947-30-1, 1949-30-1

Helm, Dr. and Mrs. MacKinley
Gift 1943-44-1, 1944-87-1, 1951-33-1, 1952-57-3
Hemsley, Mrs. Charles V.
Gift 1961-179-1
Henderson, Mr. and Mrs. J. Welles
Gift 1973-259-2, 1983-161-1
Henry, Mrs. Joseph A.
Gift F1923-4-1
Henry, Mrs. T. Charlton
Gift 1964-105-1–3
Hiesinger, Mr. and Mrs. Ulrich W.
Gift 1981-66-1
Hilprecht, Sallie Crozer
Collection (gift of Elsie Robinson Paumgarten) 1945-57-191, 196
Hinchman, Anne
Bequest 1952-82-12–15
Hinchman, Margaretta S.
Bequest 1955-96-1, 7–11
Hoffman, Miss Elizabeth D.
Gift 1976-199-1
Hogue, Mrs. Robert M.
Gift 1943-50-1
Hornor, Caleb W.
Gift 1956-39-1–2, 1967-79-5–6, 1968-44-1
Hornor, Peter T.
Gift 1956-39-1–2, 1956-40-1–2, 1967-79-5–6, 1968-44-1
Horter, Mrs. Earle
Gift 1950-40-1
Horwitz, Martin
Gift 1975-180-1–2, 1976-244-1, 1976-245-1
Houston, Mr. and Mrs. S. F.
Gift 1914-26
Howe, George
Gift 1949-57-1
Hubbard, Theodora Kimball
Gift 1928-112-1
Hunt, Rebecca Mandeville Rozet
Gift 1935-13-21–22, 24–26, 33–34, 46–47
Hyde, James H.
Gift 1948-27-1
Ide, Dora Donner
Gift 1961-215-1, 1965-90-1
Ingersoll, Miss Anna Warren
Bequest 1985-85-2, 1989-51-1
Gift 1942-45-1, 1950-27-1, 1958-12-1, 1964-108-1, 1975-150-1
Ingersoll, Charles E.
Gift 1931-7-1
Ingersoll, Mr. and Mrs. Paul M.
Gift 1967-158-1, 1980-129-1
Ingersoll, R. Sturgis
Bequest 1973-254-1
Funds contributed 1954-10-1
Gift 1939-53-1, 1942-45-1
Ingersoll, Mr. and Mrs. R. Sturgis
Gift 1938-38-1, 1941-103-1–5, 1942-1-1, 1944-88-1, 1950-6-1, 1953-136-1, 1964-30-1, 1966-190-1
Jaffe, Mr. and Mrs. Josef
Gift 1971-220-1
James, Mr. and Mrs. Samuel
Gift 1975-86-1
Jaquette, John J.
Gift 1962-218-1
Jaquette, Mrs. William A.
Gift 1962-217-1
Jaquette, Dr. William A., Jr.
Gift 1962-219-1
Jefferys, Mrs. C. P. Beauchamp
Gift 1966-53-1–2

Johnson, Eldridge R.
Gift 1922-87-1
Johnson, John G.
Collection cat. 1–42, 44–229, 231–80, 282–95, 297–709, 711–96, 798–869, 871–953, 955–62, 964–68, 971–86, 988, 990–1020, 1026–33, 1035–44, 1047–60, 1062–78, 1080–1116, 1163–87; inv. 3–4, 35–36, 54, 60–61, 77, 155, 162–63, 170–75, 183, 194a, 198, 203, 212, 220, 309–10, 319, 325, 333, 335, 337, 339, 344, 347, 353, 368, 377, 387, 408–9, 415, 421, 424, 432, 446, 448, 456–58, 705, 716, 723, 729, 732, 742, 1258, 1275–76, 1282, 1290–92, 1295, 1305, 1321, 1329, 1336, 1350–51, 1368, 1390, 1404, 1410, 1438, 1694, 1729, 1739, 1850, 1855, 2034a, 2051, 2055–56, 2059, 2073, 2088, 2095, 2100–101, 2265, 2322, 2438, 2493, 2518–19, 2585, 2692, 2700, 2749, 2753, 2773, 2811, 2814, 2818, 2822, 2827–30, 2832, 2836, 2840–43, 2846–49, 2856, 2862, 2922–24, 2926, 2932, 2943–44, 2954, 2956, 2976, 3023–24
Gift W1900-1-2–5, W1903-1-5, W1904-1-52, W1905-1-1, W1906-1-7, 10, W1907-1-21, 25
Joiner, Rev. Dr. Franklin
Gift 1958-92-1
Jones, Constance A.
Bequest 1988-27-50, 114, 1988-72-18–19
Jones, Linda
Gift 1978-40-1
Kaplan, Dr. and Mrs. Richard
Gift 1967-271-1
Keating, Elizabeth Ellen
Bequest F1920-1-1–2
Keedwell, Mrs. Albert
Gift 1972-43-1
Keehmle (Ozeas, Ramborger, Keehmle)
Collection 1919-162–64, 1921-34-96–102, 104, 119, 223
Kendall, Diana
Gift 1978-40-1
Kidd, Mrs. Elizabeth
Gift 1942-65-1
Kienbusch, Carl Otto Kretzschmar von
Bequest 1977-167-1032, 1039–44, 1083–87
Kimball, Fiske
Fund 1965-65-1
Kimball, Fiske and Marie
Bequest 1955-86-14–19
Gift 1972-267-1
Kimball, Marie
Fund 1965-65-1
Kimmig, Miss Helen A.
Gift 1961-179-1
King, Miss Georgiana Goddard
Gift 1934-10-1
Kistler, Mrs. John S.
Gift 1967-99-1
Kline, Franz
Gift of the artist 1961-223-1
Koecker, Leonora L.
Bequest 1942-37-2–3, 5
Korman, Mr. and Mrs. Leonard
Funds contributed 1987-31-1
Krumbhaar, Hermann, and Dr. Edward Krumbhaar
Gift 1921-69-1–2
Krumbhaar, Peter D.
Gift 1969-289-1, 1971-151-1
Kuh, Katherine
Gift 1972-100-1
Kulicke, Barbara
Gift 1973-71-1–2

Kulicke family
    Gift 1969-86-1—5
Kurtz, Elaine
    Gift of the artist 1982-32-1
Lamborn, Robert H.
    Collection 1903-872—80, 882—89, 891—92, 894, 897, 900—916, 918—20, 922—36, 938—44, 946
Langston, Bryant W.
    Gift 1961-77-1
Larner, Chester Waters
    Bequest 1977-258-1
Lauck, Gerald M.
    Gift 1942-65-1
Lea, Arthur H.
    Bequest F1938-1-1—49, 51, 117
Lee, James
    Gift 1982-32-1
Lefft, Dr. and Mrs. Harold
    Gift 1965-214-1
Lefton, Mrs. Al Paul
    Gift 1972-264-1
Lerner, Morris
    Gift 1973-76-1
Levy, Dr. and Mrs. Richard W.
    Gift 1968-182-1, 1969-167-1
Lewisohn, Sam A.
    Gift 1944-85-1
Lionni, Leonard
    Gift 1942-65-1
Lippincott, Walter
    Collection 1923-59-1—2, 4—17
    Gift 1923-59-3
Lloyd, Mr. and Mrs. H. Gates
    Gift 1974-232-1
Lloyd, Mrs. H. Gates
    Funds contributed 1982-121-1, 1984-79-1, 1984-118-1
    Gift 1956-5-1, 1966-57-1—4, 1973-154-1
Locks, Gene
    Funds contributed 1975-120-1
    Gift 1974-77-1, 1991-139-1
Longstreth, Thatcher
    Gift 1975-70-1
Longstreth, Walter
    Gift 1968-41-1
Lorber, Dr. Herman
    Gift 1944-95-1—2, 4
Lorimer, Graeme
    Gift 1975-182-1
Lowe, Sue Davidson
    Gift 1968-69-53
Ludington, Wright S.
    Gift 1951-3-1
Ludington, Wright S. (nieces and nephews of)
    Gift 1980-139-1—2
Luria, Dr. and Mrs. Milton
    Gift 1976-37-1
The M. L. Annenberg Foundation
    Gift 1955-51-1
The Mabel Pew Myrin Trust
    Funds contributed 1980-135-1, 1983-90-1—11
McBrien, Frederick R.
    Funds contributed 1975-120-1
McCarter, Henry
    Bequest 1944-44-2—3, 1964-151-1, 1972-238-3, 13, 15, 18, 189
McCarthy, Dr. and Mrs. Daniel
    Gift 1942-87-1
McCarthy, Mrs. Daniel J.
    Gift 1953-142-1—4, 6—26, 1954-21-1—23, 25—27, 1954-63-1—2, 4—9, 11, 1955-1-1—23, 1955-1-25—28b

McCormick, Mrs. Cyrus
    Gift 1946-10-1—2
McFadden, John Howard
    Collection M1928-1-1—43
McFadden, John Howard, Jr.
    Fund 1956-118-1, 1963-180-1, 1971-164-1, 1972-250-1—4
    Gift 1946-36-1—3, 5—6, 1951-125-17—18
McFadden, Mr. and Mrs. John Howard, Jr.
    Gift 1952-97-1, 1956-13-1
Machold, Mr. and Mrs. William F.
    Gift 1975-125-1, 1978-100-1
McIlhenny, Henry P.
    Collection 1986-26-1, 4—5, 10, 17—18, 22, 24, 28—29, 32, 35—36, 38, 271—74, 276—285, 287, 401—5
    Fund 1987-73-1—2, 1990-100-1
    Funds contributed 1954-10-1
    Gift 1955-113-1, 1956-107-1, 1957-125-1, 1958-144-1, 1964-77-1—3, 1971-265-1
McIlhenny, John D.
    Collection 1943-40-38—45, 48—49, 51—55
    Fund 1938-11-1, 1966-20-2—7, 1973-253-1, W1984-57-1
McIlvain, Mrs. John Morton
    Gift 1929-48-2
McKean, Mrs. Sargent
    Gift 1950-52-1
McLean, Mr. and Mrs. Robert
    Gift 1977-202-1
McMichael, Mrs. C. Emory
    Gift 1950-51-1
McMichael, Ellen Harrison
    Gift 1942-60-1—2
Madeira, Mrs. Louis C.
    Gift 1965-205-23, 1977-288-1
Magill, Bradford S.
    Gift 1977-174-1
Magill, Mr. and Mrs. James P.
    Gift 1957-127-1, 6—7
Makler, Dr. and Mrs. Paul Todd
    Gift 1967-38-1, 1969-174-1, 1970-92-1, 1971-170-1—2, 1979-186-3
Mann, Mr. and Mrs. Fredric R.
    Gift 1955-24-1
Marceau, Henri
    Funds contributed in memory of 1970-169-1
Margini, Dr. and Mrs. Lorenzo
    Gift 1980-131-1
Marine, Mr. and Mrs. Walter S.
    Gift 1971-222-1
Marinot, Mlle Florence
    Gift 1967-98-1—3
Markoe, Mrs. Harry
    Bequest 1943-51-101
The Mark Rothko Foundation, Inc.
    Gift 1985-19-2—3
Marsh, Felicia Meyer
    Gift of the estate 1979-98-1
Marvel, Mrs. Josiah
    Gift 1962-74-1
Mason, Mrs. Frederick Thurston
    Gift 1914-365
Mastbaum, Jules E.
    Gift F1929-7-205
Mauch Chunk National Bank
    Gift 1949-56-1
Meeteer, Anne Maria
    Bequest 1938-4-1
Meirs, Mrs. Richard Waln
    Gift 1933-11-2
Melzac, Vincent
    Gift 1967-39-1

Mieger, Ernie and Lynn
    Gift 1988-33-7
Miller, Mr. and Mrs. C. Earle
    Gift 1970-15-1, 1986-97-1
Miller, N. Richard
    Gift 1966-180-1
Miller, Mr. and Mrs. N. Richard
    Funds contributed 1982-121-1
    Gift 1967-217-1, 1969-265-1, 1972-204-1, 1978-151-1—2, 1979-160-1, 1985-86-1
Miller, Percy Chase
    Gift 1945-33-1—2
Milliken, Mr. and Mrs. Gerrish H.
    Gift 1978-177-1
Mirkil, Mrs. William I.
    Gift 1961-150-1
Mitcheson, Lucie Washington
    Gift 1938-22-1, 3—10
Mitcheson, Robert Stockton Johnson
    Collection 1938-22-1, 3—10
Montferrier, Mme Florence de
    Gift 1961-180-1
Moore, Bloomfield
    Collection 1882-210, 1168—71, 1174—77, 1883-73, 82—83, 85, 89, 97—98, 101—3, 105—6, 112—15, 120—21, 131—33, 136—37, 140—41, 1889-79, 1899-957, 964—69, 976, 1007, 1011, 1029—30, 1099, 1106, 1108—9, 1120—21
    Fund 1951-31-1—5, 1966-4-1
Moore, Dr. and Mrs. Matthew T.
    Gift 1964-45-1, 1984-108-1
Morris, Mr. and Mrs. Herbert Cameron
    Bequest 1990-100-1
    Gift 1943-46-1—2, 1951-104-1, 1957-94-1
Morris, Mrs. Herbert Cameron
    Funds contributed 1954-10-1
    Gift 1943-5-1, 1945-2-1, 1946-13-1, 1946-40-1, 1947-24-1, 1948-11-1, 1964-89-1, 1977-27-1—2
Morris, Lydia Thompson
    Bequest 1932-45-18—19, 83, 116—21
    Gift 1930-73-4
Mucci, Mrs. Mary B.
    Gift 1973-201-1
Muckle, Mrs. Craig W.
    Gift 1991-182-1
Mueller, Frederic
    Gift 1978-29-1
Museum funds
    1913-455, 1949-40-1a—b, 1950-13-1, 1954-31-1, 1959-28-1
The National Collection of Fine Arts
    Gift 1972-123-1
National Endowment for the Arts
    Grant 1974-111-1, 1977-28-1, 1982-121-1, 1991-51-1
Nebinger, Robert
    Bequest 1889-110, 113, 139
The Nebinger Fund
    1949-24-1
Neville, Sheila
    Gift 1978-40-1
Nevins, J. J. (family of)
    Gift 1992-41-1
Newman, Mr. and Mrs. Philip
    Gift 1983-64-1
Newton, Francis, F. Maurice Newton, and Richard Newton, Jr.
    Gift 1962-142-1
Newton, Maurice
    Gift 1966-220-1
Norman, Mrs. Dorothy
    Gift 1959-30-1

| Accession No. | Artist | Page |
|---|---|---|
| E1924-4-32 | Whistler, James Abbott McNeill, imitator of | 304 |
| F1925-1-1 | Zurbarán, Francisco de, workshop of | 246 |
| F1925-5-1 | Sargent, John Singer | 295 |
| 1925-83-1 | Neagle, John | 289 |
| 1925-83-2 | Neagle, John | 289 |
| F1926-3-1 | Reckless, Stanley L. | 417 |
| F1926-3-2 | Reckless, Stanley L. | 417 |
| 1926-9-1 | Dodson, Sarah Paxton Ball | 268 |
| 1926-9-2 | Dodson, Sarah Paxton Ball | 268 |
| 1927-5-12 | American, unknown artist | 478 |
| 1927-52-37 | Dutch, unknown artist | 451 |
| 1927-52-38 | Dutch, unknown artist | 451 |
| 1927-52-42 | German, unknown artist | 464 |
| 1927-52-192 | Joffray | 467 |
| 1927-52-206 | French, unknown artist | 463 |
| 1927-52-209 | European, unknown artist | 460 |
| 1927-52-212 | French, unknown artist | 462 |
| 1927-52-218 | Giraud, D. | 464 |
| 1927-62-1 | American, unknown artist | 262 |
| M1928-1-1 | Bonington, Richard Parkes, follower of | 3 |
| M1928-1-2 | Constable, John | 5 |
| M1928-1-3 | Constable, John, studio of | 6 |
| M1928-1-4 | Constable, John, imitator of | 6 |
| M1928-1-5 | Cox, David | 8 |
| M1928-1-6 | Crome, John | 8 |
| M1928-1-7 | Crome, John, copy after | 9 |
| M1928-1-8 | Gainsborough, Thomas | 14 |
| M1928-1-9 | Gainsborough, Thomas | 14 |
| M1928-1-10 | Harlow, George Henry | 15 |
| M1928-1-11 | Harlow, George Henry | 15 |
| M1928-1-12 | Harlow, George Henry | 15 |
| M1928-1-13 | Hogarth, William | 15 |
| M1928-1-14 | Hogarth, William | 16 |
| M1928-1-15 | Hoppner, John, imitator of | 16 |
| M1928-1-16 | Lawrence, Sir Thomas | 18 |
| M1928-1-17 | Linnell, John | 19 |
| M1928-1-18 | Morland, George | 20 |
| M1928-1-19 | Morland, George | 19 |
| M1928-1-20 | Morland, George | 20 |
| M1928-1-21 | Raeburn, Sir Henry | 21 |
| M1928-1-22 | Raeburn, Sir Henry | 22 |
| M1928-1-23 | Raeburn, Sir Henry | 22 |
| M1928-1-24 | Raeburn, Sir Henry | 22 |
| M1928-1-25 | Raeburn, Sir Henry | 21 |
| M1928-1-26 | Raeburn, Sir Henry | 22 |
| M1928-1-27 | Raeburn, Sir Henry | 22 |
| M1928-1-28 | Raeburn, Sir Henry, follower of | 23 |
| M1928-1-29 | Reynolds, Sir Joshua | 23 |
| M1928-1-30 | Reynolds, Sir Joshua, follower of | 23 |
| M1928-1-31 | Romney, George | 26 |
| M1928-1-32 | Romney, George | 25 |
| M1928-1-33 | Romney, George | 25 |
| M1928-1-34 | Romney, George | 25 |
| M1928-1-35 | Romney, George | 25 |
| M1928-1-36 | Romney, George | 24 |
| M1928-1-37 | Romney, George | 25 |
| M1928-1-38 | Romney, George | 24 |
| M1928-1-39 | Stark, James | 26 |
| M1928-1-40 | Stubbs, George | 27 |
| M1928-1-41 | Turner, Joseph Mallord William | 28 |
| M1928-1-42 | Gordon, Sir John Watson | 15 |
| M1928-1-43 | Wilson, Richard | 30 |
| 1928-7-121 | Sully, Thomas, follower of | 302 |
| 1928-37-1 | Redfield, Edward Willis | 417 |
| 1928-63-1 | Alexander, John White | 320 |
| 1928-63-2 | Blakelock, Ralph A. | 264 |
| 1928-63-3 | Cassatt, Mary Stevenson | 266 |
| 1928-63-4 | Chase, William Merritt | 266 |
| 1928-63-5 | Dougherty, Paul | 349 |
| 1928-63-6 | Eakins, Thomas | 270 |
| 1928-63-7 | Johnson, Eastman | 286 |
| 1928-63-8 | Rosen, Charles | 420 |
| 1928-63-9 | Thayer, Abbott Handerson | 302 |
| 1928-63-11 | Wyant, Alexander Helwig | 305 |
| 1928-112-1 | West, Benjamin, copy after | 30 |
| F1929-1-1 | Röchling, Carl | 174 |
| F1929-7-205 | Guillaume, Albert | 366 |
| 1929-48-2 | American, unknown artist | 477 |
| 1929-79-1 | Davies, Arthur Bowen | 345 |
| 1929-79-2 | Davies, Arthur Bowen | 344 |
| 1929-126-14 | English, unknown artist | 460 |
| 1929-126-15 | Hervé, Henry | 465 |
| 1929-136-148 | Lapp, Jan Willemsz., follower of | 69 |
| 1929-184-1 | Eakins, Thomas | 273 |
| 1929-184-2 | Eakins, Thomas | 277 |
| 1929-184-3 | Eakins, Thomas | 270 |
| 1929-184-4 | Eakins, Thomas | 276 |
| 1929-184-5 | Eakins, Thomas | 273 |
| 1929-184-6 | Eakins, Thomas | 278 |
| 1929-184-7 | Eakins, Thomas | 277 |
| 1929-184-8 | Eakins, Thomas | 269 |
| 1929-184-9 | Eakins, Thomas | 269 |
| 1929-184-10 | Eakins, Thomas | 277 |
| 1929-184-11 | Eakins, Thomas | 275 |
| 1929-184-12 | Eakins, Thomas | 275 |
| 1929-184-14 | Eakins, Thomas | 269 |
| 1929-184-15 | Eakins, Thomas | 275 |
| 1929-184-16 | Eakins, Thomas | 276 |
| 1929-184-17 | Eakins, Thomas | 276 |
| 1929-184-18 | Eakins, Thomas | 269 |
| 1929-184-19 | Eakins, Thomas | 275 |
| 1929-184-20 | Eakins, Thomas | 275 |
| 1929-184-21 | Eakins, Thomas | 276 |
| 1929-184-22 | Eakins, Thomas | 275 |
| 1929-184-23 | Eakins, Thomas | 277 |
| 1929-184-24 | Eakins, Thomas | 272 |
| 1929-184-25 | Eakins, Thomas | 270 |
| 1929-184-27 | Eakins, Thomas | 271 |
| 1929-184-28 | Eakins, Thomas | 270 |
| 1929-184-29 | Eakins, Thomas | 279 |
| 1929-184-30 | Eakins, Thomas | 275 |
| 1929-184-31 | Eakins, Thomas | 270 |
| 1929-184-32 | Eakins, Thomas | 273 |
| 1929-184-33 | Eakins, Thomas | 272 |
| 1929-184-34 | Eakins, Thomas | 272 |
| 1929-184-35 | Eakins, Thomas | 270 |
| 1929-184-36 | Eakins, Thomas | 276 |
| 1930-7-1 | Inness, George | 285 |
| 1930-32-3 | Eakins, Thomas | 274 |
| 1930-32-4a | Eakins, Thomas | 272 |
| 1930-32-4b | Eakins, Thomas | 272 |
| 1930-32-5 | Eakins, Thomas | 269 |
| 1930-32-6 | Eakins, Thomas | 270 |
| 1930-32-7a | Eakins, Thomas | 273 |
| 1930-32-7b | Eakins, Thomas | 273 |
| 1930-32-8 | Eakins, Thomas | 274 |
| 1930-32-9 | Eakins, Thomas | 278 |
| 1930-32-10 | Eakins, Thomas | 271 |
| 1930-32-11a | Eakins, Thomas | 271 |
| 1930-32-11b | Eakins, Thomas | 271 |
| 1930-32-12 | Eakins, Thomas | 274 |
| 1930-32-13 | Eakins, Thomas | 274 |
| 1930-32-14 | Eakins, Thomas | 278 |
| 1930-32-15a | Eakins, Thomas | 278 |
| 1930-32-15b | Eakins, Thomas | 278 |
| 1930-32-16 | Eakins, Thomas | 276 |
| 1930-32-17 | Eakins, Thomas | 271 |
| 1930-32-18a | Eakins, Thomas | 271 |
| 1930-32-18b | Eakins, Thomas | 271 |
| 1930-46-16 | American, unknown artist | 475 |
| 1930-50-2 | Eichholtz, Jacob | 279 |
| 1930-50-3 | Eichholtz, Jacob | 279 |
| 1930-54-1 | Peale, Charles Willson, attributed to | 292 |
| 1930-67-1 | Carles, Arthur Beecher | 336 |
| 1930-73-4 | American, unknown artist | 257 |
| 1930-105-1 | Eakins, Thomas | 272 |
| 1931-7-1 | Picasso, Pablo Ruiz | 410 |
| 1931-40-1 | Redfield, Edward Willis | 417 |
| 1931-64-1 | Borie, Adolphe | 328 |
| E1932-1-1 | Poussin, Nicolas | 151 |
| 1932-8-1 | Duplessis, Joseph-Siffred, attributed to | 451 |
| 1932-13-1 | Eakins, Thomas | 277 |
| 1932-45-18 | American, unknown artist | 477 |
| 1932-45-19 | American, unknown artist | 477 |
| 1932-45-83 | Dantzig, Meyer | 268 |
| 1932-45-116 | Jones, H. Bolton | 286 |
| 1932-45-117 | Craig, Thomas Bigelow | 268 |
| 1932-45-118 | Waugh, Samuel Bell, follower of | 304 |
| 1932-45-119 | Waugh, Samuel Bell | 304 |
| 1932-45-120 | Dantzig, Meyer | 268 |
| 1932-45-121 | Linford, Charles | 287 |
| 1932-48-1 | Craig, Thomas Bigelow | 267 |
| 1932-49-1 | Tyson, Carroll Sargent, Jr. | 437 |
| 1933-11-2 | Wayne, Hattie | 304 |
| 1933-82-4 | Fromentin, Eugène | 137 |
| 1934-10-1 | Hawthorne, Charles Webster | 370 |
| 1935-6-1 | Borie, Adolphe | 328 |
| 1935-9-1 | Sully, Thomas | 300 |
| 1935-10-95 | Flemish, unknown artist | 56 |
| 1935-10-96 | Flemish, unknown artist | 56 |
| 1935-10-97 | Flemish, unknown artist | 56 |
| 1935-10-98 | Flemish, unknown artist | 56 |
| 1935-13-21 | Birch, Thomas | 480 |
| 1935-13-22 | Birch, Thomas | 480 |
| 1935-13-24 | American, unknown artist | 255 |
| 1935-13-25 | American, unknown artist | 255 |
| 1935-13-26 | American, unknown artist | 259 |
| 1935-13-33 | American, unknown artist | 478 |
| 1935-13-34 | American, unknown artist | 477 |
| 1935-13-46 | American, unknown artist | 478 |
| 1935-13-47 | French, unknown artist | 463 |
| 1935-14-2 | Italian, unknown artist | 466 |
| 1935-17-1 | English, unknown artist | 457 |
| 1935-17-2 | English, unknown artist | 457 |
| 1935-17-3 | English, unknown artist | 457 |
| 1935-17-4 | English, unknown artist | 458 |
| 1935-17-5 | English, unknown artist | 457 |
| 1935-17-6 | English, unknown artist | 454 |
| 1935-17-7 | English, unknown artist | 459 |
| 1935-17-8 | English, unknown artist | 457 |
| 1935-17-9 | English, unknown artist | 456 |
| 1935-17-10 | English, unknown artist | 459 |
| 1935-17-11 | English, unknown artist | 459 |
| 1935-17-12 | English, unknown artist | 458 |
| 1935-17-13 | English, unknown artist | 456 |
| 1935-17-14 | English, unknown artist | 455 |
| 1935-17-15 | English, unknown artist | 458 |
| 1935-17-16 | English, unknown artist | 456 |
| 1935-17-17 | English, unknown artist | 456 |
| 1935-17-18 | English, unknown artist | 454 |
| 1935-17-19 | English, unknown artist | 454 |
| 1935-17-20 | English, unknown artist | 454 |
| 1935-17-21 | English, unknown artist | 454 |
| 1935-17-22 | English, unknown artist | 454 |
| 1935-17-23 | English, unknown artist | 459 |
| 1935-28-1 | West, Benjamin, copy after | 30 |
| 1935-46-1 | Watkins, Franklin Chenault | 441 |
| 1936-1-1 | Anshutz, Thomas Pollock | 263 |
| E1936-1-1 | Cézanne, Paul | 115 |
| 1936-1-2 | Chase, William Merritt | 266 |
| 1936-1-3 | Perot, Annie Lovering | 293 |

| | | |
|---|---|---|
| 1936-6-1 | English, unknown artist 455 | |
| 1936-6-2 | English, unknown artist 456 | |
| 1936-6-3 | English, unknown artist 456 | |
| 1936-6-4 | English, unknown artist 456 | |
| 1936-6-5 | English, unknown artist 455 | |
| 1936-6-6 | English, unknown artist 458 | |
| 1936-6-7 | English, unknown artist 459 | |
| 1936-6-8 | English, unknown artist 455 | |
| 1936-6-9 | English, unknown artist 459 | |
| 1936-6-10 | English, unknown artist 458 | |
| 1936-6-11 | English, unknown artist 458 | |
| 1936-6-12 | English, unknown artist 457 | |
| 1936-6-13 | English, unknown artist 458 | |
| 1936-6-14 | English, unknown artist 455 | |
| 1936-6-15 | English, unknown artist 459 | |
| 1936-10-1 | Sully, Thomas 300 | |
| 1936-17-1 | Paxton, William McGregor 290 | |
| 1936-22-9 | Stuart, Gilbert, copy after 500 | |
| 1936-22-10 | Stuart, Gilbert, copy after 500 | |
| 1936-22-12 | Stuart, Gilbert, copy after 500 | |
| 1936-26-1 | Soutman, Pieter Claesz., attributed to 97 | |
| 1936-35-1 | Breckenridge, Hugh Henry 331 | |
| 1936-50-1 | Cooper, Colin Campbell 267 | |
| 1936-50-2 | Cooper, Colin Campbell 267 | |
| W1937-1-1 | Cézanne, Paul 115 | |
| W1937-2-1 | Degas, Hilaire-Germain-Edgar 128 | |
| 1937-14-1 | Peale, Anna Claypoole 495 | |
| 1937-18-1 | Hamilton, John McLure 366 | |
| 1937-31-1 | Torres-Garcia, Joaquin 435 | |
| F1938-1-1 | French, unknown artist 135 | |
| F1938-1-2 | Pignoni, Simone 226 | |
| F1938-1-3 | Lely, Sir Peter 18 | |
| F1938-1-4 | Italian, unknown artist 208 | |
| F1938-1-5 | European, unknown artist 248 | |
| F1938-1-6 | Italian, active Bologna, unknown artist 207 | |
| F1938-1-7 | Italian, unknown artist 207 | |
| F1938-1-8 | Flemish, unknown artist 57 | |
| F1938-1-9 | Italian, active Bologna, unknown artist 205 | |
| F1938-1-10 | Tosini, Michele, follower of 235 | |
| F1938-1-11 | Italian, active Florence, unknown artist 206 | |
| F1938-1-12 | French, unknown artist 135 | |
| F1938-1-13 | Wilson, Richard, follower of 31 | |
| F1938-1-14 | Italian, unknown artist 206 | |
| F1938-1-15 | Italian, active Florence, unknown artist 206 | |
| F1938-1-16 | Strozzi, Bernardo 232 | |
| F1938-1-17 | Italian, unknown artist 206 | |
| F1938-1-18 | Italian, active Bologna, unknown artist 206 | |
| F1938-1-19 | Cigoli, copy after 187 | |
| F1938-1-20 | Diaz de la Peña, Narcisse-Virgile 130 | |
| F1938-1-21 | Italian, active Siena, unknown artist 204 | |
| F1938-1-22 | Teniers, David, II, follower of 101 | |
| F1938-1-23 | Cecco Bravo, attributed to 186 | |
| F1938-1-24 | Italian?, unknown artist 208 | |
| F1938-1-25 | Casteels, Pieter, II, imitator of 42 | |
| F1938-1-26 | Veronese, Paolo, copy after 236 | |
| F1938-1-27 | Richards, William Trost 295 | |
| F1938-1-28 | Moucheron, Isaac de, imitator of 78 | |
| F1938-1-29 | Italian, active Florence, unknown artist 206 | |
| F1938-1-30 | Italian, unknown artist 205 | |
| F1938-1-31 | Diaz de la Peña, Narcisse-Virgile 130 | |
| F1938-1-32 | Cecco Bravo 186 | |
| F1938-1-33 | Italian, unknown artist 205 | |
| F1938-1-34 | Caravaggio, copy after 186 | |
| F1938-1-35 | Spranger, Bartholomeus, follower of 97 | |

| | | |
|---|---|---|
| F1938-1-36 | Italian, active Verona?, unknown artist 207 | |
| F1938-1-37 | European, unknown artist 248 | |
| F1938-1-38 | Italian, unknown artist 207 | |
| F1938-1-39 | Frediani, Vincenzo di Antonio 193 | |
| F1938-1-40 | Pignoni, Simone, follower of 226 | |
| F1938-1-41 | Bassano, Leandro, follower of 179 | |
| F1938-1-42 | Italian, unknown artist 207 | |
| F1938-1-43 | Beccafumi, Domenico, follower of 179 | |
| F1938-1-44 | Italian, unknown artist 207 | |
| F1938-1-45 | Reni, Guido, copy after 228 | |
| F1938-1-46 | Reschi, Pandolfo 228 | |
| F1938-1-47 | Italian, unknown artist 207 | |
| F1938-1-48 | Richards, William Trost 294 | |
| F1938-1-49 | Pignoni, Simone, follower of 226 | |
| F1938-1-51 | Italian, unknown artist 209 | |
| F1938-1-117 | Herzog, Hermann 283 | |
| 1938-2-1 | American, unknown artist 475 | |
| 1938-4-1 | Peale, James 497 | |
| 1938-8-1 | Sully, Thomas 299 | |
| 1938-11-1 | West, Benjamin, copy after 30 | |
| 1938-14-1 | Hamilton, John McLure 366 | |
| 1938-22-1 | Murphy, John Francis 288 | |
| 1938-22-3 | Lawson, Ernest 385 | |
| 1938-22-4 | Wyant, Alexander Helwig 305 | |
| 1938-22-5 | Lathrop, William Langson 384 | |
| 1938-22-6 | Sartain, William 296 | |
| 1938-22-7 | Jongkind, Johan Barthold, attributed to 66 | |
| 1938-22-8 | Jongkind, Johan Barthold 66 | |
| 1938-22-9 | Inness, George 285 | |
| 1938-22-10 | Robinson, Théodore 295 | |
| 1938-25-1 | Lambdin, James Reid 287 | |
| 1938-29-1 | Miles, Edward 468 | |
| 1938-29-2 | Miles, Edward 468 | |
| 1938-29-3 | Miles, Edward 469 | |
| 1938-29-4 | Miles, Edward 469 | |
| 1938-29-5 | Miles, Edward 469 | |
| 1938-29-6 | English, unknown artist 453 | |
| 1938-29-7 | English, unknown artist 457 | |
| 1938-29-8 | Miles, Edward 470 | |
| 1938-29-9 | Miles, Edward 469 | |
| 1938-29-10 | Miles, Edward 469 | |
| 1938-29-11 | Miles, Edward 468 | |
| 1938-29-12 | Miles, Edward 468 | |
| 1938-29-13 | Miles, Edward 469 | |
| 1938-29-14 | Miles, Edward 469 | |
| 1938-29-15 | Miles, Edward 469 | |
| 1938-29-16 | Miles, Edward 470 | |
| 1938-29-17 | Miles, Edward 468 | |
| 1938-38-1 | Rousseau, Henri-Julien-Félix 422 | |
| 1939-3-1 | Tucker, Allen 435 | |
| 1939-7-16 | Hawthorne, Charles Webster 371 | |
| 1939-7-17 | Turner, Helen Maria 435 | |
| 1939-7-18 | Schofield, Walter Elmer 425 | |
| 1939-11-1 | Eakins, Susan MacDowell 269 | |
| 1939-12-1 | Wagner, Frederick 440 | |
| 1939-53-1 | Horter, Earl 372 | |
| 1940-10-1 | Cushman, George Hewitt 487 | |
| 1940-10-2 | Cushman, George Hewitt 487 | |
| 1940-17-27 | Zuloaga y Zabaleta, Ignacio 445 | |
| 1940-18-1 | Garber, Daniel 359 | |
| 1940-46-1 | Henri, Pierre 464 | |
| 1941-2-1 | Pippin, Horace 412 | |
| 1941-22-1 | Borie, Adolphe 328 | |
| 1941-78-1 | Inman, Henry 284 | |
| 1941-79-1 | Russian, unknown artist 423 | |
| 1941-79-2 | Russian, unknown artist 423 | |
| 1941-79-3 | Burliuk, David Davidovich 333 | |
| 1941-79-4 | Palmov, Viktor Nikandrovich 407 | |
| 1941-79-29 | Grigoriev, Boris Dmitryevich 363 | |
| 1941-79-38 | Burliuk, David Davidovich 333 | |

| | | |
|---|---|---|
| 1941-79-47 | Burliuk, David Davidovich 332 | |
| 1941-79-48 | Burliuk, David Davidovich 333 | |
| 1941-79-66 | Graham, John D. 363 | |
| 1941-79-67 | Roerich, Nicholas Konstantinovich 420 | |
| 1941-79-68 | Grigoriev, Boris Dmitryevich 363 | |
| 1941-79-69 | Burliuk, David Davidovich 333 | |
| 1941-79-70 | Campendonk, Heinrich 334 | |
| 1941-79-71 | Roerich, Nicholas Konstantinovich 419 | |
| 1941-79-74 | Chanler, Robert Winthrop 340 | |
| 1941-79-76 | Burliuk, David Davidovich 332 | |
| 1941-79-77 | Archipenko, Gela Forster 321 | |
| 1941-79-79 | Vasilieff, Nicholas 438 | |
| 1941-79-80 | Chernoff, Vadim Anatolievich 340 | |
| 1941-79-81 | Melchers, Julius Gari 394 | |
| 1941-79-82 | Burliuk, David Davidovich 333 | |
| 1941-79-89 | Burliuk, David Davidovich 333 | |
| 1941-79-94 | Burliuk, David Davidovich 333 | |
| 1941-79-95 | Burliuk, David Davidovich 332 | |
| 1941-79-98 | Manievich, Abraham Anshelovich 390 | |
| 1941-79-99 | Grigoriev, Boris Dmitryevich 363 | |
| 1941-79-100 | Jacovleff, Alexander 374 | |
| 1941-79-101 | Kádár, Béla 377 | |
| 1941-79-102 | Hausch, Aleksandr F. 370 | |
| 1941-79-103 | Kádár, Béla 376 | |
| 1941-79-105 | Kádár, Béla 376 | |
| 1941-79-106 | Burliuk, David Davidovich 333 | |
| 1941-79-107 | Cickowsky, Nikolai Stepanovich 342 | |
| 1941-79-108 | Cickowsky, Nikolai Stepanovich 341 | |
| 1941-79-109 | Vasilieff, Nicholas 438 | |
| 1941-79-110 | Vasilieff, Nicholas 438 | |
| 1941-79-111 | Schattenstein, Nikol Ovseyvich 424 | |
| 1941-79-112 | Burliuk, David Davidovich 332 | |
| 1941-79-113 | Vasilieff, Nicholas 438 | |
| 1941-79-115 | Palmov, Viktor Nikandrovich 407 | |
| 1941-79-116 | Cickowsky, Nikolai Stepanovich 341 | |
| 1941-79-117 | Vasilieff, Nicholas 438 | |
| 1941-79-119 | Archipenko, Alexander Porfirevich 321 | |
| 1941-79-120 | Grigoriev, Boris Dmitryevich 363 | |
| 1941-79-138 | Kádár, Béla 377 | |
| 1941-79-139 | Pippin, Horace 412 | |
| 1941-79-144 | Anisfeld, Boris 320 | |
| 1941-79-147 | Grigoriev, Boris Dmitryevich 364 | |
| 1941-79-148 | Roerich, Svyatoslav Nikolaievich 420 | |
| 1941-79-149 | Cickowsky, Nikolai Stepanovich 341 | |
| 1941-79-150 | Grigoriev, Boris Dmitryevich 363 | |
| 1941-79-151 | Sprinchorn, Carl 431 | |
| 1941-79-153 | Russian, unknown artist 250 | |
| 1941-79-335 | Schattenstein, Nikol Ovseyvich 425 | |
| 1941-79-336 | Lund, Henrik 389 | |
| 1941-99-19 | Hamilton, John McLure 366 | |
| 1941-103-1 | Blume, Peter 327 | |
| 1941-103-2 | Dickinson, Preston 348 | |
| 1941-103-3 | Sloan, John 428 | |
| 1941-103-4 | Carles, Arthur Beecher 337 | |
| 1941-103-5 | Carles, Arthur Beecher 337 | |
| 1942-1-1 | Biddle, George 325 | |
| 1942-14-1 | Kelly, Leon 380 | |
| 1942-15-1 | Maurer, Alfred Henry 394 | |
| 1942-17-1 | Watkins, Franklin Chenault 441 | |
| 1942-31-1 | Sully, Thomas 301 | |
| 1942-31-2 | Sully, Thomas 301 | |
| 1942-31-3 | Sully, Thomas 301 | |
| 1942-37-2 | Sully, Thomas 300 | |
| 1942-37-3 | American, unknown artist 478 | |
| 1942-37-5 | Collas, Louis-Antoine 449 | |
| 1942-45-1 | McCarter, Henry 389 | |
| 1942-60-1 | Hovenden, Thomas 284 | |
| 1942-60-2 | Israëls, Jozef 65 | |

| | | |
|---|---|---|
| 1950-134-512a | Jawlensky, Alexey von 374 | |
| 1950-134-512b | Jawlensky, Alexey von 375 | |
| 1950-134-513 | Lebduska, Lawrence H. 385 | |
| 1950-134-514 | Lebduska, Lawrence H. 386 | |
| 1950-134-519 | Stella, Joseph 431 | |
| 1950-134-520 | Stevens, Frances Simpson 432 | |
| 1950-134-523 | Wilkie, John 305 | |
| 1950-134-524 | Williams, Edith Clifford 444 | |
| 1950-134-526a | Wyckoff, Sylvester 306 | |
| 1950-134-526b | Wyckoff, Sylvester 306 | |
| 1950-134-527 | Italian, active Florence, unknown artist 200 | |
| 1950-134-528 | Arrigo di Niccolò 177 | |
| 1950-134-529 | Italian, unknown artist 206 | |
| 1950-134-532 | Piero di Miniato, attributed to 226 | |
| 1950-134-533 | American, unknown artist 259 | |
| 1950-134-534 | American, unknown artist 262 | |
| 1950-134-535 | American, unknown artist 257 | |
| 1950-134-538 | American, unknown artist 255 | |
| 1950-134-813 | Middle American, unknown artist 396 | |
| 1950-134-814 | Middle American, unknown artist 316 | |
| 1950-134-815 | Mexican, unknown artist 316 | |
| 1950-134-817 | Cabrera, Miguel, attributed to 307 | |
| 1950-134-823 | Mexican, unknown artist 315 | |
| 1950-134-824 | Mexican, unknown artist 315 | |
| 1950-134-826 | Middle American, unknown artist 317 | |
| 1950-134-827 | Mexican, unknown artist 316 | |
| 1951-2-1 | Eichholtz, Jacob 279 | |
| 1951-3-1 | Shahn, Ben 426 | |
| 1951-27-1 | Stettheimer, Florine 432 | |
| 1951-28-1 | Berman, Eugène 324 | |
| 1951-31-1 | Blackburn, Morris Atkinson 326 | |
| 1951-31-2 | Feininger, Lyonel 357 | |
| 1951-31-3 | Heliker, John Edward 371 | |
| 1951-31-4 | Pittman, Hobson L. 413 | |
| 1951-31-5 | Shahn, Ben 426 | |
| 1951-33-1 | Meza, Guillermo 396 | |
| 1951-44-1 | Sully, Thomas 301 | |
| 1951-69-1 | Lagrange, Jacques 383 | |
| 1951-79-1 | Eakins, Thomas 276 | |
| 1951-84-1 | Harnett, William Michael, copy after 281 | |
| 1951-84-2 | Picabia, Francis 409 | |
| 1951-104-1 | Laurencin, Marie 384 | |
| 1951-105-1 | Sharp, John 426 | |
| 1951-109-1 | Monet, Claude 147 | |
| 1951-120-1 | Cantú, Federico 335 | |
| 1951-120-4 | Soriano, Juan 429 | |
| 1951-125-17 | Puyl, Louis François Gérard van der 88 | |
| 1951-125-18 | Sandby, Paul 26 | |
| W1952-1-1 | Master of Montelabate 217 | |
| 1952-3-1 | Larue, André-Léon, attributed to 467 | |
| 1952-16-1 | Miró, Joan 397 | |
| 1952-46-1 | Lemoine, Jacques-Antoine-Marie 467 | |
| 1952-57-3 | Lazo, Agustin 385 | |
| 1952-61-4 | Braque, Georges 329 | |
| 1952-61-5 | Braque, Georges 330 | |
| 1952-61-6 | Braque, Georges 330 | |
| 1952-61-8 | Braque, Georges 331 | |
| 1952-61-13 | Delaunay, Robert 347 | |
| 1952-61-22 | Derain, André 347 | |
| 1952-61-23 | Domela, César 349 | |
| 1952-61-26a | Frelinghuysen, Suzy 358 | |
| 1952-61-26b | Frelinghuysen, Suzy 358 | |
| 1952-61-28 | Gallatin, Albert Eugene 359 | |
| 1952-61-29 | Gallatin, Albert Eugene 359 | |
| 1952-61-34 | Gris, Juan 364 | |
| 1952-61-35 | Gris, Juan 364 | |
| 1952-61-36 | Gris, Juan 364 | |
| 1952-61-38a | Gris, Juan 365 | |
| 1952-61-38b | Gris, Juan 365 | |

| | | |
|---|---|---|
| 1952-61-39 | Gris, Juan 365 | |
| 1952-61-40 | Gris, Juan 365 | |
| 1952-61-41 | Gris, Juan 365 | |
| 1952-61-46 | Hartung, Hans 369 | |
| 1952-61-51 | Knaths, Karl 381 | |
| 1952-61-57 | Léger, Fernand 386 | |
| 1952-61-58 | Léger, Fernand 386 | |
| 1952-61-63 | Léger, Fernand 387 | |
| 1952-61-64 | Léger, Fernand 387 | |
| 1952-61-72 | Lissitzky, El 388 | |
| 1952-61-76 | Mason, Alice Trumbull 391 | |
| 1952-61-77 | Masson, André 392 | |
| 1952-61-78 | Masson, André 392 | |
| 1952-61-79 | Matisse, Henri 392 | |
| 1952-61-81 | Metzinger, Jean 395 | |
| 1952-61-82 | Miró, Joan 397 | |
| 1952-61-83 | Miró, Joan 397 | |
| 1952-61-85 | Miró, Joan 398 | |
| 1952-61-87 | Mondrian, Piet 399 | |
| 1952-61-88 | Mondrian, Piet 399 | |
| 1952-61-89 | Mondrian, Piet 399 | |
| 1952-61-90 | Mondrian, Piet 399 | |
| 1952-61-91 | Ozenfant, Amédée 407 | |
| 1952-61-93 | Picasso, Pablo Ruiz 410 | |
| 1952-61-94 | Picasso, Pablo Ruiz 411 | |
| 1952-61-95 | Picasso, Pablo Ruiz 411 | |
| 1952-61-96 | Picasso, Pablo Ruiz 411 | |
| 1952-61-97 | Picasso, Pablo Ruiz 411 | |
| 1952-61-98 | Picasso, Pablo Ruiz 411 | |
| 1952-61-99 | Picasso, Pablo Ruiz 412 | |
| 1952-61-120 | Taeuber-Arp, Sophie 433 | |
| 1952-61-121 | Torres-Garcia, Joaquin 435 | |
| 1952-61-122 | Torres-Garcia, Joaquin 435 | |
| 1952-61-124 | Doesburg, Theo van 348 | |
| 1952-61-126 | Wallace, John 440 | |
| 1952-65-1 | Savage, Edward, copy after 296 | |
| 1952-82-12 | Biddle, George 325 | |
| 1952-82-13 | Kantor, Morris 377 | |
| 1952-82-14 | Kantor, Morris 378 | |
| 1952-82-15 | Kantor, Morris 378 | |
| 1952-97-1 | Raeburn, Sir Henry 22 | |
| 1952-98-1 | Duchamp, Marcel 352 | |
| 1953-11-18 | Sully, Thomas 302 | |
| 1953-111-1 | Johnson, Eastman 286 | |
| 1953-119-1 | Susan, Robert 433 | |
| 1953-120-1 | Eakins, Thomas 278 | |
| 1953-125-20 | Landis, John 287 | |
| 1953-136-1 | Soutine, Chaim 429 | |
| 1953-142-1 | Ahrens, Ellen Wetherald 474 | |
| 1953-142-2 | Augustin, Jean-Baptiste-Jacques 448 | |
| 1953-142-3 | Augustin, Jean-Baptiste-Jacques 448 | |
| 1953-142-4 | Meyer, Jeremiah 468 | |
| 1953-142-6 | Bridport, Hugh 482 | |
| 1953-142-7 | Bridport, Hugh 482 | |
| 1953-142-8 | Brunton, Violet 449 | |
| 1953-142-9 | Clark, Alvan, Jr. 486 | |
| 1953-142-10 | Cooper, Samuel 449 | |
| 1953-142-11 | Cooper, Samuel, copy after 449 | |
| 1953-142-12 | Cooper, Samuel, attributed to 449 | |
| 1953-142-13 | Cooper, Samuel 449 | |
| 1953-142-14 | Cosway, Richard 449 | |
| 1953-142-15 | Cosway, Richard 450 | |
| 1953-142-16 | Cosway, Richard 450 | |
| 1953-142-17 | Cosway, Richard 450 | |
| 1953-142-18 | Cosway, Richard 450 | |
| 1953-142-19 | Cosway, Richard 450 | |
| 1953-142-20 | Debillemont-Chardon, Gabrielle 451 | |
| 1953-142-21 | Engleheart, George 452 | |
| 1953-142-22 | Engleheart, George 452 | |
| 1953-142-23 | Engleheart, George 452 | |
| 1953-142-24 | Engleheart, George 452 | |
| 1953-142-25 | Engleheart, George 452 | |

| | | |
|---|---|---|
| 1953-142-26 | Field, Robert 489 | |
| W1954-1-1 | Daumier, Honoré 126 | |
| 1954-10-1 | Daumier, Honoré 126 | |
| 1954-21-1 | Monogrammist P. D. 470 | |
| 1954-21-2 | French, unknown artist 464 | |
| 1954-21-3 | Fraser, Charles 489 | |
| 1954-21-4 | Rymsdyck, Andreas van 472 | |
| 1954-21-5 | Hawley, Margaret Foote 490 | |
| 1954-21-6 | Hills, Laura Coombs 491 | |
| 1954-21-7 | Edridge, Henry 452 | |
| 1954-21-8 | Hoskins, John, attributed to 465 | |
| 1954-21-9 | Hoskins, John 465 | |
| 1954-21-10 | Høyer, Cornelius 465 | |
| 1954-21-11 | Barry, John 448 | |
| 1954-21-12 | Humphrey, Ozias 465 | |
| 1954-21-13 | Inman, Henry 491 | |
| 1954-21-14 | Jean, Philip 466 | |
| 1954-21-15 | Johnson, Jeanne Payne 492 | |
| 1954-21-16 | Lane, John 467 | |
| 1954-21-17 | Malbone, Edward Greene 494 | |
| 1954-21-18 | Malbone, Edward Greene 493 | |
| 1954-21-19 | Malbone, Edward Greene 494 | |
| 1954-21-20 | Malbone, Edward Greene 494 | |
| 1954-21-21 | Marchant, Edward Dalton 494 | |
| 1954-21-22 | Oliver, Isaac, copy after 470 | |
| 1954-21-23 | Oliver, Isaac, attributed to 470 | |
| 1954-21-25 | Peale, James 496 | |
| 1954-21-26 | Peale, Raphaelle 497 | |
| 1954-21-27 | Peale, Raphaelle 497 | |
| 1954-30-1 | Davis, Stuart 345 | |
| 1954-31-1 | American, unknown artist 260 | |
| 1954-42-1 | Ahrens, Ellen Wetherald 474 | |
| 1954-42-2 | Archambault, Anna Margaretta 478 | |
| 1954-42-3 | Archambault, Anna Margaretta 478 | |
| 1954-42-4 | Baer, William Jacob 479 | |
| 1954-42-5 | Barrett, Lisbeth S. 479 | |
| 1954-42-6 | Baum, Walter Emerson 479 | |
| 1954-42-7 | Baxter, Martha Wheeler 479 | |
| 1954-42-8 | Baxter, Martha Wheeler 479 | |
| 1954-42-9 | Baxter, Martha Wheeler 479 | |
| 1954-42-10 | Beckington, Alice 480 | |
| 1954-42-11 | Benton, Margaret Peake 480 | |
| 1954-42-12 | Bill, Sally Cross 480 | |
| 1954-42-13 | Bill, Sally Cross 480 | |
| 1954-42-14 | Bliss, Alma Hirsig 481 | |
| 1954-42-15 | Boardman, Rosina Cox 481 | |
| 1954-42-16 | Boericke, Johanna Magdalene 481 | |
| 1954-42-17 | Boericke, Johanna Magdalene 481 | |
| 1954-42-18 | Bonsall, Mary Waterman 481 | |
| 1954-42-19 | Borda, Katharine K. 481 | |
| 1954-42-20 | Boyle, Sarah Yocum McFadden 481 | |
| 1954-42-21 | Bush, Ella Shepard 482 | |
| 1954-42-22 | Carew, Berta 483 | |
| 1954-42-23 | Cariss, Marguerite Feldpauche 486 | |
| 1954-42-24 | Debillemont-Chardon, Gabrielle 451 | |
| 1954-42-25 | Debillemont-Chardon, Gabrielle 451 | |
| 1954-42-26 | Chase, Violet Thompson 486 | |
| 1954-42-27 | Collier, Grace 486 | |
| 1954-42-28 | Coolidge, Bertha 486 | |
| 1954-42-29 | Coolidge, Bertha 486 | |
| 1954-42-30 | Cowan, Sarah Eakin 486 | |
| 1954-42-31 | Daggett, Grace E. 487 | |
| 1954-42-32 | Dalrymple, Lucille Stevenson 487 | |
| 1954-42-33 | Day, Martha B. Willson 487 | |
| 1954-42-34 | Dunn, Marjorie Cline 488 | |
| 1954-42-35 | Ely, Frances Campbell 488 | |
| 1954-42-36 | Fenderson, Annie M. 488 | |
| 1954-42-37 | Fenderson, Annie M. 488 | |
| 1954-42-38 | Fenderson, Annie M. 488 | |
| 1954-42-39 | Fisher, Howell Tracy 489 | |
| 1954-42-40 | Fisher, Howell Tracy 489 | |
| 1954-42-41 | Fisher, Howell Tracy 489 | |

| | | |
|---|---|---|
| 1959-91-21 | Carew, Berta 483 | |
| 1959-91-22 | Carew, Berta 483 | |
| 1959-91-23 | Carew, Berta 484 | |
| 1959-91-24 | Pollock, L. 497 | |
| 1959-91-26 | Carew, Berta 484 | |
| 1959-91-27 | Carew, Berta 484 | |
| 1959-91-28 | Carew, Berta 484 | |
| 1959-91-29 | Carew, Berta 484 | |
| 1959-91-30 | Carew, Berta 484 | |
| 1959-91-31 | Carew, Berta 482 | |
| 1959-91-32 | Carew, Berta 483 | |
| 1959-91-33 | Carew, Berta 484 | |
| 1959-91-34 | Carew, Berta 483 | |
| 1959-91-35 | Carew, Berta 482 | |
| 1959-91-36 | Carew, Berta 483 | |
| 1959-91-37 | Trueworthy, Jessie 502 | |
| 1959-91-38 | Carew, Berta 485 | |
| 1959-91-39 | Carew, Berta 484 | |
| 1959-91-40 | McKerwin 493 | |
| 1959-91-41 | Carew, Berta 485 | |
| 1959-91-42 | Carew, Berta 485 | |
| 1959-91-43 | Carew, Berta 485 | |
| 1959-91-44 | Carew, Berta 485 | |
| 1959-91-45 | Carew, Berta 485 | |
| 1959-91-46 | Carew, Braley Colman 486 | |
| 1959-91-47 | Brugger, Dorothy 482 | |
| 1959-91-52 | Italian, unknown artist 466 | |
| 1959-91-53 | Italian, unknown artist 466 | |
| 1959-102-1 | Wyeth, Andrew Newell 444 | |
| 1959-133-1 | Chagall, Marc 339 | |
| 1960-23-3 | Frelinghuysen, Suzy 359 | |
| 1960-57-1 | Drew-Bear, Jessie 350 | |
| 1960-78-1 | Sully, Thomas 300 | |
| 1960-78-2 | Sully, Thomas 300 | |
| 1960-109-1 | Stuart, Gilbert Charles, attributed to 298 | |
| 1961-21-1 | Stuart, Gilbert Charles, copy after 298 | |
| 1961-37-1 | Petitot, Jean 470 | |
| 1961-48-1 | Monet, Claude 147 | |
| 1961-48-2 | Monet, Claude 148 | |
| 1961-48-3 | Monet, Claude 146 | |
| 1961-64-1 | Blackburn, Morris Atkinson 326 | |
| 1961-77-1 | Karfiol, Bernard 378 | |
| 1961-78-1 | Speight, Francis 430 | |
| 1961-150-1 | Pissarro, Camille 150 | |
| 1961-171-1 | Sully, Thomas 299 | |
| 1961-179-1 | German, unknown artist 464 | |
| 1961-180-1 | Leonid 387 | |
| 1961-195-1 | Lievens, Jan, attributed to 69 | |
| 1961-215-1 | Robert, Hubert 155 | |
| 1961-223-1 | Kline, Franz 381 | |
| 1961-226-1 | Wollaston, John, attributed to 305 | |
| W1962-1-1 | Kuhn, Walt 382 | |
| 1962-49-1 | Konolyi, Mary Barnwell 382 | |
| 1962-74-1 | Collet, Édouard 116 | |
| 1962-126-1 | Peale, Charles Willson 290 | |
| 1962-142-1 | Aman-Jean, Edmond-François 108 | |
| 1962-193-1 | Sargent, John Singer 295 | |
| 1962-193-2 | Sully, Thomas 299 | |
| 1962-205-1 | Demuth, Charles 347 | |
| 1962-205-2 | Demuth, Charles 347 | |
| 1962-206-1 | Forain, Jean-Louis 133 | |
| 1962-217-1 | Trott, Benjamin 501 | |
| 1962-218-1 | Trott, Benjamin 501 | |
| 1962-219-1 | Robinson, John 471 | |
| 1963-75-1 | Peale, Charles Willson 496 | |
| 1963-75-2 | Peale, Charles Willson, attributed to 292 | |
| 1963-75-3 | American, unknown artist 256 | |
| 1963-75-4 | American, unknown artist 256 | |
| 1963-116-1 | Boudin, Eugène-Louis 111 | |
| 1963-116-2 | Cézanne, Paul 114 | |
| 1963-116-3 | Cézanne, Paul 114 | |
| 1963-116-4 | Cézanne, Paul 114 | |
| 1963-116-5 | Cézanne, Paul 113 | |
| 1963-116-6 | David, Jacques-Louis, follower of 127 | |
| 1963-116-8 | Goya y Lucientes, Francisco José de 240 | |
| 1963-116-9 | Manet, Édouard 143 | |
| 1963-116-10 | Manet, Édouard 143 | |
| 1963-116-11 | Monet, Claude 148 | |
| 1963-116-12 | Spierincks, Karel Philips, attributed to 97 | |
| 1963-116-13 | Renoir, Pierre-Auguste 153 | |
| 1963-116-14 | Renoir, Pierre-Auguste 153 | |
| 1963-116-15 | Renoir, Pierre-Auguste 154 | |
| 1963-116-16 | Renoir, Pierre-Auguste 153 | |
| 1963-116-17 | Renoir, Pierre-Auguste 153 | |
| 1963-116-18 | Sisley, Alfred 157 | |
| 1963-116-19 | Gogh, Vincent Willem van 59 | |
| 1963-116-21 | Cézanne, Paul 113 | |
| 1963-117-1 | Degas, Hilaire-Germain-Edgar 128 | |
| 1963-171-1 | Raeburn, Sir Henry 22 | |
| 1963-180-1 | Hofmann, Hans 372 | |
| 1963-181-1 | Bonnard, Pierre 327 | |
| 1963-181-2 | Bonnard, Pierre 328 | |
| 1963-181-3 | Boudin, Eugène-Louis 111 | |
| 1963-181-4 | Braque, Georges 331 | |
| 1963-181-5 | Brook, Alexander 331 | |
| 1963-181-6 | Cézanne, Paul 114 | |
| 1963-181-9 | Chagall, Marc 338 | |
| 1963-181-10 | Chagall, Marc 339 | |
| 1963-181-11 | Chagall, Marc 339 | |
| 1963-181-12 | Chagall, Marc 339 | |
| 1963-181-13 | Chagall, Marc 338 | |
| 1963-181-14 | Chagall, Marc 339 | |
| 1963-181-16 | Chagall, Marc 340 | |
| 1963-181-18 | Corot, Jean-Baptiste-Camille 117 | |
| 1963-181-19 | Courbet, Gustave 122 | |
| 1963-181-20 | Courbet, Gustave 122 | |
| 1963-181-21 | Courbet, Gustave 123 | |
| 1963-181-22 | Courbet, Gustave 123 | |
| 1963-181-23 | Courbet, Gustave 123 | |
| 1963-181-25 | Eakins, Thomas 276 | |
| 1963-181-26 | Ensor, James 355 | |
| 1963-181-29 | Gatch, Lee 360 | |
| 1963-181-30 | Gordey, Ida 362 | |
| 1963-181-31 | Gwathmey, Robert 366 | |
| 1963-181-32 | Hassam, Childe 282 | |
| 1963-181-38 | Kroll, Leon 382 | |
| 1963-181-45 | Matisse, Henri 393 | |
| 1963-181-47 | Miró, Joan 398 | |
| 1963-181-48 | Modigliani, Amedeo 398 | |
| 1963-181-51 | Pascin, Jules 408 | |
| 1963-181-53 | Picasso, Pablo Ruiz 412 | |
| 1963-181-58 | Renoir, Pierre-Auguste 153 | |
| 1963-181-59 | Renoir, Pierre-Auguste 154 | |
| 1963-181-60 | Ritman, Louis 419 | |
| 1963-181-61 | Rouault, Georges 421 | |
| 1963-181-62 | Rouault, Georges 421 | |
| 1963-181-64 | Rousseau, Henri-Julien-Félix 422 | |
| 1963-181-65 | Rousseau, Henri-Julien-Félix 422 | |
| 1963-181-66 | Rubin, Reuven 423 | |
| 1963-181-68 | Sheeler, Charles 427 | |
| 1963-181-69 | Soyer, Raphael 430 | |
| 1963-181-70 | Sterne, Maurice 432 | |
| 1963-181-71 | Soutine, Chaim 430 | |
| 1963-181-72 | Soutine, Chaim 430 | |
| 1963-181-73 | Soutine, Chaim 430 | |
| 1963-181-74 | Utrillo, Maurice 437 | |
| 1963-181-76 | Vuillard, Édouard 439 | |
| 1963-181-77 | Vuillard, Édouard 440 | |
| 1963-191-1 | Feke, Robert 280 | |
| 1963-192-1 | Cox, Jan 343 | |
| 1963-214-1 | Mingorance, Juan 396 | |
| 1963-215-1 | Francesco di Giorgio, follower of 192 | |
| 1964-30-1 | Riopelle, Jean-Paul 418 | |
| 1964-31-1 | Sully, Thomas 302 | |
| 1964-32-1 | Hankins, Abraham P. 367 | |
| 1964-45-1 | Watkins, Franklin Chenault 441 | |
| 1964-46-1 | Picasso, Pablo Ruiz 410 | |
| 1964-61-1 | Branchard, Emile Pierre 329 | |
| 1964-77-1 | Matisse, Henri 393 | |
| 1964-77-2 | Rouault, Georges 421 | |
| 1964-77-3 | Vuillard, Édouard 440 | |
| 1964-89-1 | Picasso, Pablo Ruiz 412 | |
| 1964-103-1 | Gainsborough, Thomas 13 | |
| 1964-104-1 | Prendergast, Maurice B. 415 | |
| 1964-105-1 | Stuart, Gilbert Charles 298 | |
| 1964-105-2 | Peale, Charles Willson 291 | |
| 1964-105-3 | Peale, Charles Willson 291 | |
| 1964-106-1 | Carles, Arthur Beecher 336 | |
| 1964-106-2 | Keene, Paul 378 | |
| 1964-106-3 | Remenick, Seymour 418 | |
| 1964-106-4 | Remenick, Seymour 418 | |
| 1964-106-5 | Remenick, Seymour 418 | |
| 1964-107-1 | Matisse, Henri 393 | |
| 1964-108-1 | Braque, Georges 331 | |
| 1964-109-1 | Picasso, Pablo Ruiz 412 | |
| 1964-110-1 | Blake, William 3 | |
| 1964-111-1 | Sully, Thomas 299 | |
| 1964-114-1 | Manet, Édouard 144 | |
| 1964-116-1 | Prendergast, Maurice B. 415 | |
| 1964-116-2 | Luks, George B. 388 | |
| 1964-116-3 | Davies, Arthur Bowen 345 | |
| 1964-116-4 | Lawson, Ernest 385 | |
| 1964-116-5 | Sloan, John 428 | |
| 1964-116-6 | Henri, Robert 371 | |
| 1964-116-7 | Glackens, William 361 | |
| 1964-117-1 | Hankins, Abraham P. 367 | |
| 1964-117-2 | Hankins, Abraham P. 367 | |
| 1964-117-3 | Hankins, Abraham P. 366 | |
| 1964-117-4 | Hankins, Abraham P. 367 | |
| 1964-117-5 | Hankins, Abraham P. 367 | |
| 1964-151-1 | Tanguy, Kay Sage 434 | |
| 1964-181-1 | Tanguy, Yves 434 | |
| 1964-210-1 | Peale, James 292 | |
| 1964-210-2 | Peale, James 292 | |
| 1965-48-1 | Otis, Bass 289 | |
| 1965-49-1 | West, Benjamin 29 | |
| 1965-65-1 | Vouet, Simon, studio of 162 | |
| 1965-85-1 | Lagrenée, Louis, the Elder, attributed to 141 | |
| 1965-85-2 | Rousseau, Pierre-Étienne-Théodore 155 | |
| 1965-90-1 | Pannini, Giovanni Paolo 224 | |
| 1965-117-10 | Borie, Adolphe 328 | |
| 1965-158-1 | Lueders, Jimmy C. 388 | |
| 1965-170-1 | Strater, Henry 432 | |
| 1965-205-23 | Paxton, W. 408 | |
| 1965-208-1 | László, Philip A. de 384 | |
| 1965-209-1 | Durand, John 269 | |
| 1965-209-2 | Britton, William 265 | |
| 1965-209-3 | American, unknown artist 257 | |
| 1965-209-4 | American, unknown artist 259 | |
| 1965-209-5 | American, unknown artist 260 | |
| 1965-209-6 | Raleigh, Charles Sidney 294 | |
| 1965-214-1 | França, Manuel Joachim de 280 | |
| 1965-218-1 | Richenberg, Robert 418 | |
| 1966-4-1 | Smith, T. Henry 297 | |
| 1966-20-2 | English, unknown artist 453 | |
| 1966-20-3 | Daniel of Bath, Joseph, or Abraham Daniel of Bath, attributed to 450 | |
| 1966-20-4 | English, unknown artist 453 | |
| 1966-20-5 | English, unknown artist 453 | |
| 1966-20-6 | Daniel of Bath, Joseph, or Abraham Daniel of Bath, attributed to 450 | |

1971-219-1 Sugai, Kumi 433
1971-220-1 Wasserman, Burton 441
1971-222-1 Weinstone, Howard 443
1971-262-1 English or Irish, unknown artist 10
1971-263-1 Davie, Alan 344
1971-264-1 Mitchell, Joan 398
1971-264-2 Parker, Raymond 407
1971-265-1 David, Jacques-Louis 127
1971-266-1 Rattner, Abraham 415
1971-271-1 American, unknown artist 262
1971-272-1 Ward, Edward Matthew, copy after 28
1971-272-2 German, unknown artist 169
1971-272-3 Mason, William Sanford 287
E1972-1-1 West, Benjamin 29
E1972-2-1 Dossi, Battista 191
W1972-2-1 Tissot, James-Jacques-Joseph 158
E1972-3-1 Franque, Joseph 134
1972-30-1 Davis, Gene 345
1972-30-2 Davis, Gene 345
1972-43-1 Tuttle, Adrianna 502
1972-50-1 Gainsborough, Thomas 14
1972-50-2 Romney, George 25
1972-50-3 Raeburn, Sir Henry 21
1972-53-1 Shields, Alan 427
1972-54-1 Davis, Gene 345
1972-100-1 Stieglitz, Edward 297
1972-121-1 Biddle, George 325
1972-121-2 Biddle, George 325
1972-121-3 Biddle, George 325
1972-121-4 Biddle, George 326
1972-123-1 Saÿen, Henry Lyman 424
1972-124-1 Partridge, Nehemiah 289
1972-124-2 Partridge, Nehemiah 289
1972-125-1 Herbin, Auguste 372
1972-131-1 Omwake, Leon William, Jr. 404
1972-156-1 Wesselmann, Tom 443
1972-201-1 American, unknown artist 255
1972-204-1 Vedova, Emilio 439
1972-227-1 Monet, Claude 146
1972-227-2 Monet, Claude, imitator of 148
1972-237-1 Canadé, Vincent 334
1972-237-2 Canadé, Vincent 335
1972-237-4 Canadé, Vincent 335
1972-237-5 Canadé, Vincent 334
1972-237-6 Canadé, Eugene George 334
1972-237-7 Maurer, Alfred Henry 394
1972-237-8 Cook, Howard Norton 342
1972-237-11 Mexican, unknown artist 396
1972-238-3 Pittman, Hobson L. 413
1972-238-13 Pittman, Hobson L. 413
1972-238-15 Pittman, Hobson L. 413
1972-238-18 Pittman, Hobson L. 413
1972-238-189 Pittman, Hobson L. 413
1972-239-1 Mané-Katz 390
1972-250-1 Cipriani, Giovanni Battista 188
1972-250-2 Cipriani, Giovanni Battista 188
1972-250-3 Cipriani, Giovanni Battista 188
1972-250-4 Cipriani, Giovanni Battista 188
1972-252-21 Neilson, Raymond Perry Rodgers 401
1972-262-1 American, unknown artist 258
1972-262-2 American, unknown artist 257
1972-262-3 Greenwood, Ethan Allen 280
1972-262-4 Greenwood, Ethan Allen 280
1972-262-5 Moulthrop, Reuben 288
1972-262-6 Moulthrop, Reuben 288
1972-262-7 Earl, Ralph 279
1972-262-8 Lovejoy, E. W. 287
1972-262-9 American, unknown artist 261
1972-262-10 Hathaway, Rufus 283
1972-264-1 Aldewerelt, Hermanus van 31
1972-267-1 Beckmann, Max 324
E1973-1-1 Pratt, Matthew 294

1973-70-1 Formicola, John 358
1973-71-1 Dash, Robert 344
1973-71-2 Kahn, Wolf 377
1973-73-2 Zakanitch, Robert 444
1973-76-1 Bernard, Émile 324
1973-129-1 Gogh, Vincent Willem van 59
1973-130-1 Salinas, Juan Pablo 243
1973-131-1 Danziger, Fred 344
1973-133-1 Havard, James 370
1973-134-1 Dessner, Murray 348
1973-154-1 English, unknown artist 458
1973-200-1 Jackson, Martin 374
1973-201-1 Garber, Daniel 360
1973-202-38 Watkins, Franklin Chenault 442
1973-202-50 Watkins, Franklin Chenault 442
1973-250-1 Cushman, George Hewitt 487
1973-252-1 Winterhalter, Franz Xaver 174
1973-253-1 Pacecco de Rosa 222
1973-254-1 Watkins, Franklin Chenault 442
1973-256-1 Glarner, Fritz 361
1973-256-3 Tchelitchew, Pavel 434
1973-256-4 Eilshemius, Louis Michel 354
1973-256-5 Eilshemius, Louis Michel 354
1973-256-7 Vordemberge-Gildewart, Friedel 439
1973-256-8 Francés, Esteban 358
1973-256-9 Valverde, Joaquin 438
1973-258-1 Phillips, Ammi 293
1973-258-2 Phillips, Ammi 293
1973-258-3 Prior, William Matthew 294
1973-258-4 American, unknown artist 260
1973-258-5 American, unknown artist 261
1973-258-6 American, unknown artist 262
1973-259-2 Bannard, Walter Darby 323
1973-263-1 Phillips, Ammi 293
1973-263-2 Phillips, Ammi 293
1973-264-1 Beechey, Sir William, copy after 2
1974-10-1 Sander, Ludwig 424
1974-41-2 Conarroe, George W. 267
1974-41-3 Conarroe, George W. 267
1974-41-4 American, unknown artist 255
1974-41-5 American, unknown artist 255
1974-77-1 Rohrer, Warren 420
1974-98-1 Beach, Thomas 2
1974-98-2 Cotes, Francis, imitator of 8
1974-110-1 Lichtenstein, Roy 388
1974-111-1 Pearlstein, Philip 408
1974-112-1 Goodman, Sidney 362
1974-159-1 Guardi, Francesco 197
1974-160-1 English, unknown artist 12
1974-161-1 Beechey, Sir William 2
1974-161-2 Hoppner, John, attributed to 16
1974-178-17 Balthus 322
1974-178-18 Balthus 322
1974-178-19 Bosos 329
1974-178-20 Boudin, Eugène-Louis 111
1974-178-21 Capraro, Vincent 335
1974-178-22 Carles, Arthur Beecher 337
1974-178-23 de Kooning, Willem 346
1974-178-24 de Kooning, Willem 346
1974-178-25 de Kooning, Willem 346
1974-178-26 Dickinson, Edwin Walter 348
1974-178-27 Dickinson, Edwin Walter 348
1974-178-28 Etting, Emlen 356
1974-178-29 Ferrandier, Gisele 357
1974-178-30 Foss, Olivier 358
1974-178-31 Giacometti, Alberto 361
1974-178-32 Harnett, William Michael 281
1974-178-33 Jean, Felix 375
1974-178-34 Lansner, Fay 383
1974-178-35 Matisse, Henri 392
1974-178-36 Miró, Joan 397
1974-178-37 Miró, Joan 397

1974-178-38 Monet, Claude 148
1974-178-39 Okada, Kenzo 403
1974-178-40 Peto, John Frederick 293
1974-178-41 Pollock, Jackson 414
1974-178-42 Pousette-Dart, Richard 415
1974-178-43 Remenick, Seymour 418
1974-178-44 Remenick, Seymour 418
1974-178-45 Rivers, Larry 419
1974-178-46 Roger, Suzanne 420
1974-178-47 Sekoto, G. 426
1974-178-48 Sekoto, G. 426
1974-178-50 Watkins, Franklin Chenault 442
1974-179-1 Castellon, Federico 338
1974-229-1 Johnson, Eastman 286
1974-231-2 Horter, Earl 372
1974-232-1 Pollock, Jackson 414
1974-233-1 Ricciardi, Cesare A. 418
E1975-1-1 Corinth, Lovis 343
W1975-1-1 Gauffier, Louis 138
W1975-1-2 Gauffier, Louis 138
1975-38-1 Moses, Ed 400
1975-40-1 Street, Robert 297
1975-40-2 Street, Robert 297
1975-53-1 Gaughan, Tom 360
1975-54-1 Ferszt, Ed 357
1975-70-1 Culverhouse, Johan Mengels 268
1975-78-1 Chimès, Thomas 340
1975-79-1 Glarner, Fritz 361
1975-79-3 Lenbach, Franz von 171
1975-81-1 Avery, Milton 322
1975-81-2 Bruce, Patrick Henry 332
1975-81-4 Frankenthaler, Helen 358
1975-81-5 Irwin, Robert 374
1975-81-6 Johns, Jasper 376
1975-81-8 Liberman, Alexander 388
1975-81-9 Louis, Morris 388
1975-81-10 Marcus, Marcia 390
1975-81-11 Martin, Agnes 391
1975-81-12 Noland, Kenneth 402
1975-81-13 Poons, Larry 414
1975-81-14 Rauschenberg, Robert 416
1975-81-15 Smith, Richard 429
1975-82-1 Chimes, Thomas 340
1975-82-2 Chimes, Thomas 340
1975-83-1 De Forest, Roy 346
1975-83-3 Davis, Ron 345
1975-86-1 Winner, William E. 305
1975-90-1 Eakins, Thomas 274
1975-119-1 Prendergast, Maurice B. 415
1975-120-1 Keyser, Robert 380
1975-125-1 Bordley, Judge John Beale 264
1975-150-1 Goya y Lucientes, Francisco José de 239
1975-163-1 Schock, Maya 425
1975-164-1 Blackburn, Morris Atkinson 326
1975-165-1 Stegeman, Charles 431
1975-165-2 André, Françoise 320
1975-169-1 Dawson, Manierre 345
1975-170-1 Ozenfant, Amédée 407
1975-180-1 Oakley, Violet 403
1975-180-2 Emerson, Edith 355
1975-182-1 Moran, Thomas 288
1976-34-1 Leighton, Sir Frederic 18
1976-35-1 Bateman, Ronald C. 323
1976-37-1 Newman, Carl 401
1976-98-1 Curtiss, Deborah 344
1976-99-1 Palmore, Tommy Dale 407
1976-152-1 Sefarbi, Harry 425
1976-152-2 Sefarbi, Harry 425
1976-154-1 Chimes, Thomas 341
1976-156-1 Brush, George de Forest 265
1976-164-1 Thayer, Abbott Handerson 302